Computer Concepts 2013

COMPREHENSIVE

Parsons :: Oja

COURSE TECHNOLOGY
CENGAGE Learning·

New Perspectives on Computer Concepts, 2013, Comprehensive

June Jamrich Parsons, Dan Oja

Executive Editor: Marie Lee

Senior Product Manager: Kathy Finnegan

Product Managers: Katherine C. Russillo, Leigh Hefferon

Associate Acquisitions Editor: Amanda Lyons

Developmental Editor: Katherine C. Russillo

Associate Product Manager: Julia Leroux-Lindsey

Editorial Assistant: Jacqueline Lacaire

Marketing Manager: Jennifer Stiles

Senior Content Project Manager: Jennifer Goguen McGrail

Photo Research: Bill Smith Group

Art Director: GEX Publishing Services

Cover Designer: Roycroft Design

Cover Art: © Masterfile

BookOnCD Technician: Keefe Crowley

BookOnCD Development: MediaTechnics Corp.

Prepress Production: GEX Publishing Services

For product information and technology assistance, contact us at
Cengage Learning Customer & Sales Support, 1-800-354-9706

For permission to use material from this text or product,
submit all requests online at cengage.com/permissions.
Further permissions questions can be e-mailed to
permissionrequest@cengage.com.

Some of the product names and company names used in this book have been used for identification purposes only and may be trademarks or registered trademarks of their respective manufacturers and sellers.

Microsoft and the Office logo are either registered trademarks or trademarks of Microsoft Corporation in the United States and/or other countries. Course Technology, Cengage Learning is an independent entity from the Microsoft Corporation, and not affiliated with Microsoft in any manner. All screenshots are courtesy of Microsoft unless otherwise noted.

Disclaimer: Any fictional data related to persons or companies or URLs used throughout this book is intended for instructional purposes only. At the time this book was printed, any such data was fictional and not belonging to any real persons or companies.

Library of Congress Control Number: 2011944792

ISBN-13: 978-1-133-19056-1
ISBN-10: 1-133-19056-1

Course Technology
20 Channel Center Street
Boston, MA 02210
USA

Cengage Learning is a leading provider of customized learning solutions with office locations around the globe, including Singapore, the United Kingdom, Australia, Mexico, Brazil and Japan. Locate your local office at:
international.cengage.com/global

Cengage Learning products are represented in Canada by Nelson Education, Ltd.

To learn more about Course Technology, visit **www.cengage.com/coursetechnology**

To learn more about Cengage Learning, visit **www.cengage.com**

Purchase any of our products at your local college store or at our preferred online store **www.cengagebrain.com**

Printed in the United States of America
1 2 3 4 5 6 7 16 15 14 13 12

CONTENTS AT A GLANCE

TABLE OF CONTENTS

ORIENTATION

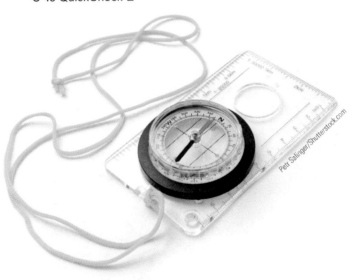

Petr Salinger/Shutterstock.com

CHAPTER 1

COMPUTERS AND DIGITAL BASICS

Oleksiy Mark /Shutterstock.com

CHAPTER 2

COMPUTER HARDWARE

Alexander Kalina/Shutterstock.com

almagami /Shutterstock.com

CHAPTER 5

LOCAL AREA NETWORKS

CHAPTER 8

DIGITAL MEDIA

Irina Silayeva/Shutterstock.com

CHAPTER 10

INFORMATION SYSTEMS ANALYSIS AND DESIGN

CHAPTER 11

DATABASES

CHAPTER 12

COMPUTER PROGRAMMING

AirOne/Shutterstock.com

NEW PERSPECTIVES LABS

STUDENT EDITION LABS*

*Available with the NP2013 CourseMate.

Africa Studio/Shutterstock.com

Preface

Connect the Concepts. We live in a digital world and pick up bits and pieces of information about computers and other digital devices. But *understanding* digital devices in a way expected of a college graduate requires a framework of concepts that organizes information into hierarchies and relationships. It is, in a sense, **THE SOCIAL NETWORK OF LEARNING**.

New Perspectives on Computer Concepts 2013 is designed to help students connect the dots to visualize and internalize a framework for technology concepts that's applicable to academic research, career preparation, and today's digital lifestyles.

Ensure Success. Developed by digital textbook pioneers, NP2013 is a time-tested and fully interactive teaching and learning environment that supplies **TOOLS FOR SUCCESS**. The printed book, CourseMate Web site, interactive multimedia eBook, and assessment tools offer an engaging, multi-layered technology platform that supports diverse teaching and learning styles.

New for This Edition. NP2013 is offered in **THREE FORMATS:** printed textbook, eBook CD, and CourseMate eBook. You can use the text alone or bundle it with one of the multimedia interactive eBooks. Or use the interactive eBooks by themselves. They contain page-for-page material from the printed textbook, plus videos, animated diagrams, software tours, computer-scored assessment, and results tracking.

PRINTED TEXTBOOK	EBOOK CD	COURSEMATE
Orientation Chapter	All the features of the printed textbook	All the features of the printed textbook
Section Concept Maps	Videos and animated diagrams	Videos and animated diagrams
Learning Objectives	Software tours	Software tours
Learning Objectives Checkpoints	Computer-scored and tracked QuickChecks, Interactive Summaries, Situation Questions, and Concept Maps	Computer-scored QuickChecks, Interactive Summaries, Situation Questions, and Concept Maps
Chapter Opener Try It!s	Practice Tests	Computer-scored and tracked Pre-Quizzes and Chapter Quizzes
Section QuickChecks	New Perspectives Labs with scored and tracked QuickChecks	Student Edition Labs
Issues	WebTrack results tracking	Audio Overviews
Information Tools	Instructor annotations	Audio Flashcards
Technology in Context	Chirps	Games
Key Terms		Engagement Tracker
Interactive Summary		
Interactive Situation Questions		
Concept Maps		

CREATE YOUR OWN LEARNING PLAN

It's easy! Use the NP2013 printed textbook, NP2013 CourseMate Web site, or NP2013 eBook CD in **ANY WAY THAT'S RIGHT FOR YOU**. The Orientation helps you get acquainted with the extensive array of NP2013 technology at your command.

Your eBook CD Plan—Seven Easy Steps

1. Get started with the **EBOOK CD** and work on the Chapter opener **TRY IT ACTIVITY** for a hands-on introduction to the chapter topics.

2. Read a chapter and complete the **QUICKCHECKS** at the end of each section.

3. Use **CHIRPS** while you're reading to send questions to your instructor.

4. Work with **NEW PERSPECTIVES LABS** to apply your knowledge.

5. Complete **REVIEW ACTIVITIES** using your digital textbook.

6. Take a **PRACTICE TEST** to see if you're ready for the exam.

7. Transmit your results to your instructor on **WEBTRACK**.

Your CourseMate Plan—Eight Steps Online

1. Log in to the NP2013 CourseMate to take the **PRE-QUIZ** and gauge what you already know.

2. Listen to an **AUDIO OVERVIEW** of chapter highlights.

3. Read a chapter in the online eBook.

4. Work with the **EBOOK ACTIVITIES AND PRACTICE TESTS** to assess your understanding.

5. Have some fun reviewing with **ONLINE GAMES**.

6. Use **AUDIO AND TECHTERM FLASHCARDS** to review terminology from the chapter.

7. Check the **DETAILED LEARNING OBJECTIVES** to make sure you've mastered the material.

8. Take the **QUIZZES** so your instructor can see your progress; your scores are automatically recorded by the Engagement Tracker.

Gladskikh Tatiana/Shutterstock.com

THE BOOK

NP2013 gives you the straight story on today's technology. The style has been carefully honed to be clear, concise, and visual.

Easy to read

Each chapter is divided into five **SECTIONS**, beginning with a **CONCEPT MAP** that provides a visual overview of concepts. **FAQS** answer commonly asked questions about technology and help you follow the flow of the presentation.

Keeps you on track

QUICKCHECKS at the end of each section give you a chance to find out if you understand the most important concepts. As you read the chapter, look for the answers to the questions posed as Learning Objectives, then try your hand at the **LEARNING OBJECTIVES CHECKPOINTS** at the end of each chapter to make sure you've retained the key points. Additional review activities include **KEY TERMS**, **INTERACTIVE CHAPTER SUMMARIES**, **INTERACTIVE SITUATION QUESTIONS**, and **CONCEPT MAPS**.

Helps you explore

The **ISSUE** section in each chapter highlights controversial aspects of technology. In the **TECHNOLOGY IN CONTEXT** section, you'll discover how technology plays a role in careers such as film-making, architecture, banking, and fashion design. The **INFORMATION TOOLS** section helps you brush up on digital research techniques and apps. Work with **ISSUE AND INFORMATION TOOLS TRY ITS** to apply the concepts you learned as you explore technology controversies and hone your information literacy skills.

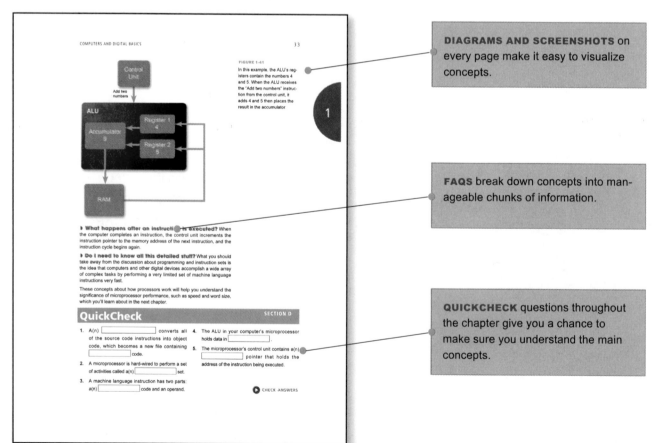

DIAGRAMS AND SCREENSHOTS on every page make it easy to visualize concepts.

FAQS break down concepts into manageable chunks of information.

QUICKCHECK questions throughout the chapter give you a chance to make sure you understand the main concepts.

THE INTERACTIVE MULTIMEDIA EBOOK CD

The **NP2013 EBOOK CD** is a digital version of your textbook with multimedia and interactive activities designed to enhance your learning experience.

Works alone or with the printed book

Every page of the eBook CD **MIRRORS THE PRINTED TEXTBOOK**, so use the tool that's most convenient and that best suits your learning style.

Brings concepts to life

In the eBook CD, photos turn into **VIDEOS**. Illustrations become **ANIMATED DIAGRAMS**. Screenshots activate guided **SOFTWARE TOURS**, so you can see how applications and operating systems work even if they aren't installed on your computer.

Makes learning interactive

As you read each chapter, be sure to complete the computer-scored **QUICKCHECKS** at the end of each section. When you complete a chapter, try the interactive, **COMPUTER-SCORED ACTIVITIES**. Take some **PRACTICE TESTS** to gauge how well you'll perform on exams.

You can master hundreds of computer concepts using the **NEW PERSPECTIVES LABS**. Use **WEBTRACK** to easily transmit your scores to your instructor. If you have questions as you're reading, use **CHIRPS** to send questions anonymously to your instructor.

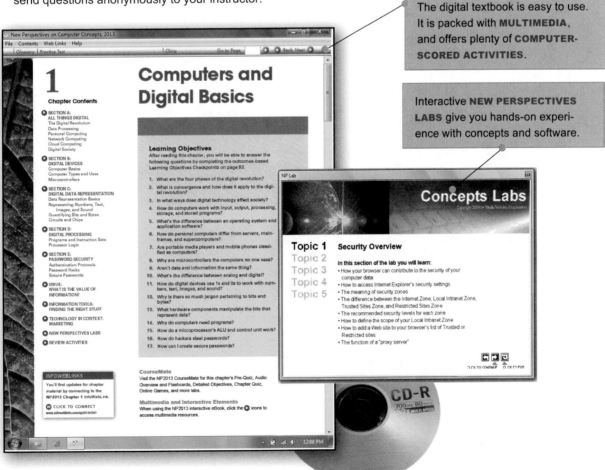

The digital textbook is easy to use. It is packed with **MULTIMEDIA**, and offers plenty of **COMPUTER-SCORED ACTIVITIES**.

Interactive **NEW PERSPECTIVES LABS** give you hands-on experience with concepts and software.

THE NP2013 COURSEMATE WEB SITE WITH EBOOK

The NP2013 CourseMate Web site is packed full of information and includes an interactive, multimedia eBook plus activities to accompany each chapter. Follow the directions in Section E of the Orientation chapter to sign up for an account and access the NP2013 CourseMate.

Lets you study anywhere

CourseMate includes an **ONLINE EBOOK**, so you can access your textbook from any computer that's connected to the Internet.

Gives you options

Want to find out where to focus your study time? Start with a **PRE-QUIZ**. Looking for a fun way to review? Try an **ONLINE GAME** that packages chapter concepts into an entertaining quiz show or action game. When you're ready for some serious exam preparation, work with the **CHAPTER QUIZZES** to see how well you understand key concepts. Need some last-minute review? Load up your portable music player with a **CHAPTER OVERVIEW** and **AUDIO FLASHCARDS**.

Now you can listen to Audio Overviews and Flashcards on your computer or study while you are out and about by downloading them to your portable music player.

Reinforces your understanding

STUDENT EDITION LABS give you hands-on experience with key concepts and skills. **DETAILED LEARNING OBJECTIVES** help you determine if you've mastered all the requirements for completing a chapter.

Keeps track of your progress

CourseMate's **ENGAGEMENT TRACKER** records the time you spend on various activities, saves your scores, and shares them with your instructor.

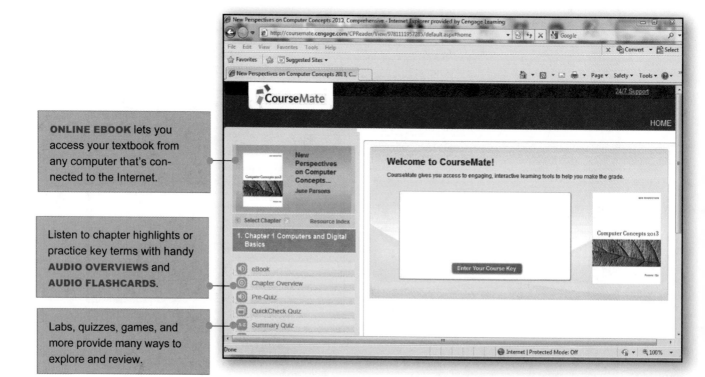

ONLINE EBOOK lets you access your textbook from any computer that's connected to the Internet.

Listen to chapter highlights or practice key terms with handy **AUDIO OVERVIEWS** and **AUDIO FLASHCARDS**.

Labs, quizzes, games, and more provide many ways to explore and review.

INSTRUCTOR RESOURCES

New Perspectives' instructional resources and technologies provide instructors with a wide range of tools that enhance teaching and learning. These tools and more can be accessed from the NP Concepts Community Web site www.cengage.com/ct/npconcepts.

The **NP CONCEPTS COMMUNITY SITE** is designed to be an instructor's one-stop point of access for **TEACHING TOOLS** and **TECHNICAL SUPPORT**.

Instructor's Manual: Help is only a few keystrokes away

The special Instructor's Manual offers bullet-point lecture notes for each chapter, plus classroom activities and teaching tips, including how to effectively use and integrate CourseMate Web site content, interactive multimedia eBook content, and labs.

Technology Guide

Do you need to learn how to use WebTrack, the eBook CD, and the CourseMate Web site with integrated eBook? We now offer instructors a Technology Guide that provides step-by-step instructions for collecting WebTrack data, adding your own annotations to the digital textbook, exporting student scores, and much more.

WebTrack

Monitoring student progress is easy. With WebTrack's store-and-forward system, a student can transmit scores to an instructor, who can download them at any time. Newly downloaded scores are consolidated with previous scores and can be displayed, printed, or exported in a variety of report formats.

Chirps

Would you like to know the questions students have while reading their textbooks? Chirps let you find out! Similar to tweets, our Chirps feature allows students to send questions to instructors from within the eBook CD. Instructors can also use Chirps as an in-class polling system, or as an asynchronous polling tool for online students. To learn about this versatile new NP technology, refer to the Technology Guide.

ANNOTATIONS! Instructors can create their own text, graphical, or video annotations that students will see as they read their digital textbook. Find out more about this innovative feature in the Technology Guide.

Web TrackIII

WebTrackIII Instructor's Page

WEBTRACKIII is now available as a portable app that instructors can carry on a USB flash drive and use on their classroom, office, or home computer.

Clicker Questions

Are you wondering if your students are awake in class? Use the clicker questions supplied with the Instructor's Manual and included in the NP2013 PowerPoint presentations. Each question is numbered so you can collect results using Chirps or a third-party course polling system.

Course Presenter

Instructors can deliver engaging and visually impressive lectures for each chapter with the professionally designed Course Presenter. Course Presenter is a PowerPoint presentation enhanced with screentours, animations, and videos.

Engagement Tracker

For courses that take advantage of the activities on the NP2013 CourseMate Web site, the Engagement Tracker monitors student time on tasks and records scores that help instructors keep track of student progress.

BlackBoard Learning System™ Content

Blackboard
www.blackboard.com

We offer a full range of content for use with the BlackBoard Learning System to simplify using NP2013 in distance education settings.

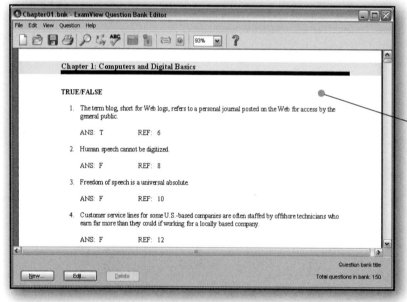

ExamView test banks for *New Perspectives on Computer Concepts 2013* make test creation easy.

ExamView: Testbanks and powerful testing software

With ExamView, instructors can generate printed tests, create LAN-based tests, or test over the Internet. Examview testbanks cover the same material as Practice Tests and Test Yourself testbanks, but the questions are worded differently so the ExamView testbanks contain a unique collection of questions for graded tests and exams.

SAM

SAM (Skills Assessment Manager) is a robust assessment, training, and project-based system that enables students to be active participants in learning valuable Microsoft Office skills. A set of testbank questions ties directly to each applicable chapter in this book. Let SAM be an integral part of your students' learning experience! Please visit www.cengage.com/samcentral.

FROM THE AUTHORS

Many of today's students have substantially more practical experience with digital devices than their counterparts of 15 years ago, but even these students may lack a cohesive framework for their knowledge. Our new Concept Map feature throughout the chapters is designed to help students organize technology-related facts, terms, and experiences.

The goal of *New Perspectives on Computer Concepts* is to bring every student up to speed with computer basics, and then go beyond basic computer literacy to provide students with technical and practical information that every college-educated person would be expected to know.

In producing the 2013 edition of this very popular textbook, we incorporated significant technology trends that affect computing and everyday life. Concerns for data security, personal privacy, and online safety, controversy over digital rights management, interest in open source software and portable applications, the popularity of the iPad, and the skyrocketing sales of Macs are just some of the trends that have been given expanded coverage in this edition of the book.

Whether you are an instructor or a student, we hope that you enjoy the learning experience provided by our text-based and technology-based materials.

ACKNOWLEDGEMENTS

The book would not exist—and certainly wouldn't arrive on schedule—were it not for the efforts of our media, editorial, and production teams. We thank Kate Russillo for her developmental edit and tireless work on every detail of the project; Suzanne Huizenga for a miraculously detailed copy edit; Marie L. Lee for her executive leadership of the New Perspectives series; Jennifer Goguen McGrail for managing production; artist Derek Bedrosian for great illustrations; Julia Leroux-Lindsey for managing the book's ancillaries; Jacqueline Lacaire for assisting the editorial team; and our brilliant sales reps for encouraging instructors to adopt this book for their intro courses.

The MediaTechnics team worked tirelessly and we can't offer enough thanks to Donna Mulder for managing the lab revisions and revising the screentours; Tensi Parsons for her extraordinary devotion to desktop publishing; Keefe Crowley for his versatile skills in producing the online and CD eBooks, creating videos, taking photos, and maintaining the InfoWebLinks site; Chris Robbert for his clear narrations; and Debora Elam, Kevin Lappi, Joseph Smit, Nikki Smit, Marilou Potter, Michael Crowley, and Kelsey Schuch for checking and double-checking the alpha and beta CDs.

We also want to give special thanks to Bob Metcalf for giving us permission to use his original sketch of the Ethernet; and The University of Illinois for supplying photos of PLATO.

In addition, our thanks go to the New Perspectives Advisory Committee members and reviewers listed on the next page, who have made a tremendous contribution to New Perspectives. Thank you all!

June Parsons and Dan Oja

ACADEMIC, TECHNICAL, AND STUDENT REVIEWERS

Thank you to the many students, instructors, Advisory Committee members, and subject-matter experts who provided valuable feedback and who have influenced the evolution of New Perspectives on Computer Concepts:

Dr. Nazih Abdallah, University of Central Florida; Beverly Amer, Northern Arizona University; Ken Baldauf, Florida State University; Dottie Baumeister, Harford Community College; Paula Bell, Lock Haven University of Pennsylvania; Mary Burke, Ocean County College; Barbara Burns, St. Johns River Community College; Mary Caldwell, Rollins College; Chuck Calvin, Computer Learning Centers; Wendy Chisholm, Barstow College; Linda Cooper, Macon State College; Dave Courtaway, Devry University, Ponoma; Becky Curtin, William Rainey Harper College; Eric Daley, University of New Brunswick; Sallie Dodson, Radford University; Leonard Dwyer, Southwestern College of Business; Robert Erickson, University of Vermont; Mark Feiler, Merritt College; Alan Fisher, Walters State Community College; Pat Frederick, Del Mar College; Michael Gaffney, Century College; John Gammell, St. Cloud State University; Ernest Gines, Tarrant Count College SE; Ione Good, Southeastern Community College; Tom Gorecki, College of Southern Maryland; Steve Gramlich, Pasco-Hernando Community College; Michael Hanna, Colorado State University; Dorothy Harman, Tarrant County College Northeast; Bobbye Haupt, Cecil Community College; Heith Hennel, Valencia Community College; Gerald Hensel, Valencia Community College; Patti Impink, Macon State College; Bob Irvine, American River College; Ernie Ivey, Polk Community College; Joanne Lazirko, University of Wisconsin; Stan Leja, Del Mar College; Martha Lindberg, Minnesota State University; Richard Linge, Arizona Western College; Terry Long, Valencia Community College; Karl Smart Lyman, Central Michigan University; Dr. W. Benjamin Martz, University of Colorado, Colorado Springs; Deann McMullen, Western Kentucky Community and Technical College; Dori McPherson, Schoolcraft College; Saeed Molki, South Texas College; Robert Moore, Laredo Community College; Ed Mott, Central Texas College; Cindi Nadelman, New England College; Karen O'Connor, Cerro Coso Community College; Dr. Rodney Pearson, Mississippi State University; Catherine Perlich, St. Thomas; Tonya Pierce, Ivy Tech College; David Primeaux, Virginia Commonwealth University; Ann Rowlette, Liberty University; Lana Shyrock, Monroe County Community College; Betty Sinowitz, Rockland Community College; Martin Skolnik, Florida Atlantic University; Karl Smart, Central Michigan University; Jerome Spencer, Rowan University; Ella Strong, Hazard Community and Technical College; Gregory Stefanelli, Carroll Community College; Shane Thomas, Victor Valley College Martha; J. Tilmann, College of San Mateo; Michael Wiemann, Blue River Community College; Kathy Winters, University of Tennessee, Chattanooga; John Zamora, Modesto Junior College; Mary Zayac, University of the Virgin Islands; Matt Zullo, Wake Tech Community College; Student Reviewers Kitty Edwards and Heather House; Technical Reviewers Jeff Harrow, Barbra D. Letts, John Lucas, Ramachandran Bharath, and Karl Mulder.

Computer Concepts 2013

Parsons :: Oja

Orientation

Chapter Contents

Multimedia and Interactive Elements
When using the NP2013 interactive eBook, click the icons to
access multimedia resources.

Apply Your Knowledge
The information in this chapter will give you the background to:

- Start your computer, use the keyboard, and operate the mouse
- Work with Windows or Mac OS
- Use word processing software
- Carry out research on the Web using a search engine and other resources such as Wikipedia
- Send e-mail
- Take effective steps to guard your privacy and safety online
- Use eBook CD resources, such as pre-assessments, practice tests, labs, and interactive summaries
- Access the NP2013 CourseMate Web site for labs, quizzes, CourseCasts, and online games

Try It!

WHAT DO I NEED TO GET STARTED?

To complete the activities in Sections A, B, and C, you'll need access to a computer, Internet access, your e-mail address, and your instructor's e-mail address. To complete optional Sections D and E, you'll need access to the eBook CD or CourseMate eBook.

To be sure you have what you need, use the following checklist. Check off the boxes for each item that you have.

☐ Access to a computer. If you're using your own computer, you might need a user ID and password to log in. Don't write your password down, but make sure you know what it is.

☐ Access to a school computer network. You might need a user ID and password if you use a lab computer or access your school's network. Check with your instructor or lab manager to learn how your school handles network access.

☐ An interactive, digital version of the textbook, such as the eBook CD or the CourseMate eBook. The eBook CD requires a CD or DVD drive. If your computer does not have this type of drive, check with your instructor. CourseMate eBook versions of your textbook require a browser. Your school network might provide access to the eBook CD or CourseMate eBook from lab computers.

☐ Your e-mail address. Your instructor should explain how you can obtain an e-mail address if you don't already have one. Write your e-mail address here:

_____

☐ Your instructor's e-mail address. To correspond with your instructor, you'll need your instructor's e-mail address. Write it here:

_____

☐ Your instructor's WebTrack address. If your instructor will be collecting your scores with WebTrack, make sure you have your instructor's WebTrack address. Write it here:

_____

NEW PERSPECTIVES

Computer Concepts 2013

Parsons :: Oja

© Cengage Learning

Getting Started

WHEN YOU USE the *New Perspectives on Computer Concepts* textbook, you will not only learn about computers; you'll also use computers as learning tools. Section A is designed to get computer novices quickly up to speed with computing basics, such as turning on computer equipment, working with Windows or Mac OS, using a mouse and computer keyboard, and accessing Help. Read through this section while at a computer so that you can do the TRY IT! activities.

COMPUTER EQUIPMENT

▶ **What do I need to know about my computer?** Computers come in many packages, including small handheld smartphones, sleek tablets, portable notebooks, and stationary desktop models. A computer runs software applications (also called programs) that help you accomplish a variety of tasks. The desktop or notebook computer system you're likely to use for school or work consists of several devices.

▶ **What are the important components of my computer system?** Your computer is housed in a case called a system unit that contains circuitry, including the microprocessor that is the "brain" of your computer and memory chips that temporarily store data. It also contains storage devices, such as a hard disk drive.

Your computer system includes basic hardware devices that allow you to enter information and commands, view work, and store information for later retrieval. Devices for entering information include a keyboard and mouse or touchpad. A display device, sometimes called a monitor, allows you to view your work. A printer produces "hard copy" on paper. Speakers output music, movie soundtracks, and various sounds that help you pay attention to what happens on the screen.

▶ **Where are the important components of a desktop computer system?** A desktop computer is designed for stationary use on a desk or table. Figure 1 shows the key components of a desktop computer system.

PC OR MAC?

Microcomputers are sometimes divided into two camps: PCs and Macs. PCs are manufactured by companies such as Dell, Lenovo, Acer, and Hewlett-Packard. Macs are manufactured by Apple.

Most PCs and some Macs use an operating system called Microsoft Windows. The eBook CD is designed for use with computers that run Microsoft Windows.

To determine whether your computer runs Windows, look for screens similar to those shown in Figure 4 on page O-6. If you have a Mac that does not run Windows, you can go to *www.infoweblinks. com* and download a MacPac to convert your CD to a format that runs on your Mac. You'll find full instructions on the site.

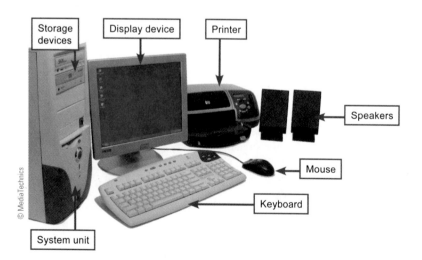

FIGURE 1

A desktop computer system includes several components that can be connected by cables or wirelessly.

▶ Where are the important components of a notebook computer system? Notebook computers (sometimes called laptops) are small, lightweight computers designed to be carried from place to place. The components of a notebook computer system, except the printer, are housed in a single unit, as shown in Figure 2.

LCD screen

Touchpad

Speakers

Keyboard

Storage devices

© MediaTechnics

A notebook computer includes a flat-panel screen, keyboard, speakers, and touchpad in the same unit that contains the microprocessor, memory, and storage devices. An external mouse is sometimes used instead of the touchpad.

▶ How do I identify my computer's storage devices? Your computer contains a hard disk housed inside the system unit. It is also likely to have a USB connector and some type of drive that works with CDs and DVDs. Figure 3 can help you identify your computer's storage devices and their uses.

© MediaTechnics

You should use the hard disk to store most of your data; but to transport or back up data, you can use CDs, DVDs, or USB flash drives.

CD drive

CD drives can play CD-ROMs, but can't change the data they contain. CD drives can store data on CD-Rs, CD+Rs, or CD-RWs.

DVD drive

DVD drives play CD-ROMs and DVD-ROMs. Most of today's DVD drives can write data on CD-Rs, CD-RWs, DVD-Rs, and DVD-RWs.

USB flash drive

A USB flash drive is about the size of a highlighter and plugs directly into the computer system unit.

HOW TO TURN YOUR COMPUTER ON AND OFF

▶ How do I turn it on? A notebook computer typically has one switch that turns on the entire system. Look for the switch along the sides of the computer or above the keyboard. When using a desktop computer, turn on the monitor, printer, and speakers before you turn on the system unit.

Most computers take a minute or two to power up, and you might be required to log in by entering a user ID and password. Your computer is ready to use when the Windows or Mac OS desktop (Figure 4 and Figure 5 on the next two pages) appears on the computer screen and you can move the arrow-shaped pointer with your mouse.

▶ How do I turn it off? Your computer is designed to turn itself off after you initiate a shutdown sequence. When using a Windows computer, click the on-screen Start button, select Shut Down or Turn Off Computer, and follow the instructions on the screen. When using a Mac, click the Apple icon in the upper-left corner of the screen and select Shut Down.

After the computer shuts off, you can turn off the monitor, speakers, and printer. When using computers in a school lab, ask about the shutdown procedure. Your lab manager might ask that you log out but do not turn the computer off.

TRY IT!

Turn your computer on

1. Locate the power switch for any devices connected to your computer and turn them on.

2. Locate the power switch for your computer and turn it on.

3. If a message asks for your user ID and/or password, type them in, and then press the **Enter** key on your computer's keyboard.

4. Wait for the desktop to appear.

Orientation

WINDOWS BASICS

▶ **What is Windows?** Microsoft Windows is an example of a type of software called an operating system. The operating system controls all the basic tasks your computer performs, such as running application software, manipulating files on storage devices, and transferring data to and from printers, digital cameras, and other devices. The operating system also controls the user interface—the way software appears on the screen and the way you control what it does.

▶ **What is the Windows desktop?** The Windows desktop is the base of operations for using your computer. It displays small pictures called icons that help you access software, documents, and the components of your computer system. The design of the Windows desktop depends on the version of Windows you're using. Figure 4 shows the important elements of Windows XP, Windows Vista, and Windows 7.

FIGURE 4

Windows desktop components as they appear in Windows XP (top), Windows Vista (middle), and Windows 7 (bottom).

Desktop icons can represent programs, documents, folders, or other electronic tools.

The **taskbar** contains the Start button and Notification area. Taskbar buttons help you keep track of programs that are in use.

The **Start button** displays the Start menu, which lists programs installed on your computer.

The **Start menu** lists application and utility programs installed on your computer.

The **Notification area** displays the current time and the status of programs, devices, and Internet connections.

MAC OS X BASICS

▶ What is Mac OS? Mac OS is the operating system used on many of today's Macintosh computers. The most recent version of this operating system is Mac OS X, featured in Figure 5.

▶ How similar are the Mac and Windows desktops? The Mac and Windows desktops have many similarities, such as the use of icons, menus, and rectangular on-screen windows. However, there are notable differences in the two desktops, such as the Mac desktop's dock, Apple icon, and fixed menu bar. If you switch between computers running Windows and Mac OS X, you should be aware of these differences.

▶ What is the dock? The dock is a collection of icons that represent programs, files, and other activities. Usually the dock is located at the bottom of the screen, but it can be configured to appear on the left side or right side of the screen if that better suits the way you work. You can add icons to the dock for programs you use frequently so they are easily accessible.

▶ What is the Apple icon? The Apple icon is the first icon on the menu bar located at the top of the Mac desktop. It is always visible, regardless of the program you're using. Clicking the Apple icon displays a menu that you can use to configure preferences for your computer display and devices. The Apple icon menu also includes options for logging out and shutting down your computer.

▶ How does the fixed menu bar work? The Mac desktop contains a menu bar that remains at the top of the screen. The options on this menu bar change according to the program you are using. In contrast, the menus for Windows programs are incorporated into individual program windows; so if you have more than one window open, each program window displays a menu.

FIGURE 5

The Mac OS X desktop includes icons, a fixed menu bar, and a dock.

Desktop icons can represent devices, programs, documents, folders, or other electronic tools.

The **dock** displays icons for frequently used programs and files.

The **menu bar** contains the Apple icon and menu options for the active program.

The **Apple icon** is used to display a menu of options for setting preferences, moving the dock, logging in, and shutting down.

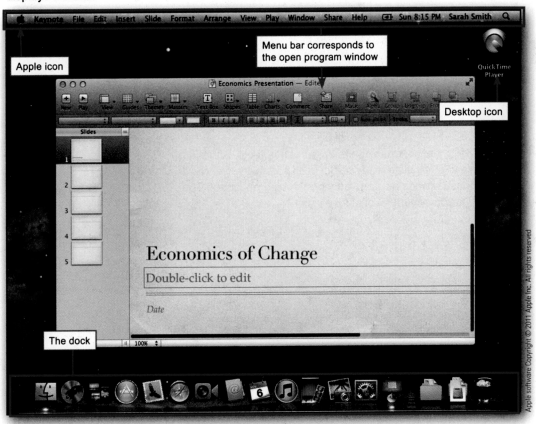

MOUSE BASICS

▶ **What is a mouse?** A mouse is a device used to manipulate items on the screen, such as the buttons and icons displayed on the Windows desktop. The mouse controls an on-screen pointer. The pointer is usually shaped like an arrow ⌖, but it can change to a different shape, depending on the task you're doing. For example, when the computer is busy, the arrow shape turns into an hourglass ⌛ or circle ◯, signifying that you should wait for the computer to finish its current task before attempting to start a new task.

PC-compatible mice have at least two buttons located on top of the mouse. Most mice also include a scroll wheel mounted between the left and right mouse buttons. Your mouse might include additional buttons on the top or sides (Figure 6).

▶ **How do I use a mouse?** Hold the mouse in your right hand as shown in Figure 7. When you drag the mouse from left to right over your mousepad or desk, the arrow-shaped pointer on the screen moves from left to right. If you run out of room to move the mouse, simply pick it up and reposition it. The pointer does not move when the mouse is not in contact with a flat surface.

FIGURE 6

For basic mousing, you only need to use the mouse buttons; but the scroll wheel is also handy.

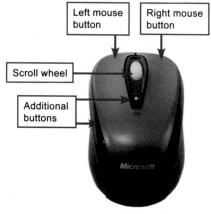

Spike Mafford/Photodisc/Getty Images

There are several ways you can manipulate on-screen objects. Although you might not be able to manipulate every object in all possible ways, you'll soon learn which mouse actions are allowed for each type of control. The following list describes your repertoire of mouse actions.

Action	How to	Result
Click	Press the left mouse button once, and then immediately release it.	Select an object
Double-click	Press the left mouse button twice in rapid succession without moving the body of the mouse.	Activate an object
Right-click	Press the right mouse button once, and then immediately release it.	Display a shortcut menu
Drag	Hold the left mouse button down while you move the mouse.	Move an object

FIGURE 7

Rest the palm of your right hand on the mouse. Position your index finger over the left mouse button and your middle finger over the right mouse button.

TRY IT!

Use your mouse

1. With your computer on and the desktop showing on the screen, move your mouse around on the desk and notice how mouse movements correspond to the movement of the arrow-shaped pointer.

2. Move the mouse to position the pointer on the Start button or Apple icon.

3. Click the left mouse button to open the Start menu or Apple menu.

4. Click the **Start** button or **Apple** icon again to close the Start menu.

KEYBOARD BASICS

▶ What are the important features of a computer keyboard?

You use the computer keyboard to input commands, respond to prompts, and type the text of documents. An insertion point that looks like a flashing vertical bar indicates where the characters you type will appear. You can change the location of the insertion point by using the mouse or the arrow keys. Study Figure 8 for an overview of important computer keys and their functions.

A The **Esc** (Escape) key cancels an operation.

B **Function** keys activate commands, such as Save, Help, and Print. The command associated with each key depends on the software you are using.

C The **Print Screen** key prints the contents of the screen or stores a copy of the screen in memory that you can print or manipulate with graphics software.

D The **Windows** key on a PC opens the Start menu.

E The **Page Up** key displays the previous screen of information. The **Page Down** key displays the next screen of information.

F The **Backspace** key deletes one character to the left of the insertion point.

G The **Insert** key switches between insert mode and typeover mode.

H The **Home** key takes you to the beginning of a line or the beginning of a document, depending on the software you are using.

I The **Tab** key can move your current typing location to the next tab stop or the next text-entry box.

J The **Caps Lock** key capitalizes all the letters you type when it is engaged, but does not produce the top symbol on keys that contain two symbols. This key is a toggle key, which means that each time you press it, you switch between uppercase and lowercase modes.

K The **Shift** key capitalizes letters and produces the top symbol on keys that contain two symbols.

L You hold down the **Ctrl** key while pressing another key. On a Mac, the Command key, marked with an Apple or ⌘ symbol, works the same way. The result of Ctrl or Alt key combinations depends on the software you are using.

M You hold down the **Alt** key while you press another key.

N The **Enter** key is used to indicate that you have completed a command or want to move your typing position down to the next line.

O The **Delete** key deletes the character to the right of the insertion point.

P The **End** key takes you to the end of a line or the end of a document, depending on the software you are using.

Q The **right-click** key accomplishes the same task as right-clicking a mouse button, and usually opens a shortcut menu.

R The **arrow** keys move the insertion point.

S The **numeric keypad** produces numbers or moves the insertion point, depending on the status of the Num Lock key shown by indicator lights or a message on the screen.

© Media Technics

Orientation

What do Alt and Ctrl mean? The Alt and Ctrl keys work with the letter keys. If you see <Ctrl X>, Ctrl+X, [Ctrl X], Ctrl-X, or Ctrl X on the screen or in an instruction manual, it means to hold down the Ctrl key while you press X. For example, Ctrl+X is a keyboard shortcut for clicking the Edit menu, and then clicking the Cut option. A keyboard shortcut allows you to use the keyboard rather than the mouse to select menu commands.

What if I make a mistake? Everyone makes mistakes. The first rule is don't panic! Most mistakes are reversible. The hints and tips in Figure 9 should help you recover from mistakes.

> **TERMINOLOGY NOTE**
>
> Mac keyboard shortcuts use the Command key ⌘ and the Option key ⌥ instead of the Ctrl or Alt keys.

FIGURE 9

Most mistakes are easy to fix.

What Happened	What to Do
Typed the wrong thing	Use the Backspace key to delete the last characters you typed.
Selected the wrong menu	Press the Esc key to close the menu.
Opened a window you didn't mean to	Click the X button in the upper corner of the window.
Computer has "hung up" and no longer responds to mouse clicks or typed commands	Hold down the Ctrl, Shift, and Esc keys, and then follow instructions to close the program.
Pressed the Enter key in the middle of a sentence	Press the Backspace key to paste the sentence back together.

WORKING WITH WINDOWS SOFTWARE

How do I start Windows programs? When using Windows, you can click the Start button to launch just about any software that's installed on your computer. The Start menu includes a list of recently accessed programs. Clicking the All Programs option displays a list of every program installed on your computer. You can run a program from this list simply by clicking it. Follow the instructions in the TRY IT! box to start Microsoft Paint (assuming it is installed on your computer).

TRY IT!

Start Microsoft Paint

1. Make sure your computer is on and it is displaying the Windows desktop.

2. Click the **Start** button to display the Start menu.

3. Click **All Programs** to display a list of all software installed on your computer.

4. Click **Accessories**, and then click **Paint**.

5. Wait a few seconds for your computer to display the main screen for Microsoft Paint, shown below in Windows XP and Vista (top) or Windows 7 (bottom). Leave Paint open for use with the next TRY IT!.

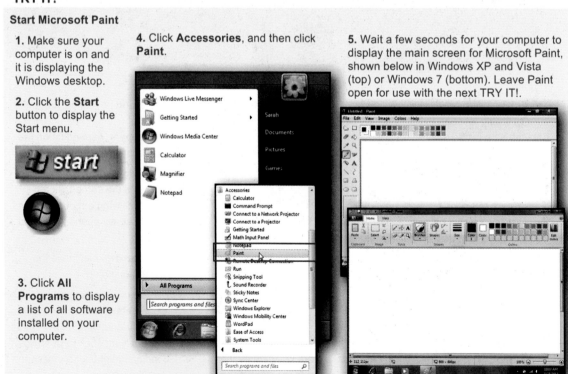

▶ **How do I tell the software what I want to do?** Word processing, photo editing, and other software designed for use on computers running the Windows operating system is referred to as Windows software. Most Windows software works in a fairly uniform way and uses a similar set of controls.

Each software application appears within a rectangular area called a window, which can include a title bar, a menu bar, a ribbon, a workspace, and the various controls shown in Figure 10.

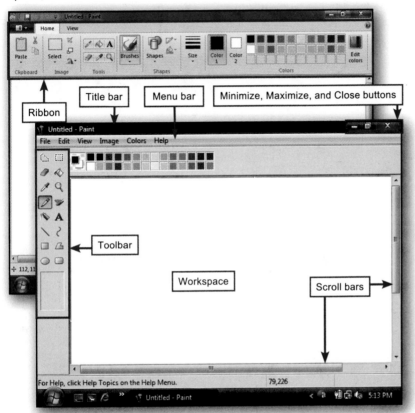

If you're unfamiliar with Windows controls, take a few minutes to complete the steps in the TRY IT! box below.

FIGURE 10

The **title bar** displays the title of the software, the name of the current data file, and the window sizing buttons.

The **Minimize button** shrinks the window to a button at the bottom of the screen.

The **Maximize button** stretches the window to fill the screen.

The **Close button** closes the window and exits the program.

A **menu bar** displays the titles of menus you can click to select commands.

A **toolbar** displays a series of tools for accomplishing various tasks.

A **ribbon** combines the options of a menu and toolbars into a single set of controls.

A **scroll bar** can be clicked or dragged to see any material that does not fit in the displayed window.

The **workspace** is the area in which your document or drawing is displayed.

Orientation

TRY IT!

Use the toolbar or ribbon

1. As shown below, click the **Brushes** button on the Paint toolbar or ribbon.

2. Move the pointer to the workspace, hold down the left mouse button, and drag the mouse to paint a shape.

3. Release the mouse button when the shape is complete.

Use the ribbon or menu bar

1. Click the arrow next to **Rotate**, then click **Flip vertical**.

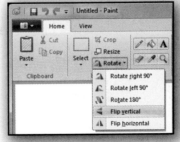

In old versions of Paint, click **Image**, click **Flip/Rotate**, click **Flip Vertical**, then click the **OK** button.

Your shape is now upside down.

Use the sizing buttons

1. Click the [] **Minimize** button.

2. The Paint window shrinks down to a button on the taskbar at the bottom of the screen.

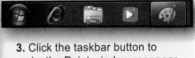

3. Click the taskbar button to make the Paint window reappear.

4. Click the [x] **Close** button to close the Paint program and remove its window from the screen. If you see a message asking if you want to save changes, click the Don't Save button.

WORKING WITH MAC SOFTWARE

▶ **How do I start programs on the Mac?** When using Mac OS X, you can click icons in the dock to easily start programs. For programs that are not in the dock, you can click the Finder icon and then click the Applications option. If you need to brush up on Mac controls, follow the instructions in the TRY IT! box below.

TRY IT!

Find out which programs are in the dock

1. Position the mouse pointer over each of the icons in the dock and wait for the program name to appear.

Use Finder to start a program

1. Click the ⚏ **Finder** icon on the left side of the dock.

2. When the Finder window (similar to the one at right) appears, click the **Applications** option.

3. Double-click the **iCal** option to start the iCal calendar program and display the iCal window shown at right.

Select Applications.

Select iCal.

iCal window

Use a menu and dialog box

1. Click **iCal** on the menu bar at the top of the screen.

2. Click **Preferences** to display a dialog box.

3. Click the ▼ button next to *Start week on* to change the day to Monday.

4. Click the ⊗ **Close** button to close the Preferences dialog box.

Close a program

1. Click **iCal** on the menu bar.

2. Click **Quit iCal** to close the window and terminate the application.

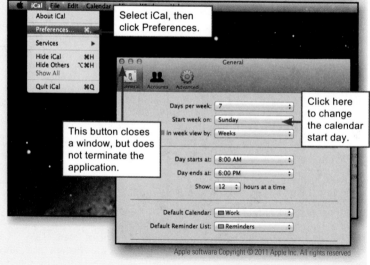

Select iCal, then click Preferences.

This button closes a window, but does not terminate the application.

Click here to change the calendar start day.

HELP

▶ How can I get help using software? If you've had problems using software, you're not alone! Everyone has questions at one time or another. Most software offers several sources of help, such as the following:

▶ **Message boxes.** When using software, it is important to pay attention to any message boxes displayed on the screen. Make sure you carefully read the options they present. If the box doesn't seem to apply to what you want to do, click its Cancel button to close it. Otherwise, set the options the way you want them, and then click the OK button to continue.

▶ **User manual.** Whether you're a beginner or a power user, the manual that comes with software can be an excellent resource. User manuals can contain quick-start guides, tutorials, detailed descriptions of menu options, and tips for using features effectively. Many manuals are offered online along with tools you can use to browse through them or look for the answer to a specific question.

▶ **Help menu.** The Help menu provides access to on-screen documentation, which can contain detailed instructions, tips, and FAQs. Answers to specific questions can be found by entering search terms, consulting the index, or browsing through a table of contents (Figure 11).

FIGURE 11

Clicking the 🔘 Help button or the Help menu produces a list of help options, where you can enter search terms or browse through topics.

Orientation

QuickCheck   SECTION A

1. The case that holds a computer's circuitry and storage devices is called a(n) [   ] unit.

2. Instead of using the on/off switch to turn off a computer, you should instead use the Shut Down option from the Start menu or Apple menu. True or false? [   ]

3. On the Mac desktop, the [   ] displays a row of program icons.

4. Some programs include a ribbon of commands, whereas other programs present commands on a(n) [   ] bar.

5. The [   ] key can be used to delete the last character you typed.

▶ CHECK ANSWERS

Documents, Browsers, and E-mail

TO COMPLETE ASSIGNMENTS for your course, you should be able to work with documents, browsers, and e-mail. Section B walks you through the basics.

CREATING DOCUMENTS

▶ **How do I create and save a document?** To create a document, simply type text in the workspace provided by word processing software such as Microsoft Word, OpenOffice Writer, LibreOffice Writer, or Apple iWork Pages. The flashing vertical insertion point (Figure 12) indicates your place in the document. Figure 13 explains how to save a document.

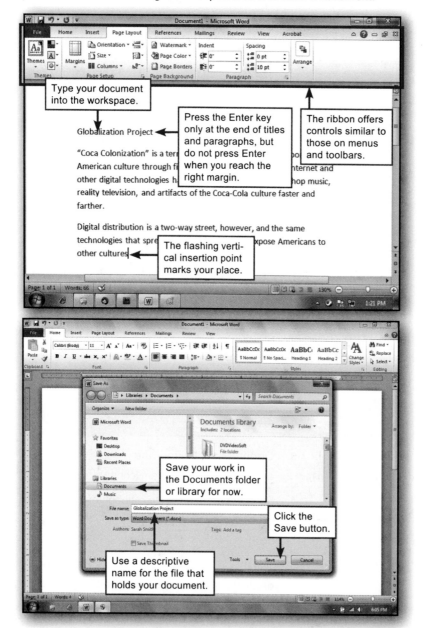

FIGURE 12

When typing text, you can use the following keys to move within a document and make revisions:

▶ **Backspace:** Delete the character to the left of the insertion point. On Macs, hold down the Fn key while pressing the Delete key.

▶ **Delete:** Delete the character to the right of the insertion point.

▶ **Enter:** End a paragraph and begin a new line.

▶ **Arrow keys:** Move the insertion point up, down, right, or left.

FIGURE 13

It is a good idea to save your document every few minutes, even if it is not finished. When you save a document, use the 💾 Save icon at the top of the screen. Your computer is probably configured to save documents on the hard disk in a library called Documents or a folder called My Documents. There is no need to change that until you gain more experience. File names can be several words long; just do not use the * / \ " ' : symbols in the file name.

O-14

FIGURE 14

▶ **How do I print a document?** To print a document, simply click the File tab, File menu, or Office button and then select Print. Your computer displays a window containing a series of print options. If you want to print a single copy of your document, these options should be correct, so you can click the Print or OK button to send your document to the printer.

▶ **Can I send a document to my instructor?** You can e-mail a document by using the Send option accessed from the File tab, File menu, or Office button (Figure 14). To do so, you must know your instructor's e-mail address. Documents that you send along with e-mail messages are referred to as attachments. You'll learn more about e-mail later in the Orientation, but keep this option in mind because it is a handy way to submit assignments, such as projects and term papers.

▶ **How do I find my documents again in the future?** If you want to revise a document sometime in the future, simply start your word processing software; click the File tab, File menu, or Office button; and then click Open. Your computer should display a list of documents stored in the Documents folder. Locate the one you want to revise and double-click it.

▶ **What should I do when I'm done?** When you're ready to quit, you can close the document by clicking the Close option from the File tab, File menu, or Office button. When you want to close your word processing software, click the [X] Close button (Windows) or click the program name on the menu bar and then select Quit (Mac).

To e-mail a document:

▶ In Word 2010, click the File tab, select Save & Send, and then select Send as Attachment (shown below).

▶ In Word 2007, click the Office button, point to Send, and then select E-mail.

▶ In Word 2003, OpenOffice Writer, or LibreOffice Writer, click File, and then select Send or Send To.

▶ In iWork Pages, click the Share tab and then select the e-mail option.

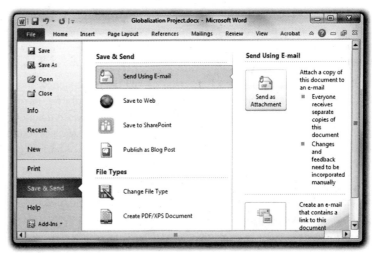

TRY IT!

Create a document

1. Click the **Start** button (Windows), or click the **Finder** icon and select the **Applications** option (Mac).

2. Look for Microsoft Word, LibreOffice Writer, or iWork Pages. Click the name of your word processing software to open it.

3. Click the workspace to position the insertion point in the upper-left corner.

4. Type a paragraph. Refer to Figure 12 for keys to use while typing and revising your work.

5. When the first paragraph is complete, press the **Enter** key to begin a new paragraph.

6. Type a second paragraph of text.

Save a document

1. Click the [icon] **Save** icon located near the top of the window.

2. Make sure the Documents library or folder is selected. If not, click the [▶] button next to your user name at the top of the window and then click the Documents folder from the list. (Or use the [▼] button next to the Save In box to display a list of folders.)

3. In the *File name* box, type a name for your document.

4. Click the **Save** button.

5. When the Save As dialog box closes, your document is saved.

Print a document, close it, and exit your word processing application

1. Click the **File** tab, **File** menu, or **Office** button and then click **Print**.

2. Make sure the page range is set to **All**.

3. Make sure the number of copies is set to **1**.

4. Click the **Print** or **OK** button and wait a few seconds for the printer to produce your document.

5. Close the document by clicking the **File** tab, **File** menu, or **Office** button and then clicking **Close**. The workspace should become blank.

6. Exit your word processing software by clicking the [X] **Close** button (Windows), or by clicking the program name on the menu bar and then selecting **Quit** (Mac).

INTERNET AND WEB BASICS

▶ **What is the Internet?** The Internet is the largest computer network in the world, carrying information from one continent to another in the blink of an eye (Figure 15). The computers connected to this network offer many types of resources, such as e-mail, instant messaging, social networking, popular music downloads, and online shopping.

▶ **What is the Web?** Although some people use the terms *Internet* and *Web* interchangeably, the two are not the same. The Internet refers to a communications network that connects computers all around the globe. The Web—short for World Wide Web—is just one of the many resources available over this communications network.

The Web is a collection of linked and cross-referenced information available for public access. This information is accessible from Web sites located on millions of computers. The information is displayed as a series of screens called Web pages. You'll use the Web for general research and for specific activities designed to accompany this textbook. To use the Web, your computer must have access to the Internet.

▶ **How do I access the Internet?** Most digital devices can be configured to connect to the Internet over telephone, cell phone, satellite, or cable television systems. Internet access can be obtained from school computer labs, local service providers such as your cable television company, and national Internet service providers such as AOL, AT&T, Comcast, Verizon, and EarthLink.

To expedite your orientation, it is assumed that your computer has Internet access. If it does not, consult your instructor, or ask an experienced computer user to help you get set up.

▶ **How do I know if my computer has Internet access?** The easiest way to find out if your computer can access the Internet is to try it. You can quickly find out if you have Internet access by starting software called a browser that's designed to display Web pages.

Browser software called Internet Explorer is supplied with Microsoft Windows. Mac OS X includes a browser called Safari. Other browsers, such as Firefox and Chrome, are also available. Follow the steps in the TRY IT! box to start your browser.

HOW TO USE A WEB BROWSER AND SEARCH ENGINE

▶ **How do I use a browser?** A browser lets you enter a unique Web page address called a URL, such as *www.google.com*. You can also jump from one Web page to another by using links. Links are usually underlined; and when you position the arrow-shaped mouse pointer over a link, it changes to a hand shape.

FIGURE 15

The Internet communications network stretches around the globe.

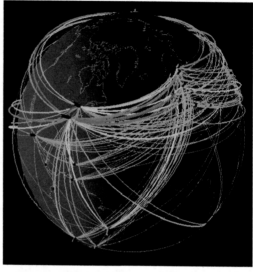

Courtesy of Stephen G. Eick

TRY IT!

Start your browser

1. Click the icon for your browser. It is usually located near the Start button or on the dock.

2. Your computer should soon display the browser window.

If your computer displays a Connect to box, click the **Dial** button to establish a dial-up connection over your telephone line.

You'll need to cancel the browser command and consult an experienced computer user if:

• Your computer displays a "working off line" message.

• Your computer displays an Internet Connection Wizard box.

Although browsers offer many features, you can get along quite well using the basic controls shown in Figure 16.

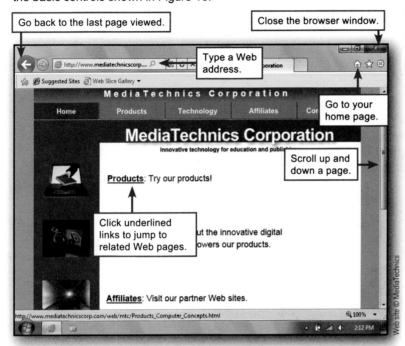

Go back to the last page viewed.

Close the browser window.

Type a Web address.

Go to your home page.

Scroll up and down a page.

Click underlined links to jump to related Web pages.

FIGURE 16

Using a Browser

A full Web address might look like this:

http://www.mediatechnicscorp.com

It is not necessary to type the *http://*. So to access the MediaTechnics Corporation page shown here, you would type:

www.mediatechnicscorp.com

When typing a Web address, do not use any spaces, and copy uppercase and lowercase letters exactly.

▶ **How do I find specific information on the Web?** If you're looking for information and don't know the Web site where it might be located, you can use a search engine to find it. Follow the steps in the TRY IT! box to "google it" by using the Google search engine.

TRY IT!

Use a search engine

1. Make sure the browser window is open.

2. Click the Address box and type:

www.google.com

3. Press the **Enter** key. Your browser displays the Web page for the Google search engine.

4. Click the blank search box and then type **national parks**.

Google™ | Advanced Search Preferences
national parks

5. Press the **Enter** key. Google displays a list of Web pages that relate to national parks.

6. Click the underlined **National Park Service** link. Your browser displays the Park Service's home page.

7. Leave your browser open for the next TRY IT!.

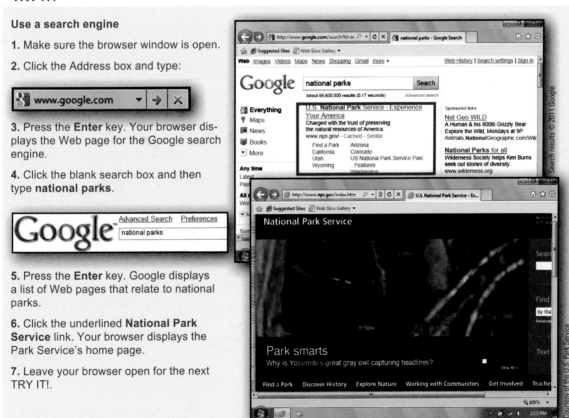

▶ **What are the best sources of information on the Web?**
The best sources of information are easy to access, dependable, and
preferably free. Sites such as Wikipedia, Answers.com, WhatIs.com, and
HowStuffWorks are great sources for general information and researching topics for computer courses.

When you're looking for information on the Web, remember that virtually
anyone can post anything. Consequently, some information you encounter
might not be accurate.

To check the quality of information provided by a Web site, you can cross-
check facts with other sites. Be sure to check when the material was posted
or updated to determine if it is current. You might also consider the information source. Blogs, tweets, Facebook posts, and YouTube videos often
express opinions rather than facts.

▶ **How does Wikipedia work?** Wikipedia is an encyclopedia that is
written and maintained by the people who use it. More than 10 million in-
depth articles on a vast range of topics have been submitted and updated
by users, many of them experts. Wikipedia information tends to be accurate
because users are continually reading the articles and correcting inaccurate or biased information. However, some vandalism occurs and from time
to time a few articles contain false or misleading information.

Most Wikipedia articles include a History tab that tracks changes. Check
the date of the last change to determine if the information is current. Articles
also include a Discussion tab that can help you spot controversial aspects
of the information. Use the TRY IT! below to see how Wikipedia works.

TRY IT!

Check out Wikipedia

1. In the Address bar of your
browser, type **www.wikipedia.
org** and then press the **Enter** key.

2. When the Wikipedia window
appears, enter **cyberspace** in
the search box and then press
Enter.

3. Read a bit of the article to get
an idea of its scope and detail. Do
you detect any bias in the article?

4. Click the **View history** tab.
Look at the last few updates.
Does this
article seem up to date?

5. Click the **Discussion** tab. What
is the status of the article? Does
it contain controversial statements? Can you envision how you
might use Google or other Web
resources to explore specific controversies?

6. Click the **Article** tab to return
to the Cyberspace article.

7. You can leave your browser
open for the next TRY IT!.

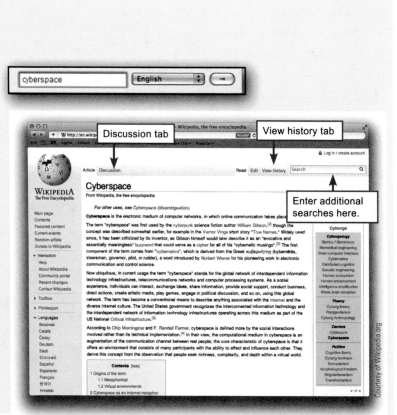

WORKING WITH E-MAIL

▶ **What is e-mail?** E-mail is a form of communication that relies on computer networks, such as the Internet, to transmit messages from one computer to another. Like regular mail, e-mail messages are sent to a mailbox where they are kept until the recipient retrieves the message. Messages might arrive at their destination within seconds, or might not arrive for a few hours. Once sent, e-mail messages cannot be recalled.

▶ **What do I need to use e-mail?** To send and receive e-mail, you need an Internet connection, an e-mail account, and software that enables you to compose, read, and delete e-mail messages. An e-mail account consists of an e-mail address (Figure 17), a password, and a mailbox. You can usually obtain an e-mail account from your Internet service provider, your school, or a Webmail provider, such as Hotmail, Yahoo! Mail, or Gmail.

Webmail providers store your mail online. To access your mail, simply use your browser. In contrast, local mail, such as Microsoft Outlook, transfers mail to your computer and requires you to use special e-mail software instead of a browser.

▶ **How do I get a Webmail account?** Registering for a Webmail account is easy and many online e-mail providers offer free basic service. Work with the TRY IT! below to see how.

FIGURE 17

E-mail Addresses

An e-mail address consists of a user ID followed by an @ symbol and the name of a computer that handles e-mail accounts. Ask your instructor for his or her e-mail address. It is likely similar to the following:

instructor@school.edu

When typing an e-mail address, use all lowercase letters and do not use any spaces.

TRY IT!

Get a Web-based e-mail account

1. In the Address bar of your browser, enter **www.gmail.com**.

2. When the Gmail window appears, click the button labeled **Create an account**.

3. Follow the directions to enter your first name, last name, and login name.

4. Click the **check availability!** button. If the login name you want is already in use, you'll have to try a different one, again clicking the **check availability!** button.

5. When you've selected a valid login name, continue down the page to create a password. Try not to use a name, date, or any dictionary word as your password.

6. Continue down the page to complete the rest of the registration form.

7. Before finalizing your registration, review the information you've entered and jot down your login name and password.

8. Read the Terms of Service. If you agree, click the **I accept** button. That's it! You now have a Gmail account.

New to Gmail? It's free and easy.

Create an account »

About Gmail   New features!

Get started with Gmail

First name: John
Last name: Adams
Desired Login Name: JohnXAdams @gmail.com
Examples: JSmith, John.Smith
(check availability!)

You might have to try several login names to find one that is available.

JohnXAdams is available

Choose a password: ••••••••••   Password strength: **Strong**
Minimum of 8 characters in length.
Re-enter password: ••••••••••

Try to choose a strong password.

☑ Remember me on this computer.

Creating a Google Account will enable Web History. Web History is a feature that will provide you with a more personalized experience on Google that includes more relevant search results and recommendations. Learn More
☐ Enable Web History.

You can uncheck this box for better privacy.

By clicking on 'I accept' below you are agreeing to the Terms of Service above and both the Program Policy and the Privacy Policy.

(I accept. Create my account.)

Orientation

▶ **Is Webmail better than local e-mail?** Both Web-based and local e-mail have their advantages and disadvantages. Webmail accounts are definitely easier to set up and you can use them from any computer with an Internet connection. Webmail accounts are also ideal for "throw-away" accounts.

▶ **What is a throw-away e-mail account?** Whether you use local mail or Webmail for your regular correspondence, you might consider creating one or two throw-away accounts for occasions when you have to give an e-mail address, but you don't want any continued correspondence from that source. Later in the chapter, you'll learn more about how e-mail scams and online marketing contribute to all the junk e-mail you receive. Your throw-away e-mail address can become the recipient for lots of those messages, and eventually you can simply delete the throw-away account and all the junk it contains.

▶ **How do I create and send an e-mail message?** Many e-mail systems are available, and each uses slightly different software, making it impossible to cover all options in this short orientation. You might want to enlist the aid of an experienced computer user to help you get started. The steps in the TRY IT! box pertain to Gmail, but other e-mail packages work in a similar way.

> ### E-MAIL PRIVACY
>
> E-mail messages are not necessarily private; their contents might be seen during system maintenance or repair, and commercial e-mail archives are subject to search by government agencies.
>
> Free Web-based mail is typically searched as you write it by digital bots that look for keywords, like *vacation* or *pet*, to display related advertising. If you want more privacy, consider private e-mail providers and local e-mail software.

TRY IT!

Create and send e-mail

1. If Gmail is not open, open your browser and type **www.gmail.com** in the address box. Log in to your Gmail account.

2. Click the **Compose Mail** button to display a form like the one below.

3. Follow steps 4 through 6 as shown below.

7. When your message is complete, click the **Send** button and Gmail sends the message.

8. You can continue to experiment with e-mail. When done, use the **Sign out** option under the link for your user name, then close your browser.

Note: With some local e-mail configurations, the Send button places the e-mail in an Outbox and you have to click the **Send/Receive** button on the toolbar to ship the message out from your computer.

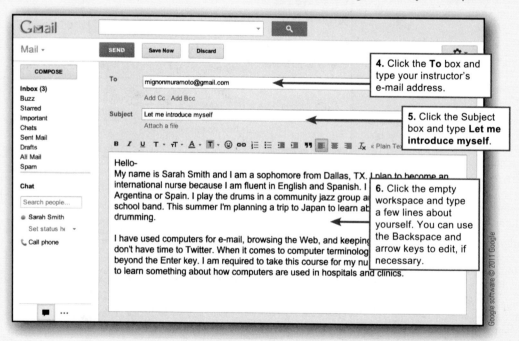

4. Click the **To** box and type your instructor's e-mail address.

5. Click the Subject box and type **Let me introduce myself**.

6. Click the empty workspace and type a few lines about yourself. You can use the Backspace and arrow keys to edit, if necessary.

Google software © 2011 Google

▶ **How do I get my e-mail?** As with sending mail, the way you get mail depends on your e-mail system. In general, clicking the Send/Receive button collects your mail from the network and stores it in your Inbox. Your e-mail software displays a list of your messages. The new ones are usually shown highlighted or in bold type. You can click any message to open it, read it, and reply to it, as shown in Figure 18.

▶ **How do I log off?** When working with a Webmail account, it is important to use the Log out or Sign out link before you close your browser. Taking this extra step makes your e-mail less vulnerable to hackers.

FIGURE 18

When e-mail software displays your Inbox, you can:

▶ Open a message and read it.

▶ Reply to a message.

▶ Delete unwanted messages (a good idea to minimize the size of your mailbox).

▶ Forward a message to someone else.

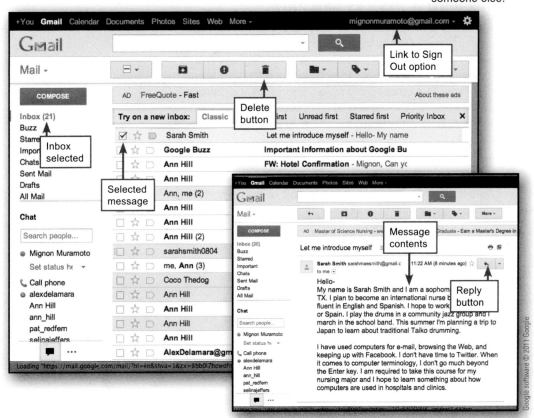

Orientation

QuickCheck

1. Documents that you send along with e-mail messages are referred to as [＿＿＿＿] .

2. Popular [＿＿＿＿] software includes Internet Explorer, Chrome, and Firefox.

3. When looking for information on the Web, you can use a(n) [＿＿＿＿] engine to produce a list of links to Web pages that might contain the information you seek.

4. An e-mail [＿＿＿＿] looks something like student@school.edu.

5. To access Webmail, you use a browser; but to access [＿＿＿＿] e-mail, you use e-mail software such as Microsoft Outlook.

 CHECK ANSWERS

Security and Privacy

AS WITH MOST OTHER facets of modern life, the digital world has its share of troublemakers, scam artists, and identity thieves. Section C offers some tips on navigating through the sometimes rough neighborhoods of cyberspace, while keeping your data safe and your identity private.

SECURING YOUR DIGITAL DEVICES AND DATA

▶ **What's at risk if my computer or phone is stolen?** The value of a stolen computer or phone is not so much in the hardware as in the data it contains. With stolen data such as your bank account numbers and PINs, a thief can wipe out your checking and savings accounts. With your credit card numbers, a thief can go on a spending spree. Even worse, a criminal can use stolen data to assume your identity, run up debts, get into legal difficulties, ruin your credit rating, and cause you no end of trouble.

▶ **How can I protect my data from theft?** Never leave your devices unattended. If a thief steals your computer or phone, you can make it difficult to access your data by setting up a password. Until the password is entered, your data is off limits. Thieves will not be able to get beyond the login screen and should not be able to easily access your data.

Use security tools to protect your phone. Keep it locked while not in use and consider subscribing to a tracking service that allows you to use a Web site to find your phone, lock it, or erase it.

Many new computers are shipped with a standard administrator password that everyone knows. If you are the only person using your computer, you can use the administrator account for your day-to-day computing, but create a secure password (Figure 19) for this account as soon as you can.

Your computer might also include a preset guest account with a nonsecure password such as *guest*. You should disable this guest account or assign it a secure password.

FIGURE 19

To create a secure password:

▶ Use at least eight characters, mixing numbers with letters, as in *2by4lumber*.

▶ Do not use your name, the name of a family member, or your pet's name.

▶ Do not use a word that can be found in the dictionary.

▶ Do not forget your password!

TRY IT!

Check the accounts on your computer

1. To access accounts on Windows, click the **Start** button, then select **Control Panel**.

For Windows Vista and Windows 7, select **User Accounts and Family Safety**, select **User Accounts**, and then select **Manage another account**. (You might be required to enter an administrator password.) For Windows XP, select **User Accounts**.

On a Mac, click the **Apple** icon, select **System Preferences**, and **Accounts**.

2. Check the password protection on all accounts. If you are working on a school lab computer, do not make changes to the account settings. If you are using your own computer, click the Administrator account and make sure it has a secure password.

AVOIDING VIRUSES

▶ **What's so bad about viruses?** The term *virus* has a technical meaning, but is loosely used when referring to malicious programs that circulate on infected downloads, in e-mail attachments, and on the Internet. This malware, as it is sometimes called, can steal your data, destroy files, or create network traffic jams. It might display an irritating message to announce its presence, or it might work quietly behind the scenes to spread itself to various files or mail itself out to everyone in your e-mail address book.

After a virus takes up residence in a computer or phone, it is often difficult to disinfect all your files. Rather than wait for a virus attack, you can take steps to keep your digital devices virus free.

▶ **How can I steer clear of malware?** It helps to avoid risky behaviors, such as downloading pirated software, opening e-mail attachments from unknown senders, installing random social networking plug-ins, installing non-approved apps, and participating in illegal file sharing.

Antivirus software protects digital devices from malware (Figure 20). Because fewer viruses target Macs, OS X users who don't engage in risky online activities sometimes opt to work without antivirus software.

If you use antivirus software, configure it to run continuously whenever your computer is on. You should make sure your antivirus software is set to scan for viruses in incoming files and e-mail messages. At least once a week, your antivirus software should run a full system check to make sure every file on your computer is virus free.

As new viruses emerge, your antivirus software needs to update its virus definition file. It gets this update as a Web download. If you've selected the auto update option, your computer should automatically receive updates as they become available.

FIGURE 20

Popular Antivirus Software

Norton AntiVirus Plus
McAfee VirusScan
Kaspersky Anti-Virus
F-Secure Anti-virus
Panda Antivirus
Trend Micro Antivirus
AVG Anti-Virus
avast! Free Antivirus

TRY IT!

Get familiar with your antivirus software

1. In Windows, click the **Start** button, and then select **All Programs**. On the Mac, use **Finder** to access the Applications folder. Look for antivirus software (refer to Figure 20 for a list). Open your antivirus software by clicking it.

Can't find any? If you are using your own computer and it doesn't seem to have antivirus software, you can connect to an antivirus supplier's Web site and download it.

2. Each antivirus program has unique features. The figure on the right shows the main screen for avast! Free Antivirus software. Explore your antivirus software to make sure it is configured to do the following:

• Scan incoming e-mail.

• Run continuously in the background—a feature sometimes called Auto Protect.

• Block malicious scripts.

3. Check the date of your last full system scan. If it was more than one week ago, you should check the settings that schedule antivirus scans.

4. Check the date when your computer last received virus definitions. If it was more than one week ago, you should make sure your antivirus software is configured to receive automatic live updates.

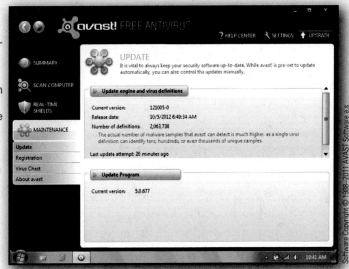

Orientation

PREVENTING INTRUSIONS

▶ Is the Internet risky? The Internet offers lots of cool stuff: music, movies, online shopping and banking, and much more. Most Internet offerings are legitimate, but some downloads contain viruses, and shady characters called hackers control programs that lurk about waiting to infiltrate your digital devices. If a hacker gains access to your phone or computer, he or she can look through your files and steal personal information.

An infiltrated computer can be used as a launching platform for viruses and network-jamming attacks, or turned into a server for pornography and other unsavory material. Hackers have even found ways to turn thousands of infiltrated computers into "zombies," link them together, and carry out coordinated attacks to disrupt online access to Microsoft, Bank of America, and other Internet businesses.

▶ How do hackers gain access? Intruders gain access by exploiting security flaws in your device's operating system, browser, and e-mail software. Companies, such as Microsoft, Apple, and HTC, constantly produce software updates to fix these flaws. As part of your overall security plan, you should download and install security updates as they become available.

▶ Do I need a firewall? Firewall software and Internet security suites, such as those listed in Figure 21, provide a protective barrier between a computer and the Internet. If your computer is directly connected to the Internet, it should have active firewall software. If your computer connects to a local area network for Internet access, the network should have a device called a router to block infiltration attempts.

When a firewall is active, it watches for potentially disruptive incoming data called probes. When a probe is discovered, your firewall displays a warning and asks what to do. If the source looks legitimate, you can let it through; if not, you should block it (Figure 22).

▶ Where do I get a firewall? Mac OS X and Windows include built-in firewalls. Third-party Internet security suites also include firewall modules.

FIGURE 21

Popular Firewall Software and Internet Security Suites

Emsisoft Online Armor

McAfee Internet Security

ZoneAlarm Internet Security

Norton Internet Security

Mac OS X Firewall

Agnitum Outpost Firewall

Windows Firewall

Comodo Firewall Pro

Kaspersky Internet Security

Trend Micro Titanium Internet Security

FIGURE 22

When your firewall software encounters new or unusual activity, it asks you what to do.

TRY IT!

Check your Windows computer's firewall

1. Click the **Start** button, then click **Control Panel**. For Windows Vista, click the **Security** link; for Windows 7, click the **System and Security** link; or for Windows XP, double-click the **Security Center** icon. Click the **Windows Firewall** link.

2. If the Windows firewall is not active, you should check to see if a third-party firewall is protecting your computer.

3. Click the **Start** button, click **All Programs**, and then look through the program list for firewalls such as those in Figure 21. If you find a firewall listed, start it and explore to see if it has been activated.

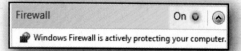

Check your Mac computer's firewall

1. Click the **Apple** icon, and then select **System Preferences**.

2. Click the **Security** icon and then click the **Firewall** button.

3. If the firewall is off, click the Start button if you want to activate it.

4. If the Start button is grayed out, click the lock at the bottom of the page and then enter an administrator name and password.

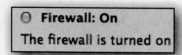

BLOCKING SPYWARE AND POP-UP ADS

▶ **Are some Web sites dangerous?** When you access Web sites, data is transferred to your device and displayed by your browser. Most of this data is harmless, but malicious HTML scripts, rogue ActiveX components, and spyware have the potential to search your device for passwords and credit card numbers, monitor your Web-browsing habits for marketing purposes, block your access to legitimate Web sites, or surreptitiously use your device as a staging area for illicit activities.

Spyware is the most insidious threat. It often piggybacks on pop-up ads and activates if you click the ad window. Some spyware can begin its dirty work when you try to click the Close button to get rid of an ad.

▶ **How can I block spyware?** The first line of defense is to never click pop-up ads—especially those with dire warnings, such as those in Figure 23, about your computer being infected by a virus or spyware! To close an ad, right-click its button on the taskbar at the bottom of your screen, and then select the Close option from the menu that appears. Most browsers can be configured to block spyware and pop-up ads (Figure 24). Your antivirus software might offer similar options.

▶ **What other steps can I take to browse the Web safely?** Most browsers include security features. You should take some time to become familiar with them. For example, Internet Explorer allows you to specify how you want it to deal with ActiveX components. You can also specify how to deal with HTML scripts, cookies, security certificates, and other Web-based data. If you don't want to be bothered by these details, however, Internet Explorer offers several predefined configurations for Medium, Medium-High, and High security. Most Internet Explorer users set security and privacy options to Medium-High.

FIGURE 23

Some pop-up ads contain fake warnings about viruses, spyware, and intrusion attempts.

FIGURE 24

Check your browser's settings to make sure it is blocking pop-up ads.

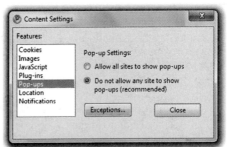

TRY IT!

Check Internet security and privacy options

1. Start your browser and look for its security settings.

Internet Explorer: Click **Tools**, then select **Internet Options**. Click the **Security** tab. Normally, your security setting should be Medium High. Click the **Privacy** tab. Your privacy setting should be Medium. If your version of IE offers a Pop-up Blocker, make sure its box contains a check mark so that it is activated.

Firefox: Click **Tools**, select **Options**, and then click **Content**. Make sure there is a check mark in the box for **Block pop-up windows**.

Safari: Click **Safari** on the menu bar. Make sure there is a check mark next to **Block Pop-Up Windows**.

Chrome: Click the **Wrench** (Tools) icon, select **Options**, and then click **Under the Hood** and click the **Content settings** button. Under Pop-ups, make sure that the **Do not allow** option is selected.

2. If your browser does not seem to offer antispyware and pop-up blocking, you can use the Start button to see if one of the security suites listed in Figure 21 has been installed. If your computer seems to have no antispyware or ad-blocking software, you might want to download some and install it.

PROTECTING E-COMMERCE TRANSACTIONS

▶ Is online shopping safe? Online shopping is generally safe. From time to time, shoppers encounter fake storefronts designed to look like legitimate merchants but that are actually set up to steal credit card information. You can avoid these fakes by making sure you enter correctly spelled URLs when connecting to your favorite shopping sites.

▶ How safe is my credit card information when I'm shopping online? Online shopping has about the same level of risk as using your credit card for a telephone order or giving it to a server when you've finished eating in a restaurant. Anyone who handles your card can copy the card number, jot down the expiration date, and try to make unauthorized charges.

That's not to say that credit cards are risk free. Credit cards are surprisingly vulnerable both online and off. Thieves can break in to merchant computers that store order information. Thieves might even pick up your credit card information from discarded order forms. Despite these risks, we continue to use credit cards.

Many people are concerned about their credit card data getting intercepted as it travels over the Internet. As you wrap up an online purchase and submit your credit card information, it is transmitted from your computer to the merchant's computer. Software called a packet sniffer, designed for legitimately monitoring network traffic, can be used by unscrupulous hackers to intercept credit card numbers and other data traveling over the Internet.

▶ How can I keep my credit card number confidential? When you submit credit card information, make sure the merchant provides a secure connection for transporting data. Normally, a secure connection is activated when you're in the final phases of checking out—as you enter your shipping and credit card information into a form and click a Submit button to send it.

A secure connection encrypts your data. Even if your credit card number is intercepted, it cannot be deciphered and used. To make sure you have a secure connection, look for the lock icon. The Address box should also display a URL that begins with *https://* (Secure HTTP) or contains *ssl* (Secure Sockets Layer).

TRY IT!

Identify a secure connection

1. Start your browser and connect to the site **www.bestbuy.com**.

2. Select any item and use the **Add to Cart** button to place it in your online shopping cart.

3. Click the **Checkout** button, then at the next screen click the **Checkout as Guest** button to reach the screen where you enter your billing information.

4. At the Billing Address screen, do you see any evidence that you're using a secure connection?

5. Close your browser so that you don't complete the transaction.

AVOIDING E-MAIL SCAMS

▶ **What are e-mail scams?** From time to time, you hear about con artists who have bilked innocent consumers out of their life savings. The Internet has its share of con artists, too, who run e-mail scams designed to collect money and confidential information from unsuspecting victims. E-mail scams are usually distributed in mass mailings called spam.

▶ **What do I need to know about spam?** The Internet makes it easy and cheap to send out millions of e-mail solicitations. In the United States, the CAN-SPAM Act requires mass-mail messages to be labeled with a valid subject line. Recipients are supposed to be provided with a way to opt out of receiving future messages.

Legitimate merchants and organizations comply with the law when sending product announcements, newsletters, and other messages. Unscrupulous spammers ignore the law and try to disguise their solicitations as messages from your friends, chat room participants, or co-workers (Figure 25).

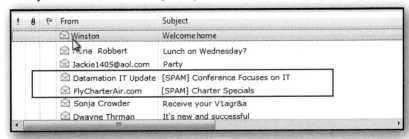

FIGURE 25

Some e-mail systems use spam filters to flag suspected spam by adding [SPAM] to the subject line. Spam filters are not perfect, however. Some spam is not flagged and occasionally legitimate mail is mistaken for spam.

▶ **Is spam dangerous?** Some mass mailings contain legitimate information, including daily or weekly newsletters to which you've subscribed. Many mass mailings, however, advertise illegal products. Others are outright scams to get you to download a virus, divulge your bank account numbers, or send in money for products you'll never receive.

Beware of e-mail containing offers that seem just too good to be true. Messages about winning the sweepstakes or pleas for help to transfer money out of Nigeria (Figure 26) are scams to raid your bank account.

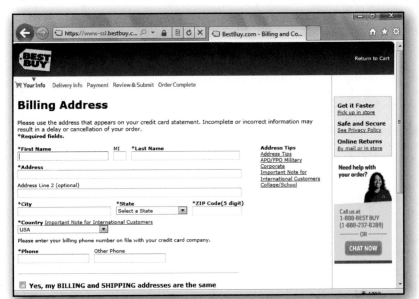

FIGURE 26

Many variations of this African money-transfer fraud—complete with deliberate grammatical errors—have circulated on the Internet for years. Victims who respond to these preposterous e-mails have found their bank accounts raided, their credit ratings destroyed, and their reputations ruined. According to the FBI, some victims have even been kidnapped!

Orientation

▶ What's phishing? Phishing (pronounced "fishing") is a scam that arrives in your e-mailbox looking like official correspondence from a major company, such as Microsoft, PayPal, eBay, MSN, Yahoo!, or AOL. The e-mail message is actually from an illegitimate source and is designed to trick you into divulging confidential information or downloading a virus.

Links in the e-mail message often lead to a Web site that looks official, where you are asked to enter confidential information such as your credit card number, Social Security number, or bank account number.

The following are examples of phishing scams you should be aware of:

▶ A message from Microsoft with an attachment that supposedly contains a security update for Microsoft Windows. Downloading the attachment infects your computer with a virus.

▶ A message that appears to come from PayPal, complete with official-looking logos, that alerts you to a problem with your account. When you click the Billing Center link and enter your account information, it is transmitted to a hacker's computer.

▶ A message that's obviously spam, but contains a convenient opt-out link. If you click the link believing that it will prevent future spam from this source, you'll actually be downloading a program that hackers can use to remotely control your computer for illegal activities.

▶ How do I avoid e-mail scams? If your e-mail software provides spam filters, you can use them to block some unsolicited mail from your e-mailbox. Spam filters are far from perfect, however, so don't assume everything that gets through is legitimate. Use your judgment before opening any e-mail message or attachment.

Never reply to a message that you suspect to be fraudulent. If you have a question about its legitimacy, check whether it's on a list of known scams. Never click a link provided in an e-mail message to manage any account information. Instead, use your browser to go directly to the company's Web site and access your account as usual. Microsoft never sends updates as attachments. To obtain Microsoft updates, go to *www.microsoft.com* and click the Security button, then select Security & Updates.

TRY IT!

Arm yourself against e-mail scams

1. Start your browser and connect to the site **www.millersmiles.co.uk**. Browse through the list of recent phishing attacks.

2. Open your e-mail software and find out if it includes spam filters. You can usually find this information by clicking **Help** on the menu bar and then typing **spam filter** in the search box.

3. Explore your options for configuring spam filters. If you use Windows Live Mail, you can find these settings by clicking the **Menus** button and then clicking **Safety options**. Check the settings for spam filters on the Options tab (shown at right), and then check the settings on the Phishing tab.

Spam filters sometimes catch legitimate mail and group it with junk mail. You might want to keep tabs on your spam filters when they are first activated to make sure they are set to a level that eliminates most unwanted spam without catching too much legitimate mail.

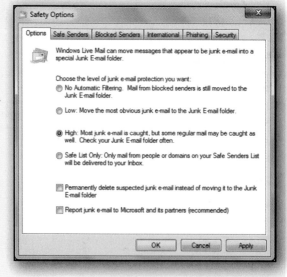

PROTECTING YOUR PRIVACY

▶ **How much information about me has been collected online?** Information about you is stored in many places and has the potential to be consolidated by government agencies, private businesses, and criminals. Some databases are legitimate—those maintained by credit bureaus and medical insurance companies, for example. By law, you have the right to ask for a copy of these records and correct any errors you find. Many other databases, such as those maintained at e-commerce sites and those illegally acquired by hackers, are not accessible, and you have no way of checking the data they contain.

▶ **What's the problem with having my personal information in a few databases?** The problem is that many companies share their databases with third parties. Your personal data might start in a single legitimate database, but that data can be sold to a continuous chain of third parties who use it to generate mass mailings that clog up your Inbox with marketing ploys, unwanted newsletters, and promotions for useless products.

▶ **Can I control who collects information about me?** To some extent, you can limit your exposure to future data collection by supplying personal data only when absolutely necessary. When filling out online forms, consider whether you want to or need to provide your real name and address. Avoid providing merchants with your e-mail address even if you're promised a $5 coupon or preferred customer status. A small reward might not be worth the aggravation of an Inbox brimming with spam and e-mail scams. You should also be careful when using public computers (Figure 27).

▶ **Can I opt out?** Some mass e-mailings give you a chance to opt out so that you don't receive future messages. Opting out is a controversial practice. On mailings from reputable businesses, clicking an opt-out link might very well discontinue unwanted e-mail messages. However, opting out does not necessarily remove your name from the database, which could be sold to a third party that disregards your opt-out request.

Scammers use opt-out links to look for "live" targets, perhaps in a database that contains lots of fake or outdated e-mail addresses. By clicking one of these opt-out links, you've played right into the hands of unscrupulous hackers—this action lets them know that your e-mail address is valid.

Most experts recommend that you never use opt-out links, but instead go to the sender's Web site and try to opt out from there. If you are tempted to use an opt-out link directly from an e-mail message, carefully examine the link's URL to make sure you'll connect to a legitimate Web site.

TRY IT!

Check your privacy

1. Start your browser and go googling by connecting to **www.google.com**. Enter your name in the Search box. What turns up?

2. Connect to **www.peopledata.com**. Enter your name and state of residence. Click the **Search** button. Notice all the information that's offered.

3. Connect to **www.ciadata.com** and scroll down the page to view the kind of information anyone can obtain about you for less than $100.

4. Read about your rights to view credit reports at the Federal Trade Commission site:
    www.ftc.gov/bcp/menus/consumer/credit/rights.shtm

FIGURE 27

Using public computers poses security risks from people looking over your shoulder, spyware that collects your keystrokes, and the footprint you leave behind in cookies and temporary Internet pages.

AP Photo/Darren Hauck

To minimize risks when using public computers:

▶ Be sure to log out from all sites and close all browser windows before quitting.

▶ Delete cookies and browser history.

▶ Avoid using public computers for financial transactions such as filing your taxes.

▶ Reboot the computer before you quit.

▶ If you're using your own portable apps from a USB drive, make sure your computer is running antivirus software.

Orientation

SAFE SOCIAL NETWORKING

▶ What's the risk at sites like Twitter, Facebook, and LinkedIn? A prolific Twitter user with 650 followers had a nasty surprise one morning. She discovered that private messages she'd sent to specific friends were showing up on her public feed for everyone to see. Although this is an extreme example of how things can go wrong on social networking sites, embarrassing incidents are all too frequent.

The more information you reveal at social networking sites, the more you increase your susceptibility to identity theft, stalking, and other embarrassing moments, such as when a prospective employer happens to see those not-so-flattering photos of you on your spring break.

▶ How do I stay safe and keep my stuff private when using social networking sites? The first rule of social networking safety is never share your Social Security number, phone number, or home address. Unfortunately, everyone has access to Web-based tools for finding addresses and phone numbers, so withholding that information provides only a thin security blanket.

Most social networking sites depend on references and friends-of-friends links to establish a trusted circle of contacts. *Trusted* is the key word here. When using social networking sites, make sure you understand what information is being shared with friends, what information is available to strangers on the site, and what data is available publicly to search engines.

Be careful about revealing personal information at social networking sites, blogs, chat rooms, and Twitter. Many online participants are not who they appear to be. Some people are just having fun with fantasy identities, but others are trying to con people by telling hard luck stories and faking illnesses. Resist the temptation to meet face to face with people you've met online without taking precautions, such as taking along a group of friends.

▶ And what about the site itself? Social networking sites, like any online business, are always looking for ways to make a profit. Every participant is a valuable commodity in a database that can be used for marketing and research. Before you become a member, read the site's privacy policy to see how your personal data could be used. Remember, however, that privacy policies can change, especially if a site goes out of business and sells its assets.

You should also find out if you can remove your data from a site. Although most sites allow you to deactivate your information, some sites never actually remove your personal information from their databases, leaving it open to misuse in the future.

TRY IT!

Check your social networking sites

1. Log in to any social networking site you use.

2. Locate the site's privacy policy and read it. Are you comfortable with the ways in which the site protects your personal information?

3. If you are not familiar with the site's options for designating who can view your personal data, find out how you can limit its public exposure.

4. Find out if you can delete your data from the site.

ONLINE PRIVACY AND SAFETY GUIDELINES

▶ **What should I do?** Online safety and privacy are an important aspect of computer use today. The average consumer has to remain constantly vigilant to detect if his or her personal data has been misused or has fallen into the wrong hands.

Cyberthreats are becoming more troubling. Who would imagine that the webcam at the top of your notebook computer screen could be remotely controlled by hackers to capture video of you without your knowledge?

If you recognize that anything on the Web or in e-mail messages is not necessarily private, you've got the right outlook. You can use the guidelines in Figure 28 to keep track of your personal data and stay safe online.

FIGURE 28

Online Privacy and Safety Guidelines

▶ Use a password to protect your data in case your computer is stolen.

▶ Don't leave your digital devices unattended in public places.

▶ Run antivirus software and keep it updated.

▶ Install software service packs and security patches as they become available, but make sure they are legitimate.

▶ Install and activate firewall software, especially if your computer is directly connected to the Internet by an ISDN, DSL, satellite, or cable connection.

▶ Do not publish or post personal information, such as your physical address, passwords, Social Security number, phone number, or account numbers, on your Web site, in your online resume, in your blog, or in other online documents.

▶ Be wary of contacts you make in public chat rooms and social networking sites.

▶ Don't click pop-up ads.

▶ Install and activate antispyware and ad-blocking software.

▶ Do not reply to spam.

▶ Ignore e-mail offers that seem too good to be true.

▶ Establish a throw-away e-mail account and use it when you have to provide your e-mail address to marketers and other entities whom you don't want to regularly correspond with.

▶ Make sure you control who has access to the data you post at social networking sites.

▶ Do not submit data to a social networking site until you've read its privacy policy and have made sure that you can remove your data when you no longer want to participate.

▶ Avoid using opt-out links in mass mailings unless you are certain the sender is legitimate.

▶ When using public computers, avoid financial transactions if possible. Make sure you log out from password-protected sites. Delete cookies and Internet history. Reboot the computer at the end of your session.

▶ Regard e-mail messages as postcards that can be read by anyone, so be careful what you write!

▶ Cover the webcam on your computer with a piece of tape when it is not in use.

Orientation

QuickCheck

1. Internet security suites usually include antivirus and antispyware tools. True or false? [_____]

2. [_____] software can block intrusion attempts such as hacker probes.

3. Most Web browsers include settings for blocking pop-up ads. True or false? [_____]

4. E-mail scams are usually distributed in mass mailings called [_____].

5. Using opt-out links is the most secure and dependable way to reduce the amount of spam you receive. True or false? [_____]

 CHECK ANSWERS

eBook CD

ELECTRONIC VERSIONS of your textbook are designed to be portable, interactive learning environments. This section offers a hands-on overview of the popular NP2013 interactive eBook CD.

EBOOK CD BASICS

▶ **What is the eBook CD?** The eBook CD is a multimedia version of your textbook with photos that come to life as videos, diagrams that become animations, screenshots that open to guided software tours, and computer-scored activities that can help improve your test scores.

▶ **What's the most effective way to use the eBook CD?** You can use the eBook CD in place of a printed textbook for all of your reading and studying. As you work through a chapter, you'll be able to view the multimedia elements in context and take QuickChecks at the end of each section. If your eBook CD is bundled with a printed book, you can use them interchangeably. Each page in the eBook CD is the same as the corresponding page in the printed textbook.

▶ **How do I start the eBook CD?** To start the eBook CD on any Windows computer, follow the instructions in the TRY IT! box below. If you have an OS X Mac, skip to the instructions on the next page.

> **QUESTIONS?**
>
> Additional FAQs about the eBook CD are posted at *www.infoweblinks.com* under the Technical Support link. You'll find information on topics such as what to do if the CD doesn't start, and how to use the eBook CD in a computer without a CD drive.

TRY IT!

Start the eBook CD

1. Insert the eBook CD into your computer's CD or DVD drive, label side up.

2. Wait a few seconds until the eBook CD has loaded.

3. When the main Computer Concepts screen appears, proceed to step 4.
- If an Autoplay box appears, select *Run eBook CD.exe*.
- If the CD does not start automatically, click the Start button, click Computer, and then double-click the CD or DVD drive icon.

The eBook CD allows you to save your scores for QuickChecks, practice tests, and other activities, but for this session you do not need to track this data.

4. To disable tracking for now, make sure the box next to *Save Tracking data* is empty. If the box contains a check mark, click the box to empty it.

5. Click the **OK** button. The Tracking Options dialog box closes and the eBook CD displays the first page of Chapter 1.

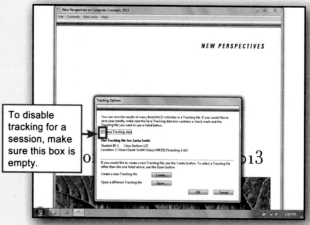

To disable tracking for a session, make sure this box is empty.

❱ **What if I have a Mac?** If you have a Mac that runs Parallels or Boot Camp, that means you have access to the Windows operating system on your Mac. Boot up your Mac in Windows mode and then use the eBook CD just as you would on a Windows computer.

If your Mac runs only OS X, you can still access the digital textbook by performing a simple conversion process. It takes just a few minutes; and when the process is complete, you'll have all the eBook CD files on your Mac's hard drive. You can launch the book right from there, or you can copy the files to a CD or USB flash drive if that is more convenient.

❱ **How do I convert the eBook CD so it works on a Mac?** Make sure you have the NP2013 eBook CD, then use your browser to connect to *www.mediatechnicscorp.com/pub/samples/NP2013MacPac.htm* and follow the instructions. When the MacPac page appears, you might want to print out the instructions so that you can easily follow them.

The MacPac file is about the size of two or three iTunes songs, so it does not take long to download it. Once the file is downloaded, follow the rest of the instructions to get your Mac eBook ready to go.

❱ **How do I start the NP2013 eBook on my Mac?** The setup process puts an NP2013 eBook folder icon on your desktop. The TRY IT! below guides you through the startup process.

TRY IT!

Start the Mac eBook CD

THESE INSTRUCTIONS ARE FOR MAC OS X USERS ONLY!

1. Make sure you have an NP2013 eBook folder icon on your Mac desktop. If not, refer to the material at the top of this page for instructions on how to convert your eBook CD to run on the Mac.

2. Double-click the **NP2013 eBook** folder icon.

3. When the Finder window appears, look for the NP2013 eBook program.

NOTE: You might also have an *eBookCD.exe* program, but that is NOT the program that runs on the Mac. That is the Windows version of the eBook CD.

4. Double-click **NP2013 eBook** and your digital textbook should open and display the Tracking Options dialog box.

The eBook CD allows you to save your scores for QuickChecks, practice tests, and other activities, but for this session you do not need to track this data.

5. To disable tracking for now, make sure the box next to *Save Tracking data* is empty. If the box contains a check mark, click the box to empty it.

6. Click the **OK** button. The Tracking Options dialog box closes and the eBook displays the first page of Chapter 1.

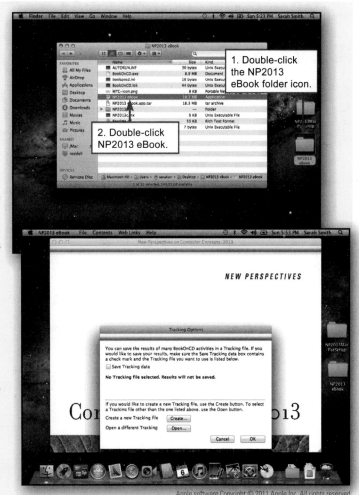

▶ How do I navigate through the book? The eBook CD menu and toolbar, near the top of the screen, contain tools you can use for navigation. The Next and Back buttons turn one page at a time. To get to the first page of any chapter, you can select it from the Contents menu.

The eBook CD pages mirror the pages in the printed book. So if you want to take the QuickCheck that's on page 21 of your printed textbook, for example, you can use the Go to Page option on the toolbar to jump right to it.

▶ What are the other menu and navigation options? The menu bar includes a Web Links menu that opens your browser and connects to InfoWebLinks. The menu bar also includes a Help menu where you can access instructions and troubleshooting FAQs. The Glossary button provides access to definitions for key terms. An Annotation button appears when your instructor has posted comments or lecture notes. If your instructor has not posted annotations, the button will not appear.

▶ How do I exit the eBook CD? When you have completed a session and want to close the eBook CD, you can click the [X] button in the upper-right corner of the title bar (Windows). On Mac OS X, you can click NP2013 eBook CD on the menu bar and select Quit. Figure 29 helps you locate the Close button and eBook CD navigation tools.

> **TERMINOLOGY NOTE**
>
> The eBook CD requires Adobe Flash Player for displaying labs. The Flash Player is installed on most computers. If the eBook CD cannot find your Flash Player when it starts, you'll be directed to go online to download and install it.

FIGURE 29

Key Features of the eBook CD Menu Bar and Toolbar

The Contents menu takes you to the first page of any chapter you select.

The Glossary button helps you look up key terms.

The Back button displays the previous page.

The Next button displays the next page.

To jump to a specific page, enter the page number in the box, then click the ⊙ button.

The Close button closes the eBook CD on Windows computers.

TRY IT!

Open a chapter and navigate the eBook CD

1. Click **Contents** on the menu bar. The Contents menu appears.

2. Click **Chapter 2**.

3. When Chapter 2 appears, click the **Next** button twice until you see page 56.

4. Click the **Back** button twice to go back to the first page of Chapter 2.

5. Click the white box on the right side of Go to Page. Type **89**, then click the **Go to Page** ⊙ button.

6. Click the ◉ **Go to Page** button. Now you should be back at the first page of Chapter 2.

7. Scroll down the page until you can see the Chapter Contents listing. As shown at right, you can use this list to quickly jump to Sections A, B, C, D, or E; Issues; Technology in Context; NP Labs; and Review Activities.

8. Click ◉ **Section D** to jump to Section D.

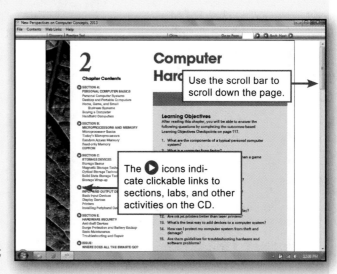

Use the scroll bar to scroll down the page.

The ◉ icons indicate clickable links to sections, labs, and other activities on the CD.

MULTIMEDIA AND COMPUTER-SCORED ACTIVITIES

▶ **What kinds of multimedia are included in the eBook CD?** Figures in your book marked with the ▶ icon morph into multimedia tours, animations, and videos. A tour takes you on a guided software tour—even if you don't have the software installed on your computer! Animations and videos visually expand on the concepts presented in the text.

▶ **How do I access screentours and other multimedia?** To access multimedia elements, simply click the ▶ icon while using the eBook CD.

▶ **Which activities are computer scored?** Figure 30 lists the eBook CD activities that are computer scored. You can use these activities to gauge how well you remember and understand the material you read in the textbook.

Suppose you're reading Chapter 2. Work with the TRY IT! below to see how multimedia and computer-scored activities work.

FIGURE 30

eBook CD Computer-scored Activities

- **Interactive Summary**
- **Interactive Situation Questions**
- **Interactive Practice Tests**
- **Concept Map**
- **QuickChecks**
- **Lab QuickChecks**

TRY IT!

Explore multimedia and computer-scored activities

1. Use the **Go to Page** control to jump to page 79.

2. On page 79, Figure 2-27 contains an ▶ icon. Click any line of the figure caption to launch the video.

3. When you want to stop the video, click any blank area of the eBook CD page. To restart the video, click the ▶ icon again.

4. Now, try a computer-scored QuickCheck. Use the **Go to Page** control to get to page 87 and scroll down the page until you can see the entire set of QuickCheck questions.

5. Click the answer box for question 1, and then type your answer. Most answers are a single word. Upper- and lowercase have no effect on the correctness of your answer.

6. Press the **Tab** key to jump to question 2, and then type your answer. Don't worry if you don't know the answer; you haven't actually read Chapter 2 yet. Just make a guess for now.

7. When you have answered all the questions, click the ▶ CHECK ANSWERS icon. The computer indicates whether your answer is correct or incorrect.

8. Continue to click **OK** to check the rest of your answers.

9. When you've reviewed all your answers, the computer presents a score summary. Click **OK** to close the dialog box.

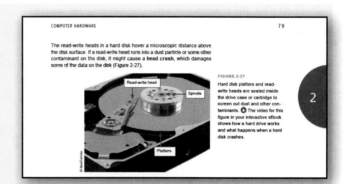

COMPUTER HARDWARE   79

The read-write heads in a hard disk hover a microscopic distance above the disk surface. If a read-write head runs into a dust particle or some other contaminant on the disk, it might cause a head crash, which damages some of the data on the disk (Figure 2-27).

Read-write head
Spindle
Platters

FIGURE 2-27

Hard disk platters and read-write heads are sealed inside the drive case or cartridge to screen out dust and other contaminants. ▶ The video for this figure in your interactive eBook shows how a hard drive works and what happens when a hard disk crashes.

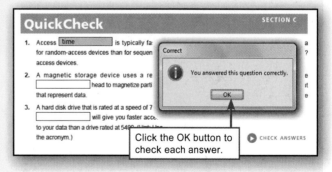

QuickCheck   SECTION C

1. Access [time] is typically fa... for random-access devices than for sequen... access devices.

2. A magnetic storage device uses a re... head to magnetize parti... that represent data.

3. A hard disk drive that is rated at a speed of 7... will give you faster acce... to your data than a drive rated at 540... the acronym.)

Correct

You answered this question correctly.

[OK]

Click the OK button to check each answer.

▶ CHECK ANSWERS

NEW PERSPECTIVES LABS

▶ **What about labs?** Your eBook CD includes New Perspectives Labs that give you hands-on experience applying concepts and using software discussed in each chapter. Labs in the eBook CD are divided into topics, and each topic ends with a QuickCheck so that you can make sure you understand key concepts.

In addition to lab QuickChecks, each New Perspectives Lab also includes a set of assignments located on the Lab page of each chapter. Your instructor might require you to complete these assignments. You can submit them on paper, on disc, or as an e-mail message, according to your instructor's directions.

▶ **How do I launch a lab?** First, navigate to the lab page using the New Perspectives Labs option from the Chapter Contents list, or type in the corresponding page number from the printed book. Click the lab's ▶ icon to start it, as explained in the TRY IT! below.

TRY IT!

Open a New Perspectives Lab

1. Click **Contents** on the eBook CD menu bar and select **Chapter 1**.

2. Scroll down to the Chapter Contents list and click ▶ **New Perspectives Labs**.

3. When the New Perspectives Labs page appears, click ▶ **OPERATING A PERSONAL COMPUTER**.

4. The lab window opens. Click the ⬆ button to view objectives for Topic 1.

5. Click the ⬆ button again to view page 1 of the lab. Read the information on the page, and then continue through the lab, making sure to follow any numbered instructions.

6. After page 8, you will encounter the first QuickCheck question. Click the correct answer, and then click the **Check Answer** button. After you find out if your answer was correct, click the ⬆ button to continue to the next question. Complete all the QuickCheck questions for Topic 1.

7. For this TRY IT! you don't have to complete the entire lab. When you are ready to quit, click the ⬆ button.

8. Click the ⬆ button again. Your Lab QuickCheck results are displayed.

9. Click the **OK** button to return to the eBook CD.

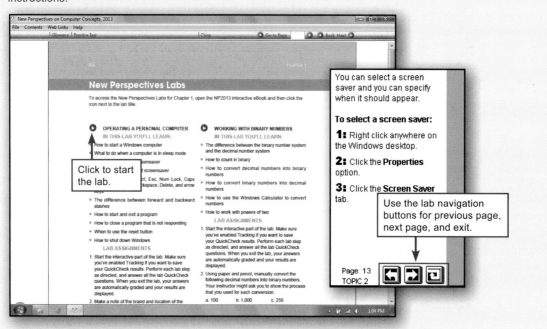

TRACKING YOUR SCORES

▶ **Can I save scores from QuickChecks, labs, and other activities?** To save your scores, you have to create a Tracking file. The file can be located on a rewritable CD, your computer's hard disk, a USB flash drive, or a network drive where you have permission to store files.

▶ **How do I make a Tracking file?** The Tracking Options dialog box lets you create a Tracking file and designate where you want to store it. Work with the TRY IT! below to create a Tracking file.

TRY IT!

Create a Tracking file

1. Make sure your eBook CD is open.

2. Click **File** on the eBook CD menu bar, then click **Change Tracking Options**.

3. When the Tracking Options dialog box appears, click the **Create** button.

4. When the Create Tracking File dialog box appears, enter the requested data (see illustration at right), then click **Continue**. The Save As (Windows) or Save (Mac) dialog box appears.

5. Use the dialog box to specify the location and name for your Tracking file. (See the illustration at right for Windows or the illustration below for Macs.)

6. After selecting a name and location for your Tracking file, click the **Save** button.

7. Back at the Tracking Options dialog box, make sure there is a check mark in the box labeled *Save Tracking data*, then click the **OK** button. Now your Tracking file is ready to receive your scores.

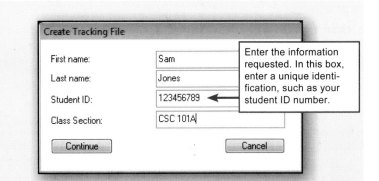

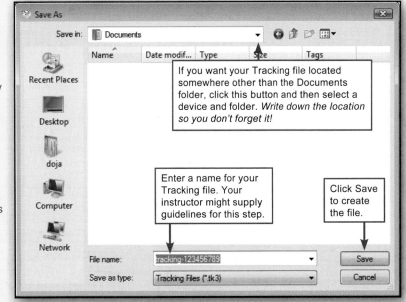

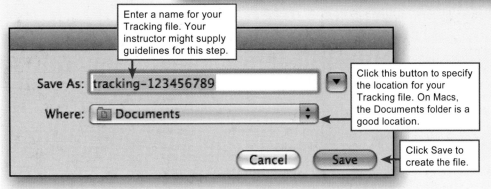

Enter the information requested. In this box, enter a unique identification, such as your student ID number.

If you want your Tracking file located somewhere other than the Documents folder, click this button and then select a device and folder. Write down the location so you don't forget it!

Enter a name for your Tracking file. Your instructor might supply guidelines for this step.

Click Save to create the file.

Enter a name for your Tracking file. Your instructor might supply guidelines for this step.

Click this button to specify the location for your Tracking file. On Macs, the Documents folder is a good location.

Click Save to create the file.

Orientation

How do I get scores into my Tracking file? Whenever the *Save Tracking data* box is checked, all scored activities are automatically saved in your Tracking file. In the previous TRY IT!, you activated tracking; so until you go back into Tracking Options and remove the check mark from *Save Tracking data*, your scores will be saved.

What happens if I do an activity twice? While tracking is active, all your scores are saved. If you do an activity twice, both scores are saved. Your scores are dated, so you and your instructor can determine which scores are the most recent.

Can I review my scores? You can see all your scores in a Tracking Report.

Can I delete or change my scores? No. Your Tracking data is encrypted and cannot be changed.

Work with the TRY IT! below to see how easy it is to save scores and view your Tracking Report.

TRY IT!

Complete a Practice Test

To start tracking your scores, you can complete a Practice Test.

1. Click the **Practice Test** button located on the eBook CD toolbar.

2. The first question of a ten-question Practice Test appears. Answer the question, then click the **Next** button.

3. Answer the remaining questions, then click the **Check Answers** button.

4. When you see your score summary, click the **OK** button. You can then step through each of your answers or view a study guide.

5. Click the **Study Guide** button. A browser window opens to display each Practice Test question, your answers, and the corresponding page numbers in your textbook.

6. Close the Study Guide by clicking the button on your browser window (Windows), or by clicking the browser name in the Mac menu bar and then selecting **Quit** (Mac).

7. Click the **Close** button on the Practice Test window to close it and save your scores.

View the contents of your Tracking file

1. Click **File** on the eBook CD menu bar.

2. Click **View Tracking Report**. Your computer opens your browser and displays a summary score for the Practice Test you completed. The list of summary scores grows as you save additional Practice Tests, QuickChecks, Interactive Summaries, Interactive Situation Questions, and Lab QuickChecks.

3. To close the Tracking Report, close the browser window (Windows) or the TextEdit window (Mac).

Thursday, February 15   9:11:13 AM

New Perspectives on Computer Concepts

Name:	Sam Jones
Student ID:	123456789
Class Section:	CSC 101A
Tracking file:	Documents\tracking-123456789.tk3

Correct:	8
Points Possible:	10
Score:	80.00%

#	Question	Your Answer	Scored As	Review Page
1	The _____ conversion process allows photos, sounds, and other media to travel over the Internet as ASCII text e-mail attachments.	MIME	Correct	34
2	A URL never contains a(n) _____	B	Correct	26
3	Personal computer systems typically include the following devices EXCEPT _____.	A	Incorrect	10
	Personal computers are available as desktop computers, tablet computers, or			

Sunday, August 24   7:16:33 PM

Tracking Report

New Perspectives on Computer Concepts

Name:	Sam Jones
Student ID:	123456789
Class Section:	CSC 101A
Tracking file:	Macintosh HD:Users Sam:Documents:tracking-123456789.tk3

#	Activity	Date	Time	Points Earned	Points Possible	Score
1	NP2013 Chapter 01 Practice Test	8/24	7:16 PM	8	10	80.00%

▶ How do I submit scores from my Tracking file? You can use the Submit Tracking Data option on the File menu to send your scores to your instructor. The files are sent over an Internet service called WebTrack.

▶ Are the scores erased from my Tracking file when they are sent? No. Your scores remain in your file—a copy is sent to your instructor. If your instructor's computer malfunctions and loses your data, you can resubmit your Tracking file. It is a good idea to back up your Tracking file using the Back Up Tracking File option on the File menu.

▶ What are chirps? A chirp is a short message, similar to a Twitter-style tweet. You can use chirps to send queries to your instructor. Your instructor might also use chirps as a classroom polling system. Chirps work through WebTrack.

TRY IT!

Send your Tracking data and send a chirp

1. Click **File** on the eBook CD menu bar, then click **Submit Tracking Data**.

2. Make sure your instructor's WebTrack address is correctly displayed in the Tracking Data Destination dialog box, then click **Continue**.

3. Your computer opens a browser window, makes an Internet connection, and contacts the WebTrack server.

4. When the WebTrack screen appears, make sure the information displayed is correct, then click the **Submit** button.

5. When you see a message that confirms your data has been submitted, you can close the browser window.

6. To send a chirp, click the **Chirp** button on the eBook CD toolbar.

7. When the Chirps panel appears, enter your message in the box labeled *Your message*.

8. Click the **Send** button.

9. Close your eBook CD.

Make sure your instructor's WebTrack ID is entered here.

Enter your question here.

QuickCheck

1. Figures in the book marked with an & sign morph into multimedia screentours, animations, and videos. True or false? [　　　　　]

2. When you use the NP2013 eBook CD, a(n) [　　　　　] button appears if your instructor has posted comments or lecture notes.

3. To save your scores, you have to create a(n) [　　　　　] file.

4. New Perspectives [　　　　　] are divided into topics and each topic ends with a QuickCheck.

5. WebTrack provides a way to submit scores to your instructor. True or false? [　　　　　]

 CHECK ANSWERS

Orientation

NP2013 CourseMate Web Site

THE INTERNET offers access to information that's useful to just about everyone, and New Perspectives students are no exception. When you purchase access to the New Perspectives NP2013 CourseMate Web site, you'll find targeted learning materials to help you understand key concepts and prepare for exams.

WEB SITE RESOURCES

▶ **What's on CourseMate?** The New Perspectives NP2013 CourseMate Web site includes an interactive eBook, quizzes, games, and even audio files that you can download to your iPod or other portable device. Figure 31 highlights the features you'll find on the NP2013 CourseMate.

FIGURE 31

NP2013 CourseMate Features

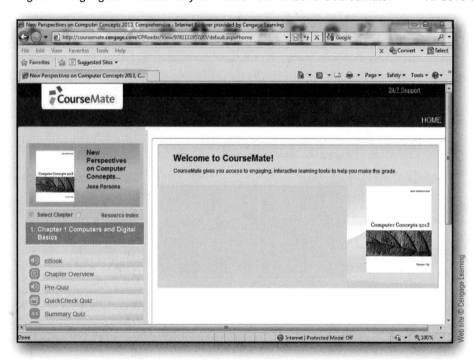

eBook
The NP2013 interactive, multimedia eBook gives you access to your textbook from any computer connected to the Internet.

Detailed Objectives
Access an expanded version of the Learning Objectives that are included at the beginning of each chapter.

Pre-Quiz
Before starting a chapter, take the pre-quiz to find out how to best focus your study time.

TechTerm Flashcards
Make sure you understand all of the technical terms presented in the chapter.

Audio Overview
Listen to a five-minute audio presentation of chapter highlights on your computer or download the files to your MP3 player to study on the go.

Audio Flashcards
Interact with downloadable audio flashcards to review key terms.

Projects
Ideas for term papers, group projects, and assignments.

Quizzes
Check your understanding and ability to apply concepts.

Student Edition Labs
Get hands-on practice with key topics presented in a chapter.

Games
Have some fun while refreshing your memory about key concepts that might appear on the exam.

Glossary
Get a quick overview of all the key terms presented in each chapter.

WEB SITE ACCESS

▶ **How do I access the NP2013 CourseMate?** You can get to the site by opening your browser and typing *www.cengagebrain.com.*

▶ **Do I need a password?** The first time you connect to CengageBrain, sign up for an account. When you have completed the short registration process, enter the ISBN for your book, and if you have an access code, enter it, too. Your materials are added to your dashboard for easy access. Click the link for the NP2013 CourseMate. From there, you can click links to each chapter's activities and information.

TRY IT!

Access the NP2013 CourseMate

1. Start your browser.

2. Click the address box and type:

Make sure to use all lowercase letters, insert no spaces, and use the / slash, not the \ slash.

3. Press the **Enter** key. The CengageBrain screen is displayed.

4. If you are accessing CengageBrain for the first time, click the **Sign Up** tab and follow the instructions to create your account.

5. Once you've created a CengageBrain account, you can log in by entering your user name and password, then clicking the **log in** button.

6. In the *Have Another Product to Register?* box, enter your CourseMate access code, click **Register**, and follow the links to add it to your bookshelf.

7. Once the title is added, you can look for the link to the CourseMate on the right side of the dashboard. The NP2013 CourseMate Welcome screen contains links to activities for each chapter of the textbook. Click the **Select Chapter** button to access Chapter 1. Your browser displays links to activities for the first chapter in your textbook.

8. You can always return to the Welcome screen by clicking the Home button on the right side of your screen. Click the **Home** button now.

First-time users can click this link to set up a CengageBrain account.

Once you have a CengageBrain account, you can enter your user name and password to access the site.

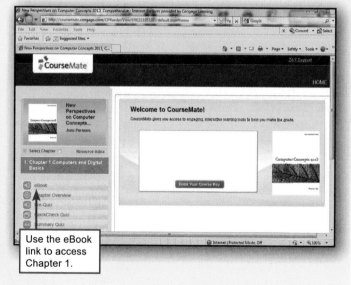

Use the eBook link to access Chapter 1.

Orientation

COURSEMATE WEB SITE TOUR

▶ How do I use the resources at the NP2013 Web site?

The NP2013 CourseMate Web site is designed to help you review chapter material, prepare for tests, and extend your understanding of various topics.

▶ Each eBook chapter contains text and figures from the printed textbook, videos, guided software tours, and InfoWebLinks.

▶ Before beginning a chapter, try the Pre-Quiz activity to find out where to focus your study time.

▶ The Audio Overview presents a high-level introduction to chapter high-lights. Use it as an orientation or as a quick refresher before an exam.

▶ If you like a challenge, use the online games as a review activity; you'll get high scores if you understand the chapter material.

▶ Quizzes are a great way to make sure that you understand and can apply key concepts presented in a chapter.

▶ For last-minute review, load up your iPod with the Audio Flashcards. You can listen to them for a quick refresher on your way to the test!

▶ Can I submit scores from CourseMate activities to my instructor?

Your results from various CourseMate activities are automatically recorded for your instructor using the Engagement Tracker. You do not have to take any additional steps to send scores.

Follow the steps in the box below to explore the NP2013 CourseMate and find out how to view a summary of your scores.

> **STUDY TIP**
>
> Activities in the NP2013 eBook are for your own practice. They are computer-scored, but your scores are not sent to the Engagement Tracker.

TRY IT!

Explore the NP2013 CourseMate

1. Connect to the NP2013 CourseMate, and use the **Select Chapter** button to access Chapter 1.

2. To listen to a CourseCast on your computer, click the **Audio Overview** link. You might have to wait a bit for the overview to begin, depending on the speed of your Internet connection.

3. You can get an idea of where you need to focus your study time by taking a Pre-Quiz. Click the Pre-Quiz link and take the quiz.

4. Click the **Games** link and select one of the games. Try your hand at a few questions, and then go back to the Chapter 1 page.

5. Click the **Quiz** link. Complete a quiz and then click the **Done** button.

6. Check your answers and note your score. You can click the magnifying glass icon to see more details for each question. Your score is saved by the Engagement Tracker.

7. Look for the link to the eBook and click it. Use the Next page and Previous page buttons to navigate page by page.

8. Jump to page 6 and scroll down the page, if necessary, until you can see Figure 1-4.

9. Click to start the software tour.

10. When the tour ends, make sure that you can see the CourseMate menu.

> **STUDY TIP**
>
> If you would like to store a CourseCast on your computer or portable music player, right-click the link, click Download Audio, and then select a location for the CourseCast file. When you are ready to continue the tour, close the audio window.

Online games provide a fun way to review chapter material.

STUDENT EDITION LABS

▶ **How do I access Student Edition Labs?** Student Edition Labs help you review the material presented in the textbook and extend your knowledge through demonstrations and step-by-step practice.

TRY IT!

Work with Student Edition Labs

1. Make sure you're connected to the NP2013 CourseMate, and use the **Select Chapter** button to access Chapter 1.

2. Click the link for **Student Edition Labs**.

3. Take a few minutes to walk through the section **Guide to Student Edition Labs**.

4. Click **Select a Lab** and then click **Understanding the Motherboard** to start the lab.

5. Complete the first section of the lab, including the Intro, Observe, Practice, and Review activities.

6. When you've completed the review activity, a report containing your results is displayed. Use the Print button to print your report, or return to the NP2013 CourseMate.

7. Exit the lab by clicking the **Exit** button in the upper-right corner of the lab window.

The first time you work with the Student Edition Labs, you can find out how to use them effectively by stepping through the introduction, Guide to Student Edition Labs.

Select each link in order to complete all the lab activities.

Use the audio control buttons to start, pause, or rewind the narration.

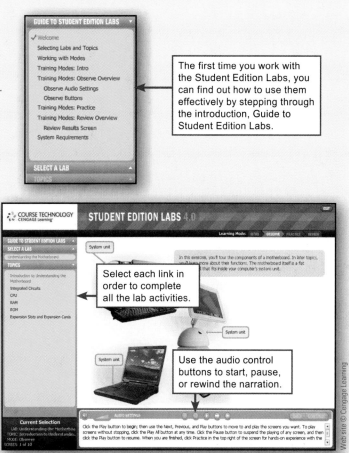

Orientation

QuickCheck

1. To access the NP2013 CourseMate, you need a user name and password. True or false? [_____]

2. The [_____] Tracker automatically records your scores.

3. When you're at the NP2013 CourseMate, you can use the [_____] button to display the Welcome screen.

4. The Audio [_____] is a five-minute audio presentation of chapter highlights.

5. The Student Edition [_____] help you review through demonstrations and step-by-step practice.

 CHECK ANSWERS

NEW PERSPECTIVES

Computer Concepts 2013

Parsons :: Oja

1

Chapter Contents

INFOWEBLINKS

You'll find updates for chapter
material by connecting to the
NP2013 Chapter 1 InfoWebLink.

Ⓦ CLICK TO CONNECT
www.infoweblinks.com/np2013/ch01

Computers and Digital Basics

Learning Objectives

After reading this chapter, you will be able to answer the
following questions by completing the outcomes-based
Learning Objectives Checkpoints on page 53.

1. What are the four phases of the digital revolution?

2. What is convergence and how does it apply to the digital revolution?

3. In what ways does digital technology affect society?

4. How do computers work with input, output, processing, storage, and stored programs?

5. What's the difference between an operating system and application software?

6. How do personal computers differ from servers, mainframes, and supercomputers?

7. Are portable media players and mobile phones classified as computers?

8. Why are microcontrollers the computers no one sees?

9. Aren't data and information the same thing?

10. What's the difference between analog and digital?

11. How do digital devices use 1s and 0s to work with numbers, text, images, and sound?

12. Why is there so much jargon pertaining to bits and bytes?

13. What hardware components manipulate the bits that represent data?

14. Why do computers need programs?

15. How do a microprocessor's ALU and control unit work?

16. How do hackers steal passwords?

17. How can I create secure passwords?

CourseMate

Visit the NP2013 CourseMate for this chapter's Pre-Quiz, Audio
Overview and Flashcards, Detailed Objectives, Chapter Quiz,
Online Games, and more labs.

Multimedia and Interactive Elements

When using the NP2013 interactive eBook, click the ▶ icons to
access multimedia resources.

1

Apply Your Knowledge The information in this chapter will give you the background to:

- Inventory the digital devices you own
- Put digital technology in the context of history, pop culture, and the global economy
- Read computer ads with an understanding of technical terminology

- Select secure passwords for protecting your computer and Internet logins
- Use a password manager to keep track of all your passwords
- Use digital devices with an awareness of how they might infringe on your privacy

Try It!

WHAT'S MY DIGITAL PROFILE?

The average American consumer owns more than 24 digital devices. Before you begin Chapter 1, take an inventory of your digital equipment to find the brands, models, and serial numbers. Tuck this information in a safe place. It can come in handy when you need to call technical support, arrange for repair services, or report missing equipment.

1. Fill in the following table for any digital equipment you own, rent, lease, or use.

	Brand	Model	Serial Number
Computer			
Keyboard			
Mouse			
Monitor			
Printer			
Digital camera			
Digital music player			
Internet or network device			
Mobile phone			
Game console			
Other (list)			

3

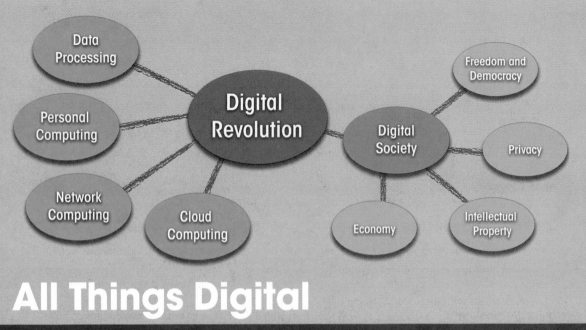

All Things Digital

WE LIVE IN THE INFORMATION AGE: a period in history when information is easy to access and affects many aspects of everyday life, from the economy to politics and social relationships. The importance of information is not new. It has always been a powerful tool. Scrolls treasured by monks during the Middle Ages, scientific knowledge collected during the Renaissance, and intelligence data collected during the Cold War were all critical in shaping world events. The Information Age is unique because of its underlying technology based on digital electronics. Section A offers an overview of the digital revolution that ushered in the Information Age.

THE DIGITAL REVOLUTION

▶ **What is the digital revolution?** The **digital revolution** is an ongoing process of social, political, and economic change brought about by digital technology, such as computers and the Internet.

Like the agricultural and industrial revolutions, the digital revolution offers advantages, but requires adaptations. Digital innovations challenge the status quo and require societies to make adjustments to traditions, lifestyles, and legislation.

The technology driving the digital revolution is based on digital electronics and the idea that electrical signals can represent data, such as numbers, words, pictures, and music. Without digital electronics, computers would be huge machines, priced far beyond the reach of individuals; your favorite form of entertainment would probably be foosball, and you'd be listening to bulky vacuum tube radios instead of carrying sleek iPods (Figure 1-1).

FIGURE 1-1

The digital revolution has a profound effect on everyday life.

▶ What is the significance of digitization? **Digitization** is the process of converting text, numbers, sound, photos, and video into data that can be processed by digital devices. The significant advantage of digitization is that things as diverse as books, movies, songs, conversations, documents, and photos can all be distilled down to a common set of signals that do not require separate devices.

Before digitization, a phone conversation required a telephone handset and dedicated phone lines. Viewing photos required a slide projector and screen. Reading required a paper book. Viewing movies required a film projector. Once digitized, however, conversations, photos, books, and movies can all be managed by a single device or transmitted over a single set of communication lines.

You can pull a photo down from a Web site, store it on your computer's hard disk, make a copy of it on a flash drive, send it to a friend as an e-mail attachment, add it to a report, print it, combine it with other photos to make a slide show, burn the slide show to a CD, and watch the slide show on your home theater system.

You can use a digitized photo in so many ways. In contrast, if you just have a photo print, you can make a copy of it with a photo copier, send it by snail mail, or frame it, but not much else. Digitization creates versatility.

The digital revolution has evolved through four phases, beginning with big, expensive, standalone computers, and progressing to today's digital world in which small, inexpensive digital devices are everywhere (Figure 1-2).

FIGURE 1-2

As the digital revolution progressed, technology changed, as did the way we used it.

Expired	Tired	Uninspired	Desired
Data processing	Personal computing	Network computing	Cloud computing
Big corporate and government computers	Desktop computers	Notebook computers	iPhone, Droid X, and iPad-like devices
Custom applications	Standalone applications	Monolithic software suites	Handheld apps and cloud-based apps
CB radios	Dial-up Internet access	Cable, satellite Internet access	3G, Wi-Fi Internet access
ARPANET	AOL and CompuServe	The Web and virtual worlds	Social media
Arcade games	2-D action games	3-D multiplayer games	Touch screen microgames for handheld devices

DATA PROCESSING

▶ When did the digital revolution begin? Some historians mark the 1980s as the beginning of the digital revolution, but engineers built the first digital computers during World War II for breaking codes and calculating missile trajectories. In the 1950s, computers were marketed for business applications, such as payroll and inventory management.

▶ What was computing like back then? In this first phase of the digital revolution, computers were huge, complex, and expensive devices. They existed in limited numbers, primarily housed in big corporations and government agencies. Computers were operated by trained specialists. Each computer installation required specialized software. The idea that computers might be used by ordinary people in their homes was only a glimmer of an idea in the minds of science fiction writers.

Back then, processing components for computers were housed in closet-sized cabinets that did not usually include a keyboard or display device. Computers were accessed using the keyboard and display screen of a terminal. Terminals had little processing capability of their own, so they were simply used to enter data and view results produced by software that ran on the main computer.

During the antiestablishment era of the 1960s, the digital revolution was beginning to transform organizations, but ordinary people had little direct contact with computers. As with many new technologies, computers were initially viewed with suspicion by consumers, who were uncomfortable with the idea of giant machine "brains." Computers seemed remote. They were housed out of sight in special facilities and were inaccessible to ordinary people. Computers also seemed impersonal. Instead of names, computers used Social Security numbers to uniquely identify people (Figure 1-3).

Throughout the first phase of the digital revolution, businesses adopted computers with increasing enthusiasm as benefits for cutting costs and managing mountains of data became apparent. Computers and data processing became crucial tools for effective business operations.

▶ What is data processing? **Data processing** is based on an input-processing-output cycle. Data goes into a computer, it is processed, and then it is output. For example, a batch of employee time cards are entered into a payroll computer system; the payroll data is processed to calculate take-home pay, deductions, and taxes; paychecks are output (Figure 1-4).

FIGURE 1-3

In the 1950s and 1960s, data used by government and business computers was coded onto punched cards that contained the warning "Do not fold, tear, or mutilate this card." Similar slogans were used by protesters who were concerned that computers would have a dehumanizing effect on society.

Do not fold, bend, spindle, or mutilate

FIGURE 1-4

Data processing is the computing model for the first phase of the digital revolution. The concept of large computers performing tasks based on the input-processing-output cycle represents the primary way computers were used from the 1940s through the 1970s. Data processing installations still exist today, but other technologies emerged, making computing available to a more diverse group of users. ▶ See an example of data processing.

Input ⟶ Process ⟶ Output

PERSONAL COMPUTING

▶ **When did digital devices become available to consumers?** Digital devices were first available to consumers in the 1970s when handheld calculators and digital watches hit store shelves. The first personal computers made their debut in 1976, but sales got off to a slow start. Without compelling software applications, personal computers, such as the Apple II, seemed to offer little for their $2,400 price.

As the variety of software increased, however, consumer interest grew. In 1982, *TIME* magazine's Man of the Year award went to the computer, an indication that these digital machines had finally gained a measure of popular acceptance.

▶ **What is personal computing?** The model for the second phase of the digital revolution, **personal computing** is characterized by small, standalone computers powered by local software. **Local software** refers to any software that is installed on a computer's hard drive.

During this phase of the digital revolution, computers were not connected to networks, so they were essentially self-contained units that allowed users to interact with installed software. On the business front, large computers continued to run payroll, inventory, and financial software. Some managers used personal computers and spreadsheet software to crunch numbers for business planning.

If you owned a computer back in the second phase of the digital revolution, it was probably a small standalone machine with a display device that looked like an old-fashioned television (Figure 1-5).

FIGURE 1-5

The most popular uses for personal computers were word processing and gaming; sound systems and graphics capabilities were primitive. The Internet wasn't open to public use, so computing was not a social experience.

▶ **How long was the second phase of the digital revolution?** In 1982, computers had gained recognition in *TIME* magazine, but fewer than 10% of U.S. households had a computer. Working on a standalone computer wasn't for everyone.

People without an interest in typing up corporate reports or school papers, crunching numbers for accounting, or playing computer games weren't tempted to become active soldiers in the digital revolution. Social scientists even worried that people would become increasingly isolated as they focused on computer activities rather than social ones. Computer ownership increased at a gradual pace until the mid-1990s, and then it suddenly accelerated into the third phase of the digital revolution.

NETWORK COMPUTING

▶ **What caused the sudden upswing in computer ownership during the 1990s?** The third phase of the digital revolution materialized as computers became networked and when the Internet was opened to public use. A **computer network** is a group of computers linked together to share data and resources.

Network technology existed before the Internet became popular, but those networks were mainly deployed to connect computers within a school or business. Networks were complicated to set up and unreliable. As the third phase of the digital revolution unfolded, network technology became consumer-friendly, allowing homeowners to connect multiple computers, exchange files, and, most importantly, share an Internet connection.

The **Internet** is a global computer network originally developed as a military project, and was then handed over to the National Science Foundation for research and academic use. When restrictions on commercial use of the Internet were lifted in 1995, companies such as AOL and CompuServe became popular services for access to e-mail and the World Wide Web. Internet access was a major factor contributing to the upswing in computer ownership during the 1990s.

▶ **What about the Web?** When historians look back on the digital revolution, they are certain to identify the Web as a major transformative influence. The **Web** (short for *World Wide Web*) is a collection of linked documents, graphics, and sounds that can be accessed over the Internet.

A key aspect of the Web is that it adds content and substance to the Internet. Without the Web, the Internet would be like a library without any books or a railroad without any trains. Online storefronts, auction sites, news, sports, travel reservations, and music downloads made the Web a compelling digital technology for just about everyone.

▶ **So what was computing like?** During the period from 1995–2010, computing was characterized by the Web, e-mail, multiplayer games, music downloads, and enormous software applications, such as Microsoft Office, Norton's Internet Security Suite, and Corel Digital Studio (Figure 1-6).

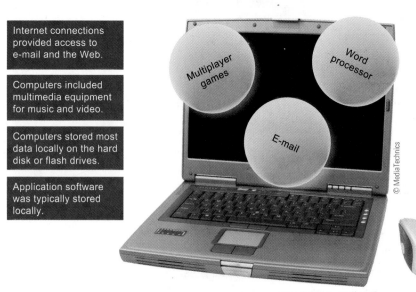

Internet connections provided access to e-mail and the Web.

Computers included multimedia equipment for music and video.

Computers stored most data locally on the hard disk or flash drives.

Application software was typically stored locally.

FIGURE 1-6

Computers were the primary devices for accessing the Internet prior to 2010, but applications, media, and data remained on the local hard disk.

CLOUD COMPUTING

▶ Is the Web dead? A 2010 *Wired* magazine cover announced "The Web is Dead." That pronouncement was premature, but Facebook, Twitter, and Google Apps have sent computing in new directions. Local applications are being eclipsed by cloud computing, which characterizes the fourth phase of the digital revolution.

▶ What is cloud computing? Cloud computing provides access to information, applications, communications, and storage over the Internet. Before cloud computing, your computer typically ran software based locally. For example, to use a word processor, you might fire up the latest edition of Microsoft Word, which you'd installed on your computer's hard disk. Prior to the cloud, you stored data locally, too. E-mail, documents, photos, and music all resided on your computer's hard disk or flash drive.

With cloud computing, all that changes. You can use your browser to access word processing applications that run from the Internet, instead of software that you have installed on your local hard disk. You can use online applications to manage your e-mail, create floor plans, produce presentations, and carry out a host of other activities. You can store your data in the cloud, too, making it available no matter what computer you're using as long as it has an Internet connection.

The cloud gets its name from diagrams like the one in Figure 1-7 that show Internet-based applications, storage, and other services outlined by a cloud-like shape designed to help you visualize the idea that cloud services are "out there" somewhere on the Internet.

▶ What is convergence? The expansion of cloud computing is due in part to **convergence**, a process by which several technologies with distinct functionalities evolve to form a single product. Your computer plays movies. Your cell phone has a camera. Your clock has a radio. Your watch functions as a compass. You can store data on your iPod touch. All these are examples of technological convergence.

Convergence worked its magic on cell phones, computers, portable media players, digital cameras, GPSs, watches, and e-book readers. Now you get features from all of them by purchasing a single digital device. Whether you purchase a full-size computer, a sophisticated mobile phone, or even a game console, you typically have access to software, music, photos, ebooks, movies, communications, and the Web (Figure 1-8).

In 2010, the average consumer owned more than 24 digital devices. With convergence on a roll, you can expect that number to dwindle, as consumers discover the versatility of today's multipurpose digital devices.

Convergence is important to the digital revolution because it created sophisticated mobile devices whose owners demand access to the same services available from full-size computers on their desks. Your smartphone isn't usually in range of the cable modem in your house, so it needs a different way to access the Internet. Your iPad is too small for a huge hard disk, so it needs an alternative place to store data and applications. You can see how these mobile devices require a solution such as cloud computing to provide a full spectrum of digital services.

FIGURE 1-7

The "cloud" represents Internet-based services, such as applications and social media, that are available from computers and handheld digital devices.

FIGURE 1-8

High-end mobile phones such as the iPhone and Droid X offer a huge selection of applications and Internet access.

▶ **What role do social media play?** The fourth phase of the digital revolution turned the worry of social isolation on its head; instead of computers decreasing human interaction, social media encourage interpersonal communications and relationships. **Social media** are cloud-based applications designed for social interaction and consumer-generated content. They include social networking services, wikis, blogging services, photo sharing services, and microblogging sites (Figure 1-9).

FIGURE 1-9

Social media include many popular services.

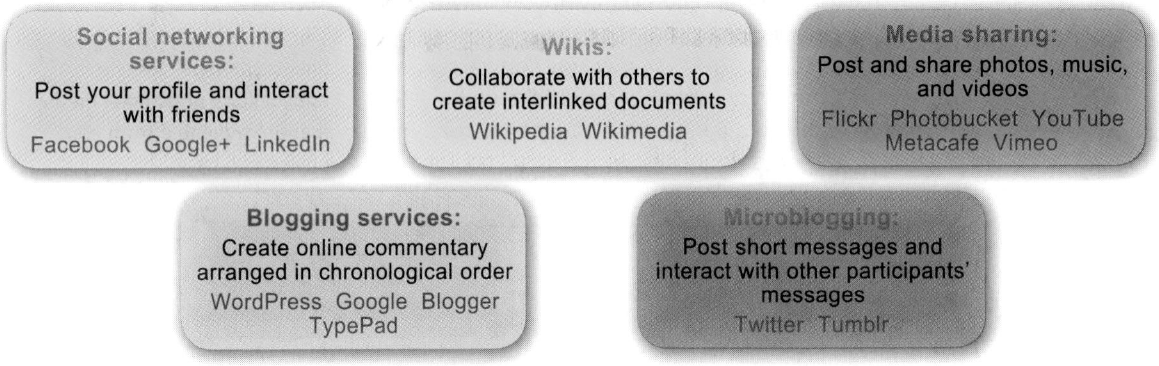

Social networking services:
Post your profile and interact with friends
Facebook Google+ LinkedIn

Wikis:
Collaborate with others to create interlinked documents
Wikipedia Wikimedia

Media sharing:
Post and share photos, music, and videos
Flickr Photobucket YouTube Metacafe Vimeo

Blogging services:
Create online commentary arranged in chronological order
WordPress Google Blogger TypePad

Microblogging:
Post short messages and interact with other participants' messages
Twitter Tumblr

Myspace, Facebook, and Twitter became some of the first popular social networking services. Myspace lost steam in 2008, but Facebook and Twitter marched ahead. By 2011, Facebook had 750 million users and Twitter had 200 million. Many factors influenced the popularity of these sites, but one important factor is their ease of use. As cloud-based services, there is no software to install and there are no updates to worry about. Getting started is as simple as registering your name and creating a password.

▶ **How is today's computing different from the past?** Using computers during the fourth phase of the digital revolution, you're likely to have a mobile device that accesses the Internet using a cell phone service provider.

The touch screen on your mobile device gives you access to apps that play music, show movies, report news and sports scores, help you find the nearest Starbucks, and all kinds of other fun stuff. You occasionally use Google or Wikipedia to access information; and when you need to produce a document, you head over to Google to access its cloud-based word processor. You spend lots of time maintaining your profiles on social networking services and interacting with friends through cloud-based social media.

DIGITAL SOCIETY

▶ **How does digital technology affect freedom and democracy?** Freedom of speech is the cornerstone of democracy. It can be defined as being able to speak freely without censorship or fear of reprisal. The concept is not limited to speaking, but includes all forms of expression, including writing, art, and symbolic actions. The more inclusive term *freedom of expression* is sometimes used instead of *freedom of speech*.

Freedom of speech is not an absolute. Most societies prohibit or repress some types of expression, such as hate speech, libel, pornography, and flag burning. Although freedom of expression is guaranteed under the U.S. Constitution, the European Convention on Human Rights, and the Universal Declaration of Human Rights, these documents recognize the necessity for some restrictions, which might vary from one society to the next.

Incidents ranging from the controversy over teaching evolution in schools to the Arab world's fury over cartoons of Mohammed illustrate that societies draw the freedom of speech line in different places. The types of expression that are allowed or prohibited in a particular country are, in many respects, a reflection of its culture (Figure 1-10).

Digital technologies and communications networks make it easy to cross cultural and geographic boundaries. News, television shows, music, and art from all over the globe are accessible on the Internet. The Internet has the potential to expand freedom of speech by offering every person on the planet a forum for personal expression using personal Web sites, blogs, chat groups, social media, and collaborative wikis. Anonymous Internet sites such as Freenet and **anonymizer tools** that cloak a person's identity even make it possible to exercise freedom of speech in situations where reprisals might repress it.

Internet information that seems innocuous in some cultures is not acceptable in others. Governments, parents, and organizations sometimes find it necessary to censor the Internet by limiting access and filtering content.

Despite attempts to censor and filter speech on the Internet, it seems clear that digital technology opens the door to freedom of expression in unprecedented ways. Limitations on Internet speech are likely to change, too, as technology evolves and as societies come to grips with the balance between freedom and responsibility.

FIGURE 1-10

The 1960 movie *Inherit the Wind* was based on the trial of John Scopes, who was accused of violating a state law that prohibited teaching evolution in state-funded schools.

▶ Has digital technology changed the way we view privacy?

Citizens of free societies have an expectation of privacy, which in the words of Supreme Court Justices Warren and Brandeis is "the right to be let alone." Digital technology use has exerted substantial pressure to diminish privacy by making it possible to easily collect and distribute data about individuals without their knowledge or consent.

Privacy also encompasses confidentiality—the expectation that personal information will not be collected or divulged without permission. Internet marketers have a whole bag of tricks for surreptitiously getting personal information, and hackers are adept at breaking into sensitive databases to obtain confidential information.

Surveillance is viewed by many people as an invasion of privacy. Tracking technologies embedded in cars, clothing, passports, and devices such as cell phones make it much too easy to track people without their knowledge.

In the United States, the expectation of privacy is derived from Fourth Amendment protections against unreasonable searches and seizures. The Fourth Amendment was formulated long before the digital revolution. Today's lawmakers struggle to strike the right balance between privacy and competing principles, such as free speech or free trade.

Some individuals dismiss the erosion of privacy saying, "I have nothing to hide, so I don't care." There was a time when even they typically didn't want stores, hackers, and curious onlookers to have access to data about what they buy, read, and watch; who they call; where they travel; and what they say.

Social media, however, encourage participants to reveal personal details online, and that information is being captured, aggregated, reposted, and distributed publicly. Privacy advocates fear that these digital technologies are fundamentally changing our expectation of what is private and what is not.

▶ How does digital technology affect intellectual property? Intellectual property refers to the ownership of certain types of information, ideas, or representations. It includes patented, trademarked, and copyrighted material, such as music, photos, software, books, and films. In the past, such works were difficult and expensive to copy.

Digital technology has made it easy to produce copies with no loss in quality from the original. Pirating—illegal copying and distribution of copyrighted material—is simple and inexpensive. It has caused significant revenue loss for software publishers, recording studios, and film producers. The fight against piracy takes many forms, from passing strict anti-piracy laws; to scrambling, encryption, and digital rights management schemes that physically prevent copying; to anti-piracy videos (Figure 1-11).

Don't copy that (what? what? why?)

Digital technology adds complexity to intellectual property issues. For example, artists used to think nothing of cutting out various photos from magazines and pasting them together to form a collage. It is even easier to download digital images from the Web and paste them into reports, add them to Web pages, and incorporate them into works of art. Without permission, however, such digital cut and paste is not allowed.

FIGURE 1-11

Most moviegoers have seen the rock-video style "Don't Copy" trailer. Consumer education is one front in the war against piracy. ▶ You can view this video from your interactive eBook.

Some films contain scenes that parents would rather their children not see. Even some scenes from family-oriented Harry Potter films might be too intense for young viewers. So, why not simply edit them out digitally to make a new DVD that the little tykes can watch? Such modifications are not allowed under current U.S. law, even for private viewing.

In the U.S., it is legal to make a backup copy of software CDs or DVDs that you own. However, if a CD, for example, is copy protected to prevent you from making a copy, it is against the law to break the copy protection. So, legally you have a right to a backup, but you don't have the right to circumvent the copy protection to legally create one!

Bucking protectionist trends are **open source** projects that promote copying, free distribution, peer review, and user modification. Linux is an open-source computer operating system that can be modified and freely distributed. Open source application software includes the popular LibreOffice suite, Firefox Web browser, and Thunderbird e-mail.

Digital technology makes it possible to copy and modify films, music, software, and other data, but a tricky balancing act is required to allow consumers flexibility to use data while protecting the income stream to artists, performers, and publishers.

▶ What effect does digital technology have on the economy? Digital technology is an important factor in global and national economies, in addition to affecting the economic status of individuals. **Globalization** can be defined as the worldwide economic interdependence of countries that occurs as cross-border commerce increases and as money flows more freely among countries.

In a global economy, consumers gain access to a wide variety of products, including technology products manufactured in locations scattered all over the globe.

Global communications technology offers opportunities for teleworkers in distant countries. Customer service lines for U.S.-based companies, such as IBM, Dell, and Hewlett-Packard, are often staffed by offshore technicians who earn far more than they could if working for a company in their home country.

Globalization, fueled by digital technology, has controversial aspects, however. Worker advocates object to the use of cheap offshore labor that displaces onshore employees.

Some individuals are affected by the **digital divide**, a term that refers to the gap between people who have access to technology and those who do not. Typically, digital have-nots face economic barriers. They cannot afford computers, cell phones, and Internet access, or they are located in an economically depressed region where electricity is not available to run digital devices, power satellite dishes, and pick up Internet signals (Figure 1-12).

Globalization is an ongoing process that will have far-reaching effects on people in countries with developed technologies and those with emerging economies. Digital technology will be called upon to open additional economic opportunities without disrupting the lifestyles of currently prosperous nations.

▶ **So what's the point?** Learning about digital technology is not just about circuits and electronics, nor is it only about digital gadgets, such as computers and portable music players. Digital technology permeates the very core of modern life. Understanding how this technology works and thinking about its potential can help you comprehend many issues related to privacy, security, freedom of speech, and intellectual property. It will help you become a better consumer and give you insights into local and world events.

As you continue to read this textbook, don't lose sight of the big picture. On one level, in this course you might be simply learning about how to use a computer and software. On a more profound level, however, you are accumulating knowledge about digital technology that applies to broader cultural and legal issues that are certain to affect your life far into the future.

FIGURE 1-12

The digital divide is narrowing as the prices of digital devices fall, and as inexpensive handheld devices acquire more features.

AP Photo/Pavel Rahman

1

QuickCheck

SECTION A

1. Data [ ] was the computing technology behind the first phase of the digital revolution.

2. [ ] software refers to any software that is installed on a computer's hard drive.

3. A computer [ ] is a group of computers linked together to share data and resources.

4. The process of converting text, numbers, sound, photos, or video into data that can be processed by a computer is called [ ].

5. [ ] computing provides access to information, applications, communications, and storage over the Internet.

 CHECK ANSWERS

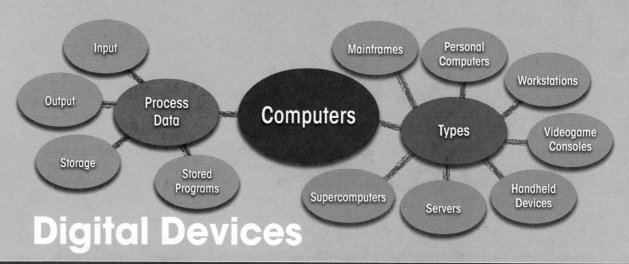

Digital Devices

WHETHER YOU REALIZE IT or not, you already know a lot about the devices produced by the digital revolution. You've picked up information from commercials and news articles, from books and movies, from friends and coworkers—perhaps even from using a variety of digital devices and trying to figure out why they don't always work! Section B provides an overview that's designed to help you start organizing what you know about digital devices, beginning with computers.

COMPUTER BASICS

▶ **What is a computer?** The word *computer* has been part of the English language since 1646; but if you look in a dictionary printed before 1940, you might be surprised to find a computer defined as a person who performs calculations! Prior to 1940, machines designed to perform calculations were referred to as calculators and tabulators, not computers. The modern definition and use of the term *computer* emerged in the 1940s, when the first electronic computing devices were developed.

Most people can formulate a mental picture of a computer, but computers do so many things and come in such a variety of shapes and sizes that it might seem difficult to distill their common characteristics into an all-purpose definition. At its core, a **computer** is a multipurpose device that accepts input, processes data, stores data, and produces output, all according to a series of stored instructions (Figure 1-13).

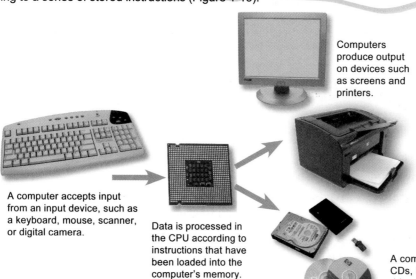

Computers produce output on devices such as screens and printers.

A computer accepts input from an input device, such as a keyboard, mouse, scanner, or digital camera.

Data is processed in the CPU according to instructions that have been loaded into the computer's memory.

A computer uses disks, CDs, DVDs, and flash drives to permanently store data.

FIGURE 1-13

A computer can be defined by its ability to accept input, process data, store data, and produce output, all according to a set of instructions from a computer program.

What is input? Computer **input** is whatever is typed, submitted, or transmitted to a computer system. Input can be supplied by a person, by the environment, or by another computer. Examples of the kinds of input that computers can accept include words and symbols in a document, numbers for a calculation, pictures, temperatures from a thermostat, audio signals from a microphone, and instructions from a computer program. An input device, such as a keyboard or mouse, gathers data and transforms it into a series of electronic signals for the computer to store and manipulate.

What is output? **Output** is the result produced by a computer. Some examples of computer output include reports, documents, music, graphs, and pictures. Output devices display, print, or transmit the results of processing.

What does *process data* mean? Technically speaking, **data** refers to the symbols that represent facts, objects, and ideas. Computers manipulate data in many ways, and this manipulation is called **processing**. Some of the ways that a computer can process data include performing calculations, modifying documents and pictures, keeping track of your score in a fast-action game, drawing graphs, and sorting lists of words or numbers (Figure 1-14).

In a computer, most processing takes place in a component called the **central processing unit** or **CPU.** The CPU of most modern computers is a **microprocessor**, which is an electronic component that can be programmed to perform tasks based on data it receives. You'll learn more about microprocessors later in the chapter. For now, visualize a microprocessor as the little black box that's the brain of a digital device.

How do computers store data? A computer stores data so that it will be available for processing. Most computers have more than one place to put data, depending on how the data is being used. **Memory** is an area of a computer that temporarily holds data waiting to be processed, stored, or output. **Storage** is the area where data can be left on a permanent basis when it is not immediately needed for processing.

Data is typically stored in files. A computer file, usually referred to simply as a **file**, is a named collection of data that exists on a storage medium, such as a hard disk, CD, DVD, or flash drive. A file can contain data for a term paper, Web page, e-mail message, or music video. Some files also contain instructions that tell the computer how to perform various tasks.

What's so significant about a computer's ability to store instructions? The series of instructions that tells a computer how to carry out processing tasks is referred to as a **computer program**, or simply a program. These programs form the **software** that sets up a computer to do a specific task. When a computer "runs" software, it performs the instructions to carry out a task.

Take a moment to think about the way you use a simple handheld calculator to balance your checkbook each month. You're forced to do the calculations in stages. Although you can store data from one stage and use it in the next stage, you cannot store the sequence of formulas—the program—required to balance your checkbook. Every month, therefore, you have to perform a similar set of calculations. The process would be much simpler if your calculator remembered the sequence of calculations and just asked you for this month's checkbook entries.

FIGURE 1-14

An unsorted list is input into the computer, where it is processed in the CPU and output as a sorted list.

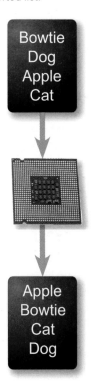

The idea of a **stored program** means that a series of instructions for a computing task can be loaded into a computer's memory. These instructions can easily be replaced by a different set of instructions when it is time for the computer to perform another task. This ability to switch programs makes computers multipurpose machines.

The stored program concept allows you to use your computer for one task, such as word processing, and then easily switch to a different type of computing task, such as editing a photo or sending an e-mail message. It is the single most important characteristic that distinguishes a computer from other simpler and less versatile digital devices, such as watches, calculators, and pocket-sized electronic dictionaries.

▶ **What kinds of software do computers run?** Computers run two main types of software: application software and system software. A computer can be applied to many tasks, such as writing, number crunching, video editing, and online shopping. **Application software** is a set of computer programs that helps a person carry out a task. Word processing software, for example, helps people create, edit, and print documents. Personal finance software helps people keep track of their money and investments. Video editing software helps people edit video footage to create home movies and professional films. Software applications are sometimes referred to as **apps**, especially in the context of handheld devices.

Whereas application software is designed to help a person carry out a task, the primary purpose of **system software** is to help the computer system monitor itself in order to function efficiently. An example of system software is a computer **operating system** (OS), which is essentially the master controller for all the activities that take place within a computer. Although an operating system does not directly help people perform application-specific tasks, such as word processing, people do interact with the operating system for certain operational and storage tasks, such as starting programs and locating data files.

COMPUTER TYPES AND USES

▶ **Are computers categorized in any way?** At one time it was possible to define three distinct categories of computers. Mainframes were housed in large, closet-sized metal frames. Minicomputers were smaller, less expensive, and less powerful computers that were able, nevertheless, to provide adequate computing power for small businesses. Microcomputers were clearly differentiated from computers in other categories because their CPUs consisted of a single microprocessor chip.

Today, microprocessors are no longer a distinction between computer categories because just about every computer uses one or more microprocessors as its CPU. The term *minicomputer* has fallen into disuse and the terms *microcomputer* and *mainframe* are used with less and less frequency.

Computers are versatile machines, but some computers are better suited than others for certain tasks. Categorizing computers is a way of grouping them according to criteria such as usage, cost, size, and capability. Experts don't necessarily agree on the categories or the devices placed in each category, but commonly used computer categories include personal computers, servers, mainframes, supercomputers, and handhelds.

> **TERMINOLOGY NOTE**
>
> The term *personal computer* is sometimes abbreviated as *PC*. However, *PC* can also refer to a specific type of personal computer that descended from the original IBM PC and runs Windows software.
>
> In this book, *PC* refers to IBM PC descendants. It is not used as an abbreviation for *personal computer*.

▶ What is a personal computer? A **personal computer** is a microprocessor-based computing device designed to meet the computing needs of an individual. It typically includes a keyboard and screen, and provides access to a wide variety of local and cloud-based applications.

Personal computers are available as desktop or portable models, and in a variety of shapes, sizes, and colors. You'll learn more about the wide variety of personal computers in the Hardware chapter. For now, simply remember that computers like those pictured in Figure 1-15 are classified as personal computers.

▶ What is a workstation? The term **workstation** has two meanings. It can simply refer to an ordinary personal computer that is connected to a network. A second meaning refers to powerful desktop computers used for high-performance tasks, such as medical imaging and computer-aided design, that require a lot of processing speed. Workstations, such as the one pictured in Figure 1-16, typically cost a bit more than an average personal computer.

▶ Is an Xbox a personal computer? A **videogame console**, such as Nintendo's Wii, Sony's PlayStation, or Microsoft's Xbox, is not generally referred to as a personal computer because of its history as a dedicated game device. Videogame consoles originated as simple digital devices that connected to a TV set and provided only a pair of joysticks for input.

Today's videogame consoles contain microprocessors that are equivalent to any found in a fast personal computer, and they are equipped to produce graphics that rival those on sophisticated workstations. Add-ons such as keyboards, DVD players, and Internet access make it possible to use a videogame console for activities similar to those for which you'd use a personal computer. Despite these features, videogame consoles like the one in Figure 1-17 fill a specialized niche and are not considered a replacement for a personal computer.

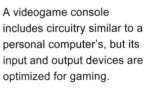

▶ What makes a computer a server? In the computer industry, the term *server* has several meanings. It can refer to computer hardware, to a specific type of software, or to a combination of hardware and software. In any case, the purpose of a **server** is to serve computers on a network (such as the Internet or a home network) by supplying them with data.

Any software or digital device, such as a computer, that requests data from a server is referred to as a **client**. For example, on the Internet, a server might respond to a client's request for a Web page. Servers also handle the steady stream of e-mail that travels among clients from all over the Internet. A server might also allow clients within a home, school, or business network to share files or access a centralized printer.

Client computers can download and upload files from servers. The term **download** refers to the process of copying a file from a server to your own client computer. For example, you can say "I had to download the file before I could install it." The term can also refer to the file that you download, as in "I had to delete the download because it was infected with a virus."

Upload refers to the process of copying files from your client computer to a server. As with the term *download*, *upload* can also refer to the file you have uploaded.

Remarkably, just about any personal computer, workstation, mainframe, or supercomputer can be configured to perform the work of a server. That fact should emphasize the concept that a server does not require a specific type of hardware. Nonetheless, computer manufacturers such as IBM, SGI, HP, and Dell offer devices called servers (Figure 1-18) that are especially suited for storing and distributing data on a network.

FIGURE 1-18

Some servers look like personal computer tower units, whereas others are housed in industrial-looking cases.

© MediaTechnics

© John Kershaw/Alamy

Server prices vary, depending on configuration, but tend to be more similar to workstation prices than personal computer prices. Despite impressive performance on server-related tasks, these machines do not offer features such as sound cards, DVD players, and other fun accessories, so they are not a suitable alternative to a personal computer.

▶ What's so special about a mainframe computer? A **mainframe computer** (or simply a mainframe) is a large and expensive computer capable of simultaneously processing data for hundreds or thousands of users. Mainframes are generally used by businesses or governments to provide centralized storage, processing, and management for large amounts of data. Mainframes remain the computer of choice in situations where reliability, data security, and centralized control are necessary.

The price of a mainframe computer typically starts at $100,000 and can easily exceed $1 million. Its main processing circuitry is housed in a closet-sized cabinet (Figure 1-19); but after large components are added for storage and output, a mainframe computer system can fill a good-sized room.

FIGURE 1-19

This IBM z9 mainframe computer weighs 2,807 pounds and is about 6.5 feet tall.

Courtesy of International Business Machines Corporation. Unauthorized use not permitted.

▶ How powerful is a supercomputer? A computer falls into the **supercomputer** category if it is, at the time of construction, one of the fastest computers in the world (Figure 1-20).

FIGURE 1-20

In 2011, a Japanese computer named K was the fastest supercomputer. Using more than 68,544 processors housed in 672 red cabinets, the K clocks peak performance speeds of 8.16 petaflops, more than 8 quadrillion operations per second.

Because of their speed, supercomputers can tackle complex tasks and compute-intensive problems that just would not be practical for other computers. A **compute-intensive** problem is one that requires massive amounts of data to be processed using complex mathematical calculations. Molecular calculations, atmospheric models, and climate research are all examples of projects that require massive numbers of data points to be manipulated, processed, and analyzed.

Common uses for supercomputers include breaking codes, modeling worldwide weather systems, and simulating nuclear explosions. One impressive simulation, which was designed to run on a supercomputer, tracked the movement of thousands of dust particles as they were tossed about by a tornado.

At one time, supercomputer designers focused on building specialized, very fast, and very large CPUs. Today, most supercomputer CPUs are constructed from thousands of microprocessors. Of the 500 fastest supercomputers in the world, the majority use microprocessor technology.

FIGURE 1-21

High-end mobile phones and similar handheld devices allow you to install your choice of application software.

▶ Are handheld devices computers? Handheld digital devices include familiar gadgets such as iPhones, iPads, iPods, Garmin GPSs, Droids, and Kindles. These devices incorporate many computer characteristics. They accept input, produce output, process data, and include storage capabilities. Handheld devices vary in their programmability and their versatility.

Handheld devices can be divided into two broad categories: those that allow users to install software applications (apps) and those that do not. A handheld device that allows you to install applications can be classified as a **handheld computer** to distinguish it from the dedicated handheld devices that do not offer apps.

iPod touch devices, for example, offer access to a wide range of apps that include games, ebook readers, maps, comics, recipes, and news. Many high-end mobile phones can also be classified as handheld computers (Figure 1-21).

MICROCONTROLLERS

▶ **What is a microcontroller?** Have you ever wondered how a guided missile reaches its target or how your refrigerator knows when to initiate a defrost cycle? What controls your microwave oven, digital video recorder, washing machine, and watch? Many common appliances and machines are controlled by embedded microcontrollers. A **microcontroller** is a special-purpose microprocessor that is built into the machine it controls. A microcontroller, such as the one in Figure 1-22, is sometimes called a computer-on-a-chip or an embedded computer because it includes many of the elements common to computers.

© mbed

FIGURE 1-22

A microcontroller is a self-contained chip that can be embedded in an appliance, vehicle, or other device.

▶ **How does a microcontroller work?** Consider the microcontroller in a Sub-Zero refrigerator. It accepts user input for desired temperatures in the refrigerator and freezer compartments. It stores these desired temperatures in memory. Temperature sensors collect additional input of the actual temperatures. The microcontroller processes the input data by comparing the actual temperature to the desired temperature. As output, the microcontroller sends signals to activate the cooling motor as necessary. It also generates a digital readout of the refrigerator and freezer temperatures.

▶ **Is a microcontroller really a computer?** Recall that a computer is defined as a multipurpose device that accepts input, produces output, stores data, and processes it according to a stored program. A microcontroller seems to fit the input, processing, output, and storage criteria that define computers. Some microcontrollers can even be reprogrammed to perform different tasks.

Technically, a microcontroller could be classified as a computer, just as ebook readers and portable media players can be. Despite this technicality, however, microcontrollers tend to be referred to as processors rather than as computers because in practice they are used for dedicated applications, not as multipurpose devices.

❱ **Why are microcontrollers significant?** Microcontrollers can be embedded in all sorts of everyday devices, enabling machines to perform sophisticated tasks that require awareness and feedback from the environment (Figure 1-23).

FIGURE 1-23

A microcontroller is usually mounted on a circuit board and then installed in a machine or appliance using wires to carry input and output signals.

When combined with wireless networks, devices with embedded processors can relay information to Web sites, cell phones, and a variety of data collection devices. Machines and appliances with embedded processors tend to be smarter about their use of resources—such as electricity and water—which makes them environmentally friendly.

Perhaps the most significant effect of microcontrollers is that they are an almost invisible technology, one that doesn't require much adaptation or learning on the part of the people who interact with microcontrolled devices. However, because microcontrollers remain mostly out of sight and out of mind, it is easy for their use to creep into areas that could be detrimental to quality of life, privacy, and freedom.

The GPS chip in your cell phone, for example, can be useful if you're lost and need 911 assistance, but it could potentially be used by marketers, law enforcement, and others who want to track your location without your consent.

QuickCheck   SECTION B

1. A computer is a digital device that processes data according to a series of [ ] instructions called a program or software.

2. Computer data is temporarily stored in [ ], but is usually transferred to [ ] where it can be left on a more permanent basis.

3. [ ] computers are available in desktop and portable models.

4. A digital device, such as a computer, is called a(n) [ ] when it requests data from a server.

5. A(n) [ ] is a special-purpose microprocessor that is built into the machine it controls.

▶ CHECK ANSWERS

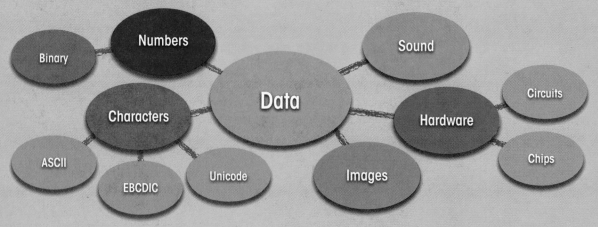

Digital Data Representation

SECTION **C**

COMPUTERS AND OTHER DIGITAL DEVICES work with all sorts of "stuff," including text, numbers, music, images, speech, and video. The amazing aspect of digital technology is that it distills all these different elements down to simple pulses of electricity and stores them as 0s and 1s. Understanding the data representation concepts presented in Section C will help you grasp the essence of the digital world and get a handle on all the jargon pertaining to bits, bytes, megahertz, and gigabytes.

DATA REPRESENTATION BASICS

▶ **What is data?** As you learned earlier in the chapter, *data* refers to the symbols that represent people, events, things, and ideas. Data can be a name, a number, the colors in a photograph, or the notes in a musical composition.

▶ **Is there a difference between data and information?** In everyday conversation, people use the terms *data* and *information* interchangeably. Nevertheless, some technology professionals make a distinction between the two terms. They define data as the symbols that represent people, events, things, and ideas. Data becomes information when it is presented in a format that people can understand and use. As a general rule, remember that (technically speaking) data is used by machines, such as computers; information is used by humans.

▶ **What is data representation?** **Data representation** refers to the form in which data is stored, processed, and transmitted. For example, devices such as mobile phones, iPods, and computers store numbers, text, music, photos, and videos in formats that can be handled by electronic circuitry. Those formats are data representations. Data can be represented using digital or analog methods.

▶ **What's the difference between analog and digital?** For a simple illustration of the difference between analog and digital, consider the way you can control the lights in a room using a traditional light switch or a dimmer switch (Figure 1-24).

A traditional light switch has two discrete states: on and off. There are no in-between states, so this type of light switch is digital. A dimmer switch, on the other hand, has a rotating dial that controls a continuous range of brightness. It is, therefore, analog.

Digital data is text, numbers, graphics, sound, and video that have been converted into discrete digits such as 0s and 1s. In contrast, **analog data** is represented using an infinite scale of values.

FIGURE 1-24

A computer is a digital device, more like a standard light switch than a dimmer switch.

▶ **How does digital data work?** Imagine that you want to send a message by flashing a light. Your light switch offers two states: on and off. You can use sequences of ons and offs to represent various letters of the alphabet. To write down the representation for each letter, you can use 0s and 1s. The 0s represent the off state of your light switch; the 1s indicate the on state. For example, the sequence on on off off would be written as 1100, and you might decide that sequence represents the letter *A*.

Digital devices are electronic and so you can envision data flowing within these devices as pulses of light. In reality, digital signals are represented by two different voltages, such as +5 volts and 0 volts. They can also be represented by two different tones as they flow over a phone line. Digital data can also take the form of light and dark spots etched onto the surface of a CD or the positive and negative orientation of magnetic particles on the surface of a hard disk.

The 0s and 1s used to represent digital data are referred to as binary digits. It is from this term that we get the word *bit—bi*nary digi*t*. A **bit** is a 0 or 1 used in the digital representation of data.

REPRESENTING NUMBERS, TEXT, IMAGES, AND SOUND

▶ **How do digital devices represent numbers?** Numeric data consists of numbers that can be used in arithmetic operations. For example, your annual income is numeric data, as is your age. Digital devices represent numeric data using the binary number system, also called base 2.

The **binary number system** has only two digits: 0 and 1. No numeral like 2 exists in this system, so the number two is represented in binary as 10 (pronounced *one zero*). You'll understand why if you think about what happens when you're counting from 1 to 10 in the familiar decimal system. After you reach 9, you run out of digits. For ten, you have to use the digits 10—zero is a placeholder and the 1 indicates one group of tens.

In binary, you just run out of digits sooner—right after you count to 1. To get to the next number, you have to use the 0 as a placeholder and the 1 indicates one group of twos. In binary, then, you count 0 (zero), 1 (one), 10 (one zero), instead of counting 0, 1, 2 in decimal. If you need to brush up on binary numbers, refer to Figure 1-25 and to the lab at the end of the chapter.

Decimal (Base 10)	Binary (Base 2)
0	0
1	1
2	10
3	11
4	100
5	101
6	110
7	111
8	1000
9	1001
10	1010
11	1011
1000	1111101000

FIGURE 1-25

The decimal system uses ten symbols to represent numbers: 0, 1, 2, 3, 4, 5, 6, 7, 8, and 9. The binary number system uses only two symbols: 0 and 1.

The important point to understand is that the binary number system allows digital devices to represent virtually any number simply by using 0s and 1s. Digital devices can then perform calculations using these numbers.

❚ How do digital devices represent words and letters?

Character data is composed of letters, symbols, and numerals that are not used in arithmetic operations. Examples of character data include your name, address, and hair color. Just as Morse code uses dashes and dots to represent the letters of the alphabet, a digital computer uses a series of bits to represent letters, characters, and numerals. Figure 1-26 illustrates how a computer can use 0s and 1s to represent the letters and symbols in the text *HI!*

Digital devices employ several types of codes to represent character data, including ASCII, EBCDIC, and Unicode. **ASCII** (American Standard Code for Information Interchange, pronounced "*ASK ee*") requires only seven bits for each character. For example, the ASCII code for an uppercase *A* is 1000001. ASCII provides codes for 128 characters, including uppercase letters, lowercase letters, punctuation symbols, and numerals.

A superset of ASCII, called **Extended ASCII**, uses eight bits to represent each character. For example, Extended ASCII represents the uppercase letter *A* as 01000001. Using eight bits instead of seven bits allows Extended ASCII to provide codes for 256 characters. The additional Extended ASCII characters include boxes and other graphical symbols. Figure 1-27 lists the Extended ASCII character set.

FIGURE 1-26

A computer treats the letters and symbols in the word *HI!* as character data, which can be represented by a string of 0s and 1s.

01001000   01001001 00100001

FIGURE 1-27

The Extended ASCII code uses eight 1s and 0s to represent letters, symbols, and numerals. The first 32 ASCII characters are not shown in the table because they represent special control sequences that cannot be printed. The two blank entries are space characters.

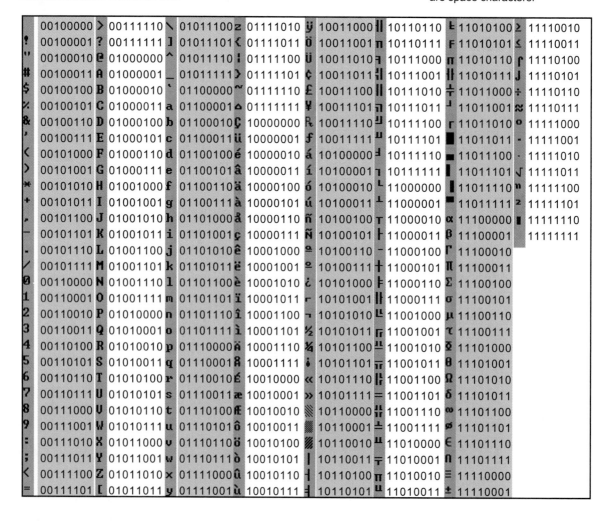

An alternative to the 8-bit Extended ASCII code, called **EBCDIC** (Extended Binary-Coded Decimal Interchange Code, pronounced *EB seh dick*), is usually used only by older, IBM mainframe computers.

Unicode (pronounced "*YOU ni code*") uses sixteen bits and provides codes for 65,000 characters—a real bonus for representing the alphabets of multiple languages. For example, Unicode represents an uppercase *A* in the Russian Cyrillic alphabet as 0000010000010000.

▶ **Why do ASCII and Extended ASCII provide codes for 0, 1, 2, 3, 4, 5, 6, 7, 8, and 9?** While glancing at the table of ASCII codes in Figure 1-27, you might have wondered why the table contains codes for 0, 1, 2, 3, and so on. Aren't these numbers represented by the binary number system? A computer uses Extended ASCII character codes for 0, 1, 2, 3 , etc. to represent numerals that are not used for calculations. For example, you don't typically use your Social Security number in calculations, so it is considered character data and represented using Extended ASCII. Likewise, the numbers in your street address can be represented by character codes rather than binary numbers.

▶ **How can bits be used to store images?** Images, such as photos, pictures, line art, and graphs, are not small, discrete objects like numbers or the letters of the alphabet. Images have to be digitized in order for digital devices to work with them.

Images can be digitized by treating them as a series of colored dots. Each dot is assigned a binary number according to its color. For example, a green dot might be represented by 0010 and a red dot by 1100, as shown in Figure 1-28. A digital image is simply a list of color numbers for all the dots it contains.

▶ **How can bits be used to store sound?** Sound, such as music and speech, is characterized by the properties of a sound wave. You can create a comparable wave by etching it onto a vinyl platter—essentially how records were made in the days of jukeboxes and record players. You can also represent that sound wave digitally by sampling it at various points, and then converting those points into digital numbers. The more samples you take, the closer your points come to approximating the full wave pattern. This process of sampling, illustrated in Figure 1-29, is how digital recordings are made.

FIGURE 1-28

An image can be digitized by assigning a binary number to each dot.

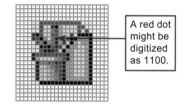

A red dot might be digitized as 1100.

FIGURE 1-29

A sound wave can be sampled at fraction-of-a-second time intervals. Each sample is recorded as a binary number and stored.

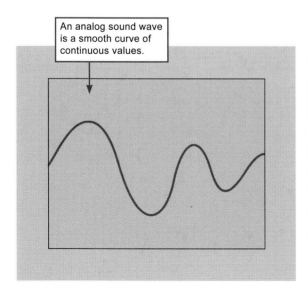

An analog sound wave is a smooth curve of continuous values.

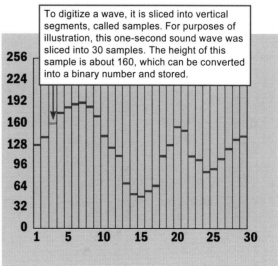

To digitize a wave, it is sliced into vertical segments, called samples. For purposes of illustration, this one-second sound wave was sliced into 30 samples. The height of this sample is about 160, which can be converted into a binary number and stored.

QUANTIFYING BITS AND BYTES

▶ **How can I tell the difference between bits and bytes?**
The ads for digital devices typically include lots of abbreviations relating to bits and bytes. A few key concepts can help you understand what these abbreviations mean. Even though the word *bit* is an abbreviation for *binary digit*, it can be further abbreviated, usually as a lowercase *b*.

On older digital devices, bits were handled in groups, and terminology from that era is still used. A group of eight bits is called a **byte** and is usually abbreviated as an uppercase *B*.

Transmission speeds are typically expressed in bits, whereas storage space is typically expressed in bytes. For example, a cable Internet connection might transfer data from the Internet to your computer at 8 mega*bits* per second. In an iPod ad, you might notice that it can store up to 60 giga*bytes* of music and video.

▶ **What do the prefixes *kilo-*, *mega-*, *giga-*, and *tera-* mean?** When reading about digital devices, you'll frequently encounter references such as 50 kilobits per second, 1.44 megabytes, 2.8 gigahertz, and 2 terabytes. *Kilo*, *mega*, *giga*, *tera*, and similar terms are used to quantify digital data.

In common usage, *kilo*, abbreviated as K, means a thousand. For example, $50K means $50,000. In the context of computers, however, 50K means 51,200. Why the difference? In the decimal number system we use on a daily basis, the number 1,000 is 10 to the third power, or 10^3. For digital devices where base 2 is the norm, a kilo is precisely 1,024, or 2^{10}. A **kilobit** (abbreviated Kb or Kbit) is 1,024 bits. A **kilobyte** (abbreviated KB or Kbyte) is 1,024 bytes. Kilobytes are often used when referring to the size of small computer files.

The prefix *mega* means a million, or in the context of bits and bytes, precisely 1,048,576 (the equivalent of 2^{20}). A **megabit** (Mb or Mbit) is 1,048,576 bits. A **megabyte** (MB or MByte) is 1,048,576 bytes. Megabytes are often used when referring to the size of medium to large computer files.

In technology lingo, the prefix *giga* refers to a billion, or precisely 1,073,741,824. As you might expect, a **gigabit** (Gb or Gbit) is approximately 1 billion bits. A **gigabyte** (GB or GByte) is 1 billion bytes. Gigabytes are typically used to refer to storage capacity.

Computers—especially mainframes and supercomputers—sometimes work with huge amounts of data, and so terms such as *tera* (trillion), *peta* (thousand trillion), and *exa* (quintillion) are also handy. Figure 1-30 summarizes the terms commonly used to quantify computer data.

> **TERMINOLOGY NOTE**
>
> What's a kibibyte? Some computer scientists have proposed alternative terminology to dispel the ambiguity in terms such as *mega* that can mean 1,000 or 1,024. They suggest the following prefixes:
>
> Kibi = 1,024
>
> Mebi = 1,048,576
>
> Gibi = 1,073,741,824

Bit	One binary digit	Gigabit	2^{30} bits
Byte	8 bits	Gigabyte	2^{30} bytes
Kilobit	1,024 or 2^{10} bits	Terabyte	2^{40} bytes
Kilobyte	1,024 or 2^{10} bytes	Petabyte	2^{50} bytes
Megabit	1,048,576 or 2^{20} bits	Exabyte	2^{60} bytes
Megabyte	1,048,576 or 2^{20} bytes		

FIGURE 1-30

Quantifying Digital Data

CIRCUITS AND CHIPS

❱ **How do digital devices store and transport all those bits?** Because most digital devices are electronic, bits take the form of electrical pulses that can travel over circuits in much the same way that electricity flows over a wire when you turn on a light switch. All the circuits, chips, and mechanical components that form a digital device are designed to work with bits.

At the simplest level, you can envision bits as two states of an electric circuit; the state used for a 1 bit would be on and the state for a 0 bit would be off. In practice, the 1 bit might be represented by an elevated voltage, such as +5 volts, whereas a 0 bit is represented by a low voltage, such as 0.

❱ **What's inside?** If it weren't for the miniaturization made possible by digital electronic technology, computers, cell phones, and portable media players would be huge, and contain a complex jumble of wires and other electronic gizmos. Instead, today's digital devices contain relatively few parts—just a few wires, some microchips, and one or more circuit boards.

❱ **What's a computer chip?** The terms *computer chip*, *microchip*, and *chip* originated as technical jargon for integrated circuit. An **integrated circuit** (IC), such as the one pictured in Figure 1-31, is a super-thin slice of semiconducting material packed with microscopic circuit elements, such as wires, transistors, capacitors, logic gates, and resistors.

Semiconducting materials (or semiconductors), such as silicon and germanium, are substances with properties between those of a conductor (like copper) and an insulator (like wood). To fabricate a chip, the conductive properties of selective parts of the semiconducting material can be enhanced to essentially create miniature electronic pathways and components, such as transistors.

FIGURE 1-31

The first computer chips contained fewer than 100 miniaturized components, such as diodes and transistors. The chips used as the CPUs for today's computers and cutting edge graphics cards contain billions of transistors.

Integrated circuits are packaged in protective carriers that vary in shape and size. Figure 1-32 illustrates some chip carriers, including small rectangular DIPs (dual in-line packages) with caterpillar-like legs protruding from a black, rectangular body; and pincushion-like PGAs (pin-grid arrays).

A DIP has two rows of pins that connect the IC circuitry to a circuit board.

A PGA is a square chip package with pins arranged in concentric squares, typically used for microprocessors.

FIGURE 1-32

Integrated circuits can be used for microprocessors, memory, and support circuitry. They are housed within a ceramic carrier. These carriers exist in several configurations, or chip packages, such as DIPs and PGAs.

▶ **How do chips fit together?** The electronic components of most digital devices are mounted on a circuit board called a system board, motherboard, or main board. The **system board** houses all essential chips and provides connecting circuitry between them. Figure 1-33 illustrates circuit boards for two digital devices. Although one device is a full-size computer and the other is an iPhone, they both have chips for processing, memory, input, and output.

FIGURE 1-33

The electronic components of computers and handheld devices have many similar elements, including microchips and circuit boards. Circuit boards are usually green, whereas microchips are usually black.

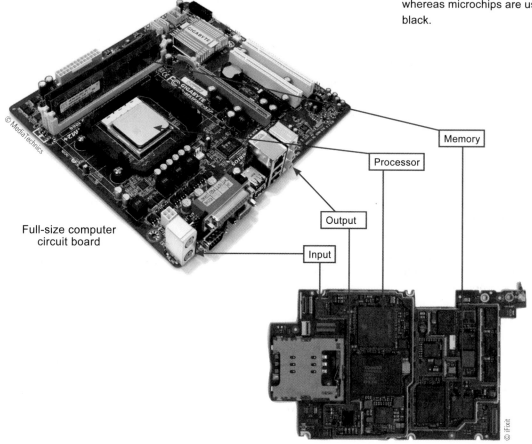

Full-size computer circuit board

Memory

Processor

Output

Input

iPhone circuit board (enlarged)

QuickCheck   SECTION C

1. Data [_____] refers to the format in which data is stored, processed, and transferred.

2. Digital devices often use the [_____] number system to represent numeric data.

3. Most computers use Unicode or Extended [_____] code to represent character data. (Hint: Use the acronym.)

4. KB is the abbreviation for [_____].

5. Integrated circuits are fabricated from [_____] materials that have properties of a conductor and an insulator.

▶ CHECK ANSWERS

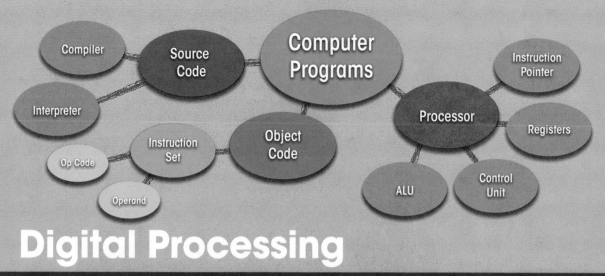

Digital Processing

COMPUTERS AND OTHER DIGITAL DEVICES process data, but how do they know what to do with it? The instructions you issue aren't 0s and 1s that a digital device can work with. So what goes on inside the box? Section D explains the programs that make digital devices tick. You'll discover that although digital devices appear to perform very complex tasks, under the hood they are really performing some very simple operations, but doing them at lightning speed.

PROGRAMS AND INSTRUCTION SETS

▶ **How do digital devices process data?** Computers and dedicated handheld devices all work with digital data under the control of a computer program. Let's take a closer look at programs to see how they are created and how digital devices work with them.

▶ **Who creates programs?** Computer programmers create programs that control digital devices. These programs are usually written in a high-level **programming language**, such as C, BASIC, COBOL, or Java.

Programming languages use a limited set of command words such as *Print*, *If*, *Write*, *Display*, and *Get* to form sentence-like statements designed as step-by-step directives for the processor chip. An important characteristic of most programming languages is that they can be written with simple tools, such as a word processor, and they can be understood by programmers. A simple program to select a song on your iPod might contain the statements shown in Figure 1-34.

```
Display Playlist
Get Song
Play Song
```

FIGURE 1-34

The program for an iPod displays a list of songs that the user can choose to play. A program works behind the scenes to display the list, get your selection, process it, and play the song.

The human-readable version of a program, like the one above, created in a high-level language by a programmer is called **source code**. However, just as a digital device can't work directly with text, sounds, or images until they have been digitized, source code has to be converted into a digital format before the processor can use it.

29

How does source code get converted? The procedure for translating source code into 0s and 1s can be accomplished by a compiler or an interpreter. A **compiler** converts all the statements in a program in a single batch, and the resulting collection of instructions, called **object code**, is placed in a new file (Figure 1-35). Most of the program files distributed as software contain object code that is ready for the processor to execute.

FIGURE 1-35

A compiler converts statements written in a high-level programming language into object code that the processor can execute.
▶ Watch a compiler in action.

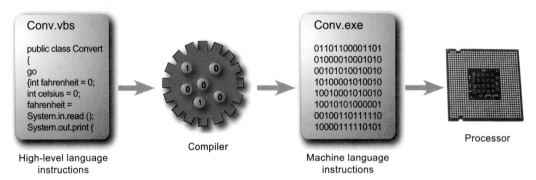

As an alternative to a compiler, an **interpreter** converts and executes one statement at a time while the program is running. After a statement is executed, the interpreter converts and executes the next statement, and so on (Figure 1-36).

FIGURE 1-36

An interpreter converts high-level statements one at a time as the program is running.
▶ Watch an interpreter in action.

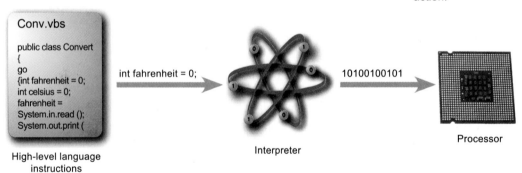

Compilers and interpreters don't simply convert the characters from source code into 0s and 1s. For example, in the first line of the iPod program, Display Playlist, a compiler would not simply convert the *D* into its ASCII equivalent. No, computers are a little trickier than that.

What does the conversion process produce? A microprocessor is hard-wired to perform a limited set of activities, such as addition, subtraction, counting, and comparisons. This collection of preprogrammed activities is called an **instruction set**. Instruction sets are not designed to carry out any specific task, such as word processing or playing music. Instead, an instruction set is designed to be general purpose so that programmers can use it in creative ways for the wide variety of tasks performed by all kinds of digital devices.

Each instruction has a corresponding sequence of 0s and 1s. For example, 00000100 might correspond to *Add*. The list of codes for a microprocessor's instruction set, called **machine language**, can be directly executed by the processor's circuitry. A set of machine language instructions for a program is called **machine code**.

A machine language instruction has two parts: the op code and the operands. An **op code**, which is short for *operation code*, is a command word for an operation such as add, compare, or jump. The **operand** for an instruction specifies the data, or the address of the data, for the operation. In the following instruction, the op code means add and the operand is 1, so the instruction means add 1.

A single high-level instruction very often converts into multiple machine language instructions. Figure 1-37 illustrates the number of machine language instructions that correspond to a simple high-level program.

```
#include <stdio.h>
int main ()
{
int i;

for (i=1; i<=100; i=i+1)
  printf("%d\t",i);
return(0);
}
```

```
00100111101111011111111111100000
10101111101111110000000000010100
10101111101001000000000000100000
10101111101001010000000000100100
10101111101000000000000000011000
10101111101000000000000000011100
10001111101011000000000000011100
10001111101110000000000000011000
00000001110011100000000000011001
00100101110010000000000000000001
00101001000000010000000001100101
10101111101010000000000000011100
00000000000000000111110000010010
00000011000011111110010000010000 1
00010100001000001111111111110111
10101111101110010000000000011000
00111100000000100000100000000000
10001111101001010000000000011000
00001100000010000000000001101100
00100100100001000000000100000000
```

FIGURE 1-37

The source code program on the left prints numbers from 1 to 100. This source code is converted to machine language instructions shown in the right column that the computer can directly process.

To summarize what you should now know about programs and instruction sets, a programmer creates human-readable source code using a programming language. A compiler or interpreter converts source code into machine code. Machine code instructions are a series of 0s and 1s that correspond to a processor's instruction set.

PROCESSOR LOGIC

▶ **What happens inside a computer chip?** A microprocessor contains miles of microscopic circuitry and millions of miniature components divided into different kinds of operational units, such as the ALU and the control unit.

The **ALU** (arithmetic logic unit) is the part of the microprocessor that performs arithmetic operations, such as addition and subtraction. It also performs logical operations, such as comparing two numbers to see if they are the same. The ALU uses **registers** to hold data that is being processed, just as you use a mixing bowl to hold the ingredients for a batch of cookies.

The microprocessor's **control unit** fetches each instruction, just as you get each ingredient out of a cupboard or the refrigerator. Data is loaded into the ALU's registers, just as you add all the ingredients to the mixing bowl. Finally, the control unit gives the ALU the green light to begin processing, just as you flip the switch on your electric mixer to begin blending the cookie ingredients. Figure 1-38 illustrates a microprocessor control unit and an ALU preparing to add 2 + 3.

FIGURE 1-38

The control unit fetches the ADD instruction, then loads data into the ALU's registers where it is processed.

▶ What happens when a computer executes an instruction?
The term **instruction cycle** refers to the process in which a computer executes a single instruction. Some parts of the instruction cycle are performed by the microprocessor's control unit; other parts of the cycle are performed by the ALU. The steps in this cycle are summarized in Figure 1-39.

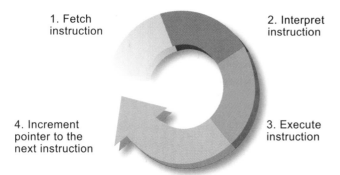

1. Fetch instruction

2. Interpret instruction

4. Increment pointer to the next instruction

3. Execute instruction

FIGURE 1-39

The instruction cycle includes four activities.

▶ What role does the control unit play? The instructions that a computer is supposed to process for a particular program are held in memory. When the program begins, the memory address of the first instruction is placed in a part of the microprocessor's control unit called an instruction pointer. The control unit can then fetch the instruction by copying data from that address into its instruction register. From there, the control unit can interpret the instruction, gather the specified data, or tell the ALU to begin processing. Figure 1-40 helps you visualize the control unit's role in processing an instruction.

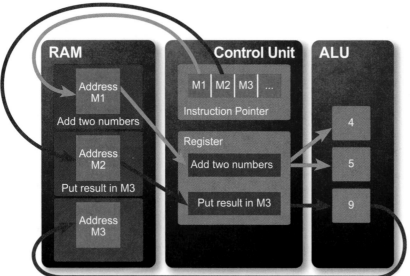

FIGURE 1-40

The control unit's instruction pointer indicates M1, a location in memory. The control unit fetches the "Add two numbers" instruction from M1. This instruction is then sent to the ALU. The instruction pointer then changes to M2. The processor fetches the instruction located in M2, moves it to a register, and executes it.
▶ See how it works.

▶ When does the ALU swing into action? The ALU is responsible for performing arithmetic and logical operations. It uses registers to hold data ready to be processed. When it gets the go-ahead signal from the control unit, the ALU processes the data and places the result in an accumulator. From the accumulator, the data can be sent to memory or used for further processing. Figure 1-41 on the next page helps you visualize what happens in the ALU as the computer processes data.

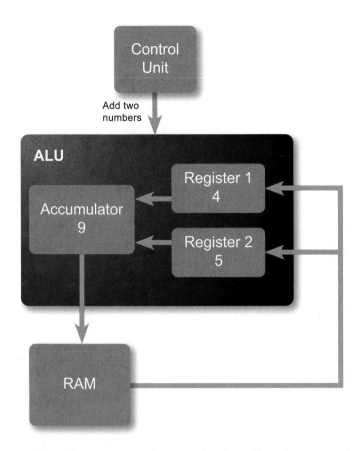

FIGURE 1-41

In this example, the ALU's registers contain the numbers 4 and 5. When the ALU receives the "Add two numbers" instruction from the control unit, it adds 4 and 5 then places the result in the accumulator.

1

▶ **What happens after an instruction is executed?** When the computer completes an instruction, the control unit increments the instruction pointer to the memory address of the next instruction, and the instruction cycle begins again.

▶ **Do I need to know all this detailed stuff?** What you should take away from the discussion about programming and instruction sets is the idea that computers and other digital devices accomplish a wide array of complex tasks by performing a very limited set of machine language instructions very fast.

These concepts about how processors work will help you understand the significance of microprocessor performance, such as speed and word size, which you'll learn about in the next chapter.

QuickCheck
SECTION D

1. A(n) [_____] converts all of the source code instructions into object code, which becomes a new file containing [_____] code.

2. A microprocessor is hard-wired to perform a set of activities called a(n) [_____] set.

3. A machine language instruction has two parts: a(n) [_____] code and an operand.

4. The ALU in your computer's microprocessor holds data in [_____].

5. The microprocessor's control unit contains a(n) [_____] pointer that holds the address of the instruction being executed.

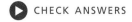 CHECK ANSWERS

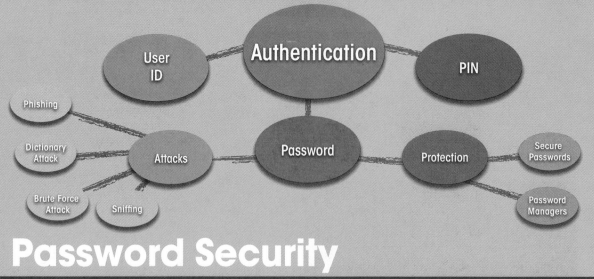

Password Security

SECTION E

USER IDS, passwords, and personal identification numbers (PINs) are a fact of everyday life in the information age. They are required for activities such as using ATMs and debit cards, logging into Windows, accessing wireless networks, making an iTunes purchase, instant messaging, reading e-mail, and file sharing. Many Web sites encourage you to sign up for membership by choosing a user ID and password. Section E provides information about selecting secure passwords and managing the mountain of passwords you collect and tend to forget.

AUTHENTICATION PROTOCOLS

▶ **What is an authentication protocol?** Security experts use the term **authentication protocol** to refer to any method that confirms a person's identity using something the person knows, something the person possesses, or something the person is. For example, a person might know a password or PIN. A person might possess an ATM card or a credit card. A person can also be identified by **biometrics**, such as a fingerprint, facial features (photo), or a retinal pattern (Figure 1-42).

Authentication protocols that use more than one means of identification are more secure than others. Two-factor authentication, which verifies identity using two independent elements of confirmation such as an ATM card and a PIN, is more secure than single-factor authentication, such as a password. Computer-related security is primarily based on passwords associated with user IDs. The level of protection offered by single-factor authentication depends on good password selection and management on the part of users.

▶ **What is a user ID?** A **user ID** is a series of characters—letters and possibly numbers or special symbols—that becomes a person's unique identifier, similar to a Social Security number. It is also referred to as a user name, login, screen name, online nickname, or handle. User IDs are typically public. Because they are not secret, they do not offer any level of security.

The rules for creating a user ID are not consistent throughout all applications, so it is important to read instructions carefully before finalizing your user ID. For example, spaces might not be allowed in a user ID. Hence, the underline in brunhilde_jefferson is used instead of a space. There might be a length limitation, so Ms. Jefferson might have to choose a short user ID, such as bjeffe. It is becoming common to use your e-mail address as a user ID; it is unique and easy to remember.

FIGURE 1-42

Biometric authentication protocols include retinal scans that identify unique patterns of blood vessels in the eye.

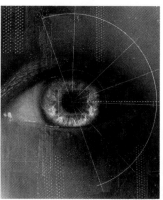

Some computers that host password-protected resources don't differentiate between uppercase and lowercase letters, and would consider the user IDs B_Jefferson and b_jefferson to be the same. Other computers are **case sensitive** and differentiate between uppercase and lowercase. On such computers, if Ms. Jefferson selected Brun_Jeff as her user ID, she would not be able to gain access by typing brun_jeff. To avoid such problems, most people stick to lowercase letters for their user IDs.

▶ What is a password? A **password** is a series of characters that verifies a user ID and guarantees that you are the person you claim to be. Although you might be assigned a password, typically you are asked to provide your own. In some situations you might be given a temporary password, and then asked to change it as soon as you successfully log in for the first time. Passwords and user IDs are typically created on a registration or enrollment screen similar to the one in Figure 1-43.

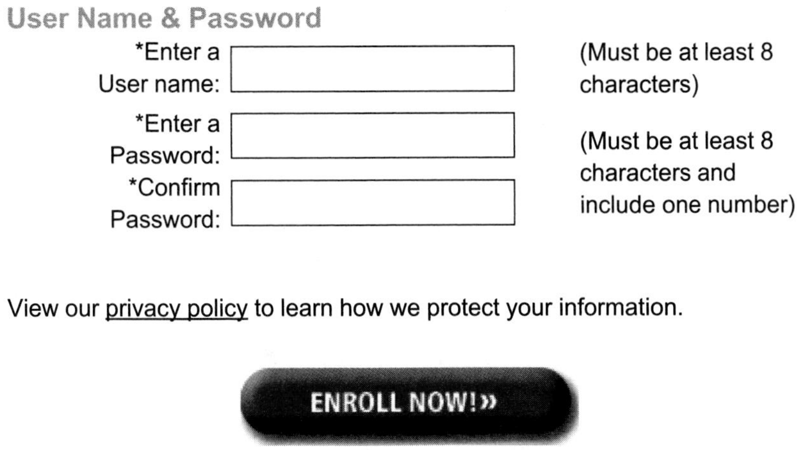

User Name & Password

*Enter a User name:	_____	(Must be at least 8 characters)
*Enter a Password:	_____	(Must be at least 8 characters and include one number)
*Confirm Password:	_____	

View our privacy policy to learn how we protect your information.

ENROLL NOW!»

FIGURE 1-43

When you create an account, you are typically asked to enter a user ID and password.

▶ What if I forget my password? Login screens for many applications provide a "forgot my password" link. Clicking this link checks your identity using your answer to a personal question. If your identity checks out, your password is e-mailed to you. A personal question provides an alternative authentication protocol to ensure that you are not a hacker pretending to be a legitimate user who has lost a password.

Personal questions and answers are usually set up at the same time you create an account. After selecting a password, you are required to choose a question that you must answer before your forgotten password is e-mailed to you. This question might be something like: *What is your mother's maiden name?*, *What is your favorite color?*, or *Where were you born?* You should be careful about the question you choose because public information like your mother's maiden name or the town of your birth can be researched by any hacker.

▶ What is the difference between a password and a PIN? Both passwords and PINs are classified as *something-the-user-knows* authentication methods. In practice, PINs tend to be a short sequence of numbers that can be entered using a numeric keypad, whereas passwords tend to be longer sequences of letters, numbers, and special characters that require a full qwerty keyboard for entry. PINs are typically used with two-factor authentication protocols, whereas passwords are used in conjunction with single-factor authentication protocols.

For example, ATMs require a bank card (something you possess) and a PIN (something you know). In contrast, passwords are associated with single-factor authentication used for networks, Web sites, and other situations in which the hardware for dealing with ID cards is not available.

PASSWORD HACKS

▶ **How serious is password theft?** To a hacker, obtaining the password for a specific user ID can be even more rewarding than a burglar figuring out the combination to a house safe. Once hackers get into a user account, a wealth of personal information can be at their fingertips. This information could be anything from juicy e-mail gossip to Social Security numbers, credit card numbers, bank account numbers, health data, and other private details. When someone gains unauthorized access to your personal data and uses it illegally, it is called **identity theft**. Victims of this increasingly common crime often don't realize what has happened until it's too late.

TERMINOLOGY NOTE

Hacker can refer to a skilled programmer or to a person who manipulates computers with malicious intent. The terms *black hat* and *cracker* are also used to refer to a malicious or criminal hacker.

Armed with your password and other personal data, a cybercriminal can rack up bills using your credit card, apply for a mortgage using your financial data, create fake accounts in your name, send embarrassing e-mail messages, or wreak havoc on your bank account. Once a thief breaks into an online account, he or she can also change your password and you will no longer be able to log in. Password theft is serious and pervasive, so it is important to understand how hackers get passwords and how you can protect yours.

▶ **How can hackers get my password?** Hackers employ a whole range of ways to steal passwords. Some primitive means include shoulder surfing, which is looking over your shoulder as you type in your password, and dumpster diving, which is going through your trash.

Password thieves can easily find your password if you write it down on a yellow sticky note hidden under your keyboard or in plain sight on top of your monitor. If a hacker doesn't have physical access to your work area but your computer is connected to a network, your password can be discovered by a hacker using a remote computer and software tools that systematically guess your password, intercept it, or trick you into revealing it.

A **dictionary attack** helps hackers guess your password by stepping through a dictionary containing thousands of the most commonly used passwords. Password dictionaries can be found on black hat sites and packaged with password-cracking software, such as John the Ripper. Unfortunately, dictionary attacks are often enough to break a password because many users choose passwords that are easy to remember and likely to be in the most commonly used list (Figure 1-44).

FIGURE 1-44

Some of the most commonly used passwords are included in the dictionaries packaged with password-cracking software. These passwords (listed in order of popularity) should not be used.

12345	internet	jordan	alex	newyork	jonathan
abc123	service	michael	apple	soccer	love
password	canada	michelle	avalon	thomas	marina
computer	hello	mindy	brandy	wizard	master
123456	ranger	patrick	chelsea	Monday	missy
tigger	shadow	123abc	coffee	asdfgh	monday
1234	baseball	andrew	dave	bandit	monkey
a1b2c3	donald	bear	falcon	batman	natasha
qwerty	harley	calvin	freedom	boris	ncc1701
123	hockey	changeme	gandalf	dorothy	newpass
xxx	letmein	diamond	golf	eeyore	pamela
money	maggie	matthew	green	fishing	pepper
test	mike	miller	helpme	football	piglet
carmen	mustang	ou812	linda	george	poohbear
mickey	snoopy	tiger	magic	happy	pookie
secret	buster	trustno1	merlin	iloveyou	rabbit
summer	dragon	12345678	molson	jennifer	rachel

The **brute force attack** also uses password-cracking software, but its range is much more extensive than the dictionary attack. Because it exhausts all possible combinations of letters to decrypt a password, a brute force attack can run for days to crack some passwords.

If hackers can't guess a password, they can use another technique called **sniffing**, which intercepts information sent out over computer networks. Sniffing software is used legitimately by network administrators to record network traffic for monitoring and maintenance purposes. The same software can also be used for illicit activities. If your user ID and password travel over a network as unencrypted text, they can easily fall into the hands of a password thief.

An even more sophisticated approach to password theft is **phishing**, in which a hacker poses as a legitimate representative of an official organization such as your ISP, your bank, or an online payment service in order to persuade you to disclose highly confidential information. Mostly through e-mail or instant messaging, a fake customer representative or administrator asks you to visit a Web page to confirm billing information or verify your account by providing your password, credit card number, or Social Security number.

If you examine phishing messages more closely, you might realize that the Web sites referred to are fake. However, seasoned hackers try to make the URLs look as close as possible to the official Web sites they claim to represent (Figure 1-45).

FIGURE 1-45

A fake Web site can look very similar to the real thing, but this fraudulent site originates in Korea. Do you notice that the URL is *www.paypvl.com* instead of the legitimate *www.paypal. com*? You should avoid clicking links in e-mail messages that attempt to get you to confirm or renew account data.

As users became better at identifying phishing messages, password thieves resorted to the use of keyloggers. Short for *keystroke logging*, a **keylogger** is software that secretly records a user's keystrokes and sends the information to a hacker. A keylogger is a form of malicious code called a Trojan horse, or Trojan. Trojans are computer programs that seem to perform one function while actually doing something else. They can be embedded in e-mail attachments, software downloads, and even files. Trojans are discussed in more detail in the security section of the Software chapter.

SECURE PASSWORDS

▶ **How do I create a secure password?** With password theft becoming more and more widespread, security experts recommend using a strong, secure password for financial transactions such as those that involve PayPal, iTunes, or bank accounts. A strong, secure password is one that is easy to remember but difficult to crack. Figure 1-46 offers guidelines for selecting secure passwords and avoiding ones that are easily crackable.

FIGURE 1-46

Tips for Creating Secure Passwords

▶ Use passwords that are at least eight characters in length. The longer the password, the tougher it is to crack.

▶ Use a combination of letters, numbers, and special characters such as $, #, if permitted.

▶ Use uppercase and lowercase letters if the hosting computer is case sensitive.

▶ Use a passphrase based on several words or the first letters of a verse from a favorite poem or song. For example, the words from the nursery rhyme "Jack and Jill went up the hill" can be converted to jjwuth. You can then insert special characters and numbers, and add some uppercase letters to create a password that still makes sense to you personally, such as J&J w^th!ll. This type of password appears random to anyone else but you.

▶ Do not use a password based on public information such as your phone number, Social Security number, driver's license number, or birthday. Hackers can easily find this information, and other personal facts such as names of your spouse, children, or pets.

▶ Avoid passwords that contain your entire user ID or part of it. A user ID of bjeffe coupled with a password of bjeffe123 is an easy target for password thieves.

▶ Steer clear of words that can be found in the dictionary, including foreign words. Dictionary attacks can utilize foreign language dictionaries. Even common words spelled backwards, such as *drowssap* instead of *password*, are not tricky enough to fool password-cracking software.

▶ **How do I protect my password?** Once you have selected a strong password, you must take steps to keep it safe. Do not share your password with anyone. Avoid writing down a password. If possible, memorize it. If you must write down a password, do not leave it in an obvious place such as under your keyboard or mouse pad. Recording passwords in an unencrypted file stored on your computer is risky, too, especially if you have more than one password. A hacker who gains access to that file can use the passwords to access all your accounts.

If you think one of your passwords has been compromised, change it immediately. Even if you have no evidence of password tampering, security experts recommend that you change passwords periodically, say every six months. When you change your passwords, do not just make a slight variation to your current one. For example, do not change just4Me1 to just4Me2. You should not reuse your old passwords either, so it's best to keep a password history list.

Aside from good password maintenance habits, computer maintenance is also essential. Make sure that your entire computer is protected by security software, which is explained in the Software chapter.

▶ **How do I deal with all my passwords and user IDs?** You can accumulate many passwords and user IDs—for logging in to Windows, accessing online banking, using e-mail, shopping online, downloading music, and getting into your Facebook account. The more passwords and user IDs you have, the more difficult they become to remember.

How many times have you had to click on the "I forgot my password" link when you logged in to an online account? Your passwords provide the most protection if they are unique, but accessing even 25 different Web sites that require 25 different user IDs and 25 corresponding passwords requires quite a memory. To add to the confusion, you must also regularly change passwords to your critical accounts!

Instead of using 25 different user IDs and passwords, you need some way to reduce the number of things you have to memorize. First, strive to select a unique user ID that you can use for more than one site. Remember that people with your name who selected user IDs before you might have already taken the obvious user IDs. For example, when John Smith selects a user ID, you can bet that other people have already used johnsmith, jsmith, and john_smith. To keep his user ID unique, John might instead select jsl2wm (the first letters in "John Smith loves 2 watch movies").

Next, you can maintain two or three tiers of passwords—the top level for high security, the second level for medium security, and the third level for low security. If you do not have too many accounts, you can opt for just two tiers—for high and low security. You can then select two passwords. Use the high-security password for accessing critical data, such as online banking, for managing an online stock portfolio, or for your account at an online bookstore that stores a copy of your billing and credit card information.

Use your low-security password in situations where you don't really care if your security is compromised. Some places on the Internet want you to establish an account with a user ID and password just so that they can put you on a mailing list. At other sites, your user ID and password provide access to information, but none of your critical personal or financial data is stored there. It is not necessary to change your low-security password very often. Figure 1-47 provides more information about tiered passwords.

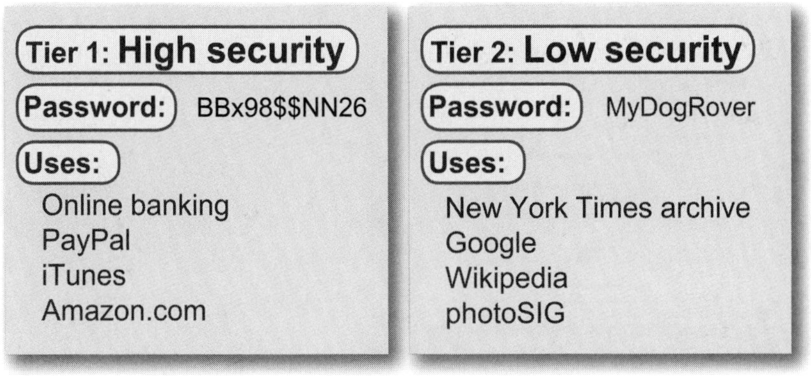

FIGURE 1-47

Tiered passwords reduce the number of user IDs and passwords that you have to remember; however, the disadvantage is that a hacker who discovers one of your passwords will be able to use it to access many of your accounts.

(Tier 1: **High security**)

(Password:) BBx98$$NN26

(Uses:)
Online banking
PayPal
iTunes
Amazon.com

(Tier 2: **Low security**)

(Password:) MyDogRover

(Uses:)
New York Times archive
Google
Wikipedia
photoSIG

▶ Can my computer help me to remember passwords?

Your computer's operating system, Web browser, or other software might include a password manager to help you keep track of user IDs and passwords. A **password manager** (sometimes called a keychain) stores user IDs with their corresponding passwords and automatically fills in login forms. For example, when you register at a Web site while using a browser such as Internet Explorer, the browser stores your new ID and password in an encrypted file on your computer's hard disk. The next time you visit the Web site, your ID and password are automatically filled in on the login screen (Figure 1-48).

The drawback to password managers that are built into browsers, operating systems, or other software is that if you switch to different software or to a different computer, you will not have access to the stored passwords. For example, if you typically work with the Safari browser on your MacBook Air, it stores your passwords; but if you use a public computer in a coffee shop, your passwords are not accessible from that machine.

Standalone password manager software offers a more inclusive approach to creating and retrieving passwords.

▶ What is password manager software?

A standalone password manager is a software application that feeds passwords into login forms regardless of the software you're using. As with built-in password managers, a standalone password manager stores user IDs and passwords in an encrypted file. You can access this file using a master password. This type of password manager can be moved from one computer to another, for example, if you purchase a new computer.

A standalone password manager can also generate secure "nonsense passwords." You don't have to worry if the passwords are difficult to remember because the password manager software can keep track of them (Figure 1-49).

FIGURE 1-48

Checking the "Remember me" box saves your user ID and password for the next time you log in, but you have to be using the same browser.

FIGURE 1-49

Password managers help you keep track of all your passwords. ▶ If you've never used a password manager and want to see how one works, start the guided tour for this figure in your interactive eBook.

In addition to generating and tracking your passwords, most password manager software provides other features, such as password strength meters and form fillers.

A password strength meter indicates whether your passwords are secure enough—a feature that is useful if you've created your own passwords, rather than using your password manager to generate them.

Form fillers automatically enter data into online Web forms such as those that request billing data when you order at an online shopping site. Many form fillers also match a Web form's URL against a set of valid URLs that you have provided in order to avoid sending data to a fake Web site that you have been lured to visit by a phishing message. When entering passwords, form fillers are not collecting your password from the keyboard; therefore, a hacker's keylogger cannot secretly record keystrokes.

There are several free, shareware, or open source password managers, such as KeePass, RoboForm, and SurfSecret KeyPad. Some password manager software is portable, which means that it does not have to be installed on a computer before it is used. Instead, you can carry it around on a USB flash drive so that your passwords are available wherever you use a computer, such as in your school lab, at the library, or at work. When you remove the flash drive, your portable password manager leaves no traces of passwords behind (Figure 1-50).

For extra protection against intruders who might search your computer for passwords, a flash drive that contains a password manager can be unplugged when you are not accessing password-protected sites. You can also remove the flash drive from your computer when you're out so that your nosy roommate can't snoop through your computer files.

▶ **Should I store passwords in the cloud?** New password management techniques are being developed, but some offer their own set of potential security problems. For example, Web-based password managers can be attractive targets for password thieves. By breaking into a single site, a password thief could harvest thousands of passwords. As new password management technologies appear, make sure you evaluate them carefully before trusting them with your valuable data.

FIGURE 1-50

Some password managers are portable so that you can carry them with you on a USB flash drive.

1

QuickCheck

1. An authentication [_____] is any method that confirms a person's identity using something the person knows, something the person possesses, or something the person is.

2. On a(n) [_____] -sensitive server, the user ID BJP is different than bjp.

3. A(n) [_____] attack can guess your password if you are using common passwords or everyday words.

4. A(n) [_____] scam looks like a request from your bank or an online payment service, but is actually a hacker who wants you to disclose your user ID and password.

5. Most browsers include a built-in password [_____] that remembers the user IDs and passwords you use when logging in to Web sites or online e-mail.

▶ CHECK ANSWERS

Issue: What Is the Value of Information?

THE GUERILLA Open Access Manifesto begins, "Information is power. But like all power, there are those who want to keep it for themselves. The world's entire scientific and cultural heritage, published over centuries in books and journals, is increasingly being digitized and locked up by a handful of private corporations."

Written by Aaron Swartz, the manifesto makes a case for free access to information, particularly scientific information that has the potential to benefit society. To publicize his views, Swartz took action, allegedly downloading nearly 5 million articles, editorials, reviews, and other material from the prestigious JSTOR academic database. He was arrested on felony charges.

Shortly after the Swartz story broke, another open access advocate, Gregg Maxwell, uploaded more than 18,000 articles from Philosophical Transactions of the Royal Society to a file sharing site. The articles, all dated prior to 1923 and previously available by subscription, became accessible to the general public for free.

In explaining his actions, Maxwell wrote, "The liberal dissemination of knowledge is essential to scientific inquiry. More than in any other area, the application of restrictive copyright is inappropriate for academic works: there is no sticky question of how to pay authors or reviewers, as the publishers are already not paying them. And unlike 'mere' works of entertainment, liberal access to scientific work impacts the well-being of all mankind. Our continued survival may even depend on it."

Certainly there are expenses associated with operating academic databases such as JSTOR, but the researchers who write academic articles are typically not paid for their contributions. Money to support their research often comes from public funding collected from taxpayers. Yet academic databases typically charge access fees to read full-text articles.

Schools and libraries often pay a per-year fee that provides students and faculty with free access to academic publications, but members of the general public trying to access such information from their home or work computers hit a paywall that becomes a barrier to access. Open access advocates want information to be freely available, and technologies of the Information Age seem on the way to making that a reality.

Information purveyors such as JSTOR and *The New York Times* argue that free data is unsustainable. Gathering, storing, and distributing information entail costs that need to be passed on to consumers. Information has value that consumers should be willing to pay for.

A U.S. Department of the Navy report suggests that information has value whether or not it is free; however, the value of information increases when it is easy to access, organized, current, and reliable.

On the surface, information available from the Web might seem free, but there are hidden costs such as intrusive advertising, surreptitious tracking, and personal data collection that erode privacy.

Information from the Web might seem free, but there are hidden costs...

Public release of massive numbers of documents onto the Internet is becoming more common as open access advocates take action. Sometimes information, such as Sarah Palin's e-mails and FBI files on the Roswell UFO incident, can be obtained through the Freedom of Information Act (FOIA) and other legitimate channels.

When legitimate routes fail, documents and databases are sometimes released through backdoor channels. Climategate and WikiLeaks are notorious examples of leaked data.

Open access is a complex concept that requires intelligent compromise among the interests of individuals, businesses, and government agencies. Individuals want to retain their privacy, businesses want to retain their income stream, and governments want to maintain security. Yet, all parties would like as much information as possible in order to make informed decisions and take constructive action.

Try It! Explore the value of information, paywalls, and data leaks by working on the following activities.

1 Despite the widespread belief that digital information should be free, the popularity of iTunes and ebook readers, such as the Kindle, demonstrate that consumers are willing to pay for some digital content accessed from the Internet. Make a list of digital content that you currently pay for.

2 A paywall blocks access to documents, news articles, and other content until the consumer pays an access or registration fee. Notable publications such as *The New York Times* and *The Wall Street Journal* have instituted paywalls with varying degrees of success. Use a search engine to answer two questions about paywalls:

a. What is the reason that premium newspapers and magazines believe that paywalls are necessary?

b. How successful are paywalls based on the number of consumers who actually pay for access to content in online newspapers and magazines?

3 Paywalls are not the only barrier that blocks access to information. Individuals, corporations, and governments hold personal, proprietary, and classified information that is not available for public access. That information sometimes goes public. Explore some of the most notorious data leaks by filling in the following table.

Leak	Contents	Date	Number of Documents
CRU Climate Data			
U.S. Diplomatic Cables			
War Diary: Afghanistan War Logs			
War Diary: Iraq War Logs			

4 Many countries have legislation similar to the United States Freedom of Information Act, which provides a legitimate channel for requesting the release of proprietary and classified information. Declassified data is posted on Web sites for public access. The FBI maintains a fascinating site called The Vault, where you can read dossiers about Marilyn Monroe, Malcolm X, and the Roswell UFO incident.

Head over to The Vault (*vault.fbi.gov*), browse through the documents for a topic that interests you, and record the most surprising piece of information you find.

INFOWEBLINKS

You can check the **NP2013 Chapter 1** InfoWebLink for updates to these activities.

W CLICK TO CONNECT
www.infoweblinks.com/np2013/ch01

What Do You Think?

ISSUE

1. From what you have learned, do you think that academic research articles should be available for free?

2. Do you agree with magazine and news companies that quality content requires a paywall?

3. Do you support efforts to make information accessible through back channels such as WikiLeaks?

Information Tools: Finding the Right Stuff

You're looking for information. Where you start depends on how you plan to use the information. The sources you need for a class research paper often differ from information sources for personal use.

Information sources can be roughly divided into two categories: those that serve academic audiences and those that serve consumers.

Find these sources using Google Scholar and academic databases/directories such as DOAJ

Scholarly and academic sources

- Written by experts
- Intended for academic or professional readers
- Peer-reviewed by other experts before publication
- Contain original research, theoretical analysis, or best practices
- Carefully documented by footnotes or endnotes
- Published by academic publishers, professional associations, or university presses
- Include academic books, academic journals, papers, conference proceedings, dissertations, textbooks, and monographs in printed or digital format

Use these sources for class papers, theses, essays, and dissertations

Find these sources using Google Web, Google News, and product Web sites

Consumer-level sources

- Written by reporters, bloggers, or practitioners
- Intended for the general public
- Usually reviewed by an editor before publication
- Sometimes open to public comment after publication 👍 Like
- Printed or displayed in color with included photos
- Often published in for-profit publications that include advertising
- Include trade books, magazines, encyclopedias, press releases, trade journals, blogs, news sites, and online forums

Use these sources for product information, troubleshooting, news, and topic overviews

HELP!

Can't access what you need for a research project? Here are some common problems encountered by students, and solutions that help you find the resources you need for a paper that earns you an A.

PROBLEM: Web search engines, such as Google, sometimes miss many of the articles most relevant for a college-level research project because articles are often locked behind paywalls or firewalls that don't allow search engine access. SOLUTION: Go directly to a journal's Web site and search there.

PROBLEM: Many scholarly journals display only abstracts to the general public; viewing the full text of articles requires a subscription or download fee. SOLUTION: Use your library's online database to locate articles that are included in the physical collection. You might have to go to the library to read the articles or ask for the full article from inter-library loan.

PROBLEM: Access to academic search engines and databases, such as LexisNexis, requires subscriptions. SOLUTION: Your school might provide registered students with free access to journal databases if you log in from a computer on the school network or from within the library.

Try It! Research about computers and technology relies on information from a broad base of sources. Let's explore these sources by comparing what they offer. Some searches will produce information suitable for academic projects, such as term papers, while other searches tend to produce information suitable for personal use, such as figuring out if someone is hacking into your home network.

To record the results of this comparison, write down (or screen capture) one example that you get from each source, and then describe an academic project or personal use for which that information would be suitable. As an example, suppose that you search for "cloud computing" using Google Scholar and one of the results is

Introduction to parallel algorithms and architectures
T Leighton - sce.uhcl.edu
... Catalog Description: This course covers parallel computations using popular interconnection networks such as arrays, trees, hypercubes, and permutation networks such as the star and the pancake networks, as well as grid and **cloud computing**. ...
Cited by 2996 - Related articles - View as HTML - Library Search - All 5 versions

This information is academic and could be suitable as one of the sources for a term paper about cloud computing for a computer science course. Okay, now see what you can do with the rest.

1. Check Wikipedia for general information about "cloud computing."

2. Search for academic and trade books about cloud computing at Amazon Books.

3. Search for conference proceedings about cloud computing at the ACM Digital Library.

4. Search an open access database such as DOAJ (see sidebar) for a recent paper about cloud computing.

5. Search an academic database (see sidebar) for an abstract about cloud computing.

6. Search Science.gov for a full text article about cloud computing.

7. Search an online computer magazine, such as *Wired*, for a recent article about cloud computing.

8. Use a search engine, such as Google or Bing, to locate a recent press release about cloud computing.

9. Search Amazon Electronics for cloud computing products and customer reviews.

10. Search a technology news site (see sidebar) for the latest industry news about cloud computing.

Computer and Technology Academic Databases

Odysci Academic Search

DOAJ (Directory of Open Access Journals)

Science.gov

TDG Scholar

Microsoft Academic Search

IEEE Xplore

CiteSeerX

ACM (Association for Computing Machinery) Digital Library

Computer and Technology News Sites

Huffington Post Tech

Engadget

TechCrunch

Ars Technica

Google News Technology

WSJ All Things Digital

CNET News

Tom's Hardware

Darren Hubley/Shutterstock.com

Technology in Context: Marketing

WALKING OUT THE GATE of ancient Pompeii, you might have come across an eye-catching sign extolling the virtues of a popular tavern in the next town. The sign was a clever bit of marketing designed to target thirsty travelers and drum up business. Throughout the centuries, handbills, newspaper ads, television commercials, radio spots, and mass mail campaigns were all important tools of the marketing industry. Now, computers have opened new vistas for communicating with consumers.

The American Marketing Association defines marketing as an organizational function and a set of processes for creating, communicating, and delivering value to customers and for managing customer relationships in ways that benefit the organization and its stakeholders. A person-in-the-street definition might simply be that marketing is an attempt to sell products.

Computers first played a role in marketing as a research tool for quickly crunching numbers from consumer surveys and sales figures. Statistics derived from that data helped companies focus development efforts on the most promising products and market them effectively. Marketing research data made one fact very clear: Even the most effective advertising cannot convince everyone to buy a particular product. A costly prime-time television ad, for example, might be seen by millions of viewers, but many of them have no interest in the advertised product. To better target potential buyers, marketers turned to direct marketing.

Direct marketing attempts to establish a one-to-one relationship with prospective customers rather than waiting for them to learn about a product from general, impersonal forms of advertising, such as billboards, radio spots, television commercials, and newspaper ads. The first direct marketing techniques included personalized let-

ters, catalogs, and telemarketing. Customer names, addresses, and phone numbers were mined from computer databases maintained by mailing list brokers. Lists could be tailored in rudimentary ways to fit target markets. Selling snow tires? Get a list of consumers in northern states. Looking for Peace Corps volunteers? Get a list of college students.

"Dear Carmen Smith, you might already have won…" Just about everyone in America has received a personalized sweepstakes mailing. Initially, personalized names were crudely inserted using dot matrix printers, but today high-speed laser printers dash off thousands of personalized letters per hour and use graphics capabilities to affix signatures that appear to have been hand-signed in ink.

Telemarketing is a technique for telephone solicitation. Computerized autodialers make it possible for telemarketers to work efficiently. An autodialer is a device that can dial telephone numbers stored in a list. It can also generate and dial telephone numbers using a random or sequential number generator.

A smart autodialer, called a predictive dialer, increases a telemarketer's efficiency even more by automatically calling several numbers at the same time and only passing a call to the marketer when a person answers.

If you've picked up the telephone only to hear silence or a disconnect, it was likely an autodialer that connected to more than one person at the same time and dropped your call. Predictive dialers eliminate telemarketing time that would be otherwise wasted with busy signals, answering machines, and so on.

The Internet opened up dramatic new horizons in direct marketing by providing an inexpensive conduit for collecting information about potential customers and distributing targeted direct marketing. According to author Jim Sterne, "The Internet and the World

THE SATURDAY EVENING POST   June 14, 1942

It's easy to make Sodas and Sparkling Drinks at home!

CANADA DRY WATER

FREE!

CANADA WORLD FAMOUS DRY WATER

Image Courtesy of The Advertising Archives

Wide Web have become the most important new communication media since television, and ones that are fundamentally reshaping contemporary understanding of sales and marketing." Today, a vast amount of information flows over the Internet and marketers are trying to harness that information to most efficiently communicate their messages to prospective customers.

E-commerce Web sites offer a global distribution channel for small entrepreneurs as well as multinational corporations. Consumers can locate e-commerce sites using a search engine. Some search engines allow paid advertising to appear on their sites. Clever marketers use search engine optimization techniques to get their Web sites to the top of search engine lists.

Another way to drive traffic to an e-commerce site is banner advertising that clutters up Web pages with inviting tag lines for free products. Clicking the ad connects consumers to the site. The cost of placing a banner ad depends on the click-through rate—the number of consumers who click an ad. Sophisticated banner ad software displays the banner ad across an entire network and monitors click-through rates. Not only does this software keep track of click throughs for billing purposes, it can automatically adjust the sites that carry each ad to maximize click-through rates.

Internet marketing is often associated with the tidal wave of spam that's currently crashing into everyone's Inbox. These mass spam e-mails, however bothersome, are a very crude form of direct marketing. Typically, spammers use unscrubbed mailing lists containing many expired, blocked, and invalid e-mail addresses. This hit-or-miss strategy is cheap. Ten million e-mail addresses can be rented for as low as $100 and server bandwidth provided by e-mail brokers costs about $300 per million messages sent.

Marketing professionals regard massive e-mail spamming with some degree of scorn because most

lists don't narrow the focus to the most promising customers. Worse yet, consumers react by installing spam filters. Some spammers try to evade spam filters. More than one Web site offers marketers a free service that analyzes mass e-mail solicitations using a spam filter simulator. If the solicitation can't get through the filter, the service offers suggestions on what to change so the message slips through.

In contrast to gratuitous spammers, marketing professionals have learned that opt-in mailing lists have much higher success rates. Consumers who have asked for information more often appreciate receiving it and act on it. Opt-in consumers are also more willing to divulge information that develops an accurate profile of their lifestyle so marketers can offer them the most appropriate products.

When given a choice, however, consumers tend to opt out, and marketers responded by surreptitiously collecting data from free apps, Web sites, Facebook pages, and the content of Web-based e-mail messages. Privacy advocates attacked this practice, and savvy consumers have found tools and techniques to minimize the amount of personal data that is harvested behind the scenes.

Most consumers would agree that the marketing industry needs professionals who are socially responsible. In describing the qualifications for marketing professionals, the Bureau of Labor Statistics states the obvious when it says, "Computer skills are vital because marketing, product promotion, and advertising on the Internet are increasingly common."

In preparing for a marketing career, a knowledge of computers, the Web, and the Internet are important. Equally important is preparation in statistical analysis, psychology, and ethics, along with coursework that covers legal and regulatory aspects of the technology-driven marketing industry.

New Perspectives Labs

To access the New Perspectives Labs for Chapter 1, open the NP2013 interactive eBook and then click the icon next to the lab title.

▶ OPERATING A PERSONAL COMPUTER

IN THIS LAB YOU'LL LEARN:

- How to start a Windows computer
- What to do when a computer is in sleep mode
- How to deactivate a screensaver
- How to select a different screensaver
- How to use the Alt, Ctrl, Esc, Num Lock, Caps Lock, Windows, Fn, Backspace, Delete, and arrow keys
- The difference between forward and backward slashes
- How to start and exit a program
- How to close a program that is not responding
- When to use the reset button
- How to shut down Windows

LAB ASSIGNMENTS

1. Start the interactive part of the lab. Make sure you've enabled Tracking if you want to save your QuickCheck results. Perform each lab step as directed, and answer all the lab QuickCheck questions. When you exit the lab, your answers are automatically graded and your results are displayed.

2. Make a note of the brand and location of the computer you're using to complete these lab assignments.

3. Use the Start button to access your computer's Control Panel folder. Describe the status of your computer's power saver settings.

4. Preview the available screensavers on the computer you use most frequently. Select the screensaver you like the best and describe it in a few sentences.

5. What is the purpose of an Fn key? Does your computer keyboard include an Fn key? Explain why or why not.

6. In your own words, describe what happens when you (a) click the Close button; (b) hold down the Ctrl, Alt, and Del keys; (c) press the reset button; and (d) select the Shut Down option.

▶ WORKING WITH BINARY NUMBERS

IN THIS LAB YOU'LL LEARN:

- The difference between the binary number system and the decimal number system
- How to count in binary
- How to convert decimal numbers into binary numbers
- How to convert binary numbers into decimal numbers
- How to use the Windows Calculator to convert numbers
- How to work with powers of two

LAB ASSIGNMENTS

1. Start the interactive part of the lab. Make sure you've enabled Tracking if you want to save your QuickCheck results. Perform each lab step as directed, and answer all the lab QuickCheck questions. When you exit the lab, your answers are automatically graded and your results are displayed.

2. Using paper and pencil, manually convert the following decimal numbers into binary numbers. Your instructor might ask you to show the process that you used for each conversion.

   a. 100   b. 1,000   c. 256
   d. 27   e. 48   f. 112
   g. 96   h. 1,024

3. Using paper and pencil, manually convert the following binary numbers into decimal numbers. Your instructor might ask you to show the process that you used for each conversion.

   a. 100   b. 101   c. 1100
   d. 10101 e. 1111   f. 10000
   g. 1111000 h. 110110

4. Describe what is wrong with the following sequence:

   10 100 110 1000 1001 1100 1110 10000

5. What is the decimal equivalent of 2^0? 2^1? 2^8?

Key Terms

Make sure you understand all the boldfaced key terms presented in this chapter. With the NP2013 interactive eBook, you can use this list of terms as an interactive study activity. First, try to define a term in your own words, and then click the term to compare your definition with the definition presented in the chapter.

ALU, 31
Analog data, 22
Anonymizer tools, 11
Application software, 16
Apps, 16
ASCII, 24
Authentication protocol, 34
Binary number system, 23
Biometrics, 34
Bit, 23
Brute force attack, 37
Byte, 26
Case sensitive, 35
Central processing unit, 15
Character data, 24
Client, 18
Cloud computing, 9
Compiler, 30
Compute-intensive, 19
Computer, 14
Computer network, 8
Computer program, 15
Control unit, 31
Convergence, 9
CPU, 15
Data, 15
Data processing, 6
Data representation, 22
Dictionary attack, 36
Digital data, 22
Digital divide, 13
Digital revolution, 4
Digitization, 5

Download, 18
EBCDIC, 25
Extended ASCII, 24
File, 15
Gigabit, 26
Gigabyte, 26
Globalization, 12
Handheld computer, 19
Identity theft, 36
Input, 15
Instruction cycle, 32
Instruction set, 30
Integrated circuit, 27
Intellectual property, 12
Internet, 8
Interpreter, 30
Keylogger, 37
Kilobit, 26
Kilobyte, 26
Local software, 7
Machine code, 30
Machine language, 30
Mainframe computer, 18
Megabit, 26
Megabyte, 26
Memory, 15
Microcontroller, 20
Microprocessor, 15
Numeric data, 23
Object code, 30
Op code, 31
Open source, 12
Operand, 31

Operating system, 16
Output, 15
Password, 35
Password manager, 40
Personal computer, 17
Personal computing, 7
Phishing, 37
Processing, 15
Programming language, 29
Registers, 31
Semiconducting materials, 27
Server, 18
Sniffing, 37
Social media, 10
Software, 15
Source code, 29
Storage, 15
Stored program, 16
Supercomputer, 19
System board, 28
System software, 16
Unicode, 25
Upload, 18
User ID, 34
Videogame console, 17
Web, 8
Workstation, 17

1

Interactive Summary

To review important concepts from this chapter, fill in the blanks to best complete each sentence. When using the NP2013 interactive eBook, click the Check Answers buttons to automatically score your answers.

SECTION A: The [_____] revolution is an ongoing process of social, political, and economic change brought about by technologies such as computers and networks. The [_____] is a global computer network originally developed as a military project, adapted for research and academic use, and then for commercial use. [_____], a form of electronic communication, was an application for the masses and finally a reason to buy a computer and join the digital revolution. Another aspect of the digital revolution is [_____], a process by which several technologies with distinct functionalities

evolve to form a single product. Technology has the potential to spread ideas, such as freedom and democracy, but it might have a chilling effect on [_____], or "the right to be left alone." It might also affect intellectual [_____] because digital technology has made it easy to produce copies with no loss in quality from the original. Technology-driven [_____] has an effect on the economy, as consumers gain access to products and services from countries other than their own. Activists worry about the digital [_____] that separates people who have access to technology and those who do not.

▶ CHECK ANSWERS

SECTION B: A(n) [_____] is a multipurpose device that accepts input, processes data, stores data, and produces output according to a series of stored instructions. The data a computer is getting ready to process is temporarily held in [_____]. This data is then processed in the central processing [_____]. The series of instructions that tells a computer how to carry out processing tasks is referred to as a computer [_____], which forms the [_____] that sets up a computer to do a specific task. Data is typically stored in a(n) [_____] which is a named collection of data that exists on a storage medium, such as a hard disk, CD, DVD, Blu-ray disc, or USB flash drive. The idea of a(n) [_____] program means that a series of instructions for a computing task can be loaded into a computer's memory. [_____] software is a set of computer programs that helps a person carry out a task. [_____] software helps the computer system monitor itself in order to function efficiently. For

example, a computer [_____] system (OS) is essentially the master controller for all the activities that take place within a computer. Computers can be grouped into categories. A(n) [_____] computer is a type of microcomputer designed to meet the needs of an individual. The term [_____] can refer to an ordinary personal computer that is connected to a network or to a powerful desktop computer designed for high-performance tasks. A(n) [_____] is, at the time of its construction, one of the fastest computers in the world. A(n) [_____] computer is large, expensive, and capable of simultaneously processing data for hundreds or thousands of users. Small, portable digital devices that allow you to install apps can be classified as [_____] computers. A(n) [_____] is a special-purpose microprocessor that can control a device, such as a refrigerator or microwave oven.

▶ CHECK ANSWERS

SECTION C: [_____] data is processed, stored, and transmitted as a series of 1s and 0s. Each 1 or 0 is called a(n) [_____] . A series of eight 0s and 1s, called a(n) [_____] , represents one character—a letter, number, or punctuation mark. Data becomes [_____] when it is presented in a format that people can understand and use. [_____] data consists of numbers that might be used in arithmetic operations. It can be represented digitally using the [_____] number system. [_____] data is composed of letters, symbols, and numerals that are not used in arithmetic operations. Computers represent this type of data using [_____] , EBCDIC, or Unicode. Data is quantified using terms such as [_____] or kibibyte (1024 bytes), and prefixes, such as [_____] or mebi (1,048,576), and giga or [_____] (1,073,741,824). The bits that represent data travel as electronic pulses through [_____] circuits, sometimes called computer chips. These chips are made from [_____] materials and are housed in chip carriers that can be plugged into the [_____] board of a digital device. ▶ CHECK ANSWERS

SECTION D: Software is usually written in high-level languages, such as C, BASIC, COBOL, and Java. The human-readable version of a program, created in a high-level language by a programmer, is called [_____] code. A(n) [_____] or an interpreter converts this high-level code into [_____] code. A microprocessor is hard-wired to perform a limited set of activities, such as addition, subtraction, counting, and comparisons. This collection of preprogrammed activities is called a(n) [_____] set. Each instruction begins with a(n) [_____] code, which is a command word for an operation such as add, subtract, compare, or jump. Most instructions also include a(n) [_____] that specifies the data, or the address of the data, for the operation. The processor's ALU uses [_____] to hold data that is being processed. The processor's [_____] unit fetches each instruction, sends data to the registers, and then signals the ALU to begin processing. ▶ CHECK ANSWERS

SECTION E: Passwords and user IDs are the most common authentication [_____] . Password theft has become a serious security problem that has led to many cases of [_____] theft, when unauthorized individuals gain access to personal data. Hackers guess, discover, and steal passwords using a variety of techniques. A(n) [_____] attack tries passwords from a list of commonly used passwords. A(n) [_____] force attack tries every possible combination of letters and numbers. [_____] intercepts information sent out over computer networks. [_____] uses fraudulent Web sites or e-mail messages to fool unsuspecting readers into entering passwords and other personal information. A(n) [_____] is software that secretly records a user's keystrokes and sends them to a hacker. To keep passwords safe, you should consider using tiered passwords or standalone password [_____] software that generates secure passwords and keeps track of which password corresponds to each site you access. ▶ CHECK ANSWERS

Interactive Situation Questions

Apply what you've learned to some typical computing situations. When using the NP2013 interactive eBook, you can type your answers, and then use the Check Answers button to automatically score your responses.

1. Suppose that you walk into an office and see the devices pictured to the right. You would probably assume that they are the screen, keyboard, and mouse for a(n) [_____] computer, workstation, or server.

2. You receive an e-mail message asking you to join a circle of friends. You assume that the message was generated in conjunction with an online [_____] network, such as Facebook, and if you become a member, you will be able to socialize online.

3. You're planning a trip to Finland, but when you access the hotel site, the prices are listed in euros. To find the price in U.S. dollars, you access a currency converter from your portable phone. That's an example of [_____] computing, representative of the fourth phase of the digital revolution.

4. You're visiting an antique shop and notice a collection of old-fashioned radios. They actually feature a dial for tuning in different radio stations. You immediately recognize this as a(n) [_____] device because it deals with an infinite scale of values, rather than discrete values.

5. While attending a meeting at work, you hear one of the executives wondering if "unit code" would be helpful. After a moment of puzzlement, you realize that the executive really meant [_____] , and that it would allow your company software to be translated into the Cyrillic alphabet used by the Russian language.

6. You have a storage device that offers 2 GB of storage space. It is currently empty. Your friend wants to give you a large digital photo that's 16 MB. Will it fit on your storage device? [____]

7. Your bank is giving customers the choice of using a four-digit PIN or a password that can contain up to ten letters and numbers. The [_____] is more secure, so that's what you decide to use.

8. You need to select a password for your online PayPal account. Which of the following passwords would be the LEAST secure: jeff683, hddtmrutc, gargantuan, fanhotshot, bb#ii22jeffry, or high348? [_____]

▶ CHECK ANSWERS

Interactive Practice Tests

Practice tests that consist of ten multiple-choice, true/false, and fill-in-the-blank questions are available in your NP2013 interactive eBook. Test questions are selected at random from a large test bank, so each time you take a test, you'll receive a different set of questions. Your tests are scored immediately, and you can print study guides that help you find the correct answers for any questions that you missed.

▶ CLICK TO START

Learning Objectives Checkpoints

Learning Objectives Checkpoints are designed to help you assess whether you have achieved the major learning objectives for this chapter. You can use paper and pencil or word processing software to complete most of the activities.

1. List the four phases of the digital revolution.

2. Define the term *convergence* and provide examples of at least five devices that are converging.

3. Describe at least two social, political, and economic effects of the digital revolution.

4. Draw a diagram to explain how a computer makes use of input, processing, storage, memory, output, and stored programs.

5. Describe the difference between system software, an operating system, application software, and a computer program.

6. List, briefly describe, and rank (in terms of computing capacity) the characteristics of each computer category described in Section B of this chapter.

7. List the characteristics that handheld computers and dedicated handheld devices have in common with personal computers, and list factors by which they differ.

8. Define the term *microcontroller* and provide three examples of devices in which microcontrollers are found.

9. Explain the technical difference between data and information.

10. Provide three examples of digital devices and three examples of analog devices.

11. List the ASCII representation for *B* and the binary representation for 18; draw a stepped waveform showing a digital sound; and draw a diagram showing how color is represented in a graphic.

12. List and define all the chapter terms, such as *bit, byte,* and *kibibyte,* that pertain to quantifying data.

13. Use the terms *integrated circuits, microprocessor,* and *system board* in a meaningful sentence.

14. Describe how compilers and interpreters work with high-level programming languages, source code, and object code.

15. Make a storyboard showing how a microprocessor's ALU would add the numbers 2 and 8.

16. Explain how hackers use dictionary and brute force attacks.

17. Provide examples of five secure passwords and five passwords that might be easy to crack.

Study Tip: Make sure you can use your own words to correctly answer each of the purple focus questions that appear throughout the chapter.

Concept Map

Fill in the blanks to show that you understand the relationships between programming concepts presented in the chapter.

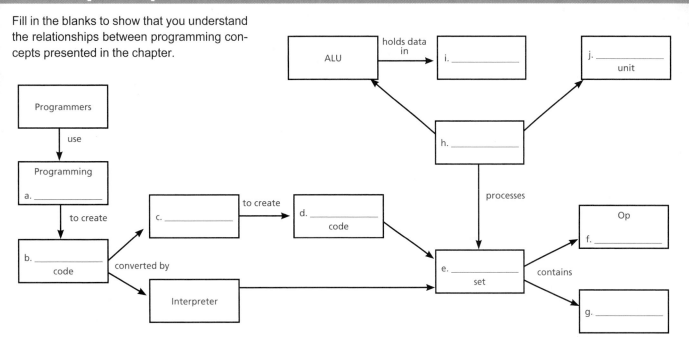

► CHECK ANSWERS

2

Chapter Contents

INFOWEBLINKS

You'll find updates for chapter
material by connecting to the
NP2013 Chapter 2 InfoWebLink.

Ⓦ CLICK TO CONNECT
www.infoweblinks.com/np2013/ch02

Computer Hardware

Learning Objectives

After reading this chapter, you will be able to answer the
following questions by completing the outcomes-based
Learning Objectives Checkpoints on page 117.

1. What are the components of a typical personal computer
    system?
2. What is a computer form factor?
3. Is a home computer more or less desirable than a game
    console or small business computer?
4. What's the best way to select a computer?
5. Are PCs and Macs compatible?
6. Is it a good idea to upgrade an old computer?
7. How does a microprocessor work?
8. Why are some computers faster than others?
9. Why does a computer need memory?
10. What is the best type of storage for my data?
11. What factors affect a computer's screen display?
12. Are ink jet printers better than laser printers?
13. What's the best way to add devices to a computer system?
14. How can I protect my computer system from theft and
    damage?
15. Are there guidelines for troubleshooting hardware and
    software problems?

CourseMate

Visit the NP2013 CourseMate for this chapter's Pre-Quiz, Audio
Overview and Flashcards, Detailed Objectives, Chapter Quiz,
Online Games, and more labs.

Multimedia and Interactive Elements

When using the NP2013 interactive eBook, click the ▶ icons to
access multimedia resources.

2

Apply Your Knowledge The information in this chapter will give you the background to:

- Identify all the components of a typical personal computer system
- Purchase a new computer based on features, performance, and price
- Upgrade your current computer
- Change your computer's boot settings in EEPROM

- Select a microprocessor based on performance specifications
- Select storage devices for your computer
- Change the resolution of your monitor
- Install peripheral devices
- Perform basic maintenance on your computer and troubleshoot hardware problems

Try It!

HOW POWERFUL IS MY COMPUTER?

As you read Chapter 2, you'll learn that some computers are more powerful than others because they can store more data and process data faster. To find out how your home, work, or lab computer stacks up, you'll need to know a few of its specifications. Check your computer's specifications by starting your computer and then doing the following:

1. Windows: Click the **Start** button, then click **Control Panel**.

Select the **System** icon or link to open the System Properties dialog box. (If you're in Category View, click System and Maintenance first.)

If you see a window with tabs, make sure the General tab is displayed.

MAC OS X: Click the 🍎 **Apple** icon on the menu bar located at the top of the desktop. Select **About this Mac**.

2. Record information about your computer similar to the information provided for the sample computer in the table below.

3. Then, just to get an idea of the other equipment you've got attached to your Windows computer, click the link or icon for **Device Manager**. (You might have to click the Hardware tab first.) For more information about your Mac hardware, click the More Info button.

4. Browse through the list. When you're done, close all the dialog boxes.

5. If your computer has Windows 7, click **Check the Windows Experience Index**. Make a note of your computer's base score and subscores, then click the link to find out what the numbers mean.

	Sample Computer	Your Computer
Computer Manufacturer	Dell	
Computer Model	Studio 17	
Processor Manufacturer	Intel	
Processor Type	Core i7	
Processor Speed	1.60 GHz	
Operating System	Windows 7	
RAM Capacity	6 GB	

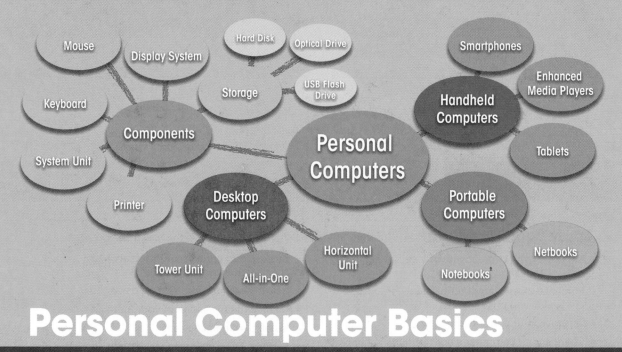

Personal Computer Basics

WHETHER YOU ARE SHOPPING for a new computer, using your trusty laptop, or troubleshooting a system glitch, it is useful to have some background about computer system components and how they work. Section A begins with a framework for understanding the vast number of options available for putting together a personal computer system, and then wraps up with some tips on interpreting the jargon in computer ads and negotiating the digital marketplace.

PERSONAL COMPUTER SYSTEMS

▶ **What are the components of a typical personal computer system?** The centerpiece of a personal computer system is, of course, a personal computer. In addition, most systems include peripheral devices. The term **peripheral device** designates input, output, and storage equipment that might be added to a computer system to enhance its functionality. Popular peripheral devices include printers, digital cameras, scanners, game controllers, and speakers.

A personal computer system usually includes the components shown in Figure 2-1. These components are described briefly on the next page. They are defined and discussed in more detail later in the chapter.

FIGURE 2-1

A typical personal computer system includes the system unit and a variety of storage, input, and output devices. ▶ The components of a typical desktop system are shown here. To compare the components of desktops with portable computers, watch the video for this figure in your interactive eBook.

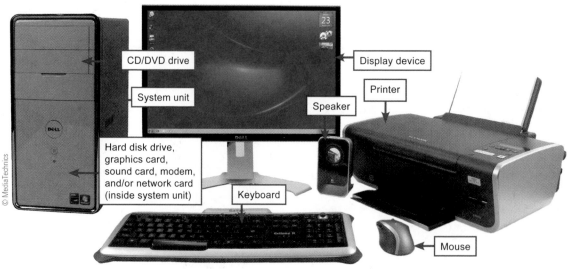

▶ **System unit.** The **system unit** is the case that holds the computer's main circuit boards, microprocessor, memory, power supply, and storage devices. Depending on the computer design, the system unit might also include other built-in devices, such as a keyboard and speakers.

▶ **Keyboard.** Most personal computer systems are equipped with a keyboard as the primary input device.

▶ **Mouse.** A mouse is an input device designed to manipulate on-screen graphical objects and controls.

▶ **Hard disk drive.** A hard disk drive is the main storage device on a personal computer system. It is usually mounted inside the computer's system unit and can store billions of characters of data. A small external light indicates when the drive is reading or writing data.

▶ **Optical drive.** An optical drive is a storage device that works with CDs, DVDs, Blu-ray discs, or some combination of these storage media. Optical drives are handy for playing audio CDs, DVD movies, and Blu-ray movies. They can also be used to store computer data on writable CDs, DVDs, and Blu-ray discs.

FIGURE 2-2

Computers provide sockets called ports for solid state storage such as these SD cards and USB flash drives.

▶ **Other storage.** In the past, personal computers included a low-capacity storage device called a floppy disk drive. Today, these drives have been replaced by solid state storage options, such as USB flash drives and memory cards (Figure 2-2).

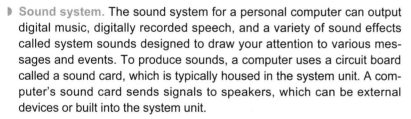

© MediaTechnics

▶ **Sound system.** The sound system for a personal computer can output digital music, digitally recorded speech, and a variety of sound effects called system sounds designed to draw your attention to various messages and events. To produce sounds, a computer uses a circuit board called a sound card, which is typically housed in the system unit. A computer's sound card sends signals to speakers, which can be external devices or built into the system unit.

▶ **Display system.** A personal computer display system consists of two parts. Circuitry, called a graphics card, converts raw digital data into images that can be shown on a display device. Display devices, often called computer screens or monitors, present visual output, such as documents, photos, and videos. Display devices are usually integrated with the system unit of portable computers, but exist as standalone devices for computers that spend most of their time on a desk.

▶ **Network and Internet access.** Many personal computer systems include built-in circuitry for wired or wireless connections to a computer network. Networking circuitry is useful for constructing a home network or connecting to public networks in coffee shops and airports.

▶ **Printer.** A computer printer is an output device that produces computer-generated text or graphical images on paper.

TERMINOLOGY NOTE

The word *peripheral* is a relatively old part of computer jargon that dates back to the days of mainframes when the CPU was housed in a giant box and all input, output, and storage devices were housed separately. Technically speaking, a peripheral is any device that is not part of the CPU.

In the world of personal computers, however, the use of the term *peripheral* varies and it is often used to refer to any components that are not housed inside the system unit. Many personal computer owners do not think of a hard disk drive as a peripheral device, but technically it is one.

DESKTOP AND PORTABLE COMPUTERS

▶ **What is the significance of different computer designs?** The industrial design principle that "form follows function" applies to computers. If you need a computer that's functional for mobile applications, you would not consider hauling around a large, heavy unit designed to remain on a desk. Instead, you would look for a computer "form" that suits your mobile "function."

In the computer industry, the term **form factor** refers to the size and dimensions of a component, such as a system board or system unit. Personal computers are available in all sorts of form factors; some are small and some are large; some are designed to remain on a desk, whereas others are designed to be portable.

▶ **What are the characteristics of desktop computers?** A **desktop computer** fits on a desk and runs on power from an electrical wall outlet. The main component of a typical desktop computer is a system unit that houses the processor, memory, storage devices, display circuitry, and sound circuitry. A desktop computer's keyboard, mouse, and display screen are typically separate components that are connected to the main unit by cables or wireless technology (Figure 2-3).

A tower unit can be placed on the desk or on the floor.

The circuitry for this desktop all-in-one model is integrated into the case that holds the screen.

FIGURE 2-3

A desktop computer fits on a desk and is tethered to a wall outlet.

The first personal computers were desktop models, and this style remains popular for offices, schools, and homes. Because their components can be manufactured economically, desktop computers typically provide the most computing power for your dollar. The price of an entry-level desktop computer starts at US$300 or a bit less. Desktops with average performance cost $500–$700 and a souped up desktop equipped for gaming can cost over $3,000.

A desktop computer's system unit can be housed in a vertical case or a horizontal case. Most horizontal units are placed under the display device to save desk space. A vertical system unit can be placed on a desk, on the floor, or in a cubbyhole beneath the desk. The case for a vertical system unit is often referred to as a tower.

A **tower case** provides plenty of space for gamers and "modders" who want to enhance their machines by adding storage devices, lighted power cables, or accelerated graphics cards. Tower units are also the form factor of choice for computer owners who might want to upgrade components in the future because it is easy to get inside the case and swap out parts.

Some manufacturers eliminate the separate system unit by incorporating computer circuitry in the back of a flat-panel screen. Dubbed an **all-in-one computer**, this form factor is handy, but has limited space for expansion.

▶ **How do portable computers differ from desktops?** A **portable computer** is a small, lightweight personal computer with screen, keyboard, storage, and processing components integrated into a single unit that runs on power supplied by an electrical outlet or a battery. Portable computers are ideal for mobile uses because they are easy to carry and can be used outdoors, in airports, and in classrooms without the need for a nearby electrical outlet. Portable computers are classified as notebooks and netbooks.

▶ **What is a notebook computer?** A **notebook computer** (also referred to as a laptop) is a small, lightweight portable computer that opens like a clamshell to reveal a screen and keyboard. Notebook computers tend to cost a bit more than desktop computers with similar computing power and storage capacity.

Notebook computers are popular with students because they don't take up too much space in crowded dorm rooms and they are fairly easy to carry around campus. On average, a notebook computer weighs about five pounds. The price of an entry-level notebook computer starts around $400. Consumers often spend between $700 and $1,000, however, to get the features and performance they want. A fully loaded notebook computer with widescreen display can cost more than $2,000 (Figure 2-4).

FIGURE 2-4

A notebook computer is small and lightweight, giving it the advantage of portability. It can be plugged into an electrical outlet, or it can run on battery power.

FIGURE 2-5

Netbooks are scaled-down versions of standard notebook computers. They are lightweight, small, and very portable.

▶ **What is a netbook?** A **netbook** is a small version of a notebook computer, typically with a 10" screen. Classified as subnotebooks and sometimes referred to as mini-laptops, these small form factor computers are typically only seven or eight inches wide and weigh about two pounds. The small form factor doesn't have space for a CD or DVD drive, but one can be connected externally if needed to install software or play DVDs. Some netbooks run Windows, but Linux is also a popular operating system for these fully functional computers priced under $300 (Figure 2-5).

HOME, GAME, AND SMALL BUSINESS SYSTEMS

▶ **What's the significance of designations, such as home, small business, or game systems?** When studying computer ads and browsing vendor Web sites, you're likely to see some computer systems designated as home systems, whereas others are designated as game systems or small business systems. These designations are created by computer vendors to help consumers sort through the sometimes mind-boggling variety of configuration options.

▶ **What differentiates a home computer from other types?** The idea of a home computer system probably developed because Microsoft offered Home and Professional versions of the Windows operating system. Windows Home version targeted less sophisticated users and originally was not meant to be used extensively for networking.

Today, the term **home computer system** encompasses a vast array of computer configurations designed to accommodate consumers who use computers for personal tasks. These systems also work for dual-use environments where a computer might be needed for general computing activities and also for home office tasks. Netbooks, as well as notebooks, and many desktop computers are marketed as home computer systems.

The prices and features of home computer systems vary. Basic, inexpensive home systems offer adequate, but not super-charged, support for most computer applications, including Web browsing, e-mail, working with photos, downloading music, and working with general productivity applications, such as word processing. Software applications run at an acceptable speed, but graphics and games might be a bit slow.

A basic home computer system can also function for home office tasks with the addition of accounting software or other business applications.

Upscale home computer systems include cutting-edge computers, large-screen displays, 3-D Blu-ray players, and entertainment components to stream music throughout the house and display movies in a home theater (Figure 2-6).

FIGURE 2-6

Many high-end home computers are configured to function as the command center for watching movies and listening to music.

Movies, games, and music come to life with cutting-edge 3-D graphics and mind-blowing audio. Experience amazing visuals and incredible sound.

- 3-D Blu-Ray at home or on the go

- 2nd generation Intel Core processors

- Razor-sharp graphics

- High-fidelity JBL speakers and Waves MaxxAudio

- Hi-Def Webcam

Maximum Entertainment. Experience.

Volodymyr Vasylkiv /Shutterstock.com

▶ **What's so great about a gaming computer?** Some of the most cutting-edge computers are designed for gaming. Not only do these machines feature the fastest processors, they are also stuffed with memory, include state-of-the-art sound capabilities, and feature multiple graphics processors (Figure 2-7).

Although some manufacturers produce gaming notebook computers, most serious gamers tend to select desktop models because they are easier to customize and offer a little more power per dollar. The technophile features of a gaming computer come with a steep price premium. Computers start at $1,000 and quickly climb past the $3,000 price point.

FIGURE 2-7

Game systems are high-powered and expensive.

Aurora: Alienware Built. Gamer Approved.

The new Alienware Aurora: Overwhelm the enemy with overclocked power and expandability with the most upgradable desktop in its class.

• Factory-overclocked, liquid-cooled processors

• Ultraperformance dual graphics and optional high definition (HD) 3-D gaming

• Chassis designed for easy and optional thermal control

▶ **What are the characteristics of small business computers?** Computers marketed for small business applications tend to be middle-of-the-line models pared down to essentials. A medium-speed processor, moderate amount of RAM, and sensible disk capacity are adequate for basic business applications, such as word processing, spreadsheet analysis, accounting, and e-mail. Easy networking options allow small business computers to connect with other computers in an office environment.

Tower and all-in-one units are popular for in-office use, whereas notebook computers are a practical solution for employees who are on the go.

With price tags under $1,000, small business computers like those advertised in Figure 2-8 remain cost-effective because they are not loaded with memory, fancy graphics cards, or audio systems, which are typical on home computers. Small business computers might not include a CD or DVD drive and often do not include speakers.

FIGURE 2-8

Small business owners want a cost-effective solution without bells and whistles.

BusinessClass 400 Desktop.

Reliable, Expandable Solution for Small Businesses

From its scalable design to its versatility, the latest MTC BusinessClass computers can be configured to meet all your business requirements. Whether your business is migrating to the cloud or staying anchored to the ground, the BusinessClass 400 provides a strong foundation for a wide range of business applications.

• Scalable design: Just the right size for the modern office, with choices of network options

• Business dedicated: No extraneous software, no demoware, just the basic operating system allows your tech team to easily install your business desktop

• Affordable: Put your investment where you need it; in processing power, storage, and connectivity

• Backed by solid MTC service and warranty

BUYING A COMPUTER

▶ **How do I get started?** The process of buying your own computer system is not cut and dried. Some experts advocate assessing your computing needs first, whereas other experts suggest researching features and prices. The trick is to do your homework for the entire system before jumping into a purchase of any one component. Remember that you will be purchasing peripherals, software, and accessories in addition to a computer. To prepare for a computer purchase, you should complete the following activities:

▶ Browse through computer magazines and online computer stores to get a general idea of features and prices.

▶ Decide on a budget and stick to it.

▶ Make a list of the ways you plan to use your computer.

▶ Select a platform.

▶ Decide on a form factor.

▶ Select peripherals, software, and accessories.

▶ **Where can I find product information?** You can start by looking at ads in current computer magazines, such as *Wired*, *PCWorld*, and *Macworld*. You might visit computer stores online or in a nearby mall to get a general idea of prices and features.

▶ **How can I make sense of all the jargon in computer ads?** Computer ads are loaded with jargon and acronyms, such as RAM, ROM, GHz, GB, and USB. You're sure to spot lots of this computer lingo in ads like the one in Figure 2-9.

When you complete this chapter, you should be able to sort out the terminology used in a typical computer ad. For terms you encounter that are not covered in this textbook, you can google the term or refer to online dictionaries and encyclopedias, such as Webopedia, Whatis.com, or Wikipedia.

▶ **What can I expect to pay for a new computer?** Computers are sold at price points ranging from a few hundred dollars to several thousand dollars. Computer price points can be roughly grouped into three categories.

A computer priced higher than $1,200 is the computer equivalent of a luxury automobile. Computers in this price range contain one or more fast processors, a generous amount of RAM, and a copious amount of disk space. These computers contain state-of-the-art components and should not have to be replaced as quickly as less expensive computers. Computer game enthusiasts and anyone planning to work extensively with video editing, graphics, and desktop publishing are likely to require a high-end computer.

Computers that retail for between $500 and $1,200 might be considered the four-door sedans of the computer marketplace because a majority of buyers select computers in this price range. These popular computers lack the flashy specifications of their state-of-the-art cousins, but provide ample computing power to meet the needs of an average user.

FIGURE 2-9

A typical computer ad provides specifications and lots of computer jargon.

- Intel Core i7-2630M processor 2.0 GHz 1066 MHz FSB
- 6 MB L2 cache
- 6 GB DDR3-800 MHz dual channel SDRAM
- 750 GB SATA HD (7200 rpm)
- 8x CD/DVD burner (Dual Layer DVD+/-R)
- 15.6" High Def (720p) LCD display screen
- 1 GB NVIDIA GeForce graphics card
- Harman/Kardon speakers
- Integrated 1.3 megapixel Webcam
- 4 USB ports
- 1 IEEE 1394 port
- HDMI graphics ports
- 5-in-1 Media card reader
- Wireless networking 802.11 g/n
- 1 GB Ethernet
- Windows 7 Home Premium 64-bit operating system
- Home/small business software bundle
- 1-year limited warranty

© MediaTechnics

In the computer industry, the equivalent of a compact car is a sub-$500 computer. The technology in these computers is usually a year or two old and you can expect reduced processor speed, memory capacity, and drive capacity. Nevertheless, budget computers feature many of the same components that owners coveted in their state-of-the-art computers a few years back. You might have to replace a budget computer sooner than a more expensive computer, but it should be serviceable for typical applications.

▶ **Why is it important to figure out how I'm going to use my new computer?** Computers can help you perform such a wide variety of tasks that it can be impossible to predict all the ways you might use your new machine in the future. You can, however, make a list of the ways you plan to immediately use your computer and that list can help you think about the features you'll need.

Some computer-based activities require more processing or storage capacity than others. Therefore, if you have some ideas about your computer usage, you're more likely to buy the right computer and not have to purchase expensive upgrades for it later. Figure 2-10 offers some guidelines to help you evaluate how your plan for using a computer might affect your purchase decision.

FIGURE 2-10

Consider these factors to narrow down the mind-boggling number of choices offered to computer shoppers.

Usage Plan	Purchase Recommendation
You plan to use your computer for popular activities such as e-mail and Facebook, browsing the Web, playing a few games, managing your finances, downloading digital music, and writing school papers.	A mid-priced computer with standard features might meet your needs.
You're on a budget.	A budget-priced computer will handle the same applications as a mid-priced computer, but some tasks might run more slowly.
You plan to work on accounting and budgeting for a small business.	Consider one of the business systems offered by a local or an online computer vendor.
You spend lots of time playing computer games.	Buy a computer with the fastest processor and graphics card you can afford.
You plan to work extensively with video editing or desktop publishing.	Select a computer system with a fast processor, lots of hard disk capacity, and a graphics card loaded with memory.
Someone who will use the computer has special needs.	Consider purchasing appropriate adaptive equipment, such as a voice synthesizer or one-handed keyboard.
You plan to use specialized peripheral devices.	Make sure the computer you purchase can accommodate the devices you plan to use.
Your work at home overlaps your work at school or on the job.	Shop for a computer that's compatible with the computers you use at school or work.
You want to work with specific software, such as a game or graphics tool.	Make sure you select a computer that meets the specifications listed on the software box or Web site.
You're buying a new computer to replace an old one.	If you have a big investment in software, you should select a new computer that's compatible with the old one.
You want a 3-D display for games and movies.	Make sure the monitor is rated for 3-D display.

▶ How important is compatibility? Suppose that you want to do some assignments at home using the same software provided by your school lab. Maybe you want to transport data back and forth between your job and home. Or, perhaps your children want to use a computer at home that is similar to those they use at school. Computers that operate in essentially the same way and use the same software are said to be compatible. To assess whether two computers are compatible, check their operating systems. Computers with the same operating systems can typically use the same software and peripheral devices. Currently, there are three personal computer platforms: PC, Mac, and Linux.

▶ The **PC platform** is based on the design for one of the first personal computer superstars—the IBM PC. The great-grandchildren of the IBM PC are on computer store shelves today—a huge selection of personal computer brands and models manufactured by companies such as Lenovo, Hewlett-Packard, Dell, and Sony. The Windows operating system was designed specifically for these personal computers and, therefore, the PC platform is sometimes called the Windows platform.

▶ The **Mac platform** is based on a proprietary design for a personal computer called the Macintosh (or Mac), manufactured almost exclusively by Apple Inc. The Mac lineup includes the iMac, MacBook Air, MacBook Pro, and Mac mini, all running the Mac OS operating system.

▶ The **Linux platform** uses a standard PC or Mac to run the Linux operating system. A variety of software is available for this platform, though it tends to be more specialized but not as polished as software for Windows and Mac operating systems.

> **TERMINOLOGY NOTE**
>
> Computers that are compatible with the PC platform are usually referred to simply as PCs. Computers in the Mac platform are referred to as Macs.

At one time, the PC, Mac, and Linux platforms were not compatible because of hardware and operating system differences. Application software designed for Macs did not typically work on other platforms and vice versa.

The compatibility situation has changed because most Mac computers now use the same microprocessor as PCs. If you have a Mac computer with an Intel processor (sometimes called an Intel Mac), you can install Windows on it and run Windows software. You can also configure it to run Linux software.

The ability to run Windows offers Mac owners access to software from the PC and Mac platforms, and makes it possible to use the Mac OS to run one application, then switch to Windows to run another application. This capability can come in handy, for example, if a parent who uses Windows software is sharing a computer with an elementary-school student who is working with Macs at school.

▶ What about software? Most computers are sold with a preinstalled operating system, which typically includes a Web browser and e-mail software. Some computers are bundled with application software that you can use to create documents, crunch numbers, and produce presentations. Check the software situation carefully. The trend today is for manufacturers to install trial software that you can use free for a few months. To continue using the software beyond the trial period, however, you have to pay for it. Such software is "included" but not "free." Buyer beware.

If you're purchasing a computer to do a task that requires specialized software, you should factor its price into the cost of your computer system. Check the specifications listed on the software box to make sure your new computer has enough memory and processing speed to run it.

HANDHELD COMPUTERS

❱ **What types of handheld computers are available?** Handheld computers are small, portable devices that allow you to install application software, usually referred to as apps. Three types of handheld computers are available: enhanced media players, smartphones, and tablets.

❱ **What is an enhanced media player?** An **enhanced media player** is a handheld device, such as the iPod Touch, designed for playing music and videos, and offers a camera, access to the Internet, and a variety of apps. Enhanced media players do not typically include mobile phone capabilities.

Media players are great for listening to music and watching videos on the go. They're handy entertainment devices for traveling because you can use them without worrying that you're depleting the battery in your mobile phone. Enhanced media players typically feature a 3.5" screen, with overall dimensions about the size of an index card (Figure 2-11).

❱ **What is a smartphone?** A **smartphone** is an enhanced mobile phone that typically also functions as a portable media player and has the capability to access the Internet. Smartphones, such as the iPhone and Droid X, that allow you to install apps are classified as handheld computers. Smartphones are similar in size and appearance to enhanced media players, but generally cost a bit more and require a mobile service contract for voice calls.

❱ **What is a tablet computer?** A **tablet computer** is a handheld computer that is essentially a large version of an enhanced media player. First popularized by the Apple iPad, tablets are also offered by other companies, including Samsung and Motorola. Tablet prices range upward from $400 depending on brand and features.

Tablets are smaller than most notebook computers and weigh considerably less, in part because they have no keyboard, trackpad, or DVD drive. A virtual keyboard, displayed on the screen, can be supplemented by an auxiliary keyboard. A trackpad and mouse are not necessary; the touch screen handles most input and provides output (Figure 2-12).

Tablets can generally access the Internet using Wi-Fi networks or cellular data service. Many people use a tablet as a second computer; one that's handy for a quick Web search. In the business world, tablets are used by insurance adjusters who do most of their work at the scene of accidents and natural disasters, real estate agents who need access to data while out with clients, and health care workers who are moving quickly from one patient to the next.

FIGURE 2-11

Enhanced media players, such as this iPod Touch, range in price from $150–$400, depending on storage capacity.

FIGURE 2-12

Tablet computers typically cost about $500, feature a 10" screen, and weigh about one pound.

▶ **Are there compatibility issues with handheld computers?** As with full-size computers, the world of handheld computers includes several non-compatible platforms that affect your selection of apps.

When purchasing apps, you are limited to those designed for your device. Android apps do not work on iPhones, iPods, or iPads. Windows Phone apps run on many Nokia phones, but not on iPhones, Palm, or BlackBerry devices. Handheld computer platforms are summarized in Figure 2-13.

Platform	Source	Devices
iPhone	Apple	iPhone, iPad, iPod Touch
Android	Google	Droid, ATRIX, HKC, HTC phones Samsung Galaxy, Acer ICONIA, Motorola XOOM, Toshiba Thrive tablets
Windows Phone	Microsoft	Zune media player Nokia smartphones
webOS	Hewlett-Packard	Palm smartphones
RIM BlackBerry OS	Research In Motion	BlackBerry smartphones

FIGURE 2-13

Handheld Computer Platforms

QuickCheck   SECTION A

1. A computer [   ] unit houses the main circuit board, microprocessor, storage devices, and network card.

2. Personal computers are available in a variety of [   ] factors, such as tower units and all-in-one units.

3. The iPad is an example of a classification of handheld computers called [   ].

4. Small [   ] computers are typically middle-of-the-line models that are not loaded with memory, fancy graphics cards, or audio systems.

5. There are three personal computer [   ]: PC, Mac, and Linux.

▶ CHECK ANSWERS

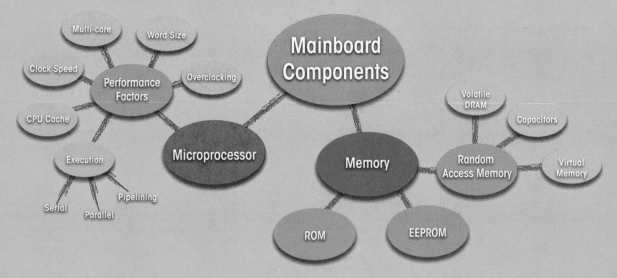

Microprocessors and Memory

A TYPICAL COMPUTER AD contains a long list of specifications that begin with microprocessor speed and memory capacity (Figure 2-14). Section B explains how microprocessors and memory affect computer performance and price.

MICROPROCESSOR BASICS

▶ **What exactly is a microprocessor?** As you learned in Chapter 1, a microprocessor (sometimes simply referred to as a processor) is an integrated circuit designed to process instructions. It is the most important, and usually the most expensive, component of a computer.

▶ **What does it look like?** Looking inside a computer, you can usually identify the microprocessor because it is the largest chip on the system board, although it might be hidden under a cooling fan. Most of today's microprocessors are housed in a pin grid array chip package, as shown in Figure 2-15.

▶ **What makes one microprocessor perform better than another?** A microprocessor's performance is affected by several factors, including clock speed, bus speed, word size, cache size, instruction set, number of cores, and processing techniques.

▶ **What do MHz and GHz have to do with computer performance?** A specification, such as 2.3 GHz, that you see in a computer ad indicates the speed of the **microprocessor clock**—a timing device that sets the pace for executing instructions. Most computer ads specify the speed of a microprocessor in gigahertz. **Gigahertz** (GHz) means a billion cycles per second.

A cycle is the smallest unit of time in a microprocessor's universe. Every action a processor performs is measured by these cycles. It is important, however, to understand that the clock speed is not equal to the number of instructions a processor can execute in one second. In many computers, some instructions occur within one cycle, but other instructions might require multiple cycles. Some processors can even execute several instructions in a single clock cycle.

FIGURE 2-14

A computer ad typically specifies the amount and type of RAM.

- Intel Core i7 2820QM processor 2.3 GHz 1600 MHz FSB
- 6 MB L3 cache
- 4 GB DDR2-800 MHz dual channel SDRAM
- 1 TB SATA HD (7200 rpm)
- 16X max. DVD+/-R/RW SuperMulti drive

FIGURE 2-15

Although a microprocessor is sometimes mistakenly referred to as a computer on a chip, it can be more accurately described as a CPU on a chip because it contains—on a single chip—circuitry that performs essentially the same tasks as the central processing unit of a classic mainframe computer.

67

A specification such as 1.6 GHz means that the microprocessor's clock operates at a speed of 1.6 billion cycles per second. If you are curious about the speed of the processor in your computer, Figure 2-16 can help you find it.

You might expect a computer with a 1.6 GHz processor to perform slower than a computer with a 2.3 GHz processor. This is not necessarily the case. Clock speed comparisons are only valid when comparing processors within the same chip family. As you might expect, a 1.87 GHz i7 840QM processor is faster than a 1.6 GHz i7 720QM processor.

Suppose, however, that you're shopping for a notebook computer and you have the option of an Intel i7 720QM 1.6 GHz processor or an i5 520M 2.4 GHz processor. You might be surprised that the i7 1.6 GHz processor is faster than the i5 2.4 GHz processor. Why? Because factors other than clock speed contribute to the overall performance of a microprocessor. In multi-core processors, the number of cores affects performance.

▶ What's a multi-core processor? A microprocessor that contains circuitry for more than one processing unit is called a **multi-core processor**. More cores usually produce faster performance. The 2.4 GHz i5 processor has two cores, giving it the equivalent of 4.8 GHz performance (2.4 x 2). The 1.6 GHz i7 processor has four cores, giving it the equivalent of 6.4 GHz performance (1.6 x 4).

FIGURE 2-16

You can discover your computer processor's specs using operating system utilities or third-party software, such as CPU-Z. If you are using a Mac, click the Apple icon and then select About This Mac. When using Windows, click the Control Panel button to access System Information.

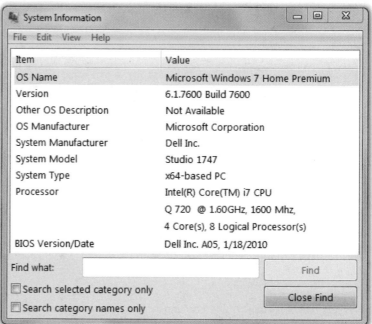

▶ What is FSB? FSB stands for **front side bus**, a term that refers to the circuitry that transports data to and from the microprocessor. A fast front side bus moves data quickly and allows the processor to work at full capacity. FSB speed (technically its frequency) is measured in megahertz. **Megahertz** means one million cycles per second. Today's computers have FSB speeds ranging from 1000 MHz to 1600 MHz. Higher numbers indicate faster FSB speeds.

TERMINOLOGY NOTE

Other terms for *front side bus* include *system bus* and *memory bus*.

▶ How does the cache size affect performance? **CPU cache** (pronounced "cash") is special high-speed memory that allows a microprocessor to access data more rapidly than from memory located elsewhere on the system board. A large cache can increase computer performance.

CPU cache is structured into several levels. Level 1 cache (L1) is the fastest, whereas Level 2 (L2) and Level 3 (L3) are slightly slower, but still faster than accessing main memory or disk storage. Cache capacity is usually measured in megabytes.

▶ What impact does word size have on performance? **Word size** refers to the number of bits that a microprocessor can manipulate at one time. Word size is based on the size of registers in the ALU and the capacity of circuits that lead to those registers. A **64-bit processor**, for example, has 64-bit registers and processes 64 bits at a time.

A large word size gives processors the ability to handle more data during each processing cycle—a factor that leads to increased computer performance. Today's personal computers typically contain 32-bit or 64-bit processors.

▶ **How does an instruction set affect performance?** As chip designers developed various instruction sets for microprocessors, they added increasingly complex instructions, each requiring several clock cycles for execution. A microprocessor with such an instruction set uses **CISC** (complex instruction set computer) technology. A microprocessor with a limited set of simple instructions uses **RISC** (reduced instruction set computer) technology.

A RISC processor performs most instructions faster than a CISC processor. It might, however, require more of these simple instructions to complete a task than a CISC processor requires for the same task.

Most processors in today's personal computers use CISC technology. Many processors used in handheld devices, such as iPods, Droids, and BlackBerrys, are ARM (advanced RISC Machine) processors.

▶ **Can a microprocessor execute more than one instruction at a time?** Some processors execute instructions "serially"—that is, one instruction at a time. With **serial processing**, the processor must complete all steps in the instruction cycle before it begins to execute the next instruction. However, using a technology called **pipelining**, a processor can begin executing an instruction before it completes the previous instruction. Many of today's microprocessors also perform **parallel processing**, in which multiple instructions are executed at the same time. Pipelining and parallel processing, illustrated in Figure 2-17, enhance processor performance.

FIGURE 2-17

Microprocessor designers have developed techniques for serial processing, pipelining, and parallel processing.

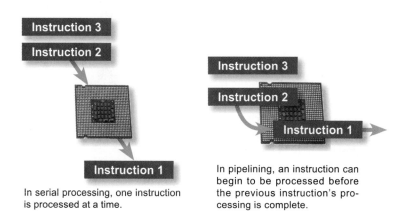

In serial processing, one instruction is processed at a time.

In pipelining, an instruction can begin to be processed before the previous instruction's processing is complete.

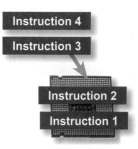

In parallel processing, multiple instructions can be processed at the same time.

To get a clearer picture of serial, pipelining, and parallel processing technology, consider an analogy in which computer instructions are pizzas. Serial processing executes only one instruction at a time, just like a pizzeria with one oven that holds only one pizza.

Pipelining is similar to a pizza conveyor belt. A pizza (instruction) starts moving along the conveyor belt into the oven; but before it reaches the end, another pizza starts moving along the belt.

Parallel processing is similar to a pizzeria with a large oven. Just as this oven can bake more than one pizza at a time, a parallel processor can execute more than one instruction at a time.

❯ **With so many factors to consider, how can I compare micro-processor performance?** Various testing laboratories run a series of tests to gauge the overall speed of a microprocessor. The results of these tests—called **benchmarks**—can then be compared to the results for other microprocessors. The results of benchmark tests are usually available on the Web and published in computer magazine articles.

Windows 7 offers a set of benchmarks called the Windows Experience Index that scores a computer's overall performance, and the performance of components such as its processor, memory, graphics, and storage system (Figure 2-18).

FIGURE 2-18

To access the Windows Experience Index, enter "Windows Index" in the Start menu's Search box.

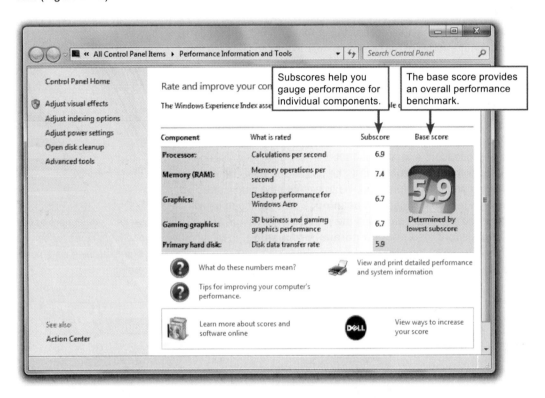

❯ **What do the Windows Experience Index scores mean?** Windows determines the performance subscores for five computer components: processor speed, memory transfer speed, ability to display the Aero desktop, 3-D animated graphics performance, and disk drive data transfer rate. Scores range from a low of 1.0 to a high score of 7.9.

The base score is determined by the lowest subscore because the component with the worst performance sets the limit on overall performance. Computers with a base score lower than 3.0 might be fine for basic applications, but base scores above 6.0 are desirable for computers used for multiplayer and 3-D games, teleconferencing, and HDTV playback.

TODAY'S MICROPROCESSORS

▶ **Which companies produce most of today's popular microprocessors?** Intel is the world's largest chipmaker and supplies a sizeable percentage of the microprocessors that power computers of all types. In 1971, Intel introduced the world's first microprocessor—the 4004. Intel's 8088 processor powered the original IBM PC. Since the debut of the IBM PC in 1985, Intel has introduced numerous microprocessors that have been used by most major computer manufacturers.

AMD (Advanced Micro Devices) is Intel's chief rival in the PC chip market. AMD's Phenom processors are direct competitors to Intel's Core 2 Quad line; AMD's Athlon X2 processors compete directly with Intel's Core 2 Duo processors (Figure 2-19). AMD processors are less expensive than comparable Intel models and have a slight performance advantage according to some benchmarks.

ARM processors are designed and licensed by ARM Holdings, a British technology company founded by Acorn Computers, Apple Inc., and VLSI Technology. Its RISC processors are used in many mobile phones and other handheld devices, such as the Apple iPad.

▶ **Which microprocessor is best for my PC?** The microprocessor that's best for you depends on your budget and the type of work and play you plan to do. The microprocessors marketed with the current crop of computers can handle most business, educational, and entertainment applications. You'll want to consider the fastest processor offerings if you typically engage in processing-hungry activities, such as 3-D animated computer games, desktop publishing, multitrack sound recording, or video editing.

▶ **Can I replace my computer's microprocessor with a faster one?** It is technically possible to upgrade your computer's microprocessor, but computer owners rarely do so. The price of the latest, greatest microprocessor can often get you more than halfway to buying an entirely new computer system. Technical factors also discourage microprocessor upgrades. A microprocessor operates at full efficiency only if all components in the computer can handle the faster speeds. In many cases, installing a new processor in an old computer can be like attaching a huge outboard engine to a canoe. In both cases, too much power can lead to disaster.

▶ **What is overclocking?** **Overclocking** is a technique for increasing the speed of a computer component, such as a processor, graphics card, system board, or memory. When successful, overclocking can increase the processing power of a slow component to match that of a faster, more expensive component. Overclocking is popular with gamers who want to squeeze every bit of processing speed out of their computers.

▶ **Why doesn't everyone overclock?** Overclocking is very risky. Additional electrical power pumped into a component increases heat output. Overclocked components can overheat and even catch fire. To maintain safe operating temperatures, an overclocked computer might require a supplemental cooling system.

FIGURE 2-19

Today's Popular Server, Desktop, and Mobile Microprocessor Families

Processor	Application
INTEL	
Core i7 and i5	Desktops and Notebooks
Pentium	Desktops
Celeron	Desktops and Notebooks
Xeon	Servers and Workstations
Itanium	Servers
Atom	Netbooks and Handhelds
AMD	
Phenom	Desktops
Athlon	Desktops and Notebooks
Sempron	Desktops and Notebooks
Turion	Notebooks
Opteron	Servers and Workstations
ARM	
ARM7	Analog phones
ARM9	Digital phones
Cortex-A	Handhelds

2

RANDOM ACCESS MEMORY

▶ **What is RAM? RAM** (random access memory) is a temporary holding area for data, application program instructions, and the operating system. In a personal computer, RAM is usually several chips or small circuit boards that plug into the system board within the computer's system unit. A computer's RAM capacity is invariably included in the list of specifications in personal computer ads (Figure 2-20).

The amount of RAM in a computer can affect the overall price of a computer system. To understand how much RAM your computer needs and to understand computer ad terminology, it is handy to have a little background on how RAM works and what it does.

▶ **Why is RAM so important?** RAM is the "waiting room" for the computer's processor. It holds raw data waiting to be processed as well as the program instructions for processing that data. In addition, RAM holds the results of processing until they can be stored more permanently on a hard disk, CD, or flash drive.

In addition to data and application software instructions, RAM also holds operating system instructions that control the basic functions of a computer system. These instructions are loaded into RAM every time you start your computer, and they remain there until you turn off your computer.

▶ **How does RAM work?** In RAM, microscopic electronic parts called **capacitors** hold the bits that represent data. You can visualize the capacitors as microscopic lights that can be turned on or off. A charged capacitor is "turned on" and represents a "1" bit. A discharged capacitor is "turned off" and represents a "0" bit. Each bank of capacitors holds eight bits—one byte of data. A RAM address on each bank helps the computer locate data, as needed, for processing (Figure 2-21).

FIGURE 2-20

A computer ad typically specifies the amount and type of RAM.

- Intel Core i7 2820QM processor 2.3 GHz 1600 MHz FSB
- 6 MB L3 cache
- 4 GB DDR2-800 MHz dual channel SDRAM
- 1 TB SATA HD (7200 rpm)
- 16X max. DVD+/-R/RW SuperMulti drive

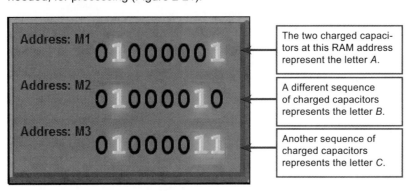

The two charged capacitors at this RAM address represent the letter *A*.

A different sequence of charged capacitors represents the letter *B*.

Another sequence of charged capacitors represents the letter *C*.

FIGURE 2-21

Each RAM location has an address and uses eight capacitors to hold the eight bits that represent a byte. ▶ Your interactive eBook shows you how RAM works with bits that represent data.

In some respects, RAM is similar to a chalkboard. You can use a chalkboard to write mathematical formulas, erase them, and then write an outline for a report. In a similar way, RAM can hold numbers and formulas when you balance your checkbook, and then can hold the outline of your English essay when you use word processing software. RAM contents can be changed just by changing the charge of the capacitors.

Unlike disk storage, most RAM is **volatile**, which means it requires electrical power to hold data. If the computer is turned off, if the battery runs out of juice, or if a desktop computer is accidentally unplugged or experiences a power failure, all data stored in RAM instantly and permanently disappears. This type of RAM is technically classified as **dynamic RAM** (DRAM) but it is commonly referred to simply as RAM.

TERMINOLOGY NOTE

RAM is classified as memory, whereas a computer's hard disk or solid state drive is classified as storage. Don't confuse the two. Memory is temporary; storage is more permanent. Computers typically have much less memory than storage capacity.

▶ **How much RAM does my computer need?** RAM capacity is expressed in gigabytes. Today's personal computers typically feature 2–8 GB of RAM. For good basic performance, a computer running Windows 7 should have at least 1 GB of RAM. Games, desktop publishing, graphics, and video applications tend to run more smoothly with at least 2 GB of RAM.

The amount of RAM your computer needs depends on the software you use. RAM requirements are routinely specified on the outside of a software package (Figure 2-22).

▶ **Can my computer run out of memory?** Suppose that you want to work with several programs and large graphics at the same time. Will your computer eventually run out of memory? The answer is "probably not." Today's personal computer operating systems are quite adept at allocating RAM space to multiple programs.

If a program exceeds its allocated space, the operating system uses an area of the hard disk, called **virtual memory**, to store parts of programs or data files until they are needed. By selectively exchanging the data in RAM with the data in virtual memory, your computer effectively gains almost unlimited memory capacity.

Too much dependence on virtual memory can slow down your computer's performance, however, because getting data from a mechanical device, such as a hard disk drive, is much slower than getting data from an electronic device, such as RAM. To minimize virtual memory use, load up your computer with as much RAM as possible.

▶ **How do I add RAM?** First, check how much RAM is currently installed, and then check the maximum RAM limit to make sure RAM can be added. Check your computer documentation or the manufacturer's Web site for information on the type and speed of RAM required.

Most of today's personal computers use SDRAM (synchronous dynamic RAM), which is fast and relatively inexpensive. SDRAM (shown in Figure 2-23) is further classified as DDR, DDR2, or DDR3. Make sure that you purchase the right type.

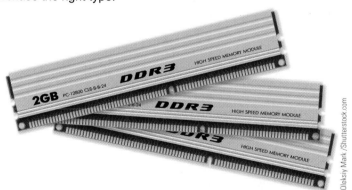

▶ **What about RAM for handheld computers?** Handheld computers commonly have about 512 MB of RAM, which is far less than the amount in desktop or notebook computers. Handheld apps are simpler than the applications designed for more powerful devices, so they require less memory. Apps run within the standard memory limits, so there is no need to add RAM to handheld devices.

FIGURE 2-22

Minimum RAM requirements are typically displayed on the package of a software product.

Minimum System Requirements:
- Windows 7 or Vista
- 1 GB of RAM
- 450 MB hard drive space
- CD drive for installation
- Mouse
- Internet connection (optional)
- Printer (optional)
- Scanner or digital camera with 32-bit twain interface (optional)

FIGURE 2-23

SDRAM is the most popular type of RAM in today's computers. It is typically available on a small circuit board. When adding memory to a computer, follow the manufacturer's instructions carefully.

READ-ONLY MEMORY

▶ **How is ROM different from RAM? ROM** (read-only memory) is a type of memory circuitry that holds the computer's startup routine. ROM is housed in a single integrated circuit—usually a fairly large, caterpillar-like DIP package—which is plugged into the system board.

Whereas RAM is temporary and volatile, ROM is permanent and non-volatile. ROM holds "hard-wired" instructions that are a permanent part of the circuitry and remain in place even when the computer power is turned off. This is a familiar concept to anyone who has used a handheld calculator that includes various hard-wired routines for calculating square roots, cosines, and other functions. The instructions in ROM are permanent, and the only way to change them is to replace the ROM chip.

▶ **If a computer has RAM, why does it need ROM too?** When you turn on your computer, the microprocessor receives electrical power and is ready to begin executing instructions. As a result of the power being off, however, RAM is empty and doesn't contain any instructions for the microprocessor to execute. Now ROM plays its part. ROM contains a small set of instructions called the **ROM BIOS** (basic input/output system). These instructions tell the computer how to access the hard disk, find the operating system, and load it into RAM. After the operating system is loaded, the computer can understand your input, display output, run software, and access your data.

EEPROM

▶ **Where does a computer store its basic hardware settings?** To operate correctly, a computer must have some basic information about storage, memory, and display configurations. For example, your computer needs to know how much memory is available so that it can allocate space for all the programs you want to run.

RAM goes blank when the computer power is turned off, so configuration information cannot be stored there. ROM would not be a good place for this information, either, because it holds data on a permanent basis. If, for example, your computer stored the memory size in ROM, you could never add more memory—well, you might be able to add it, but you couldn't change the size specification in ROM.

To store some basic system information, your computer needs a type of memory that's more permanent than RAM, but less permanent than ROM. EEPROM is just the ticket.

EEPROM (electrically erasable programmable read-only memory) is a non-volatile chip that requires no power to hold data. EEPROM replaces CMOS technology that required power from a small battery integrated into the system board.

When you change the configuration of your computer system—by adding RAM, for example—the data in EEPROM must be updated. Some operating systems recognize such changes and automatically perform the update. You can manually change EEPROM settings by running your computer's setup program, as described in Figure 2-24 on the next page.

```
┌────────────────────────────────────────────────────────────────┐
│                   PhoenixBIOS Setup Utility                      │
│ ┌──────┬──────────┬──────────┬────────┬───────┐                  │
│ │ Main │ Advanced │  Power   │  Boot  │  Exit │                  │
│ └──────┴──────────┴──────────┴────────┴───────┘                  │
│  System Time:       [10:40:48]              │ Item Specific Help │
│  System Date:       [03/03/2013]            │                    │
│  Language:          [English  (US) ]        │ <Tab>, <Shift-Tab>,│
│                                             │ or <Enter> selects │
│  CPU Type:          Intel (R) Core (TM) i7  │ field.             │
│                     CPU                     │                    │
│  CPU Speed:         1.60GHz                 │                    │
│                                             │                    │
│  HDD1/SSD1:         TOSHIBA MK5055GSX (S2)  │                    │
│  ODD:               MATSHITADVD-RAM UJ890ES │                    │
│                                             │                    │
│  Total Memory Size: 4096 MB                 │                    │
│                                             │                    │
│  System BIOS Version: 1.20                  │                    │
│  EC Version:          5.30                  │                    │
│                                             │                    │
│ F1   Help     ↑↓ Select Item   -/+   Change Values  F5  Setup    │
│ Esc  Exit     ←→ Select Menu   Enter Select Submenu F10 Save/Exit│
└────────────────────────────────────────────────────────────────┘
```

BIOS software © Phoenix Technologies

FIGURE 2-24

EEPROM holds computer configuration settings, such as the date and time, hard disk capacity, number of floppy disk drives, and RAM capacity. To access the EEPROM setup program, hold down the F1 key as your computer boots. But be careful! If you make a mistake with these settings, your computer might not be able to start.

2

If you mistakenly enter the setup program, follow the on-screen instructions to exit and proceed with the boot process. The Esc (Escape) key typically allows you to exit the setup program without making any changes to the EEPROM settings.

▶ **What information about memory performance is most important?** Even though ROM and EEPROM have important roles in the operation of a personal computer, RAM capacity really makes a difference you can notice. With lots of RAM, you'll find that documents scroll faster, games respond more quickly, and many graphics operations take less time than with a computer that has a skimpy RAM capacity.

Most ads specify RAM capacity, speed, and type. Now when you see the specification "2 GB Dual Channel DDR2 SDRAM (max. 4 GB)" in a computer ad, you'll know that the computer's RAM capacity is 2 gigabytes (enough to run Windows 7) and that it uses dual-channel, double data rate SDRAM. You'll also have important information about the maximum amount of RAM that can be installed in the computer—4 GB, which is more than enough for the typical computer owner who does a bit of word processing, surfs the Web, and plays computer games.

QuickCheck

1. A personal computer with an Intel Core i7 microprocessor is likely to operate at a speed of 2.3 [_____] . (Hint: Use the abbreviation.)

2. A(n) [_____] side bus is circuitry that transports data to and from the processor.

3. 4004, 8088, Athlon, and Pentium are all types of [_____] .

4. *DDR2*, *virtual*, and *volatile* are terms that apply to [_____] . (Hint: Use the acronym.)

5. The instructions for loading the operating system into RAM when a computer is first turned on are stored in [_____] . (Hint: Use the acronym.)

▶ CHECK ANSWERS

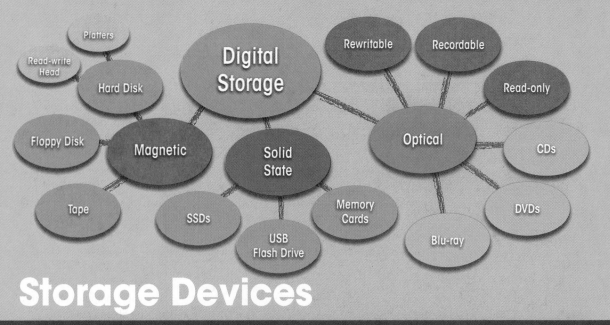

Storage Devices

COMPUTER MANUFACTURERS typically try to entice consumers by configuring computers with a variety of storage devices, such as a hard disk drive, solid-state card readers, and some sort of CD or DVD drive. What's the point of having so many storage devices? As it turns out, none of today's storage technologies is perfect.

In this section, you'll find guidelines that can make you a smart storage technology buyer and owner. The storage technologies you'll learn about are now used in a variety of devices—from digital cameras to player pianos—so an understanding of storage technology can be useful even outside the boundaries of personal computing.

STORAGE BASICS

▶ **What are the basic components of a data storage system?** A data storage system has two main components: a storage medium and a storage device. A **storage medium** (*storage media* is the plural) is the disk, tape, CD, DVD, paper, or other substance that contains data. A **storage device** is the mechanical apparatus that records and retrieves data from a storage medium. Storage devices include hard disk drives, CD drives, DVD drives, Blu-ray drives, and flash drives. The term *storage technology* refers to a storage device and the media it uses.

▶ **How does a storage device interact with other computer components?** You can think of your computer's storage devices as having a direct pipeline to RAM. Data gets copied from a storage device into RAM, where it waits to be processed. After data is processed, it is held temporarily in RAM, but it is usually copied to a storage medium for more permanent safekeeping.

As you know, a computer's processor works with data that has been coded into bits that can be represented by 1s and 0s. When data is stored, these 1s and 0s must be converted into some kind of signal or mark that's fairly permanent, but can be changed when necessary.

Obviously, the data is not literally written as "1" or "0." Instead, the 1s and 0s must be transformed into something that can remain on the surface of a storage medium. Exactly how this transformation happens depends on the storage technology. For example, hard disks store data in a different way than CDs. Three types of storage technologies are commonly used for personal and handheld computers: magnetic, optical, and solid state.

> **TERMINOLOGY NOTE**
>
> The process of storing data is often referred to as writing data or saving a file because the storage device writes the data on the storage medium to save it for later use.
>
> The process of retrieving data is often referred to as reading data, loading data, or opening a file.

2

▶ **Which storage technology is best?** Each storage technology has its advantages and disadvantages. If one storage system was perfect, we wouldn't need so many storage devices connected to our computers! To compare storage devices, it is useful to apply the criteria of versatility, durability, speed, and capacity.

▶ **How can one storage technology be more versatile than another?** The hard disk drive sealed inside a computer's system unit is not very versatile; it can access data only from its fixed disk platters. More versatile devices can access data from several different media. For example, a DVD drive is versatile because it can access computer DVDs, DVD movies, audio CDs, computer CDs, and CD-Rs.

▶ **What makes a storage technology durable?** Most storage technologies are susceptible to damage from mishandling or environmental factors, such as heat and moisture. Some technologies are more susceptible than others to damage that could cause data loss. CDs and DVDs tend to be more durable than hard disks, for example.

▶ **What factors affect storage speed?** Quick access to data is important, so fast storage devices are preferred over slower devices. **Access time** is the average time it takes a computer to locate data on the storage medium and read it. Access time for a personal computer storage device, such as a disk drive, is measured in milliseconds (thousandths of a second). One millisecond (ms) is one-thousandth of a second. Lower numbers indicate faster access times. For example, a drive with a 6 ms access time is faster than a drive with an access time of 11 ms.

Access time is best for random-access devices. **Random access** (also called direct access) is the ability of a device to "jump" directly to the requested data. Hard disk, CD, DVD, Blu-ray, and solid state drives are random-access devices, as are the memory cards used in digital cameras. Old-fashioned tape drives, on the other hand, used slower **sequential access** by reading through the data from the beginning of the tape. The advantage of random access becomes clear when you consider how much faster and easier it is to locate a song on a CD (random access) than on a cassette tape (sequential access).

Data transfer rate is the amount of data a storage device can move per second from the storage medium to the computer. Higher numbers indicate faster transfer rates. For example, a hard disk drive with a 57 Mps (megabytes per second) data transfer rate is faster than one with a 50 MBps transfer rate.

▶ **What's important about storage capacity?** In today's computing environment, higher capacity is almost always preferred. Storage capacity is the maximum amount of data that can be stored on a storage medium, and it is measured in bytes; usually in gigabytes (GB) or terabytes (TB).

Storage capacity is directly related to **storage density**, the amount of data that can be stored in a given area of a storage medium, such as the surface of a disk. The higher the storage density, the more data is stored. Storage density can be increased by making the particles representing bits smaller, by layering them, packing them closer together, or standing them vertically (Figure 2-25).

FIGURE 2-25

Vertical storage produces higher storage capacities than horizontal storage.

With horizontal storage, particles are arranged end to end, and use of the disk surface is not optimized.

With vertical storage, particles stand on end so that many more can be packed on the disk surface.

MAGNETIC STORAGE TECHNOLOGY

▶ **What is magnetic storage technology?** **Magnetic storage** stores data by magnetizing microscopic particles on a disk or tape surface. The particles retain their magnetic orientation until that orientation is changed, thereby making disks fairly permanent but modifiable storage media.

Data stored magnetically can be easily changed or deleted simply by changing the magnetic orientation of the appropriate particles on the disk surface. This feature of magnetic storage provides lots of flexibility for editing data and reusing areas of a storage medium containing unneeded data.

▶ **How does a hard disk drive work?** As the main storage device on most computers, a **hard disk drive** contains one or more platters and their associated read-write heads. A **hard disk platter** is a flat, rigid disk made of aluminum or glass and coated with magnetic iron oxide particles.

More platters mean more data storage capacity. The platters rotate as a unit on a spindle, making thousands of rotations per minute. Personal computer hard disk platters are typically 3.5" in diameter, with storage capacities ranging from 40 GB to 2 TB.

Each platter has a read-write head that hovers just a few microinches above the surface. A **read-write head** mechanism in the disk drive magnetizes particles to write data, and senses the particles' polarities to read data. Figure 2-26 shows how a computer stores data on magnetic media.

> **TERMINOLOGY NOTE**
>
> You might hear the term *fixed disk* used to refer to hard disks. You often see the terms *hard disk* and *hard disk drive* used interchangeably, although technically *hard disk* refers to the platters sealed inside the hard disk drive.

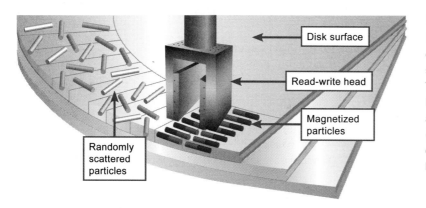

Disk surface

Read-write head

Magnetized particles

Randomly scattered particles

FIGURE 2-26

Before data is stored, particles on the surface of the disk are scattered in random patterns. The disk drive's read-write head magnetizes the particles, and orients them in a positive (north) or negative (south) direction to represent 0 and 1 bits.

▶ **Why are hard disk drives so popular?** Hard disk technology is the preferred type of main storage for most personal computers for three reasons. First, it provides lots of storage capacity. Second, it provides fast access to files. Third, a hard disk is economical. The cost of storing 1 gigabyte of data is about fifteen cents.

▶ **What's the downside of hard disk storage?** Hard disks are not as durable as many other storage technologies. Data stored on magnetic media can be unintentionally altered by magnetic fields, dust, mold, smoke particles, heat, and mechanical problems with a storage device. Over time, magnetic media gradually lose their magnetic charge, resulting in lost data. Some experts estimate that the reliable life span of data stored on magnetic media is about three years. They recommend that you refresh your data every two years by recopying it.

The read-write heads in a hard disk hover a microscopic distance above the disk surface. If a read-write head runs into a dust particle or some other contaminant on the disk, it might cause a **head crash**, which damages some of the data on the disk (Figure 2-27).

Read-write head

Spindle

Platters

© MediaTechnics

FIGURE 2-27

Hard disk platters and read-write heads are sealed inside the drive case or cartridge to screen out dust and other contaminants. ▶ The video for this figure in your interactive eBook shows how a hard drive works and what happens when a hard disk crashes.

To help prevent contaminants from contacting the platters and causing head crashes, a hard disk is sealed in its case. A head crash can be triggered by jarring the hard disk while it is in use. Although hard disks have become considerably more rugged in recent years, you should handle and transport them with care. You should also make backup copies of the data stored on your hard disk in case of a head crash.

▶ What should I know about selecting a hard disk drive?
Computer ads typically specify the capacity, access time, and speed of a hard disk drive. So "1 TB 8 ms 7200 RPM HD" means a hard disk drive with 1 terabyte capacity, access time of 8 milliseconds, and speed of 7,200 revolutions per minute. Ads rarely specify the amount of data that a hard drive can transfer, but the average data transfer rate is about 57,000 KBps (also expressed as 57 MBps or MB/s).

Hard disk access times of 6 to 11 ms are not uncommon, whereas a CD takes about half a second to spin up to speed and find data. Hard disk drive speed is sometimes measured in revolutions per minute (rpm). The faster a drive spins, the more rapidly it can position the read-write head over specific data. For example, a 7,200 rpm drive is able to access data faster than a 5,400 rpm drive.

Computer ads use acronyms such as ATA, EIDE, SCSI, and DMA to describe the type of circuitry used to transfer data between the hard disk and other components on the computer's system board. Some are slightly faster than others, but for most buyers this specification is not a significant factor.

TERMINOLOGY NOTE

Data transfer rates can be specified in bits or bytes, so read the specifications carefully.

50 Mbps or MB/s means 50 mega*bits* per second.

50 MBps or MB/s means 50 mega*bytes* per second.

Also stay alert for the difference between kilo (K) and mega (M), remembering that mega is 1,000 times more than kilo.

▶ **Can I use a second hard disk drive to increase storage space?** You can increase the storage capacity of your computer by adding a second hard disk drive, which can also provide a backup for your primary drive. Hard disk drives are available as internal or external units. Internal drives are inexpensive and can be easily installed in a desktop computer's system unit. External drives are slightly more expensive and connect to a desktop or notebook computer using a cable (Figure 2-28).

FIGURE 2-28

External hard drives offer a low-cost way to beef up the storage capacity of a personal computer.

▶ **Do computers still store data on tapes?** Next time you watch a movie from the 1950s or 1960s that shows a computer, look for the big reels of tape used as storage devices. Tape storage, once used to store mainframe data and also used for personal computer backups, is too slow for modern computing.

▶ **What is floppy disk technology?** At one time, just about every personal computer included a floppy disk drive (Figure 2-29) that stored data on **floppy disks** (also called floppies or diskettes). This storage technology is no longer used because a floppy disk's 1.44 MB capacity is not sufficient for today's media-intensive applications.

Many MP3 music files and photos are too large to fit on a floppy. In the past, floppy disks were extensively used to distribute software. CDs and DVDs offer more capacity for distributing the huge files for today's software applications. Web downloads offer more convenience.

FIGURE 2-29

A standard floppy disk drive reads and writes data on a 3.5" floppy disk.

OPTICAL STORAGE TECHNOLOGY

▶ **How do CD, DVD, and Blu-ray technologies differ?** Today, most computers come equipped with one or more drives designed to work with CD, DVD, and Blu-ray technologies.

▶ **CD** (compact disc) technology was originally designed to hold 74 minutes of recorded music. The original CD standard was adapted for computer storage with capacity for 650 MB of data. Later improvements in CD standards increased the capacity to 80 minutes of music or 700 MB of data.

▶ **DVD** (digital video disc or digital versatile disc) is a variation of CD technology that was originally designed as an alternative to VCRs, but was quickly adopted by the computer industry to store data. The initial DVD standard offered 4.7 GB (4,700 MB) of data storage; that's about seven times as much capacity as a CD. Subsequent improvements in DVD technology offer even more storage capacity. A double layer DVD has two recordable layers on the same side and can store 8.5 GB of data.

▶ **Blu-ray** is a high-capacity storage technology with a 25 GB capacity per layer. The name *Blu-ray* is derived from the blue-violet colored laser used to read data stored on Blu-ray discs. DVD technology uses a red laser; CD technology uses a near infrared laser.

▶ **How do CD, DVD, and Blu-ray drives work?** CD, DVD, and Blu-ray technologies are classified as **optical storage**, which stores data as microscopic light and dark spots on the disc surface. The dark spots, shown in Figure 2-30, are called **pits**. The lighter, non-pitted surface areas of the disc are called **lands**.

Optical drives contain a spindle that rotates the disc over a laser lens. The laser directs a beam of light toward the underside of the disc. The dark pits and light lands on the disc surface reflect the light differently. As the lens reads the disc, these differences are translated into the 0s and 1s that represent data (Figure 2-31).

2

FIGURE 2-30

As seen through an electron microscope, the pits on an optical storage disc look like small craters. Each pit is less than 1 micron (one-millionth of a meter) in diameter—1,500 pits lined up side by side are about as wide as the head of a pin.

Courtesy of IBM

FIGURE 2-31

CD, DVD, and Blu-ray drives use a laser to read data from the underside of a disc.

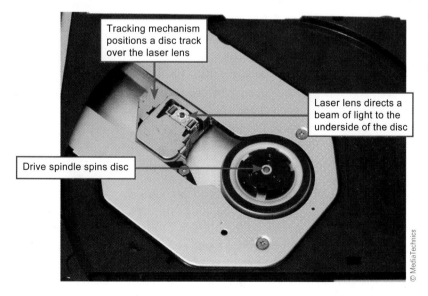

Tracking mechanism positions a disc track over the laser lens

Laser lens directs a beam of light to the underside of the disc

Drive spindle spins disc

© MediaTechnics

The surface of an optical disc is coated with clear plastic, making the disc quite durable and less susceptible to environmental damage than data recorded on magnetic media. An optical disc, such as a CD, is not disrupted by humidity, fingerprints, dust, magnets, or spilled soft drinks. Scratches on the disc surface can interfere with data transfer, but a good buffing with toothpaste can erase the scratch without damaging the underlying data. An optical disc's useful life is estimated to be more than 30 years. Figure 2-32 illustrates the layers of an optical disc.

FIGURE 2-32

CDs, DVDs, and Blu-ray discs are constructed with one or more layers of recording surface sandwiched between protective plastic.

▶ **How fast are CD, DVD, and Blu-ray drives?** The original CD drives could access 150 kilobytes per second (150 KBps) of data. The next generation of drives doubled the data transfer rate and were consequently dubbed "2X" drives. Transfer rates seem to be continually increasing. A 52X CD drive, for example, transfers data at 7,800 KBps, which is still relatively slow compared to an average hard disk drive's transfer rate of 57,000 KBps.

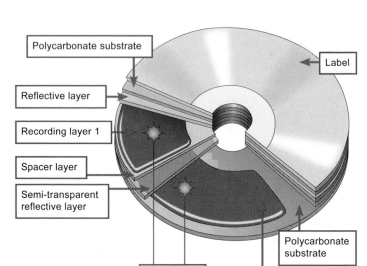

The speed of a DVD drive is measured on a different scale than a CD drive. A 1X DVD drive is about the same speed as a 9X CD drive. Today's DVD drives typically have 24X speeds for a data transfer rate of about 3,600 KBps.

Blu-ray drive speed is measured on an even different scale. A 1X Blu-ray drive transfers data at 4,500 KBps.

▶ **What's the significance of ROM, R, and RW?** Optical technologies are grouped into three categories: read-only, recordable, and rewritable.

TERMINOLOGY NOTE

The letter *D* in acronyms for optical media such as CDs and DVDs formally means *disc*. In common usage, however, you will often see it spelled *disk*.

▶ **Read-only technology** (ROM) stores data permanently on a disc, which cannot be subsequently added to or changed. Read-only discs, such as CD-ROMs, CDDAs, DVD-Video, and DVD-ROMs, are typically pre-pressed during mass production and used to distribute software, music, and movies.

▶ **Recordable technology** (R) uses a laser to change the color in a dye layer sandwiched beneath the clear plastic disc surface. The laser creates dark spots in the dye that are read as pits. The change in the dye is permanent, so data cannot be changed once it has been recorded.

▶ **Rewritable technology** (RW) uses phase change technology to alter a crystal structure on the disc surface. Altering the crystal structure creates patterns of light and dark spots similar to the pits and lands on a CD. The crystal structure can be changed from light to dark and back again many times, making it possible to record and modify data much like on a hard disk. The term *rerecordable* (RE) is sometimes used instead of *rewritable*.

❭ What are my choices for CD, DVD, and Blu-ray media?
Several CD and DVD formats are currently popular for use in personal computers. Figure 2-33 summarizes available optical media formats.

FIGURE 2-33

Optical Storage Media

CDDA	(compact disc digital audio)	The format for commercial music CDs. Music is typically recorded on audio CDs by the manufacturer, but can't be changed by the consumer. Commonly known as audio CDs.
DVD-Video	(digital versatile disc video)	The format for commercial DVDs that contain feature-length films.
CD-ROM	(compact disc read-only)	The original optical format for computer data. Data is stamped on the disc at the time it is manufactured. Data cannot be added, changed, or deleted from these discs.
DVD-ROM	(digital versatile disc read-only)	Contains data stamped onto the disc surface at the time of manufacture. Like CD-ROMs, the data on DVD-ROMs is permanent, so you cannot add or change data.
CD-R	(compact disc recordable)	Stores data using recordable technology. The data on a CD-R cannot be erased or modified once you record it. However, most CD-R drives allow you to record your data in multiple sessions. For example, you can store two files on a CD-R disc today, and add data for a few more files to the disc at a later time.
DVD+R DVD-R	(digital versatile disc recordable)	Stores data using recordable technology similar to a CD-R, but with DVD storage capacity.
CD-RW	(compact disc rewritable)	Stores data using rewritable technology. Stored data can be recorded and erased multiple times, making it a very flexible storage option.
DVD+RW DVD-RW	(Digital versatile disc rewritable)	Stores data using rewritable technology similar to CD-RW, but with DVD storage capacity.
BD-ROM	(Blu-ray disc read-only memory)	Used to store commercial movies.
BD-R	(Blu-ray disc recordable)	Stores data using recordable technology; can be written to once.
BD-RE	(Blu-ray disc rerecordable)	Stores data using rewritable technology so data can be recorded and erased multiple times.

❭ Are rewritable CD, DVD, or Blu-ray drives an acceptable replacement for a hard disk? A rewritable CD, DVD, or Blu-ray drive is a fine addition to a computer system, but is not a good replacement for a hard disk drive. Unfortunately, the process of accessing, saving, and modifying data on a rewritable disc is relatively slow compared to the speed of hard disk access.

❭ Can I use a single drive to work with any CD, DVD, or Blu-ray media? Most CD drives can read CD-ROM, CD-R, and CD-RW discs, but cannot read DVDs or BDs. Most DVD drives can read CD and DVD formats. Storing computer data and creating music CDs require a recordable or rewritable device.

> **TERMINOLOGY NOTE**
>
> Even though *CD-ROM* and *ROM BIOS* both contain the word *ROM*, they refer to quite different technologies. ROM BIOS is a chip on the system board that contains permanent instructions for the computer's boot sequence. A CD-ROM drive is an optical storage device that's usually installed in one of the system unit's drive bays.

SOLID STATE STORAGE TECHNOLOGY

▶ **What is solid state storage?** **Solid state storage** (sometimes called flash memory) is a technology that stores data in erasable, rewritable circuitry, rather than on spinning disks or streaming tape. It is widely used in portable consumer devices, such as digital cameras, portable media players, iPads, and cell phones. It is also used as an alternative for hard disk storage in some notebook computers and netbooks.

Some solid state storage is removable and provides fairly fast access to data. It is an ideal solution for storing data on mobile devices and transporting data from one device to another.

▶ **How does solid state storage work?** Solid state storage contains a gridwork of circuitry. Each cell in the grid contains two transistors that act as gates to hold the 1s and 0s that represent data (Figure 2-34).

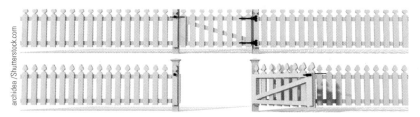

archidea /Shutterstock.com

Very little power is required to open or close the gates, which makes solid state storage ideal for battery-operated devices, such as digital cameras and media players. Once the data is stored, it is **non-volatile**—the chip retains the data without the need for an external power source.

Solid state storage provides fast access to data because it includes no moving parts. This storage technology is very durable—it is virtually impervious to vibration, magnetic fields, or extreme temperature fluctuations. On the downside, the capacity of solid state storage does not currently match that of hard disks. The cost per megabyte of solid state storage is slightly higher than for magnetic or optical storage.

▶ **What are my options for solid state storage?** Several types of solid state storage are available to today's consumers: memory cards, solid state drives, and USB flash drives.

▶ **When should I use memory cards?** A **memory card** is a flat, solid state storage medium commonly used to transfer files from digital cameras and media players to computers. The term *memory card* might lead you to believe that it is similar to random access memory (RAM), but these cards are non-volatile, so they retain data even when they are disconnected from computers and other devices.

The formats for memory cards include CompactFlash, MultiMedia, Secure Digital (SD), xD-Picture Cards, and SmartMedia. A **card reader** is a device that reads and writes data on solid state storage. Sometimes referred to as 5-in-1, 7-in-1, or all-in-one card readers, these combination devices work with multiple types of solid state storage formats (Figure 2-35).

Because digital photography is so popular, many notebook and desktop computers have a built-in card reader to make it simple to transfer photos from your camera to your computer. Moving data in the other direction, a computer can download MP3 or iTunes music files and store them on a solid state memory card. That card can be removed from the computer and inserted into a portable media player, so you can listen to your favorite tunes while you're on the go.

FIGURE 2-35

Most personal computers are equipped with a card reader for transferring data to and from solid state memory cards.

Card reader

© MediaTechnics

Memory card

▶ **Do I need a solid state drive?** A **solid state drive** (SSD) is a package of flash memory that can be used as a substitute for a hard disk drive. Some solid state drives are about the same size as a microprocessor chip, whereas others are about the size of a small hard disk drive (Figure 2-36).

SSDs are widely used as the main storage device in handheld computers, such as iPhones and iPads. Some notebook computers and netbooks also include an SSD instead of a hard disk drive.

When shopping for a netbook or notebook computer, you might have the choice of a hard disk drive or SSD. An SSD is an attractive option for customers who use computers in rugged conditions. Currently, solid state drives are not a popular option for adding storage capacity to existing computers.

▶ **What is the best use for USB flash drives?** A **USB flash drive** is a portable storage device that plugs directly into a computer's system unit using a built-in connector.

Also called thumb drives, pen drives, jump drives, keychain drives, or UFDs, USB flash drives are about the size of a highlighter pen and so durable that you can literally carry them on your key ring. USB flash drives have capacities ranging from 16 MB to 256 GB.

USB flash drive data transfer speeds average 10–35 MBps (10,000–35,000 KBps). At these speeds, flash drives are slower than hard disk drives, so you might notice a bit of hesitation, especially when working with large files.

Files stored on a USB flash drive can be opened, edited, deleted, and run just as though those files were stored on magnetic or optical media. You might say that USB flash drives are the new floppy disks because not only can you access files as if they were stored on disks, but you can carry them from one computer to another and you can run software from them, too.

A USB flash drive is typically used for storing data files and programs that you want to use on various computers; for example, on your home computer and at work or in a school lab. When a USB flash drive is inserted, your computer automatically detects it. Macs display a flash drive icon on the desktop. Windows detects the flash drive and displays the AutoPlay window shown in Figure 2-37 so that you can quickly access files.

FIGURE 2-36

Like hard disk drives, SSDs offer fast data transfer rates and are fixed in place. Although they use the same technology as USB flash drives, SSDs cannot be easily removed from a computer.

FIGURE 2-37

To view the files and programs stored on a USB flash drive, insert it into the computer. Windows displays the AutoPlay window that you can use to quickly view the files stored on the USB device.

STORAGE WRAP-UP

▶ **Can I add storage to my computer?** You can increase storage capacity by adding hard drives and you can add storage flexibility by installing additional types of storage devices.

External storage devices, such as external hard disk drives, CD drives, DVD drives, and USB flash drives, simply plug into connectors built into your computer's system unit. They can be easily detached when you want to move your computer or if your external drive contains a backup that you want to store away from your computer.

Before you disconnect any storage device, make sure you understand the manufacturer's instructions for doing so. On PCs, you usually have to use the Safely Remove Hardware icon on the Windows taskbar. Macs usually provide an eject icon next to the drive listing.

As an alternative to an external drive, you can install storage devices inside your computer's system unit case in "parking spaces" called **drive bays**. An external drive bay provides access from outside the system unit—a necessity for a storage device with removable media, such as floppy disks, CDs, and DVDs.

Internal drive bays are located deep inside the system unit and are designed for hard disk drives, which don't use removable storage media. Most desktop computers include several internal and external bays. Notebook computers typically include a drive bay for a CD/DVD drive (Figure 2-38).

An empty drive bay located on the side of a notebook computer

© MediaTechnics

FIGURE 2-38

Some notebook computers provide bays for one hard disk drive and one CD or DVD drive.

© MediaTechnics

Most desktop computers have several drive bays, some accessible from outside the case, and others—designed for hard disk drives—without any external access. Empty drive bays are typically hidden from view with a face plate.
▶ Watch the video for this figure to find out how to install internal and external drives.

❯ **What are the relative advantages and disadvantages of each type of computer storage device?** Earlier in the chapter, you read that no storage technology is perfect. While hard disk drives offer fast and inexpensive access, they are not the most durable technology. CD and DVD technology is durable, but slow, and flash drive storage is expensive when compared per gigabyte to other storage media. The table in Figure 2-39 summarizes the relative advantages and disadvantages of each storage technology covered in this section.

FIGURE 2-39

Storage Technology Comparison

2

Storage Type	Cost of Device	Capacity	Data Transfer Rate	Technology	Removable
USB Flash Drive	$$	2–256 GB	Medium	Solid state	Yes
CD-RW	$	700 MB	Slow	Optical	Yes
DVD+RW	$	8.5 GB	Slow	Optical	Yes
Blu-ray	$$$$	50 GB	Slow	Optical	Yes
Floppy Disk	$	1.44 MB	Glacial	Magnetic	Yes
Hard Drive (Internal)	$$$	80 GB–2 TB	Fast	Magnetic	No
Hard Drive (External)	$$$	80 GB–2 TB	Fast	Magnetic	Yes
Solid State Drive (Internal)	$$$	32 GB–256 GB	Fast	Solid state	No

QuickCheck

SECTION C

1. Access [_____] is typically faster for random-access devices than for sequential-access devices.

2. A magnetic storage device uses a read-[_____] head to magnetize particles that represent data.

3. A hard disk drive that is rated at a speed of 7200 [_____] will give you faster access to your data than a drive rated at 5400. (Hint: Use the acronym.)

4. CD-R technology allows you to write data on a disc, and then change that data. True or false? [_____]

5. A(n) [_____] uses the same storage technology as a USB flash drive, but is not designed to be removable. (Hint: Use the acronym.)

▶ CHECK ANSWERS

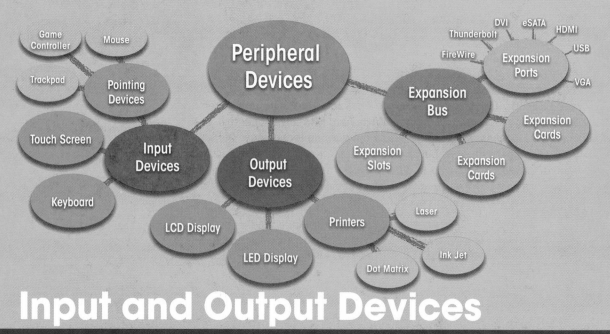

Input and Output Devices

SECTION **D**

THIS SECTION provides an overview of the most popular input and output devices for personal computers. After a survey of input devices, display devices, and printers, you'll take a look at the computer's expansion bus so that you'll be able to select, install, and use all kinds of peripherals.

BASIC INPUT DEVICES

▶ **What devices can I use to get data into a computer?** Most computer systems include a keyboard and pointing device, such as a mouse, for basic data input. Touch-sensitive screens offer an additional input option. Other input devices, such as scanners, digital cameras, and graphics tablets, are handy for working with graphical input. Microphones and electronic instruments provide input capabilities for sound and music.

▶ **What's special about a computer keyboard's design?** The design of most computer keyboards is based on the typewriter's qwerty layout, which was engineered to keep the typewriter's mechanical keys from jamming. In addition to a basic typing keypad, desktop and notebook computer keyboards include a collection of keys such as Alt, Ctrl, and Print Screen, designed for computer-specific tasks.

Most desktop computer keyboards include a calculator-style numeric keypad, plus an editing keypad with keys such as End, Home, and Page Up, to efficiently move the screen-based insertion point. You can even find tiny keyboards on handheld devices—entering text and numbers is an important part of most computing tasks.

▶ **What does a pointing device do?** A **pointing device** allows you to manipulate an on-screen pointer and other screen-based graphical controls. The most popular external pointing devices for personal computers include mice and game controllers. External pointing devices, such as those in Figure 2-40, can be connected to the computer with a cable or with a wireless connection.

▶ **Which pointing device should I choose?** Most desktop computer systems include a **mouse** as the primary pointing device. Many computer owners also add a mouse to their notebook computers.

Game controllers come in many styles, such as joysticks, steering wheels, and wands. Game controllers also serve as adaptive devices for people with physical disabilities who cannot use a keyboard or mouse.

FIGURE 2-40

An optical mouse uses an onboard chip to track a light beam as it bounces off a surface, such as a desk, clipboard, or mouse pad.

Game controllers can include several sticks and buttons for arcade-like control when playing computer games.

88

2

▶ When do I need a trackpad? A **trackpad** (or touchpad) is a touch-sensitive surface on which you can slide your fingers to move the on-screen pointer. Trackpads also include buttons that serve the same function as mouse buttons. Trackpads are typically supplied with notebook and net-book computers so that it is not necessary to carry a mouse as an extra component.

The act of moving your fingers on the surface of a trackpad is called a ges-ture. On a standard trackpad, sliding a single finger moves the pointer. With a multi-touch trackpad, additional gestures are possible (Figure 2-41).

FIGURE 2-41

Touchpad Gestures

Zoom in: Move two fingers apart to zoom in and enlarge photos or documents.

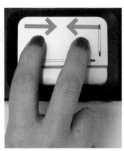

Zoom out: Move two fingers closer to each other to reduce the size of images or documents.

Horizontal scrolling: Move two fingers to the right or left.

Vertical scrolling: Move two fingers up or down.

Rotate: Turn two fingers on the trackpad to rotate an image.

Tap: Tapping the trackpad performs the same function as clicking a mouse button.

Two-finger tap: Tapping the trackpad with two fingers generates a right-click.

Swipe: Move three fingers horizontally to step through a series of photos, album covers, or windows.

© MediaTechnics

▶ How does a touch screen work? Tablet computers, handheld devices, retail store self-checkouts, and information kiosks collect input from a **touch screen**, which overlays a display screen. The most commonly used touch screen technology is a transparent panel coated with a thin layer of electrically conductive material that senses a change in the electri-cal current when touched. This "resistive" technology is fairly durable. It is not susceptible to dust or water, but it can be damaged by sharp objects. Processing technology can interpret a single touch or more complex input such as handwriting.

The coordinates for a touch event are processed in essentially the same way as a mouse click. For example, if you touch your iPad screen at the location of a button labeled Calendar, the area you touch generates coor-dinates and sends them to the processor. The processor compares the coordinates to the image displayed on the screen to find out what is at the coordinates, and then responds—in this case, by opening your appointment calendar. A popular use for touch screens is to display a **virtual keyboard** on the screen of a handheld device, as shown in Figure 2-42.

FIGURE 2-42

A virtual keyboard can be dis-played on a touch screen to collect typed input.

© Media Technics

DISPLAY DEVICES

▶ **What are my options for display devices?** A computer display device that simply displays text and images is classified as an output device. Touch-sensitive screens, however, can be classified as both input and output devices because they accept input and display output. Two technologies are commonly used for computer display devices: LCD and LED.

An **LCD display** (Figure 2-43) produces an image by filtering light through a layer of liquid crystal cells. Modern LCD (liquid crystal display) technology is compact, lightweight, and provides an easy-to-read display. LCDs are standard equipment on notebook computers. Standalone LCDs, referred to as LCD monitors or flat panel displays, are popular for desktop computers. The advantages of LCD monitors include display clarity, low radiation emission, portability, and compactness. Most new computers ship with LCD displays.

The source of the light that filters through the LCD is referred to as backlighting. In a standard LCD screen, the source of this light is typically a series of cold cathode fluorescent lamps (CCFLs), which are not environmentally friendly. Gradually, CCFL backlighting technology is being replaced by low-power light-emitting diodes (LEDs). A computer screen that uses this technology is sometimes referred to as an **LED display**.

▶ **Can I watch DVDs and television on a computer display?** Computer display devices can be equipped with NTSC (standard American television) or HDTV (high-definition television) circuitry so they accept television signals from an antenna or a cable. This technology lets you switch between your computer desktop and television stations, or simultaneously view computer data and television on the same display device using split-screen or picture-in-picture format.

▶ **What factors affect image quality?** Image quality is a factor of screen size, dot pitch, width of viewing angle, response rate, resolution, and color depth. Screen size is the measurement in inches from one corner of the screen diagonally across to the opposite corner. Screen sizes range from 11" on netbooks to 60" or more for home entertainment systems.

Dot pitch (dp) is a measure of image clarity. A smaller dot pitch means a crisper image. Technically, dot pitch is the distance in millimeters between like-colored **pixels**—the small dots of light that form an image. A dot pitch between .26 and .23 is typical for today's display devices.

A display device's **viewing angle width** indicates how far to the side you can still clearly see the screen image. With a wide viewing angle of 170 degrees or more, you can view the screen from various positions without compromising image quality.

Response rate is the time it takes for one pixel to change from black to white then back to black. Display devices with fast response rates display a crisp image with minimal blurring or "ghosting" of moving objects. Response rate is measured in milliseconds (ms). For gaming systems, a response rate of 5 ms or less is desirable.

The number of colors a monitor can display is referred to as **color depth** or bit depth. Most PC display devices have the capability to display millions of colors. When set at 24-bit color depth (sometimes called True Color), your PC can display more than 16 million colors—and produce what are considered photographic-quality images.

FIGURE 2-43

LCD screens are used with most desktop and portable computers.

Andrey Burmakin /Shutterstock.com

TERMINOLOGY NOTE

A computer display device is sometimes referred to as a *monitor*.

▶ What should I know about screen resolution? The number of horizontal and vertical pixels that a device displays on the screen is referred to as **screen resolution**. Standard resolutions are optimized for a 4:3 aspect ratio in which the width is slightly larger than the height. Widescreen displays with 16:9 aspect ratios carry a W designation. Common screen resolutions are listed in Figure 2-44.

HDTV broadcast systems use resolutions of 1280 x 720 (720p) or 1920 x 1080 (1080p). For HDTV compatibility, make sure your computer monitor is compatible with one of these formats.

▶ Should I set my computer on its highest resolution? At higher resolutions, text and other objects appear smaller, but the computer can display a larger work area, such as an entire page of a document. At lower resolutions, text appears larger, but the work area is smaller. Enlarged text sometimes looks blurry because a letter that required one row of dots might now require additional dots to fill it in. Most displays have a recommended resolution at which images are clearest and text is crispest.

The two screens in Figure 2-45 help you compare a display set at 1280 x 800 resolution with a display set at 800 x 600 resolution.

FIGURE 2-44

Common Screen Resolutions

VGA	640 x 480
SVGA	800 x 600
XGA	1024 x 768
SXGA	1280 x 1024
UXGA	1600 x 1200
WUXGA	1920 x 1200
WQXGA	2560 x 1600

FIGURE 2-45

The screen on the left shows 1280 x 800 resolution. Notice the size of text and other screen-based objects. The screen on the right shows 800 x 600 resolution. Text and other objects appear larger on the low-resolution screen, but you see a smaller portion of the screen desktop.

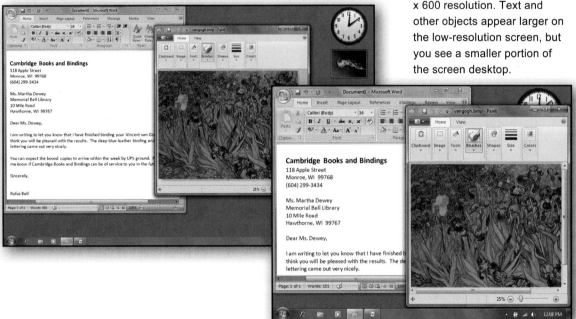

▶ What are the components of a typical computer display system? In addition to a display device, such as a monitor, a computer display system also requires graphics circuitry that generates the signals for displaying an image on the screen. One type of graphics circuitry, referred to as **integrated graphics**, is built into a computer's system board. A second option, called **dedicated graphics**, is graphics circuitry mounted on a small circuit board called a **graphics card** (or video card) like the one in Figure 2-46.

A graphics card typically contains a **graphics processing unit** (GPU) and special video memory, which stores screen images as they are processed but before they are displayed. Lots of video memory is the key to lightning-fast screen updating for fast action games, 3-D modeling, and graphics-intensive desktop publishing. In addition to video memory, most graphics cards contain special graphics accelerator technology to further boost performance.

FIGURE 2-46

A graphics card is a small circuit board that plugs into the system board.

Lusoimages /Shutterstock.com

PRINTERS

❱ **What printer technologies are available for personal computers?** Printers are one of the most popular output devices available for personal computers. Today's best-selling printers typically use ink jet or laser technology in multifunction devices that can also serve as scanners, copiers, and fax machines.

❱ **How does an ink jet printer work?** An **ink jet printer** has a nozzle-like print head that sprays ink onto paper to form characters and graphics. The print head in a color ink jet printer consists of a series of nozzles, each with its own ink cartridge. Most ink jet printers use CMYK color, which requires only cyan (blue), magenta (pink), yellow, and black inks to create a printout that appears to have thousands of colors. Alternatively, some printers use six or eight ink colors to print midtone shades that create slightly more realistic photographic images.

FIGURE 2-47

Ink jet printers spray ink from a series of ink cartridges.

Ink jet printers, such as the one in Figure 2-47, outsell all other types of printers because they are inexpensive and produce both color and black-and-white printouts. They work well for most home and small business applications. Small, portable ink jet printers meet the needs of many mobile computer owners.

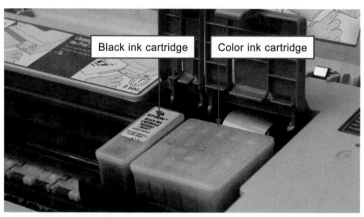

Black ink cartridge

Color ink cartridge

© Media Technics

Ink jet technology also powers many photo printers, which are optimized to print high-quality images produced by digital cameras and scanners.

❱ **How do laser printers compare to ink jet printers?** A **laser printer** uses the same technology as a photocopier to paint dots of light on a light-sensitive drum. Electrostatically charged ink is applied to the drum and then transferred to paper. Laser technology is more complex than ink jet technology, which accounts for the higher price of laser printers.

A basic laser printer like the one in Figure 2-48 produces only black-and-white printouts. Color laser printers are available, but are somewhat more costly than basic black-and-white models. Laser printers are often the choice for business printers, particularly for applications that produce a high volume of printed material.

Toner cartridge

© Media Technics

FIGURE 2-48

Laser printers electrostatically collect toner on a drum, then the toner is transferred onto paper. ❱ Find out more about laser printers by watching the video for this figure in your interactive eBook.

▶ **What is a dot matrix printer?** When PCs first appeared in the late 1970s, dot matrix printers were the technology of choice, and they are still available today. A **dot matrix printer** produces characters and graphics by using a grid of fine wires. As the print head noisily clatters across the paper, the wires strike a ribbon and paper in a pattern prescribed by your PC (Figure 2-49).

FIGURE 2-49

Unlike laser and ink jet technologies, a dot matrix printer actually strikes the paper and, therefore, can print multipart carbon forms.

Print head contains a matrix of thin wires

Characters are formed from a pattern of dots created as the wires strike an inked ribbon

© MediaTechnics

Dot matrix printers can print text and graphics—some even print in color using a multicolored ribbon. Today, dot matrix printers are used primarily for "back-office" applications that demand low operating cost and dependability, but not high print quality.

▶ **What features should I look for in a printer?** Printers differ in resolution, speed, duty cycle, operating costs, duplex capability, memory, and networkability.

▶ **Resolution.** The quality or sharpness of printed images and text depends on the printer's resolution—the density of the gridwork of dots that create an image. Printer resolution is measured by the number of dots printed per linear inch, abbreviated as dpi. At normal reading distance, a resolution of about 900 dpi appears solid to the human eye, but a close examination reveals a dot pattern. If you want magazine-quality printouts, 900 dpi is sufficient resolution. If you are aiming for resolution similar to expensive coffee-table books, look for printer resolution of 2,400 dpi or higher.

▶ **Print speed.** Printer speeds are measured either by pages per minute (ppm) or characters per second (cps). Color printouts typically take longer than black-and-white printouts. Pages that contain mostly text tend to print more rapidly than pages that contain graphics. Typical speeds for personal computer printers range between 6 and 30 pages of text per minute. A full-page 8.5 x 11 photo can take about a minute to print.

▶ **Duty cycle.** In addition to printer speed, a printer's **duty cycle** determines how many pages a printer is able to churn out. Printer duty cycle is usually measured in pages per month. For example, a personal laser printer has a duty cycle of about 3,000 pages per month (ppm)—that means roughly 100 pages per day. You wouldn't want to use it to produce 5,000 campaign brochures for next Monday, but you would find it quite suitable for printing ten copies of a five-page outline for a meeting tomorrow.

▶ **Operating costs.** The initial cost of a printer is only one of the expenses associated with printed output. Ink jet printers require frequent replacements or refills for relatively expensive ink cartridges. Laser printers require toner cartridge refills or replacements. Dot matrix printers require replacement ribbons. When shopping for a printer, you can check online resources to determine how often you'll need to replace printer supplies and how much they are likely to cost.

▶ **Duplex capability.** A **duplex printer** can print on both sides of the paper. This environmentally friendly option saves paper but can slow down the print process, especially on ink jet printers that pause to let the ink dry before printing the second side.

▶ **Memory.** A computer sends data for a printout to the printer along with a set of instructions on how to print that data. **Printer Command Language** (PCL) is the most widely used language for communication between computers and printers, but **PostScript** is an alternative printer language that many publishing professionals prefer. Data that arrives at a printer along with its printer language instructions require memory. Laser printers do not start printing until all the data for a page is received. You can add memory to most laser printers if necessary for your print jobs.

FIGURE 2-50

When you replace printer components, check to see if the manufacturer has a recycle program.

▶ **Networkability.** If your personal computer system is not networked to other computers in your house, apartment, or dorm, you can attach a printer directly to your computer. If your computer is part of a network, you can share your printer with other network users, who essentially send their print jobs to your computer's printer for output. Another way to configure network printing for multiple users is to purchase a network-enabled printer that connects directly to the network, rather than to one of the computers on a network. The network connection can be wired or wireless. The advantage of a network-ready printer is that it can be placed in a location convenient for all the network users.

▶ **Should I refill or recycle?** Ink and toner cartridges are expensive and you can save some money by refilling them yourself or taking them to an ink refilling station at a local office store. Remanufactured and discount printer supplies are available online, too. Before you try one of these options, read the instructions and warranty for your printer. Inexpensive printer supplies don't always get stellar ratings from consumers. If cartridge and toner refills are not available, find out how to responsibly recycle them (Figure 2-50).

INSTALLING PERIPHERAL DEVICES

▶ **How does a computer move data to and from peripheral devices?** When you install a peripheral device, you are basically creating a connection for data to flow between the device and the computer. Within a computer, data travels from one component to another over circuits called a **data bus**.

One part of the data bus, referred to as the local bus or internal bus, runs between RAM and the microprocessor. The segment of the data bus to which peripheral devices connect is called the **expansion bus** or external bus. As data moves along the expansion bus, it can travel through expansion slots, expansion cards, ports, and cables (Figure 2-51).

FIGURE 2-51

The expansion bus connects the computer system board to peripheral devices.

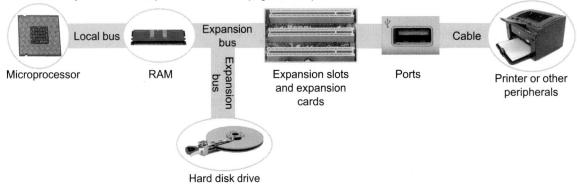

Microprocessor   Local bus   RAM   Expansion bus   Expansion slots and expansion cards   Ports   Cable   Printer or other peripherals

Hard disk drive

▶ **What's an expansion slot?** An **expansion slot** is a long, narrow socket on the system board into which you can plug an expansion card. An **expansion card** is a small circuit board that gives a computer the capability to control a storage device, an input device, or an output device. Expansion cards are also called expansion boards, controller cards, or adapters.

Expansion slots are typically used for installing high-end graphics cards in desktop computers configured for gaming, desktop publishing, and graphics applications. Figure 2-52 shows how to plug an expansion card into an expansion slot.

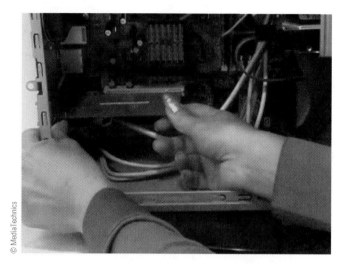

FIGURE 2-52

An expansion card simply slides into an expansion slot. Before you install an expansion card, be sure to unplug the computer and ground yourself—that's technical jargon for releasing static electricity by using a special grounding wristband or by touching both hands to a metal object. ▶ Your interactive eBook explains how to install expansion cards in a desktop computer.

▶ **What is an expansion port?** An **expansion port** is any connector that passes data into and out of a computer or peripheral device. It is similar to an electrical outlet because you can plug things in to make a connection.

Expansion ports are usually incorporated in the system board. Computer system units are designed with openings that make these ports accessible from outside the case.

As shown in Figure 2-53, the built-in ports supplied with today's computers usually include graphics ports for connecting display devices, an Ethernet port for connecting to a wired network, eSATA and FireWire ports for high-speed external data storage, audio ports for microphone and speakers, and USB ports for connecting a mouse, keyboard, printer, and other peripheral devices.

FIGURE 2-53

When this system board is installed in a computer, the expansion ports will be accessible from outside the system unit.

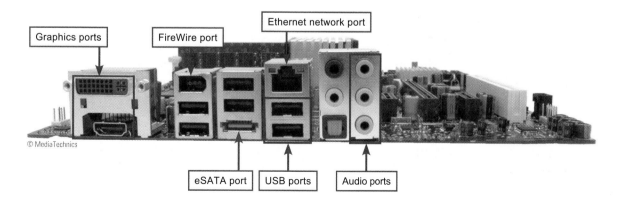

Graphics ports

FireWire port

Ethernet network port

eSATA port

USB ports

Audio ports

© MediaTechnics

▶ **Is it difficult to install a new peripheral device?** At one time, installing computer peripherals required a screwdriver and extensive knowledge of ports, slots, boards, and various electronic gizmos. Today, most peripheral devices connect to an external **USB** (universal serial bus) port, located on the front, sides, or back of the computer system unit (Figure 2-54).

Many kinds of peripheral devices—including mice, scanners, and joysticks—are available with USB connections. Transmitters for wireless devices, such as wireless mice, also plug into USB slots. Several types of storage devices, such as USB flash drives and external hard disk drives, use USB connections, too.

▶ **What if I run out of USB ports?** You can easily add USB ports to your computer by using an inexpensive **USB hub**, which contains several auxiliary USB ports. The hub plugs into one of your computer's USB ports and you can then insert multiple USB devices into the ports supplied by the hub.

Self-powered USB hubs require power from an external power supply, such as a wall outlet. Bus-powered USB hubs (sometimes called unpowered hubs) draw their power from the computer. A bus-powered USB hub can be used for low-power devices, such as card readers and mice. A self-powered USB hub is required if the hub is used for connecting scanners, printers, and some external hard drives. Figure 2-55 illustrates how a USB hub can be used to connect several devices to a single USB port on a computer.

FIGURE 2-54

A USB connector is shaped like a flat rectangle. Make sure you know which side of the plug is up; the top is usually labeled with the USB logo.

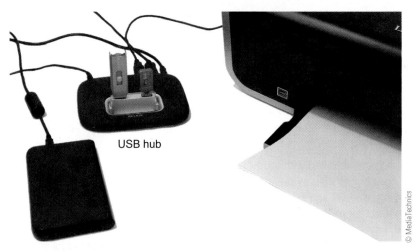

USB hub

FIGURE 2-55

This self-powered USB hub connects two USB flash drives, an external hard drive, and a printer to a single USB port that is connected to a computer.

▶ **When do I use other kinds of ports?** **FireWire** ports (also called IEEE 1394 ports) are used for external storage devices and for transferring data from digital video cameras to a computer. **Thunderbolt** and **eSATA** are high-speed ports used for connecting external storage devices.

VGA (Video Graphics Array), **DVI** (Digital Visual Interface), and **HDMI** (High-Definition Multimedia Interface) ports are designed for audiovisual devices. They are primarily used for connecting a monitor to a desktop computer, and for connecting an external monitor to a notebook computer. Figure 2-56 illustrates ports that can be used for connecting display devices.

VGA   DVI   HDMI

FIGURE 2-56

A variety of ports are available for connecting an external monitor to a desktop or notebook computer.

▶ What is hot-plugging? When you connect or disconnect a peripheral device while the computer is operating, you are **hot-plugging**, a practice that's allowed with USB and FireWire devices. Before you unplug a device, such as a USB flash drive, however, your computer might require notification. In Windows, you can give notification using the Safely Remove Hardware icon in the notification area of the taskbar. With a Mac, hold down the Control key, click the device icon, and then select Eject (Figure 2-57).

FIGURE 2-57

Before removing USB devices when the computer is operating, issue a notification. For Windows (left), use the Safely Remove Hardware icon. On Macs (below), hold down the Control key, click the device icon, and select Eject.

▶ Why do some peripheral devices include a disk or CD? Some devices require software to establish communication with your computer. The directions supplied with your peripheral device include instructions on how to install the software. Typically, you use the installation CD one time to get everything set up, and then you can put the CD away in a safe place. You'll learn more about this software, called a device driver, in the next chapter.

Long-time computer techies probably remember the days when installing a peripheral device meant messing around with little electronic components called dip switches and a host of complex software settings called IRQs.

Fortunately, today's computers include a feature called **Plug and Play** that automatically takes care of these technical details. Plug and Play detects new devices that are connected to a computer and attempts to establish the settings necessary for sending data between them.

Plug and Play works quite well for most popular peripheral devices. If your computer does not recognize a newly connected device or is unable to correctly exchange data with it, check the manufacturer's Web site for a device driver update, or call the manufacturer's technical support department.

QuickCheck

SECTION D

1. On a multi-touch trackpad, you can use various _____ to move the pointer, zoom, and scroll.

2. A widescreen computer display has a 16:9 _____ ratio.

3. One type of graphics circuitry, referred to as _____ graphics, is built into a computer's system board.

4. Most ink jet printers use _____ color that requires four ink colors. (Hint: Use the acronym.)

5. A(n) _____ port provides one of the fastest, simplest ways to connect peripheral devices. (Hint: Use the acronym.)

▶ CHECK ANSWERS

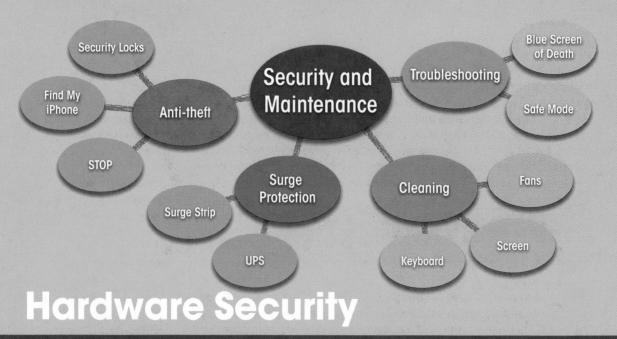

- Security Locks
- Find My iPhone
- Anti-theft
- STOP
- Surge Strip
- Surge Protection
- UPS
- **Security and Maintenance**
- Troubleshooting
- Blue Screen of Death
- Safe Mode
- Cleaning
- Fans
- Screen
- Keyboard

Hardware Security

THE INFORMATION that computers contain and process has become practically priceless to every PC owner. Just about everyone depends on a computer for information and communication. A stolen computer, even if it's low-priced, can be a huge loss if it holds valuable financial data or months of research. A broken PC can easily cost hundreds of dollars to repair, especially if the data is damaged and needs to be recovered. For trouble-free computer use, it is important to secure and regularly maintain your computer equipment, just as you would your home and car.

ANTI-THEFT DEVICES

▶ **What can I do to prevent my computer from being stolen?** Computers are prime targets for thieves. Many security breaches have been traced to stolen computers. The portability of notebook, netbook, and tablet computers makes them particularly easy for a thief to grab, just as a wallet or a handbag would be. Figure 2-58 contains important tips for protecting your portable computer from theft.

- ▶ Never leave your portable computer unattended, especially when you are at a coffee shop, the library, or the airport.
- ▶ If you have to leave your portable computer in your car, never leave it in plain view. Lock it up in the trunk or cover it up.
- ▶ Carry your portable computer in an inconspicuous carrying case.
- ▶ Record your portable computer's make, model, and serial number and store them away from the computer. Many recovered computers cannot be returned to their owners because this tracking information is not supplied to police.
- ▶ Consider securing your portable computer with an anti-theft device.

▶ **How do computer anti-theft devices work?** Several computer anti-theft devices are available. Most can be used for both desktop and notebook computers.

The Kensington Security Slot is a security mechanism that's factory-installed on many personal computers. It is a small, reinforced oblong hole into which you can insert a special lock that can be attached to a cable. The cable can be fastened to a desk to prevent theft as shown in Figure 2-59.

FIGURE 2-58

Tips for Preventing Computer Theft

FIGURE 2-59

The Kensington Security Slot is an industry standard way to secure a computer to a desk.

© MediaTechnics

98

▶ **If my computer is stolen, can authorities recover it?** Your chances of recovering a stolen computer improve if you have taken some steps in advance, such as recording the computer's serial number, affixing a tracking label, or installing tracking software.

STOP (Security Tracking of Office Property) plates leave an indelible tattoo on your computer equipment, which contains a unique ID number registered in the international STOP database.

Tracking and recovery software, such as CyberAngel and LoJack for Laptops, secretly sends a message as soon as a thief uses a stolen computer to log on to the Internet. This message contains the computer's exact location and is directed to a tracking or monitoring center.

Apple's Find My iPhone system can be used to track missing iPhones, iPods, and iPads (Figure 2-60).

Find My iPhone can locate a missing phone and remotely lock it or delete its contents.

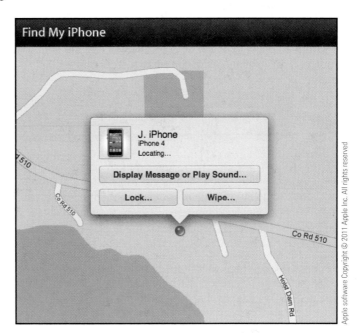

SURGE PROTECTION AND BATTERY BACKUP

▶ **What is a power surge?** To ensure that your computer stays in good running condition, it is essential to protect it from power surges. A **power surge** is a sudden increase in electrical energy affecting the current that flows to electrical outlets. Power surges often occur before or after power failures, which also put your computer and data at risk.

Computers and peripheral devices require stable current and are particularly sensitive to sudden bursts of electrical energy. A powerful surge can ruin computer circuitry. Smaller surges can slowly damage your computer's circuit boards and other electrical components. Over time, even small, repeated power surges can shorten your PC's life.

Power surges originate from a number of sources: downed power lines, power grid switching by the electric company, faulty wiring, and large appliances like refrigerators and air conditioners powering on and off. Lightning causes extremely large power surges and consequently poses a real threat to your computer equipment.

▶ **How can I protect my computer from power surges?** You can protect your computer equipment from power surges by plugging it into a surge strip instead of directly into a wall outlet. For added protection during thunderstorms, shut down your computer, turn off all your peripheral devices, and unplug the surge strip and all computer-related cables from wall outlets, including the cable for your modem.

▶ **What is a surge strip and how does one work?** A **surge strip** (also called a surge suppressor or surge protector) is a device that contains electrical outlets protected by circuitry that blocks surges. Some surge strips also have sockets for modem connections that prevent surges from traveling down telephone or cable lines and into your computer.

A surge strip like the one in Figure 2-61 monitors the electrical current that passes from an outlet to all the devices plugged into the strip. When it detects a surge, it redirects the extra current to a grounded circuit.

© MediaTechnics

FIGURE 2-61

Surge strips should be connected directly to a wall outlet. Plugging one surge strip into another surge strip reduces their effectiveness.

A big power surge can burn out a surge strip while it tries to protect your equipment. Some surge strips have an indicator light that warns you if the surge strip is no longer functioning properly. Check the manufacturer's documentation to determine if you should discard the depleted strip, reset it, or install a new fuse.

▶ **What is a UPS?** A **UPS** (uninterruptible power supply) is a device that not only provides surge protection, but also furnishes desktop computers and network devices with battery backup power during a power outage.

If your desktop computer is connected to a UPS when a power outage occurs, the battery backup allows you to save what you're doing and properly shut down your computer. Depending on your system's configuration, a UPS with a high-performance battery might give you enough backup power to keep your computer up and running for several hours, allowing you to continue to work during the entire power outage.

Portable computers run on battery power and so the data you're working on is not immediately affected by a power outage. However, if you want to access your local area network or Internet connection, you might consider plugging your network devices and Internet modem into a UPS so that they continue to operate during an outage.

As shown in Figure 2-62, most UPSs have two types of sockets: one type offers battery backup plus surge protection, and the other offers only surge protection. The surge-only sockets are for printers, which use so much power that they can quickly drain the battery. At the Web site for American Power Conversion, you'll find tips for choosing a UPS based on your system's configuration and the amount of run time you want during a power outage.

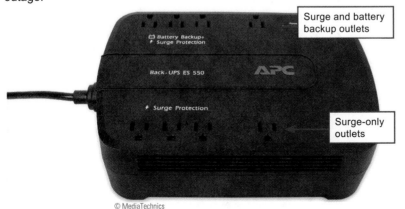

Surge and battery backup outlets

Surge-only outlets

© MediaTechnics

FIGURE 2-62

An uninterruptible power supply (UPS) not only protects electronic equipment from power surges, it also provides battery power during power outages.

BASIC MAINTENANCE

▶ Can I prevent hardware problems? Computer component failures can be caused by manufacturing defects and other circumstances beyond your control. You can, however, undertake some preventive maintenance to extend the life of your computer equipment, just as regular tune-ups lengthen the life of your car.

Preventive maintenance can save you more than the cost of repairs; you also save the time you would've lost while tracking down problems and arranging for repairs. Regularly cleaning your computer components and peripheral devices helps to keep them in good condition.

▶ How do I clean the keyboard? Always shut down your computer before you clean your keyboard so that you don't inadvertently type in commands that you don't want your system to execute. Also, disconnect the keyboard and remember where the connection is located. Flip the keyboard over and shake it gently to get rid of debris that became lodged between the keys. A can of compressed air is also effective for removing debris. A vacuum cleaner can suck away the keys on your keyboard, so be very careful if you use one to clean your keyboard.

You can use cotton swabs just slightly moistened with a mild cleaning fluid to clean the sides of keys. Wipe the tops of the keys with a soft cloth, again slightly dampened with a mild cleaning solution. Allow your keyboard to dry before you reconnect it. Keep drinks away from your computer to avoid spilling liquids onto the keyboard. Figure 2-63 provides more information on cleaning your computer keyboard.

© MediaTechnics

FIGURE 2-63

Carefully use a cotton swab and a can of compressed air or a vacuum cleaner to remove dust and debris from your keyboard. Sticky liquids are difficult to remove. That can of pop? Keep it away from your keyboard. ▶ Watch the video in your interactive eBook to see how to safely clean your computer keyboard.

▶ How do I get dust and fingerprints off my computer screen?
Dust and fingerprint smudges can easily accumulate on display screens and make them quite difficult to read. You should clean screens, especially touch screens, on a regular basis. It's always best to turn off your display device before you clean because a blank screen will reveal all the smudges, dust, and dirt.

Follow the manufacturer's instructions for cleaning your display screens, using the recommended cleaning product. Spray the cleaner on a lint-free, soft cloth, but never directly on the screen. Don't scrub. The membrane covering many screens is delicate and can be easily damaged.

▶ **Should I be concerned about my computer's operating temperature?** High-performance processors, hard drives, graphics cards, and several other computer components generate a lot of heat. Overheating can shorten the lifespan of internal components and chips.

Most desktop computers have a fan mounted on the power supply that runs continuously to maintain the proper temperature inside of the system unit. Additional cooling fans might also be used to cool the microprocessor or graphics card. Notebook computers also have cooling fans, but the fans come on only after the processor reaches a certain temperature (Figure 2-64).

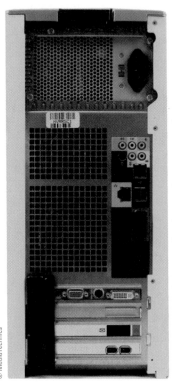

It is important to be aware of the ventilation around your computer system and ensure that the fans are able to draw air from the room and blow it across the internal components. If your computer is in an enclosed space, such as a cabinet, you might need to cut out a hole at the back to give your PC some room to "breathe."

You should also be aware of the temperature in the room in which your computer resides. Several vendors sell cooling mats containing fans that can be placed under your notebook computer (Figure 2-65).

© MediaTechnics

Dust particles, dirt, and pet hair can collect on and around a computer's cooling fans and impede their performance. You should regularly use a can of compressed air or a vacuum cleaner hose to clean out debris from the vents and fans.

Exercise extreme caution when cleaning inside your computer's system case. First, make sure that you've turned off the computer and all connected devices. Do not touch the system board, and be sure not to knock any cables loose.

▶ **Are there any other components that need TLC?** To avoid read or write errors, you want your optical drives to function properly. Retailers provide cleaning kits for many types of storage devices and media. Also examine your CDs and DVDs for scratches and fingerprints. Clean them with a soft cloth slightly dampened with water. If the smudges don't come off, a little isopropyl alcohol might help.

▶ **What is a good computer maintenance routine?** Aside from cleaning your computer equipment on a regular basis, you should do the preventive maintenance tasks listed in Figure 2-66. You'll learn how to do these tasks in later chapters.

FIGURE 2-66

Tips for Regular Computer Maintenance

▶ Back up your files regularly, particularly those that are most important to you. You might want to perform daily incremental backups of critical data and monthly backups of all your files. You should also test your backup procedures periodically.

▶ Run utilities that ensure peak performance for your hard disk drive. In Windows, these utilities include Disk Cleanup and Disk Defragmenter. It's best to do this maintenance on a weekly basis.

▶ Delete your browser's history and cache files on a monthly basis in order to free up space for your temporary files. The free space results in faster downloads from the Internet.

▶ Apply the latest operating system, driver, and security updates.

▶ Scan your computer for viruses and spyware once a week.

▶ Keep antivirus and spyware definitions updated.

TROUBLESHOOTING AND REPAIR

▶ **How can I tell if something is wrong with my computer?** There are several telltale signs that your computer is in trouble. The most obvious one is failure to power up. A loud beep at startup time can also indicate a problem. If your computer's screen remains blank or error messages appear, you might have a hardware problem.

Hardware problems can also show up as unexpected restarts at random intervals, or as a peripheral device that stops working. Some problems are intermittent and might seem to be resolved only to come back when they are least convenient to deal with.

Many seasoned Windows users have encountered the **blue screen of death** (also called BSoD) that suddenly replaces the usual graphical screen display with an enigmatic error message written in white text against a blue background. The blue screen of death indicates that the operating system has encountered an error from which it cannot recover, and the computer no longer accepts any commands.

Hardware problems can quickly escalate and some can eventually make your computer non-functional or make your data impossible to access. Any computer problem that prevents you from working as usual should be taken seriously. A little time spent troubleshooting can save you lots of annoyance down the road.

How do I troubleshoot a hardware problem? You might be able to solve many hardware problems by simply following the basic guidelines for troubleshooting listed in Figure 2-67.

FIGURE 2-67

Troubleshooting Tips

- Stay calm and don't jump to any conclusions until you've thought everything through.
- Write down all error messages and any other information that goes with them.
- Make sure all components are plugged in and that there are no loose cables. For example, if your display device's cable is loose, the indicator light will be off and your screen will be blank.
- If you can, try to duplicate the problem by going through the same steps that led you to it.
- Look for troubleshooting and repair tips in your user's manual, on your vendor's Web site, or even through a search engine. If you search the Internet by typing in the error message number or keywords in the error message, you might discover that at least one person has already found a solution to your problem.
- Run your antispyware and antivirus software. Lurking viruses, worms, Trojan horses, and spyware (discussed in the next chapter) can cause strange and unexplainable occurrences in your computer system. For example, spyware can cause your computer to keep displaying a pop-up ad no matter how you try to close it.
- A simple reboot of your computer might clear up the problem. Windows always requires a reboot when it displays the blue screen of death. However, a more serious problem underlying the BSoD will not be resolved with a reboot. To reboot a PC, hold down the Ctrl, Alt, and Del keys at the same time. When the next screen appears, click the red Shut Down button in the lower-right corner.

Troubleshooting and diagnostic tools can help you find the source of a problem and fix it. For example, Windows offers interactive troubleshooting tools formatted as a series of simple questions, answers, and recommendations (Figure 2-68). You might have to borrow a computer to run these tools if your computer is totally out of commission.

FIGURE 2-68

To access a Windows trouble-shooter, enter "troubleshoot" in the Start menu's Search box, then select the Troubleshooting option.

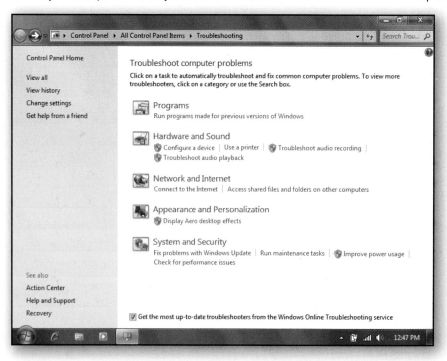

▶ **What is Safe Mode?** If Windows encounters a critical problem that is keeping it from operating normally, it starts up in Safe Mode the next time you reboot your computer. **Safe Mode** is a limited version of Windows that allows you to use your mouse, screen, and keyboard, but no other peripheral devices (Figure 2-69). While in Safe Mode, you can use the Control Panel's Add/Remove Programs option to uninstall recently added programs or hardware that might be interfering with the operation of other components.

FIGURE 2-69

To enter Safe Mode, you can press the F8 function key as your PC boots.

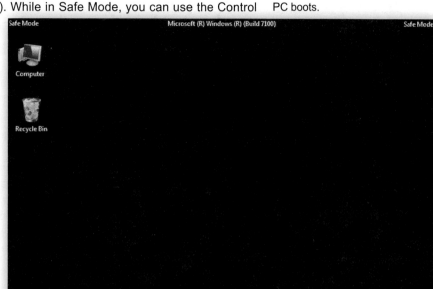

▶ **What if I can't solve the problem myself?** If you are unable to fix a hardware problem yourself, you might have to call the technical support center for the device or component that is malfunctioning. You can also consider asking for help from a knowledgeable person or from computer repair professionals like the Geek Squad.

When seeking outside technical help, make sure you've checked your warranty, and know the purchase date, serial number, brand, model, and operating system. You should also have a written copy of error messages and a description of the steps that led to the problem.

Once the problem is resolved, write down the solution. You never know when you might need it again!

QuickCheck

SECTION E

1. A power [_____] is a sudden increase or spike in electrical energy, affecting the current that flows to electrical outlets.

2. A(n) [_____] can provide power to keep your computer, network, and Internet connection operational during a power outage. (Hint: Use the acronym.)

3. If your computer's built-in fans don't provide an adequate level of cooling, you can place it on a chill mat. True or false? [_____]

4. When using Windows, you can troubleshoot hardware problems by logging in to the BSoD. True or false? [_____]

5. [_____] Mode is a stripped-down version of Windows that is designed for troubleshooting.

▶ CHECK ANSWERS

Issue: Where Does All the Ewaste Go?

IN THE WEST AFRICAN nation of Ghana, smoldering piles of discarded computers and monitors ring a mucky river, polluted beyond recovery. Teenage boys play soccer in a toxic haze. When their break is over, they get back to work smashing monitors, ripping out the innards, and tossing the plastic cases into a smoking pyre of oozing plastic.

In Guiyu, China, thousands of women huddle over primitive stoves "cooking" circuit boards to retrieve trace amounts of gold. Toxic fumes from the cooking process cloud the air; a toddler showing symptoms of lead poisoning plays listlessly with the carcasses of discarded mice and cell phones.

It is called ewaste, e-garbage, or technotrash—all the unwanted and outdated computers, monitors, printers, cell phones, disk drives, disks, CDs, and DVDs. According to the Environmental Protection Agency (EPA), 3 million tons of it is discarded every year. In the United States alone, almost eight printer cartridges are discarded every second, and millions of CDs and DVDs end up in landfills every year.

Some illegal ewaste originates in legitimate recycling centers...

Computers and other electronic gear contain toxic substances such as lead, cadmium, and mercury. When discarded equipment is buried in landfills, these substances can leach into groundwater and streams. When burned, electronic components can emit toxic dioxin.

Ewaste is a global problem. As countries struggle to deal with discarded electronic components, an alarming amount of ewaste is shipped to developing countries where villagers, working for pennies a day, are exposed to toxic chemicals as they attempt to reclaim resalable metals from discarded equipment. Throughout the emerging world, ugly ewaste dumps defile the landscape and have yet unknown health effects.

Where does all this ewaste originate? Every country generates ewaste, but the bulk of it comes from prosperous, technology-forward countries such as the United States, Great Britain, Germany, Japan, France, and China. Despite laws that ban ewaste transhipping, loopholes allow discarded but working electronics to be shipped as "donations." Tons of donations arrive every day in port cities, such as Hong Kong, where they follow a shadowy route to unregulated workshops and dump sites.

Some illegal ewaste originates in legitimate recycling centers, where consumers assume electronic components will be handled in environmentally friendly ways. Many recycling centers do not process materials on site. Instead, they ship the ewaste to third parties. Without careful monitoring, that ewaste can be diverted to offshore locations where it piles up, waiting to be disassembled by backstreet laborers ungoverned by environmental protection regulations.

Developed countries have strict environmental regulations designed to prevent toxic substances from polluting air, land, and water. Proper disposal is expensive, however. In countries with high labor costs and stringent environmental regulations, the value of compounds retrieved from ewaste does not cover the cost of extraction.

The high cost of properly processing ewaste makes gray market options attractive. Ewaste can be handled more cost-effectively in emerging countries where environmental regulations are ignored, wages are pitiful, and workers are not covered by health and safety laws.

So, who is responsible for ewaste sweatshops and pollution? Is it consumers in developed countries who deposit unwanted gear at recycling stations that don't carry out the recycling process in-house, or is it the recycling firms that ship ewaste to third parties? Is it the firms that ship ewaste to emerging countries or the governments that can't close the loopholes on ewaste transhipping?

Perhaps the responsibility lies with emerging countries that are unable to control ewaste sweatshops and ignore the resulting environmental and human casualties.

Wherever the blame lies, consumers who are aware of the problem can become more responsible in the way they dispose of unwanted gear, to keep it out of landfills at home and offshore.

Try It! Explore the ewaste issue. Watch a video of the Ghana crisis and explore the steps you can take to minimize the number of electronic components that end their life in landfills and toxic waste dumps.

1 A group of graduate journalism students from the University of British Columbia investigated the illicit ewaste industry. Their story is presented in a Frontline World report located at *www.pbs.org/frontlineworld/stories/ghana804/video/video_index.html*. Watch the video. Where do the researchers drop off the ewaste and where does it end up?

2 Many computers, mobile phones, and other electronic components pile up in landfills because their owners are unaware of potential environmental hazards and simply toss them in the garbage. Use Web sites such as Earth911.com, or search for "recycling computers" and add your city name as in "recycling computers Chicago." Where is the nearest drop-off location for old notebook computers? Would you be charged a fee, and if so, how much?

3 Before donating or discarding a computer, you should erase all the data it contains. Simply deleting files is not sufficient to prevent data from being recovered. Connect to *www.pcworld.com* and search for "erase hard drive." What are three ways you can securely prevent access to the data on a hard disk?

4 Consumers can select "green" products and purchase equipment from environment-friendly manufacturers. Check out Greenpeace's Green Ranking. What is the ranking for the company that manufactured your computer?

5 You might wonder if the computer you are currently using is environmentally friendly. The Green Electronics Council rates specific computer models as bronze, silver, or gold. Connect to the EPEAT site (*www.epeat.net*), click Search the Registry, and then drill down to find your computer. What is the rating for your computer brand and model?

	BRONZE	SILVER	GOLD	Total
Desktops	1	83	132	216
Displays	0	352	308	660
Integrated Desktop Computers	0	51	27	78
Notebooks	50	635	1018	1703
Thin Clients	0	21	4	25
Workstation Desktops	0	0	20	20
Workstation Notebooks	0	2	7	9
Totals	51	1144	1516	2711

INFOWEBLINKS

You can check the **NP2013 Chapter 2** InfoWebLink for updates to these activities.

W CLICK TO CONNECT
www.infoweblinks.com/np2013/ch02

What Do You Think?

ISSUE

1. Have you ever thrown away an old computer or other electronic device?

2. Do you research products before you purchase them to find out if they are environmentally friendly throughout their life cycle?

3. Would it be fair for consumers to pay a recycling tax on electronic equipment that they purchase?

Information Tools: Making the Cut

Searching Bing, Google Scholar, or academic databases produces mountains of links. How do you select and save the most relevant bits of information? The first step is to decide which information is relevant enough to make the cut. To decide, ask yourself the following three questions:

1. IS IT RELEVANT? Read the search engine synopsis carefully. With Google and other search engines, the synopsis shows your search terms in the context of the article. Academic databases display a standard synopsis. Don't waste your time linking to articles that are not relevant to your research topic.

The zen of **overclocking**

B Colwell - Computer, 2004 - ieeexplore.ieee.org
Every once in a while, some- thing comes along in the computer industry that really surprises me. The first time this happened was in the early 1980s, when the first personal computing stores showed up in shop- ping malls. The second time was when I took the first Internet browser ....
Cited by 13 - Related articles - All 4 versions

2. WHAT'S THE MAIN IDEA? Link to articles that seem relevant and skim them to pick up the main idea. Academic databases typically connect you to an abstract that provides a short summary. You can get an overview of an article's key terms using Web apps such as Wordle to create a word cloud.

3. ARE THERE LINKS TO ADDITIONAL MATERIAL?
The first part of a full-text journal article summarizes historical research and typically includes lots of citations. Some of these ideas might be worth tracking down for your own research. The bibliography can help you locate specific material mentioned in the article.

> Overclocked parts that are pushed to their limits also tend to have a reduced functional lifespan or even worse, if improperly done, can be destroyed completely [1]. In this experiment we will overclock an Intel processor. Its original frequency is 2.13 GHz, we will try to hit 3.20 GHz which is about 50% increase in CPU frequency

> Bibliography
> [1]http://compreviews.about.com/od/cpus/l/aaOverclock.htm

For more sources, jump to resources mentioned in the bibliography.

NOTE-TAKING TIPS

- Use a word processor or bookmarking tool.
- Be sure to identify information that is not your own; one technique is to put it inside quotation marks. Another technique is to apply a highlight color.
- Always capture the URL of a source document so that you can return to it if you eventually include it in your paper and need a full citation.
- Make sure that you add your own identifier to each piece of information; use your notes as topic headers, which will help you group and organize the information.
- Articles most relevant to your research topic require careful reading and note taking. For less relevant articles, simply make a note of the main idea and URL, just in case it becomes relevant later in your research process.

Try It! As you find information that is relevant to your research topic, you need a way to record it and keep track of it. Note-taking tools help you record important ideas; the trick is to keep your notes in good order. Many students use word processors to take notes. Bookmarking tools offer another option. Here's a chance to explore these tools and make a word cloud.

Many scholars record their notes in a word processing document. This method offers flexibility for copying snippets of text as well as entering summary notes.

1. Use your favorite word processing software to create a blank document called Project [Your Name] Chapter 2, then complete the rest of the steps.

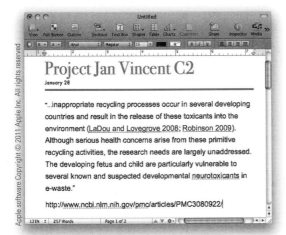

2. Use an academic database to search for a journal article about ewaste. Read the conclusion, highlight the most important idea, and copy it to your Project document using quotation marks to show that it is original material. Capture the Web address (URL) in your Project document. Add a phrase in your own words that summarizes the main idea.

3. Find three pieces of information that support the idea you selected in step 2. This information can be found in the journal article or another source. Copy the passages into your Project document (don't forget the quotation marks) along with the corresponding URLs.

4. Use a search engine, such as Google or Bing, to locate a magazine article about ewaste. Read the article, highlight the paragraph containing the most important idea, copy it to your Project document, and put it in quotation marks. Also capture the URL.

5. Search for ewaste in Wikipedia. Highlight one of the main ideas. Copy the text, add quotation marks, and capture the URL in your Project document.

A bookmarking tool helps you collect and recall key pieces of information by storing the source URL and important snippets that you highlight. Dedicated bookmarking apps offer tools that automate the process of collecting information and URLs from online sources. Many bookmarking services are Web apps, so your data remains in the cloud and is accessible to you from any computer connected to the Internet.

6. Register for a free account on a bookmarking service such as WebNotes or Diigo. Use that tool to capture the same information as you collected in steps 2–5. Don't forget to add your own tags that summarize each idea. Export your bookmarks if the tool offers a way to do so, then import the bookmarks into your Project document. If you can't export and import, then instead take a screenshot of your bookmarks and paste it into your Project document.

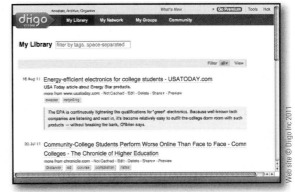

7. Search Wikipedia for the article about ewaste. Copy the entire article, then go to *www.wordle.com* and paste the text to create a word cloud. Take a screenshot of your word cloud and paste it into your Project document.

Technology in Context: Military

IN THE BOOK ENGINES OF THE MIND, Joel Shurkin writes, "If necessity is the mother of invention, then war can be said to be its grandmother." The military, an early pioneer in computer and communication technologies, continues to be the driving force behind technologies that have revolutionized everyday life.

During World War II, the U.S. military initiated a classified research program, called Project PX, to develop an electronic device to calculate artillery firing tables; by hand, each table required weeks of grueling calculations.

Project PX produced ENIAC (Electronic Numerical Integrator And Computer), one of the first general-purpose electronic computers. When ENIAC was completed in 1946, the war was over, but ENIAC's versatile architecture could be used for other calculations, such as designing hydrogen bombs, predicting weather, and engineering wind tunnels. ENIAC's technology evolved into the computers used today.

After Project PX, the military continued to support computer research. Like most large corporations, the military used mainframe computers to maintain personnel, inventory, supply, and facilities records. This data was distributed to terminals at other locations through rudimentary networks.

Because all data communication flowed through the mainframe, a single point of failure for the entire system was a possible risk. A malfunction or an enemy "hit" could disrupt command and control, sending the military into chaos. Therefore, the armed forces created the Advanced Research Projects Agency (ARPA) to design a distributed communications system that could continue operating without a centralized computer.

The result was ARPANET, which paved the way for the data communications system we know today as the Internet. ARPANET was activated in 1967, but the .mil domain that designates U.S. military Web sites was not implemented until 1984.

The U.S. Department of Defense (DoD) currently maintains several data communications networks, including SIPRNet, a classified (secret-level) network, and NIPRNet, which provides unclassified services. The DoD's public Web site, called DefenseLINK, provides official information about defense policies, organizations, budgets, and operations.

Computers and communications technology have also become an integral part of high-tech military operations. U.S. Apache helicopters, for example, are equipped with computer-based Target Acquisition Designation Sights, laser range finder/designators, and Pilot Night Vision Sensors.

The U.S. Army's BCT Modernization project includes high-tech vehicles, sensors, and equipment, coordinated by a network of computers, software, and radios. According to United States Army General George W. Casey Jr., "The network links Soldiers on the battlefield with space-based and aerial sensors, robots, and command posts. This provides the situational awareness necessary to apply lethal and non-lethal force with the precision demanded by the security environment."

BCT, which stands for Brigade Combat Team, includes "software-defined" radios that are less vulnerable to cyberthreats than conventional radios. Soldiers can use these radios to communicate voice and data.

A small handheld device with a touch-sensitive screen allows soldiers to control unmanned robots and drones. A solar backpack supplements the battery-powered device. BCT equipment also includes wearable devices, such as helmet-mounted displays and communications devices.

The military has conducted research in computer simulations that are similar to civilian computer games. "Live" military training is dangerous—weapons are deadly and equipment costs millions of dollars. With computer simulations, however, troops can train in a true-to-life environment without physical harm or equipment damage.

Photo Courtesy of U.S. Army

Flying an F-16 fighter, for example, costs thousands of dollars an hour, but flying an F-16 simulator costs only a few hundred dollars per hour. The military uses simulators to teach Air Force pilots to fly fighter jets, Navy submarine officers to navigate in harbors, and Marine infantry squads to handle urban combat. Military trainers agree that widespread use of computer games helps prepare troops to adapt quickly to simulations.

A 24-year-old preflight student at Pensacola Naval Air Station modified the Microsoft Flight Simulator game to re-create a T-34C Turbo Mentor plane's controls. After logging 50 hours on the simulator, the student performed so well on a real plane that the Navy used his simulation to train other pilots.

Today, a growing cadre of computer and communications specialists is needed to create and maintain increasingly complex military systems such as the Defense Department's Distributed Common Ground System (DCGS) for sharing surveillance imagery and intelligence.

Armies once depended primarily on their infantry divisions, but today's high-tech armies also depend on database designers, computer programmers, and network specialists. Even previously low-tech military jobs, such as mechanics and dietitians, require some computer expertise. Happily, new recruits are finding military computer systems easy to learn, based on their knowledge of civilian technologies, such as the Internet and computer games.

Although most citizens recognize that an adequate national defense is necessary, the cost of defense-related equipment, personnel, and cutting-edge research remains controversial. In a 1961 speech, President Dwight Eisenhower warned "We must guard against the acquisition of unwarranted influence, whether sought or unsought, by the military-industrial complex."

Some socially motivated citizens and pacifists tried to withhold tax dollars from the military-industrial complex that Eisenhower cautioned against. In retrospect, however, military funding contributed to many technologies we depend on today.

For example, detractors tried to convince the government that Project PX was doomed to failure; but without ENIAC research, computers might not exist today. Skeptics saw no future for the fruits of ARPANET research; but it led to the Internet, which has changed our lives significantly.

New Perspectives Labs

To access the New Perspectives Lab for Chapter 2, open the NP2013 interactive eBook and then click the icon next to the lab title.

▶ BENCHMARKING

IN THIS LAB YOU'LL LEARN:

- Which computer performance factors can be measured by benchmark tests

- How to run a test that identifies a computer's processor type, RAM capacity, and graphics card type

- How to run benchmarking software that analyzes a computer's processor speed and graphics processing speed

- How to interpret the results of a benchmark test

- How to compare results from benchmark tests that were performed on different system configurations

- When benchmark tests might not provide accurate information on computer performance

LAB ASSIGNMENTS

1. Start the interactive part of the lab. Make sure you've enabled Tracking if you want to save your QuickCheck results. Perform each lab step as directed, and answer all the lab QuickCheck questions. When you exit the lab, your answers are automatically graded and your results are displayed.

2. Use the System Information utility to analyze the computer you typically use. If you are using a Windows 7 computer, also check the results of the Windows Experience Index. Provide the results of the analysis along with a brief description of the computer you tested and its location (at home, at work, in a computer lab, and so on).

3. Based on the Processor Benchmarks table above,

PROCESSOR BENCHMARKS		
Processor	Quake III Arena	PCMark
"Supernova EE"	548	5198
"Pulsar FX"	551	5020

which fictional processor appears to be faster at graphics processing? Which processor appears to be better at overall processing tasks?

4. Explain why you might perform a benchmark test on your own computer, but get different results from those stated in a computer magazine, which tested the same computer with the same benchmark test.

5. Use a search engine on the Web to find benchmark ratings for one of Intel's Core processors and one of AMD's Athlon 64 processors. Are the benchmarks different? What would account for the benchmark results?

Key Terms

Make sure you understand all the boldfaced key terms presented in this chapter. With the NP2013 interactive eBook, you can use this list of terms as an interactive study activity. First, try to define a term in your own words, and then click the term to compare your definition with the definition presented in the chapter.

2

64-bit processor, 68
Access time, 77
All-in-one computer, 58
Benchmarks, 70
Blue screen of death, 103
Blu-ray, 81
Capacitors, 72
Card reader, 84
CD, 81
CISC, 69
Color depth, 90
CPU cache, 68
Data bus, 94
Data transfer rate, 77
Dedicated graphics, 91
Desktop computer, 58
Dot matrix printer, 93
Dot pitch, 90
Drive bays, 86
Duplex printer, 94
Duty cycle, 93
DVD, 81
DVI, 96
Dynamic RAM, 72
EEPROM, 74
Enhanced media player, 65
eSATA, 96
Expansion bus, 94
Expansion card, 95
Expansion port, 95
Expansion slot, 95
FireWire, 96
Floppy disks, 80
Form factor, 58
Front side bus, 68
Game controllers, 88
Gigahertz, 67
Graphics card, 91
Graphics processing unit, 91
Hard disk drive, 78

Hard disk platter, 78
HDMI, 96
Head crash, 79
Home computer system, 60
Hot-plugging, 97
Ink jet printer, 92
Integrated graphics, 91
Lands, 81
Laser printer, 92
LCD display, 90
LED display, 90
Linux platform, 64
Mac platform, 64
Magnetic storage, 78
Megahertz, 68
Memory card, 84
Microprocessor clock, 67
Mouse, 88
Multi-core processor, 68
Netbook, 59
Non-volatile, 84
Notebook computer, 59
Optical storage, 81
Overclocking, 71
Parallel processing, 69
PC platform, 64
Peripheral device, 56
Pipelining, 69
Pits, 81
Pixels, 90
Plug and Play, 97
Pointing device, 88
Portable computer, 59
PostScript, 94
Power surge, 99
Printer Command Language, 94
RAM, 72
Random access, 77
Read-only technology, 82
Read-write head, 78

Recordable technology, 82
Response rate, 90
Rewritable technology, 82
RISC, 69
ROM, 74
ROM BIOS, 74
Safe Mode, 105
Screen resolution, 91
Sequential access, 77
Serial processing, 69
Smartphone, 65
Solid state drive, 85
Solid state storage, 84
Storage density, 77
Storage device, 76
Storage medium, 76
Surge strip, 100
System unit, 57
Tablet computer, 65
Thunderbolt, 96
Touch screen, 89
Tower case, 58
Trackpad, 89
UPS, 100
USB, 96
USB flash drive, 85
USB hub, 96
VGA, 96
Viewing angle width, 90
Virtual keyboard, 89
Virtual memory, 73
Volatile, 72
Word size, 68

Interactive Summary

To review important concepts from this chapter, fill in the blanks to best complete each sentence. When using the NP2013 interactive eBook, click the Check Answers buttons to automatically score your answers.

SECTION A: The core of a personal computer system includes the computer system _____, display device, keyboard, and mouse. Personal computers come in several varieties of _____ factors. A(n) _____ computer fits on a desk, runs on power from an electrical wall outlet, and can be housed in a horizontal case or vertical _____ case. A(n) _____ computer is a small, lightweight personal computer with screen, keyboard, storage, and processing components integrated into a single unit that runs on power supplied by an electrical outlet or a battery. Two categories of these computers are notebook computers and _____. Personal comput-

ers are sometimes designated as home, small business, or game systems to help consumers select the computer that's right for their needs. Although the Mac platform was not previously _____ with the PC platform, the situation has changed now that Intel Macs use the same _____ as PCs. Consumers can sometimes save money by installing upgrades after purchase; however, replacing a(n) _____ is difficult and not recommended. Handheld computers include enhanced media players, smartphones, and _____ computers, such as the iPad. To know which apps are available for a handheld, it is important to know its platform.

 CHECK ANSWERS

SECTION B: The microprocessor and memory are two of the most important components in a computer. The microprocessor is a(n) _____ circuit, which is designed to process data based on a set of instructions. Microprocessor performance can be measured by the speed of the microprocessor _____. A specification such as 3.33 GHz means that the microprocessor operates at a speed of 3.33 _____ cycles per second. Other factors affecting overall processing speed include word size, cache size, instruction set complexity, parallel processing, and pipelining. Most personal computers only contain one main microprocessor, but today's multi- _____ processors contain the circuitry for multiple microprocessors.

Computers contain various kinds of memory. Random _____ memory is a special holding area for data, program instructions, and the _____ system. It stores data on a temporary basis until the processor makes a data request. RAM is different from disk storage because it is _____, which means that it can hold data only when the computer power is turned on. Computers also contain read- _____ memory, which is a type of memory that provides a set of "hard-wired" instructions that a computer uses to boot up. A third type of memory, called by its acronym _____, is a non-volatile chip that contains configuration settings, such as hard disk size and RAM capacity.

CHECK ANSWERS

SECTION C:

Today's personal computers use a variety of storage technologies. [_____] storage technologies, such as hard disks, store data as magnetized particles. A hard disk drive provides multiple [_____] for data storage that are sealed inside the drive case to prevent airborne contaminants from interfering with the read-write heads. Hard disks are less durable than many other types of storage, so it is important to make a copy of the data they contain. [_____] storage technologies store data as a series of [_____] and lands on the surface of CDs, DVDs, or BDs. Storage technologies, such as CD-[_____], are often used for distributing software, but you cannot alter the disc's contents. [_____] technology allows you to write data on a CD, DVD, or BD, but you cannot delete or change that data. Rerecordable or [_____] technology allows you to write and erase data on a CD, DVD, or BD. [_____] state storage technologies, such as USB flash drives, store data by activating electrons in a microscopic grid of circuitry.

▶ CHECK ANSWERS

SECTION D:

Most computer systems include a keyboard and some type of [_____] device for basic data [_____]. For output, most computers include a display device. [_____] technology produces an image by filtering light through a layer of liquid crystal cells. Image quality for a display device is a factor of resolution, screen size, dot [_____], viewing angle width, response [_____], and color [_____]. A typical computer display system consists of the display device and a(n) [_____] card. For printed output, most personal computer owners select [_____] jet printers, although [_____] printers are a popular option when low operating costs and high duty cycle are important. A(n) [_____] matrix printer is sometimes used for back-office applications and printing multipart forms. Installing a peripheral device is not difficult when you remember that it uses the [_____] bus to make a connection between the computer and peripheral device. Many of today's peripherals connect to a(n) [_____] port. If the right type of port is not built into your computer, you might have to add a(n) [_____] card.

▶ CHECK ANSWERS

SECTION E:

For trouble-free computer use, it is important to secure and regularly [_____] your computer equipment. Anti-theft devices include computer locks and tie-down brackets. Computers can be protected from power [_____] by connecting to a surge strip. A(n) [_____] power supply can also protect against surges, plus it can supply backup power in case of a power outage. Keeping your computer's [_____] vents free of dust can help to keep its temperature within operational levels. You can also clean dust off the screen and shake dirt out of the keyboard. Problems such as the blue screen of [_____] require troubleshooting. Windows offers interactive troubleshooting tools formatted as a series of simple questions, answers, and recommendations. Booting into [_____] Mode can also be a helpful step in the troubleshooting process.

▶ CHECK ANSWERS

Interactive Situation Questions

Apply what you've learned to some typical computing situations. When using the NP2013 interactive eBook, you can type your answers, and then use the Check Answers button to automatically score your responses.

1. Suppose you're reading a computer magazine and you come across the ad pictured to the right. By looking at the specs, you can tell that the microprocessor was manufactured by which company? [_____]

2. The capacity of the hard disk drive in the ad is [_____] GB and the memory capacity is [_____] GB.

3. The computer in the ad appears to have a(n) [_____] controller card for the hard disk drive.

4. You are thinking about upgrading the microprocessor in your four-year-old computer, which has a 2.6 GHz Pentium microprocessor and 512 MB of RAM. Would it be worthwhile to spend $500 to install an Intel Core i5 processor? Yes or no? [_____]

5. You're in the process of booting up your computer and suddenly the screen contains an assortment of settings for date and time, hard disk drive, and memory capacity. From what you've learned in this chapter, you surmise that these settings are stored in [_____] , and that they are best left unmodified.

6. You're looking for a portable storage device that you can use to transport a few files between your home computer and your school computer lab. The school lab computers have no floppy disk drives, but do have USB ports. You should be able to transport your files using a USB [_____] drive.

**SUP-R GAME DESKTOP
MODEL EEXL**

- Intel® Core™ i7
- 6 GB Tri-Channel DDR3
- 500 GB - SATA-II (7200 rpm)
- 16x CD/DVD burner
- 21.5" HD widescreen monitor
- NVIDIA® GeForce™
- Creative Sound Blaster® X-Fi Titanium
- Altec Lansing speakers
- Gigabit Ethernet port
- 3-year limited warranty
- Windows 7

$949

7. You're frustrated about using the keys on your cell phone to enter long e-mail addresses, so you decide to get a new smartphone with a touch screen that displays a(n) [_____] keyboard.

8. Suppose that you want to purchase a new monitor. A(n) [_____] screen offers a more environmentally friendly choice than a(n) [_____] screen.

9. Suppose that you volunteer to produce a large quantity of black-and-white leaflets for a charity organization. It is fortunate that you have access to a(n) [_____] printer with a high duty cycle and low operating costs.

 CHECK ANSWERS

Interactive Practice Tests

Practice tests that consist of ten multiple-choice, true/false, and fill-in-the-blank questions are available in the NP2013 interactive eBook. Test questions are selected at random from a large test bank, so each time you take a test, you'll receive a different set of questions. Your tests are scored immediately, and you can print study guides that help you find the correct answers for any questions that you missed.

▶ CLICK TO START

Learning Objectives Checkpoints

Learning Objectives Checkpoints are designed to help you assess whether you have achieved the major learning objectives for this chapter. You can use paper and pencil or word processing software to complete most of the activities.

1. Draw a sketch of your computer system and label at least six of its components. Make a table with three columns, labeled Input, Output, and Storage/Memory. Page through the chapter and for each device you encounter, place it in one or more of the columns as appropriate.

2. Draw a set of quick sketches that show each of the following form factors: desktop tower, desktop horizontal, small form factor desktop, notebook, tablet, and netbook. List the advantages of each form factor.

3. Create a short consumer brochure that lists five characteristics that would help consumers choose among a home, game, or small business computer system.

4. List important factors to consider when shopping for a new computer. Describe the three price points for personal computers and indicate which price point best fits your computing needs.

5. Explain how Intel Macs are changing the old idea that PCs and Macs are not compatible.

6. List at least six computer upgrades and rank each as easy, moderate, or difficult for computer owners to perform.

7. Refer to Section D of Chapter 1 and create a sequence of sketches that shows what happens in a microprocessor's ALU and control unit when an instruction is processed.

8. List and describe the factors that affect microprocessor performance. Name three companies that produce microprocessors, and list some of the models that each company produces.

9. List four types of memory and briefly describe how each one works.

10. Describe the advantages and disadvantages of magnetic storage, optical storage, and solid state storage using criteria such as versatility, durability, capacity, access time, and transfer rate.

11. Summarize what you know about how a graphics card can affect a display device's resolution.

12. Compare and contrast the technologies and applications for ink jet, laser, and dot matrix printers.

13. Create your own diagram to illustrate how the data bus connects RAM, the microprocessor, and peripheral devices. Explain the hardware compatibility considerations, device drivers, and procedures involved in installing a peripheral device.

14. List ways you can protect your computer system hardware from theft and damage.

15. Think about the last time you had a problem with computer hardware or software. Would any of the steps in Figure 2-67 have helped you solve the problem faster? If not, what guidelines would you add to the list in the figure?

Study Tip: Make sure you can use your own words to correctly answer each of the purple focus questions that appear throughout the chapter.

2

Concept Map

Fill in the blanks to show the hierarchy of system unit components.

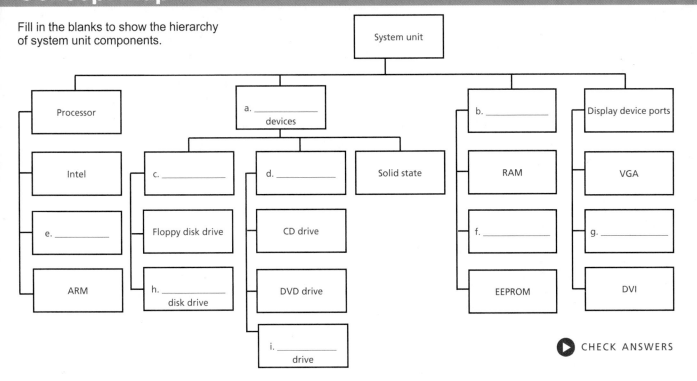

CHECK ANSWERS

3

Software

Chapter Contents

INFOWEBLINKS

You'll find updates for chapter material by connecting to the **NP2013 Chapter 3** InfoWebLink.

W CLICK TO CONNECT
www.infoweblinks.com/np2013/ch03

Learning Objectives

After reading this chapter, you will be able to answer the following questions by completing the outcomes-based Learning Objectives Checkpoints on page 181.

1. What are the most popular types of application software?

2. What basic utilities are typically included with Windows and Mac operating systems?

3. How do iPhones provide adaptive utilities for people who can't see the screen?

4. Why is it important to know where to locate the version numbers for device drivers?

5. How can word processing software help improve your writing?

6. How does spreadsheet software work?

7. How is the data in a database stored and accessed?

8. What are key features of presentation software?

9. What is the difference between Web apps and mobile apps?

10. What kinds of files are typically included in local applications software?

11. Is installing downloaded software different from installing software from a distribution CD?

12. What are software patches and service packs?

13. How do I uninstall software on Windows and Macs?

14. What is a EULA?

15. What are the differences between proprietary software, commercial software, shareware, open source software, freeware, and public domain software?

16. What's malware?

17. How does antivirus software work?

CourseMate
Visit the NP2013 CourseMate for this chapter's Pre-Quiz, Audio Overview and Flashcards, Detailed Objectives, Chapter Quiz, Online Games, and more labs.

Multimedia and Interactive Elements
When using the NP2013 interactive eBook, click the ▶ icons to access multimedia resources.

Apply Your Knowledge The information in this chapter will give you the background to:

- Find, view, and update device drivers for printers and other devices
- Use word processing software
- Use a spreadsheet
- Select new software for your computer
- Use Web apps
- Install mobile apps

- Download and install local software
- Work with portable application software
- Find open source software
- Read a software license so that you know how to use it legally
- Uninstall software
- Install and use antivirus software

Try It!

IS MY SOFTWARE UP TO DATE?

Chapter 3 introduces you to basic concepts about computer software. Before you begin reading, take a glance at the software installed on your home, work, or school computer. Want to know if your software is up to date? You can use the "About" feature of any software package to find its version number.

1. Windows: Click the **Start** button. Click the **All Programs** option to display a list of installed software. Point to items in the list that have a ▶ symbol to see a sublist of software programs.

Mac: Click the 🙂 **Finder** icon and then click **Applications** from the list on the left side of the Finder window.

2. As you read through the list of installed software, jot down the names of any that you're not familiar with. When you read the chapter, you might find out what they do.

3. Open any one of your applications.

4. To find the current version of the application in Windows, click the **Help** menu, then click **About**. For Microsoft Office applications, click **File**, then click **Help**. On the Mac, click the program name from the menu bar at the top of the screen, then select **About**.

5. A dialog box appears. It contains a version number like 6.0 or 7.0, and it might also contain a service pack number like SP2. You'll learn the significance of version numbers and service packs when you read the chapter.

6. Close the About window. Close the program by clicking the ✖ button (Windows) or clicking the program name on the menu bar, and then selecting **Quit** (Mac).

7. Check the version numbers for other software that is installed on your computer. Do some programs provide more information than others in the About window?

About Internet Explorer

Windows® Internet
Explorer 9

Version: 9.0.7930.16406
Cipher Strength: 256-bit
Product ID: 03201-997-8992687-00057
Update Versions: beta

Warning: This computer program is protected by copyright law and international treaties. Unauthorized reproduction or distribution of this program, or any portion of it, may result in severe civil and criminal penalties, and will be prosecuted to the maximum extent possible under the law.

©2010 Microsoft Corporation   OK

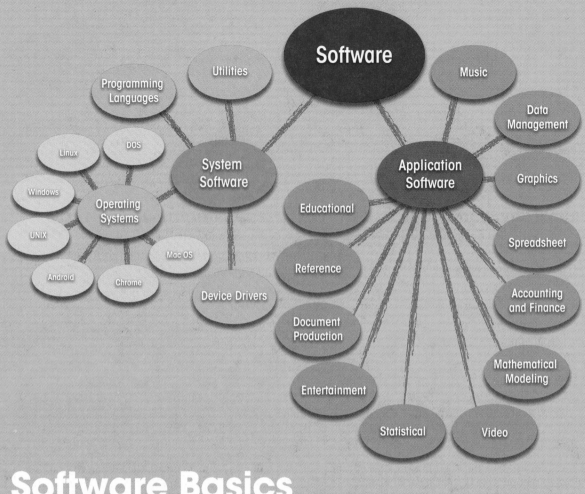

Software Basics

SECTION **A**

SOFTWARE determines the tasks a digital device can help you accomplish. Some software helps you create documents, while other software helps you block viruses or fine-tune computer performance. Section A helps you categorize application software, utilities, and device drivers.

SOFTWARE CATEGORIES

▶ **What is software?** As you learned in Chapter 1, the instructions that tell a computer how to carry out a task are referred to as a computer program. These programs form the software that prepares a computer to do a specific task, such as document production, photo editing, virus protection, file management, or Web browsing.

▶ **How is software categorized?** The two main categories are application software and system software. Application software is designed to help people accomplish real-world tasks, whereas system software is designed for computer-centric tasks. For example, you would use application software to edit a photo or write a term paper, but you would use system software to diagnose a problem with your hard disk drive or Internet connection.

There are thousands of useful software applications designed for personal use or business use. Let's start off with a look at some popular application categories and utilities.

TERMINOLOGY NOTE

The term *software* was once used for all non-hardware components of a computer. In this context, *software* referred to computer programs and to the data the programs used. It could also refer to any data that existed in digital format, such as documents or photos. Using today's terminology, however, the documents and photos you create are usually referred to as data files rather than as software.

120

MUSIC SOFTWARE

▶ What are the basic capabilities of music software?

Music software offers many ways to work with music, sound effects, and narration from your desktop, notebook, or handheld computer. The most popular music software capabilities are listed in Figure 3-1.

- ▶ Download music and other sound files
- ▶ Play music and sound files
- ▶ Create playlists
- ▶ Transfer music to handheld devices
- ▶ Convert audio CDs into digital music
- ▶ Record music and narrations

- ▶ Edit volume, speed, and quality of digital recordings
- ▶ Crop and mix recordings
- ▶ Stream radio music to your computer
- ▶ Identify songs playing on the radio
- ▶ Voice training

FIGURE 3-1

Music software may offer some, but not all, of these features. For example, some music software offers extensive playback features, but no way to make recordings. You might have to use more than one music software product to complete a project.

▶ What's the most popular music software?

The premier music software, iTunes, can be used by anyone who wants to listen to digital music (Figure 3-2).

FIGURE 3-2

iTunes helps you collect digital music and arrange it into playlists; you can also use it to pull music from audio CDs and convert it into a format supported by your portable media player.

If you want tools that allow you to record, edit, and mix digital audio, you can turn to **audio editing software**, also called recording or mixing software. Your operating system might supply audio editing software, such as Windows Sound Recorder, or you can download software, such as the ProStudio app or open source Audacity (Figure 3-3).

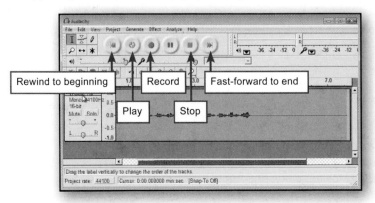

FIGURE 3-3

Audio editing software provides controls much like those on a tape recorder. Menus offer additional digital editing features, such as speed control, volume adjustments, clipping, and mixing.

VIDEO SOFTWARE

▶ What do I need to work with video on my digital devices?

The most popular video software plays movies on your computer or hand-held device. As with digital music, the source of videos is usually an online store such as iTunes or Netflix, or a movie sharing site such as YouTube. Another popular video application is video editing software.

▶ What can video editing software do?

Video editing software provides a set of tools for creating video productions from raw footage. Professional versions are used by video production studios, whereas simpler, consumer-level software is designed for the casual user.

The popularity of video editing can be attributed to consumer-level video editing software, such as Windows Live Movie Maker and Apple iMovie, now included with just about every new computer. Consumer-level video editing software provides a set of tools for video production tasks, such as these:

- ▶ Transfer footage from camera to computer hard disk
- ▶ Split video into smaller clips
- ▶ Rearrange clips
- ▶ Add still photos
- ▶ Add transitions between clips
- ▶ Add soundtracks
- ▶ Add titles and captions
- ▶ Add special effects
- ▶ Alter colors
- ▶ Zoom in and out
- ▶ Export in formats for e-mail, Web pages, or desktop viewing

Despite an impressive array of features, video editing software is relatively easy to use, as explained in Figure 3-4.

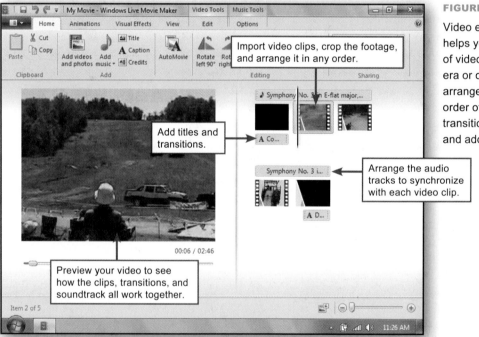

FIGURE 3-4

Video editing software helps you import a series of video clips from a camera or other video source, arrange the clips in the order of your choice, add transitions between clips, and add an audio track.

▶ Can it produce discs for DVD players?

After producing a video that plays on your computer, you might want to transfer it to a DVD that you can use in a standard DVD or Blu-ray player connected to a television or projector. **DVD authoring software** offers tools for creating DVDs with Hollywood-style menus. Examples of DVD authoring software include Roxio Creator, ULead DVD MovieFactory, and Apple iDVD.

GRAPHICS SOFTWARE

▶ **What kind of software do I need to work with drawings, photos, and other pictures?** In computer lingo, the term **graphics** refers to any picture, drawing, sketch, photograph, image, or icon that appears on your computer screen. **Graphics software** is designed to help you create, manipulate, and print graphics.

Some graphics software products specialize in a particular type of graphic, while others allow you to work with multiple graphics formats. If you are really interested in working with graphics, you will undoubtedly end up using more than one graphics software product.

The graphics captured by digital cameras and smartphones can be best edited using paint or photo editing software (Figure 3-5). To create graphics from scratch, you can use drawing software, 3-D graphics software, or CAD software.

Paint software (sometimes called a raster graphics editor) provides a set of electronic pens, brushes, and paints for painting images on the screen. A simple program called Microsoft Paint is included with Windows. More sophisticated paint software products include Corel Painter and Paint.NET. Many graphic artists, Web page designers, and illustrators use paint software as their primary computer-based graphics tool.

Photo editing software, such as Adobe Photoshop, includes features specially designed to fix poor-quality photos by modifying contrast and brightness, cropping out unwanted objects, and removing red eye. Photos can also be edited using paint software, but photo editing software commonly offers tools and wizards that simplify common photo editing tasks.

Drawing software provides a set of lines, shapes, and colors that can be assembled into diagrams, corporate logos, and schematics. The drawings created with tools such as Adobe Illustrator, CorelDRAW, and Autodesk SketchBook tend to have a flat cartoon-like quality, but they are very easy to modify and look good at just about any size. Figure 3-6 illustrates a typical set of tools provided by drawing software.

FIGURE 3-5

Use paint or photo editing software for working with images from digital cameras, smartphones, or scanners.

Phase4Photography /Shutterstock.com

3

FIGURE 3-6

Drawing software provides tools for creating and manipulating graphics.

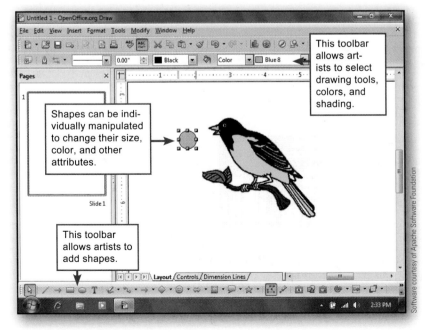

This toolbar allows artists to select drawing tools, colors, and shading.

Shapes can be individually manipulated to change their size, color, and other attributes.

This toolbar allows artists to add shapes.

Software courtesy of Apache Software Foundation

3-D graphics software provides a set of tools for creating wireframes that represent three-dimensional objects. A wireframe acts much like the framework for a pop-up tent. Just as you would construct the framework for the tent and then cover it with a nylon tent cover, 3-D graphics software can cover a wireframe object with surface texture and color to create a graphic of a 3-D object (Figure 3-7).

© MediaTechnics

FIGURE 3-7

3-D graphics software provides tools for creating a wireframe that represents a 3-D object. Some 3-D software specializes in engineering-style graphics, while other 3-D software specializes in figures.

© Ralf Juergen Kraft/Shutterstock

CAD software (computer-aided design software) is a special type of 3-D graphics software designed for architects and engineers who use computers to create blueprints and product specifications. AutoCAD is one of the best-selling professional CAD products. TurboCAD is a low-cost favorite. Scaled-down versions of professional CAD software provide simplified tools for homeowners who want to redesign their kitchens, examine new landscaping options, or experiment with floor plans (Figure 3-8).

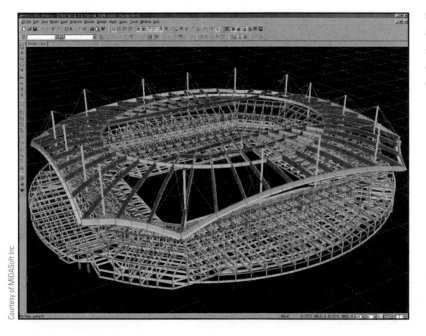

Courtesy of MIDASoft Inc.

FIGURE 3-8

CAD software is used extensively for architectural, engineering, and mechanical drawings.

MAPPING AND LOCATION-BASED SOFTWARE

▶ **What are mapping applications?** A **mapping application** typically displays satellite, aerial, or street maps used to locate places and get directions between two addresses. Google Maps is one of the most extensive mapping applications, and its core technology is the basis for many other mapping and location-based products (Figure 3-9).

FIGURE 3-9

With Google Maps, you can view a street map, satellite image, or street view.

3

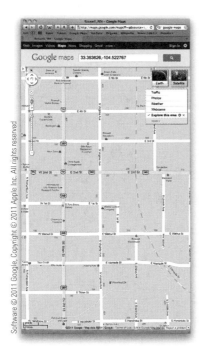

▶ **What is location-based software?** **Location-based software** is able to access your current location and use it to show you the closest shops, restaurants, and theaters, as well as information about each location. Want to find the nearest ATM? Need turn-by-turn directions to the airport? Want to hook up with friends who are nearby? Would you like some user reviews about the Mexican restaurant you just spotted? There are location-based apps designed to answer those questions and more (Figure 3-10).

Location-based software is available for desktop, notebook, and handheld computers. Mobile devices typically pinpoint your location using the built-in GPS (Global Positioning System) or by triangulating your distance from nearby cell towers. Desktop and notebook computers can determine your location based on your Internet service provider and nearby private computer networks.

▶ **Is it safe?** When devices record your location, there is the possibility of abuse. Stay alert for devices and software applications that track your location. In some cases, you can turn tracking off temporarily or permanently. In other cases, tracking may not be under your control; you'll have to decide whether the service you receive from the device or software is worth relinquishing your privacy.

FIGURE 3-10

Yelp uses the GPS signal built into your mobile phone to pinpoint your position and offer suggestions for nearby restaurants, banks, museums, and other attractions.

BUSINESS AND "NUMBER CRUNCHING" SOFTWARE

▶ **Do businesses use specialized software?** *Business software* is a broad term that includes vertical and horizontal market software.

▶ **What is vertical market software? Vertical market software** is designed to automate specialized tasks in a specific market or business. Examples include hospital patient management and billing software, construction industry job estimating software, and student record management. Today, almost every business has access to some type of specialized vertical market software designed to automate, streamline, or computerize key business activities.

▶ **What is horizontal market software? Horizontal market software** is generic software that just about any kind of business can use. For example, many small and medium-size businesses use QuickBooks to keep track of income and expenses, pay bills, and track inventory.

Payroll software is another example of horizontal market software. Almost every business has employees and must maintain payroll records. No matter what type of business uses it, payroll software must collect similar data and make similar calculations to produce payroll checks and W-2 forms.

Accounting software and project management software are additional examples of horizontal market software. **Accounting software** helps a business keep track of the money flowing into and out of various accounts. **Project management software** is an important tool for planning large projects, scheduling project tasks, and tracking project costs.

▶ **How about other "number crunching" software?** Businesses use a variety of "number crunching" software applications for planning and analysis. Spreadsheets, featured in Section B, are an important tool that can be used to create numeric models by simply entering values, labels, and formulas.

Statistical software is designed for analyzing large sets of data to discover relationships and patterns. Products such as IBM SPSS Statistics and StatSoft STATISTICA are helpful tools for summarizing survey results, test scores, sales data, experiment results, or population data. Most statistical software includes graphing capability so that you can display and explore your data visually.

Mathematical modeling software provides tools for solving a wide range of math, science, and engineering problems. Students, teachers, mathematicians, and engineers, in particular, appreciate how products such as Mathcad and Mathematica help them recognize patterns that can be difficult to identify in columns of numbers (Figure 3-11).

FIGURE 3-11

Mathematical modeling software helps you visualize complex formulas. Here the points from a sphere are graphed onto a plane to demonstrate the principles behind the Astronomical Clock of Prague.

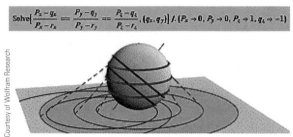

DESKTOP PUBLISHING SOFTWARE

▶ What is desktop publishing software? **Desktop publishing software** (DTP software) takes word processing to the next level by providing professional tools for producing typeset-quality documents.

DTP software is available in consumer-level and professional-level versions. Adobe InDesign is the choice of professional layout artists, with Scribus and QuarkXPress as alternatives. Microsoft Publisher is an example of a consumer-level option.

▶ How does DTP software differ from word processing software? The main difference is that word processing software is document-based, whereas DTP software is frame based. When you use word processing software, each page is basically one box into which you enter text and paste images. When the box becomes full, your software adds another page and the text flows onto it.

DTP software allows you to create a page using multiple frames; some frames can hold text, while other frames can hold titles, graphics, and tables. To achieve a pleasing layout, you can move, resize, and overlap frames. You can also link frames so that text flows seamlessly from one frame to another on the same page or over to a different page. Because this software maximizes the flexibility for placing elements on a page, it is sometimes referred to as page layout software.

▶ Do I need DTP software? Today's word processing software typically provides an adequate feature set for the document production needs of most individuals.

DTP software is usually used in a production environment for publishing paperback and hardcover books. In a typical production environment, an author uses word processing software to create a document, edit it, and check spelling. The electronic version of the document then goes to a desktop publishing technician who imports the document into desktop publishing software, where the text can be formatted into columns and linked to flow from one page to another (Figure 3-12).

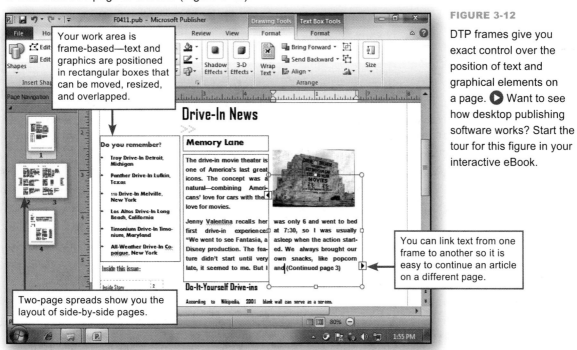

FIGURE 3-12

DTP frames give you exact control over the position of text and graphical elements on a page. ▶ Want to see how desktop publishing software works? Start the tour for this figure in your interactive eBook.

PERSONAL FINANCE SOFTWARE

❱ What software is available for managing my money?

Money management software offers a variety of tools for tracking cash flow and investments. In this software category, **personal finance software**, such as Intuit Quicken, is designed to keep track of income, expenses, assets, and liabilities using a simple checkbook-like user interface. Options for handhelds include Mint and Jumsoft Money.

Personal finance software also automates routine tasks, such as budgeting, investing, check writing, and bill paying. Many personal financial software products provide direct links to online banking services, so you can use them to check account balances, transfer funds, and pay bills.

Personal finance software produces reports and graphs that show you where your money goes. For example, you can analyze various aspects of your cash flow, such as how much you spent on entertainment last month and how that compares to previous months (Figure 3-13).

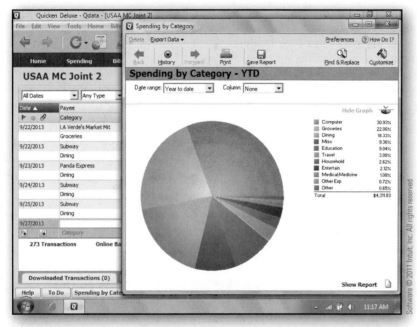

FIGURE 3-13

Personal finance software offers lots of tools to help you get a handle on the money that comes in and goes out.

Tax preparation software is a specialized type of personal finance software designed to help you gather your annual income and expense data, identify deductions, and calculate tax payments. Popular products, such as Intuit TurboTax, even accept data directly from personal finance software to eliminate hours of tedious data entry.

When using tax preparation software, make sure you have the current version and updates. Tax laws are constantly changing; you don't want to miss out on any changes that let you keep more of the money you earn. Before submitting your return, proofread it to make sure the numbers make sense.

Your tax preparation software includes a feature that files your return electronically. That option not only eliminates paper forms and the late night trip to the post office on April 15, but it speeds up your refund, too.

UTILITY SOFTWARE

▶ What is utility software? A type of system software called **utility software** is designed to help you monitor and configure settings for your digital gear, its operating system, or application software.

Like all system software, utilities focus on computer-centric tasks such as blocking viruses or diagnosing hard disk errors, rather than real-world tasks such as document production or accounting.

A set of basic utilities is included with your device's operating system. Your iPhone utilities are accessed from the Settings icon. In Windows, you can access these utilities from the Control Panel; with a Mac, click the Apple icon and select System Preferences. These are some of the most useful operating system utilities for Windows and Mac computers:

▶ Back up hard disk

▶ Change the desktop background

▶ Adjust screen resolution

▶ Adjust mouse and trackpad sensitivity

▶ Change keyboard and language

▶ Troubleshoot problems

▶ Manage user accounts and passwords

▶ Monitor network connectivity

▶ Uninstall software

▶ Monitor the device's power settings

▶ Adjust speaker volume

▶ Check print status

▶ Where can I get other utilities? Third-party software companies offer additional products that extend and improve upon those supplied by the operating system. You can download these products from the Web or from an app store.

▶ What are must-have utilities? A PDF reader, such as Adobe Reader, is an essential utility that displays documents stored in standard PDF files. **PDF** (Portable Document Format) is a standard format for exchanging files, so most people will assume that your computer has PDF capability (Figure 3-14).

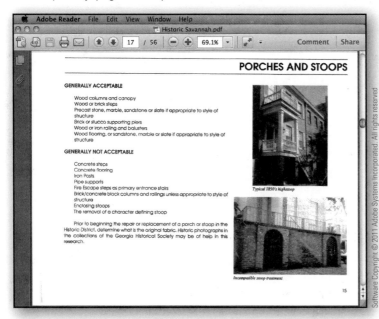

FIGURE 3-14

Documents from expensive DTP software and other applications can be output in PDF format. You don't have to have the DTP software to view these documents; you can simply open them using a PDF reader.

▶ **How about adaptive utilities?** Computers offer opportunities for individuals with physical challenges. **Adaptive utilities** alter a device's user interface to create an accessible environment by providing closed captions, text-to-speech, speech-to-text, or large screen text. These capabilities are usually included with operating system utilities.

Individuals who cannot read the screen have the biggest challenge when it comes to computers. Screen readers that narrate the text displayed on a computer screen offer only rudimentary accessibility. Imagine the jumble of text, advertising, and sidebars displayed on a typical Web page; making sense out of a narrated version of that chaos is not easy.

Touch screen capabilities, combined with screen readers, are a next step toward better accessibility. For example, the iPhone includes an accessibility feature for people who can't see the screen (Figure 3-15).

▶ **What else?** Another popular category of utility software is **system utilities** that can track down and fix disk errors, repair corrupted files, and give your device a performance-enhancing tune-up.

System utilities for handheld computers include apps such as System Activity Monitor, which displays memory usage, available storage space, CPU usage, Wi-Fi and cellular addresses, and battery level. Similar utilities for desktops, notebooks, and netbooks include TuneUp Utilities, System Mechanic, and Advanced System Optimizer (Figure 3-16).

FIGURE 3-15

The iPhone Accessibility screen includes a VoiceOver option that speaks a description of anything you touch on the screen.

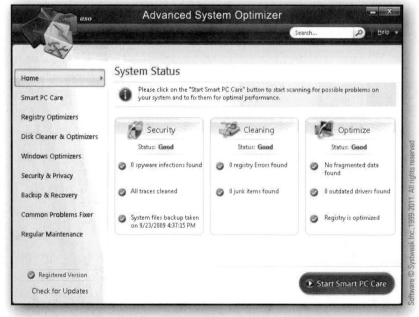

FIGURE 3-16

Utility software includes diagnostics that track down file errors and other problems that prevent computers from running at peak efficiency.

DEVICE DRIVERS

What is a device driver? A **device driver** is software that helps a peripheral device establish communication with a computer. This type of system software is used by printers, monitors, graphics cards, sound cards, network cards, modems, storage devices, mice, and scanners. Once installed, a device driver automatically starts when it is needed. Device drivers usually run in the background, without opening a window on the screen.

Suppose you connect a new printer to your computer. You might also have to install a printer driver or select a preinstalled driver. After the device driver is installed, it runs in the background to send data to the printer whenever you initiate a print job. The printer driver signals you only if it runs into a problem, such as if the printer is not connected or it runs out of paper.

On a Mac, you can click the Apple icon, select About this Mac, and then select More info to look at a list of devices connected to your computer. By selecting a device, you can view information about it, including the driver version number. Check the manufacturer's Web site to find out if your version is current.

On a PC, if you need to update a device driver or change its settings, you can usually access the driver by using the Start menu's Control Panel option and opening the System icon. Then use the Device Manager option to view a list of your computer system hardware and corresponding device drivers, as shown in Figure 3-17.

FIGURE 3-17

The Windows Device Manager offers access to device drivers. You can check if they are working and change settings. You can also check the device driver's version number and compare it with the most recent version posted online.

3

QuickCheck   SECTION A

1. The category of software that is designed for computer-centric tasks is [＿＿＿＿＿] software.

2. [＿＿＿＿＿] software helps you carry out tasks such as creating documents, editing graphics, and locating nearby restaurants.

3. [＿＿＿＿＿] market software is designed to automate specialized business tasks, such as hospital billing.

4. System [＿＿＿＿＿] software can help you track down and fix disk errors, repair corrupted files, and improve device performance.

5. A(n) [＿＿＿＿＿] driver is designed to help a peripheral device establish communication with a computer.

 CHECK ANSWERS

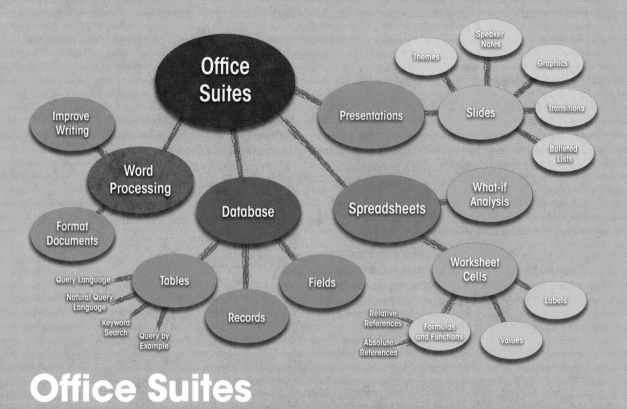

Office Suites

OFFICE SUITES, such as Microsoft Office and Google Docs, are popular with individual computer owners and in business environments. They are sometimes referred to as **productivity software** because they offer features that really help get work done. Section B highlights productivity software applications in office suites.

OFFICE SUITE BASICS

▶ **What is an office suite?** An **office suite** is a collection of programs that typically include word processing, spreadsheet, presentation, and database modules. Suites may also include e-mail and contact managers, calendars, project management, and drawing modules.

In the context of office suites, the term **module** refers to a component, such as a word processing module. Modules can be run as individual programs, but all of the modules in an office suite have a standard set of controls, making it easy to transfer your expertise on one module to the others.

▶ **What are the most popular office suites?** Popular office suites include Google Docs, iWork, LibreOffice, Microsoft Office, Microsoft Office 365, and Zoho Office Suite (Figure 3-18).

FIGURE 3-18

Popular office suites contain a similar set of modules.

Name	Modules	Platform
Google Docs	Word processing, spreadsheet, presentation	Online (Free)
iWork	Word processing, spreadsheet, presentation	Mac ($$)
LibreOffice	Word processing, spreadsheet, presentation, database, drawing	Windows, Mac, Linux (Free)
Microsoft Office	Word processing, spreadsheet, presentation, database, mail/calendar	Windows, Mac, Linux ($$)
Microsoft Office 365	Word processing, spreadsheet, presentation	Online (Free)
Zoho Office Suite	Word processing, spreadsheet, presentation, calendar, and more	Online (Free)

WORD PROCESSING

▶ How can my computer help me with my writing? Whether you are writing a ten-page paper, generating software documentation, designing a brochure for your new startup company, or writing a dissertation, you will probably use the word processing module of an office suite.

Word processing software has replaced typewriters for producing many types of documents, including reports, letters, memos, papers, and book manuscripts. Word processing packages, such as Microsoft Word, iWork Pages, and LibreOffice Writer, give you the ability to create, spell-check, edit, and format a document on the screen before you commit it to paper.

A typical word processor window displays a work area, called a workspace, that represents a blank piece of paper. The window also includes controls for viewing and formatting the document (Figure 3-19).

FIGURE 3-19

No matter which word processor you use, it includes elements similar to those shown in this Microsoft Word example.

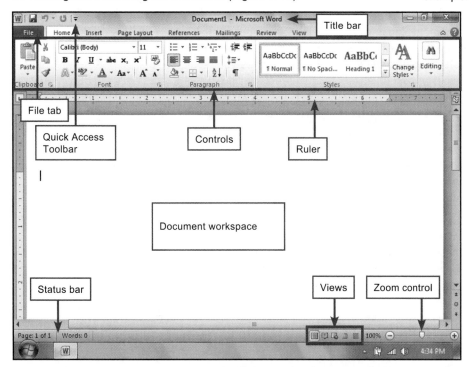

▶ How does word processing software help me turn my ideas into sentences and paragraphs? Word processing software makes it easy to let your ideas flow because it automatically handles many tasks that might otherwise distract you. For example, you don't need to worry about fitting words within the margins. A feature called **word wrap** determines how your text flows from line to line by automatically moving words down to the next line as you reach the right margin.

Imagine that the sentences in your document are ribbons of text; word wrap bends the ribbons. Changing the margin size just means bending the ribbon in different places. Even after you type an entire document, adjusting the size of your right, left, top, and bottom margins is simple.

▶ Can word processing software help me break bad writing habits? You can use the **Search and Replace** feature to hunt down mistakes that you habitually make in your writing. For example, if you tend to overuse the word *typically*, you can use Search and Replace to find each occurrence of *typically*, and then decide whether you should substitute a different word, such as *usually* or *ordinarily*.

▶ Can word processing software improve my writing?

Because word processing software tends to focus on the writing process, it offers several features that can improve the quality of your writing.

Your word processing software is likely to include a **thesaurus**, which can help you find a synonym for a word so that you can make your writing more varied and interesting. A **grammar checker** reads through your document and points out potential grammatical trouble spots, such as incomplete sentences, run-on sentences, and verbs that don't agree with nouns.

Your word processing software might also be able to analyze the reading level of your document using a standard **readability formula**, such as the Flesch-Kincaid reading level. You can use this analysis to find out if your writing matches your target audience, based on sentence length and vocabulary.

Most word processing software includes a **spelling checker** that marks misspelled words in a document You can easily correct a misspelled word as you type, or you can run the spelling checker when you finish entering all the text. Some software even has autocorrecting capability as you type that automatically changes a typo, such as *teh*, to the correct spelling (*the*).

Although your software's spelling checker helps you correct misspellings, it cannot guarantee an error-free document. A spelling checker works by comparing each word from your document to a list of correctly spelled words stored in a data file called a **spelling dictionary**. If the word from your document is in the dictionary, the spelling checker considers the word correctly spelled. If the word is not in the dictionary, the word is counted as misspelled.

Spelling checkers can't tell if you misuse a word, such as if you use the phrase *pear of shoes* instead of *pair of shoes*. Also, spelling checkers flag many proper nouns and scientific, medical, and technical words because they are not included in the spelling checker's dictionary. Make sure you proofread, even after using a spelling checker (Figure 3-20).

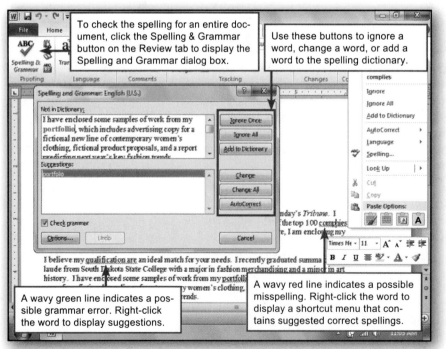

FIGURE 3-20

Word processing software can check your spelling and grammar. ▶ Refer to your interactive eBook for an overview of using your word processor's thesaurus, spelling checker, grammar checker, and readability statistics.

▶ How do I get my documents to look good? The term **document formatting** refers to the way that all the elements of a document—text, pictures, titles, and page numbers—are arranged on the page.

The final format of your document depends on how and where you intend to use it. A school paper, for example, simply needs to be printed in standard paragraph format—perhaps double spaced and with numbered pages. A brochure, newsletter, or corporate report, on the other hand, might require more ambitious formatting, such as columns, headers, and graphics.

The look of your final document depends on several formatting factors, such as page layout, paragraph style, and font.

▶ **Page layout** refers to the physical position of each element on a page. In addition to paragraphs of text, these elements might include margins, page numbers, **header** text that you specify to automatically appear in the top margin of every page, and **footer** text that you specify to automatically appear in the bottom margin of every page.

▶ **Paragraph style** includes the alignment of text within the margins and the space between each line of text. The spacing between lines of text is called **leading** (pronounced "LED ding"). Most documents are single spaced or double spaced, but you can adjust line spacing in 1 pt. increments. **Paragraph alignment** refers to the horizontal position of text—whether it is aligned at the left margin, aligned at the right margin, or **fully justified** so that the text is aligned evenly on both the right and left margins (Figure 3-21).

▶ A **font** is a set of letters that share a unified design. Font size is measured as **point size**, abbreviated pt. One point is about 1/72 of an inch.

Instead of individually selecting font and paragraph style elements, word processing software typically allows you to select a **style** that lets you apply several font and paragraph characteristics with a single click (Figure 3-22).

FIGURE 3-21

Your document looks more formal if it is fully justified than if it has an uneven, ragged-right margin.

> The study in question produced results that appear consistent with the findings from earlier research, with the exception of Miller and Candlewood's classic experiment with digital and genetic markers.

Fully justified text

> Once upon a time, very long ago, a motley crew of pirates sailed into a sheltered Caribbean harbor ringed with jagged rocks and scrubby vegetation.

Left-aligned text

3

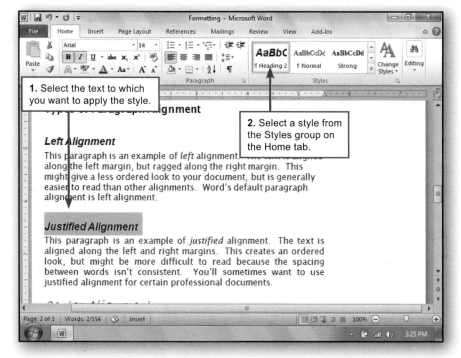

FIGURE 3-22

In this document, headings were formatted by selecting a style with a single click instead of individually selecting a font color, font size, and font style. Now if the Heading style is changed to green, for example, all the headings will automatically change from black to green. ▶ Your interactive eBook walks you through the process of defining and using styles.

SPREADSHEETS

▶ **What is a spreadsheet?** A **spreadsheet** uses rows and columns of numbers to create a model or representation of a real situation. For example, your bank statement is a type of spreadsheet because it is a numerical representation of cash flowing into and out of your bank account.

Spreadsheet software, such as Microsoft Excel, iWork Numbers, Google Docs Spreadsheets, or LibreOffice Calc, provides tools to create electronic spreadsheets. It is similar to a smart piece of paper that automatically adds up columns of numbers written on it.

You can make other calculations, too, based on simple equations that you create or more complex, built-in formulas. As an added bonus, spreadsheet software can turn your data into colorful graphs. It also includes special data-handling features that allow you to sort data, search for data that meets specific criteria, and print reports.

Spreadsheet software was initially popular with accountants who dealt with paper-based spreadsheets, but found the electronic version far easier to use and less prone to errors than manual calculations. Other people soon discovered the benefits of spreadsheets for projects that require repetitive calculations, such as budgeting, computing grades, tracking investments, calculating loan payments, and estimating project costs.

Because it is so easy to experiment with different numbers, spreadsheet software is particularly useful for **what-if analysis**. You can use what-if analyses to answer questions such as "What if I get an A on my next two economics exams? But what if I get only Bs?" or "What if I invest $100 a month in my retirement plan? But what if I invest $200 a month?"

▶ **What does a computerized spreadsheet look like?** You use spreadsheet software to create an on-screen **worksheet**. A worksheet is based on a grid of columns and rows. Each **cell** in the grid can contain a value, label, or formula. A **value** is a number that you want to use in a calculation. A **label** is any text used to describe data (Figure 3-23).

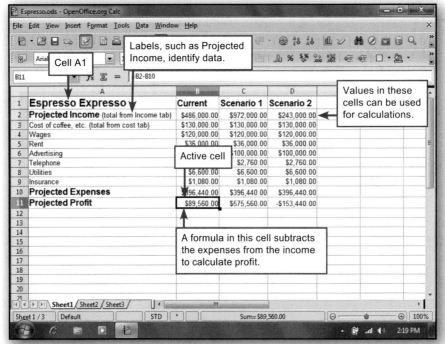

FIGURE 3-23

In a worksheet, each column is lettered and each row is numbered. The intersection of a column and a row is called a cell. Each cell has a unique cell reference, or address, derived from its column and row location. For example, A1 is the cell reference for the upper-left cell in a worksheet because it is in column A and row 1. You can designate the active cell by clicking it. Once a cell is active, you can enter data into it.

▶ Click for an overview of spreadsheet software.

▶ Are there formatting options? You can format the labels and values on a worksheet in much the same way as you would format text in a word processing document. You can change fonts and font size, select a font color, and select font styles, such as bold, italics, and underline.

▶ How does spreadsheet software work? The values contained in a cell can be manipulated by formulas placed in other cells. A **formula** works behind the scenes to tell the computer how to use the contents of cells in calculations. You can enter a simple formula in a cell to add, subtract, multiply, or divide numbers. More complex formulas can be designed to perform just about any calculation you can imagine. Figure 3-24 illustrates how a formula might be used in a simple spreadsheet to calculate savings.

3

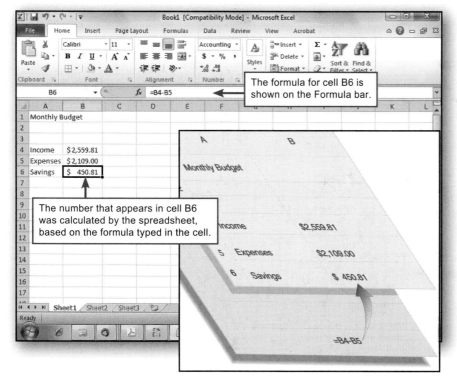

FIGURE 3-24

When a cell contains a formula, it displays the result of the formula rather than the formula itself. To view and edit the formula, you use the Formula bar. You can think of the formula as working behind the scenes to perform calculations and then to display the result.

▶ Why is it important to use a formula such as =B4-B5 instead of a formula with the actual numbers? To find out, start the tour for this figure in your interactive eBook.

FIGURE 3-25

Functions are special formulas provided by spreadsheet software.

A formula, such as =D4-D5+((D8/B2)*110), can contain **cell references** (like D4 and D5), numbers (like 110), and **mathematical operators**, such as the multiplication symbol (*), the division symbol (/), the addition symbol, and the subtraction symbol. Parts of a formula can be enclosed in parentheses to indicate the order in which the mathematical operations should be performed. The operation in the innermost set of parentheses—in this case, (D8/B2)—should be performed first.

You can enter a formula from scratch by typing it into a cell, or you can use a built-in preset formula called a **function**, provided by the spreadsheet software. To use a function, you simply select one from a list, as shown in Figure 3-25, and then indicate the cell references of any values you want to include in the calculation.

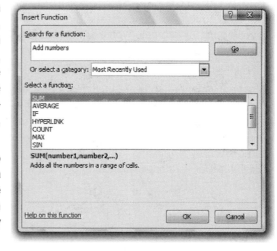

▶ What happens when I modify a worksheet? When you change the contents of any cell in a worksheet, all the formulas are recalculated. This **automatic recalculation** feature ensures that the results in every cell are accurate for the information currently entered in the worksheet.

Your worksheet is also automatically updated to reflect any rows or columns that you add, delete, or copy within the worksheet. Unless you specify otherwise, a cell reference is a **relative reference**—that is, a reference that can change from B4 to B3, for example, if row 3 is deleted and all the data moves up one row.

If you don't want a cell reference to change, you can use an absolute reference. An **absolute reference** never changes when you insert rows, or copy or move formulas. Understanding when to use absolute references is one of the key aspects of developing spreadsheet design expertise. Figure 3-26 and its associated tour provide additional information about relative and absolute references.

FIGURE 3-26

As shown in the examples, a relative reference within a formula can change when you change the sequence of a worksheet's rows and columns. An absolute reference is anchored so that it always refers to a specific cell. ▶ For some dynamic examples of absolute and relative references, watch the tour for this figure in your digital textbook.

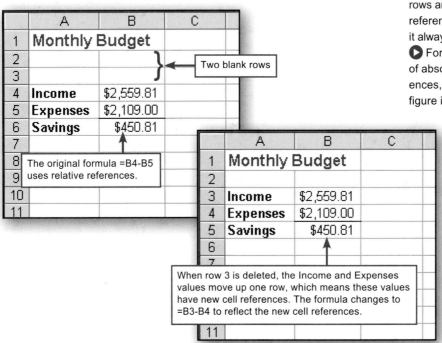

▶ How will I know which formulas and functions to use when I create a worksheet? To create an effective and accurate worksheet, you must understand the calculations and formulas that are involved. If, for example, you want to create a worksheet that calculates your final grade in a course, you need to know the grading scale and understand how your instructor plans to weight each assignment and test.

Most spreadsheet software includes a few templates or wizards for pre-designed worksheets, such as invoices, income-expense reports, balance sheets, and loan payment schedules. Additional templates are available on the Web. These templates are designed by professionals and contain all the necessary labels and formulas. To use a template, you simply plug in the values for your calculation.

DATABASES

▶ **What is a database?** The term *database* has evolved from a specialized technical term into a part of our everyday vocabulary. In the context of modern usage, a **database** is simply a collection of data that is stored on one or more computers.

A database can contain any sort of data, such as a university's student records, a library's card catalog, a store's inventory, an individual's address book, or a utility company's customers. Databases can be stored on personal computers, network servers, Web servers, mainframes, and even handheld computers.

▶ **What is database software?** **Database software** helps you enter, find, organize, update, and report information stored in a database. Microsoft Access, FileMaker Pro, and LibreOffice Base are three examples of popular database software for personal computers. Oracle and MySQL are popular server database software packages.

> **TERMINOLOGY NOTE**
>
> Database software is also referred to as database management software (DBMS).

▶ **How does a database store data?** Database software stores data as a series of records, which are composed of fields that hold data. A **record** holds data for a single entity—a person, place, thing, or event. A **field** holds one item of data relevant to a record. You can envision a record as a Rolodex card or an index card. A series of records is often presented as a table arranged in rows and columns (Figure 3-27).

FIGURE 3-27

A single database record is similar to a Rolodex card or an index card. A series of records is usually depicted in table format.

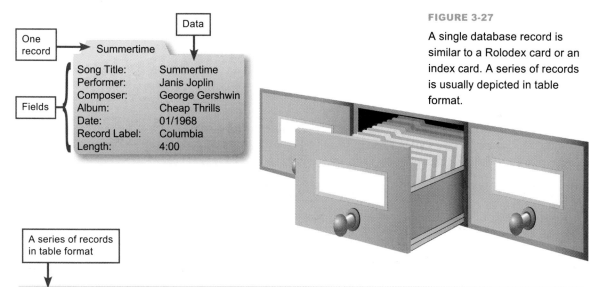

Song Title	Performer	Composer	Album	Date	Label	Length
Chasing Pirates	Norah Jones	Jones	The Fall	11/17/2009	Blue Note	2:40
Even Though	Norah Jones	Jones, Harris	The Fall	11/17/2009	Blue Note	3:52
Summertime	Janis Joplin	George Gershwin	Cheap Thrills	08/12/1968	Columbia	4:00
Summertime	Sarah Vaughan	George Gershwin	Compact Jazz	06/22/1987	PolyGram	4:34

❱ Can a database hold different kinds of records? Some database software provides tools to work with more than one collection of records, as long as the records are somehow related to each other.

For example, suppose MTV maintains a database pertaining to jazz music. One series of database records might contain data about jazz songs. It could contain fields such as song title, performer, and length. Another series of records might contain biographical data about jazz performers, including the performer's name, birth date, and hometown. It might even include a field for the performer's photo.

These two sets of records can be related by the name of the performing artist, as shown in Figure 3-28.

FIGURE 3-28

The two sets of records are related by the Performer field. The relationship allows you to select Norah Jones from the Jazz Performers table and locate two of her songs in the Jazz Songs table.

JAZZ PERFORMERS

Performer	Birth Date	Hometown
Ella Fitzgerald	04/25/1917	Newport News, VA
Norah Jones	03/30/1979	New York, NY
Billie Holiday	04/07/1915	Baltimore, MD
Lena Horne	06/30/1917	Brooklyn, NY

JAZZ SONGS

Song Title	Performer	Composer	Album	Date	Label	Length
Chasing Pirates	Norah Jones	Jones	The Fall	11/17/2009	Blue Note	2:40
Even Though	Norah Jones	Jones, Harris	The Fall	11/17/2009	Blue Note	3:52
Summertime	Janis Joplin	George Gershwin	Cheap Thrills	08/12/1968	Columbia	4:00
Summertime	Sarah Vaughan	George Gershwin	Compact Jazz	06/22/1987	PolyGram	4:34

❱ How do I create a database? Database software provides the tools you need to define fields for a series of records. Figure 3-29 shows a simple form you might use to specify the fields for a database.

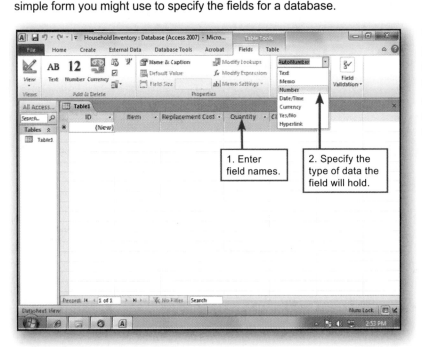

1. Enter field names.

2. Specify the type of data the field will hold.

FIGURE 3-29

Database software provides tools for specifying fields for a series of records. ▶ Your interactive eBook shows you how to use database software to create a handy household database.

▶ When can I enter data? After you've defined fields for a series of records, you can enter the data for each record. Your database software provides a simple-to-use data entry form that allows you to easily fill in the data for each field.

Instead of typing data into a database, you can also import data from a commercial database, such as a customer mailing list. You can even download databases from the Web, and then import the data into fields you have defined with your database software.

▶ How do I locate specific data? Many databases contain hundreds or thousands of records. If you want to find a particular record or a group of records, scrolling through every record would take a very long time. Instead, you can enter a **query** that describes the information you want to find. Queries can take several forms:

▶ A **query language**, such as SQL (Structured Query Language), provides a set of commands for locating and manipulating data. To locate all performances of *Summertime* before 1990 from a Jazz Songs database, you might enter a query such as:

Select * from JazzSongs where SongTitle = 'Summertime' and Date < '1990'

▶ A **natural language query** is a question stated in a language such as English, rather than an esoteric query language.

Who performed Summertime before 1990?

▶ A **keyword search**, popular with search engines such as Google, is simply a collection of words relevant to your search:

Summertime song performer <1990

▶ A **query by example** (QBE) simply requires you to fill out a form with the type of data you want to locate. Figure 3-30 illustrates a query by example for *Summertime* performances before 1990.

▶ How can I use database search results? Your database software can typically help you print reports, export data to other programs (such as to a spreadsheet where you can graph the data), convert the data to other formats (such as HTML so that you can post the data on the Web), and transmit data to other computers.

Whether you print, import, copy, save, or transmit the data you find in databases, it is your responsibility to use it appropriately. Never introduce inaccurate information into a database.

Respect copyrights, giving credit to the person or organization that compiled the data. You should also respect the privacy of the people who are the subject of the data. Unless you have permission to do so, do not divulge names, Social Security numbers, or other identifying information that might compromise someone's privacy.

FIGURE 3-30

When you query by example, your database software displays a blank form on the screen, and you enter examples of the data that you want to find.

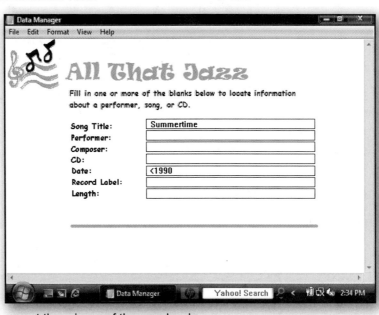

PRESENTATIONS

▶ **What is presentation software?** **Presentation software** supplies the tools for combining text, photos, clip art, graphs, animations, and sound into a series of electronic slides that can be shown on a computer screen or projector (Figure 3-31).

Popular presentation software products include Microsoft PowerPoint, iWork Keynote, LibreOffice Impress, and Google Docs Presentations.

▶ **What are the best features of presentation software?** Presentation software highlights include:

▶ Bulleted lists to summarize the points in your presentation

▶ Graphics to make your presentation visually interesting

▶ Transitions between slides to keep your audience's attention

▶ Speaker notes to help you remember what to say

▶ Themes and templates to give your slides a professional appearance

▶ Conversion routines to package presentations as PDF files and YouTube videos

FIGURE 3-31

A computer-based presentation consists of a series of slides created with presentation software. ▶ Click to find out how to use presentation software.

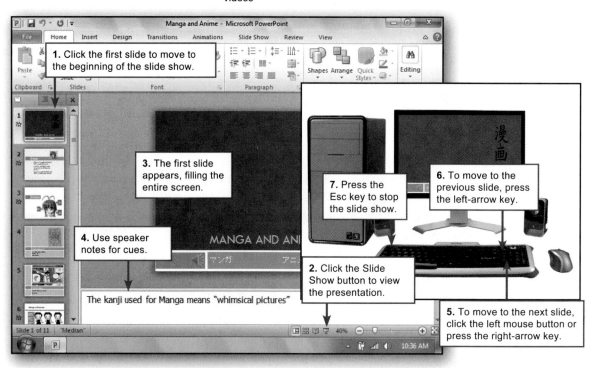

QuickCheck

1. Word processing applications offer [ ] style options including margins, leading, and alignment.

2. [ ] software is useful for performing "what-if" analyses.

3. When entering formulas, you can use relative references and [ ] references.

4. When using database software, you can search for data by entering a keyword or natural language [ ] .

5. Each database record is composed of many [ ] .

 CHECK ANSWERS

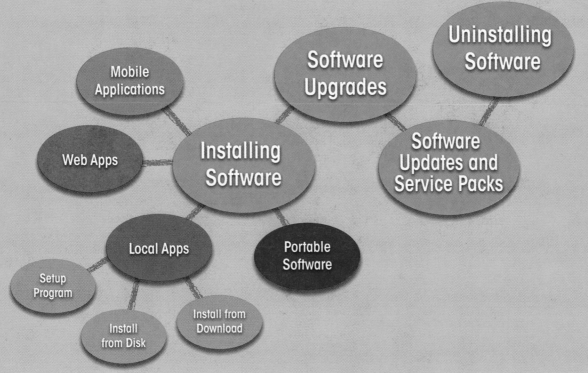

Installing Software and Upgrades

IT'S SURPRISING HOW QUICKLY your collection of software can grow as you discover new applications for school, work, and play. You can use some software without installing it, but other software has to be installed before you can use it. **Software installation** is the process of placing a program into a computer so that it can be run or executed. As you read Section C, you'll find out how to access and install software on handheld and full-size computers. You'll also learn how to eliminate software you no longer need.

WEB APPS

▶ **What are Web apps?** A **Web application** (or Web app) is software that is accessed with a Web browser. Instead of running locally, much of the program code for the software runs on a remote computer connected to the Internet or other computer network.

Web apps are examples of cloud computing. You might be familiar with some frequently used Web apps, such as Hotmail, Google Docs, and Turnitin (Figure 3-32), but there are thousands more.

Many Web apps are associated with consumer sites, such as the Color Visualizer at the Sherwin-Williams Web site that uses a photo of your house to help you select paint colors. Other Web apps, such as the XE Universal Currency Converter, have dedicated sites.

FIGURE 3-32

Turnitin is a Web app that compares any text you paste in or upload with a database of existing works. Used by instructors and students, the program is accessed from a browser. The Turnitin program runs from a Web server and delivers results back to the user's browser.

▶ Do I have to install Web apps? Most Web apps require no installation at all on your local computer or handheld device. Your device must, however, have a Web browser and an Internet connection.

To access a Web app, simply go to its Web site. You might have to register before your first use, and then log in using your registered user name and password for subsequent visits (Figure 3-33).

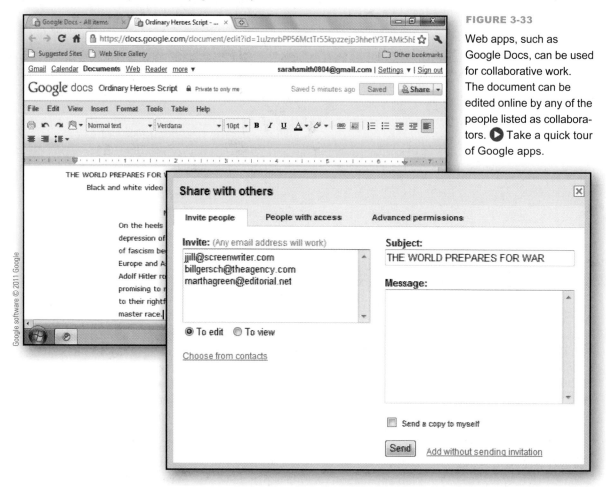

FIGURE 3-33

Web apps, such as Google Docs, can be used for collaborative work. The document can be edited online by any of the people listed as collaborators. ▶ Take a quick tour of Google apps.

▶ What are the advantages and disadvantages of Web apps? Web apps are truly handy, but consider their advantages and disadvantages before entrusting them with your work:

➕ You can access Web apps from any device that has a browser and an Internet connection, including full-size computers, smartphones, tablet computers, and enhanced media players.

➕ Your data is usually stored on the app's Web site, so you can access data even when you are away from your main computer.

➕ Web apps are always up to date; you don't have to install updates because the latest version is the one posted at the Web site where you access the app.

➕ Web apps don't require storage space, so you don't have to worry about them accumulating on your hard disk or SSD.

➖ Web apps tend to have fewer features than applications that require installation.

➖ If the site hosting the app shuts down, you will not be able to access the application or your data.

➖ Your data might be more vulnerable to exposure or loss because it is out of your control; make local backups, if possible.

MOBILE APPS

❱ **What are mobile apps?** A **mobile app** is designed for a handheld device, such as a smartphone, tablet computer, or enhanced media player. They are typically small, focused applications sold through an online app store. Many apps are free or cost less than US$5.00. There are lots of them, and they are fun (Figure 3-34)!

Mobile apps range from simple utilities that turn the device into a flashlight, to more sophisticated apps for entertainment and learning.

❱ **How do mobile apps differ from Web apps?** Most handheld devices can use both Web apps and mobile apps. The difference between the two is that Web apps are accessed using a browser, whereas mobile apps run from the handheld device, so they have to be downloaded and installed. Games and entertainment seem to dominate mobile apps, whereas shopping and social apps dominate the Web apps category.

❱ **How do I install mobile apps?** The first step is to head over to the app store for your device. iPhone, iPad, and iPod Touch owners can find apps for their devices at the online Apple App Store; Droid owners can go to the Android Market. Most handheld devices have an icon that takes you directly to the app store for your device's platform.

At the app store, select an app and pay for it, if necessary. Touching the Download button retrieves the file and installs it automatically. The installation process places the app's program file on the storage device and creates an icon that you can use to launch the app (Figure 3-35).

❱ **What is jailbreaking?** iPads, iPhones, and iPods are only allowed to download apps from the official iTunes App Store. Apps are available from other sources, but using them requires an unauthorized change to the device's software called a **jailbreak**.

Software that helps you jailbreak a device is available from several Web sites. After downloading and installing the jailbreak software, your device will be able to install apps from a variety of sources other than the iTunes App Store.

The jailbreak lasts until you accept a software update from Apple. Updates wipe out the jailbreak software, forcing you to reinstall it.

❱ **Can I jailbreak an Android device?** Android phones are not limited to a single app store, so there is no need to jailbreak them to access more apps. There are various ways to make unauthorized modifications to any mobile device to overcome limitations imposed by mobile service providers. The process is called **rooting**, but most consumers have no need to root their mobile devices.

Once an app is downloaded, an icon automatically appears on the desktop. You can start the app by touching the icon. Some apps require an Internet connection to run.

LOCAL APPLICATIONS

❯ **How do local apps work?** Local applications are installed on a computer's hard disk. When you install a local application, all of its files are placed in the appropriate folders on your computer's hard disk, and then your computer performs any software or hardware configurations necessary to make sure the program is ready to run.

The installation process typically adds an icon to the desktop that you can click to launch the program; on Windows computers, the program is also added to the list of programs accessible from the Start menu (Figure 3-36).

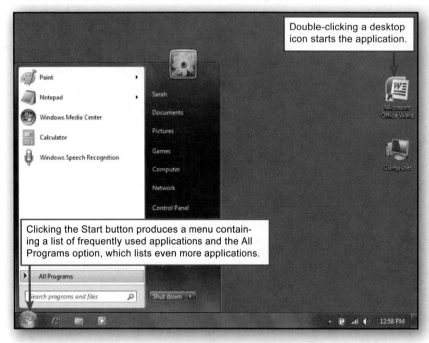

FIGURE 3-36

When using a Windows computer, you can usually start application software using the Start menu or a desktop icon. ▶ Use your interactive eBook to take a tour of ways to start programs and create desktop shortcuts.

❯ **What happens during installation?** Most local applications contain a **setup program** that guides you through the installation process. During the installation process, the setup program usually performs the following activities:

❯ Copies application files from distribution media (CDs or DVDs) or downloads files to specified folders on the hard disk

❯ Reconstitutes files that have been distributed in compressed format

❯ Analyzes the computer's resources, such as processor speed, RAM capacity, and hard disk capacity, to verify that they meet or exceed the minimum system requirements

❯ Analyzes hardware components and peripheral devices to select appropriate device drivers

❯ Looks for any system files and players, such as Internet Explorer or Windows Media Player, that are required to run the program but are not supplied on the distribution media or download

❯ Updates necessary system files, such as the Windows Registry and the Windows Start menu, with information about the new software

TERMINOLOGY NOTE

The *Windows Registry* is a database that keeps track of your computer's peripheral devices, software, preferences, and settings. You'll learn more about the Registry in the operating system chapter. The important concept to understand is that when you install software on a computer with the Windows operating system, information about the software is recorded in the Registry.

❱ What's included in a typical software package? Whether it's on a CD or downloaded from the Web, today's software is typically composed of many files, as shown in Figure 3-37.

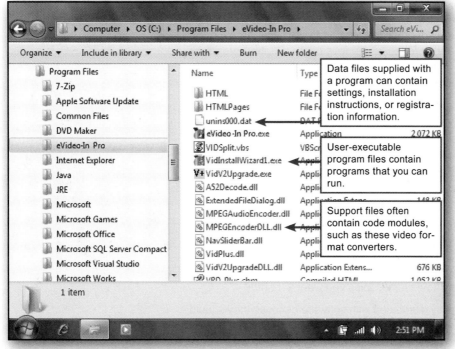

FIGURE 3-37

All of the files listed on the right side of the screen are supplied as part of a video editing software application.

(Annotations within figure:)

Data files supplied with a program can contain settings, installation instructions, or registration information.

User-executable program files contain programs that you can run.

Support files often contain code modules, such as these video format converters.

❱ What is the purpose of these files? At least one of the files included in a software package is an **executable file** designed to be started by users or automatically launched by the operating system. These programs are sometimes referred to as EXE files (pronounced "E-X-E") because of the .exe file extension appended to the program name. Figure 3-38 can help you visualize how multiple files work together as one software application.

FIGURE 3-38

The main executable file provides the primary set of instructions for the computer to execute and calls various support programs and data files as needed.

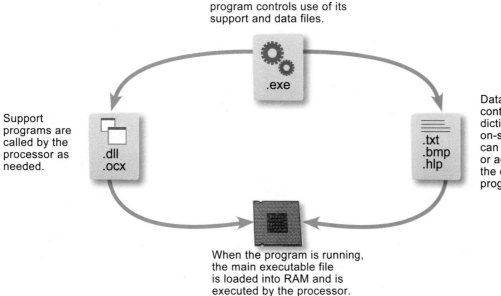

The main executable program controls use of its support and data files.

.exe

Support programs are called by the processor as needed.

.dll
.ocx

Data files containing dictionaries or on-screen help can be opened or accessed by the executable program.

.txt
.bmp
.hlp

When the program is running, the main executable file is loaded into RAM and is executed by the processor.

▶ How about Mac software? A Mac software application is usually distributed as a bundle of programs and support modules with an .app extension. The .app package contains similar sorts of files as a Windows application.

▶ Why does software require so many files? The use of a main executable file plus several support programs and data files offers a great deal of flexibility and efficiency for software developers. Support programs and data files from existing programs can usually be modified by developers for other programs without changing the main executable file.

Modular programming techniques are of interest mainly to people who create computer programs; however, these techniques affect the process of installing and uninstalling software. It is important, therefore, to remember that most computer software consists of many files; some contain user-executable programs or support programs, whereas other files contain data used by the program.

▶ Are all the files used by an application included with the installation? With some operating systems, including Windows, one software program might share some common files with other software. These shared files are often supplied by the operating system and perform routine tasks, such as displaying the Print dialog box, which allows you to select a printer and specify how many copies you want to print.

Shared files are not ordinarily distributed with software because they should already exist on your computer. The installation routine attempts to locate these files. It then notifies you if any files are missing, and provides instructions for installing them.

▶ Are all the software files installed in the same folder? Most executable files and data files for new software are placed in the folder you specify. Some support programs for the software, however, might be stored in other folders, such as Windows\System. The location for these files is determined by the software installation routine. Figure 3-39 maps out the location of files for a typical Windows software installation.

FIGURE 3-39

When you install software, its files might end up in different folders. Files for this video editing software product are installed in two folders.

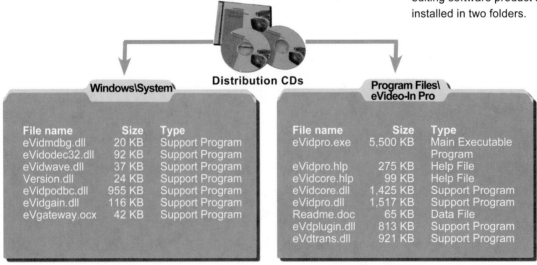

Distribution CDs

Windows\System

File name	Size	Type
eVidmdbg.dll	20 KB	Support Program
eVidodec32.dll	92 KB	Support Program
eVidwave.dll	37 KB	Support Program
Version.dll	24 KB	Support Program
eVidpodbc.dll	955 KB	Support Program
eVidgain.dll	116 KB	Support Program
eVgateway.ocx	42 KB	Support Program

Program Files\ eVideo-In Pro

File name	Size	Type
eVidpro.exe	5,500 KB	Main Executable Program
eVidpro.hlp	275 KB	Help File
eVidcore.hlp	99 KB	Help File
eVidcore.dll	1,425 KB	Support Program
eVidpro.dll	1,517 KB	Support Program
Readme.doc	65 KB	Data File
eVdplugin.dll	813 KB	Support Program
eVdtrans.dll	921 KB	Support Program

❭ How do I install local applications from CDs and DVDs?

The process of installing a local application from distribution CDs or DVDs is very straightforward. You insert the CD or DVD and close the tray. A setup program should autostart and then guide you through the process of selecting the hard disk location for the program files and acknowledging the license agreement. Figure 3-40 shows what to expect when you use a setup program to install local applications from CDs or DVDs.

FIGURE 3-40

Installing from Distribution Media

3

1 Insert the first distribution CD or DVD. The setup program should start automatically. If it does not, look for a file called *Setup.exe* and then run it.

© MediaTechnics

2 Read the license agreement, if one is presented on the screen. By agreeing to the terms of the license, you can proceed with the installation.

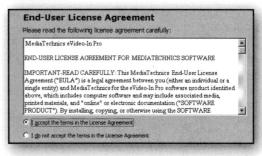

3 Select the installation option that best meets your needs. If you select a full installation, the setup program copies all files and data from the distribution medium to the hard disk of your computer system. A full installation gives you access to all features of the software.

If you select a custom installation, the setup program displays a list of software features for your selection. After you select the features you want, the setup program copies only the selected program and data files to your hard disk. A custom installation can save space on your hard disk.

- ◉ **Full Installation**
- ○ **Custom Installation**

4 Follow the prompts provided by the setup program to specify a folder to hold the new software program. You can use the default folder specified by the setup program or a folder of your own choosing. You can also create a new folder during the setup process.

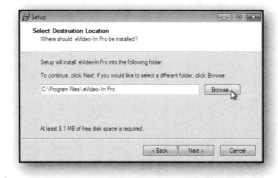

5 If the software includes multiple distribution CDs, insert each one in the specified drive when the setup program prompts you to do so.

6 When the setup is complete, start the program you just installed to make sure it works.

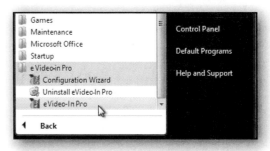

❱ How do I install downloaded software? The installation process is slightly different for Windows software that you download. Usually all the files needed for the new software are **zipped** to consolidate them into one large file, which is compressed to decrease its size and reduce the download time. As part of the installation process, this downloaded file must be reconstituted, or **unzipped**, into the original collection of files.

It is a good idea to store original unzipped files for downloaded software on a CD or in a hard disk folder that you back up periodically. If your computer's hard drive malfunctions, you can use these files to reconstitute your software without having to download all of it again. Figure 3-41 maps out the process of downloading and installing local apps.

FIGURE 3-41

Installing Downloaded Software

1 At the distribution Web site, locate any information pertaining to installing the software. Read it. You might also want to print it. $\longrightarrow$ **2** Click the download link.

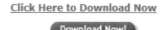

3 If you are downloading from a trusted site and have antivirus software running, click the Run button in the File Download dialog box. $\longrightarrow$ **4** Wait for the download to finish. Usually, the setup program included in the download starts automatically.

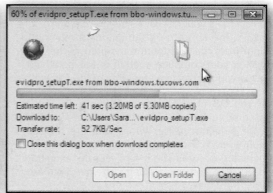

5 Use the setup program to specify a folder to hold the new software program. You can use the default folder specified by the setup program or a folder of your own choosing. You can also create a new folder during the setup process. $\longrightarrow$ **6** Wait for the setup program to uncompress the downloaded file and install the software in the selected directory. During this process, respond to the license agreement and other prompts. When the installation is complete, test the software to make sure it works.

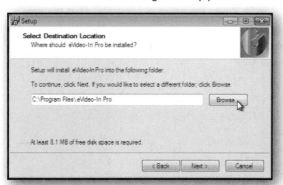

PORTABLE SOFTWARE

▶ What is portable software? **Portable software** is designed to run from removable storage, such as a CD or USB flash drive. Program files are not installed on the hard disk, no configuration data is stored on the hard disk, and no entries need to be made in the Windows Registry. When the media containing the portable software is removed from the computer, no trace of it is left there.

The CD version of this textbook is an example of portable software. To use it, you simply insert the CD containing the program files. Other examples of portable applications include LibreOffice Portable, Thunderbird (e-mail), Firefox (browser), and FileZilla (upload and download), which are designed to run from USB flash drives.

▶ How do I install portable software? Portable software is so simple to install that it is sometimes referred to as install-free software. Installation is simply a matter of getting program files to the media on which they are supposed to run. For example, suppose that you want to run LibreOffice Portable from a USB flash drive. You can download the LibreOffice Portable zip file and then simply unzip it so that the files end up on the USB flash drive (Figure 3-42).

FIGURE 3-42

Portable software is designed so that you can simply copy files to a hard disk or flash drive and run the program without additional installation. ▶ Find out how to work with portable software from your USB flash drive.

Download the program files to your flash drive.

SOFTWARE UPGRADES AND UPDATES

▶ **What are updates, patches, and service packs?** Periodically, software publishers replace older versions of a software product with a new version that's sometimes referred to as a **software upgrade**. To keep these upgrades straight, each one carries a version or revision number. For example, version 1.0 might be replaced by a newer version, such as version 2.0. Upgrading to a new version usually involves a fee, but it is usually less costly than purchasing the new version off the shelf.

A **software update** (sometimes called a software patch) is a small section of program code that replaces part of the software you currently have installed. The term **service pack**, which usually applies to operating system updates, is a set of patches designed to correct problems and address security vulnerabilities. Software updates and service packs are usually free. They are typically numbered using decimal places; for example, an update might change version 2.0 to version 2.01.

▶ **How do I get updates?** Many software applications allow you to set your preferences for how you would like to receive notifications and updates. You can periodically check for updates at the publisher's Web site, or use the software's Automatic Update option that downloads and installs updates without user intervention. The advantage of Automatic Update is convenience. The disadvantage is that changes can be made to your computer without your knowledge.

Most popular software can be configured to check the Web to see if an update is available and gives you the option of downloading and installing it (Figure 3-43).

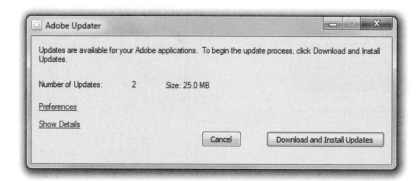

FIGURE 3-43

If you prefer not to have software updates automatically installed, look for an option or preference that lets you choose which updates to install and decide when to install them. ▶ Work with the tour to find out how to manually launch updates.

▶ **When should I update or upgrade my software?** It is always a good idea to install updates and service packs when they become available. The revised code they contain often addresses security vulnerabilities, and the sooner you patch up those holes, the better.

Version upgrades are a slightly different story. Many savvy computer owners wait to upgrade for a few weeks or months after new software versions become available. The reason they wait is to find out how other users like the new version. If Internet chatter indicates some major flaws, it can be prudent to wait until the publisher is able to address them with patches.

▶ **How do I install an upgrade?** A new version upgrade usually installs in a similar way as you installed the original version, by activating a setup program, displaying a license agreement, and adding updated entries to your computer's Start menu. To combat piracy, many software publishers require users to enter a validation code to complete an upgrade.

UNINSTALLING SOFTWARE

▶ How do I know what software is installed on my computer? Mac users can find a list of installed software by opening the Applications folder from the Dock. When working with a PC, there are several places you can look to see what software is installed. The All Programs menu lists most installed applications. A few applications might not appear on this list if they were installed in a non-standard way.

▶ How do I get rid of software? The Windows operating system includes an **uninstall routine**, which deletes the software's files from various folders on your computer's hard disk. The uninstall routine helps you decide what to do with shared files that are used by more than one program. Typically, you should leave the shared files in place.

The uninstall routine also removes references to the program from the desktop and from operating system files, such as the file system and the Windows Registry (Figure 3-44).

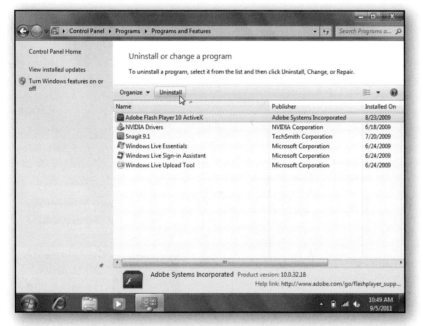

FIGURE 3-44

Always use the Uninstall utility when removing Windows software to make sure all files are properly deleted. ▶ Make sure you know how to uninstall software by watching the tour for this figure in your interactive eBook.

▶ What about uninstalling Mac software? Most Mac users simply use Finder to locate the program's .app file and move it to the trash. This process can leave some support files on the hard disk, however. Some Mac programs include a more thorough uninstall routine, which is usually listed in the Utilities folder.

QuickCheck   SECTION C

1. Most _____ applications require no installation and are accessed through a browser.

2. A(n) _____ program guides you through the installation process.

3. Usually all the files for downloaded software are _____ into one compressed file.

4. _____ software can be copied to a flash drive and run without additional installation.

5. A(n) _____ pack is a set of patches that correct problems and address security vulnerabilities.

▶ CHECK ANSWERS

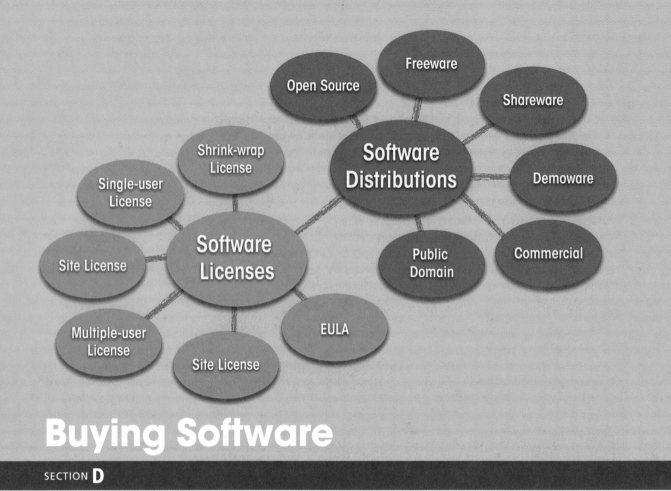

Buying Software

SAVVY SOFTWARE SHOPPERS have a good sense of what to buy and where to find it. Section C offers some shopping tips for expanding the software accessible from your handheld or full-size computer. The section ends with a discussion of software copyrights—important information that will help you understand the difference between legal and illegal software use.

CONSUMER BASICS

▶ **What are the most essential applications and utilities to have on a handheld device?** Most smartphones and other handheld computers include a basic set of apps including a calendar, clock, calculator, notepad, e-mail, and browser. Your device might also supply social networking, photo, video, music, and game apps (Figure 3-45).

▶ **What about a full-size computer?** In addition to an operating system, your computer should have browser software, an e-mail client, word processing software, a security suite, a graphics viewer, and software that lets you burn files onto CDs and DVDs.

You will probably also want compression software that lets you shrink big graphics files before e-mailing them, graphics software for editing photos, and some type of diagnostic software for troubleshooting hardware and software problems. For entertainment, you might want music software, as well as a few computer games.

FIGURE 3-45

Just about every digital device includes a set of preinstalled applications.

▶ **Should I use the apps and utilities that come with the operating system?** Most operating systems include a handful of small applications and a good variety of useful utility software. You'll want to thoroughly explore what your operating system has to offer before you spend money on third-party software. Figure 3-46 contains a list of the most frequently used apps and utilities offered by the Microsoft Windows operating system.

Software	Function
Internet Explorer	Browse the Web
Windows Explorer	Keep track of files and folders; shrink file size
WordPad	Perform basic word processing
Notepad	Perform basic text editing
Calculator	Add, subtract, and calculate basic functions
Paint	Edit bitmap images, such as photos
Sound Recorder	Digitize music and voice input from a microphone
Windows Media Player	Play music and videos
Backup	Make backups of hard disk files
Disk Defragmenter	Arrange data on hard disk for optimal efficiency
Security Center	Set security levels for Internet and network access
Windows Firewall	Block intrusion attempts
Windows Movie Maker	Edit videos
Windows Photo Gallery	View digital photos

FIGURE 3-46

The Windows operating system includes many useful applications and utilities. You can evaluate these offerings before considering whether to supplement them with third-party versions.

▶ **How do I know if an application will work on my device?** If you're like the majority of digital device owners, you want more applications and utilities than those supplied out of the box. You can choose from any applications that are compatible with your device.

Most Web apps work on any device with a compatible browser. Mobile, local, and portable apps specify device requirements, such as model number, memory capacity, and storage space. **System requirements** specify the operating system and minimum hardware capacities necessary for a software product to work correctly (Figure 3-47).

FIGURE 3-47

System requirements typically can be found on the software box or posted on the download site.

System Requirements

Operating Systems: Windows 7/Vista/XP
Processor: Intel Pentium or Core or equivalent
Memory: 1 GB or more
Hard Disk Space: 10 MB for installation
Network Protocol: TCP/IP
Network Connection: 10/100 Ethernet LAN/WAN,
cable modem, DSL router, ISDN router, or dial-up modem

eCourse Internet Works
2013 eCourseWare Corp. All rights reserved. eCourse is a registered trademark of eCourseWare Corp.

SOFTWARE COPYRIGHTS AND LICENSES

▶ **What is a software copyright?** After you purchase a software package, you might assume that you can install it and use it in any way you like. In fact, your purchase entitles you to use the software only in certain prescribed ways. In most countries, computer software, like a book or movie, is protected by a copyright.

A **copyright** is a form of legal protection that grants the author of an original work an exclusive right to copy, distribute, sell, and modify that work. Purchasers do not have this right except under the following special circumstances described by copyright laws:

▶ The purchaser has the right to copy software from distribution media or a Web site to a computer's hard disk in order to install it.

▶ The purchaser can make an extra, or backup, copy of the software in case the original copy becomes erased or damaged, unless the process of making the backup requires the purchaser to defeat a copy protection mechanism designed to prohibit copying.

▶ The purchaser is allowed to copy and distribute sections of a software program for use in critical reviews and teaching.

Most software displays a **copyright notice**, such as © *2013 eCourse Corporation*, on one of its screens. This notice is not required by law, however, so programs without a copyright notice are still protected by copyright law. People who circumvent copyright law and illegally copy, distribute, or modify software are sometimes called software pirates, and their illegal copies are referred to as **pirated software**.

▶ **Can I tell if software is pirated?** Software pirates are getting more and more aggressive, and pirated software is not always easy to identify. Some unsuspecting consumers have inadvertently obtained pirated software, even when paying full price from a reputable source. Widespread pirating of Microsoft products has led to preventive measures such as Certificates of Authenticity and expensive-to-duplicate holographic images on CD labels.

If you suspect that software is pirated, it is best not to buy it or install it. If you have questions about a product's authenticity, you can contact the Software & Information Industry Association (SIIA) or the legitimate software publisher. According to the SIIA, the following tips can help you spot pirated software:

▶ Software sold in a clear CD-ROM jewel case with no accompanying documentation, license, registration card, or Certificate of Authenticity

▶ Software marked as an "Academic" product, but not purchased through an authorized dealer

▶ Software marked as "OEM" or "For Distribution Only With New PC Hardware"

▶ Software CD-ROMs with handwritten labels

▶ Backup discs that you receive from a computer retailer containing handwritten labels

▶ Poor graphics and coloring of labels, disc jackets, or documentation

▶ Multiple programs from many different publishers on a single CD-ROM (commonly referred to as compilation CDs)

▶ If a computer retailer loads software on your PC and you request the original manual, but the dealer responds by telling you to purchase a third-party book (e.g., *Photoshop for Dummies*)

▶ Photocopied manuals

> **What is a software license?** In addition to copyright protection, computer software is often protected by the terms of a software license. A **software license**, or license agreement, is a legal contract that defines the ways in which you may use a computer program.

Software licenses can impose additional restrictions on software use, or they can offer additional rights to consumers. For example, most software is distributed under a **single-user license** that limits use to one person at a time. However, some software publishers offer licenses for multiple users to schools, organizations, and businesses.

A **site license** is generally priced at a flat rate and allows software to be used on all computers at a specific location. A **multiple-user license** is priced per user and allows the allocated number of people to use the software at any time. A **concurrent-use license** is priced per copy and allows a specific number of copies to be used at the same time.

> **Where is the license?** For personal computer software, you can find the license on the outside of the package, on a separate card inside the package, on the CD packaging, in one of the program files, or at the software publisher's Web site.

Most legal contracts require signatures before the terms of the contract take effect. This requirement becomes unwieldy with software—imagine having to sign a license agreement and return it before you can use new software. To circumvent the signature requirement, software publishers use two techniques to validate a software license: shrink-wrap licenses and EULAs.

> **What is a shrink-wrap license?** When you purchase boxed computer software, the distribution media are usually sealed in an envelope, a plastic box, or shrink wrapping. A **shrink-wrap license** goes into effect as soon as you open the packaging.

> **What is a EULA?** A **EULA** (end-user license agreement) is displayed on the screen when you first install software. After reading the software license on the screen, you can indicate that you accept the terms of the license by clicking a designated button—usually labeled OK, I agree, or I accept. If you do not accept the terms, the software does not load and you will not be able to use it (Figure 3-48).

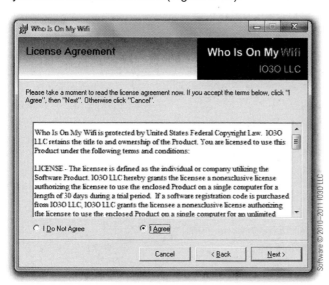

FIGURE 3-48

When you agree to the terms of an on-screen license agreement, you are essentially signing a contract to abide by the terms stated in the agreement.

▶ **When I accept a software license, what am I agreeing to do?** Software licenses are often lengthy and written in legalese, but your legal right to use the software continues only as long as you abide by the terms of the software license. Therefore, you should understand the software license for any software you use. To become familiar with a typical license agreement, you can read through the one in Figure 3-49.

Software License Agreement

Important - READ CAREFULLY: This License Agreement ("Agreement") is a legal agreement between you and eCourse Corporation for the software product, eCourse GraphWare ("The SOFTWARE"). By installing, copying, or otherwise using the SOFTWARE, you agree to be bound by the terms of this Agreement. The SOFTWARE is protected by copyright laws and international copyright treaties. The SOFTWARE is licensed, not sold.

GRANT OF LICENSE. This Agreement gives you the right to install and use one copy of the SOFTWARE on a single computer. The primary user of the computer on which the SOFTWARE is installed may make a second copy for his or her exclusive use on a portable computer.

OTHER RIGHTS AND LIMITATIONS. You may not reverse engineer, decompile, or disassemble the SOFTWARE except and only to the extent that such activity is expressly permitted by applicable law.

The SOFTWARE is licensed as a single product; its components may not be separated for use on more than one computer. You may not rent, lease, or lend the SOFTWARE.

You may permanently transfer all of your rights under this Agreement, provided you retain no copies, you transfer all of the SOFTWARE, and the recipient agrees to the terms of this Agreement. If the software product is an upgrade, any transfer must include all prior versions of the SOFTWARE.

You may receive the SOFTWARE in more than one medium. Regardless of the type of medium you receive, you may use only one medium that is appropriate for your single computer. You may not use or install the other medium on another computer.

WARRANTY. eCourse warrants that the SOFTWARE will perform substantially in accordance with the accompanying written documentation for a period of ninety (90) days from the date of receipt. TO THE MAXIMUM EXTENT PERMITTED BY APPLICABLE LAW, eCourse AND ITS SUPPLIERS DISCLAIM ALL OTHER WARRANTIES AND CONDITIONS EITHER EXPRESS OR IMPLIED, INCLUDING, BUT NOT LIMITED TO, IMPLIED WARRANTIES OF MERCHANTABILITY, FITNESS FOR A PARTICULAR PURPOSE, TITLE, AND NON-INFRINGEMENT, WITH REGARD TO THE SOFTWARE PRODUCT.

FIGURE 3-49

When you read a software license agreement, look for answers to the following questions:

▶ Am I buying the software or licensing it?

▶ When does the license go into effect?

▶ Under what circumstances can I make copies?

▶ Can I rent the software?

▶ Can I sell the software?

▶ Does the software publisher provide a warranty?

▶ Can I loan the software to a friend?

▶ **Are all software licenses similar?** From a legal perspective, there are two categories of software: public domain and proprietary. **Public domain software** is not protected by copyright because the copyright has expired, or the author has placed the program in the public domain, making it available without restriction. Public domain software may be freely copied, distributed, and even resold. The primary restriction on public domain software is that you are not allowed to apply for a copyright on it.

Proprietary software has restrictions on its use that are delineated by copyright, patents, or license agreements. Some proprietary software is distributed commercially, whereas some of it is free. Based on licensing rights, proprietary software is distributed as commercial software, demoware, shareware, freeware, and open source software.

▶ What is commercial software? Commercial software is usually sold in computer stores or at Web sites. Although you buy this software, you actually purchase only the right to use it under the terms of the software license. A license for commercial software typically adheres closely to the limitations provided by copyright law, although it might give you permission to install the software on a computer at work and on a computer at home, provided that you use only one of them at a time.

▶ What is demoware? Some commercial software is available as a trial version, sometimes called demoware. **Demoware** is distributed for free and often comes preinstalled on new computers, but it is limited in some way until you pay for it.

Demoware publishers can use a variety of techniques to limit the software. It might remain functional for a set number of days before expiring and requiring payment. It might run for a limited amount of time—for example, 60 minutes—each time you launch it. Demoware could be configured so that you can run it for only a limited number of times. Or, key features, such as printing, might be disabled.

Demoware publishers usually take steps to prevent users from uninstalling and reinstalling the demo to circumvent time limitations. Users who want to unlock the full version of a demo can do so by following links to the software publisher's Web site and using a credit card to purchase a registration code. The software can then be restarted and used without further interruption after the registration code is entered.

▶ Is shareware the same as demoware? The characteristics of shareware sound very similar to those of demoware. **Shareware** is copyrighted software marketed under a try-before-you-buy policy. It typically includes a license that permits you to use the software for a trial period. To use it beyond the trial period, you are supposed to pay a registration fee. The original idea behind shareware was that payment would be on the honor system. Unlike feature- or time-limited demoware, shareware was supposed to be fully-functioning software.

Shareware was conceived as a low-cost marketing and distribution channel for independent programmers. Thousands of shareware programs are available, encompassing just about as many applications as commercial software. A shareware license usually encourages you to make copies of the software and distribute them to others. Copying, considered a bad thing by commercial software publishers, can work to the advantage of shareware authors, but only if users pay for the product. Unfortunately, many shareware authors collect only a fraction of the money they deserve for their programming efforts.

Today, many shareware authors use demoware techniques to limit their programs until payment is received. The term *shareware* is used today to refer to programs distributed by independent programmers, whereas *demoware* tends to be used when referring to trial versions of software from big software firms, such as Microsoft, Adobe Systems, and Symantec.

3

▶ What is open source software?

Open source software makes uncompiled program instructions—the source code—available to programmers who want to modify and improve the software. Open source software may be sold or distributed free of charge in compiled form, but it must, in every case, also include the source code.

Linux is an example of open source software, as is FreeBSD—a version of UNIX designed for personal computers. LibreOffice—a full-featured productivity suite—is another popular example of open source software. You can search for open source applications at the *sourceforge.net* Web site.

Despite the lack of restrictions on distribution and use, open source software is copyrighted and is not in the public domain. Many open source characteristics also apply to free software (not to be confused with freeware, which you are not supposed to modify or resell). Both open source and free software can be copied an unlimited number of times, distributed for free, sold, and modified.

The philosophies behind open source and free software are slightly different, but their licenses are really quite similar. Two of the most common open source and free software licenses are BSD and GPL. The **BSD license** originated as the Berkeley Software Distribution license for a UNIX-like operating system. The license is simple and short (Figure 3-50).

The **GPL** (General Public License) was developed for a free operating system called GNU. The GPL is slightly more restrictive than the BSD license because it requires derivative works to be licensed. That means if you get a really cool computer game that's licensed under a GPL and you modify the game to create a new level, you have to distribute your modification under the GPL. You cannot legally market your modification under a commercial software license. There are currently three versions of the GPL. Their differences are of interest primarily to software developers.

FIGURE 3-50

Open source and free software applications are plentiful. ▶ Click to find out how to participate in open source software development projects and download free open source software.

© 2006 by the Open Source Initiative

Software	Function
LibreOffice	Productivity
Thunderbird	E-mail
Firefox	Browser
Pidgin	Instant messenger
GIMP	Graphics editing
Gallery	Photo viewer
Blender	3-D modeling and game design
Audacity	Sound editing and effects
MediaPortal	PC/TV media center
7-Zip	Compression
ClamWin	Antivirus

3

▶ What about freeware? **Freeware** is copyrighted software that—as you might expect—is available for free. It is fully functional and requires no payment for its use. Because the software is protected by copyright, you cannot do anything with it that is not expressly allowed by copyright law or by the author. Typically, the license for freeware permits you to use the software, copy it, and give it away, but does not permit you to alter it or sell it. Many utility programs, device drivers, and some games are available as freeware.

▶ What if my software requires activation? **Product activation** is a means of protecting software from illegal copying by requiring users to enter a product key or activation code before the software can be used. Activation is usually part of the software installation process, but it can also occur when demoware times out. Failure to enter a valid code prohibits the program from launching. The information you enter is either checked against a database or used to create a hash value.

Checking an activation code against a database makes sure that the code you've entered has not been used before. If the code is a duplicate, the license for that copy of the software is being used by someone else and you will have to call customer service to straighten out the problem.

A **hash value** is a unique number derived from encoding one or more data sets, such as names, serial numbers, and validation codes. Product validation can create a hash value based on your validation code and your computer's internal serial number, effectively tying the software to use on one specific computer.

Validation codes are very important. You should keep a list of them in a safe place, along with other configuration information for your computer system.

▶ Should a software license affect my purchase decision? Before purchasing software, make sure the license allows you to use the software the way you want to. If you plan to install the software on more than one computer or introduce modifications, make sure the license allows you to do so.

Some commercial software, such as security software, requires annual renewal. If you don't want to pay the fee every year, you might consider freeware or open source security software instead. Informed consumers tend to make better buying decisions. Just remember that many software programs exist and you can usually find alternatives with similar features offered under various licensing terms.

QuickCheck   SECTION D

1. Before purchasing software, you should check the [_____] requirements.

2. [_____] law allows you to make an extra, or backup, copy of software as long as you do not defeat any copy protection mechanisms.

3. A(n) [_____] use license is priced per copy and allows a specific number of copies to be used at the same time.

4. [_____] that expires after a set period of time is often factory-installed on new computers.

5. LibreOffice, Firefox, and Linux are examples of [_____] source software that can be legally modified and redistributed.

▶ CHECK ANSWERS

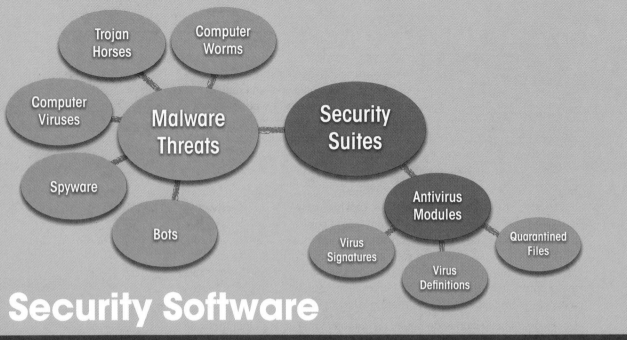

Security Software

THE DAYS WHEN VIRUSES were the greatest threat to computers are long gone. Today, a virus is just one of many categories of malicious software, or malware, that can wreak havoc on computer systems, networks, and even handheld devices. Section E explains how you can use security software to combat malicious software that threatens your computer.

SECURITY SOFTWARE BASICS

▶ **What is security software?** **Security software** is designed to protect computers from various forms of destructive software and unauthorized intrusions. Security software can be classified into various types: antivirus, antispyware, anti-spam, and firewalls. Each type focuses on a specific security threat.

▶ **What devices are at risk?** Windows computers have the highest risk of contracting a virus or unwanted intrusions, but any device that receives e-mail, accesses the Web, and runs apps is potentially vulnerable.

Apple computers and handheld devices are not targeted as often as Windows and Android devices, but the incidence of attacks is growing across all platforms. Jailbreaking a phone increases its vulnerability (Figure 3-51).

▶ **What are malware threats?** The terms **malicious software** and **malware** refer to any computer program designed to surreptitiously enter a computer, gain unauthorized access to data, or disrupt normal processing operations. Malware includes viruses, worms, Trojans, bots, and spyware.

Malware is created and unleashed by individuals referred to as hackers, crackers, black hats, or cybercriminals. Some malware is released as a prank. Other malware is created to distribute political messages or to disrupt operations at specific companies.

In an increasing number of cases, malware is unleashed for monetary gain. Malware designed for identity theft or extortion has become a very real threat to individuals and corporations.

FIGURE 3-51

This smartphone's security was breached, letting a hacker surreptitiously record conversations.

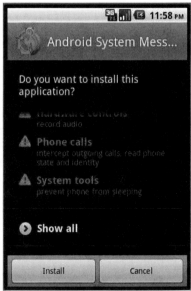

▶ **What is a virus?** A **computer virus** is a set of program instructions that attaches itself to a file, reproduces itself, and spreads to other files. A common misconception is that viruses spread themselves from one computer to another. They don't. Viruses can replicate themselves only on the host computer.

A key characteristic of viruses is their ability to lurk in a computer for days or months, quietly replicating themselves. While this replication takes place, you might not even know that your computer has contracted a virus; therefore, it is easy to inadvertently spread infected files to other people's computers.

In addition to replicating itself, a virus usually delivers a payload, which can be as harmless as displaying an annoying message or as devastating as trashing the data on your computer's hard disk. It can corrupt files, destroy data, or otherwise disrupt computer operations. A trigger event, such as a specific date, can unleash some viruses. Viruses that deliver their payloads on a specific date are sometimes referred to as time bombs. Viruses that deliver their payloads in response to some other system event are referred to as logic bombs.

Viruses spread when people exchange infected files on disks and CDs, as e-mail attachments, and on file sharing networks, social networking sites, and download sites.

▶ **What is a worm?** A **computer worm** is a self-replicating program designed to carry out some unauthorized activity on a victim's computer. Worms can spread themselves from one computer to another without any assistance from victims.

Worms can enter a computer through security holes in browsers and operating systems, as e-mail attachments, and by victims clicking on infected pop-up ads or links contained in e-mails. For example, a mass-mailing worm called Ackantta is hidden in an attachment to an e-mail message that's a fake Twitter invitation. Clicking the attachment activates the worm.

A **mass-mailing worm** spreads by sending itself to every address in the address book of an infected computer. Your friends receive these messages and, thinking that they are from a trusted source, open the infected attachment, spreading the worm to their computers and on to their friends.

Although e-mail is currently the primary vehicle used to spread worms, hackers have also devised ways to spread worms over file sharing networks, instant messaging links, and mobile phones.

▶ **What is a Trojan horse?** A **Trojan horse** (sometimes simply called a Trojan) is a computer program that seems to perform one function while actually doing something else. Unlike a worm, a Trojan is not designed to spread itself to other computers. Also differing from viruses and worms, Trojans are not typically designed to replicate themselves. Trojans are standalone programs that masquerade as useful utilities or applications, which victims download and install unaware of their destructive nature.

Trojans are notorious for stealing passwords using a keylogger that records keystrokes as you log in to your computer and various online accounts. Another type of Trojan called a **Remote Access Trojan** (RAT) has backdoor capabilities that allow remote hackers to transmit files to victims' computers, search for data, run programs, and use a victim's computer as a relay station for breaking into other computers.

TERMINOLOGY NOTE

A spoofed address is one that is misleading or incorrect. In the case of e-mail, it is not the actual address of the person or computer that sent the e-mail message. Spoofed addresses make it difficult or impossible to trace mail back to the sender.

▶ What is a bot? Any software that can automate a task or autonomously execute a task when commanded to do so is called an intelligent agent. Because an intelligent agent behaves somewhat like a robot, it is often called a **bot**.

Good bots perform a variety of helpful tasks such as scanning the Web to assemble data for search engines like Google. Some bots offer online help, while others monitor online discussions for prohibited behavior and language. Bad bots, on the other hand, are controlled by hackers and designed for unauthorized or destructive tasks. They can be spread by worms or Trojans. Most bad bots are able to initiate communications with a central server on the Internet to receive instructions. A computer under the control of a bad bot is sometimes referred to as a **zombie** because it carries out instructions from a malicious leader.

Like a spider in its web, the person who controls many bot-infested computers can link them together into a network called a **botnet**. Experts have discovered botnets encompassing more than 1 million computers. Botmasters who control botnets use the combined computing power of their zombie legions for many types of nefarious tasks such as breaking into encrypted data, carrying out denial-of-service attacks against other computers, and sending out massive amounts of spam.

TERMINOLOGY NOTE

A denial-of-service attack is designed to generate a lot of activity on a network by flooding its servers with useless traffic—enough traffic to overwhelm the server's processing capability and essentially bring all communications and services to a halt.

▶ What is spyware? **Spyware** is a type of program that secretly gathers personal information without the victim's knowledge, usually for advertising and other commercial purposes. Once it is installed, spyware starts monitoring Web-surfing and purchasing behavior, and sends a summary back to one or more third parties. Just like Trojans, spyware can monitor keystrokes and relay passwords and credit card information to cybercriminals.

Spyware can get into a computer using exploits similar to those of Trojans. It can piggyback on seemingly legitimate freeware or shareware downloads. You can also inadvertently allow spyware into your computer by clicking innocuous but infected pop-up ads or surfing through seemingly valid and secure Web sites that have been compromised by hackers.

▶ What does malware do? Once viruses, worms, bots, Trojans, and spyware enter your computer, they can carry out a variety of unauthorized activities, such as those listed in Figure 3-52.

FIGURE 3-52

Malware Activities

- ▶ Display irritating messages and pop-up ads
- ▶ Delete or modify your data
- ▶ Encrypt your data and demand ransom for the encryption key
- ▶ Upload or download unwanted files
- ▶ Log your keystrokes to steal your passwords and credit card numbers
- ▶ Propagate malware and spam to everyone in your e-mail address book or your instant messaging buddy list
- ▶ Disable your antivirus and firewall software
- ▶ Block access to specific Web sites and redirect your browser to infected Web sites
- ▶ Cause response time on your system to deteriorate
- ▶ Allow hackers to remotely access data on your computer
- ▶ Allow hackers to take remote control of your machine and turn it into a zombie
- ▶ Link your computer to others in a botnet that can send millions of spam e-mails or wage denial-of-service attacks against Web sites
- ▶ Cause network traffic jams

Michael D Brown/Shutterstock.com

▶ **How do I know if my computer is infected?** Watch out for the symptoms of an infected computer listed in Figure 3-53.

FIGURE 3-53

Symptoms of Infection

▶ Irritating messages or sounds
▶ Frequent pop-up ads, at times with pornographic content
▶ The sudden appearance of a new Internet toolbar on your browser's home page
▶ An addition to your Internet favorites list that you didn't put there
▶ Prolonged system startup
▶ Slower than usual response to mouse clicks and keyboard strokes
▶ Browser or application crashes
▶ Missing files
▶ Your computer's security software becomes disabled and cannot be restarted
▶ Periodic network activity when you are not actively browsing or sending e-mail
▶ Your computer reboots itself frequently

Some malware does a good job of cloaking itself, so victims are unaware of its presence. Cloaking techniques are great defense mechanisms because when victims aren't aware of malware, they won't take steps to eradicate it. Many victims whose computers were part of massive botnets never knew their computers were compromised.

Some hackers cloak their work using rootkits. The term **rootkit** refers to software tools used to conceal malware and backdoors that have been installed on a victim's computer. Rootkits can hide bots, keyloggers, spyware, worms, and viruses. With a rootkit in place, hackers can continue to exploit a victim's computer with little risk of discovery. Rootkits are usually distributed by Trojans.

▶ **How do I avoid security threats?** The Orientation section at the beginning of this book listed some techniques for safe computing. That list is worth repeating (Figure 3-54).

FIGURE 3-54

Avoiding Security Threats

▶ Install and activate security software on any digital device that is at risk.
▶ Keep software patches and operating system service packs up to date.
▶ Do not open suspicious e-mail attachments.
▶ Obtain software only from reliable sources; and before running it, use security software to scan for malware.
▶ Do not click pop-up ads—to make an ad go away, right-click the ad's taskbar button and select the Close option.
▶ Avoid unsavory Web sites.
▶ Disable the option *Hide extensions for known file types in Windows* so you can avoid opening files with more than one extension, such as a file called *game.exe.zip*.

▶ **What's a virus hoax?** Some virus threats are very real, but you're also likely to get e-mail messages about so-called viruses that don't really exist. A **virus hoax** usually arrives as an e-mail message containing dire warnings about a supposedly new virus on the loose. When you receive an e-mail message about a virus or any other type of malware, don't panic. It could be a hoax.

You can check one of the many hoaxbuster or antivirus software Web sites to determine whether you've received a hoax or a real threat. The Web sites also provide security or virus alerts, which list all of the most recent legitimate malware threats. If the virus is a real threat, the Web site can provide information to determine whether your computer has been infected. You can also find instructions for eradicating the virus. If the virus threat is a hoax, by no means should you forward the e-mail message to others.

▶ **What if my computer gets infected?** If you suspect that your computer might be infected by a virus or other malware, you should immediately use security software to scan your computer and eradicate any suspicious program code.

SECURITY SUITES

▶ **What is a security suite?** A **security suite** integrates several security modules to protect against the most common types of malware, unauthorized access, and spam. Security suites might include additional features such as Wi-Fi detection that warns of possible intrusions into your wireless network, and parental controls for monitoring and controlling children's Internet usage. A security suite, like the one in Figure 3-55, typically includes antivirus, firewall, and antispyware modules.

FIGURE 3-55

The Norton security suite includes modules for scanning viruses, detecting spyware, and activating a firewall against unauthorized intrusions.
▶ Take a tour of these modules by using your interactive eBook.

▶ **What are the advantages and disadvantages of a security suite?** A security suite costs less than purchasing standalone security modules. In addition, a single interface for accessing all of the security suite's features is much less complex than having to learn how to configure and run several different products.

When installing a security suite, you might be required to uninstall or disable all other antivirus, antispyware, and firewall software on your computer. Most security suites cannot run concurrently with standalone security products, and overlapping security coverage from two similar products can cause glitches. Therefore, one disadvantage of security suites is that you become dependent on your security package's vendor, which becomes the sole protector of your computer from malicious code.

▶ Where can I purchase a security suite? The most popular security suites include Symantec Norton Internet Security, McAfee Internet Security Suite, avast!, and Trend Micro Titanium Maximum Internet Security. They can be purchased in most office, electronics, and computer stores, or downloaded from the Web.

It is also worth looking into your Internet service provider's free security offerings. For example, Comcast provides its customers with Norton security products, all accessible through Comcast's Security Web page.

A security suite is often preinstalled on a new computer. However, it is usually demoware, so you have the option of purchasing it after the trial period, normally 60 days. Typically, there is also an annual subscription fee for continued use and regular updates. When you renew your subscription, you might have an option to upgrade to a newer version for an extra $10–$20. There are also open source and freeware versions of security software, which do not require annual subscription fees.

ANTIVIRUS MODULES

▶ What is antivirus software? **Antivirus software** is a type of utility software that looks for and eradicates viruses, Trojan horses, worms, and bots. Some antivirus software also scans for spyware, although several security software publishers offer spyware detection as a separate module. Antivirus software is included in security suites or available as a standalone module (Figure 3-56). Antivirus software is available for all types of computers and data storage devices, including handhelds, personal computers, USB flash drives, and servers.

FIGURE 3-56

Free antivirus software is available, so computer owners have no excuse for leaving their computers unprotected.

Software Copyright © 1988–2011 AVAST Software a.s.

▶ How does antivirus software work? Modern antivirus software attempts to identify malware by searching your computer's files and memory for virus signatures. A **virus signature** is a section of program code, such as a unique series of instructions, that can be used to identify a known malicious program, much as a fingerprint is used to identify an individual.

Antivirus software scans for virus signatures in programs, data files, incoming and outgoing e-mail and attachments, and inbound instant message attachments. Antivirus software can also watch for unusual activity such as a considerably large number of e-mail messages being sent out from your computer by a mass-mailing worm or bot.

Most antivirus programs can also scan for virus signatures in zip files, which is important when downloading zipped software and receiving zipped e-mail attachments.

▶ **How do I activate and deactivate my antivirus software?** Installation and activation procedures vary for each virus protection product. However, once you have installed your antivirus software, the best and safest practice is to keep it running full time in the background so that it checks every e-mail message as it arrives and scans all files the moment you access them. The scanning process requires only a short amount of time, which creates a slight delay in downloading e-mail and opening files.

When installing some application or utility software, you might be instructed to deactivate your antivirus software. You can usually right-click the icon on your computer's taskbar that corresponds to your antivirus software and then select the exit or disable option. Do not forget to reactivate your antivirus software as soon as the installation is completed.

▶ **How should I configure my antivirus software?** For the most extensive protection from malware, you should look for and enable the following features of your antivirus software:

- ▶ Start scanning when the computer boots.
- ▶ Scan all programs when they are launched and document files when they are opened.
- ▶ Scan other types of files, such as graphics, if you engage in some risky computing behaviors and are not concerned with the extra time required to open files as they are scanned.
- ▶ Scan incoming mail and attachments.
- ▶ Scan incoming instant message attachments.
- ▶ Scan outgoing e-mail for worm activity such as mass-mailing worms.
- ▶ Scan zipped (compressed) files.
- ▶ Scan for spyware, sometimes called pups (potentially unwanted programs).
- ▶ Scan all files on the computer's hard disk at least once a week.

▶ **How do I keep my antivirus software up to date?** Two aspects of your antivirus software periodically need to be updated. First, the antivirus program itself might need a patch or update to fix bugs or improve features. Second, the list of virus signatures must be updated to keep up with the latest malware developments.

Virus signatures and other information that antivirus software uses to identify and eradicate malware are stored in one or more files usually referred to as **virus definitions** (or a virus database). Antivirus program updates and revised virus definitions are packaged into a file that can be manually or automatically downloaded. If your antivirus software is part of a security suite, the update might also include patches for other security software modules, such as the spyware module or firewall.

Most antivirus products are preconfigured to regularly check for updates, download them, and install them without user intervention. If you would rather control the download and installation process yourself, you can configure your antivirus software to alert you when updates are ready. In any case, you should manually check for updates periodically just in case the auto-update function has become disabled.

▶ How often should I run a system scan? Most experts recommend that you configure your antivirus software to periodically scan all the files on your computer. With the proliferation of malware attacks, it's best to schedule a weekly system scan. Because a full system scan can significantly slow down your computer, schedule the scan for a time when you are not usually using your computer, but it is turned on.

You can also run a manual scan of your entire computer or of specific files. For example, suppose you download a program and you want to make sure it is virus-free before you install and run it. You can use Windows Explorer to locate and right-click the downloaded file, then select the Scan option from the pop-up menu (Figure 3-57).

▶ What does *quarantine* mean? If, during the scanning process, your virus protection software identifies a virus, worm, Trojan horse, or bot in a file or an attachment, it can try to remove the infection, put the file into quarantine, or simply delete the file.

In the context of antivirus software, a **quarantined file** contains code that is suspected of being part of a virus. For your protection, most antivirus software encrypts the file's contents and isolates it in a quarantine folder, so it can't be inadvertently opened or accessed by a hacker. If the infected file ends up on a quarantine list, your antivirus software might give you the option of trying to disinfect the file or deleting it.

▶ How dependable is antivirus software?
Today's antivirus software is quite dependable, but not infallible. A fast-spreading worm can reach your computer before a virus definition update arrives, some spyware can slip through the net, and cloaking software can hide some viral exploits.

Despite occasional misses, however, antivirus software and other security software modules are constantly weeding out malware that would otherwise infect your computer. It is essential to use security software, but also important to take additional precautions, such as making regular backups of your data.

FIGURE 3-57

Before installing and running a downloaded file, you can scan it by right-clicking the file name and selecting the Scan option.

QuickCheck   SECTION E

1. A computer [＿＿＿＿＿＿＿] can lurk in a computer for days or months, quietly replicating itself.

2. A mass-mailing [＿＿＿＿＿＿＿] spreads to other computers by sending itself to all the addresses stored in the local e-mail client.

3. A group of zombie computers controlled by a hacker is called a(n) [＿＿＿＿＿＿＿].

4. A virus [＿＿＿＿＿＿＿] is a unique section of malicious code that can be identified by antivirus software.

5. A(n) [＿＿＿＿＿＿＿] file is suspected of containing a virus, so your antivirus software usually encrypts the file and stores it in a special folder.

▶ CHECK ANSWERS

Issue: How Serious Is Software Piracy?

Péter Gudella/Shutterstock.c

SOFTWARE IS EASY TO STEAL. You don't have to walk out of a Best Buy store with a box of expensive software under your shirt. You can simply copy the software from your friend's computer. It seems so simple that it couldn't be illegal. But it is.

Piracy takes many forms. End-user piracy includes friends loaning distribution discs to each other and installing software on more computers than the license allows. Although it is perfectly legal to lend a physical object, such as a sweater, to a friend, it is not legal to lend digital copies of software and music because, unlike a sweater that can be worn by only one person at a time, copies of digital things can be simultaneously used by many people.

Software counterfeiting is the large-scale illegal duplication of software distribution media, and sometimes even its packaging. According to Microsoft, many software counterfeiting groups are linked to organized crime and money-laundering schemes that fund a diverse collection of illegal activities, such as smuggling, gambling, extortion, and prostitution. Counterfeit software is sold in retail stores and through online auctions—often the packaging looks so authentic that buyers have no idea they have purchased illegal goods.

Internet piracy uses the Web as a way to illegally distribute unauthorized software. In Net jargon, the terms *appz* and *warez* (pronounced as "wares" or "war EZ") refer to pirated software. Some warez have even been modified to eliminate serial numbers, registration requirements, expiration dates, or other forms of copy protection. Web sites, file sharing networks, and auction sites sell or distribute hundreds of thousands of pirated software products.

In many countries, including the United States, software pirates are subject to civil lawsuits for monetary damages and criminal prosecution, which can result in jail time and stiff fines. Nonetheless, software piracy continues to have an enormous impact. According to a Business Software Alliance (BSA) and IDC Piracy Study, $130 billion of software was

Web sites, file sharing networks, and auction sites sell or distribute hundreds of thousands of pirated software products.

legitimately purchased worldwide, but software worth a whopping $53 billion was pirated.

Is software piracy really damaging? Who cares if you use a program without paying for it? According to industry experts, software piracy has a negative effect on the economy. Software production makes a major contribution to the United States economy, employing more than 250,000 people and accounting for billions of dollars in corporate revenue. It fuels economic development in countries such as India and China. A BSA economic impact study concluded that lowering global piracy by 10 percentage points in the next four years would add more than 500,000 jobs and $141 billion in worldwide economic growth.

Decreases in software revenues can have a direct effect on consumers, too. When software publishers are forced to cut corners, they tend to reduce customer service and technical support. As a result, you, the consumer, get put on hold when you call for technical support, find fewer free technical support sites, and encounter customer support personnel who are only moderately knowledgeable about their products. The bottom line—software piracy negatively affects customer service.

As an alternative to cutting support costs, some software publishers might build the cost of software piracy into the price of the software. The unfortunate result is that those who legitimately license and purchase software pay an inflated price.

Try It! What is the extent of piracy and is there any way to stop it? Explore the issue by completing the Try It! activities. Your instructor can specify how to submit your findings.

① Analysts fear that the Internet is a major factor in piracy growth. As Internet access becomes more widely available, piracy is likely to increase, rather than decrease. Access to high-speed Internet connections makes it much easier to quickly download large software files. To find out if piracy is increasing, connect to *www.bsa.org* and look at the most recent Global Piracy Study, and then answer the following questions:

a. What time period does the study cover?

b. Did software piracy increase or decrease during this time period, and if so, by how much?

c. Which regions had the highest and lowest piracy rates?

d. Which countries had the three highest piracy rates, and what percentage of software is pirated in these countries?

② As a justification of high piracy rates, some observers point out that people in many countries simply might not be able to afford software priced for the U.S. market. Find the current retail price for Microsoft Office in the United States. Next, find the average annual income for Bangladesh. Divide the price by the average annual income to calculate the percentage of a Bangladeshi's income that would be required to purchase Microsoft Office. What is percentage of a Bangladeshi's income would he or she have to pay to get Microsoft Office at full retail U.S. price?

③ The incidence of piracy seems to be higher among small businesses and individual users than corporations and government agencies. According to one study, two-thirds of college and university students see nothing unethical about swapping or downloading digital copyrighted software, music, and movie files without paying for them, and more than half of the people surveyed for the study believe it is acceptable to do so in the workplace. Perhaps education is part of the solution; more publicity about the cost of piracy might encourage people to stop using illegal software. Search YouTube for "software piracy" or "anti-piracy ads," and then complete the following:

a. List the titles and links for three of the ads that you consider most effective.

b. List the title and link for an anti-piracy video that college students would consider "lame."

④ The software industry wants you to report piracy. Do a Web search for "report piracy" and list five sites where you can report individuals or businesses that use or distribute illegal copies of software.

INFOWEBLINKS

You can check the **NP2013 Chapter 3** InfoWebLink for updates to these activities.

W CLICK TO CONNECT
www.infoweblinks.com/np2013/ch03

What Do You Think?   ISSUE

1. Do you believe that software piracy is a serious issue?

2. Do you know of any instances of software piracy?

3. Do you think that most software pirates understand that they are doing something illegal?

4. Should software publishers try to adjust software pricing for local markets?

Information Tools: **Organizing Your Writing**

You can organize a research paper, report, or essay simply by rearranging entries you made in the document containing your research notes. Your bookmarking application might include a feature to arrange your bookmarks and accompanying notes. These tools can be clumsy, however, if your notes are extensive. Dealing with hundreds of notes, you might have trouble seeing the big picture.

Organization tools help you visualize relationships between important pieces of information and supporting detail. They also help you determine the order in which you'll present concepts when you begin to write. Tools that writers find useful include outlines, concept maps, and Smart Art shapes.

OUTLINES. Most word processors include an outline feature that you can use to devise the basic structure of a research paper. You can rearrange outline points using your word processor's Move function. Pay attention to make sure the outline numbering adjusts correctly.

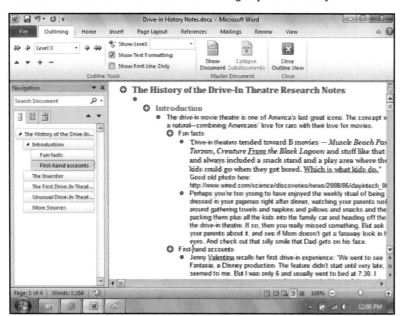

Microsoft Word offers an Outline view in which you can collapse or expand outline levels. This feature is useful for long outlines. For example, suppose you want to organize main ideas; you can collapse the detail so that supporting points are not displayed. Dedicated outline apps, such as OmniOutliner and ThinkBook, offer similar features.

CONCEPT MAPS. If you like to work with concepts visually, check out concept mapping software, such as Mind Map, Tufts' VUE, and SmartDraw, or Web apps, such as Cacoo and bubbl.us.

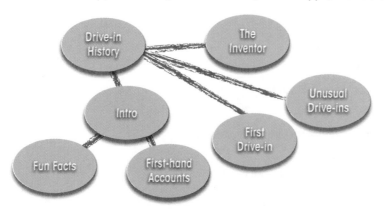

Concept maps typically use bubbles to represent ideas. Lines connect the bubbles to show related concepts. You can customize your concept maps to show a sequence by mapping from left to right.

SMART ART Shapes. You can use Microsoft Excel's SmartArt shapes to organize the structure for a research paper. Just looking through the SmartArt options can give you ideas about the overall structure and the structure of subsections.

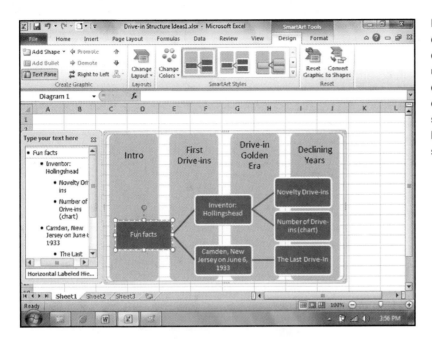

Excel's Smart Art Tools feature contains a variety of pre-designed diagrams that you can use to visualize how the pieces of your report fit together. You can enter text directly on the shapes, or in the outline box located on the left side of the screen.

Try It! Suppose you are working with a team to improve the organization of a Wikipedia article on gray wolves. To begin this project, copy the entire Wikipedia article on gray wolves into a new document named Wolf Project [Your Name] Chapter 3.

1. Use outline view and make each of the headings an outline level.

2. Add or modify headings and move material so that the article is organized into the sections listed in the sidebar.

3. Enter the headings as nodes in a concept map created with the diagramming tool of your choice. Add three subpoints to each node.

4. Use an Excel SmartArt diagram to show how you visualize the points made in the "Relation with humans" section.

New Organization for Gray Wolves Article

Naming and etymology

Range and habitat

Physical characteristics

Behavior

Conservation efforts

Relation with humans

Technology in Context: Journalism

IN THE ANCIENT WORLD, news spread by word of mouth, relayed by bards and merchants who traveled from town to town—in essence, they were the first reporters to broadcast the news. The news business is all about gathering and disseminating information quickly. Technology has played a major role in news reporting's evolution from its bardic roots to modern 24-hour news networks and Web sites.

Johann Gutenberg's printing press (ca. 1450), the first technological breakthrough in the news business, made it feasible to publish news as printed notices tacked to walls in the town square. As paper became more economical, resourceful entrepreneurs sold broadsheets to people eager for news, and the concept of a newspaper was born. The first regularly published newspapers appeared in Germany and Holland in 1609, and the first English newspaper, the *Weekly News*, was published in 1622.

But the news spread slowly. In the early 1800s, it took four weeks for newspapers in New York to receive reports from London. With the advent of the telegraph in 1844, however, reporters from far-flung regions could wire stories to their newspapers for publication the next day. The first radio reporters in the 1920s offered live broadcasts of sports events, church services, and variety shows. Before the 1950s, black-and-white newsreels shown in movie theaters provided the only visual imagery of news events, but television gave viewers news images on a nightly basis.

Technology has benefited print journalism, too. For decades, typesetters transferred reporters' handwritten stories into neatly set columns of type. Today, reporters use computers and word processing software to tap out their stories and run a preliminary check of spelling and grammar.

Stories are submitted by computer network to editors, who also use word processing software to edit stories to fit time and space constraints. The typesetting process has been replaced by desktop publishing software and computer to plate (CTP) technology. Digital pages produced with desktop publishing software are sent to a raster image processor (RIP), which converts the pages into dots that form words and images. After a page has been RIPed, a plate-

setter uses lasers to etch the dots onto a physical plate, which is then mounted on the printing press to produce printed pages. CTP is much faster and more flexible than typesetting, so publishers can make last-minute changes to accommodate late-breaking stories.

Personal computers have also added a new dimension to the news-gathering process. Reporters were once limited to personal interviews, observation, and fact gathering at libraries, but can now make extensive use of Internet resources and e-mail. Web sites and online databases provide background information on all sorts of topics. Other resources include newsgroups and chat rooms, where reporters can monitor public opinion on current events and identify potential sources.

Most major networks maintain interactive Web sites that offer online polls and bulletin boards designed to collect viewers' opinions. Although online poll respondents are not a representative sample of the population, they can help news organizations gauge viewer opinions and determine whether news coverage is comprehensive and effective.

News organizations also accept news, images, and videos from amateur "citizen journalists" who happen upon news events armed with a cell phone or digital camera. And even CNN now reports on news stories that originate on blogs such as *slashdot.org*.

E-mail has changed the way reporters communicate with colleagues and sources. It's often the only practical method for contacting people in remote locations or distant time zones, and it's useful with reluctant sources, who feel more comfortable providing information under the cloak of anonymous Hotmail or Yahoo! accounts. Vetting e-mail sources—verifying credentials such as name, location, and occupation—can be difficult, however, so reporters tend not to rely on these sources without substantial corroboration.

For broadcast journalism, digital communications play a major role in today's live-on-the-scene television reporting. Most news organizations maintain remote production vans, sometimes called satellite news gathering (SNG) trucks, that travel to the site of breaking news, raise their antennas, and begin to broadcast. These complete mobile production facilities include camera control units, audio and video recording equipment, and satellite or microwave transmitters.

On-the-scene reporting no longer requires a truck full of equipment, however. Audiovisual editing units and video cameras have gone digital, making them easier to use and sized to fit in a suitcase. A new breed of backpack journalists carry digital video cameras, notebook computers, and mobile phones.

Backpack journalists can transfer video footage to their notebook computers and then edit the footage with consumer-level video editing software. The resulting video files are compressed and sent to newsroom technicians, who decompress the videos and then broadcast them—all in a matter of seconds.

One drawback of backpack journalists' use of digital cameras and compression is that the video quality usually isn't as crisp as images filmed with studio cameras. News organizations with high standards were once hesitant to use this lower quality video, but have found that viewers would rather see a low-

quality image now than a high-quality image later. To many viewers, a few rough edges just make the footage seem more compelling—more like you are there.

A memorable tour de force in SNG was the brainchild of David Bloom, an NBC reporter embedded with the U.S. Army 3rd Infantry Division during Operation Iraqi Freedom. He helped modify an M-88 tank recovery vehicle into a high-tech, armored SNG vehicle. The $500,000 Bloommobile featured a gyrostabilized camera that could produce jiggle-free video as the tank blasted over sand dunes at 50 mph. Tragically, Bloom died while covering the conflict; but many viewers vividly remember his exhilarating reports as the Bloommobile raced down desert roads, trundled along with Army supply convoys, and narrowly escaped enemy fire.

Video-enabled mobile phones ushered in another era of news gathering. Citizen journalists who are on the spot during news-making events simply point, shoot, and e-mail footage to media Web sites, such as CNN.com and FOXNews.com. During the tragic 2008 terrorist attacks in Mumbai, eyewitness accounts and updates flooded over social networking sites such as Facebook and Twitter. The first images of the attacks spread through social networking sites minutes before they appeared on mainstream news channels.

Computers, the Internet, and communications technology make it possible to instantly broadcast live reports across the globe, but live reporting is not without controversy. Reporters and amateur journalists who arrive at the scene of a disaster with microphones, cameras, or cell phones in hand have little time for reflection, vetting, and cross-checking, so grievous errors, libelous images, or distasteful video footage sometimes find their way into news reports.

Jeff Gralnick, former executive producer for ABC News, remarks, "In the old days, we had time to think before we spoke. We had time to write, time to research and time to say, 'Hey, wait a minute.' Now we don't even have the time to say, 'Hey, wait a nanosecond.' Just because we can say it or do it, should we?" Technology has given journalists a powerful arsenal of tools for gathering and reporting the news, but has also increased their accountability for accurate, socially responsible reporting.

New Perspectives Labs

To access the New Perspectives Lab for Chapter 3, open the NP2013 interactive eBook and then click the icon next to the lab title.

 INSTALLING AND UNINSTALLING SOFTWARE

IN THIS LAB YOU'LL LEARN:

* How to use a setup program to install Windows application software from a distribution CD

* The difference between typical, compact, and custom installation options

* How to specify a folder for a new software installation

* How to install downloaded software

* How to install an upgrade

* How to uninstall a Windows application

* What happens, in addition to deleting files, when you uninstall a software application

* How to locate the program that will uninstall a software application

* Why you might not want to delete all of the files associated with an application

LAB ASSIGNMENTS

1. Start the interactive part of the lab. Make sure you've enabled Tracking if you want to save your QuickCheck results. Perform each lab step as directed, and answer all the lab QuickCheck questions. When you exit the lab, your answers are automatically graded and your results are displayed.

2. Browse the Web and locate a software application that you might like to download. Use information supplied by the Web site to answer the following questions:

   a. What is the name of the program and the URL of the download site?

   b. What is the size of the download file?

   c. According to the instructions, does the download file appear to require manual installation, or does it automatically install itself when the download is complete?

3. On the computer you regularly use, look through the list of programs (For Windows, click Start, then select All Programs to see a list of them. For Macs, click the Applications folder located on the Dock.) List the names of any programs that include their own uninstall routines.

4. (Windows only) On the computer you regularly use, open the Control Panel and then select the Uninstall a Program option. List the first ten programs shown.

Key Terms

Make sure you understand all the boldfaced key terms presented in this chapter. With the NP2013 interactive eBook, you can use this list of terms as an interactive study activity. First, try to define a term in your own words, and then click the term to compare your definition with the definition presented in the chapter.

3

Absolute reference, 138
Automatic recalculation, 138
Bot, 164
Botnet, 164
BSD license, 160
Cell, 136
Cell references, 137
Commercial software, 159
Computer virus, 163
Computer worm, 163
Concurrent-use license, 157
Copyright, 156
Copyright notice, 156
Database, 139
Demoware, 159
Device driver, 131
Document formatting, 135
EULA, 157
Executable file, 147
Field, 139
Font, 135
Footer, 135
Formula, 137
Freeware, 161
Fully justified, 135
Function, 137
GPL, 160
Grammar checker, 134
Graphics, 123
Hash value, 161
Header, 135
Jailbreak, 145
Keyword search, 141
Label, 136
Leading, 135
Malicious software, 162
Malware, 162

Mapping application, 125
Mass-mailing worm, 163
Mathematical operators, 137
Mobile app, 145
Module, 132
Multiple-user license, 157
Natural language query, 141
Office suite, 132
Open source software, 160
Page layout, 135
Paragraph alignment, 135
Paragraph style, 135
PDF, 129
Pirated software, 156
Point size, 135
Portable software, 151
Product activation, 161
Productivity software, 132
Proprietary software, 159
Public domain software, 158
Quarantined file, 169
Query, 141
Query by example, 141
Query language, 141
Readability formula, 134
Record, 139
Relative reference, 138
Remote Access Trojan, 163
Rooting, 145
Rootkit, 165
Search and Replace, 133
Security suite, 166
Service pack, 152
Setup program, 146
Shareware, 159
Shrink-wrap license, 157
Single-user license, 157

Site license, 157
Software installation, 143
Software license, 157
Software update, 152
Software upgrade, 152
Spelling checker, 134
Spelling dictionary, 134
Spreadsheet, 136
Spyware, 164
Style, 135
System requirements, 155
System utilities, 130
Thesaurus, 134
Trojan horse, 163
Uninstall routine, 153
Unzipped, 150
Utility software, 129
Value, 136
Virus definitions, 168
Virus hoax, 166
Virus signature, 167
Web application, 143
What-if analysis, 136
Word wrap, 133
Worksheet, 136
Zipped, 150
Zombie, 164
*See page 180 for a list of key software applications.

Interactive Summary

To review important concepts from this chapter, fill in the blanks to best complete each sentence. When using the NP2013 interactive eBook, click the Check Answers buttons to automatically score your answers.

SECTION A: Computer software can be grouped into two main categories. _____ software is designed for computer-centric tasks, whereas _____ software is designed to help people accomplish real-world tasks. These two main categories can be further divided into subcategories. Popular software categories include music, video, and graphics. Mapping and _____-based software on desktop and mobile computing devices helps consumers find the nearest ATM or turn-by-turn directions to the airport. For businesses, _____ market software is designed to automate specialized tasks in a specific market or business. _____ market soft-

ware is generic software that can be used by just about any kind of business. _____ software is designed to help you monitor and configure settings for your computer system equipment, the operating system, or application software. A(n) _____ reader is an essential utility that displays documents in a standard format for exchanging files. _____ utilities alter a device's user interface to create an accessible environment for people who cannot see the screen or have other barriers to access. Device _____ are a type of system software that helps a computer establish communication with peripheral devices.

▶ CHECK ANSWERS

SECTION B: Office suites are sometimes referred to as _____ software because they offer features that really help get work done. Word _____ software assists you with composing, editing, designing, printing, and electronically publishing documents. When you want to change margins, headers, and footers, you can use _____ layout tools. To change the spacing between lines or the alignment of text, you can use tools to adjust _____ style. _____ software is similar to a smart piece of paper that automatically adds up the columns of numbers you write on it. You can use it to make other calculations, too, based on simple equations that you write or more complex, built-in formulas. Because it is so

easy to experiment with different numbers, this type of software is particularly useful for _____ analyses. _____ software helps you store, find, organize, update, and report information stored in one or more tables. Data is stored in _____, which form records. When two sets of records are _____, database software allows you to access data from both tables at the same time. A(n) _____ language such as SQL describes the information you want to find in a set of records. _____ software supplies tools for creating a series of electronic slides that can be shown on a computer screen or projector.

▶ CHECK ANSWERS

SECTION C:

The process of [ ] software places a program into a computer so that it can be executed or run. [ ] apps are examples of cloud computing and are accessed from a browser. [ ] apps are installed on a local handheld device by downloading from an app store. Some Apple devices have to use a designated app store unless they are [ ] by an unauthorized change to the device's software. Local applications typically include a(n) [ ] program that guides you through the installation process. The main program is stored in a(n) [ ] file that might call additional programs as necessary. For downloaded software, the first step in the installation process is usually to [ ] the distribution file that was compressed to conserve space and reduce download time. In contrast to local applications, [ ] software is designed to run from removable storage, such as a CD or USB flash drive. On PCs, these apps require no entries in the Windows Registry. Software publishers regularly update their software to add new features, fix bugs, and update its security. A software [ ] is a small section of program code that replaces part of the software you currently have installed. The term *service* [ ], which usually applies to operating system updates, is a set of patches that correct problems and address security vulnerabilities. To remove software from a Windows PC, it is important to use a(n) [ ] routine, rather than simply deleting program files.

▶ CHECK ANSWERS

SECTION D:

Most new computers include an operating system, essential utilities, and some basic application software. When shopping for additional utilities and apps, check the system [ ] to make sure your device has the correct operating system and necessary hardware capacity. Software is protected by copyright, and illegal copying or distribution is sometimes referred to as software [ ]. [ ] software, such as commercial software, is protected by copyright that grants to its author an exclusive right to copy, distribute, sell, and modify that work. Public [ ] software is not protected by copyright. A software [ ] can extend or limit the rights granted by copyright. Demoware and [ ] are distributed free of charge, but require payment for continued use. Freeware is copyrighted software that can be used for free, but cannot be altered or resold. [ ] source software is distributed with its source code, and can be modified, sold, and redistributed.

▶ CHECK ANSWERS

SECTION E:

Security software can be classified into various types: antivirus, antispyware, anti-spam, and firewalls. Each type focuses on a specific security threat. A computer [ ] is a set of program instructions that attaches itself to a file, reproduces itself, and spreads to other files. A computer [ ] is a self-replicating program designed to carry out some unauthorized activity on a victim's computer. In the context of computing, a Trojan [ ] is a computer program that seems to perform one function while actually doing something else. For example, it might steal passwords using a type of program called a [ ] that records keystrokes. A Remote Access Trojan sets up [ ] capabilities that allow remote hackers to access files on victims' computers. [ ] programs can turn computers into zombies and link them together into [ ]. [ ] is a type of program that secretly gathers personal information without the victim's knowledge, usually for advertising and other commercial purposes. To combat malware, it is important to use [ ] software that looks for virus signatures. Most computer owners obtain this software as one module in a security [ ].

▶ CHECK ANSWERS

Software Key Terms

3-D graphics software, 124
Accounting software, 126
Adaptive utilities, 130
Antivirus software, 167
Audio editing software, 121
CAD software, 124
Database software, 139
Desktop publishing software, 127
Drawing software, 123
DVD authoring software, 122
Graphics software, 123

Horizontal market software, 126
Location-based software, 125
Mathematical modeling software, 126
Money management software, 128
Music software, 121
Paint software, 123
Payroll software, 126
Personal finance software, 128
Photo editing software, 123
Presentation software, 142
Project management software, 126

Security software, 162
Spreadsheet software, 136
Statistical software, 126
Tax preparation software, 128
Vertical market software, 126
Video editing software, 122
Word processing software, 133

Interactive Situation Questions

Apply what you've learned to some typical computing situations. When using the NP2013 interactive eBook, you can type your answers, and then use the Check Answers button to automatically score your responses.

1. You're using an app on your iPhone to find the nearest bike repair shop. This _____-based app works because it can triangulate your whereabouts based on the built-in GPS or your distance from nearby cell towers.

2. Suppose that you've been hired to organize a professional skateboard competition. When you consider how you'll need to use computers, you realize that you must collect information on each competitor and keep track of every competitive event. With at least two types of related records, you'll probably need to use _____ software.

3. Imagine that you just purchased a new software package. You insert the distribution CD, but nothing happens. No problem—you can manually run the _____ program, which will start the install routine.

4. Your friend has an iPod touch that's loaded with all kinds of applications; but every time there's a software update, your friend grumbles about "redoing stuff." You guess that your friend's iPod is _____.

5. You download an open source software program from the Web. You assume that the download includes the uncompiled _____ code for the program as well as the _____ version.

6. You're in the process of receiving some e-mail messages when your antivirus software displays an alert. You assume that it has discovered a virus _____ in an attachment for one of the e-mail messages. The message also states that the file has been _____; that is, moved to an area where it cannot cause more harm.

 CHECK ANSWERS

Interactive Practice Tests

Practice tests that consist of ten multiple-choice, true/false, and fill-in-the-blank questions are available in the NP2013 interactive eBook. Test questions are selected at random from a large test bank, so each time you take a test, you'll receive a different set of questions. Your tests are scored immediately, and you can print study guides that help you find the correct answers for any questions that you missed.

 CLICK TO START

Learning Objectives Checkpoints

Learning Objectives Checkpoints are designed to help you assess whether you have achieved the major learning objectives for this chapter. You can use paper and pencil or word processing software to complete most of the activities.

1. List seven categories of application software.

2. List at least ten functions performed by utilities included with Windows and Mac operating systems.

3. Provide an example of an adaptive utility on the iPhone.

4. Explain why you might want to locate the version number for a device driver.

5. Describe three ways that word processing software can help improve your writing.

6. Draw a sketch of a simple worksheet and label the following: columns, rows, cell, active cell, values, labels, formulas, and Formula bar. Explain the difference between an absolute reference and a relative reference, giving an example of each.

7. Describe four ways to query a database.

8. List at least six key features of presentation software.

9. Describe the difference between Web apps and mobile apps.

10. List and describe the two main types of files included in a local software installation.

11. Write a set of step-by-step instructions for installing software from a distribution CD, and another set of instructions for installing downloaded software.

12. Explain the purpose of a software patch and describe how it differs from a service pack.

13. Describe the difference between uninstalling software on Macs and on Windows.

14. Read the license agreement in Figure 3-49 and answer each of the questions in the corresponding figure caption.

15. Explain the differences between proprietary software, commercial software, shareware, open source software, freeware, and public domain software.

16. Create a table that summarizes the differences between various types of malware based on their method of distribution and exploits.

17. Draw a story board to illustrate how antivirus software works.

Study Tip: Make sure you can use your own words to correctly answer each of the purple focus questions that appear throughout the chapter.

3

Concept Map

Fill in the blanks to show the hierarchy of software described in this chapter.

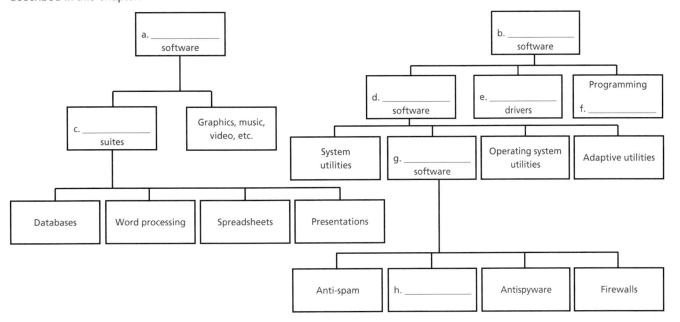

CHECK ANSWERS

4

Operating Systems and File Management

Chapter Contents

INFOWEBLINKS

You'll find updates for chapter material by connecting to the **NP2013 Chapter 4** InfoWebLink.

Ⓦ CLICK TO CONNECT
www.infoweblinks.com/np2013/ch04

Learning Objectives

After reading this chapter, you will be able to answer the following questions by completing the outcomes-based Learning Objectives Checkpoints on page 243.

1. What are system resources?
2. How do multitasking, multithreading, and multiprocessing work?
3. What is a memory leak?
4. When do users interact with the operating system?
5. How do GUIs differ from command line interfaces?
6. What happens during the boot process?
7. Which operating systems are typically used on personal computers, on servers, and on handheld devices?
8. What is a virtual machine?
9. Do operating systems put limits on the names that can be used for files?
10. What is a file specification or path?
11. What is a native file format?
12. Are there guidelines for managing files so that they are easy to locate and back up?
13. What happens behind the scenes when a computer stores a file?
14. What is the best backup device?
15. How does backup software work?
16. How do restore points, bare-metal restore, disk imaging, virtual machines, boot disks, and recovery disks relate to backup?
17. Is it possible to back up data on handheld devices?

CourseMate

Visit the NP2013 CourseMate for this chapter's Pre-Quiz, Audio Overview and Flashcards, Detailed Objectives, Chapter Quiz, Online Games, and more labs.

Multimedia and Interactive Elements

When using the NP2013 interactive eBook, click the ▶ icons to access multimedia resources.

Apply Your Knowledge
The information in this chapter will give you the background to:

- Find out which processes are running on your computer
- Use Windows, Mac OS, DOS, and Linux
- Maintain an efficient organization of files on your computer
- Use extensions to identify the software needed to open a file
- Convert files from one format to another

- Open, save, rename, move, copy, and delete files
- Burn a CD, DVD, or BD
- Defragment your computer's hard disk
- Shred computer files so they cannot be read
- Make a backup of the data that is stored on your computer's hard disk or on your handheld device
- Get up and running after a hard disk failure

Try It!

IS MY COMPUTER'S HARD DISK GETTING FULL?

Your computer's hard disk stores a high percentage of the programs you use and the data files you create. You might wonder if your hard disk is getting full. To find out, follow the steps below.

Windows:

1. Start your computer and make sure you can see the Windows desktop.

2. Click the **Start** button, and then select Computer (or My Computer if you're using Windows XP).

3. Right-click your **(C:)** drive to display a pop-up menu.

4. Click **Properties**. A Local Disk Properties dialog box should appear containing statistics about your computer's hard disk.

5. For the properties indicated by red underlines in the figure at right, jot down the statistics for used space, free space, and capacity. Then sketch in the slices of the pie chart for your computer.

6. Also, use the blank provided to jot down the file system used by your computer. You'll learn the significance of your computer's file system when you read the chapter.

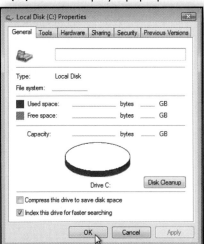

Mac:

1. Start your computer and make sure you can see the Mac OS X desktop, dock, and toolbar.

2. Locate the desktop icon labeled **Macintosh HD** and right-click it. (If your mouse has only one button, hold down the Ctrl key and click it.)

Macintosh HD

3. Select **Get Info** from the pop-up menu.

4. For the properties indicated by red underlines in the figure at right, jot down the statistics for capacity, available space, and used space in GB and bytes.

5. Also, jot down the file system shown on the Format line. You'll learn the significance of the file system when you read the chapter.

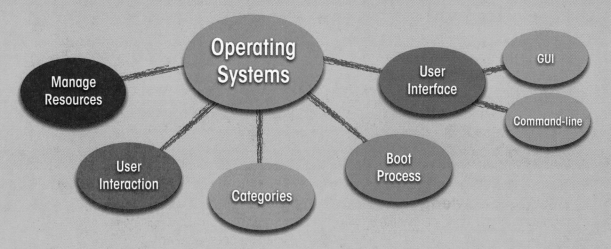

Operating System Basics

AN OPERATING SYSTEM is an integral part of virtually every computer system. It fundamentally affects how you can use your computer. Can you run two programs at the same time? Can you connect your computer to a network? Does your computer run dependably? Does all your software have a similar look and feel, or do you have to learn a different set of controls and commands for each new program you acquire? To answer questions like these, it is helpful to have a clear idea about what an operating system is and what it does. Section A provides an overview of operating system basics.

OPERATING SYSTEM ACTIVITIES

▶ **What is an operating system?** An operating system (abbreviated OS) is a type of system software that acts as the master controller for all activities that take place within a computer system. It is one of the factors that determines your computer's compatibility and platform.

Most personal computers are sold with a preinstalled operating system, such as Microsoft Windows or Mac OS (Figure 4-1). A third operating system called Linux is typically used for high-end workstations and servers, but can also be installed on personal computers. A variety of other operating systems, such as Google Chrome OS, DOS, UNIX, and OpenSolaris, are also available.

FIGURE 4-1

Windows (left) is typically pre-installed on IBM-compatible computers manufactured by companies such as Dell and Hewlett-Packard. Mac OS (middle) is preinstalled on Apple Macintosh computers. Linux (right) is an open source operating system that's available as a free download.

▶ Is the Windows operating system the same as Windows software? No. Although it is true that an operating system is software, terms such as *Windows software*, *Mac software*, or *Linux software* are used to refer to application software. Windows software, for example, refers to applications designed to run on computers that have Microsoft Windows installed as the operating system. A program called Microsoft Word for Windows is an example of Windows software.

▶ What does an operating system do? Your computer's operating system provides an environment for running software and controlling peripheral devices.

Your computer's operating system, application software, and device drivers are organized similar to the chain of command in an army. You issue a command using application software. Application software tells the operating system what to do. The operating system tells the device drivers, device drivers tell the hardware, and the hardware actually does the work. Figure 4-2 illustrates this chain of command for printing a document or photo.

FIGURE 4-2

A command to print a document is relayed through various levels of software, including the operating system, until it reaches the printer.

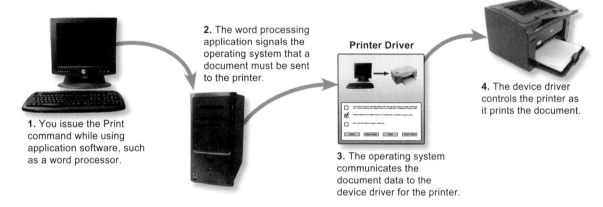

2. The word processing application signals the operating system that a document must be sent to the printer.

Printer Driver

4. The device driver controls the printer as it prints the document.

1. You issue the Print command while using application software, such as a word processor.

3. The operating system communicates the document data to the device driver for the printer.

The operating system interacts with application software, device drivers, and hardware to manage a computer's resources. In the context of a computer system, the term **resource** refers to any component that is required to perform work.

The processor is a computer's main resource. RAM (random access memory), storage space, and peripheral devices are also resources. While you interact with application software, your computer's operating system is busy behind the scenes with resource management tasks such as those listed in Figure 4-3.

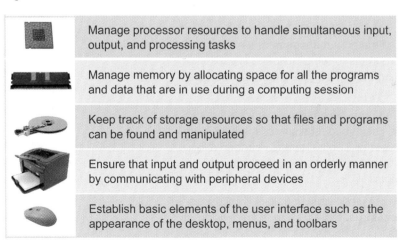

Manage processor resources to handle simultaneous input, output, and processing tasks

Manage memory by allocating space for all the programs and data that are in use during a computing session

Keep track of storage resources so that files and programs can be found and manipulated

Ensure that input and output proceed in an orderly manner by communicating with peripheral devices

Establish basic elements of the user interface such as the appearance of the desktop, menus, and toolbars

FIGURE 4-3

Operating System Tasks

❯ How do operating systems manage processor resources?

Every cycle of a computer's microprocessor is a resource for accomplishing tasks. Many activities—called processes—compete for the attention of your computer's microprocessor. Commands are arriving from programs you're using, while input is arriving from the keyboard and mouse. At the same time, data must be sent to the display device or printer, and Web pages are arriving from your Internet connection.

To manage all these competing processes, your computer's operating system must ensure that each process receives its share of microprocessor cycles. You can check the processes that are being executed by the microprocessor if you suspect that a program did not close properly or that malware is working behind the scenes (Figure 4-4).

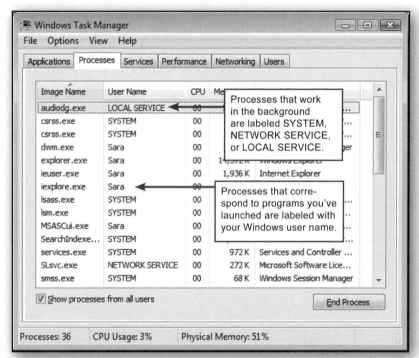

FIGURE 4-4

The Windows operating system displays a list of processes when you hold down the Ctrl, Shift, and Esc keys. On the Mac, look for the Activity Monitor in the Utilities folder listed under Applications. Most processes are legitimate programs that run in the background to carry out tasks for the operating system, device drivers, and applications. Occasionally a bot or worm launches rogue processes. If you want to know if a process is legitimate, you can google it. ▶ Use your interactive eBook to find out how to access information about the processes on your computer.

❯ How do operating systems handle so many processes?

During a typical computing session, your computer might run an average of 50 processes. Ideally, the operating system should be able to help the microprocessor switch seamlessly from one process to another. Depending on the capabilities of the operating system and computer hardware, processes can be managed by multitasking, multithreading, and multiprocessing.

Multitasking provides process and memory management services that allow two or more tasks, jobs, or programs to run simultaneously. Most of today's operating systems, including the OS on your personal computer and iPhone, offer multitasking services.

Within a single program, **multithreading** allows multiple parts, or threads, to run simultaneously. For example, one thread for a spreadsheet program might be waiting for input from the user while other threads perform a long calculation in the background. Multithreading can speed up performance on single or multiple processor computers.

Many new computers include multi-core processors or multiple processors. An operating system's **multiprocessing** capability supports a division of labor among all the processing units.

▶ How does an operating system manage memory? A microprocessor works with data and executes instructions stored in RAM—one of your computer's most important resources. When you want to run more than one program at a time, the operating system has to allocate specific areas of memory for each program, as shown in Figure 4-5.

Sometimes, an application requests memory, but never releases it, a condition called a **memory leak**. Memory 'leaks' away into this application's reserved area, eventually preventing other programs from accessing enough memory to function properly. Those programs can crash, and the operating system might display error messages, such as "General Protection Fault" or "Program Not Responding." Your computer can sometimes recover from a memory leak if you access Task Manager (PCs) or Activity Monitor (Macs) to close the corrupted program.

▶ How does the OS keep track of storage resources? Behind the scenes, an operating system acts as a filing clerk that stores and retrieves files from your computer's hard drive and other storage devices. It remembers the names and locations of all your files and keeps track of empty spaces where new files can be stored. Later in the chapter, you'll explore file storage in more depth and learn how the operating system affects the way you create, name, save, and retrieve files.

▶ Why does the operating system get involved with peripheral devices? Every device connected to a computer is regarded as an input or output resource. Your computer's operating system communicates with device driver software so that data can travel smoothly between the computer and peripheral resources. If a peripheral device or driver is not performing correctly, the operating system makes a decision about what to do—usually it displays an on-screen message to warn you of the problem.

Your computer's operating system ensures that input and output proceed in an orderly manner, using buffers to collect and hold data while the computer is busy with other tasks. By using a keyboard buffer, for example, your computer never misses one of your keystrokes, regardless of how fast you type or what else is happening in your computer at the same time.

▶ Are different operating systems needed for different computing tasks? One operating system might be better suited to some computing tasks than others. To provide clues to their strengths and weaknesses, operating systems are informally categorized and characterized using one or more of the following terms:

A **single-user operating system** expects to deal with one set of input devices—those that can be controlled by one user at a time. Operating systems for handheld computers and some personal computers fit into the single-user category. DOS is an example of a single-user operating system.

A **multiuser operating system** allows a single, centralized computer to deal with simultaneous input, output, and processing requests from many users. One of its most difficult responsibilities is to schedule all the processing requests that a centralized computer must perform. IBM's z/OS is one of the most popular multiuser operating systems.

A **server operating system** provides tools for managing distributed networks, e-mail servers, and Web hosting sites. Mac OS X Server, Windows Server 2008 R2, and Linux are examples of server operating systems. Technically, multiuser operating systems schedule requests for processing on a centralized computer, whereas a server operating system simply

FIGURE 4-5

The operating system allocates a specific area of RAM for each program that is open and running. The operating system is itself a program, so it requires RAM space, too.

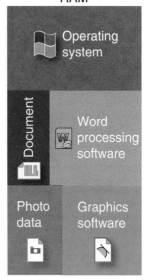

RAM

4

routes data and programs to each user's local computer where the actual processing takes place. In practice, however, today's server operating systems can be configured for centralized or distributed processing.

A **desktop operating system** is designed for a desktop or notebook personal computer. The computer you use at home, at school, or at work is most likely configured with a desktop operating system, such as Microsoft Windows or Mac OS. Typically, these operating systems are designed to accommodate one user at a time, but also provide networking capability. Today's desktop operating systems invariably provide multitasking capabilities so that users can run more than one application at a time.

A **handheld operating system** (also called a mobile operating system) is designed for devices, such as smartphones and tablet computers. These systems include modules for mobile connectivity and alternative input and output, such as touch screens.

▶ **Do I ever interact directly with the OS?** Although its main purpose is to control what happens behind the scenes, many operating systems provide utilities that you can use to control your computer equipment and customize your work environment. For example, Microsoft Windows offers its users controls to do the following activities:

▶ **Launch programs.** When you start your computer, Windows displays graphical objects, such as icons, the Start button, and the Programs menu, which you can use to start programs.

▶ **Manage files.** A useful utility, called Windows Explorer, allows you to view a list of files, move them to different storage devices, copy them, rename them, and delete them.

▶ **Get help.** Windows offers a Help system you can use to find out how various commands work.

▶ **Customize the user interface.** The Windows Control Panel, which is accessible from the Start menu, provides utilities that help you customize your screen display and work environment.

▶ **Configure equipment.** The Control Panel also provides access to utilities that help you set up and configure your computer's hardware and peripheral devices (Figure 4-6).

FIGURE 4-6

Many Windows utilities can be accessed from the Control Panel. You'll find it by clicking the Start button. Classic View displays Control Panel utilities as icons; Category View (shown here) organizes the utilities into groups. ▶ Use your interactive eBook to take a tour of handy Control Panel options.

USER INTERFACES

▶ **What is a user interface?** A **user interface** can be defined as the combination of hardware and software that helps people and computers communicate with each other. A personal computer's user interface includes a display device, mouse, and keyboard that allow you to view and manipulate your computing environment. It also includes software elements, such as icons, menus, and toolbar buttons.

▶ **How does the operating system affect the user interface?** The operating system's user interface defines the so-called look and feel of compatible software. For example, application software that runs under Mac OS uses a standard set of menus, buttons, and toolbars based on the operating system's user interface. Originally, computers had a **command-line interface** that required users to type memorized commands to run programs and accomplish tasks.

Command-line user interfaces can be accessed from most operating systems, including Windows and Mac OS. Experienced users and system administrators sometimes prefer to use a command-line interface for troubleshooting and system maintenance. Figure 4-7 illustrates the use of a command-line interface.

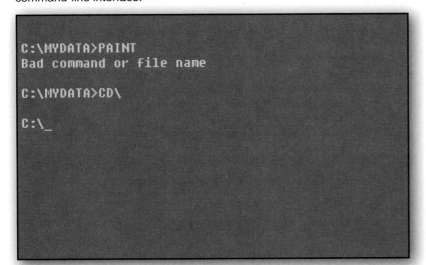

```
C:\MYDATA>PAINT
Bad command or file name

C:\MYDATA>CD\

C:\_
```

FIGURE 4-7

A command-line user interface requires users to type commands. Here the prompt C:\ MYDATA> means the computer is looking at the MYDATA folder of drive C. The user has tried to start a program called Paint, but that program does not exist in the current folder, so the computer has produced the error message "Bad command or file name."

Most computers today feature a graphical user interface, abbreviated as GUI and pronounced as "gooey" or "gee you eye." A **graphical user interface** provides a way to select menu options and manipulate graphical objects displayed on the screen using a mouse or gesture.

GUIs were originally conceived at the prestigious Xerox PARC research facility. In 1984, Apple turned the idea into a commercial success with the launch of its popular Macintosh computer, which featured a GUI operating system and applications. Graphical user interfaces didn't really catch on in the PC market until the 1992 release of Windows 3.1.

▶ **What are the basic elements of a GUI?** GUIs are based on graphical objects that can be manipulated using a touch, mouse, or other input device. Each graphical object represents a computer task, command, or real-world object.

Icons and windows can be displayed on a screen-based **desktop**. An **icon** is a small picture that represents a program, file, or hardware device. A **window** is a rectangular work area that can hold a program, data, or controls (Figure 4-8 on the next page).

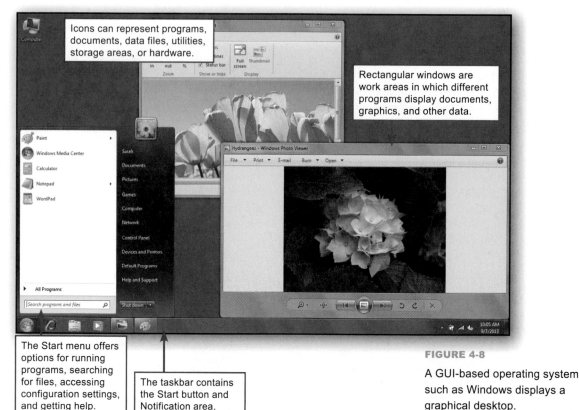

Icons can represent programs, documents, data files, utilities, storage areas, or hardware.

Rectangular windows are work areas in which different programs display documents, graphics, and other data.

The Start menu offers options for running programs, searching for files, accessing configuration settings, and getting help.

The taskbar contains the Start button and Notification area.

FIGURE 4-8

A GUI-based operating system such as Windows displays a graphical desktop.

FIGURE 4-9

Buttons and command options can be arranged on menu bars, toolbars, taskbars, or ribbons (shown top to bottom).

A **button** is a graphic—usually rectangular in shape—that can be clicked to make a selection. Buttons can be arranged in a **menu bar**, **toolbar**, **task-bar**, or **ribbon** (Figure 4-9).

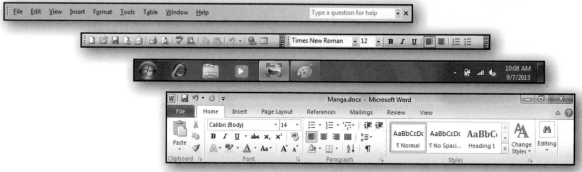

▶ **What's the point of menus and dialog boxes?** Menus were developed as a response to the difficulties many people experienced trying to remember command words and syntax for command-line user interfaces. A **menu** displays a list of commands or options. Each line of the menu is referred to as a menu option or a menu item. Menus are popular because you simply choose the command you want from a list. Also, because all the commands on the list are valid, it is not possible to invoke invalid commands that generate errors.

You might wonder how a menu can present all the commands you might want to use. Obviously, there are many possibilities for combining command words so there could be hundreds of menu options. Two methods are generally used to present a reasonably sized list of options: submenus and dialog boxes.

A **submenu** is an additional set of commands that the computer displays after you make a selection from the main menu. Sometimes a submenu displays another submenu, providing even more command choices (Figure 4-10).

FIGURE 4-10

Menu options with a ▶ symbol lead to submenus.

4

Instead of leading to a submenu, some menu options lead to a dialog box. A **dialog box** displays the options associated with a command. You fill in the dialog box to indicate specifically how you want the command carried out. As shown in Figure 4-11, dialog boxes appear when you click a dialog box launcher or when you click a menu item that ends with an ellipsis.

FIGURE 4-11

Dialog boxes appear when you select corresponding menu items from the ribbon or from a menu.

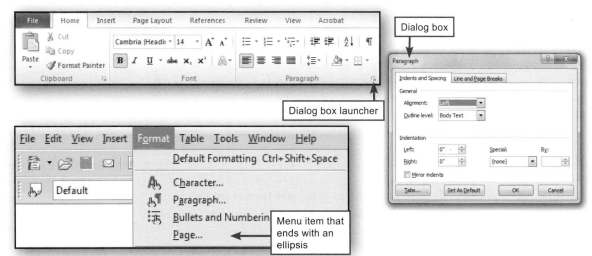

FIGURE 4-12

Dialog box controls offer a variety of ways to enter specifications for tasks you'd like the software to carry out.

Dialog boxes display controls that you manipulate with a mouse to specify settings and other command parameters. Figure 4-12 explains how to use some of the dialog box controls that you are likely to encounter in Windows, Mac, or Linux environments.

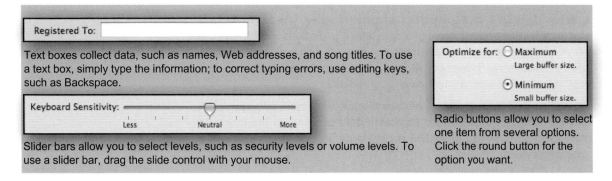

▶ **How similar are the user interfaces for Windows, Mac OS, and Linux?** All of the popular desktop operating systems use graphical user interfaces that are more similar than they are different. Regardless of whether you use Windows, Mac OS, or Linux, you'll encounter a fairly standard set of on-screen controls. They might differ in their visual design, but it is easy to determine how to use them. In the next section of the chapter, you'll learn more about the similarities and differences in today's popular operating systems.

THE BOOT PROCESS

▶ **Where is the operating system stored?** In some digital devices, such as handhelds and videogame consoles, the entire operating system is small enough to be stored in ROM (read-only memory). For most other computers, the operating system program is quite large, so most of it is stored on a hard disk.

During the boot process, the operating system kernel is loaded into RAM. The **kernel** provides essential operating system services, such as memory management and file access. The kernel stays in RAM all the time your computer is on. Other parts of the operating system, such as customization utilities, are loaded into RAM as they are needed.

▶ **What is the boot process?** The sequence of events that occurs between the time that you turn on a computer and the time that it is ready for you to issue commands is referred to as the **boot process**, or booting your computer.

Your computer's small **bootstrap program** is built into special ROM circuitry housed in the computer's system unit. When you turn on a computer, the ROM circuitry receives power and begins the boot process by executing the bootstrap program. Six major events happen during the boot process:

❶ Power up. When you turn on the power switch, the power light is illuminated, and power is distributed to the computer circuitry.

❷ Start boot program. The microprocessor begins to execute the bootstrap program that is stored in ROM.

❸ Power-on self-test. The computer performs diagnostic tests of several crucial system components.

❹ Identify peripheral devices. The computer identifies the peripheral devices that are connected and checks their settings.

❺ Load operating system. The operating system is copied from the hard disk to RAM.

❻ Check configuration and customization. The microprocessor reads configuration data and executes any customized startup routines specified by the user.

▶ **Why doesn't a computer simply leave the operating system in memory?** Most of a computer's memory is volatile DRAM, which cannot hold any data when the power is off. Although a copy of the operating system is housed in RAM while the computer is in operation, this copy is erased as soon as the power is turned off.

In addition to RAM, computers have non-volatile memory circuitry, such as ROM and EEPROM, which can store data even when the power is off. Typically, ROM and EEPROM are not large enough to store an entire operating system.

> **TERMINOLOGY NOTE**
>
> The term *boot* comes from the word *bootstrap*, which is a small loop on the back of a boot. Just as you can pull on a big boot using a small bootstrap, your computer boots up by first loading a small program into memory, and then it uses that small program to load a large operating system.

Given the volatility of RAM and the insufficient size of ROM and EEPROM, computer designers decided to store the operating system on a computer's hard disk or solid state drive. During the boot process, a copy of the operating system is transferred into RAM, where it can be accessed quickly whenever the computer needs to carry out an input, output, or storage operation (Figure 4-13).

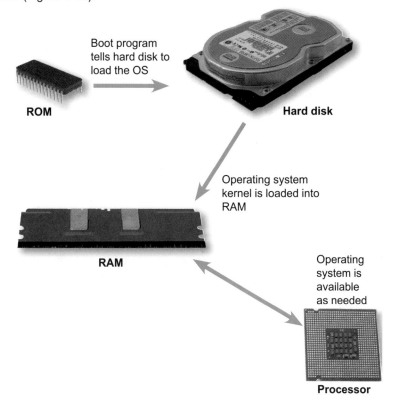

FIGURE 4-13

The bootstrap program copies the operating system into RAM, where it can be directly accessed by the processor to carry out input, output, or storage operations.

Boot program tells hard disk to load the OS

ROM

Hard disk

Operating system kernel is loaded into RAM

RAM

Operating system is available as needed

Processor

▶ How do I know when the operating system is loaded?
The operating system is loaded and the boot process is complete when the computer is ready to accept your commands. Usually, the computer displays an operating system prompt or a main screen. The Windows operating system, for example, displays the Windows desktop when the boot process is complete.

QuickCheck   SECTION A

1. An operating system manages a computer's _____ , such as RAM, storage, and peripherals.

2. Most personal computer operating systems have _____ capabilities so that they can simultaneously run two or more tasks, jobs, or programs.

3. The core part of an operating system is called its _____ .

4. Most computers today have _____ user interfaces.

5. During the _____ process, a program stored in ROM tells the hard disk to load the operating system into RAM.

▶ CHECK ANSWERS

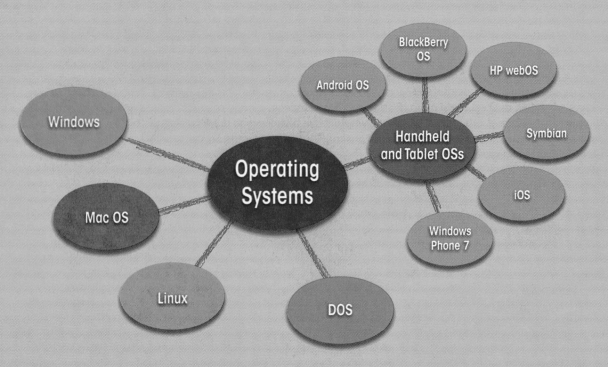

Today's Operating Systems

CONSUMERS CAN SELECT from several operating systems for their personal computers and handheld devices. What makes these operating systems different? What are their strengths and weaknesses? Section B offers an operating system overview designed to give you a basic familiarity with their features.

MICROSOFT WINDOWS

▶ What's the best-selling operating system? Microsoft

Windows is installed on more than 80% of the world's personal computers. The Windows operating system gets its name from the rectangular work areas that appear on the screen-based desktop. Each work area window can display a different document or program, providing a visual model of the operating system's multitasking capabilities (Figure 4-14).

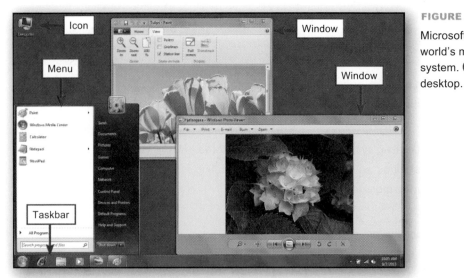

FIGURE 4-14

Microsoft Windows 7 is the world's most popular operating system. ▶ Tour the Windows desktop.

▶ **What do I need to know about the evolution of Windows?** The first versions of Windows, including Windows 3.1, were sometimes referred to as operating environments rather than operating systems because they required DOS to supply the operating system kernel. Windows operating environments hid the DOS command line with a point-and-click graphical user interface. Windows operating environments evolved into today's comprehensive operating systems, which do not require the DOS kernel.

From its inception, the Windows operating system was designed to run on Intel or Intel-compatible microprocessors. As those chips evolved from 16-bit to 32-bit, and then to 64-bit architectures, Windows evolved to keep pace.

Windows developers also added and upgraded features, such as networking and the file system. They refined the user interface by attempting to make it more visually attractive and easier to use. Since its introduction in 1985, Windows has evolved through several versions, listed in Figure 4-15.

▶ **What are the strengths of Windows?** The number and variety of programs that run on Windows are unmatched by any other operating system, a fact that contributes to Windows being the most widely used desktop operating system. For the best selection of software, especially for games and vertical market business software, Windows is the operating system of choice.

The variety of hardware platforms that run Windows is also a significant strength. You can use a desktop computer, notebook, netbook, or handheld computer and see a familiar set of Windows icons and menus. Features such as handwriting recognition contribute to the versatility of Windows, allowing it to control smartphones and tablet computers with touch screens.

The Windows user community is also a strength. A vast amount of documentation, including tutorials and troubleshooting guides, can be found online and on the shelves of most bookstores. Microsoft's official site, *www.microsoft.com*, includes thousands of pages of easily searchable information. Third-party sites, such as Paul Thurrott's *www.winsupersite.com*, also offer tips, tools, and troubleshooting guides.

When it comes to hardware and peripheral devices, Windows offers excellent support in the form of built-in drivers and Plug and Play functionality. Many of the fastest graphics cards and the coolest joysticks are offered exclusively for the Windows platform. With the largest user base of any platform, Windows computer owners are the target market for the majority of personal computer manufacturers.

FIGURE 4-15

Windows Timeline

2012 Windows 8
Provided smooth transition to HTML apps and enhanced security features.

2009 Windows 7
Featured 64-bit support, enhanced desktop and taskbar features, and touch-screen capabilities.

2007 Windows Vista
Featured 64-bit support, enhanced security, and more flexible file management.

2001 Windows XP
Featured an updated user interface, used the Windows 2000 32-bit kernel, and supported FAT32 and NTFS file systems.

2000 Windows Me
The last Windows version to use the original Windows kernel that accesses DOS.

2000 Windows 2000
Billed as a "multipurpose network OS for businesses of all sizes" and featured enhanced Web services.

1998 Windows 98
Increased stability was a big feature of this Windows version, which also included the Internet Explorer browser.

1995 Windows 95
Featured a revised user interface. Supported 32-bit processors, dial-up networking, and long file names.

1993 Windows NT
Provided management and security tools for network servers and the NTFS file system.

1992 Windows for Workgroups
Provided peer-to-peer networking, e-mail, group scheduling, and file and printer sharing.

1992 Windows 3.1
Introduced program icons and the file folder metaphor.

1990 Windows 3.0
Introduced graphical controls.

1987 Windows 2.0
Introduced overlapping windows and expanded memory access.

1985 Windows 1.0
Divided the screen into rectangular windows that allowed users to work with several programs at the same time.

4

▶ **What are Windows' weaknesses?** Windows has been criticized for two major weaknesses: reliability and security. The reliability of an operating system is usually gauged by the length of time it operates without glitches. Unfortunately, Windows tends to become unstable with more frequency than other operating systems.

Slow system response, programs that stop working, and error messages can be symptoms of a Windows malfunction. Rebooting usually clears the error condition and returns a computer to normal functionality, but the time wasted shutting down and waiting for a reboot adds unnecessary frustration to the computing experience.

Of the major desktop operating systems, Windows has the reputation for being the most vulnerable to viruses, worms, and other attacks. One reason for Windows' vulnerability is because its huge user base makes it the biggest target.

Further, Microsoft is a hip adversary for anti-establishment hackers. Even so, Windows has many security holes that are found and exploited. Although Microsoft is diligent in its efforts to patch security holes, its programmers are always one step behind the hackers; and while users wait for patches, their computers are vulnerable.

▶ **What's the difference between desktop, server, and embedded versions of Microsoft Windows?** Microsoft offers several versions, called editions, of the Windows operating system for various markets. Desktop editions, such as Home, Professional, and Ultimate, are designed for personal computers. Server editions are designed for LAN, Internet, and Web servers. Embedded editions are designed for handheld devices, such as mobile phones. Figure 4-16 categorizes some of the most popular Windows offerings.

FIGURE 4-16

Microsoft offers several versions of Windows designed for different computing tasks and equipment.

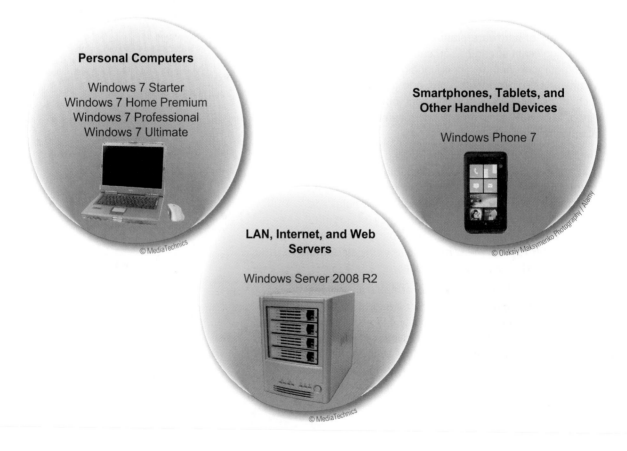

Personal Computers

Windows 7 Starter
Windows 7 Home Premium
Windows 7 Professional
Windows 7 Ultimate

© MediaTechnics

Smartphones, Tablets, and Other Handheld Devices

Windows Phone 7

© Oleksiy Maksymenko Photography / Alamy

LAN, Internet, and Web Servers

Windows Server 2008 R2

© MediaTechnics

MAC OS

▶ **Is Mac OS similar to Windows? Mac OS** stands for Macintosh Operating System and it is the operating system designed for Apple Computer's Macintosh line of computer systems. Although Mac OS was developed several years before Windows, both operating systems feature multiple rectangular work areas to reflect multitasking capabilities. Both operating systems also provide basic networking services.

Unique features of the Mac desktop include the Apple icon, the Dock, and an application menu bar fixed at the top of the screen. Figure 4-17 illustrates some basic features of the Mac desktop.

▶ **What do I need to know about the evolution of Mac OS?** Like Windows, Mac OS has been through a number of revisions. The original Classic Mac OS was introduced in 1984 and designed for a line of Macintosh computers based on the Motorola 68000 microprocessor.

In 2001, Classic Mac OS was rewritten to run on Macintosh computers containing PowerPC microprocessors produced by IBM. The new Mac OS was called Mac OS X (the X can either be pronounced as "ten" or the letter "X"). Mac OS X was much more sophisticated than its predecessor, with better memory management and multitasking capabilities.

In 2006, Macintosh hardware changed significantly with the switch from PowerPC to Intel processors. Mac OS X was again rewritten. The first version of Mac OS X to support the Intel architecture was Mac OS X version 10.4.4, sometimes referred to as Tiger. In 2011, Apple released Mac OS X 10.7 (Lion), which is installed on most of today's Macs (Figure 4-18).

FIGURE 4-17

You can tell when you're using Mac OS by the Apple logo that appears on the menu bar. The Mac OS X interface includes all the standard elements of a GUI, including icons, menus, windows, and taskbars.
▶ Tour the Mac OS desktop and compare it to the Windows desktop.

4

FIGURE 4-18

Mac OS X Timeline

2011	**Mac OS X 10.7 (Lion)** Integrated iPad-style gestures and App Store.
2009	**Mac OS X 10.6 (Snow Leopard)** Enhanced version to increase efficiency and reliability.
2007	**Mac OS X 10.5 (Leopard)** Supported both Intel and PowerPC processors; full support for 64-bit applications.
2006	**Mac OS X 10.4.4 (Tiger Intel)** First OS for Intel Macs.
2001	**Mac OS X 10.1 - 10.4 (Cheetah)** Desktop editions for PowerPC; new kernel based on UNIX-like, open source code.

❱ What are the strengths of Mac OS? Mac OS X has a reputation for being an easy-to-use, reliable, and secure operating system. Back when PC owners were struggling with an inscrutable command-line operating system, Macintosh owners were breezing along with a point-and-click GUI. According to industry observers, Macintosh developers have always been in the lead when it comes to intuitive user interface design.

The operating system kernel of Mac OS X is based on UNIX and includes industrial-strength memory protection features that contribute to a low incidence of errors and glitches. Mac OS X inherited a strong security foundation from UNIX that tends to limit the number of security holes and the damage that can be done by hackers who manage to slip in.

Another factor that contributes to the security of computers running Mac OS is that fewer viruses are designed to target Macs because the user base is much smaller than the Windows user base.

Regardless of the relative security of computers running Mac OS X, Macintosh owners should practice safe computing by applying software and OS patches as they become available, activating wireless network encryption, not opening suspicious e-mail attachments, and not clicking links embedded in e-mail messages.

In addition to reliability and security, Mac OS X offers dual boot options and a good virtual machine platform.

❱ What is dual boot? Mac OS X on an Intel Mac offers the ability to run Windows and Windows application software in addition to software designed for the Macintosh. Software called Boot Camp is a **dual boot** utility that can switch between Mac OS X and Windows. When booting, you can select either Mac OS X or Windows (Figure 4-19). To change operating systems, you have to reboot.

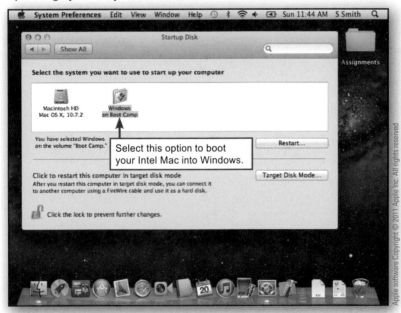

FIGURE 4-19

On a Macintosh computer with Boot Camp, you can boot into Mac OS X or into Windows. ❱ See how it works!

❱ What is a virtual machine? Mac OS X is also a good platform for **virtual machine** (VM) technologies that allow you to use one computer to simulate the hardware and software of another. Each virtual machine has its own simulated processor (or core processor), RAM, video card, input and output ports, and operating system. Each machine can run most software that's compatible with the virtual OS platform.

Popular virtual machine software such as VMware and Parallels Desktop can run on most computers with Intel microprocessors, including Intel Macs, PCs, and generic Linux computers. The computer boots into its native OS such as Mac OS, but users can create a virtual machine running guest operating systems, such as Windows. The virtual machine's desktop appears in a window on the host desktop (Figure 4-20).

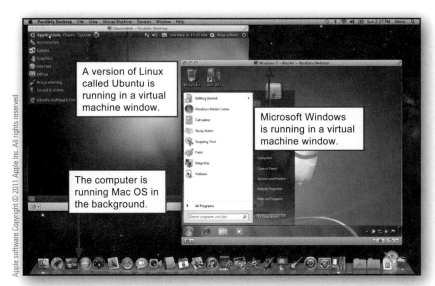

A version of Linux called Ubuntu is running in a virtual machine window.

Microsoft Windows is running in a virtual machine window.

The computer is running Mac OS in the background.

FIGURE 4-20

On a Mac with virtual Windows and Linux, switching from one operating system to another is as simple as selecting a window. When switched to the Windows work area, you can run games, business software, and other applications designed for the Windows OS. By clicking the Linux work area, you could run Linux applications from its vast collection of open source software. After returning to the Mac OS X desktop, you could run your collection of high-end graphics and multimedia iLife software designed exclusively for the Macintosh.

▶ **What are the weaknesses of Mac OS?** The weaknesses of Mac OS include a somewhat limited selection of software and its use of resource forks. A decent collection of software is available for computers that run Mac OS, although the selection is not as vast as the Windows collection. Many of the most prolific software publishers produce one version of their software for Windows and another, similar version for Mac OS.

Macintosh computer owners might find that many popular software titles are not available for Mac OS X. The selection of games, for example, is much sparser than for Windows, although it should be noted that the selection of graphics software for Mac OS X is as good as or better than the selection available for Windows.

▶ **What is a resource fork?** In most operating systems, a file is a single unit that contains data or program code. Files maintained by the Macintosh operating system, however, can have two parts, called forks. The **data fork** is similar to files in other operating systems. It contains data, such as the text for a document, the graphics for a photo, or the commands for a program. The **resource fork** is a companion file that stores information about the data in the data fork, such as the file type and the application that created it.

Although resource forks have advantages on their native Macintosh platform, they can be a nuisance when files are transferred to other platforms. When you copy a file from a Mac to a Windows computer, for example, you end up with two files, one for the data fork and one for the resource fork. The resource fork begins with a period and can usually be ignored or deleted from the Windows directory.

UNIX AND LINUX

▶ **Are UNIX and Linux the same?** The **UNIX** operating system was developed in 1969 at AT&T's Bell Labs. It gained a good reputation for its dependability in multiuser environments, and many versions of it became available for mainframes and microcomputers.

In 1991, a young Finnish student named Linus Torvalds developed the **Linux** (pronounced "LIH nucks") operating system. Linux was inspired by and loosely based on a UNIX derivative called MINIX, created by Andrew Tanenbaum. Linux is frequently used as an operating system for servers. It is not as popular for desktop applications as Windows or Mac OS.

▶ **What are the strengths of Linux?** Linux is rather unique because it is distributed along with its source code under the terms of a GPL (General Public License), which allows everyone to make copies for their own use, to give to others, or to sell. This licensing policy has encouraged programmers to develop Linux utilities, software, and enhancements. Linux is primarily distributed over the Web.

Linux shares several technical features with UNIX, such as multitasking and multiuser capabilities. It is also secure and reliable. The Android, Symbian, and Chromium operating systems for handheld devices are built on the Linux kernel.

▶ **What are the weaknesses of Linux?** Linux typically requires more tinkering than the Windows and Mac desktop operating systems. The comparatively limited number of programs that run under Linux also discourages many nontechnical users. A constantly growing collection of high-quality open source software is becoming available for the Linux platform, but many of these applications are targeted toward business and technical users.

▶ **How do I get Linux?** A **Linux distribution** is a download that contains the Linux kernel, system utilities, graphical user interface, applications, and an installation routine. Beginner-friendly Linux distributions include Fedora, Mandriva, openSUSE, and Ubuntu (Figure 4-21).

FIGURE 4-21

Linux users can choose from several graphical interfaces. Pictured here is the popular Ubuntu graphical desktop. ▶ With your interactive eBook, you can tour Linux and compare it to using Windows and Mac OS.

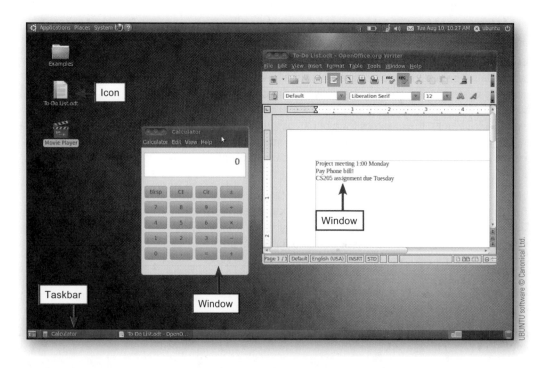

UBUNTU software © Canonical Ltd.

DOS

▶ Why do I keep hearing about DOS? Old-timers in the computer industry sometimes reminisce about DOS. It was the first operating system that many of them used, and its cryptic command-line user interface left an indelible impression.

DOS (which rhymes with "toss") stands for Disk Operating System. It was developed by Microsoft—the same company that later produced Windows—and introduced on the original IBM PC in 1982. Although IBM called this operating system PC-DOS, Microsoft marketed it to other companies under the name MS-DOS.

DOS software, such as VisiCalc, used command-line interfaces and rustic menus that users controlled with the keyboard's arrow keys (Figure 4-22).

FIGURE 4-22

When using VisiCalc, you could press the slash key (/) to call up the main menu, which simply listed the first letter of each command. For example, F was the Format command; so if you wanted to format a cell, you pressed F to see a list of letters, such as *C*, *L*, and *R*—the commands for centering, left alignment, and right alignment.

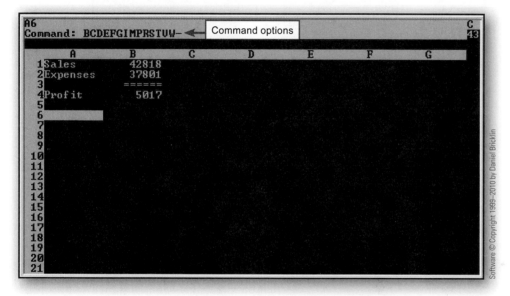

After more than 20 years, remnants of DOS still linger in the world of personal computers because it provided part of the operating system kernel for Windows versions 3.1, 95, 98, and Me.

During the peak of its popularity, thousands of software programs were produced for computers running DOS. You can occasionally find some of these programs on the Internet, and run them using the Command Prompt option accessed from the Windows Start menu. DOS also offers handy troubleshooting utilities, such as Ping, Tracert, Copy, Msconfig, and Netstat, that are used by tech-savvy computer users.

HANDHELD AND TABLET OPERATING SYSTEMS

▶ **What are the options for handheld operating systems?**
Six operating systems dominate the realm of handheld computers: iOS, Symbian, BlackBerry OS, Android OS, Windows Phone 7, and HP webOS, which are shown in Figure 4-23.

FIGURE 4-23

Operating systems for mobile devices feature graphical user interfaces with touch screen input.

iOS

Symbian^3

BlackBerry OS

Android OS

Windows Phone 7

HP webOS

iOS (formerly iPhone OS) is a version of Mac OS X written for the iPhone's ARM processor and optimized for touch-screen communications applications. iOS is also the operating system used for Apple's iPod Touch and iPad tablet computer. It was the first handheld OS to offer routines that manage gesture inputs, such as using your fingers to "squeeze" an on-screen graphic into a smaller size. It also includes apps for stock quotes, maps, and weather reports. iOS is an open platform, which means that programs, called iPhone apps, can be created by third-party programmers.

Symbian is a popular handheld operating system used with Nokia and Ericsson smartphones. In 2010, Symbian became available as an open source operating system, giving developers a free platform to use for developing Symbian mobile applications.

BlackBerry OS is a proprietary operating system produced by RIM, the Canadian company that developed the BlackBerry smartphone. A key feature of BlackBerry OS is its ability to work with corporate e-mail software systems produced by Microsoft and IBM.

Android OS is an open source operating system developed by Google and designed for mobile devices, such as smartphones and netbooks. It is based on the Linux kernel. Users can select from a variety of applications or create their own. Android runs on popular HTC and Motorola phones, as well as on several netbooks, tablet computers, and ebook readers.

Windows Phone 7 replaced Windows Mobile OS in 2010. It features a series of "tiles" that represent applications, contacts, links, or media. With the initial release, multitasking is limited to running only one third-party program at a time.

HP webOS was developed for popular Palm brand PDAs (personal digital assistants) and smartphones. It is based on a system of "cards" that represent applications in a multitasking environment. It is designed to seamlessly interact with social networking sites, such as Facebook and Twitter. In 2011, HP announced that it would discontinue production of all webOS devices. When this book went to print, the future of this operating system was unknown.

▶ **What about tablet operating systems?** Today's tablet computers, such as the iPad and XOOM, use handheld operating systems. Tablets are essentially a physically larger version of handheld smartphones and enhanced media players, so similar hardware support and user interface capabilities are provided by the operating system.

▶ **Are operating systems for handheld devices similar to desktop operating systems?** Operating systems for handheld and desktop devices provide many similar services, such as scheduling processor resources, managing memory, loading programs, managing input and output, and establishing the user interface. But because handheld devices tend to be used for less sophisticated tasks, their operating systems are somewhat simpler and significantly smaller.

Today's handheld operating systems typically support touch screens and include a standard set of apps for e-mail, browsing, playing media, mapping, and scheduling.

4

QuickCheck

1. Microsoft Windows featured the first graphical user interface. True or false? [   ]

2. VMware and Parallels Desktop are examples of [   ] machine technology that can be used to run Windows software on a Mac.

3. An open source operating system called [   ] is the foundation for several handheld operating systems, such as Symbian and Android OS.

4. A resource [   ] is a companion file created by Mac OS to store information about a file and its data.

5. Android OS and iOS are examples of operating systems used for handheld devices. True or false? [   ]

▶ CHECK ANSWERS

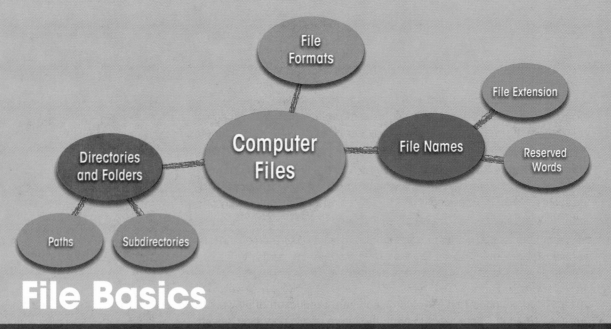

File Basics

SECTION **C**

COMPUTER FILES IN DIGITAL format offer a compact and convenient way to store documents, photos, videos, and music. Computer files have several characteristics, such as a name, format, location, size, and date. To make effective use of computer files, you'll need a good understanding of these file basics, and that is the focus of Section C.

FILE NAMES AND EXTENSIONS

▶ **What is a computer file?** As you learned in Chapter 1, a computer file—or simply a file—is defined as a named collection of data that exists on a storage medium, such as a hard disk, CD, DVD, or USB flash drive. A file can contain a group of records, a document, a photo, music, a video, an e-mail message, or a computer program.

▶ **What are the rules for naming files?** Every file has a name and might also have a file extension. When you save a file, you must provide a valid file name that adheres to specific rules, referred to as **file-naming conventions**. Each operating system has a unique set of file-naming conventions. Figure 4-24 lists file-naming conventions for the current versions of Windows and Mac OS.

▶ **Is there a maximum length for file names?** DOS and Windows 3.1 limited file names to eight characters. With that limitation, it was often difficult to create descriptive file names. A file name such as *HseBud13* might be used for a file containing a household budget for 2013. With such cryptic file names, it was not always easy to figure out what a file contained. As a result, files were sometimes difficult to locate and identify. Today, most operating systems allow you to use longer file names.

Current versions of Windows and Mac OS support file names up to 255 characters long. In practice, some of the 255 characters are used for the file's drive letter, folder designation, and extension, so the name you assign to a file should be much shorter. A file name limitation of 255 characters gives you the flexibility to use descriptive file names, such as *Household Budget 2013*, so that you can easily identify what a file contains.

▶ **What is a file extension?** A **file extension** (sometimes referred to as a file name extension) is an optional file identifier that is separated from the main file name by a period, as in *Paint.exe*. File extensions provide

FIGURE 4-24

Windows File-naming Conventions

Case sensitive	No
Maximum length of file name	File name, path, and extension cannot exceed 255 characters
Spaces allowed	Yes
Numbers allowed	Yes
Characters not allowed	* \ : < > | " / ?
File names not allowed	Aux, Com1, Com2, Com3, Com4, Con, Lpt1, Lpt2, Lpt3, Prn, Nul

Macintosh File-naming Conventions

Case sensitive	No
Maximum length of file name	File name, path, and extension cannot exceed 255 characters
Spaces allowed	Yes
Numbers allowed	Yes
Characters not allowed	: (the colon)

204

clues to a file's contents. For example .exe files (Windows) and .app files (Mac OS) contain computer programs.

▶ Why are certain characters not allowed in a file name? If an operating system attaches special significance to a symbol, you might not be able to use it in a file name. For example, Windows uses the colon (:) character to separate the device letter from a file name or folder, as in *C:Music*. A file name that contains a colon, such as *Report:2010*, is not valid because the operating system would become confused about how to interpret the colon. When you use Windows applications, avoid using the symbols : * \ < > | " / and ? in file names.

▶ What are reserved words? Some operating systems also contain a list of **reserved words** that are used as commands or special identifiers. You cannot use these words alone as a file name. You can, however, use these words as part of a longer file name. For example, under Windows, the file name *Nul* would not be valid, but you could name a file something like *Nul Committee Notes.docx* or *Null Set.exe*.

▶ What else should I know about creating file names? Some operating systems are case sensitive, but not those you regularly work with on personal computers. Feel free to use uppercase and lowercase letters in file names that you create on PCs and Macs.

You can also use spaces in file names. That's a different rule than for e-mail addresses, where spaces are not allowed. You've probably noticed that people often use underscores or periods instead of spaces in e-mail addresses such as Madi_Jones@msu.edu. That convention is not necessary in file names, so a file name such as *Letter to Madi Jones* is valid.

FILE DIRECTORIES AND FOLDERS

▶ How do I designate a file's location? To designate a file's location, you must first specify the device where the file is stored. As shown in Figure 4-25, each of a PC's storage devices is identified by a device letter—a convention that is specific to DOS and Windows. The main hard disk drive is usually referred to as drive C. A device letter is usually followed by a colon, so C: is typically the designation for a hard disk drive.

Although the hard disk drive on a Windows computer is designated as drive C, device letters for CD, DVD, and USB flash drives are not standardized. For example, the CD writer on your computer might be assigned device letter E, whereas the CD writer on another computer might be assigned device letter R.

Macs do not use drive letters. Every storage device has a name. The main hard disk is called Macintosh HD, for example.

▶ What is a disk partition? A **disk partition** is a section of a hard disk drive that is treated as a separate storage unit. Most computers are configured with a single hard disk partition that contains the operating system, programs, and data. However, it is possible to create more than one hard disk partition. For example, a PC owner might set up one partition for operating system files and another partition for programs and data. This arrangement sometimes can speed up the process of disinfecting a computer that has been attacked by malicious software.

Partitions can be assigned drive letters. In the example above, the operating system files would be stored in partition C. The program and data file partition would probably be designated as drive D. Partitions are not the

FIGURE 4-25

The Windows operating system labels storage devices with letters, such as C: and F:.

Drive letter assignments are based on conventions that date back to the first PCs. The original IBM PCs shipped with a single floppy disk drive and it was designated drive A. An enhanced PC later shipped with two floppy disk drives, designated A and B. When hard disk drives were eventually added to PC systems, they were designated drive C.

same thing as folders. Partitions are more permanent, and a special utility is required to create, modify, or delete them.

▶ **Do I have to remember where I put each file?** Your computer's operating system maintains a list of files called a **directory** for each storage disk, CD, DVD, BD, or USB flash drive. The main directory is referred to as the **root directory**. On a PC, the root directory is identified by the device letter followed by a backslash. For example, the root directory of the hard disk would be C:\. A root directory can be subdivided into smaller lists. Each list is called a **subdirectory**.

▶ **What is a folder?** When you use Windows, Mac OS, or a Linux graphical file manager, each subdirectory is depicted as a **folder**. Folders help you envision your files as if they were stored in a filing cabinet. Each folder can hold related items; for example, a set of documents, sound clips, financial data, or photos for a school project. Windows provides a folder called My Documents that you might use to hold reports, letters, and so on. You can also create and name folders to meet your needs, such as a folder called QuickBooks to hold your personal finance data.

Folders can be created within other folders. You might, for example, create a Jazz folder within the Music folder to hold your jazz collection, and another folder named Reggae to hold your reggae music collection.

A folder name is separated from a drive letter and other folder names by a special symbol. In Microsoft Windows, this symbol is the backslash (\). For example, the folder for your reggae music (within the Music folder on drive C) would be written as C:\Music\Reggae. Other operating systems use a forward slash (/) to separate folders.

A computer file's location is defined by a **file specification** (sometimes called a **path**), which on a PC includes the drive letter, folder(s), file name, and extension. Suppose that you have stored an MP3 file called *Marley One Love* in the Reggae folder on your hard disk. Its file specification is shown in Figure 4-26.

FIGURE 4-26

A file specification provides the name and location of a file.

C:\Music\Reggae\Marley One Love.mp3

| Drive letter | Primary folder | Secondary folder | File name | File extension |

▶ **What's the significance of a file's size?** A file contains data, stored as a group of bits. The more bits, the larger the file. **File size** is usually measured in bytes, kilobytes, or megabytes. Knowing the size of a file can be important. Compared to small files, large files fill up storage space more quickly, require longer transmission times, and are more likely to be stripped off e-mail attachments by a mail server. Your computer's operating system keeps track of file sizes and supplies that information when you request a listing of files.

▶ **Is the file date important?** Your computer keeps track of the date that a file was created or last modified. The **file date** is useful if you have created several versions of a file and want to make sure you know which version is the most recent. It can also come in handy if you have downloaded several versions of a software package, such as your printer's device driver, and you want to make sure to install the latest version.

FILE FORMATS

▶ **What is a file format?** The term **file format** refers to the organization and layout of data that is stored in a file. As you might expect, music files are stored differently than text files or graphics files; but even within a single category of data, there are many file formats. For example, graphics data can be stored in file formats such as BMP, GIF, JPEG, or PNG.

The format of a file usually includes a header, data, and possibly an end-of-file marker. A **file header** is a section of data at the beginning of a file that contains information about a file, such as the date it was created, the date it was last updated, its size, and its file type.

The remaining contents of a file depend on whether it contains text, graphics, audio, or multimedia data. A text file, for example, might contain sentences and paragraphs interspersed with codes for centering, boldfacing, and margin settings. A graphics file might contain color data for each pixel, followed by a description of the color palette. Figure 4-27 illustrates the format for a Windows bitmap (BMP) file and contrasts it with the format of a GIF file.

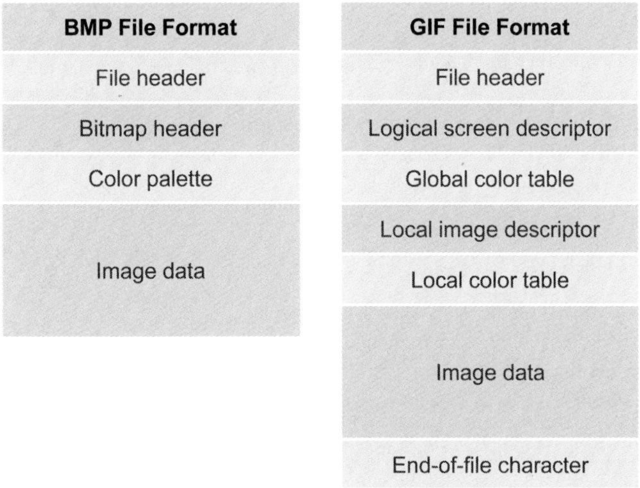

BMP File Format	GIF File Format
File header	File header
Bitmap header	Logical screen descriptor
Color palette	Global color table
	Local image descriptor
Image data	Local color table
	Image data
	End-of-file character

FIGURE 4-27

Although BMP and GIF file formats contain graphics, the file layouts differ.

▶ **Is a file extension the same as a file format?** No. Although a file extension is a good indicator of a file's format, it does not really define the format. You could use the Rename command to change a QuickTime movie called *Balloons.mov* to *Balloons.docx*. Despite the .docx extension, the file is still in QuickTime format because the data elements in the file are arranged in a specific configuration unique to QuickTime.

▶ **What should I know about file formats?** Each software application works with specific file formats. When you use the Open dialog box, most applications automatically comb through your files to display a list of files that are stored in file formats they can use.

Some operating systems also do a fairly good job of shielding users from the intricacies of file formats. For example, Windows uses a file association list to link file formats with corresponding application software so that when you double-click a file name, your computer automatically opens a software application that works with the correct file format.

With all this help from the operating system and your application software, it might seem that knowing about file formats is unimportant. However, understanding file formats is useful for accomplishing tasks such as those listed in Figure 4-28.

FIGURE 4-28

Understanding file formats helps you perform the following tasks:

▶ Figure out the correct format for e-mail attachments that you send to friends or colleagues.

▶ Find the right player software for music and media files that you download from the Web.

▶ Discover how to work with a file that doesn't seem to open.

▶ Convert files from one format to another.

▶ Which file formats am I most likely to encounter? A Windows software program typically consists of at least one executable file with an .exe file extension. It might also include a number of support programs with extensions such as .dll, .vbx, and .ocx. Configuration and startup files usually have .bat, .sys, .ini, and .bin extensions. In addition, you'll find files with .hlp and .tmp extensions. Files with .hlp extensions hold the information for a program's Help utility.

Files with .tmp extensions are temporary files. When you open a data file with software applications, such as word processors, spreadsheets, and graphics tools, your operating system makes a copy of the original file and stores this copy on disk as a temporary file. It is this temporary file that you work with as you view and revise a file.

To the uninitiated, the file extensions associated with programs and the operating system might seem odd. Nevertheless, executable and support files—even so-called temporary files—are crucial for the correct operation of your computer system. You should not manually delete them. The table in Figure 4-29 lists file extensions associated with the Windows operating system and executable files.

FIGURE 4-29

Executable File Extensions

Type of File	Description	Extension
Batch file	A sequence of operating system commands executed automatically when the computer boots	.bat
Configuration file	Information about programs the computer uses to allocate the resources necessary to run them	.cfg .sys .mif .bin .ini
Help	The information displayed by on-screen Help	.hlp
Temporary file	A sort of scratch pad that contains data while a file is open, but is discarded when you close the file	.tmp
Support program	Program instructions executed along with the main .exe file for a program	.ocx .vbx .vbs .dll
Program	The main executable files for a computer program	.exe .com .app (Mac OS)

The list of data file formats is long, but becoming familiar with the most popular formats (shown in Figure 4-30) and the type of data they contain is useful, whether you are using a PC or Mac.

FIGURE 4-30

Data File Extensions

Type of File	Extensions
Text	.txt .dat .rtf .doc (Microsoft Word 2003) .docx (Word 2007 and 2010) .odt (OpenDocument text) .wpd (WordPerfect) .pages (iWork)
Sound	.wav .mid .mp3 .m4p .aac .au .ra (RealAudio)
Graphics	.bmp .tif .wmf .gif .jpg .png .eps .ai (Adobe Illustrator)
Animation/video	.flc .swf .avi .mpg .mp4 .mov (QuickTime) .rm (RealMedia) .wmv (Windows Media Player)
Web page	.htm .html .asp .vrml .php
Spreadsheet	.xls (Microsoft Excel 2003) .xlsx (Excel 2007 and 2010) .ods (OpenDocument spreadsheet) .numbers (iWork)
Database	.accdb (Microsoft Access) .odb (OpenDocument database)
Miscellaneous	.pdf (Adobe Acrobat) .pptx (Microsoft PowerPoint 2007 and 2010) .qxp (QuarkXPress) .odp (OpenDocument presentations) .zip (WinZip) .pub (Microsoft Publisher)

How do I know which files a program will open? A software application can open files that exist in its **native file format**, plus several additional file formats. For example, Microsoft Word opens files in its native DOCX (.docx) format, plus files in formats such as HTML (.htm or .html), Text (.txt), and Rich Text Format (.rtf).

Within the Windows environment, you can discover which formats a particular software program can open by looking at the list of file types in the Open dialog box, as shown in Figure 4-31.

FIGURE 4-31

An application's Open dialog box usually displays a list of file formats the program can open. You can also look for an Import option on the File menu.

4

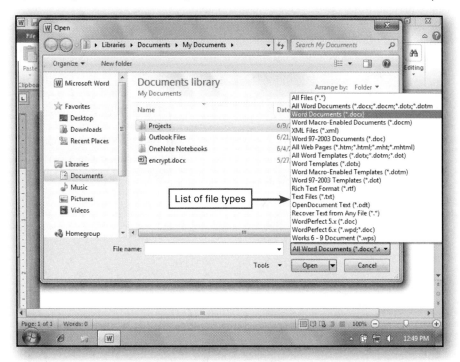

Why can't I open some files? Suppose you receive an e-mail attachment called *Cool.tif*. "Aha!," you say to yourself, "My Photoshop software ought to open that file." You try—several times—but all you get is an error message. When a file doesn't open, one of three things probably went wrong:

- The file might have been damaged—a techie would call it corrupted—by a transmission or disk error. Although you might be able to use file recovery software to repair the damage, it is usually easier to obtain an undamaged copy of the file from its original source.

- Someone might have inadvertently changed the file extension. While renaming the *Cool* file, perhaps the original .bmp extension was changed to .tif. If you have a little time, you can change the file extension and try to open the file. If a file contains a graphic, chances are that it should have the extension for one of the popular graphics formats, such as .bmp, .gif, .jpg, .tif, or .png. Otherwise, you should contact the source of the file to get accurate information about its real format.

- Some file formats exist in several variations, and your software might not have the capability to open a particular variation of the format. You might be able to open the file if you use different application software. For example, Photoshop might not be able to open a particular file with a .tif file extension, but Corel PaintShop Pro might open it.

▶ What if all my software fails to open a particular file format? Although a computer might be able to discover a file's format, it might not necessarily know how to work with it. Just as you might be able to identify a helicopter, you can't necessarily fly it without some instructions. Your computer also requires a set of instructions to use most file formats. These instructions are provided by software. To use a particular file format, you must make sure your computer has the corresponding software.

Many files downloaded from the Web require special player or reader software. For example, PDF files require software called Adobe Reader, Flash video files require the Adobe Flash Player, and OGG music files require a player such as Winamp. Suppose you download a file with an .ogg extension and none of your current software works with this file format (Figure 4-32).

FIGURE 4-32

A download from the music group Epoq is in OGG format. To play the file, you'll need software that works with the OGG file format.

Typically, you can follow a link from the Web page that supplied your file download to find a site from which you can download the necessary player or reader software. When such a link is not provided, you can google the file type or extension. Several Web sites provide lists of file formats and corresponding software. By looking up a file extension in one of these lists, you can find out what application software you'll need to download and install.

▶ How do I know what kinds of file formats I can send to other people? Unless you know what application software is installed on your friends' computers, you won't know for certain whether they can open a particular file you've sent. There's a good chance, however, that your friends can open files saved in common document formats such as Microsoft Word's DOCX or Adobe Reader's PDF format; graphics formats such as PNG, TIFF, or JPEG; and music formats such as MP3 and WAV. You should check with the recipient before sending files in less common, proprietary formats, such as Adobe Illustrator's AI format and QuarkXPress's QXP format.

▶ Is it possible to convert a file from one format to another? Perhaps you created a Word document on your PC, but you need to convert it into a format that's usable by your colleague who is using LibreOffice Writer. Or suppose you want to convert a Word document into HTML format so that you can post it on the Web. You might also want to convert a BMP graphic into JPEG format so that you can include it on a Web page.

The easiest way to convert a file from one format to another is to find application software that works with both file formats. Open the file using that software, and then use the Export option, or the Save As dialog box, to select a new file format, assign the file a new name, and save it (Figure 4-33).

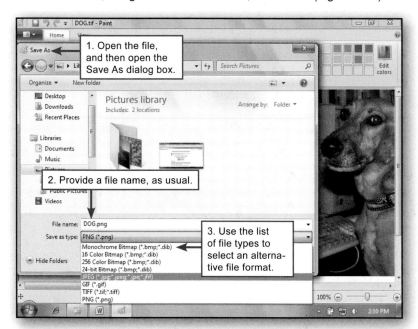

FIGURE 4-33

An easy way to convert a file from one format to another is to open it with an application that supports both file formats, and then use the Save As dialog box to select an alternative file format. ▶ Discover the native file formats for Adobe Reader and Windows Paint. Your interactive eBook also shows you how to adjust the Windows setting for showing or hiding file extensions.

▶ Will a converted document be identical to the original?
Many file formats convert easily to another format, and the resulting file is virtually indistinguishable from the original. Some conversions, however, do not retain all the characteristics of the original file. When you convert a DOCX file into HTML format, for example, the HTML page does not contain any of the headers, footers, superscripts, page numbers, special characters, or page breaks that existed in the original DOCX file.

When you need a conversion routine for an obscure file format, or if you need to make conversions between many different file formats, consider specialized conversion software, available through commercial or shareware outlets.

QuickCheck

1. .bmp, .docx, .exe, and .mov are examples of file [   ] .

2. When using Windows, you cannot use a(n) [   ] word, such as Aux, as a file name.

3. A disk [   ] is a section of a hard disk drive that is treated as a separate storage unit.

4. A software application automatically stores files in its [   ] file format unless you specify otherwise.

5. When you convert a DOCX file into HTML format, the resulting file is virtually indistinguishable from the original. True or false? [   ]

 CHECK ANSWERS

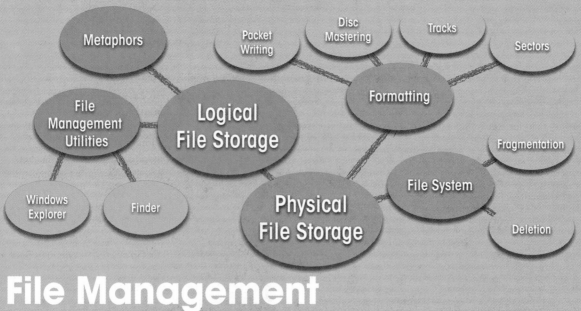

File Management

SECTION D

FILE MANAGEMENT ENCOMPASSES any procedure that helps you organize your computer-based files so that you can find and use them more efficiently. Depending on your computer's operating system, you can organize and manipulate files from within an application program or by using a special file management utility provided by the operating system. Section D offers an overview of application-based and operating system-based file management.

APPLICATION-BASED FILE MANAGEMENT

▶ How does a software application help me manage files? Applications generally provide a way to open files and save them in a specific folder on a designated storage device. Additional file management capabilities include deleting, copying, and renaming files.

Some applications also allow you to add tags for a file. A **file tag** in the context of Windows is a piece of information that describes a file. Tags are particularly handy for files that contain photos because you can describe the location, note camera settings, and name people pictured in the shot. Figure 4-34 illustrates the process of saving a file and adding tags.

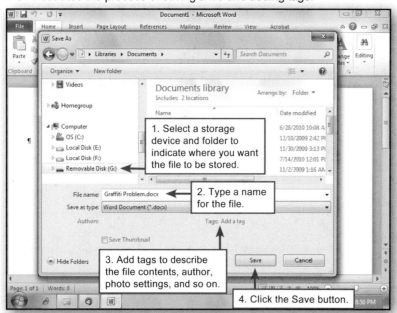

FIGURE 4-34

The Save As dialog box is used to name a file and specify its storage location. Here a file called Graffiti Problem is being saved on a USB flash drive.
▶ Learn more about the Save As dialog box and sort out the differences between it and the Save option.

❱ What's the difference between the Save option and the Save As option? Most applications provide a curious set of options on the File menu. In addition to the Save As option, the menu contains a Save option. The difference between the two options is subtle, but useful.

The Save As option allows you to select a name and storage device for a file, whereas the Save option simply saves the latest version of a file under its current name and at its current location.

A potentially confusing situation occurs when you try to use the Save option for a file that doesn't yet have a name. Because you can't save a file without a name, your application displays the Save As dialog box, even though you selected the Save option. The flowchart in Figure 4-35 can help you decide whether to use the Save or Save As command.

❱ What other options are available in the Save As dialog box? When you use application software, activities such as opening files and saving files require the software to interact with the operating system's file management system. When you create a file, the operating system needs to know its name. When you look for a file, the application software has to check with the operating system to get a list of available files.

You might have noticed that the Open and Save dialog boxes look the same for most of the applications that you use. That is because today's application software typically calls on the operating system to provide these dialog boxes. So, when you use Audacity, Adobe Illustrator, or other third-party Windows software, the Open and Save dialog boxes are essentially the same. Figure 4-36 illustrates some of the file management tasks you can accomplish while using the Save As dialog box.

FIGURE 4-35

Should I use the Save or Save As command?

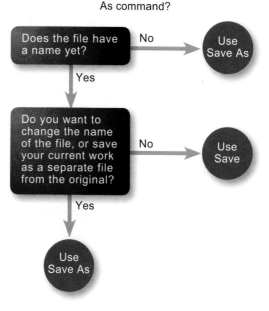

4

FIGURE 4-36

The Save As command of most Windows applications uses a standard dialog box provided by the operating system, so you can carry out a wide variety of file and folder tasks such as creating, renaming, and deleting files.

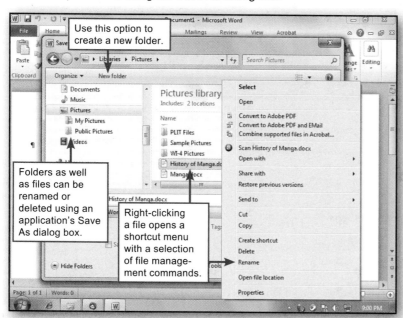

FILE MANAGEMENT UTILITIES

❱ How does the operating system help me manage files?

Although most application software gives you access to commands you can use to save, open, rename, and delete individual files, you might want to work with groups of files or perform other file operations that are inconvenient within the Open or Save dialog boxes.

Most operating systems provide a **file management utility** that gives you the big picture of the files you have stored on your disks and helps you work with them. For example, Mac OS X provides a file management utility called Finder. Windows 7 provides a file management utility called Windows Explorer that can be accessed from the folder icon on the taskbar or from the first six buttons on the Start menu. Utilities such as these help you view a list of files, find files, move files from one place to another, make copies of files, delete files, discover file properties, and rename files (Figure 4-37).

FIGURE 4-37

Windows Explorer can be tailored to show files as lists (top), icons (middle), or tiles (bottom).

▶ The tour for this figure in your interactive eBook shows you how to start Windows Explorer and use it to view files.

FILE MANAGEMENT METAPHORS

▶ **How can a file management utility help me visualize my computer's file storage?** File management utilities often use some sort of storage metaphor to help you visualize and mentally organize the files on your disks and other storage devices. These metaphors are also called **logical storage models** because they are supposed to help you form a mental (logical) picture of the way in which your files are stored.

▶ **What storage metaphors are typically used for personal computers?** After hearing so much about files and folders, you might have guessed that the filing cabinet is a popular metaphor for computer storage. In this metaphor, each storage device corresponds to one of the drawers in a filing cabinet. The drawers hold folders and the folders hold files.

Another storage metaphor is based on a hierarchical diagram that is sometimes referred to as a tree structure. In this metaphor, a tree represents a storage device.

The trunk of the tree corresponds to the root directory. The branches of the tree represent folders. These branches can split into small branches representing folders within folders. The leaves at the end of a branch represent the files in a particular folder. Figure 4-38 illustrates the tree lying on its side so that you can see the relationship to the metaphor shown in Figure 4-39.

The tree structure metaphor offers a useful mental image of the way in which files and folders are organized. It is not, however, particularly practical as a user interface. Imagine the complexity of the tree diagram from Figure 4-38 if it were expanded to depict branches for hundreds of folders and leaves for thousands of files.

For practicality, storage metaphors are translated into more mundane screen displays. Figure 4-39 shows how Microsoft programmers combined the filing cabinet metaphor to depict a tree structure in the Windows Explorer file management utility.

FIGURE 4-38

You can visualize the directory of a disk as a tree on its side. The trunk corresponds to the root directory, the branches to folders, and the leaves to files.

FIGURE 4-39

Windows Explorer borrows folders from the filing cabinet metaphor and places them in a hierarchical structure similar to a tree on its side.

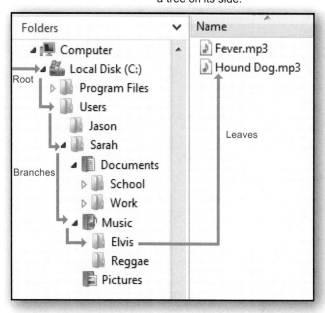

4

WINDOWS EXPLORER

▶ **How do I use a file management utility?** As an example of a file management utility, take a closer look at **Windows Explorer**, a utility program bundled with the Windows operating system and designed to help you organize and manipulate the files stored on your computer.

The Windows Explorer window is divided into several window panes. The pane on the left side of the window lists each of the storage devices connected to your computer, plus several important system objects, such as Desktop and Computer.

An icon for a storage device or other system object can be expanded by clicking its corresponding ▷ symbol. Expanding an icon displays the next level of the storage hierarchy—usually a collection of folders.

A device icon or folder can be opened by clicking directly on the icon rather than on the ▷ symbol. Once an icon is opened, its contents appear in the pane on the right side of the Windows Explorer window. Figure 4-40 illustrates how to manipulate the directory display.

FIGURE 4-40

Windows Explorer makes it easy to drill down through the levels of the directory hierarchy to locate a folder or file.
▶ Learn how to navigate through the hierarchy of folders by watching the tour for this figure in your interactive eBook.

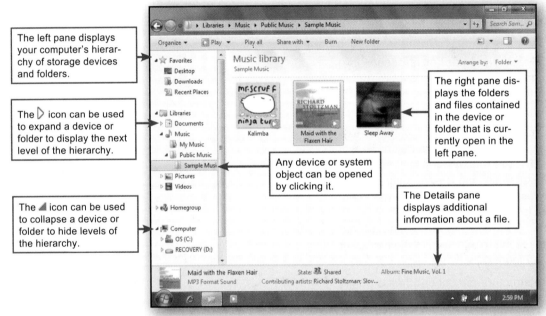

The left pane displays your computer's hierarchy of storage devices and folders.

The ▷ icon can be used to expand a device or folder to display the next level of the hierarchy.

The ◢ icon can be used to collapse a device or folder to hide levels of the hierarchy.

The right pane displays the folders and files contained in the device or folder that is currently open in the left pane.

Any device or system object can be opened by clicking it.

The Details pane displays additional information about a file.

▶ **What can I do with the folders and files that are listed in Windows Explorer?** In addition to locating files and folders, Windows Explorer helps you manipulate files and folders in the following ways:

▶ Rename. You might want to change the name of a file or folder to better describe its contents.

▶ Copy. You can copy a file from one device to another—for example, from a USB drive to the hard disk drive. You can also make a copy of a document so that you can revise the copy and leave the original intact.

▶ Move. You can move a file from one folder to another or from one storage device to another. When you move a file, it is erased from its original location, so make sure you remember the new location of the file. You can also move an entire folder and its contents from one storage device to another storage device, or move it to a different folder.

▶ Delete. You can delete a file when you no longer need it. You can also delete a folder. Be careful when you delete a folder because most file management utilities also delete all the files within a folder.

▶ Can I work with more than one file or folder at a time?
To work with a group of files or folders, you must first select them. You can accomplish this task in several ways. You can hold down the Ctrl key (Command key on the Mac) as you click each item. This method works well if you are selecting files or folders that are not listed consecutively.

As an alternative, you can hold down the Shift key while you click the first item and the last item you want to select. By using the Shift key method, you select the two items that you clicked and all the items in between. After a group of items is selected, you can use the same copy, move, or delete procedure that you would use for a single item.

▶ What are personal folders?
Windows offers a set of preconfigured personal folders, such as My Documents and My Music, for storing your personal data files. Windows also supplies preconfigured Public folders, such as Public Documents and Public Pictures, that can be used to store files you want to share with other network users (Figure 4-41).

▶ What is a library?
In addition to folders, Windows 7 offers libraries that are handy for organizing and accessing files that you use for projects. A **library** is similar to a folder only in the sense that it can be used to group similar files; however, a library doesn't actually store files. Instead, it contains a set of links to files that are stored on various devices and in various folders.

Macs also have a Library folder, but its purpose is quite different from the Windows Library folder. The Mac Library folder is used for system files and should not be used for your data files.

To understand how you might use libraries in Windows, think about a collection of music files. Some files might be stored on your hard disk in the My Music folder. Other music might be stored on an external hard drive in a folder called Jazz. Your Music library can contain links to the music files in both folders so that you can access them all from the same list (Figure 4-42).

FIGURE 4-41

Windows supplies a set of preconfigured personal folders and a corresponding set of Public folders.

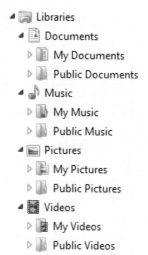

FIGURE 4-42

A library is not a "real" location; it is more like an index in a book because it points to the location of a file.

▶ Find out how to use libraries to organize files for your projects.

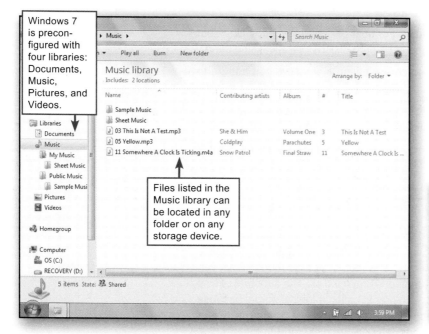

Windows 7 is preconfigured with four libraries: Documents, Music, Pictures, and Videos.

Files listed in the Music library can be located in any folder or on any storage device.

TERMINOLOGY NOTE

In Windows, libraries and personal folders have similar names, which can be confusing. Personal folders are labeled with "My" as in My Documents. The name of the corresponding library is simply Documents.

FILE MANAGEMENT TIPS

A file management utility provides tools and procedures to help you keep track of your program and data files, but these tools are most useful when you have a logical plan for organizing your files and when you follow some basic file management guidelines. Consider the following tips for managing files on your own computer. When working with files on lab computers, follow the guidelines from your instructor or lab manager.

▶ **Use descriptive names.** Give your files and folders descriptive names, and avoid using cryptic abbreviations.

▶ **Maintain file extensions.** When renaming a file, keep the original file extension so that it can be opened with the correct application software.

▶ **Group similar files.** Separate files into folders based on subject matter. For example, store your creative writing assignments in one folder and your MP3 music files in another folder.

▶ **Organize your folders from the top down.** When devising a hierarchy of folders, consider how you want to access files and back them up. For example, it is easy to specify one folder and its subfolders for a backup. If your important data is scattered in a variety of folders, however, making backups is more time consuming.

▶ **Consider using default folders.** You should use personal folders, such as My Documents and My Music, as your main data folders. Add subfolders to these personal folders as necessary to organize your files.

▶ **Use Public folders for files you want to share.** Use the Public folders for files that you want to share with other network users.

▶ **Do not mix data files and program files.** Do not store data files in the folders that hold your software—on Windows systems, most software is stored in subfolders of the Program Files folder; on Macs, in the Applications folder.

▶ **Don't store files in the root directory.** Although it is acceptable to create folders in the root directory, it is not a good practice to store programs or data files in the root directory of your computer's hard disk.

▶ **Access files from the hard disk.** For best performance, copy files from USB drives or CDs to your computer's hard disk before accessing them.

▶ **Follow copyright rules.** When copying files, make sure you adhere to copyright and license restrictions.

▶ **Delete or archive files you no longer need.** Deleting unneeded files and folders helps keep your list of files from growing to an unmanageable size.

▶ **Be aware of storage locations.** When you save files, be sure to specify the correct storage device and folder.

▶ **Back up!** Back up your folders regularly.

PHYSICAL FILE STORAGE

▶ **Is data stored in specific places on a disk?** So far, you've seen how an operating system such as Windows can help you visualize computer storage as files and folders. This logical storage model, however, has little to do with what actually happens on your disk. The structure of files and folders you see in Windows Explorer is called a logical model because it is supposed to help you create a mental picture. A **physical storage model** describes what actually happens on the disks and in the circuits. As you will see, the physical model is quite different from the logical model.

Before a computer can store a file on a disk, CD, DVD, or BD, the storage medium must be formatted. The **formatting** process creates the equivalent of electronic storage bins by dividing a disk into **tracks** and then further dividing each track into **sectors**.

Tracks and sectors are numbered to provide addresses for each data storage bin. The numbering scheme depends on the storage device and the operating system. On hard disks, tracks are arranged as concentric circles; on CDs, DVDs, and BDs, one or more tracks spiral out from the center of the disk (Figure 4-43).

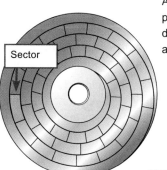

FIGURE 4-43

A process called formatting prepares the surface of a disk to hold data in storage areas called sectors.

4

▶ **How does a disk get formatted?** Today, most hard disks are preformatted at the factory. CDs, DVDs, and BDs are formatted by the utilities that you use when you copy data files to them. Before you write data to a CD, DVD, or BD, you usually have the option of formatting it for mastering or for packet writing (Figure 4-44).

▶ **Disc mastering** is the process of creating a CD, DVD, or BD by selecting all the files and then copying them in a single session. The process can take some time—especially when burning a full DVD or BD. Mastered discs are compatible with the largest number of computer optical drives and standalone players. Mastering also works well if you want to burn several copies of a disc.

▶ **Packet writing** is a recording technology that lets you record in multiple sessions. For example, you can copy a few files to a CD during one session, and then at a later date record additional files to the same CD. In Windows terminology, CDs, DVDs, and BDs formatted for packet writing are referred to as Live File System discs.

Packet writing is faster and more flexible than mastering, but discs created with packet writing might not work on all computers. A process called closing helps make the discs more compatible; but once a disc is closed, no more data can be added to it.

FIGURE 4-44

CDs and DVDs can be created using mastering or packet-writing techniques. Mastering creates discs that can be used more reliably on a wide variety of computers and standalone players. Packet writing is more flexible for discs that you plan to use only on your own computer.

▶ **How does the operating system keep track of a file's location?** The operating system uses a **file system** to keep track of the names and locations of files that reside on a storage medium, such as a hard disk. Different operating systems use different file systems. For example, Mac OS X uses the Macintosh Hierarchical File System Plus (HFS+). Ext3fs (Third Extended File System) is the native file system for Linux. Microsoft Windows 7, NT, 2000, XP, and Vista use a file system called NTFS (New Technology File System).

To speed up the process of storing and retrieving data, a disk drive usually works with a group of sectors called a **cluster** or a block. The number of sectors that form a cluster varies, depending on the capacity of the disk and the way the operating system works with files. A file system's primary task is to maintain a list of clusters and keep track of which are empty and which hold data. This information is stored in a special index file. If your computer uses NTFS, the index file is called the Master File Table (MFT).

Each of your disks contains its own index file so that information about its contents is always available when the disk is in use. Unfortunately, storing this crucial file on disk also presents a risk because if the index file is damaged by a hard disk head crash or corrupted by a virus, you'll generally lose access to all the data stored on the disk. Index files become damaged all too frequently, so it is important to back up your data.

When you save a file, your PC's operating system looks at the index file to see which clusters are empty. It selects one of these empty clusters, records the file data there, and then revises the index file to include the new file name and its location.

A file that does not fit into a single cluster spills over into the next contiguous (meaning adjacent) cluster, unless that cluster already contains data. When contiguous clusters are not available, the operating system stores parts of a file in noncontiguous (nonadjacent) clusters. Figure 4-45 helps you visualize how an index file, such as the MFT, keeps track of file names and locations.

FIGURE 4-45

Each colored cluster on the disk contains part of a file. *Bio.txt* is stored in contiguous clusters. *Jordan.wks* is stored in noncontiguous clusters. A computer locates and displays the *Jordan.wks* file by looking for its name in the Master File Table.

Master File Table

File	Cluster	Comment
MFT	1	Reserved for MFT files
DISK USE	2	Part of MFT that contains list of empty sectors
Bio.txt	3, 4	Bio.txt file stored in clusters 3 and 4
Jordan.wks	7, 8, 10	Jordan.wks file stored noncontiguously in clusters 7, 8, and 10
Pick.bmp	9	Pick.bmp file stored in cluster 9

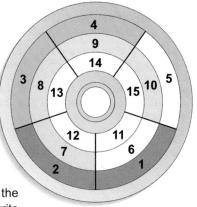

When you want to retrieve a file, the operating system looks through the index for the file name and its location. It moves the disk drive's read-write head to the first cluster that contains the file data. Using additional data from the index file, the operating system can move the read-write heads to each of the clusters containing the remaining parts of the file.

▶ What happens when a file is deleted? When you click a file's icon and then select the Delete option, you might have visions of the read-write head somehow scrubbing out the clusters that contain data. That doesn't happen. Instead, the operating system simply changes the status of the file's clusters to "empty" and removes the file name from the index file. The file name no longer appears in a directory listing, but the file's data remains in the clusters until a new file is stored there.

You might think that this data is as good as erased, but it is possible to purchase utilities that recover a lot of this supposedly deleted data. Law enforcement agents, for example, use these utilities to gather evidence from deleted files on the computer disks of suspected criminals.

To delete data from a disk in such a way that no one can ever read it, you can use special **file shredder software** that overwrites supposedly empty sectors with random 1s and 0s. This software is handy if you plan to donate your computer to a charitable organization, and you want to make sure your personal data no longer remains on the hard disk.

▶ Can deleted files be undeleted? The Windows Recycle Bin and similar utilities in other operating systems are designed to protect you from accidentally deleting hard disk files you actually need. Instead of marking a file's clusters as available, the operating system moves the file to the Recycle Bin folder. The deleted file still takes up space on the disk, but does not appear in the usual directory listing.

Files in the Recycle Bin folder can be undeleted so that they again appear in the regular directory. The Recycle Bin can be emptied to permanently delete any files it contains.

▶ How does a disk become fragmented? As a computer writes files on a disk, parts of files tend to become scattered all over the disk. These **fragmented files** are stored in noncontiguous clusters. Drive performance generally declines as the read-write heads move back and forth to locate the clusters containing the parts of a file. To regain peak performance, you can use a **defragmentation utility**, such as Windows Disk Defragmenter, to rearrange the files on a disk so that they are stored in contiguous clusters (Figure 4-46).

FIGURE 4-46

Defragmenting a disk helps your computer operate more efficiently. Consider using a defragmentation utility at least once a month to keep your computer running in top form. ▶ Your interactive eBook shows you how to defragment your computer's hard disk and how to find out how much space is available for storing files.

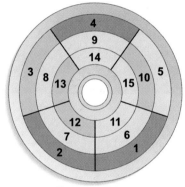

Fragmented disk

On the fragmented disk (left), the purple, orange, and blue files are stored in noncontiguous clusters.

When the disk is defragmented (right), the sectors of data for each file are moved to contiguous clusters.

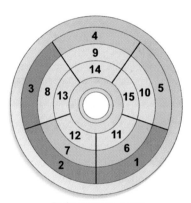

Defragmented disk

QuickCheck   SECTION D

1. Suppose you open a file and edit it, and then want to save it with a different name. You can use the Save option from the File menu. True or false? [   ]

2. [   ] file storage models, such as a filing cabinet or tree metaphor, help you visualize the organization of your computer files.

3. Windows 7 offers a preconfigured Documents [   ] that's designed to hold links to document files stored in various folders.

4. A hard disk stores data in concentric circles called [   ], which are divided into wedge-shaped [   ].

5. The acronyms NTFS, HFS+, and MFT pertain to [   ] file storage models.

 CHECK ANSWERS

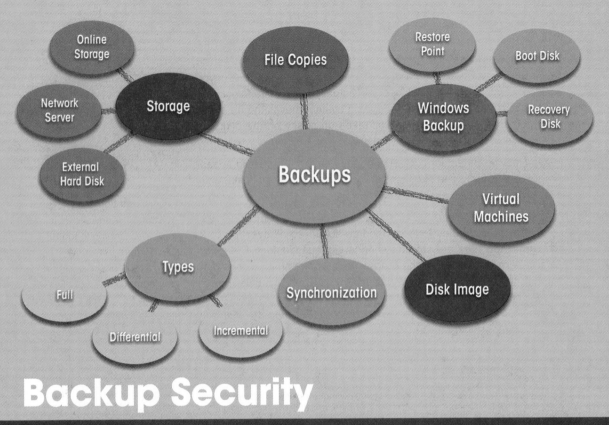

Backup Security

COMPUTER EXPERTS UNIVERSALLY recommend that you back up your data. It sounds pretty basic, right? Unfortunately, this advice tells you what to do, not how to do it. It fails to address some key questions, such as: Do I need special backup equipment and software? How often should I make a backup? How many of my files should I back up? What should I do with the backups? In this section, you'll find the answers to your questions about backing up data that's stored on personal and handheld computers.

BACKUP BASICS

▶ Why do I need to make backups? Have you ever mistakenly copied an old version of a document over a new version? Has your computer's hard disk drive gone on the fritz? Did a virus wipe out your files? Did your smartphone fail? These kinds of data disasters are not rare; they can happen to everyone.

You can't always prevent data disasters, so you should have a **backup** that stores the files needed to recover data that's been wiped out by operator error, viruses, or hardware failures. Backups allow you to **restore** data from a backup to the original storage location or to a replacement device.

▶ How often should I back up my data? Your backup schedule depends on how much data you can afford to lose. If you're working on an important project, you might want to back up the project files several times a day. Under normal use, however, most people schedule a once-a-week backup. If you work with a To Do list, use it to remind yourself when to make a backup or verify that your automated backup has been completed.

▶ How can I be sure that my backup works? You should test your backup by trying to restore one file. Restore the test file to a different drive or folder to avoid overwriting the original file.

▶ Where should I store my backups? You can choose to store backups on local devices such as an external hard disk or a USB flash drive, or you might consider storing your backup on a server in a local network or on an Internet-based server (Figure 4-47).

FIGURE 4-47

The device that holds your backups depends on what you want to back up.

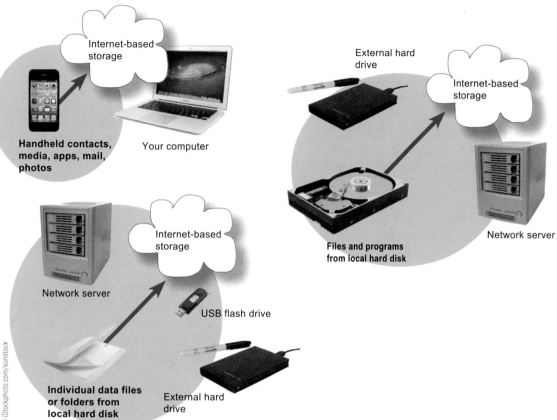

Internet-based storage

Handheld contacts, media, apps, mail, photos

Your computer

External hard drive

Internet-based storage

Files and programs from local hard disk

Network server

Network server

Internet-based storage

USB flash drive

Individual data files or folders from local hard disk

External hard drive

© iStockphoto.com/sunstock

▶ What's better: online backups or local backups? There are advantages and disadvantages for each. Local storage is the traditional route. Your backups are under your control, but they are vulnerable to theft and damage.

If your backups are local, keep them in a safe place. Don't leave them on your computer desk because a fire or flood that damages your computer could also wipe out your backups. In addition, a thief who steals your computer might also scoop up nearby equipment and media. Storing your backups at a different location is the best idea. If off-site storage isn't practical, at least move them to a room apart from your computer.

Web sites that offer storage space for backups are called **online backup services**. The cost of these services usually depends on the amount of storage space that's allocated to you.

Before depending on remote backups, however, be aware that the speed for backing up and restoring your data is only as fast as your Internet connection. Also, remote data is more prone to snooping by employees, hackers, and overzealous government agents; you might want to encrypt your remote backup data, but make sure you don't lose your encryption key or your backup data will be useless.

You should also be aware that a backup service might close down without giving much notice to its users. Use an additional backup location for your really important files.

TERMINOLOGY NOTE

Online backup services are also referred to as remote backup services or managed backup services.

FILE COPIES

▶ What's the easiest way to back up my important data?
The most important files on your computer contain the documents, images, and other data that you've created. These files are unique and might be difficult to reproduce. An easy way to back up your important data is simply by copying selected files to a USB flash drive or to an external hard disk. To copy important files manually, you can use the Copy and Paste commands supplied by your computer's file management software.

▶ Which data files should I back up?
If your strategy is to back up important data files, the procedure can be simplified if you've stored all these files in one folder and its subfolders. For example, Windows users might store their data files in the preconfigured folders for their user accounts.

Folders such as My Documents, My Music, and My Pictures are all stored as subfolders of your user folder. With your data files organized under the umbrella of a single folder, you are less likely to omit an important file when you make backups.

Some applications, such as financial software, create files and update them without your direct intervention. If you have the option during setup, make sure these files are stored in one of your personal folders. Otherwise, you must discover the location of the files and make sure they are backed up with the rest of your data.

In addition to data files you create, a few other types of data files might be important to you. Consider making backups of the files listed in Figure 4-48.

FIGURE 4-48

Back up these files in addition to your documents, graphics, and music files.

- **E-mail folders.** If you're using local e-mail software, your e-mail folder contains all the messages you've sent and received, but not deleted. Check the Help menu on your e-mail program to discover the location of these files.

- **E-mail address book.** Your e-mail address book might be stored separately from your e-mail messages. To find the file on a Windows computer, use the Search or Find option on the Start menu to search for "Address Book" (XP) or "Contacts" (Windows 7 and Vista).

- **Favorite URLs.** If you're attached to the URLs you've collected in your Favorites or Bookmarks list, you might want to back up the file that contains this list. To find the file, search your hard disk for "Favorites" or "Bookmarks." As an alternative method, check your browser for an option that exports your favorite URLs.

- **Internet connection information.** Your ISP's phone number and IP address, your user ID, and your password are often stored in an encrypted file somewhere in the Windows\System folder. Your ISP can usually help you find this file.

- **Downloads.** If you paid to download software, you might want to back it up so that you don't have to pay for it again. Downloaded software usually arrives in the form of a compressed .zip file. For backup purposes, the .zip file should be all you need.

- **Validation codes and other configuration information.** If you keep a running list of validation or activation codes that correspond to your software, then it is important to copy this information in case your hard disk crashes and you have to reinstall your software.

▶ How do I restore files from my data file backups?
Restoring from a data file backup is easy. You simply copy files from your backup to your hard disk. If, for example, you inadvertently delete an important file and discover that you have done so only after you've cleaned out your computer's Recycle Bin, then you can retrieve the file from your backup.

▶ Are file backups sufficient protection against data disasters?
Your computer system contains programs and configuration settings in addition to your data files. Your computer setup is unique and you can't capture it by simply backing up your data files. If you want to be able to restore your computer to its current state, you need to back up all of its files using synchronization software, backup software, imaging software, or virtual machine technology.

SYNCHRONIZATION

▶ **What is synchronization?** **Synchronization** compares the content of files on two devices and makes them the same. It can be used for backup because it dynamically maintains a parallel set of files on your computer's hard disk and your backup device.

▶ **How does synchronization software work?** A program called Time Machine supplied with Mac OS X is a good example of synchronization software. It works by first making a backup of every file from the computer's primary storage device. Every hour, Time Machine checks the files on your computer's primary storage device and synchronizes any files that have been changed. This procedure ensures that your backup is never more than an hour old.

The number of backups you can retain—days', weeks', or months' worth—depends on the capacity of your storage device, the size of your data files, and the frequency at which you make changes. For best results, use an external hard disk drive that's at least the same capacity as your computer's internal hard disk. Time Machine and similar synchronization software can store backups on network file servers and on Internet-based storage services.

▶ **Can I restore individual files from these backups?** Yes. Time Machine displays a window for each hour's backup. You can go back in time to any hour or day, select a file, and restore it to your computer's primary storage device.

▶ **What about restoring the entire computer?** Suppose your computer's hard disk fails and you have to replace it. Once you've installed a new, blank hard disk, you can insert the Mac OS setup CD and select the Time Machine option to restore the operating system, programs, preferences, and data files that existed at the time of the last Time Machine backup. Figure 4-49 explains the elements of Time Machine's interface.

FIGURE 4-49

Time Machine saves hourly backups for the past 24 hours, daily backups for the past month, and weekly backups for data older than a month. When the backup device runs out of space, Time Machine deletes the oldest weekly backup.

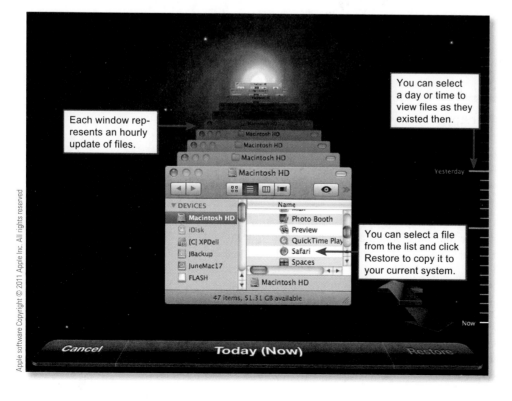

Each window represents an hourly update of files.

You can select a day or time to view files as they existed then.

You can select a file from the list and click Restore to copy it to your current system.

WINDOWS BACKUP

▶ **What does backup software do?** Microsoft supplies its customers with backup software designed to make backups of data and program files. **Backup software** is a set of utility programs designed to back up and restore some or all of the files on a computer's primary storage device. Backup software usually includes options that make it easy to schedule periodic backups, define a set of files that you want to regularly back up, and automate the restoration process.

Backup software differs from most copy and synchronization routines because it typically compresses all the files for a backup and places them in one large file. Under the direction of backup software, this file can be spread across multiple discs if necessary. The backup file is indexed so that individual files can be located, uncompressed, and restored.

▶ **How do I use backup software?** To use backup software, you specify which files you want to back up, select the location of the backup device, and select the days and times for automatic backups to proceed. Because the backup process uses system resources, most people schedule backups for times when their computer is on, but when they are not typically using it (Figure 4-50).

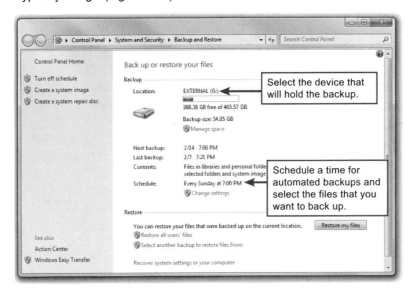

FIGURE 4-50

Microsoft Windows 7 includes backup software. ▶ Discover how to use it to back up your computer's hard disk.

▶ **What is a full backup?** When you set up your backup software, you might have a choice between full, differential, and incremental backups. A **full backup** makes a fresh copy of every file in the folders you've specified for the backup. A full backup does not necessarily contain every file on your computer. A full backup might contain only your data files, for example, if those are the files you want to regularly back up.

▶ **What is a differential backup?** A **differential backup** makes a backup of only those files that were added or changed since your last full backup session. After making a full backup of your important files, you can make differential backups at regular intervals. If you need to restore all your files after a hard disk crash, first restore the files from your full backup, and then restore the files from your latest differential backup.

▶ **What is an incremental backup?** An **incremental backup** backs up files that were added or changed since the last backup—not necessarily the files that changed from the last full backup, but the files that changed since any full or incremental backup (Figure 4-51 on the next page).

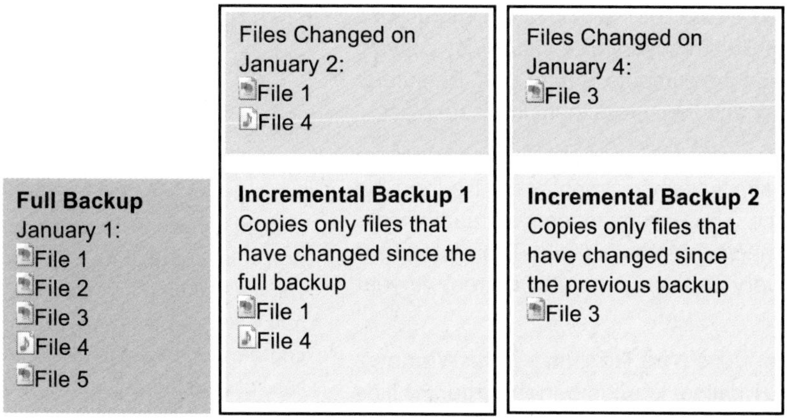

Full Backup January 1:	Files Changed on January 2:	Files Changed on January 4:
File 1	File 1	File 3
File 2	File 4	
File 3		
File 4	**Incremental Backup 1**	**Incremental Backup 2**
File 5	Copies only files that have changed since the full backup	Copies only files that have changed since the previous backup
	File 1	File 3
	File 4	

FIGURE 4-51

Incremental backups record only files that have changed since the previous backup. To restore files after a hard disk crash, first load all the files from the full backup, and then load each incremental backup, starting with the oldest and ending with the most recent.

4

▶ **How do I avoid backing up files that contain viruses?**
Viruses can damage files to the point that your computer can't access any data on its hard disk. It is really frustrating when you restore data from a backup only to discover that the restored files contain the same virus that wiped out your original data. If your antivirus software is not set to constantly scan for viruses on your computer system, you should run an up-to-date virus check as the first step in your backup routine.

▶ **How do I get backup software started after a hard disk crash?** Backup software includes modules for restoring files. To restore a single file or a few files, simply start the backup software, make sure the backup device is connected, and use the Restore module to locate and retrieve the file you want. If, however, your hard disk fails, the backup process can become more complex.

Whatever backup software you use, remember that it needs to be accessible when you want to restore your data. If your hard drive crashes and the only copy of your backup software exists on your backup media, you will be in a Catch-22 situation. You won't be able to access your backup software until you restore the files from your backup, but you won't be able to restore your files until your backup software is running!

To recover from a hard disk crash, you have to get your computer booted up so that you can run your backup software. If your computer won't boot from the hard disk, you can use a boot disk or a recovery disk.

▶ **What is a boot disk?** A **boot disk** is a removable storage medium containing the operating system files needed to boot your computer without accessing the hard disk. CDs, DVDs, and even USB flash drives can be used as boot disks. With current versions of Windows, the Windows installation CD is configured as a boot disk and can be used if your computer does not boot normally. When you insert the installation CD, you'll have the option of repairing Windows or reinstalling it. Try the repair option first.

▶ **What is a recovery disk?** A **recovery disk** (sometimes referred to as a recovery CD) is a bootable CD, DVD, or other media that contains a complete copy of your computer's hard disk as it existed when the computer was new. It contains the operating system, device drivers, utilities, and even software that was bundled with your computer.

You can use a recovery disk to return your computer to its factory default state. However, a recovery disk will not restore your data files, any software that you installed, or any configuration settings you've made since you unwrapped your computer from its shipping box.

▶ Where can I get a recovery disk? The installation instructions for new computers explain how to make a recovery disk, usually by copying files stored in a **recovery partition** on the computer's hard disk. Be sure to create your recovery disks right away and then store them in a safe place.

Recovery partitions are convenient for restoring a corrupted device driver or software module because you can simply copy or reinstall the file from the recovery partition to the main partition. The files in the recovery partition are not accessible, however, if your computer's hard disk fails. Therefore, don't be misled into thinking that a recovery partition can help you restore your computer after a hard disk failure.

▶ What about backing up the Windows Registry? The **Windows Registry**, or Registry as it is usually called, is an important group of files used by the Windows operating system to store configuration information about all the devices and software installed on a computer system. If the Registry becomes damaged, your computer might not be able to boot up, launch programs, or communicate with peripheral devices. It is a good idea to have an extra copy of the Registry in case the original file is damaged.

As simple as it sounds, backing up the Registry can be a problem because the Registry is always open while your computer is on. Some software that you might use for backups cannot copy open files. If you use such software, it might never back up the Registry. To get periodic copies of your computer's Registry settings, you can create restore points.

▶ What is a restore point? A **restore point** is a snapshot of your computer settings. Restore points are essentially backups of the Windows Registry. If a hard disk problem causes system instability, you might be able to roll back to a restore point when your computer was operational.

Restore points are set automatically when you install new software. You can manually set restore points, too. For example, you might want to set a restore point before updating a program, setting up a network, or installing new hardware (Figure 4-52).

TERMINOLOGY NOTE

The contents and capabilities of recovery disks vary. Some are designed to restore your computer to its like-new state and wipe out all your data. Others attempt to restore user settings, programs, and data. Before you depend on a recovery disk, make sure you know what it contains and how to use it in case of a system failure.

FIGURE 4-52

Restore points can be set by entering "Create a Restore Point" in the Start menu Search box, and then accessing the System Protection tab. ▶ Use this figure in your interactive eBook to learn how to work with restore points.

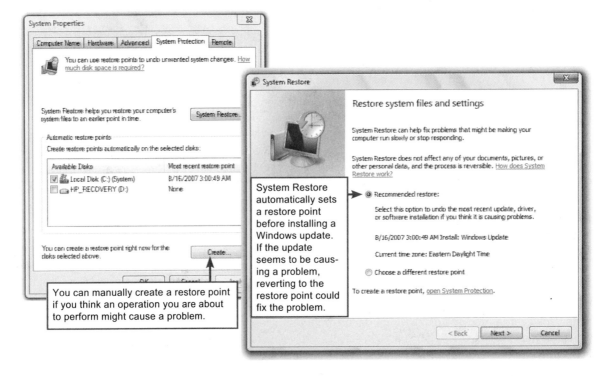

System Restore automatically sets a restore point before installing a Windows update. If the update seems to be causing a problem, reverting to the restore point could fix the problem.

You can manually create a restore point if you think an operation you are about to perform might cause a problem.

DISK IMAGES AND BARE-METAL RESTORE

▶ **Can I restore my computer in one simple operation?**
Restoring a Windows computer usually entails several steps that can require a boot disk, a recovery disk, backup disks, and file backups. The objective of this extended and sometimes frustrating process is to get optical and hard drive device drivers running so the computer can access its storage devices to get the operating system running, which can then run backup and restore software.

Some backup systems streamline the process by restoring a computer's operating system, device drivers, settings, and data in a single step—a process called **bare-metal restore**.

Bare-metal restore backup software stores the operating system, boot program, drivers, software applications, and data necessary to restore a backed up system to an entirely new computer, without requiring intermediate steps to install the operating system and device drivers. Bare-metal restore software usually works with a disk image.

▶ **What is a disk image?** A **disk image** is a bit-by-bit copy of the data from all sectors of a disk. Disk imaging utilities create an exact clone of the original disk, unlike most backup software that makes file-by-file copies. The advantage of disk imaging is that it includes all the data from a disk, even boot information and other data locked by the operating system.

The disadvantage of disk imaging is that it copies data from the entire disk; it generally cannot be configured like traditional backup software to copy only selected files. Disk imaging takes time and is best used while other applications are not running. It is valuable for periodic backups, but cumbersome for daily backups.

Popular Mac disk imaging utilities include SuperDuper! and Carbon Copy Cloner. Popular Windows disk imaging utilities include Paragon Drive Backup, Norton Ghost, and Acronis True Image (Figure 4-53).

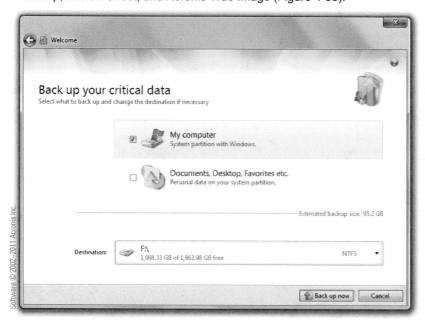

FIGURE 4-53

Disk imaging software, such as Acronis True Image, creates a bit-by-bit copy of all the data on your computer's hard disk that can be used to restore all operating system, program, and data files.

VIRTUAL MACHINES

❱ Are there any other backup options? Today's trend toward the use of virtual machines offers another option for backups. Reinstalling an operating system on a blank hard disk can be tricky, but you can avoid that hassle if you run your operating system as a virtual machine.

For example, if you run Windows as a virtual machine on a Mac, you can simply back up the entire Windows machine as one folder or file. If a virus or corrupted file begins to disrupt the operation of Windows, instead of reformatting your hard disk and reinstalling Windows, you can simply copy the image of your Windows virtual machine from your backup device to your primary storage device and continue working (Figure 4-54).

FIGURE 4-54

When you run Windows as a virtual machine, the Windows operating system, program files, and settings, along with your data files, are stored in a folder. The entire Windows computer runs essentially like any other software application on the host machine.

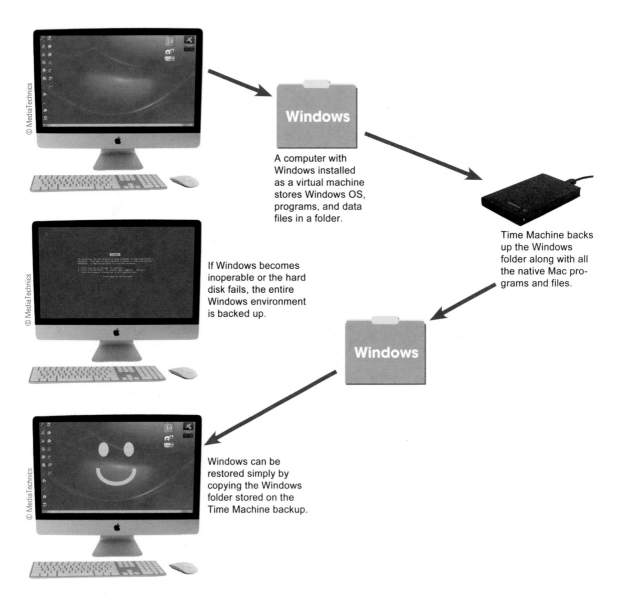

A computer with Windows installed as a virtual machine stores Windows OS, programs, and data files in a folder.

If Windows becomes inoperable or the hard disk fails, the entire Windows environment is backed up.

Time Machine backs up the Windows folder along with all the native Mac programs and files.

Windows can be restored simply by copying the Windows folder stored on the Time Machine backup.

HANDHELD BACKUP

▶ What about my handheld device? Handheld devices are usually backed up by synching them to a desktop or notebook computer. The procedure is a legacy from the days of personal digital assistants that used synchronization as a mechanism to update contacts and appointments from a handheld device to those on a desktop computer.

Synching is usually initiated by tethering your handheld device to a full-size computer using a USB cable. Synchronization software examines files on both devices and asks you which files you want to sync.

iPhones, iPods, and iPads synch with iTunes software, and you have the option to encrypt the backup to prevent your data from exposure if your computer falls victim to an unauthorized intrusion (Figure 4-55).

FIGURE 4-55

iTunes creates a backup of the data stored on your iPad, iPod, or iPhone.

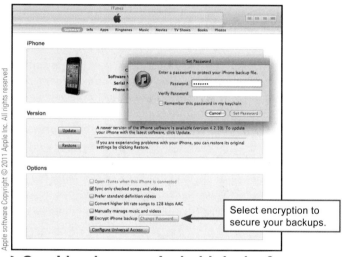

Select encryption to secure your backups.

© MediaTechnics

▶ Can I back up my Android device? Android devices generally do not include backup software, but several backup apps are available. Look for apps such as Titanium Backup, Astro file Manager, and My Backup Pro at your favorite app store. The backup data from your Android device is typically stored in the cloud at a Web site maintained by the backup app provider. Some apps also give you the option of storing your backup on an SD memory card.

To back up your files and apps to a computer, you might have to root your Android device using software, such as Nandroid, and use its recovery feature. The process is not authorized and can potentially ruin your phone, so most owners settle for the backups generated by standard backup apps.

QuickCheck   SECTION E

1. _____ software, such as Time Machine, keeps your backup files up to date with the original files on your hard disk.

2. One of the best devices for home backup is a(n) _____ hard drive.

3. A(n) _____ backup makes copies of only those files that have changed since your last full backup.

4. A(n) _____ point is essentially a backup of the settings in the Windows Registry.

5. A bare-_____ restore includes the operating system, boot program, drivers, software applications, and data necessary to rebuild a replacement hard disk in one easy operation.

▶ CHECK ANSWERS

Issue: Cyberterrorists or Pranksters?

SOME COMPUTER CRIMES require no special digital expertise. Setting fire to a computer doesn't require the same finesse as writing a stealthy virus, but both can have the same disastrous effect on data. Old-fashioned crimes, such as arson, that take a high-tech twist because they involve a computer can be prosecuted under traditional laws.

Traditional laws do not, however, cover the range of possibilities for computer crimes. Suppose a person unlawfully enters a computer facility and steals backup drives. That person might be prosecuted for breaking and entering. But would common breaking and entering laws apply to a person who remotely accesses a corporate computer system without authorization? And what if a person copies a data file without authorization? Has that file really been stolen if the original remains on the computer?

Many countries have computer crime laws that specifically define computer data and software as personal property. These laws also define as crimes the unauthorized access, use, modification, or disabling of a computer system or data. But laws don't necessarily stop criminals. If they did, we wouldn't have to deal with malicious code and intrusions.

One of the first computer crime cases involved a worm unleashed on the ARPANET in 1988 that quickly spread through government and university computer systems. The worm's author, Robert Morris, was convicted and sentenced to three years of probation, 400 hours of community service, and a US$10,000 fine.

A 1995 high-profile case involved a computer hacker named Kevin Mitnick, who was accused of breaking into dozens of corporate, university, government, and personal computers. Although vilified in the media, Mitnick had the support of many hackers and other people who believed that the prosecution grossly exaggerated the extent of his crimes. Nonetheless, Mitnick was sentenced to 46 months in prison and ordered to pay restitution in the amount of $4,125 during his three-year period of supervised release.

Forbes reporter Adam L. Penenberg took issue with the 46-month sentence imposed by Judge Mariana Pfaelzer and wrote, "Mitnick's crimes were curiously innocuous. He broke into corporate computers, but no evidence indicates that he destroyed data. Or sold anything he copied. Yes, he pilfered software—but in doing so left it behind. This world of bits is a strange one, in which you can take something and still leave it for its rightful owner. The theft laws designed for payroll sacks and motor vehicles just don't apply to a hacker."

The USA PATRIOT Act and the Cybersecurity Enhancement Act carry stiff penalties for cybercrimes—ranging from ten years to life in prison. CNET editor, Robert Vamosi questions the harshness of such penalties: "What bothers me most is that here in the United States, rapists serve, on average, ten years in prison. Yet if, instead of assaulting another human being, that same person had released a virus on the Net, the criminal would get the same or an even harsher sentence."

This world of bits is a strange one, in which you can take something and still leave it for its rightful owner.

Modern society has an ambivalent attitude toward computer hackers. On the one hand, they are viewed as evil cyberterrorists who are set on destroying the glue that binds together the Information Age.

From this perspective, hackers are criminals who must be hunted down, forced to make restitution for damages, and prevented from creating further havoc.

From another perspective, hackers are viewed more as Casper the Friendly Ghost in our complex cybermachines—as moderately bothersome entities whose pranks are tolerated by the computer community, along with software bugs and hardware glitches.

Seen from this perspective, a hacker's pranks are part of the normal course of study that leads to the highest echelons of computer expertise. "Everyone has done it," claims one hacking devotee, "even Bill Gates and Steve Jobs."

Try It! Which perspective is right? Are hackers dangerous cyber-terrorists or harmless pranksters? Before you make up your mind about computer hacking and cracking, here's more for you to explore.

1 After the publicity from Kevin Mitnick's trial, consumers might expect corporate databases to be rigorously guarded; but hacking incidents continue to escalate. To find information about recent data breaches, check the Wikipedia article on data breaches or sites such as DatalossDB (*datalossdb.org*). What were the three largest data breaches in the past five years, how many accounts were exposed, and did you have accounts with any of the breached organizations?

2 Data breaches are a major source of information used for identity theft. You probably know basic steps to take to avoid identity theft, but there's always more to learn. Check sites such as *www.identity-theft.org/protect.htm* or the National Crime Prevention Council's online booklet *Preventing Identity Theft*. What are five identity-protection techniques that you didn't know about before this project?

3 In 2010, a mysterious computer worm spread across the Internet and targeted industrial equipment that happened to be used in Iran's nuclear program. According to one security expert, Stuxnet was designed to probe the security of a wide variety of crucial industrial plants throughout the world and gauge potential weaknesses for future cyberwarfare attacks. Use Web resources to learn more about Stuxnet and recent attacks against RSA, a cyber security company, and Google's Gmail system. What is the difference between cyber-warfare and cybercrime?

4 The media labeled an attack against the country of Estonia a "cyber war." Use Web resources to explore this incident. How might a similar incident affect your country?

5 The world of cybercrime has a jargon all its own. What do the following terms mean?

a. Zero-day attack	e. Denial of service
b. Data diddling	f. Man-in-the-middle
c. Salami shaving	g. Dead drop
d. Vandalism	h. Honeypot

INFOWEBLINKS

You can check the **NP2013 Chapter 4** InfoWebLink for updates to these activities.

W CLICK TO CONNECT
www.infoweblinks.com/np2013/ch04

What Do You Think?

ISSUE

1. Should a computer virus distribution sentence carry the same penalty as manslaughter?

2. Should it be a crime to steal a copy of computer data while leaving the original data in place and unaltered?

3. Should hackers be sent to jail if they cannot pay restitution to companies and individuals who lost money as the result of a prank?

4. Do you think that a hacker would make a good computer-security consultant?

Information Tools: Fact Checking

skvac/Shutterstock

These days, you have to be a skeptic. Bloggers have opinions that are not always based on facts. Scam artists say anything to get your money. Even reputable journalists sometimes make mistakes.

Before you form an opinion, make a decision, or take action based on what you read, see, or hear, you can easily use your computer or smartphone to verify facts and look up background information.

Search Google. You can use Google or a similar search engine to find information from all corners of the Web. You can search for information in specific formats, such as videos, images, and news reports. Check out Google Scholar for links to authoritative information in peer-reviewed journals, theses, and other professional publications. Remember that you can formulate searches such as "Define zero-day attack" to learn the meaning of technical terms and find the meaning of acronyms.

Search within sites. Rather than conducting a wide-ranging Google search, you can go to a specific Web site and search within it. Search Wikipedia for definitions and topic overviews. Search a news site for articles and video footage about current events. Start at Snopes.com or hoaxbusters.org to identify e-mail scams. Try LexisNexis for links to authoritative primary and secondary source material.

When you check facts or use them in your own research papers, primary sources tend to be more reliable than secondary or tertiary sources. How can you tell the difference?

PRIMARY SOURCES	SECONDARY SOURCES	TERTIARY SOURCES
Original material such as speeches, interviews, letters, photos, e-mail messages, tweets, artwork, diaries, laws, database reports, and accounting records	Reviews, critiques, panel discussions, biographies, and other sources that analyze, summarize, or otherwise repackage information from primary sources	A list or compilation of material that pertains to a topic; from sources that include bibliographies, dictionaries, almanacs, indexes, time lines, and inventory lists
Example: A video of Apple's CEO announcing a new music product for the iPhone and iPad	Example: An article on Google News that describes Apple's new music product	Example: Apple's e-commerce site that lists and sells all versions of its new music product

FACT CHECKING TIPS

- **Two sources are better than one.** Cross-check facts between two or more sites.
- **Use common sense.** Claims that seem outlandish require extra verification.
- **Understand your priorities.** For example, you can go to YouTube and view the trailer for *Live Free or Die Hard*. That might be fun, but it might not be relevant for a term paper on cyberterrorism.
- **Use primary sources when possible.** Go to the original text of a speech, check the product manufacturer's Web site, or watch the video clip.
- **Use reputable sources.** The Web contains billions of documents; few of them follow strict journalistic standards for accuracy. Check the author's credentials, look at the general quality of the Web site, and make sure the information is up to date.

- **Maintain a list of the sites you frequently use for fact checking.** You can create a Fact Check folder in your browser's Bookmarks or Favorites list.
- **Nail down your search terms.** When using voice search on your mobile phone, think about an exact set of keywords before you launch Speak Now.

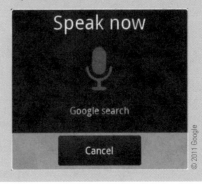
© 2011 Google

Try It! Fact checking can be fun and it can lead you to all sorts of intriguing factoids as well as to substantive information. Practice your fact-checking skills by completing the following activities.

1 After investigating a worm that infiltrated U.S. Army networks, the NSA (National Security Agency) and Department of Defense banned USB flash drives from military computers. From which one of the following sources are you most likely to obtain primary source information about the USB flash drive ban?

Under Worm Assault, Military Bans Disks, USB Drives | Danger ...
www.wired.com/dangerroom/2008/11/army-bans-usb-d/ - Cached

Nov 19, 2008 – Under Worm Assault, Military Bans Disks, USB Drives ...
The ban comes from the commander of U.S. Strategic Command, according to an...

[PDF] USB Storage Drives
www.nsa.gov/ia/_files/factsheets/I731-002R-2007.pdf

File Format: PDF/Adobe Acrobat - Quick View
of devices not described by other policy settings". To allow administrators to ...
www.nsa.gov. Information ... cameras, and USB hard drives. Windows. Linux ..

Judging the cyber war terrorist threat : The New Yorker
www.newyorker.com/reporting/2010/11/.../101101fa_fact_hersh

Subscribe to New Yorker ... by Seymour M. Hersh ... N.S.A. unit commanders,
facing penetration of their bases' secure networks, concluded that the break-in
was caused by a disabling thumb drive...

2 Suppose that you receive an e-mail message warning of a zero-day cyberwar worm called Storm that is spreading rapidly. The message warns that your security software doesn't yet have the ability to identify and quarantine this virus. According to the e-mail, it is your civic duty to stop this virus by following a set of instructions to alter the Windows Registry or Mac OS kernel. Of the following options, which would be the best way to find out if this warning is legitimate?

a. Use Google to search for "Storm worm."

b. Go to the Web site Snopes.com and search for "Storm."

c. Reply to the e-mail and ask for the app's security certificate.

3 Suppose you're gathering information for a term paper about enforcement efforts to catch cybercriminals, and you come across the following short article posted on a security blog. Operation Shady RAT sounds intriguing; but before you add material from this article to your research notes, you should do a fact check by answering the questions in the diagram below.

Operation Shady RAT Exposed

the passwords necessary to gain entry. Data gathered from this server revealed hundreds of active targets and terabytes of illicit data waiting to be claimed by hackers.

c. Are these statistics accurate?

Victims ranged from the U.S. Olympic Committee to government agencies in the U.S., Canada, India, South Korea, Taiwan, Pakistan, and Vietnam.

d. Is this list of victims correct?

Dmitri Alperovitch of McAfee, the security firm spearheading the investigation, describes the discovery "even we were surprised by the enormous diversity of the victim organizations and were taken aback by the audacity of the perpetrators."

e. Check the primary source: Is this quote correct?

a. Was the sting operation called Shady RAT?

In a massive sting operation called Shady RAT, a U.S. security firm raided the command and control server used by a group of Romania-based hackers.

b. Were the hackers based in Romania?

An extensive investigation led up to the discovery of the clandestine server and

© Thinkstock LLC

Technology in Context: Law Enforcement

SIRENS WAIL. Blue lights flash. A speeding car slows and pulls off to the side of the road. It looks like a routine traffic stop, but the patrol car is outfitted with a mobile data computer. The police officers on this high-tech force have already checked the speeding car's license plate number and description against a database of stolen cars and vehicles allegedly used in kidnappings and other crimes.

Mounted in the dashboard of marked and unmarked police cars, a mobile data computer resembles a notebook computer with its flat-panel screen and compact keyboard. Unlike a consumer-grade notebook, however, the computers in police cruisers use hardened technology designed to withstand extreme conditions, such as high temperatures in parked vehicles. The dashboard-mounted computer communicates with an office-based server using a wireless link, such as short-range radio, mobile phone technology, or Wi-Fi. With this wireless link, police officers can access data from local, state, and national databases.

One national database, the National Crime Information Center (NCIC), is maintained by the FBI and can be accessed by authorized personnel in local, state, and federal law enforcement agencies. The system can process more than 5 million queries per day related to stolen vehicles, wanted criminals, missing persons, violent gang members, stolen guns, and members of terrorist organizations. The officers who pulled over the speeding car received information from the NCIC that the car was stolen, so they arrested the car's occupant and took him to the police station for booking.

At the police station, digital cameras flash and the suspect's mug shot is automatically entered into an automated warrants and booking system. The system stores the suspect's complete biographical and arrest information, such as name, aliases, addresses, Social Security number, charges, and arrest date. The system also checks for outstanding warrants against the suspect, such as warrants for other thefts. Booking agents can enter those charges into the system, assign the new inmate to a cell, log his or her personal items, and print a photo ID or wrist band.

Automated warrants and booking systems have been proven to increase police productivity. New York City's system handles more than 300,000 bookings per year, with gains in productivity that have put nearly 300 officers back into action investigating crimes and patrolling neighborhoods.

As part of the booking process, the suspect is fingerprinted. A standard fingerprint card, sometimes called a ten-print card, contains inked prints of the fingers on each hand, plus name, date of birth, and other arrest information. Now, however, instead of using ink, a biometric scanning device can electronically capture fingerprints. Text information is entered using a keyboard and stored with digital fingerprint images.

The fingerprint information can be transmitted in digital format from local law enforcement agencies to the FBI's Integrated Automated Fingerprint Identification System (IAFIS). This biometric identification system uses digital imaging technology and sophisticated algorithms to analyze fingerprint data. IAFIS can classify arriving prints for storage or search for a match in its database containing 66 million criminal prints, 25 million civilian prints, and prints from 73,000 known and suspected terrorists.

Conventional crimes, such as car theft, are often solved by using standard investigative techniques with information from computer databases. To solve cybercrimes, however, the special skills of computer forensic investigators are often required.

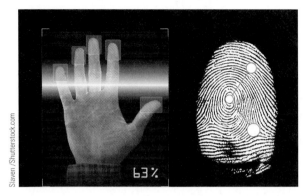

Slaven./Shutterstock.com

Computer forensics is the scientific examination and analysis of data located on computer storage media, conducted to offer evidence of computer crimes in court. Computer crimes can be separated into two categories. The first includes crimes that use computers, such as transmitting trade secrets to competitors, reproducing copyrighted material, and distributing child pornography. The second includes crimes targeted at computers, such as denial-of-service attacks on servers, Web site vandalism, data theft, and destructive viruses. Computer forensics can be applied to both categories.

Whether investigators suspect that a computer is the origin of a cyber-attack or contains evidence, the first step in the forensic process is to use disk imaging software to make an exact replica of the information stored on the hard disk. The disk image is collected on a write-once medium that cannot be altered with planted evidence, and the forensic scientist begins analyzing the disk image data with simple search software that looks through files for keywords related to the crime. In the case of the Gap-Toothed Bandit who was convicted for robbing nine banks, analysis of the disk image revealed word processing files containing notes he handed to tellers demanding money.

Criminals typically attempt to delete files with incriminating evidence, but a good forensic scientist can retrieve data from deleted files with undelete software or data recovery software. Temporary Internet or cache files can also yield evidence, pointing law enforcement officers to Web sites the suspect visited that might be fronts for illegal activity.

When a computer is a target of a cyber-attack, forensic investigators use three techniques to track the source. The first option is to make an immediate image of the server's hard disk and look through its log files for evidence of activity coming from unauthorized IP addresses. A second technique is to monitor the intruder by watching login attempts, changes to log files, and file access requests. Sophisticated intruders might be able to detect such monitoring, however, and cover their tracks. A third technique is to create a honeypot—an irresistible computer system or Web site containing fake information that allows investigators to monitor hackers until identification is possible.

Despite the many techniques and tools available to forensic investigators, they have three main constraints. First, they must adhere to privacy regulations and obtain warrants to set up wiretaps or gather information from ISPs about their customers. Second, they must scrupulously document their procedures so that the evidence they produce cannot be discredited in court as planted or fabricated. Third, forensic investigators must examine a wide range of alternatives pertaining to the crime, such as the chance that an IP or e-mail address used to commit a cybercrime might belong to an innocent bystander being spoofed by the real hacker.

Privacy, documentation, and evidentiary constraints cost forensic investigators time, and failure to adhere to strict standards can sometimes allow criminals to avoid conviction and penalties. But even within these constraints, careful forensic investigation is an important aspect of catching and convicting high-tech criminals.

4

New Perspectives Labs

To access the New Perspectives Labs for Chapter 4, open the NP2013 interactive eBook and then click the icon next to the lab title.

▶ MANAGING FILES

IN THIS LAB YOU'LL LEARN:

- How to access Windows Explorer
- How to expand and collapse the directory structure
- How to rename or delete a file or folder
- The basic principles for creating an efficient directory structure for your files
- How to create a folder
- How to select a single file or a group of files
- How to move files from one folder to another

LAB ASSIGNMENTS

1. Start the interactive part of the lab. Make sure you've enabled Tracking if you want to save your QuickCheck results. Perform each lab step, and answer all the lab QuickCheck questions.

2. Use Windows Explorer to look at the directory of the disk or USB flash drive that currently contains most of your files. Draw a diagram showing the hierarchy of folders. Write a paragraph explaining how you could improve this hierarchy, and draw a diagram to illustrate your plan.

3. On a blank USB flash drive, create three folders: Music, Web Graphics, and Articles. Within the Music folder, create four additional folders: Jazz, Reggae, Rock, and Classical. Within the Classical folder, create two more folders: Classical MIDI and Classical MP3. If you have Internet access, go on to #4.

4. Use your browser software to connect to the Internet, and then go to a Web site, such as *www. zdnet.com* or *www.cnet.com*. Look for a small graphic (perhaps 100 KB or less) and download it to your Web Graphics folder. Next, use a search engine to search for "classical MIDI music." Download one of the compositions to the Music\ Classical\Classical MIDI folder. Open Windows Explorer and expand all the directories for your USB flash drive. Open the Music\Classical\ Classical MIDI folder and make sure your music download appears. Capture a screenshot. Follow your instructor's directions to submit this screenshot as a printout or an e-mail attachment.

▶ BACKING UP YOUR COMPUTER

IN THIS LAB YOU'LL LEARN:

- How to work with restore points
- How to create a recovery disk
- How to create a disk image
- How to make a Windows backup
- How to restore files from a backup

LAB ASSIGNMENTS

1. Start the interactive part of the lab. Make sure you've enabled Tracking if you want to save your QuickCheck results. Perform each lab step as directed, and answer all the lab QuickCheck questions. When you exit the lab, your answers are automatically graded and your results are displayed.

2. Describe where most of your data files are stored, and estimate how many megabytes of data (not programs) you have in all these files. Next, take a close look at these files and estimate how much data (in megabytes) you cannot afford to lose. Would your data fit on a USB flash drive? If so, what capacity?

3. Start the backup software that is provided for your computer, specify its name, and list which of the following features it provides: file backup, system image, disk image, automatic backup, manual backup. If an automatic backup is available, list the userdefinable options for selecting backup intervals, days, and times.

4. Explore your computer to discover how its recovery disk is provided. For example, is it a partition, a download, or a utility? Use the built-in Help provided by your computer manufacturer or go to its Web site to learn how to make a recovery disk. Write a short summary of the procedure.

Key Terms

Make sure you understand all the boldfaced key terms presented in this chapter. With the NP2013 interactive eBook, you can use this list of terms as an interactive study activity. First, try to define a term in your own words, and then click the term to compare your definition with the definition presented in the chapter.

4

Android OS, 203
Backup, 222
Backup software, 226
Bare-metal restore, 229
BlackBerry OS, 202
Boot disk, 227
Boot process, 192
Bootstrap program, 192
Button, 190
Cluster, 219
Command-line interface, 189
Data fork, 199
Defragmentation utility, 221
Desktop, 189
Desktop operating system, 188
Dialog box, 191
Differential backup, 226
Directory, 206
Disc mastering, 219
Disk image, 229
Disk partition, 205
DOS, 201
Dual boot, 198
File date, 206
File extension, 204
File format, 207
File header, 207
File management utility, 214
File shredder software, 220
File size, 206

File specification, 206
File system, 219
File tag, 212
File-naming conventions, 204
Folder, 206
Formatting, 219
Fragmented files, 221
Full backup, 226
Graphical user interface, 189
Handheld operating system, 188
HP webOS, 203
Icon, 189
Incremental backup, 226
iOS, 202
Kernel, 192
Library, 217
Linux, 200
Linux distribution, 200
Logical storage models, 215
Mac OS, 197
Memory leak, 187
Menu, 190
Menu bar, 190
Microsoft Windows, 194
Multiprocessing, 186
Multitasking, 186
Multithreading, 186
Multiuser operating system, 187
Native file format, 209
Online backup service, 223

Packet writing, 219
Path, 206
Physical storage model, 218
Recovery disk, 227
Recovery partition, 228
Reserved words, 205
Resource, 185
Resource fork, 199
Restore, 222
Restore point, 228
Ribbon, 190
Root directory, 206
Sectors, 219
Server operating system, 187
Single-user operating system, 187
Subdirectory, 206
Submenu, 191
Symbian, 202
Synchronization, 225
Taskbar, 190
Toolbar, 190
Tracks, 219
UNIX, 200
User interface, 189
Virtual machine, 198
Window, 189
Windows Explorer, 216
Windows Phone 7, 203
Windows Registry, 228

Interactive Summary

To review important concepts from this chapter, fill in the blanks to best complete each sentence. When using the NP2013 interactive eBook, click the Check Answers buttons to automatically score your answers.

SECTION A: An operating system interacts with application software, device drivers, and hardware to manage a computer's [_____], such as the processor, memory, and input/output devices. To allow two or more programs to run simultaneously, an OS can offer [_____] services. Within a single program, [_____] allows multiple parts, or threads, to run simultaneously. An operating system's [_____] capability supports a division of labor among all the processing units. An operating system might have to deal with a memory [_____], a situation caused by an application that requests memory, but never releases it. Operating systems are informally categorized and characterized using one or more of the following terms: A(n) [_____] -user operating system expects to deal with one set of input devices—those that can be controlled by one person at a time. A(n) [_____] -user operat-

ing system is designed to deal with input, output, and processing requests from many users. A(n) [_____] operating system provides management tools for distributed networks, e-mail servers, and Web site hosting. A(n) [_____] operating system is one that's designed for a personal computer. A(n) [_____] operating system is designed for devices such as iPhones and Droids.

In addition to behind-the-scenes activities, operating systems also provide tools, called operating system [_____], that you can use to control and customize your computer equipment and work environment. Many operating systems also influence the "look and feel" of your software, or what's known as the user [_____]. The core part of an operating system is called the [_____], which is loaded into RAM during the [_____] process.

▶ CHECK ANSWERS

SECTION B: Popular [_____] operating systems include Microsoft Windows, Mac OS, and Linux. The first versions of Windows were sometimes referred to as operating [_____] rather than operating systems because they required DOS to supply the operating system kernel. Windows has evolved to keep pace with 16-bit, 32-bit, and [_____] -bit architectures. Its strengths include a huge library of Windows [_____], support for a variety of peripheral devices, and plenty of documentation. Two of the weakest features of Microsoft Windows are reliability and [_____].

Mac OS evolved from the original Classic Mac OS designed for [_____] computers based on the Motorola 68000 microprocessor. In 2001, Mac OS X was released for Apple's new line of computers using IBM's PowerPC processor. OS X was again revised for a line of computers using [_____] pro-

cessors. These Macs can be set up to dual [_____] Mac OS and Windows. Intel Macs also offer a good platform for [_____] machine technologies that allow you to use one computer to simulate the hardware and software of another. One of the potential problems with Mac OS is its use of [_____] forks, which make cross-platform file sharing clumsy. Linux is a(n) [_____] source operating system that is used extensively for servers. One of the reasons it has not become a popular desktop OS is that it requires a bit more technical savvy than Windows or Mac OS. Developed by Microsoft and supplied on the original IBM PCs, [_____] was one of the first operating systems for personal computers. Today's handheld operating systems include [_____] used on the iPhone, iPad, and iPod Touch.

▶ CHECK ANSWERS

SECTION C: A computer [_____] is a named collection of data that exists on a storage medium, such as a hard disk, CD, DVD, or BD. Every file has a name and might also have a file extension. The rules that specify valid file names are called file-naming [_____]. These rules typically do not allow you to use certain characters or [_____] words in a file name. A file [_____] is usually related to a file format—the arrangement of data in a file and the coding scheme used to represent the data. A software program's [_____] file format is the default format for storing files created with that program. A file's location is defined by a file [_____] (sometimes called a path), which includes the storage device, folder(s), file name, and extension. In Windows, storage devices are identified by a drive letter, followed by a(n) [_____]. An operating system maintains a list of files called a directory for each storage disk, USB flash drive, tape, CD, or DVD. The main directory of a disk is referred to as the [_____] directory, which can be subdivided into several smaller lists called subdirectories that are depicted as [_____].

▶ CHECK ANSWERS

SECTION D: File [_____] encompasses any procedure that helps you organize your computer-based files so that you can find them more effectively. [_____]-based file management uses tools provided with a software program to open and save files. Additional tools might also allow you to create new folders, rename files, and delete files. The Save and Save As dialog boxes are examples of these file management tools. Most operating systems provide file management [_____] that give you the "big picture" of the files you have stored on your disks. The structure of folders that you envision on your disk is a(n) [_____] model, which is often represented by a storage [_____], such as a tree structure or filing cabinet. Windows [_____] is an example of a file management utility provided by an operating system. Windows Explorer allows you to find, rename, copy, move, and delete files and folders. In addition, it allows you to perform these file management activities with more than one file at a time. The way that data is actually stored is referred to as the [_____] storage model. Before a computer stores data on a disk, CD, or DVD, it creates the equivalent of electronic storage bins by dividing the disk into [_____], and then further dividing the disk into [_____]. This dividing process is referred to as [_____]. Each sector of a disk is numbered, providing a storage address that the operating system can track. Many computers work with a group of sectors, called a(n) [_____], to increase the efficiency of file storage operations. An operating system uses a file [_____] to track the physical location of files.

▶ CHECK ANSWERS

SECTION E: A backup is a copy of one or more files that have been made in case the original files become damaged. A good backup plan allows you to [_____] your computing environment to its pre-disaster state with a minimum of fuss. Your personal backup plan depends on the files you need to back up, the hardware you have available to make backups, and your backup software. In any case, it is a good idea to back up the Windows [_____] and make sure your files are free of [_____]. Backups should be stored in a safe place, away from the computer. Personal computer backups are typically recorded on [_____] hard drives, USB flash drives, network servers, and online storage services. An easy way to create a backup of important data files is to use Finder or Windows [_____] to simply copy files to a USB flash drive. [_____] compares files on two devices and makes them the same. Backup software differs from most copy routines because it [_____] all the files for a backup into one large file. A(n) [_____] backup saves time by backing up only those files that have been changed since the last backup. Restoring a Windows computer usually requires several steps, such as reinstalling the operating system, before a backup can be restored. The process can be simplified by using a backup system that offers bare-[_____] restore.

▶ CHECK ANSWERS

4

Interactive Situation Questions

Apply what you've learned to some typical computing situations. When using the NP2013 interactive eBook, you can type your answers, and then use the Check Answers button to automatically score your responses.

1. While using several Windows programs at the same time, your computer displays an error message that refers to a program that is not responding. You recognize this message as one that might result from a(n) [_____] leak and decide to close the non-responding program using the Ctrl, Shift, and Esc key combination.

2. Your friend wants to open a window on his Mac computer in which he can run Microsoft Windows and play some games designed for the Windows platform. You tell your friend to create a(n) [_____] machine using software such as Parallels Desktop.

3. Suppose you are using Microsoft Word and you want to open a file. When your software lists the documents you can open, you can expect them to be in Word's [_____] file format, which is DOCX.

4. Can you use a Windows application, create a document, and store it using the file name *I L*ve NY*? Yes or no? [_____]

5. When you want to work with several files—to move them to different folders, for example—it would be most efficient to use a file management utility, such as Windows [_____] or the Mac Finder.

6. When specifying a location for a data file on your hard disk, you should avoid saving it in the [_____] directory.

7. Your computer seems to be taking longer to store and retrieve files. You use a(n) [_____] utility to rearrange the files in contiguous clusters.

8. You have an old computer that you will donate to a school, but you want to make sure its hard disk contains no trace of your data. To do so, you use file [_____] software that overwrites empty sectors with random 1s and 0s.

9. You just finished copying data files to an external USB hard disk. Before you depend on these files as a backup, you should test to make sure you can [_____] the data in the event of a hard disk crash.

10. Your hard disk crashed for some unknown reason. Now when you switch on the computer power, all you get is an "Error reading drive C:" message. You use a(n) [_____] CD that contains the operating system files and device drivers needed to start your computer without accessing the hard disk.

▶ CHECK ANSWERS

Interactive Practice Tests

Practice tests that consist of ten multiple-choice, true/false, and fill-in-the-blank questions are available in the NP2013 interactive eBook. Test questions are selected at random from a large test bank, so each time you take a test, you'll receive a different set of questions. Your tests are scored immediately, and you can print study guides that help you find the correct answers for any questions that you missed.

▶ CLICK TO START

Learning Objectives Checkpoints

Learning Objectives Checkpoints are designed to help you assess whether you have achieved the major learning objectives for this chapter. You can use paper and pencil or word processing software to complete most of the activities.

1. List and describe the four main resources that an operating system manages.

2. Explain the significance of multitasking, multithreading, and multiprocessing.

3. Explain the term *memory leak*, and describe what you can do if one occurs on your PC.

4. Describe five tasks for which you must interact directly with the operating system.

5. Describe the basic elements of a graphical user interface and contrast them with the elements of a command-line interface.

6. Watch your computer while it boots, and then revise the list on page 192 so that it reflects what happens when your computer boots.

7. List four operating systems used on personal computers, two operating systems used on servers, and four operating systems used on handheld devices. List advantages and disadvantages of the three most popular personal computer operating systems.

8. Explain the difference between dual booting and virtual machine technology. Give examples of tasks that might benefit from dual booting or virtual machine capability.

9. Make a list of five file names that are valid under the file-naming conventions for your operating system. Also, create a list of five file names that are not valid, and explain the problem with each one.

10. Pick any five files on the computer that you usually use, and write out the full path for each one.

11. Describe the significance of file formats. List at least ten common formats and their extensions. Make a list of at least 20 file extensions you find on the computer you use most often. Group these extensions into the following categories: system files, graphics files, sound files, text files, other.

12. Demonstrate that you can manage files on a computer by looking at the files on your computer and locating at least five files or folders that should be renamed or relocated to improve the organization and make it easier to locate information on your computer.

13. Describe what happens in the MFT when a file is stored or deleted. Explain what it means when a file is fragmented.

14. Discuss the pros and cons of using an external hard drive, USB flash drive, network server, or online storage service for backups.

15. Describe the way backup software deals with the files in the backup. Explain the differences between full, differential, and incremental backups.

16. Describe the significance of restore points, bare-metal restore, disk imaging, virtual machines, boot disks, and recovery disks.

17. Describe the basic technique for backing up an iPhone, iPad, or iPod Touch.

Study Tip: Make sure you can use your own words to correctly answer each of the purple focus questions that appear throughout the chapter.

Concept Map

Fill in the blanks to illustrate the hierarchy of OS resource management activities.

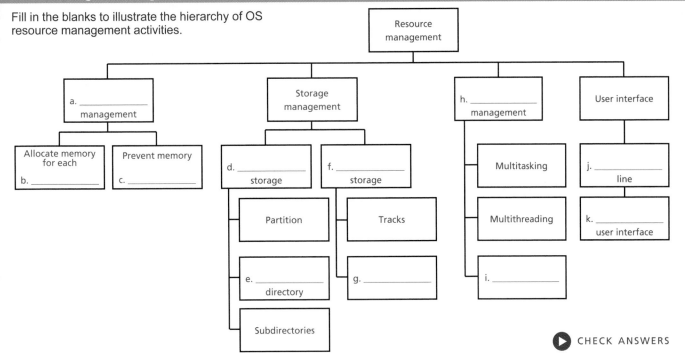

CHECK ANSWERS

5

Chapter Contents

INFOWEBLINKS

You'll find updates for chapter material by connecting to the **NP2013 Chapter 5** InfoWebLink.

Ⓦ CLICK TO CONNECT
www.infoweblinks.com/np2013/ch05

Local Area Networks

Learning Objectives

After reading this chapter, you will be able to answer the following questions by completing the outcomes-based Learning Objectives Checkpoints on page 299.

1. What are PANs, LANs, MANs, and WANs?
2. What are the advantages and disadvantages of LANs?
3. Which devices are included in a typical LAN?
4. What is the purpose of a communications protocol?
5. Why do most networks transmit digital rather than analog signals?
6. How does data find its way over a network to a specified destination?
7. What are the characteristics of Ethernet that make it a popular network technology?
8. How are data signals sent wirelessly?
9. What are the major differences between Bluetooth and Wi-Fi?
10. How do you configure a router for your LAN?
11. What sort of security is available for wireless routers?
12. How do you join a wireless network?
13. What are the easiest ways to share files on a LAN?
14. What are the threats to LAN security?
15. How does encryption work?

CourseMate
Visit the NP2013 CourseMate for this chapter's Pre-Quiz, Audio Overview and Flashcards, Detailed Objectives, Chapter Quiz, Online Games, and more labs.

Multimedia and Interactive Elements
When using the NP2013 interactive eBook, click the ▶ icons to access multimedia resources.

Apply Your Knowledge The information in this chapter will give you the background to:

- Select equipment for building a local area network
- Assemble a basic network
- Configure a network router
- Use a Bluetooth device

- Share files, printers, and an Internet connection over a network
- Join a Wi-Fi network using a smartphone or other handheld device
- Troubleshoot problems with your network
- Implement measures to secure your network
- Use encryption software

Try It!

IS MY COMPUTER CONNECTED TO ANY NETWORKS?

Chapter 5 introduces computer networks and explains how handy they are for sharing files and accessing the Internet at home, at school, or in a business. Your computer might be connected to a home network or it might have access to a campus network or a local wireless hotspot. To discover the networks that your computer can access, complete the following steps:

1. Windows: Click **Start**, then select **Control Panel**. For **Windows 7** and **Vista**, click the **View network status and tasks** link. For **XP**, double-click the **Network Connections** icon.

   Mac: Click the ⬛ **Apple** icon on the menu bar, and select **System Preferences**. Click the **Network** icon.

2. Study the information displayed by your computer. How many networks are listed? _____

3. To view the status of a network in Windows 7, look for **Connections:** and click the link next to it. For Windows Vista, click the **View Status** link. For Windows XP, right-click a network, then select **Status** from the pop-up menu. For Macs, click a network.

4. Using applicable red lines shown on the screen at right, write down the status information for one network. Windows XP and Mac users: Your OS doesn't supply all the information; fill in as much information as you can.

5. After recording the information, close the dialog boxes. You'll learn more about network status as you read this chapter.

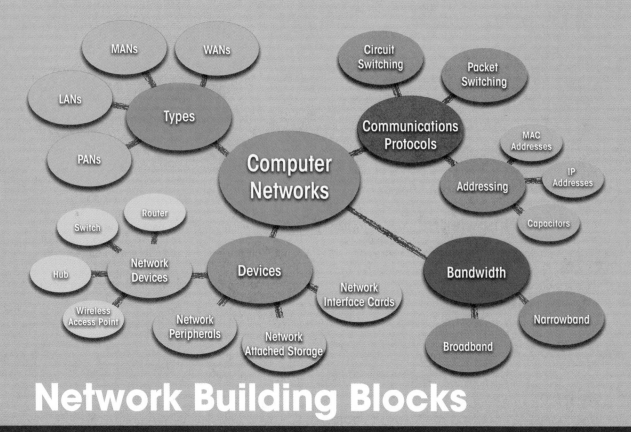

Network Building Blocks

TODAY, NETWORKS ARE EVERYWHERE and everyone wants to be connected. If you understand the network building blocks introduced in Section A, working with network technologies will be a piece of cake.

NETWORK CLASSIFICATIONS

▶ **What's the purpose of a network?** In the early years of personal computers, networks were scarce. Most personal computers functioned as standalone units, and computing was essentially a solitary activity in which one person interacted with one computer.

Some computer engineers, however, had the foresight to anticipate that personal computers could be networked to provide advantages not available with standalone computers. One of the most significant network ideas was conceived by Bob Metcalfe in 1976. His plan for transporting data between computers, shown in Figure 5-1, has become a key element in just about every computer network.

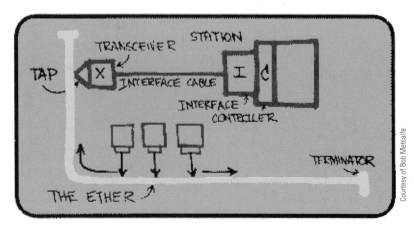

FIGURE 5-1

In 1976, Bob Metcalfe drew this diagram of network technology, which he called Ethernet.

Courtesy of Bob Metcalfe

246

▶ **How are computer networks classified?** Networks can be classified according to their size and geographic scope.

PAN (personal area network) is a term sometimes used to refer to the interconnection of personal digital devices or consumer electronics within a range of about 30 feet (10 meters) and without the use of wires or cables. For example, a PAN could be used to wirelessly transmit data from a computer to a handheld device or printer; it could also transmit data from a computer to a home theater projection device.

A **LAN** (local area network) is a data communications network that connects personal computers within a very limited geographical area—usually a single building. LANs use a variety of wired and wireless technologies. School computer labs and home networks are examples of LANs.

A **MAN** (metropolitan area network) is a public high-speed network capable of voice and data transmission within a range of about 50 miles (80 km). Examples of MANs include local Internet service providers, small cable television companies, and local telephone companies.

A **WAN** (wide area network) covers a large geographical area and usually consists of several smaller networks, which might use different computer platforms and network technologies. The Internet is the world's largest WAN. Networks for nationwide banks, large cable television companies, and multi-location superstores can also be classified as WANs.

▶ **Why is geographic scope important?** Localized networks normally include a small number of computers, which can be connected using basic equipment. As the area of network coverage expands, the number of workstations grows, specialized devices are sometimes required to boost signals, and the diversity of devices requires sophisticated management tools and strategies.

The focus of this chapter is on LANs because you are most likely to encounter this type of network in a school lab or small business. Also, if you intend to set up or upgrade a network in your home or dorm room, you will be working with LAN technologies (Figure 5-2).

© iStockphoto.com/sturti

FIGURE 5-2

The computer network in a dorm room is a LAN.

LAN ADVANTAGES AND DISADVANTAGES

▶ **Why are LANs advantageous?** Today, the pervasiveness of LANs and other types of networks has dramatically changed the face of computing by offering **shared resources**—hardware, software, and data made available for authorized network users to access. LANs offer the following advantages:

▶ **LANs enable people to work together.** Using groupware and other specialized network application software, several people can work together on a single document, communicate by e-mail and instant messaging, take part in multiplayer computer games, and participate in online conferences and Webcasts (Figure 5-3).

FIGURE 5-3

LANs can be used for intra-LAN collaboration, or they can be connected to other networks for broader participation.

▶ **Sharing networked software can reduce costs.** Although purchasing and installing a single software copy for an entire LAN might be technically possible, it is generally not allowed under the terms of a single-user license agreement. However, software site licenses for network use are usually less expensive than purchasing single-user versions of a product for each network user.

▶ **Sharing data on a LAN can increase productivity.** To transfer data between standalone computers, a file is usually copied to some type of removable storage media, and then carried or mailed to the other computer where it is copied onto the hard disk. LANs can provide authorized users with access to data stored on network servers or workstations.

▶ **Sharing networked hardware can reduce costs.** In an office environment, for example, a single expensive high-speed color printer can be purchased and attached to a LAN, instead of the costly alternative of purchasing color printers for each employee who wants to generate color printouts.

▶ **Sharing networked hardware can provide access to a wide range of services and specialized peripheral devices.** A LAN can allow multiple users to access Internet services, including Voice over IP, through a single Internet connection. Networked peripheral devices, such as scanners, photo printers, plotters, and high-capacity storage devices, can be accessed by any authorized LAN users. In a home environment, a LAN can offer access to surveillance and monitoring devices from inside or outside the home. LANs can control entertainment devices, and supply them with downloaded music and videos (Figure 5-4).

FIGURE 5-4

Music and video can stream over a LAN to projectors, speakers, and televisions when devices are equipped for wireless networking.

A wireless projector streams video signals from a remote PC.

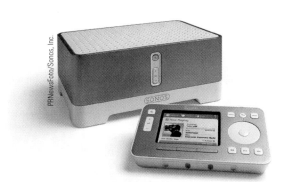

A wireless receiver connects to an audio system, so you can listen to music from your PC in any room.

A wireless media player can stream video to your television, and play digital music on your stereo system.

▶ **Do LANs have disadvantages?** One disadvantage of LANs is that when a network malfunctions, all the resources you're accustomed to accessing are unavailable until the network is repaired.

Another disadvantage of LANs is their vulnerability to unauthorized access. Whereas a standalone computer is vulnerable to on-premises theft or access, network computers are vulnerable to unauthorized access from many sources and locations.

Through unauthorized use of a LAN workstation, intruders can access data stored on the network server or other workstations. LANs connected to the Internet are vulnerable to intrusions from remote computers in distant states, provinces, or countries. Unsecured wireless connections can be tapped from any computers within range of the wireless signal.

LANs are also more vulnerable than standalone computers to malicious code. Whereas the most prevalent threat to standalone computers is disk-borne viruses, networks are susceptible to an ever-increasing number of worms, Trojan horses, and blended threats. If a worm gets through LAN security, every computer on the network is at risk.

Most computer owners are enthusiastic about the benefits provided by LANs and believe that those benefits outweigh the risks of intrusions and viruses—especially if their computers can be protected by security tools, such as antivirus software and firewalls. You'll learn more about LAN security threats and countermeasures later in this chapter.

NETWORK DEVICES

▶ What devices can be attached to a network? You can think of a network as a spider web with many interconnecting points. Each connection point on a network is referred to as a **node**. A network node usually contains a computer, networked peripheral, or network device.

▶ How do computers connect to LANs? A personal computer connected to a network is sometimes called a workstation. Other classes of computers, such as mainframes, supercomputers, servers, and handhelds, can also connect to LANs.

To connect to a LAN, a computer requires network circuitry, sometimes referred to as a **network interface card** (NIC). Network circuitry is built into the main system board of most personal computers. If not, a NIC can be added to a slot in the system board or to a USB port.

▶ What is a networked peripheral? A **networked peripheral**, or network-enabled peripheral, is any device that contains network circuitry to directly connect to a network. Printers, scanners, and storage devices are examples of devices that can be equipped to directly connect to a network instead of connecting to a workstation.

A storage device that directly connects to a network is called **network attached storage** (NAS). Networked peripherals are sometimes described as being "network ready" or as having "built-in networking." Some devices offer networking as an optional add-on.

▶ What are network devices? A **network device** (sometimes referred to as a network appliance) is any electronic device that broadcasts network data, boosts signals, or routes data to its destination.

The most important network device is a **router**, which acts as a central distribution point for getting data to its destination. Network devices also include hubs, switches, gateways, bridges, wireless access points, and repeaters. You will learn more about these devices later in the chapter. In the meantime, study Figure 5-5 for an example of a LAN that connects a variety of computers, networked peripherals, and network devices.

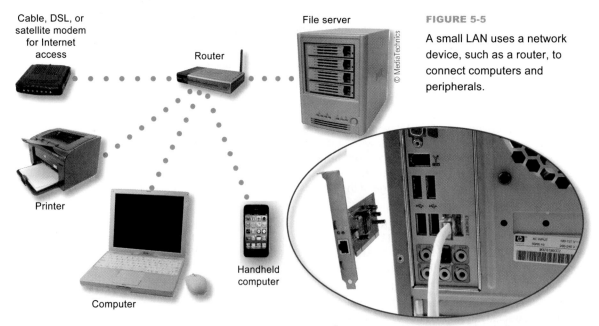

Cable, DSL, or satellite modem for Internet access

Router

File server

Printer

Computer

Handheld computer

© Media Technics

FIGURE 5-5

A small LAN uses a network device, such as a router, to connect computers and peripherals.

Every device on a network requires built-in network circuitry or a network interface card.

NETWORK LINKS

▶ **What connects network nodes?** Data in a network with wired connections travels from one device to another over cables. A network without wires transports data through the air, eliminating the need for cables.

A **communications channel**, or link, is a physical path or a frequency for signal transmissions. You're probably familiar with channels, such as 101.5, on your car radio that carry the signals from your favorite radio station. Links in a computer network are also considered communications channels.

▶ **Do networks require special cables?** Wired network devices are usually connected using Category 5 (Cat 5) or Category 6 (Cat 6) cables terminated at each end with a plastic **RJ45 connector** (Figure 5-6).

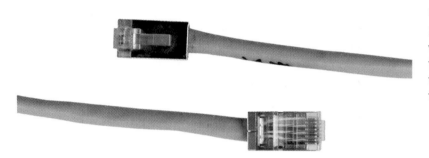

FIGURE 5-6

Network cables are terminated with plastic RJ45 connectors that are similar to, but larger than, the connectors used for telephones.

Network cables contain four pairs of copper wires. Each pair of wires is independently insulated and then twisted together, which is why network cable is sometimes referred to as twisted-pair cable. Shielded twisted-pair (STP) cable contains shielding, which reduces signal noise that might interfere with data transmitted over unshielded twisted-pair (UTP) cable. The shielded cable is not significantly more expensive. Cat 5 and Cat 6 cables have a maximum length of 328 feet (100 meters).

MANs and WANs often use optical fiber cables to carry network signals. An **optical fiber cable** is composed of many strands of glass tubes that are not much wider than a human hair. Data signals speed through these tubes as rays of light.

▶ **What's bandwidth?** Network links must move data and move it quickly. **Bandwidth** is the transmission capacity of a communications channel. Just as a four-lane freeway can carry more traffic than a two-lane street, a high-bandwidth communications channel can carry more data than a low-bandwidth channel. For example, the coaxial cable that brings you more than 100 channels of cable TV has a higher bandwidth than your home telephone line.

The bandwidth of a channel carrying digital data is usually measured in bits per second (bps). For example, your wireless LAN might be rated for an average speed of 27 Mbps. The bandwidth of a channel carrying analog data is typically measured in hertz (Hz). For example, the copper wires that carry voice-grade telephone signals are often described as having 3,000 Hz bandwidth.

High-bandwidth communications systems, such as cable TV and DSL, are sometimes referred to as **broadband**, whereas systems with less capacity, such as dial-up Internet access, are referred to as **narrowband**. Broadband capacity is essential for networks that support many users, and those that carry lots of audio and video data, such as music and movie downloads.

TERMINOLOGY NOTE

Hz is an abbreviation for hertz, which refers to the number of times a wave oscillates, or peaks, per second. Telephone signals are transmitted in the 1,200 Hz range. Many wireless networks transmit a 2.4 GHz signal that peaks 2.4 billion times per second.

COMMUNICATIONS PROTOCOLS

▶ **What is a protocol?** A protocol is a set of rules for interacting and negotiating. In some respects, it is like signals between the pitcher and catcher in a baseball game. Before the ball is thrown, the catcher and pitcher use hand signals to negotiate the speed and style of the pitch.

In the context of networks, a **communications protocol** refers to a set of rules for efficiently transmitting data from one network node to another. Just as a pitcher signals the catcher in baseball, two computers on a network might negotiate their communications protocols through a process called **handshaking**. The transmitting device sends a signal that means "I want to communicate." It then waits for an acknowledgement signal from the receiving device. The two devices negotiate a protocol that both can handle. The sounds you hear as two fax machines connect are examples of handshaking.

The best-known communications protocol is probably TCP/IP. It is the protocol that regulates Internet data transport and has become a standard for LANs as well.

▶ **What can communications protocols do?** Protocols set standards for encoding and decoding data, guiding data to its destination, and mitigating the effects of interference. Specifically, protocols are responsible for the following aspects of network communications:

▶ Dividing messages into packets

▶ Affixing addresses to packets

▶ Initiating transmission

▶ Regulating the flow of data

▶ Checking for transmission errors

▶ Acknowledging receipt of transmitted data

▶ **How does data travel over a network?** In 1948, Claude Shannon, an engineer at the prestigious Bell Labs, published an article describing a communications system model applicable to networks of all types, including today's computer networks.

In Shannon's model, data from a source, such as a network workstation, is encoded and sent as signals over a communications channel to a destination, such as a network printer, storage device, server, or workstation. When data arrives at its destination, it is decoded. Transmission signals can be disrupted by interference called noise, which has the potential to corrupt data, making it erroneous or unintelligible (Figure 5-7).

FIGURE 5-7

A communications system basically sends information from a source to a destination. Although the path between the source and destination might appear to be straight in the diagram, the data can pass through several devices, which convert it to electrical, sound, light, or radio signals; beam it up to satellites; route it along the least congested links; or clean up parts of the signal that have been distorted by noise.

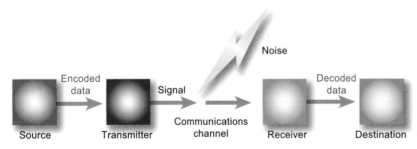

▶ **What kind of signals travel over computer networks?** When data is transmitted over a network link, it usually takes the form of an electromagnetic signal. You can think of these signals as waves that ripple through cables or through the air. Digital signals are transmitted as bits using a limited set of frequencies. Analog signals can assume any value within a specified range of frequencies. Figure 5-8 helps you visualize the difference between digital and analog waves.

▶ **How can a network detect if a signal has been corrupted?** Digital networks—those that transmit digital signals—can be easily monitored to determine if interference has corrupted any signals. At its most primitive level, digital equipment is sensitive to only two frequencies—one that represents 1s and one that represents 0s.

Suppose that a 0 is sent as -5 volts and a 1 is sent as +5 volts. What if, during transmission, some interference changes the voltage of a "perfect" 1 from +5 volts to +3 volts? When the signal is received, the receiving device realizes that +3 volts is not one of the two valid voltages. It guesses that a 1 bit (+5 volts) was actually transmitted, and cleans the signal by reestablishing its voltage to +5. Correcting errors is one of the responsibilities of protocols.

▶ **What's a packet?** When you send a file or an e-mail message, you might suppose that it is transmitted as an entire unit to its destination. This is not the case. Your file is actually chopped up into small pieces called packets.

A **packet** is a parcel of data that is sent across a computer network. Each packet contains the address of its sender, the destination address, a sequence number, and some data. When packets reach their destination, they are reassembled into the original message according to the sequence numbers (Figure 5-9).

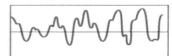

▶ **Why not just send an entire message?** Some communications networks, such as the telephone system, use a technology called **circuit switching**, which essentially establishes a dedicated, private link between one telephone and another for the duration of a call. This type of switching provides callers with a direct pipeline over which a stream of voice data can flow. Unfortunately, circuit switching is rather inefficient. For example, when someone is on hold, no communication is taking place—yet the circuit is reserved and cannot be used for other communications.

A more efficient alternative to circuit switching is **packet switching** technology, which divides a message into several packets that can be routed independently to their destination. Messages divided into equal-size packets are easier to handle than an assortment of small, medium, large, and huge files.

Packets from many different messages can share a single communications channel, or circuit. Packets are shipped over the circuit on a first-come, first-served basis. If some packets from a message are not available, the system does not need to wait for them. Instead, the system moves on to send packets from other messages. The end result is a steady stream of data (Figure 5-10).

FIGURE 5-10

Packet switching networks (bottom) provide a more efficient communications system than circuit switching networks (top). To see the differences between these technologies in action, click the Start icons in your interactive eBook.

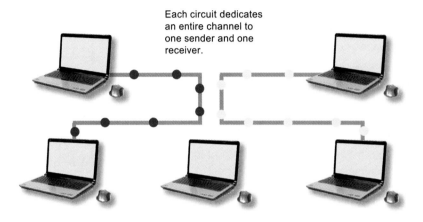

Each circuit dedicates an entire channel to one sender and one receiver.

CIRCUIT SWITCHING NETWORK

▶ CLICK TO START

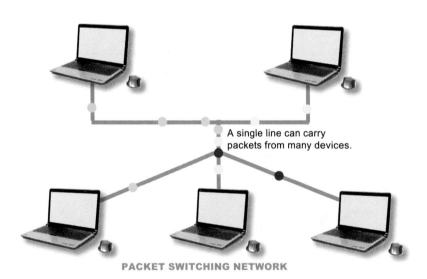

A single line can carry packets from many devices.

PACKET SWITCHING NETWORK

▶ CLICK TO START

▶ **How are packets routed to their destinations?** Every packet that travels over a network includes the address of its destination device, similar to the way a letter contains the address of a house or mailbox. Communications protocols specify the proper format for addresses within a network. When a packet reaches a network node, a routing device examines the address and sends the packet along to its destination.

▶ **How do devices get an address?** Network addresses are a potential source of confusion. Network devices can have a variety of addresses used for different purposes. Two commonly used addresses are MAC addresses and IP addresses.

▶ **What is a MAC address?** In the context of networking, *MAC* stands for Media Access Control. A **MAC address** is a unique number assigned to a network interface card when it is manufactured. MAC addresses are used for some low-level network functions and can also be employed to establish network security.

▶ What is an IP address? An **IP address** is a series of numbers used to identify a network device. IP addresses were originally used on the Internet, but now are the standard for assigning addresses to devices in virtually every type of computer network.

IP addresses are assigned to network computers, servers, peripherals, and devices. When written, an IP address such as 204.127.129.1 is separated into four sections by periods for the convenience of human readers. Each section is called an **octet** because in binary it is represented by eight bits.

▶ Where do IP addresses come from? IP addresses can be assigned by Internet service providers or system managers. Assigned IP addresses are semi-permanent and stay the same every time you boot your computer. If you use an assigned IP address, you have to enter it when you configure your network access.

IP addresses can also be obtained through **DHCP** (Dynamic Host Configuration Protocol), a protocol designed to automatically distribute IP addresses. Most computers are preconfigured to get an IP address by sending a query to the network device acting as the DHCP server.

The IP address assigned by DHCP is good for that session. The next time you boot up, you might be assigned a different address. The fact that your IP address changes each time you boot up isn't a problem. Your network keeps track of your IP address behind the scenes; and unlike an e-mail address, your IP address is not publicized as a permanent address that people use to send files and messages to you.

▶ What happens when data reaches its destination? Even on a small home network, packets might not travel from the source directly to their destination. Like travelers routed from one airline hub to another, network traffic often travels through intermediary routing devices.

When data reaches its destination, it is checked for errors one last time and then the packets are reassembled into their original configuration. Tracking data is appended or stripped off, depending on the application, and then the newly delivered file is ready to be stored or viewed on the destination device.

QuickCheck   SECTION A

1. A dorm-room network covers a limited area and is an example of a(n) [_____] area network.

2. Each connection point on a network is referred to as a network [_____].

3. Communications [_____], such as TCP/IP, set standards for encoding and decoding data, guiding data to its destination, and mitigating the effects of noise.

4. A(n) [_____] switching network establishes a dedicated connection between two devices, whereas a(n) [_____] switching network divides messages into small parcels and handles them on a first-come, first-served basis.

5. IP addresses can be assigned by an ISP or system manager, or can be automatically obtained from a(n) [_____] server. (Hint: Use the acronym.)

▶ CHECK ANSWERS

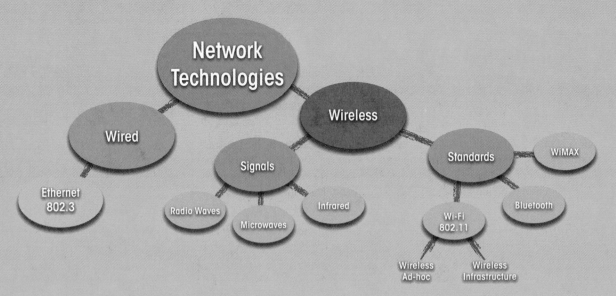

Wired and Wireless Technologies

NETWORK DEVICES CAN BE CONNECTED using wired or wireless technologies. When should you use wired connections? How do they stack up against wireless connections? This section compares the two technologies side by side.

WIRED BASICS

▶ **What is wired technology?** Wired network technology uses cables to connect network devices. Familiar technologies such as telephone and cable television make extensive use of wired connections. Much of the Internet infrastructure is also wired. Before wireless technologies became available, local area networks were exclusively wired.

Today, wired connections are used less frequently for home, school, and business networks. They remain the network technology of choice, however, for LANs that require fast and secure connectivity.

▶ **What are the advantages of wired technology?** Wired connections are fast, secure, and simple to configure. Wired connections transfer data over cables, which typically have high bandwidth and are shielded against interference.

The speed of a wired connection is useful when accessing large files from a local server. Wired connections also offer a faster infrastructure for playing multiplayer computer games within a LAN (Figure 5-11). For Internet-based multiplayer games, however, the speed of the Internet connection rather than the LAN is usually the limiting factor.

Wired connections are more secure than their wireless counterparts because a computer can only join a network if it is physically connected by a cable. When you set up a wired connection, you don't have to worry about hackers intercepting your data from the sidewalk outside your house, or your neighbor stumbling across your files because your wireless signal reaches past your property line.

FIGURE 5-11

Discerning multiplayer game players prefer a fast wired connection when playing head to head on a LAN.

© Caro / Alamy

▶ **What are the disadvantages of wired connections?** The cables that offer speed and security for a wired connection are also its main weakness. Devices tethered to cables have limited mobility. Desktop computers tend to be better candidates for wired connections, whereas notebook computers and handheld devices can retain their mobility when they are not tethered to a cable.

Cables are unsightly, tend to get tangled, and collect dust. Running cables through ceilings, walls, and floors can be tricky or banned by your landlord. Some building codes prohibit network cables from running through air conditioning and heating ducts. When drilling holes for network cables, installers should take care to avoid electrical wires and other hazards.

ETHERNET

▶ **What is Ethernet?** **Ethernet** is a wired network technology that is defined by IEEE 802.3 standards. It was first deployed in 1976 and has since emerged as the dominant standard for wired connections in local area networks.

▶ **Why is Ethernet so popular?** Ethernet's success is attributable to several factors:

▶ Ethernet is easy to understand, implement, manage, and maintain.

▶ As a nonproprietary technology, Ethernet equipment is available from a variety of vendors, and market competition keeps prices low.

▶ Current Ethernet standards allow extensive flexibility in network design to meet the needs of small and large installations.

▶ Ethernet is compatible with popular Wi-Fi wireless technology, so it is easy to mix wired and wireless devices on a single network.

▶ **How does Ethernet work?** Ethernet simultaneously broadcasts data packets to all network devices. A packet is accepted only by the device to which it is addressed (Figure 5-12).

> **TERMINOLOGY NOTE**
>
> IEEE (Institute of Electrical and Electronics Engineers) is a nonprofit professional association dedicated to advancing technological innovation. The organization publishes standards, which in networking ensure that devices interoperate.

FIGURE 5-12

On an Ethernet, a packet is broadcast to every device, but is accepted only by the device to which it is addressed.

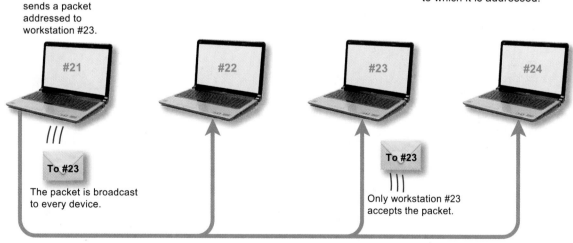

This workstation sends a packet addressed to workstation #23.

The packet is broadcast to every device.

Only workstation #23 accepts the packet.

▶ How fast is Ethernet? The original Ethernet standard carried data over a coaxial cable at 10 Mbps. Ethernet encompasses a family of LAN technologies that offer various data transmission rates as shown in Figure 5-13. Today, most personal computers and LAN equipment work with Gigabit Ethernet.

Ethernet Standard	IEEE Designation	Speed
10BaseT Ethernet	IEEE 802.3	10 Mbps
Fast Ethernet	IEEE 802.3u	100 Mbps
Gigabit Ethernet	IEEE 802.3z	1,000 Mbps
10 Gigabit Ethernet	IEEE 802.3ae	10 Gbps
40/100 Gigabit Ethernet	IEEE 802.3ba	40 or 100 Gbps

FIGURE 5-13

Ethernet Standards

FIGURE 5-14

Most computers have a built-in Ethernet port. You can determine the speed of your computer's Ethernet adapter using networking utilities.

▶ How can I tell if a device is Ethernet ready? Many computers have a built-in Ethernet port located on the system case. The port looks very similar to an oversized telephone jack. If you have such a port, the next step is to determine its speed, as explained in Figure 5-14.

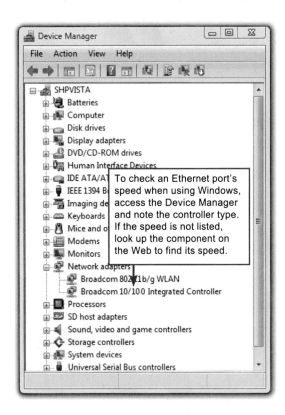

To check an Ethernet port's speed when using Windows, access the Device Manager and note the controller type. If the speed is not listed, look up the component on the Web to find its speed.

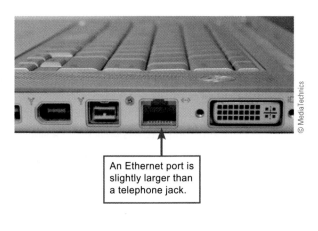

An Ethernet port is slightly larger than a telephone jack.

FIGURE 5-15

Ethernet Adapters

Ethernet adapter for expansion slot

▶ What if a computer doesn't have an Ethernet port? If your computer has no Ethernet port, you can purchase and install an **Ethernet adapter** (also called an Ethernet card or NIC). A USB Ethernet adapter plugs into a USB port and can be used with a notebook or desktop computer. You also have the option of installing an Ethernet card in an expansion slot inside the system unit of a desktop computer. Figure 5-15 illustrates some popular network adapters.

Ethernet adapter for USB port

WIRELESS BASICS

▶ **What is wireless technology?** Wireless network technology transports data from one device to another without the use of cables or wires. Although we use the term *wireless connection*, there is no physical connection between wireless devices in a network. Their connection is conceptual in the sense that data can travel between "connected" devices.

Networks of all sizes, from PANs to LANs and WANs, can use wireless technologies, such as radio signals, microwaves, and infrared light.

▶ **How do radio signals transport data?** Most wireless connections transport data as RF signals (radio frequency signals). **RF signals**—commonly called radio waves—are sent and received by a **transceiver** (a combination of a transmitter and a receiver) that is equipped with an antenna. Workstations, peripheral devices, and network devices can be equipped with transceivers to send and receive data on wireless networks (Figure 5-16).

▶ **How do microwaves transport data?** **Microwaves** (the waves themselves, not your oven!) provide another option for transporting data wirelessly. Like radio waves, microwaves are electromagnetic signals, but they behave differently.

Microwaves can be aimed in a single direction and have more carrying capacity than radio waves. However, microwaves cannot penetrate metal objects and work best for line-of-sight transmission when a clear path exists between the transmitter and receiver. Microwave installations usually provide data transport for large corporate networks.

▶ **How does infrared transport data?** Today, most people are familiar with television remote controls that use **infrared light** beams. Infrared can also carry data signals, but only for short distances and with a clear line of sight. Its most practical use seems to be for transmitting data between devices connected to a PAN.

▶ **What are the advantages of wireless connections?** The main advantage of wireless connections is mobility. Wireless devices are not tethered to network cables, so battery-operated workstations can be easily moved from room to room, or even outdoors. With wireless networks, there are no unsightly cables, and power spikes are much less likely to run through cables to damage workstations.

▶ **Do wireless networks have disadvantages?** In the past, wireless network equipment was more expensive than equivalent wired equipment. With the current popularity of wireless technologies, however, prices have equalized. When compared to wired networks, the main disadvantages of wireless networks are speed, range, licensing, and security.

▶ **Why is wireless slower than wired?** Wireless signals are susceptible to interference from devices such as microwave ovens, cordless telephones, and baby monitors. When interference affects a wireless signal, data must be re-transmitted, and that takes extra time.

5

FIGURE 5-16

Wireless equipment often sports an antenna for transmitting and receiving data signals. The antenna is not always visible; it can be incorporated within the body of the device.

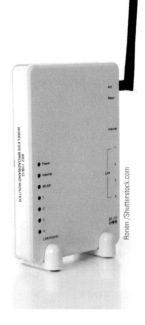

Ronen /Shutterstock.com

Despite interference, wireless connections are fast enough for most applications, such as sharing files and browsing the Web. But when lots of computer game players compete against each other over a LAN, a fast, wired connection is desirable.

▶ **What limits the range of a wireless network?** The range of a wireless signal can be limited by the type of signal, the transmitter strength, and the physical environment. Just as radio stations fade as you move away from their broadcasting towers, data signals fade as the distance between network devices increases. Signal range can also be limited by thick walls, floors, or ceilings.

As signal strength decreases, so can speed. A weak signal usually means slow data transfers. You can monitor network signal strength from your computer's desktop (Figure 5-17).

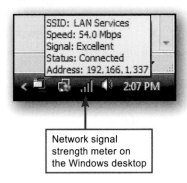

Network signal
strength meter on
the Windows desktop

FIGURE 5-17

On wireless connections, signal strength varies depending on distance from a transmitter and obstacles that might interfere with the signal.

▶ **What's wrong with wireless security?** Wireless signals float through the air and penetrate walls. The signals that carry your wireless data can be accessed from outside your premises. Someone outside of your house, for example, could surreptitiously join your network, access files, and piggyback on your Internet connection. To make wireless data useless to intruders, it should be encrypted. Later in the chapter, you'll learn how to use encryption to secure data sent over wireless connections.

▶ **How does licensing affect wireless connections?** Government agencies, such as the Federal Communications Commission (FCC), regulate signals that are sent through the air. To broadcast at most frequencies, including those used by radio and television stations, a license is required. Only certain frequencies are unlicensed and available for public use.

Unlicensed frequencies include 2.4 GHz and 5.8 GHz used by cordless telephones and baby monitors, and the 460 MHz frequency used for two-way CB (Citizens Band) radios. Wireless connections use unlicensed frequencies so that they can be set up without applying to the FCC for permission. The few unlicensed frequencies are crowded, however, and neighboring networks that are forced to use the same frequencies pose security risks.

▶ **What are the most popular technologies for wireless connections?** By far the most popular wireless LAN technology is Wi-Fi. Additional wireless technologies such as Bluetooth, Wireless USB (WUSB), and Wireless HD (WiHD) are useful for PANs that include wireless game controllers, MP3 players, televisions, printers, digital cameras, and scanners. Other wireless technologies, such as WiMAX, are MAN or WAN technologies commonly used for fixed Internet access. Let's take a brief look at Bluetooth technology and then examine Wi-Fi in more detail.

BLUETOOTH

▶ **What is Bluetooth?** **Bluetooth** is a short-range wireless network technology that's designed to make connections between two devices. Bluetooth is not commonly used to connect a collection of workstations into a LAN. Instead, Bluetooth connectivity replaces the short cables that would otherwise tether a mouse, keyboard, game controller, or similar device to a computer.

Bluetooth can be used to link devices in a PAN, connect home entertainment system components, provide hands-free cell phone operation in an automobile, connect game controllers to videogame base stations, synchronize handheld devices with desktop computers, and link a cell phone to a wireless headset (Figure 5-18).

Bluetooth operates at the unlicensed 2.4 GHz frequency, so it is open to public use.

▶ **How does Bluetooth work?** Bluetooth links devices through a process called pairing. **Pairing** creates a persistent link between two devices, usually through the exchange of an authentication code called a passkey.

Devices equipped with Bluetooth capability can be set into **discovery mode**, in which they are open for pairing. Two devices in discovery mode can "discover" each other and exchange passkeys. Once pairing is complete, the two devices can share data without exchanging passkeys again.

▶ **What are the speed and range of Bluetooth?** Bluetooth offers peak transmission rates of only 3 Mbps, and devices should be within about 30 feet of each other. It is one of the slowest wireless technologies, so it is suitable for sending small bursts of data, rather than large files.

▶ **Can I tell if my computer has Bluetooth?** Bluetooth is built into many desktop, portable, and handheld computers. If your computer does not have built-in Bluetooth, you can plug a Bluetooth antenna into a USB port. You can look for the Bluetooth logo on your computer's task bar (Windows) or menu bar (Mac). Figure 5-19 illustrates Bluetooth icons and what they mean.

FIGURE 5-18

Bluetooth technology is used for wireless keyboards and mice, but it is also the technology used for wireless headsets and devices like Motorola's Bluetooth headset, which clips to a motorcycle helmet so you don't miss important cell phone calls.

Norman Chan / Shutterstock.com

© iStockphoto.com/muratkoc

FIGURE 5-19

Bluetooth status icons appear on an iMac's menu bar at the top of the screen.

© MediaTechnics

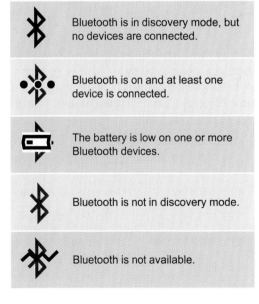

✳	Bluetooth is in discovery mode, but no devices are connected.
✦	Bluetooth is on and at least one device is connected.
🔋	The battery is low on one or more Bluetooth devices.
✳	Bluetooth is not in discovery mode.
✳	Bluetooth is not available.

WI-FI

▶ **What is Wi-Fi? Wi-Fi** refers to a set of wireless networking technologies defined by IEEE 802.11 standards. A Wi-Fi device transmits data as radio waves over 2.4 GHz or 5.8 GHz frequencies. Wi-Fi is compatible with Ethernet, so you can use the two technologies in a single network.

▶ **How does Wi-Fi work?** You can set up Wi-Fi in two ways. One option is to use **wireless ad-hoc protocol** in which devices broadcast directly to each other (Figure 5-20).

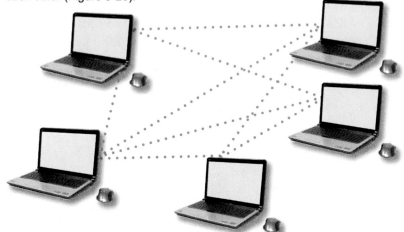

FIGURE 5-20

Wireless ad-hoc networks are conceptually simple, but provide few security safeguards. This type of connection is best limited to occasional use when you want to temporarily connect two computers to share a few files.

A second option uses **wireless infrastructure protocol** in which a centralized broadcasting device coordinates communication among network devices (Figure 5-21). Later in the chapter, you will see how this configuration offers more security than ad-hoc connections.

FIGURE 5-21

Wireless infrastructure networks use a centralized device to handle data that travels from one device to another.

▶ **How fast are Wi-Fi connections?** Wi-Fi encompasses several standards, designated by letters *b*, *a*, *g*, *n*, and *y*. Some of these standards are cross compatible, which means that you can use them on the same network. Figure 5-22 summarizes the specifications for each Wi-Fi standard.

FIGURE 5-22

Wi-Fi Standards

IEEE Designation	Frequency	Typical Speed	Range	Pros/Cons
IEEE 802.11b	2.4 GHz	5 Mbps	100–300 feet	Original standard
IEEE 802.11a	5 GHz	27 Mbps	25–75 feet	Not compatible with 802.11b, g, or n
IEEE 802.11g	2.4 GHz	27 Mbps	100–150 feet	Faster than, but compatible with, 802.11b
IEEE 802.11n	2.4/5 GHz	144 Mbps	100–150 feet	Faster than, but compatible with, b and g
IEEE 802.11y	3.6–3.7 GHz	27 Mbps	3 miles	Use: wide-area commercial base stations

▶ **How do the speed and range of Wi-Fi compare to other network technologies?** With wired connections, the rated speed and range are usually quite close to actual performance. Wireless connection speed and range, however, are often theoretical maximums because signals can easily deteriorate. Although Wi-Fi 802.11n is capable of 600 Mbps speeds, its actual performance is normally 144 Mbps, which is far slower than Gigabit Ethernet.

In a typical office environment, Wi-Fi's actual range varies from 25 to 150 feet (8 to 45 meters). Thick cement walls, steel beams, and other environmental obstacles can drastically reduce this range to the point that signals cannot be reliably transmitted. Wi-Fi signals can also be disrupted by interference from electronic devices operating at the same frequency, such as 2.4 GHz cordless telephones.

Wi-Fi speed and range can be improved with various technologies. For example, **MIMO** (multiple-input multiple-output) technology uses two or more antennas to essentially send multiple sets of signals between network devices (Figure 5-23).

▶ **How can I tell if a device is Wi-Fi ready?** Although some devices have a small antenna that reveals their wireless communications capabilities, the antenna and transceiver for most notebook computers, handheld devices, and network peripherals are hidden inside the case.

Most Macs have built-in Wi-Fi capability. In some versions of Mac OS, wireless networking is handled by an Apple rendition of Wi-Fi called **AirPort**. In newer versions of Mac OS, wireless networking is referred to as Wi-Fi.

For other computers and peripherals, you usually have to check the device's documentation or on-screen utilities to discover if it has Wi-Fi capability (Figure 5-24).

FIGURE 5-23

MIMO-equipped devices usually have more than one antenna.

5

FIGURE 5-24

Check the hardware listings to see if your computer has Wi-Fi capability. With Windows, use the Start menu to access Device Manager and look for a wireless or WLAN adapter.

▶ **Can I add Wi-Fi?** Today, most computers come equipped with Wi-Fi circuitry. Computers without Wi-Fi or those with slow Wi-Fi protocols can be upgraded using a **Wi-Fi adapter** (also called a Wi-Fi card or wireless network controller).

Wi-Fi cards that plug into an expansion slot can be used to upgrade desktop computers. Wi-Fi adapters that plug into USB ports can be used to upgrade any type of computer. Figure 5-25 illustrates these two types of Wi-Fi adapters.

FIGURE 5-25

Wi-Fi Adapters

Wi-Fi adapter in an
expansion slot

USB Wi-Fi adapter

QuickCheck   SECTION B

1. Today's most popular wired network technology is [   ] and is defined by IEEE 802.3 standards.

2. A short-range, wireless network technology primarily used for PANs is called [   ].

3. [   ] is today's most popular wireless network technology for LANs.

4. In a network that includes Wi-Fi wireless [   ] connections, a centralized device broadcasts data to all of the workstations.

5. Wi-Fi capability on some Macs is handled by the [   ] network utility.

▶ CHECK ANSWERS

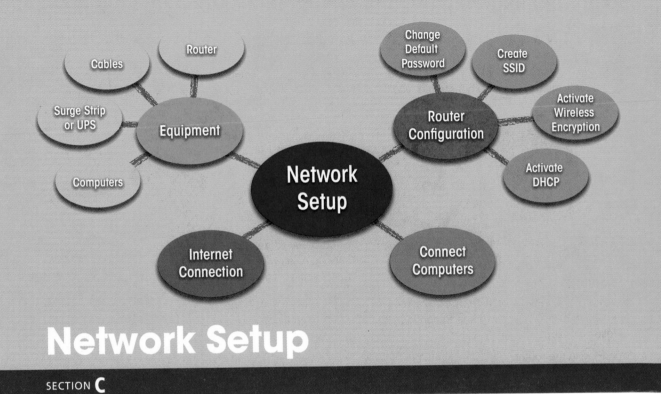

Network Setup

SETTING UP A NETWORK is easy. Whether you want to set up a simple home network to access the Internet, a lightning-fast network for playing games with your friends, or a serviceable network for your small business, use this section as a guide.

SETUP OVERVIEW

▶ **What is the basic plan?** A versatile and secure network should be configured with a centralized network device that supports both wired and wireless connections. Figure 5-26 illustrates a general network plan that can be modified by switching out workstations, printers, or file servers.

FIGURE 5-26

The plan for your network hinges on a centralized router that supports wired and wireless connections.

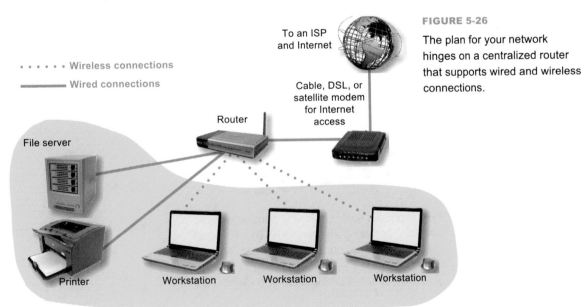

▶ **What equipment do I need?** Network equipment is widely available and fairly inexpensive. To get started, you'll need the gear shown in Figure 5-27.

FIGURE 5-27

Wireless Networking Equipment

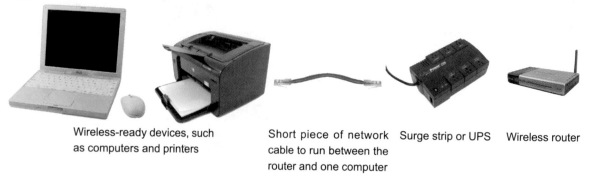

Wireless-ready devices, such as computers and printers

Short piece of network cable to run between the router and one computer

Surge strip or UPS

Wireless router

▶ **What's the general procedure for setting up a network?** The key to setting up a network is to configure the router, which involves the following steps:

- ▶ Plug in the router.
- ▶ Connect the router to a computer.
- ▶ Configure the router.
- ▶ Access the router setup utility.
- ▶ Create a new router password.
- ▶ Enter an SSID for the network.
- ▶ Activate WEP, WPA, or PSK and create an encryption key.
- ▶ Connect an Internet access device.
- ▶ Set up the wireless workstations.

ROUTER INSTALLATION

▶ **What kind of router do I need?** Look for a Wireless-N router like the one in Figure 5-28 that includes a Gigabit Ethernet switch. The wireless capacity handles Wi-Fi connections, whereas the Ethernet capacity handles wired connections.

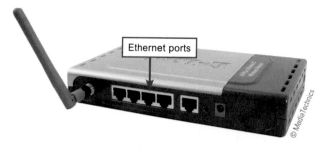

Ethernet ports

© MediaTechnics

FIGURE 5-28

Most wireless routers (note the antenna) also include ports for wired Ethernet connections.

Make sure the number of Ethernet ports is sufficient for the number of wired devices that you intend to connect. For most home networks, four Ethernet ports are sufficient; you'll likely need one for your Internet connection, one for a network printer, and perhaps one for a file server. If you have lots of friends who like to play games over a wired connection, you might want additional Ethernet ports.

In the previous section, you learned that there are several variations of Wi-Fi, including 802.11a, 802.11b, 802.11g, and 802.11n. Most Wireless-N routers allow you to connect devices that use any of these Wi-Fi standards.

▶ **What's the difference between a router and a switch?** In addition to routers, there are several types of network devices, including hubs, switches, gateways, bridges, wireless access points, and repeaters. Each device serves a slightly different purpose.

Modern network equipment often combines the functions of two or more network devices, such as a router that also functions as a switch and a gateway. For a typical home network, all that's needed is a wireless router that includes an Ethernet switch and Internet gateway. Extended networks in businesses and organizations might need additional devices, such as those described in Figure 5-29.

FIGURE 5-29

Network devices serve different purposes.

Network Device	Purpose	
Hub	Extends a wired network by adding additional ports	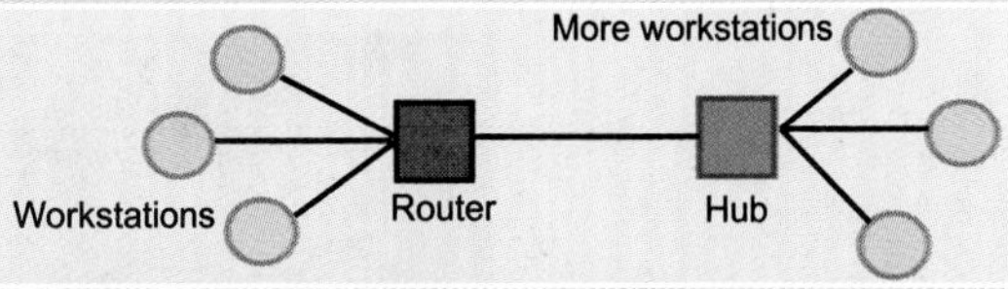
Switch	Intelligently facilitates communication among multiple devices on a network	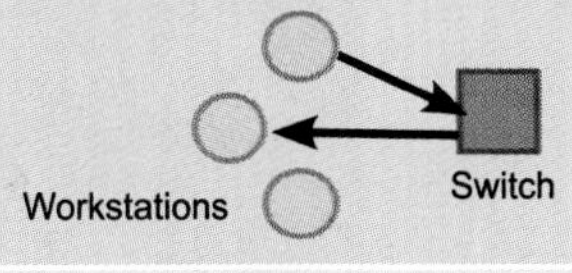
Gateway	Joins two different types of networks, such as your home network and the Internet	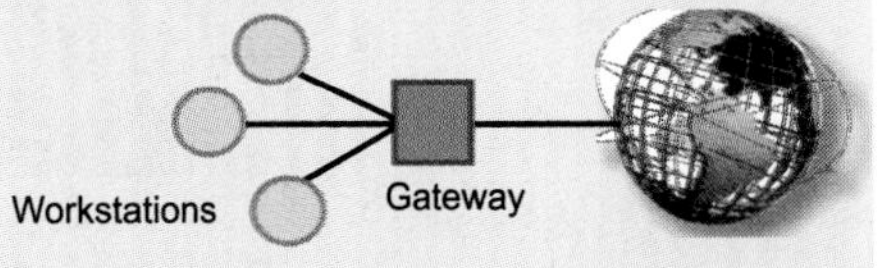
Bridge	Connects two similar networks	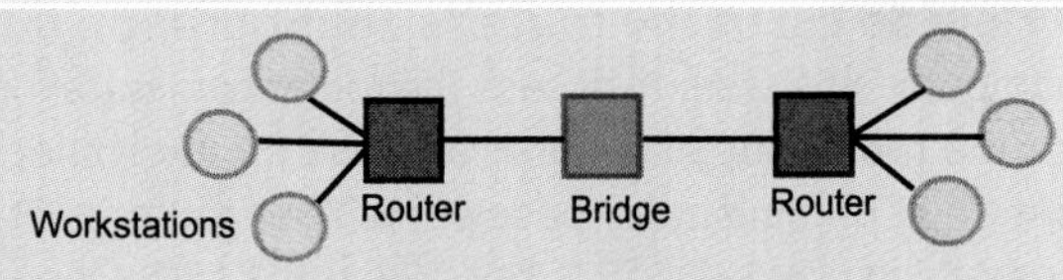
Repeater	Extends the range of a network by restoring signals to maximum strength and retransmitting them	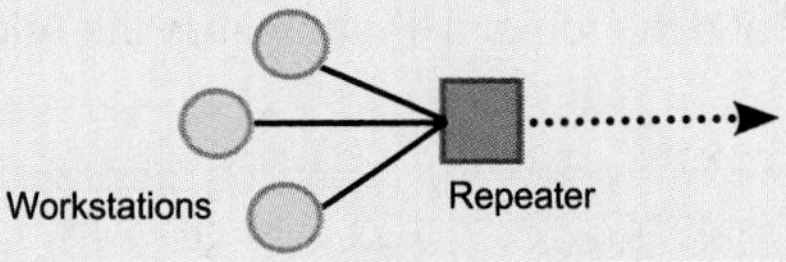
Wireless access point (WAP)	Allows wireless devices to connect to a wired network	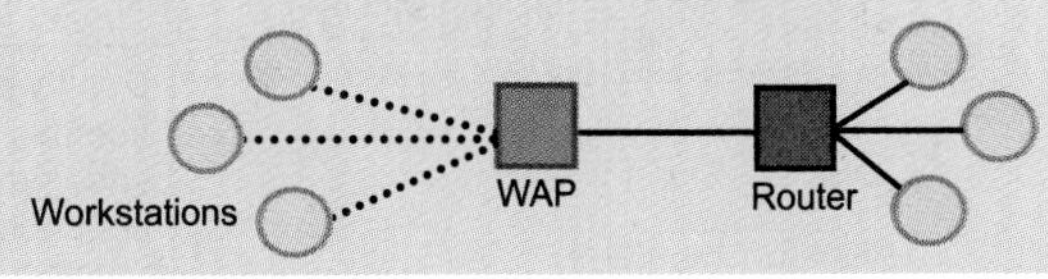

▶ **How do I power up a router?** Place the router in a central location relative to the network devices. Connect the router to a power outlet through a surge strip or UPS.

A UPS will keep your network operational during a power outage. Your ability to access the Internet during a power outage depends on the power situation at your Internet service provider, however. A network that consists of battery-operated notebook computers and a router connected to a UPS should be able to run for several hours during a blackout.

Some routers power up as soon as they are plugged in, whereas other routers have an on/off switch. Make sure your router is powered on by confirming that the power light is lit.

ROUTER CONFIGURATION

▶ How do I access the router? Before using your network, you should adjust the router's configuration settings to make sure your network is secure. The configuration settings are stored in the router's EEPROM memory. You'll need to log in to the configuration software to adjust the settings.

A router has no screen or keyboard of its own; so to access the router's configuration software, you have to connect a computer to the router. The easiest way to make this connection is with a short Ethernet cable (Figure 5-30). The wired connection is detected automatically by the computer's networking utilities, and that connection can provide a direct link to the router without any additional setup.

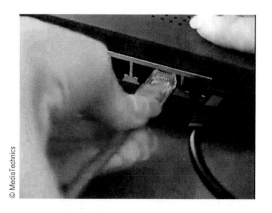

© Media Technics

FIGURE 5-30

To connect a computer to the router, plug an Ethernet cable into one of the router's ports. Plug the other end of the cable into a computer.

▶ How do I start the router's configuration utility? You can use your computer's browser to access the router configuration utility. Documentation for the router supplies an IP address for the router and might also supply a default administrator password. Your router's IP address is likely to be something like 192.168.1.1 or 192.168.1.100. Open your browser and type http:// and the router's IP address in the Address line (Figure 5-31).

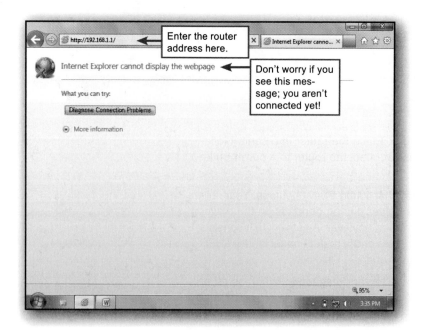

FIGURE 5-31

To access your router's configuration utility, open a browser and enter the router address.

▶ How do I change the default password? Your first step after logging on to your router's configuration utility is to change the default password so that hackers can't gain access to your network and reconfigure it for their own malevolent schemes.

Locate the setting for the administrator password and create a new one (Figure 5-32). Follow the recommendations in earlier chapters for creating a strong password. This password is only used to configure the router. It does not need to be conveyed to network users who simply want to set up their computers to send and receive data over the network.

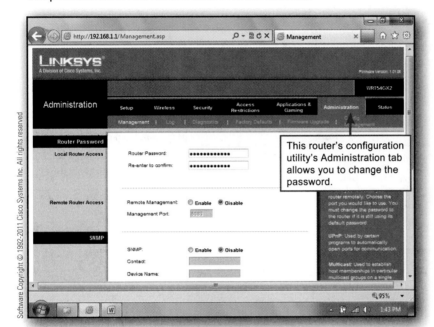

This router's configuration utility's Administration tab allows you to change the password.

FIGURE 5-32

Change the default password for your router when you install a wireless network. ▶ Your digital textbook shows you how to access router settings and change the default password.

▶ What is an SSID? An **SSID** (service set identifier) is the name of a wireless network. In areas where there are overlapping wireless networks, such as in a city or on a college campus, SSIDs help you log in to the right network, rather than a network run by a hacker who will try to suck important information off your computer as soon as you connect.

▶ How do I set the SSID? Most routers ship with an SSID predefined by the manufacturer. Predefined SSIDs are typically very simple and publicly known.

As shown in Figure 5-33, use the router configuration software to change the default SSID. When you create an SSID, think of it as a user ID, rather than a password. Examples of SSIDs would be Cabin, Acme Company, Java Joe Coffee Shop, Planters Inn of Miami, or Alpha Kappa Delta Phi.

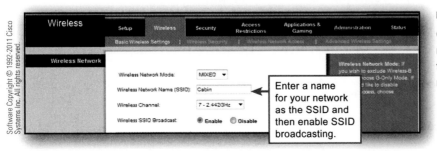

Enter a name for your network as the SSID and then enable SSID broadcasting.

FIGURE 5-33

Create an SSID for your network so that it can be differentiated from other nearby networks.

▶ Should I broadcast my SSID? When SSID broadcasting is turned on, any wireless device passing by can see that a network exists. Legitimate users can easily find the network and connect to it. With SSID broadcasting turned off, the public can't see it. Unfortunately, hackers armed with the right tools can see the network even if the SSID is not broadcast.

Turning off SSID is a very weak form of security. Experts disagree about broadcasting your network's SSID. If you believe the potential for drive-by hacking is high, then you might not want to broadcast the SSID. In any case, SSID should be left on until you configure the rest of the devices that you plan to use on your network.

▶ How do I set the addresses for my network workstations? Each workstation requires a unique address for sending and receiving data. When you configure your router to act as a DHCP server, it will automatically assign an address to each workstation that joins your network. Figure 5-34 illustrates how to set up DHCP.

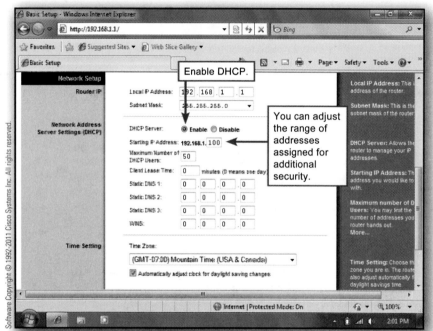

FIGURE 5-34

Enable DHCP so that the router automatically assigns an IP address to each workstation.

▶ Do I need to take any special steps to secure my network? Networks with wireless connections are much more susceptible to unauthorized access and use than networks that have only wired connections. A wireless router is not secure until you activate encryption.

▶ How does encryption secure my network? Preventing Wi-Fi signal interception is difficult, but encrypting transmitted data makes it useless to intruders. **Wireless encryption** scrambles the data transmitted between wireless devices and then unscrambles the data only on devices that have a valid encryption key. Several types of encryption are available; some are more effective than others.

▶ What are the options for wireless encryption? The original wireless encryption protocol was called **WEP** (Wired Equivalent Privacy) because it was designed to provide a level of confidentiality similar to that of a wired network. WEP is very easy to bypass, so it is a weak security measure.

WPA (Wi-Fi Protected Access) and its follow-up version, WPA2, offer stronger protection by making sure that packets have not been intercepted or tampered with in any way. **PSK** (pre-shared key), also referred to as personal mode, is a type of WPA used on most home networks.

▶ Which type of encryption should I use? All devices on a network must use the same encryption protocol. If you have even one device on your network that only supports WEP, for example, you will have to use WEP for the entire network. Although WEP is fairly easy for hackers to neutralize, it is better than leaving a network totally unprotected. If available, you'll get better security with WPA2 or PSK2.

▶ How do I activate encryption? To activate encryption, open the router's configuration software. Earlier in the chapter, you learned that most wireless routers can be configured by opening a browser and entering the router's IP address. Use the router configuration utilities to select an encryption protocol. In addition, you must create a wireless encryption key.

A **wireless encryption key** (sometimes referred to as a network security key) is the basis for scrambling and unscrambling the data transmitted between wireless devices. All workstations use the same key to scramble and unscramble data.

The key is similar to a password, only it is often longer. Instructions for creating a valid key are usually given in the router's documentation or on-screen Help file. For example, you might be limited to using only numbers 0 to 9 and letters A to F. Alternatively, you might be allowed to use a passphrase, such as notrespassingthismeansu, as the key.

Don't use a key or passphrase that's easy for an intruder to guess. Remember the key or passphrase you use to configure the router. Later, when you set up computers and other network devices, you will enter the same key so that every device on your network can encrypt and decrypt the data flowing on the network. Figure 5-35 illustrates how to activate wireless encryption.

FIGURE 5-35

The configuration utility used to set up wireless security is supplied by the router manufacturer. In this example, encryption is being configured for a Linksys router.

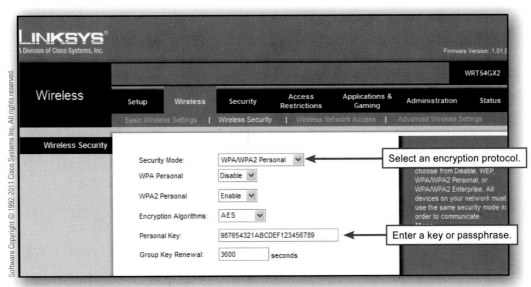

INTERNET CONNECTION

▶ **How do I connect my network to the Internet?** When you've completed the steps to configure the router password, SSID, DHCP, and encryption, make sure you save the configuration settings, then you can close the browser.

Before you connect additional computers to your network, you can connect the router to your Internet service. In the next chapter, you'll survey all the options for Internet connections; but assuming you have Internet service, you can link the router to it.

Your Internet service provider supplies a device called a modem that is designed to carry data to and from the Internet. This device typically has a standard Ethernet port that can be connected to a router (Figure 5-36).

FIGURE 5-36

Your Internet modem should have an Ethernet port.

▶ **Is there a special router port for Internet connections?** Most routers supply a WAN port designed for an Internet connection. The WAN port looks like a standard Ethernet port (Figure 5-37).

FIGURE 5-37

Look for a port labeled "WAN" or "Internet" on your router. If one does not exist, then use any of the other Ethernet ports.

▶ **How do I connect the ports?** Plug a standard network cable into the router's WAN port and connect the other end of the cable into the Internet modem. Turn the modem on and wait a few seconds for it to communicate with the router.

To test the connection, open a browser on the computer that you used to configure the router. You should have Internet access (Figure 5-38). If not, check with your Internet service provider for additional instructions.

FIGURE 5-38

After you connect the router to the Internet modem, your computer should be able to connect to the Internet and browse to your favorite Web sites.

DEVICE CONNECTION

▶ **How do I make a wireless connection with a Windows computer?** Simply turn on any Windows computer with wireless capability and make sure that it is in range of your router. Windows should automatically find the network SSID and ask you to enter the wireless encryption key or passphrase (Figure 5-39).

FIGURE 5-39

Windows automatically senses nearby networks and displays their SSIDs. If you choose to connect, you must enter the correct encryption key for the router.

5

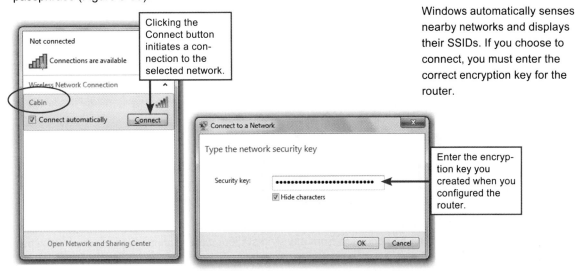

▶ **How about connecting a Mac?** Like Windows, Macs automatically sense available networks and give you the option of connecting to them. Make sure that AirPort or Wi-Fi wireless networking is turned on, then enter the encryption key when asked for the password (Figure 5-40).

FIGURE 5-40

To make sure AirPort or Wi-Fi is on, click the Apple icon, select System Preferences, and then select Network.

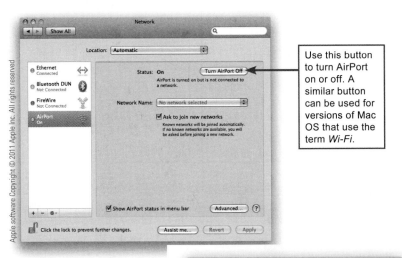

▶ Will my phone, tablet, and media player connect to the network? Any device that has Wi-Fi capability should be able to connect to your network. All use a similar procedure.

First, make sure that Wi-Fi is enabled, then wait for the device to sense the network. When asked, enter the encryption key (Figure 5-41).

FIGURE 5-41

On an iPhone, use the Settings icon to make sure Wi-Fi is enabled. When your phone is within range of a network, you'll see the SSID and can enter the encryption key to join.

▶ How can I set up a printer for network access? There are three ways to set up a printer so it can be accessed from any workstation. You can set up printer sharing using a workstation printer, set up printer sharing using a print server, or install a printer with built-in networking (Figure 5-42).

FIGURE 5-42

The easiest way to connect a printer to your network is to purchase a network-ready printer that connects to the router.

Printer attaches to one workstation

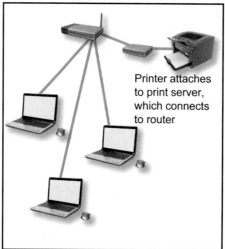

Printer attaches to print server, which connects to router

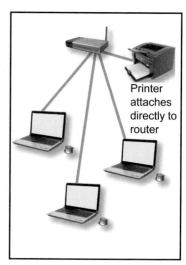

Printer attaches directly to router

QuickCheck

SECTION C

1. For flexibility using wired and wireless connections, choose a Wireless-N router with a Gigabit [   ] switch.

2. To keep your network devices powered on during an electrical outage, you can connect your router to a(n) [   ] . (Hint: Use the acronym.)

3. A(n) [   ] is the name given to a wireless network.

4. WEP, WPA, and PSK are examples of wireless [   ] .

5. To access a router's configuration utility, you can open a(n) [   ] and enter its network address in the address bar.

 CHECK ANSWERS

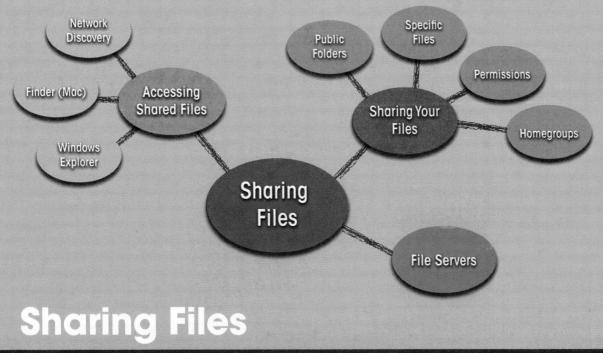

Sharing Files

LANS HAVE BECOME an integral part of computing environments at home, at school, and at work. Many LANs are installed solely for distributing access to an Internet connection. That facet of LANs will be discussed in the next chapter. What else can you do with a LAN? Section D provides practical tips on how to share files.

FILE SHARING BASICS

❚ **What is file sharing?** **File sharing** allows files containing documents, photos, music, and other data to be accessed from computers other than the one on which they are stored.

On a home network, file sharing allows you to view and copy photos, for example, from your desktop computer to a tablet computer. Or, you can access your course syllabus from the server in your school lab.

❚ **How does file sharing work?** Once your network gives you access to other computers on the network, you can view a list of files stored there. If you have permission, you can open files, view them, edit them, and save them back to the original location. You can also copy them to your own computer and work with them there.

❚ **Are there restrictions on file sharing?** Your ability to share files with other devices on a network depends on several factors:

❚ Which devices your computer can discover

❚ Whether other network devices can discover your computer

❚ Whether you are allowed to access files on other computers

❚ What you are allowed to do with files on other computers

❚ Whether you allow other computers to access files on your computer

❚ Which files you allow others to access

❚ What others are allowed to do with the files they can access

ACCESSING SHARED FILES

▶ How can I see all of the devices that are connected to my network? To see a list of devices on your network, you can use your operating system's file management utility. For example, Windows 7 users can use Windows Explorer or the Start menu's Network option to access shared resources. Mac users can access other devices on a network by using Finder (Figure 5-43).

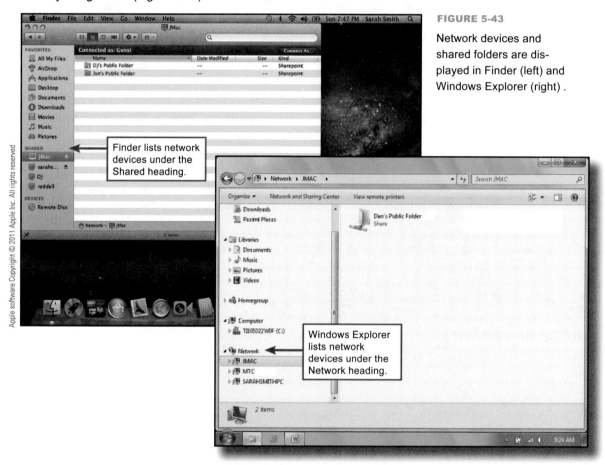

FIGURE 5-43

Network devices and shared folders are displayed in Finder (left) and Windows Explorer (right) .

Finder lists network devices under the Shared heading.

Windows Explorer lists network devices under the Network heading.

▶ What if other network devices aren't listed? The network utilities provided by operating systems such as Windows and Mac OS automatically detect other devices when network discovery is turned on. **Network discovery** is a setting that affects whether your computer can see other computers on a network, and whether your computer can be seen by others.

Network discovery is usually turned on as a standard setting. If you connect to a network and don't get a list of other devices, check your computer's network discovery setting.

▶ How do I access folders located on other computers? You can double-click any folder to open it. Folders on some computers require a valid password for access. Your file sharing user ID and password are usually the same as the password you use to log in to your computer.

▶ How do I access files? Files on other computers can be accessed just as you would access files on your own computer. Double-click a file to open it. As with all files, your computer must have software that is able to open the file. For example, to open *MySong.band*, your computer has to have software that opens GarageBand files.

SHARING YOUR FILES

▶ **Do I have to turn file sharing on?** Yes. On Windows and Mac OS X, a global setting can be used to turn file sharing on or off (Figure 5-44).

FIGURE 5-44

If you want to share files, make sure that the global file sharing setting is turned on.

5

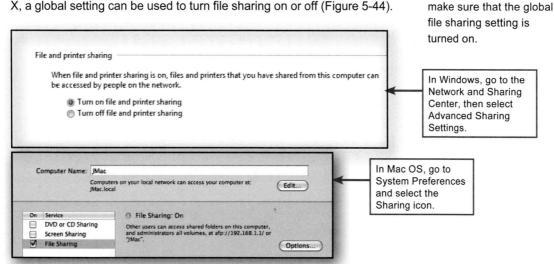

In Windows, go to the Network and Sharing Center, then select Advanced Sharing Settings.

In Mac OS, go to System Preferences and select the Sharing icon.

▶ **How do I specify which of my files can be shared by other workstations?** When you activate file sharing, files in Public folders can be accessed by other network users. You can also make specific files shareable.

▶ Public folders. A **Public folder** is designed to hold files and folders that you want to share with other people on your network. Windows 7 and Mac OS are preconfigured with Public folders—for example, the Public Documents folders in Windows. When you want to share a file or folder, simply store it in a Public folder.

▶ Specific files. You can designate any file or folder on your computer as shared. This option is the most versatile, but the least secure.

Figure 5-45 illustrates two methods for sharing files in Windows.

FIGURE 5-45

You can share files in your Public folders, or designate specific files that you want to share.

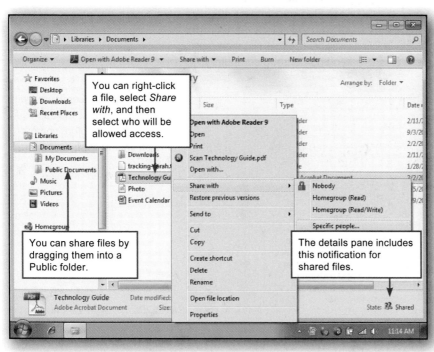

You can right-click a file, select *Share with*, and then select who will be allowed access.

You can share files by dragging them into a Public folder.

The details pane includes this notification for shared files.

▶ **How secure is file sharing?** File sharing poses security risks that have several dimensions. Shared files are subject to misuse, inadvertent modifications, and intentional alterations by those who have access to them. In addition, security holes in file sharing routines are notorious for providing Internet-based hackers with unauthorized access to computers. If you don't need to share files, turn off file sharing globally. If you want the convenience of sharing files, limit what you share and who you share it with by doing the following:

▶ Assign permissions to files.

▶ Limit sharing to specific people.

▶ Remove sharing from files you no longer want to share.

▶ Use a homegroup if your network is composed of Windows computers.

▶ **How do I assign permissions?** Use your computer's sharing utilities to select shared folders and assign permissions to files or folders.

▶ **Read and write permission** allows access for opening, viewing, modifying, or deleting files.

▶ **Read permission** allows authorized people to open a file and view it, but they cannot modify it or delete it.

▶ **Write only permission** works like a drop box, allowing people to put files in one of your folders, but not open, copy, or change any files that you have stored there (Figure 5-46).

FIGURE 5-46

On a Mac, permissions can be easily changed by clicking a user or group of users and selecting the level of access from a list.

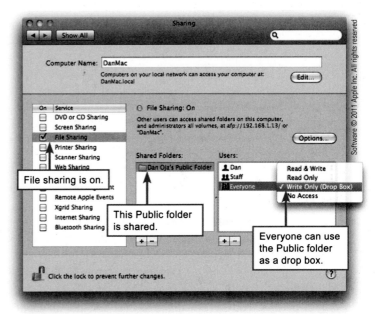

▶ **What is a homegroup?** A homegroup is a collection of trusted Windows computers that automatically share files and folders. Access to the homegroup can be protected by password. To join a homegroup, double-click the Homegroup option in Windows Explorer's navigation pane. Figure 5-47 shows how to access files stored on homegroup computers.

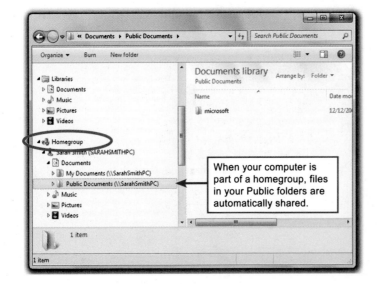

FIGURE 5-47

Windows 7 is preconfigured with a Homegroup that you can use to quickly link to other computers on your network and share files.

FILE SERVERS

▶ **What is a file server?** A **file server** is a computer whose primary purpose is to be a repository for files that can be accessed by network workstations. A file server can reside on any personal computer. For example, you might designate one of your old desktop computers as a file server and use it to store lots of big video files that you don't want clogging up your local hard disk.

A file server connects to a LAN's router just like any other network device. You can also purchase a computing device advertised as a server. A server normally has no monitor or keyboard; its system unit contains a microprocessor, memory, high-capacity hard disk, and built-in network adapter. File servers are available as tower units or rack-mounted blade servers (Figure 5-48).

FIGURE 5-48

Servers are sold as tower units (left) or as rack-mountable units (right), typically used for business applications.

▶ **Are file servers a good idea for home networks?** Whereas file servers are an essential component of most business networks, in many home networks, files are stored on workstations in shared folders rather than on a file server. A potential problem with this arrangement is that workstations must be turned on in order to access their files over a network.

If you find yourself running all over the house turning on computers in order to find files, your network could be more effective with a file server. File servers are designed to run continuously day and night, so they are always on and their files are always accessible.

Another reason to consider a file server for a home network is backup. Rather than purchasing external hard disk drives for each workstation's backup, one low-cost file server can supply enough space to back up files for several workstations.

▶ **Do file servers require any special setup?** If you're using a file server without its own keyboard or monitor, server configuration software is accessible using a browser. The process is similar to configuring a router. To configure a file server, open a browser from any workstation, enter the file server's IP address, and provide the administrator ID and password. The server's documentation can provide additional setup advice.

NETWORK TROUBLESHOOTING

▶ **What if my network stops working?** If network discovery and file sharing are on, but you cannot share files, your network might not be functioning properly.

Network problems can stem from a variety of sources. Symptoms of network malfunctions are slow response time, intermittent outages, failure to access files from one workstation, and non-availability of network services to all workstations.

To troubleshoot network problems, you have to consider the possibility of a problem with a workstation's hardware or settings; network links including cables and wireless signal strength; or network devices such as routers, servers, or network adapters. When troubleshooting network problems, consider the following possibilities:

▶ Cables. Make sure all network cables are firmly connected. If only one workstation is not accessing the network, you can try swapping cables with another workstation.

▶ Signal strength. For wireless connections, check signal strength. If the signal is weak, move the workstation closer to the router, if possible.

▶ Security. Make sure you are using the correct password and that your password has not expired.

▶ Interference. If you have intermittent network outages, look for sources of interference, such as cordless phones, baby monitors, or construction equipment.

▶ Network devices. Make sure your network hub, switch, router, or wireless access point is plugged in and functioning properly. Check the activity lights to determine if data is being sent and received.

▶ Settings. Make sure the network is enabled and then use the Control Panel (Windows) or System Preferences (Mac) to check the drivers for your network equipment.

▶ Switches. Many portable computers include a physical switch that turns wireless networking on or off. Make sure this switch is in the On position for networking.

▶ **Can I monitor network activity?** Most computer operating systems provide tools for monitoring the number of packets sent, received, and dropped from your network connection. This information helps you determine if data is flowing over your network. On Windows computers, you can monitor network activity from the Network and Sharing Center. On Macs, you can view this information using the Network Utility application (Figure 5-49).

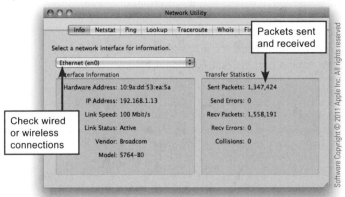

FIGURE 5-49

Look for the Network Utility in the Utility folder of any Mac. It provides lots of handy information. Use the Info tab to check if your network connection is sending and receiving packets.

▶ **Where can I find troubleshooting utilities?** Several third-party vendors offer network monitoring and troubleshooting utilities, but check your operating system first. Windows 7, for example, offers a set of basic troubleshooters from the Network and Sharing Center (Figure 5-50).

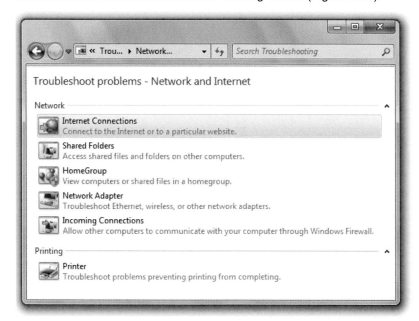

FIGURE 5-50

To access the network trouble-shooters in Windows 7, go to the Network and Sharing Center and click *Troubleshoot problems*.

5

▶ **Can I reboot my network?** Yes. When a network is not functioning correctly, you can try rebooting it. First, make sure all applications on workstation computers are closed. Then turn off the router and your Internet modem. To restart, first turn on the Internet modem. If it has a ready-to-send (RTS) status light or similar indicator, make sure it is lit. Next, turn on your network router. Give the router a few seconds to boot, then check your network connections by trying to access another workstation or the Internet.

QuickCheck   SECTION D

1. Network _____ is a setting that affects whether your computer can see other computers on a network, and whether your computer can be seen by others.

2. A(n) _____ folder is designed to hold files and folders that you want to share with other people on your network.

3. With Windows 7, users can join a(n) _____ that automatically allows them to share files located in Public folders.

4. A(n) _____ server is a computer whose primary purpose is to be a repository for files that can be accessed by network workstations.

5. Many notebook computers have a physical _____ that turns wireless networking on or off.

▶ CHECK ANSWERS

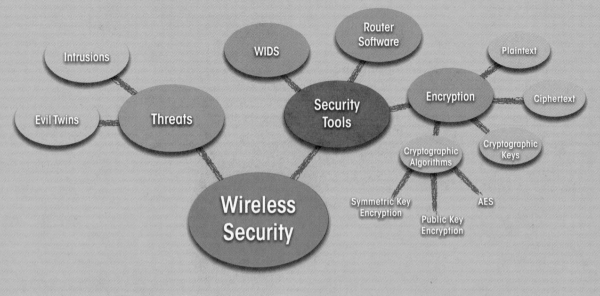

Wireless Security

JUST HOW IMPORTANT is encryption for Wi-Fi connections? Earlier in the chapter, you learned how to activate wireless encryption on your network router. In this section, you'll find out why you don't want to skip that important step.

WI-FI SECURITY

▶ **What are the threats to my network?** Networks with wired or wireless connections are vulnerable to a variety of threats, including viruses, theft, and equipment failure. Many threats can be handled using techniques for standalone computers. Network equipment should be connected to power strips to prevent damage from power spikes. Data should be backed up in case of a hard drive failure, and workstations should be protected by antivirus software.

▶ **Why are wireless connections more vulnerable than wired connections?** Wireless signals are broadcast through the air; and like the signals from a radio station, they can be picked up by any device equipped with a receiver tuned to the right frequency.

Wired connections funnel data through a cable, not through the air. Barring sophisticated eavesdropping techniques, wired signals can be intercepted only by physically tapping into the cable or router.

▶ **Is it easy to tap into wireless signals?** When network discovery is turned on, any Wi-Fi enabled device within range of your network can see its SSID. In addition, most devices indicate whether the network is secured by encryption (Figure 5-51).

FIGURE 5-51

Any Wi-Fi enabled device can detect wireless connections.

The lock icon indicates a network secured with WEP, WPA, or other wireless encryption.

Armed with basic information about a network's SSID and security status, hackers can set up two exploits. First, networks that aren't secured are open targets for hackers to steal data, spread viruses, and create a launching pad for spam.

Hackers can also set up an "evil twin"; a network with the same or similar SSID that's designed to fool users into thinking they are logging onto a legitimate network. Hackers lurking on the evil twin network can extract passwords and credit card information from unsuspecting users.

Hackers also use more sophisticated tools to uncover information about your network, such as the type of router you use, the channels on which it transmits, and the type of security you have in place (Figure 5-52).

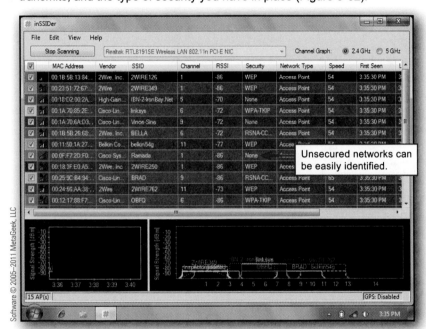

FIGURE 5-52

Software tools such as InSSIDer help locate and identify secured and unsecured networks. Once logged on to an unsecured wireless network, hackers are free to do anything from stealing the network owner's credit card or bank information to attacking computers in other networks.

▶ How does that information help hackers? When hackers see a network secured with weak WEP encryption, they know it is an easy target. If there are not unsecured networks in the area, networks with WEP encryption are the easiest to breach.

Suppose a hacker learns that you've installed a Cisco Systems router on your network and that you've activated WPA-TKIP encryption. That network should be pretty secure unless you forgot to change the default administrator password. Hackers know the standard passwords for every type of router, and it's easy for them to try it just in case you forgot to change it.

Sophisticated hacking tools can also pinpoint the location of a network using GPS tracking. Bank of America might not use BofA as its SSID, but a hacker looking for a juicy target might be able to determine that a network called FI998 is broadcasting from the building that houses a local Bank of America branch.

▶ **Can I tell if someone is hacking my network?** Yes. Your network router maintains a list of clients that are accessing your network using wired or wireless connections. You can view a list of current connections as in Figure 5-53, or you can set up your router software to maintain a log over a period of hours or days.

FIGURE 5-53

Router software keeps track of everyone who is accessing a network, and it can be used to uncover intrusions.

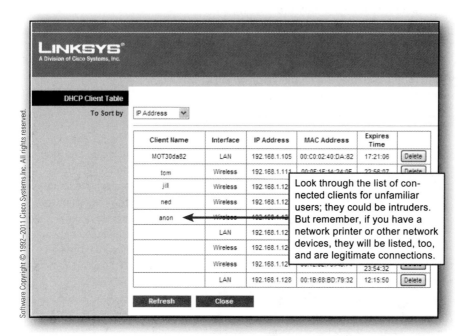

You can also use a wireless intrusion detection system (WIDS) to spot unusual activity on your network. Software, such as Who's On My WiFi and AirSnare, can compile a list of computers that are connected to your network and warn you when unknown computers have joined (Figure 5-54).

FIGURE 5-54

WIDS software runs in the background, periodically scans your network, and alerts you if unknown computers are detected.

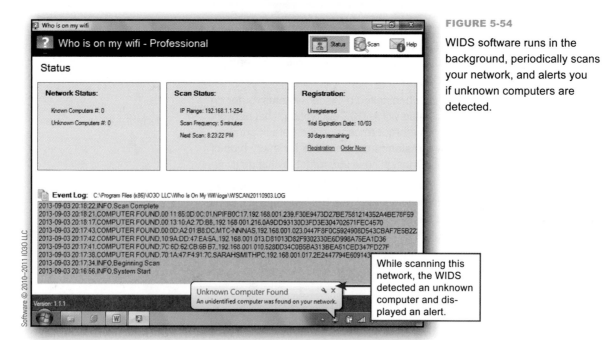

ENCRYPTION

▶ **Exactly what is encryption? Encryption** transforms a message in such a way that its contents are hidden from unauthorized readers. Encryption is designed to keep messages secret. In the context of computing, encryption can be used in many ways, including the following:

▶ Scrambling data sent over wired or wireless networks to prevent intrusions

▶ Securing credit card numbers and other personal information transferred from shoppers' computers to e-commerce sites

▶ Encrypting computer files and databases so that data they contain is unusable if the device containing the data is lost or compromised

▶ Scrambling the contents of e-mail messages to maintain privacy

▶ **How does encryption work?** An original message—one that has not yet been encrypted—is referred to as **plaintext** or cleartext. An encrypted message is referred to as **ciphertext**. The process of converting plaintext into ciphertext is called encryption. The reverse process—converting ciphertext into plaintext—is called **decryption**.

Messages are encrypted by using a cryptographic algorithm and key. A **cryptographic algorithm** is a procedure for encrypting or decrypting a message. A **cryptographic key** (usually just called a key) is a word, number, or phrase that must be known to encrypt or decrypt a message.

For example, Julius Caesar made extensive use of an encryption method called simple substitution, which could have been used to turn the plaintext message "Do not trust Brutus" into "GRQRWWUXVWEUXWXV." The cryptographic algorithm was to offset the letters of the alphabet. The key was 3 (Figure 5-55).

FIGURE 5-55

The algorithm for Caesar's encryption technique was to offset the letters of the alphabet—in this case, by three letters. A simple transformation table was used to encrypt or decrypt a message. For example, if a *G* appears in the encrypted message, it would be a *D* in the original unencrypted message.

CIPHERTEXT LETTERS:

D E F G H I J K L M N O P Q R S T U V W X Y Z A B C

EQUIVALENT PLAINTEXT LETTERS:

A B C D E F G H I J K L M N O P Q R S T U V W X Y Z

▶ **What's the difference between strong and weak encryption?** Caesar's simple substitution key is an example of **weak encryption** because it is easy to decrypt even without the algorithm and key. Unauthorized decryption is sometimes referred to as breaking or cracking a code. You could crack Caesar's code in several ways.

You could discover the key by making 25 different transformation tables, each with a different offset (assuming that the encryption method uses the letters of the alphabet in sequence and not at random). You could also analyze the frequency with which letters appear—in English documents, *E*, *T*, *A*, *O*, and *N* appear most frequently—and you can piece together the message by guessing the remaining letters.

Strong encryption is loosely defined as "very difficult to break." **AES** (Advanced Encryption Standard), the technology used for WPA2, is one of the strongest cryptographic algorithms. With continuous advances in technology, however, strong encryption is a moving target. Several encryption methods that were considered impossible to break ten years ago have recently been cracked.

▶ **How long does it take to break strong encryption?** Encryption methods can be broken by the use of expensive, specialized, code-breaking computers. The cost of these machines is substantial, but not beyond the reach of government agencies, major corporations, and organized crime. Encryption methods can also be broken by standard computer hardware—supercomputers, mainframes, workstations, and even personal computers. These computers break codes using a brute force attack, which consists of trying all possible keys (Figure 5-56).

The length of a computer-readable encryption key is measured in bits. A 32-bit key, for example, could be one of 4.2 billion (2^{32}) numbers. Surprisingly, it would be possible to try all these numbers and discover the key in less than a day by using an average personal computer.

To discover a 40-bit key, you would have to try about 1 trillion possible combinations—a week's worth of processing time on a personal computer. 768-bit encryption—once thought to be unbreakable by any computer in the private sector—requires a lot of computing power, but has been broken by combining the power of many personal computers connected over the Internet. Most encryption today uses a 128-bit key, which is secure from casual hackers.

Another way to understand how the length of a key affects the strength of encryption is to consider this guideline: Beginning with a 40-bit key, each additional bit doubles the time it would take to discover the key. If a personal computer takes one week to crack a 40-bit key, it takes two weeks to crack a 41-bit key, four weeks to crack a 42-bit key, and eight weeks to crack a 43-bit key. A 128-bit key takes $2^{(128-40)}$ times longer to crack than a 40-bit key—that's 309,485,009,821,345,068,724,781,056 times longer!

▶ **What's public key encryption?** Caesar's encryption method is an example of **symmetric key encryption** in which the key used to encrypt a message is also used to decrypt the message. Symmetric key encryption is used to encrypt stationary data, such as corporate financial records. It is also used to encrypt the data that travels over wireless LANs.

Symmetric keys are not practical for e-mail and other situations in which the person receiving encrypted data does not have the key beforehand. E-mailing the key would be a major security problem because of the potential for a hacker to intercept it.

Public key encryption (PKE) eliminates the key-distribution problem by using one key to encrypt a message, but another key to decrypt the message. Figure 5-57 illustrates how public key encryption works.

FIGURE 5-56

To discover a four-digit PIN by brute force, a criminal must try, at most, 10,000 possibilities. Finding the key to computer data encrypted using a 32-bit key would involve about 4.2 billion possibilities.

Kathleen Finlay / Radius Images/Masterfile

FIGURE 5-57

Public key encryption uses two keys. A public key can only encrypt a message. A private key is required to decrypt the message.

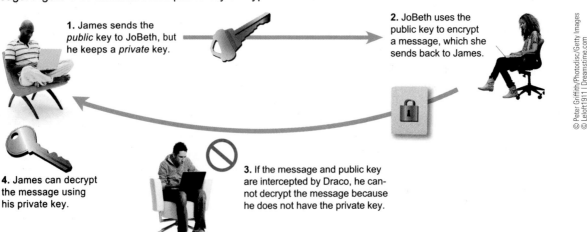

1. James sends the *public* key to JoBeth, but he keeps a *private* key.

2. JoBeth uses the public key to encrypt a message, which she sends back to James.

3. If the message and public key are intercepted by Draco, he cannot decrypt the message because he does not have the private key.

4. James can decrypt the message using his private key.

© Peter Griffith/Photodisc/Getty Images
© Lelott1911 | Dreamstime.com

Public key encryption is a crucial technology for e-commerce and e-mail. When you use a secure connection to transmit a credit card number, the server sends a public key to your browser. Your browser uses this public key to encrypt the credit card number. After it is encrypted, no one—not even you—can use the public key to decrypt the message. The encrypted message is sent to a Web server, where the private key is used to decrypt it.

When personal computer users want to encrypt e-mail or other documents, they turn to public key encryption software, such as PGP (Pretty Good Privacy), GnuPG, or AxCrypt. When you first use PKE software, it generates a private key and a public key. You must keep your private key hidden. You can then e-mail the public key to the people you have authorized to send encrypted messages to you.

The people who receive your public key can store it and use their PKE software to encrypt messages. When they send these messages to you, you can decrypt them using your private key. Figure 5-58 contains an example of a public key generated by PGP software.

```
-----BEGIN PGP PUBLIC KEY BLOCK-----

Version: 5.0

mQCNAi44C30AAAEEAL1r6BylvuSAvOKIk9ze9yCK+ZPPbRZrpXlRFBb
e+U8dGPMb9XdJS4L/cy1fXr9R9j4EfFsK/rgHV6i2rE83LjWrmsDPRPSaiz
z+EQTlZi4AN99jiBomfLLZyUzmHMoUoE4shrYgOnkc0u101ikhieAFje77j
/F3596pT6nCx/9/AAURtCRBbmRyZSBCYBNhcmQgPGFiYWNhcmRAd2
VsbC5zZi5jYS51cz6JAFUCBRAuOA6O7zYZz1mqos8BAXr9AgCxCu8C
wGZRdpfSs65r6mb4MccXvvfxO4TmPi1DKQj2FYHYjwYONk8vzA7XnE5
aJmk5J/dChdvflU7NvVifV6of=GQv9

-----END PGP PUBLIC KEY BLOCK-----
```

FIGURE 5-58

PGP software generates a huge public key. Each person's public key is unique. You can e-mail this key to anyone who might want to send you an encrypted message.

QuickCheck

1. The term [＿＿＿＿＿＿] *twin* refers to a network with the same or a similar SSID that's designed to fool users into thinking they are logging on to a legitimate network.

2. A cryptographic [＿＿＿＿＿＿] is a word, number, or phrase that must be known to encrypt or decrypt a message.

3. A cryptographic [＿＿＿＿＿＿] is the process used to encrypt or decrypt a message.

4. [＿＿＿＿＿＿] key encryption uses one key to encrypt a message, but another key to decrypt the message.

5. [＿＿＿＿＿＿] key encryption uses the same key to encrypt a message as it does to decrypt the message.

▶ CHECK ANSWERS

Issue: Who's Tracking You?

IN THE MOVIE *Harry Potter and the Prisoner of Azkaban*, Harry acquires a magical item called the Marauder's Map, which shows the location of every teacher and student at the Hogwarts School of Witchcraft and Wizardry.

In the context of Harry Potter, tracking technology seems fun; but real-life tracking technologies have a dark side, which privacy advocates fear might be misused by governments, corporations, and possibly criminals to monitor the daily activities of ordinary people.

According to the EFF (Electronic Frontier Foundation), "Tracking is the retention of information that can be used to connect records of a person's actions or reading habits across space, cyberspace, or time."

Two broad categories of tracking are behavioral tracking and locational tracking. Behavioral tracking accumulates information about what you do: the Web sites you visit, the merchandise you purchase online, and the people with whom you correspond. Locational tracking records your physical location: where you live and work, where and when you shop, and the route you take to get to school.

Tracking made headlines in 2011 when Pete Warden and Alasdair Allan discovered that iPhones collect and store date-stamped information that triangulates the phone's location. A simple software application called iPhone Tracker can retrieve this data and display it on a map.

The iPhone tracking story spread like wildfire over the mainstream media, blogs, and social networks. Privacy advocates pointed out that government agencies, disgruntled spouses, parents, and criminals

Copyright © ©Warner Bros/courtesy Everett Collection/Everett Collection

could easy trace a person's whereabouts.

Apple responded with a press release explaining the need to collect location data for LBS (location-based service) applications to work efficiently. The press release also apologized for a "bug" that allowed tracking data to be collected even when location-based service was turned off.

The technology that makes it easy for a cell phone to track your movements can be incorporated into other handheld devices and tucked into vehicles, identification badges, pet collars, clothing, and even tiny chips that can be implanted under the skin. Tracking is controversial, especially when it occurs without the consent or control of the trackee.

Privacy advocates want strict protocols for collecting, using, storing, and distributing location information. They face opposition, however, from law enforcement officials who would like to explore ways location technology can be used to track criminals and prevent terrorism.

Commercial interest in tracking technology for marketing and advertising is also high and consumers seem willing to give up some privacy for the convenience offered by location-based services, such as Yelp and Gowalla.

The outcome of conflicting interests will determine if location-tracking technology can be implemented in such a way that the rights and privacy of individuals are protected.

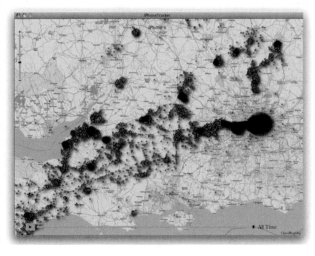

Try It! Locational tracking is kind of creepy. The idea that someone can pinpoint where you regularly use your desktop computer is one thing, but knowing that someone might be tracking your movements as you travel from home to school, to the mall, to the doctor, and to the movies might give you more than a moment of concern. Explore tracking technologies to arm yourself with knowledge that can help protect your privacy.

5

1 Just how detailed is the data about your location? As an experiment, a German privacy advocate named Malte Spitz obtained his personal records from his cell phone carrier, which in six months had amassed over 35,000 usage data points. Spitz made the information public and you can trace his movements on an interactive map at *www.zeit.de/ datenschutz/malte-spitz-data-retention*. What did Mr. Spitz do on Christmas day, December 25?

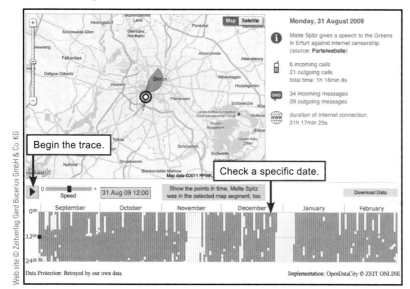

2 Privacy advocates support Do Not Track regulations. You can explore this concept by looking for "Do Not Track" at *www.eff.org* or Wikipedia. What are the similarities and differences between Do Not Track and Do Not Call?

3 The location of digital devices can be pinpointed using three different, but complementary, technologies: GPS, cell-tower triangulation, and WPS. Use Wikipedia and other online resources to explore these technologies. How would you describe each technology?

4 Tracking usually happens behind the scenes, often without a user's knowledge or approval. However, information that people intentionally post online can also be used to track their locations. Think about the information that you post on your social networking and media sharing sites. How might that information be used to determine your location or track your movements?

ISSUE

What Do You Think?

1. Do you worry about behavioral tracking based on your Internet use?

2. Do you have a device that can track your physical location?

3. Do you support efforts to institute Do Not Track?

Information Tools: Wikipedia

Wikipedia describes itself as "a multilingual, web-based, free-content encyclopedia project based on an openly editable model." Each Wikipedia article is compiled by volunteers who write, edit, and comment without pay. Except for entries prone to vandalism or disruption, Wikipedia articles can be edited by anyone who visits the site. Every edit and comment is tracked, and contributors are asked to conform to guidelines for style and content.

Wikipedia is a controversial resource for information and facts. Some librarians disapprove of its use, and many instructors discourage students from citing Wikipedia as a research source in footnotes or endnotes.

Said one librarian: "I do not allow students to use Wikipedia as a source. Since it can be edited by anyone, one cannot verify if the information is correct." However, that statement is in itself disinformation. The information in Wikipedia articles can and should be fact-checked just as you would check information from any other source.

A contrasting viewpoint is that Wikipedia offers some of the most dependable information available anywhere because it is vetted by a large and diverse audience.

Three core content principles shape the information that is acceptable for Wikipedia articles. Those principles are neutral point of view (NPOV), verifiability, and no original research (NOR).

Neutral Point of View (NPOV)

Avoid stating opinions as facts.

Avoid stating seriously contested assertions as facts.

Avoid presenting uncontested assertions as mere opinion.

Use non-judgmental language.

Accurately indicate the relative prominence of opposing views.

No Original Research (NOR)

Avoid any facts, allegations, ideas, and stories for which no reliable published source exists.

Verifiability

Any quotation or statement that might be challenged must be substantiated by an inline citation to a reputable source.

Many professionals and students make extensive use of Wikipedia as a resource for learning the meaning of technology terms and for getting an overview of a topic. At the college level, Wikipedia can be a useful research tool, if you follow these guidelines:

▶ Do not quote Wikipedia directly.

▶ Cross-check before using facts from Wikipedia articles.

▶ Follow links in, citations, or use Google to locate original sources for information you want to include in your research papers.

▶ Don't list Wikipedia articles in bibliographies; work with original sources.

▶ Never "lift" citations from the References section of a Wikipedia article; use citations only if you have examined the source document.

▶ Make sure that you go beyond Wikipedia to research your topic in sufficient depth.

Try It! Wikipedia includes tools that help you gauge the accuracy and neutrality for most of its articles. Exploring these tools will make you a more professional Wikipedia researcher.

1 Wikipedia is not Facebook or Twitter; articles are much more substantive than a tweet or status. Connect to the pages Wikipedia: List of bad ideas and Wikipedia: Avoiding Common Mistakes. What is an "AfD"?

2 Wikipedia articles are usually written by more than one author, and articles are revised by yet another set of contributors. Just to get an idea of the amount of revision that takes place on Wikipedia, connect to the Angry Birds article and click the View History tab. How many revisions were made in the last week?

3 Wikipedia articles undergo constant revisions and some are controversial. If you have doubts about the material presented in an article, you can look at the discussion tab. Connect to the Wikipedia article Hacker (term) and click the Discussion tab. What is the major controversy behind this article?

4 While looking at the Hacker article, click the Edit tab. Scroll down, if necessary, until you can see the text for the first paragraph. This text is marked up with symbols that create bold text, links, citations, and headings when the full article is displayed. List three of the symbols used for markup.

5 Although the general public is free to make contributions to Wikipedia, new contributors are encouraged to review the site's tutorial about editing, and experiment with the sandbox area before making edits to live pages. Connect to *en.wikipedia.org/wiki/Wikipedia:Tutorial/Editing* and follow the steps on the Editing tab to use the sandbox, and then record your answers to the following questions:

a. What is the five-step editing process?

b. Continue with the editing tutorial by clicking the Formatting tab. How do you specify the text you want in a heading?

c. Continue to the Wikipedia Links tab. How would you create a bold link to the Wikipedia page about Ethernet?

6 Use Wikipedia to lookup a technology topic related to the network concepts presented in this chapter. Read the article and use Wikipedia resources to answer the following questions:

a. In your opinion, what were the three most important facts in the article?

b. Did the article contain any statements that appear to violate the NPOV or NOR principles?

c. What topics are contributors discussing about the article?

d. Select two statements from the article that include references. Follow the reference links. Do the references clearly support the corresponding statements in the Wikipedia article?

5

Article   Discussion   Read Edit View history   Search   🔍

Angry Birds   ⊕

From Wikipedia, the free encyclopedia
(Redirected from Angry birds)

Angry Birds is a puzzle video game developed by Finnish computer game developer Rovio Mobile. Inspired primarily by a sketch of stylized wingless birds, the game was first released for Apple's iOS in December 2009.[1] Since that time, over 12 million copies of the game have been purchased from Apple's App Store,[2] which has prompted the company to design versions for other touchscreen-based smartphones, such as those using the Android operating system, among others.

In the game, players use a slingshot to launch birds at pigs stationed on or within various structures, with the intent of destroying all the pigs on the playfield. As players advance through the game, new birds appear, some with special abilities that can be activated by the player. Rovio Mobile has supported *Angry Birds* with numerous free updates that add additional game content, and the company has even released stand-alone holiday and promotional

	Angry Birds
Developer(s)	Rovio Mobile
Publisher(s)	Chillingo/Clickgamer (iOS, PSP/PlayStation 3) Rovio Mobile (Maemo, Symbian^3, Android Microsoft Windows, Mac OS X)
Producer(s)	Raine Mäki, Harro Grönberg, Mikko Häkkinen

INFOWEBLINKS

You can check the **NP2013 Chapter 5** InfoWebLink for updates to these activities.

Ⓦ **CLICK TO CONNECT**
www.infoweblinks.com/np2013/ch05

Technology in Context: Education

THE FIRST EDUCATIONAL application of computers emerged in the 1960s, when huge mainframes with clunky interfaces introduced students to computer-aided instruction (CAI). Based on operant conditioning research by B. F. Skinner and Ivan Pavlov—remember dogs salivating when a bell rings?—CAI uses basic drill and practice: The computer presents a problem, the student responds, and the computer evaluates the response.

Studies in the 1970s indicated that CAI systems, such as PLATO (Programmed Logic for Automated Teaching Operations), improved student test scores, but students found the mainframe's monochrome display and the CAI's regimented drill format boring. Recent incarnations of CAI, such as an alien-invader style elementary math program, use snazzy graphics and arcade formats to grab learners' attention.

Courtesy of the University of Illinois at Urbana-Champaign Archive

Educators looking for ways to harness computers' interactive and programmable nature arrived at the idea of computer-based training (CBT). CBT is formatted as a series of tutorials, beginning with a pretest to see whether students have the prerequisite skills and ending with a CAI-style drill and practice test to determine whether students can move on to the next tutorial segment. Today, CBT is a popular approach to learning how to use computer software.

Another educational approach, called computer-aided learning (CAL), uses the computer more as a source of information than an assessment mechanism. Students using CAL make decisions about their level of expertise, what material is relevant, and how to pace their own learning. Exploratory CAL environments include Seymour Papert's Logo programming language; students can investigate geometry concepts by using Logo to program a graphical turtle on the screen.

In addition to CAI, CBT, and CAL, simulations have become a popular educational tool. The computer mimics a real-world situation through a narrative description or with graphics. Students are given options and respond with a decision or an action. The computer evaluates each response and determines its consequences. Oregon Trail, a simulation popular with elementary school students, describes events that beset a group of pioneers traveling in a wagon train. Students respond to each event, while learning a little about history, money-handling skills, conservation, and decision making.

Most educators believe that computers can help create an individualized and interactive learning environment, which can make learning more effective and efficient. Although 99% of American public schools have computers and 93% of students use them in some way, these statistics can be deceiving. The reality falls far short of the ideal situation in which every student has access to a computer throughout the school day.

The challenge is to figure out how to achieve the computers' potential in an educational setting when supplying computers for every student is often cost prohibitive. Compromise solutions have been tried with varying degrees of success. Some schools have installed learning labs where students go for scheduled lab time. In elementary schools, often a few computers are placed in special work areas of classrooms and used for small group projects or individual drill and practice. Some schools have relegated most computers to the library, where they are connected to the Internet and used for research. In some classrooms, a single computer can be used as an effective presentation device.

A few schools without the budget for enough desktop computers have opted for inexpensive PDAs instead. "Students need to use technology just as you and I do, not just one hour a day," says one teacher in support of PDAs. Students use standard PDA software for educational tasks: tracking nutritional intake for health class, collecting data from experiments in biology class, graphing functions in math class, translating phrases for French class, and maintaining to-do lists. The biggest drawback to more widespread educational use of PDAs, however, is a lack of software specifically designed for education. The proliferation of sub-US$250 netbooks might offer a software-rich alternative to PDAs.

Pioneering PDA projects led to a bevy of experiments under the umbrella of mLearning, a buzzword for *mobile learning* and defined as learning that happens across locations, or that takes advantage of learning opportunities offered by portable technologies.

Some schools—primarily colleges—have tackled the problem of computer access by requiring all incoming first-year students to purchase notebook computers. Many colleges, for example, provide Internet connections in dorm rooms and library study carrels or offer campuswide Wi-Fi service. Students can tote their notebook computers to class and take notes. They can contact instructors via e-mail, use the Internet as a research resource, and run educational software.

Another educational use of computers can be seen in distance education (DE) courses (also called distance learning). Historically, distance education meant correspondence study or courses delivered by radio or television, but the meaning has been broadened to encompass any educational situation in which students and instructors aren't in the same place. Therefore, most DE courses today require students to have access to a computer and an Internet connection. DE courses are offered to K through 12 students, college students, military personnel, businesspeople, and the general public.

Most students who choose DE courses do so because they want to learn at their own pace, at a convenient time, and in a location close to home. Single parents who deal with the realities of child care, working professionals who cannot relocate to a college town, and physically disabled students find distance education handy. Distance education has the potential of increasing the pool of students for a course by making it financially feasible; for example, an advanced Kanji course could be offered at a Midwestern university with only ten on-campus Japanese majors if enough distance education students can boost enrollment.

The Internet hosts a wide variety of DE courses, both credit-earning and noncredit courses. Several learning management systems (LMSs), such as Blackboard and Moodle, help teachers prepare and manage DE courses. These systems are popular with degree-granting institutions that offer credit-earning DE courses in their course catalogs (subject to the usual course fees and requirements).

Learning management software typically runs from a server maintained by a school system, college, or university. Using Web browsers, teachers access the LMS to post an online syllabus, develop Web pages with course content, create a database of questions for online assessment, manage e-mail, set up online discussion groups, and maintain a gradebook. Students using Internet-connected computers and standard Web browsers can access course materials, submit assignments, interact with other students, and take tests.

Computers and the Internet have opened opportunities for lifelong learning. Prospective students can use a search engine to easily find non-credit courses and tutorials for a wide range of topics, including pottery, dog grooming, radio astronomy, desktop publishing, and drumming. Some tutorials are free, and others charge a small fee.

In a society that promotes learning as a lifelong endeavor, the Internet has certainly made it possible for students of all ages to pursue knowledge and skills simply by using a computer and an Internet connection.

5

New Perspectives Labs

To access the New Perspectives Lab for Chapter 5, open the NP2013 interactive eBook and then click the icon next to the lab title.

▶ LOCAL AREA NETWORKS

IN THIS LAB YOU'LL LEARN:

- When to use wired connections and when to use wireless connections
- The equipment needed to create a LAN
- How to install a router
- How to open the router configuration utility
- How to change a router's default password
- How to create an SSID
- The advantages and disadvantages of WEP, WPA, and WPA2 encryption
- How to enable wireless encryption
- How to set DHCP to automatically hand out local addresses
- How to check network settings from a PC or Mac
- How to connect to a wireless network
- How to connect a LAN to the Internet
- How to connect to a mobile hotspot

LAB ASSIGNMENTS

1. Start the interactive part of the lab. Perform each lab step as directed, and answer all the lab QuickCheck questions.

2. Use your computer's networking utilities to find out if your computer is equipped for wired or wireless connections. Make a note of the type and specifications of any network adapters installed in your computer.

3. Using the information you gathered from assignment 2, draw a sketch showing how your computer could be linked into a LAN.

4. Examine the networking utilities installed on your computer. If you are using Windows, you might find utilities such as Network Connections and Wireless Network Setup Wizard. Look at each utility and write a one-paragraph description for each.

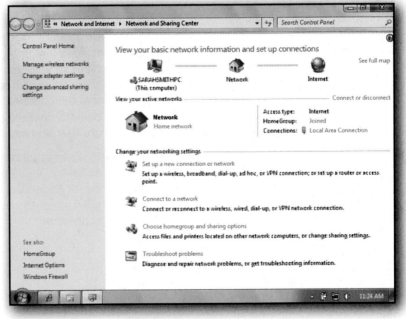

Key Terms

Make sure you understand all the boldfaced key terms presented in this chapter. With the NP2013 interactive eBook, you can use this list of terms as an interactive study activity. First, try to define a term in your own words, and then click the term to compare your definition with the definition presented in the chapter.

5

AES, 285
AirPort, 263
Bandwidth, 251
Bluetooth, 261
Bridge, 267
Broadband, 251
Ciphertext, 285
Circuit switching, 253
Communications channel, 251
Communications protocol, 252
Cryptographic algorithm, 285
Cryptographic key, 285
Decryption, 285
DHCP, 255
Discovery mode, 261
Encryption, 285
Ethernet, 257
Ethernet adapter, 258
File server, 279
File sharing, 275
Gateway, 267
Handshaking, 252
Homegroup, 278
Hub, 267

Infrared light, 259
IP address, 255
LAN, 247
MAC address, 254
MAN, 247
Microwaves, 259
MIMO, 263
Narrowband, 251
Network attached storage, 250
Network device, 250
Network discovery, 276
Network interface card, 250
Networked peripheral, 250
Node, 250
Octet, 255
Optical fiber cable, 251
Packet, 253
Packet switching, 253
Pairing, 261
PAN, 247
Plaintext, 285
PSK, 271
Public folder, 277
Public key encryption, 286

Repeater, 267
RF signals, 259
RJ45 connector, 251
Router, 250
Shared resources, 248
SSID, 269
Strong encryption, 285
Switch, 267
Symmetric key encryption, 286
Transceiver, 259
WAN, 247
Weak encryption, 285
WEP, 271
Wi-Fi, 262
Wi-Fi adapter, 264
Wireless encryption, 270
Wireless encryption key, 271
Wireless access point, 267
Wireless ad-hoc protocol, 262
Wireless infrastructure protocol, 262
WPA, 271

Interactive Summary

To review important concepts from this chapter, fill in the blanks to best complete each sentence. When using the NP2013 interactive eBook, click the Check Answers buttons to automatically score your answers.

SECTION A:

Networks can be classified by geographical scope as PANs, [_____], MANs, and WANs. LANs allow people to share network resources, such as files, printers, and Internet connections. LAN technologies are standardized by the [_____] organization. Each connection point on a network is referred to as a(n) [_____] and can contain computers, networked [_____], or network devices. Computers connected to a network require network circuitry, often housed on a network [_____] card (NIC). Network nodes are linked by communications channels. High-bandwidth channels are referred to as [_____], whereas low-band-width channels are referred to as [_____]. Communications [_____], such as TCP/IP, divide messages into [_____], handle addressing, and manage routing. Most computer networks use packet-switching technology, rather than [_____] -switching technology. Computers on a network have a variety of addresses; the two most common are IP addresses and [_____] addresses. IP addresses can be assigned or they can be automatically distributed by [_____].

▶ CHECK ANSWERS

SECTION B:

Wired networks are fast, secure, and simple to configure, but installing [_____] can be a nuisance. [_____] is a fast and secure wired network technology defined by IEEE 802.3 standards. Most wireless routers transport data using [_____] frequency signals. The most popular wireless technology is Wi-Fi, but [_____] is used for PANs and other short-range connections. Wi-Fi is defined by the IEEE [_____] standards, and there are versions denoted by the letters *a*, *b*, *g*, *n*, and *y*. Computers on a Wi-Fi network must have wireless circuitry, such as a Wi-Fi adapter. Wireless networks can be set up as [_____] networks in which devices broadcast directly to each other. Alternatively, a wireless [_____] network uses a centralized broadcasting device, such as a wireless [_____] point or a wireless router. On some Macs, Wi-Fi capability is referred to as [_____].

▶ CHECK ANSWERS

SECTION C:

Most LANs support both wired and wireless connections because they include a(n) [_____] that has a Wi-Fi antenna and [_____] ports. LANs can include other network devices, such as hubs, switches, gateways, bridges, and repeaters. After you plug in a router and connect it to a computer, you should configure the router by changing the default administrator [_____]. To access the configuration utility, open a(n) [_____] and enter the router's IP address. You should also create a(n) [_____] so your network has a name. If your network uses a wireless router, you should also activate wireless [_____] to enhance security. Once the router is configured, you can connect it to an Internet modem. Wi-Fi equipped computers and handheld devices can join your LAN, but they have to enter the wireless encryption [_____].

● CHECK ANSWERS

SECTION D:

You can access other computers in a LAN, and those computers can see yours if network [_____] is turned on. In addition, the global setting for file [_____] has to be turned on. If you have permission, you can open files from other computers on the network, view them, edit them, and save them back to the original location. You can also [_____] files to your own computer and work with them there. You can share folders and files on your own computer if you want to allow other workstations to access them, but sharing is a(n) [_____] risk. You should assign [_____] to limit who can access your files and whether they are allowed to modify and delete them. Windows users can set up a(n) [_____] to create a trusted collection of computers that can share files. If you have many files that need to be accessed from various workstations, you might want to add a(n) [_____] server to the network. Network problems can stem from a variety of sources. Symptoms of network malfunctions are slow response time, intermittent outages, failure to access files from one workstation, and non-availability of network services to all workstations. To troubleshoot network problems, you have to consider the possibility of a problem with a workstation's hardware or settings; network links including cables and wireless signal strength; or network devices such as routers, servers, or NICs. Network problems can sometimes be solved if you [_____] the network by turning off the router and Internet modem, then restarting them.

● CHECK ANSWERS

SECTION E:

Compared to wired networks, wireless networks are much more susceptible to unauthorized access and use. Hackers have an easy time intercepting signals by cruising through a business district or neighborhood with a Wi-Fi enabled notebook computer. Software tools help hackers identify the type of [_____] you have, the channels on which it transmits, and the type of security you have in place. Hackers use exploits such as the evil [_____] to steal passwords and account numbers. If a hacker can guess the administrator password, your network could get hijacked and be used to spread spam and malware. An original message—one that has not yet been encrypted—is referred to as [_____] or cleartext. An encrypted message is referred to as [_____]. Messages are encrypted by a cryptographic [_____], which is a specific procedure for encrypting or decrypting a message. A cryptographic [_____] is a word, number, or phrase that must be known to encrypt or decrypt a message. [_____] key encryption uses the same key to encrypt and decrypt a message. [_____] key encryption eliminates the key-distribution problem by using one key to encrypt a message, but another key is used to decrypt the message.

 CHECK ANSWERS

Interactive Situation Questions

Apply what you've learned to some typical computing situations. When using the NP2013 interactive eBook, you can type your answers, and then use the Check Answers button to automatically score your responses.

1. You just bought a new Blu-ray player and it mentions that you can access the Internet to view Netflix movies. You assume that the player is equipped with [_____] so that it can connect wirelessly to your LAN's router .

2. You're setting up an Ethernet wired network using a router. To access the router and its configuration software, you open your [_____] and type the router's IP address.

3. You're trying to figure out if your computer has a built-in Ethernet port. You see the port pictured to the right. Is that the port you should use for your RJ45 connector? Yes or no? [_____]

4. You install an 802.11b network, but it seems to stop working at various times. To begin troubleshooting, you look for any devices, such as cordless phones, that use the [_____] GHz frequency.

5. Your computer is connected to a LAN, and you want easy access to files stored on several other computers on the LAN. Because all of the computers use Windows, you can set up a(n) [_____] .

6. You arrive at work and one of your co-workers tells you that the router is down. Is it correct to surmise that your workstation will not be able to access other workstations, but will be able to access the Internet? Yes or no? [_____]

7. You have a small network in your house that uses a wireless router. For the past week, you've seen a black SUV parked outside and its occupant seems to be using a notebook computer. The first step you should take to discover if this person has hacked into your network is: a) knock on the car window and ask; b) call the police; or c) use your router utilities to check who is connected to your network. [_____]

8. You've set up a network using some new equipment and a few old Wi-Fi adapters given to you by your roommates. One of the adapters is equipped only for WEP, whereas all the other adapters support WPA2. Your roommate tells you that in order to use all the adapters, you'll have to disable wireless encryption. Is your roommate right? [_____]

 CHECK ANSWERS

Interactive Practice Tests

Practice tests that consist of ten multiple-choice, true/false, and fill-in-the-blank questions are available in the NP2013 interactive eBook. Test questions are selected at random from a large test bank, so each time you take a test, you'll receive a different set of questions. Your tests are scored immediately, and you can print study guides that help you find the correct answers for any questions that you missed.

 CLICK TO START

Learning Objectives Checkpoints

Learning Objectives Checkpoints are designed to help you assess whether you have achieved the major learning objectives for this chapter. You can use paper and pencil or word processing software to complete most of the activities.

1. Describe the characteristics of PANs, LANs, MANs, and WANs, plus provide an example of each.

2. List five advantages and three disadvantages of computer networks.

3. Create a list of network devices mentioned in this chapter. Write a brief description of each one.

4. Draw a diagram of Shannon's communications model and explain how it relates to communications protocols. Apply Shannon's model to a Wi-Fi LAN by indicating which real-world devices would exist at various points in the model to originate data, encode it, transmit signals, and so on.

5. Explain the difference between an analog signal and a digital signal. Explain why most modern communications systems use digital signals.

6. Explain the difference between packet switching and circuit switching. Describe the differences between IP addresses and MAC addresses.

7. List five characteristics of Ethernet that make it a popular network standard.

8. List the technologies that carry wireless signals and give an example of where each is commonly used.

9. Describe the differences between Wi-Fi and Bluetooth technologies, and give two examples of where you would expect to find each in use.

10. Draw a storyboard to illustrate the steps you would take to set up a LAN and configure the router so that you can use wired and wireless connections.

11. List four kinds of wireless encryption and indicate which ones provide the best security.

12. Suppose you've set up a wireless router. Create a quick guide that instructs authorized users how to join it using their smartphones.

13. Describe the steps required to turn on file sharing for one specific file that is stored on your computer.

14. Make a list of security concerns that are related to local area networks. Describe the steps that you would take to secure your LAN.

15. Describe the difference between symmetric encryption and public key encryption. List five uses for each one.

Study Tip: Make sure you can use your own words to correctly answer each of the purple focus questions that appear throughout the chapter.

Concept Map

Fill in the blanks to show the hierarchy of LAN technologies.

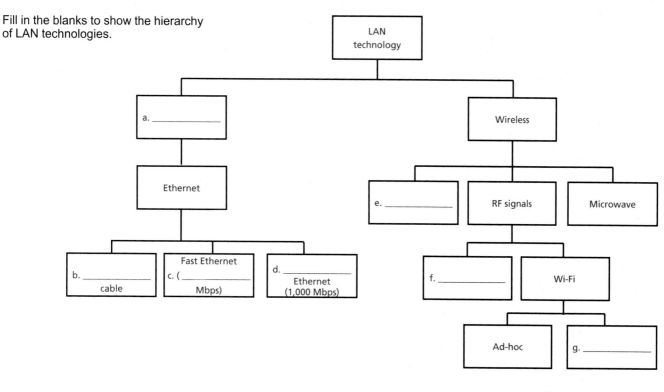

CHECK ANSWERS

6

The Internet

Chapter Contents

INFOWEBLINKS

You'll find updates for chapter
material by connecting to the
NP2013 Chapter 6 InfoWebLink.

Ⓦ CLICK TO CONNECT
www.infoweblinks.com/np2013/ch06

Learning Objectives

After reading this chapter, you will be able to answer the
following questions by completing the outcomes-based
Learning Objectives Checkpoints on page 357.

1. Who created the Internet?
2. How does the Internet work?
3. What is TCP/IP?
4. What are the differences between static IP addresses,
   dynamic IP addresses, private IP addresses, and
   domain names?
5. Can I find the actual speed of my Internet connection?
6. What is the best type of Internet service?
7. Is there a difference between portable Internet access
   and mobile Internet access?
8. How do cell phones and other handheld devices access
   the Internet?
9. How do chat, instant messaging, and other Internet-
   based communications work?
10. How does Voice over IP work?
11. What are grid and cloud computing?
12. How is FTP different from file sharing technologies
    such as BitTorrent?
13. How do hackers break into computers?
14. How can I protect my computer from intrusions?

CourseMate
Visit the NP2013 CourseMate for this chapter's Pre-Quiz, Audio
Overview and Flashcards, Detailed Objectives, Chapter Quiz,
Online Games, and more labs.

Multimedia and Interactive Elements
When using the NP2013 interactive eBook, click the ▶ icons to
access multimedia resources.

Apply Your Knowledge The information in this chapter will give you the background to:

- Find your computer's Internet address
- Get a domain name for your Web site
- Measure the speed of your Internet connection
- Select the best Internet access services for your location and budget
- Access the Internet from a Wi-Fi hotspot
- Access the Internet from a mobile phone
- Use Internet services such as instant messaging, chat, FTP, Voice over IP, and BitTorrent
- Protect your computer from online intrusions

Try It!

HOW FAST AND DEPENDABLE IS MY INTERNET CONNECTION?

You can access the Internet in various ways—using your phone line, your cable TV connection, or a personal satellite dish. Is your Internet connection fast enough for activities such as downloading DVDs and playing online multiplayer games? You can discover the speed of your Internet connection by doing the following steps:

1. Windows: Click the **Start** button, point to **All Programs**, click **Accessories**, and then select **Command Prompt** from the list. This action opens a "DOS box." Type **Ping www.google.com** and then press the **Enter** key.

  Mac: Click the **Finder** icon, select **Applications**, **Utilities**, and **Terminal**. This action opens the Terminal window. Type **Ping -c 4 www.google.com** and then press the **Enter** key.

2. Your computer makes four attempts to access Google and measures the time required for each attempt. Fill in the blanks below with the Ping statistics for your computer. When you read the chapter, you'll learn how those statistics stack up for video-conferencing, Voice over IP, and online multiplayer gaming.

3. Close the DOS box or Terminal window.

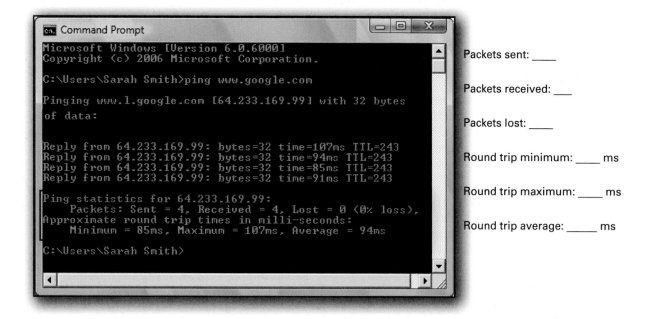

Packets sent: _____

Packets received: _____

Packets lost: _____

Round trip minimum: _____ ms

Round trip maximum: _____ ms

Round trip average: _____ ms

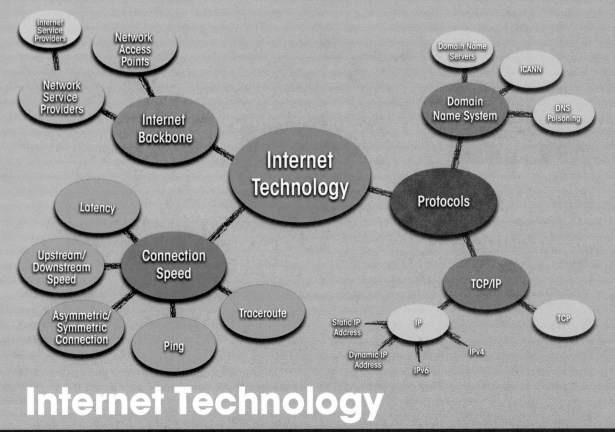

Internet Technology

TO MOST PEOPLE, the Internet seems old hat. Even people who haven't used the Internet know a lot about it from watching the news, reading magazines, and watching movies. Using the Internet is actually pretty easy. Browsing Web sites, shopping at Amazon.com, sending e-mail, and tweeting? No problem. But what makes the Internet "tick"? How can one network offer so much information to so many people? Section A pulls back the curtain and gives you a glimpse of what happens behind the scenes on the Net.

BACKGROUND

▶ **How did the Internet get started?** The history of the Internet begins in 1957 when the Soviet Union launched Sputnik, the first man-made satellite. In response to this display of Soviet superiority, the U.S. government resolved to improve its scientific and technical infrastructure. One of the resulting initiatives was the Advanced Research Projects Agency (ARPA).

ARPA swung into action with a project designed to help scientists communicate and share valuable computer resources. The ARPANET, created in 1969, connected computers at UCLA, Stanford Research Institute, University of Utah, and University of California at Santa Barbara (Figure 6-1).

In 1985, the National Science Foundation (NSF) used ARPANET technology to create a larger network, linking not just a few mainframe computers, but entire LANs at each site. Connecting two or more networks creates an internetwork, or internet. The NSF network was an internet (with a lowercase *i*). As this network grew throughout the world, it became known as the Internet (with an uppercase *I*).

FIGURE 6-1

An original diagram of the ARPANET included four nodes, depicted as circles.

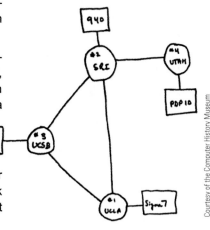

▶ How did the Internet become so popular? Early Internet pioneers used primitive command-line user interfaces to send e-mail, transfer files, and run scientific calculations on Internet supercomputers. Finding information was not easy and access was limited to a fairly small group of educators and scientists.

In the early 1990s, software developers created new user-friendly Internet access tools, and Internet accounts became available to anyone willing to pay a monthly subscription fee.

▶ How big is the Internet today? With an estimated 500 million nodes and more than 2 billion users, the Internet is huge. Although exact figures cannot be determined, it is estimated that the Internet handles more than an exabyte of data every day. An exabyte is 1.074 billion gigabytes, and that's a nearly unimaginable amount of data.

INTERNET INFRASTRUCTURE

▶ How is the Internet structured? Surprisingly, the Internet is not owned or operated by any single corporation or government. It is a data communications network that grew over time in a somewhat haphazard configuration as networks connected to other networks and to the Internet backbone.

▶ What is the Internet backbone? The **Internet backbone** is a network of high-capacity routers and fiber-optic communications links that provides the main routes for data traffic across the Internet. At one time, the Internet backbone and interconnected networks might have resembled a spine with ribs connected along its length. Today, however, it more resembles a map of interstate highways with many junctures and redundant routes.

▶ How does the backbone tie the Internet together? Backbone links and routers are maintained by **network service providers** (NSPs), such as AT&T, British Telecom, Deutsche Telekom, Sprint, and Verizon.

NSP equipment and links are tied together by **network access points** (NAPs), so that, for example, data can begin its journey on a Verizon link and then cross over to a Sprint link, if necessary, to reach its destination.

NSPs supply Internet connections to large Internet service providers, such as EarthLink, AOL, AT&T, and Comcast. An **Internet service provider** (ISP) is a company that offers Internet access to individuals, businesses, and smaller ISPs. Figure 6-2 shows a simplified conceptual diagram of the Internet backbone and its components.

FIGURE 6-2

The Internet backbone includes high-speed routers and high-speed fiber-optic links. Parts of the backbone maintained by different communications companies are connected at network access points (NAPs).

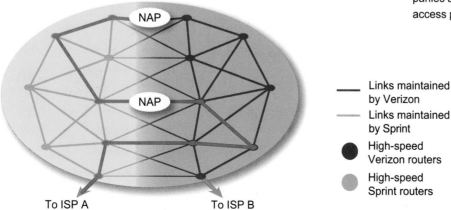

Links maintained by Verizon

Links maintained by Sprint

● High-speed Verizon routers

● High-speed Sprint routers

▶ **What kinds of network devices are part of an ISP?** An ISP operates routers, communication equipment, and other network devices that handle the physical aspects of transmitting and receiving data between their subscribers and the Internet. Many ISPs also operate e-mail servers to handle incoming and outgoing mail for their subscribers. Some ISPs have Web servers for subscriber Web sites.

An ISP might operate a server that translates an address, such as *www. google.com*, into a valid IP address, such as 208.50.141.12. ISPs can also maintain servers for online discussions, instant messaging, music file sharing, FTP, streaming video, and other file transfer services (Figure 6-3).

FIGURE 6-3

ISP Equipment

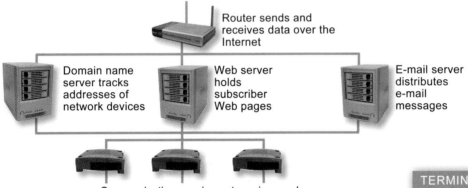

Router sends and receives data over the Internet

Domain name server tracks addresses of network devices

Web server holds subscriber Web pages

E-mail server distributes e-mail messages

Communications equipment receives and transmits signals to subscribers

▶ **How does my computer fit into the structure of the Internet?** To communicate with an ISP, your computer uses some type of communications device, such as a modem. A **modem** contains circuitry that converts the data-carrying signals from your computer to signals that can travel over various communications channels. The kind of modem you use depends on whether you are connecting to a dial-up, wireless, cable, satellite, or DSL Internet service.

A standalone computer can communicate with an ISP directly through a modem, or through a combination of a router and modem. If your computer is part of a network, the network's router communicates with a modem to handle the Internet connection. Figure 6-4 illustrates the difference between standalone and LAN Internet access.

> **TERMINOLOGY NOTE**
>
> The word *modem* is derived from the words *modulate* and *demodulate*. In communications lingo, modulation means changing the characteristics of a signal, as when a dial-up modem changes a digital pulse into an analog audio signal that travels over telephone lines. Demodulation means changing a signal back to its original state.

FIGURE 6-4

Your computer can connect to the Internet as a standalone device or part of a LAN. Your data first travels to your ISP, then to an NSP and out over the Internet backbone.

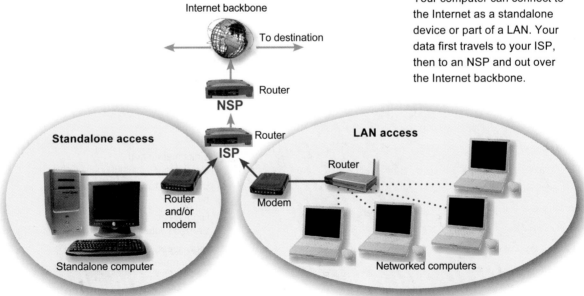

Internet backbone

To destination

Router

NSP

Router

ISP

Standalone access

Router and/or modem

Standalone computer

LAN access

Router

Modem

Networked computers

INTERNET PROTOCOLS, ADDRESSES, AND DOMAINS

▶ What protocols are used by the Internet? The Internet uses a variety of communications protocols to support basic data transport and services, such as e-mail, Web access, and downloading. Figure 6-5 briefly describes some of the main protocols used on the Internet.

FIGURE 6-5

Protocols Used on the Internet

6

Protocol	Name	Function
TCP	Transmission Control Protocol	Creates connections and exchanges packets of data
IP	Internet Protocol	Provides devices with unique addresses
UDP	User Datagram Protocol	An alternative data transport to TCP used for DNS, Voice over IP, and file sharing
HTTP	Hypertext Transfer Protocol	Exchanges information over the Web
FTP	File Transfer Protocol	Transfers files between local and remote host computers
POP	Post Office Protocol	Transfers mail from an e-mail server to a client Inbox
SMTP	Simple Mail Transfer Protocol	Transfers e-mail messages from client computers to an e-mail server
VoIP	Voice over Internet Protocol	Transmits voice conversations over the Internet
IRC	Internet Relay Chat	Transmits text messages in real time between online users
BitTorrent	BitTorrent	Distributes files using scattered clients rather than a server

▶ How significant is TCP/IP? **TCP/IP** is the primary protocol suite responsible for message transmission on the Internet. A **protocol suite** is a combination of protocols that work together. **TCP** (Transmission Control Protocol) breaks a message or file into packets. **IP** (Internet Protocol) is responsible for addressing packets so that they can be routed to their destination. From a practical perspective, TCP/IP provides a protocol standard for the Internet that is public, free, extensible, and easy to implement.

▶ Does the Internet use a special addressing scheme? In the previous chapter, you learned that IP addresses can be assigned to LAN workstations. IP addresses originated on the Internet as part of the TCP/IP protocol. IP addresses are used to uniquely identify computers on the Internet as well as on LANs. In the context of the Internet, IP addresses are sometimes referred to as TCP/IP addresses or Internet addresses.

▶ How do IP addresses work on the Internet? Every device on the Internet has an assigned IP address such as 128.110.192.40. In binary, the addresses are 32 bits long, but they are usually written as decimal numbers and divided by periods into four groups called octets.

The numbers in each octet correspond to network classes. For example, an IP address that begins with a number between 128 and 191 corresponds to a Class B network, such as a large college campus. When delivering a packet of data, Internet routers use the first octet to get a general idea of where to send the packet. The rest of the IP address is used to drill down to the exact destination.

▶ Do octets correspond to the parts of e-mail or Web site addresses? E-mail addresses such as *imastudent@uga.edu* and Web site addresses such as *http://www.uga.edu* are separated into parts with periods, similar to the octets in an IP address. The octets do not, however,

TERMINOLOGY NOTE

32-bit IP—referred to as IPv4—offers about 4 billion unique addresses. When even more addresses are needed, IPv6 can offer billions and billions of addresses. An IPv6 address is 128 bits and usually written as eight groups of four hexadecimal digits, such as 2001:0db8:0: 0:1319:8a2e:0370:57ab.

map to the parts of a Web site address or an e-mail address. So, although *http://www.uga.edu* has an IP address of 128.192.1.9, the first octet, 128, does not correspond to *http://*. Nor does the second octet map to *www*.

▶ **Do I need a permanent IP address?** A computer can have a permanently assigned **static IP address** or a temporarily assigned **dynamic IP address**. As a general rule, computers on the Internet that act as servers use static IP addresses. ISPs, Web sites, Web hosting services, and e-mail servers that always need to be found at the same address require static IP addresses. Most other Internet users have dynamic IP addresses. Figure 6-6 illustrates a tool you can use to find your IP address.

FIGURE 6-6

You can find your computer's IP address on a Mac (left) using System Preferences or in Windows (right) using the Network and Sharing Center. ▶ Your interactive eBook shows why Web-based utilities can't always identify your computer's IP address.

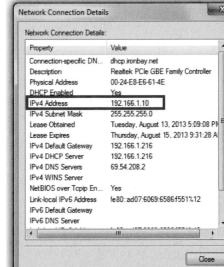

▶ **Why doesn't everyone have a static IP address?** The use of 12-digit addresses such as 128.192.100.100 provides approximately 4.3 billion unique addresses, but many of these are reserved for special purposes and devices, leaving a meager number of IP addresses for billions of Internet users. To avoid running out of static IP addresses, dynamic addresses are used whenever possible. Dynamic IP addresses can be handed out as necessary and reused as needed.

▶ **How do I get a dynamic IP address?** Every ISP controls a unique pool of IP addresses, which can be assigned to subscribers. If you have the type of Internet connection that requires a modem to make a telephone connection, for example, your ISP's DHCP server assigns a temporary IP address to your computer for use as long as it remains connected. When you end a session, that IP address goes back into a pool of addresses that can be distributed to other subscribers when they log in.

Your computer is rarely assigned the same dynamic IP address it had during a previous session. As an IP nomad with no permanent address, you can't feasibly run a Web site or perform other server-related activities on your computer. For example, if you try to run an online store, its address would change every time you connect to the Internet and customers would not be able to find it.

If you want to operate a server, your ISP should be able to supply you with a service plan that includes a static IP address and adequate bandwidth for server activity.

▶ How does a dynamic IP address relate to an always-on connection? Most high-speed Internet connections use always-on technology. An **always-on connection** is linked to your ISP and is online whenever your computer and modem are on, even if you are not actively accessing the Internet. An always-on connection can have a static or dynamic IP address. With an always-on connection, your dynamic IP address might remain the same unless you turn off your modem, or your service provider might randomly change your IP address from time to time.

Always-on connections are convenient. You don't have to wait for a connection to be established before using your browser or sending e-mail. If you have an always-on connection, however, you should be aware that it poses a security risk. With an always-on connection, your computer is connected to the Internet for long periods of time with the same IP address, making it particularly vulnerable to hackers. In Section E, you'll learn how routers and firewalls can protect computers that have always-on Internet connections.

▶ What's a domain name? Although IP addresses work for communication between computers, people find it difficult to remember long strings of numbers. Therefore, most Internet servers also have an easy-to-remember name, such as *nike.com*. By convention, you should type domain names using all lowercase letters.

The official term for this name is *fully qualified domain name (FQDN)*, but most people just refer to it as a **domain name**. A domain name is a key component of Web page addresses and e-mail addresses (Figure 6-7).

FIGURE 6-7

Domain names are part of the addresses for servers that handle e-mail and Web sites.

Web address   E-mail address

A domain name ends with an extension that indicates its **top-level domain**. For example, in the domain name *msu.edu*, *edu* indicates that the computer is maintained by an educational institution. Country codes also serve as top-level domains. Canada's top-level domain is ca; the United Kingdom's is uk; Australia's is au; the European Union uses eu as a top-level domain. Some of the most commonly used top-level domains are listed in Figure 6-8.

FIGURE 6-8

Top-level Domains

Domain	Description
biz	Unrestricted use; usually for commercial businesses
com	Unrestricted use; usually for commercial businesses
edu	Restricted to North American educational institutions
gov	Restricted to U.S. government agencies
info	Unrestricted use
int	Restricted to organizations established by international treaties
mil	Restricted to U.S. military agencies
mobi	Available for sites that cater to mobile devices such as smartphones
net	Unrestricted use; traditionally for Internet administrative organizations
org	Unrestricted use; traditionally for professional and nonprofit organizations

▶ **How are domain names related to IP addresses?** Every domain name corresponds to a unique IP address that has been entered into a huge database called the **Domain Name System** (DNS). Any computer that hosts this database is referred to as a **domain name server**.

A domain name, such as *travelocity.com*, must be converted into an IP address before packets can be routed to it. Figure 6-9 illustrates what happens when you type *www.travelocity.com* into your browser.

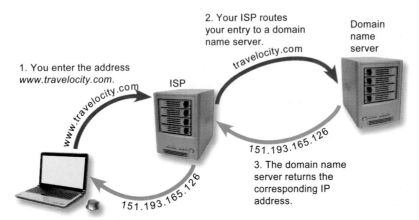

1. You enter the address *www.travelocity.com*.

ISP

2. Your ISP routes your entry to a domain name server.

travelocity.com

Domain name server

151.193.165.126

3. The domain name server returns the corresponding IP address.

151.193.165.126

FIGURE 6-9

A domain name request is routed through your ISP to your designated domain name server, which searches through its database to find a corresponding IP address. The IP address can then be attached to packets, such as requests for Web pages.

▶ **Why don't I notice a pause when I enter a domain name?** Although it seems as if you might have to wait quite a while to receive an IP address after you enter a domain name, that is not the case. Popular domain names are "cached" at your ISP; so in practice, you usually don't have to wait for an IP address from a domain name server.

▶ **The DNS seems technical; why worry about it?** The DNS is at the heart of the Internet. There are currently 13 domain name server systems that translate or "resolve" human-readable domain names into IP addresses. The DNS keeps track of every domain and every static IP address worldwide. When new addresses are added, they take a day or two to "propagate," or arrive, at all the domain name servers. Until domain names are added to the DNS database, new sites can be accessed only by entering their numeric IP addresses.

If a domain name server malfunctions or is hacked, Internet users can get directed to the wrong Web site. This misdirection, called **DNS cache poisoning**, has been used by governments to keeps citizens away from Web sites that supply politically or culturally inflammatory information. DNS cache poisoning is also a tool of hackers who want to direct users to sites infected with worms or keyloggers (Figure 6-10).

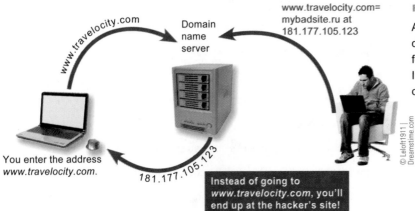

www.travelocity.com

Domain name server

www.travelocity.com= mybadsite.ru at 181.177.105.123

You enter the address *www.travelocity.com*.

181.177.105.123

Instead of going to *www.travelocity.com*, you'll end up at the hacker's site!

© Leloft1911 | Dreamstime.com

FIGURE 6-10

After a hacker poisoned this domain name server, requests for Travelocity are routed to the IP address of the hacker's malicious site.

▶ **Do I need my own domain name?** For client-style Internet activities, such as Web browsing, e-mail, and chat, you do not need your own domain name. You might, however, want a domain name if you plan to operate your own Web server or if you establish a Web site using a server provided by a Web site hosting service.

▶ **How do I get a domain name?** An organization called **ICANN** (Internet Corporation for Assigned Names and Numbers) is recognized by the United States and other governments as the global organization that coordinates technical management of the Internet's Domain Name System.

ICANN supervises several for-profit Accredited Domain Registrars, which handle domain name requests. You can select a domain name and register it for a minimal annual fee—currently between US$10 and $50, depending on the registration service (Figure 6-11).

FIGURE 6-11

The first step in registering a domain name is to find out whether the name is currently in use or reserved for future use. If a domain name is not available, consider using a different top-level domain, such as biz instead of com. After you've found an available domain name, you can continue the registration process by filling out a simple online form. ▶ You can learn more about selecting a domain name when you access this figure in your interactive eBook.

CONNECTION SPEED

▶ **How fast is the Internet?** Data travels over the Internet at an incredible speed. On average, data usually arrives at its destination in less than a second after it is sent. Data transport can slow down, however, when usage peaks during breaking news events, or when denial-of-service attacks break through security. Such slow-downs are temporary, however, and usually last only a few hours.

The elapsed time for data to make a round trip from point A to point B and back to point A is referred to as **latency**. Latency generally averages less than 100 ms (milliseconds) in North America. Latency increases slightly for overseas transmissions. If you want to play online multiplayer games, it is best to have less than 100 ms latency. Good-quality Voice over IP and videoconferencing require latency rates of 200 ms or less.

▶ **Can I measure speed and latency?** You can use a local Internet utility called **Ping** (Packet Internet Groper), which sends a signal to a specific Internet address and waits for a reply. When a reply arrives, Ping reports that the computer is online and displays the elapsed time for the round-trip message. You can use Ping before playing online games, using Voice over IP, joining an online videoconference, or streaming a Netflix movie to make sure you have adequate speed for everything to run smoothly.

Ping also shows whether packets were lost in transmission. Packets can become lost when signal interference or network congestion overwhelms Internet servers and routers. Lost packets can cause jitter in Voice over IP communications and videoconferencing. Too many lost packets during an online gaming session can cause the game to stutter or stall. And if packets don't arrive in the correct order, your game character might seem to act randomly for a few seconds.

Another utility called **Traceroute** records a packet's path in addition to its round-trip speed. You can use Traceroute to analyze the latency of your data as it hops from one Internet router to the next (Figure 6-12).

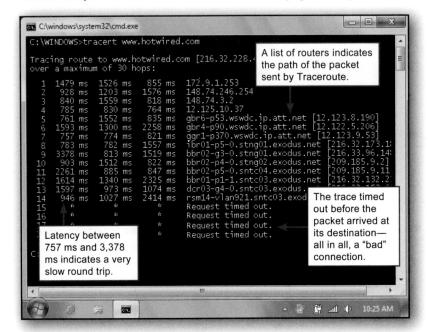

FIGURE 6-12

In this example, Traceroute is used to monitor an Internet connection between a small lakeside cabin in northern Michigan and the HotWired Web site. The satellite connection has extremely high latency and timed out before the Web site could be accessed. ▶ Click to learn how to launch Ping and Traceroute from the Windows command line and interpret the results.

▶ How fast is a typical Internet connection? The connection speeds advertised by ISPs refer to the amount of data that travels between a subscriber's computer and an ISP within a given time period. Connection speed is measured in Kbps (kilobits per second) or Mbps (megabits per second).

Slow dial-up connections top out at 56 Kbps. High-speed (also called broadband) connections at 10,000 Kbps (10 Mbps) are common. High-speed connections can display graphics quickly, show smoothly streaming video, handle net-based videoconferences, and deliver high-quality Voice over IP.

▶ What factors affect connection speed? Your connection speed depends on whether you connect to your ISP using a telephone, cable television, satellite, or wireless link. Actual speed can differ from maximum speed because links are susceptible to interference that can hinder signals. Upstream speed can also differ from downstream speed.

▶ What are upstream and downstream speeds? Upstream speed is the rate of data that is uploaded from your computer to the Internet. **Downstream speed** is the rate of data downloaded to your computer. Many ISPs limit these speeds to make sure everyone gets an equal share of the bandwidth. Usually, upstream speed is slower than downstream speed.

When upstream speeds differ from downstream speeds, you have an **asymmetric Internet connection**. When upstream and downstream speeds are the same, you have a **symmetric Internet connection**. Asymmetric connections discourage subscribers from setting up Web and e-mail servers that would transmit lots of upstream data. For most users, however, an asymmetric connection is sufficient.

You can use an Internet-based utility, such as Speedtest.net, to see if your Internet connection achieves the speed advertised by your ISP (Figure 6-13).

FIGURE 6-13

Speed tests measure the average number of bits that are transmitted per second, whereas utilities such as Ping and Traceroute measure the time required for a packet to make a round trip from your computer and back. ▶ Click to learn how to use Speedtest.net to compare the speed of your Internet connection with your ISP's advertised speed.

▶ **What are my connection options?** Consumers have several options for connecting to the Internet. **Fixed Internet access** links your computer to an ISP from a stationary point, such as a wall socket or roof-mounted antenna. **Portable Internet access** allows you to easily move your access device, as in the case of vehicle-mounted satellite dishes that can be deployed when the vehicle is parked. **Mobile Internet access** allows you to use the Internet as you are on the go, such as using a cell phone to collect your e-mail while you are traveling by train.

You're not necessarily limited to a single Internet access option. Many consumers find it convenient to maintain fixed Internet access for home use, but use a portable or mobile method of Internet access while out and about. In Sections B and C you'll learn more about Internet access options.

QuickCheck

1. TCP/ [_____] is the primary protocol suite used on the Internet.

2. 204.127.129.1 is an example of an IPv4 address. True or false? [_____]

3. A(n) [_____] name server maintains a database of IP addresses that correspond to addresses such as *www.nike.com*.

4. If you ping Google from your computer and get a result of 46 ms, you have a relatively slow Internet connection. True or false? [_____]

5. Most ISPs offer [_____] Internet connections, meaning the downstream speed is faster than the upstream speed.

▶ CHECK ANSWERS

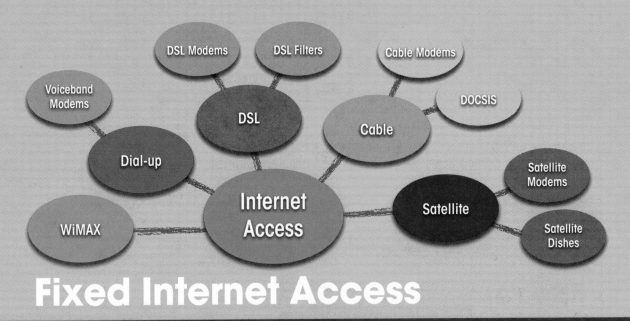

Fixed Internet Access

ONE OF THE MOST challenging aspects of the Internet is selecting a service provider. In this section of the chapter, you'll learn about fixed Internet access, which is typically your main link to the Internet. You'll learn to evaluate the pros and cons of various fixed Internet options, and discover why online interactive game players shun satellite Internet connections but love cable Internet service. Plus, you'll find out which types of Internet access work best for Voice over IP.

DIAL-UP CONNECTIONS

▶ **What is a dial-up connection?** A **dial-up connection** is a fixed Internet connection that uses a voiceband modem and telephone lines to transport data between your computer and your ISP. ISPs, such as NetZero, AOL, and EarthLink, still offer dial-up Internet access. The service typically costs less than $10 per month, but access speed is slow.

▶ **How does a dial-up connection work?** When you use a dial-up connection, your computer's modem places a regular telephone call to your ISP. When the ISP's computer answers your call, a dedicated circuit is established between you and your ISP—just as though you had made a voice call and someone at the ISP had picked up the phone.

The circuit remains connected for the duration of your call and provides a communications link that carries data between your computer and the ISP. As your data arrives at the ISP, a router sends it out over the Internet (Figure 6-14).

FIGURE 6-14

When you use a dial-up connection to access the Internet, your data travels over local telephone lines to your ISP, which sends it onto the Internet.

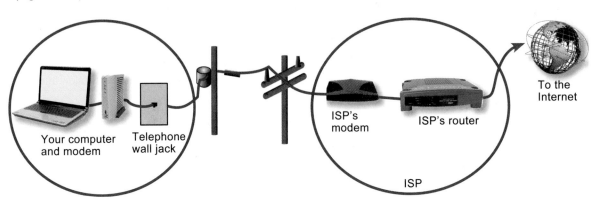

Your computer and modem — Telephone wall jack

ISP's modem — ISP's router — To the Internet

ISP

How does a voiceband modem work? The signals that represent data bits exist in your computer as digital signals. The telephone system, however, expects to work with human voices, so it carries analog audio signals. A **voiceband modem**—usually referred to simply as a modem—converts the signals from your computer into audible analog signals that can travel over telephone lines. A modem transmits a 1,070 Hz tone for a 0 data bit and a 1,270 Hz tone for a 1 data bit.

When your computer's modem initiates a connection, it sends a signal that is equivalent to picking up the receiver of a telephone to get a dial tone. It then dials the ISP by emitting a series of tones—the same tones you'd produce if you punched in the ISP's number using a phone keypad.

The modem then waits for the ISP's modem to answer the call. After the ISP's modem answers, the two modems begin to negotiate communications protocols, such as transmission rate. The series of beeps, tones, and whooshing sounds you hear when you connect to your ISP is the sound of your modem "talking" to the ISP's modem. This process of negotiation is sometimes called handshaking. When the negotiation is complete, data transmission can begin (Figure 6-15).

FIGURE 6-15

When you transmit data, your voiceband modem modulates the signal that carries your data. A modem at the other end of the transmission demodulates the signal.

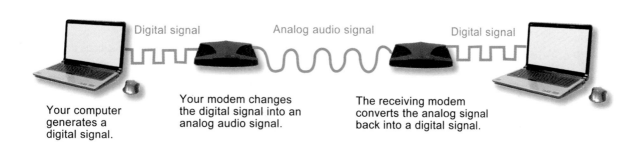

Your computer generates a digital signal.

Your modem changes the digital signal into an analog audio signal.

The receiving modem converts the analog signal back into a digital signal.

How fast is a voiceband modem? Modem speeds are measured in bits per second. (If you're a stickler for details, you'll realize that bps is actually a measure of capacity, but everyone calls it speed.) Most modems use a standard called V.90 to provide a theoretical maximum speed of 56 Kbps. Actual data transfer speeds are affected by factors such as the quality of your phone line and connection. Even with an excellent connection, however, a 56 Kbps modem tops out at about 44 Kbps.

Dial-up connections are asymmetrical; 44 Kbps is a typical download speed for a 56 Kbps modem. For uploads, the data rate drops to about 33 Kbps or less.

Can I use an analog modem if my phone service is digital? In many areas of the world, the telephone system uses digital rather than analog signals to send voice conversations. You can still use an analog modem because the sounds it emits are transported just as if they were voices.

Digital telephone systems open up the possibilities for digital data transport options such as ISDN and DSL. ISDN service offered slightly faster service than dial-up but has today been replaced by DSL.

DSL

▶ What is DSL? DSL (digital subscriber line) is a high-speed, digital, always-on, Internet access technology that runs over standard phone lines. It is one of the fastest Internet connections that's affordable to individual consumers.

Several variations of this technology exist. ADSL (asymmetric DSL) offers faster speeds for downloads than for uploads. SDSL (symmetric DSL) offers the same speed for uploads as for downloads. HDSL (high bit rate DSL), VDSL (very high bit rate DSL), and DSL lite are also available.

▶ How does DSL work? DSL data is transmitted to and from your local telephone switching station in pure digital form, bypassing the bottleneck of analog-to-digital-to-analog conversion and escaping the requirement to use the narrow bandwidth allocated to voice transmissions. The result is fast data transmission over standard copper telephone cable.

DSL uses some fairly sophisticated technology to superimpose digital signals over the unused frequency spectrum of an ordinary telephone line. A DSL connection can simultaneously carry voice and data, if permitted by your DSL provider. Voice and data signals travel over telephone lines to your telephone company's local switching station. There, the voice signals are separated from the data signals. Voice signals are routed to the regular telephone system; data signals are routed to your ISP and then to the Internet (Figure 6-16).

> **TERMINOLOGY NOTE**
>
> The acronym *xDSL* refers to the entire group of DSL technologies (including SDSL, HDSL, and so on). xDSL is not a separate variation of DSL.

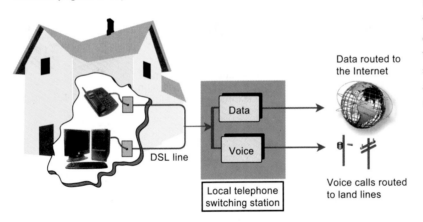

FIGURE 6-16

Voice and data signals travel over DSL to a special device at the local telephone switching station, where they are divided and routed to an ISP or to the regular telephone network.

▶ How fast is DSL? The speed of a DSL connection varies according to the characteristics of your telephone line and your distance from the telephone company's switching station. Current DSL technology can transport data at speeds up to 6 Mbps downstream for a distance of about 1.25 miles (2 km).

DSL signals deteriorate over distance, however. For DSL to work, your connection has to be within about 3 miles (5 km) of your telephone company's switching station. The distance requirement only pertains to the distance between you and the switching station. Once the signal arrives at the switch and is handed off to the ISP, it can travel the Internet backbone anywhere in the world.

▶ **How do I get DSL service?** The first step is to find out if DSL is available in your area. Contact your telephone company or check its Web site (Figure 6-17).

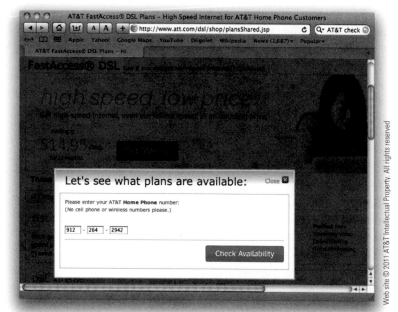

<blockquote>
FIGURE 6-17

To find out if DSL is available in your area, check with local carriers and national carriers, such as AT&T.
</blockquote>

6

▶ **What equipment do I need for DSL?** Most DSL installations can be handled by consumers. Your DSL service provider will supply you with the necessary instructions and equipment. DSL installations typically require a modem and filters.

A **DSL modem** (Figure 6-18) is a device that connects a computer to a telephone line and converts computer data signals into signals compatible with DSL. DSL is digital, so data doesn't need to be changed into analog signals and then back to digital as it does when you use a dial-up connection. DSL signals have to be modulated, however, so they can travel on non-voice frequencies.

Petr Malyshev/Shutterstock.com

FIGURE 6-18

A DSL modem connects your computer to a telephone wall jack. You can plug the modem into your computer's USB or Ethernet port.

A **DSL filter** (Figure 6-19) prevents voiceband signals from interfering with DSL signals. Professionally installed business DSL systems typically use a single external filter. Self-installed DSL kits provide filters that you connect to every device in your home that uses the telephone line.

Raymond Kasprzak/Shutterstock.com

FIGURE 6-19

A DSL filter connects to lines used for handsets, answering machines, and similar devices. For example, to filter a telephone, unplug the phone, plug the filter into the wall jack, and plug the phone cable into the filter.

CABLE INTERNET SERVICE

▶ **What is cable Internet service?** **Cable Internet service** is a means of distributing always-on broadband Internet access over the same infrastructure that offers cable television service. Local and national cable companies, such as Comcast, Cox, and Charter, offer cable Internet service for a monthly subscription. Of all Internet services, cable Internet currently offers the fastest access speeds.

▶ **How does cable Internet service work?** The cable television system was originally designed for remote areas where TV broadcast signals could not be received in an acceptable manner with an antenna. These systems were called community antenna television, or CATV. The CATV concept was to install one or more large, expensive satellite dishes in a community, catch TV signals with these dishes, and then send the signals over a system of cables to individual homes.

The topology of a CATV system looks a lot like the physical topology for a computer network. And that is just what is formed when your cable TV company becomes your Internet provider. Your computer becomes part of a neighborhood LAN joined by wiring for the cable TV infrastructure.

▶ **Are television and data signals carried over the same cable?** CATV coaxial and fiber-optic cables have plenty of bandwidth to carry television signals for hundreds of channels in addition to digital data. CATV cables provide bandwidth for television signals, incoming data signals, and outgoing data signals (Figure 6-20).

TV CHANNELS

Downstream Data

Upstream Data

FIGURE 6-20

A CATV cable has enough bandwidth to support TV channels and data flowing downstream as well as data flowing upstream.

▶ **How fast is cable Internet service?** Most cable Internet service is asymmetric, with upload speeds considerably slower than download speeds to discourage subscribers from setting up public Web servers. A standard home service plan offers speeds of 12 Mbps for downloads and 2 Mbps for uploads. Some premium plans offer even faster connections with speeds of 50 Mbps for downloads and 10 Mbps for uploads.

Cable signals are not particularly vulnerable to environmental interference, but data transport speeds are affected by subscriber use. The cable you share with your neighbors has a certain amount of bandwidth. As more and more neighbors use the service, it might seem to get slower and slower.

As an analogy, consider the luggage conveyor belt in an airport, which moves at a constant speed. If you have three pieces of luggage and you are the only passenger on the plane, your bags arrive one right after another. However, if you just arrived on a full 747, your bags are intermixed with those of hundreds of other passengers, and it takes longer to collect them.

Your cable company's network carries packets at a constant speed. However, if many of your neighbors are sending and receiving packets at the same time, your packets seem to arrive more slowly. Cable Internet subscribers notice that their connection speed seems slower during peak usage times.

▶ Do I need special equipment for cable Internet service?
When you set up your computer for cable Internet service, you are essentially linking to the cable network's Ethernet-style LAN that connects a neighborhood of cable subscribers. The two requirements for this type of connection are circuitry to handle Ethernet protocols and a **cable modem**, which converts your computer's signal into one that can travel over the CATV network.

Most subscribers rent a cable modem from their cable company, and the rental fee is included in the monthly bill. Third-party cable modems manufactured by Linksys, Motorola, D-Link, and other companies can be purchased from electronics stores, but it is a good idea to check with your cable company first to make sure the modem you select is compatible.

A cable modem can plug directly into a coaxial cable wall jack. If you need to connect your cable set-top box and cable modem to a single wall jack, you can use a cable splitter as shown in Figure 6-21.

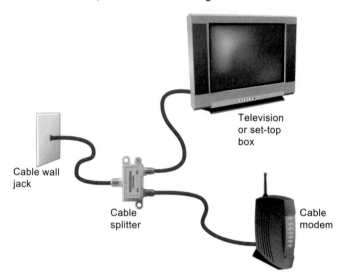

Television or set-top box

Cable wall jack

Cable splitter

Cable modem

FIGURE 6-21

If your home has only one CATV cable outlet, you might need to use a splitter to link it to your cable modem and television. If you have multiple cable outlets, you can connect your cable modem directly to any one of them.

Most cable modems have USB and Ethernet ports, and you can use one or the other. Some cable companies instruct subscribers to connect the modem directly to a computer. However, as you'll learn in the Internet Security section, the safest way to connect your computer to a cable modem is through a router.

▶ How secure are cable Internet connections? In the early days of cable Internet service, some cable Internet subscribers were unpleasantly surprised when they happened to open Windows Network Neighborhood, only to be greeted with a list of their neighbors' computers! When you boot a PC, Windows automatically connects to available LANs and looks for shared files, folders, and printers on LAN workstations. Because cable Internet service uses LAN technology, computers in different households were treated as workstations on a shared LAN.

Today, most cable companies use DOCSIS-compliant cable modems that block crossover traffic between subscribers. **DOCSIS** (Data Over Cable Service Interface Specification) is a data transport technology that includes security filters. DOCSIS secures your computer from your neighbors, but it does not close up all the security holes that are opened when you use an always-on connection. When you use cable Internet service, be sure your computer is running security software.

SATELLITE INTERNET SERVICE

▶ **What is satellite Internet service?** Most people are familiar with services that provide access to television programming over a personal satellite dish. Many companies that provide satellite TV also offer Internet access. **Satellite Internet service** is a means of distributing always-on, high-speed asymmetric Internet access by broadcasting signals to and from a personal satellite dish. In many rural areas, satellite Internet service is the only alternative to a dial-up connection.

▶ **How does satellite Internet service work?** Satellite Internet service uses a geostationary satellite to transmit computer data directly to and from a satellite dish owned by an individual (Figure 6-22).

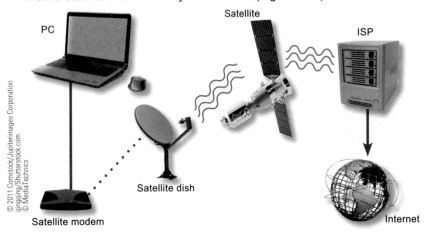

FIGURE 6-22

Satellite Internet services can be beamed to customers whose property offers an unobstructed view of the orbiting satellite. Signals are captured by a satellite dish and relayed to a satellite modem connected to a computer.

▶ **How fast is satellite Internet service?** Satellite service typically averages 1.0 to 1.5 Mbps for downloads but only 100 to 256 Kbps for uploads. Satellite signals can be slowed or blocked by adverse weather conditions, such as rain and snow, which makes this type of data transport less reliable than wired Internet access services, such as cable and DSL.

Satellite data transport is subject to latency delays of one second or more, which occur as your data is routed between your computer and a satellite that orbits 22,200 miles above the Earth. Latency might not pose much of a problem for general Web surfing and downloading files, but it can become a showstopper for interactive gaming that requires quick reactions, and for Voice over IP.

As with cable Internet service, satellite data transport speeds might seem to decline during peak usage hours because the satellite's bandwidth is shared among all users.

▶ **Does satellite Internet service require special equipment?** A satellite dish and modem are the two pieces of equipment required for satellite Internet access. If you already have a dish for satellite television, you might need a second dish for Internet services. The satellites that carry Internet signals are not the same as those that carry television signals.

A **satellite modem** is a device that modulates the data signals from a computer into a frequency band that can be carried to the satellite dish, where it is converted to another frequency, amplified, and transmitted. The modem connects to the satellite dish using two coaxial cables: one to transmit and one to receive. The modem then can be connected to the Ethernet port of a computer, or for better security, to a router.

Satellite modem front (left) and rear (right)

FIXED WIRELESS SERVICE

▶ What is fixed wireless Internet service? **Fixed wireless Internet service** (also called wireless broadband service) is designed to offer Internet access to homes and businesses by broadcasting data signals over areas large enough to cover most cities and outlying areas.

Fixed wireless technologies are MAN (metropolitan area network) standards, in contrast to technologies such as Wi-Fi, which are LAN (local area network) standards. One of the most well-known fixed wireless standards is WiMAX, currently offered by a variety of local service providers.

▶ What is WiMAX? **WiMAX**, which stands for Worldwide Interoperability for Microwave Access, is an Ethernet-compatible network standard designated as IEEE 802.16. Its popularity is growing because it offers an alternative to wired technologies, such as DSL and cable Internet service, that require expensive infrastructures.

WiMAX can be deployed in rural areas where cable service is not available and where customers are too far away from a telephone switching station for DSL service. In an urban environment, WiMAX can offer healthy competition to other Internet service providers.

▶ How does WiMAX work? A WiMAX system transmits data to and from WiMAX antennas mounted on towers. A single tower, such as the one in Figure 6-23, can serve a large geographical area.

Towers can transmit data to subscribers, they can relay data to other towers using microwave links, and they can connect directly to the Internet backbone by cable. Within 3 miles/8 km of the tower, signals are strong enough to be picked up by subscribers on a non-line-of-sight device, similar to a Wi-Fi access point. Beyond that range, a line-of-sight antenna is required.

FIGURE 6-23

A WiMAX tower broadcasts signals over a wide area. Subscribers close to the tower can use non-line-of-sight modems to pick up the signal.

▶ What is the speed of WiMAX? Under ideal conditions, WiMAX can transmit data at 70 Mbps. Actual speed, however, is affected by distance, weather, and usage. Current services claim speeds of 1 to 5 Mbps for downloads. WiMAX can be distributed as symmetrical or asymmetrical service.

Fixed wireless technologies have less latency than satellite Internet service and can usually offer connection speeds suitable for online gaming, Voice over IP, and teleconferencing.

▶ What equipment do I need for WiMAX access? Your wireless service provider typically supplies a wireless modem that you connect to your computer. The modem includes a transceiver to send and receive signals to a wireless point of access, usually located on a nearby communications tower. Subscribers on the outlying edges of the network's range might also require an antenna mounted on a window or roof, and a line-of-sight range to the WiMAX tower.

FIXED INTERNET CONNECTION ROUNDUP

▶ **What's the best Internet connection for my PC?** The best Internet connection depends on your budget, what's available in your area, and what you do while connected. For fixed Internet access, cable Internet service is usually the first choice, when available. If cable Internet service is not available, or proves slower or less dependable than expected, the next choice would be DSL or fixed wireless service, if available.

If several fixed Internet services are offered in your area, the table in Figure 6-24 can help you evaluate their requirements, costs, advantages, and disadvantages.

FIGURE 6-24

Fixed Internet Access Options

	Dial-up	DSL	Cable	Satellite	WiMAX
Download speed (max.)	56 Kbps	384 Kbps– 6 Mbps	5–50 Mbps	1–1.5 Mbps	70 Mbps
Upload speed (max.)	33 Kbps	128 Kbps– 6 Mbps	256 Kbps– 10 Mbps	100–256 Kbps	70 Mbps
Download speed (actual)	44 Kbps	2–5 Mbps	3–10 Mbps	400–800 Kbps	1–5 Mbps
Latency	100–200 ms	10–20 ms	10–20 ms	1–3 seconds	10–50 ms
Short video (72 MB) download	4 hours	5 minutes	3.2 minutes	24 minutes	6.4 minutes
Requirements	Telephone line, ISP, voiceband modem	Computer located within 3 miles of local telephone switch; DSL modem	CATV service that provides Internet access; cable modem	Clear view of southern sky; satellite dish and modem	WiMAX modem, line-of-sight to WiMAX tower for distances > 3 miles
Monthly fee	$	$$	$$	$$	$$
Installation cost	$0	$	$	$$	$
Always-on	N	Y	Y	Y	Y

QuickCheck

1. Dial-up and DSL Internet access use the telephone cables already installed in a home or business. True or false? _____

2. Always-on connections are not a security risk because they use DOCSIS. True or false? _____

3. The two requirements for cable Internet service are circuitry to handle _____ protocols and a cable modem.

4. Satellite Internet service typically has a high _____ rate, which is unsuitable for some online gaming and Voice over IP.

5. _____, which adheres to IEEE 802.16 standards, is one of the most promising fixed wireless Internet technologies.

▶ CHECK ANSWERS

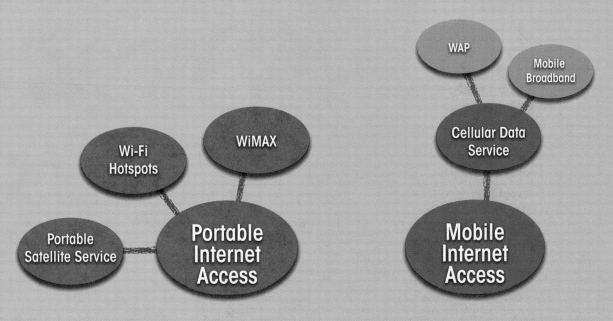

Portable and Mobile Internet Access

WHEN YOU'RE ON THE GO and away from your fixed Internet connection, you are not necessarily cut off from your e-mail and other Internet activities. Portable and mobile Internet technologies can provide Internet access while you visit friends, commute to work or school, or take a vacation. In this section, you'll find out what's available for portable and mobile access today and what's on the drawing board for the future.

INTERNET TO GO

▶ **What is portable Internet access?** Portable Internet access can be defined as the ability to easily move your Internet service from one location to another. It is portable in the sense that a hot plate is portable. It is light and compact enough to easily carry, even though you have to remain in one spot when it comes time to use it. Portable Internet access services include Wi-Fi, portable satellite, and portable WiMAX.

▶ **What is mobile Internet access?** Mobile Internet access offers a continuous Internet connection as you are walking or riding in a bus, car, train, or plane. It is very similar in concept to cellular phone service that allows you to move freely within coverage areas as the signal for your connection is seamlessly handed off from one tower to the next. Mobile Internet access includes Wi-Fi, mobile WiMAX, and cellular broadband service (Figure 6-25).

FIGURE 6-25

Using mobile Internet access, you can find the location of the nearest coffee shop.

WI-FI HOTSPOTS

▶ **What is a Wi-Fi hotspot?** In addition to being popular for home networks, Wi-Fi is also used for public networks operated by merchants, hotels, schools, and municipalities. If your computer is equipped for Wi-Fi, as are most of today's notebooks, netbooks, and smartphones, you have a portable means of accessing the Internet by carrying your digital device to any Wi-Fi hotspot.

A **Wi-Fi hotspot** is an area in which the public can access a Wi-Fi network that offers Internet service. You can find hotspots in locations such as coffee shops, RV parks, hotels, community centers, college campuses, and airports. Wi-Fi hotspot availability is expanding even in small towns and rural areas. Web sites such as *wi-fi.jiwire.com* help you find Wi-Fi hotspots in a specific location.

Some Wi-Fi hotspots offer free service that might or might not require a password; others require a service plan or one-time use fee. These fees can be expensive.

▶ **How fast is hotspot access?** The speed of a hotspot is related to the speed of the wired line that connects it to the Internet. A hotspot that goes through a 1 Mbps DSL line will be slower than a hotspot that goes through a 22 Mbps cable Internet connection. You can typically expect speeds of 2–8 Mbps, but speed can vary depending on your distance from the access point, the number of people logged in, and interference from other networks.

▶ **How do I access a Wi-Fi hotspot?** Accessing a Wi-Fi hotspot is similar to making a wireless connection to a LAN. In a typical scenario, you might take your notebook computer—equipped with Wi-Fi capability—to your local Starbucks cafe. You buy a cup of cappuccino, sit down in a comfortable chair, and switch on your computer.

Your computer's networking utilities automatically sense a Wi-Fi network and establish a connection. Windows users can access Connect to a Network to view a list of available networks and connect to one as shown in Figure 6-26.

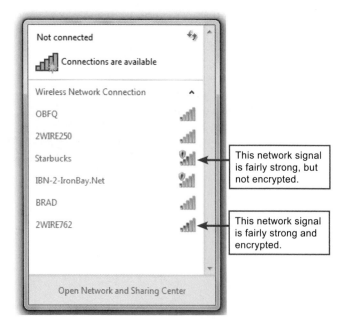

FIGURE 6-26

When using a Windows computer, enter "Connect to a Network" in the Start menu's search box to view a list of available networks, including Wi-Fi hotspots. Secure networks are safest. Networks that do not have security enabled are indicated with a yellow shield.

▶ **Is hotspot access secure?** Public hotspots are not typically protected by WPA or other encryption because it is not feasible to hand out passwords and user IDs to every person who wants access. Hotspots are not secure, and Wi-Fi eavesdroppers can easily tap into most of the data that flows over the network.

When using a Wi-Fi hotspot for simple browsing activities such as checking sports scores, reading Google news, and looking for directions, your security risk is fairly low if your computer's antivirus software is up to date.

Your security risk is also low when you are accessing secured Web sites that have addresses beginning with HTTPS. These secured sites, typically used for online banking and credit card purchases, encrypt the data that you enter to keep it safe from eavesdroppers.

When you log in to unsecured sites while using public Wi-Fi hotspots, however, a wireless eavesdropper could potentially snag your user ID and password information, then use it later to access your accounts. Logging in to your Webmail account, for example, could be risky if your user ID and password are transmitted over an unsecured connection.

Eavesdroppers might also be able to access the files on your computer if you have file sharing turned on. When using public networks, you should turn file sharing off. Windows 7 users can select the Public network option after connecting to a Wi-Fi hotspot (Figure 6-27).

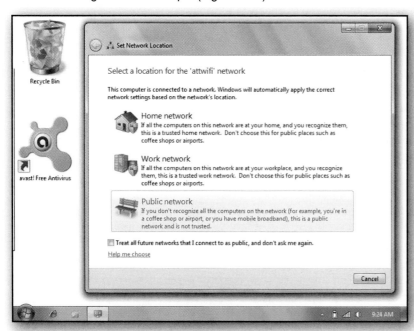

FIGURE 6-27

When connected to a public Wi-Fi hotspot, turn off file sharing to keep your data secure from eavesdroppers.

▶ **Can I use public hotspots for mobile Internet access?** Although Wi-Fi is popular for portable Internet access, public hotspots do not typically provide acceptable mobile Internet access because you can only remain connected within range of the network's hotspot.

The current model for using most Wi-Fi hotspots is that you enter the area of coverage, find a location with a strong signal, and remain there while accessing the Internet. Wi-Fi handoffs from one Wi-Fi network to another are clumsy and prone to packet loss, which is unacceptable for Voice over IP or streaming video applications. Later in this section, you'll read about cellular-based hotspots that you can set up privately to get mobile Internet access.

PORTABLE AND MOBILE WIMAX

▶ What is portable WiMAX? WiMAX can be used as a portable technology because Internet access is available to subscribers anywhere within a tower's coverage area. WiMAX subscribers who use non-line-of-sight modems with an integrated antenna (Figure 6-28) can easily relocate their modems anywhere within the service provider's coverage area. One WiMAX service provider encourages its customers to "Just plug in and jump online anywhere within the service area."

WiMAX-equipped computers make portable Internet access even easier. Just as many notebook computers are equipped with Wi-Fi circuitry, manufacturers can also add WiMAX circuitry and antennas, eliminating the need for an external modem.

▶ What are the pros and cons of portable WiMAX? The big bonus of portable WiMAX is that you use the same Internet service provider whether you are at home or on the road. You do not need supplemental service contracts or day passes as you do for Wi-Fi hotspots. On the downside, WiMAX is not yet in widespread use and coverage is limited.

▶ What about mobile WiMAX? Mobile WiMAX is an up-and-coming standard destined to be deployed by ISPs and cell phone carriers because it is designed to offer Internet access with seamless hand off from the coverage area of one tower to the coverage area of another tower. Mobile WiMAX could make it possible for you to deal with a single service provider for all your cell phone and Internet access needs.

PORTABLE SATELLITE SERVICE

▶ What if I travel to remote areas? WiMAX and Wi-Fi hotspots provide coverage in cities and small towns, but do not typically extend out to sparsely populated areas. If you plan to remain in a single remote location, fixed satellite Internet service is a good option. If, however, Internet access is required as you travel to various remote locations to hike, ski, or conduct research, then portable satellite technology is available.

▶ How does portable satellite technology work? For portable satellite Internet service, a satellite dish is typically mounted on a vehicle. The disk is stowed while the vehicle is in motion, but can be quickly deployed when the vehicle stops.

Like a fixed satellite dish, a portable dish transmits signals to and receives signals from a geostationary satellite. If a fixed satellite dish moves out of alignment, signals can no longer be captured dependably. The challenge with mobile satellite service is to make sure the dish is correctly aimed from the location where it is used. High-end portable satellite systems have self-aiming hardware that automatically deploys and rotates the dish until it locks onto the satellite signal (Figure 6-29).

▶ How fast is portable satellite service? Portable satellite service providers advertise download speeds of 400 Kbps to 5 Mbps and upload speeds of 50 to 500 Kbps. Larger dishes offer faster speeds. Portable satellites work well for browsing the Web and checking e-mail.

FIGURE 6-28

WiMAX modems are easy to transport and can be plugged in anywhere within the coverage area of a WiMAX tower.

Carlos Cordero Perez/La Nacion de Costa Rica/Newscom

FIGURE 6-29

A vehicle-mounted satellite dish can be deployed from a control panel inside the vehicle. As with fixed satellite service, however, latency becomes a factor for real-time applications such as videoconferencing, streaming movies, and online gaming.
▶ See how it works.

CELLULAR DATA SERVICE

▶ How can I use my cell phone service to access the Internet? In many countries, including the U.S., cell phone coverage is extensive and the technology is truly mobile; you can use cell phone service while walking or in a moving vehicle. The hand off as you travel from one cell area to another is seamless.

Using cell phone technology to access the Internet offers mobility that is not possible with other wired or wireless computer network technologies. And though in the past cellular-based Internet access was slower than dial-up, new technologies offer speeds that are more competitive with high-speed broadband offerings.

▶ How fast is cellular data transport? Data transport speed depends on the technology of the cellular system. Cellular technology is classified by the following generations:

▶ **1G (First-generation)** technology was analog and offered few features beyond voice communications.

▶ **2G** replaced analog technology with digital technology and added support for basic data transport in the form of text messages. Sending computer data over a 1G or 2G system required a voiceband modem to convert digital data into audible signals. Transmission rates were glacially slow.

▶ **3G** technologies offered by many of today's cellular service providers support digital transmission for both voice and data. 3G technologies have speeds ranging from 200 Kbps to 5 Mbps, so they are similar to satellite Internet service, and can potentially match DSL speeds. Cellular phone companies use a variety of 3G technologies, such as EDGE, EV-DO, and HSUPA.

▶ **4G** technology is the next step forward in mobile technology. It is designed to provide peak data rates of 100 Mbps while a device is in motion, or 1 Gbps rates when a device is stationary. Interim 4G technologies such as LTE (Long Term Evolution) have been deployed since 2009, but full-scale availability of 4G is not expected for several years.

▶ Can I get to the Internet from any cell phone? Most cellular service providers offer e-mail and Internet services. Basic phones can access a limited number of specially designed Web sites using WAP.

▶ What is WAP? WAP (Wireless Application Protocol) is a communications protocol that provides Internet access from handheld devices, such as cell phones.

WAP-enabled devices contain a microbrowser that displays simplified versions of popular Web sites, such as CNN, Google, Yahoo!, ESPN, UPS, FedEx, The Weather Channel, and MapQuest. WAP devices also include e-mail software formatted for small, low-resolution screens (Figure 6-30).

FIGURE 6-30

The advantages of WAP-enabled devices include their portability and low price. The disadvantage is their small, low-res screens. Although various schemes for scrolling over a full-sized Web page have been tried, most WAP users stick to Web sites specially designed for small screen devices.

© Alex Segre/Alamy

6

▶ **Can I use a cell phone to access regular Web sites and other Internet services?** Accessing the "real" Internet requires a different approach than is offered by WAP. For the real Internet, cellular service providers offer data services, sometimes referred to as **mobile broadband**. Broadband access requires a fast connection, a data service subscription, and mobile broadband equipment.

Broadband data access is not available in all of a cellular service provider's coverage area. Coverage maps can give you an idea of the service area, but actual coverage and speeds can vary. Where broadband coverage is not available, your device might operate at a much slower speed or might not have access to data services.

▶ **What is a data service plan?** Most cellular service providers offer a data service plan for accessing the Internet. Prices for these plans range from $20 per month and up. Less expensive plans typically limit the amount of data you can send and receive, treating megabytes like minutes. Make sure you understand the terms of your service contract. Some data service contracts prohibit users from streaming or downloading music, movies, or games; making Voice over IP phone calls; and using file sharing networks.

▶ **What equipment do I need for mobile broadband Internet access?** With a data service plan, there are five ways to take advantage of mobile broadband: using a handheld PDA or smartphone, using a mobile broadband card in a PC, using a mobile broadband-enabled computer, using a cell phone as a modem, or using a cell phone as a wireless hotspot.

▶ **How do I access the Internet with a handheld device?** You can use a smartphone to access the Internet by subscribing to a data service plan offered by a mobile phone provider such as AT&T, Verizon, or Sprint.

Many handheld devices also have built-in Wi-Fi and can access the Internet when in range of a Wi-Fi LAN or hotspot. When the device senses the Wi-Fi network, it gives you the opportunity to connect and enter the network password if one is required. Once connected, your handheld device can access the Internet at Wi-Fi speeds.

Smartphones typically include browser and e-mail software (Figure 6-31). Some devices, such as the iPhone, include specialized software to access popular Web sites such as Google Maps and YouTube.

FIGURE 6-31

Many smartphones offer a large color screen, and can connect to Wi-Fi hotspots and cellular data services to access the Internet.

▶ **How do I access the Internet with a cellular wireless modem?** Most cellular service providers offer wireless modems for broadband data access (Figure 6-32). The modem slides into the USB port of your notebook computer and is installed following the manufacturer's instructions.

After the card has been installed, you can use it to connect to the Internet and use your usual set of tools, including your Web browser and e-mail software. With your notebook computer's full-size screen, you'll have the "real" Internet experience.

▶ **What is a mobile broadband-enabled computer?** Just as many notebook computers come with Wi-Fi circuitry for accessing wireless LANs and hotspots, some manufacturers offer netbook and tablet computers with built-in circuitry for mobile broadband access. Although these configurations reduce installation hassles, they are not in demand because they may limit consumers to one mobile broadband provider.

▶ **How do I use a phone as a modem?** Some cell phones connect to your computer and act as a wireless modem to transmit data over the Internet. Data speed depends on the phone's technology.

To make the connection, obtain a data cable that's compatible with your phone from your cellular service provider or an electronics outlet. Follow the manufacturer's instructions for installing the cable and setting up a modem connection.

When you want to access the Internet, plug your cellular phone into your computer (Figure 6-33) and connect through your mobile data service. As with other connection options for desktop and notebook computers, you can use your usual suite of Internet software.

▶ **What is MiFi?** MiFi is a brand name for a compact, mobile, wireless router offered by Novatel Wireless. The term is sometimes applied to similar routers produced by other manufacturers. These routers connect to a mobile carrier's broadband data service and provide a wireless hotspot for up to five devices.

With MiFi, you can easily assemble a small network just about anywhere. For example, you can use your mobile network even when you are traveling in an RV or train. A MiFi router like the one in Figure 6-34 is about the size of a cell phone and runs on batteries.

FIGURE 6-32

It looks like a USB flash drive, but it is a modem that gives your computer Internet access using a cell phone network.

6

FIGURE 6-33

Using a data cable, your cellular phone can become a modem for your notebook computer.

FIGURE 6-34

MiFi routers run on batteries, so they can be used to construct portable networks. These routers are packaged with a cellular data plan for accessing the Internet.

❿ Can I use my phone as a wireless hotspot? Some cell phones, such as the Droid X and iPhone, can act as a Wi-Fi hotspot by becoming the router for a wireless network. You can set up your phone's mobile hotspot anywhere you have data service, but hotspot capability might entail additional monthly service charges.

When in Wi-Fi hotspot mode, your mobile phone can provide portable Internet access to other Wi-Fi enabled devices, such as notebook computers, iPods, iPads, and other smartphones.

Setting up a mobile Wi-Fi hotspot is similar to setting up a router for a private Wi-Fi network. You begin by entering an SSID as the unique network name, then select an encryption method, such as WPA2, to secure the data flowing over the network. When your hotspot is configured and active, other Wi-Fi enabled devices can connect to access the Internet and share files (Figure 6-35).

FIGURE 6-35

Some cell phones can be deployed as the router and modem for a small wireless network that you can use while traveling in a car or an RV.

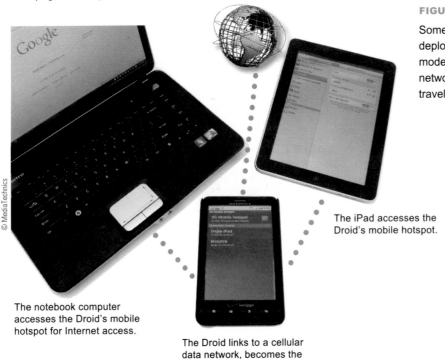

© MediaTechnics

The iPad accesses the Droid's mobile hotspot.

The notebook computer accesses the Droid's mobile hotspot for Internet access.

The Droid links to a cellular data network, becomes the router for this network, and creates a Wi-Fi hotspot with links to the Internet.

QuickCheck   SECTION C

1. _____ Internet access can be defined as the ability to use the Internet while walking or traveling in a moving vehicle.

2. A Wi-Fi _____ is an area in which the public can access a Wi-Fi network that offers Internet service.

3. _____ G technologies include EV-DO, HSUPA, and EDGE.

4. WAP devices have been replaced by devices that use mobile _____ technologies offering the full Internet experience.

5. Portable _____ technology can be used to access the Internet from remote locations where there are no cable, WiMAX, or cellular networks.

 CHECK ANSWERS

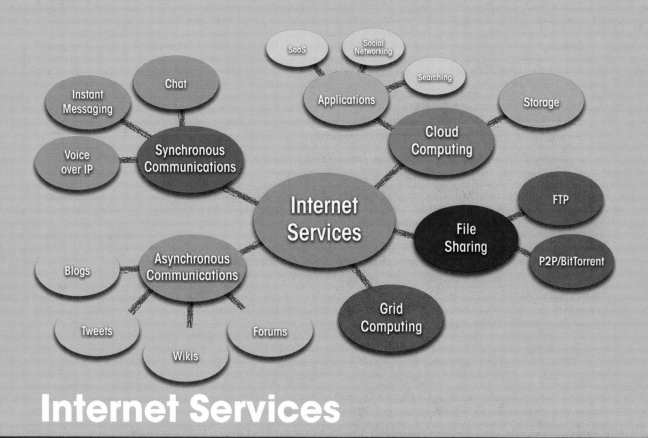

Internet Services

AN INTERNET CONNECTION offers access to a global data communications system. You know that protocols such as TCP/IP and UDP handle basic data transport; but additional protocols, sometimes referred to as application protocols, make possible a variety of useful Internet applications, such as cloud computing, real-time messaging, Voice over IP, blogging, tweeting, grid computing, FTP, and file sharing.

CLOUD COMPUTING

▶ **How does cloud computing relate to the Internet?** There's a lot of buzz about cloud computing these days, and its scope continues to evolve. Cloud computing is a concept, rather than a specific technology. It is the idea that consumers use their computers or handheld devices to access applications, storage, and other computing resources supplied by Internet-based servers, rather than from their local devices.

Under the umbrella of this broad definition, cloud computing encompasses most Internet-enabled activities including Webmail, Google searching, social networking, blogging, and photo sharing. The concept of cloud computing is that apps and data are available any time, from anywhere, and on any device (Figure 6-36).

FIGURE 6-36

Google Apps provides a glimpse of what cloud computing has to offer. Users can access productivity applications as well as their e-mail, blog, and social networking service from a desktop computer or a handheld device. Files created with these applications are also stored in the cloud for easy access.

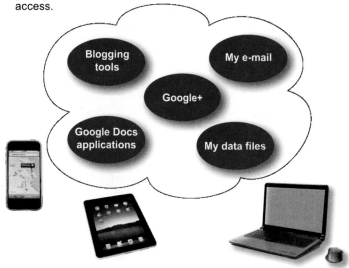

329

▶ How does cloud computing work? Cloud computing depends on a grid of servers, storage devices, and protocols that offer Internet-accessible computing services ranging from consumer-level media sharing to office productivity applications and complex corporate data processing.

These resources are maintained by Internet service companies, such as Google, Amazon, Apple, and Microsoft. For example, Apple maintains a 500,000-square-foot facility for its iCloud data center. Unveiling the new data center, Apple founder Steve Jobs said "We're going to move the digital hub, the center of your digital life, into the cloud."

Servers in a cloud data center host a variety of applications. Using an Internet connection, consumers can access these services for free or for a fee. The term **software as a service** (SaaS) refers to a model in which consumers access applications from a cloud provider over the Internet, usually by using a browser. Whereas some SaaS applications are free, most are offered through paid subscriptions or corporate leases.

▶ How does the cloud work for enterprise applications? Many years ago, when the Internet was just becoming popular, Victoria's Secret publicists came up with the innovative idea of holding an online fashion show. Only minutes after the show began, however, the host servers crashed as millions of viewers tried to access the Victoria's Secret site.

If today's cloud resources had been available, those viewers wouldn't have been disappointed. Victoria's Secret could have used Amazon's Elastic Compute Cloud, which instantly scales to respond to spikes in customer traffic.

Cloud computing offers Internet-based resources such as servers, software, and storage space on demand. The concept is similar to a temporary employment agency that provides office assistants, accountants, programmers, and other temporary workers as a business needs them. With cloud computing, Internet resources can be contracted as needed, and released when they are no longer needed.

Cloud computing helps businesses save money and offers scalable solutions that can quickly meet changing needs. For example, a startup e-commerce business might not have any idea of the server capacity that will be required to handle its Web site traffic. The business can contract with a cloud service to obtain server capacity that scales as necessary to handle customers (Figure 6-37).

FIGURE 6-37

Apps.gov is an initiative to supply cloud computing services to all U.S. government agencies. It includes a wide range of business and productivity applications, along with services such as Web hosting and secure storage.

REAL-TIME MESSAGING

▶ **What is real-time messaging?** A network-based **real-time messaging system** allows people to exchange short messages while they are online. One-on-one messaging is referred to as **instant messaging** (IM) and group communications are referred to as **chat**.

Every day, millions of people use messaging systems, such as Facebook Chat, Yahoo! Messenger, Apple iChat, and Windows Live Messenger, to communicate with friends, family, and coworkers. Some systems offer voice messaging and video options, so that participants can speak to each other using computer-based microphones and cameras.

▶ **How does real-time messaging work?** Most messaging is based on a client/server model that uses a server to handle communication packets between the participants (clients). When participants log on, they connect to the messaging server, which authenticates their user IDs and passwords. The server then sends back a list of participants who are currently online.

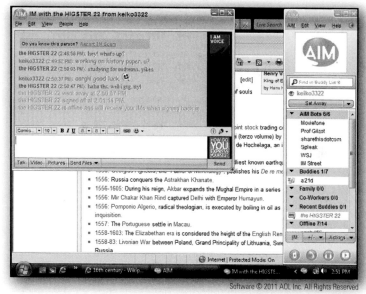

Messages are typed into client software (Figure 6-38), which uses messaging protocols to break the message into packets and ship them to the server for distribution or directly to the recipient. Some protocols encrypt messages before they are transmitted. Messaging and chat protocols include IRC (Internet Relay Chat), MSNP (Microsoft Notification Protocol), and Jabber.

VOICE OVER IP

▶ **What is Voice over IP?** **VoIP** (Voice over Internet Protocol), or Voice over IP, is a technology in which a broadband Internet connection is used to place telephone calls instead of the regular phone system. It is based on SIP (Session Initiation Protocol), so VoIP software is sometimes referred to as a SIP client.

The earliest VoIP connections were computer-to-computer connections. Both the person initiating the call and the person receiving the call had to have computers with microphones and headsets or speakers. You could only call people who were using the same VoIP software and who happened to be online when you wanted to call them. These early VoIP systems worked more like instant messaging with voice than a traditional phone call.

You can still use VoIP to make calls from one computer to another, but today VoIP systems, offered by companies such as AT&T, Comcast, magic-Jack, Skype, and Vonage, allow you to use a standard telephone handset to make or receive calls. They also allow you to receive calls from landline telephones and to place calls to these telephones.

▶ **How do today's VoIP systems work?** Today's VoIP systems convert voice communications to data packets. An IP address is attached to each packet. If you are calling a friend with computer-based VoIP, for example, your friend's IP address will be attached to the packets. If you are calling a land line or other destination without its own IP address, your VoIP packets will carry an IP address of a service that can route your packets to their destination using land lines where necessary.

How do I set up VoIP? If you want to set up free computer-to-computer VoIP, you and the people you communicate with can download and install freeware or open source VoIP clients, such as Google Talk or Blink. You can also use any messaging service that supports audio transmission. For the most basic setup, you can simply use your computer's built-in microphone and speakers instead of connecting a phone handset.

When you subscribe to a VoIP service, follow your service provider's setup instructions. For example, magicJack provides a small USB device that you plug into your computer, then connect to a telephone. Vonage supplies you with an adapter that you connect to your Internet modem.

Can I use VoIP on a cell phone? Cell phones that offer Wi-Fi as well as cellular phone service can be used to make VoIP calls if permitted by your service provider. When you are within range of a Wi-Fi hotspot, the call is routed through the Internet as a VoIP call. If no hotspot is in range, the call is routed through the standard cellular service. To get VoIP on your cell phone, find and install a compatible mobile VoIP app.

Do I need a high-speed Internet connection for VoIP? In addition to the speed of your Internet connection, VoIP audio quality is affected by jitter and packet loss. **Jitter** measures the variability of packet latency. Network traffic and interference can delay some packets and create erratic data flow. If the variation between packets exceeds 5 ms, VoIP quality is likely to be poor.

Packet loss refers to data that never reaches its destination or gets discarded because it arrives too late to be of any use. Packet loss of less than 2% is required for acceptable VoIP (Figure 6-39).

You can test your Internet connection to determine if it is suitable for VoIP by connecting to Web sites such as *myspeed.visualware.com*.

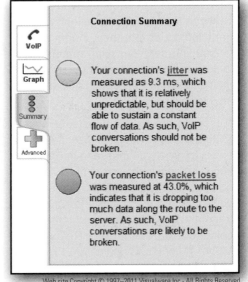

FORUMS, WIKIS, BLOGS, AND TWEETS

What about asynchronous communications? Instant messaging, chat, and VoIP are forms of **synchronous communications**; the people communicating have to be online at the same time and the conversation happens in real time. The Internet also supports several types of asynchronous communications, including Internet forums, wikis, blogs, and tweets.

The basic idea behind **asynchronous communications** is that one person posts a message using the Internet. That message can later be read by designated recipients or by the public, depending on the limitations set by the poster.

How do forums work? An **Internet forum** is a Web-based online discussion site where participants post comments to discussion threads. Those comments can be read at a later time by other participants. Most forums have a moderator who monitors discussion threads, weeds out disruptive participants, and handles membership requests.

▶ Are forums the same as wikis? No. Forums allow participants to comment on the material posted by other participants, but those comments are separate posts and the original post is not modified. A **wiki** allows participants to modify posted material.

Wikipedia is the best known wiki. Participants can post material pertaining to a topic, and other participants can modify it. Wikis can also include discussion pages where participants comment on topic material. For example, in a wiki topic about climate change, the discussion page might contain comments pointing out statements in the original post that cannot be verified.

▶ How do blogs work? A **blog** (short for Web log) is similar to an online diary; it is maintained by a person, a company, or an organization, and contains a series of entries on one or more topics. Blog entries are text-based, but can also include graphics and video. They are typically displayed in reverse chronological order on one long Web page.

FIGURE 6-40

Technorati helps you locate popular blogs or write one yourself.

Most blogs are open to the public, so blogging has become a form of personal journalism; a way to make your views public. They have been used extensively for political commentary. Some bloggers have been tapped as commentators on headline news shows on CNN and FOX. To set up your own blog, you can use a blog hosting service such as Blogger or WordPress. For a list of popular blogs, check out Technorati (Figure 6-40).

▶ What's a tweet? A **tweet** is a short message of 140 characters or less, posted to the Twitter Web site (Figure 6-41). Twitter is sometimes referred to as a microblogging service because tweets are similar to blog entries, except for their length. Your tweets are displayed in reverse chronological order on your profile page. By default, your tweets are open to the public, but you can restrict access to a list of approved viewers. Viewer comments on your tweets are also posted on your profile page.

FIGURE 6-41

Twitter is the platform for short messages called tweets.

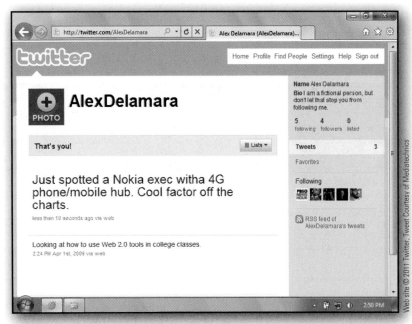

Twitter participants can subscribe to other people's tweets, a process referred to as "following." When you are a follower, you can quickly access tweets from the people you are following to find out what they are doing and thinking.

GRID COMPUTING

▶ **What is a grid computing system?** In the days when the Internet was really taking off, computer scientists noticed that thousands of computers connected to the Internet sit idle for hours while the people who own them are in meetings, talking on the telephone, sleeping, or otherwise occupied. If these idle processing cycles could be harnessed, they could supply a tremendous amount of computing power.

A **grid computing system** is a network of computers harnessed together to perform processing tasks. Grid computing systems can be public or private. Some grid systems use computers connected to the Internet as resources; others operate on private networks.

▶ **What is a distributed grid?** Distributed grids (sometimes referred to as CPU scavenging grids) tap into thousands of PCs and Macs with Internet connections whose owners donate their computers' idle hours to a grid processing task. Grid management software divides computational problems into pieces that are farmed out to computers on the grid for processing.

Each computer on the grid runs grid client software that contains the program necessary to process a piece of the problem. In this manner, complex calculations or tasks can be performed in parallel by using as many computers as are available on the grid. Results are sent back to the grid management software for consolidation. Figure 6-42 illustrates the basic architecture of a grid computing system.

▶ **Where are distributed grid systems used?** Because of their scalability, low cost, and high performance, distributed grids play a central role in scientific high-performance computing. One of the most famous examples of a distributed grid is the SETI@home project, which analyzes radio telescope data to search for signals that might originate from extraterrestrial life. People who wish to donate their computers' idle processing cycles to the SETI@home project can download and install grid client software (Figure 6-43) that processes signals when the computer is idle.

FIGURE 6-42

A distributed grid uses a diverse variety of computers as generic and equal resources.

A server running grid management software farms out pieces of a problem to computers in the grid.

Computers in the grid run grid client software and send results back to the server.

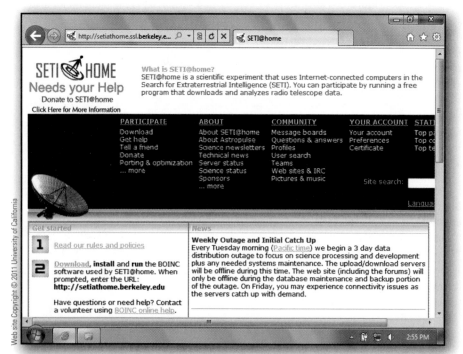

FIGURE 6-43

SETI@home consists of a grid management system and millions of privately owned personal computers whose owners donate idle processing time to the project. The SETI@home grid management system receives and stores raw data from the Arecibo radio telescope in Puerto Rico, divides this data into small segments for analysis, and farms out each segment to one of the privately owned computers.

FTP

▶ **What is FTP? FTP** (File Transfer Protocol) provides a way to transfer files from one computer to another over any TCP/IP network, such as a LAN or the Internet. The purpose of FTP is to make it easy to upload and download computer files without having to deal directly with the operating system or file management system of a remote computer. FTP also allows authorized remote users to change file names and delete files.

▶ **Do I need to use FTP?** Many people use FTP without even knowing it. When you download an updated device driver from a technical support site, access a document in PDF format from a corporate Web site, or pull down an MP3 file from your favorite music site, FTP is in action—although the mechanics of it are incorporated into other applications.

People who use FTP are often sharing large files stored on a file server in conjunction with a project. Files can be uploaded to the server by one participant and downloaded by others. An alternative to FTP, sending files as e-mail attachments, is not practical with very large files or for participants with slow Internet connections.

▶ **How does FTP work?** An **FTP server** typically resides on a computer containing files that remote users might want to access. The server runs software that listens on ports 20 and 21 for requests coming in from other computers. When a request arrives, the server makes sure the user who made the request has rights to access the file. If the request is valid, the file is transferred over the Internet as a series of packets to the requesting computer, where it is saved in a designated location on a local storage device.

▶ **How can I access FTP servers?** You can access FTP servers with FTP client software or with a browser. To use a Web browser to download a file, simply enter the address of the FTP server as shown in Figure 6-44.

FIGURE 6-44

A browser can provide access to FTP downloads. ▶ Click to see how it works.

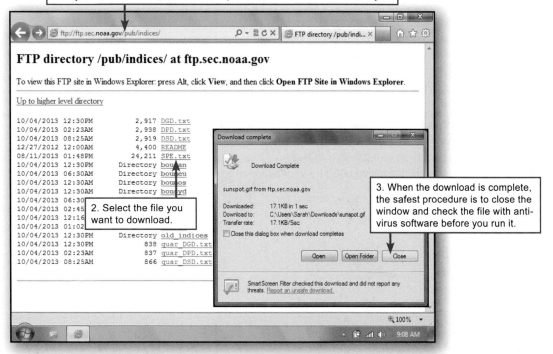

1. Enter the address of the FTP server in the browser's address bar. At an anonymous FTP server, a user ID and password would not be necessary.

2. Select the file you want to download.

3. When the download is complete, the safest procedure is to close the window and check the file with anti-virus software before you run it.

Not every FTP server is accessible from a browser, and those that are might work only for downloading files, not uploading them. If you plan to work extensively with FTP, you should get FTP client software. An **FTP client**, such as WS_FTP, CuteFTP, or open-source FileZilla, offers an easy-to-use interface for accessing FTP servers.

Convenient features of FTP clients allow you to save a list of server addresses and their corresponding user IDs and passwords, so you can connect to an FTP server with one click. FTP clients also allow you to download more than one file at a time, and they can pick up where they left off if the transfer is interrupted by a glitch in your Internet connection (Figure 6-45).

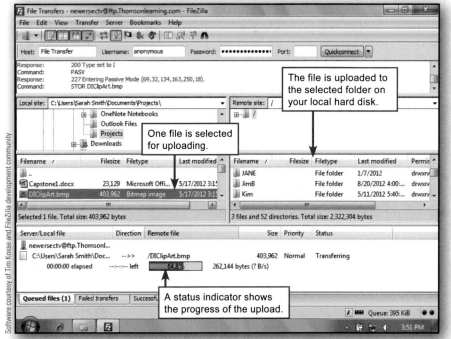

FIGURE 6-45

FTP clients such as FileZilla make it easy to upload and download files from an FTP server. ▶ Use your interactive eBook to find out how to use an FTP client to upload and download files from an FTP site.

▶ **Does FTP include security to prevent unauthorized access?** Some FTP sites require remote users to log in before accessing files. A login ID and password can be obtained from the FTP site operator. Access rights can be configured in various ways to allow or prevent remote users from changing file names, deleting files, uploading files, or downloading files.

▶ **What is anonymous FTP?** Anonymous FTP can be accessed by logging in without a password by using the user ID "anonymous." Some anonymous sites request users to enter their e-mail addresses as a password, but rarely is that piece of information used for verification or tracking.

FILE SHARING NETWORKS

▶ **What is file sharing?** File sharing, sometimes called **P2P file sharing**, allows users to obtain files from other users located anywhere on the Internet. In the late 1990s, file sharing burst onto the national scene when college students became aware of a technology called Napster that provided free access to hit songs. Today, file sharing networks such as BitTorrent facilitate movie and music downloads.

▶ **What is BitTorrent?** **BitTorrent** is a file sharing protocol that distributes the role of a file server across a collection of dispersed computers. BitTorrent is, in some sense, an offshoot of grid computing concepts, in which an ad-hoc collection of personal computers located anywhere on the Internet can cooperate to complete a task normally handled by monolithic servers or supercomputers.

A BitTorrent network is designed to reduce the bandwidth bottleneck that occurs when many people attempt to download the same very large file, such as a feature-length film, application software, or an interactive 3-D computer game.

▶ **How does BitTorrent work?** Suppose that 100 computers request Johnny Depp's film *Dark Shadows* at about the same time. A server breaks the movie file into pieces and begins to download those pieces to the first computer that requested the movie.

As more computers request the file, they become part of a "swarm" that uses peer-to-peer technology to exchange file pieces with each other. After the server has downloaded all the file pieces to the swarm, its job is complete and it can service other requests. The swarm continues to exchange file pieces until every computer in the swarm has the entire file (Figure 6-46).

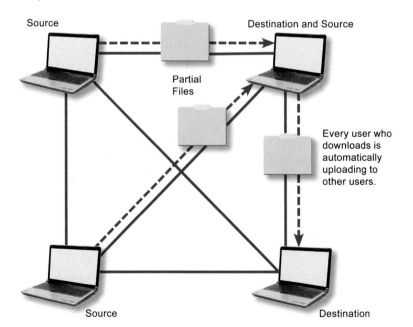

FIGURE 6-46

BitTorrent protocols dissect files into small chunks that might reside on different computers. Source computers have received parts of a file from a server. They then distribute these parts to other computers in the swarm.

▶ **How do I use BitTorrent?** BitTorrent client software is currently available from several Web sites. After installing the client, you can use it to download from any BitTorrent-enabled site simply by clicking the file you want. The BitTorrent client handles the entire file-swapping procedure. After getting the entire file, good etiquette requires clients to remain connected to the swarm so that they can "seed" file pieces to others.

▶ **Are BitTorrent and similar file swapping networks legal?** File sharing originated on FTP-style servers, which held huge collections of popular music stored as digital MP3 files that could be easily downloaded and played on a computer or transferred to CDs. Free distribution of music without the copyright holder's permission is illegal, and file sharing server operators quickly encountered the legal ramifications of their computers' shady dealings.

Peer-to-peer file sharing networks and distributed technologies like BitTorrent have legitimate uses for distributing music, images, videos, and software with the approval of copyright holders. Peter Jackson's production diaries for *King Kong* have been posted for download using BitTorrent technology. Universal Studios and several independent film companies have released movie trailers with BitTorrent technology. The technology itself is not illegal; it is the use of the technology that is subject to legal scrutiny.

▶ **Is BitTorrent safe?** Because BitTorrent files are assembled from little segments that come from a jumble of computers, they would seem on first thought to be bad candidates for distributing malware. Intelligent hackers would realize that their malicious code could easily be chopped up, too, and that pieces of it might not be delivered. And yet, BitTorrent files have become a source of adware and spyware. If you use BitTorrent, make sure your computer is protected with a security software suite that offers good spyware protection.

QuickCheck   SECTION D

1. _____ computing offers Internet-based computer resources on demand so that individuals and businesses can contract for access as these resources are needed.

2. Instant messaging, chat, and VoIP are classified as _____ communications because both parties have to be online.

3. VoIP quality can be affected by _____ that results from too much packet latency.

4. On some sites, _____ FTP can be used to upload and download files even if you don't have an account on the FTP server.

5. _____ is a peer-to-peer file sharing protocol that uses a "swarm" of computers to exchange chunks of data that can eventually be assembled into complete files.

▶ CHECK ANSWERS

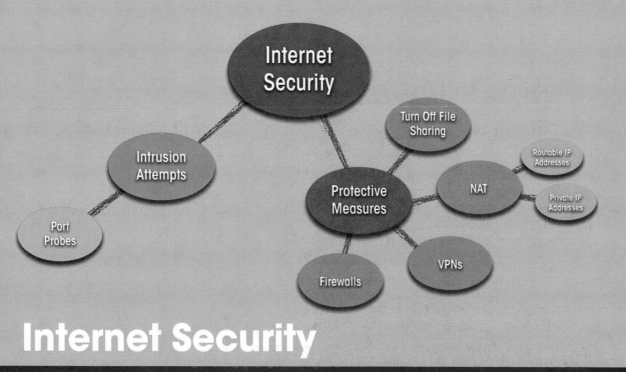

Internet Security

WHEN COMPUTERS are connected to a network, the risk of intrusion has to be taken seriously. With Internet-based connections, billions of people are just an IP address away from your computer and its valuable, personal, and confidential data. Section E explains the mechanics of intrusion attempts, and offers some practical advice for securing your computer against unauthorized access.

INTRUSION ATTEMPTS

▶ **Should I worry about intrusions?** Suppose you live in a really dangerous neighborhood where gangs roam the streets, painting every available surface with graffiti, and randomly attacking residents. Burglars creep from house to house looking for unlocked doors and windows, and occasionally trying to pick a lock or two. Dark figures sift through your garbage cans searching for scraps of information that can be pieced together to steal your identity (Figure 6-47).

Unfortunately, this dangerous neighborhood has many similarities to the Internet where gangs of hackers deface Web sites, look for backdoors left open by network administrators, crack passwords to gain access to your data, and probe ports looking for ways to sneak bots into your computer.

Your Internet connection puts you right in the middle of this dangerous neighborhood any time you are connected—and with always-on connections like DSL and cable Internet service, that means any time your computer is turned on.

In the context of computers, an **intrusion** is any access to data or programs by hackers, criminals, or other unauthorized persons. As the result of an intrusion, data can be stolen or altered, system configurations can be changed to allow even more intrusions, and software can be surreptitiously installed and operated under the remote control of a hacker.

Without any visible sign or warning, hackers can infiltrate your computer to obtain personal information or use your computer as a launching pad for attacks on other machines. Yes, you should worry about intrusions!

FIGURE 6-47

The Internet offers a wealth of useful tools and services, but it can be a very dangerous neighborhood.

Paul Edmondson

339

▶ How do hackers use the Internet to infiltrate my computer? One of the most common ways of gaining unauthorized access to a network-based computer is by looking for open ports. A **communications port** is the doorway that allows a computer to exchange data with other devices. A port is not a physical circuit or mechanism, but rather an abstract concept of a door, opening, or portal through which data flows.

Network services, such as the Web, FTP, and e-mail, operate from ports. For example, Web requests use port 80. If a port is open and listening for requests—on any computer, even your own—a hacker can exploit it like an unlocked door to gain access to your computer. Hackers are continuously canvassing the Internet and probing ports to find their next victims.

A **port probe** (or port scan) is the use of automated software to locate computers that have open ports and are vulnerable to unauthorized access. Software called a port scanner goes to a randomly selected IP address and systematically checks for a response from each port. Open ports can then be further tested to gauge their suitability for exploitation.

You might scoff at your computer's vulnerability to port probes. After all, there are millions and millions of computers on the Internet and a limited number of hackers. The chances of your computer becoming a target would seem to be slim, but the opposite is true.

Port scanning software can examine more than 30,000 computers per minute. If you use security software to monitor port probes on an unprotected computer, you would see probes within seconds of going online. According to researchers, the average "survival time" for an unprotected computer to remain uncompromised is only nine minutes.

▶ How do I know if ports are open? You can check your computer for open ports using software tools such as Steve Gibson's ShieldsUP! at *www.grc.com*. You can initiate an "innocent" port probe to discover vulnerabilities. A security report like the one in Figure 6-48 is your goal.

FIGURE 6-48

Your computer's ports are most secure if they don't even appear to exist when probed using a port scanner. ▶ Use your interactive eBook to see how ShieldsUP! checks your computer's ports and learn what the results mean.

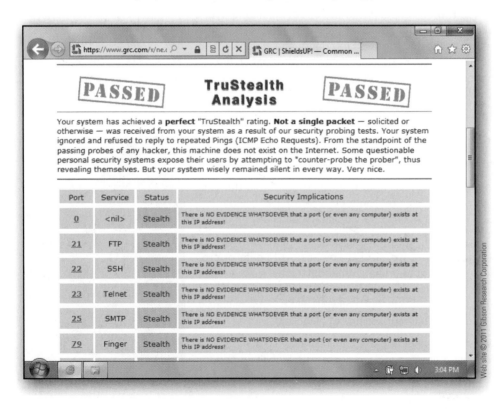

Port	Service	Status	Security Implications
0	<nil>	Stealth	There is NO EVIDENCE WHATSOEVER that a port (or even any computer) exists at this IP address!
21	FTP	Stealth	There is NO EVIDENCE WHATSOEVER that a port (or even any computer) exists at this IP address!
22	SSH	Stealth	There is NO EVIDENCE WHATSOEVER that a port (or even any computer) exists at this IP address!
23	Telnet	Stealth	There is NO EVIDENCE WHATSOEVER that a port (or even any computer) exists at this IP address!
25	SMTP	Stealth	There is NO EVIDENCE WHATSOEVER that a port (or even any computer) exists at this IP address!
79	Finger	Stealth	There is NO EVIDENCE WHATSOEVER that a port (or even any computer) exists at this IP address!

SECURING PORTS

▶ **How do I secure the ports on my computer?** One of the easiest steps to enhance your computer's security is to turn it off when you aren't using it. When your computer is turned off, its ports are inactive and they are not vulnerable to intrusions. Putting your computer into sleep mode or activating a screensaver is not sufficient protection. Your computer must be shut down and turned off.

You should also keep your computer up to date with the latest operating system security patches and service packs. Operating systems are closely linked to port activity. Known vulnerabilities in Windows and Internet Explorer can be exploited to access ports or launch additional attacks once a port is breached.

Operating system developers provide useful security tools to their customers. Microsoft's security site is *www.microsoft.com/security*. Apple's security site is *ssl.apple.com/support/security/*.

When operating system developers, such as Microsoft and Apple, produce security patches, they are available for download. You can configure your operating system to automatically check for and install patches (Figure 6-49).

FIGURE 6-49

To configure a Windows 7 computer for Automatic Updates, type "Security Center" in the Start menu's Search box.

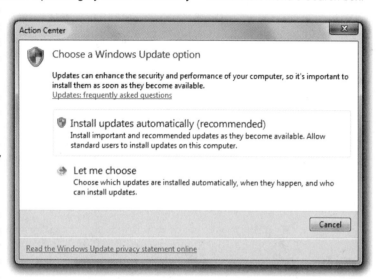

▶ **What about firewall protection?** In the context of networking, a **firewall** is software or hardware designed to filter out suspicious packets attempting to enter or leave a computer.

Firewall software helps keep your computer secure in several ways. It ensures that incoming information was actually requested and is not an unauthorized intrusion. It blocks activity from suspicious IP addresses and—best of all—it reports intrusion attempts so that you can discover whether hackers are trying to break into your computer.

You can use firewall software to open and close ports on your computer. Although it might seem safest to close all the ports, doing so would prevent you from accessing many Internet services, such as the Web, e-mail, instant messaging, and FTP.

Most firewall software is preconfigured to block only unnecessarily open ports targeted by hackers. Windows 7 includes firewall software that you can access and configure from the Security Center (Figure 6-50).

FIGURE 6-50

Windows 7 includes a built-in firewall that can be activated to monitor intrusion attempts. Do not enable it, however, if your antivirus software firewall is activated.

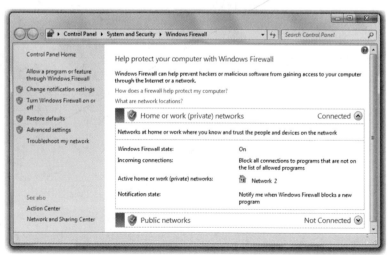

▶ What other security options should I use? Sharing printers or files on a LAN or the Internet requires open ports so the data can be transferred to and from your computer. Those open ports can be a potential entryway for hackers. If no one else needs access to your printer, do not configure it for sharing. If you also don't need to share files with other network users, you can turn off file and printer sharing (Figure 6-51).

FIGURE 6-51

When you turn off file sharing, your files cannot be accessed by other network users.

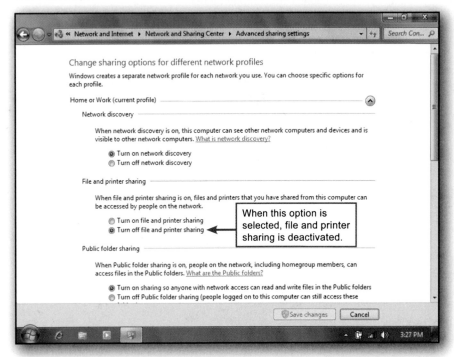

NAT

FIGURE 6-52

▶ How does a router affect security? One of the most effective steps you can take to secure your computer from intrusions is to install a router. In the chapter on networking, you learned that a router can tie a LAN together and provide a portal to the Internet. Even if you have only one computer, however, a router can offer excellent security.

A router monitors the IP addresses of packets on a LAN. Packets with local addresses (green) are kept within the LAN. Packets with external addresses (red) are routed out to the Internet. ⊙ See how it works.

▶ How does a router work? Routers are intended to work within LANs to monitor and direct packets being transported from one device to another. A router can also connect to the Internet through a DSL, cable, or satellite modem.

Routers are handy because they screen IP addresses to keep locally addressed packets within the LAN so that they are delivered without traveling a circuitous route over the Internet and back (Figure 6-52).

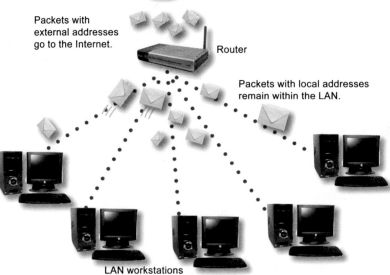

Packets with external addresses go to the Internet.

Router

Packets with local addresses remain within the LAN.

LAN workstations

Your router has its own IP address, typically obtained from your Internet service provider's DHCP server. (Recall that a DHCP server assigns dynamic IP addresses to devices that request them.) It is also possible for your router to have a fixed IP address set up by you or an installer. The key point about your router's IP address is that it is routable. A **routable IP address** is one that can be accessed by packets on the Internet.

When you connect your computer to a router and request an IP address, your router answers your request, not the ISP. Most routers are configured to assign private IP addresses. A **private IP address** is a non-routable IP address that can be used within a LAN, but not for Internet data transport.

When the IP addressing scheme was devised, three ranges of addresses were reserved for internal or private use: 10.0.0.0 to 10.255.255.255, 172.16.0.0 to 172.31.255.255, and 192.168.0.0 to 192.168.255.255. If your computer has a private IP address, its real address is essentially hidden from hackers (Figure 6-53).

FIGURE 6-53

The computers in a LAN have non-routable IP addresses.

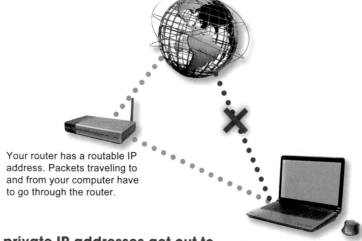

Your router has a routable IP address. Packets traveling to and from your computer have to go through the router.

Your computer has a non-routable address such as 192.168.1.1. That address is not routable; your computer is not reachable directly from the Internet.

▶ **But how do packets with private IP addresses get out to the Internet?** Let's review the scenario. You have a router connected to an Internet device, such as a DSL or cable modem. The router has a routable IP address, visible to any device (and hackers) on the Internet. Your router isn't vulnerable to attacks because it doesn't store any data. You've connected your computer to a router. Your computer has been assigned a private IP address.

Network address translation (NAT) is the process your router uses to keep track of packets and their corresponding private or public IP addresses. Jeff Tyson writing for HowStuffWorks offers a useful analogy for how NAT works:

> "NAT is like the receptionist in a large office. Let's say you have left instructions with the receptionist not to forward any calls to you unless you request it. Later on, you call a potential client and leave a message for that client to call you back. You tell the receptionist that you are expecting a call from this client and to put her through. The client calls the main number to your office, which is the only number the client knows. When the client tells the receptionist that she is looking for you, the receptionist checks a lookup table that matches your name with your extension. The receptionist knows that you requested this call, and therefore forwards the caller to your extension."

A router and the receptionist perform essentially similar tasks. Your private IP address is like a private telephone extension in an office. Your router's public IP address is like the main switchboard number. Your router screens incoming packets and only lets one through to your private extension if you've requested it.

When you use the Internet, you initiate every valid transaction; you ask for a Web site, you ask to retrieve your mail, or you request a file from an FTP server. Only those requests that you initiate are valid.

Suppose you want to download a file. You send a packet containing your request to the FTP server at 69.32.167.20. The packet goes to your router, which replaces your address with its own and makes an internal note that you initiated this FTP request. When the FTP server responds, it sends a packet addressed to the router. The router receives the packet, checks its internal note to see who made the original request, and then ships the FTP packet to your computer (Figure 6-54).

FIGURE 6-54

A router using NAT essentially cloaks your computer and makes it invisible from the Internet.

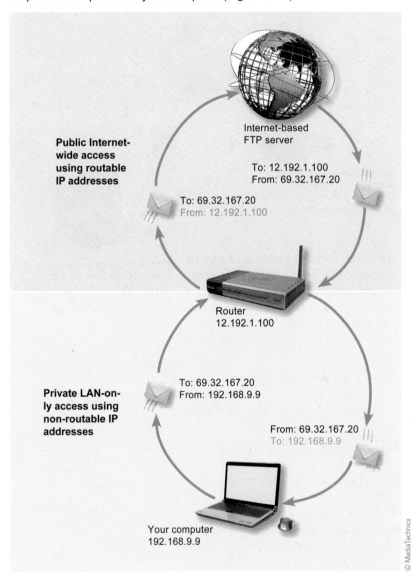

Internet-based
FTP server

To: 12.192.1.100
From: 69.32.167.20

To: 69.32.167.20
From: 12.192.1.100

Public Internet-wide access using routable IP addresses

Router
12.192.1.100

To: 69.32.167.20
From: 192.168.9.9

From: 69.32.167.20
To: 192.168.9.9

Private LAN-only access using non-routable IP addresses

Your computer
192.168.9.9

© Media Technics

VIRTUAL PRIVATE NETWORKS

▶ Is it possible to secure connections for remote users? Sales representatives and telecommuters often access corporate networks from home or from a customer's office by using a secured connection called a **virtual private network** (VPN). You might find a VPN useful when using public computers because it can encrypt the data you transmit, keeping passwords and account numbers safe from hackers.

▶ Who sets up VPNs? On the corporate end, setting up a secure VPN is not a trivial task and it is typically handled by specialists in the corporation's information technology department. Access to a corporate VPN is usually by invitation only. Employees who need to access a VPN are given the necessary instructions, addresses, and passwords to make connections.

For personal use, you can install personal VPN software such as StrongVPN, WiTopia, or HotSpotVPN. Using a VPN provides an important layer of security when you use public networks, such as Wi-Fi hotspots.

▶ How would I use a personal VPN? Once you've installed VPN software, you'll see its icon in the taskbar. Clicking the icon establishes a connection to the VPN server. When your computer sends or receives data, the VPN software encrypts it and sends it to a special VPN server that decrypts the data and sends it to its destination. Figure 6-55 illustrates how a personal VPN operates.

▶ How important is a VPN? A personal VPN is an important tool when using public networks, but it is not a complete solution. To recap the most important security precautions, you should turn your computer off when not in use, make sure all your computer's unnecessary ports are closed, activate firewall software, turn off file and printer sharing, and install a router. Taking these precautions might not make your computer invincible, but they offer very strong protection against intruders who might steal your identity or hijack your computer for various shady activities.

FIGURE 6-55

A personal VPN offers security for the data that you transmit from public Wi-Fi hotspots.

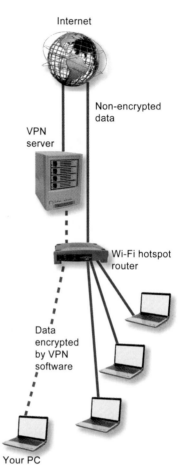

6

QuickCheck   SECTION E

1. Hackers use [_____] scanning software to look for computers connected to the Internet that are vulnerable to intrusions.

2. [_____] software monitors network activity, blocks packets from suspicious IP addresses, and reports intrusion attempts.

3. One of the best defenses against intrusions is to install a(n) [_____] between your standalone computer or LAN and your Internet connection device.

4. A(n) [_____] IP address is a nonroutable IP address that can be used within a LAN, but not for Internet data transport.

5. When using a public Wi-Fi hotspot, you can use a personal [_____] to encrypt data that travels from your computer. (Hint: Use the acronym.)

▶ CHECK ANSWERS

Issue: What's a Revolution Without the Internet?

HE CALLED IT REVOLUTION 2.0. From his computer in Cairo, Wael Ghonim, a Google executive-turned-activist, maintained Facebook pages that inspired protests and eventually ended the Egyptian government headed by Hosni Mubarak.

The revolution in Egypt showed the power of the Internet to profoundly influence politics. In an interview, Ghonim said, "If you want to free a society, just give them the Internet."

The Egyptian revolution made extensive use of social media, such as Facebook, Twitter, and blogs. A Web page dedicated to an Egyptian citizen who was beaten to death by police called for demonstrations on January 25.

Word spread from this site to Facebook and Twitter, prompting hundreds of thousands to march in the streets of Cairo. It was the beginning of widespread demonstrations, strikes, and protests.

The Egyptian government quickly became aware of the Internet's role and took action. On January 27, Egyptian networks began disappearing from the Internet's global routing table, shutting down Internet access to and from Egypt.

Analysis of the event showed that Egypt's ISPs shut down one after another. First, Telecom Egypt, then Raya Telecom, followed by three other ISPs. Analysts speculate that a government agent phoned the ISPs one after another and ordered them to shut down.

According to a Renesys report, "Approximately 3,500 individual BGP routes were withdrawn, leaving no valid paths by which the rest of the world could continue to exchange Internet traffic with Egypt's service providers."

BGP (Border Gateway Protocol) uses a list of routes to transmit data from one router to another. With BGP routes withdrawn, data packets traveling to and from Egypt fell into a digital black hole. As an analogy, imagine the Postmaster General instructing post offices to shred all the mail instead of delivering it.

@Ghonim
Wael Ghonim

Revolution 2.0: Mission Accomplished
#Jan25

53 minutes ago via web   ☆ Favorite   ↻ Retweet   ↩ Reply

Retweeted by Crossbays and 100+ others

Egypt was not the first country to shut down the Internet, nor was it the last. During the Tunisian revolution, the government blocked access to sites and filtered out dissenting messages in e-mail and blogs.

When Iranian dissidents took to the streets, the Internet remained in operation, but at drastically reduced speed. In Libya, the Internet became a pawn in the conflict between Gaddafi's government and protesters. Rather than a total blackout, however, Gaddafi slowly throttled back on service during critical periods, but periodically restored service.

The idea that Internet communications can be turned off might seem surprising when you consider that the Internet was designed to function even when many of its nodes malfunction or experience denial-of-service attacks.

The Internet as a whole continued to function during the Egyptian revolution, but packets that normally might have routed through Egypt were routed through other countries. Yet, within Egypt, and between Egypt and other countries, there was no service.

The outcome of revolutions in the past century often hinged on who controlled radio and television stations. Today, the outcome of social unrest balances on who controls the Internet—not only because of its role in communication and social media, but because it is the technology essential for banking, national infrastructure, and the stock market.

The effect of an Internet shutdown in any technological society would be chaos. Major communications channels would be unavailable. Banks would close. Credit card payments could not be processed. Airports and train stations would be mobbed by people forced to make travel reservations in person. An Internet outage could even have a cascading effect on the electrical grid, knocking out power to homes and businesses.

Despite the ensuing chaos, governments seem willing to cut off the Internet. Where might it happen next?

Try It! The Internet has become so integrated into our everyday lives that we take it for granted. That is a mistake. Our dependence on the Internet makes us vulnerable to cyberthreats that have far greater repercussions than leaving us without access to ESPN sports scores. Here's your chance to explore the relationship between the Internet and fundamental principles of democracy.

6

Work Projects Administration Poster Collection, Prints & Photographs Division, Library of Congress, LC-USZC2-921

In the play, *It Can't Happen Here*, based on a 1935 Sinclair Lewis novel, a populist candidate is elected President of the United States. He makes sweeping changes to the Constitution, abolishes Congress, and forms a jackbooted secret police force. Protesters are thrown in jail while most Americans reassure themselves that "fascism can't happen here."

① Watching events in the Arab world and the extensive role of social media, we might be reassured that democracy is safe in America. We all have social media accounts; we're masters of the Information Age. But will the Internet be there if and when we need it? Could an unpopular president use a "kill switch" to censor information about demonstrations and protests?

② Even if the government doesn't have the power to turn off the entire Internet, suppose it has the power to shut down particular sites, but makes a mistake and inadvertently turns off a big swath of the Internet. Search for "DHS Operation Save the Children 84,000 kill switch." What happened?

③ Suppose the U.S. government has the legal authority to shut down the Internet. You might wonder if it is technically possible to do so. Egypt had only a handful of ISPs; in the U.S., there are many more. But are there chokepoints where the U.S. Internet infrastructure is vulnerable? See what you can find when you search for "Internet Shutdown technically possible U.S. DNS." Pay attention to the origin of the sites you visit; some are likely to contain opinions and misinformation.

INFOWEBLINKS

You can check the **NP2013 Chapter 6** InfoWebLink for updates to these activities.

Ⓦ CLICK TO CONNECT
www.infoweblinks.com/np2013/ch06

ISSUE

What Do You Think?

1. Does it seem plausible that your government would attempt to shut down the Internet to curtail civil unrest?

2. Do you use the Internet to access political news?

3. Should your government have legal power to shut down the Internet?

4. Have you experienced an Internet outage that lasted longer than 24 hours?

Information Tools: Citations

You can use other people's ideas in your own research papers and presentations, but you must cite the source for any information that is not common knowledge. A citation is a formal reference to a published work, like this:

"It Can't Happen Here." *Encyclopædia Britannica*. *Encyclopædia Britannica Online*. Encyclopædia Britannica, 2011. Web. 13 Sep. 2011. <http://www.britannica.com/EBchecked/topic/297133/It-Cant-Happen-Here>.

A collection of citations is called a bibliography.

Use an approved citation style, such as MLA, APA, or Chicago. Several Web sites, such as the Purdue Online Writing Lab, include detailed style guides.

Papers on technology topics frequently contain material from books, magazines, journals, news reports, press releases, and court decisions. Make sure you understand the citation data that you need to collect for each of these formats, both in print and online.

Articles from Print Sources

Author, article title, periodical title, date of publication, page numbers

Books

Author, book title, edition, publisher, place and date of publication, ISBN

If referencing a section of a book, note page numbers, chapter title, and chapter author, if applicable.

Journals

Same information as a periodical with the addition of the volume and issue numbers

Legal Decisions

Case name; the volume, abbreviation, and page reference for the legal reporter where the case was reported; the date of the case

Web Pages

Author, title of Web page, title of Web site, complete URL, date of publication (sometimes there will not be a publication date; some citation styles use "n.d." in this case), sponsoring organization (look for it on the copyright line at the bottom of the page), date visited

A publication might have several unique identifying numbers. Stay alert so that you use the correct one.

ISBN (International Standard Book Number): A unique number given to a book or monograph

DOI (Digital Object Identifier): A unique number typically assigned to journal articles and other online documents

LCCN (Library of Congress Control Number): A unique number assigned to each publication in the Library of Congress

Desktop software such as EndNote, RefWorks, and Zotero helps you create citations and manage all the citations for your bibliographies.

Mobile apps, such as QuickCite, read bar codes and accept manual entries to automatically create citations on the go.

Try It! Let's go beyond the basics and work with some advanced citation tools. Use any word processor and start a document called Citation Project [Your Name], and then complete the following steps:

1 Suppose that you'd like to include information from press releases in a research paper. How do you format the citations? Use a search engine to look for "How do I cite a press release." Next, search for a recent press release from Apple. Create a citation for the press release and save it in your Citation Project document.

2 Some academic directories/databases provide citation information for the resources it lists. BibTeX, illustrated at right, is a common format.

Open an academic directory of technology articles, such as Microsoft Academic Search, TDG Scholar, ACM Digital Library, or Odysci. Search for BitTorrent articles and select one. Look for the Bib or BibTeX icon and then click it. Notice that each element of the reference is clearly labeled. Copy the BibTeX data and paste it into your Project document; you'll find out how to format this citation data in the next steps.

> Make sure you collect data for the article itself, not simply the directory that lists the article.

3 Microsoft Word includes a built-in bibliography manager that helps you format citations. To access the citation feature, select References, choose the MLA style, and click Insert Citation. Select Add New Source, then fill in the form. If you have access to Microsoft Word, use its Citation feature to create an MLA citation for the BibTeX data you found for step 2 above.

4 You can use free Web-based citation formatters, such as BibMe, Citation Machine, NoodleBib Express, or EasyBib, to format citations in MLA, APA, or other approved styles. Connect to a Web-based citation formatter, choose Online Journal as the source, select the MLA citation style, and enter the BibTeX data you collected for step 2 above. Paste the formatted citation into your Citation Project document.

5 For some books, Web sites, and journal articles, you can use their ISBN, URL, or DOI instead of manually entering the citation data. Connect to a Web-based citation formatter, such as those listed in step 4. Enter the ISBN 978-1437755824 and use the AutoCite button to search for the citation. Produce the MLA citation, copy it, and paste it into your Citation Project document.

6 The AutoCite button does not always locate the right article. Use EasyBib's Journal tab to Enter the DOI 10.1007/978-3-642-03521-0_9. Describe the result.

> When using automated citation formatters based on ISBN or DOI, look carefully at the citation that is produced to ensure that it contains all required citation information.

BibTeX Citation

@article{Thomas:2011:WWE:1982701.1982999,

author = {Thomas, Christopher and Sheth, Amit},

title = {Web Wisdom: An essay on how Web 2.0 and Semantic Web can foster a global knowledge society},

journal = {Comput. Hum. Behav.},

issue_date = {July, 2011},

volume = {27},

issue = {4},

month = {July},

year = {2011},

issn = {0747-5632},

pages = {1285--1293},

numpages = {9},

url = {http://dx.doi.org/10.1016/j.chb.2010.07.023},

doi = {http://dx.doi.org/10.1016/j.chb.2010.07.023},

acmid = {1982999},

publisher = {Elsevier Science Publishers B. V.},

address = {Amsterdam, The Netherlands, The Netherlands},

keywords = {Human and social computation, Problem solving, Social networking},

}

6

Technology in Context: Banking

H. F. Davis/Topical Press Agency/Getty Images

FOR MOST OF HISTORY, banks used low-tech methods to track one of the world's most cherished commodities—wealth. Checking accounts were in widespread use as early as 1550, when Dutch traders began depositing money with cashiers for safekeeping. The use of printed checks became popular in England in the late 18th century—so popular that banks found it difficult to process a steadily increasing stream of checks, including those drawn on accounts from other banks.

An unverified story that has become part of bank lore describes the origin of a solution to the check processing problem. As the story goes, a London bank messenger stopped for coffee and got to talking with a messenger from another bank. Realizing that they were delivering checks drawn on each other's banks, the two messengers decided to exchange checks there in the coffee house. This event evolved into a system of check clearinghouses where representatives from various banks met periodically to exchange checks and reconcile totals in cash. By 1839, British clearinghouses were annually processing in excess of £954 million of checks—equivalent to $250 billion in today's money.

Bank clearinghouses were described in an essay, *The Economy of Machinery and Manufactures*, written by computer pioneer Charles Babbage in 1832. He also included a reference to the "possibility of performing arithmetical calculations by machinery"

along with a description of the Difference Engine, then under construction in his workshop.

This dream of automated check clearing did not, however, become reality until more than a century later when S. Clark Beise, senior vice president at Bank of America, contracted with Stanford Research Institute (SRI) to develop a computer system to automate check processing. SRI completed a prototype in 1955 that used mechanical sorting equipment to queue up each check and MICR (Magnetic Ink Character Recognition) technology to read check numbers. In 1959, the first ERMA (Electronic Recording Machine-Accounting) system went into service. With ERMA handling calculations, nine employees could handle the job that once required 50 people. By 1966, 32 regional ERMA systems operated by Bank of America were processing more than 750 million checks per year. ERMA and similar check processing technologies quickly integrated with bank transaction processing systems to become the bedrock of today's banking technology.

Output from check sorting machines can be submitted to the Automated Clearing House (ACH) network, which offers a secure, batch-oriented data exchange system that can be accessed by financial institutions. On a daily basis, banks submit check data and receive a report of balances due to other banks. These balances can be reconciled by electronic funds transfer over the Federal Reserve's Fedwire telecommunications network.

An upswing in check fraud during the 1960s made it increasingly difficult to cash checks at local merchants. As an alternative to trying to cash checks at banks and local merchants, automated teller machines (ATMs) were first installed in the 1970s. A typical ATM connects to a bank's front-end processor—a computer that maintains account balances for in-network customers and monitors suspicious activity. The front-end processor is separated from the bank's main computer system for security.

Some ATMs exchange data with the front-end processor by using dedicated dial-up telephone lines. Other ATMs use always-on leased lines. Legacy protocols, such as SNA and 3270 bisync, are being replaced by the standard Internet Protocol (IP) that can be routed through more affordable connections, such as cable, ISDN, DSL, or Internet VPN.

ATMs are expensive—about $50,000 to purchase a machine, install it, and operate it for one year. Banks have offset this cost by charging transaction fees and reducing the number of bank tellers. Once a promising entry-level occupation, bank tellers today earn less than $30,000 per year. Although tellers continue to accept deposits, process withdrawals, and cash payroll checks, they are increasingly pressed into customer service roles—opening new accounts, issuing ATM cards, resolving disputed transactions, and assisting customers who have lost bank cards or checkbooks. Despite this shift in job description, the number of bank teller jobs is expected to fall at least 10% in the next few years.

ATMs offer access to bank services from convenient locations where customers shop, eat, and hang out with friends. The Internet takes banking convenience one step further and provides around-the-clock account access from PCs in customers' homes, schools, and workplaces. Today, most banks and credit unions offer some type of online banking (also called home banking, Internet banking, or electronic banking).

Basic online banking services allow customers to access checking account and bank card activity, transfer funds between checking and savings accounts, view electronic images of checks and deposit slips, download and print monthly statements, and reorder checks. Customers can also pay bills online by scheduling payment dates and amounts. Many credit card and utility companies offer e-billing

services that automatically forward electronic bills to customers' online banking accounts. For monthly fixed-amount bills, such as car loans, online banking offers automatic payment options that deduct funds from specified checking or savings accounts.

For managing assets more effectively, online banking sites also offer sophisticated tools, including account aggregation, stock quotes, rate alerts, and portfolio management programs. Most online banking sites are also compatible with personal finance software, such as AceMoney and Quicken, so that transaction data can be shuttled between customers' local computers and their online banking services.

A cadre of customer support personnel staff online help desks for customers with questions about online banking. Web masters, computer security specialists, and network technicians are also part of banking's new job corps.

Online banking services are typically housed on a well-secured Web server, and customers are not allowed direct access to the computer system that actually processes transactions. Customer privacy is maintained by the use of passwords and connections that encrypt data as it is sent to and from customers' computers.

Successful banks are built on good business decisions. Bank managers are increasingly working with business intelligence tools to look for trends in customer behavior, analyze competing financial institutions, and examine current business practices. Tools for these activities include data warehouses that collect and organize data, data mining software that organizes and analyzes data in a meaningful way, and statistical tools that formulate comparisons and trendlines.

Today, banking depends on multi-layered technologies that incorporate check processing equipment, transaction processing systems, business intelligence software, ACH networks, Fedwire, ATM networks, the Internet, and Web servers. Many banking practices originated from batch check processing, and only gradually have banks begun to move to more modern online transaction processing (OLTP) systems that store scanned images of checks and instantly update accounts when a purchase is made or a bill is paid.

6

New Perspectives Labs

To access the New Perspectives Labs for Chapter 6, open the NP2013 interactive eBook and then click the icon next to the lab title.

▶ TRACKING PACKETS

IN THIS LAB YOU'LL LEARN:

- How Ping and Traceroute work
- How to use the Ping and Traceroute utilities supplied by Windows
- How to interpret Ping and Traceroute reports to determine the speed and reliability of your Internet connection
- How to access and use a graphical Traceroute utility
- How to find and use Web-based Ping and Traceroute utilities
- The advantages and disadvantages of Web-based Ping and Traceroute utilities
- How to access the Internet Traffic Report Web site and interpret its data and graphs
- How to use Internet traffic data, Ping, and Traceroute to pinpoint problems with your Internet connection

LAB ASSIGNMENTS

1. Start the interactive part of the lab. Make sure you've enabled Tracking if you want to save your QuickCheck results. Perform each lab step as directed, and answer all the lab QuickCheck questions. When you exit the lab, your answers are automatically graded and your results are displayed.

2. Use the Ping utility that's supplied by Windows to ping *www.abcnews.com*. Record the IP address for the ABC News site, plus the minimum, maximum, and average times. For each time, indicate whether it would be considered poor, average, or good.

3. Use the Tracert command at the Windows command prompt to trace a packet between your computer and *www.excite.com*. Print the Traceroute report listing transmission times. Circle any pings on the report that indicate high latency.

4. Locate a Web-based Ping utility and use it to ping *www.gobledegok.com*. Indicate the address for the Web site where you found the Ping utility. Explain the Ping results.

5. Connect to the Internet Traffic Report Web site, make a note of the date and time, and then answer the following questions:

   a. What is the traffic index for Asia?

   b. How does the index for Asia compare with the traffic index for North America?

   c. During the previous 24 hours in Europe, what was the period with the worst response time?

▶ SECURING YOUR CONNECTION

IN THIS LAB YOU'LL LEARN:

- How to use Windows utilities, online utilities, and firewall software to check the security of your Internet connection
- Why an unauthorized intruder might want to gain access to your computer
- The significance of communications ports as an intrusion risk factor
- How to use the Netstat utility to check your computer's open ports
- How to use an online utility to get a hacker's view of your computer
- Why Windows file and printer sharing can make your computer files vulnerable
- How to adjust settings for file and printer sharing
- How firewalls protect computers from intrusions
- How to adjust firewall settings

LAB ASSIGNMENTS

1. Start the interactive part of the lab. Make sure you've enabled Tracking if you want to save your QuickCheck results. Perform each lab step as directed, and answer all the lab QuickCheck questions. When you exit the lab, your answers are automatically graded and your results are displayed.

2. Use the Netstat utility to scan any computer that you typically use. Write out the Netstat report or print it. To print the report, copy it to Paint or Word, and then print. Explain what the Netstat report tells you about that computer's security.

3. Connect to *www.grc.com* and access the ShieldsUP! tests. Test the shields and probe the ports for the same computer you used for Assignment 2. Explain the similarities and differences between the ShieldsUP! report and the Netstat report for this computer. Which report indicates more security risks? Why?

4. In the lab, you learned how to adjust settings for Windows file and printer sharing. Without actually changing the settings, determine the status of file and printer sharing on your computer. Report your findings and indicate whether these settings are appropriate for network access and security.

5. Record the firewall settings on your computer. Indicate whether the settings are optimal for the way you use your computer on networks.

Key Terms

Make sure you understand all the boldfaced key terms presented in this chapter. With the NP2013 interactive eBook, you can use this list of terms as an interactive study activity. First, try to define a term in your own words, and then click the term to compare your definition with the definition presented in the chapter.

6

Always-on connection, 307
Anonymous FTP, 336
Asymmetric Internet connection, 310
Asynchronous communications, 332
BitTorrent, 337
Blog, 333
Cable Internet service, 316
Cable modem, 317
Chat, 331
Communications port, 340
Dial-up connection, 312
DNS cache poisoning, 308
DOCSIS, 317
Domain name, 307
Domain name server, 308
Domain Name System, 308
Downstream speed, 310
DSL, 314
DSL filter, 315
DSL modem, 315
Dynamic IP address, 306
Firewall, 341
Fixed Internet access, 311
Fixed wireless Internet service, 319
FTP, 335

FTP client, 336
FTP server, 335
Grid computing system, 334
ICANN, 309
Instant messaging, 331
Internet backbone, 303
Internet forum, 332
Internet service provider, 303
Intrusion, 339
IP (IPv4 and IPv6), 305
Jitter, 332
Latency, 309
MiFi, 327
Mobile broadband, 326
Mobile Internet access, 311
Modem, 304
Network access points, 303
Network address translation, 343
Network service providers, 303
P2P file sharing, 337
Packet loss, 332
Ping, 309
Port probe, 340
Portable Internet access, 311
Private IP address, 343

Protocol suite, 305
Real-time messaging system, 331
Routable IP address, 343
Satellite Internet service, 318
Satellite modem, 318
Software as a service, 330
Static IP address, 306
Symmetric Internet connection, 311
Synchronous communications, 332
TCP, 305
TCP/IP, 305
Top-level domain, 307
Traceroute, 310
Tweet, 333
Upstream speed, 310
Virtual private network, 345
Voiceband modem, 313
VoIP, 331
WAP, 325
Wi-Fi hotspot, 322
Wiki, 333
WiMAX, 319

Interactive Summary

To review important concepts from this chapter, fill in the blanks to best complete each sentence. When using the NP2013 interactive eBook, click the Check Answers buttons to automatically score your answers.

SECTION A: The Internet infrastructure is based on high-capacity communications links referred to as the Internet [   ], tied together at network [   ] points where data can cross over from one NSP's equipment to another's. An Internet [   ] provider offers Internet access to individuals, businesses, and smaller ISPs. The Internet uses several communications protocols, including [   ], which breaks a message or file into packets, and [   ], which is responsible for addressing packets. Every device on the Internet has an IP address. 204.127.128.1 is a(n) [   ]-bit IPv4 address. [   ] IP addresses are permanently assigned to computers, whereas [   ] IP addresses are temporarily assigned by a DHCP server. Most high-speed Internet connections use [   ] technology, and even dynamic IP addresses might seem permanent because they don't change unless you turn off your modem or your ISP has an outage. A(n) [   ] name server converts numeric IP addresses into familiar names, such as Travelocity.com. The speed of an Internet connection measured by utilities such as Ping and Traceroute refers to [   ], the elapsed time for data to make a round trip from point A to point B. The speed advertised by Internet service providers is a measure of the amount of data that travels between two points in a given amount of time. Many Internet connections are [   ], meaning the downstream speed is different than the upstream speed.

▶ CHECK ANSWERS

SECTION B: A(n) [   ] connection is a fixed Internet connection that uses a(n) [   ] modem and telephone lines to transport data between your computer and your ISP. Most modems use a standard called V.90 to provide a theoretical maximum speed of [   ] Kbps. [   ] is a high-speed, digital, always-on Internet access technology that runs over standard phone lines. [   ] Internet service is a means of distributing always-on broadband Internet access over the same infrastructure that offers cable television service. Satellite Internet service is a means of distributing always-on, high-speed asymmetric Internet access by broadcasting signals to and from a personal satellite [   ]. Fixed wireless Internet technologies are [   ] area network standards, in contrast to technologies such as Wi-Fi, which are local area network standards. One of the most well-known wireless wide area network standards is [   ], an Ethernet-compatible network standard designated as IEEE 802.16.

▶ CHECK ANSWERS

SECTION C: [   ] Internet access can be defined as the ability to easily move your Internet service from one location to another. [   ] Internet access offers a continuous Internet connection as you are walking or riding in a bus, car, train, or plane. Wi-Fi is an example of portable Internet access technology that allows public access to the Internet within the network's area of coverage, called a Wi-Fi [   ]. Portable WiMAX and portable satellite offer additional Internet access options in the portable category. Cellular phone service providers offer two ways to access the Internet. [   ] is a communications protocol that provides limited access to e-mail and Internet information from handheld devices with small screens and cell phone keypads. Mobile [   ] services using EV-DO, EDGE, and HSUPA technologies offer faster access using conventional browsers and e-mail clients.

▶ CHECK ANSWERS

SECTION D: [_____] computing is the idea that consumers use their computers or handheld devices to access applications, storage, and other computing resources supplied by Internet-based servers, rather than from their local devices. Network-based one-on-one messaging is usually referred to as [_____] messaging and group communications are referred to as [_____] . Most messaging is based on a client/server model that uses a server to handle communication packets between the participants. Voice over Internet [_____] is a technology in which a broadband Internet connection is used to place telephone calls instead of the regular phone system. In contrast to synchronous communications technologies, such as IM and VoIP, [_____] communications technologies, such as blogs, do not require participants to be online at the same time. [_____] is sometimes referred to as microblogging because messages are limited to 140 characters or less.

A grid computing system is a network of computers harnessed together to perform processing tasks. One of the most famous examples of a grid system is the SETI@home project, but grid technology has also been used to crack codes, analyze earthquake data, and crunch numbers for medical research. File Transfer [_____] provides a way to transfer files from one computer to another over any TCP/IP network, such as a LAN or the Internet. The purpose of FTP is to make it easy to upload and download computer files without having to deal directly with the [_____] system or file management system of a remote computer. [_____] file sharing uses protocols that allow users to obtain files from other users located anywhere on the Internet. [_____] is an example of file sharing technology that links clients in a "swarm" for distributing files.

▶ CHECK ANSWERS

SECTION E: In the context of computers, a(n) [_____] is any access to data or programs by hackers, criminals, or other unauthorized persons. As the result of an intrusion, data can be stolen or altered, system configurations can be changed to allow even more intrusions, and software can be surreptitiously installed and operated under the remote control of a hacker. One of the most common ways of gaining unauthorized access to a network-based computer is by looking for open [_____] . A port [_____] is the use of automated software to locate computers that have open ports and are vulnerable to unauthorized access. One of the easiest steps to enhance your computer's security is to turn it off when you aren't using it. You should also keep your computer up to date with the latest operating system security [_____] and service packs. You can also install [_____] software designed to filter out suspicious packets attempting to enter or leave a computer. One of the most effective steps you can take to secure your computer from intrusions is to set up a(n) [_____] , which assigns private IP addresses to the computers it controls. The process a router uses to keep track of packets and their corresponding private or public IP addresses is called [_____] address translation. Corporations try to limit intrusions by setting up virtual [_____] networks that offer encrypted connections for access to a remote server.

▶ CHECK ANSWERS

6

Interactive Situation Questions

Apply what you've learned to some typical computing situations. When using the NP2013 interactive eBook, you can type your answers, and then use the Check Answers button to automatically score your responses.

1. A news article states that hackers tried to redirect unsuspecting users to infected sites using a technique called [   ] cache poisoning. (Hint: Use the acronym.)

2. You're installing a high-speed Internet connection. The modem has a cable like the one shown at right. This modem is designed to connect to a computer's [   ] port.

3. Your Internet access seems very slow one day. You might be able to use a networking utility called [   ] to discover the source of the slowdown.

4. Suppose that you decide to open a little Web store to sell handcrafted pottery. Your Web site will need a(n) [   ] IP address, and you'll want to register a(n) [   ] name.

5. You frequently use public Wi-Fi hotspots in cafes and other locations. To keep your passwords and other confidential data safe, you work with your employer to install a(n) [   ] that encrypts the data you transmit over the Internet. (Hint: Use the acronym.)

6. Suppose you have installed a cable modem on a standalone PC. To secure your computer, you should activate [   ] software to filter packets entering and leaving your computer.

© MediaTechnics

7. Your friend, a film student, has created a 20-minute short film that she wants to distribute to friends. The file is much too large to be an e-mail attachment and she doesn't have access to a(n) [   ] server. You suggest that she try posting it at a(n) [   ] P2P file sharing site where a swarm of computers can assist with the downloads.

8. Your friend wants you to follow her tweets and asks if you have a(n) [   ] account.

9. Your friend is setting up a cable Internet connection. You recommend that she connect a router between her computer and the cable modem, and explain that network [   ] translation can help to secure her computer against intrusions.

▶ CHECK ANSWERS

Interactive Practice Tests

Practice tests that consist of ten multiple-choice, true/false, and fill-in-the-blank questions are available in the NP2013 interactive eBook. Test questions are selected at random from a large test bank, so each time you take a test, you'll receive a different set of questions. Your tests are scored immediately, and you can print study guides that help you find the correct answers for any questions that you missed.

▶ CLICK TO START

Learning Objectives Checkpoints

Learning Objectives Checkpoints are designed to help you assess whether you have achieved the major learning objectives for this chapter. You can use paper and pencil or word processing software to complete most of the activities.

1. Make a timeline of events associated with the evolution of the Internet.

2. Draw a conceptual diagram illustrating the Internet backbone, NAPs, NSPs, routers, and ISPs. Extend the diagram to show how computers on a LAN access the Internet through a single DSL modem.

3. List at least five protocols used on the Internet and describe what they are used for.

4. Explain the differences between static IP addresses, dynamic IP addresses, private IP addresses, and domain names.

5. Describe the difference between Ping and Traceroute by giving an example of when each would be used.

6. List the advantages and disadvantages of dial-up, cable, DSL, satellite, and fixed wireless Internet services. List the Internet access methods in which upstream transmission rates differ from downstream rates.

7. List the options for mobile and portable Internet access, and explain their strengths and weaknesses.

8. Explain the advantages of mobile broadband services compared to WAP service.

9. Give examples of synchronous and asynchronous communications offered on the Internet.

10. Explain how Voice over IP works, and compare it to cell phone and land line services.

11. List two examples of distributed grid computing and two examples of cloud computing.

12. Draw diagrams to illustrate how FTP, the original Napster, and BitTorrent work.

13. Make a list of security concerns that are related to Internet access.

14. Make a checklist of steps you can take to secure your computer from Internet-based intrusions.

Study Tip: Make sure you can use your own words to correctly answer each of the purple focus questions that appear throughout the chapter.

6

Concept Map

Fill in the blanks to show the hierarchy of Internet access options.

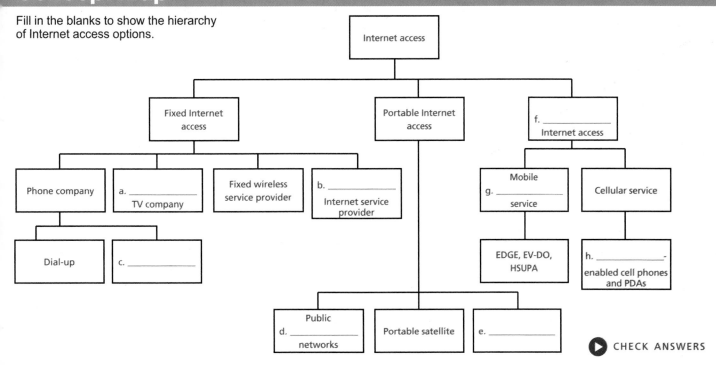

CHECK ANSWERS

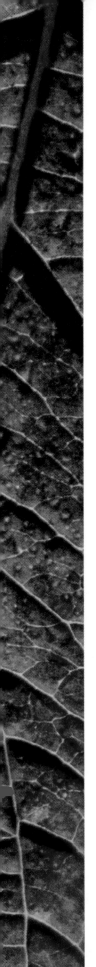

7

Chapter Contents

INFOWEBLINKS

You'll find updates for chapter
material by connecting to the
NP2013 Chapter 7 InfoWebLink.

Ⓦ CLICK TO CONNECT
www.infoweblinks.com/np2013/ch07

The Web and E-mail

Learning Objectives

After reading this chapter, you will be able to answer the
following questions by completing the outcomes-based
Learning Objectives Checkpoints on page 419.

1. What is HTML?
2. How does the Web work?
3. What does a browser do?
4. Where do cookies come from?
5. What tools are available for creating Web pages?
6. How do I create a simple Web page?
7. What makes some Web pages interactive?
8. How do search engines work?
9. What is a search operator?
10. What is the correct way to cite Web pages?
11. How do online shopping carts work?
12. How safe is online shopping?
13. Is Webmail better than client-based local e-mail?
14. How do HTML and MIME formats relate to e-mail?
15. What are the security risks of using the Web?

CourseMate

Visit the NP2013 CourseMate for this chapter's Pre-Quiz, Audio
Overview and Flashcards, Detailed Objectives, Chapter Quiz,
Online Games, and more labs.

Multimedia and Interactive Elements

When using the NP2013 interactive eBook, click the ▶ icons to
access multimedia resources.

7

Apply Your Knowledge
The information in this chapter will give you the background to:

- Use a browser to view Web pages and the source documents from which they are constructed
- Install browser plug-ins necessary to work with a variety of graphics, sound, and video files
- Create your own Web pages using a text editor and HTML tags
- Use a search engine to locate information on the Web

- Formulate advanced search queries
- Capture text and graphics from the Web
- Know how to keep your credit card information safe when shopping online
- Work with Webmail or local e-mail, attachments, and HTML mail formats
- Protect yourself from spam, spyware, cookie exploits, phishing, and pharming

Try It!

WHAT'S MY BROWSER STATUS?

Chapter 7 focuses on the World Wide Web, or "Web" for short. The most important software tool for accessing the Web is called a browser. To learn about the browser on your computer, follow these steps:

1. Make sure your computer is on and displaying the desktop.

2. Which browser do you usually use to access the Web? _____
If you don't know, look for browser icons on your desktop. Popular browsers include Internet Explorer, Safari, Firefox, and Chrome.

3. What is the URL that your browser uses as your home page? _____
The home page is the first Web page displayed and the one displayed when you click the Home button.

4. What is the version number for the browser you are using? _____
To find your browser's version number, click **Help** or the Tools icon and then click **About** (Windows), or click your browser's name on the Mac title bar and then select **About**. For Google Chrome, click the Wrench icon on the toolbar and then select **About**. Your browser's version number should be displayed in a dialog box. After you write down the version number, close the dialog box.

5. Find the most recent version for your browser by going to its Web site:

www.mozilla.org/products/firefox
www.google.com/chrome
www.microsoft.com/windows/ie
www.apple.com/safari

6. Are you using the most recent version of your browser? _____
Unless you want to download the most recent version of your browser and have permission to do so, exit the download area and close your browser.

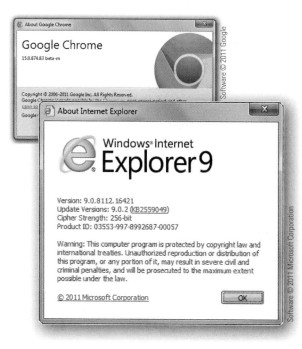

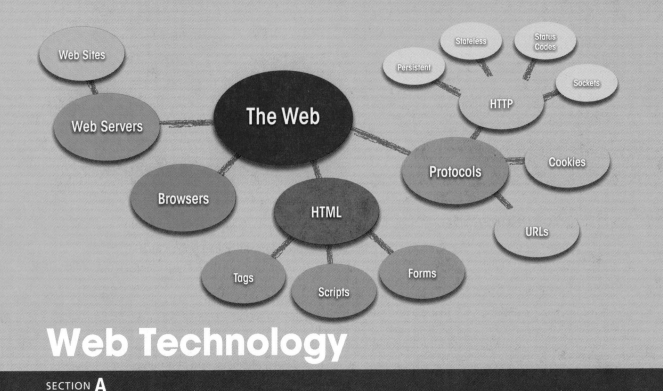

Web Technology

IN 1990, a British scientist named Tim Berners-Lee developed specifications for URLs, HTML, and HTTP; a group of technologies designed to help researchers share information by creating access to a sort of "web" of electronic documents. Berners-Lee's free Web software appeared on the Internet in 1991, but the Web didn't take off until 1993 when Marc Andreessen and his colleagues at the University of Illinois created Mosaic, a graphical browser. Andreessen later formed his own company and produced a browser called Netscape, which put the Web into the hands of millions of Web surfers. In Section A, you'll peel back the layers of Web technologies to take a look at what happens behind your browser window.

WEB BASICS

▶ **What is the Web?** One of the Internet's most captivating attractions, the **Web** (short for *World Wide Web*) is a collection of document, image, video, and sound files that can be linked and accessed over the Internet using a protocol called HTTP.

The concept of interlinking documents to access them pre-dates the Web by almost half a century. In 1945, an engineer named Vannevar Bush described a microfilm-based machine called the Memex that linked associated information or ideas through "trails."

The idea of linked documents resurfaced in the mid-1960s when Harvard graduate Ted Nelson coined the term **hypertext** to describe a computer system that could store literary documents, link them according to logical relationships, and allow readers to comment and annotate what they read. Nelson sketched the diagram in Figure 7-1 to explain his idea of a computer-based "web" of "links."

▶ **What are Web 2.0 and Web 3.0?** Originally, material for the Web was posted as a series of documents that could be accessed using a browser. That model evolved with the introduction of wikis, blogs, and social

FIGURE 7-1

Ted Nelson's early sketch of project Xanadu—a distant relative of the Web—used the terms *links* and *web*.

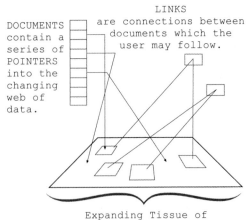

DOCUMENTS contain a series of POINTERS into the changing web of data.

LINKS are connections between documents which the user may follow.

Expanding Tissue of Text, Data, and Graphics

Courtesy of Ted Nelson "Xanadu®" is a registered trademark of Project Xanadu.

networking. These Web-based applications are sometimes characterized as **Web 2.0**. Cloud computing and other new technologies are likely to further change the way we use the Web, and those innovations are referred to as **Web 3.0**. Although Web 2.0 and Web 3.0 sound like new versions of the Web, they use the same Internet communications infrastructure as the "old" Web.

▶ **What is a Web site?** A **Web site** typically contains a collection of related information organized and formatted so it can be accessed using software called a browser. You are probably familiar with informational Web sites such as HowStuffWorks, CNN, ESPN, and Wikipedia. Web sites can also offer Web-based applications, such as Google Docs, and social networking, such as Facebook.

The activities that take place at Web sites are under the control of Web servers. A **Web server** is an Internet-based computer that accepts requests from browsers. Servers collect the requested information and transmit it back in a format that the browser can display in the form of a Web page.

▶ **What is a Web page?** A **Web page** is the product or output of one or more Web-based files displayed in a format similar to a page in a book. Unlike book pages, however, Web pages can dynamically incorporate videos, sounds, and interactive elements.

A Web page can be based on a document stored as a file or it can be assembled on the fly from information stored in a database. For example, a course syllabus that you view on the Web is probably written with a word processor and stored as a document on a Web server.

In contrast, the Web page you view about a newly released album on iTunes is assembled from a database that contains the album title, artist name, track list, price, release date, album cover art, and other product information.

▶ **How do I access a Web page?** Your main tool for accessing Web pages is browser software, such as Microsoft Internet Explorer, open-source Mozilla Firefox, Google Chrome, or Apple Safari. A **Web browser** (commonly referred to as a browser) is client software that displays Web page elements and handles links between pages. When using a browser, you can access a Web page by clicking a **hypertext link** (usually referred to simply as a link) or by typing a URL (Figure 7-2).

▶ **What is a URL?** Every Web page has a unique address called a **URL** (Uniform Resource Locator, pronounced "You Are ELL"). For example, the URL for the Cable News Network (CNN) Web site is *http://www.cnn.com*. Most URLs begin with http:// to indicate the Web's standard communications protocol. When typing a URL, the http:// can be omitted, so *www.cnn.com* works just as well as *http://www.cnn.com*.

TERMINOLOGY NOTE

The process of accessing a Web site is sometimes referred to as surfing the Web and visitors are called Web surfers.

7

FIGURE 7-2

Browsers display Web pages and the links they contain. When the mouse pointer hovers over a link, it changes from an arrow shape to a hand shape. ▶ For an overview of browser controls, refer to this figure in the digital version of your textbook.

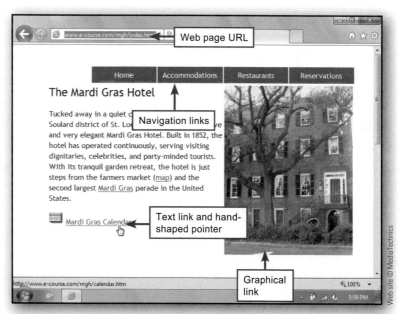

TERMINOLOGY NOTE

A URL is a type of URI (Uniform Resource Identifier). Other types of URIs include Social Security numbers and ISBNs that identify books. Some writers refer to Web addresses as URIs.

Most Web sites have a main page that acts as a doorway to the rest of the pages at the site. This main page is sometimes referred to as a home page, although this term can also refer to the page displayed by your browser each time it opens. The URL for a Web site's main page is normally short and to the point, like *www.cnn.com*.

The pages for a Web site are grouped into folders, which are reflected in the URL. For example, the CNN site might include weather information at *www.cnn.com/weather/* and entertainment information at *www.cnn.com/showbiz/*.

The file name of a specific Web page always appears last in the URL. Web page file names usually have an .htm or .html extension, indicating that the page was created with Hypertext Markup Language. You'll learn more about HTML later in the chapter. Figure 7-3 identifies the parts of a URL.

FIGURE 7-3

The URL for a Web page indicates the computer on which it is stored, its location on the Web server, its file name, and its extension.

http://www.cnn.com/showbiz/movies.htm

Web protocol standard   Web server name   Folder name   File name and file extension

▶ What are the rules for correctly typing a URL? A URL never contains spaces, even after a punctuation mark, so do not type any spaces within a URL. An underline symbol is sometimes used to give the appearance of a space between words, for example *www.detroit.com/top_10.html*.

Be sure to use the correct type of slash—always a forward slash (/)—and duplicate the URL's capitalization exactly. Some Web servers are case sensitive. On these servers, typing *www.cmu.edu/Info.html* (with an uppercase *I*) will not locate the Web page that's stored on the Web server as *www.cmu.edu/info.html* (with a lowercase *i*).

HTML

▶ What is HTML? HTML (Hypertext Markup Language) is a set of specifications for creating documents that a browser can display as a Web page. HTML is called a **markup language** because authors mark up documents by inserting special instructions, called **HTML tags**, that specify how the document should appear when displayed on a computer screen or printed.

Tim Berners-Lee developed the original HTML specifications in 1990. These specifications have been revised several times by the World Wide Web Consortium (W3C). The current version, **HTML5**, was introduced in 2010.

XHTML is a markup language very similar to HTML, but it can be customized with tags that describe the data in databases. XHTML is more rigidly structured than HTML and a bit more complex, however, so XHTML documents are required to be "well-formed" by adhering to a strict set of syntax rules.

▶ How do HTML tags work? HTML tags are incorporated into an **HTML document**, which is similar to a word processing file, but has an .htm or .html extension. HTML tags, such as <hr /> and <b>, are enclosed in angle brackets and embedded in the document. These tags are instructions for the browser. When your browser displays a Web page on your computer screen, it does not show the tags or angle brackets. Instead, it attempts to follow the tags' instructions.

▶ **So HTML documents look a lot different from Web pages, right?** Exactly. An HTML document is like a screenplay, and your browser is like a director who makes a screenplay come to life by assembling cast members and making sure they deliver their lines correctly.

As the HTML "screenplay" unfolds, your browser follows the instructions in an HTML document to display lines of text on your computer screen in the right color, size, and position.

If the screenplay calls for a graphic, your browser collects it from the Web server and displays it. Although the HTML screenplay exists as a permanent file, the Web page you see on your computer screen exists only for the duration of the "performance."

Technically speaking, you can distinguish HTML documents (the screenplay) from Web pages (the performance). However, in everyday conversation, the term *Web page* is often used for the HTML document as well as the Web page displayed on the screen.

An HTML document is sometimes referred to as a **source document** because it is the source of the HTML tags used to construct a Web page. You can view the HTML source documents for most Web pages if you are curious about how they were constructed. Figure 7-4 illustrates the difference between an HTML source document and the Web page it produces.

FIGURE 7-4

An HTML document (top) contains text and HTML tags. Formatting tags are used to change font size and separate paragraphs. Other tags add graphics and links to a page. The HTML document produces a Web page (bottom).
▶ Refer to your interactive eBook to see more examples of HTML source code.

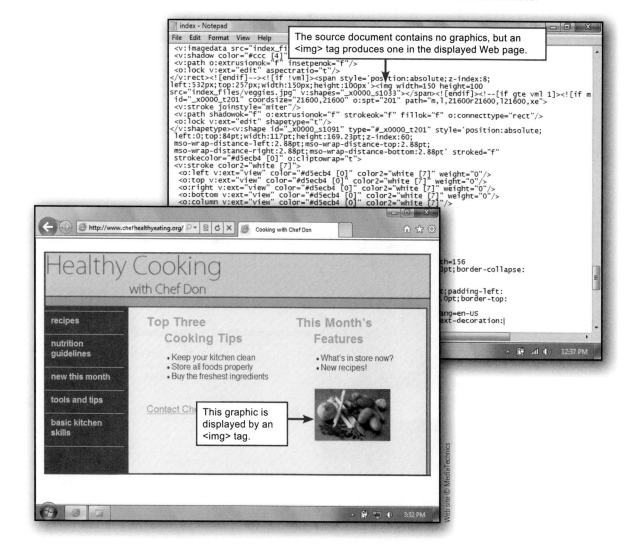

HTTP

❯ How does HTTP work? **HTTP** is a protocol that works with TCP/IP to get Web resources to your desktop. A Web resource can be defined as any chunk of data that has a URL, such as an HTML document, a graphic, or a sound file.

HTTP includes commands called methods that help your browser communicate with Web servers. GET is the most frequently used HTTP method. The GET method is typically used to retrieve text and graphics files necessary for displaying a Web page. This method can also be used to pass a search query to a file server. HTTP transports your browser's request for a Web resource to a Web server. Next, it transports the Web server's response back to your browser.

An HTTP exchange takes place over a pair of sockets. A **socket** is an abstract concept that represents one end of a connection. Although a packet switching network doesn't actually make point-to-point connections between network nodes, many people find it handy to visualize network connections as a communication line with a doorway-like socket at each end. For HTTP, sockets routinely are associated with port 80 on the client and server.

In an HTTP exchange, your browser opens a socket on your PC, connects to a similar open socket at the Web server, and issues a command, such as "send me an HTML document." The server receives the command, executes it, and sends a response back through the socket. The sockets are then closed until the browser is ready to issue another command. Figure 7-5 demonstrates the messages that flow between your browser and a Web server to retrieve an HTML document.

FIGURE 7-5

HTTP messages flow between a browser and a Web server. For an animated view of how HTTP works, take a look at this figure in your interactive eBook.

1. The URL in the browser's Address box contains the domain name of the Web server that your browser contacts.

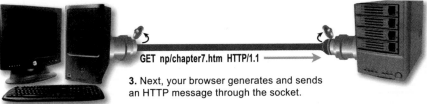

Address www.infoweblinks.com/np/chapter7.htm

2. Your browser opens a socket and connects to a similar open socket at the Web server.

GET np/chapter7.htm HTTP/1.1

3. Next, your browser generates and sends an HTTP message through the socket.

4. The server sends back the requested HTML document through the open sockets.

HTTP/1.1 200 OK
Date: Fri 24 Dec 2012
Content-Type: text.htm
Content-Length: 1354
<html>
<body>
<h1>NP InfoWebs</h1>

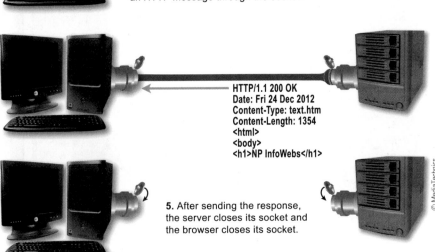

5. After sending the response, the server closes its socket and the browser closes its socket.

© Media Technics

▶ CLICK TO START

▶ Is each Web page element retrieved separately? HTTP initially allowed only one request and response per session. As a result, a browser could open a session and request an HTML document; but as soon as the document was sent, the session was closed. To make additional requests—for example, to request a graphic for the page—the browser had to open another session.

A **persistent HTTP connection** reuses the same HTTP connection to send and receive multiple requests. Today's browsers use persistent connections to obtain text, images, and audio for a Web page during a single session.

▶ What if an element cannot be found? A Web server's response to a browser's request includes an **HTTP status code** that indicates whether the browser's request could be fulfilled. The status code 200 means that the request was fulfilled—the requested HTML document, graphic, or other resource was sent. Anyone who surfs the Web has encountered the "404 Not Found" message. Your browser displays this message when a Web server sends a 404 status code to indicate that the requested resource does not exist (Figure 7-6).

FIGURE 7-6

When a broken link points to a nonexistent HTML document, your browser produces a 404 Not Found error. When a broken link points to a nonexistent graphic or other non-HTML file, your browser usually displays one of the broken link icons shown below.

Courtesy of the Department of Energy

▶ What is a Web cache? When your browser fetches pages and graphics to form a Web page, it stores that material on your computer in temporary files sometimes referred to as a **Web cache** or browser cache.

A Web cache comes in handy if you switch back and forth between pages or sites. Rather than fetch the entire page and all its graphics again, your browser can simply load them from the local cache. Files are deleted from the Web cache within days or weeks, depending on your browser's settings.

A potential problem with your Web cache is that it stores Web page elements from all the sites you've visited. If you use a public or lab computer, the Web page elements are stored there and can be viewed by others. To maintain your privacy, you might consider deleting these files periodically, adjusting browser settings to limit the time these files remain on your computer, or limiting the amount of space they can use on the hard disk.

WEB BROWSERS

▶ What are the most popular browsers? Netscape Navigator was one of the first browsers with a graphical user interface. It has been superseded by today's popular browsers, such as Mozilla Firefox, Microsoft Internet Explorer, Apple Safari, and Google Chrome. Browsers have many similarities, as you can see from examining their toolbars in Figure 7-7.

FIGURE 7-7

Popular browsers include Firefox, Internet Explorer, Safari, and Chrome.

Mozilla Firefox. In 1998, Netscape source code became open source software, managed by an organization known as Mozilla. The organization's main product, a browser called Mozilla, was all but ignored by most computer owners. In 2004, however, a new version of Mozilla, dubbed Firefox, rapidly gained popularity because it offered effective security features.

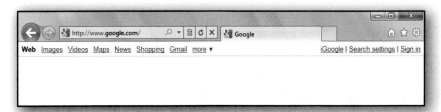

Microsoft Internet Explorer (IE). The program code for the original IE 1.0 browser was licensed from a Netscape spin-off called Spyglass. Originally developed for Windows, IE has evolved through ten versions since 1995 and is also available for Mac OS, Linux, and several versions of UNIX.

Apple Safari. In 2003, Apple introduced a browser called Safari, which is now included with Macintosh computers and available for PCs. Safari has the distinction of being the first browser to pass the Acid2 test, which means that it follows W3C standards and can correctly display all complying Web pages.

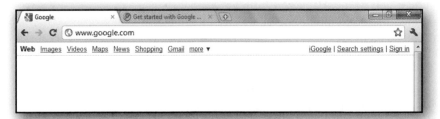

Google Chrome. Developed in 2008, Chrome was engineered specifically to support Web-based e-mail and similar online applications.

▶ Should I upgrade my browser when new versions become available? It is a good idea to upgrade when a new version of your browser becomes available. Because most browser updates are free, you can get up-to-date functionality simply by spending a few minutes downloading and installing an update.

The problem with using an old browser is that some Web pages depend on new HTML features supported only by the latest browser versions. Without the latest upgrade, you might encounter errors when your browser tries to display a page, but cannot interpret some of the HTML. In other cases, your browser might display the Web page without errors, but you will not see all the intended effects.

Another important reason to upgrade is for increased security. As hackers discover and take advantage of security holes, browser publishers try to patch the holes. Upgrades normally contain patches for known security holes, although new features might sometimes open new holes.

▶ Why do I have to download software to view some Web pages? Browsers were originally limited to displaying documents in HTML format and graphics files in GIF and JPEG formats. Today, however, many additional formats are used for the graphics, sound, and video included in Web pages. Browsers do not have built-in support for all these formats.

If your browser does not have built-in support for a file format required to display or play a Web page element, you can download the necessary software. For example, to read a PDF file, you might be directed to the Adobe Web site to download Adobe Reader software that handles PDF files. To display an animation, you might need Adobe's Flash software. The software your browser calls upon to work with additional file formats is referred to as a plug-in, add-on, or player.

▶ What is a plug-in? A **plug-in** is a program that extends a browser's ability to work with file formats. Most plug-ins can be downloaded from the Web. Plug-ins come in different versions for different browsers. When looking for plug-ins, let your browser do the searching and it will find the correct version.

The process of installing a plug-in application creates an association between the browser and a file format, such as PDF, SWF, or MOV. Whenever your browser encounters one of these file formats, it automatically runs the corresponding plug-in, which in turn opens the file.

You can download, install, and delete plug-ins for your browser. Figure 7-8 shows a list of plug-ins installed for use with Internet Explorer.

7

FIGURE 7-8

You can usually find a list of plug-ins installed for use with your browser. If you use Internet Explorer, look for a Manage Add-ons option on the Tools menu. ▶ For more information about managing plug-ins, refer to this figure in your interactive eBook.

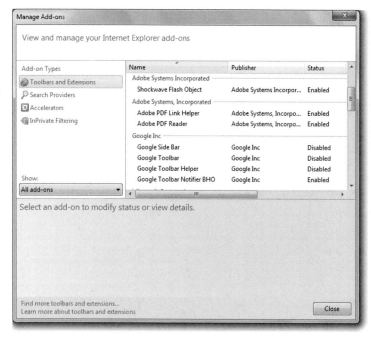

COOKIES

▸ **What is a cookie?** A **cookie** (technically an HTTP cookie) is a small chunk of data generated by a Web server and stored in a text file on your computer's hard disk. Cookies allow a Web site to store information on a client computer for later retrieval. Web sites use cookies to:

▸ Monitor your path through a site to keep track of the pages you viewed or the items you purchased.

▸ Gather information that allows a Web server to present ad banners targeted to products you previously purchased at that Web site.

▸ Collect personal information you submit to a Web page, and retain it for the next time you visit the Web site.

▸ **Why do Web sites need to use cookies?** In many respects, cookies are the solution for problems caused by HTTP's **stateless protocol**, which maintains no record of the pages you visit at a Web site.

Suppose that you use your browser to visit a popular online music store. You search for your favorite bands, listen to some sample tracks, and put a few albums in your shopping cart.

Because HTTP is a stateless protocol, each time you connect to a different Web page at the site, the server regards it as a new visit. Cookies enable the server to keep track of your activity and compile a list of your purchases.

▸ **What's in a cookie?** Cookies can contain any information that's collected by the host site, such as a customer number, Web page URL, shopping cart number, or access date (Figure 7-9).

▸ **How do cookies work?** When your browser connects to a site that uses cookies, it receives an HTTP "Set-cookie" message from the Web server. This cookie message contains information that your browser stores on your computer's hard disk. The server that creates a cookie can request it any time your browser is accessing a Web page from the Web site server.

▸ **How long do cookies stay on my computer?** A Web developer can program a cookie to time out after a designated date. When a cookie reaches the end of its predefined lifetime, your Web browser simply erases it. Some cookies have no expiration date or a date far into the future, so cookies tend to accumulate on your computer's hard disk.

▸ **Can I see the cookies stored on my computer?** You can view a list of cookies stored on your computer, but first you must find them. Refer to your browser documentation to discover which folder holds your cookies (Figure 7-10).

FIGURE 7-9

When you look at a cookie stored on your computer, most of the information is unintelligible. This cookie is called ppkcookie, its value is "hello," and it was created at *www.quirksmode.org*. The cookie contains an expiration date, but it is encoded so you can't decipher it.

ppkcookie1hellowww.
quirksmode.org/1600
18273273602981171 51
14706012829810307*

© MediaTechnics

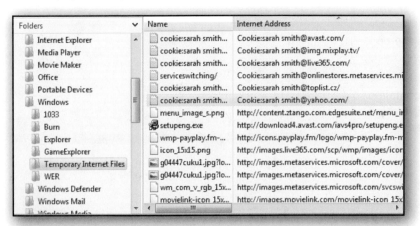

FIGURE 7-10

Internet Explorer typically stores cookies as individual files in the AppData\Local\Microsoft\Windows\Temporary Internet Files folder. The information after the @ symbol indicates the domain name of the site that created the cookie.

WEB PAGE AUTHORING

▶ **What tools can I use to create Web pages?** You can create HTML documents for Web pages with an HTML conversion utility, online Web authoring tools, Web authoring software, or a text editor.

An **HTML conversion utility** adds HTML tags to a document, spreadsheet, or other text-based file to create an HTML document that can be displayed by a browser. For example, you can work with Microsoft Word to create a standard DOCX file and then use Word's Save As Web Page option to convert the document into HTML format. The HTML conversion process sometimes produces an unusual result, however, because some of the features and formatting in your original document might not be possible within the world of HTML.

A second option for Web page authors is to use a set of online Web page authoring tools. These template-like tools are provided by some ISPs and other companies that host Web pages for individuals and businesses. Working with these tools is quite simple—you type, select, drag, and drop elements onto a Web page (Figure 7-11).

FIGURE 7-11

Many Web hosting sites, such as Google, offer subscribers online tools for creating Web pages. ▶ For a tour of online Web page authoring, activate this figure in your interactive eBook.

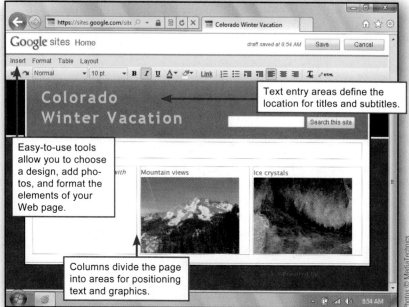

A third option for creating Web pages is a special category of software, referred to as **Web authoring software** or HTML editors, which provides tools specifically designed to enter and format Web page text, graphics, and links. Popular Web authoring products include Adobe Dreamweaver, and open source KompoZer and Amaya.

▶ **How do I create a Web page with a text editor?** You can use a text editor like Notepad (Windows) or TextEdit (Mac) to create simple HTML documents or to make quick modifications to more complex pages. The first step in the process is to open the editor. Then you can enter text and HTML tags.

▶ **How do I start an HTML document?** The framework for an HTML document consists of two sections: the head and the body. The head section begins with <!DOCTYPE html> and <head> tags. It may also include information that defines global properties, including the Web page title that appears in the browser title bar and information about the page that can be used by search engines.

The body section of an HTML document begins with the <body> HTML tag. This section of the document contains text, HTML tags that format the text, plus a variety of links to graphics, sounds, and videos. Figure 7-12 contains basic HTML for a Web page. You can use it as a template for creating your own pages.

FIGURE 7-12

Using a text editor to create an HTML document requires attention to details, such as including all necessary quotation marks and brackets.

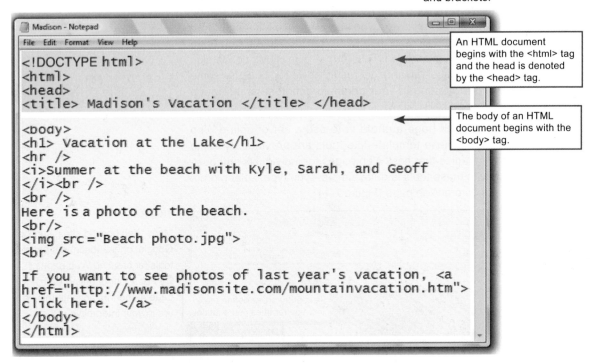

An HTML document begins with the <html> tag and the head is denoted by the <head> tag.

The body of an HTML document begins with the <body> tag.

◗ How do I specify the text and graphics for a Web page?

In the body section of your HTML document, you can enter text and HTML tags to format fonts and spacing. You can also specify the images you want to appear on the page, and you can create clickable links to other Web pages. The table in Figure 7-13 provides a list of basic HTML tags that you can use to create your own HTML documents; the HTML lab at the end of the chapter goes into more detail on the use of these tags.

FIGURE 7-13

Basic HTML Tags

HTML Tag	Use	Example
<b> <i>	Bold or italicize text	<b> Hello </b>
<h1> <h2> ... <h6>	Change font size; h1 is largest	<h1> Chapter 1 </h1>
<h1 style="color: ">	Change font color	<h1 style="color:green"> Fir Trees </h1>
<hr />	Include a horizontal line (no end tag)	Section 2 <hr />
** **	Line break (no end tag)	This is line one. This is line two.
<p>	Paragraph break	<p>It was the best of times, it ...of comparison only. </p>
<ol> <ul> <li>	Numbered list <ol>; bulleted list <ul>; list items <li>	<ol> <li>First item</li> <li> Second item</li> </ol>
<a href="URL">	Link to another Web page	<a href="www.news.com/today.htm"> Click here </a>
<img src="File">	Include an image	<img src="Photo.jpg">
<table>, <tr>, <td>	Create tables, table rows, and cells	<table>

▶ How do I get my Web pages on the Internet? Whether you work with a text editor or another authoring tool, save your HTML document with an .htm or .html extension.

Creating a Web page is not the end of the publishing process. Additional steps include testing your pages, transferring them to a Web server, and testing all your links (Figure 7-14).

FIGURE 7-14

Your Web page isn't live until it's posted.

1. Test each page locally. When you complete the first draft of a Web page, you should test it to verify that every element is displayed correctly by any browsers that visitors to your Web page might use.

You can accomplish this task without connecting to the Web. Simply open a browser, and then enter the local file name of the HTML document you created for your Web page. Repeat this process for any other browsers you expect visitors to use.

One caution: Your hard disk drive is much faster than most Internet connections, so the text and graphics for your Web page are displayed faster during your local test than for someone viewing your page over the Internet.

2. Transfer pages to a Web server. Whether you're publishing a single page, a series of pages, or an entire Web site, you must put your pages on a Web server—a process called posting.

To post Web page files manually, you can use a file transfer utility such as FileZilla or WS_FTP.

Web authoring software provides a menu option that automates the process of posting HTML documents and associated media files.

3. Test all pages and links. After you post your pages on a Web server, make sure you can access each page, and then test the links between your pages as well as any links to pages on other sites.

4. Update your pages to keep them current. Periodically, you should review the information on your Web pages and verify that the links connect to pages that still exist.

HTML SCRIPTS

▶ Is it possible to add programs to a Web page? Standard HTML provides a way to display text and graphics on a Web page and link to other Web pages; but because it isn't a programming language, HTML does not provide a way to perform complicated tasks or respond to user actions.

A series of program instructions called an **HTML script** can be embedded directly into the text of an HTML document or in a file referenced from an HTML document. Scripts are not displayed by the browser; instead, they instruct the browser to perform specific actions or respond to specific user actions.

▶ What is the purpose of a script? Scripts allow Web pages to become more interactive and incorporate activities that would otherwise require a computer program. Scripts enable e-commerce sites to verify credit card information. They also make it possible to create interactive Web pages that include fill-in forms. Scripts work with cookies to deliver custom Web pages, such as those Amazon.com generates each time you return to the site. Scripts don't replace normal HTML—they extend and enhance it.

As an example of scripting, consider what happens when you use online forms. **HTML forms** can collect user input for e-commerce orders, site registrations, opinion polls, and so on. The information you enter into an

HTML form is held in the memory of your computer, where your browser creates temporary storage bins that correspond to the input field names designated by the form's HTML tags (Figure 7-15).

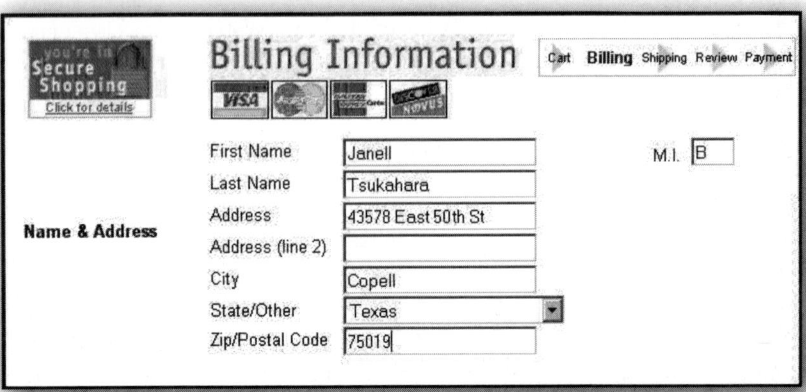

© MediaTechnics

FIGURE 7-15

The data from this form is held in memory until you click the Submit button. Then, your browser sends the data to a specially designed script on an HTTP server where it can be processed and stored.

▶ Do scripts run on my local computer or on a Web server?

Scripts can run on a client or a server. A **server-side script** consists of statements that run on a server. Server-side scripts accept data submitted by a form, process that data, and then generate a custom HTML document that is sent to the browser for display.

Pages produced dynamically by server-side scripts can often be identified because they contain question marks (?) in the URL displayed in the Address bar of your browser. Server-side scripts can be written using a variety of programming and scripting languages, such as Perl, PHP, C, C++, C#, and Java.

A **client-side script** consists of scripting statements that run on your local computer. The script is executed by the browser, which must have the capability to deal with the programming language used to write the script.

Popular languages for client-side scripts include VBScript and JavaScript. Most of today's browsers can handle JavaScript, but only IE has the built-in capability to execute VBScript. Client-side scripts often take the form of Java applets, Flash objects, and ActiveX controls.

▶ What is a Java applet?

A **Java applet** is an application written in the Java programming language. A programmer or Web page author places a reference to a Java applet in an HTML document using the <object> HTML tag. When working with a Web page that contains an <object> tag, your browser downloads the applet and executes its instructions. The applet is not installed on your computer, so it does not leave a permanent footprint.

You might wonder if a Java applet could contain a virus that would take up residence in your computer system or a worm that would spread over your network. Applets are fairly safe because they cannot open, modify, delete, or create files on your computer; they cannot make network connections except to the originating site; and they are not allowed to launch other programs.

▶ What is Flash content?

Most people associate Flash with a popular video standard, but Flash objects can include interactive elements. **ActionScript** is a programming language for the Adobe Flash Player. It is used to create sophisticated applications that can be launched from Web pages and viewed using the Flash browser plug-in or the standalone Flash Player. The Flash Player has some security holes, but users can minimize risks by installing updates as they become available.

▶ What is an ActiveX control? An **ActiveX control** is a compiled computer program that can be referenced from within an HTML document, downloaded, installed on your computer, and executed within the browser window.

ActiveX controls can be used on the server side, too, but consumers typically encounter the client-side version when their browsers display a security warning and ask for permission to proceed with installation (Figure 7-16).

FIGURE 7-16

Web surfers who use Internet Explorer sometimes encounter the Security Warning dialog box for ActiveX components. If the component is supplied by a trusted source, then it should be safe to install it.

Most ActiveX controls are safe. However, an ActiveX control is a full-fledged program, which gives it the potential to include routines that alter or delete data on your computer's hard disk. ActiveX controls include digital certificates to increase their security. A **digital certificate** is an electronic attachment to a file that verifies the identity of its source.

▶ Is it easy to create Java applets, Flash objects, and ActiveX controls? Scripts are somewhat more difficult to write and test than HTML documents, so scripts are the domain of professional Web designers. A basic understanding of scripts, however, along with a grasp of HTML, HTTP, cookies, browsers, and hypertext, is essential for understanding how the Web works.

QuickCheck   SECTION A

1. Ted Nelson coined the term [   ] to describe a web of linked documents, similar to Web pages.

2. Every Web page has a unique address called a(n) [   ] . (Hint: Use the acronym.)

3. The main protocol for sending and receiving Web content is [   ] . (Hint: Use the acronym.)

4. The basic markup language used on the Web is [   ] . (Hint: Use the acronym.)

5. [   ] were developed because HTTP is a stateless protocol; so each time you connect to a different page, the Web server regards it as a new connection.

▶ CHECK ANSWERS

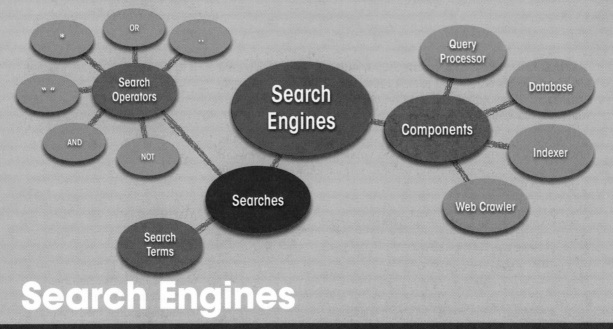

Search Engines

THE WEB ENCOMPASSES hundreds of millions of pages stored on servers scattered all over the globe. To use this information, however, you have to find it. Modern Web surfers depend on search engines to wade through the tsunami of information stored on the Web. In Section B, you'll find out how Web search engines work so that you can use them more efficiently.

SEARCH ENGINE BASICS

▶ What is a Web search engine? A **Web search engine** (commonly referred to simply as a search engine) is a program designed to help people locate information on the Web by formulating simple keyword queries. In response to a query, the search engine displays results, or "hits," as a list of relevant Web sites, accompanied by links to source pages and short excerpts containing the keywords (Figure 7-17).

FIGURE 7-17

A query for *mountain bike* returns a list of links to relevant sites.

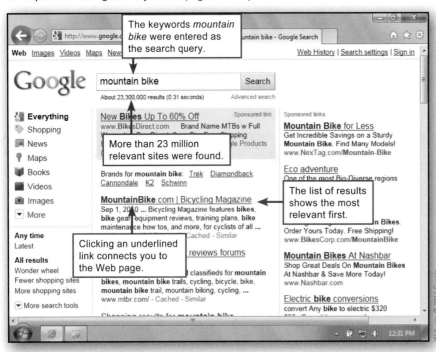

Popular search engines are located at Web sites such as *www.google.com*, *www.yahoo.com*, *www.bing.com*, and *www.ask.com*. The search engines at these sites build the equivalent of a book index. Just as an index helps readers turn to a page on which they can find a particular word or concept, a search engine helps Web surfers link to pages that contain information they seek. Unlike a book, however, the information on the Web is too vast to catalog manually, so search engine software does it autonomously.

▶ **What is the difference between a search engine and a search engine site?** It is easy to think of *www.google.com* as a search engine; but to be precise, it is a Web site that offers access to a search engine. A search engine is the program that works behind the scenes to gather, index, find, and rank information from the Web.

Some sites, including Google, use their own proprietary search engines, but other sites use third-party search technology. For example, Microsoft's Bing search engine is the underlying technology for Yahoo! searches.

Search engine technology can also be incorporated in e-commerce, informational, and corporate sites, most often taking the form of query toolbars used to search within a single Web site (Figure 7-18).

FIGURE 7-18

Many Web sites use search engine technology for searching within the site rather than searching the entire Web.

Courtesy of the U.S. Food and Drug Administration

▶ **How do search engines work?** A search engine contains four components:

▶ Web crawler: Combs the Web to gather data that's representative of the contents of Web pages

▶ Indexer: Processes the information gathered by the crawler into a list of keywords and URLs stored in a database

▶ Database: Stores billions of index references to Web pages

▶ Query processor: Allows you to access the database by entering key terms, and then produces a list of Web pages that contain content relevant to your query

Let's take a look at each of these components to find out how they affect your ability to mine information from the Web.

▶ **What is a Web crawler?** A **Web crawler** (also referred to as a Web spider) is a computer program that is automated to methodically visit Web sites. Web crawlers can be programmed to perform various activities as they visit sites; but in the context of search engines, Web crawlers download Web pages and submit them to an indexing utility for processing.

▶ How much of the Web does a Web crawler cover? A Web crawler begins with a list of URLs to visit. After copying the material at a specified URL, the Web crawler looks for hypertext links and adds them to the list of URLs to visit. To cover the Web as efficiently as possible, a Web crawler can run multiple processes in parallel. Sophisticated algorithms keep processes from overlapping or getting stuck in loops.

High-performance Web crawlers can visit hundreds of millions of Web pages a day. Those pages, however, are only a fraction of the Web. Researchers estimate that the most extensive search engines cover less than 20% of the Web. Each search engine seems to focus on a slightly different collection of Web sites. The same search entered into different search engines can produce different results, so it is sometimes worthwhile to try alternative search engines.

Web crawlers generally do not gather material from the invisible Web, which encompasses pages that require password-protected logins and pages that are dynamically generated with server-side scripts.

The potential volume of dynamically generated pages, such as all the possible pages that Amazon.com could generate from its inventory database, is just too great to feasibly index. To access information related to e-commerce merchandise or library catalogs, you might have to go directly to the merchant's or library's Web site and use its local search tools.

▶ How frequently do Web crawlers revisit sites? When you query a search engine, you want the results to be up to date so that you don't waste time trying to link to pages that have changed or been deleted. Search engines use various algorithms to refresh their indexes.

The number of times a search engine's crawler visits a Web page varies, depending on several factors such as how often the page tends to change and its popularity. Obscure pages might be visited only once a month, whereas the pages at a news site would be visited daily (Figure 7-19).

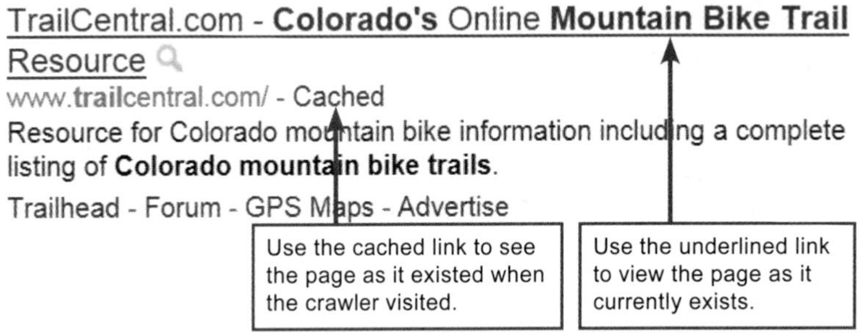

TrailCentral.com - **Colorado's** Online **Mountain Bike Trail Resource** 🔍
www.**trailcentral**.com/ - Cached
Resource for Colorado mountain bike information including a complete listing of **Colorado mountain bike trails**.
Trailhead - Forum - GPS Maps - Advertise

© 2011 Google

Use the cached link to see the page as it existed when the crawler visited.

Use the underlined link to view the page as it currently exists.

FIGURE 7-19

Google's crawler collects entire Web pages, so its database contains a copy of the page as it existed when the crawler last visited.

▶ How do search engine indexers work? A **search engine indexer** is software that pulls keywords from a Web page and stores them in an index database. The purpose of the indexer is to make pages easy to find based on their contents. For example, a Web page at a mountain biking site might contain information about bikes, gear, riding, and trail maps. Keywords that might help catalog this page for future access include *mountain*, *bike*, *trail*, *directions*, *gear*, *front range*, *advice*, *bikepacking*, and *bunny hop*.

▶ Which Web sites are shown at the top of the results list? A search engine's **query processor** looks for your search terms in the search engine's indexed database and returns a list of relevant Web sites. The order in which Web sites are listed in response to a search depends on relevancy criteria, such as keyword matches and link popularity.

TERMINOLOGY NOTE

The words you enter for your search can be referred to as queries, search criteria, search terms, or keywords.

If a search is based on multiple keywords, pages that contain the most matching words are listed first. **Link popularity** is a measure of the quality and quantity of the links from one Web page to others. Pages with links to and from popular sites tend to get high relevancy ratings.

◗ Can a search engine be manipulated into giving a high ranking to a page? Web sites can be added to a search engine index in several ways. Sites can automatically get discovered by a search engine's Web crawler, they can be submitted to a search engine by Web masters who manage various Web sites, they can be submitted for a paid placement, or they can be submitted as banner or pop-up ads.

Most search engines make it easy to submit the URL for a Web site, so that Web masters don't have to wait for their sites to be discovered by a Web crawler. Manual submissions are added to the crawler's list of sites to visit and the site will eventually be indexed.

Disreputable Web site operators are constantly trying to devise schemes, such as manipulating meta keywords, to move their Web sites up to the top of search engine query results. A **meta keyword** is entered into a header section of a Web page when it is created and is supposed to describe the page contents.

Keyword stuffing is an unethical practice in which meta keywords are manipulated to gain high relevancy rankings. For example, a Web page author might include meta keywords such as *sex* (which happens to be the most frequently used search term) even though the term has little to do with the information on the page.

Socially responsible search engine sites take steps to foil practices that manipulate rankings and make their policies on paid ads clear to users. When you use a search engine, read its About page to learn its ad placement policies and discover whether or not you can trust the search results to be unbiased.

◗ What are sponsored links? Some search engines accept paid ads, which are bumped to the top positions on the results list. Other search engines also accept paid ads, but place them in a clearly marked area (Figure 7-20).

FIGURE 7-20

Sponsored links on Google are paid ad placements that appear when users make queries using relevant keywords.

FORMULATING SEARCHES

▶ **How do I formulate a basic search?** Most search engines work with keyword queries in which you enter one or more words, called **search terms**, related to the information you want to find. For example, if you're interested in Batman comics, you can simply type the obvious: *Batman* (Figure 7-21).

FIGURE 7-21

▶ For tips on effective searching, work with the tour for this figure in your interactive eBook.

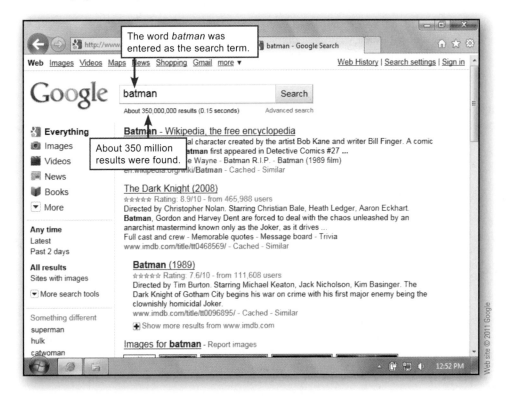

When formulating queries, keep the simple guidelines from Figure 7-22 in mind.

FIGURE 7-22

Tips for Effective Queries

▶ Most search engines are not case sensitive, so you don't have to use the Shift key when entering proper names.

▶ Search engines generally ignore common words, such as *and*, *a*, and *the*, so don't bother to include them in your query.

▶ The top search engines use stemming technology that looks for plurals and other variations of the search terms you enter. For example, if you enter *diet*, the search engine also looks for pages with terms such as *diets*, *dietary*, and *dietician*.

▶ Order matters. A search for *time machine* produces different results than a search for *machine time*.

▶ Location matters. If your search engine is able to determine your location, results might be affected. Most search engines give you an option for changing your location or hiding it.

▶ Search engines build on your previous searches. If you formulate several Batman-related searches, and then search for *dark night*, your search engine might assume that you are looking for information about the Batman movie *Dark Knight* instead of astronomy information. Google uses this predictive technology unless you clear your Web history.

▶ How do I get more targeted results? Narrowing a search can reduce the number of results and produce a more targeted list. For example, the query *first appearance Batman comic book* produces more than a million results, and those listed first link to information about when Batman first appeared in the May 1939 issue of *Detective Comics*.

Search engine queries rarely produce fewer than a thousand results. A game called Googlewhacking illustrates just how hard it is to create a narrowly targeted query. Googlewhacking challenges you to type a two-word query that produces one and only one result. Try it! You need to choose two fairly unrelated words, but they cannot be totally unrelated or you'll get no results. You can view some successful Googlewhacks at *www.googlewhack.com/tally.pl*.

▶ What are search operators? A **search operator** is a word or symbol that describes a relationship between search terms and thereby helps you create a more focused query. Figure 7-23 provides a quick overview of how to use search operators when formulating searches.

FIGURE 7-23

Search Operators

AND	When two search terms are joined by *AND*, both terms must appear on a Web page before it can be included in the search results. The query *railroad AND cars* will locate pages that contain both the words *railroad* and *cars*. Your search results might include pages containing information about old railroad cars, about railroad car construction, and even about railroads that haul automobiles (cars). Some search engines use the plus symbol (+) instead of the word *AND*.
OR	When two search terms are joined by *OR*, either one or both of the search words could appear on a page. Entering the query *railroad OR cars* produces information about railroad fares, railroad routes, railroad cars, automobile safety records, and even car ferries.
NOT	The search term following *NOT* must not appear on any of the pages found by the search engine. Entering *railroad NOT cars* would tell the search engine to look for pages that include *railroad* but not the term *cars*. In some search engines, the minus sign (-) can be used instead of the word *NOT*.
" "	To search for an exact phrase, enter it in quotes. For example, *"Dynamic Duo."*
*	The asterisk (*) is sometimes referred to as a wildcard character. It allows a search engine to find pages with any derivation of a basic word. For example, the query *medic** would not only produce pages containing the word *medic*, but also *medics*, *medicine*, *medical*, *medication*, and *medicinal*.
..	Google lets you use two dots to specify a range of numbers, dates, episodes, or prices. For example, to view Batman episodes 5, 6, 7, and 8, you can enter *Batman episodes 5..8*.

❯ What is an advanced search? Many search engines provide ways to make your searches more precise and obtain more useful results. You might be able to use advanced search options to limit your search to material written in a specific language or stored in a specific file format. You might be able to specify a date, eliminate results from adult sites, and stipulate whether to look for your search terms in the title, URL, or body of the Web page (Figure 7-24).

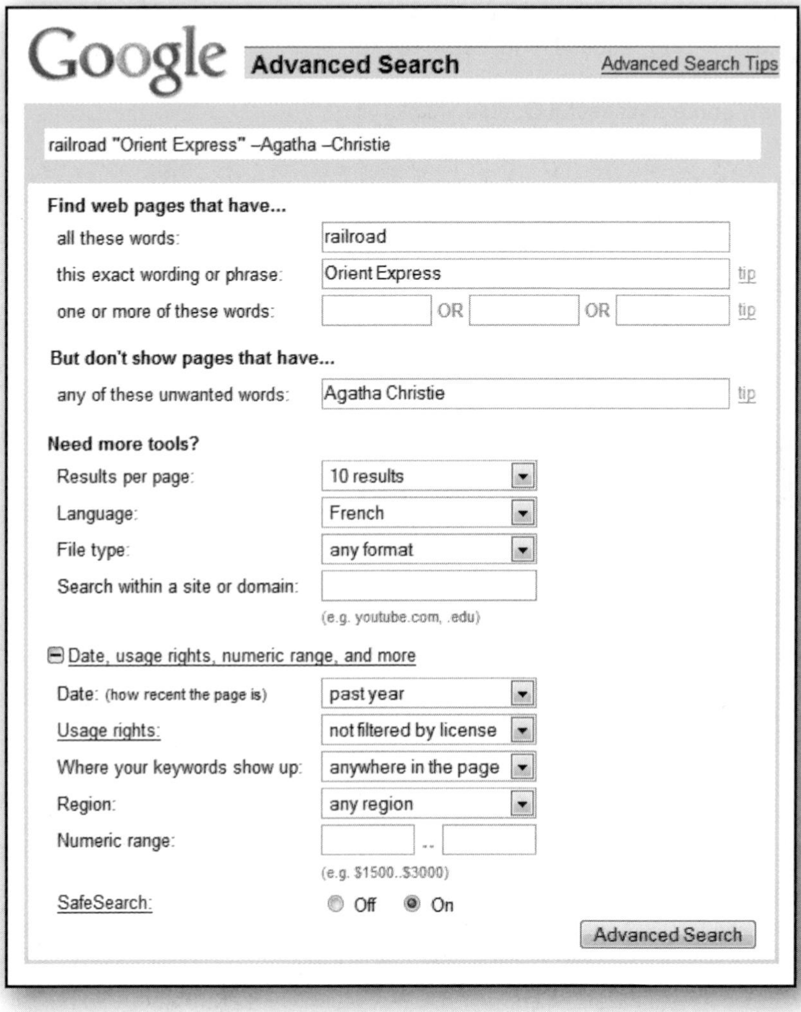

FIGURE 7-24

Many search engines provide forms designed to enhance the search process. These forms are accessible by clicking an Advanced Search link, which is located on the main page of the search engine Web site.

Some search engine sites offer separate searches for academic works, images, videos, news, e-commerce merchandise, and blogs. Look for links to these specialized searches at your favorite search engine sites.

In addition to using search engines, you can also find Web-based information using a **metasearch engine** that searches a series of other search engines and compiles the search results. Popular metasearch sites include *www.polymeta.com*, *www.dogpile.com*, and *www.webcrawler.com*.

▶ Are the top results really the most relevant? The links listed on the first page of search results are very often the most relevant, but Figure 7-25 explains how a little detective work can help you home in on the best links to explore.

FIGURE 7-25

Studying search engine results helps you select the best links.

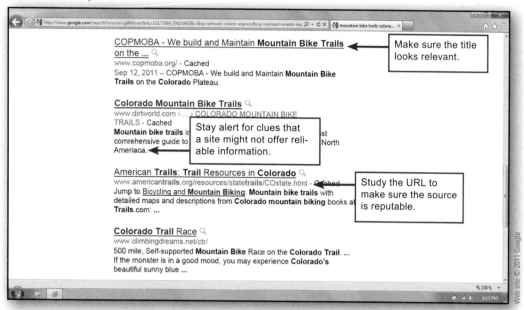

▶ Do search engines keep records of my queries? Considering that a major search engine can receive upward of 100 million queries every day, the surprising answer to this question is "yes." Search engines at major sites such as Google, AOL, MSN, Bing, and Yahoo! save massive numbers of searches made by site visitors.

Industry analysts believe that some sites retain user queries for at least 30 days, and that at least one search engine site has retained every search ever made at the site.

In 2006, AOL released a database of queries for research purposes. Figure 7-26 illustrates a small section of this database for queries made by users interested in mountain bikes.

FIGURE 7-26

A database of 20 million AOL queries is available to the public. For example, many people, including user 1404131, entered queries about mountain bikes. From the database you could also discover other queries made by this user.

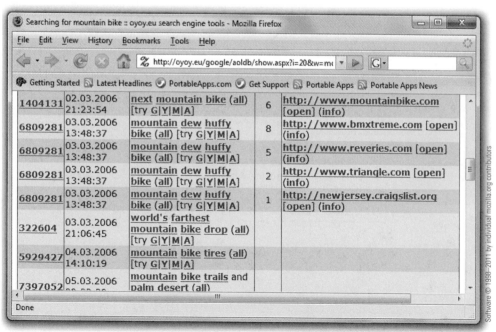

Privacy advocates question the wisdom of search engines retaining queries. They can't identify any beneficial uses for such data and fear that it is
of potential benefit only to marketing companies. Anyone who uses search
engines should be aware that the content of their searches could become
public.

▶ What kind of information does a search engine store?
Although your queries do not contain your name, you are assigned a
unique ID number that is stored in a cookie on your computer. In addition to
storing an ID number, search engines store the IP address from which the
query was initiated, the date and time of the query, the search terms, and
URLs for any Web sites accessed from the results list.

▶ What can I do to keep my searches confidential? Your
search-engine-assigned ID number is stored in a cookie and remains the
same as long as the cookie remains on your computer. If you frequently
delete your cookies as explained in Section E, a search engine's query
database is unlikely to collect enough information to link back to you.

You can block cookies from a specific search engine site, and that setting
will force the search engine to assign a different ID number to you for each
session. You can also download and use a cookie anonymizer that sets
your Google ID number to 0.

Anonymizer sites, such as *www.torproject.org*, act as relay stations to forward your searches to Google or other search engines without leaving a
trail back to a cookie or IP address. These sites claim to delete all activity
logs every day or two, but they are the subject of law enforcement scrutiny.

USING WEB-BASED SOURCE MATERIAL

▶ Can I copy text and graphics that I find on Web pages?
Most browsers provide a Copy command that allows you to copy a section
of text from a Web page, which you can then paste into one of your own
documents. To keep track of the source for each text section, you can highlight the Web page's URL in the Address box, use the Copy command, and
then paste the URL into your document (Figure 7-27).

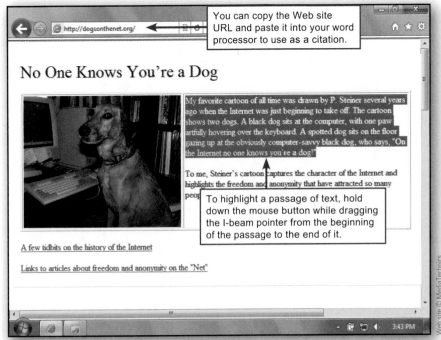

FIGURE 7-27

To copy a passage of text
from a Web page, high-
light the text, right-click it,
then select Copy. Next,
switch to your own docu-
ment and use the Paste
option. ▶ For a demon-
stration of this process, go
to your interactive eBook.

▶ **How do I cite sources?** Presenting someone else's work as your own is plagiarism. If you copy text, pictures, or other works from a Web page, make sure you give credit to the original author. Information that identifies the source of a quotation or excerpted work is called a citation. Written documents, such as reports and projects, generally include footnotes, endnotes, or in-line citations formatted according to a standard style, such as MLA, APA, or Chicago.

When compiling the citation for online sources, be sure to provide sufficient information so readers can locate the source. Also, include the date when you accessed the source and the full URL. According to APA style, a citation to a Web-based source should provide a document title or description; author name if available; the date of publication, update, or retrieval; and a URL.

▶ **Do I need permission to use material?** In the United States, the Fair Use Doctrine allows limited use of copyrighted material for scholarship and review without obtaining permission. For scholarly reports and projects, for example, you can use a sentence or paragraph of text without obtaining permission if you include a citation to the original source.

Photos and excerpts from music and videos can be used within the context of critique, but their use purely as decorative elements for a document would, in most cases, not be considered fair use.

Some Web sites clearly state allowable uses for material on the site. Look for a link to Terms of Use. For example, the YouTube Web site contains a collection of videos submitted by amateurs and semi-professionals, who retain the copyright to their materials. The Terms of Use section of the site allows the public to access, use, reproduce, distribute, create derivatives of, display, and perform user-submitted works. Even with such broad terms of use, however, it is essential to cite the original source of the material if you incorporate it in your own work.

▶ **How do I get permission?** To obtain permission to use text, photos, music, videos, and other elements you find on the Web, contact the copyright holder by e-mail, and explain what you want to use and how you plan to use it. You can often find contact information on the Web site, if not for the copyright holder, at least for a Web master who can direct you to the copyright holder.

7

QuickCheck SECTION B

1. A search engine's [_____] pulls keywords from a Web page and stores them in a database.

2. When you enter search terms, the search engine's [_____] processor looks for the terms in the search engine's database.

3. *AND, OR, NOT,* and .. are examples of search [_____].

4. Most search engines keep track of users by assigning a unique ID number, which is stored in a(n) [_____] on the hard disk of the user's computer.

5. To keep track of the Web pages where you obtained information or images, you can highlight the Web page's [_____], copy it, and then paste it into a list of sources. (Hint: Use the acronym.)

▶ CHECK ANSWERS

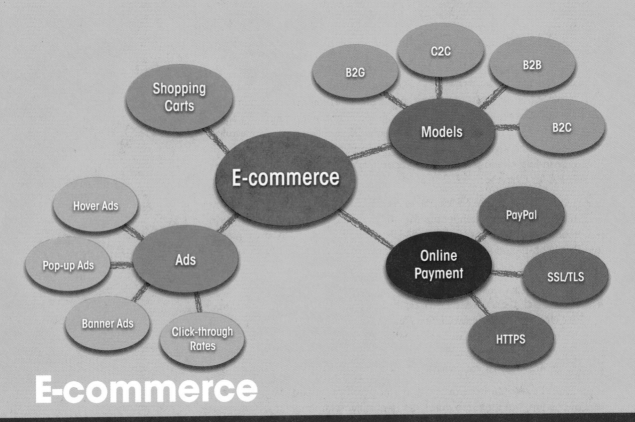

E-commerce

ONE OF THE MOST POPULAR activities on the Web is shopping. Online shopping has the same allure as catalogs—you can shop at your leisure, anonymously, and in your pajamas. But the economics of the Web provide opportunities that go beyond retail catalogs. The Internet was opened to commercial use in 1991. Since then, millions of businesses have set up shop at Web sites. This section of the chapter focuses on e-commerce and the technologies a typical shopper might encounter on the Web.

E-COMMERCE BASICS

▶ **What is e-commerce?** Although the experts don't always agree on its definition, the term **e-commerce** typically refers to business transactions that are conducted electronically over a computer network. It encompasses all aspects of business and marketing enabled by Internet and Web technologies.

E-commerce wares include many kinds of physical products, digital products, and services. Physical products offered at e-commerce sites include such goods as clothing, shoes, skateboards, and cars. Most of these products can be shipped to buyers through the postal service, a parcel delivery service, or a trucking company.

Increasingly, e-commerce goods include digital products, such as news, music, movies, databases, software, and all types of knowledge-based items. The unique feature of these products is that they can be transformed into bits and delivered over the Internet. Consumers can get them immediately upon completing their orders, and there are no shipping costs.

E-commerce merchants also peddle services, such as online medical consultation, distance education, or custom sewing. Some of these services can be carried out by computers. Others require human agents. Services can be delivered electronically, as in the case of a distance education course, or they might produce some physical product, such as a custom-fit boat cover.

▶ **What are the most common e-commerce business models?**
E-commerce activities are classified as **B2C** (business-to-consumer), **C2C** (consumer-to-consumer), **B2B** (business-to-business), and **B2G** (business-to-government), as described in Figure 7-28.

FIGURE 7-28

B2C and C2C e-commerce offer consumers many types of goods and services.

Eric Bean/Getty Images
Don Farrall/Getty Images
Comstock/Getty

B2C: Online storefronts offer goods, merchandise, and services to consumers.

C2C: Consumers sell to each other at popular auction and list sites such as eBay and craigslist.

B2B and B2G: Businesses sell goods and services to other businesses or to the government.

▶ **Is e-commerce more profitable than offline business?**
E-commerce enhances traditional business models by offering efficiency and opportunities for automation, computerization, and digitization. As with a traditional brick-and-mortar business, profit in an e-commerce business is the difference between income and expenses.

One of the advantages of e-commerce is its ability to increase profit margins by cutting costs. For example, a typical catalog order placed over the phone costs the merchant $2.50, whereas an online transaction costs about 35 cents. A hotel reservation made online costs the innkeeper 80% less than a booking by phone. A withdrawal or deposit costs a bank about a dollar when handled by a teller, about 25 cents on an ATM, and only a penny on the Web.

E-commerce merchants also generate income by hosting advertising space for marketers, who are creating increasingly hard-to-avoid styles of online advertisements, such as banner and pop-up ads. A **banner ad** is an advertisement embedded at the top of a Web page. A **hover ad** overlays the content on a Web page, sometimes obscuring it until you click the ad or its timer expires and the ad disappears. A **pop-up ad**, such as the one in Figure 7-29, is an advertisement that appears in a separate window when you connect to a Web page. If you click a banner, hover, or pop-up ad, your browser connects directly to the advertiser's Web site, where you can find product information and make a purchase.

Banner, hover, and pop-up ads earn revenue for hosting merchants based on the **click-through rate**—the number of times that site visitors click the ad to connect to the advertiser's site. The hosting merchant is paid a small fee for each clickthrough. Click-through rates have declined in recent years because most consumers simply ignore ads or install **ad-blocking software** to prevent ads from appearing on their screens. Recent versions of most browsers include a configurable feature to block pop-up ads.

FIGURE 7-29

Pop-up ads appear as separate windows.

▶ **Who benefits from e-commerce?** Both merchants and consumers benefit from e-commerce because niche goods and small merchants can reach a global customer base. At online music shops and bookstores, for example, you can find obscure titles and alternative music that brick-and-mortar merchants haven't the space or inclination to stock.

Merchants are always looking for ways to attract customers. The Web and its search engines give small merchants without a budget for national advertising a way to be found by customers. When you're looking for handmade chainmail, for example, you're unlikely to find it at your local Walmart, but chances are good that you can find a chainmail merchant on the Web.

E-COMMERCE SITE TECHNOLOGY

▶ What makes online shopping so special? E-commerce offers some unique advantages over brick-and-mortar stores and mail-order catalogs. Customers can easily search for specific merchandise. They can configure products online, see actual prices, and build an order over several days.

E-commerce customers can easily compare prices among multiple vendors using Web sites such as Bizrate, Nextag, and PriceGrabber. Many sites also offer product reviews written by consumers.

E-commerce seems simple from the perspective of a shopper who connects to an online store, browses the electronic catalog, selects merchandise, and then pays for it. Behind the scenes, an e-commerce site uses several technologies to display merchandise, keep track of shoppers' selections, collect payment data, protect customers' privacy, and prevent credit card numbers from falling into the wrong hands.

▶ Are there different e-commerce models? There are two popular models for e-commerce stores. The first is the B2C model pioneered by Amazon.com. The second is the C2C model represented by online auction sites such as eBay, and online classified advertisement sites such as craigslist.

▶ What are the important elements of a B2C e-commerce site? Most B2C sites are operated by a single merchant. The business has an inventory of products, such as DVDs, books, clothing, and other merchandise. A key element of this model is that the inventory is usually quite large and contains multiple quantities of each item; for example, Amazon's inventory includes huge quantities of *Twilight Saga* DVDs. Customers can select several items from the inventory by placing them in shopping carts.

▶ How is a B2C inventory stored? The inventory for a B2C store can be quite large and it would be impractical to create individual Web pages for each item. Instead, inventory items, along with their prices and descriptions, are entered into a database. When you browse through the merchandise at an online store, the site's Web servers and database servers interact to pull information from the database and convert it to Web pages that can be displayed in a browser.

When you view products at a large-scale B2C site, the product pages have been produced on the fly by server-side CGI, PHP, or ASP scripts. The next time you shop online, pay attention to the Address bar of your browser. When product pages are displayed, you'll probably see a ? symbol somewhere in the URL, and the URL might also include *cgi*, *php*, or *asp*, all indicating the Web page you're viewing was assembled by a server-side script from the information in a database (Figure 7-30).

FIGURE 7-30

Product pages that contain a ? symbol are constructed from a database on the fly by server-side scripts.

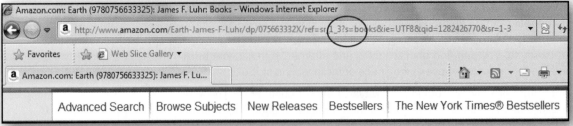

Amazon.com: Earth (9780756633325): James F. Luhr: Books - Windows Internet Explorer

http://www.amazon.com/Earth-James-F-Luhr/dp/075663332X/ref=sr_1_3?s=books&ie=UTF8&qid=1282426770&sr=1-3

Favorites | Web Slice Gallery ▼

Amazon.com: Earth (9780756633325): James F. Lu...

Advanced Search | Browse Subjects | New Releases | Bestsellers | The New York Times® Bestsellers

Web site © 1996–2011, Amazon.com, Inc

▶ How do shopping carts work? If you've done any shopping online, you've probably used an **online shopping cart**—a cyberspace version of the metal cart you wheel around a store and fill up with merchandise.

As mentioned earlier, HTTP is a stateless protocol, which maintains no record of your browser's previous interactions and handles each browser request based entirely on information that comes with it. Under these circumstances, you might wonder how it is possible for an online retail store to remember the items you put in your shopping cart.

Most shopping carts work because they use cookies to store information about your activities on a Web site. Cookies work with shopping carts in one of two ways, depending on the e-commerce site. An e-commerce site might use cookies as a storage bin for all the items you load into your shopping cart, as shown in Figure 7-31.

FIGURE 7-31

Shopping cart items can be stored in a cookie.

1. When you click the Add to Cart button, the merchant's server sends a message to your browser to add that item number to the cookie, which is stored on your computer.

ITEM # B7655

2. When you check out, the server asks your browser for all the cookie data that pertains to your shopping cart items.

3. Your browser sends those cookies along with a request for an order summary.

Your order:

1 Blender $29.95

1 Wok $38.49

4. The Web server uses the cookies to look up products in its database and produce a Web page listing the items you want to purchase.

Some e-commerce sites use cookies simply as a way to uniquely identify each shopper. These sites generate a unique ID number that is stored along with your item selections in a server-side database (Figure 7-32).

FIGURE 7-32

Shopping cart items can be stored in a server-side database.

1. When you connect to a merchant's site, the server assigns you a unique shopping cart ID number and sends it to your browser in a cookie.

DATABASE

WEB SERVER

 CART # 2098-2

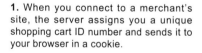

🛒 CART # 2098-2

ITEM # B7655

3. The Web server stores this number and your merchandise selection in the merchant's server-side database.

WEB SERVER

 CART # 2098-2

2. When you select an item to purchase, your browser reads your shopping cart ID number from the cookie, and then sends this number to the merchant's Web server.

Order for CART # 2098-2

1 Blender   B7655 $29.95

1 Wok   GJK4-31 $38.49

4. When you check out, your browser sends your shopping cart number to the server, which retrieves all your selections from the merchant's database.

▶ **How do C2C sites work?** At C2C auction and online classified advertising e-commerce sites, consumers offer goods and services to other consumers. The key characteristic of C2C sites is that the merchandise is generally individual items, such as a used boat, a collectible stuffed bear, or an antique flower vase. Each item is unique and sellers individually enter information that becomes the product Web page.

C2C sites are hosted by an e-commerce provider such as eBay or craigslist. The host site offers tools for sellers to auction or sell items. Sellers are provided with a way to enter item descriptions, prices, and photos. They might also be provided with tools to track bids, purchases, and other activity. Buyers are provided with tools to locate products and contact sellers with questions. Host sites might also maintain ratings for buyers and sellers to help participants avoid shady deals.

▶ **How do sellers enter product information?** Sellers can enter product information by filling in an online form and uploading photos as shown in Figure 7-33.

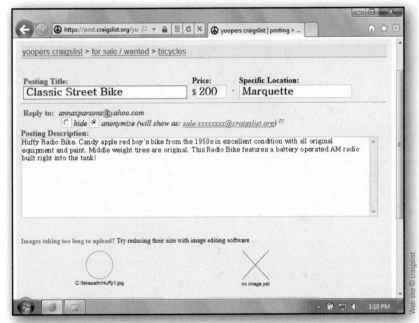

FIGURE 7-33

The craigslist Web site provides a form for entering product descriptions and photos.

▶ **How is product data stored?** Product data is stored in a database at the host site in much the same way as product data is stored at a B2C e-commerce site. Shoppers can enter queries to locate products from the database (Figure 7-34); matching descriptions and photos are retrieved and displayed as Web pages.

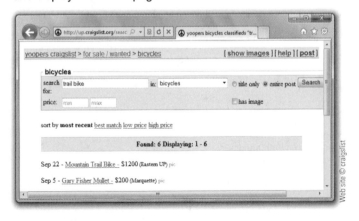

FIGURE 7-34

Buyers can find products by entering search terms.

How do buyers contact sellers? Another key characteristic of a C2C site is that buyers interact directly with individual sellers; so if you purchase a used boat advertised on craigslist, you'll likely be interacting with a different seller than when you purchase a classic street bike. C2C sites have to provide a way for buyers and sellers to interact while protecting the privacy of both parties.

Many C2C sites use e-mail forwarding to protect participants' privacy. When you register with a C2C host, you usually receive an e-mail account tied to your user ID. Your e-commerce correspondence is forwarded from that account to your regular e-mail account, which effectively hides your real name and e-mail address from the buyers or sellers you work with at the C2C site (Figure 7-35).

7

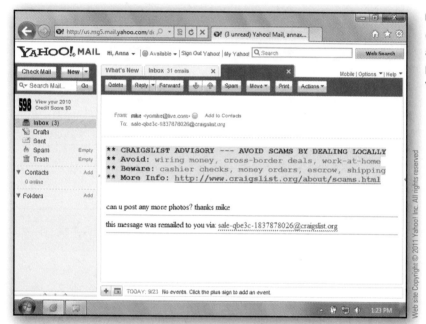

FIGURE 7-35

Communication between sellers and buyers is mediated through protected e-mail forwarding provided by the C2C host provider.

ONLINE PAYMENT

How can I pay for merchandise from online shopping and auction sites? The most popular ways to make online payments include submitting your credit card number directly to a merchant and using a third-party payment service such as PayPal.

Is it safe to use my credit card online? Online shoppers are justifiably worried that personal information and credit card numbers supplied in the course of an e-commerce transaction might be hijacked and used inappropriately. Many shoppers worry that hackers might use packet sniffers to intercept credit card numbers traveling over the Internet.

To protect your credit card from packet sniffers, you should engage in electronic transactions only over a secure connection. A **secure connection** encrypts the data transmitted between your computer and a Web site. Even if a hacker can capture the packets containing payment data, your encrypted credit card number is virtually useless for illicit purposes. Technologies that create secure connections include SSL/TLS and HTTPS.

TERMINOLOGY NOTE

Secure connections differ from secure Web sites. A secure connection encrypts the data transmitted between your computer and a Web site. A secure Web site, such as an online banking site, uses password security to prevent unauthorized access to pages on the site.

▶ What is SSL/TLS? SSL (Secure Sockets Layer) and its successor **TLS** (Transport Layer Security) are protocols that encrypt data traveling between a client computer and an HTTP server. These encryption protocols create a secure connection using a specially designated port. Secure connections commonly use port 443; port 80 is generally used for unsecured HTTP communications.

▶ What is HTTPS? HTTPS (Hypertext Transfer Protocol Secure) is a combination of HTTP and SSL/TLS that provides a secure connection for Web-based transactions. Web pages that provide a secure connection start with https: instead of http:.

▶ How do I know if a connection is secure? Your browser helps you identify when you are using a secure connection. Figure 7-36 explains.

FIGURE 7-36

Look for https or a padlock icon to ensure you have a secure connection.

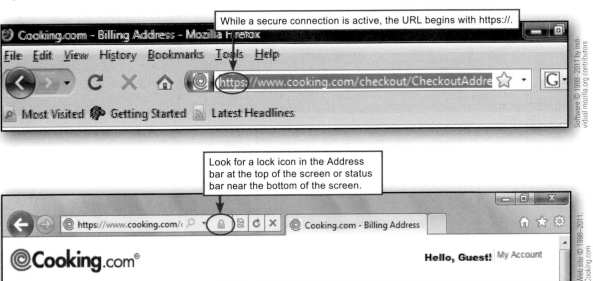

While a secure connection is active, the URL begins with https://.

Look for a lock icon in the Address bar at the top of the screen or status bar near the bottom of the screen.

▶ What if the connection is not secure? Pay attention to your browser's Address bar. It can warn you when connections might not be secure by displaying a warning or turning the Address bar yellow (suspicious site) or red (dangerous site). If you link to a site that generates a security warning, do not enter personal data. The following conditions can generate security warnings:

▶ Expired security certificate. HTTPS checks the Web server's security certificate. If the certificate is out of date, the site might not be legitimate.

▶ Suspected phishing site. Browsers check URLs against a list of sites that have been reported to be fakes.

▶ Partially secured. Some items on the page are not secured by HTTPS (Figure 7-37).

FIGURE 7-37

Google Chrome indicates that some items on this page are not secure. Each browser has a slightly different system of warnings. Check your browser's Help pages to become familiar with its warning system.

▶ **What is a person-to-person payment?** A **person-to-person payment** (sometimes called a P2P payment, an online payment, or a third-party payment) offers an alternative to credit cards. It can be used to pay for online auction items and to wire money over the Internet. The online service called PayPal, now owned by eBay, pioneered person-to-person payments. PayPal's model has since been copied by several other service providers.

▶ **How does a person-to-person payment work?** The process begins when you open an account at a person-to-person payment service. You receive a user ID and password that enable you to access your account to make purchases and deposit additional funds. Money can be sent to anyone who has an e-mail account, as shown in Figure 7-38.

FIGURE 7-38

PayPal and other online payment systems offer a method for transferring funds without revealing your credit card number to the payee.

1. To use a person-to-person payment service, simply log in to your account, enter the recipient's e-mail address, and indicate the payment amount.

2. The recipient immediately receives an e-mail notification of your payment.

3. The recipient connects to the payment site to pick up the money by transferring the funds to his or her checking or payment account, requesting a check, or sending the funds to someone else.

▶ **Are person-to-person payments safe?** The major advantage of person-to-person payments is that the payment service is the only entity that sees your credit card number—merchants, auction dealers, and other payment recipients never receive your credit card number and, therefore, can't misuse it or store it on an unsecured computer. Consumer advocates recommend using these services with caution and keeping your account balances low.

QuickCheck

1. Online auction sites such as eBay are examples of B2G e-commerce. True or false? [ ]

2. One factor in the e-commerce economic model is ad revenue based on [ ] rates, the number of times that site visitors click an ad to connect to the advertiser's Web site.

3. Most online shopping carts work because they use [ ] to store information about your activities at a Web site.

4. Product pages at e-commerce sites with URLs that contain a(n) [ ] symbol, cgi, php, or asp are most likely assembled by a server-side script from the information in a database.

5. Web sites that provide a secure connection have URLs that begin with https: instead of http:. True or false? [ ]

 CHECK ANSWERS

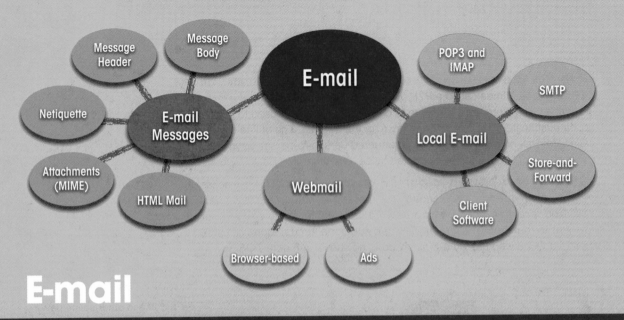

E-mail

THE INTERNET REALLY TOOK OFF when people discovered electronic mail. More than 250 billion e-mail messages speed over the Internet each day. This section of the chapter offers background information about how e-mail works—in particular, the difference between Webmail and client-based local e-mail.

E-MAIL OVERVIEW

▶ **Exactly what is e-mail?** The term *e-mail* can refer to a single message or to the entire system of computers and software that transmits, receives, and stores e-mail messages. An **e-mail message** is an electronic document transmitted over a computer network.

The computers and software that provide e-mail services form an **e-mail system**. At the heart of a typical e-mail system is an **e-mail server**—a computer that essentially acts as a central post office for a group of people. E-mail servers run special e-mail server software, which provides an electronic mailbox for each person, sorts incoming messages into these mailboxes, and routes outgoing mail over the Internet to other e-mail servers.

E-mail messages have a standard format that consists of a **message header** and the message body as shown in Figure 7-39.

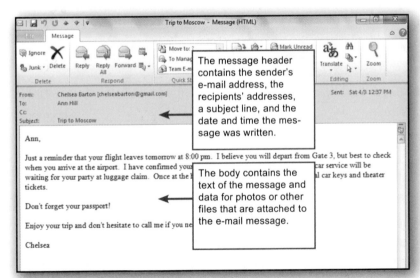

FIGURE 7-39

A basic message header contains the information for To, From, Subject, and Date fields. Additional fields can contain addresses for sending copies, priority levels, and tracking information.

▶ How do I get access to e-mail? To use an e-mail system, you need an Internet connection, an e-mail account, and software to compose e-mail messages.

▶ Internet connection. As you learned in earlier chapters, Internet connections are available from telephone, cable, satellite, and cellular service providers. Wi-Fi hotspots and local area networks at home, school, or work can also provide Internet access. Any of these connections work for e-mail, though a dial-up connection will respond slowly when sending or receiving messages with photos or other large files attached.

▶ E-mail account. Obtaining an **e-mail account** gets your electronic mailbox set up on an e-mail server. Your ISP might play the role of postmaster, set up your e-mail account, and provide you with e-mail software. You can also obtain an e-mail account from a Webmail service, such as Hotmail, Gmail, or Yahoo!.

▶ E-mail software. The software you use to send, receive, and manage messages is called **e-mail client software**. It is available for desktop, notebook, tablet, and handheld computers. E-mail software can be installed locally on a hard drive, as a portable app on a USB flash drive, or accessed from the Web through a browser. E-mail systems based on local client software are referred to as **local e-mail**. Systems that provide access to e-mail through a browser are called **Webmail**.

Whether you use local e-mail or Webmail, your e-mail account has a unique **e-mail address**. Like the address on a letter, an e-mail address provides the information necessary to route messages to a specified mailbox. An e-mail address consists of a user ID (also called a user name), followed by the @ sign and the name of the e-mail server that manages the user's electronic post office box. For example, the address ann_smith@mtc.com refers to the e-mail account for Ann Smith on the e-mail server named mtc.com.

▶ How do I select an e-mail address? In order for e-mail to be routed correctly, each e-mail address must be unique. Gmail can have only one AnnSmith user ID, which explains the existence of e-mail addresses such as AnnSmith256@gmail.com and ASmithTraverseCity@gmail.com. You can, however, use the same user ID for e-mail accounts on different servers. For example, AlexZ@msu.edu and AlexZ@hotmail.com are perfectly acceptable for a student who has e-mail accounts on a school server and at Hotmail.

E-mail addresses can sometimes tell you a bit about the person who holds the account. The first part of an e-mail address often corresponds to the account holder's name, nickname, or online persona. For example, the address cat_lover32@hotmail.com probably belongs to a person who likes cats. You should be aware of the image that e-mail addresses can project and select one that won't be embarrassing when you correspond with prospective employers.

The second part of an e-mail address is the e-mail server's domain name, which can provide information about the account holder's job or school. An account for jwatson@ibm.com probably belongs to an IBM employee. An account for rbutler@uga.edu probably belongs to a student at the University of Georgia. You can't control the server domain name, but you can establish several e-mail accounts so that your work server handles business mail and a generic provider, such as Gmail, handles your private mail.

LOCAL E-MAIL

▶ How does local e-mail work? When you use local e-mail, an Internet-based e-mail server stores your incoming messages until you launch your e-mail client and get your mail. Messages are then downloaded to a folder on a local storage device that serves as your e-mail Inbox. This telecommunications technique is sometimes referred to as **store-and-forward**.

Using your e-mail client, you can read your mail at your leisure. You can also compose new mail and reply to messages. This outgoing mail can be temporarily stored in an Outbox or it can be sent immediately.

The protocols **POP3** (Post Office Protocol version 3) or **IMAP** (Internet Message Access Protocol) are used to manage your incoming mail. POP3 deletes messages from the server after they are downloaded, whereas IMAP leaves messages on the server until you specifically delete them. **SMTP** (Simple Mail Transfer Protocol) handles outgoing mail.

Keep these protocols in mind when setting up local e-mail because the server you specify for outgoing mail might be different than the server for incoming mail (Figure 7-40).

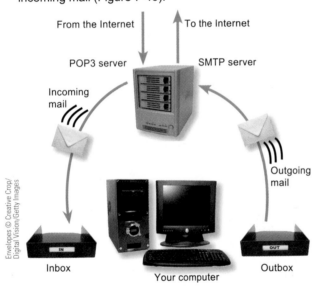

FIGURE 7-40

Outgoing mail can be stored in your Outbox until you connect to the Internet and send it to the SMTP server. Incoming mail can be stored on a POP3 server until it is downloaded to the Inbox on your hard disk.

▶ What are the advantages of local e-mail? Because local e-mail stores your Inbox and Outbox on your computer, you can compose and read mail offline. You are required to go online only to transfer outgoing mail from your Inbox to the e-mail server, and to receive incoming messages. On a slow dial-up connection or in situations where you are charged for dial-up service by the minute, local e-mail might be preferable to Webmail.

Local e-mail also works well with broadband always-on connections, such as DSL, cable Internet, or satellite Internet. When using these connections, you can remain online throughout the entire process of collecting, reading, and sending mail. By configuring your e-mail client to send messages immediately, messages can be sent as they are composed instead of remaining in your Outbox and being sent as a batch.

The major advantage of local e-mail is control. Once your messages are transferred to your computer's hard disk, you can control access to them. With this control, however, comes the responsibility for maintaining backups of your important e-mail messages.

▶ How do I set up local e-mail? To set up local e-mail, the first step is selecting a local e-mail client. Macs include a mail client called Mail. Microsoft Outlook is one of the most popular e-mail clients for Windows. Its pared-down cousin, Windows Live Mail, can be downloaded for free as part of the Windows Live Essentials suite. Thunderbird, a free open source e-mail client, is another popular alternative, and several other very serviceable e-mail clients are available as shareware.

After installing an e-mail client, you can configure it for the e-mail service you're using. Your e-mail provider can supply the information needed for this task. That information can include the following:

▶ Your e-mail user ID, which is the first part of your e-mail address (for example, in AlexHamilton@gsu.edu, the user ID is AlexHamilton)

▶ Your e-mail password, if required to access the e-mail server

▶ An address for the outgoing (SMTP) server, such as *mail.viserver.net* or *smtp.mailisus.com*

▶ An address for the incoming (POP3) server, such as *mail.gsu.edu* or *pop.mailserver.net*

▶ Port numbers for incoming and outgoing servers, which are usually Port 110 (incoming) and Port 25 or 587 (outgoing)

▶ Whether the servers require secure authentication

▶ The type of connection security used by the servers: STARTTLS or SSL/TLS

To configure a local e-mail client such as Thunderbird, look for an Account Settings option on the Tools menu. When using Microsoft Outlook 2010, click the File tab and then click the Add Account button (Figure 7-41).

FIGURE 7-41

When configuring local e-mail, the incoming and outgoing servers might require different settings. ▶ This figure in your interactive eBook guides you through the process of configuring a local e-mail account.

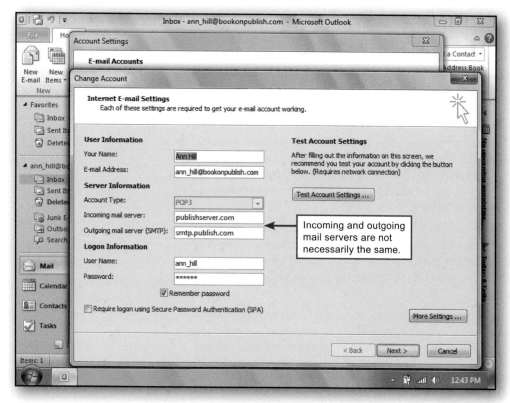

WEBMAIL

▶ **How does Webmail work?** Webmail is typically a free service accessed using a browser. Most Webmail services also can be accessed using a local e-mail client, such as Microsoft Outlook, if you prefer a local client's feature set and do not want to remain online while reading and composing messages.

In a classic Webmail configuration, your Inbox is stored on the Web; and because messages are sent immediately, an Outbox is not needed. When you want to read or send mail, use a browser to go to your e-mail provider's Web site and log in. The controls for reading, composing, and managing messages are all presented in the browser window. While reading and composing mail, you generally must remain online (Figure 7-42).

© Creative Crop/Digital Vision/Getty Images

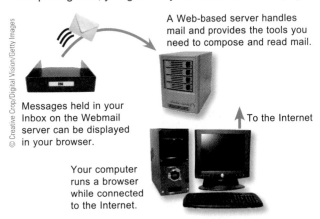

A Web-based server handles mail and provides the tools you need to compose and read mail.

Messages held in your Inbox on the Webmail server can be displayed in your browser.

To the Internet

Your computer runs a browser while connected to the Internet.

FIGURE 7-42

The key characteristic of Webmail is that your messages remain on the Web server, rather than being downloaded to your computer.

▶ **What are the pros and cons of Webmail?** Webmail is ideal for people who travel because accounts can be accessed from any computer connected to the Internet. Accessing e-mail from a public computer can be a security risk, however. If possible, reboot the computer before logging in to your e-mail account. Avoid entering sensitive information, such as your credit card number, in case your keystrokes are being monitored by malicious software lurking on the public computer. Be sure to log off when your session is finished. Log out of Windows and shut down the computer if you are allowed to do so.

Even when accessing Webmail from your home, security can be an issue. Unfortunately, Webmail services are the target of many malicious exploits, which can work their way into your computer through various security holes. When using Webmail, your computer must be protected by security software, and your computer will be more secure if you log out of your e-mail account when you are not using it.

Webmail can be accessed from mobile devices when your computer is not handy. If you opt to use mobile mail, read the options offered by your e-mail service provider and make sure you understand how to sync your mobile e-mail with the mail you view on your computer so that you don't miss an important message.

Free Webmail is supported by advertising, so expect to see advertisements. Today's sophisticated ad servers can search the content of an incoming message looking for keywords and then use them to display targeted ads in your e-mail window. For example, suppose you receive an e-mail message about a trip to Moscow. When viewing the message, you'll also be presented with ads about Moscow hotels, flights to Moscow, and similar promotions. Some Webmail services offer an ad-free option for a monthly fee.

How do I get a Webmail account? Getting a Webmail account is an automated process that you can complete online. Begin by using a browser to access a Webmail site such as *www.gmail.com, www.hotmail. com,* or *www.yahoomail.com.* Selecting the Sign Up or Register option produces an on-screen form. When you submit the completed form, your e-mail account is created and ready for immediate use (Figure 7-43).

FIGURE 7-43

You can use a browser to access your Webmail account. ▶ This figure in your interactive eBook takes you on a tour of Gmail.

A Webmail account is handled by services such as Gmail. You'll use a browser to read and compose messages.

Is Webmail the same as HTML mail? No. **HTML mail** is a term used for e-mail messages containing HTML tags that produce bold, italicized, and underlined text; fancy fonts; embedded graphics; and various font sizes. Most e-mail software offers a setting for choosing HTML or plain, unformatted ASCII text.

You should be aware that HTML formatted e-mail messages can distribute viruses and open security holes that leave your computer vulnerable to hackers. When working with HTML mail, make sure your antivirus software is checking incoming messages. Figure 7-44 illustrates an e-mail message written in HTML format.

FIGURE 7-44

An e-mail message in HTML format can include graphics in addition to a variety of fonts and font colors.

The text in HTML mail can be formatted using a selection of fonts, font sizes, colors, and other attributes.

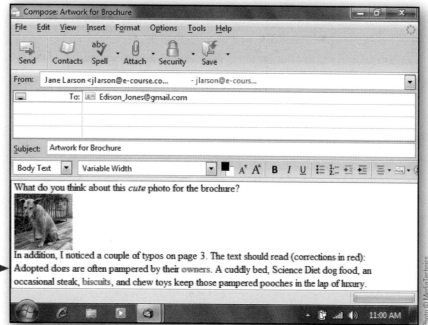

E-MAIL ATTACHMENTS

▶ What is an e-mail attachment? Originally, e-mail messages were stored in a plain and simple format called ASCII text. No fancy formatting was allowed—no variation in font type or color, no underlining or boldface, and, of course, no pictures or sounds. Although you cannot technically insert a digital photo or sound file into a plain ASCII e-mail message, you can send these kinds of files as e-mail attachments.

Any file that travels with an e-mail message is called an **e-mail attachment**. A conversion process called **MIME** (Multipurpose Internet Mail Extensions) provides a clever way of disguising digital photos, sounds, and other media as plain ASCII code that can travel over the Internet with text-based e-mail data. An electronic message incorporated in the e-mail header provides your e-mail software with information that allows it to reconstruct the attachment into its original form (Figure 7-45).

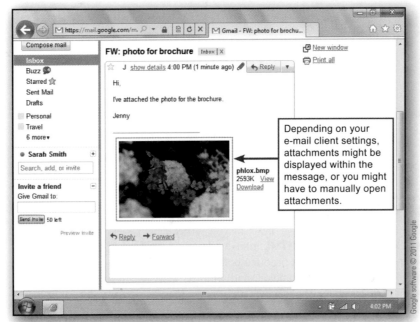

FIGURE 7-45

Attachments ride along with e-mail messages. ▶ For more tips about attachments, refer to this figure in your interactive eBook.

Depending on your e-mail client settings, attachments might be displayed within the message, or you might have to manually open attachments.

▶ What should I know about attachments? When working with attachments, keep the following points in mind:

▶ **Don't send huge attachments.** Try to limit the size of attachments to 50 KB or less for recipients who have dial-up connections. If necessary, use a compression program, such as WinZip, to shrink the attachment.

▶ **Explain all attachments.** To reassure recipients that an attachment is legitimate, include the file name of the attachment, what the attachment contains, and the name of the software you used to create it.

▶ **Don't open suspicious attachments.** If an attachment arrives from an unknown source, don't open it because it might contain a virus.

▶ **You can save attachments.** By right-clicking an attachment, you can save it as a separate file.

▶ **You might have to download a plug-in or player.** Attachments can contain text, music, video, and other types of files stored in a variety of file formats. To open some files, you might need to download a plug-in or player.

NETIQUETTE

▶ Is e-mail different from other types of communication?

In some respects, e-mail is similar to an old-fashioned letter because its message is conveyed without the facial expressions, voice inflections, and body gestures that accompany face-to-face conversations. When composing a message, it is important to carefully consider your audience and the message you want to convey.

By understanding netiquette, you can avoid some of the pitfalls and problems of e-mail communications. **Netiquette** is online jargon for Internet etiquette. It is a series of customs or guidelines for maintaining civilized and effective communications in online discussions and e-mail exchanges (Figure 7-46).

FIGURE 7-46

Principles of Netiquette

▶ **Put a meaningful title on the subject line.** The subject line of your message should clearly describe the contents of your e-mail message.

▶ **Use uppercase and lowercase letters.** An e-mail message that's typed in all uppercase means that you're shouting.

▶ **Check spelling.** Most e-mail software offers a Check Spelling command. Use it.

▶ **Be careful what you send.** E-mail is not private, nor is it secure. Treat your messages as though they are postcards that can be read by anyone. Remember that all laws governing copyright, slander, and discrimination apply to e-mail.

▶ **Be polite.** Avoid wording that could sound inflammatory or argumentative. If you would not say it face-to-face, don't say it in e-mail.

▶ **Be cautious when using sarcasm and humor.** The words in your e-mail arrive without facial expressions or voice intonations, so a sarcastic comment can easily be misinterpreted.

▶ **Notify recipients of viruses.** If you discover that your computer sent out infected attachments, use antivirus software to remove the virus, and then notify anyone to whom you recently sent mail.

▶ **Use smileys and text messaging shorthand cautiously. Smileys** are symbols such as :-) that represent emotions. They can help convey the intent behind your words, but use them only in casual messages.

▶ **Use the Bcc function for group mailings.** By placing e-mail addresses for secondary recipients in the Bcc box, the recipients of your message won't have to scroll through a long list of addresses before reaching the meat of your message.

▶ **Don't send replies to all recipients.** Use the Reply All command only when there is a very specific need for everyone listed in the To, Cc, and Bcc boxes to receive the message.

QuickCheck   SECTION D

1. The [_____] of an e-mail message contains recipient addresses, the subject line, and the file names of any e-mail attachments.

2. For most client-based e-mail systems, a(n) [_____] server handles outgoing mail, and a(n) [_____] server or an IMAP server handles incoming mail. (Hint: Use the acronyms.)

3. HTML mail is the same as Webmail. True or false? [_____]

4. Attachments to e-mail messages are encoded in [_____] format. (Hint: Use the acronym.)

5. The rules and suggestions regarding electronic communications such as e-mail are referred to as [_____].

 CHECK ANSWERS

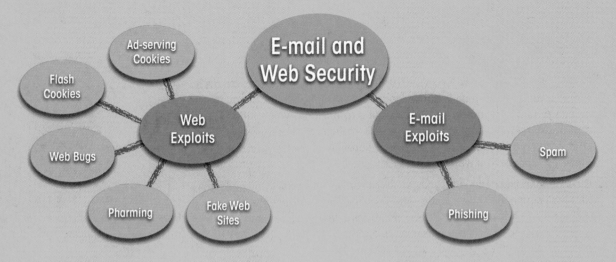

Web and E-mail Security

THE WEB AND E-MAIL abound with spam and scams engineered to monitor your online activities and collect confidential information, such as credit card numbers, passwords, and bank account numbers. You were introduced to spyware in an earlier chapter. Now you'll learn about specific spam and spyware exploits, and find out how to minimize the risk they pose to computer security and your privacy.

COOKIE EXPLOITS

▶ **Can cookies be a security risk?** Cookies have built-in safeguards designed to reduce their abuse, but marketers, hackers, and pranksters have discovered loopholes that twist cookies to serve the dark side. One of the most prevalent cookie exploits involves ad-serving cookies, and Flash cookies pose another potential threat.

▶ **What is an ad-serving cookie?** When you connect to a Web site, you expect it to store an innocuous cookie on your computer's hard disk. Some Web sites, however, feature banner ads supplied by third-party marketing firms. If you click the ad, this third party can surreptitiously create an ad-serving cookie and use it to track your activities at any site containing banner ads from that third party.

The marketing firms that distribute **ad-serving cookies** claim that the data in their cookies is used simply to select and display ads that might interest you, but privacy advocates worry that shopper profiles can be compiled, sold, and used for unauthorized purposes. Figure 7-47 on the next page illustrates how third parties use ad-serving cookies.

FIGURE 7-47

Ad-serving Cookies

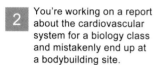

1 You purchase a birth-day gift for a friend at PlusSize.com.

You receive a routine shopping cart cookie from the PlusSize site.

You also receive an ad-serving cookie from UglyAds.com, a firm that runs ads on the PlusSize site.

2 You're working on a report about the cardiovascular system for a biology class and mistakenly end up at a bodybuilding site.

At the Workout site, UglyAds.com reads the ad-serving cookie and changes it to show you've also been to a bodybuilding site.

3 Many e-commerce sites you now visit display banner ads for weight-loss products.

At a third site, the UglyAds cookie is read again, but this time it interacts with the UglyAds server. Based on your previous browsing, it determines that you are a potential customer for weight-loss products.

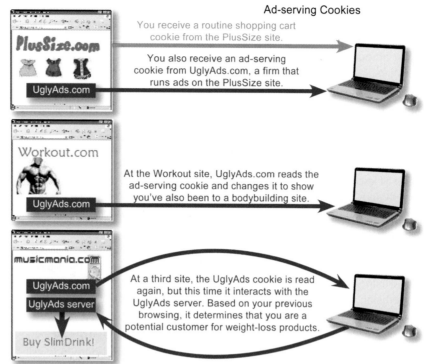

▶ **Can I turn off cookies to foil ad-serving exploits?** Most browsers include security settings that allow you to block first-party cookies or third-party cookies (Figure 7-48).

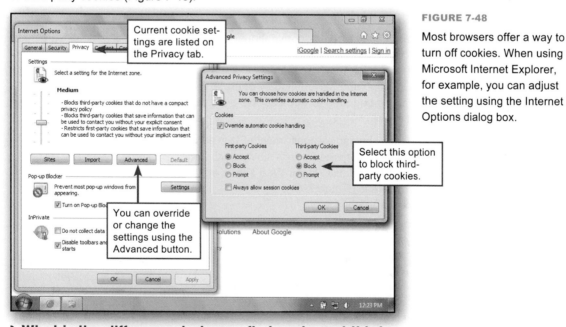

FIGURE 7-48

Most browsers offer a way to turn off cookies. When using Microsoft Internet Explorer, for example, you can adjust the setting using the Internet Options dialog box.

Current cookie settings are listed on the Privacy tab.

Select this option to block third-party cookies.

You can override or change the settings using the Advanced button.

▶ **What is the difference between first-party and third-party cookies?** A **first-party cookie** is created by the Web site that you are visiting. If you visit Amazon.com, for example, and it sets a cookie for your shopping cart, that is classified as a first-party cookie.

A **third-party cookie** is one that is set by an affiliated site. These sites are usually associated with marketing and advertising, so most third-party cookies are not desirable.

▶ Which cookies should I disable? If you disable all cookies, you might not be able to make online purchases, participate in online training classes, use Webmail, or register for premium services at search engine sites. Rather than block all cookies, blocking third-party cookies eliminates most ad cookies without disabling cookies required for legitimate Web activities.

You can also block cookies from specific sites. For example, if you'd rather not have your favorite search engine compile and store your searches, you can block its cookies.

▶ Should I delete cookies? Some privacy advocates suggest deleting cookies periodically, rather than blocking them. By deleting cookies, you can still interact with online shopping carts and take part in other activities that require cookies, but deleted third-party cookies won't be able to communicate with their handlers. The downside of deleting cookies is it might disrupt your attempts to opt out of various cookie schemes.

An opt-out function allows you to refuse to participate in an activity or promotion. Similar to the National Do Not Call Registry, several third-party advertising companies, such as DoubleClick, ZEDO, and the Network Advertising Initiative (NAI), now provide users with an opt-out mechanism to disallow ad-serving cookies.

Opting out creates an opt-out cookie. If you delete all the cookies on your computer, the opt-out cookie will also be deleted and third-party ads will again start appearing when you use your browser.

▶ What is a Flash cookie? A **Flash cookie**, also called a local shared object, is the Flash equivalent of a conventional Web cookie. Flash cookies are set and used by Adobe's Flash Player, which is installed on practically every computer to run movies, videos, and games.

Because so many computer users delete or block conventional cookies, some marketers now use Flash cookies as an alternative way to track and target consumers. In the context of running Flash animations, Flash cookies can collect and store personal data, and surreptitiously operate your computer's built-in camera. It is not a bad idea to put a sticker over your computer's camera when it is not in use.

▶ Can I avoid Flash cookies? You can manually delete Flash cookies from your computer after locating the #Shared Objects file in which they are stored. You can also visit the Adobe Flash Player Web site to adjust your computer's settings for Flash cookies (Figure 7-49).

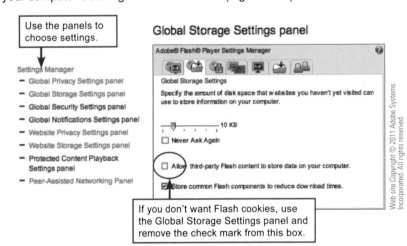

FIGURE 7-49

To access settings for Flash cookies, use your browser to locate the Adobe Flash Player Settings Manager Web page.

What is a Web bug? A **Web bug** or clear GIF is a 1x1 pixel graphic embedded in a Web page or e-mail message. It is almost invisible due to its size, and is designed to track who's reading the Web page or e-mail message. Web bugs on a Web page can generate third-party ad-serving cookies.

Unlike cookies that are generated when you click a banner ad, you don't have to click anything to receive a third-party cookie generated by a Web bug. When you view a Web bug infested page, an HTTP set-cookie request automatically goes to a third-party server, which can be the site of a marketer or hacker. The site can set a cookie on your computer for later retrieval, or log the IP address of your computer.

Is there any way to avoid Web bugs? A drastic solution is to turn off all the graphics displayed by your browser, but that step makes the Web much less interesting. A better solution is to download a Web bug detector that works with your browser to test graphics on every Web page you visit and flag clear GIF images that might be used to set third-party cookies. Clear GIFs are also used legitimately for alignment purposes on Web pages, however, so not all clear GIFs are malware. Undesirable clear GIFs can be eliminated by Web bug detectors included in antispyware.

Antispyware is a type of security software designed to identify and neutralize Web bugs, ad-serving cookies, and other spyware. Antispyware such as Spy Sweeper, Ad-Aware, Spybot Search & Destroy, SpywareBlaster, and Microsoft Security Essentials can offer some degree of protection against browser parasites and other Web-based nuisances. Avoid responding to or downloading spyware from pop-up ads, however. Those ads often lead to infected software.

Can I surf the Internet anonymously? In addition to tracking cookies, Web sites can track IP addresses of computers that connect to their sites. IP addresses can sometimes be traced back to individuals, especially those who have fixed IP addresses or always-on connections that retain the same IP address for long periods of time.

Individuals who prefer not to leave a trail of their Internet activities surf through an **anonymous proxy service**, which uses an intermediary, or proxy, server to relay Web page requests after masking the originating IP address (Figure 7-50).

Proxy service is similar to a VPN in some respects because they both encrypt data being sent over the Internet. An anonymous proxy service, however, is limited to use with your browser, whereas a VPN can be used with any network application. If you use a VPN, you don't need a proxy service.

A tradeoff to the anonymity offered by anonymous proxies is that they tend not to operate at the same speed as your regular browser. In addition, some Web sites and discussion groups block access from proxy servers because they have been used to spam the site or flood it with traffic. Also, anonymous proxies can be compromised by malicious third parties or monitored under court order, so anonymity is never assured.

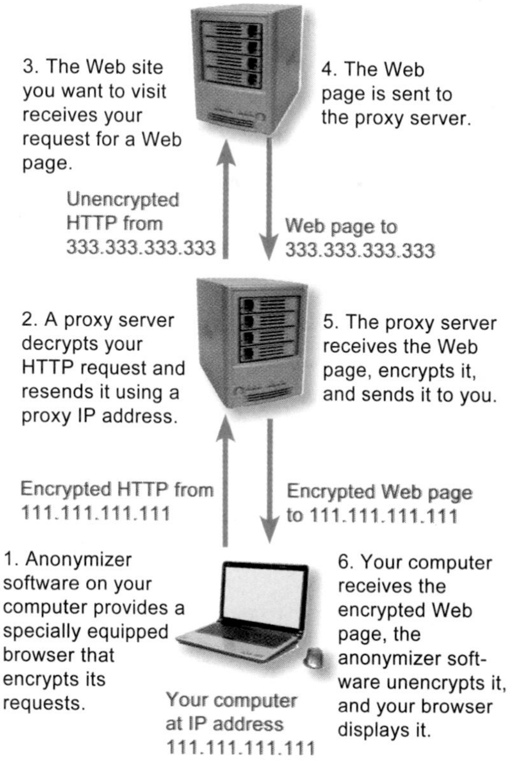

3. The Web site you want to visit receives your request for a Web page.

4. The Web page is sent to the proxy server.

Unencrypted HTTP from 333.333.333.333

Web page to 333.333.333.333

2. A proxy server decrypts your HTTP request and resends it using a proxy IP address.

5. The proxy server receives the Web page, encrypts it, and sends it to you.

Encrypted HTTP from 111.111.111.111

Encrypted Web page to 111.111.111.111

1. Anonymizer software on your computer provides a specially equipped browser that encrypts its requests.

Your computer at IP address 111.111.111.111

6. Your computer receives the encrypted Web page, the anonymizer software unencrypts it, and your browser displays it.

FIGURE 7-50

An anonymous proxy server relays your Web page requests after stripping off your IP address. ▶ To see this process in action, activate this figure in your interactive eBook.

SPAM

▶ What is spam? One of e-mail's main disadvantages is **spam**—unwanted electronic junk mail about medical products, low-cost loans, and fake software upgrades that arrives in your online mailbox. Today's proliferation of spam is generated by marketing firms that harvest e-mail addresses from mailing lists, membership applications, and Web sites.

▶ Is spam dangerous? In the past, spam flooding your Inbox with unsolicited and often pornographic messages was merely an annoyance. These days, however, spam has turned into another major hacking tool for cybercriminals. Spam sometimes contains Web bugs, viruses, worms, or keyloggers that can wreak havoc on your computer or steal personal information such as passwords. Spam can also be used for phishing scams, which are described later in this section.

▶ Can spam be blocked before it gets to my mailbox? With millions of copies of some spam floating around the Internet, it would seem possible to identify and delete it before individuals have to contend with it. Most ISPs make an effort to block spam by blacklisting known spam servers. However, this method often results in blocking e-mail from legitimate ISPs that just happen to have been the source for dubious e-mail traffic.

▶ What can I do about spam? First, you can be aware of spam and delete it without responding to it. You can also install and configure spam filters. A **spam filter** is a type of utility software that captures unsolicited e-mail messages before they reach your Inbox. It works by checking the text of e-mail headers and messages against a series of rules.

For example, a rule such as *The message header contains viagra, v1agra, v.a.gra, or vi@gra* would help identify spam that's trying to hawk cheap pharmaceuticals.

Spam filters periodically download updated rules to catch the latest spams. Some spam filters also allow consumers to create their own rules to target spam that gets through the standard filters (Figure 7-51).

FIGURE 7-51

Spam filters include standard rules that block common spams, but you can create your own rules for spam that standard filters miss. ▶ Activate this figure in your interactive eBook to find out how to create customized spam filters.

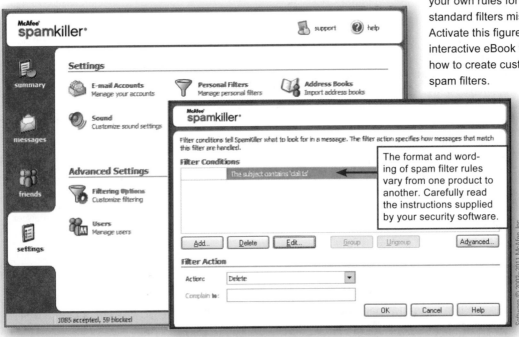

The format and wording of spam filter rules vary from one product to another. Carefully read the instructions supplied by your security software.

Software © 2003–2011 McAfee, Inc.

Spam filters are available as standalone software, but often are included in e-mail clients and security suites. Spam filters tend to slow down the process of downloading mail and they sometimes trash legitimate mail. Periodically, you should look in the junk e-mail folder used by your spam filters to retrieve any mail that's not junk.

In addition to using spam filters, you can avoid being a spam victim by following guidelines in Figure 7-52.

FIGURE 7-52

Guidelines for Avoiding Spam

▶ Never reply to spam when you receive it.

▶ Don't click links in e-mail messages, even if it's an opt-out link.

▶ Give your e-mail address only to people from whom you want to receive e-mail. Be wary of providing your e-mail address at Web sites, entering it on application forms, or posting it in public places such as online discussion groups.

▶ Use a disposable e-mail address when you register for online sites. You can use this disposable address to get your confirmation number for online purchases you've made, but don't use it for regular e-mail correspondence.

▶ If your e-mail provider offers a way to report spam, use it.

▶ When spam gets out of hand, consider changing your e-mail account so that you have a different e-mail address.

PHISHING

▶ **What is phishing?** Phishing is an e-mail based scam that's designed to persuade you to reveal confidential information such as your bank account number or Social Security number. Unlike pharming attacks (which you'll read about in a moment), phishing scams require that you reply to an e-mail message or click an embedded Web site link for the scam to unfold.

If you've used e-mail for any length of time, you've probably encountered the granddaddy of all phishing scams: a letter from a Nigerian political refugee who wants to move a large sum of money to a bank in your country and needs a bank account (yours!) to stash it for a few days. Of course you'll get a percentage for your trouble. Don't even think about it. According to the FBI, several gullible individuals have been lured abroad where they've been kidnapped and even killed.

More innocuous but potentially damaging spam scams start with an e-mail message that appears to come from a legitimate organization such as a bank, an online payment service, an online store, or even your ISP. The message directs you to click a link to verify confidential data. The link connects you to a bogus site cleverly disguised to look very much like a legitimate Web site. There you are urged to enter your bank account number, PIN, password, credit card number, or other data.

> **TERMINOLOGY NOTE**
>
> Fake sites, URLs, and even e-mail addresses are often referred to as spoofed, and the process of misdirection is called spoofing.

▶ **How do I avoid phishing scams?** If you don't want to become a phishing victim, be suspicious of e-mail messages that supposedly come from banks, ISPs, online payment services, operating system publishers, and online merchants. Even if the messages appear to be legitimate, do not click links in the messages, but instead go to the Web site using your browser and link to your account as you normally would. If your account needs updating, you should see instructions about how to proceed.

FAKE SITES

▶ **What is a fake site?** A fake, or fraudulent, Web site looks legitimate, but has been created by a third party to be a very clever replica of a legitimate Web site, such as eBay or even the White House.

Many fake Web sites are bogus storefronts designed exclusively for collecting credit card numbers from unwary shoppers. These sites might have the trappings of a real site. They might even offer a secure connection for transmitting your credit card number. When your data is received, however, it is stored in a database that belongs to a hacker, who can use the data for unauthorized transactions.

Some fake sites are not fake storefronts; rather, they are official-sounding sites, such as government agencies, that actually contain sexually explicit material. Other bogus sites simply present totally fabricated information or stories designed to fool the user. Fake sites are a key part of illegitimate pharming schemes.

▶ **What is pharming? Pharming** is an exploit that redirects users to fake sites by poisoning a domain name server with a false IP address. Pharming and phishing are similar in many respects; both take advantage of fake sites. Phishing links, however, often lead to fake sites with URLs that are just slightly different from those of legitimate sites. Hackers depend on victims not paying close attention to the discrepancy when they click links.

Pharming is more sophisticated than phishing because the link appears to be for a legitimate URL. Even a close examination of the URL will not reveal anything suspicious because the URL's IP address has been changed at the domain name server.

▶ **How can I recognize a pharming attack?** Pharming is more surreptitious and tougher to detect than most other hacker schemes. Antipharming tools are emerging in response to growing security threats posed by fake sites. Mainstream browsers now include routines that compare IP addresses to a list of known fake sites and warn you of suspicious sites. Make sure your antipharming and antiphishing filters are activated (Figure 7-53).

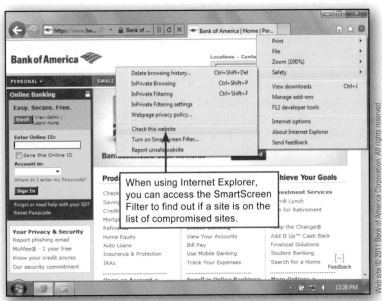

FIGURE 7-53

Most browsers include features that can help you avoid pharming and phishing attacks. Find out which features are available and use them.

▶ What's the best defense against all the bad stuff on the Web and in e-mail? First, understand that there is no perfect defense. Then understand that you should do all you can to safeguard your computer and your privacy. Use the list in Figure 7-54 as a starting point.

▶ Use antispyware utilities to clean up any spyware that might have infiltrated your computer.

▶ Run antispyware continuously just as you do antivirus software.

▶ Set your browser to reject third-party cookies.

▶ Register to reject Flash cookies.

▶ Make sure your browser's antispoofing tools are activated; or install a third-party antispoofing tool to help you identify fake Web sites.

▶ Set up a disposable e-mail address at a site such as Hotmail or Gmail and use it when you don't want to disclose your primary e-mail address.

▶ Do not click links in untrusted e-mail or pop-up ads, and never respond to e-mail offers, especially those that seem too good to be true.

FIGURE 7-54

Guidelines for Secure and Private Web Surfing

7

QuickCheck

SECTION E

1. A Web [＿＿＿＿＿＿] embedded in an e-mail message or a Web page can be activated when you view an infested page.

2. If you don't want your IP address tracked as you surf the Web, you can use an anonymous [＿＿＿＿＿＿] service.

3. A spam [＿＿＿＿＿＿] can be configured with rules that block messages containing text such as *viagra* or *v1@gra*.

4. A(n) [＿＿＿＿＿＿] exploit redirects users to fake sites by poisoning a Domain Name Server with a false IP address.

5. The Adobe site provides a Settings Manager that can be used to control [＿＿＿＿＿＿] cookies and prevent your computer's camera from being activated without your knowledge.

▶ CHECK ANSWERS

Issue: Who's Reading Your E-mail?

WHEN YOU DROP an envelope into the corner mailbox, you probably expect it to arrive at its destination unopened, with its contents kept safe from prying eyes.

When you make a phone call, you might assume that your conversation will proceed unmonitored by wiretaps or other listening devices. Can you also expect an e-mail message to be read only by the person to whom it is addressed?

Your e-mail messages can go public in any number of ways. The recipient of your e-mail can forward it to one or more people—people you never intended for it to reach. Your e-mail messages could pop up on a technician's screen in the course of system maintenance, updates, or repairs.

Employers routinely monitor employee e-mail. Government agencies tasked with maintaining national security monitor all types of electronic communications. Schools and organizations sometimes monitor messages that flow over their e-mail systems. You might wonder if such open access to your e-mail is legal. The answer in most cases is yes.

In the United States, the Electronic Communications Privacy Act of 2000 prohibits the use of intercepted e-mail as evidence unless a judge approves a search warrant. That doesn't mean the government isn't reading your mail.

Heightened security concerns after the September 11, 2001 terrorist attacks resulted in a clear pattern of legislation characterized by the American Civil Liberties Union (ACLU) as allowing the federal government to "conduct dragnet surveillance of Americans' international telephone calls and e-mails en masse, without a warrant, without suspicion of any kind, and with only very limited judicial oversight."

According to the American Management Association, 43% of U.S. businesses monitor employee e-mail. Employees generally have not been successful in defending their rights to e-mail privacy because courts have ruled that an employee's right to privacy does not outweigh a company's rights and interests.

You should use your e-mail account with the expectation that some of your mail will be read by someone other than the intended recipient.

Courts seem to agree that because a company owns and maintains its e-mail system, it has the right to monitor the messages carried by the system.

Like employees of a business, students who use a school's e-mail system cannot be assured of e-mail privacy. When a Caltech student was accused of sexually harassing a female student by sending lewd e-mail to her and her boyfriend, investigators retrieved all the student's e-mail from the archives of the e-mail server. The student was expelled from the university even though he claimed that the e-mail had been spoofed to make it look as though he had sent it, when it had actually been sent by someone else.

Why would an employer want to know the contents of employee e-mail? Why would a school be concerned with the correspondence of its students? It is probably true that some organizations simply snoop on the off chance that important information might be discovered.

Most organizations, however, have legitimate reasons for monitoring e-mail. An organization that owns an e-mail system can be held responsible for the consequences of actions related to the contents of e-mail messages on that system. For example, a school has a responsibility to protect students from harassment. If it fails to do so, it can be sued along with the author of the offending e-mail message.

You should use your e-mail account with the expectation that some of your mail will be read by someone other than the intended recipient. Think of your e-mail as a postcard, rather than a letter, and save your controversial comments for face-to-face conversations.

Try It! We all use e-mail. Should we be nervous about sending messages such as: "When we meet at the airport, we'll have some time to kill before our flight, so you can tell me your explosive news then." Explore the issue to find out just how cautious you need to be.

1 Many schools and businesses have e-mail privacy policies, which explain the conditions under which you can and cannot expect your e-mail to remain private. Locate your school's e-mail privacy policy. Was it easy to find and what does it say?

2 Webmail services, such as Gmail and Yahoo! Mail, display ads that are related to the content of each e-mail message. For example, if you are e-mailing a friend about spring break in Cancun, your Webmail service might display ads for hotels and other travel deals. To explore how e-mail ad servers work, send a few e-mail messages to yourself that include notable keywords, such as *Cancun*, *motorcycle*, *Chevy Volt*, *diabetes*, or *CIA*. What kinds of ads appear?

3 With increasing frequency, government agencies, such as the U.S. Department of Justice (DOJ), have tried to force e-mail service providers to hand over e-mail messages. The legal debate about e-mail privacy hinges on the Fourth Amendment to the U.S. Constitution. Exactly what does the Fourth Amendment say and how does it relate to the government reading your e-mail?

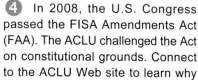

Rich Koele/Shutterstock.com

4 In 2008, the U.S. Congress passed the FISA Amendments Act (FAA). The ACLU challenged the Act on constitutional grounds. Connect to the ACLU Web site to learn why the ACLU believes that the FAA is unconstitutional. What is the name of the lawsuit challenging the FAA and what is the status of that suit?

5 Google, Yahoo!, and other e-mail service providers receive requests from government agencies, such as the U.S. Department of Justice, to hand over e-mail messages. Some requests are based on a search warrant; others are not. Most e-mail service providers have privacy policies that describe the circumstances under which e-mail messages would be handed over. Find the policy for your e-mail service. How will your service provider respond to government requests to hand over your messages?

What Do You Think?

ISSUE

1. Do you think most people believe that their e-mail is private?

2. Do you agree with Caltech's decision to expel the student who was accused of sending harassing e-mail to another student?

3. Should the laws be changed to make it illegal for employers to monitor e-mail without court approval?

4. Would you have different privacy expectations regarding an e-mail account at your place of work as opposed to an account you purchase from an e-mail service provider?

Information Tools: Your Own Words

PLAGIARISM. Buying a term paper from a company or an individual and turning it in as your own. Copying words directly from someone else's print or online work. Paraphrasing without attribution. That's plagiarism.

COMMON KNOWLEDGE. To avoid plagiarism in your written work, you should include citations for any statements that are not common knowledge. Common knowledge includes ideas and facts that can be found in many places and are known by many people. Material that is based on the work, ideas, or statements of other people is not common knowledge and needs a citation for its source. Include a citation for:

▶ Any statement that refers to a research study or is based on its conclusions

▶ Any statement or graph that includes statistics

▶ Any word-for-word spoken or written quotations

▶ Any statement that restates or summarizes another person's original ideas

PARAPHRASING. Citations are required even when you paraphrase. Changing the words of an original source is not sufficient. You must cite the source whenever you borrow ideas as well as words.

Acceptable paraphrasing should not be too close to the original wording, yet you must be careful not to change the idea behind the original wording. Your paraphrase also requires a citation to the original source. Suppose you find this passage on Carla Charmer's blog that contains material you'd like to include in a mid-term report:

> A Michigan man who accessed his wife's e-mail account while she was allegedly carrying on an affair faces up to five years in prison. He is being prosecuted for violating a state law typically used against hackers and identity thieves. It is shocking that a person could be charged with a felony for reading his spouse's e-mail.

There are several ways in which you can use this material. Some ways are more ethical than others.

A Michigan man faces five years in prison on charges that he violated a state law by reading his wife's e-mail without permission.	Common knowledge. Okay to use without a citation to the original source.
It is shocking that a person could be charged with a felony for reading his wife's e-mail. A Michigan man who read his wife's e-mail while she was supposedly having an affair faces up to five years in prison for violating a state law usually used for identity thieves and hackers.	This paraphrase is too close to the original and should include a citation.
It came as quite a shock that a Michigan man could be charged with a felony and face up to five years in the slammer simply for reading his wife's e-mail while she was supposedly having an affair with another man.	This paraphrase is unique and maintains the basic idea of the original, but still requires a citation.
Blogger Carla Charmer found it "shocking that a person could be charged with a felony for reading his spouse's e-mail."	This use of a direct quotation includes an in-context citation, but could also use a more complete citation in MLA, APA, or Chicago style.

Try It! Explore the differences between original and plagiarized material by answering the following questions.

1 Which of these statements would not need a citation because it is common knowledge?

a. While it is fairly easy to build a slow crawler that downloads one or a few pages per second for a short period of time, building a high-performance system that can download hundreds of millions of pages over several weeks presents a number of challenges in system design, I/O and network efficiency, and robustness and manageability.

b. Search engines, such as Google, include software called a Web crawler that visits Web sites and indexes the material it finds there. This material can later be accessed by entering keywords at a search engine site.

c. Experimental results show that a distributed Web crawler can more effectively visit Web pages than a single Web crawler.

2 Which of these statements would need a citation because they refer to statements based on statistics?

a. The main problem search engines have to deal with is the size and rate of change of the Web, with no search engine indexing more than one-third of the publicly available Web.

b. Back in 2004, the average working day consisted of dealing with 46 phone calls, 15 internal memos, 19 items of snail mail, and 22 e-mails.

c. Search engines deal with a vast amount of material. The process of collecting and organizing that material becomes ever greater as the Web expands.

3 Which of these statements should have citations because they refer to a research study or its conclusions?

a. We ran a crawl of over 100 million Web pages on about 5 million hosts. The crawl was performed over a period of 18 days; however, the crawler was not continuously in operation during this time. Of the 138 million pages cataloged, more than 400,000 produced a 403 error that access was forbidden.

b. Given the current size of the Web, even large search engines cover only a portion of the publicly available part. A report from the Websonite Group indicates that large-scale search engines index no more than 40% to 70% of the indexable Web.

c. You can study the Web all you want, but there will still be more to learn.

> "Can ordinary Americans like you and me sue the government for illegally spying on them? When it comes to the NSA surveillance program, the government itself says the answer is no. After all, since it's a secret program, you don't really know if you're being spied on. And if you don't know you're being spied on, you have no standing to sue."

4 Use a search engine to find the above quotation, then do the following:

a. Create an MLA citation for the original source.

b. Create an acceptable paraphrase for the quotation using an in-context citation.

c. Write at least two sentences on the same topic that would be common knowledge and not need a citation.

5 Plagiarism scanning services, such as Turnitin and Viper, make it easy for instructors to check the originality of your work. Before turning in a paper, you can make sure you've cited all relevant sources by running your document through the student version of Turnitin or a free plagiarism scanner such as Viper, Grammarly, Dustball, or Dupli Checker. Copy a page of text from one of your original documents and submit it to a plagiarism checker, then do the same for a page that you copy out of Wikipedia. What are the results?

INFOWEBLINKS

You can check the **NP2013 Chapter 7** InfoWebLink for updates to these activities.

W CLICK TO CONNECT
www.infoweblinks.com/np2013/ch07

Technology in Context: Fashion Industry

MIT Media Lab/Photo by Lynn B

FASHION IS BIG BUSINESS. Worldwide, clothing sales generate more than $340 billion in revenue. Shoes, accessories, and jewelry bump the industry's revenue even higher. Competition is tough as designers, manufacturers, and retailers compete for customer dollars.

In the fashion industry, trends change quickly. As the saying goes, "Today's style is tomorrow's markdown." Fashion industry players look for every competitive advantage. It is no surprise that technology plays a major role in this glitzy industry.

Fashion begins with designers, such as Miuccia Prada, John Galliano, and Marc Jacobs. Their runway extravaganzas set off fashion trends that eventually work their way to retail stores. Fashion runways went high-tech in 1999 when lingerie manufacturer Victoria's Secret produced a Webcast watched by over 1 million viewers. Bravo television's *Project Runway* show has been one of the top iPod downloads. Fashion podcasts and blogs abound on the Web, as do fashion sites packed with news about the latest trends.

Although runway fashions are often conceived with a sketch and stitched by hand, designs are adapted for the ready-to-wear market by using computer-assisted design (CAD) tools, such as pattern-making software.

Garments are constructed by sewing together sections of fabric that form arms, fronts, backs, collars, and so forth. The set of templates used to cut fabric sections is called a pattern. Pattern-making is a tricky 3-D challenge because flat pieces of fabric eventually become garments shaped to conform to curved body contours. Pattern-making software helps designers visualize how flat pieces fit together and drape when sewn. Once a master pattern is complete, pattern-making software automatically generates a set of patterns for each garment size.

Fashion requires fabric, and computers play a major role in fabric design and manufacturing. Computer

software, such as ArahWeave, lets fabric designers experiment with colors, yarns, and weaves while viewing detailed, realistic on-screen samples. Fabric designs can be stored in a variety of formats for weaving machines. A few older mechanical weaving machines are controlled by punched cards. Digital fabric designs can be transferred to punched cards with a dedicated card punch machine.

Most of today's weaving mills use computerized machinery that directly accepts digital input to control threads and patterns. Networks tie looms to CAD stations and to the Internet. Fabric designs can be stored in XML format, transmitted to a fabric manufacturer over the Internet, and used directly by computerized weaving machines.

Clothing production, warehousing, and shipping are also highly automated. Benetton's high-tech facility at Castrette, Italy can produce over 110 million gar-

©Lifetime Television/Courtesy Everett Co/Everett Collection

ments per year. Its automated distribution center uses a workforce of only 24 people to handle 40,000 boxes of merchandise daily. RFID tags—sometimes called smart labels—can be attached to individual garments or to packing boxes as an important tool for controlling inventory.

RFID technology uses an inexpensive, tiny computer chip with a built-in antenna and the capacity to store between 64 and 128 bits of data about a garment—its SKU number, size, model, dye lot, manufacturing date, and so on. Tags can be attached to a garment or its label. An RFID reader that can retrieve data from tags is used to track merchandise from the manufacturing plant through the distribution chain to the retailer.

RFID tags are becoming popular for all types of merchandise. Businesses that use them can save time and money. For example, RFID tags can reduce the time it takes to do a physical inventory by a factor of 10. Privacy advocates, however, are worried because these tags remain active even after you bring your merchandise home. Could a thief circle your house with an RFID scanner to find out what's inside? Could a stalker follow your movements by tracking the RFID tag embedded in your sweater?

Next time you buy a garment, check to see if an RFID tag is attached. It would normally be sewn into a seam and may carry a warning "Remove before wearing."

In response to competition from offshore companies, U.S. clothing manufacturers pioneered Quick Response (QR)—a business model for compressing supply chains to quickly obtain raw materials, such as fabric, yarn, buttons, and zippers. Sophisticated software tools, such as the Sourcing Simulator, simplify QR planning.

Online shopping has become routine, but one drawback of catalog and online ordering is the cost associated with restocking returned merchandise. Can an online customer find out how a garment will fit and look before ordering it? Can in-store customers find their correct size without trying multiple sizes?

In 1998, Lands' End introduced My Virtual Model technology that allows shoppers to create a custom model of themselves by choosing from a variety of hair colors and styles, face shapes, and body types. The model can "try on" clothes to show online customers how they would look when wearing the garments.

More recently, a company called Unique Solutions is setting up full-body scanners in malls all over the country. According to the company's Web site, the scanning process takes about 15 seconds and produces 200,000 data points that can be used to match your body's contours with actual clothing sizes for different brands.

No discussion of fashion and computers would be complete without highlighting wearable technology. MIT's Media Lab has been a hotbed of wearable technology development. A recent student project uses a Webcam, a battery-powered projector, and an Internet-enabled mobile phone, and allows wearers to use hand gestures in 3-D space to conjure up information from the phone and project it on any surface.

Some wearables have even emerged from the laboratory and onto store shelves.

Originally popular with Secret Service agents, the SCOTTEVEST is a jacket with pockets for cell phone, MP3 player, iPad, and built-in wiring to connect these devices into a personal area network (PAN). Available as a jacket or vest and in men's and women's sizes, the jacket and vest can now be purchased by civilians.

With a growing emphasis on the use of technology in fashion design and manufacturing, fashion degree programs at colleges and technical schools have added courses such as computer-aided fashion design, computer-based pattern drafting, pattern grading and computer-aided drafting, and wearable computers.

7

New Perspectives Labs

To access the New Perspectives Labs for Chapter 7, open the NP2013 interactive eBook and then click the icon next to the lab title.

▶ BROWSER SECURITY & PRIVACY

IN THIS LAB YOU'LL LEARN:

- How to adjust the security settings for Internet Explorer's security zones
- How your browser can help you avoid phishing scams
- Why Web-based images and active content can pose a security risk
- The safest way to close pop-up ads and the most effective way to block them
- How to adjust security settings for active content
- How to delete or block Flash cookies
- How to secure the camera and microphone on your computer
- How to allow or prevent Web sites from determining your location

LAB ASSIGNMENTS

1. Perform each lab step as directed, and answer all the lab QuickCheck questions.
2. Identify which browser you usually use and look at its security settings. Does your browser allow you to select an overall security level, such as low, medium, or high?
3. Look at your browser's security settings and record the current settings for its phishing filter, pop-up blocker, ActiveX controls, JavaScript, and Java. Would you make any changes to these settings?
4. Connect to the Flash Player Settings Manager and count the number of Flash cookies you have. Next, record the security settings for your computer's camera and microphone.

▶ WORKING WITH COOKIES

IN THIS LAB YOU'LL LEARN:

- How Web servers use cookies
- Why cookies might pose a threat to your privacy
- How to locate, view, block, and delete cookies
- How to limit the space allocated to cookies created by Internet Explorer
- What a session cookie is
- How to set cookie prompts and use the cookie prompt dialog box
- How to take advantage of P3P and Compact Privacy Policies
- The differences between first-party and third-party cookies

LAB ASSIGNMENTS

1. Perform each lab step as directed, and answer all the lab QuickCheck questions.
2. Use your browser to look at the cookies on your computer. Indicate how many cookies are currently stored. Examine the contents of one cookie, and indicate whether you think it poses a threat to your privacy.
3. Indicate the name and version of the browser you generally use. Next, look at your browser's cookie settings. Describe how you would adjust these settings to produce a level of privacy protection that is right for your needs.
4. Adjust your browser settings so that you are prompted whenever a Web server attempts to send a cookie to your computer. Go to your favorite Web sites and watch for third-party cookies. When you receive a message from a third-party Web site, record the name of the third-party site and the contents of the cookie it is attempting to send. Finally, indicate whether you would accept such a cookie.

▶ WORKING WITH HTML

IN THIS LAB YOU'LL LEARN:

- How to use a text editor such as Notepad to create a basic HTML document
- Which HTML tags to use to format text
- How to use HTML for numbered and bulleted lists
- How to add graphics to your Web pages
- How to add hyperlinks to a Web page
- Methods for testing Web pages locally
- How to post your Web page

LAB ASSIGNMENTS

1. Perform each lab step as directed, and answer all the lab QuickCheck questions.
2. Use a text editor such as Notepad to create a Web page that contains your name as the title and at least two paragraphs of text.
3. Use the heading, bold, and horizontal rule HTML tags to add interest to your page.
4. Add at least one hyperlink to the page, making sure that you include explanatory link text.
5. Select a graphic to add to your page. Make sure that it is stored in a file that's not too big to load quickly. Designate alternative text for the graphic for accessibility.
6. Test your Web page locally. Print your HTML document and then make a screen capture of your Web page as it appears in the browser.
7. If your instructor so specifies, post your Web page to a Web site, test it, and supply the page's URL to your instructor using e-mail.

Key Terms

Make sure you understand all the boldfaced key terms presented in this chapter. With the NP2013 interactive eBook, you can use this list of terms as an interactive study activity. First, try to define a term in your own words, and then click the term to compare your definition with the definition presented in the chapter.

ActionScript, 372
ActiveX control, 373
Ad-blocking software, 385
Ad-serving cookies, 400
Anonymous proxy service, 403
Antispyware, 403
B2B, 385
B2C, 385
B2G, 385
Banner ad, 385
C2C, 385
Click-through rate, 385
Client-side script, 372
Cookie, 368
Digital certificate, 373
E-commerce, 384
E-mail account, 393
E-mail address, 393
E-mail attachment, 398
E-mail client software, 393
E-mail message, 392
E-mail server, 392
E-mail system, 392
First-party cookie, 401
Flash cookie, 402
Hover ad, 385
HTML, 362
HTML conversion utility, 369
HTML document, 362
HTML forms, 371
HTML mail, 397
HTML script, 371

HTML tags, 362
HTML5, 362
HTTP, 364
HTTP status code, 365
HTTPS, 390
Hypertext, 360
Hypertext link, 361
IMAP, 394
Java applet, 372
Keyword stuffing, 377
Link popularity, 377
Local e-mail, 393
Markup language, 362
Message header, 392
Meta keyword, 377
Metasearch engine, 380
MIME, 398
Netiquette, 399
Online shopping cart, 387
Persistent HTTP connection, 365
Person-to-person payment, 391
Pharming, 406
Phishing, 405
Plug-in, 367
POP3, 394
Pop-up ad, 385
Query processor, 376
Search engine indexer, 376
Search operator, 379
Search terms, 378
Secure connection, 389
Server-side script, 372

Smileys, 399
SMTP, 394
Socket, 364
Source document, 363
Spam, 404
Spam filter, 404
SSL, 390
Stateless protocol, 368
Store-and-forward, 394
Third-party cookie, 401
TLS, 390
URL, 361
Web, 360
Web 2.0, 361
Web 3.0, 361
Web authoring software, 369
Web browser, 361
Web bug, 403
Web cache, 365
Web crawler, 375
Web page, 361
Web search engine, 374
Web server, 361
Web site, 361
Webmail, 393
XHTML, 362

Interactive Summary

To review important concepts from this chapter, fill in the blanks to best complete each sentence. When using the NP2013 interactive eBook, click the Check Answers buttons to automatically score your answers.

SECTION A: The Web, one of the Internet's hottest attractions, is a collection of document, image, video, and sound files that can be linked and accessed over the Internet via the [   ] protocol. The Web is an interlinked collection of information; whereas the [   ] is the communications system used to transport Web information from computers that store it to client computers that request it. An Internet-based computer that stores and distributes Web files is called a Web [   ]. It can host one or more Web [   ] such as *www.wikipedia.com* or *www.facebook.com* containing HTML [   ] documents, which can be accessed and displayed using client software called a Web [   ]. Each Web page has a unique address called a(n) [   ]. [   ] Markup Language is a set of specifications for creating documents that a browser can display as a Web page. To create HTML documents, you can use a variety of Web authoring tools, such as a text [   ], HTML conversion utility, online Web authoring tool, or Web authoring software. To enable your Web pages to perform tasks beyond what HTML can do, you can add programs by embedding a(n) [   ] in your HTML document, or by coding a Java [   ], [   ] content, or a(n) [   ] control, which you can refer to in your document.

▶ CHECK ANSWERS

SECTION B: To sift through massive amounts of information available on the Web and locate pertinent information about a topic, Web surfers utilize programs called search [   ]. These special programs have four major components. A Web [   ], also called a Web spider, is automated to methodically visit Web sites and gather Web pages. A search engine [   ] culls keywords from the gathered pages and stores them in a(n) [   ]. The search engine's query [   ] accepts one or more words called search [   ], looks them up in the database, and produces a list of relevant Web sites. There are a number of ways to narrow searches and produce more targeted results, such as using [   ] operators or putting exact phrases in [   ]. The order in which Web sites are returned in response to your query is dependent on relevancy criteria, such as keyword matches and [   ] popularity.

▶ CHECK ANSWERS

SECTION C: Any business transaction that is conducted electronically over a computer network is typically referred to as a(n) [   ] transaction. The most common business models are business-to-[   ], consumer-to-consumer, business-to-business, and business-to-government. E-commerce merchants cut costs by taking advantage of the efficiencies and opportunities offered by [   ], computerization, and digitization. They also increase their profits by providing space for third-party hover, pop-up, and [   ] ads on their Web pages. Online stores use [   ] to track customers' online shopping carts. B2C e-commerce sites usually store product descriptions in a(n) [   ]. Product information is assembled into Web pages on the fly by [   ]-side scripts. Online purchases can be paid for by submitting a credit card number directly to a merchant or using a person-to-[   ] payment service, such as PayPal.

▶ CHECK ANSWERS

SECTION D: E-mail is an electronic version of the postal system that transmits messages from one computer to another, usually over the [   ]. Obtaining an e-mail [   ] gets your electronic mailbox set up on an e-mail server. The software you use to send, receive, and manage messages is called e-mail [   ] software. E-mail systems based on client software that's installed locally are referred to as [   ] e-mail. Systems that provide access to e-mail through a(n) [   ] are called Webmail. Two protocols are typically used to manage your incoming mail. [   ] deletes messages after they are downloaded, whereas [   ] leaves messages on the server until you specifically delete them. The protocol that handles outgoing mail is [   ].

[   ] mail is a term used for e-mail messages that contain tags that produce bold, italicized, and underlined text; fancy fonts; embedded graphics; and various font sizes. Any file that travels with an e-mail message is called an e-mail attachment. A conversion process called [   ] provides a clever way of disguising digital photos, sounds, and other media as plain ASCII code that can travel over the Internet as e-mail attachments. Attachments can harbor computer [   ]. Do not open attachments from an unknown source. [   ] is online jargon for Internet etiquette. It is a series of customs or guidelines for maintaining civilized and effective communications in online discussions and e-mail exchanges.

▶ CHECK ANSWERS

SECTION E: When you surf the Web or work with your e-mail, you need to be aware of potential spyware exploits, such as [   ] cookies from third parties. While browsers and marketing firms are now providing opt-out mechanisms to block third-party cookies, it is not as easy to turn off all kinds of cookies. [   ] cookies, also called local shared objects, are used as an alternative to conventional cookies, and most users are not aware of their existence. Web [   ], or clear GIFs, are practically invisible 1x1 pixel graphics embedded in a Web page or e-mail message that can be used to set cookies for third-party Web sites. [   ] redirects users to fake sites by tampering with the information in a(n) [   ] name server. While these attacks don't need any action on your part to be effective, [   ] scams require you to respond to an e-mail message or click an embedded link in your e-mail. [   ] is unsolicited e-mail that you can avoid by practicing safe e-mail techniques such as using a spam [   ]. You can also use a(n) [   ] e-mail address to receive confirmation for online purchases without getting added to a spam mailing list. A safe bet for combating most forms of spyware is using a type of security software called [   ].

▶ CHECK ANSWERS

Interactive Situation Questions

Apply what you've learned to some typical computing situations. When using the NP2013 interactive eBook, you can type your answers, and then use the Check Answers button to automatically score your responses.

1. Suppose that you are about to check out at an online store, but you don't see any indication that your transaction data will be protected by a secure connection. It would be best, under these circumstances, to use PGP software to encrypt your shipping and billing data. True or false? [_____]

2. Your friend, who is a little computer phobic, is going to be creating his first Web page and asks you to recommend some software for the task. Which one requires the least knowledge of HTML tags: Notepad or Microsoft Word? [_____]

3. Suppose you visit a Web site that has eye-catching pages. You want to know how these pages were formatted, so you use one of the options on your browser's menu to take a look at the HTML [_____] document.

4. Suppose you click a link at a Web site and get a message that the file cannot be displayed because it is in PDF format. To view the file, you need an updated version of your browser. True or false? [_____]

5. Suppose you're performing a local test of a Web page you created. All the page elements appear to be correctly positioned and formatted. You're also happy to discover that your large graphics files are displayed quite quickly by your browser. Can you expect similar performance after you post the page on a Web site? Yes or no? [_____]

6. You'd prefer not to have the search engine you use maintain accumulative records of your searches. You can block [_____] from a specific search engine site, and that setting will force the search engine to assign a different ID number to you for each session.

7. You're getting ready for a week-long trip. You'd rather not take your computer, but you'll have access to public computers. Rather than use Webmail while you're away from home, you decide to use your familiar POP e-mail [_____] software by storing it and your e-mail files on a portable USB flash drive.

8. One of your relatives wants to try online shopping, but is suspicious that her credit card number might get stolen from a merchant's server by a hacker using a packet sniffer. Is it correct to tell her that she can best avoid these potential rip-offs by using a secure connection, such as HTTPS? Yes or no? [_____]

9. Your Inbox is getting more and more unsolicited messages with "fisd foos" in the header. You decide to generate a new rule for your security software's spam [_____] to block those irritating messages.

10. You're looking through a list of cookies stored on your computer, but you don't remember visiting sites such as bannerbank, hotlog, and ad.bb. You can assume that these cookies were created by [_____], such as ad-serving cookies.

▶ CHECK ANSWERS

Interactive Practice Tests

Practice tests that consist of ten multiple-choice, true/false, and fill-in-the-blank questions are available in the NP2013 interactive eBook. Test questions are selected at random from a large test bank, so each time you take a test, you'll receive a different set of questions. Your tests are scored immediately, and you can print study guides that help you find the correct answers for any questions that you missed.

▶ CLICK TO START

Learning Objectives Checkpoints

Learning Objectives Checkpoints are designed to help you assess whether you have achieved the major learning objectives for this chapter. You can use paper and pencil or word processing software to complete most of the activities.

1. Explain the relationship between an HTML source document and a Web page. List five HTML tags and describe how each is used.

2. Draw a multi-panel cartoon that shows how a Web server and browser interact. Include the following terms: *Web server*, *browser*, *HTTP*, *HTML*, *port*, *socket*, *HTML document*, *graphic file*, and *URL*.

3. Briefly sketch the evolution of Web browsers. Describe how browsers use plugins.

4. Explain why cookies are useful in an environment that is based on a stateless protocol, and provide some concrete examples of their use.

5. Describe the advantages and disadvantages of each type of Web page development tool discussed in this chapter.

6. Create a short tutorial explaining how to create, test, and post a Web page using a text editor such as Notepad or TextEdit.

7. Explain the purpose of HTML scripts and the differences between server-side scripts and client-side scripts.

8. Create a comic-strip like sequence of diagrams that illustrates how the following technologies interact: Web crawler, search engine database, indexer, query processor.

9. Use a search engine and search operators to formulate a search for information about your favorite era in history. Can you make a more targeted search to find out what kind of slang was used during that time period?

10. List the four most commonly used styles of citation and demonstrate how to correctly format a citation to a Web page using each style.

11. Explain two ways that shopping carts can work with cookies.

12. List three threats to the security of credit card numbers and other sensitive data during e-commerce transactions. Describe how the following e-commerce technologies work: SSL/TLS, HTTPS, and person-to-person payment systems.

13. Create a table that compares and contrasts local mail with Webmail.

14. List the advantages and disadvantages of HTML formatted mail. Explain how MIME works.

15. Make a list of security and privacy concerns discussed in this chapter. Describe each one and then list procedures and technologies available to make your online experience more secure and private.

Study Tip: Make sure you can use your own words to correctly answer each of the purple focus questions that appear throughout the chapter.

7

Concept Map

Fill in the blanks to show the hierarchy of Web technology concepts presented in this chapter.

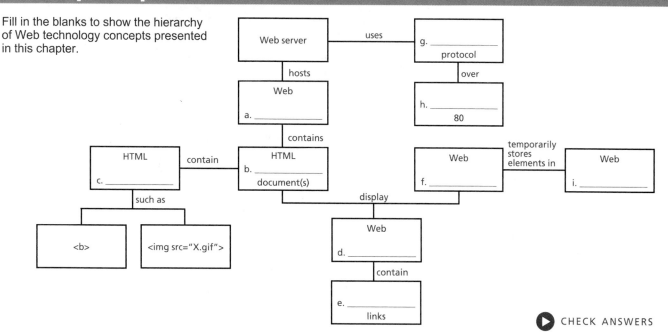

CHECK ANSWERS

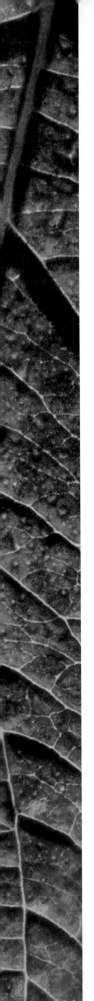

8

Chapter Contents

INFOWEBLINKS

You'll find updates for chapter material by connecting to the **NP2013 Chapter 8** InfoWebLink.

Ⓦ CLICK TO CONNECT
www.infoweblinks.com/np2013/ch08

Digital Media

Learning Objectives

After reading this chapter, you will be able to answer the following questions by completing the outcomes-based Learning Objectives Checkpoints on page 483.

1. How do computers and portable media players such as iPods store digital music?
2. Why are some digital audio files so huge?
3. What is the difference between digital audio and MIDI?
4. What are bitmap graphics, where are they used, and how can they be identified?
5. How are images transferred from digital cameras to computers?
6. What affects the quality of a bitmap graphic, its file size, and whether it is best suited for uses such as Web pages, e-mail attachments, printed photos, or desktop published documents?
7. Can compression play a role in reducing the size of graphics files?
8. How do vector graphics differ from bitmaps, and how does that affect the way in which they are created and used?
9. Is it possible to convert vector graphics into bitmap graphics?
10. What tools and techniques are used to create 3-D graphics?
11. What kinds of devices can be used to capture video?
12. Can analog video be converted into digital video?
13. What affects the amount of video that can be stored on a hard disk or portable media player?
14. How is digital video deployed on the Web?
15. What are the most popular digital media file formats and software players?
16. Is a special procedure required to make DVDs that work on standalone DVD players?
17. How do digital rights management technologies restrict the ways in which I can use digital media?
18. How are time shifting, place shifting, and format shifting related to digital media?

CourseMate

Visit the NP2013 CourseMate for this chapter's Pre-Quiz, Audio Overview and Flashcards, Detailed Objectives, Chapter Quiz, Online Games, and more labs.

Multimedia and Interactive Elements

When using the NP2013 interactive eBook, click the ▶ icons to access multimedia resources.

Apply Your Knowledge
The information in this chapter will give you the background to:

- Recognize digital media files by their extensions
- Play digital music and video files on your computer and transfer them to portable media players
- Add WAV or MIDI music to Web pages
- Use speech recognition software applications to manipulate software with voice commands
- Create digital photos with a camera or scanner and then edit them
- Create vector and 3-D graphics

- Process photos to make them suitable for e-mail attachments, Web pages, or printing
- Create digital video using an analog or digital camcorder
- Turn your digital video into a DVD complete with menu options for scene selection and special features
- Legally use music, video, and other digital content, including content that is controlled by digital rights management

Try It!
WHAT KINDS OF GRAPHICS, AUDIO, AND VIDEO FILES ARE ON MY COMPUTER?
You can use your computer to work with many types of media, such as photos, music, and videos. Your computer stores media that you've created and downloaded. It also stores images from Web sites you've recently visited. To discover what sort of media is stored on your computer, follow these steps:

Windows 7 and Vista:
1. Click the **Start** button. Type **pictures** into the search box as shown below. For **Windows 7**, click the **See more results** option above the search box. For **Vista**, click the **Search Everywhere** option above the search box.

2. Repeat step 1 to search for **music** and then again to search for **video**.

Windows XP:
1. Click **Start** and then select **Search**. The Search Results dialog box appears. On the left side of the Search Results window, click the button for **Pictures, Music, or Video**.

2. Click the box for **Pictures and Photos**, then click the **Search** button. Your computer shows you a list

of image files. If Windows displays a list of file names, but you'd rather see the images, click the **View** menu and select **Thumbnails**.

3. Repeat step 2 to search for **Music** and then again to search for **Video**.

Mac:
1. Click the **Finder** icon, located on the dock.

2. Use the SEARCH FOR listing on the left side of the Finder window to select **All images**. If your Mac displays file names, but you'd prefer to see the images, click the **View** menu and then select **as icons**.

3. Use the SEARCH FOR listing to select **All Movies**.

4. To find music on your Mac, type **music** in the search box, located in the upper-right corner of the Finder window.

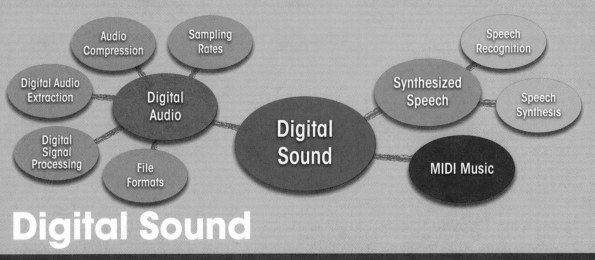

Digital Sound

COMPUTERS CAN RECORD, store, and play sounds, such as narrations, sound effects, and music. Downloading music files over the Internet is currently the most popular use of digital audio, but audio technology plays a key role in other interesting applications. This section of the chapter covers a wide-ranging selection of digital audio concepts and technologies that you're likely to find handy for personal and professional use.

DIGITAL AUDIO BASICS

▶ **What is digital audio?** **Digital audio** is music, speech, and other sounds represented in binary format for use in digital devices. Sound is produced by the vibration of matter such as a violin string or a drum head. This vibration causes pressure changes in the surrounding air, creating waves.

The smooth, continuous curve of a sound wave can be directly recorded on analog devices, such as records. To digitally record sound, samples of the sound wave are collected at periodic intervals and stored as numeric data. Figure 8-1 shows how a computer digitally samples a sound wave.

FIGURE 8-1

Sampling a Sound Wave

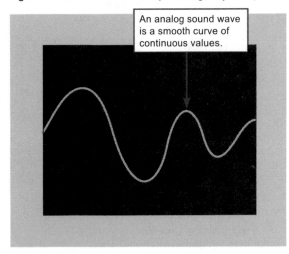

An analog sound wave is a smooth curve of continuous values.

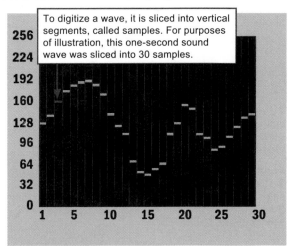

To digitize a wave, it is sliced into vertical segments, called samples. For purposes of illustration, this one-second sound wave was sliced into 30 samples.

Sample	Sample Height (Decimal)	Sample Height (Binary)
1	130	10000010
2	140	1000110
3	160	10100000
4	175	10101111

The height of each sample is converted into a binary number and stored. The height of sample 3 is 160 (decimal), so it is stored as its binary equivalent—10100000.

▶ Does sampling rate affect sound quality? Sampling rate

refers to the number of times per second that a sound is measured during the recording process. It is expressed in hertz (Hz). One thousand samples per second is expressed as 1,000 Hz or 1 kHz (kilohertz). Higher sampling rates increase the quality of the sound recording but require more storage space than lower sampling rates.

To conserve space, applications that do not require such high-quality sound use much lower sampling rates. Voice-overs and narrations are often recorded with sampling rates of 11 kHz (11,000 samples per second). This rate results in lower quality sound, but the file is about one-fourth the size of a file for the same sound recorded at 44.1 kHz. Figure 8-2 illustrates how sampling rate affects sound quality.

FIGURE 8-2

A higher sampling rate produces more true-to-life sound quality. Use your interactive eBook to compare the quality of these audio clips, which were digitized at different sampling rates. You'll have to listen carefully to notice the differences.

8

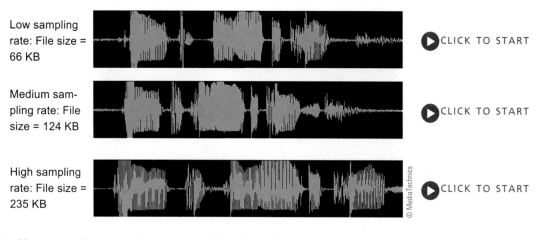

Low sampling rate: File size = 66 KB

▶ CLICK TO START

Medium sampling rate: File size = 124 KB

▶ CLICK TO START

High sampling rate: File size = 235 KB

© MediaTechnics

▶ CLICK TO START

▶ How much space is required to store an audio file? When

you sample stereo CD-quality music at 44.1 kHz, one second of music requires about 0.176 MB of storage space. Forty-five minutes of music—the length of a typical album—require about 475 MB. You might wonder how audio files rack up so much space.

The height of each sound sample is saved as an 8-bit number for radio-quality recordings, or a 16-bit number for high-fidelity recordings. The audio CDs you buy at your favorite music store are recorded at a sampling rate of 44.1 kHz, which means a sample of the sound is taken 44,100 times per second.

Sixteen bits are used for each sample. To achieve stereo effects, you must take two of these 16-bit samples. Therefore, each sample requires 32 bits of storage space (Figure 8-3).

FIGURE 8-3

To get an idea of the space required to store digital audio, just look at the number of bytes required to sample one second of music.

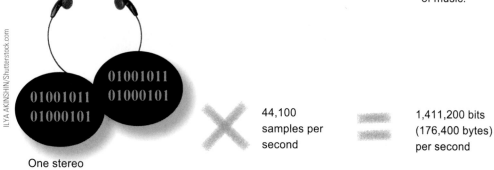

ILYA AKINSHIN/Shutterstock.com

01001011
01001011 01000101
01000101

One stereo sample = 32 bits

× 44,100 samples per second

= 1,411,200 bits (176,400 bytes) per second

▶ Is there any way to shrink audio files? Regardless of sampling rate, digital audio file size can be reduced using audio compression techniques. **Audio compression** reduces the size of a sound file by removing bits that represent extraneous noise and sounds that are beyond the frequencies of normal hearing.

In addition, general-purpose compression techniques explained later in the chapter can be applied to sound files. A compressed audio file requires less storage space than an uncompressed file and can be transmitted faster over a network. Most of the music for portable media players is stored in compressed audio file formats.

▶ How does a computer produce digital audio? Your computer's sound card is responsible for transforming the bits stored in an audio file into music, sound effects, and narrations. A **sound card** is a device that contains a variety of input and output jacks, plus audio-processing circuitry.

A desktop computer's sound card is usually plugged into an expansion slot inside the system unit. Alternatively, sound card circuitry referred to as **integrated audio** can be built into a computer's system board. Portable computers rarely feature a separate sound card because manufacturers save space by using integrated audio.

A sound card is equipped to accept input from a microphone and send output to speakers or headphones. For processing digital audio files, a sound card contains a special type of circuitry called a **digital signal processor**, which performs three important tasks:

▶ Transforms digital bits into analog waves when you play a digital audio file

▶ Transforms analog waves into digital bits when you make a sound recording

▶ Handles compression and decompression, if necessary

To play a digitally recorded sound, the bits from an audio file are transferred from disk to the microprocessor, which routes them to your computer's sound card. The digital signal processor handles any necessary decompression, and then transforms the data into analog wave signals. These signals are routed to the speakers and voilà! You have sound (Figure 8-4).

FIGURE 8-4

Most sound cards use a digital signal processor to convert bits into analog signals.

The microprocessor sends compressed digital data to the sound card.

The sound card's digital signal processor decompresses data and converts it to analog signals.

The sound card sends analog signals to speakers.

▶ What type of hardware do I need for digital audio?

Your PC outputs sound to headphones or speakers. The speakers on your notebook computer are fine for listening to music; but when you're giving presentations or showing movies, you're likely to need external speakers to generate adequate volume.

Some speakers draw power from the computer, but they are limited in volume. Speakers that plug into a wall outlet offer much more versatile audio output, especially in situations that require high volume.

Most portable computers include a built-in microphone. If you're not picky about sound quality, you'll find the bundled microphone suitable for radio-quality voice recording and sound effects destined for Web pages or presentations. For multimedia or professional audio projects, you'll want to shop for a better-quality "mic." You can connect most standard microphones to your computer through the microphone socket or USB port.

DIGITAL AUDIO FILE FORMATS

▶ How can I recognize a digital audio file?

You can recognize a digital audio file by looking at its file extension. Digital audio is stored in a variety of file formats. The table in Figure 8-5 provides an overview of the most popular digital audio formats, including **AAC** (Advanced Audio Coding), **MP3** (also called MPEG-1 Layer 3), **Ogg Vorbis**, **WAV**, and **WMA** (Windows Media Audio).

FIGURE 8-5

Popular Digital Audio File Formats

Audio Format	File Extension	Advantages	Disadvantages
AAC	.aac, .m4p, or .mp4	Very good sound quality based on MPEG-4; compressed format; used for iTunes music	Files can be copy protected so that use is limited to approved devices
MP3 (also called MPEG-1 Layer 3)	.mp3	Good sound quality even though the file is compressed; can be streamed over the Web	Might require a standalone player or browser plug-in
Ogg Vorbis	.ogg	Free, open standard; supported by some browsers; supplies audio stream for Google's WebM format	Slow to catch on as a popular standard
WAV	.wav	Good sound quality; supported in browsers without a plug-in	Audio data is stored in raw, uncompressed format, so files are very large
WMA (Windows Media Audio)	.wma	Compressed format; very good sound quality; used on several music download sites	Files can be copy protected; requires Windows Media Player 9 or above

▶ What type of software is required to play digital audio files?

To play a digital audio file, you must use audio or media player software. Audio software might be included with your computer's operating system, packaged with your sound card, installed in a handheld device, or available on the Web. Popular audio and media players include iTunes, Windows Media Player, and open source offerings such as QuickAudio and Audacity.

Audio player software tends to support several audio file formats. In the Windows environment, for example, you can use Windows Media Player to play audio formats such as WAV, WMA, and MP3.

▶ **What about Web-based audio?** Digital audio files can be embedded into a Web page using the HTML5 <audio> tag. WAV files are supported by most Web browsers, so it is a popular audio file format. Other audio formats can be delivered over the Web, but might require plug-ins.

Suppose that you want to listen to some free tracks at a jazz Web site where files are stored in Vorbis format. Firefox and Chrome offer built-in support for Vorbis audio. If you use Internet Explorer, however, you'll have to download and install a plug-in before you can listen to the jazz tracks.

Web-based digital audio is often delivered in streaming format to avoid lengthy delays while the entire audio file is downloaded. **Streaming audio** plays as its file is downloaded (Figure 8-6).

▶ **Can I convert audio files from one format to another?** Suppose you find a cool MIDI ring tone on the Web, but your iPhone won't play MIDI music. You can use audio converter software to change audio files from one format to another. Your audio player software might provide tools for opening a file stored in one format and saving it in another format. If not, a quick Google search can provide links to free audio converters.

Suppose you want your iPod to play tracks from one of your audio CDs. You can use audio software to rip tracks into a format that's supported by your iPod. *Ripping* is a slang term that refers to the process of importing tracks from a CD or DVD to your computer's hard disk. The technical term for ripping is **digital audio extraction**.

Music is stored on CDs in a digital format called CDDA. The format offers high fidelity; but as with WAV files, one minute of CDDA music requires in excess of 10 MB of storage space. During the ripping process, music in CDDA format is converted into a compressed format such as MP3, AAC, or WMA to reduce file size.

Many software tools are available for converting audio files from one format to another and ripping CD tracks. One of the most versatile tools is Apple iTunes software (Figure 8-7).

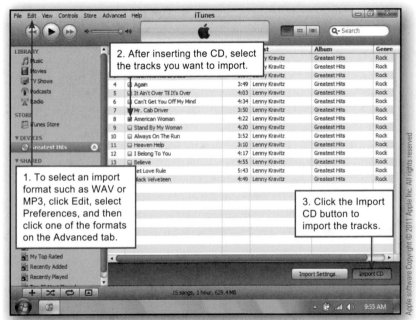

MIDI MUSIC

▶ **What is MIDI music?** Digital audio is a recording of real analog sound signals. In contrast, **synthesized sound** is an artificially created, or synthetic, sound. Synthesized sound can be classified as MIDI music or synthesized speech.

MIDI (Musical Instrument Digital Interface) specifies a standard way to store music data for synthesizers, electronic MIDI instruments, and computers. Unlike digital audio files, which contain digitized recordings of real performances, MIDI files contain instructions for creating the pitch, volume, and duration of notes that sound like various musical instruments.

MIDI music is encoded as a **MIDI sequence** and stored as a file with a .mid, .cmf, or .rol file extension. A MIDI sequence is analogous to a player-piano roll that contains punched information indicating which musical notes to play. A MIDI sequence contains instructions specifying the pitch of a note, the point at which the note begins, the instrument that plays the note, the volume of the note, and the point at which the note ends.

▶ **Is special hardware needed for MIDI music?** Most computer sound cards are equipped to generate music from MIDI files, and many can capture music data from a MIDI instrument as well.

A MIDI-capable sound card contains a **wavetable** (sometimes called a patch set), which is a set of prerecorded musical instrument sounds. The sound card accesses these sounds and plays them as instructed by the MIDI file. For example, if a sound card receives a MIDI instruction for a trumpet to play middle C, it accesses the trumpet's middle C patch and routes it to the speaker until it receives a MIDI instruction to stop the note.

▶ **What are the advantages and disadvantages of MIDI?** MIDI files are much more compact than digital audio files. Depending on the exact piece of music, three minutes of MIDI music might require only 10 KB of storage space, whereas the same piece of music stored in a high-quality, uncompressed digital audio file might require 30 MB of storage space.

FIGURE 8-8

MIDI music tends not to have the full resonance of digital audio. Use your interactive eBook to listen to these two sound clips and see if you can hear a difference.

One of the big disadvantages of MIDI is that it does not produce high-quality vocals. Another disadvantage is that it does not have the full resonance of real sound. Most musicians can easily identify MIDI recordings because they simply lack the tonal qualities of symphony-quality sound. You can compare the differences by using the CLICK TO START buttons in Figure 8-8.

● CLICK TO START

● CLICK TO START

▶ **When would I use MIDI music?** MIDI is a good choice for adding background music to multimedia projects and Web pages. Using a procedure similar to that for digital audio files, you can add a link to a MIDI file by inserting a tag such as <audio src="sousa.mid"> within an HTML document. Most browsers include built-in support for MIDI music.

You can use music composition software, such as Finale, to create your own snappy tunes or get permission to use MIDI files you find on the Web. For composing your own MIDI music, you can input notes from a MIDI instrument directly to your computer. The input is handled by music composition software (Figure 8-9), which you can also use to edit notes and combine the parts for several instruments.

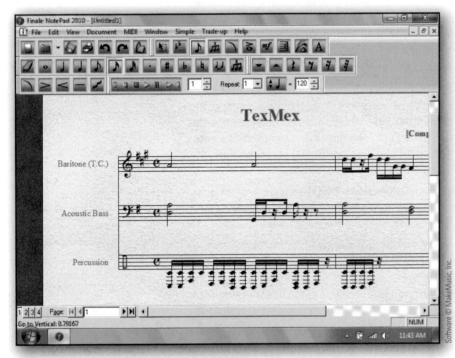

FIGURE 8-9

Music composition software provides tools for entering notes, specifying instruments, printing sheet music, and saving compositions in formats such as MIDI. ▶ You can use your interactive eBook to take a tour of music composition software and see how the TexMex music was created.

SPEECH RECOGNITION AND SYNTHESIS

▶ **What's the difference between speech synthesis and speech recognition?** Speech synthesis is the process by which machines, such as computers, produce sound that resembles spoken words. **Speech recognition** (or voice recognition) refers to the ability of a machine to understand spoken words.

Speech recognition is used to automate telephone-based services such as Directory Assistance and interactive voice response systems, such as Google Search that allow users to search Google by voice over their mobile phones.

The use of digital spectrographic analysis to identify human speakers is an emerging part of law enforcement and homeland security. Not only can digitized samples of voices be analyzed to confirm identity, but real-time voice print identification can match speakers with known recordings of their voices.

Speech synthesis is a key technology in mobile communication, such as accessing your e-mail using a cell phone—a speech synthesizer reads your e-mail messages to you. A speech synthesizer can also read a computer screen aloud, which unlocks access to computers and the Internet for individuals with visual disabilities.

▶ **How does speech synthesis work?** A basic sound unit, such as "reh" or "gay," is called a **phoneme**. Most speech synthesizers string together phonemes to form words. For example, the phonemes "reh" and "gay" produce the word "reggae." A basic speech synthesizer consists of **text-to-speech software**, which generates sounds that are played through your computer's standard sound card. As an alternative, some speech synthesizers are special-purpose hardware devices.

▶ **How does speech recognition work?** On a personal computer or smartphone, a speech recognition system collects words spoken into a microphone that's connected to the sound card. The sound card's digital signal processor transforms the analog sound of your voice into digital data. This data is then processed by speech recognition software.

Speech recognition software analyzes the sounds of your voice and converts them to phonemes. Next, the software analyzes the content of your speech. It compares the groups of phonemes to the words in a digital dictionary that lists phoneme combinations along with their corresponding English (or French, Spanish, and so on) words. When a match is found, the software can display the word on the screen or use it to carry out a command.

Speech recognition software can be integrated with word processing software so that you can enter text simply by speaking into a microphone. Going beyond word processing, speech recognition can be used to activate Windows controls instead of using a mouse. Most speech recognition software also works with your browser, allowing you to "voice surf" the Web (Figure 8-10).

FIGURE 8-10

The Windows Speech Recognition Wizard displays short text passages. As you read each passage, the computer listens to the way you pronounce each word and stores it in your speech profile.

Norman Pogson/Shutterstock.com

You can voice surf with a handheld device, too. ▶ Find out how Google Voice Search works.

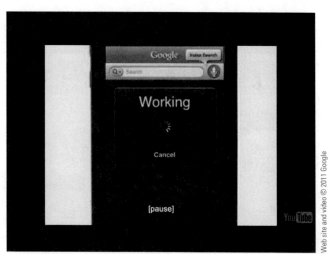

Web site and video © 2011 Google

QuickCheck

SECTION A

1. [_____] rate refers to the number of times per second that a sound is measured during the recording process.

2. When sound card circuitry is incorporated into a computer system board, it is often referred to as [_____] audio.

3. The process of ripping tracks from an audio CD to a digital format such as MP3 is called digital audio [_____].

4. MIDI sound is generated from a(n) [_____] (or patch set), which is a set of prerecorded musical instrument sounds.

5. When a telephone-based airline voice response system asks you to say your flight number, it processes your response using speech [_____] software.

 CHECK ANSWERS

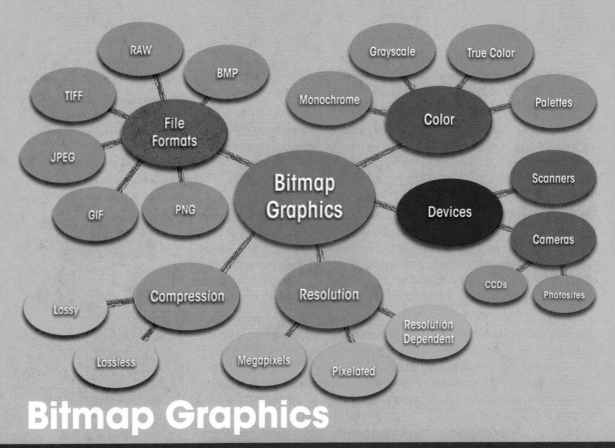

Bitmap Graphics

A DIGITAL CAMERA seems easy to use. Point it, shoot the photo, and…what next? How do you transfer digital photos from camera to computer? How can you print them? How do you get them ready to become e-mail attachments? How do you prepare them for inclusion on Web pages? To understand the wide range of possibilities for digital photos, you'll need some background information about bitmap graphics.

BITMAP BASICS

▶ **What is a bitmap graphic?** A **bitmap graphic**, also called a raster graphic or simply a bitmap, is composed of a grid of dots. The color of each dot is stored as a binary number. Think of a grid superimposed on a picture. The grid divides the picture into cells, called pixels. Each pixel is assigned a color, which is stored as a binary number. Figure 8-11 illustrates these basic characteristics of a bitmap graphic.

> **TERMINOLOGY NOTE**
>
> The term *pixel* is derived from *picture element*. It is the smallest element that can be manipulated on a computer display or printer.

FIGURE 8-11

A bitmap graphic is divided into a grid of individually colored pixels. The color number for each pixel is stored in binary format. ▶ Learn how to use Windows Paint to create bitmap graphics and see how to work pixel by pixel to edit an image.

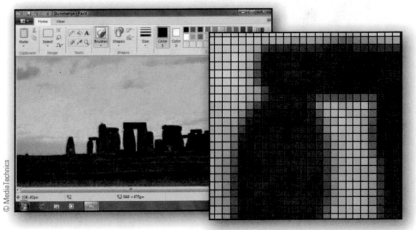

430

▶ Are there different kinds of bitmap graphics?

Many graphics file formats exist, and most graphics software offers a choice of popular formats, such as BMP, RAW, TIFF, JPEG, GIF, and PNG. Selecting the best graphics file format to use depends on what you intend to do with the image. Figure 8-12 summarizes popular formats and their uses.

FIGURE 8-12

Bitmap Graphics Formats

	Format	Use
 © MediaTechnics	**BMP**, pronounced "bee-em-pee" or "bump," is the native bitmap graphics file format of the Microsoft Windows environment. Microsoft Paint, included as part of Microsoft Windows, creates BMP graphics files. The BMP format supports True Color and can be used for a wide variety of graphics applications, such as photographs, illustrations, and graphs. BMP files are often too large for e-mail attachments. BMP graphics are not supported by most browsers, so they are not used on the Web.	Graphical elements, such as buttons and other controls for graphical user interfaces
 © MediaTechnics	**RAW** image formats contain the unprocessed pixel data generated directly by a digital camera's sensor. Up to 12 bits of data can be stored for each of the red, blue, and green values for a pixel, so RAW files are very large. Cameras that offer a RAW format also supply proprietary software to convert RAW data to JPEG or TIFF.	Photographic images before they are stored in other formats
 © MediaTechnics	**TIFF** (Tagged Image File Format), or TIF, is a flexible and platform-independent graphics file format supported by most photo-editing software packages. Scanners and digital cameras commonly store bitmaps in TIFF format because it supports True Color and can be easily converted into other graphics file formats.	Desktop publishing and any projects that require high-resolution graphics; not supported by browsers
 © MediaTechnics	**JPEG** (pronounced "JAY-peg"), which stands for Joint Photographic Experts Group, is a graphics format with built-in compression that stores True Color bitmap data very efficiently in a small file. The JPEG format is popular for Web graphics and for photos attached to e-mail messages. When creating a JPEG or converting an image to JPEG format, you can control the level of compression and the resulting file size. The compression process eliminates some image data, however, so highly compressed files suffer some quality deterioration.	General use, such as desktop publishing or Web pages, where flexibility in file size is important
 JPL/NASA	**GIF** (Graphics Interchange Format), pronounced "GIF" or "JIFF," was specifically designed to create images that can be displayed on multiple platforms, such as PCs and Macs. GIF graphics are limited to 256 colors, but the format supports simple animations. Once a popular format for Web pages, GIF is being replaced by JPEG and PNG.	Web graphics and simple animations
 © MediaTechnics	**PNG** (Portable Network Graphics), pronounced "ping," is a graphics format designed to improve on the GIF format. A PNG graphic can display up to 48-bit True Color (trillions of colors). Unlike JPEG, PNG compresses bitmap files without losing any data, so compressed images retain the same high quality as the originals. PNG was developed as a public domain format without any restrictions on its use.	Web graphics and other general uses

8

▶ Where would I encounter bitmap graphics? Bitmap graphics are used to create realistic images, such as photographs. You might also encounter bitmaps in the form of cartoons, images that appear in computer games, the desktop images displayed by your computer or smartphone, and rendered images produced by 3-D graphics software.

When you use a digital camera or camera-enabled cell phone, your photos are stored as bitmaps. A scanner produces bitmaps. The photos you send or receive as e-mail attachments are bitmaps, as are most Web page graphics.

▶ How do I create bitmap images? You can create a bitmap graphic from scratch using the tools provided by graphics software—specifically a category of graphics software referred to as paint software. You might be familiar with paint software such as Adobe Photoshop, Corel Painter, and Microsoft Paint (included with Windows).

Paint software includes tools for freehand sketching, filling in shapes, adding realistic shading, and creating effects that look like oil paints, charcoal, or watercolors. If your freehand sketching talent maxes out with stick figures, you can also create bitmap graphics by using a scanner or digital camera.

SCANNERS AND CAMERAS

▶ How do I convert a printed image into a bitmap? When you have a printed image, such as a photograph, a page from a magazine, or a picture from a book, you can use a **scanner** to convert the printed image into a bitmap graphic.

A scanner essentially divides an image into a fine grid of cells and assigns a digital value for the color of each cell. As the scan progresses, these values are transferred to your computer's hard disk and stored as a bitmap graphics file. Scanners, such as the one pictured in Figure 8-13, are inexpensive and easy to use.

© MediaTechnics

FIGURE 8-13

To scan an image, turn on the scanner and start your scanner software. Place the image face down on the scanner glass, and then use the scanner software to initiate the scan. The scanned image is saved in RAM and can then be saved on your computer's hard disk.
▶ Learn the difference between scanning an image and scanning a document into an editable word processing file.

▶ When should I use a digital camera rather than a scanner? Whereas a scanner is designed to digitize printed images, a **digital camera** creates a digital image of real objects. Although you could take a photo with a conventional camera, develop the film, and then digitize the photo with a scanner, it is much simpler to use a digital camera to take a photo in digital format, which you can then transfer directly to your computer or print directly to a photo printer.

How does a digital camera capture an image without using film? The lens of a film camera captures the light from an image onto a light-sensitive roll of film, which is developed to produce a photographic print. In a digital camera, the lens focuses light from the image onto a small image sensor called a **CCD** (charge-coupled device). A CCD contains a grid of tiny light-sensitive diodes called **photosites**.

The number of photosites depends on the size of the CCD. A one-half-inch square CCD can contain more than 500,000 photosites. Each photosite detects the brightness and color for its tiny piece of the image (Figure 8-14).

A CCD's photosites correspond to pixels. The more pixels used to capture an image, the higher its resolution, and the better the resulting picture. Cameras with larger CCDs produce higher quality images. Some cameras contain multiple CCDs, which enhance the color quality of a camera's output.

How does a digital camera store images? Some digital cameras store photos on CDs, mini CDs, or microdrives, but the most popular digital camera storage is solid state memory cards. Like RAM, memory cards can be erased and reused. Unlike RAM, however, solid state storage holds data without consuming power, so it doesn't lose data when the camera is turned off.

How can I get images out of the camera? Digital cameras allow you to preview images while they are still in the camera and delete those you don't want. The photos you want to keep can be transferred directly to a properly equipped printer or transferred to your computer's hard disk. Depending on your camera, this transfer can be achieved in several ways:

- **Card readers.** A card reader is a small device designed to read data contained in a solid state memory card. To transfer photo data from a memory card, remove it from the camera and insert it into the card reader, as shown in Figure 8-15.

- **Direct cable transfer.** If your computer and your camera have FireWire ports or USB ports, you can connect a cable between these two ports to transfer the photo data.

- **Infrared port.** Some cameras can beam photo data to your computer's infrared port. This method eliminates the need for a cable but is much slower than using FireWire or USB.

- **Media transfer.** If your camera stores data on CDs or similar optical media, you can simply remove the media from your camera and insert it into the appropriate drive of your computer.

- **Docking station.** Some camera manufacturers offer a camera docking station that connects to a computer by cable. A camera can be placed in the docking station to transfer photos to the computer's hard disk.

- **E-mail.** Cell phone photos can be transferred to a computer by e-mailing the photo to your e-mail account. The photo arrives as an attachment, which can be saved as a separate file.

FIGURE 8-14

A digital camera's CCD converts the image captured by the camera lens into a grid of colored pixels, which are stored as bits. ▶ Watch the video for this figure in your interactive eBook for an overview of digital camera features, file formats, and the process of transferring photos from a camera to your computer.

Courtesy of Learning Technology Services, University of Wisconsin-Stout

FIGURE 8-15

Card readers can be connected to your computer's USB port, built into a computer system unit, or built into a photo printer.

© MediaTechnics

▸ How do I access the memory card? Your computer treats memory cards essentially as any other storage device. After inserting a memory card, you can use Windows Explorer or Finder to copy photo files from the card to your computer's hard disk. Files copied in this way retain their original file names, such as *img00030*, which can be fairly cryptic.

You can also handle photo transfer with photo software, which might be supplied along with your camera, with your card reader, or by a standalone graphics software package, such as Adobe Photoshop. This software allows you to select a file format, specify a file name, and determine the location for each image file.

After you store your digital photos on your computer's hard disk, you can modify them, send them as e-mail attachments, print them, post them on Web pages, or archive them on a CD or DVD.

▸ What characteristics of a bitmap can I modify? Because bitmap graphics are coded as a series of bits that represent pixels, you can use graphics software to modify or edit this type of graphic by changing individual pixels.

You can modify photos to wipe out red eye or erase the "rabbit ears" that ruined an otherwise good family portrait. You can design eye-catching new pictures with images you cut and paste from several photos or scanned images. You can even retouch old photographs to eliminate creases, spots, and discoloration (Figure 8-16).

Whether you acquire an image from a digital camera or a scanner, bitmap graphics tend to require quite a bit of storage space. Although a large graphics file might provide the necessary data for a high-quality printout, these files take up space on your hard disk and can require lengthy transmission times that clog up mailboxes and make Web pages seem sluggish.

The size of the file that holds a bitmap depends on its resolution and color depth. Read on to see how these factors affect file size and how you can alter them to create smaller graphics files, suitable for e-mail attachments and Web pages.

IMAGE RESOLUTION

▸ How does resolution pertain to bitmap graphics? The dimensions of the grid that forms a bitmap graphic are referred to as its resolution. The resolution of a graphic is usually expressed as the number of horizontal and vertical pixels it contains. For example, a small graphic for a Web page might have a resolution of 150 x 100 pixels—150 pixels across and 100 pixels high.

▸ How does resolution relate to image quality? High-resolution graphics contain more data than low-resolution graphics. With more data, it is possible to display and print high-quality images that are sharper and clearer than images produced using less data. For example, a photograph of a cat taken with an inexpensive digital camera might produce a graphic with a resolution of 1600 x 1200, but a more expensive camera with 3888 x 2592 resolution contains more pixels and produces a higher-quality image.

Camera manufacturers sometimes express the resolution of digital cameras as megapixels. A **megapixel** is 1 million pixels. A camera with a resolution of 1600 x 1200 has the capability of producing photos containing 1.9 megapixels (1600 multiplied by 1200). A camera with 3888 x 2592 resolution is technically 10.1 megapixels, but might be rounded off and called a 10 megapixel camera by its manufacturer.

FIGURE 8-16

Bitmap graphics can be easily modified. Many graphics software products include wizards that help you retouch photographs.

Before

After

▶ How does resolution relate to the file size of a graphic?
Each pixel in a bitmap graphic is stored as one or more bits. The more pixels in a bitmap, the more bits needed to store the file.

▶ How does resolution relate to the physical size of an image?
A bitmap graphic is simply a collection of data. Unlike a printed photograph, a bitmap has no fixed physical size. The size at which a bitmap is displayed or printed depends on the density as well as the resolution (dimensions) of the image grid.

Imagine that each bitmap image and its grid come on a surface that you can stretch or shrink. As you stretch the surface, the grid maintains the same number of horizontal and vertical cells, but each cell becomes larger and the grid becomes less dense. As you shrink the surface, the grid becomes smaller and more dense. The graphic retains the same resolution no matter how much you stretch or shrink the graphic's physical size, as shown in Figure 8-17.

Reduced size
remains at
24 x 24 resolution

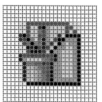

Original graphic at
24 x 24 resolution

Enlarged graphic still
has 24 x 24 resolution

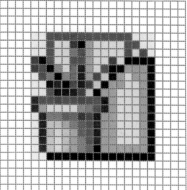

FIGURE 8-17

When a bitmap graphic is enlarged or reduced in size, it still retains its original resolution—24 x 24.

This concept of stretching and shrinking without changing resolution is important for understanding what happens when bitmaps are displayed and printed. The denser the grid, the smaller the image will appear. The density of an image grid can be expressed as dots per inch (dpi) for a printer or scanner, or as pixels per inch (ppi) on a display device.

▶ How do I specify the size of a printed image?
Most graphics software allows you to specify the size at which an image is printed without changing the resolution of the bitmap graphic. You'll get an acceptable image if you print 400 dpi or more. So, if a photo's resolution is 1600 x 800 pixels, it will look fine as a 4" x 2" print. As you enlarge the image beyond this size, it will start to appear somewhat fuzzy because the pixels will begin to become visible.

As a general rule, when you incorporate an image in a desktop-published document, or when you print photographs, you should work with high-resolution bitmaps so that you can produce high-quality output. To capture high-resolution bitmaps, use the highest resolution provided by your digital camera. When scanning an image, choose a dpi setting on your scanner that is at least as high as the dpi for the printout.

▶ How does a bitmap's resolution relate to what I see on the screen?
In Chapter 2, you learned that you can set your computer display to a particular resolution, such as 1024 x 768. When you display a bitmap graphic on the screen, each pixel of the graphic usually corresponds to one pixel on the screen. If the resolution of your graphic is 1024 x 768 and your display is set at 1024 x 768 resolution, the image

appears to fill the screen. If you view a 4.0 megapixel image on the same display device, the image is larger than the screen, and you have to scroll or change the zoom level to view it (Figure 8-18).

▶ **Can I change a graphic's file size?** The resolution and corresponding file size of a graphic might not be right for your needs. For example, if you take a photo with a 10.0 megapixel camera, it is unsuitable for a Web page. Not only would it take a long time to download, but it would be larger than most screens.

A 10.0 megapixel graphic is also not suitable for an e-mail attachment. Uploading and downloading such a large file—especially over a dial-up connection—would take much too long. Reducing the resolution of a bitmap can reduce its file size and on-screen display size. Most experts recommend that Web graphics not exceed 100 KB and that e-mail attachments not exceed 500 KB.

You can reduce the size of a bitmap by cropping it. **Cropping** refers to the process of selecting part of an image—just like cutting out a section of a photograph.

▶ **What happens if I try to change the overall resolution?** Bitmap graphics are **resolution dependent**, which means that the quality of the image depends on its resolution. If you reduce the overall resolution of an image, the computer eliminates pixels, which reduces the size of the image grid.

Suppose you reduce the resolution from 2160 x 1440 (3.1 megapixels) to 1080 x 720 (0.8 megapixels). The image grid becomes a quarter of its original size, and the file size is reduced by a similar amount. However, the computer threw away data with the pixels, which can reduce image quality.

If you attempt to enlarge a bitmap by increasing its resolution, your computer must somehow add pixels because no additional picture data exists. But what colors should these additional pixels become? Most graphics software uses a process called **pixel interpolation** to create new pixels by averaging the colors of nearby pixels.

For some graphics, pixel interpolation results in an image that appears very similar to the original. Other images—particularly those with strong curved or diagonal lines—develop an undesirable **pixelated**, or "bitmappy," jagged appearance (Figure 8-19).

FIGURE 8-18

When viewing an image larger than the screen, you must scroll to see all parts of the image or set the zoom level of your graphics software to less than 100%. You should understand, however, that changing the zoom level stretches or shrinks only the size of the image grid. It has no effect on the printed size of a graphic or the graphic's file size.

© MediaTechnics

FIGURE 8-19

When you increase the resolution of an existing graphic, the file size increases, but the quality might deteriorate.

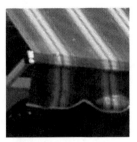

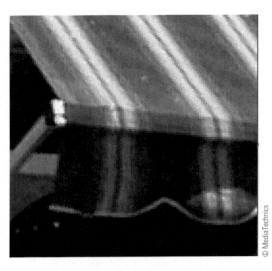
© MediaTechnics

The figure above has a resolution of 130 x 130. The figure at right was enlarged to a resolution of 260 x 260, but it has a rough, pixelated appearance.

COLOR DEPTH AND PALETTES

▶ **What is color depth?** As you learned in Chapter 2, color depth is the number of colors available for use in an image. As the number of colors increases, image quality improves, but file size also increases. You can limit color depth to decrease the file size required for a graphic. To find out how this works, first take a look at the storage requirements for various color depths.

▶ **How does color depth relate to file size?** To answer this question, consider a simple monochrome display device. Each screen pixel can be either "on" or "off." A **monochrome bitmap** is displayed by manipulating the pattern of "off" and "on" pixels displayed on the screen. To store the data for a monochrome bitmap, an "on" pixel is represented by a 1 bit. An "off" pixel is represented by a 0 bit. Each row of the bitmap grid is stored as a series of 0s and 1s, as shown in Figure 8-20.

FIGURE 8-20

Each pixel in a monochrome bitmap graphic is stored as a bit.

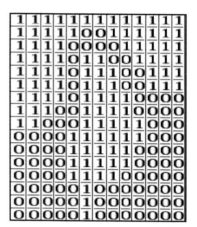

1. This image originated as a black-and-white silhouette.

2. The computer divides the picture into a matrix.

3. If a cell is white, it is coded as a 1. If a cell is black, it is coded as a 0.

Monochrome bitmaps require very little storage space. Suppose you create a full-screen monochrome bitmap with your screen resolution set to 1024 x 768. Your screen displays 786,432 pixels (that's 1,024 multiplied by 768). Each pixel is set to display a black dot or a white dot. When you store the graphic, each dot requires only one bit. Therefore, the number of bits required to represent a full-screen picture is the same as the number of pixels on the screen.

At a resolution of 1024 x 768, a full-screen graphic requires 786,432 bits of storage space. The number of bytes required to store the image is 786,432 divided by 8 (remember that there are eight bits in a byte). Your full-screen monochrome bitmap would, therefore, require only 98,304 bytes of storage space.

▶ **But what about color?** Today's color display devices require a more complex storage scheme. Each screen pixel displays a color based on the intensity of red, green, and blue signals it receives. A pixel appears white if the red, green, and blue signals are set to maximum intensity. If red, green, and blue signals are equal but at a lower intensity, the pixel displays a shade of gray. If the red signal is set to maximum intensity, but the blue and green signals are off, the pixel appears in brilliant red. A pixel appears purple if it receives red and blue signals, and so forth.

Each red, green, and blue signal is assigned a value ranging from 0 to 255: 0 represents the absence of color, and 255 represents the highest intensity level for that color. These values produce a maximum of 16.7 million colors. A graphic that uses this full range of colors is referred to as a **True Color bitmap** or a 24-bit bitmap.

You might be able to guess where the 24-bit term comes from. The data for each pixel requires three bytes of storage space—eight bits for blue, eight bits for green, and eight bits for red—for a total of 24 bits. Although True Color bitmaps produce photographic-quality images, they also produce very large files. Because each pixel requires three bytes, a 3 megapixel True Color bitmap would require a 9 MB file!

You might occasionally encounter a 32-bit bitmap. Just like a 24-bit bitmap, it displays 16.7 million colors. The extra bits are used to define special effects, such as the amount of transparency, for a pixel. These files are even larger than those containing 24-bit bitmaps. A 3 megapixel 32-bit bitmap would be about 10 MB.

Files containing full-screen 24-bit and 32-bit bitmaps are generally too large for Web pages because they require excessively long upload and download times. Earlier in the chapter, you learned that you can reduce a bitmap's file size by removing pixels. Another way to shrink a bitmap file is to reduce its color depth.

▶ **How can I reduce color depth?** To reduce the color depth of a bitmap, you can use your graphics software to work with color palettes. A **color palette** (also called a color lookup table or color map) is the digital version of a kidney-shaped artist's palette that holds the selection of colors an artist uses for a particular painting. A digital color palette allows you to select a group of colors to use for a bitmap graphic.

The advantage of a palette is that if it contains only 256 colors, you can store the data for each pixel in 8 bits instead of 24 bits, which reduces the file to a third of the size required for a True Color bitmap.

▶ **How does a color palette work?** A color palette is stored as a table within the header of a graphics file. Each palette contains a list of 256 color numbers. Each of these numbers is mapped to a 24-bit number that corresponds to the actual levels of red, green, and blue required to display the color. Figure 8-21 explains how this table works.

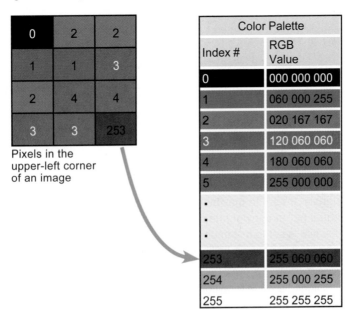

Pixels in the
upper-left corner
of an image

Color Palette	
Index #	RGB Value
0	000 000 000
1	060 000 255
2	020 167 167
3	120 060 060
4	180 060 060
5	255 000 000
.	
.	
.	
253	255 060 060
254	255 000 255
255	255 255 255

FIGURE 8-21

A color palette is a subset of all possible colors. Each color in the palette is numbered, and its number points to the full 24-bit RGB (red, green, blue) value stored in the graphics file header. The values in the lookup table are shown in decimal notation; converted into binary, a decimal number such as 255 would require eight bits.

▶ How do I select a color palette? Most graphics software offers a selection of ready-made palettes that you can choose by using the color palette or color picker tool. Ready-made palettes usually include a grayscale palette, a system palette, and a Web palette.

A **grayscale palette** uses shades of gray, or "gray scales," to display images that look similar to black-and-white photographs. Most grayscale palettes consist of 256 shades of gray. Figure 8-22 illustrates a grayscale palette and a grayscale bitmap graphic.

Grayscale bitmaps look like black-and-white photographs.

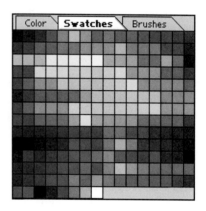

A **system palette** is the collection of colors the operating system uses for graphics that represent desktop icons and controls. Windows, for example, uses a system palette containing 20 permanent colors and 236 colors that can be changed, depending on the application.

A **Web palette** (also called a Web-safe palette or a browser palette) contains a standard set of colors used by Internet Web browsers. Because most browsers support this palette, it is regarded as a safe choice when preparing graphics for Internet distribution.

Your graphics software might offer additional palettes. They are likely to include a "woodsy" palette that works well for outdoor photographs, a pastel palette that works well with images filled with predominantly light colors, and a flesh-tone palette that's designed to work nicely for portraits. Figure 8-23 shows the collection of colors used by system and Web palettes.

The Windows system palette (left) and Web palette (right) are usually provided by graphics software.

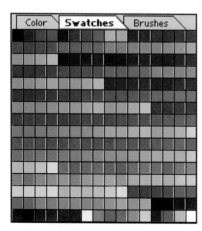
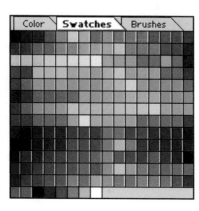

IMAGE COMPRESSION

▶ **What is image compression?** **Image compression** refers to any technique that recodes the data in an image file so that it contains fewer bits. Smaller files produced as a result of image compression require less storage space and can be transmitted more rapidly than the larger, original files. Images can be compressed using lossless or lossy compression.

▶ **What is the difference between lossless and lossy compression?** **Lossless compression** provides the means to compress a file and then reconstitute all the data into its original state. TIFF, PNG, and GIF graphics formats offer lossless compression.

In contrast, **lossy compression** throws away some of the original data during the compression process. In theory, the human eye won't miss the lost information. JPEG files are compressed using lossy compression. Most lossy compression techniques have adjustable compression levels so that you can decide how much data you can afford to lose.

▶ **How does lossless compression shrink a file without throwing away data?** Various techniques exist for lossless image compression. As a simple example, consider a type of lossless compression called run-length encoding. **Run-length encoding** (RLE) replaces a series of similarly colored pixels with a binary code that indicates the number of pixels and their colors.

Suppose that a section of a picture has 167 consecutive white pixels, and each pixel is described by one byte of data, as in a 256-color bitmap image. RLE compresses this series of 167 bytes into as few as two bytes, as shown in Figure 8-24.

FIGURE 8-24

In an uncompressed file, each pixel of a 256-color bitmap requires one byte to indicate its color. For example, a white pixel might be coded 11111111. Run-length encoding compresses graphical data by recoding like-colored pixels when they appear in a series.

1. The data for the first 167 white pixels can be compressed as 10100111 11111111. The first byte is the binary representation of 167. The second byte is the code for white.

2. The next five pixels are coded 00000101 00000000. The first byte is the binary representation of the number 5. The second byte is the code for black.

3. With compression, the first nine rows of the graphic require only 30 bytes—the binary numbers in columns 2 and 4 of this table. The uncompressed graphic requires 288 bytes.

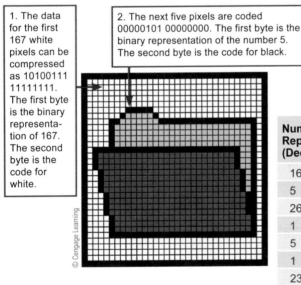

© Cengage Learning

Number of Repetitions (Decimal)	Number of Repetitions (Binary)	Pixel Color	Pixel Color (Binary)
167	10100111	White	11111111
5	00000101	Black	00000000
26	00011010	White	11111111
1	00000001	Black	00000000
5	00000101	Yellow	10100000
1	00000001	Black	00000000
23	00010111	White	11111111
2	00000010	Black	00000000
7	00000111	Yellow	10100000
18	00010010	Black	00000000
5	00000101	White	11111111
1	00000001	Black	00000000
25	00011001	Yellow	10100000
1	00000001	White	11111111
1	00000001	Black	00000000

8

▶ **What happens during lossy compression?** Lossy compression techniques discard some data from an image to shrink its file size. JPEG is a lossy version of run-length encoding that can be applied to images, such as photographs, that don't have large areas of solid color.

A True Color photograph might not have any adjoining pixels of the same color. Applying RLE to such a photo would not result in any compression whatsoever. JPEG preprocesses an image by tweaking the colors in adjoining pixels so that they are the same color whenever possible. After this preprocessing is complete, run-length encoding can be applied with more success.

For many images, lossy compression results in only a minor reduction in the sharpness of the image. The reduction in quality can be unnoticeable in many circumstances. Figure 8-25 illustrates a section of a noncompressed image and a section of that same image after JPEG compression has been applied. Can you see any difference?

FIGURE 8-25

JPEG compression can slightly adjust the colors of adjacent pixels to make them the same. These like-colored pixels can then be compressed with RLE.

© MediaTechnics

Non-compressed JPEG image

JPEG image with 35% compression

▶ **How do I compress image files?** Some graphics file formats automatically compress file data. You can also compress files using a general-purpose file compression utility.

GIF, JPEG, PNG, and TIFF file formats include compression options. Software that works with these file formats might allow you to select compression levels before saving a graphics file. For example, when saving an image in JPEG format, you might be given the option of selecting compression settings from 1 (worst quality) to 10 (best quality) as shown in Figure 8-26.

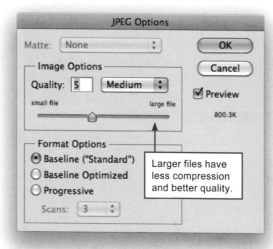

FIGURE 8-26

When saving an image in JPEG format, you can specify the level of compression.

▶ What about file formats without compression options?

Formats such as BMP and RAW do not include compression options. If you want to compress these types of image files before sending them as e-mail attachments, for example, you can do so manually using a file compression utility.

A **file compression utility** uses lossless compression to shrink one or more files into a single new file. PKZIP and WinZip are popular shareware programs that compress and decompress files. 7-Zip is a popular open source compression utility.

You can compress any kind of file, including programs and data files, graphics, and document files. BMP file sizes might shrink by as much as 70% when compressed. Files stored in formats such as PNG, GIF, and JPEG hardly shrink at all when you use compression utilities because they are already stored in compressed format.

Compressing files is sometimes called zipping, and decompressing files is sometimes called unzipping. Most file compression utilities not only zip single files, but can also zip several files into a single compressed file that can later be unzipped into the original separate files.

For example, suppose you want to send three files to your boss. The original files are called *Technology.xlsx*, *Schedule-Fall Classes.docx*, and *Insurance.bmp*. You can zip all three files into a single compressed file called *Management 212.zip* (Figure 8-27). Simply attach this one file to an e-mail and send it to your boss. When *Management 212.zip* is unzipped, it produces the three original files.

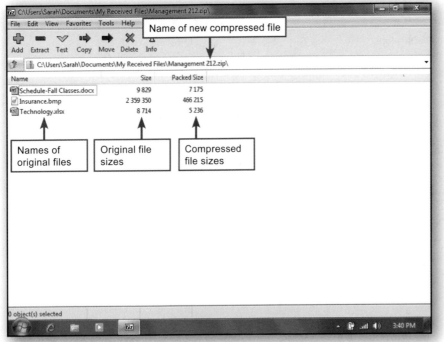

FIGURE 8-27

File compression utilities, such as open source 7-Zip, zip one or more files into a new compressed file with a .zip extension. ▶ Watch how to zip multiple files into a single compressed file, and learn how to unzip files using 7-Zip.

If you have not installed compression software such as PKZIP, you can use a feature of Windows to create compressed folders (Figure 8-28). Any files that you drag into a compressed folder are automatically compressed. You don't have to do anything special to open a file from a compressed folder. Simply double-click the file as usual, and Windows automatically decompresses the file before displaying its contents.

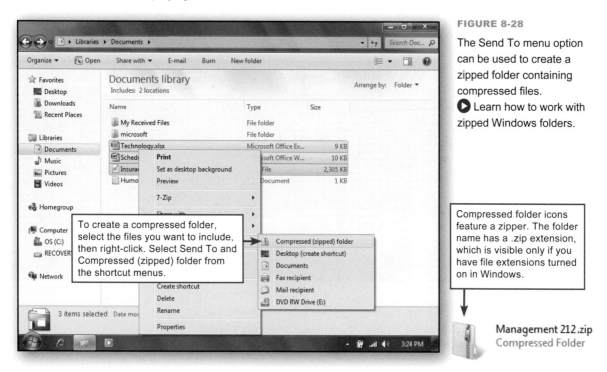

FIGURE 8-28

The Send To menu option can be used to create a zipped folder containing compressed files.
▶ Learn how to work with zipped Windows folders.

Compressed folder icons feature a zipper. The folder name has a .zip extension, which is visible only if you have file extensions turned on in Windows.

Management 212.zip
Compressed Folder

QuickCheck

SECTION B

1. A digital camera captures images on the photosites of a(n) [   ] . (Hint: Use the acronym.)

2. A characteristic of bitmap graphics is that they are resolution [   ] , so that reducing the resolution also reduces the image quality.

3. Graphics stored in True Color format require [   ] bits for each pixel.

4. The most popular True Color formats for Web graphics include [   ] and JPEG. (Hint: Use the acronym.)

5. Unlike [   ] compression, [   ] compression shrinks a file without throwing away any data.

 CHECK ANSWERS

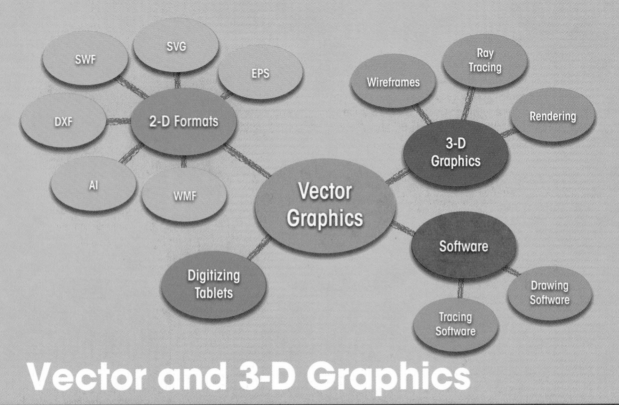

Vector and 3-D Graphics

IF YOU'VE PLAYED any computer games recently or watched an animated movie, you've seen the product of computer-generated 3-D animated graphics. This section begins with two-dimensional vector graphics. You'll find out how they differ from bitmaps and why you might want to use them. After covering the basics for two-dimensional graphics, the section progresses to static 3-D graphics and then to animated 3-D graphics.

VECTOR GRAPHICS BASICS

▶ **What is a vector graphic?** Unlike a bitmap graphic created by dividing an image into a grid of pixels, a **vector graphic** consists of a set of instructions for re-creating a picture. Instead of storing the color value for each pixel, a vector graphic file contains instructions the computer needs to create the shape, size, position, and color for each object in an image.

These instructions are similar to those a drafting teacher might give students: "Draw a 2-inch (or 112-pixel) circle. Locate this circle 1 inch down and 2 inches in from the right edge of the work area. Fill the circle with yellow."

▶ **How can I identify vector graphics?** It can be difficult to accurately identify a vector graphic just by looking at an on-screen image. Some have a flat, cartoon-like quality (Figure 8-29), but others can look fairly realistic. For a more definitive identification, you should check the file extension. Vector graphics files have file extensions such as .wmf, .ai, .dxf, .eps, .swf, and .svg.

FIGURE 8-29

The parts of a vector graphic are created as separate objects. This image was created with a series of roughly rectangular objects for the stones and a circular object for the sun. The objects are layered and can be manipulated individually. This characteristic of vector graphics gives artists flexibility in arranging and editing image elements.

▶ How do vector graphics compare with bitmap graphics?
Vector graphics are suitable for most line art, logos, simple illustrations, and diagrams that might be displayed and printed at various sizes. You should take the following distinctions into account when deciding which type of graphic to use for a specific project.

▶ **Vector graphics resize better than bitmaps.** When you change the size of a vector graphic, the objects change proportionally and maintain their smooth edges. In contrast, bitmap graphics might appear to have jagged edges after they are enlarged, as shown in Figure 8-30.

FIGURE 8-30

Unlike bitmaps, vector graphics can be resized without becoming pixelated and blurry.

8

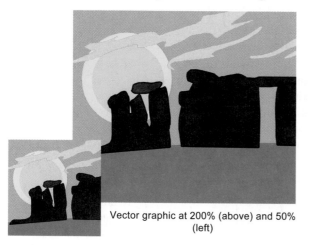

Vector graphic at 200% (above) and 50% (left)

Bitmap graphic at 200% (above) and 50% (right)

▶ **Vector graphics usually require less storage space than bitmaps.** The storage space required for a vector graphic reflects the complexity of the image. Each instruction requires storage space; so the more lines, shapes, and fill patterns in the graphic, the more storage space it requires. The Stonehenge vector graphic used as an example in this chapter requires less than 4 KB of storage space. A True Color photograph of the same image requires 1,109 KB.

▶ **Vector graphics are not usually as realistic as bitmap images.** Many 2-D vector images have a cartoon-like appearance instead of the realistic appearance you expect from a photograph. This cartoon-like characteristic of vector images results from the use of objects filled with blocks of color.

▶ **It is easier to edit an object in a vector graphic than an object in a bitmap graphic.** In some ways, a vector graphic is like a collage of objects. Each object can be layered over other objects, but moved and edited independently. You can individually stretch, shrink, distort, color, move, or delete any object in a vector graphic. Figure 8-31 illustrates the difference between vector and bitmap graphics when you try to edit out parts of the Stonehenge image.

FIGURE 8-31

Vector graphic objects are layered, so it is easy to move and delete objects without disrupting the rest of the image. In contrast, deleting a shape from a bitmap image leaves a hole because the image is only one layer of pixels.

Stones in this vector image are a separate layer that can easily be removed.

A bitmap graphic is not layered, so removing the stones leaves a hole.

▶ **What tools do I need to create vector graphics?** Neither scanners nor digital cameras produce vector graphics. Architects and engineers might use a digitizing tablet to turn a paper-based line drawing into a vector graphic. A **digitizing tablet** (sometimes called a 2-D digitizer) is a device that provides a flat surface for a paper-based drawing and a pen or mouse-like puck that you can use to click the endpoints of each line on the drawing. The endpoints are converted into vectors and stored.

Usually, vector graphics are created from scratch with vector graphics software, referred to as drawing software. Popular drawing software includes Adobe Illustrator, Corel DESIGNER, LibreOffice Draw, and open source Inkscape. Drawing software is sometimes packaged separately from the paint software used to produce bitmap graphics. In other cases, it is included with bitmap software as a graphics software suite.

Vector graphics software provides an array of drawing tools that you can use to create objects, position them, and fill them with colors or patterns. For example, you can use the filled circle tool to draw a circle filled with a solid color. You can create an irregular shape by connecting points to outline the shape. Figure 8-32 illustrates how to use drawing tools to create a vector graphic.

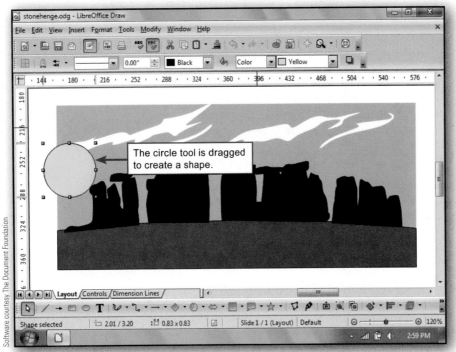

The circle tool is dragged to create a shape.

Software courtesy The Document Foundation

FIGURE 8-32

To draw a circle, select the filled circle tool, and then drag the mouse pointer to indicate the circle's location and size. A color palette allows you to select the circle color. After you create the circle object, you can move it and change its size or color. You can also create irregular shapes for objects, such as clouds, by connecting short line segments. ⊙ Learn the basics of drawing vector images by accessing this figure in your interactive eBook.

The clouds are created as a series of short line segments and filled with color.

The stones are created as a series of short line segments and filled with black.

The sun is two circles, each filled with a slightly different shade of yellow.

Vector graphics software helps you easily edit individual objects within a graphic by changing their sizes, shapes, positions, or colors. For example, the data for creating a circle for the sun is recorded as an instruction, such as CIRCLE 40 Y 200 150, which means create a circle with a 40-pixel radius, color it yellow, and place the center of the circle 200 pixels from the left of the screen and 150 pixels from the top of the screen.

If you move the circle to the right side of the image, the instruction that the computer stores for the circle changes to something like CIRCLE 40 Y 500 150, which reflects its new position at 500 pixels from the left instead of 200.

When filling a shape with color, your graphics software might provide tools for creating gradients. A **gradient** is a smooth blending of shades from one color to another or from light to dark. Gradients, as shown in Figure 8-33, can be used to create shading and three-dimensional effects.

Some vector graphics software provides tools that apply bitmapped textures to vector graphic objects, giving them a more realistic appearance. For example, you can create a vector drawing of a house, and then apply a brick-like texture derived from a bitmap photograph of real bricks. A graphic that contains both bitmap and vector data is called a **metafile**.

VECTOR-TO-BITMAP CONVERSION

▶ **Is it possible to convert a vector graphic into a bitmap?**
A vector graphic can be converted quite easily into a bitmap graphic through a process called rasterizing. **Rasterization** works by superimposing a grid over a vector image and determining the color for each pixel. This process can be carried out by graphics software, which allows you to specify the output size for the final bitmap image.

On a PC, you can rasterize a vector graphic by using the Print Screen key to take a screenshot of a vector image. On a Mac, the Command-Shift-3 key combination takes a screenshot. It is important to rasterize images at the size you ultimately need. If you rasterize a vector image at a small size and then try to enlarge the resulting bitmap image, you will likely get a poor-quality pixelated image, such as the one in Figure 8-34.

After a vector graphic is converted to a bitmap, the resulting graphic no longer has the qualities of a vector graphic. For example, if you convert the Stonehenge vector graphic into a bitmap, the sun is no longer an object that you can easily move or assign a different color.

▶ **How about converting a bitmap graphic into a vector graphic?** Converting a bitmap graphic into a vector graphic is more difficult than converting from a vector to a bitmap. To change a bitmap graphic into a vector graphic, you must use tracing software. **Tracing software** locates the edges of objects in a bitmap image and converts the resulting shapes into vector graphic objects.

Tracing software products, such as VectorEye and MagicTracer, work best on simple images and line drawings. They do not usually produce acceptable results when used on complex, detailed photos. Tracing capabilities are included in some general-purpose graphics software, but standalone tracing software offers more flexibility and usually produces better results.

FIGURE 8-33

Gradients can create the illusion of three dimensions, such as making this shape appear to be a tube.

FIGURE 8-34

When vector images are rasterized, they become bitmaps and can't be enlarged without becoming pixelated.

VECTOR GRAPHICS ON THE WEB

▶ **Do vector graphics work on the Web?** Web browsers were originally designed to support a limited number of graphics formats—GIF and JPEG—and these formats were exclusively bitmaps. Today, vector graphics such as **SVG** (Scalable Vector Graphics) and **Flash** can also be used on the Web (Figure 8-35).

FIGURE 8-35

The two most pervasive vector formats on the Web are SVG and Flash.

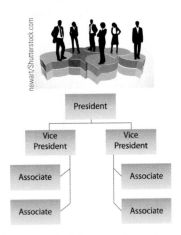

SVG is supported by most modern browsers without requiring a plug-in. It supports gradients, drop shadows, multiple levels of transparency, and animation effects, along with portability to other platforms, such as handheld computers and cellular phones.

Adobe's Flash software creates vector graphics that are stored in files with .swf extensions. Flash graphics can be static or animated. Flash plug-ins are available for most popular browsers. However, when this book went to press, the browsers supplied with iOS devices were unable to work with Flash formats.

▶ **What are the advantages of using vector graphics on the Web?** Vector graphics have several advantages:

▶ Consistent quality. On Web pages, vector graphics appear with the same consistent quality on all computer screens. This capability makes it possible for browsers to adjust the size of an image on the fly to fit correctly on a screen, regardless of its size or resolution. These adjustments don't carry any penalty in terms of image quality—a large version of a vector graphic displayed on a screen set at 1600 x 1200 resolution has the same sharp detail and smooth curves as the original image sized to fit a smaller screen set at 800 x 600 resolution. This flexibility is important for Web pages that might be viewed at different resolutions on PCs, Macs, or other platforms.

▶ Searchable. Text contained in a vector image is stored as actual text, not just a series of colored dots. This text can be indexed by search engines so that it can be included in keyword searches. For example, suppose a vector drawing was used to produce a diagram describing the service box where your telephone line enters your house. One of the components in this diagram is labeled "telephone test jack." If you enter "telephone test jack" into a search engine, the service box diagram will likely turn up in the list of search results.

▶ Compact file size. A third advantage of vector graphics on the Web is their compact file sizes. A fairly complex graphic can be stored in a file that is under 30 KB—that's kilobytes, not megabytes. These files require little storage space and can be transmitted swiftly from a Web server to your browser.

8

3-D GRAPHICS

▶ **How do vector graphics relate to 3-D graphics?** Like vector graphics, **3-D graphics** are stored as a set of instructions. For a 3-D graphic, however, the instructions contain the locations and lengths of lines that form a wireframe for a three-dimensional object.

A **wireframe** acts in much the same way as the framework of a pop-up tent. Just as you would construct the framework for the tent, and then cover it with a nylon tent cover, a 3-D wireframe can be covered with surface texture and color to create a graphic of a 3-D object.

The process of covering a wireframe with surface color and texture is called **rendering**. The rendering process, shown in Figure 8-36, outputs a bitmap image.

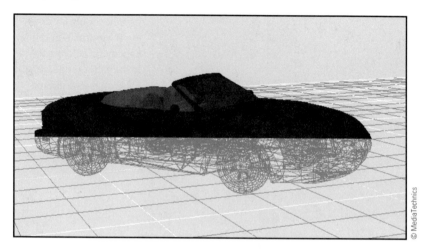

FIGURE 8-36

3-D graphics are based on a wireframe, which can be rendered into a bitmap image that looks three-dimensional.

For added realism, the rendering process can take into account the way that light shines on surfaces and creates shadows. The technique for adding light and shadows to a 3-D image is called **ray tracing**.

Before an image is rendered, the artist selects a location for one or more light sources. The computer applies a complex mathematical algorithm to determine how the light source affects the color of each pixel in the final rendered image. Figure 8-37 shows the image from the previous figure rendered with an additional light source and ray tracing.

FIGURE 8-37

Ray tracing adds realism to 3-D graphics by adding highlights and shadows that are produced by a light source.

❱ What tools do I need to create 3-D graphics? 3-D graphics software runs on most personal computers, although some architects, designers, special effects artists, and engineers prefer to use high-end workstations. A fast processor, lots of RAM, and a fast graphics card with its own video RAM all speed up the rendering process.

To create 3-D graphics, you need 3-D graphics software, such as Autodesk AutoCAD or Caligari trueSpace. This software has tools for drawing a wireframe and viewing it from any angle. It provides rendering and ray tracing tools, along with an assortment of surface textures that you can apply to individual objects. Figure 8-38 takes you on a tour of a popular 3-D graphics software package.

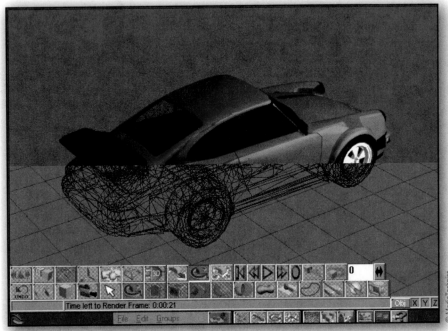

FIGURE 8-38

3-D graphics software provides tools for drawing a wireframe and then specifying colors and textures for rendering. ▶ Watch a wireframe being rendered and animated in your interactive eBook.

❱ Is it possible to animate 3-D graphics? 3-D graphics can be animated to produce special effects for movies or to create interactive, animated characters and environments for 3-D computer games. Animated special effects, such as massive battle scenes, are created by rendering a sequence of bitmaps, in which one or more objects are moved or otherwise changed between each rendering.

In traditional hand-drawn animation, a chief artist draws the keyframes, and then a team of assistants creates each of the in-between images—24 of these images for each second of animation. For 3-D computer animation, the computer creates the in-between images by moving the object and rendering each necessary image. All the images are then combined into a single file, creating essentially a digital movie.

Graphics design companies such as Pixar Animation Studios and DreamWorks use 3-D animation techniques to produce animated feature films as well as special effects. The first full-length animated 3-D movie was *Toy Story*, released in 1995 by Walt Disney Studios and Pixar. Digitally animated films, such as *Avatar* and *Happy Feet Two*, illustrate the growing sophistication of 3-D animation.

▶ Do game and movie animation require similar tools and techniques?
An important characteristic of special effects and animated films is that rendering can be accomplished during the production phase of the movie and incorporated into the final footage. In contrast, 3-D computer game animation happens in real time. Each frame that makes the image seem to move must be rendered while you are playing the game—a process that requires an incredible amount of computer power.

FIGURE 8-39

Classic computer games established building blocks for animation technologies used to create today's fast-action, visually detailed computer games, such as Call of Duty.

To give you a handle on the immensity of the processing power required to render the real-time images for computer games, consider a classic game like Doom displayed on a screen that's set at 1024 x 768 resolution (Figure 8-39). At this resolution, the screen contains 786,432 pixels (1,024 multiplied by 768). If the game is presented in 32-bit color, each frame of the animation requires 25,165,824 bits (multiply 786,432 times 32).

Computer game designers believe that on-screen animation looks smoothest at 60 frames per second, which means your computer must handle 1,509,949,440— that's more than 1 billion—bits of information every second just to display the 3-D image on the screen. In addition, the computer must process even more data to keep track of the movements of each player.

To handle all the data required for game play, your computer's main processor gets help from a graphics processor located on your computer's graphics card. These graphics processors vary in their capabilities. For the fastest graphics capability, some computers can accept two graphics cards that work in tandem as 3-D accelerators.

▶ Can I create my own animated 3-D graphics?
You can create 3-D animations on a standard PC or Mac with commercially available software; but professional 3-D software, such as Autodesk Maya and 3ds Max, is expensive and has a steep learning curve.

If you want to dabble with 3-D animations before making an expensive software investment, you might try Smith Micro Poser or DAZ Studio. Whether you use a commercial or shareware package, be prepared to spend lots of time with the manual before you are able to produce your own original animations.

QuickCheck   SECTION C

1. Vector graphics require more storage space than bitmaps, but vectors can be enlarged without becoming pixelated. True or false? [_____]

2. A process called [_____] converts vector graphics into bitmap images.

3. SVG and [_____] are two of the most popular vector formats used on the Web.

4. A 3-D image is based on an assemblage of vectors called a(n) [_____].

5. The technique of adding light and shadows to a 3-D image is called ray [_____].

 CHECK ANSWERS

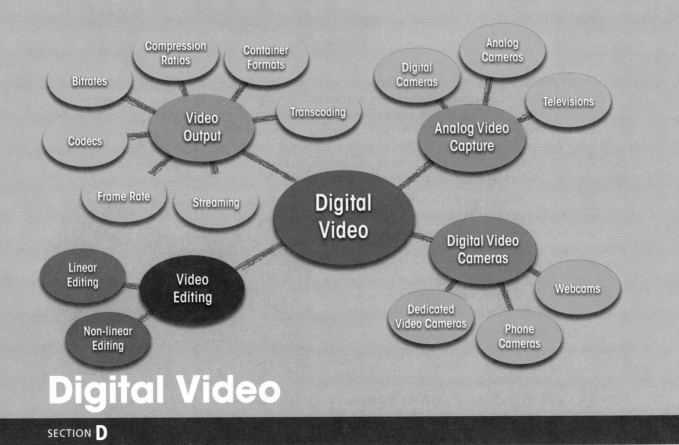

Digital Video

DIGITAL VIDEO IS EVERYWHERE. It encompasses several technologies, including those that produce theater-quality DVD movies, desktop video that you edit on your computer, and quick clips that you shoot with the camera on your smartphone. In this section, you'll take a look at what you can do with affordable, easy-to-use desktop video tools.

DIGITAL VIDEO BASICS

▶ **What is digital video?** A video is a series of still frames, like those in Figure 8-40, projected at a rate fast enough to fool the human eye into perceiving continuous motion. **Digital video** uses bits to store color and brightness data for each video frame. The process is similar to storing the data for a series of bitmap images in which the color for each pixel is represented by a binary number.

▶ **Where does digital video footage originate?** Footage for digital videos can be supplied from a digital or analog source, but analog video requires conversion. You can shoot footage with a consumer-quality camcorder, webcam, or cell phone camera. Some cameras designed for still photography can also capture short videos. Footage can also originate from a videotape, television, DVD, or even a digital video recording device.

▶ **How is digital video used?** You can use your personal computer to edit footage into videos suitable for a variety of personal and professional uses, such as video wedding albums, product sales videos, training videos, video holiday greeting cards, documentaries for nonprofit organizations, and video scrapbooks. Video that is created on a personal computer and designed to be played back on a similar device is sometimes referred to as **desktop video**.

In addition to its use to create personal videos, digital video is also used in the movie industry. Digital cinematography and editing have been used for many award-winning films, such as *Cold Mountain*, *Slumdog Millionaire*, and *Avatar*. Outside of the context of Hollywood, digital video is a core

FIGURE 8-40

A video is composed of a series of bitmap graphics, each one called a frame.

technology for HDTV, videoconferencing systems, and video messaging. Real-time video even allows deaf people to sign over cell phones.

Digital videos can be stored on a hard disk or distributed on CDs, DVDs, videotapes, memory cards, file sharing networks, or the Web. Popular software for playing digital video on computers includes Apple QuickTime Player, Windows Media Player, and Adobe Flash Player.

▶ **How do I create digital videos?** To understand how you can create your own digital videos, you'll need information about four procedures summarized in Figure 8-41 and explained in the rest of this section.

1. Produce video footage. Select equipment for filming videos and use effective filming techniques.

2. Transfer video footage to a computer. Use a cable, a video capture card, or an SD card to move video footage from cameras, videotapes, television, and DVDs to your computer's hard disk.

3. Edit video footage. Use software to select video segments, arrange them into a video, and add a soundtrack.

4. Store and play. Select digital video file formats for playback on desktop, Web, portable, and DVD platforms.

FIGURE 8-41

Creating digital videos requires a few fairly simple steps.

PRODUCING VIDEO FOOTAGE

▶ **What kinds of video cameras are available?** You can shoot video footage using standalone video cameras and cameras embedded in computers and handheld devices.

As you might expect, digital video cameras capture footage as a series of bits. Most of today's standalone digital video cameras store data on solid state memory cards, but storage options also include solid state drives, miniDVDs, digital tape, or built-in hard drives. Cameras run the gamut from sub-US$150 consumer minicams to professional quality shoulder-mount camcorders costing more than $20,000 and high-definition Hollywood-style cameras priced over $100,000 (Figure 8-42).

FIGURE 8-42

Digital video cameras are available in many sizes and prices.

▶ Can I use an analog camera? You can use an analog video camera to shoot footage that eventually becomes digital video. Analog footage is stored on tape as a continuous track of magnetic patterns. To use your computer to store and edit analog footage, you'll have to convert it into digital format.

▶ How about webcams? Another option for shooting video footage is a small, inexpensive **webcam** that is built in over the screen of a notebook computer or attached as a peripheral device (Figure 8-43). These cameras capture a series of still photos, which are stored in digital format directly on your computer's hard disk or transmitted over a network.

Webcams can be controlled by various software applications, including instant messenger clients and specialized webcam software that is bundled with new computers and add-on webcams. Webcams tend to produce low-quality video. Most webcams must remain tethered to your computer, which tends to limit your videos to "talking heads."

▶ Can I get digital footage from my cell phone camera? Most mobile phones and handheld devices include a camera. Many of these cameras are equipped to film video footage and store it on the device's internal hard drive or memory card. The video quality produced by these cameras is not usually as high as the footage produced by standalone digital video cameras, and storage space is usually more limited.

Cameras embedded in handheld devices tend to have fewer options and features than standalone cameras. For example, most cameras included with handheld devices lack the image stabilization feature common on standalone cameras that compensates for hand vibration.

▶ Do I need a fancy camera? Most people agree that an inexpensive camera is better than nothing, but the quality of your camera can make a difference in the quality of the finished footage.

A common misconception is that a cheap camera won't make a difference for videos shown on small screens at a fairly low resolution. Just the opposite is true. The higher the quality of the original video, the better the final video will look, regardless of the size of the screen on which it is shown.

▶ Does digital video require special filming techniques? When videos are processed and stored on a personal computer, some of the image data is eliminated to reduce the video file to a manageable size. Simpler videos tend to maintain better quality as they are edited, processed, and stored. Camera movements, fast actions, patterned clothing, and moving backgrounds all contribute to the complexity of a video and should be minimized. The techniques listed in Figure 8-44 can help you produce video footage that maintains good quality as it is edited and processed.

FIGURE 8-43

A Web camera can be built into a computer display device or can be attached as shown. It is designed mainly for "talking head" applications, such as online video chats and video-conferences.

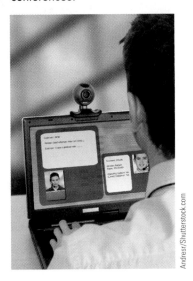

Andresr/Shutterstock.com

FIGURE 8-44

Video Filming Tips

© Media Technics

▶ Use a tripod to maintain a steady image.
▶ Move the camera slowly if it is necessary to pan from side to side.
▶ Zoom in and out slowly.
▶ Direct your subjects to move slowly, when possible.
▶ Position your shot to eliminate as much background detail and movement as possible.
▶ Ask the subjects of your video to wear solid-colored clothing, if possible.

VIDEO TRANSFER

▶ **What can I do with my video footage?** Video footage can be transferred to a computer for editing, streamed out during synchronous communications sessions, e-mailed, or uploaded to file sharing sites. Some cameras automate these transfers, whereas transferring footage from other types of cameras requires several manual steps.

▶ **What are my options for webcam footage?** The footage captured by webcams is often immediately streamed to your computer's hard disk or out over a network during a video chat session or videoconference. If you've stored webcam footage on your computer, you can view and edit it using video editing software.

▶ **How about video from handheld devices?** Video from handheld devices can be e-mailed directly to friends or to yourself. E-mailing footage to yourself is an easy way to get it to your computer for editing. Alternatively, your handheld device might store video footage on a memory card that you can transfer to your computer. Most handheld devices also allow you to directly upload videos to YouTube and other video sharing sites.

▶ **How do I transfer video footage from a video camera to my computer?** The basic method for transferring digital video footage to your computer's hard disk for editing is to remove the SD card from the camera and insert it into a card reader on your computer.

Your digital camera might provide other ways to transfer data to a computer. You can connect the camera to your computer with a cable and fire up video editing software to control the transfer. This method is used for cameras that store video on non-removable media, such as a built-in hard drive or digital videotape, but you might also use this method if you want a lengthy video divided into several smaller clips.

▶ **How do I transfer video from analog devices?** Analog video footage from TV, videotape, and analog video cameras has to be converted into digital format before it can be stored on your computer's hard disk. The process of converting analog video signals into digital format is referred to as **video capture** and requires a video capture device and software.

Your computer's graphics card might include video capture capabilities. If not, you can purchase a separate video capture device that connects to your computer's USB port or a video capture card that plugs into an expansion slot (Figure 8-45).

▶ **How much hard disk space is required to store video files?** Video files are large, but just how large depends on the video format used by your camera. Video files produced from digital tape usually are largest, whereas videos stored on memory cards are somewhat smaller, and videos from cell phones and webcams are usually small enough to e-mail.

Be prepared with several gigabytes of free space on your computer's hard disk before you begin any serious video editing. You might consider using an external hard disk drive to hold the sound files and video footage you use for assembling videos.

FIGURE 8-45

After it has been installed in your computer, a video capture card can be connected to the video-out and audio-out ports on an analog camera, television, VCR, or DVD player.

© MediaTechnics

8

VIDEO EDITING

▶ Do I need special equipment for video editing? Before camcorders went digital, editing a video consisted of recording segments from one videotape onto another tape. This process, called **linear editing**, required two VCRs at minimum. Professional video editors used expensive editing equipment, beyond the budget of most consumers.

Today's **nonlinear editing** simply requires a computer hard disk and video editing software. The advantage of nonlinear editing is that you can use a random-access device to easily edit and arrange video clips. Video editing requires lots of hard disk space, however. So before you begin an editing session, make sure your computer's hard disk has several gigabytes of available storage space. It is also a good idea to have at least 1 GB of RAM—professionals opt for at least 4 GB.

▶ How do I edit a video? After your video footage is transferred to your computer and stored on the hard disk, you can begin to arrange your video clips by using video editing software, such as Adobe Premiere, Apple Final Cut Pro, Windows Live Movie Maker, or Corel VideoStudio.

Videos are easier to edit if you divide them into several files, each containing a one- or two-minute video clip. Some video capture software automatically creates clips by detecting frame changes, such as when you turn your camera off, pause, or switch to a new scene.

Video editing software allows you to further crop tracks and add transitions between them. You can also overlay video tracks with one or more audio tracks containing music or narrations.

Your completed video consists of video tracks containing video segments and transitions, plus audio tracks containing voices and music. Figure 8-46 illustrates how to lay out video and audio tracks.

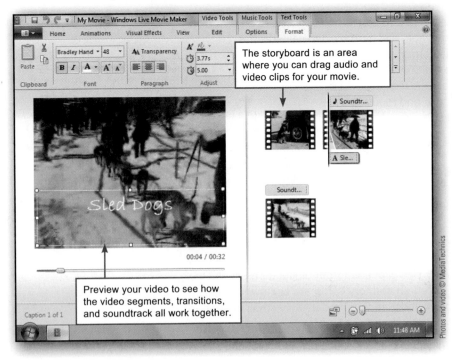

FIGURE 8-46

Simple video editing software combines video clips, sounds, and transitions into movies. ▶ Learn the basics of Windows Live Movie Maker and see how to create a short movie about sled dogs, complete with soundtrack. (This tour might take a few moments to begin. Please be patient.)

VIDEO OUTPUT

▶ How does video footage become a digital video? Your video editing software combines the data from all the video and audio files you selected into a single file, which is stored on your computer's hard disk. During the output process, you can select settings for aspect ratio, frame size, and compression so that the resulting video quality and file size are appropriate for the video's intended use.

Aspect ratio refers to the relative width and height of the video frame; widescreen is 16:9 and fullscreen is 4:3. Most computers, televisions, and handheld devices are designed for widescreen format, though the screens for a few devices, such as iPads, are sized for fullscreen formats.

Frame size corresponds to the resolution of the video window. A typical frame size for handheld devices is 320 x 480 or 480 x 600. Fullscreen computer display size is 1024 x 768, as is the iPad. DVD video has a resolution of 720 x 480; high-definition video has a resolution of 1920 x 1080.

▶ How is video compressed? Raw video requires vast amounts of storage space, so videos are usually compressed to create files that can be conveniently stored and transmitted. Video compression can be achieved by decreasing the frame rate (number of frames per second), reducing the frame size, and using techniques similar to JPEG to compress the data stored for each frame.

A **codec** (compressor/decompressor) is the software that compresses a video stream when a video is stored, and decompresses the file when the video is played. Popular codecs include MPEG, DivX, H.264, Theora, and Windows Media Video. Each codec uses a unique algorithm to shrink the size of a video file, so they are not interchangeable. When creating videos, you should use one of the codecs included in popular video players.

Video compression can be expressed as a compression ratio or as a bitrate. A **compression ratio** indicates the ratio of compressed data to uncompressed data. A video file with a high compression ratio, such as 35:1, has more compression, a smaller file size, and lower image quality than a file with a smaller compression ratio, such as 5:1.

Bitrate refers to the amount of data transferred per second as a video plays. Higher bitrates produce better quality video. Click the CLICK TO START buttons in Figure 8-47 to compare video and audio quality produced by different compression settings.

8

FIGURE 8-47

Different compression ratios can have a remarkable effect on video quality and file size.

Bitrate: 90 Kbps
Frame rate: 10
File size: 359 KB

▶ CLICK TO START

Bitrate: 448 Kbps
Frame rate: 15
File size: 1177 KB

▶ CLICK TO START

Bitrate: 928 Kbps
Frame rate: 30
File size: 2448 KB

▶ CLICK TO START

▶ How can I specify a compression level? Some entry-level video editing software allows you simply to select a use for your video, such as sending it as an e-mail attachment, posting it on the Web, publishing it on YouTube, or viewing it from your local hard disk. The software automatically applies an appropriate level of compression to the video data.

Alternatively, your software might offer the option of selecting a maximum file size. For example, if you are planning to send a video as an e-mail attachment, you might limit the size to 1 MB, and your video data will be compressed to that specified size.

Some video editing software allows you to select a bitrate for your final video. Uncompressed video files contain a huge number of bits per frame, so smooth playback requires a high bitrate, such as 340 Kbps. Compressed files contain fewer bits per frame and play back more smoothly at lower bitrates, such as 38 Kbps, offered by slower Internet connections.

As another option, your video editing software might offer you a selection of compression ratios, such as 5:1 or 35:1. You might have to experiment with compression ratios a bit to find the best balance between file size and image quality.

▶ What is the best video file format? Many video file formats are available; the format you use should be compatible with the devices on which it is played and its browser or player software. Digital video file formats are sometimes referred to as **container formats** because they hold the compressed video and audio data streams that form a video (Figure 8-48).

Figure 8-49 describes some popular video container formats—**AVI**, **MOV**, **MPEG**, **WebM**, **ASF**, **Flash video**, **VOB**, and **Blu-ray Disc Movie**.

FIGURE 8-48

Codecs and video formats are easily confused, especially because some containers have the same names as codecs. A codec, such as H.264, is software that compresses the video stream, whereas a container format, such as MOV, is a method of storing video data in a file.

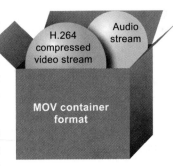

FIGURE 8-49

Popular Digital Video Formats

Format	Extension	Platform	Description and Use
AVI (Audio Video Interleave)	.avi	PC	A format sometimes used for storing digital clips from video cameras; used for desktop video on the PC platform
MOV (QuickTime Movie)	.mov	PC, Mac, UNIX, Linux	One of the most popular formats for desktop video and streaming Web videos
MPEG (Moving Picture Experts Group)	.mpg or .mpeg	PC, Mac, UNIX, Linux	Versions include MPEG-1, MPEG-2, and MPEG-4; used for desktop video and streaming Web video
WebM	.webm	PC, Mac, UNIX, Linux	Royalty-free, high-quality open format for use with HTML5
ASF (Advanced Systems Format)	.asf or .wmv	PC	Container format for Microsoft's Windows Media Video (WMV) desktop video and streaming Web video
Flash video	.flv	PC, Mac	Popular for Web-based video; requires Adobe Flash Player
VOB (Video Object)	.vob	Standalone DVD player, PC, Mac, Linux	Industry-standard format for standalone DVD players
Blu-ray Disc Movie	.bdmv	PC, Mac	A format used for storing HD video clips on Blu-ray disc

▶ Can I change videos from one format to another? Digital videos can be converted from one file format to another through a process called **transcoding**. If you want to move a video into a different file format, you can check to see if your video editing software offers a conversion, export, or transcoding option. If not, you can find transcoding software on the Web. Transcoding can cause loss of quality, so avoid transcoding an already transcoded video file.

WEB VIDEO

▶ **How do Web-based videos work?** A video for a Web page is stored on a Web server in a file. Usually, a link for the video file appears on the Web page. When you click the link, the Web server transmits a copy of the video file to your computer. If your browser has a plug-in that corresponds to the video format, the video is displayed on your computer screen.

The transfer of a digital video file from the Web to your computer can happen in one of two ways, depending on the video format. In one case, your computer waits until it downloads the entire video file before starting to play it. This technology is typically used for movie downloads.

An alternative video delivery method, called **streaming video**, sends a small segment of the video to your computer and begins to play it. While this segment plays, the Web server sends the next part of the file to your computer, and so on, until the video ends. With streaming video, your computer essentially plays the video while it continues to receive it. Videos intended to be viewed in the context of a Web page are routinely delivered by streaming video technology.

▶ **How do I post a video to YouTube or a similar file sharing site?** YouTube is a video sharing Web site that encourages members to upload, view, and rate video clips. YouTube and similar sites accept most popular video file formats directly from digital cameras, camcorders, cell phones, and webcams (Figure 8-50).

FIGURE 8-50

You can use YouTube to capture footage on your computer's webcam and upload it to the YouTube Web site.

Before uploading videos, you can edit them and save them in a standard video format, such as WebM, MPEG, MOV, AVI, WMV, or Flash video. YouTube imposes a length and time limitation, so you should check the current regulations before you finalize your video.

After your file is uploaded, it is converted into the standard formats used by YouTube. Originally, all YouTube videos were converted into Flash format. Later, a format for mobile phones was added, as was an HD widescreen format. In conjunction with the move to HTML5, WebM format was also added. In order to make YouTube videos more accessible to the deaf and hearing impaired, some videos can be automatically captioned.

▶ **How are videos added to Web pages?** On today's Web, most videos are embedded in Web pages so that they appear to play in place. For browsers that support HTML5, the <video> tag can be used to specify the name of the video file and a message to display if someone tries to access the video without the corresponding plug-in. The <object> and <iframe> tags can be used in HTML 4 or HTML5.

A simple HTML5 snippet using the <video> tag for adding a video might look like this:

```
<video src="myvideo.webm" controls>
If the video doesn't begin, you might need to download a plug-in.
</video>
```

▶ **What are the best formats for Web videos?** The HTML5 <video> tag supports several video formats, but it does not designate a common video format for all HTML5-compliant browsers. Web site developers sometimes have to provide a video in multiple formats to make it accessible to a variety of browsers and hardware devices.

At the time this book was published, there was no single video format supported by all browsers. But the Flash, Ogg Theora, H.264, and WebM formats appear to be the best candidates for widespread Web use with HTML5.

▶ **Can I incorporate videos from the Web into my own Web site and social networking pages?** There are several ways to reuse and share videos that you find on the Web. When using videos created by others, make sure you give the authors credit, adhere to originating sites' usage policies, and abide by copyright law.

Video sharing sites, such as YouTube, include tools for e-mailing videos, sharing videos on social networking sites, and including them in blogs. You can embed videos from these sites by copying HTML code into the source code for your own Web pages. You can also copy video links into e-mail messages and Web page source documents so that readers can quickly connect to the original video source on YouTube, Facebook, or other Web sites (Figure 8-51).

FIGURE 8-51

YouTube provides source code for embedding a video into your own Web page or sharing links on Facebook, Twitter, and other social networking sites.

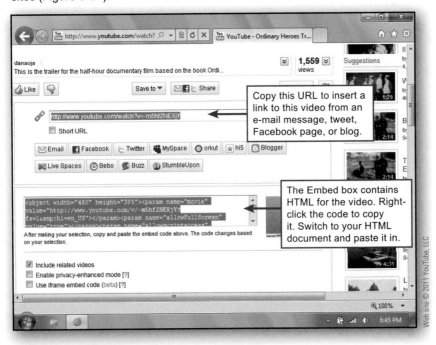

Web site © 2011 YouTube, LLC

DVD-VIDEO

▶ Can I burn my digital videos onto DVDs with interactive menus like commercial movies? Suppose you've used video editing software to create a short documentary on sled dogs. You can package the completed video footage into a professional-style DVD that can be played on computer DVD drives (if your computer is equipped with DVD player software) or standalone DVD players. It can include interactive menus with options, such as Play Video, Select a Scene, and Special Features, that viewers can select using their DVD remote controls.

▶ What equipment do I need? To create video DVDs, you need a writable DVD drive (sometimes called a DVD burner) plus software that includes tools for DVD menu creation and writing data onto a DVD-Video—a process sometimes called burning. These tools are offered by DVD authoring software, such as Adobe Encore, Sonic MyDVD, Nero, and Corel DVD MovieFactory. Many video editing software packages and suites also include tools for creating DVD menus and burning projects onto DVDs.

▶ What's the process for making a video DVD? To create a video DVD, you usually begin by selecting one or more completed videos that include soundtracks, transitions, titles, special effects, and so on. You then use DVD authoring software to design menus and buttons that viewers can use to navigate to specific parts of your video. To complete the project, you can test your project and then burn it to DVD.

▶ What are my options for creating interactive DVD menus? A DVD menu is a screen that provides viewers with navigation tools to start a video, skip to specific scenes, play special features, and link to other menus. A typical DVD menu consists of a decorative background and option buttons that viewers can select using their DVD player's remote control. Some DVD authoring software offers a selection of predesigned menu and button templates that you can easily incorporate with your videos (Figure 8-52). Your software might also provide the option to create your own backgrounds and buttons using graphics software, such as Adobe Photoshop or Microsoft Paint.

FIGURE 8-52

DVD authoring software offers a selection of backgrounds and button styles for creating DVD menus. ▶ Your interactive eBook demonstrates how to create a DVD menu and generate a standalone DVD using Windows DVD Maker.

8

❱ **Are menus easy to create?** Yes, they just require a little advance planning. As you design the menu flow, remember that you want to provide viewers with a way to return to the main menu from each submenu. You might also want viewers to return to the main menu after viewing individual clips. If a submenu offers options for outtakes or other special features, you should provide a way for viewers to return to the submenu when the special feature ends. To help visualize the way your menus will work, you can draw a diagram similar to the one in Figure 8-53.

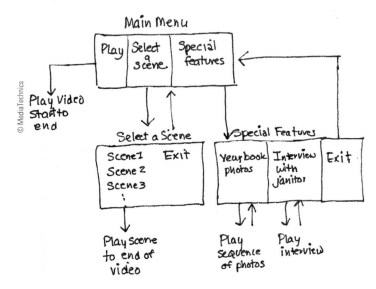

FIGURE 8-53

Sketching a diagram of the menus for your DVD can help you envision how viewers will navigate to selected scenes and special features.

❱ **How do I output my video to DVD?** To create a DVD that can be viewed on a standalone DVD player, you have to output your video in DVD-Video format, which requires video encoded with MPEG-2 and stored in VOB files. Your DVD authoring software can generate MPEG-2 video clips and menus, store them in VOB files, and lay them out on a DVD according to industry standards.

Most DVD authoring software can accomplish the MPEG encoding on the fly as it burns the DVD. However, this process takes time. So if you are burning more than one copy, or if you want to test your menu structure before burning the video onto a DVD, you might want to consider creating a DVD image.

❱ **What's a DVD image?** A **DVD image** (sometimes called a DVD volume) is essentially a prototype of your DVD, but it is stored on your computer's hard disk. If you have space to store a DVD image, it is a good idea to make one before burning a DVD. You can use a DVD image for testing. You can also use the image to burn multiple DVDs without waiting for your software to prepare the files for each burn.

❱ **Can I simply copy a desktop video to a DVD using the Copy command?** Desktop videos are usually stored in WMV or MOV format, and some standalone DVD players are not equipped to handle those formats. So, although you can use the Copy command to copy MOV and WMV files to a DVD and distribute them, these files can be viewed on most computers, but not on all DVD players.

Even copying files stored in MPEG format might not produce a DVD that works in a standalone player. The DVD-Video format specification requires a specific layout for data on the DVD surface. The method you use to copy computer data files does not produce the required layout, so most DVD players will not be able to play the video.

▶ **How do I test my DVD image?** Your DVD is ready for production and distribution if the video quality looks good and the menus work correctly. Use the tips listed below to test your DVD on your computer before you burn a DVD:

▶ Test each button to make sure it links to the correct clip.

▶ Play each clip to the end and make sure it returns to the correct menu when completed.

▶ Watch the video carefully and look for any poor quality segments with distracting artifacts, such as blurs or halos. Artifacts can sometimes be removed by revisiting your MPEG coding options.

▶ Listen to the soundtrack to make sure the audio is clear, smooth, and synchronized with the video.

▶ **Does it make a difference if I use recordable or rewritable DVDs?** Commercial DVD movies are stamped onto DVD-ROM discs during the manufacturing process—something you can't do with your computer's DVD drive. Your computer can burn data on DVD-R, DVD+R, or DVD-RW discs.

Because the DVD industry has not achieved a single media standard, some standalone DVD players—particularly those manufactured before 2004—are not able to read one or more of these disc types. DVD+R and DVD-R seem to be compatible with the widest variety of DVD players, whereas DVD-RW seems to be the least compatible. Before you distribute your DVDs, make sure you test them in a standalone DVD player.

> **TERMINOLOGY NOTE**
>
> In the world of video production, an artifact is any visible degradation in the image quality, such as shimmering where contrasting colors meet or backgrounds that become wavy during fast pans or zooms.

8

QuickCheck

1. The process of converting analog video signals into digital format is referred to as video [_____].

2. A(n) [_____] is the software that compresses a video stream when a video is stored, and decompresses the file when the video is played.

3. Compressed files contain less data per frame and play back more smoothly at lower [_____] rates.

4. Digital videos can be converted from one file format to another through a process called [_____].

5. Before you create a DVD video, it is a good idea to create a DVD [_____] on your computer's hard disk.

▶ CHECK ANSWERS

Digital Rights Management

THE SECURITY SECTIONS of earlier chapters looked at security from the user perspective. In contrast, the security section for this chapter examines the techniques used by content providers to protect digital media from unlicensed duplication and use. In this section, you'll learn about DRM technologies you may have already encountered and some that are likely to affect your ability to use digital media in the future.

CONTENT BASICS

▶ **What is "content"?** **Media content** (or simply content) includes television shows, movies, music, and books. **Digital content** is a term used for movies and other content that is stored digitally.

Content is accessed by means of a player. Keep in mind that the term *player* can refer to a hardware device or software.

▶ Software players include familiar media players, such as iTunes, Windows Media Player, and QuickTime.

▶ Hardware players include standalone devices such as CD players, VCRs, DVD players, Blu-ray players, ebook readers, and portable media players.

▶ Computer devices, such as CD, DVD, and Blu-ray drives, are also considered players, though they require software to play back content.

▶ **How do consumers expect to use media content?** Consumers expect to be able to manipulate media content so that they can use it on multiple devices at a convenient time and place (Figure 8-54 on the next page).

464

▶ **Time shifting** is the process of recording a broadcast, such as a television show, so that it can be played back at a more convenient time.

myosotisrock/Shutterstock.com

FIGURE 8-54

Consumers want to be able to engage in time, place, and format shifting.

▶ **Place shifting** allows media that originates in one place to be accessed from another place without changing the device on which it is stored.

Place shifting is often achieved using computer networks, as when you stream a movie from your computer to your Wi-Fi equipped DVD player to your Wi-Fi equipped HDTV.

▶ **Format shifting** is the process of converting media files from a format suitable for one device to a format suitable for a different kind of device.

A common use of format shifting is ripping audio tracks from a CD and converting them into MP3 format for playback on a portable media device, such as an iPod.

© MediaTechnics

▶ **What's the problem?** Pirating music and movies is a multibillion-dollar worldwide activity that is increasingly controlled by organized crime. Yet individuals also contribute to the high incidence of movie and music piracy.

File-sharing sites entice consumers with free, but illegal, downloads. Audio extraction software makes it easy to rip tracks from an audio CD and hand them out to friends.

Every hardware device and software program that interacts with digital content poses a potential vulnerability that can be exploited by pirates. Software that encrypts content can be cracked, signals that travel from one device to another can be intercepted, and when all else fails, the **analog hole** allows pirates to capture content by using a microphone to record songs as they are output to speakers or using a camcorder to film movies as they are projected in a movie theater.

Content providers use digital rights management to reduce piracy, but it can limit the way ordinary consumers use digital content that they purchase, rent, subscribe to, or download.

DRM TECHNOLOGIES

▶ **What is DRM?** **Digital rights management** (DRM) is a collection of techniques used by copyright holders to limit access to and use of digital content.

You've probably encountered DRM systems, such as Apple's FairPlay and Microsoft's Windows Media DRM, that are designed to protect music, movies, ebooks, and even television shows. DRM systems often consist of several layers of technology, which means that a movie, for example, might be protected by multiple types of DRM.

DRM technologies include authentication, proprietary media formats, encryption, and watermarks.

▶ **What is authentication?** Authentication is a very simple form of digital rights management that allows content to be accessed only by authorized individuals. It is commonly one aspect of digital rights management for cloud-based content. Very simply, you are required to log in with a valid user ID and password before you can access movies, music, or other digital content.

Authentication provides weak protection unless combined with encryption and other DRM technologies. Additional DRM is necessary to prevent customers from copying content and sharing their IDs with friends who can then access content without paying any monthly fees.

▶ **What are proprietary media formats?** Digital content that is distributed on physical media, such as CDs, DVDs, or Blu-ray discs, can be **copy protected** by proprietary media formats that intentionally vary from standard formats. Proprietary formats have been used with music CDs and with DVD movies. Figure 8-55 illustrates how a proprietary media format was used to protect music CDs.

FIGURE 8-55

Copy protected CDs contain a software program that strips out intentionally corrupted data.

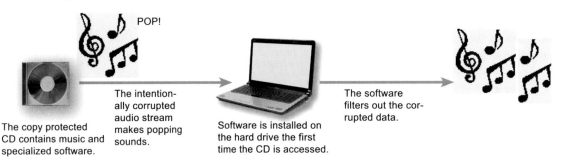

POP!

The copy protected CD contains music and specialized software.

The intentionally corrupted audio stream makes popping sounds.

Software is installed on the hard drive the first time the CD is accessed.

The software filters out the corrupted data.

▶ **How is encryption used for DRM?** Encryption is the gold standard of DRM. Data for a television show, movie, song, or ebook is encrypted so that the file cannot be viewed without a valid encryption key. Keys and decryption are usually handled behind the scenes, so users don't need to know the keys or enter them. DRM encryption can be handled by software or hardware. Software-based DRM encryption is the easier solution (Figure 8-56).

FIGURE 8-56

With software-based DRM, player software is required to decrypt encrypted content.

Player software, such as Windows Media Player or iTunes, decrypts the media file and plays it.

Software-based DRM encryption can be circumvented by routing content to a recording device as it is decrypted during playback. To close the loophole created by routing playback to a recorder, DRM encryption is also necessary within the devices used for playback.

DRM encryption technologies, such as CSS, AACS, and HDCP, are built into devices such as microprocessors, computers, DVD players, and televisions. These devices route content only to authorized devices that will not record or copy protected content (Figure 8-57).

FIGURE 8-57

With hardware-based DRM, all playback devices are required to be compliant.

8

© iStockphoto.com/Stephen Krow

▶ What are watermarks? A **digital watermark** is a pattern of bits, inserted at various places in an image or a content stream, that can be used to track, identify, verify, and control content use. Watermarks are usually imperceptible to viewers, readers, or listeners, but can be picked up by compliant devices.

Watermarks can be used to identify content owners or authorized users. For example, iTunes embeds your name in the content stream for the music and movies that you download.

Some watermarks are classified as broadcast flags. A **broadcast flag** is a set of bits inserted into the data stream that specifies how the stream can and cannot be used. A broadcast flag can:

▶ Limit the resolution or sound quality of playback

▶ Prevent fast-forwarding during commercials

▶ Limit content use to specific regions

▶ Prohibit copying or limit the number of copies that can be made (Figure 8-58)

FIGURE 8-58

Watermarks are read by devices that comply with the limitations embedded in the content stream.

Original DVD with one-copy-only watermark

Compliant DVD burner

DVD copy now contains do-not-copy watermark

Compliant DVD burner will not copy the DVD

MUSIC DRM

▶ Can I copy tracks from an old CD? Suppose you get your hands on a classic Garth Brooks CD and you'd like to add the tracks to your iTunes collection. You might assume that you can use audio extraction software to rip the tracks from the CD and save them in MP3 format.

Music CDs adhere to a standardized Red Book format, which implements DRM with a data bit that can be set to "no-copy." The Red Book no-copy bit is easy to defeat, so between 2000 and 2005, the recording industry produced copy protected CDs that did not play correctly on computers or when copied. Ripping tracks from these CDs is difficult, but not impossible. Most people prefer to avoid the aggravation and simply purchase a digital version of the music.

▶ How does DRM affect the way I can use music downloads? Downloading pulls a music file to your local device and stores it there before playing it. With downloads, you have to wait for the file to arrive; but once it is there, playback can proceed without interruption. Downloads are used at online music stores where you purchase or rent music.

Because downloaded files are stored locally, you have the potential to access them multiple times and copy them to other devices. Further, you don't have to be connected to the Internet when you want to access your music, so you can listen to downloaded music at a remote beach or with a device that doesn't have an Internet connection.

In practice, your ability to play downloaded content can be restricted by DRM that limits the devices on which you can play it, restricts your ability to make copies, or prohibits you from converting the music to a non-protected format.

Some music sites offer DRM-free downloads, but copyright law remains in effect. Technically, you might be able to make a copy and distribute it to your friends, but it is illegal to do so. Consumers should be aware that downloads from iTunes have the purchaser's name embedded in the file. If you give one of your music files to a friend, who gives it to another friend, and it eventually winds up on a file sharing network, you could be liable for copyright violation.

▶ Is streaming music protected by DRM? Streaming music is transmitted to your computer and played immediately. It is the technology used for Internet radio, subscription music services, and some services that offer cloud-based music storage (Figure 8-59).

FIGURE 8-59

Streaming music is not stored on your local device; so every time you want to listen to a song, it has to be re-streamed. Also, because the content never exists as a local file, you cannot copy it.

It is easier to protect streamed content than downloaded content, but streaming is not an effective DRM technology by itself because the stream can be captured using various software tools. Streaming music can be protected by authentication DRM that requires you to log in when you want to access music. It can also be encrypted using software-based DRM, or DRM that requires a compliant radio or other device.

MOVIE DRM

▶ Can I make a copy of a DVD movie? The first DVD players were introduced primarily as a distribution medium for mainstream movies. Based on prior experience with CD and VHS piracy, a DRM technology called CSS was built into the DVD standard from its inception.

CSS (Content Scramble System) is a digital rights management technology designed to encrypt and control the use of content stored on DVDs. It is intended to render DVD copies nonfunctional and enforces additional restrictions, such as region coding.

A key aspect of CSS is the use of an authentication key that allows a DVD disc and player to prove to each other that they are legitimately licensed to use CSS. CSS was introduced in 1996. Only four years later, tools for disabling it began to emerge. Although tools such as DeCSS are readily available, in many countries including the U.S., it is illegal to use them to circumvent DRM.

▶ Are Blu-ray movies copy protected? The primary DRM technology for Blu-ray discs is **AACS** (Advanced Access Content System). Like CSS, AACS works with an encrypted content stream. AACS, however, uses a much stronger encryption key, which makes it quite difficult for hackers to break the encryption using brute force methods.

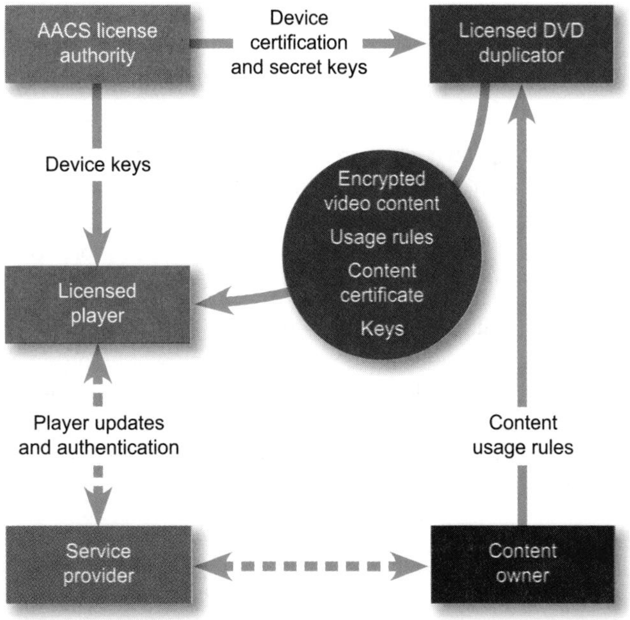

Another difference between the two methods is that CSS uses a shared set of encryption keys, and all devices of a specific model use the same key. In contrast, AACS compliant devices each contain their own unique set of keys, and these keys can be revoked if a player is found to be compromised.

The concept of authorization and revocation can be applied to hardware devices and software players to give licensing bodies the means to keep non-complying players off the market and deny further access to complying devices that have become compromised (Figure 8-60).

Despite its complexity, AACS has been broken. Just knowing the key, however, is not enough to proceed with Blu-ray copying; so as with other anti-DRM hacks, most users find it easier to simply pay to get content in the format and on the devices they desire.

FIGURE 8-60

AACS depends on authentication and revocation built into devices and content.

▶ Are movie downloads copy protected? Movie downloads tend to have more rigorous DRM protection than music downloads. Whereas music stores such as iTunes and Amazon MP3 allow you to make copies of music, change its format, and burn it to CDs for your own use, there are tighter restrictions on movies.

Downloaded movies that you rent or buy are generally protected by DRM software and hardware encryption. They require authorized devices and proprietary player software, which are all designed to deter digital pirates.

❱ What about streaming movies? The technology for streaming movies is the same as for streaming music, but movies are much longer and require more bandwidth. Movie streams are buffered when the amount of data exceeds the carrying capacity of your network connection.

For example, suppose you're streaming a Netflix movie over a basic cable Internet connection. Before the movie begins, Netflix takes a minute or so to check your connection speed and transmit the first few minutes of the movie to a memory area of your computer called a buffer. When the buffer is filled, the movie begins.

While data from the buffer is processed to display the movie, additional data is streamed to the buffer. If the buffer doesn't get filled fast enough because your Internet connection is too slow or because the Netflix server is overloaded, then the movie pauses for a period of time while it refills the buffer. During this time, you'll see a "rebuffering" or "loading" message.

Buffers open a potential hole for movie pirating, so streaming movies are usually protected by additional DRM technologies, such as encryption and HDCP. **HDCP** (High-bandwidth Digital Content Protection) is a hardware-based DRM technology that requires compliant devices for content playback. When working with HDCP-protected content, you'll have to make sure that your computer, DVD player, television, and handheld are all compliant. Look for the HDCP label when you purchase new media devices.

EBOOK DRM

❱ Are ebooks protected? Early DRM efforts for ebooks tied books to dedicated ebook readers, such as the Kindle and Nook, which were designed to decrypt ebook files and display them (Figure 8-61).

In response to consumer demand, ebook distributors expanded the platforms on which digital books can be read. Now, when you purchase a digital book from Amazon, Barnes & Noble, or iTunes, you can read it on devices that include computers, tablets, and smartphones. Ebook DRM technologies have evolved to allow this flexibility, yet retain control over copying and unauthorized distribution.

The power of digital rights management is illustrated by an incident that took place in 2009 when Amazon deleted copies of George Orwell's *1984* and *Animal Farm* that Kindle users had legitimately purchased and stored on their devices. According to an Amazon press release, those titles had been added to the Kindle store by a company that did not have the right to distribute them.

Customers were credited for their purchases, but many Kindle users were uncomfortable with the idea that Amazon was able to reach across the Internet and pull content from their personal Kindles.

ENFORCEMENT

❱ How do I know if I am breaking the law? The person who creates a film, album, television show, or book automatically receives the copyright to that work. The copyright can be transferred to a second party such as a publisher or distributor. By law, the copyright holder is the only entity that can make copies of the work and distribute them, but license agreements and usage policies might allow you to make copies under certain circumstances.

When using digital content, make sure you know the rules. Check the license agreement and usage policy to find out if you are allowed to make

FIGURE 8-61

Ebooks can be displayed on a dedicated reader, such as the Kindle, which handles digital rights.

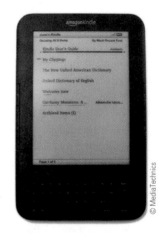

copies for your own use and if there are limitations on what you can do with those copies.

▶ **What are the penalties?** The copyright owner is entitled to recover monetary damages resulting from infringement, and any profits made from illegal sales of the work. Under U.S. law, copyright holders may also be awarded statutory damages up to $250,000. You've seen the warnings displayed while waiting for your movie to start (Figure 8-62).

▶ **Who will know if I copy a few songs?** Copyright holders periodically crack down on infringers. In the past decade, the music industry has singled out over 30,000 alleged music pirates and threatened them with astronomical fines.

FIGURE 8-62

Unauthorized copying of movies, music, and books is illegal.

A current initiative called Six Strikes takes a slightly different approach to curtailing infringement. Copyright holders, such as music companies, scan the Internet for IP addresses that initiate suspicious activity. For example, suppose the music watchdogs see your IP address participating in a swarm for *Dark Knight*. Your ISP will receive a notice about your alleged infringement and that notice will be forwarded to you.

After the fifth or sixth alert (hence the "Six Strikes" name), your ISP can institute mitigation measures, such as directing you to educational information about copyright, or temporarily reducing your Internet connection speed.

Although ISPs have agreed to participate in Six Strikes, it is unclear how aggressively they will monitor and punish their subscribers.

▶ **It sounds like I don't have to worry?** Not only is it against the law to make unauthorized copies of music, movies, and books, it is unethical. Copyright infringers have a whole host of excuses for what they do, but don't get caught up in that vibe.

Happily, the most draconian digital rights management schemes have failed. Today's digital content distributors maintain fairly reasonable prices and policies that allow consumers to download content and play it back on multiple devices. Copyright holders are watching the situation, however. If copying gets out of control, content providers will certainly crack down by raising prices, harassing consumers, and re-instituting intrusive digital rights management systems.

QuickCheck   SECTION E

1. [_____] shifting is the process of converting media files from a format suitable for one device to a format suitable for a different kind of device.

2. A digital [_____] can be inserted into a music or video file to specify the number of times a content stream can be duplicated.

3. HDCP is a(n) [_____]-based DRM technology.

4. [_____] is the primary technology used to protect DVDs, but it was cracked soon after it was introduced. (Hint: Use the acronym.)

5. Streaming movies are temporarily held in a(n) [_____] that opens a potential hole for illegal copying.

 CHECK ANSWERS

Issue: What Happened to Fair Use?

FAIR USE is the right to use portions of copyrighted material without the permission of the copyright holder for purposes such as review, criticism, or parody. Under certain circumstances, Fair Use is also a successful defense for practices, such as time shifting, in which whole works are copied for limited personal use.

Exactly what does or does not constitute Fair Use, however, is only sketched out in copyright law. The precise nature of Fair Use is shaped by court decisions covering situations and devices as disparate as vinyl records, printer toner cartridges, videotape recorders, and file sharing networks.

It seems incredible, but there once were no restrictions on copying sound recordings. "Record pirates" could legally copy and distribute, say, an Elvis Presley recording.

In 1971, the U.S. Congress passed the Sound Recording Act that prohibited copying music for commercial use. The law was not, however, aimed at prohibiting consumers from making copies for their own use.

The legal precedent that gave consumers a green light for time shifting is the landmark 1984 Betamax case in which Universal Studios attempted to hold Sony Corp. of America liable for copyright infringement by people who used video recorders to tape movies from their televisions. The U.S. Supreme Court sided with Sony and concluded that some instances of time shifting were legal.

The court's decision, however, was based on a definition of time shifting as "the practice of recording a program to view it once at a later time." Note the word "once." The Betamax case did not offer legal precedent for copying and saving content for viewing multiple times.

The proliferation of computer networks and streaming media has made place shifting a reality. You can, for example, view a cable television broadcast sent from your Wi-Fi equipped set-top box in your living room to your Wi-Fi equipped notebook out on the

"Specifically, it is not the intention of Congress to restrain the home recording, from broadcasts or from tapes or records, of recorded performances, where the home recording is for private use and with no purpose of reproducing or otherwise capitalizing commercially on it."

U.S. Judiciary Committee statement regarding the Sound Recording Act of 1971

deck. Your network, however, is transmitting a copy of the broadcast, a use of copyrighted work that is not explicitly allowed by copyright law in most countries. Therefore, unless a user agreement extends the basic rights granted by copyright law, place shifting would be considered a questionable practice.

So how about format shifting? Surely, it must be legal to rip tracks from a CD that you own, save them as an MP3 file, and play them on your iPod. Why do consumers believe that they have a right to use a legally purchased song or video in any manner they please short of redistributing it for profit?

Consumers are familiar with copyright restrictions on printed books and have an expectation that digital media can be legally used in parallel ways.

Readers expect to be able to carry a book with them to any location, read it at any time, use any type of reading light or reading glasses, loan the book to friends, and sell the book when they have finished using it.

No wonder consumers are peeved when ebook vendors and other digital content providers use DRM technology to limit how much of an ebook can be viewed, whether the text can be printed or shared, and how long it can be viewed.

Although it is convenient to focus on the "once I buy it I can use it as I like" rationale, we tend to ignore situations in which our expectations about content use are more limited. For example, we do not expect that after attending a Widespread Panic concert, we are entitled to a free DVD or video of the performance. If we pay to see a movie at a theater, we don't then expect to get the DVD or soundtrack CD for free when they are released.

From rock concerts to theaters, consumers are familiar with the idea that different venues and formats might require separate payments. Digital rights management technologies simply enforce this idea in practice.

Try It! Do you know how to legally use music, movies, ebooks, and other media? Here's a chance for you to explore Fair Use and content usage policies.

1 Fair Use is defined in Section 107 of U.S. copyright law. It includes four factors designed to determine whether a use is fair. Look up Section 107 of the U.S. Copyright Law. In your own words, what are those four factors?

2 The book *Grateful Dead: The Illustrated Trip* included concert posters and ticket images used without approval of the copyright holder. In a subsequent suit, courts decided the use was fair and transformative, based on a four-factor analysis. Look up the results of this case by searching for the article, *Grateful Dead Posters' Re-publication Held to Be a Transformative, Fair Use* by Martine Courant Rife. In your own words, what did the court say about each of the four factors?

3 "Transformative use" means that you change a work enough to make it your own. Collages, music remixes, and video parodies can fall into this category. Find an example of a transformative work on YouTube and list the original works from which it is derived. In your opinion, what makes this a transformative work?

4 Digital content providers such as iTunes, Amazon, and Google each have their own rules about how you can use the content you purchase, rent, or subscribe to. To get an idea of a typical usage policy, search for "Amazon Instant Video Usage Rules," and then answer the following questions:

a. Are you allowed to stream more than one video at a time?

b. Are you allowed to stream the same video to two devices at the same time?

c. Are you allowed to stream videos to any digital device?

d. Are you allowed to save rented content to a handheld device so that you can watch it after the viewing period has ended?

5 The Digital Millennium Copyright Act (DMCA) makes it illegal to circumvent a technological measure that controls access to a work, but this law is reviewed every three years. Search the Web for the latest DMCA review (2010 or 2013). Which changes are beneficial to consumers?

Charlie Gillett/Redferns/Getty Images

8

INFOWEBLINKS

You can check the **NP2013 Chapter 8** InfoWebLink for updates to these activities.

W CLICK TO CONNECT
www.infoweblinks.com/np2013/ch08

ISSUE

What Do You Think?

1. Have you ever had trouble using software, music CDs, or movie DVDs because of copy protection?

2. In your opinion, do sites like the iTunes Store provide consumers with enough flexibility for copying files and creating playlists?

3. Do you think digital rights management technologies are justified because of the high rate of piracy?

Information Tools: Media Attribution

You can easily copy music, photos, and video clips for use in reports, on your blog, on YouTube, and on your Facebook pages. If you are not creating a transformative work or a critical work that would be covered by Fair Use, what steps must you take to use "borrowed" content correctly?

As a general rule, assume that all images and media are copyrighted. Media elements on the Web are covered by the same copyrights as works in print and in other formats. When using copyrighted media, you should seek permission and you should provide attribution that identifies the copyright holder. Permission and attribution are not the same.

▶ **Permission** means obtaining rights for a specific use, such as on a Web site.

▶ **Attribution** means acknowledging the person who holds the copyright, usually by including a tagline under a media element or a citation in a bibliography.

You can obtain permission by asking the copyright holder. Most media sharing sites provide links to copyright holders. Supply the copyright holder with information about the item you want to use and how you intend to use it.

You might not have to contact the copyright holder for permission if the media element is covered by a license. Look for a license or rights link near the media element, or a site-use policy near the bottom of a Web page.

For academic work, such as term papers and theses, you must include attributions for any media elements that you use, even though academic work falls under the umbrella of Fair Use. As with citations for quoted and paraphrased material, media attribution helps to establish the legitimacy of your work.

You can place your photo attribution in a small font directly under the photo or on its side, or you can include it in the bibliography. Video and music attributions should be placed near the "Play" link or in a bibliography.

The copyright holder might specify the text you should use for the attribution. For example, "Courtesy IBM" or "Jerry Harris Photography."

If the wording for an attribution is not specified, then you should include the following:

▶ Copyright holder's name

▶ License type, such as "with permission" or "Creative Commons"

▶ URL (optional)

The easiest media elements to use legally have a Creative Commons license for "Attribution."

These licenses clearly specify whether the element can be used for personal or commercial use, and only require you to provide an attribution crediting the source.

NASA

Courtesy of Creative Commons

Try It! The more you learn about copyright, citations, and attributions, the more complex these topics seem. Here's your chance to track down a few more concepts pertaining to media citations and then summarize what you've learned. For this project, create a document called Chapter 8 Media Project.

8

1 Photographers sometimes give permission to use images that are not free from other copyright and legal restrictions. For example, if a photographer takes a photo of a painting, it is considered a derivative work and it is subject to the painting's copyright. Link to the Shutterstock photo site and search for photos of the Mona Lisa. Can you find any photos of the actual painting? Why do you think this is the case?

2 Some museums and libraries allow personal, educational, and non-commercial use of digital images and other media. What is the policy for personal and educational use of digital versions of works from the Smithsonian American Art Museum's collection?

3 Media elements that include images of identifiable people are subject to complex legal issues, depending on the subject, the subject's age, and the element's intended use. To be on the safe side, photos or videos that contain images of identifiable people should be used only if the license includes a model release. Link to Shutterstock and Flickr and search for images of businessmen. Which site provides clear information about model releases?

4 Go to the Flickr site and link to the Advanced Search. Enter "Pyramids" in the search field, then select the options for Creative Commons-licensed content and for content to use commercially. Select an image with an "Attribution" license. Download the smallest resolution and paste the image into your Media Project document.

Add the appropriate attribution under the Pyramids photo in your Media Project document.

5 Fill in the following table to summarize what you've learned about media attributions and citations.

Situation	Fair Use?	Is This Use Correct? Why or Why Not?
You use a photo from an online magazine in a research paper without seeking permission and you do not attribute the source.		
You use a photo from an online magazine in a research paper without seeking permission, but you do attribute the source.		
You use a photo from an online magazine in a poster for an event without seeking permission, but you attribute the source.		
You use a photo from an online magazine in a poster for an event, but you get permission to do so and follow the photographer's instructions for attribution.		
A photo from Shutterstock is royalty free, so you use it on your Facebook page.		
You use a photo from the Smithsonian American Art Museum for a background in an app that you sell on iTunes.		

Technology in Context: Film

IN 1895, eager Parisians crowded into a busy cafe to watch the first public presentation of an exciting new invention—the Cinematograph. The 10-minute film, mostly scenes of everyday life, was a smashing success and ushered in the motion picture era. Early films were short, grainy, grayscale, and silent, but technology quickly improved. In the New York debut of *The Jazz Singer* (1927), Al Jolson spoke the first words in a feature film, "Wait a minute, wait a minute. You ain't heard nothin' yet!"

Even before "talkies" and Technicolor, filmmakers sought ways to escape the bounds of reality through special effects. As early as 1925, directors such as Willis O'Brien used stop-motion photography to animate dinosaurs, giant gorillas, and sword-wielding skeletons. Special-effects technologies—miniatures, blue screens, puppets, Claymation, 3-D, and composite shots—were used with varying degrees of skill over the next 50 years. Films such as Stanley Kubrick's masterpiece, *2001: A Space Odyssey* (1968), and George Lucas's original *Star Wars* (1977) stretched these technologies to their limits, but audiences demanded even more spectacular, yet "realistic," effects.

In 1982, Disney released *TRON*, a movie about a computer programmer who becomes trapped in the depths of a computer where programs are human-like creatures that serve every whim of an evil Master Control Program. The movie included the first primitive attempts at computer-generated footage—30 minutes of computer-generated imagery (CGI) created by two Cray X-MP supercomputers.

CGI uses rendering techniques to create a 3-D scene from a 2-D image, a camera angle, and a light source. Sophisticated algorithms determine how textures, colors, and shadows appear in the rendered scene. Camera angles can be changed at will, and fantastic effects can be created by bending or stretching the image, manipulating light, creating textures, and adding movement to the scene.

Rendered scenes can be set in motion with computer animation techniques. Manual animation requires a painstaking process called in-betweening, in which an artist draws a series of incrementally different images to produce the illusion of movement. Computers can easily generate in-between images

and free up human animators for more challenging work.

A captivating animation special effect called morphing was first seen on the big screen in James Cameron's *The Abyss* (1989) and later used in *Terminator 2* (1991) and other movies. Like in-betweening, morphing starts out with animators defining the morph's start and end points—for example, in *Terminator 2*, the liquid metal face of the T-1000 robot and actor Robert Patrick's face. The start and end points are rendered into digital images, and then the computer generates all the in-between images. Human animators tweak the images by inserting small discrepancies for a touch of less-than-perfect realism in the final footage.

Although the process might sound simple, morphing complex objects realistically and believably takes a tremendous amount of time and computer power. The five-minute morphing sequence in *Terminator 2* took special-effects company Industrial Light & Magic a year to create.

Memorable computer-generated scenes from classic blockbusters include the breathtaking aerial scenes in *Spiderman*, a furry blue monster called Sully careening downhill in *Monsters, Inc.*, and the endless army of Uruk-hai marching down the valley toward Helm's Deep in *The Lord of the Rings: The Two Towers*. Spiderman's acrobatic swing through Manhattan was generated with three professional rendering products: Maya, Houdini, and RenderMan. The Uruk-hai were created with MASSIVE, a custom program that gave each computer-generated warrior a unique sequence of actions. To individually animate each of Sully's 2,320,413 blue hairs, animators developed software called Fizt, a dynamic simulator.

Rendering, morphing, and other special-effects processing require sophisticated computer systems. Pixar Animation Studios, the company that provided the technology behind *Toy Story*, *Up*, *Ratatouille*, *WALL-E*, and many other feature-length animated films, uses a cluster of computers called a renderfarm.

Toy Story took more than 800,000 computer hours to produce using the renderfarm. That might seem like a long time; but if Pixar animators had used a single-processor computer, it would have taken 43 years to finish the job!

Other CGI variations are being used for increasingly sophisticated effects. Special-effects guru John Gaeta developed bullet time and image-based rendering for *The Matrix* (1999). Bullet time produces reality-defying action sequences that slow time to a tantalizing crawl and then crank it back up to normal speed as the camera pivots rapidly around the scene. The effect requires a computer to meticulously trigger a circular array of more than 100 still cameras in sequence.

Films such as *Sky Captain and the World of Tomorrow* (2004) and *Sin City* (2005) took green screen special effects to a new level. Filmed entirely indoors on a sound stage, these movies used a technique called compositing that layers two or more video clips over each other and merges them into one image. Actors were filmed against a green background screen. During post-production, video editing software removed the background and layered in scenery created with CGI or from real footage on location.

Sin City is also notable as one of the first fully digital live action motion pictures. It was filmed in full color with high-definition digital cameras. The footage was converted to black and white, and then color was reintroduced digitally with the use of a DLP Cinema projector.

Motion capture suits were put to award-winning use for Peter Jackson's *The Lord of the Rings*. The actor who played Gollum was outfitted with sensors that tracked the position of his head, arms, and limbs. The collected data was later used by animators to create the 3-D animated Gollum that you saw on screen. Motion capture was further refined for *Avatar*, which used digital technology to capture the actors' facial expressions.

Avatar also touched off the emergence of 3-D films that had been languishing as a small niche market since the 1950s. 3-D has gone mainstream and is now available on consumer televisions and computers.

Sophisticated animation and rendering techniques now come close to producing realistic human figures. Animations were once clearly two-dimensional and far from lifelike, but CGI renderings are becoming more difficult to distinguish from real actors.

What might happen in the future is the subject of *Simone* (2002), starring Al Pacino as a washed-up director who is given a hard disk containing code for a computer-generated movie star. Pacino uses her as the leading lady in a string of hits, all the while keeping her identity secret. According to reviewer Leigh Johnson, it becomes clear that Simone, a computer-generated image, is more authentic than the people watching her. It is one of the film's main themes, expressed by Pacino's character: "Our ability to manufacture fraud now exceeds our ability to detect it."

The implications of computer-generated actors are just emerging. Not only do they blur the line between reality and fiction, but they also raise puzzling questions for actors and their agents, directors, and programmers. Is it possible to create CGI doubles for long-dead actors, such as Marilyn Monroe and James Dean? If so, who controls their use and profits from their work? Can aging actors sign contracts for use of their "young" CGI counterparts? Would it be legal and ethical for programmers to create and market virtual characters based on real actors or a compilation of the best traits of popular stars? As is often the case, new technologies present issues along with their benefits—issues you might want to consider the next time you watch a movie.

New Perspectives Labs

To access the New Perspectives Lab for Chapter 8, open the NP2013 interactive eBook and then click the icon next to the lab title.

▶ WORKING WITH BITMAP GRAPHICS

IN THIS LAB YOU'LL LEARN:

- How to identify common bitmap graphics file extensions
- How to capture an image from the Web
- How to find the properties of a graphic
- How to eliminate red eye and manipulate the brightness, contrast, and sharpness of photos
- How to make a photo look old
- How to select a palette and apply a dithering technique
- How to prepare graphics for the Web and e-mail attachments
- The effects of lossy compression

LAB ASSIGNMENTS

1. Start the interactive part of the lab. Make sure you've enabled Tracking if you want to save your QuickCheck results. Perform each lab step as directed, and answer all the lab QuickCheck questions. When you exit the lab, your answers are automatically graded and your results are displayed.

2. Use the Start button to access the All Programs menu for the computer you typically use. Make a list of the available bitmap graphics software.

3. Capture a photographic image from a digital camera, scanner, or Web page. Save it as "MyGraphic." Open the image using any available graphics software. Use this software to discover the properties of the graphic. Indicate the source of the graphic, and then describe its file format, file size, resolution, and color depth.

4. Prepare this graphics file to send to a friend as an e-mail attachment that is smaller than 200 KB. Describe the steps that were required.

5. Suppose you want to post the image from assignment 4 on a Web page. Make the necessary adjustments to file size and color depth. Describe the resulting graphic in terms of its resolution, color depth, palette, and dithering.

Key Terms

Make sure you understand all the boldfaced key terms presented in this chapter. With the NP2013 interactive eBook, you can use this list of terms as an interactive study activity. First, try to define a term in your own words, and then click the term to compare your definition with the definition presented in the chapter.

3-D graphics, 449
AAC, 425
AACS, 469
Analog hole, 465
ASF, 458
Audio compression, 424
AVI, 458
Bitmap graphic, 430
Bitrate, 457
Blu-ray Disc Movie, 458
BMP, 431
Broadcast flag, 467
CCD, 433
Codec, 457
Color palette, 438
Compression ratio, 457
Container formats, 458
Copy protected, 466
Cropping, 436
CSS, 469
Desktop video, 452
Digital audio, 422
Digital audio extraction, 426
Digital camera, 432
Digital content, 464
Digital rights management, 466
Digital signal processor, 424
Digital video, 452
Digital watermark, 467
Digitizing tablet, 446
DVD image, 462
File compression utility, 442

Flash, 448
Flash video, 458
Format shifting, 465
GIF, 431
Gradient, 447
Grayscale palette, 439
HDCP, 470
Image compression, 440
Integrated audio, 424
JPEG, 431
Linear editing, 456
Lossless compression, 440
Lossy compression, 440
Media content, 464
Megapixel, 434
Metafile, 447
MIDI, 427
MIDI sequence, 427
Monochrome bitmap, 437
MOV, 458
MP3, 425
MPEG, 458
Nonlinear editing, 456
Ogg Vorbis, 425
Phoneme, 428
Photosites, 433
Pixel interpolation, 436
Pixelated, 436
Place shifting, 465
PNG, 431
Rasterization, 447
RAW, 431

Ray tracing, 449
Rendering, 449
Resolution dependent, 436
Run-length encoding, 440
Sampling rate, 423
Scanner, 432
Sound card, 424
Speech recognition, 428
Speech synthesis, 428
Streaming audio, 426
Streaming video, 459
SVG, 448
Synthesized sound, 427
System palette, 439
Text-to-speech software, 429
TIFF, 431
Time shifting, 465
Tracing software, 447
Transcoding, 458
True Color bitmap, 438
Vector graphic, 444
Video capture, 455
VOB, 458
WAV, 425
Wavetable, 427
Web palette, 439
Webcam, 454
WebM, 458
Wireframe, 449
WMA, 425

Interactive Summary

To review important concepts from this chapter, fill in the blanks to best complete each sentence. When using the NP2013 interactive eBook, click the Check Answers buttons to automatically score your answers.

SECTION A: Music, voice, and sound effects can all be recorded and stored on a computer as [_____] audio. To digitally record sound, [_____] of the sound are collected at periodic intervals and stored as numeric data. High-quality sound is usually sampled at 44.1 [_____], and each stereo sample requires 32 bits of storage space. To conserve space, radio-quality recordings of speaking voices are often recorded at lower sampling rates. A computer's [_____] card is responsible for transforming the bits stored in an audio file into music, sound effects, and narrations. It contains digital [_____] processing circuitry that transforms bits into analog sound, records analog sounds as digital bits, and handles audio compression. Digital audio file formats include WAV, AAC, WMA, Ogg Vorbis, and MP3. Most portable media players work with MP3 format or with the [_____] format, used for .m4p files at

the iTunes Store. MIDI music is [_____] sound that is artificially created. Unlike digital audio sound files, which contain digitized recordings of real sound passages, MIDI files contain [_____] for creating the pitch, volume, and duration of notes made by musical instruments. MIDI files are typically much smaller than digital audio files for similar musical passages, so they are ideal for Web pages. However, MIDI music tends to lack the full resonance of symphony-quality sound that can be achieved with digital audio. Speech [_____] is the process by which machines, such as computers, produce sound that resembles spoken words. Speech [_____] refers to the ability of machines to "understand" spoken words.

▶ CHECK ANSWERS

SECTION B: A(n) [_____] graphic is composed of a grid of dots, and the color of each dot is stored as a binary number. Popular bitmap graphics formats include BMP, TIFF, GIF, JPEG, RAW, and PNG. Of these formats, GIF, JPEG, and PNG are supported by most Web browsers. Both scanners and cameras produce images in bitmap format. The dimensions of the grid that forms a bitmap graphic are referred to as its [_____]. High-resolution graphics typically produce better image quality than low-resolution graphics, but require more storage space. It is possible to change the resolution and/or the file size of a bitmap graphic; but because bitmaps are resolution [_____], these changes can reduce image quality. For example, enlarging a bitmap requires your computer to fill in missing pixels, which often results in a jagged or [_____] image. As

a general rule, images that you intend to print should remain at full size and resolution. When sending bitmap files as e-mail attachments, they can be [_____] in size or resolution to produce a file that is less than 500 KB. Color [_____] refers to the number of colors available for use in an image. For example, a bitmap graphic composed of 256 colors requires only [_____] bits to store the data for each pixel, whereas 24 bits are required for each pixel in a(n) [_____] Color graphic. Grayscale, system, and Web palettes use eight bits to represent each pixel. Image [_____] shrinks the size of a graphics file. [_____] compression permanently removes data, but [_____] compression shrinks files without removing any data.

▶ CHECK ANSWERS

8

SECTION C: Unlike a bitmap graphic, created by superimposing a grid of pixels over an image, a(n) [_____] graphic consists of a set of instructions for creating a picture. These graphics are created by using a type of graphics software called [_____] software. They are stored as a collection of [_____] and their corresponding sizes, colors, and positions. You can identify these graphics by their flat cartoon-like appearance and their file extensions: .wmf, .ai, .dxf, .eps, .swf, and .svg. A vector graphic can be converted into a bitmap by a process called [_____]. Once converted, however, the resulting graphic loses the object-editing qualities it had in its vector state. Two vector graphics formats, [_____] and Flash, are popular for Web-based graphics. 3-D graphics are stored as a set of instructions that contain the locations and lengths of lines that form a(n) [_____] for a 3-D object. This framework then can be covered by colored, patterned, and textured surfaces. This process, called [_____], produces a bitmap image of the 3-D object. [_____] tracing adds highlights and shadows to the image. 3-D graphics can be animated to produce special effects for movies and animated characters for 3-D computer games. ▶ CHECK ANSWERS

SECTION D: Footage for digital videos can be supplied from a digital source, or from a(n) [_____] source that requires conversion. In addition to standalone digital cameras, digital footage can also be obtained from cameras embedded in handheld devices and from [_____] built in above a computer screen. Video stored on a computer hard disk can be edited using a technique called [_____] editing, which does not require moving segments from one VCR to another. After editing, you can prepare to output your video by selecting settings for [_____] ratio, display size, and compression so that the resulting video quality and file size are appropriate for its intended use. Software, such as MPEG, DivX, Theora, and H.264, that compresses the video stream is referred to as a(n) [_____]. A compression [_____] indicates the degree of compression. A video file compressed at 35:1 has more compression, a smaller file size, and lower image quality than a file compressed at 5:1. Video and audio streams are combined into the final video file and stored using a(n) [_____] format, such as AVI, MOV, or WebM. Video can be included in HTML5-compliant Web pages using the <video> HTML [_____]. Videos can also be burned onto DVDs for playback in a standalone DVD player that requires data in [_____] format. ▶ CHECK ANSWERS

SECTION E: Digital [_____] management is a collection of techniques used by copyright holders to limit access to and use of digital content. DRM technologies can limit or prevent convenient [_____], place, and format shifting. A digital [_____] is a DRM technology inserted into the content stream in such a way that it is imperceptible to users, but can be recognized by complying devices. In the past, music CDs were [_____] protected by DRM technology, but that technology was not very effective. The major DRM technology for DVD content, called [_____], was cracked shortly after it was introduced. A somewhat more sophisticated DRM technology called [_____] is used on Blu-ray and HD-DVD. A hardware-based DRM technology called [_____] required all devices involved in content playback to be compliant. Content downloaded from online music and video stores might be protected by DRM technologies, such as Apple's [_____] and Microsoft's Windows Media DRM. [_____] content is somewhat easier to protect than downloaded content because it is never stored in a file on a local device. ▶ CHECK ANSWERS

Interactive Situation Questions

Apply what you've learned to some typical computing situations. When using the NP2013 interactive eBook, you can type your answers, and then use the Check Answers button to automatically score your responses.

1. Suppose you are creating an English-as-a-Second-Language Web page and you want to add links to sound files that pronounce English phrases. Would it be better to store the files in WAV or MIDI format? [ ]

2. Imagine that you're a musician and you are asked to synthesize some music for the opening screen of a Web site. For this project, you would most likely work with [ ] music.

3. Suppose you visit a Web site that allows you to enter sentences, and then it reads the sentences back to you. The site even gives you a choice of a female or male voice. You assume that this site uses speech [ ] technology.

4. You have an old photograph that you want to incorporate in a brochure for your antiques business. To convert the photo into digital format, you use a(n) [ ] .

© MediaTechnics

5. Imagine that you are preparing a series of bitmap graphics for a Web site. To decrease the download time for each graphic, you can remove pixels or reduce the color [ ] .

6. You've taken a photo with a high-resolution digital camera and you want to send it as an e-mail attachment. You decide to use [ ] software, such as PKZIP, to reduce the image to a more manageable size.

7. Suppose you are designing a logo for a client. You know the design will undergo several revisions, and you understand that the logo will be used at various sizes. You decide it would be best to use drawing software to create the logo as a(n) [ ] graphic.

8. After you finish arranging video clips and adding a soundtrack, you can select a video file format and a compression technique. For example, you might store the video in WebM container format and use the MPEG [ ] to compress the file.

9. After purchasing a CD of your favorite rock group, you try to rip one of the tracks to your computer and convert it to MP3 format. When you play the file on your computer, you notice loud pops in the audio that indicate that the CD was probably copy [ ] .

10. You've downloaded a movie from a new online store. You can watch it on your computer; but when you try to watch it on a large-screen television, you don't get a picture. You know the television is working, so you guess that the movie is protected by [ ] that requires all devices to be compliant. ▶ CHECK ANSWERS

Interactive Practice Tests

Practice tests that consist of ten multiple-choice, true/false, and fill-in-the-blank questions are available in the NP2013 interactive eBook. Test questions are selected at random from a large test bank, so each time you take a test, you'll receive a different set of questions. Your tests are scored immediately, and you can print study guides that help you find the correct answers for any questions that you missed.

 ▶ CLICK TO START

Learning Objectives Checkpoints

Learning Objectives Checkpoints are designed to help you assess whether you have achieved the major learning objectives for this chapter. You can use paper and pencil or word processing software to complete most of the activities.

1. Draw a diagram to show how the smooth curve of an analog sound wave is divided into samples and stored digitally.

2. Explain the relationship between sampling rate, audio quality, and file size.

3. Make a list of ten digital audio applications and indicate whether each one would use WAV or MIDI.

4. Use the file manager on your computer to locate five bitmap graphics. List the file name and extension for each one, and where possible identify whether it originated from a digital camera, scanner, or some other source.

5. Describe six ways to transfer photos from a digital camera to a computer.

6. Explain how resolution, image size, color depth, and color palettes can be manipulated to adjust the file size of a bitmap graphic. Summarize how you would prepare bitmap graphics for the following uses: e-mail attachment, Web page, desktop publishing, and printed photo.

7. Recap key points about image compression, explaining the difference between lossy and lossless compression and listing file types with built-in compression.

8. Describe differences in the ways that vector and bitmap graphics are created, stored, and used. Explain how the concept of layering relates to your ability to modify a vector graphic.

9. Describe the procedures used to convert bitmap graphics into vector graphics, and to convert vector graphics into bitmaps.

10. Make a series of quick sketches that illustrates the evolution of a 3-D graphic from wireframe to rendered image, and to ray-traced image.

11. List the devices that can be used to capture video and indicate which are analog and which are digital.

12. Explain the procedures required to capture analog video and transfer it to digital format.

13. Explain how compression affects the file size of a digital video.

14. Explain how streaming audio and video work, and contrast them with non-streaming technology.

15. Use your own words to make a list of the steps required to burn video onto a DVD that can be viewed on standalone DVD players.

16. Make a list of the file extensions that were mentioned in this chapter and group them according to digital media type: bitmap graphic, vector graphic, digital video, digital audio, and MIDI. Circle any formats that are used on the Web and put a star by formats that typically require you to download a player.

17. Explain how specific DRM technologies are used to prevent consumers from a) making a copy of a music CD, b) ripping tracks from a music CD, c) copying a DVD movie, and d) watching a streaming movie.

18. Give examples of time shifting, place shifting, and format shifting.

Study Tip: Make sure you can use your own words to correctly answer each of the purple focus questions in the chapter.

8

Concept Map

Fill in the blanks on the concept map to show the hierarchy of digital media formats.

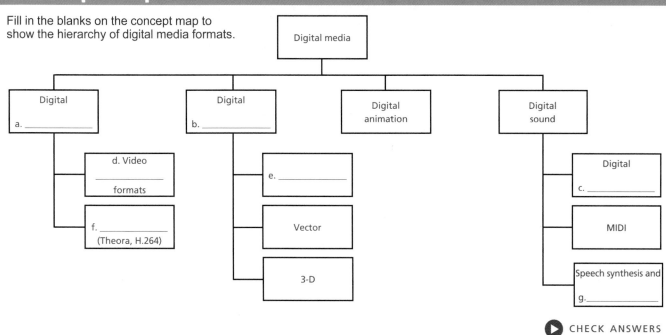

CHECK ANSWERS

9

Chapter Contents

INFOWEBLINKS

You'll find updates for chapter material by connecting to the **NP2013 Chapter 9** InfoWebLink.

Ⓦ CLICK TO CONNECT
www.infoweblinks.com/np2013/ch09

The Computer Industry: History, Careers, and Ethics

Learning Objectives

After reading this chapter, you will be able to answer the following questions by completing the outcomes-based Learning Objectives Checkpoints on page 553.

1. What are the key events in the history of computers?

2. Before digital computers and calculators, what kinds of devices were used to carry out calculations?

3. Who invented the first digital computer?

4. How long did it take for computers to become such a ubiquitous part of modern life?

5. What technical innovations characterize each of the four generations of computers?

6. Which companies are major players in the computer industry?

7. How important are the computer and IT industries in today's global economy?

8. Is the IT industry affected by outsourcing and offshoring?

9. What do consumers need to know about the life cycles of hardware and software products in order to make smart purchasing and investment decisions?

10. How can consumers take advantage of the computer industry's overlapping marketing channels?

11. What kinds of jobs are available in the computer and IT industries?

12. What qualifications are IT industry employers looking for?

13. How do computers and the Internet figure into the process of job hunting?

14. Are computer professionals faced with tricky ethical decisions?

15. How safe are computers and other digital devices?

16. What is ergonomics and how does it apply to computers?

CourseMate

Visit the NP2013 CourseMate for this chapter's Pre-Quiz, Audio Overview and Flashcards, Detailed Objectives, Chapter Quiz, Online Games, and more labs.

Multimedia and Interactive Elements

When using the NP2013 interactive eBook, click the ▶ icons to access multimedia resources.

Apply Your Knowledge The information in this chapter will give you the background to:

- Select the best marketing channel for a computer purchase
- Consider whether you'd be interested in a job as a computer professional
- Get the education, training, and certification you need for a job in the computer industry
- Use computers and the Internet to search for a job in any career field

- Create an effective digital resume
- Find the resources needed to make ethical decisions about computer use
- Set up your computer work area in a way that will help you avoid eye strain, back aches, and repetitive stress injuries

Try It!

DO I HAVE A SAFE AND HEALTHY COMPUTING ENVIRONMENT?

If you spend hours at your computer each day working, studying, chatting online, or playing games, you might begin to feel stresses and strains in your back, neck, wrist, fingers, or eyes. OSHA (Occupational Safety and Health Administration) experts on work area health and safety have identified sources for many work-related physical maladies. Often the culprit is a work area that does not fit your body. To find out how your computer work area stacks up to OSHA standards, complete the following steps. You'll learn more about setting up an ergonomic workstation in Section E.

1. If possible, ask a friend to snap a digital photo of you sitting in a position similar to the person in the illustration. Otherwise, sit at your computer while a friend compares your desk, chair, and posture to those in the illustration.

2. On the illustration, circle any of the equipment, angles, or positions that are not optimal in your work area.

3. Consider how you could change your work area to achieve OSHA standards and help prevent muscle soreness, joint pain, eye strain, and headaches.

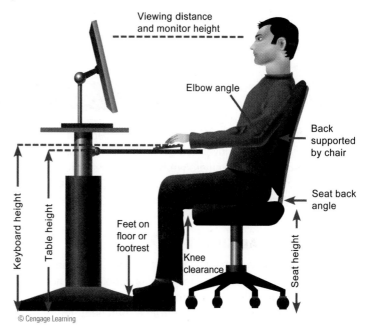

© Cengage Learning

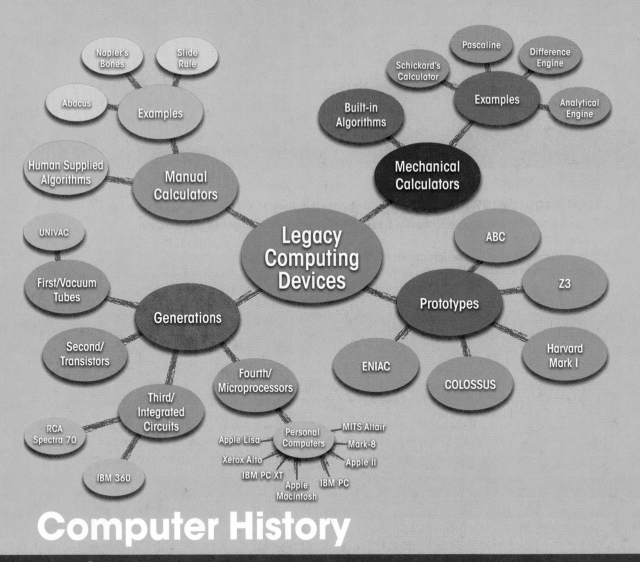

Computer History

LIKE MOST INVENTIONS throughout history, computer technology evolved as inventors tinkered with various devices. In Chapter 1, you traced how computers were used for data processing, personal computing, networking, and cloud computing. This chapter begins by tracing the evolution of computer hardware, from room-sized number crunchers to today's svelte handheld devices.

MANUAL CALCULATORS

▶ What came before computers? Even before recorded history, humans used counting aids, such as pebbles and notched sticks, to keep track of quantities—the number of sheep in a flock, for example, or the number of oil jars purchased from a merchant. Many transactions, however, required calculations.

A calculation is based on an algorithm—the step-by-step process by which numbers are manipulated. Even simple paper-and-pencil addition requires an algorithm. The steps include adding the rightmost digits first, carrying a 1 if necessary, and then moving left to any remaining digits, where the process is repeated. A **manual calculator** is a device that assists in the process of numeric calculations, but requires the human operator to keep track of the algorithm.

9

A manual calculator called an **abacus** was used in ancient Rome, Greece, India, China, and Japan. Only recently has it been replaced by handheld digital calculators. An abacus, like the one in Figure 9-1, consists of beads mounted on rods within a rectangular frame. Each bead represents a quantity—1, 5, 10, 50, and so on. To use an abacus, you must learn the algorithm for manipulating the beads.

Each of these beads represents the quantity "5."

© MediaTechnics

Each of these beads represents the quantity "10."

Each of these beads represents the quantity "1."

FIGURE 9-1

An abacus uses beads to represent numbers. This abacus shows the number 17. Using an algorithm, the beads on an abacus can be manipulated to perform arithmetic operations. ▶ Click this figure in your interactive eBook to learn how an abacus works.

Other manual calculators include the oddly named Napier's Bones and the slide rule. John Napier, the Scottish Laird of Merchiston, made two contributions to the field of mathematics. He invented logarithms and a device for multiplication and division. The device consisted of several rods, divided into ten squares, each labeled with two numbers. The rods were positioned according to the numbers in a calculation, and the result was determined by adding values shown in a specific location on the rods. These rods were often constructed out of bones, so they came to be called **Napier's Bones** (Figure 9-2).

In 1621, an English mathematician named William Oughtred used Napier's logarithms to construct the first **slide rule**. Slide rules, like the one pictured in Figure 9-2, remained in use as an essential tool for students, engineers, and scientists through the 1960s.

FIGURE 9-2

Napier's Bones (left) evolved into the slide rule (right). ▶ Watch a video showing how a slide rule works.

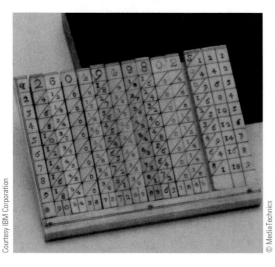

Courtesy IBM Corporation

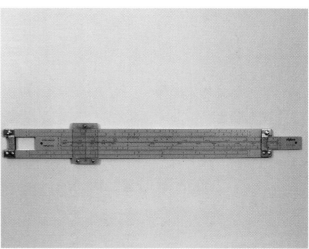

© MediaTechnics

MECHANICAL CALCULATORS

▶ When did machines begin to perform calculations?

Manual calculators require the operator to apply algorithms to perform calculations. In contrast, a **mechanical calculator** implements algorithms autonomously. With a mechanical calculator, the operator simply enters the numbers for a calculation, and then pulls a lever or turns a wheel to carry out the calculation. No thinking—or at least very little—is required.

Mechanical calculators were developed as early as 1623. **Schickard's Calculator** had a series of interlocking gears. Each of the ten spokes on a gear represented a digit. Every time a gear completed a full circle, it moved the next gear one notch to the left to "carry the 1." A similar mechanism is used to advance the mileage on the odometers of vintage cars.

In 1642, a Frenchman named Blaise Pascal developed the **Pascaline**, a mechanical device that could be used to perform addition, subtraction, multiplication, and division. A similar calculator called the **Leibniz Calculator** was created by a German baron named Gottfried Wilhelm von Leibniz in 1673. It was not until 1820, however, that Thomas **de Colmar's Arithmometer** became the first mass-produced mechanical calculator.

▶ When did calculating devices begin to operate without human power?

In 1822, an English mathematician named Charles Babbage proposed a device called the **Difference Engine** that would operate using steam power—cutting-edge technology during Babbage's lifetime. The Difference Engine was intended to quickly and accurately calculate large tables of numbers used for astronomical and engineering applications.

Blueprints for the Difference Engine called for more than 4,000 precision-engineered levers, gears, and wheels. Babbage worked on the Difference Engine until 1833, but he was unable to fabricate gears with the necessary precision to create a working version of this complex mechanical device.

In 1834, Babbage began designing a new general-purpose calculating device, called the **Analytical Engine**. Although the Analytical Engine was never completed, computer historians believe that its design embodies many of the concepts that define the modern computer, including memory, a programmable processor, an output device, and user-definable input of programs and data (Figure 9-3).

FIGURE 9-3

Babbage's Analytical Engine was designed to process programs and data stored on punched cards, much like those used in 1970s mainframe computers. The use of punched cards was probably borrowed from the cards used to control Jacquard looms.

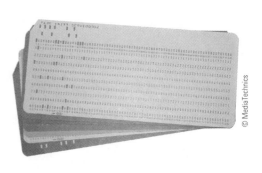

9

▶ When did calculating machines become widespread?

The U.S. Census provided incentives for the next generation of calculating machines. The process of compiling data from the 1880 census dragged on until 1887—just three years before the next census was to begin. With a surge in population, Census Bureau administrators feared that the 1890 census could not be completed before the 1900 census would begin. Clearly a faster method of tabulating census results was required.

The U.S. Census Bureau held a competition to find a way to tabulate the 1890 census. Herman Hollerith won the competition with a design for an electronic punched card tabulating device. Each card contained areas to represent fields, such as "nationality." Once punched, the cards were fed into a card reader that used an array of metal rods to electronically read data from the cards and tabulate the results. The **Hollerith Tabulating Machine** was effective. The 1890 census was tallied in six months, and only two additional years were required to complete all statistical calculations.

Hollerith incorporated The Tabulating Machine Company in 1896. In 1924, the name of the company was changed to International Business Machines, better known today as IBM. Since it was founded, IBM has become a major player in the computer industry.

The first half of the 20th century ushered in an era of growth in the business machine industry, which at that time produced typewriters and mechanical calculating devices. IBM faced tough competition from companies such as Burroughs, National Cash Register (NCR), Olivetti, and Remington. Some of these companies would later venture into the computer industry.

COMPUTER PROTOTYPES

▶ Who invented the computer?

The question "Who invented the computer?" doesn't have a simple answer because the modern digital computer evolved from a series of prototypes developed by various groups of people. A **prototype** is an experimental device that must be further developed and perfected before going into production and becoming widely available.

Between 1937 and 1942, an Iowa State University professor, John V. Atanasoff, and a graduate student, Clifford E. Berry, worked on a prototype for an electronic computer. The **Atanasoff-Berry Computer** (ABC) was the first to use vacuum tubes instead of mechanical switches for processing circuitry. Its design also incorporated the idea of basing calculations on the binary number system.

The ABC, shown in Figure 9-4, is often considered the first electronic digital computer. According to one historian, "The ABC first demonstrated in 1939 may not have been much of a computer, just as the Wrights' model was not much of an airplane, but it opened the way."

FIGURE 9-4

The Atanasoff-Berry Computer (ABC) gained national attention when it was pulled from obscurity in a 1972 patent dispute. The Sperry Rand company claimed to have a patent on digital computer architecture, but the court declared the patent claim invalid because it was based on the work of Atanasoff and Berry.

AP Photo/Frederick News-Post

While Atanasoff and Berry worked on the ABC, a German engineer named Konrad Zuse developed a computer called the **Z3**, which, like the ABC, was designed to work with binary numbers. Built in Nazi Germany during World War II, the Z3 was cloaked in secrecy, even though Hitler believed that computers had no strategic use in the war effort. Information on Zuse's invention did not surface until long after the war ended. So although Zuse was on the trail of modern computer architecture, his work had little effect on the development of computers in other areas of the world.

Even with the work of Atanasoff, Berry, and Zuse, it was not clear that computers were destined to be binary electronic devices. IBM pursued an entirely different computer architecture by sponsoring an engineer named Howard Aiken, who embarked on an audacious plan to integrate 73 IBM Automatic Accounting Machines into a single unified computing unit.

What emerged in 1939 was a mechanical computer officially named the IBM Automatic Sequence Controlled Calculator, but now usually referred to as the **Harvard Mark I** (Figure 9-5) because it was moved to Harvard University shortly after completion.

akg-images/Newscom

FIGURE 9-5

Constructed of relay switches, rotating shafts, and clutches, the Harvard Mark I sounded like a "roomful of ladies knitting." The device was 51 feet long and 8 feet tall and weighed about 5 tons.

Although the Harvard Mark I was one of the first working computers, as a prototype, it strayed considerably from the path of development leading to modern computers. The Harvard Mark I was digital but used decimal rather than binary representation, which is used by today's computers. In contrast, the ABC, with its electronic vacuum tubes and binary representation, was a much closer prototype of the generations of computers to come.

Aiken was a fine engineer but did not quite grasp the far-reaching potential of computers. In 1947, he predicted that only six electronic digital computers would be required to satisfy the computing needs of the entire United States—a sentiment that echoed an earlier statement made by Thomas J. Watson, then chairman of IBM.

▶ Were prototypes able to perform any real computing?
Some computer prototypes were pressed into service barely before they were completed. In 1943, a team of British developers created **COLOSSUS**, an electronic device designed to decode messages encrypted by the German Enigma machine.

COLOSSUS contained 1,800 vacuum tubes, used binary arithmetic, and was capable of reading input at the rate of 5,000 characters per second. COLOSSUS successfully broke the Enigma codes and gave the Allies a major advantage during World War II.

In 1943, a team headed by John W. Mauchly and J. Presper Eckert started work on ENIAC, a gigantic, general-purpose electronic computer. **ENIAC** (Electronic Numerical Integrator and Computer) was designed to calculate trajectory tables for the U.S. Army, but wasn't finished until November 1945, three months after the end of World War II.

ENIAC was over 100 feet long and 10 feet high and weighed 30 tons. This gigantic machine contained over 18,000 vacuum tubes and consumed 174,000 watts of power. It could perform 5,000 additions per second and was programmed by manually connecting cables and setting 6,000 switches—a process that generally took two days to complete.

ENIAC was formally dedicated at the Moore School of Electrical Engineering of the University of Pennsylvania on February 15, 1946, and immediately pressed into service making atomic energy calculations and computing trajectories for new missile technologies. ENIAC received several upgrades and remained in service until 1955.

GENERATIONS OF COMPUTERS

▶ What was the first commercially successful computer?

A computer called the **UNIVAC** is considered by most historians to be the first commercially successful digital computer. The first UNIVAC computer was constructed under the auspices of the Eckert-Mauchly Computer Corp. By the time the first UNIVAC was completed in 1951, the Eckert-Mauchly Computer Corp. had fallen into financial distress and been acquired by Remington Rand, one of IBM's chief rivals in the business machine arena. Forty-six UNIVAC computers were delivered to Remington Rand's customers between 1951 and 1958.

At 14.5 feet long, 7.5 feet high, and 9 feet wide, UNIVAC was physically smaller than ENIAC, but more powerful. UNIVAC could read data at the rate of 7,200 characters per second, and complete 2.25 million instruction cycles per second. (See Figure 9-6.)

AP Photo/HO

FIGURE 9-6

UNIVAC had RAM capacity of 12,000 characters (12 KB), and used magnetic tape for data storage and retrieval. The cost of a UNIVAC averaged about US$930,000—more than $7 million in today's currency. ▶ View original footage from Remington Rand Corporation showing how UNIVAC worked.

▶ **How did computers progress from room-sized behemoths to modern personal computers?** Early computers, such as the Harvard Mark I, ENIAC, and UNIVAC, used technology that required lots of space and electrical power. As technology evolved, relay switches and vacuum tubes were replaced with smaller, less power-hungry components. Most computer historians agree that computers have evolved through four distinct generations; and in each generation, computers became smaller, faster, more dependable, and less expensive to operate.

▶ **What characterized the first generation of computers?** **First-generation computers** can be characterized by their use of vacuum tubes to store individual bits of data. A **vacuum tube** is an electronic device that controls the flow of electrons in a vacuum (Figure 9-7). Each tube can be set to one of two states. One state is assigned a value of 0 and the other a value of 1.

Vacuum tubes respond more quickly than mechanical relays, resulting in faster computations, but they also have several disadvantages. They consume a lot of power, much of which is wasted as heat. They also tend to burn out quickly. ENIAC, the prototype for first-generation computers, contained about 18,000 tubes, and every tube was replaced at least once in the first year of operation.

In addition to vacuum tube technology, first-generation computers were characterized by custom application programs, made to order for the specific task the computer was to perform. Programming first-generation computers was difficult. As the computer era dawned, programmers were forced to think in 1s and 0s to write instructions in machine language.

Before the first generation ended, programmers had devised rudimentary compilers that allowed them to write instructions using assembly language op codes, such as LDA and JNZ. Assembly language was a small step forward; but like machine language, it was machine specific and required programmers to learn a different set of instructions for each computer.

Although many companies recognized the potential of machines to perform fast calculations, first-generation computers did not seem ready for prime time. That said, many business machine companies, such as IBM, Burroughs, and NCR, began research and development efforts into fledgling computer technologies. Companies in the electronics industry, such as General Electric, RCA, Control Data, and Honeywell, also showed interest in the new field of computing.

▶ **How did second-generation computers differ from first-generation computers?** **Second-generation computers** used transistors instead of vacuum tubes. First demonstrated in 1947 by AT&T's Bell Laboratories, **transistors** regulate current or voltage flow and act as a switch for electronic signals.

Transistors performed functions similar to vacuum tubes, but they were much smaller, cheaper, less power hungry, and more reliable. By the late 1950s, transistors, such as those in Figure 9-8, had replaced vacuum tubes as the processing and memory technology for most computers.

First-generation computers were packed with rows and rows of vacuum tubes, which were used to represent digital data.

Courtesy of vintchip.com

Transistors first sparked a revolution in the entertainment industry by providing a small, power-efficient technology for portable radios. Later, transistors were incorporated in computers to replace large, hot, power-hungry vacuum tubes.

© MediaTechnics

Several successful transistorized computers were manufactured by companies such as IBM, Burroughs, Control Data, Honeywell, and Sperry Rand (which was the new name given to Remington Rand after its merger with Sperry Corp.). These computers served businesses and even played major roles in the U.S. space program (Figure 9-9).

FIGURE 9-9

It was big, but not very fast. Yet, the IBM 7090 transistorized computer was used to plot the trajectories for NASA space flights.

9

In addition to the important hardware breakthrough provided by transistors, an equally important development in software differentiated second-generation computers from their first-generation ancestors.

First-generation computers didn't have operating systems as we know them today. Instead, each software application included the instructions necessary for every aspect of the computing job, including input, output, and processing activities.

Programmers were quick to realize that this style of programming was terribly inefficient. For example, although virtually every program sent results to a printer, every program was required to have its own print routine.

Computer manufacturers such as IBM developed operating systems that provided standardized routines for input, output, memory management, storage, and other resource management activities.

Early operating systems were a step in the right direction; but unfortunately, learning to use each one was like learning a new and unique programming language. It was not until the third generation of computers that portable operating systems, such as CP/M and UNIX, provided programmers with similar operating system commands across hardware platforms.

In addition to operating systems, second-generation computers also ran programming language compilers that allowed programmers to write instructions using English-like commands rather than machine language 1s and 0s or cryptic assembly language commands.

High-level languages, such as COBOL (Common Business-Oriented Language) and Fortran (Formula Translator), were available for use on second-generation computers and remain in use today. The availability of high-level computer programming languages made it possible for third parties to develop software, and that capability was instrumental in the birth of the software industry.

▶ **What are the characteristics of third-generation computers?** **Third-generation computers** became possible in 1958, when Jack Kilby at Texas Instruments and Robert Noyce at Fairchild Semiconductor independently developed integrated circuits (Figure 9-10). Integrated circuit technology made it possible to pack the equivalent of thousands of vacuum tubes or transistors onto a single miniature chip, vastly reducing the physical size, weight, and power requirements for devices such as computers.

FIGURE 9-10

Jack Kilby's original integrated circuit was a key development for creating today's small, fast, and efficient computers.

Two of the first computers to incorporate integrated circuits were the **RCA Spectra 70** and the wildly successful **IBM 360**. The first orders for IBM 360 computers were filled in 1965—a date regarded by many historians as the advent of third-generation computers.

In 1965, Digital Equipment Corp. (DEC) introduced the **DEC PDP-8**, the first commercially successful minicomputer. Minicomputers were designed to be smaller and less powerful than mainframe computers, while maintaining the capability to simultaneously run multiple programs for multiple users. Thousands of manufacturing plants, small businesses, and scientific laboratories were attracted to the speed, small size, and reasonable cost of the PDP-8.

DEC introduced a succession of minicomputers that stole a share of the mainframe market. Eventually, IBM and other mainframe makers introduced their own minicomputers, but the star for minicomputers faded as microcomputers gained processing power and networking became easier. DEC was purchased by Compaq in 1998. Compaq was later purchased by Hewlett-Packard (HP).

By 2000, the **IBM AS/400** (renamed the iSeries 400) was one of the few remaining devices that could be classified as a minicomputer. Today, demand for minicomputers is satisfied by high-end personal computers and servers, and the term *minicomputer* has generally fallen into disuse.

▶ **How did microprocessor technology affect the computer industry?** The technology for **fourth-generation computers** appeared in 1971, when Ted Hoff developed the first general-purpose microprocessor. Called the Intel 4004, this microprocessor dramatically changed the computer industry, resulting in fourth-generation microprocessor-based computer systems that were faster, smaller, and even less expensive than third-generation computers.

Microprocessor manufacturers soon flourished. Early industry leaders included Intel, Zilog, Motorola, and Texas Instruments. Intel's 4004 microprocessor (Figure 9-11) was smaller than a corn flake but matched the computing power of ENIAC.

The 4004 packed the equivalent of 2,300 transistors or vacuum tubes on a single chip and was able to perform 60,000 instructions per second. The 4004 was followed by the 8008, the first commercial 8-bit microprocessor, and then the 8080.

In 1974, Motorola released the 6800 8-bit microprocessor. A few months later, ex-Motorola engineers working at MOS Technology created the 6502, an 8-bit microprocessor that was used in the Apple II and Commodore personal computer systems.

FIGURE 9-11

The Intel 4004 microprocessor was small. Its chip (lower right) was only 1/8" by 1/16". Even in the chip carrier (top left) the microprocessor was less than 1" in length.

9

In 1976, Zilog introduced the Z80 microprocessor, an enhanced 8080 microprocessor that was used in many early computer systems. In the same year, Intel released the 8085, a further enhancement of the 8080.

Both Intel and Motorola continued development of advanced microprocessors. The Intel line, used in most Windows-compatible and Intel Mac computers, included the 8086, 8088, 80286, 80386, 80486, Pentium, Itanium, and multi-core microprocessors. The Motorola line of microprocessors grew to include the 68000 series processors used in Apple Macintosh computers, plus the PowerPC processors developed in the early 1990s and used in Macintosh computer systems until 2006.

Today, microprocessors are a key component of all types of computers—ranging from PDAs to supercomputers. Intel reigns as the world's leading microprocessor manufacturer, although microprocessors are also produced by companies such as Hitachi, Texas Instruments, Toshiba, AMD, ARM, and Motorola.

▶ **Has a fifth generation of computers emerged?** It is not clear if there is a fifth generation of computers. A Japanese artificial intelligence project in the 1980s was called fifth-generation computing, but historians do not equate this effort with the four generations mentioned so far in this chapter.

Current processor technology requires very large scale integration (VLSI) that packs millions of components on a single chip. VLSI technology is used for CPUs, GPUs, and controllers. It integrates cellular technology, Wi-Fi, and sound into all-purpose chips that power smartphones and tablet computers. Whether this technology represents the fifth generation of computers is yet to be seen.

PERSONAL COMPUTERS

▶ **Who invented the personal computer?** In the early 1970s, many hobbyists built their own computer systems based on integrated circuit and microprocessor technologies. One such system, the **Mark-8**, was developed by Jonathan A. Titus and featured in the July 1974 issue of *Radio-Electronics*. These early personal computers were not commercially produced or widely available, but they are often considered forerunners of today's personal computer.

In 1975, Ed Roberts and the MITS (Micro Instrumentation and Telemetry Systems) company announced the **MITS Altair**, which many historians believe to be the first commercial microcomputer (Figure 9-12).

The Altair was based on the Intel 8080 processor and sold as a kit for $395 or fully assembled for $650—about one-fourth the price of a 1975 Volkswagen Beetle. The Altair was a computer for the hobbyist. The kit came unassembled in a box containing a processor and 256 bytes of memory—not 256 KB, just 256 bytes. It had no keyboard, no monitor, and no permanent storage device.

Programming the Altair computer meant flipping individual switches on the front of the system unit. Output consisted of flashing lights, and the only programming language available was 8080 machine language.

FIGURE 9-12

Although it was sold as a kit, required assembly, and was too limited to perform significant computational tasks, the Altair was snapped up by hobbyists interested in learning how computers worked.

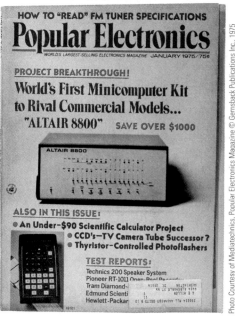

▶ What were the first personal computers? In 1976, Steve Jobs and Steve Wozniak founded Apple Computer Corporation and released the **Apple I**, a kit containing a system board with 4 KB of RAM that sold for $666.66. Other companies, such as Commodore, Atari, and RadioShack, also pursued the hobbyist market, but with preassembled computers.

In 1978, Apple introduced a preassembled computer called the **Apple II**, which featured color graphics, expansion slots, a disk drive, a 1.07 MHz 6502 processor, and 16 KB of RAM for $1,195. The Apple II, shown in Figure 9-13, was a very successful product. One of the main reasons behind its success was a commercial software program called **VisiCalc**—the first electronic spreadsheet. This program landed computers on the radar screen of business users and clearly marked a turning point where personal computers appealed to an audience beyond hobbyists.

In 1981, IBM began marketing what it called a *personal computer* or PC, based on the 8088 processor. When the PC version of VisiCalc became available, the IBM PC quickly became the top-selling personal computer, far surpassing IBM's expectations.

The $3,000 **IBM PC**, shown in Figure 9-14, shipped with a 4.77 MHz Intel 8088 processor, 16 KB of RAM, and single-sided 160 KB floppy disk drives. The IBM PC was soon followed by the **IBM PC XT**, which featured RAM upgradable to 640 KB, and a 10 MB hard disk drive.

IBM PCs were constructed with off-the-shelf parts that could be easily obtained from many electronics wholesalers. Within months, dozens of companies used these parts to produce clones of IBM-compatible computers that could run the same software and use the same expansion cards as the IBM PC and PC XT. These companies were also able to obtain essentially the same operating system used by IBM.

The IBM PC used an operating system called PC-DOS that was marketed by a young entrepreneur named Bill Gates, founder of a fledgling software company called Microsoft. Microsoft marketed a similar operating system, called MS-DOS, to PC clone makers. Many of the companies that produced IBM clones failed, but some, such as Dell and Hewlett-Packard, became major forces in the personal computer industry.

▶ How did personal computers become so successful? Although hobbyists and the business community had embraced computers, these machines were still considered difficult for the average person to use. That perception began to change in 1983, when Apple introduced a product called the **Apple Lisa**. A key feature of the Lisa was its graphical user interface—an idea borrowed from the **Xerox Alto** computer.

At $10,000, the Lisa proved too expensive for most consumers. Apple remained committed to graphical user interfaces, however, and in 1984, released the first **Apple Macintosh** (Figure 9-15). The $2,495 Macintosh featured a graphical user interface that made programs easier to use than those on the command-line-based IBM PC. The Macintosh became the computer of choice for graphical applications such as desktop publishing.

By the late 1980s, the computer industry had begun to consolidate around two primary platforms—the MS-DOS-based IBM-compatible platform and the Apple Macintosh. Although dozens of companies produced IBM-compatible systems that ran the same software and used the same hardware as the

The Apple II was the most popular computer of its time.

The IBM PC (shown here with an Epson printer), which was launched in 1981, evolved into today's popular Windows-based PCs.

The Apple Macintosh computer popularized graphical user interfaces.

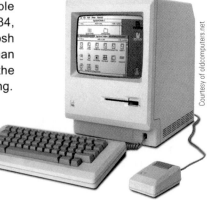

9

IBM PC, Apple attempted to keep its system proprietary. As more IBM-compatible computers were sold, the market for IBM-compatible hardware and software continued to grow.

By the mid-1990s, IBM-compatible computer systems accounted for more than 90% of all personal computer sales. The Apple Macintosh accounted for most of the remainder, with other proprietary platforms accounting for a very small percentage of new computer sales.

Even as computer sales soared, and graphical user interfaces, such as Windows 3.1, made computers easier to use, many people simply could not think of any reason to own one. They preferred to write short notes on paper rather than learn how to use a word processor. It seemed easier to punch numbers into a handheld calculator than tackle the complexities of electronic spreadsheets. Why buy a computer if it didn't offer some really enticing perks?

That attitude began to change in the late 1980s when the Internet opened to public use. In a flurry of activity, graphical browsers appeared, ISPs provided inexpensive connections, e-mail began to fly, and e-commerce sites opened their doors. By the mid-1990s, personal computers had finally achieved mass popularity.

FIGURE 9-16

The first portable computers were the size of a carry-on bag and weighed nearly 30 pounds.

▶ **What's trending?** Desktop computers had their day; and though they are still available, the trend is toward portable computing devices.

The first portable computers appeared in the early 1970s, but they were the size of a carry-on bag and weighed just as much! (See Figure 9-16.) Throughout the 1980s and 1990s, portable computers became smaller, lighter, and more popular until sometime around 2005, when they outsold desktop computers.

The Apple iPhone ushered in the era of handheld computing devices. A computer industry milestone occurred in 2011 when, for the first time, smartphones outsold desktop and notebook computers.

Courtesy of oldcomputers.net

QuickCheck   SECTION A

1. The abacus and slide rule are examples of manual calculators, which require the operator to apply a(n) [_____] to perform calculations.

2. Charles [_____] designed a general-purpose calculating device, called the Analytical Engine, that embodied many of the concepts that define the modern computer.

3. In 1965, Digital Equipment Corp. (DEC) introduced the DEC PDP-8, the first commercially successful [_____].

4. The first generation of computers can be characterized by its use of [_____] tubes to store individual bits of data, whereas second-generation computers used [_____].

5. Third-generation computers were based on [_____] circuit technology, and fourth-generation computers are characterized by [_____] technology.

▶ CHECK ANSWERS

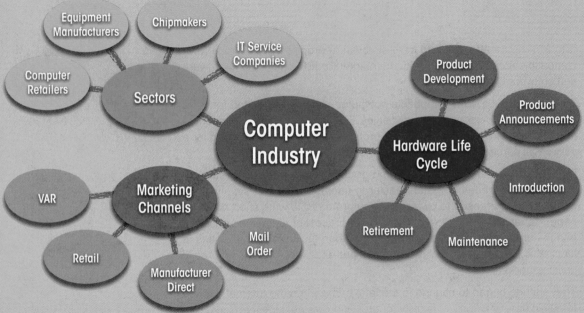

The Computer and IT Industries

SECTION **B**

BEFORE YOU VENTURE OUT to buy computers, handheld devices, peripheral devices, or software; before you commit yourself to a computer career; or before you buy stock in computer companies, you should arm yourself with some basic knowledge about the computer and information technology industries. In this section of the chapter, you'll learn about the scope and economics of these dynamic industries.

INDUSTRY OVERVIEW

▶ Is there a difference between the computer industry and the information technology industry? The term *computer industry* is used in a variety of ways. Narrowly defined, the **computer industry** encompasses those companies that manufacture computers and computer components (Figure 9-17).

The term *computer industry* is also used more broadly to include software publishers and peripheral device manufacturers.

An even broader term, **information technology industry** (or *IT industry*), is used to refer to the companies that develop, produce, sell, or support computers, software, and computer-related products. It includes companies in the computer industry, software publishers, communications service vendors such as AT&T, information services such as the LexisNexis online law library, and service companies such as HP Enterprise Services.

The terms *computer industry* and *IT industry* are sometimes used interchangeably in news reports and publications, leaving the reader to decide whether the subject is limited to computer manufacturers and distributors.

FIGURE 9-17

Manufacturers such as Apple, Dell, Hewlett-Packard, IBM, and Intel are representative of companies in the computer industry.

498

▶ **Is every company that uses computers part of the IT industry?** No. A bank uses computers to track money flowing into and out of accounts, but it is classified as part of the banking industry. A clothing store might use computers to monitor inventory, but it is classified as part of the apparel industry. Such businesses make use of information technology, but they are definitely not part of the computer industry and are not considered part of the IT industry either.

▶ **What kinds of companies are included in the IT industry?** Companies in the IT industry can be separated into several broad categories, sometimes referred to as sectors or segments, including equipment manufacturers, chipmakers, software publishers, service companies, and computer retailers.

9

Equipment manufacturers design and manufacture computer hardware and communications products, such as personal computers, mainframes, mice, monitors, storage devices, routers, scanners, and printers. Examples of these companies include computer manufacturers IBM, Dell, Lenovo, and Hewlett-Packard. Network hardware companies, such as Cisco and its subsidiary Linksys, are also examples of equipment manufacturers.

Chipmakers design and manufacture computer chips and circuit boards, including microprocessors, RAM, system boards, sound cards, and graphics cards. Intel, Texas Instruments, AMD, and Taiwan Semiconductor are examples of chipmakers.

Software publishers create computer software, including applications, operating systems, and programming languages. Examples of software companies include Microsoft, Adobe Systems, Oracle Corporation, Electronic Arts, and Computer Associates (CA).

IT service companies provide computer-related services, including business consulting, Web site design, Web hosting, Internet connections, computer equipment repair, network security, and product support. Classic examples of service companies include AOL, Google, and the computer consulting giant Accenture.

Computer retailers (sometimes called resellers) include companies that sell computer products through retail stores, direct sales representatives, mail-order catalogs, and Web sites. Well-known computer resellers include CompUSA, which operates retail stores, and mail-order retailers PC Connection and CDW.

Although some companies fit neatly into one of the above categories, other companies operate in two or more areas. For example, Dell manufactures hardware but also resells that hardware directly to individuals and businesses. The IT industry also encompasses large conglomerates with one or more divisions devoted to computer hardware, software, or services.

▶ **What about dot-coms?** The 1990s spawned a group of Internet-based companies that came to be called **dot-coms**. The dot-com moniker came from the companies' domain names, which inevitably ended with .com; many of the companies even incorporated .com into their official company names.

Amazon.com was one of the first Internet-based companies. Founded in 1995, the company's original mission statement was to "use the Internet to transform book buying into the fastest, easiest, and most enjoyable shopping experience possible." To transform book buying, Amazon.com set up a Web site where customers can buy books online without walking into a store located in a mall or shopping center.

Unless a dot-com sells computers, peripherals, or software online, it is probably not considered part of the computer industry; but experts disagree on whether dot-coms rightfully belong to the IT industry. Some experts group dot-coms under the IT umbrella because they make extensive use of computer equipment and have developed key e-commerce technologies. Other analysts classify dot-coms by their core businesses. For example, dot-coms that sell clothing would be in the apparel industry, music vendors would be in the entertainment industry, and an online stock broker would be in the financial industry.

FIGURE 9-18

Silicon Valley is home to many companies in the IT industry.

▶ **What is the significance of Silicon Valley?** The area of California called Silicon Valley that stretches south and east from San Francisco's Golden Gate Bridge was the birthplace of integrated circuits, microprocessors, and personal computers.

Today, well-known companies, such as Cisco Systems, Sun Microsystems, Google, Apple, Symantec, AMD, Oracle, and Hewlett-Packard, all have headquarters in or near California's Silicon Valley (Figure 9-18).

Although Silicon Valley has a reputation as the home of the IT industry, many top IT players are located elsewhere. Microsoft is located near Seattle, and Dell is just outside Austin.

North Carolina's Research Triangle (Raleigh-Durham-Chapel Hill) is home base for IBM's largest hardware lab and several small research startups. Software publisher Computer Associates is based in New York. Unisys, a high-end server manufacturer, has its headquarters near Philadelphia. Outsourcing and offshoring spread the computer industry to additional locations both in the United States and abroad.

▶ **What are outsourcing and offshoring?** Like companies in many industries, computer companies make significant use of outsourcing to reduce the price of materials and labor.

Outsourcing is defined as the use of components or labor from outside suppliers. Most computer companies do not manufacture all the components used to assemble their computers. Instead they depend on components from other companies, such as microprocessors from Intel,

hard drives from Seagate, and LCD panels from Samsung. Software publishers also make use of outsourcing by hiring outside firms to develop products and manufacture packaging. Outsourcing offers economies of scale and expertise to companies in the highly competitive computer industry.

Offshoring is another technique used by companies to help keep product prices competitive. **Offshoring** is defined as relocating business processes, such as development and production, to lower-cost locations in other countries.

U.S. computer companies have established manufacturing and development facilities in countries such as China, India, Malaysia, Thailand, and Mexico, where labor is inexpensive but reliable. Computer manufacturer Dell Inc. maintains a team of offshore technicians to staff customer call centers. It is common now to dial technical support and be connected to a technician on the other side of the world.

Companies such as Microsoft and Oracle make extensive use of programmers based in India, who telecommute, when necessary, using the Internet (Figure 9-19).

FIGURE 9-19

The IT industry reaches globally for programmers, call center staffers, and manufacturing facilities.

▶ Where can I find information about the IT industry?

Whether you are planning to purchase a computer, embark on a computing career, or invest in a computer company, you can dig up lots of information on IT and computer companies from a wide variety of computer and business publications (Figure 9-20).

In Print	On the Web
PCWorld	PC Magazine
Macworld	CNET News
Wired	InformationWeek
CPU	InfoWorld
Mac|Life	Wired
Smart Computing	ZDNet
	TechWeb
	Dr. Dobb's News
	Forbes.com/technology

FIGURE 9-20

IT Information Sources

ECONOMIC FACTORS

▶ How has the IT industry affected the global economy?

The IT industry has been described as the most dynamic, most prosperous, most economically beneficial industry the world has ever known. That statement might be a bit of an exaggeration, but the IT industry unquestionably has fueled the economies of many countries. Worldwide, consumers spend more than $1 trillion on information technology each year.

▶ What about the U.S. IT industry?

In the U.S., the IT industry has had its ups and downs. IBM stock, once a staple of retirement portfolios, was all but abandoned during a dot-com bubble that began in the late 1990s.

A stock market bubble refers to a sharp rise in stock values, which is later followed by a sudden decline. The so-called "dot-com bubble" was fueled by a frenzy of online business startups. Entrepreneurs seemed to believe that any Internet-based business was destined for success. Investors believed that dot-coms were the key to quick profits. Stock sold like hotcakes on the technology-specialized NASDAQ stock exchange (Figure 9-21).

Dot-com stock values soared as investors poured money into online businesses. These businesses needed equipment and employees, which had a positive effect on other sectors of the IT industry by boosting computer sales, networking equipment sales, and IT employment. Unfortunately, many dot-coms lacked experienced management teams, failed to develop realistic business plans, burned through startup capital without making a profit, and then went bankrupt.

The high rate of dot-com business failures during 2001 and 2002 was a tough jolt of reality for many stockholders. It affected a wide swath of the economy. The end of the dot-com bubble meant a decline in equipment orders, Web site hosting contracts, and IT sector job openings.

Nonetheless, strength in worldwide markets for IT equipment and services continued to buoy up the industry, and tech stocks eventually re-emerged as attractive investments. Analysts believe that well-conceived and professionally managed online businesses can be a profitable part of the IT industry.

▶ What does the future hold for the IT industry?

As with many situations involving the economy, the IT industry's future cannot be predicted with certainty. Population growth and business globalization are two important factors that have contributed to past investments in information technology.

The worldwide population more than doubled over the past 50 years, and an International Institute for Applied Systems Analysis study predicts that the population will peak at 9 billion by 2070. Keeping track of the information relating to all these people—births, deaths, marriages, property ownership, taxes, purchases, banking records, and licenses—certainly seems impossible without the use of computers.

Intense global competitive pressure keeps companies looking for ways to cut costs and raise productivity. As businesses globalize, they encounter new competitors that may use more advanced technological tools. Obtaining competitive tools can be a requirement for success, so information technology would appear to have many potential customers in the expanding global business market.

FIGURE 9-21

Dot-com Bubble Timeline

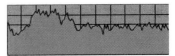

May 1997 Amazon.com stock initial public offering (IPO) kicks off the dot-com frenzy.

November 1998 theglobe.com earns $100 million during its IPO, making it the most successful stock offering in history.

March 2000 NASDAQ reaches its all-time high of 5,048; stocks are trading for an average of $55.92 per share.

December 2000 By year's end, venture capitalists have invested an estimated $20 billion in 12,450 dot-com startups.

January 2001 17 dot-coms each spend over $2 million for a 30-second ad during the Super Bowl.

June 2001 By mid-year, 345 dot-coms have closed their doors or filed for bankruptcy protection.

August 2001 theglobe.com goes out of business.

September 2002 NASDAQ bottoms out at 1,184, much lower than its 5,048 peak. Average price per share is $14.07.

August 2004 Google has a successful IPO—a sign that consumers are regaining confidence in dot-com stocks.

PRODUCT LIFE CYCLES

▶ How are new computer hardware products developed?

Two factors drive the development of new computer hardware products: marketing and technology. Hardware manufacturers introduce new products for the same reasons as their counterparts in other industries: New products are designed to attract customers and generate sales. New hardware products can also generate sales of add-ons and accessories.

New technologies spur a flurry of development activity and generate new hardware products. For example, the debut of Wi-Fi technology stimulated development of Wi-Fi hubs and cards, Wi-Fi enabled notebook computers, Internet access points in coffee shops and airports, as well as Wi-Fi access plans from companies such as T-Mobile. Apple's foray into tablet computers led to a slew of iPad-like products and accessories.

Technological breakthroughs do not necessarily adhere to a schedule, however. Companies cannot always predict when a new technology will appear, how it might be incorporated into new products, or how popular it will become. As a result, the life cycle of some hardware products is short, whereas others have a long life cycle.

▶ What are the stages in the life cycle of a typical hardware product?

In the computer industry, the life cycle of a new hardware product usually includes five stages: product development, product announcement, introduction, maintenance, and retirement, as shown in Figure 9-22.

FIGURE 9-22

Hardware Product Life Cycle

Product Development
Product development often takes place under wraps. Developers use fanciful code names, such as Sawtooth and Portola, to refer to their products. Inevitably, news of these products leaks out and causes much speculation among industry analysts.

Product Announcement
Products are often announced at trade shows and press conferences. As a consumer, you should be wary of making purchase or investment decisions based on product announcements. A product announcement can precede the actual launch by months or even years. Some products, referred to as vaporware, are announced but never produced.

Introduction
When a new product becomes available, it is usually added to the vendor's product line and featured prominently in advertisements. Initial supplies of the product generally remain low while manufacturing capacity increases to meet demand.

Maintenance
As supply and demand for a product reach an equilibrium, the manufacturer might reduce the price to keep the product attractive to buyers.

Retirement
As demand declines, a company's oldest products are discontinued. Eventually product support is discontinued as well.

▶ **How does the hardware life cycle affect me as a consumer?** Hardware manufacturers offer a range of products at various price points. Less powerful devices containing older technology are generally less expensive than devices with the latest and greatest technology.

When considering a technology purchase, look for a balance between features and price. Products at the top of the manufacturer's line might offer features and technology that are not worth the price, whereas products at the low end of the product line might not offer the features you'll require over the life of the device. For most consumers, mid-range products offer the best value (Figure 9-23).

FIGURE 9-23

A sample of computers in a typical manufacturer's product line shows a range of prices and features.

EDGE 2500 NETBOOK

- Intel® Atom Processor® 1.66 GHz
- 10" widescreen display
- 1 GB DDR2 SDRAM
- 120 GB SATA HD
- 2.75 pounds
- Wireless 802.11g Mini Card
- 1 year warranty

$249

EDGE 4500 NETBOOK

- Intel® Atom Processor® 2.00 GHz
- 12" widescreen display
- 1 GB DDR2 SDRAM
- 160 GB SATA HD
- 2.50 pounds
- Wireless 802.11g Mini Card
- 3 year warranty

$399

EDGE 8000 NETBOOK

- Intel® Atom Processor® 2.13 GHz
- 12" widescreen display
- 4 GB DDR2 RAM
- 250 GB SATA HD
- 2.50 pounds
- Wireless 802.11g Mini Card
- 3 year warranty

$575

▶ **Is the life cycle of a software product similar to that of a hardware product?** Software, like hardware, begins with an idea that is shaped by a design team and marketing experts. A team of programmers then works to produce executable programs and support modules for the new software product.

Most software products undergo extensive testing before they are released. The first phase of testing, called an **alpha test**, is carried out by the software publisher's in-house testing team. Errors, or bugs, found during the alpha test phase are fixed, and then the software enters a second testing phase called a **beta test**. Typically, a beta test is conducted by a team of off-site testers, such as a professional testing company.

Sometimes a software publisher releases a beta version of the software to individuals and companies in the general public to expose the software to the widest possible variety of computers and operating environments. Although it can be exciting to test a yet-to-be-released software package, beta versions are often "buggy" and can cause unexpected glitches in your computer. Beta testing requires a high tolerance for frustration.

Unlike computer hardware products, older versions of software normally do not remain in the vendor's product line. When a publisher offers a new version of the software that you are using, it is a good idea to upgrade; but you can wait to upgrade, however, for several months until the initial rush for technical support on the new product subsides.

Upgrading your existing software is usually less expensive than replacing it with a brand-new program. If you don't upgrade, you might find that the software publisher offers minimal technical support for older versions of the program. Also, if you let several versions go by without upgrading, you might lose your eligibility for special upgrade pricing.

MARKET SHARE

▶ **How do computer companies stack up against each other?** Industry analysts often use market share as a gauge of a company's success. **Market share** refers to a company's share, or percentage, of the total market. For example, Microsoft's share of the total personal computer operating system market is about 90%. The remaining 10% share is distributed among Apple and several Linux vendors.

In the U.S., Dell, Hewlett-Packard, and Apple have the most market share. Worldwide, Hewlett-Packard leads the pack with more than 17% market share, followed by Dell and Lenovo. Figure 9-24 illustrates market share for PC vendors.

Market share graphs for personal computer manufacturers, software publishers, operating system developers, Internet service providers, and handheld computer manufacturers provide a road map to the changing fortunes of companies in the computer industry. Competition is fierce in all segments of the industry, and market share is one indicator of a company's ability to retain customers and acquire sales from its rivals. The top companies are constantly challenged not only by their peers, but by startup companies in lower tiers of the industry.

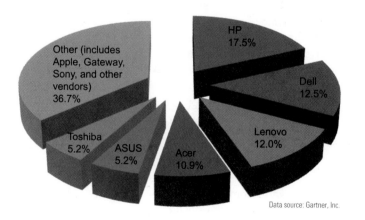

Data source: Gartner, Inc.

FIGURE 9-24

Worldwide Market Share for Personal Computer Vendors in the Second Quarter of 2011

MARKETING CHANNELS

▶ Why are computer equipment and software sold through so many outlets? Hardware manufacturers and software publishers try to reach consumers by making their products available through a variety of sources. Computer hardware and software are sold through marketing outlets called **marketing channels**. These channels, shown in Figure 9-25, include computer retail stores, mail-order/Internet outlets, value-added resellers, and manufacturer direct.

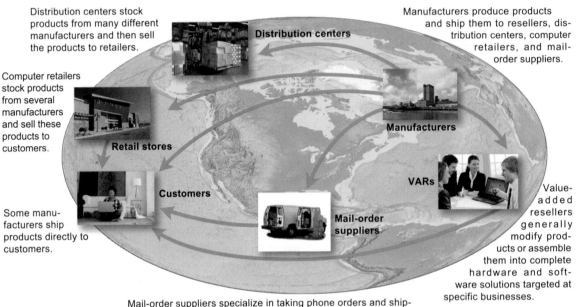

Distribution centers stock products from many different manufacturers and then sell the products to retailers.

Computer retailers stock products from several manufacturers and sell these products to customers.

Some manufacturers ship products directly to customers.

Manufacturers produce products and ship them to resellers, distribution centers, computer retailers, and mail-order suppliers.

Value-added resellers generally modify products or assemble them into complete hardware and software solutions targeted at specific businesses.

Mail-order suppliers specialize in taking phone orders and shipping products to customers using U.S. mail or courier services.

▶ Isn't a computer retail store the best channel for hardware and software products? A computer retail store specializes in the sale and support of microcomputer software and hardware. Computer retail stores tend to be small local shops with knowledgeable employees. Many computer retail stores also offer classes and training sessions, answer questions, provide technical support, and repair hardware products. Computer retail stores primarily service business customers.

▶ What about office and electronics stores? Today, computers, peripherals, and software are sold from a variety of retail outlets, including electronics stores, such as Best Buy, CompUSA, and RadioShack. Office superstores, such as Staples, OfficeMax, and Office Depot, also sell computers and accessories.

Prices and employee expertise at these outlets vary. Some offer troubleshooting and repair services, such as Best Buy's Geek Squad. Consumers should ask about a store's service facilities and policies when considering a purchase.

▶ How do mail-order channels compare to retail? Mail order is a special type of retailing in which a vendor takes orders by telephone or from an Internet site, and then ships the product directly to consumers. Mail-order suppliers, such as TigerDirect.com and CDW, generally offer low prices but might provide only limited service and support. A mail-order supplier is often the best source of products for buyers who are unlikely to need support or who can troubleshoot problems by calling a help desk.

Experienced computer users who can install components, set up software, and do their own troubleshooting are often happy with mail-order suppliers. Inexperienced computer users might not be satisfied with the assistance they receive.

▶ Do computer manufacturers and software publishers sell direct? Manufacturer direct refers to hardware manufacturers that sell their products directly to consumers without a middleman, such as a retail store. IBM has a long tradition of direct sales, and that model has been emulated by several hardware manufacturers and some software publishers. A company's sales force usually targets large corporate or educational customers, where large-volume sales can cover the sales representative's costs and commissions.

The obvious advantage of direct sales is that by cutting out the retailer, a manufacturer can make more profit on each unit sold. The disadvantage is that the manufacturer must provide customers with technical support—a potentially costly service that requires large teams of technical support personnel.

For personal computer hardware, Dell pioneered Web-based direct sales to individual customers. Its innovative Web site allows customers to select from a variety of standard models or configure their own custom builds (Figure 9-26). A just-in-time inventory model allows Dell to build each customer's computer as it is ordered, which eliminates costly inventories of computers that quickly become outdated.

FIGURE 9-26

At Dell's Web site, customers can order a custom-built computer by simply clicking to add various hardware options.
⏵ Click for more information about creating and ordering a custom-built computer.

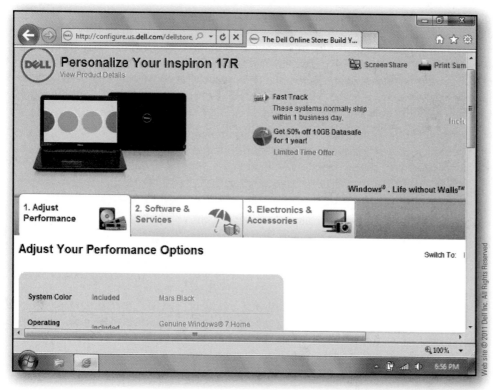

9

▶ **What's a VAR? VAR** stands for value-added reseller. A value-added reseller combines commercially available products with specialty hardware or software to create a computer system designed to meet the needs of a specific industry.

Although VARs charge for their expertise, they are often the only source for specialized computer systems. For example, if you own a video rental store and want to automate the rental process, the best type of vendor might be a VAR that offers a complete hardware and software package tailored to the video rental business. Otherwise, you must piece together the computer, scanner, printer, and software components yourself.

VARs are often the most expensive channel for hardware and software, but their expertise can be crucial to ensure that the hardware and software work correctly in a specific environment.

▶ **What's the benefit of having so many channels?** Vendors from one channel often find that vendors from other channels pirate their sales—a process referred to as **channel conflict**. In the early days of the computer industry, some manufacturers attempted to reduce channel conflict by granting exclusive territories to local computer retailers and by limiting online sales.

This practice is no longer common; although some computer manufacturers attempt to limit channel conflict by restricting the way products are advertised and sold. For example, e-commerce sites might not be allowed to advertise discount prices for some computer brands.

Although vendors lose sales to channel conflict, consumers can benefit from a variety of channels. Because the price of computer equipment and software tends to vary by channel, consumers can shop for the best price and the most appropriate level of support.

INDUSTRY REGULATION

▶ **Is the IT industry regulated in any way?** Some aspects of the IT industry are regulated by government agencies, but many aspects are self-regulated. Unlike the airline industry, which is regulated by agencies such as the Federal Aviation Administration (FAA), most countries do not have a single government agency dedicated to regulating the IT industry. The IT industry encompasses many activities, however, and consequently it is subject to regulation from a variety of broad-based government agencies, such as the FCC and FTC (Figure 9-27).

Many governments are enacting laws that restrict access to particular Internet activities and content. For example, several Caribbean countries have enacted laws that regulate online casino operators.

In 1996, the U.S. Congress enacted the Communications Decency Act, which made it illegal to put indecent material online where children might see it. Parts of this legislation were contested and ultimately nullified by the U.S. Supreme Court, but the desire for decency without censorship has not died among lawmakers.

In many countries, export restrictions affect the type of technology that can be sold to foreign governments and individuals. For example, before being exported from the United States, software and hardware products that contain certain encryption algorithms must be registered with the U.S. government. Additional government regulations that pertain to law enforcement, national security, e-commerce, and taxation can also affect the way the IT industry conducts its business and how it engineers products.

FIGURE 9-27

IT Industry Regulation

Internet activity is affected by policies of the U.S. Federal Communications Commission (FCC), which regulates interstate and international communications by television, wire, radio, satellite, and cable.

The U.S. Federal Trade Commission (FTC) and Department of Justice police the business practices of the IT industry, just as they police other industries.

9

▶ How does the IT industry perceive government regulation? Most IT industry leaders oppose regulation. They remain skeptical of government regulations that might limit their ability to explore new technologies and offer them to the public. To avoid further government intervention, the IT industry has taken steps toward self-regulation.

Several organizations provide a forum for the IT industry to examine issues, express views, work out self-governing policies, and set standards. The Information Technology Industry Council has become one of the major trade associations for computer manufacturers, telecommunications suppliers, business equipment dealers, software publishers, and IT service providers. As part of its mission, this organization provides a powerful lobbying group, which works with lawmakers to minimize legislation that might curtail technology innovation and use.

The Software & Information Industry Association, formerly known as the Software Publishers Association, has 500 member companies and organizations. This organization focuses on protecting the intellectual property of members and lobbying for a legal and regulatory environment that benefits the entire IT industry. Its anti-piracy program is instrumental in identifying and prosecuting software and Internet piracy cases.

Organizations such as the IEEE Standards Association help the IT industry standardize technology, such as microprocessor architecture and network protocols, as well as programming languages and multimedia components.

QuickCheck   SECTION B

1. IT [_____] companies offer business consulting, Web site design, Web hosting, Internet connections, computer equipment repair, network security, and product support.

2. Many computer companies make significant use of [_____] to obtain components and labor from other companies.

3. The life cycle of a new computer model typically evolves through five stages: product development, product [_____], introduction, maintenance, and retirement.

4. Software publishers sometimes offer a public [_____] version of a product for widespread testing before the product is officially released.

5. If a small business lacks the time or expertise to assemble a computer system customized for a task such as professional video editing, a(n) [_____], might offer a turn-key solution. (Hint: Use the acronym.)

▶ CHECK ANSWERS

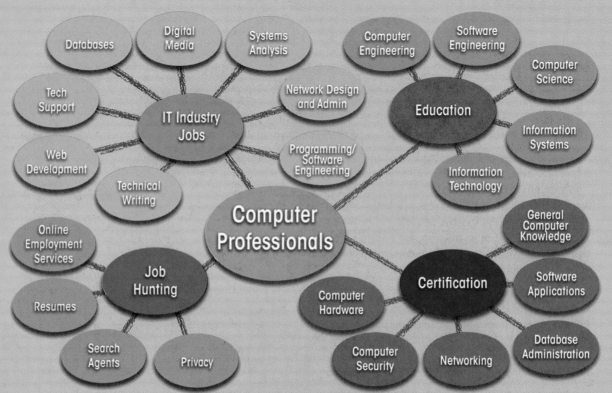

Careers for Computer Professionals

TODAY, IT SEEMS that just about everyone uses computers at work. In this part of the chapter, you'll learn about workers within the IT industry called computer professionals. Maybe you'll even get a glimpse of your own future if you're considering a career in IT.

JOBS AND SALARIES

▶ **What is a computer professional?** In 1999, the U.S. Congress crafted an amendment to the Fair Labor Standards Act that essentially defines a **computer professional** as any person whose primary occupation involves the design, configuration, analysis, development, modification, testing, or security of computer hardware or software.

▶ **What kinds of jobs are available to computer professionals?** Many computer professionals work in an IT department—the wing of a business or an organization responsible for computer, data, software, and support services. An IT department is also responsible for prioritizing an organization's information needs, modifying old systems as necessary, and creating new systems.

Historically, IT departments were part of an organization's Finance department because computers were initially deployed for accounting and inventory management functions. As computers began to assist with a wider variety of business tasks, some organizations changed their organizational charts to make the IT department a separate entity headed by a **chief information officer** (CIO), or director who reports directly to the chief executive officer or president (Figure 9-28).

FIGURE 9-28

The organizational structure of IT departments varies. This organizational structure might be found in a mid-size business.

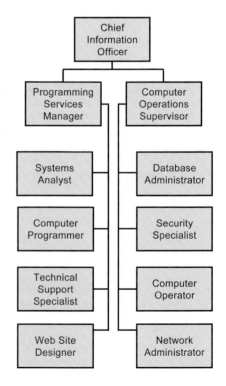

The following descriptions highlight typical responsibilities and skills for various IT department jobs:

▶ A **systems analyst** investigates the requirements of a business or an organization, its employees, and its customers in order to plan and implement new or improved computer services. This job requires the ability to identify problems and research technical solutions. Good communications skills are essential for interacting with managers and other employees.

▶ A **computer programmer** (sometimes described as a programmer/analyst) designs, codes, and tests computer programs. In addition, programmers modify existing programs to meet new requirements or eliminate bugs. Computer programming requires concentration and a good memory for the countless details that pertain to a programming project. Programming projects range from entertainment and games to business and productivity applications. Programmers get satisfaction from devising efficient ways to make a computer perform specific jobs, tasks, and routines.

▶ A **security specialist** analyzes a computer system's vulnerability to threats from viruses, worms, unauthorized access, and physical damage. Security specialists install and configure firewalls and antivirus software. They also work with management and employees to develop policies and procedures to protect computer equipment and data. Computer security is punctuated by crises when a virus hits or a security breach is discovered. A security specialist must have wide-ranging knowledge of computers and communications protocols that can be applied for a quick resolution to any crisis that occurs.

▶ A **database administrator** analyzes a company's data to determine the most effective way to collect and store it. Database administrators create databases, data entry forms, and reports. They also define backup procedures, provide access to authorized users, and supervise the day-to-day use of databases.

▶ A **network specialist/administrator** plans, installs, and maintains one or more local area networks. These specialists also provide network accounts and access rights to approved users. They troubleshoot connectivity problems and respond to requests from a network's users for new software. Network specialists/administrators might be responsible for maintaining the security of a network, plus they often pick up Web master duties to maintain an organization's Web site.

▶ A **computer operator** works with system software for network servers, mainframes, and supercomputers. Computer operators monitor computer performance, install software patches and upgrades, perform backups, and restore data as necessary.

▶ A **technical support specialist** troubleshoots hardware and software problems. Good interpersonal skills and patience are required for this job (Figure 9-29).

▶ A **Web site designer** creates, tests, posts, and modifies Web pages. A good sense of design and artistic talent are required for this job, along with an understanding of how people use graphical user interfaces. Familiarity with Web tools, such as HTML, XML, JavaScript, and ActiveX, is becoming more important for this job, as is a knowledge of computer programming and database management.

FIGURE 9-29

Some technical support specialists work in-house with company employees, whereas others provide remote phone support for customers.

Hill Creek Pictures/Getty Images

▶ Do computer professionals work outside of IT departments? In addition to jobs in IT departments, computer professionals also find work in companies that produce computer hardware and software. Some of these jobs are listed below.

▶ A **technical writer** creates documentation for large programming projects and writes the online or printed user manuals that accompany computers, peripheral devices, and software. Some technical writers work for computer magazines, writing columns about the latest hardware products, software, and automated business solutions. Good writing and communications skills are valuable for this job, as is an ability to quickly learn how to use new hardware products and software.

▶ A **computer salesperson**, or sales rep, sells computers. Sales reps might pay personal visits to potential corporate customers or staff the order desk of a mail-order computer company. Sales reps' starting salaries tend to be low but are usually supplemented by commissions. Effective sales reps have good interpersonal skills, an ability to remember technical specifications, and an understanding of business problems and solutions.

▶ A **quality assurance specialist** participates in alpha and beta test cycles of software, looking for bugs or other usability problems. This job title sometimes refers to assembly-line workers who examine and test chips, circuit boards, computers, and peripheral devices. An effective quality assurance (QA) specialist has a good eye for detail and a passion for perfection.

▶ A **computer engineer** designs and tests new hardware products, such as computer chips, circuit boards, computers, and peripheral devices.

▶ A **manufacturing technician** participates in the fabrication of computer chips, circuit boards, system units, or peripheral devices. Some of these jobs require basic screwdriver skills, whereas others require special training in microlithography.

These job descriptions are but a sample of those in IT departments and the IT industry. Additional job titles are listed in Figure 9-30.

▶ What's the outlook for computer careers? According to an Information Technology Association of America study, the U.S.-based IT workforce totaled about 10.4 million in 2000, but lost 500,000 jobs in 2001 as the dot-com bubble burst. A small but steady upswing from 2002 through 2006 brought the IT workforce close to its year 2000 peak, but the workforce again suffered cutbacks during the economic recession that began in 2008. In coming years, the highest demand may be for network, technical support, and security specialists.

As in the past, economic trends could cause significant changes in the job market. In preparing for an IT career, flexibility is the key. You should be willing to train and then retrain as new skills are needed to work with emerging technologies.

▶ What can I expect as a salary for an IT industry job? Web sites such as *www.bls.gov* provide salary data for various IT industry jobs. In addition to data from the Bureau of Labor Statistics, you can find comparative IT industry salary averages using a standard Web search engine.

FIGURE 9-30

The Information Technology Association of America (ITAA) categorizes IT jobs into eight clusters, shown in bold. Sample job titles are listed here and in the continuation of this figure on the next page.

Database Administration and Development
Database Administrator
Database Analyst
Database Developer
Database Manager
Database Security Expert
DSS (Decision Support Services)
Knowledge Architect

Digital Media
2-D/3-D Artist
Animator
Audio/Video Engineer
Designer
Media Specialist
Media/Instructional Designer
Multimedia Author
Multimedia Authoring Specialist
Multimedia Developer
Multimedia Specialist
Producer
Streaming Media Specialist
Virtual Reality Specialist

Enterprise Systems Analysis and Integration
Application Integrator
Business Continuity Analyst
Cross-enterprise Integrator
Data Systems Designer
Data Systems Manager
E-business Specialist
Information Systems Architect
Information Systems Planner
Systems Analyst
Systems Architect
Systems Integrator

Network Design and Administration
Communications Analyst
Network Administrator
Network Analyst
Network Architect
Network Engineer
Network Manager
Network Operations Analyst
Network Security Analyst
Network Specialist
Network Technician

As with almost every industry, the compensation rates for jobs in the IT industry vary. Jobs that require college degrees and certification tend to pay more than jobs that require a high school diploma and some on-the-job training. IT industry salaries also vary by geographic location. In the United States, the highest salaries tend to be offered in the Northeast and on the West Coast—two regions where the cost of living is relatively high.

▶ What are the advantages of working in the IT industry? Many technology companies offer employee-friendly working conditions that include child care, flexible hours, and the opportunity to work from home. As in any industry, the exact nature of a job depends on the company and the particular projects that are in the works. Some jobs and projects are more interesting than others.

▶ What about part-time or contract work? As with other industries, IT employs full-time, part-time, and contract workers. A **contract worker** is typically hired as a consultant. Contract workers are not official employees of a company. They might be paid by the job, rather than by the hour; they are not eligible for a company's health insurance benefits or retirement plan, and they must pay self-employment taxes.

IT businesses benefit from the ability to hire contract workers. The pool of IT contract workers offers a selection of people with specialized skills. Contract workers can be added to a company's staff when needed, instead of hiring full-time workers who might later be laid off if the company is forced to downsize.

▶ Can I work at an IT job from home? Workers in many industries are interested in **telecommuting**—using available technology to work from home or an off-site location. Telecommuters tend to be more productive and work longer hours because they have no commute time, and they are not interrupted by routine office chatter. As fuel prices climb, telecommuting looks even more attractive to workers who can save money by avoiding long commutes.

Telecommuting also has disadvantages. Some workers need supervision or they procrastinate. The home environment can be distracting, which reduces productivity. Security is also a concern—especially the security of data transmitted from home-based workers to corporate networks. Virtual private networks, encryption, and secure connections are essential for securing business data transmitted over the Internet.

The Internet and telecommunications technologies have made an impact on the availability of telecommuting opportunities for workers. It has become common for employees to collaborate through e-mail, fax, groupware, and videoconferencing. Although the majority of IT workers still commute to work, industry observers expect the number of telecommuting IT workers to increase. Programming and customer support are likely to be the first jobs with a significant number of telecommuting workers.

FIGURE 9-30 (CONTINUED)

Programming/Software Engineering
Applications Analyst
Applications Engineer
Business Analyst
Computer Engineer
OS Designer/Engineer
OS Programmer/Analyst
Program Manager
Programmer
Programmer/Analyst
Software Applications Specialist
Software Architect
Software Design Engineer
Software Engineer
Software QA Specialist
Software Tester

Technical Support
Call Center Support Rep
Customer Liaison
Customer Service Rep
Customer Support Professional
Help Desk Specialist
Help Desk Technician
PC Support Specialist
PC Systems Coordinator
Product Support Engineer
Sales Support Technician
Technical Account Manager
Technical Support Engineer
Technical Support
     Representative

Technical Writing
Desktop Publisher
Document Specialist
Documentation Specialist
Editor
Electronic Publications
     Specialist
Electronic Publisher
Instructional Designer
Online Publisher
Technical Communicator
Technical Editor
Technical Publications Manager
Technical Writer

Web Development and Administration
Web Administrator
Web Architect
Web Designer
Web Master
Web Page Developer
Web Site Developer
Web Specialist

9

EDUCATION AND CERTIFICATION

▶ Do I need a computer science degree to work in the computer industry?
Computer science is only one of many computer-related degrees that colleges and universities offer. According to the Association for Computing Machinery (ACM), there are five major computing disciplines, as described in Figure 9-31.

FIGURE 9-31

Computing Disciplines

Degree	Curriculum	Careers
Computer engineering focuses on the design of computer hardware and peripheral devices, often at the chip level.	Basic studies in calculus, chemistry, engineering, physics, computer organization, logic design, computer architecture, microprocessor design, and signal processing Students learn how to design new computer circuits, microchips, and other electronic components, plus they learn how to design new computer instruction sets and combine electronic or optical components to provide powerful, cost-effective computing.	Working at a chip manufacturer, such as Intel, Motorola, IBM, AMD, or Texas Instruments
Computer science focuses on computer architecture and how to program computers to make them work effectively and efficiently.	Courses in programming, algorithms, software development, computer architecture, data representation, logic design, calculus, discrete math, and physics Students investigate the fundamental theories of how computers solve problems, and they learn how to write application programs, system software, computer languages, and device drivers.	Computer programmers, with good possibilities for advancement to software engineers, object-oriented/GUI developers, and project managers in technical applications development Also, theorists, inventors, and researchers in fields as diverse as artificial intelligence, virtual reality, and computer games
Information systems degree programs, typically offered by a university's college of business, focus on applying computers to business problems.	Coursework in business, accounting, computer programming, communications, systems analysis, and human psychology Recommended for students who want to become computer professionals but lack strong math aptitude	Programming or technical support jobs, with good possibilities for advancement to systems analyst, project manager, database administrator, network manager, or other management positions
Information technology degree programs focus on computer equipment and software used by businesses.	Hands-on coursework with hardware, networks, Web pages, multimedia, e-mail systems, and security	Network specialists and administrators, systems analysts, and help desk technicians
Software engineering takes a disciplined approach to developing software that is reliable, efficient, affordable, user-friendly, and scalable.	Statistics, software design, programming, systems analysis, and courses from information systems and computer science curricula	Programmers, analysts, or managers on large-scale, safety-critical applications

9

▶ What are the basic qualifications for IT industry jobs?
Qualifications for most IT industry jobs include some type of higher education, certification, or computer experience. A bachelor's degree in a computer-related discipline is the most prevalent requirement, but some employers accept a two-year associate's degree.

▶ What kinds of computer jobs require only an associate's degree? Colleges, community colleges, and technical schools offer several computer-related associate's degrees, ranging from computer programming to graphic design, networking, and telecommunications.

The curriculum for these programs varies from one degree program to another, but all tend to require intensive course work. Graduates of two-year programs commonly find employment as entry-level technicians, programmers, and support personnel. Advancement opportunities might be limited, however, without additional education or certification.

▶ Do I need a graduate degree? Master's degrees in software engineering have been difficult to find, except at large research universities with well-established computer science programs. A master's degree in computer science is available at most colleges and universities that offer graduate degrees. Another option at the graduate level is to pursue a master's degree in information systems or a master's degree in business administration (MBA). Any of these graduate degrees would help you get a management position in the computer industry.

Doctoral degrees are available in software engineering, applications software engineering, systems software development, and management information systems. A doctoral degree in any of these areas would qualify you for advanced technical research or for a position as a college professor.

▶ Where can I find information on computer-related degree programs? Peterson's is a comprehensive resource for educational services. Its Web site at *www.petersons.com* has become a primary resource for locating educational programs. Peterson's maintains a searchable database of two-year, four-year, and graduate programs that prepare you for a variety of IT jobs. You can find additional information about these programs at the Web sites of various technical schools, community colleges, and universities.

▶ How important is certification? Certification alone is rarely sufficient to qualify you for a job in the IT industry. Paired with a college degree or extensive experience, however, several studies suggest that certification can improve your chances for employment, increase your credibility in the workplace, and lead to higher salaries.

Many employers view certification with some degree of skepticism, so the value of a certificate depends on where, when, and how it is obtained. Critics of certification exams, for example, maintain that a multiple-choice test cannot accurately measure a person's ability to deal with real-world equipment and software. Bottom line: Certification is only part of your total package of qualifications.

A certification exam is an objective test that verifies your level of knowledge about a particular technology or subject. Approximately 300 computer-related certification exams are offered in areas of specialty that range from desktop publishing to network installation. Most of these exams use multiple-choice format, last several hours, and require substantial testing fees (Figure 9-32).

FIGURE 9-32

Certification exams are offered in a variety of formats. Some are offered online, but most take place in authorized testing venues, such as schools.

DAJ/Getty Images

You can prepare for a certification exam with independent study materials (Figure 9-33), online tutorials, or an exam preparation class. Certification exams can be divided into several categories:

FIGURE 9-33

Your local bookstore and the Internet provide sources for independent study materials that can help you prepare for an IT certification exam.

▶ **General computer knowledge.** IC3 certification, offered by Certiport, covers basic computing knowledge and skills. General certification is also offered by the College Board's Computer Skills Placement (CSP).

The Institute for Certification of Computing Professionals (ICCP) offers generalized certification exams, such as the Information Systems CORE, leading to Certified Computing Professional certification. According to the ICCP Web site, "Professionals certified with ICCP serve as consultants, working with local, state, and federal government; in accounting and banking; in high schools, technical schools, and universities; in the manufacturing industry; in insurance and numerous other fields."

▶ **Software applications.** Many certification exams allow you to demonstrate your prowess with a specific software application. The Microsoft Office Specialist certification is perhaps the most popular, but of limited value to most computer professionals who are expected to be able to quickly learn such applications on their own. Certification in productivity applications is most valuable for entry-level secretarial and clerical positions as well as help desk personnel.

Autodesk offers the AutoCAD Certified User exam on the use of its 3-D design software. Certification is also available for popular Adobe software applications, such as Illustrator, InDesign, Photoshop, Premiere, Dreamweaver, Flash, and ColdFusion.

▶ **Database administration.** Databases require a high level of expertise, not only in the use of database software, but in the conception and design of database structures. Many computer professionals have sought certification in database systems, such as Oracle, Access, Sybase, and DB2. The most popular database certification exams include the Microsoft Certified Database Administrator and Oracle Certified Professional.

▶ **Networking.** Among computer professionals, network certification might be the most useful. Microsoft offers a corresponding MCSE certification (Microsoft Certified Systems Engineer). Network hardware certification includes the Cisco Certified Network Professional (CCNP), offered by network equipment supplier Cisco Systems. Wireless network certification, such as CCNP Wireless certification, is available too.

▶ **Computer hardware.** One of the most popular computer hardware certifications is the A+ Certification, sponsored by the Computing Technology Industry Association (CompTIA). This certification process is designed to measure the competency of entry-level computer service technicians for installing, configuring, upgrading, troubleshooting, and repairing personal computer systems. A+ Certification provides good credentials for employment in a computer store or computer repair shop.

▶ **Computer security.** With the proliferation of computer viruses and worms, computer security has become a hot niche for IT workers. CompTIA offers the Security+ Certification exam, which covers topics such as cryptography, access control, authentication, external attacks, and operational security. The International Information Systems Security Certification Consortium offers a Certified Information Systems Security Professional (CISSP) exam, which is one of the highest-paying IT certifications available.

JOB HUNTING BASICS

▶ **How do I find a job in the IT industry?** In many ways, finding a job in the IT industry is just like finding a job in any other industry. Effective job seekers begin by taking stock of their qualifications, identifying job titles relevant to their skills, identifying potential employers, and considering the geographic area in which they want to work. They then create a carefully worded resume, look for job openings, contact potential employers, and work with employment agencies and recruiting firms. Figure 9-34 summarizes the steps in a job hunt.

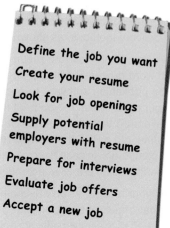

FIGURE 9-34

Job Hunting Steps

Define the job you want
Create your resume
Look for job openings
Supply potential employers with resume
Prepare for interviews
Evaluate job offers
Accept a new job

Conventional wisdom about job hunting applies to a broad spectrum of industries, such as financial, automotive, hospitality, and even entertainment. But one job hunting strategy is not necessarily effective for every job in every industry. Take a closer look at the job hunting process, and examine how hunting for an IT job might differ from conducting a job search in other industries.

▶ **How can I use the Internet to find a job?** The Internet has become an important tool for job hunters. In 1994, about 10,000 resumes were posted on the Web. Today, the Web plays host to millions of resumes.

The Internet can figure into your job hunt in several ways, including researching potential jobs and employers, posting your resume, locating job leads, and corresponding with potential employers.

Career counselors warn of placing too much emphasis on the online aspects of your job search, however. "Don't put all your eggs in the online basket" summarizes this advice.

Some job hunting experts advise IT job seekers to spend no more than 50% of their total job hunting efforts online; the other 50% should be spent making contacts with recruiters, placement agencies, career counselors, and mentors. Rather than accept that advice outright, consider it with regard to your employment needs, geographical location, and current employment situation.

▶ **Where do I start?** You should begin by defining the jobs for which you are qualified. In the IT industry, job titles are not standardized. For example, the job title for a person who provides employee or customer support over the phone might be Help Desk Operator, Customer Support Technician, Support Specialist, Personal Computer Specialist, Technology Support Specialist, or Inbound Telephone Service Consultant.

Nonstandardized job titles can pose a problem for job hunters, especially those who use search engines to locate job openings. Failure to enter one of the many titles for a job might mean that a job hunter misses a good opportunity.

Although many job search sites maintain their own lists of equivalent job titles, job hunters in the IT industry should take some time to compile their own lists of equivalent job titles and relevant search terms. You can compile such a list by entering *job titles and computer industry* into a general search engine such as Google. Connect to the sites the search produces, and take note of any job titles that seem applicable.

RESUMES AND WEB PORTFOLIOS

▶ Do I need an online resume? As a computer professional, you are expected to use technology effectively for everyday tasks. You can demonstrate this ability to prospective employers by the way you treat your resume. You can prepare your resume in formats suitable for different computer platforms and delivery methods, as shown in Figure 9-35.

FIGURE 9-35

Job seekers can format their resumes for printed output, e-mail delivery, or Web posting.

▶ **Print.** You should save one version of your resume as a beautifully formatted word processing file. You might consider using desktop publishing software to put the finishing touches on your resume before you print it on high-quality paper. Make sure that you can output the file that holds your resume into a PDF that can be read on Mac, PC, and Linux computers, in case a prospective employer asks you to send it as an e-mail attachment.

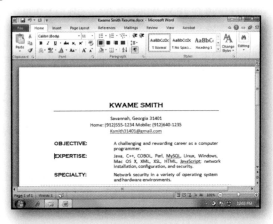

▶ **E-mail.** Before sending your resume as an attachment, try to discover the format that is easiest for your prospective employer to use. PDF is a universally accepted format. Microsoft's Rich Text Format (RTF) can be read by a variety of word processing applications. Microsoft's DOC and DOCX formats are also widely used.

Some career counselors advise against the use of e-mail attachments, suggesting that many employers never open attachments for fear of e-mail viruses. Instead of attaching your resume, you can simply paste it into the body of an e-mail message. To make sure it is formatted for maximum readability, you might want to create an ASCII version of your resume, without fancy fonts, bullets, or symbols. This ASCII version might also be useful for online job posting sites that store your resume information in a searchable database.

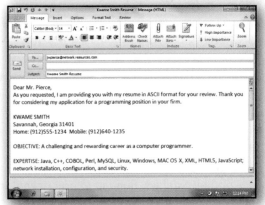

▶ **HTML and XML.** You might also want to create HTML and XML versions of your resume. You can paste the HTML version into an HTML-formatted e-mail message or post it on a Web site provided by your school or ISP. You might also consider developing an XML resume based on standard XML stylesheets. For more information, refer to *http://xmlresume.sourceforge.net*.

▶ Should an IT industry resume contain any special elements? Regardless of the industry in which you seek employment, an effective resume is clear, correct, and easy to read. When developing your resume, you can ask friends, coworkers, and career counselors to review your drafts and provide suggestions for improvement. Figure 9-36 on the next page shows a short checklist of resume writing guidelines.

In the past, tips on how to create the perfect resume applied to a conventional process in which a recruiter sifted through a pile of resumes that arrived by surface mail. Job seekers spent hours agonizing over the weight, texture, and color of the paper on which they printed their resumes.

Conventional tips about paper color, fonts, and wording remain valid for hard-copy resumes. Today, however, resumes are often stored in online databases, which are initially scanned not by human eyes, but by a computer.

How can my resume get maximum exposure in an online job database? For resumes that become part of a computer-searchable database, experts recommend that you focus on nouns, not verbs. At one time, the trend was to pepper your resume with action phrases and power verbs, such as "implemented successful solutions" and "created innovative algorithms."

When employers use a job site's search engine to locate potential employees, however, they routinely search for particular skills by entering nouns associated with programming language names, software, computer equipment, analysis methodologies, and business sectors. They might also enter buzzwords and acronyms, such as *HTML5*, *B2B*, *client/server*, *API*, and *AJAX*, which relate to specific IT tools and methods. Job seekers should try to envision the search terms that employers might enter, and then include applicable terms in their resumes.

In addition to computer-related terms, employers sometimes search for words that indicate a job applicant's personality, communication skills, and work ethic. When appropriate, adjectives such as *enthusiastic*, *team player*, *industrious*, *honest*, *capable*, and *experienced* can be effective in helping an online recruiter pull your resume from those submitted by thousands of other applicants.

What other factors are important for online resumes? Today's trend to search resumes online has implications for all job seekers, not just those in the IT industry. For example, you should avoid formatting your resume into side-by-side columns because the columns could get scrambled when transferred to an online job database.

Experience is important, but the old style of dating your tenure at a job supplies little information for online searches. Information such as "Intern IBM from 2009-2011" does not produce a hit for a recruiter searching online for "IBM >2 years." By modifying your online resume to "Intern IBM, 2 years: 2009-2011," you provide better information for electronic searches.

What is a Web portfolio? A **Web portfolio** is a hypertext version of your resume, which might contain links to relevant Web sites, such as past employers, your alma mater, and samples of your work. For example, a programmer might include a link to one of her particularly well-documented and elegant programs, or a Web designer might provide links to sites that he designed.

Should I jazz up my Web portfolio with multimedia? Current technology gives you the ability to personalize your Web portfolio with photos, your favorite music, or even video portraits that demonstrate your speaking and communications abilities.

Forget the music—it is more likely to irritate prospective employers than impress them. Photos and videos that indicate an applicant's age, gender,

FIGURE 9-36

Resume Writing Guidelines

9

Tips for an Effective Resume

Be clear and concise

- Eliminate unnecessary words, phrases, and sentences.
- Be economical with words when describing tasks, duties, titles, and accomplishments.
- Be brief and to the point without selling yourself short.

Place the most important point first

- List your qualifications by importance and relevance to the job you seek.
- Summarize skills at the top of the resume.
- Use a bold font to emphasize skills and accomplishments that are required for the position you seek.
- Include pertinent information about training, certification, and professional affiliations, but avoid personal information, such as church affiliation and hobbies, that is not directly related to the job.

Use language effectively

- Target terms and wording to prospective employers.
- Use industry jargon wherever appropriate.
- Use action verbs to maintain the reader's interest.
- Use past and present tenses consistently.
- Double-check grammar and spelling.
- When posting information in a database, use nouns that describe your skills.

ethnicity, or physical characteristics also have potential drawbacks. Decisions based on such characteristics could be viewed as discriminatory. You might want to keep such multimedia presentations on hand, but supply them only when requested.

▶ Where do I post my Web portfolio? You can post your Web portfolio on a professional network, such as LinkedIn. Just remember that your personal Web site is an open book to prospective employers. If you don't want them to know the details about your spring break, you should remove such extraneous material from your Web site and social networking site. Even if you don't mention your Web site or Facebook page to prospective employers, they can find them easily simply by entering your name in a search engine, such as Yahoo! or Google.

JOB LISTINGS

▶ Where can I find a list of job openings? To find job openings, you can begin with the usual sources of job listings: the newspaper's Help Wanted section, your school's career placement office, and your local state employment agency. You'll then move quickly to online resources, such as online newspapers, company Web sites, and employment services.

On the Web you can access the Help Wanted sections from major metropolitan newspapers. Many companies maintain Web sites that include links to information about their job openings. If you have a short list of companies that you'd like to work for, check out their Web sites.

▶ How do online employment services work? An **online employment service** maintains a database that contains thousands of job openings posted by employers. The largest employment services span just about every industry. Others are devoted to specific industries. Several online employment services specialize in the IT industry.

Employment services usually offer free access to job seekers, although you might be required to register before searching. You can search most online job databases by job title, geographic location, or company (Figure 9-37).

FIGURE 9-37

If your search turns up a job that looks promising, most employment services provide a way to apply online by sending your resume information to the employer through the employment service's Web site. To use the apply online feature, you're typically required to register with the employment service. ▶ Take a tour of ComputerJobs.com by clicking this figure in your interactive eBook.

> **Do I have to manually search every online employment service?** The Internet offers thousands of employment services, each with unique job announcements. Searching all these sites manually would be a full-time job in itself! Search agents and metasearch tools allow you to automate the search process across many sites.

A **job search agent** is an automated program that searches one or more databases and notifies you when it finds any leads that match your specified criteria. To use a job search agent, you configure it with keywords that describe the type of job you want, your geographical limitations, and salary requirements. You then launch the agent and it searches for matching job announcements. When a match is found, the search agent generates an e-mail message with the information you need to view the job posting. Most employment services provide access to free job search agents.

Some search agents work within one specific online employment service. Other search agents visit multiple employment service sites. The key advantage of a job search agent, such as the one shown in Figure 9-38, is that you don't have to be online while it works.

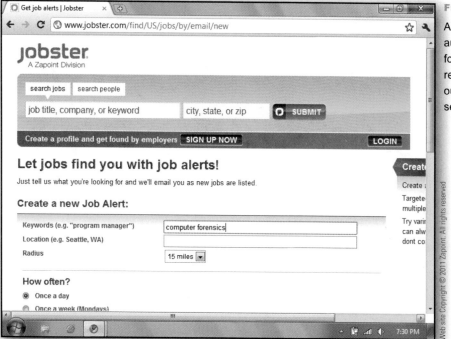

FIGURE 9-38

An online search agent autonomously searches for jobs that match your requirements. ▶ Find out how to set up a search agent to find jobs.

A **metasearch tool** is a software program that performs broad-based Web searches, such as searching more than one job database at a time. In some respects, a metasearch tool is similar to a multi-site job search agent, except that when you use a metasearch tool, you might have to remain online. Instead of notifying you by e-mail, a metasearch tool supplies a list of links to applicable job postings, similar to the links provided by a standard search engine, such as Google.

> **How well do employment services protect my privacy?** Job seekers who post their resumes at online employment services should be aware of potential threats to their privacy. Without privacy safeguards, the information in your online resume could be used to compile a profile of you, which could be misused by advertisers or individuals interested in stealing identities.

Some employment services might distribute your resume or personal information without your authorization. Sometimes employment services sell resumes to employers and pass personal information to advertisers. Before posting your resume, always check the employment service's privacy policy.

If an employment service requires you to register, follow common sense to protect your privacy. Do not, for example, provide your Social Security number. Although it is required for jobs in the United States, your Social Security number should be given only to your employer after you receive a job offer.

FIGURE 9-39

Stay alert! Protect your privacy when posting your resume and contacting prospective employers.

If your employment service allows you to set an expiration date for your resume, do so just in case you forget to manually remove it when your job search is complete.

To protect your privacy, you might also consider removing most of the contact information, such as your address and phone number, from your online resume (Figure 9-39).

You should provide an e-mail address, but not the address of the business e-mail account supplied by your employer. Also, make sure your e-mail address is not linked to a personal profile, as it is on America Online (AOL) and some other Internet provider sites.

You can open a Web-based e-mail account specifically devoted to job hunting. Consider your e-mail user ID carefully. Employers might respond better to an e-mail address such as excellentprogrammer@hotmail.com than an address such as bigbertha@hotmail.com.

Many job seekers are hesitant to post their resumes for fear that their current employers will learn they are preparing to jump ship. Some employment services allow you to block access to your resume by specific employers. You can learn about the features of each employment service by connecting to its links for Help, Privacy, and Terms of Use.

QuickCheck   SECTION C

1. The term *computer professional* was defined in an amendment to the Fair Labor Standards Act of 1999. True or false? [   ]

2. A(n) [   ] is usually paid by the job, rather than by the hour, and is not officially an employee of the company for which he or she works.

3. A student who wants to work with computers but does not have strong math aptitude might find a good fit by pursuing a(n) [   ] systems degree.

4. IC3, CCNP, and CISSP are examples of computer [   ] exams.

5. An XML or [   ] version of your resume can be easily posted online or added to the text of e-mail messages.

 CHECK ANSWERS

Professional Ethics

WHEN DISCUSSING ETHICAL ISSUES, we often do so from the perspective of the victim. It is quite possible, however, that at some time in your career, you could become the perpetrator—the copyright violator, the snoop, or the thief—perhaps without intending to cause harm. Section D presents information about professional ethics as they relate to computing and digital technologies.

ETHICS BASICS

▶ **What are professional ethics?** The term **professional ethics** refers to on-the-job choices and actions that reflect a person's values. Professional ethics define standards of conduct that specify how workers should behave, particularly in situations where doing the right thing might not have short-term rewards, or when doing something of questionable legality seems to offer attractive benefits. Situations, like the one in Figure 9-40, in which you ask yourself "What's the right thing to do?" often require you to make ethical decisions.

Professional ethics are derived from principles of right and wrong. In most modern societies, the foundation for ethical decisions and actions is based on values such as impartiality, fairness, objectivity, honesty, regard for privacy, commitment to quality, and respect for others.

▶ **How are ethics related to laws?** Laws are legislated documentation of permissible behavior based on a community's ethics. Although most laws are designed to promote ethical behavior, laws and ethics are not necessarily the same. Some behaviors are legal, but not necessarily ethical. Some laws are not ethical or their ethics are controversial. An act isn't ethical simply because it is permissible or you can get away with it. An ethical person often chooses to do more than the law requires and less than the law allows.

As computers and digital technologies play a more central role in every aspect of daily life, laws have been created to deal with computer uses and abuses. It is important to consider applicable laws as you make ethical decisions. Keep in mind, too, that laws relating to computers vary from country to country. Figure 9-41 on the next page provides a brief overview of the most significant computer laws and court decisions in the United States.

FIGURE 9-40

If your boss asks you to divulge information about your work on a competing project with a previous employer, you'll score some points with your new employer if you give over the information—but doing so might not be ethical.

523

FIGURE 9-41

Significant U.S. Computer Laws
and Court Decisions

United States Copyright Act (1976) extends copyright protection beyond print media to "original works of authorship fixed in any tangible medium of expression, now known or later developed, from which they can be perceived, reproduced, or otherwise communicated, either directly or with the aid of a machine or device."

Fair Use Doctrine, a part of the U.S. Copyright Act, generally allows copying if it is for educational or personal use, if only a portion of the original work is copied, and if it does not have a substantial effect on the market for the original work.

Sony Corp. v. Universal City Studios (1984) sets a precedent that companies are not liable for user infringements, such as using VCRs to make unauthorized copies of videotapes, so long as the technology has valid, non-infringing uses, such as copying personal home videos. In recent cases, the defense for peer-to-peer file sharing networks was based on this decision.

Computer Fraud and Abuse Act (1986 amended in 1994, 1996, 2001, and USA PATRIOT Act) makes it a criminal offense to knowingly access a computer without authorization; transmit a program, information, code, or command that causes damage; or distribute passwords that would enable unauthorized access.

Electronic Communications Privacy Act (1986) extends telephone wiretap laws by restricting government agents and unauthorized third parties from tapping into data transmissions without a search warrant. The law does not apply to data, such as e-mail, transmitted on employer-owned equipment.

Health Insurance Portability and Accountability Act (1996) requires health care providers to take reasonable procedural and technical safeguards to insure the confidentiality of individually identifiable health information.

Communications Decency Act (1996) protects ISPs from liability for defamatory statements made by customers. Prohibits material deemed offensive by local community standards from being transmitted to minors. The latter section was overturned in 2002.

Digital Millennium Copyright Act (1998) makes it illegal to circumvent copy-protection technologies, such as those used to prevent unauthorized copying of software CDs, music CDs, and movie DVDs. In addition, it is illegal to distribute any type of cracking software technology that would be used by others to circumvent copy protection. Protects ISPs against copyright infringement by subscribers if the ISP takes prompt action to block the infringement as soon as it discovers illegal activity.

Children's Online Privacy Protection Act (1998) regulates the types of data that can be collected and posted online with regard to children under the age of 13.

Gramm-Leach-Bliley Act (1999) requires financial institutions to protect the confidentiality and security of customers' personal information.

Children's Internet Protection Act (2000) requires schools and libraries that receive federal funds to implement filtering software that protects adults and minors from obscenity and pornography.

USA PATRIOT Act (2001) enhances the authority of law enforcement agents to preempt potential terrorist acts by various means, such as monitoring electronic communications without first obtaining a search warrant in situations where there is imminent danger. Offers safe harbor to ISPs that voluntarily disclose potentially threatening activities of users. Increases maximum penalties for hackers.

Homeland Security Act (2002) establishes a Department of Homeland Security with an agency to monitor threats to the communications infrastructure, including the Internet, and exempts from the Privacy Act any information about infrastructure vulnerabilities to terrorism submitted by individuals or non-federal agencies.

Sarbanes-Oxley Act (2002) establishes financial reporting regulations to prevent corporate fraud. Requires full disclosure in accounting systems and protects corporate whistleblowers.

CAN-SPAM Act (2003) establishes national standards for sending commercial e-mail by requiring senders to use a valid subject line, include the sender's legitimate physical address, and provide an opt-out mechanism.

Green v. America Online (2003) interprets sections of the Communications Decency Act to mean that ISPs are not responsible for malicious software transmitted over their services by hackers.

MGM v. Grokster (2005) refines the precedent set in the 1984 Sony Corp. v. Universal City Studios case. Companies that actively encourage infringement, as seemed to be true of peer-to-peer file sharing networks such as Grokster, can be held accountable for user infringement.

9

IT ETHICS

▶ Why are professional ethics important for IT workers?

Most computer professionals are hard-working and honest. They take pride in their work and strive to offer excellent products and services that benefit consumers. They want to do what's right. Sometimes, however, computer professionals have to cope with ethical dilemmas in which the right course of action is not entirely clear, or in which the right course of action is clear, but the consequences—such as getting fired—are not easy to face.

Ethical dilemmas in the workplace are more common than you might imagine. It is likely that you'll find yourself in an ethical quandary about some aspect of your job even before you've completed your first year. Some situations that call for an ethical decision offer you the luxury of time—you don't have to respond or act right away—so you can think about what you'll do. Other situations require an immediate response. If an immediate response is required, you'll be less likely to take action that you'll later regret if you have considered potentially compromising situations ahead of time and have prepared some general guidelines you can use if necessary.

▶ What kinds of situations in an IT career might require ethical decisions?

Situations that require computer professionals to make ethical decisions often involve software copyrights, privacy, conflict of interest, use of work computers, software quality, hacking, and social responsibility. Sometimes, computer professionals are pressured to participate in activities that border on being illegal and are clearly unethical. These marginal activities are sometimes justified with statements such as "Everyone does it." or "No one will know." Employees might be assured, "You won't be responsible." or "It's for the good of the company." Such justifications are not, however, always true or appropriate.

Outside of corporate IT departments, individual entrepreneurs sometimes get caught up in unethical activities because they make bad judgments or have not done their homework regarding applicable laws and regulations.

▶ How would software copyrights become an ethical issue?

Most computer professionals are familiar with the general principles of copyright law and the provisions of the Digital Millennium Copyright Act. They understand it is illegal to make unauthorized copies of software and other copyrighted media, such as commercial music and movies. Programmers, Web designers, and other creative professionals tend to respect intellectual property and try to adhere to copyright laws and license agreements. It is not unusual, however, to find yourself in a software copyright dilemma like the one described in Figure 9-42.

Business managers are not always familiar with current copyright restrictions or choose to ignore them. Computer professionals should stay up to date on current copyright law that applies to software and other digital media. Asking for a copy of the software license agreement is considered standard practice and can help resolve questions about the legality of copying software for use in multiple-user installations.

FIGURE 9-42

Copyrights can trigger ethical dilemmas.

Jiang Jin/SuperStock

On your first day of work, your employer hands you CDs containing the latest upgrade for Microsoft Office and asks you to install it on every computer in the organization. When you ask if the company owns a site license, your boss responds, "No, do you have a problem with that?" What would you reply? Would you risk your job by insisting that the company order enough copies for all the computers before you install it? Or would you go ahead and install the software, assuming that your boss would take responsibility for this violation of the software license agreement?

▶ What kinds of ethical issues revolve around privacy?

You know it is ethical to respect the privacy of others, but business practices can clash with privacy rights. Network technicians sometimes see the content of e-mail messages or files in the course of system maintenance or troubleshooting.

Most professionals simply try to forget what they see. However, computer professionals sometimes come across a file or an e-mail message that's troubling. It might be a message from an employee who is corresponding with a competing company about a job offer. More seriously, a message might divulge proprietary information to the competitor, harass another employee, or outline other illegal activities. If your employer has no guidelines for reporting suspicious activities, you'll have to make your own decision about what kinds of information are serious threats.

Computers are increasingly used to monitor employee activities. RFID chips embedded in ID badges can be used to track employee locations in an office or manufacturing facility. Keystroke monitors, random samples of active programs, Web browsing history, network logs, and e-mail volume offer additional ways to monitor employee activities. Some surveillance is done with employee knowledge and consent, such as when it is clearly explained in an employment contract or company policy. Other surveillance is surreptitious.

Either way, surveillance is set up by someone, often a programmer or network administrator. How would you respond if you were asked to set up a surveillance system like the one in Figure 9-43?

Employees—particularly computer professionals—should be familiar with laws and company policy applicable to privacy. Privacy laws differ from one country to the next, and most companies have unique privacy policies. Rather than assume you know the rules, make an effort to check applicable documents before you take action.

▶ How might confidentiality lead to ethical dilemmas?
Confidentiality is the obligation not to disclose willingly any information that should be kept private. Confidentiality rights apply to individuals and organizations. With respect to individuals, confidentiality means not disclosing names and associated data from databases and other information repositories.

Laws in most countries restrict the disclosure of an individual's medical or financial information. Marketers, however, currently take advantage of gray areas in these laws to use names, addresses, and phone numbers collected with consent on forms, applications, and Web sites. The ethics of such practices is doubtful.

With respect to organizations, confidentiality means protecting **proprietary information** about company finances, procedures, products, and research that competitors would find valuable. Computer professionals can find themselves in compromising situations where they are asked to disclose confidential information gathered while employed in previous jobs.

FIGURE 9-43

Privacy rights sometimes clash with safety issues or business goals.

Comstock Images/Alamy

Imagine that you're a programmer for a local public school system. One day, the superintendent of schools calls you into her office and asks if you can write software that supplies the administration with a log of Web sites visited by students and teachers. From your understanding of the school's network and Web access, you realize that it would be easy to write such monitoring software. You also realize, however, that the superintendent could use the software to track individual teachers and students as they visit Web sites. You ask the superintendent if faculty and students would be aware of the monitoring software, and she replies, "What they don't know won't hurt them." Should you write the program? Should you write the program, but start a rumor that monitoring software is being used to track faculty and student Web access? Should you pretend that it would be technically impossible to write such software? Should you tell the superintendent that federal law does not permit interception of electronic communications without consent?

9

Job mobility is one of the perks of a hot career field. The skills you pick up on one job can increase your qualifications for other jobs. For example, you might learn about multimedia production while working for an educational software company, and those skills might provide you with qualifications to switch to a higher-paying and more challenging job working for an online game company.

Using your skills as a springboard to a new job is perfectly acceptable, but disclosing confidential information is not ethical in most cases, including the one in Figure 9-44.

Many employment contracts contain a non-compete clause designed to prevent employees from divulging proprietary information to competitors or opening competing businesses. Non-compete clauses can extend beyond the period of employment and can remain in effect for a specified time after you leave a job. Most non-compete clauses, however, fail to delineate exactly what information cannot be divulged, and so ex-employees are forced to make ethical decisions about competitive information.

To avoid compromising situations, you can check the business plans of prospective employers so that you won't be working on projects that compete directly with those at your previous place of employment. You can also have a frank discussion with your new boss to outline the boundaries of the knowledge you are able to share from your old job.

▶ Can I get into trouble using my work computer for personal activities? When surveyed, a majority of computer professionals admit that they see no problem using their work computers for personal activities as long as it has no adverse effect on the employer.

It seems innocent enough to send and receive personal e-mail over your account at work or place bids on an online auction, especially if you do so during your lunch hour. Maybe it also seems okay to use your corporate e-mail server to send bulk mail to raise money for a private, nonprofit relief organization. Your employer might not agree, however.

There is a temptation to use computers, copiers, and network connections at work for personal activities; the equipment is convenient and usually cutting edge. Most companies have explicit policies about what is and what is not acceptable use. Some policies are strict, but designed to prevent conflicts like the one in Figure 9-45.

It is never a good practice to use facilities at work for personal activities, unless you have a specific agreement with your employer and your activities do not breach your employment contract. Some employment

FIGURE 9-44

Disclosures about your former employer might violate the confidentiality clause of your previous employment contract.

Suppose you take a new job and then discover that your new employer—an online game company—wants to produce online educational games that will directly compete with your previous employer's products. Your new boss wants you to lead the team that creates its first educational product, which sounds suspiciously like a rip-off of your old employer's best selling software. What should you do?

FIGURE 9-45

Personal use of your employer's equipment and computer facilities could lead to a conflict of interest.

You might believe it is perfectly fine to spend your lunch hour writing a Linux media player—not because your company can use it, but because one of your friends wants to listen to iTunes music on a Linux computer. You finish the program and realize there's a market for it. You begin selling it as shareware. The response is overwhelming. You quit your job and go into business marketing your product. Unfortunately, your old employer claims to own your software because you used company computers to develop it. How would you respond?

contracts have restrictions pertaining to intellectual property. In the most restrictive contracts, anything employees develop at work or at home using on-the-job equipment or knowledge during their tenure of employment belongs to the company.

If your contract does not limit outside development, you might still have to make an ethical decision about what rightfully belongs to your company and what you created outside of your company's sphere of influence.

▶ Why would I get involved in hacking?

Computer professionals have to keep up with the latest threats from viruses and intrusion attempts, but "knowing your enemy" can be a two-edged sword. Most computing students learning about virus and intrusion countermeasures become more than a little curious about these technologies. "Is it really so easy to design and launch viruses?" they wonder. "Are passwords easy to crack? Do I have the skill to do it?" Pursuing these questions can get students and computer professionals into sticky ethical situations like the one in Figure 9-46.

Many computer scientists have toyed with the idea of creating virus-killing programs that autonomously prowl the Internet to eradicate viruses before they cause widespread damage. Is anything wrong with that? The answer—or part of it—relates to problems with antispyware technologies. Antispyware watches network packets heading into a computer, and filters out those suspected to be parts of Trojan horses or bots.

Unfortunately, not everything caught in the antispyware net is malware. Some legitimate programs—at least their authors claim they are legitimate—are also filtered out. When antispyware applications reside on a computer's hard disk, it is a relatively easy task to update the antispyware definitions to exclude erroneously filtered but legitimate programs. An autonomous virus killer set loose on the Internet would not be so easy to modify, however, unless it contains some kind of recall mechanism or expiration date.

As of yet no one has wanted to take the responsibility for an autonomous virus killer and its potential repercussions. The legality of "good" viruses is questionable, so the decision on whether to create and distribute such programs becomes an ethical one.

▶ Am I responsible for software quality?

Most computer professionals believe that software should be thoroughly tested to produce the most reliable and accurate product possible, but what if you encounter a situation like the one in Figure 9-47?

Software development is an incredibly complex undertaking. Bugs are virtually impossible to completely eradicate, so most companies have policies that guide

FIGURE 9-46

Even an academic interest in hacking can raise sticky ethical issues.

In the course of your computing career, you might be tempted to try some passwords at a protected site. What if you get in? Should you poke around? Should you notify the system administrator that the network password is not secure? If you do so, you'll have to admit that you were doing a bit of illegal hacking, so your decision about a course of action might not be an easy one.

FIGURE 9-47

A decision to short-cut software testing should not be made lightly.

Suppose your project team has spent the better part of a year developing a new software product. The project is scheduled for release in four weeks; but to meet the deadline, you'll have to cut testing time in half. The team leader tells you to pare down the testing plan to the bare minimum. What should you do? Does the type of software you're developing make a difference in your response? What if you're working on an arcade-style game? What if it is a government project to help the IRS audit tax returns? What if it is an ambulance dispatch system or an air traffic control system?

9

developers on the number, severity, and type of bugs that are and are not acceptable when the software ships to customers. Although developers, managers, and marketers are supposed to be governed by these policies, software testing cycles are sometimes cut short when deadlines loom. Computer professionals working on such projects should think carefully about the repercussions of shortened test cycles and speak out when serious risks to users might result.

▶ **Am I responsible for how my software is used?** Technology may be neutral in and of itself, but technology can be put to use in both positive and negative ways.

Some IT projects are clearly not socially responsible. Society would be better off without spam and viruses. Filtering software and monitoring software can be misused. If you are assigned to a project of questionable social value like the one in Figure 9-48, you might have to make an ethical decision about whether to participate or look for another job.

Decisions pertaining to social responsibility are not always easy. Members of a project team might not be supplied with enough information to make value judgments about the projects to which they are assigned.

Laws and court decisions sometimes conflict with regard to whether programmers and members of software development teams are responsible for the way their software is used. In the landmark case Sony Corp. v. Universal City Studios, the U.S. Supreme Court set a precedent that Sony was not responsible when individuals used Sony Betamax recording technology to make and distribute illegal copies of movies. When applied to the IT industry, the Sony case seemed to absolve software developers from any illegal actions taken by users.

However, the Digital Millennium Copyright Act explicitly states that it is illegal to produce any product that allows individuals to circumvent copyright law or copy protection methods. Therefore, a programmer who produces software to crack Blu-ray copy protection can be held responsible when individuals use it to make illegal copies of Blu-ray movies.

Peer-to-peer file sharing networks such as eMule and BitTorrent can be held accountable for users who illegally share copyrighted music and movies—especially if such illegal sharing is encouraged and the networks are not also used for legal file sharing. As with laws governing non-technical aspects of society, like parking and speeding, ignorance of the law is not an excuse for breaking it.

FIGURE 9-48

Sorting out issues of social responsibility can be tough.

Javier Pierini/Getty Images

After graduating, your first big software development project was creating adaptive software to help people with physical handicaps use computers in productive careers. That product had clear social benefits. You've now been assigned to a project team working on automated garment production software. You have an uneasy feeling about its benefits. Will it displace hundreds of garment workers? What if those workers are domestic? Does it make a difference if those workers are offshore?

ETHICAL DECISION MAKING

▶ **How do I make ethical decisions?** Ethical decisions that you make on the job can have long-term consequences for your career and lifestyle, so it is important to approach these decisions seriously.

Take time to think about your situation before responding or taking action. As you examine the immediate situation, make sure you have a good handle on your long-term and short-term career goals. Gather the information needed for a decision, and make sure the facts are credible. Use Web resources and legal services, if necessary, to check applicable laws.

With the facts in hand, list your options and consider the advantages and disadvantages of each one. For help in defining and evaluating your options, you can use strategies, such as those listed below.

▶ **Talk to people whose judgment you respect.** Mentors and responsible friends might be willing to help you evaluate your options. Your workplace might provide access to an arbitrator, ombudsman, or counselor. Remember, however, that after you've gathered opinions and advice, you are ultimately responsible for the outcome of your decision.

▶ **Consider what the most ethical person you know would decide to do.** Think of a real-life person or fictional character who has strong values and impeccable ethical judgment. Use that person as your decision-making role model and ask yourself what he or she would do in your situation.

▶ **Think about what you would do if your actions were made public.** Ask yourself how you would feel if you made a particular decision and everyone found out about it. Would you be proud or uncomfortable? Decisions that look good only if no one knows are usually wrong. When you've made a good decision, you should feel comfortable talking about it as long as it doesn't violate confidentiality.

▶ **Look at the problem from the opposite perspective.** Put yourself in the place of other stakeholders, such as your boss, your clients, or consumers. How would you want to be treated if you were them?

▶ **Consult a code of professional ethics.** The guidelines contained in a code of professional ethics might offer a path of action suitable for your situation.

FIGURE 9-49

Many IT professional organizations offer codes of ethics.

▶ **What is a code of ethics?** A **code of ethics** is a set of guidelines designed to help professionals thread their way through a sometimes tangled web of ethical on-the-job decisions. Some codes of ethics are short and pithy, whereas others are long and detailed.

Even with a detailed code of ethics, however, don't expect a cookbook that tells you exactly what to do in a particular situation. Expect instead to be offered some general guidelines that you can apply to a specific situation. Most codes of ethics are created for a specific career field, such as medicine, accounting, or IT. Figure 9-49 contains a code of ethics from the Computer Ethics Institute.

"Ten Commandments" from the Computer Ethics Institute Professional Code

▶ Thou shalt not use a computer to harm other people.

▶ Thou shalt not interfere with other people's computer work.

▶ Thou shalt not snoop around in other people's files.

▶ Thou shalt not use a computer to steal.

▶ Thou shalt not use a computer to bear false witness.

▶ Thou shalt not use or copy software for which you have not paid.

▶ Thou shalt not use other people's computer resources without authorization.

▶ Thou shalt not appropriate other people's intellectual output.

▶ Thou shalt think about the social consequences of the program you write.

▶ Thou shalt use a computer in ways that show consideration and respect.

▶ **How effective are codes of ethics?** Professional codes of ethics are not without controversy. For example, the code published by the Computer Ethics Institute has drawn fire from critics, such as Dr. N. Ben Fairweather, the Centre for Computing and Social Responsibility's resident philosopher and research fellow, who states, "It is easy to find exceptions to the short dos and don'ts of the 'ten commandments'... indeed, every time such a short code of ethics falls into unwarranted disrepute, the whole idea of acting morally is brought into disrepute too." Dr. Fairweather seems to suggest that hard and fast rules might not apply to all situations.

9

For the situations in which these guidelines clearly apply, however, they are a valuable resource. In some cases, a code might include guidelines whose intent is not accurately reflected in their wording. For example, the Computer Ethics Institute guideline "Thou shalt not use or copy software for which you have not paid." obviously does not include public domain and open source software, or software for which your employer has paid.

Similarly, the idea that you should "think about the social consequences of the program you write" is valid, but what should you think about? This guideline does not offer helpful criteria for distinguishing between socially useful programs and those that might be damaging. When a code of ethics does not offer a complete solution, professionals might have to refer to other resources before making a decision and taking action.

Some codes of ethics attempt to offer more complete guidelines. Such a comprehensive approach can be useful, but it can sometimes become so complex that it seems to contradict itself. For example, the Association for Computing Machinery Code of Ethics and Professional Conduct contains a guideline that begins, "ACM members must obey existing local, state, province, national, and international laws unless there is a compelling ethical basis not to do so."

The code goes on, however, to offer a series of caveats that add complexity to the decision-making process: "...sometimes existing laws and rules may be immoral or inappropriate and, therefore, must be challenged. Violation of a law or regulation may be ethical when that law or rule has inadequate moral basis or when it conflicts with another law judged to be more important. If one decides to violate a law or rule because it is viewed as unethical, or for any other reason, one must fully accept responsibility for one's actions and for the consequences."

▶ **Where can I find codes of ethics for IT?** IT professionals have access to codes of ethics published by many professional organizations, such as the Computer Ethics Institute, the British Computer Society, the Australian Computer Society, and the Association for Computing Machinery (Figure 9-50).

FIGURE 9-50

The ACM posts a code of ethics at its Web site.

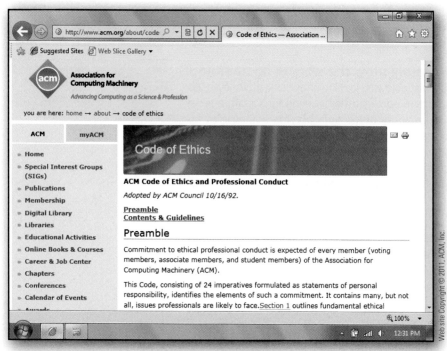

▶ **How should I apply codes of ethics to my situation?** A code of ethics can provide guidelines, but it might not offer ready answers to every dilemma that arises in the course of your career. When confronted with a difficult ethical decision, you should consider ethical guidelines, but also consider the policies of your workplace and relevant laws.

You might also seek legal advice, consult the human resources advocate at your job, or ask for advice from your union representative. Sometimes even talking to a trusted friend helps you recognize the correct course of action.

Ethical decisions can be difficult, and sometimes the results of your decision—good or bad—are not apparent right away. A decision with immediate negative repercussions might have beneficial long-term advantages that you cannot foresee. Ultimately, a decision about the right course of action is yours, and you must be willing to take responsibility for the consequences of your decision.

WHISTLEBLOWING

▶ **Should I blow the whistle on unethical practices?** A widely accepted definition of **whistleblowing** is the disclosure by an employee (or professional) of confidential information that relates to some danger, fraud, or other illegal or unethical conduct connected with the workplace, be it of the employer or of fellow employees.

A whistleblower is someone in an organization who decides to speak out against on-the-job activities that are contrary to the mission of the organization or threaten the public interest.

▶ **Is whistleblowing effective?** Whistleblowers have focused public attention on corporate abuses at Enron and WorldCom, revealed major problems in the way the FBI investigated potential terrorists prior to 9-11, and uncovered defects in the body armor supplied to the U.S. president and combat troops (Figure 9-51).

Although whistleblowing might seem effective, the consequences of whistleblowing can be extreme. Even with strong legal protection under the Sarbanes-Oxley Act, whistleblowers are often fired or forced out of their jobs. If they keep their jobs, they might be excluded from promotions and shunned by coworkers. They are sometimes branded as tattletales and have difficulty finding other jobs in their career field.

▶ **Is there any way to safely blow the whistle on unethical business practices?** Whistleblowing is risky under any circumstances. For example, a computer system administrator working for a state agency noticed his boss spent the majority of his time playing solitaire on his computer. After several e-mail messages up the chain of command were ignored, the system administrator installed Win-Spy software, which grabbed incriminating screenshots of his boss's computer several times per day over a period of several months. When the system administrator showed this evidence to his superiors, he was fired for violating his boss's privacy. His boss received only a light reprimand.

As a whistleblower, the system administrator did some things right, but he missed some important measures that might have led to a more positive outcome. Employee advocates have the following suggestions for reducing the risk of career repercussions so often experienced by whistleblowers.

FIGURE 9-51

The head of research for a company that manufactures body armor blew the whistle on his company for not notifying consumers that fibers in the company's bulletproof vests break down over time, significantly reducing their protection against gunfire.

9

▶ **Examine your motives.** Make sure your cause is significant. Don't act out of frustration or because you feel underappreciated or mistreated.

▶ **Try the normal chain of command.** Before you blow the whistle, try to correct the problem by reporting up the normal chain of command. Consider every possible way to work within the system before you take your concerns public.

▶ **Collect evidence to back up your accusations.** Gather documentary evidence that proves your case and keep it in a safe place. Do not break any laws while collecting evidence. Try to collect evidence before you draw attention to your concerns.

▶ **Record events as they unfold.** Keep detailed, dated notes about events before and after you blow the whistle. Keep in mind that your notes might become public if they are used as evidence in a trial.

▶ **Act ethically.** Do not embellish your case and do not violate any confidentiality agreements you may have. Engage in whistleblowing activities on your own time, not your employer's.

▶ **Be ready to accept repercussions.** Think through the effect your actions might have on your family. Be prepared for unemployment and the possibility of being blacklisted in your profession.

▶ **Establish a support network.** Seek out potential allies, such as elected officials, journalists, and activists who can support your cause.

▶ **Consult a lawyer.** Make sure you understand your rights as an employee.

▶ **Consider your strategy.** You might reduce the risk of repercussions if you lodge your complaint anonymously or as part of a group.

As with other ethical decisions, your resolution to become a whistleblower can have a long-term effect on your career, family, and lifestyle. Think about your situation carefully and make use of whatever resources are available to you.

QuickCheck

1. Computer professionals sometimes have to make _____ decisions in situations where the right course of action is not clear.

2. Many aspects of law that pertain to computers, software, and intellectual property are included in the _____ Millennium Copyright Act.

3. Computer professionals know that it is important to maintain _____ and privacy for data that pertains to individuals.

4. Computer professionals sometimes have difficulty evaluating whether a project is socially _____ because project team members might not be given detailed information about a product's application.

5. A(n) _____ is someone in an organization who decides to speak out against on-the-job activities that are contrary to the mission of the organization or threaten the public interest.

 CHECK ANSWERS

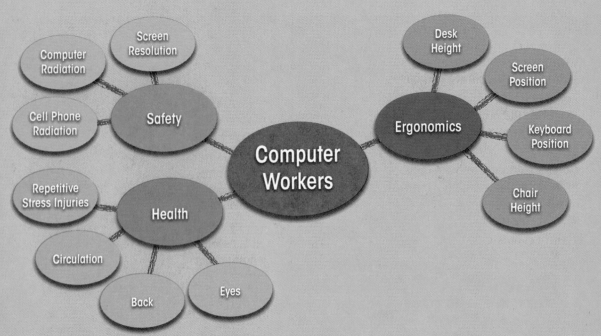

Work Area Safety and Ergonomics

MORE AND MORE WORKERS spend an entire eight-hour work day in front of a computer screen. Road warriors lug notebook computers through airports and try to get work done in the cramped confines of economy seats. It is rare to go anywhere and not see someone talking on a cell phone or plugged into a portable media player. Section E focuses on how digital lifestyles affect health.

RADIATION RISKS

▶ **What is radiation?** Although we tend to associate radiation with the fallout from nuclear blasts and debilitating cancer treatments, the term refers simply to any energy that is emitted in the form of waves or particles.

Radiation streams out of the sun in the form of heat and out of your stereo system as sound waves. Even more radiation pulses out from electrical appliances, wireless networks, cell phone towers, and electrical powerlines. Most of the radiation in your everyday world is considered safe, especially in moderation (Figure 9-52).

A few types of radiation can be harmful. **Ionizing radiation**, such as gamma rays and X-rays, contains enough electromagnetic energy to potentially alter chemical reactions in the body and disrupt molecules in human tissue. Shielding against these types of radiation is an important safety factor.

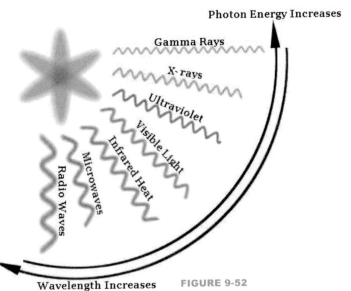

Courtesy of Body Composition Laboratory, Baylor College of Medicine

FIGURE 9-52

Some types of radiation, such as light, heat, microwaves, and radio waves, are generally considered safer than Gamma rays, X-rays, and ultraviolet light.

534

▶ What kinds of radiation are emitted by digital devices?
Every electronic device emits some type of radiation, otherwise they would be useless. The light emitted by computer screens and the signals that transmit cell phone data are essential for their use.

Although the radiation from most digital gadgets is considered harmless, researchers have raised concerns about radiation from CRT display devices and cell phones.

▶ What's the problem with CRTs? The first digital lifestyle devices to raise alarm were bulky cathode ray tube (CRT) displays, used in older computer monitors and televisions. These devices contain electronic vacuum tubes that essentially shoot a stream of high-speed electrons at the front of the screen as shown in Figure 9-53.

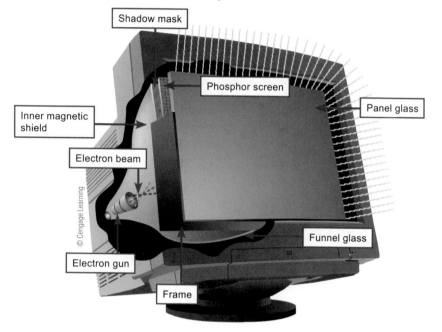

Shadow mask

Phosphor screen

Panel glass

Inner magnetic shield

Electron beam

© Cengage Learning

Funnel glass

Electron gun

Frame

FIGURE 9-53

The electron gun in a CRT sprays a beam of electrons at the screen.

Consumers became concerned that emissions from CRT devices might be a health risk, but a large collection of research carried out over the last 30 years has been unable to find a definitive link.

Most harmful X-rays from a CRT are blocked by leaded glass that forms the tube. Radiation that escapes through the tube is primarily ELF and VLF, which deteriorates over a fairly short distance. The level of emissions 20 inches (50 cm) from the screen is considerably less than emissions 10 inches away. The distance at which consumers normally use CRT devices exposes them to fairly small amounts of radiation.

▶ Do LCD screens emit radiation? Unlike a CRT, LCD display devices have no tubes and generate no X-rays. LCD devices do, however, emit low levels of radiation. Emission levels vary depending on manufacturer, brand, and model. When using an LCD, sitting at least an arm's length away from it reduces your exposure.

▶ Does a computer emit radiation? In addition to the computer's display device, the rest of the electronics in your desktop or notebook computer also emit radiation. Radiation levels increase when your computer is plugged into an external power source and when you have Wi-Fi turned on.

As with display devices, the radiation levels from your computer decrease quite quickly with distance. At an arm's length, your exposure is very small.

▶ **How much radiation is emitted from a typical cell phone?** A cell phone is a radio transmitter and receiver so it emits RF (radio frequency) energy. High levels of RF energy can heat human tissue much like the way a microwave oven heats food. Compared to a microwave oven, however, the amount of radiation emitted by a cell phone is miniscule.

Cell phone radiation can be measured by its **specific absorption rate** (SAR). In the U.S. and Canada, a phone's maximum SAR must be less than 1.6 W/kg; in Europe, the maximum level is 2.0 W/kg.

In a 2011 CNET survey of phones available in the U.S., the highest SAR was just under 1.6 W/kg. The phone with the lowest radiation level was measured at 0.19 W/kg. You can find the SAR level for your cell phone by entering its FCC ID number (look for it in the user manual) at *www.fcc.gov/oet/ea/fccid/*.

▶ **Are the current limits safe?** The scientific community continues to study and debate the amount of RF radiation that should be considered safe for long-term use. A Swedish study found evidence that long-term, extensive cell phone use significantly increases the risk of developing a brain tumor.

A contradictory study performed by the London-based Institute of Cancer Research and three British universities found that cell phone risk does not increase the incidence of brain tumors in cell phone users. Research literature is full of similar conflicting studies. Even the U.S. Food and Drug Administration (FDA) admits, "the available scientific evidence does not allow us to conclude that mobile phones are absolutely safe, or that they are unsafe."

▶ **What can I do to avoid excess cell phone radiation?** The easiest way to reduce your exposure to cell phone radiation is to use its speakerphone or a hands-free headset. Headsets, which many states require for use while driving, offer the additional benefit of reducing your chance of becoming involved in a traffic accident. Bluetooth wireless headsets emit a small amount of RF radiation, but only 10% of the radiation produced by the average cell phone.

REPETITIVE STRESS INJURIES

▶ **What is a repetitive stress injury?** Most of the health risks associated with computer use are not caused by the equipment itself, but how it is set up and used. Improper positioning of your keyboard and mouse can cause repetitive stress injuries to wrists, arms, neck, back, and shoulders.

A **repetitive stress injury** (RSI) is not a specific disease but a group of similar overuse disorders that affect tendons, muscles, and nerves. Symptoms include stiffness and minor pain in your hands, wrists, arms, or shoulders. Your symptoms might appear while you're working, or they might appear several hours or days later. With rest, these injuries tend to heal; although some problems, such as carpal tunnel syndrome, might require medical intervention.

▶ **What is carpal tunnel syndrome?** Your wrist contains eight carpal bones surrounding a large nerve that controls your thumb, index finger, and middle finger. Anything that compresses this nerve, such as arthritis or thickened tendons, can cause numbness, pain, or tingling in your fingers, a condition called carpal tunnel syndrome (Figure 9-54). At one time, it was generally accepted that keyboarding was a major cause of carpal tunnel syndrome. A recent Mayo Clinic study, however, concluded that key-

FIGURE 9-54

Carpal tunnel syndrome is a condition affecting the nerve that runs to your thumb, index finger, and middle finger.

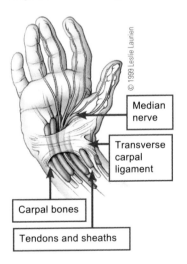

© 1999 Leslie Laurien

Median nerve

Transverse carpal ligament

Carpal bones

Tendons and sheaths

boarding does not cause carpal tunnel syndrome, though it can make the condition worse. Most computer-related hand and arm injuries are repetitive stress injuries, which can be avoided by following ergonomic guidelines.

▶ **What is ergonomics? Ergonomics** is the study of safe and efficient environments, particularly working environments. Ergonomics provides guidelines for making work environments safer and healthier.

In the U.S., the Occupational Safety and Health Administration (OSHA) sets and enforces standards for the safety and health of American workers. Although a federal law to enforce ergonomic standards in the workplace was repealed in 2001, many states have regulations designed to protect workers from repetitive stress injuries.

▶ **How should I set up my work area?** At the beginning of the chapter, you had an opportunity to evaluate the ergonomics of your current work area. The key to avoiding uncomfortable stress injuries is in the placement and use of your keyboard, mouse, monitor, desk, and chair (Figure 9-55).

FIGURE 9-55

Set up and use your computer equipment according to ergonomic guidelines to avoid repetitive stress injuries.

▶ Position the keyboard so that it is just above your lap and your elbows are able to extend past the 90 degree angle when you type. If you use an external keyboard, choose a computer desk with a keyboard tray that you can adjust so it is 1"–2" above your thighs.

▶ Angle the keyboard so that your wrists are straight when typing.

▶ If you have a wrist-rest, use it only when you are not typing; resting your palm on a wrist-rest while typing usually creates an angle in your wrist that is not efficient.

▶ Use a keyboard that fits the size of your hands and fingers. When you rest your fingers on the home keys (asdf and jkl;), there should be 1/8"–1/4" of space between them so you are not trying to type with your fingers cramped together or overextending.

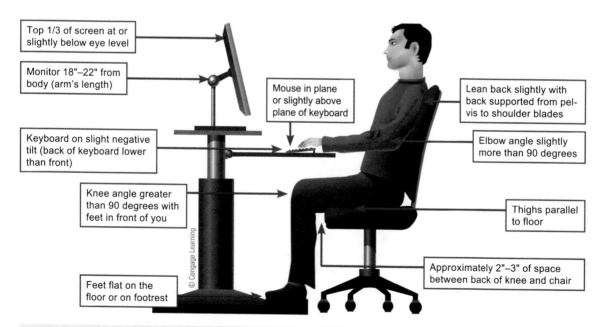

Top 1/3 of screen at or slightly below eye level

Monitor 18"–22" from body (arm's length)

Mouse in plane or slightly above plane of keyboard

Lean back slightly with back supported from pelvis to shoulder blades

Keyboard on slight negative tilt (back of keyboard lower than front)

Elbow angle slightly more than 90 degrees

Knee angle greater than 90 degrees with feet in front of you

Thighs parallel to floor

Approximately 2"–3" of space between back of knee and chair

Feet flat on the floor or on footrest

© Cengage Learning

▶ Make sure your mouse is positioned close by so that you don't have to reach for it.

▶ Keep the mouse at the same height as your keyboard to minimize arm movements.

▶ Use your mouse with a relaxed arm and wrist.

▶ When working at mouse-intensive activities, change mouse hands occasionally or change to an air mouse, trackball, or touchpad, which require a different set of muscles.

EYE STRAIN

▶ What about computer-related eye problems? Studies have found links between computer use and eye problems. The most common symptoms are sore, tired, burning, or itching eyes; watery eyes; dry eyes; blurred or double vision; headaches; difficulty shifting focus between the screen display and printed documents; and increased sensitivity to light. For many computer users, eye problems can be avoided by proper monitor placement and adjustment.

▶ What is the optimal placement for my monitor? To correctly position your monitor, sit back slightly in your chair and stretch your left arm out straight ahead of you. Your middle finger should almost touch the center of your screen as shown in Figure 9-56.

© Cengage Learning

FIGURE 9-56

You can position your monitor by stretching out your arm parallel to the ground. Your fingertips should almost touch the center of the screen.

Once the screen is set at the proper height, tilt it backwards just a bit. You should feel like you are looking down slightly at the screen. Your screen should be directly in front of you and parallel to your shoulders.

If you use two monitors, place your second monitor as close to the first monitor as possible, but angled so that when you turn your head slightly, you face it straight on. You might also consider moving it to the other side of your primary monitor periodically.

When positioning your monitor, try to minimize the amount of glare from lights or windows that is reflected on the screen. Angle the screen away from windows, but you should not end up facing a window where bright outdoor light can interfere with the way your pupils need to dilate for the brightness of your computer screen.

If glare is a problem in your work area, you can purchase an antiglare screen that fits over your computer screen. Keeping the surface of your monitor free of dust can also cut down on glare.

▶ What about placement of my notebook computer? Notebook computers present an ergonomic problem because the screen and keyboard are attached to each other. Placement becomes a compromise between the best viewing angle and the best typing height. When possible, use an external keyboard and mouse with your notebook computer to achieve a more ergonomic work area.

▶ What if I wear glasses? Bifocal and trifocal lenses tend to offer the correct focus for computer work through the bottom of the lens. Wearers raise their chins to view the screen, which puts stress on neck muscles and causes headaches. To avoid this situation, bifocal and trifocal wearers might have to lower their screens or ask their optometrist for eyewear dedicated to viewing the computer screen.

▶ How about adjusting the resolution? One of the most effective steps you can take to avoid eye strain is to adjust the resolution of your monitor so that you can easily read the text displayed on your screen. Remember that you can adjust the screen resolution or the zoom level.

Adjusting screen resolution globally affects window, icon, and text size. LCD screens have a **native resolution** that displays one pixel for each tiny light in the display matrix. Selecting a resolution lower than a screen's native resolution forces the display device to interpolate pixels and results in a slightly fuzzy display. Figure 9-57 explains.

FIGURE 9-57

To find your screen's native resolution when using Windows, check the display settings. Typically, the highest resolution available is your screen's native resolution.

9

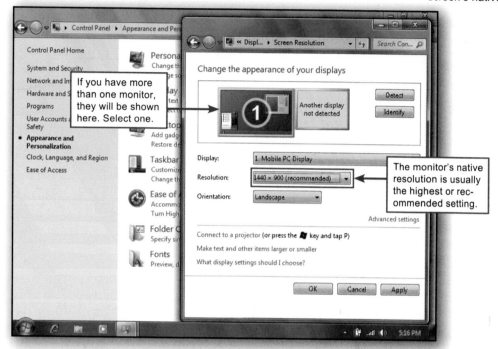

Once your monitor is set to its native resolution, you might find that the text on Web pages and in documents is too small to view comfortably. In that situation, you can adjust the zoom level within various applications. For example, you might set your browser to display larger text and set your word processor to display text at 125% or 150% (Figure 9-58).

FIGURE 9-58

If the text is too small at your monitor's native resolution, try increasing the zoom level within applications.

BACK PAIN

▶ How can computer use affect my back and spine? Back pain can be caused by many factors, including poor posture and careless lifting of heavy objects.

▶ What about posture? Doctors and physical therapists commonly use the term *flex-forward posture* to describe the sitting posture shared by many computer users. The layman's term *computer slump* refers to the same thing: sitting hunched over a computer keyboard with your neck craned forward (Figure 9-59).

Habitual slouching can lead to stiffness and muscle tenderness. Left uncorrected, the problem can cause nerve irritation that spreads down the arms and back. Back problems caused by habitual flex-forward posture are sometimes referred to as T4 syndrome, named after the fourth cervical vertebra that is most affected.

▶ How can I avoid computer-related back problems? The key to comfort while working on a computer is keeping your shoulders relaxed so that tense muscles don't generate headaches and stiffness. If the armrests on your chair make your shoulders rise, you should remove the armrests or get another chair.

Conventional wisdom about sitting straight has been challenged recently by a body of evidence that indicates the best position for computer work is with your upper torso leaning back slightly. With your torso at a 100–110 degree angle, the back of your chair helps to support your spine.

Carrying a heavy computer can also contribute to back problems. To lighten your load, try to reduce the number of peripheral devices you carry. Consider toting your computer in a backpack instead of a shoulder bag. When traveling, place your notebook computer in a wheeled carrier.

SEDENTARY LIFESTYLE

▶ Does computer use affect my overall physical fitness? People who live and work in digital cultures tend to spend many hours each day in sedentary pursuits, such as watching television and using computers. Many researchers believe that there is a link between our increasingly sedentary lifestyle and a steady climb in obesity and cardiovascular disease.

To counteract the effects of a sedentary lifestyle, it is important to exercise and eat right. A good balance of stretching and cardiovascular exercise can help you keep physically fit and has the additional benefit of helping to prevent repetitive stress injuries and back pain.

▶ What about circulatory problems? Sitting still for long periods of time, especially in positions that limit blood circulation, can be a health risk, similar to the risk of long haul air travel. A condition called deep vein thrombosis is the formation of blood clots that commonly affect veins in the legs. Symptoms include pain, swelling, and redness in the affected area.

Deep vein thrombosis requires treatment to prevent life threatening complications if the clot moves to the heart. Although the condition is not common in young people, good work habits can help you maintain healthy circulation at any age.

FIGURE 9-59

Bad posture can lead to back pain.

© Cengage Learning

9

▶ **What factors help maintain good circulation?** Your chair should not prevent good circulation to your legs. Make sure there is at least 2 inches (5 cm) of clearance between your calf and the front of your chair. Your thighs should be parallel to the ground to allow for good blood flow; if necessary, use a footrest to raise your feet and reduce pressure on the backs of your thighs.

▶ **What else can I do?** To combat potential health hazards associated with computer use, you should try to take breaks periodically—say, every 20 minutes or at least once every hour. At minimum, try the 20/20/20 break: Every 20 minutes, take 20 seconds and look 20 feet away.

Longer breaks of two to five minutes are even more effective. During a longer break, stand up to change your circulation. Rest your eyes by focusing on distant objects. Gently rotate and stretch your wrists, shoulders, and neck. **Break reminder software**, such as RSIGuard and open source Workrave, can help you remember when it's time to take a break from your work (Figure 9-60).

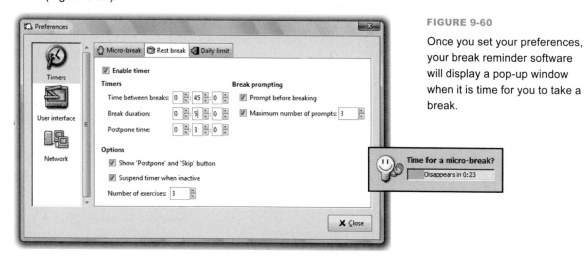

FIGURE 9-60

Once you set your preferences, your break reminder software will display a pop-up window when it is time for you to take a break.

QuickCheck   SECTION E

1. Some types of radiation, such as gamma rays and X-rays, are safer than light, heat, and microwaves. True or false? [_____]

2. Computer displays and televisions that use CRT technology emit less radiation than LCD screens. True or false? [_____]

3. If you are curious about the amount of radio frequency emitted by your cell phone, you can check its [_____] level on the FCC Web site. (Hint: Use the acronym.)

4. Carpal tunnel syndrome is an example of a(n) [_____] stress injury.

5. According to ergonomic guidelines, you should place your notebook computer in your lap when in use. True or false? [_____]

 CHECK ANSWERS

Issue: Can Computers Think?

dimitris_k /Shutterstock.com

TODAY WE THINK of computers mostly in the context of getting connected on Facebook, streaming music and video from the Web, and playing amusing little games like Angry Birds. But back behind the scenes, there are computers doing some really heavy lifting, such as estimating climate change, piecing together the human genome, and researching the beginning of the universe.

The computers that delve into these problems are the descendants of room-sized machines constructed in the 1940s and 1950s that laborously calculated ballistic tables and deciphered Nazi coded messages.

In the era when only a handful of computers existed, some visionary scientists looked toward the future and speculated that computers might rival humans in their capacity to think.

In 1950, the well-respected British mathematician Alan Turing wrote, "I believe that at the end of the century, the use of words and general educated opinion will have altered so much that one will be able to speak of machines thinking without expecting to be contradicted."

His prediction did not turn out to be correct, but it sparked a controversy that continues today: Could computers think, and how would we know if they do?

Turing described a test of machine intelligence in a 1950 article called *Computing Machinery and Intelligence*. The "Turing Test," as it is now called, is somewhat like a TV game show. In a simplified version, it pits a judge against two backstage contestants: one a computer and one a human. The judge engages each contestant in a conversation.

A computer passes the Turing Test if the judge is unable to determine which contestant is the computer and which contestant is human. According to Turing, a computer that can respond as intelligently as a human must be intelligent and must be able to think.

> *"By the time the controversy dies down...AIs will already be thousands of times smarter than us."*
>
> Ray Kurzweil commenting on IBM's Jeopardy! victory

Turing's test of machine intelligence launched the study of artificial intelligence (AI), which is now a mainstream discipline of computer science. An idea that previously existed only in the fantasy worlds of science fiction writers, such as Karel Capek, L. Frank Baum, and Isaac Asimov, became a legitimate field of scientific enquiry.

Computers have competed with humans in domain-specific showdowns. An IBM computer named Deep Blue beat chess Grand Master Garry Kasparov in a 1997 showdown. Then in 2011, an AI computer named Watson won a two-game combined-point Jeopardy! match beating two of the quiz show's biggest all-time winners.

Watson had access to four terabytes of data, including the entire content of Wikipedia.

An IBM Web page describes Watson's technology as "an application of advanced Natural Language Processing, Information Retrieval, Knowledge Representation and Reasoning, and Machine Learning technologies...At its core, Watson is built on IBM's DeepQA technology for hypothesis generation, massive evidence gathering, analysis, and scoring."

Beating two Jeopardy! experts does not make Watson intelligent, however. Jeopardy! requires contestants to answer questions in the form of "Who is..." or "What is...". Carrying out a sustained conversation, staying on topic, and responding sensibly require more sophistication; but that is not to say that Watson could not acquire those abilities through additional programming and learning.

Whether or not you believe that computers might eventually be able to think, consider Ray Kurzweil's prediction, "By the time the controversy dies down and it becomes unambiguous that nonbiological intelligence is equal to biological human intelligence, the AIs will already be thousands of times smarter than us." But not to worry. Kurzweil continues, "Ultimately, we will vastly extend and expand our own intelligence by merging with these tools of our own creation."

Try It! From science fiction to real life, artificial intelligence is fascinating. Yes, you can talk to an AI today! Have fun exploring while you compile your findings in a document called AI Project.

Thomas Watson was the founder of IBM and namesake for the computer that bested human opponents in Jeopardy! Notice the THINK sign; an intriguing motto for a computer company.

1 In 1990, Hugh Loebner sponsored the first real-world Turing Test, pledging a $100,000 prize to the first winner. In addition, an annual prize of $2,000 is awarded to the most human-like computer entered in the contest. Check the Web site for the Loebner Prize in Artificial Intelligence to see if the competition is still active. Look for a transcript of the conversation during the competition; copy and paste a section of it into your AI Project document (make sure to include its URL). Add your own answers to the questions and think about how they differ from the computer's answers.

2 You can usually spot artificial intelligence programs because they tend to offer vague answers and sometimes try to change the subject when they don't understand a question. These programs are called chatterbots. Find an online chatterbot, such as Jabberwacky, ELIZA, A.L.I.C.E., or Web Hal, and have a chat. Provide the URL for your chatterbot and write a short paragraph of your impressions. What did you ask that it answered intelligently? Give an example of a question for which you received a weird answer.

3 CAPTCHA technology turned the Turing Test inside out, and is sometimes classified as a reverse Turing Test. What is the main goal of CAPTCHA and is it really a reverse Turing Test? Use search terms such as *CAPTCHA*, *reverse turing test*, and *cracked* to find out.

4 Even if a computer can eventually pass the Turing Test, not everyone would agree that it can think. Philosopher John Searle, for example, attempted to refute the Turing Test using the now famous Chinese Room thought experiment. What can you find out about Searle's Chinese Room and how it applies to machine intelligence?

5 Alan Turing's original test of machine intelligence was based on a game with players A, B, and C. Use the Web to locate a PDF file of Turing's original paper, *Computing Machinery and Intelligence*. Find out how Turing described each of the three players and how he described the point of the original game. How did Turing propose to change this game to determine if a computer could be considered intelligent?

INFOWEBLINKS

You can check the **NP2013 Chapter 9** InfoWebLink for updates to these activities.

W CLICK TO CONNECT
www.infoweblinks.com/np2013/ch09

What Do You Think?

ISSUE

1. Does the Turing Test of machine intelligence make sense to you?

2. If a computer can beat human contestants in Jeopardy!, is it showing signs of intelligence?

3. Do you believe that computers might someday have the capacity to think?

Information Tools: Provenance

If you've watched Antiques Roadshow, you know that the Beatles signed many album covers, which today are worth between $8,000 and $10,000. However, an album with the right provenance, such as the first American album cover signed by the Beatles before their Ed Sullivan Show debut, could be worth up to $150,000.

The term *provenance* refers to the origins of an object and its history. It is commonly used in the antique business, but it can also be applied to printed documents, and to electronic information including Web sites, photos, videos, and posts on social networking pages.

In the context of information, provenance provides clues that help you evaluate accuracy and reliability. Provenance also helps you track down permission to use and reuse articles, quotes, photos, videos, and music. The questions below can help you establish the provenance of electronic information.

▶ What is the top-level domain? Recognizing .edu, .com, .org, and other top-level domains helps to classify the person, organization, or business that is responsible for the site.

▶ What else can the URL tell you? The Web page title or site name can help you identify whether the information is provided by a Web site, blog, tweet, forum, news aggregator, or social network post.

▶ Who sponsors the site? Check the site copyright or About page to determine who or what is the site sponsor.

▶ What kind of resources are provided? Take an inventory of the objects (text, images, animations, videos, ads, links, comments, ratings) included and note those that are most relevant.

▶ Has the information been peer reviewed? See the box below for a description of reviews.

▶ Are there ads on the page? Pay attention to peripheral objects, such as ads, because they might offer clues you'll later use to determine the validity of information.

▶ Who produced the content and what are their credentials? Look for the names of authors, photographers, designers, and others who produced content. Google their names to link to their biographies, social pages, or other work.

▶ Did the material originate at the site, or was it reposted, republished, or retweeted? Redistributed material might be altered; you can refer to the original material to ensure its accuracy.

▶ Is the material a mashup or derivative work? Stay alert for doctored photos and parodies.

▶ Is the material date-appropriate? Check the date when the material was created or posted.

▶ Is there a Contact link that you can use to get additional information or obtain permission to use content from the site?

▶ Take note of the site's access policy. Does it require a login or a paid subscription?

Peer-reviewed information is usually found in scholarly sources, such as journals. Articles reviewed by topic experts before publication produce information that is typically accurate and backed by facts or research.

Public reviewed information can be found in popular media, such as news magazines, blogs, and social network sites. Articles with comments made by readers after publication are often opinionated, but can be useful for understanding divergent viewpoints.

Ratings are found on blogs, social networks, and commercial sites. Likes, stars, and other anonymous ratings have little meaning in the context of evaluating information.

Try It! On November 29, 2010, the U.S. space agency NASA announced that it would hold a press conference the following Thursday "to discuss an astrobiology finding that will impact the search for evidence of extraterrestrial life." The announcement led to widespread speculation that NASA had discovered proof of extraterrestrial life.

At the press conference, microbiologist Felisa Wolfe-Simon explained that her research team had isolated bacteria that could subsist on arsenic instead of phosphorus, which was considered essential for all terrestrial life forms.

Although the announcement wasn't as spectacular as receiving a radiotelescope message "Hello, earthlings," the idea that arsenic could sustain life rocked the scientific community and caused all manner of misunderstanding in the popular press. Had Wolfe-Simon's team found some weird form of alien life? Readers who wanted reliable information about the discovery had to carefully choose their news sources. Let's see how provenance can help separate reliable reports from sensationalized trash.

1️⃣ Use a search engine to find the original NASA press release by entering "NASA Wolfe-Simon press release." Make sure you have the primary-source document by examining the URL. How does the press release define *astrobiology*?

2️⃣ The press conference was held on December 2, 2010. Search the Web and locate what you think is the most reliable source of the information that was presented at the press conference. Based on the provenance of the site you've chosen, explain why you selected it.

Alien Life on Earth?

Rick Whitacre/Shutterstock.com

3️⃣ In the aftermath of the press conference, blogs, Twitter, and YouTube carried a full spectrum of commentary, from wacky "arsenic-eating" conjectures of amateur scientists to very technical critiques from mainstream researchers. Search YouTube for a video that relates to Wolfe-Simon's research. Watch the video, read the public comments, and check the provenance of the video itself. Based on the provenance, explain how comfortable you would be including the information presented in a term paper.

4️⃣ Wolfe-Simon's research was immediately criticized. An especially strong blog post from Rosie Redfield called it "Lots of flim-flam, but very little reliable information." Find Rosie's post and determine its provenance based on the criteria listed on the facing page. Would you characterize this blog as authoritative or wacky? Why?

5️⃣ On December 2, 2010, the Web site for *Science* Magazine published a paper authored by Wolfe-Simon and members of her team. The article was later published in the print version of *Science* Magazine. Find the article online and determine if Wolfe-Simon's paper was peer reviewed. What does the peer review or lack of it tell you about the validity of Wolfe-Simon's claim that arsenic rather than phosphorus can sustain life?

Tim Boyle/Newsmakers/Getty Images

Technology in Context: Travel

RAMON STOPPELENBURG LEFT his home in the Netherlands with a backpack, a digital camera, a laptop computer, and a cell phone. He left behind the one thing most travelers would never be caught without—money! Instead, he set up a Web site called Let Me Stay For a Day. Every few days, Ramon updated his Web site with a journal entry, a picture or two, and his travel itinerary. After viewing the Web site, more than 3,600 people from 72 different countries offered money, meals, and lodging.

Using the Web as his travel agent, Ramon traveled through 17 countries, wrote more than 500 journal entries, took more than 7,000 photographs, and spent exactly zero of his own money. Ramon Stoppelenburg's adventure might be unconventional, but it demonstrates the growing role that computers play in the travel industry.

Since the 1960s, computer-based GDSs (global distribution systems) have managed and distributed travel-related information, such as flight schedules, ticket prices, and passenger itineraries. GDSs were originally proprietary systems installed in airports and used only by authorized airline employees. Today, GDSs are used by travel agents, hotel employees, and airline ticketing clerks. They also provide the power behind some travel-related Web sites.

The SABRE system, one of the oldest and largest GDSs, caters primarily to travel industry professionals. In 1953, American Airlines president C. R. Smith happened to be seated next to IBM sales representative R. Blair Smith on a flight from Los Angeles to New York. Their chance meeting led to the devel-

opment of the Semi-Automatic Business Research Environment—commonly known as SABRE. When SABRE went online in 1964, it became the first e-commerce system in the world, allowing American Airlines agents in airport terminals to automate up to 26,000 passenger reservation transactions per day. Other airlines quickly followed suit, and competing GDSs were launched by United Airlines, TWA, and Amadeus, a partnership of European Airlines.

Before SABRE, flight reservations required cumbersome manual transactions. Travel agents used teletypes to communicate with airlines to reserve seats and generate tickets. Processing a round-trip reservation could take up to three hours and involved as many as 12 people.

Today, SABRE and other GDSs manage information from hundreds of airlines, thousands of hotels, and a multitude of other travel-related organizations, such as car rental companies, cruise lines, and tour operators. Travel agents can use these systems to compare fare information, generate itineraries, and print tickets instantly. Schedule and rate changes are available immediately—no waiting for new rates to be printed and distributed.

Although GDSs are still in demand, some experts believe that their early popularity is now contributing to their demise. Most GDSs were built before the Internet and the Web were invented, and the hardware and software they rely on is now considered outdated. Compared to modern information systems, GDSs are difficult and expensive to maintain, and their use often requires special training. The information stored on a GDS was historically available only to professional travel agents.

The use of GDSs has been affected by a fundamental change in the travel industry characterized by a shift away from marketing through tour guides and travel agents. Many travel-related companies now prefer to market directly to consumers through Web sites and telephone sales. Some GDSs have been modified for consumer-level Web accessibility. These GDSs now provide the power behind popular travel Web sites such as Expedia.com and Travelocity.com.

GDS-powered Web sites offer consumers the same information that was previously available only to travel professionals who subscribed to a GDS ser-

9

vice. Consumers can search for flights, compare fares, research travel destinations, and find hotel and car rental fees from one easy-to-use Web site. The GDS components of these systems continue to use old hardware and software, however, and the ongoing cost of maintenance is high.

In 2001, five airlines—American, Continental, Delta, Northwest, and United—launched a travel-related Web site called Orbitz.com. Unlike other travel Web sites, this site was not powered by a traditional GDS. Instead, Orbitz.com was built from the ground up, using modern hardware and software. Like GDS-based sites, Orbitz.com maintains information about flights, fares, hotels, rental cars, and cruises. Consumers can search for travel deals and discounts or research specific destinations.

Even before Orbitz. com went live, it was the subject of criticism and lawsuits. For example, the American Society of Travel Agents (ASTA) claimed that Orbitz. com could publish special pricing not available through the standard fare schedules. If travel agents were unable to access the special online pricing, the ASTA predicted that consumers would eventually stop using the services of travel agencies to book flights, rental cars, and other travel services.

The Department of Transportation Inspector General investigated Orbitz and its effect on the travel business, but found no evidence of anti-competitive behavior. The investigation concluded that Orbitz would provide valuable services to consumers and promote competition in the travel marketplace. Orbitz.com opened to much fanfare in June 2001 and quickly became one of the most popular travel-related Web sites.

Web-based travel services represented one of the few bright spots on the e-commerce landscape after the dot-com bubble burst. Online travel sites appear to be flourishing.

Going a step beyond Orbitz, travel consolidators such as Kayak.com use metasearch technology to search hundreds of airline, hotel, and cruise sites to help customers find the best deals. Revenues garnered from ad clickthroughs keep these sites in business and travel planners benefit from the convenience of using a single site to search for travel deals.

Hotel and transportation reservations are one aspect of the travel-related services found on the Internet. The Web provides an abundance of trip planning information. Google Maps and MapQuest provide road maps and driving directions between cities all over the globe. Popular travel Web sites, such as Frommers and Fodors, provide information that helps travelers plan where to eat, where to stay, and what to see.

The Web also offers travelogues, reviews, blogs, and message boards with postings from individual travelers. Web sites and blogs, such as TripAdvisor and Epinions.com, encourage tourists and business travelers to post reviews about favorite restaurants, events, hotels, and tourist attractions.

Computers aren't used only for planning travel. Many travelers opt to take handheld and portable devices on the road, or stop at local Internet cafes and spend some time browsing the Web or sending e-mail messages. Web-based e-mail services such as Hotmail, Gmail, and Yahoo! Mail make it simple and inexpensive to keep in touch with friends, family, clients, and colleagues while on the road.

Travelers with digital cameras can send vacation photos to friends and relatives by e-mail or post the photos on a personal Web site. Tourists can download street maps and sightseeing information to their PDAs or iPhones, calculate exchange rates, and even use their digital devices to translate simple phrases from one language to another.

New Perspectives Labs

To access the New Perspectives Lab for Chapter 9, open the NP2013 interactive eBook and then click the icon next to the lab title.

 ONLINE JOB HUNTING

IN THIS LAB YOU'LL LEARN:

- How to register with an online employment service
- How to submit your resume online
- Why the file that you use for your printed resume might not be appropriate for posting online
- The characteristics of an ASCII document
- How to convert a formatted resume to an ASCII resume
- How to fix an ASCII resume so that it presents information in an easy-to-read format
- How to post an ASCII resume at an employment service
- How to enter a job search by keyword or category
- Creative ways to use keywords in a search specification
- How to configure a search agent
- How to find information on salaries, employers, and places to live

LAB ASSIGNMENTS

1. Start the interactive part of the lab. Make sure you've enabled Tracking if you want to save your QuickCheck results. Perform each lab step as directed, and answer all the lab QuickCheck questions. When you exit the lab, your answers are automatically graded and your results are displayed.

2. Write a paragraph that describes your ideal job. Next, create a list of search specifications that you could enter at an online employment service to find job openings for your ideal job. Connect to an online employment service and enter your search specifications. Describe the results. If your results were not satisfactory, try modifying your search specifications. Record what seems to be the most effective search, and, if possible, print the job listings that resulted from your search.

3. Using word processing or desktop publishing software, create a one-page resume that highlights your current skills and experience. Print this resume. Convert the resume into an ASCII document, tidy up the format, and then print it.

4. Use the Web to find information about the corporate culture at Microsoft. Summarize your findings, and list each Web site you visited to find information.

5. Use the Web to compare Macon, GA to San Diego, CA in terms of salaries, cost of living, job opportunities, and other factors. Write a one-page summary of the strengths and weaknesses of each city, and then explain which city you would prefer to live in. List the URLs for any Web sites you used for this assignment.

Key Terms

Make sure you understand all the boldfaced key terms presented in this chapter. With the NP2013 interactive eBook, you can use this list of terms as an interactive study activity. First, try to define a term in your own words, and then click the term to compare your definition with the definition presented in the chapter.

9

Interactive Summary

To review important concepts from this chapter, fill in the blanks to best complete each sentence. When using the NP2013 interactive eBook, click the Check Answers buttons to automatically score your answers.

SECTION A: Even before recorded history, humans used various [_____] aids, such as pebbles and notched sticks, to keep track of quantities. By 1200, a(n) [_____] calculator, called the abacus, had appeared in China. In Europe, a popular calculating device called Napier's Bones was transformed into the slide rule in 1621, and became the calculating tool of choice in Europe and later the Americas. Manual calculators require the operator to apply a(n) [_____] to perform calculations. In contrast, [_____] calculators, such as the Pascaline and de Colmar's Arithmometer, are designed to carry out calculations autonomously. In 1822, an English mathematician named Charles [_____] proposed to build a device, called the Difference Engine, that would oper-

ate using steam power. He also designed a second device, called the [_____] Engine, which embodied many of the concepts that define the modern computer. In the 1930s and 1940s, several [_____] computers were developed, including the Atanasoff-Berry Computer, Z3, Harvard Mark I, COLOSSUS, and ENIAC. Most of these early computers used [_____] tubes, which paved the way for the architecture of first-generation computers, such as UNIVAC. Second-generation computers were smaller and less power hungry because they used [_____]. Third-generation computers were even smaller because they used [_____] circuits. The key technology for fourth-generation computers, including personal computers, is the [_____]. ▶ CHECK ANSWERS

SECTION B: The [_____] industry encompasses those companies that manufacture computers. A broader term, *IT industry*, is typically used to refer to the companies that develop, produce, sell, or support computers, software, and computer-related products. A high rate of dot-com business failures during 2001 and 2002 meant a decline in equipment orders, Web site hosting contracts, and IT sector job openings. During that time, strength in worldwide markets for IT equipment and services continued to buoy up the industry. The life cycle of a typical hardware product includes product development, product announcement, introduction, [_____], and retirement. The life cycle of a software product is similar, except that old versions of a software product do not typically remain in the publisher's product line. During development, software products usually undergo a(n) [_____] test, and then they might be released for a public [_____] test. Soon after a new version of a software product is released, the publisher discontinues sales of

the old version. Hardware and software products are sold through marketing [_____], such as retail stores, mail-order/Internet outlets, value-added resellers, and manufacturer direct. Retail stores and VARs tend to have the highest prices. In most countries, including the United States, the IT industry is not regulated by a dedicated government agency. Instead, the IT industry is subject to broad-based [_____] that pertains to anti-monopoly laws, communications rules, and gambling restrictions. To avoid government regulations that target technology companies, the IT industry has attempted to regulate itself by creating organizations to set standards and disseminate information to technology companies, government, and the general public.

▶ CHECK ANSWERS

SECTION C: A computer [ ] is defined as any person whose primary occupation involves the design, configuration, analysis, development, modification, testing, or security of computer hardware or software. The IT industry encompasses a wide variety of jobs for computer professionals, and the career outlook appears to be relatively positive. Salaries and working conditions are quite favorable. Computer professionals work full-time or part-time jobs, and some are [ ] workers, who arrange to work for a company on a temporary basis, usually as consultants for particular projects. Although these workers are usually highly paid, they are not official employees of a company and are not eligible for company health care or retirement benefits. Education is an important key to most high tech jobs. Computer [ ] degree programs focus on the design of computer hardware and peripheral devices. Computer [ ] degree programs focus on digital computer architecture and how to program computers to make them work effectively and efficiently. Information [ ] degree programs focus on applying computers to business problems. In addition to a college degree, [ ] provides job applicants with marketable credentials pertaining to skill and knowledge of specific software or hardware. Finding a job in the IT industry is similar to finding any job. Preparing a resume is essential, and it can be supplemented by a Web [ ] with links to relevant Web sites, such as past employers, your alma mater, and samples of your work. Job seekers can make use of online search [ ] and [ ] tools that can be automated to search one or more job databases. Before posting a resume at an online employment service, you should always check the employment service's [ ] policy.

▶ CHECK ANSWERS

SECTION D: Computer professionals sometimes encounter situations in which the right course of action requires a decision based on evaluating what's right and wrong. Professional [ ] refers to on-the-job choices and actions that reflect a person's values. Ethical decisions should take into account applicable [ ], such as the Digital Millennium Copyright Act. Laws and ethics are not the same thing, however, and sometimes following the letter of the law does not result in ethical behavior. Situations that require computer professionals to make ethical decisions often involve software copyrights, privacy, conflict of interest, use of work computers, software quality, hacking, and social [ ]. Ethical decisions made on the job can have long-term career effects. Many IT organizations have [ ] of ethics designed to help computer professionals make tough decisions. Additional help in making ethical decisions can also be obtained from knowledgeable friends, mentors, lawyers, and workplace counselors. Computer professionals who are compelled to become [ ] and speak out against on-the-job activities that threaten the public interest should understand the potential legal and career risks before they proceed.

▶ CHECK ANSWERS

SECTION E: As computers and other digital devices became a fixture in modern workplaces and everyday life, questions were raised about health risks associated with computer use. All electronic devices emit various types of [ ] in the form of light, heat, and radio waves. Some consumer watchdogs have suggested that cathode ray [ ] in display devices pose a potential health risk because they generate X-rays. Researchers have explored the link between cell phones and brain cancer with inconclusive results; however, government standards limit emissions to 1.6 W/kg, measured by [ ]. To avoid [ ] stress injuries, equipment and furniture in a computer work area should be arranged according to [ ] guidelines. Taking frequent rest breaks while using a computer can also help to avoid eye strain and stress injuries. [ ] reminder software can help workers remember when to take a break. Television and digital gadgets seem to contribute to a sedentary lifestyle. To counteract health problems associated with sitting for long periods of time, regular exercise and good nutrition are essential.

▶ CHECK ANSWERS

9

Interactive Situation Questions

Apply what you've learned to some typical computing situations. When using the NP2013 interactive eBook, you can type your answers, and then use the Check Answers button to automatically score your responses.

1. Suppose that you were an accountant in 1979, and you wanted to use a state-of-the-art personal computer and software for your work. You would probably have selected an Apple II computer and [   ] software.

2. You work as a manufacturing technician in a chip fabrication plant. Your aunt asks if you're in the IT industry. Your response: [   ]

3. When you call your computer manufacturer for technical support, you aren't surprised by the lilting accents of the technicians because many call centers operate in other countries, a practice called [   ].

4. You receive an e-mail from a software publisher that offers to supply you with a free copy of a new operating system if you become part of a beta test program. You are hesitant about participating because beta software versions often contain [   ] that can cause unexpected glitches in your computer.

5. After studying and gaining practical experience on how to analyze a computer system's vulnerability to threats from viruses, worms, unauthorized access, and physical damage, you are ready for a job as a(n) [   ] specialist.

6. You accepted a project with an IT company as a(n) [   ] worker, fully realizing that you will not be considered an official employee of the company, nor will you be eligible for the company's health care or retirement benefits.

7. Your friend is not strong in math, but really wants to work with computers. You suggest that your friend consider a(n) [   ] systems degree.

8. To supplement your computer science degree, you decide to take a(n) [   ] exam to become a Microsoft Certified Systems Engineer.

9. As part of your job hunting activities, you plan to create your resume in several different [   ] , for use in the body of an e-mail message, as a Web page, and as a printed document.

10. You're working with a friend on an assignment and she proudly shows you a program she's developing to shut down hate sites on the Web. Her plan gives you an uneasy feeling. You'll have to make a(n) [   ] decision about what to do.

11. You've discovered your company's accounting system was intentionally modified to disguise certain expenses. You're contemplating what might happen if you become a(n) [   ] , and expose this unethical practice.

12. You want to make sure your computer is set up so that you can avoid disabling musculoskeletal injuries, like carpal tunnel syndrome. You can look for [   ] guidelines on the Web, which offer advice on how to position your computer monitor and where to place lighting.

● CHECK ANSWERS

Interactive Practice Tests

Practice tests that consist of ten multiple-choice, true/false, and fill-in-the-blank questions are available in the NP2013 interactive eBook. Test questions are selected at random from a large test bank, so each time you take a test, you'll receive a different set of questions. Your tests are scored immediately, and you can print study guides that help you find the correct answers for any questions that you missed.

● CLICK TO START

Learning Objectives Checkpoints

Learning Objectives Checkpoints are designed to help you assess whether you have achieved the major learning objectives for this chapter. You can use paper and pencil or word processing software to complete most of the activities.

1. Create a timeline of the historical computer events described in Section A.

2. Supply examples of counting aids, manual calculators, and mechanical calculators, and then explain the differences that characterize each.

3. Define how the term *prototype* applies to the history of computing, and list at least five computer prototypes that were developed between 1937 and 1951.

4. Discuss the key developments that changed the personal computer's target market from a small group of hobbyists to a diverse population.

5. Describe the hardware, software, and operating system characteristics for each of the four generations of computers.

6. Make a list of the computer companies mentioned in the chapter. What was the contribution of each company to the evolution of computers, from the prototypes of the 1940s to the personal computers that we use today?

7. Describe the role of the computer and IT industries in today's global economy.

8. Define the terms *outsourcing* and *offshoring*, and then explain how they relate to the IT industry.

9. List five stages in the life cycle of a typical computer hardware product, then explain the similarities and differences that exist in the life cycle of a software product.

10. List the various marketing channels that exist in the computer industry, and explain the advantages and disadvantages of each channel for consumers.

11. Define the term *computer professional*, and list at least eight job titles that it encompasses. Summarize the current job outlook and working conditions for computer professionals.

12. Explain in your own words the focuses of computer engineering, computer science, information technology, software engineering, and information systems degree programs.

13. List four ways in which the Internet can figure into your job search. Suppose you have a version of your resume in DOCX, PDF, ASCII, and HTML formats. Explain the circumstances under which you would use each of these versions.

14. Make a list of the situations described in this chapter that required a computer professional to make an ethical decision. Make a list of the resources mentioned in this chapter that can help computer professionals resolve ethical issues.

15. List and briefly describe the major health risks that have been associated with computer use.

16. Draw a diagram showing ergonomic placement for equipment and furniture in a computer work area.

Study Tip: Make sure you can use your own words to correctly answer each of the purple focus questions that appear throughout the chapter.

Concept Map

Fill in the blanks to show the hierarchy of computer generations described in this chapter.

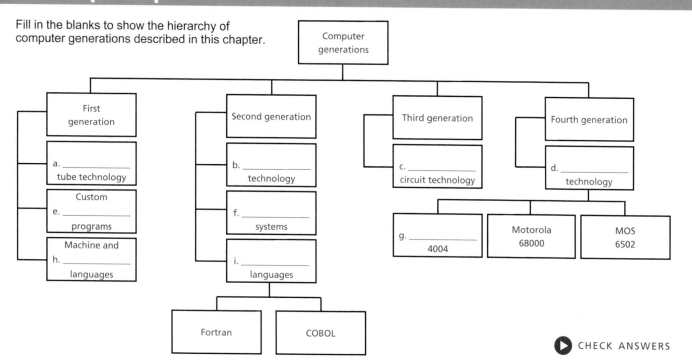

CHECK ANSWERS

10

Information Systems Analysis and Design

Chapter Contents

INFOWEBLINKS

You'll find updates for chapter
material by connecting to the
NP2013 Chapter 10 InfoWebLink.

Ⓦ CLICK TO CONNECT
www.infoweblinks.com/np2013/ch10

Learning Objectives

After reading this chapter, you will be able to answer the
following questions by completing the outcomes-based
Learning Objectives Checkpoints on page 607.

1. Why are information systems such an important aspect
   of everyday life?
2. How do information systems help organizations carry
   out their missions?
3. How do organizations use computers for strategic, tactical, and operational planning?
4. Can information systems solve structured, semi-
   structured, and unstructured problems?
5. How can information systems help organizations
   respond to competition?
6. What kinds of information systems do organizations
   typically use?
7. What is an SDLC?
8. How do systems analysts use the PIECES framework?
9. What kinds of tools do systems analysts use for scheduling information systems projects and documenting
   system requirements?
10. Are most large corporate information systems handled
    by a centralized mainframe computer?
11. Are most information systems custom built?
12. How dependable are corporate information systems?
13. How does a new information system go live without
    disrupting business operations?
14. Can you measure how well an information system is
    performing?
15. How vulnerable are information systems to threats that
    could cause them to fail?
16. Do corporations and government agencies do a good
    job of protecting data that pertains to individuals?

CourseMate

Visit the NP2013 CourseMate for this chapter's Pre-Quiz, Audio
Overview and Flashcards, Detailed Objectives, Chapter Quiz,
Online Games, and more labs.

Multimedia and Interactive Elements

When using the NP2013 interactive eBook, click the ▶ icons to
access multimedia resources.

Apply Your Knowledge The information in this chapter will give you the background to:

- Use a TPS, MIS, DSS, or expert system
- Participate in developing a new information system
- Understand DFDs and other types of diagrams used to model information systems
- Use documentation and help desk resources for an information system

- Create a simple decision support worksheet
- Remain alert for phishing attacks and other exploits to the information systems you commonly use
- Develop a realistic level of confidence in information systems operated by organizations, corporations, and government agencies

Try It!

HOW EFFECTIVE IS MY INFORMATION SYSTEM?

One of the first steps in the systems analysis process is to uncover problems and opportunities with computer systems currently in use. Systems analysts work on large organizational projects, but you can use some of their techniques to analyze your personal computer. Apply the PIECES framework to your computer system to complete the table below. You'll learn more about PIECES when you read the chapter.

P	Performance	List any tasks your computer performs slowly or software that doesn't respond as quickly as you would like.	
I	Information	List any examples of applications that don't provide you with the right information at the right time or in the most usable format.	
E	Economics	List any computing tasks that seem to cost too much.	
C	Control	List any computing tasks that make it difficult to control unauthorized access to your data.	
E	Efficiency	List any tasks that seem to take longer than necessary.	
S	Service	List any computing tasks that seem too complex or inconvenient.	

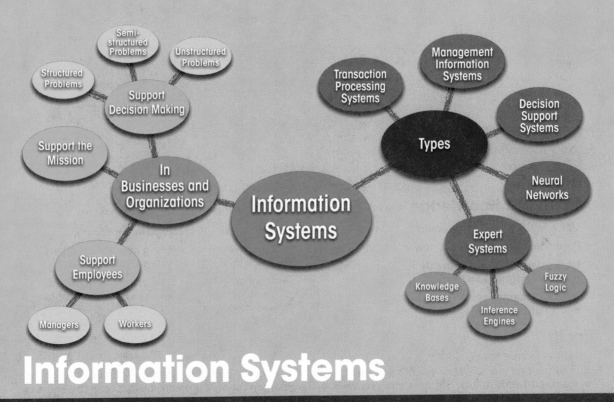

Information Systems

YOU ARE PROBABLY a member of an organization, such as a student club, fraternity or sorority, sports team, or political party. You also deal with all kinds of organizations every day: your school, stores, banks, and government agencies. Most organizations use information systems to operate more effectively, gather information, and accomplish tasks. In this section, you'll review some basic concepts about organizations and find out how information systems enhance organizational activities.

INFORMATION SYSTEMS IN ORGANIZATIONS

▶ **What is an information system?** An **information system** collects, stores, and processes data to provide useful, accurate, and timely information, typically within the context of an organization (Figure 10-1).

Although an information system does not necessarily have to be computerized, today most information systems rely on computers and communications networks to store, process, and transmit information with far more efficiency than would be possible using manual systems. In this textbook, the term *information system* refers to a system that uses computers and usually includes communications networks.

▶ **What's the official definition of *organization*?** An **organization** is a group of people working together to accomplish a goal. Organizations have accomplished amazing feats, such as sending astronauts into space, providing live television coverage of global events, and inventing freeze-dried ice cream. They also accomplish all kinds of day-to-day, routine tasks, such as offering banking services, selling merchandise, improving the environment, and policing neighborhoods.

Any organization that seeks profit by providing goods and services is called a **business**. Some organizations are formed to accomplish political, social, or charitable goals that do not include amassing profit. Such an organization is known as a **nonprofit organization**.

FIGURE 10-1

Information systems encompass many aspects of an organization.

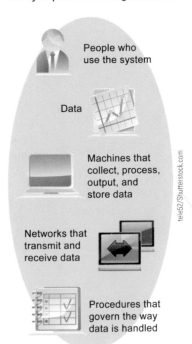

People who use the system

Data

Machines that collect, process, output, and store data

Networks that transmit and receive data

Procedures that govern the way data is handled

tele52/Shutterstock.com

▶ **What is a mission statement?** Every organization has a goal or plan that's referred to as its **mission**. All activities that take place in an organization, including those that involve computers, should contribute to this mission.

The written expression of an organization's mission is called a mission statement. A **mission statement** describes not only an organization's goals, but also the way in which those goals will be accomplished.

▶ **Who uses information systems?** An information system is used by the people in an organization and its customers. You've undoubtedly used many information systems—for example, when registering for classes, getting cash from an ATM, and purchasing merchandise on the Web. You might even work for a business or nonprofit organization where you access an information system as part of your job.

Not everyone in an organization uses an information system in the same way. An information system must support the needs of people who engage in many different organizational activities.

To coordinate the activities of employees, most organizations use a hierarchical structure. An **organizational chart**, such as the one in Figure 10-2, depicts the hierarchy of employees in an organization.

10

FIGURE 10-2

An Organizational Chart

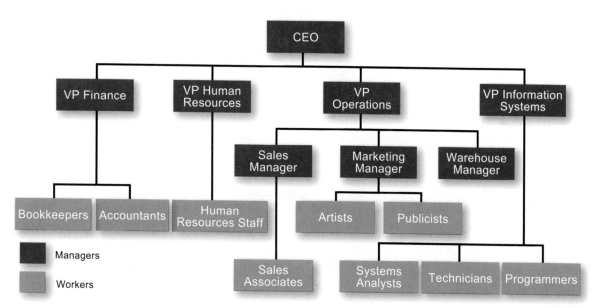

▶ **How are employees classified?** In many organizations, and most businesses, employees can be classified as workers or managers. **Workers** are the people who directly carry out the organization's mission. For example, they assemble cars, write newspaper articles, sell merchandise, answer telephones, lay bricks, cut trees, fix engines, or perform other types of labor. Workers routinely produce and collect data for information systems. For example, as checkout clerks ring up sales, their cash registers store each item in a database.

Managers determine organizational goals and plan how to achieve those goals. They approve new products, authorize new construction, and supervise workers. Executive managers plan an organization's long-range goals for profitability, market share, membership levels, and so on. This emphasis on long-range and future goals is referred to as **strategic planning**.

Mid-level managers are responsible for figuring out how to achieve long-range goals through sales, marketing, or new product development. They set incremental goals that can be achieved in a year or less—a process referred to as **tactical planning**.

Low-level managers are responsible for scheduling employees, ordering supplies, and other activities that make day-to-day operations run smoothly—a process referred to as **operational planning**. Information systems can provide some or all of the data needed for strategic, tactical, and operational planning.

▶ **How do information systems help the people in an organization?** An information system can help people perform their jobs more quickly and effectively by automating routine tasks, such as reordering inventory, taking customer orders, or sending out renewal notices. Information systems can also help people solve business and organizational problems.

One of the major functions of an information system is to help people make decisions in response to problems. According to Herbert Simon, who was well known for his insights into organizational behavior, the decision-making process has three phases, shown in Figure 10-3.

Reza Estakhrian
© Ryan McVay/PhotoDisc/Getty Images
© Antonio Mo/PhotoDisc/Getty Images

Phase 1: Recognize a problem or a need to make a decision.

Phase 2: Devise and analyze possible solutions to the problem.

Phase 3: Select an action or a solution.

FIGURE 10-3

The three decision-making phases are usually clear cut, leading to decisions that are objective, standardized, and based on factual data.

▶ **What kinds of problems need to be solved?** All problems are not alike, but they can be classified into three types: structured, semi-structured, and unstructured (Figure 10-4).

FIGURE 10-4

Problem Classifications

Type of Problem	Example	Methodology
A **structured problem** is an everyday, run-of-the-mill, routine problem. When you make decisions in response to structured problems, the procedure for obtaining the best solution is known, the objective is clearly defined, and the information necessary to make the decision is easy to identify.	Which customers should receive overdue notices?	The information for this decision is usually stored in a file cabinet or computer system. The method for reaching a solution is to look for customers with outstanding balances, and then check whether the due dates for their payments fall before today's date.
A **semi-structured problem** has a known procedure for arriving at a solution; however, the process might involve some degree of subjective judgment. Also, some of the information regarding the problem might not be available, might lack precision, or might be uncertain.	How many mountain bikes should a store stock for the holidays?	The decision can be based on the previous year's sales; but because future consumer spending is uncertain, determining the appropriate amount of holiday inventory might require some guesswork.
An **unstructured problem** requires human intuition as the basis for finding a solution. Information relevant to the problem might be missing, and few parts of the solution can be tackled using concrete models. If experts are presented with a problem, but they disagree on a solution, it is likely an unstructured problem.	Should Saks Fifth Avenue stock Japanese-inspired evening gowns?	The purchasing agent for women's clothing makes this decision based on her intuition of customer taste and fashion trends.

10

▶ Can an information system solve all three types of problems? Traditionally, information systems have contributed most to solving structured problems, but tools have emerged to help people tackle semi-structured and unstructured problems as well. Despite these tools and the data they provide, many semi-structured and unstructured problems continue to be solved based on "guesstimates."

An information system's ability to assist with problem solving and decision making depends on the data it collects and makes available. Some information systems collect and store **internal information** generated by the organization itself. Other information systems store or provide access to **external information** generated by sources outside the organization. Later in this section, you'll learn how different types of information systems deal with internal and external information.

▶ Do organizations require different kinds of information systems? Because organizations have different missions and face different problems, they require different kinds of information systems. A small business might require a basic information system for accounting, inventory, and payroll. A large business might require an **enterprise information system** that supports a variety of business activities such as inventory management, point-of-sale cash registers, e-commerce, payroll, and managerial planning.

An information system or its components can be classified as a transaction processing system, management information system, decision support system, or expert system.

TRANSACTION PROCESSING SYSTEMS

▶ What's a transaction? In an information system context, a **transaction** is an exchange between two parties that is recorded and stored in a computer system. When you order a product at a Web site, buy merchandise in a store, or withdraw cash from an ATM, you are involved in a transaction.

▶ What is a transaction processing system? A **transaction processing system** (TPS) provides a way to collect, process, store, display, modify, or cancel transactions. Most transaction processing systems allow many transactions to be entered simultaneously.

The data collected by a TPS is usually stored in databases, and can be used to produce a regularly scheduled set of reports, such as monthly bills, weekly paychecks, annual inventory summaries, and daily manufacturing schedules. Figure 10-5 lists some examples of business transaction processing systems.

FIGURE 10-5

Business Transaction Processing Systems

Payroll

Accounting

Airline reservations

Inventory

Point of sale

Cellular phone billing

In the 1970s, early transaction processing systems, such as banking and payroll applications, used **batch processing** to collect and hold a group of transactions until the end of a day or pay period, when the entire batch was processed. Batch processing proceeds without human intervention, until all transactions are completed or until an error occurs.

In contrast to batch processing, most modern transaction processing systems use **online processing**—a real-time method in which each transaction is processed as it is entered. Such a system is often referred to as an **OLTP system** (online transaction processing system).

OLTP uses a **commit or rollback strategy** to ensure that each transaction is processed correctly. This strategy is crucial because most transactions require a sequence of steps, and every step must succeed for the transaction to be completed.

▶ **How does commit or rollback work?** If you withdraw cash from an ATM, the bank's computer must make sure your account contains sufficient funds before it deducts the withdrawal from your account and allows the ATM to deliver cash. If the ATM is out of cash, however, the transaction fails, and the withdrawal should not be deducted from your account.

A TPS can commit to a transaction and permanently update database records only if every step of the transaction can be successfully processed. If even one step fails, however, the entire transaction fails and a rollback returns the records to their original state. Figure 10-6 diagrams the processes that take place in a typical TPS, and the video that accompanies the figure provides additional information about commit or rollback.

FIGURE 10-6

A transaction processing system is characterized by its ability to:

▶ Collect, display, and modify transactions

▶ Store transactions

▶ List transactions

⏵ Scroll down and start the video to see how a TPS processes an ATM transaction.

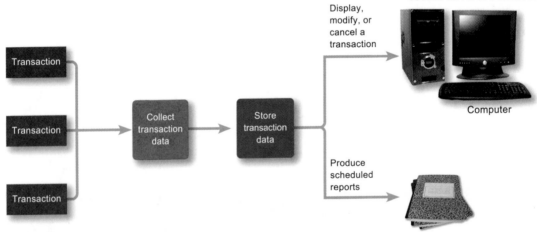

▶ **What are the limitations of transaction processing systems?** Although a TPS excels at maintaining transaction data entered by clerical personnel and online customers, its reporting capabilities are limited. A typical TPS generates **detail reports**, which provide a basic record of completed transactions. However, managers need more sophisticated reports to help them understand and analyze data. These reports are usually created by a management information system.

10

MANAGEMENT INFORMATION SYSTEMS

▶ **What is a management information system?** The term *management information system* is used in two contexts. It can be a synonym for the term *information system*, or it can refer to a specific category or type of information system.

We'll use the term **management information system** (MIS, pronounced "em-eye-ess") in this second context to refer to a type of information system that uses the data collected by a transaction processing system, and manipulates that data to create reports used by managers to make routine business decisions in response to structured problems. As Figure 10-7 shows, an MIS is characterized by the production of periodic reports that managers use for structured and routine tasks.

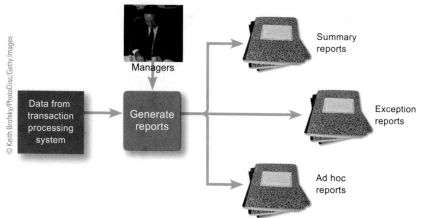

© Keith Brofsky/PhotoDisc/Getty Images

One of the major goals of an MIS is to increase the efficiency of managerial activity. Different levels of management have different information needs. In response to these different needs, an MIS can produce scheduled reports or ad hoc reports. An **ad hoc report** (sometimes called a demand report) is a customized report, generated to supply specific information not available in scheduled reports. These reports are normally used by upper-level managers to gather data pertaining to specific business problems.

Scheduled reports, such as monthly summaries and exception reports, are used by various levels of management, follow a fixed format, and are produced according to a preset timetable. A **summary report** combines, groups, or totals data. For example, a summary report might show total annual sales for the past five years. Summary reports are useful in tactical and strategic planning. An **exception report** contains information that is outside normal or acceptable ranges (Figure 10-8).

FIGURE 10-7

A management information system is characterized by its ability to:

▶ Produce routine and on-demand reports

▶ Provide useful information for managerial activities

▶ Increase managerial efficiency

▶ Provide information used for structured, routine decisions

⏵ Use your interactive eBook to find out how ATM data would be used in an MIS.

FIGURE 10-8

Exception reports help managers take action, such as reordering inventory. Managers also use exception reports to analyze potential problems, such as continued inventory shortages or an excessive number of customers making late payments.

```
              Low Inventory-May 30
   Item#  Description   Minimum    Current     Vendor
                        Quantity   Quantity
   J506   Qualo-bag        12         10        REI
   05D-8  Sm. Backpack     48         22        REI
   B99A   Med. Backpack    48         40        REI
   L2020  Canteen          24          3        ZB Ind.
   D2990  Flashlight       36          8        ZB Ind.
   6-334  Tent stakes     112         24        Granot
```

▶ How does an MIS differ from a TPS? Whereas a TPS simply records data, an MIS can consolidate data by grouping and summarizing it. For example, most modern library systems contain both a TPS and an MIS, which serve different functions, as Figure 10-9 explains.

FIGURE 10-9

A library's TPS performs different functions than its MIS.

TPS

Purpose: Track books by maintaining a database of titles, checkout dates, and so forth.
Users: Library patrons locate books and librarians check books in and out.
Key characteristic: Manage transactions as books are checked in and out.

MIS

Purpose: Provide librarians with summary and exception reports needed to manage the collection.
Users: Librarians request and analyze reports.
Key characteristics: Summary reports indicate how many books are checked out each day, each week, each month, or each year; exception reports list long-overdue books.

▶ What are the limitations of a management information system? A traditional MIS is based on the data collected by a transaction processing system. Sometimes, however, the MIS software that generates reports is not flexible enough to provide managers with the exact information needed. Further, an MIS usually cannot create models or projections—two important strategic planning tools. Today's competitive business environment calls for more sophisticated data manipulation tools, such as those that decision support systems provide.

DECISION SUPPORT SYSTEMS

▶ What's a decision support system? A **decision support system** (DSS) helps people make decisions by directly manipulating data, analyzing data from external sources, generating statistical projections, and creating data models of various scenarios. A DSS provides tools for routine decisions, non-routine decisions, structured problems, and even semi-structured problems in which a decision might be based on imprecise data or require guesstimates.

A special type of decision support system, called an **executive information system** (EIS), is designed to provide senior managers with information relevant to strategic management activities—such as setting policies, planning, and preparing budgets—based on information from internal and external databases.

A decision support system derives its name from the fact that it *supports* the decision maker; that is, it provides the tools a decision maker needs to analyze data. A DSS does not make decisions, however. That task remains the responsibility of the human decision maker.

Decision makers use DSSs to design decision models and make queries. A **decision model** is a numerical representation of a realistic situation, such as a cash-flow model of a business that shows how income adds to cash accounts and expenses deplete those accounts. A **decision query** is a question or set of instructions describing data that must be gathered to make a decision.

A DSS typically includes modeling tools, such as spreadsheets, so that managers can create a numerical representation of a situation and explore what-if alternatives. DSS statistical tools help managers study trends before making decisions. In addition, a DSS usually includes data from an organization's transaction processing system, and it might include or access external data, such as stock market reports, as shown in Figure 10-10.

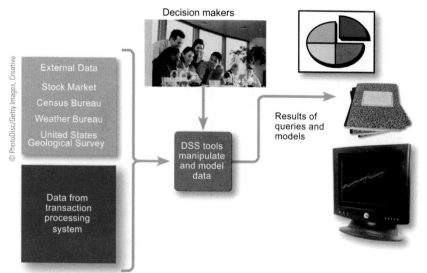

Decision makers

Results of queries and models

© PhotoDisc/Getty Images, Creative

External Data
Stock Market
Census Bureau
Weather Bureau
United States
Geological Survey

Data from transaction processing system

DSS tools manipulate and model data

FIGURE 10-10

A decision support system is characterized by its ability to:

⯈ Support, rather than replace, managerial judgment

⯈ Create decision models

⯈ Improve quality of decisions

⯈ Help solve semi-structured problems

⯈ Incorporate external data

⯈ Use your interactive eBook to learn how a DSS helps decision makers at a fast food franchise.

⯈ **What kinds of decisions can a DSS handle?** A DSS can be used to tackle diverse problems because it contains a good selection of decision support tools. Directors of a disaster-relief organization might use a DSS to set fund-raising targets based on internal data from its accounting system and previous donations recorded by its TPS system.

A disaster relief DSS can also incorporate external information based on national fund-raising trends and current economic statistics pertaining to employment and disposable income. This data can be manipulated to examine what-if scenarios, such as "What if donations continue to decrease, but we are faced with another disaster similar to the 2011 tsunami in Japan?"

⯈ **What are the limitations of a DSS?** A DSS helps people manipulate the data needed to make a decision but does not actually make a decision. Instead, a person must analyze the data and reach a decision. A DSS is not a substitute for human judgment. Therefore, a DSS is appropriate in situations where it is used by trained professionals.

Many organizations, however, would like an alternative in which not every decision needs to be made by a highly paid expert. The major limitation of most decision support systems is they require users to have in-depth knowledge of the business problem that underlies the decision, plus a good background on what-if models and statistics.

When organizations want an information system to make decisions without direct guidance from an experienced decision maker, they turn to expert systems.

EXPERT SYSTEMS AND NEURAL NETWORKS

▶ **What is an expert system?** An **expert system**, sometimes referred to as a knowledge-based system, is a computer system designed to analyze data and produce a recommendation, diagnosis, or decision based on a set of facts and rules, as shown in Figure 10-11.

The facts and rules for an expert system are usually derived by interviewing one or more experts, and then incorporated into a **knowledge base**. The knowledge base is stored in a computer file and can be manipulated by software called an **inference engine**. The process of designing, entering, and testing the rules in an expert system is referred to as **knowledge engineering**.

▶ **What kinds of decisions can an expert system make?** An expert system is not a general-purpose problem solver or decision maker. Each expert system is designed to make decisions in a particular area or domain.

An expert system created for use at the Campbell Soup Company captured the knowledge of an expert cooking-vat operator to help less experienced employees troubleshoot problems that might arise during the cooking and canning process.

Other expert systems have been developed to locate mineral deposits, diagnose blood diseases, evaluate corporate financial statements, underwrite complex insurance policies, order a customized personal computer, and recommend stock purchases.

▶ **How are expert systems built?** Expert systems can be created with a computer programming language, but an expert system shell offers a set of tools designed to simplify the development process. An **expert system shell** is a software tool containing an inference engine and a user interface that developers use to enter facts and rules for a knowledge base. An expert system shell also has tools for testing a knowledge base to make certain it produces accurate decisions.

▶ **Can an expert system deal with uncertainty?** Expert systems are designed to deal with data that is imprecise, or with problems that have more than one solution. Using a technique called **fuzzy logic**, an expert system can deal with imprecise data by working with confidence levels.

Suppose an expert system is helping you identify a whale you spotted off the California coast. The expert system asks, "Did you see a dorsal fin?" You're not sure. You think you saw one, but it could have been a shadow. If the expert system is using fuzzy logic, it will let you respond with something like "I'm 85% certain I saw a dorsal fin." Based on the confidence level of your answer to this and other questions, the expert system might be able to tell you that it is "pretty sure," maybe 98% confident, that you saw a gray whale.

▶ **How does an expert system work?** When it is time to make a decision, the inference engine begins analyzing the available data by

FIGURE 10-11

A simple expert system, such as this automechanic expert, collects information about car trouble by asking questions. Answers are analyzed according to a set of facts and rules to produce a repair recommendation.

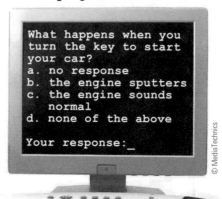

What happens when you turn the key to start your car?
a. no response
b. the engine sputters
c. the engine sounds normal
d. none of the above

Your response:_

© Media Technics

RULE 1:
IF you turn the key and there is no response,
THEN the battery is dead and you should recharge the battery.

RULE 2:
IF you turn the key and the engine sputters,
THEN you might be out of gas and you should check the fuel gauge.

RULE 3:
IF you turn the key and the engine sounds normal,
THEN the transmission might be malfunctioning. Check the position of the shift lever.

RULE 4:
IF none of the above choices applies to the problem,
THEN the expert system will ask additional questions.

following the rules in the knowledge base. If the expert system needs additional data, it checks external databases, looks for the data in a transaction processing system, or asks the user to answer questions. Figure 10-12 outlines the flow of information in an expert system and summarizes its capabilities.

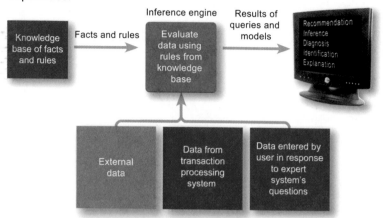

10

FIGURE 10-12

An expert system is characterized by its ability to:

▶ Replicate the reasoning of a human expert

▶ Work with internal or external data

▶ Produce a recommendation or decision

▶ Watch how an expert system determines if a student should be admitted to graduate school.

▶ Is it possible to build an expert system without an expert?

An expert system begins with a set of facts and rules. But if the rules are not known, a computer can "learn" how to make decisions based on hundreds or thousands of lightning-fast trial-and-error attempts. A **neural network** uses computer circuitry to simulate the way a brain might process information, learn, and remember.

A neural network could be connected to a digital projector that displays photos of people's faces. Which faces are males and which are females? The neural network begins with a list of criteria with no values attached. "Hair length" might be one criterion, but the neural network is not programmed to expect that females usually have longer hair than men. Based on the evidence, a neural network begins to establish its own criteria—its own rules—about the data.

Neural networks have been successfully implemented in many business and financial applications where identification and trend analysis are important. A useful application of neural networks takes place in video surveillance systems, such as one that analyzes video footage of busy central London streets, watching for faces that match those of known terrorists (Figure 10-13).

FIGURE 10-13

Neural networks have been developed for a variety of applications, including surveillance.

© Jeremy Horner/CORBIS

QuickCheck

1. Effective [_____] systems are designed to support goals that help an organization carry out its mission statement.

2. Executive managers typically engage in [_____] planning, whereas mid-level managers are responsible for [_____] planning.

3. [_____] processing holds a group of transactions for later processing, whereas [_____] processing handles each transaction as it is entered.

4. A(n) [_____] collects data from a TPS and uses it to create scheduled and ad hoc reports. (Hint: Use the acronym.)

5. A(n) [_____] system uses an inference engine to process rules and produce a diagnosis, recommendation, or decision.

▶ CHECK ANSWERS

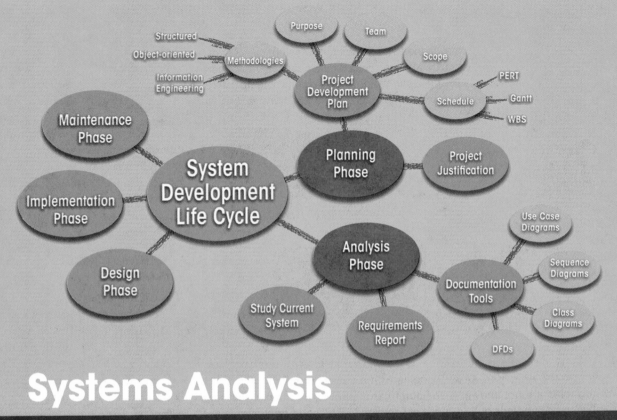

Systems Analysis

WHETHER YOU ARE PART OF a team that is developing a complex corporate information system, or you are developing a small information system for your own use, you will be more likely to succeed if you analyze the purpose of the information system, carefully design the system, test it thoroughly, and document its features. In this section of the chapter, you'll learn about information system planning and analysis.

SYSTEM DEVELOPMENT LIFE CYCLE

▶ **What is a system development life cycle?** An information system progresses through several phases as it is developed, used, and finally retired. These phases encompass a **system development life cycle**, usually referred to as the SDLC. Figure 10-14 illustrates a typical sequence of SDLC phases.

FIGURE 10-14

System Development Life Cycle

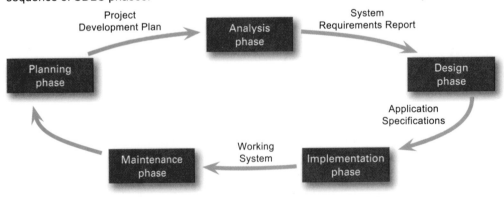

▶ **How does the SDLC apply to systems analysis and design?** The SDLC provides a general outline of how an information system evolves. **Systems analysis and design** is a discipline that focuses on developing information systems according to the phases of an SDLC.

The scope of systems analysis and design encompasses the people, procedures, computers, communications networks, and software involved with handling information in an organization. It is much broader than software engineering, which is one of the main tasks later in the SDLC.

PLANNING PHASE

▶ How does an information system project begin? Creating an information system can be compared to building a house. You don't just grab a hammer and start nailing pieces of wood together. It is important to have a plan. Initial plans for an information system are developed during the planning phase.

▶ What does the planning phase entail? The **planning phase** for an information system project includes the activities listed in Figure 10-15. The goal of these activities is to create a **Project Development Plan**. Before the project proceeds beyond the planning phase, the Project Development Plan is usually reviewed and approved by management. This planning document includes:

▶ A short description of the project, including its scope

▶ A justification for the project, which includes an estimate of the project costs and potential financial benefits

▶ A list of project team participants

▶ A schedule for the project, including an outline of its phases

▶ Who supervises the project? Depending on the scope of the problem and the expertise of the professional staff, an information systems project can be managed by an in-house information technology department or outsourced to a development firm.

A system development project team, or project team for short, is assigned to analyze and develop an information system. The project team has a leader, sometimes referred to as the project manager, who supervises the project team's work flow and output.

▶ Who participates in the process of building an information system? The composition of a project team depends on the scope of the project. Large and complex projects tend to have sizeable project teams, and a majority of team members are systems analysts or other computer professionals. Smaller projects tend to have fewer members on the project team, and a higher percentage of team members are likely to be users rather than computer professionals.

In addition to the project team, other members of an organization might be asked to participate in various phases of the project. A widely accepted technique called **joint application design** (JAD) is based on the idea that the best information systems are designed when end users and systems analysts work together on a project as equal partners.

JAD provides a structured methodology for planning and holding a series of meetings, called JAD sessions, in which users and analysts jointly identify problems and look for solutions.

FIGURE 10-15

10

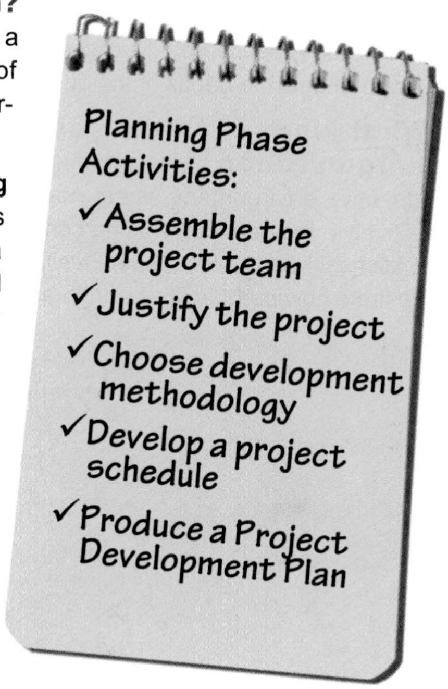

Planning Phase Activities:

✓ Assemble the project team

✓ Justify the project

✓ Choose development methodology

✓ Develop a project schedule

✓ Produce a Project Development Plan

TERMINOLOGY NOTE

As described in Chapter 9, systems analysts are responsible for analyzing information requirements, designing new information systems, and supervising their implementation. Systems analysts also create specifications for application software, and then give those specifications to computer programmers, who, in turn, create software to meet those specifications.

❱ **Why are new information systems developed?** The justification for a new information system usually emerges from a serious problem with the current system, a threat to the organization's success, or an opportunity to improve an organization's products or services through technology.

If the current information system is manual, for example, it might not be cost effective, efficient, or competitive. Computerized information systems can become obsolete when hardware becomes outdated, or when the software no longer meets the needs of the business mission.

❱ **What kinds of threats and opportunities can affect an organization?** Most organizations exist in a rapidly changing and competitive environment, where many opportunities and threats can be effectively handled only by using computers. A well-known business analyst, Michael Porter, created the Five Forces model, shown in Figure 10-16, to illustrate how opportunities and threats can affect an organization.

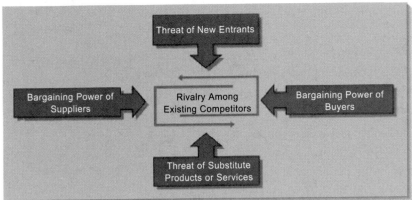

FIGURE 10-16

Michael Porter's Five Forces model illustrates the factors that affect competition among business rivals. ▶ Watch the video to find out how these forces affect such diverse products as videogames, fur coats, and televisions.

❱ **How can an information system help an organization respond to threats and opportunities?** To be successful in its mission, an organization must respond effectively to opportunities and threats. An organization has a choice of three fundamental responses:

❱ Make improvements. An organization can become better at what it does by cutting costs, lowering prices, improving its products, offering better customer service, and so on. Computers often provide ways to make businesses run more efficiently, and they can supply timely information that helps improve customer service. For example, to deal with rapidly fluctuating oil prices and competition from other oil companies, Hess Corporation installed an information system designed to maximize profitability by supporting instantaneous price changes across the entire enterprise, including more than 1,300 retail gas stations.

❱ Change the industry. An organization can change the nature of an industry. Computers and related technologies, such as the Internet, often make such changes possible. For example, Amazon.com pioneered the idea of selling books on the Web, which was a major change to an industry that sold books from mall-based stores.

❱ Create new products. An organization can create a new product, such as flavored potato chips, or a new service, such as overnight package delivery. Although creativity and invention usually spring from the minds of people, computers can contribute to research and development efforts by collecting and analyzing data, helping inventors create models and explore simulations, and so on.

A new information system might be only one aspect of a larger plan to evolve an organization into a stronger, more competitive entity. The business community has embraced several business practices, summarized in Figure 10-17, that use information systems as a key component for transforming organizations.

FIGURE 10-17

Business Practices Glossary

BI (Business Intelligence): An integrated set of technologies and procedures used to collect and analyze data pertaining to sales, production, and other internal operations of a business in order to make better business decisions.

BPR (Business Process Reengineering): An ongoing iterative process that helps businesses rethink and radically redesign practices to improve performance, as measured by cost, quality, service, and speed.

CRM (Customer Relationship Management): A technique for increasing profitability by improving the relationship between a company and its customers. It helps a business increase sales by identifying, acquiring, and retaining customers. It can also cut costs by automating sales, marketing, and customer service. Information systems make it possible to collect and process the large volumes of customer data required for CRM and to efficiently transform this data into useful information.

EAI (Enterprise Application Integration): The use of networked, compatible software modules and databases to provide unrestricted sharing of data and business processes throughout an organization; for example, between CRM and BI systems.

EDI (Electronic Data Interchange): The ability to transfer data between different companies using networks, such as the Internet, which enables companies to buy, sell, and trade information.

ERP (Enterprise Resource Planning): A system of business management that integrates all facets, or resources, of a business, including planning, manufacturing, sales, and marketing. An information system running special ERP software is a key technology that allows a business to track the information necessary to monitor its resource use.

JIT (Just In Time): A manufacturing system in which the parts needed to construct a finished product are produced or arrive at the assembly site just when they are needed. JIT tends to reduce costs by eliminating substantial warehousing costs and obsolete parts.

MRP (Manufacturing Resource Planning): Calculates and maintains an optimum manufacturing plan based on master production schedules, sales forecasts, inventory status, open orders, and bills of material. If properly implemented, it improves cash flow and increases profitability. MRP provides businesses with the ability to be proactive rather than reactive in the management of their inventory levels and material flow.

TQM (Total Quality Management): A technique initiated by top management that involves all employees and all departments, and focuses on quality assurance in every product and service offered to customers.

10

▶ **How does the project team identify problems and opportunities?** Justifying a project often involves identifying problems and opportunities within an organization's current information system. By eliminating problems and taking advantage of opportunities, an organization can become more competitive.

Project team members can identify problems and opportunities using a variety of techniques, such as interviews and data analysis. For example, James Wetherbe's **PIECES framework** helps classify problems in an information system. Each letter of PIECES stands for a potential problem, as shown in Figure 10-18.

FIGURE 10-18

Wetherbe's PIECES

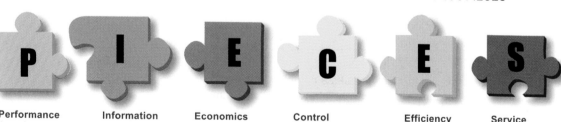

Performance
A performance problem means that an information system does not respond quickly enough to users or takes too long to complete processing tasks.

Information
An information problem means that users don't receive the right information at the right time in a usable format.

Economics
An economics problem means that the system costs too much to operate or use.

Control
A control problem means that information is available to unauthorized users, or that authorized users are not given the authority to make decisions based on the information they receive.

Efficiency
An efficiency problem means that too many resources are used to collect, process, store, and distribute information.

Service
A service problem means that the system is too difficult or inconvenient to use.

What is a system development methodology? As part of the planning phase, the project team selects one or more methodologies that provide structure for the development effort. Earlier in the chapter you learned that the SDLC delineates the phases of system development.

A system development methodology specifies what takes place in each phase; it encompasses the activities, procedures, methods, best practices, deliverables, and automated tools that system developers follow to complete the SDLC. In short, a system development methodology guides developers through the phases of system development.

There are many standard system development methodologies. **Structured methodology** focuses on the processes that take place within an information system. **Information engineering methodology** focuses on the data an information system collects before working out ways to process that data. **Object-oriented methodology** treats an information system as a collection of objects that interact to accomplish tasks.

How is the project schedule developed? Project scheduling begins in the planning phase, but stretches throughout the entire project. Project managers organize the work into tasks and milestones, which can be scheduled and assigned. As tasks are completed, the schedule is updated and adjusted. Industry standard tools for scheduling and project management include PERT, WBS, and Gantt charts.

PERT (Program Evaluation and Review Technique) is a method for analyzing the time needed to complete each project task and identifying the minimum time needed to complete the total project. A PERT diagram uses arrows to map the sequence of tasks in a project (Figure 10-19).

FIGURE 10-19

PERT chart elements are arranged to show which tasks must be completed before subsequent dependent tasks can begin. By tracing paths through the diagram, project managers can determine the best-case and worst-case scheduling scenarios. The longest path through the tasks, shown in purple, is called the critical path.

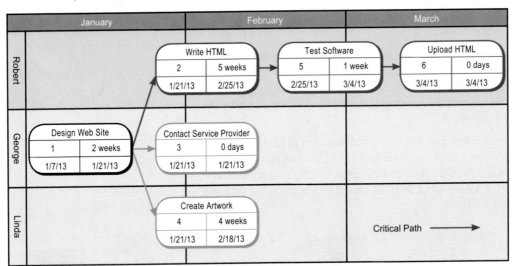

A **WBS** (work breakdown structure) breaks a complex task into a series of subtasks. The hierarchy of tasks can be shown as a hierarchical diagram, but it can also be formatted as a simple outline. A WBS can be activity-oriented to list tasks, or deliverable-oriented to list project milestones (Figure 10-20 on the next page).

A **Gantt chart** uses bars to show the timing of development tasks as they occur over time. Each bar on the chart represents a task; the length of a bar indicates the task's expected duration (Figure 10-21 on the next page).

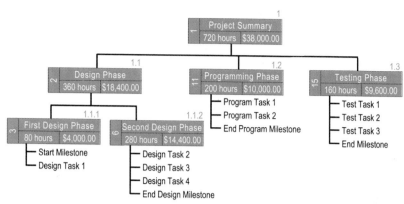

FIGURE 10-20

The top element on a WBS chart represents the entire project. At the next level, the project is broken down into subtasks, and those tasks are in turn broken down into even smaller tasks.

10

▶ Do computers offer tools for planning phase activities? Project management software is an effective tool for planning and scheduling. It helps managers track and visualize the complex interactions between tasks using tools such as Gantt charts, PERT, and WBS. Popular project management offerings include open source software, such as Open Workbench, and commercial software, such as Microsoft Project.

FIGURE 10-21

Gantt charts indicate the duration of each task. They can also show milestones and compare planned completion dates with actual completion dates.

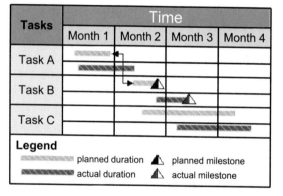

ANALYSIS PHASE

▶ What happens in the analysis phase? The analysis phase begins after the project team selects a development methodology, draws up the Project Development Plan, and receives permission to proceed from management. The goal of the **analysis phase** is to produce a list of requirements for a new or revised information system. Tasks for the analysis phase are listed in Figure 10-22.

▶ Why study the current system? Most new information systems are designed to replace a system or process that is already in place. It is important to study the current system to understand its strengths and weaknesses before designing a new system.

FIGURE 10-22

▶ How does the project team discover what happens in the current system? Some members of the project team might have first-hand experience with the current system. They can often provide an overview of the system and identify key features, strengths, and weaknesses. To obtain additional information about the current system, project team members can observe the system in action and interview people who use the system.

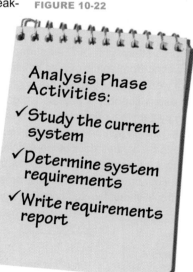

▶ How does the project team determine what the new system should do? System requirements are the criteria for successfully solving problems identified in an information system. These requirements guide the design and implementation for a new or updated information system. They also serve as an evaluation checklist at the end of the development project, so they are sometimes called **success factors**. A new or updated information system should meet requirements defined by the project team.

The project team determines requirements by interviewing users and studying successful information systems that solve problems similar to those in the current system. Another way to determine requirements is to construct a prototype as an experimental or trial version of an information system.

Often the prototype is not a fully functioning system because it is designed to demonstrate only selected features that might be incorporated into a new information system. A systems analyst shows the prototype to users, who evaluate which features of the prototype are important for the new information system.

▶ **What does the project team do with system requirements?** After the project team studies the current system and then determines what the new system should do, system requirements are incorporated into a document called a **System Requirements Report** that describes the objectives for an information system.

Figure 10-23 outlines the content of a System Requirements Report, which includes narrative descriptions and diagrams showing the new system's users, data, processes, objects, and reports. When management approves the report, the project can move on to the design phase.

DOCUMENTATION TOOLS

▶ **How does the project team document system requirements?** The project team can use a variety of tools to diagram the current system and produce documentation that is also useful in later phases of the SDLC. Documentation tools vary according to development methodology. For example, a project team following a structured methodology will use different documentation tools than a project team using object-oriented methodology.

To understand some of the most popular documentation tools, consider a project to develop an information system for a for-profit organization that offers business seminars and workshops throughout the world. The new information system must keep track of workshop schedules and student enrollments. Students have to be able to select workshops, and instructors must be supplied with a roster of students.

▶ **What are structured documentation tools?** The core documentation tool for project teams using structured methodology is the **data flow diagram** (DFD), which graphically illustrates how data moves through an information system.

You can think of a DFD as a map that traces the possible paths for data traveling from entities (such as students) to processes (such as enrolling in a workshop) or storage areas (such as databases). In DFD terminology, an **external entity** is a person, organization, or device outside the information system that originates or receives data. A **data store** is a filing cabinet, disk, or tape that holds data. A **process** is a manual or computerized routine that changes data by performing a calculation, updating information, sorting a list, and so on. An arrow symbolizes a **data flow** and indicates how data travels from entities to processes and data stores. Each of these elements is represented on a DFD by a symbol, as shown in Figure 10-24.

FIGURE 10-23

A System Requirements Report describes the objectives for a new information system.

Title Page

Table of Contents

Executive Summary

Introduction
▶ Project background
▶ Problems and opportunities that prompted the project
▶ Brief description of the current system

Findings
▶ Description of the scope of the proposed project
▶ List of general requirements for the proposed information system

Recommendations
The rationale for developing or not developing the proposed system

Time and Cost Estimates
An estimate of the time and cost required to implement additional phases of the project

Expected Benefits
A description of the benefits that can be expected if the project team's recommendations are followed

Appendices
Diagrams, interviews, and other documentation gathered by the project team

FIGURE 10-24

Data Flow Diagram Symbols

Student		Workshop enrollment	Workshop title
An external entity is represented by a square labeled with a noun.	A process is represented by a rounded rectangle, which is numbered and labeled with a verb phrase.	A data store is represented by an open rectangle labeled with the name of a data file.	A data flow is represented by an arrow labeled with a description of the data.

▶ **What does a DFD look like?** In a completed DFD, data flow arrows show the path of data to and from external entities, data stores, and processes. Figure 10-25 explains how to read a DFD.

FIGURE 10-25

To read a DFD, begin at any one of the square entities and follow the arrows to trace the flow of data. The label on each data flow arrow identifies the data that moves through the system. Arrows moving into a process indicate input data. Arrows that emerge from a process show output. Rectangular data stores represent data that is stored in databases.

10

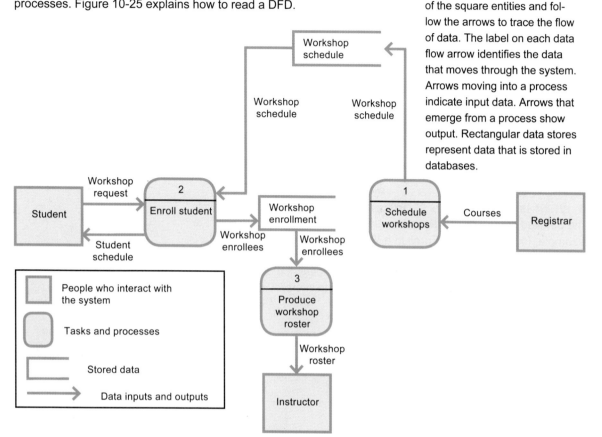

▶ **How do documentation tools differ for object-oriented analysis and design?** Structured documentation tools such as DFDs help analysts decide how to design databases and write applications that allow people to interact with those databases. In contrast, object-oriented design tools provide blueprints for creating data objects and the routines that allow people to interact with those objects. The current standard for object-oriented documentation is referred to as **UML** (Unified Modeling Language). Three of the most frequently used UML tools include use case diagrams, sequence diagrams, and class diagrams.

▶ **What is a use case diagram?** A **use case diagram** documents the users of an information system and the functions they perform. In object-oriented jargon, the people who use the system are called **actors**. Any task an actor performs is called a **use case**. Figure 10-26 shows a simple use case diagram for a workshop registration system.

▶ **What is the composition of an object?** A key element of object-oriented development is defining objects. In the registration example, a student interacts with two objects: a Workshop object and a Section object. A **class diagram** provides the name of each object, a list of each object's attributes, a list of methods, and an indication of the cardinality between objects. An attribute is simply any data element that is stored as part of an object. A method is any behavior that an object is capable of

FIGURE 10-26

A use case diagram for a workshop registration system depicts two use cases—one in which a student enrolls in a workshop and one in which the student drops the workshop.

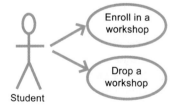

performing. Cardinality refers to the number of associations that can exist between objects. You'll find detailed definitions of object-oriented terms, such as classes, attributes, and methods, in Chapter 12. Figure 10-27 illustrates a class diagram for the workshop registration system.

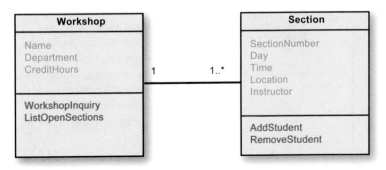

FIGURE 10-27

This class diagram shows each object's attributes (in green) and methods (in blue). The cardinality between objects (indicated by 1 and 1..*) means that each workshop may have one or more sections.

▶ **What is a sequence diagram?** A **sequence diagram** depicts the detailed sequence of interactions that take place for a use case. For example, for the use case Enroll in a Workshop, a student might inquire which workshops are offered and then select a workshop based on a list of open workshop sections. Figure 10-28 shows a sequence diagram for the Enroll in a Workshop use case and explains how to interpret it.

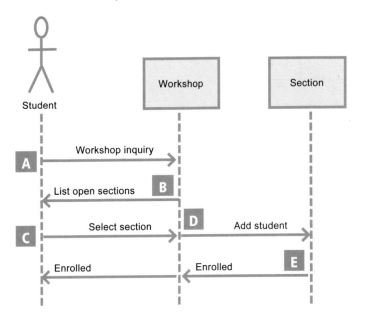

FIGURE 10-28

Sequence Diagram for the *Enroll in a Workshop* Use Case

A A student enters the title or number of a workshop that he or she wants to take.

B The Workshop object displays a list of sections that are open.

C The student selects a section.

D The student is added to the workshop roster for the section.

E The student receives confirmation of the enrollment.

▶ **Are diagramming tools computerized?** Maintaining documentation can become a complex task as the project progresses and system requirements are revised. A **CASE tool** (computer-aided software engineering tool) is a software application designed for documenting system requirements, diagramming current and proposed information systems, scheduling development tasks, and developing computer programs.

Commercial CASE tools such as Visible Analyst and open source tools such as ArgoUML automate many of the routine housekeeping tasks required for systems analysis and design, such as changing the name of a data element on one diagram and making sure the change is reflected in other diagrams and program code. Figure 10-29 on the next page explains some of the features of CASE tools.

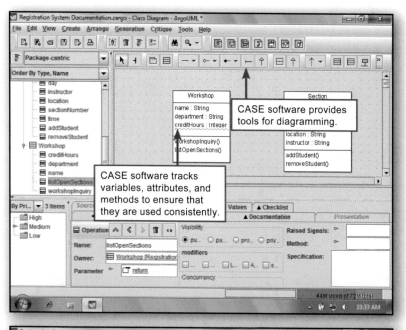

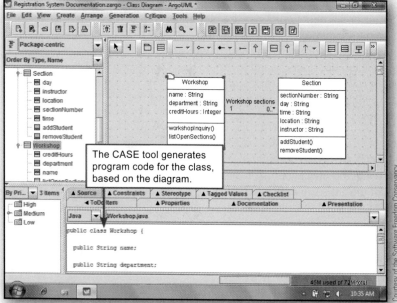

FIGURE 10-29

CASE tools help project team members manage all the details of system documentation. The top screen shows how the CASE tool helps developers create diagrams. The bottom screen shows how the CASE tool generates program code. ▶ See how CASE software is used to document a course registration system.

10

QuickCheck   SECTION B

1. In the planning phase, one of the main goals is to produce a Project [＿＿＿＿＿＿] Plan.

2. In Wetherbe's PIECES framework, the "S" represents a(n) [＿＿＿＿＿＿] problem that means the system is too difficult or inconvenient to use.

3. A(n) [＿＿＿＿＿＿] diagram shows the time needed to complete each project task and the critical path for the entire project. (Hint: Use the acronym.)

4. To fulfill the main objective of the [＿＿＿＿＿＿] phase, the project team produces a System Requirements Report for a new or revised information system.

5. Data [＿＿＿＿＿＿] diagrams are used with structured methodology, whereas object-oriented methodology uses tools such as use case, class, and sequence diagrams.

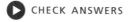 CHECK ANSWERS

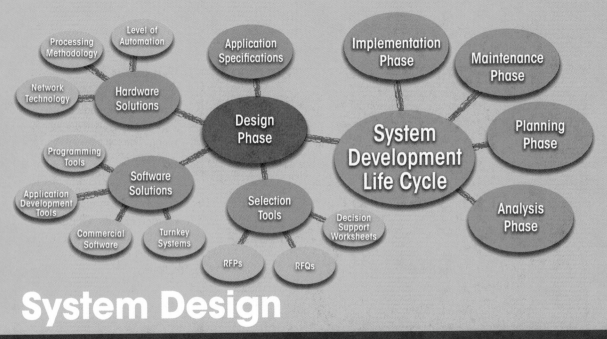

System Design

MANY ASPECTS of designing an information system resemble the process of building a house. After an architect analyzes the number of bedrooms, bathrooms, and closets needed, the next step is figuring out how to arrange them. Should all the rooms be on the same floor? Where will the closets be located? Where will the doors be placed to create the best traffic pattern? As the architect answers these questions, the design for the house begins to emerge. In Section C, you'll learn how a project team applies the same approach to design a new information system.

DESIGN PHASE

▶ What happens in the design phase? In the analysis phase, the project team determines *what* the new information system must do. In the **design phase** of the SDLC, the project team must figure out *how* the new system will fulfill the requirements specified in the System Requirements Report. The activities that normally take place during the design phase for an information system are listed in Figure 10-30.

▶ How does the project team come up with solutions? There might be more than one way to solve the problems and meet the requirements identified in the analysis phase of the SDLC. Some potential solutions might be better than others. They might be more effective, less costly, or less complex. Therefore, it is not a good idea to proceed with the first solution that comes to mind. The project team should instead identify several potential hardware and software solutions by brainstorming and researching case studies at Web sites and in computer publications.

▶ What kinds of hardware solutions are available? A myriad of hardware options are available for information systems. Servers and personal computers are the most commonly used components; but in some information systems, handheld devices, mainframes, or even supercomputers play a role. The project team has to consider the overall architecture based on level of automation, processing methodology, and network technology.

FIGURE 10-30

Design Phase Activities:

✓ Identify potential solutions

✓ Evaluate solutions and select the best

✓ Select hardware and software

✓ Develop application specifications

✓ Obtain approval to implement the new system

▶ **Level of automation.** The project team should consider the pros and cons of different levels of automation because they affect all aspects of the planned information system. A point-of-sale system with a low level of automation might require the checkout clerk to enter credit card numbers from a keypad.

At a higher level of automation, a magnetic strip reader automates the process of entering a credit card number. A further level of automation is achieved by using a pressure-sensitive digitizing pad and stylus to collect customer signatures (Figure 10-31). With signatures in digital format, the entire transaction record becomes electronic, and the business does not need to deal with paper credit card receipts.

10

FIGURE 10-31

Automation alternatives can affect many aspects of an information system. A credit card number can be stored using a few bytes. Storing a digitized signature, however, might require far more disk space, a special type of database software, and specialized input devices. The project team should consider the pros and cons of different levels of automation because they affect all aspects of the planned information system.

▶ **Processing methodology.** An information system can be designed for **centralized processing**, in which data is processed on a centrally located computer. An alternative option is **distributed processing**, in which processing tasks are distributed to servers and workstations.

Typically, centralized processing requires a more powerful computer—usually a mainframe—to achieve the same response speed as distributed processing. Distributed processing in a client/server or peer-to-peer environment is very popular because it provides high levels of processing power at a low cost. However, these distributed architectures present more security problems than a single, centralized computer—a factor that the project team must consider within the context of selecting a solution.

▶ **Network technology.** An information system, by its very nature, is designed to serve an entire organization. That organization includes many people who work in different rooms, different buildings, and perhaps even different countries.

Virtually every information system requires a network, so the project team must examine network alternatives, such as LANs, extranets, intranets, the Internet, and cloud computing models. Many information systems require a complex mixture of networks, such as a LAN in each branch office connected to a company intranet, with customers accessing selected data using the Internet.

▶ **What kinds of software solutions are available?** The project team might consider software alternatives, such as whether to construct the system from scratch in a programming language, use an application development tool, purchase commercial software, or select a turnkey system (Figure 10-32).

▶ Programming tools. Creating an information system from scratch using a programming language can take many months or years. It is usually costly, but offers the most flexibility for meeting the system requirements.

As an analogy, baking a cake from scratch allows you some flexibility in the ingredients you choose—margarine instead of shortening, for example. However, baking from scratch requires a lot of time and work to sift the flour; mix the sugar, eggs, shortening, and milk; and so forth.

The project team can analyze the costs and benefits of developing an information system from scratch. If it appears to be a feasible solution, the team can also select a programming language to use.

▶ Application development tools. An **application development tool** is essentially a type of software construction kit containing building blocks that can be assembled into a software product. Application development tools include expert system shells and database management systems.

An application development tool is the programmer's "cake mix," which contains many of the ingredients necessary for quickly and easily developing the modules for an information system. Although application development tools usually speed up the development process, they might not offer the same level of flexibility as a programming language.

▶ Commercial software. Commercial software for an information system is usually a series of preprogrammed software modules, supplied by a software developer or value added reseller (VAR).

Commercial software eliminates much of the design work required with programming languages or application development tools. However, commercial software requires extensive evaluation to determine how well it meets the system requirements. Following through with the cake analogy, commercial software is equivalent to buying a pre-made cake that you simply slice and serve.

Commercial software is available for standard business functions, such as human resource management, accounting, and payroll. It is also available for many vertical market businesses and organizations, such as law offices, video stores, medical offices, libraries, churches, e-commerce, and charities. Although most commercial software has some customization options, in many cases, it cannot be modified to exactly meet every system requirement, which necessitates adjustments in an organization's procedures. The project team must decide if the benefits of commercial software can offset the cost and inconvenience of procedural changes.

▶ Turnkey systems. A **turnkey system** is essentially an "information system in a box," which consists of hardware and commercial software designed to offer a complete information system solution. In terms of the cake analogy, a turnkey system is like going out to dinner and simply ordering your choice of cake for dessert.

A turnkey system might seem like a quick and easy solution, and it looks attractive to many project teams. Like commercial software, however, a turnkey system must be extensively evaluated to determine whether it can satisfy system requirements.

FIGURE 10-32

Software Alternatives

Programming Languages
Pros: Can be exactly tailored to system requirements
Cons: Require development time and expertise

Application Development Tools
Pros: Require less time than programming languages
Cons: Might limit developers in the way they implement some system features

Commercial Software
Pros: Little or no programming required, so require minimal development time
Cons: Software features might not exactly match business needs; might require extensive customization

Turnkey Systems
Pros: Minimal effort required to select and set up equipment and software
Cons: Require time and expertise to evaluate

EVALUATION AND SELECTION

▶ **How does the team choose the best solution?** The project team devises a list of criteria for comparing each potential solution. This list includes general criteria related to costs, benefits, and development time. The list also includes technical criteria, such as the flexibility of the solution and its adaptability for future modifications and growth. Finally, the list includes functional criteria that indicate how well the solution satisfies the specified requirements.

Each criterion is assigned a weight to indicate its importance. The project team then evaluates the criteria for each solution and assigns raw scores. A raw score of 10, for example, might indicate a highly valued feature.

The raw score for each criterion is multiplied by the weight, and these weighted scores are added to produce a total score for each solution. Sound complicated? It isn't, especially if the project team uses a **decision support worksheet**. Take a few moments to study Figure 10-33, and you'll quickly see how it works.

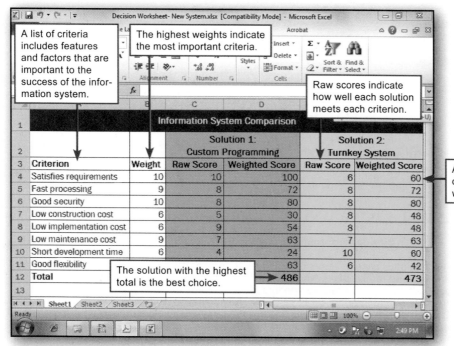

FIGURE 10-33

A spreadsheet program, such as Microsoft Excel, can be used to produce a decision support worksheet for comparing potential solutions.

▶ **How does the project team find the right hardware and software for the new information system?** After the project team selects a solution, the next task is to select the hardware and software needed to implement the solution. Sometimes more than one vendor sells the hardware and software necessary for the new system, so an organization might have a choice of vendors.

The method for selecting the hardware, software, and vendor depends on the project team's understanding of what is required for the solution. Sometimes the team knows exactly what brand, model, or version of hardware and software are required. At other times, the team has a general understanding but needs vendor help selecting specific products. RFPs and RFQs (described on the next page) help the team collect information for these important decisions.

▶ **What's an RFP?** A **request for proposal** (RFP) is a document that describes the information system problem and the requirements for the solution. An RFP essentially asks a vendor to recommend hardware and software for the solution, and to describe the vendor's qualifications for implementing the solution. A project team usually issues an RFP when its members believe that a vendor has valuable knowledge and experience in the solution area. Look at the sample RFP in Figure 10-34.

FIGURE 10-34

RFP Excerpt

RFP for the University Library Information System

The purpose of this request for proposal (RFP) and subsequent vendor presentations is to identify a vendor with whom the University will negotiate a contract to supply, install, and support an integrated library system. This system must be capable of supporting an online public access catalog, cataloging and authority control, acquisitions and serials control, circulation, and reserve. It should be capable of supporting media booking, interlibrary loan and document delivery, and preservation control. Proposals are due 10 August 3:00pm, Purchasing Dept.

A letter of intent to propose should be received by the University by 5:00pm CDT, July 13, 2013. Letters should be sent to the following address:

▶ **What's an RFQ?** A **request for quotation** (RFQ) is a request for a formal price quotation on a list of hardware and software. A project team issues an RFQ to vendors when it knows the make and model of the equipment and the titles of the software packages needed but wants to compare prices from different vendors. Compare the RFQ in Figure 10-35 with the RFP in the previous figure.

FIGURE 10-35

RFQ Excerpt

City Hall Information System RFQ

The Information Technology Office is seeking qualified vendors for the quotation of network equipment required for the expansion of the city hall facility. A list of hardware and software is provided below. Prospective vendors MUST provide the total price including shipping charges and the applicable sales tax. Any deviation from the specifications MUST be noted on the quotation and a written explanation is strongly encouraged to support the substitutions. Bids submitted with equipment other than those stated in the specifications may be rejected.

Part Description	Part Number	Quantity	Price
1. Cisco Catalyst 3750 24 10/100/1000T + 4 SFP Enhanced Multilayer Switch	WS-C3750G-24TS-E	1	
2. Cisco Catalyst 3750 24 10/100/1000T + 4 SFP Standard Multilayer Switch	WS-C3750G-24TS-S	2	

▶ **How does the project team evaluate an RFP or RFQ?** The project team can evaluate RFPs or RFQs by constructing a decision table similar to the one used for evaluating solutions. The basis for choosing hardware and software includes general criteria, such as cost and delivery time.

The project team should also consider the vendor's reliability, expertise, and financial stability. Technical criteria for hardware might include processing speed, reliability, upgradability, maintenance costs, and warranty. Technical criteria for software might include reliability, compatibility, and the availability of patches to fix program errors.

10

APPLICATION SPECIFICATIONS

▶ **What happens after the project team selects a solution?** Exactly what happens next in the system design phase depends on the type of solution selected. If a turnkey solution is selected, the next step might be to get approval to move into the implementation phase of the SDLC.

In contrast, if the project team selects a solution that requires custom programming, the team's systems analysts will create a set of **application specifications** that describe the way the information system's software should interact with users, store data, process data, and format reports.

This part of the SDLC is sometimes referred to as the detailed design phase because its goal is to create very detailed specifications for the completed information system, such as a detailed description of the process for discontinuing an inventory item in Figure 10-36.

```
BEGIN
FIND item in INVENTORY with matching inventory-ID
IF record cannot be found
    DISPLAY "No inventory item matches the Inventory ID."
ELSE
    READ item record
    SET discontinued-item to YES
    WRITE item record
    DISPLAY "Item [inventory-ID] is now marked as
    discontinued."
ENDIF
END
```

FIGURE 10-36

This excerpt from a project team's application specifications describes in detail the process for discontinuing an inventory item.

Detailed application specifications can be developed only after selecting the hardware and software for an information system. For example, the specifications for a program that runs on a Windows-based LAN might require quite a different user interface and processing model than a program that runs on an application server that is accessed via the Internet.

▶ **What is the importance of application specifications?** Application specifications are a key element in developing an effective information system. Not only do these specifications serve as a blueprint for the new system, but they play a critical role in ensuring that the development process proceeds efficiently.

▶ **Can projects fail?** Some projects fail because of constant, unmanaged demand for changes, even before the system is implemented. This failure to constrain change is often referred to as **feature creep** because new features tend to creep into the development process with a snowballing effect on other features, costs, and schedules.

It might be important to change some specifications during the development process because of changes in business needs, laws, or regulations. Proposed changes should be managed within a formal process that includes written **change requests**, which detail the scope of a proposed change and can be evaluated by project team members.

▶ **What happens to the completed specifications?** Application specifications are similar to the pages of an architectural blueprint that show the detailed plan for electrical wiring or plumbing. In a large information systems project, the specifications are given to a programming team or application developer who creates the software.

In a small information systems project, you as the user might develop your own specifications. Then you might give the specifications to a programmer or, if you have the expertise, you might create the software yourself.

▶ **When can the project team actually begin to build the new information system?** In the design phase of the SDLC, the project team chooses a solution, selects hardware and software, and designs detailed application specifications. Before the solution is implemented, the project team typically must seek approval from management.

The approval process might be fairly informal, simply involving a discussion with the CIO. In contrast, some organizations require a much more formal process for obtaining approval, in which the project team submits a written proposal that's supplemented by presentations to management and user groups. After the project team's proposal is approved, the project can move to the next phase of development.

QuickCheck   SECTION C

1. In the [_____] phase of the SDLC, a project team identifies several potential solutions and then selects the one that offers the most benefits at the lowest cost.

2. A(n) [_____] development tool is essentially a software construction kit containing building blocks that can be assembled into the software for an information system.

3. The project team can develop and send out a(n) [_____] to ask vendors for prices on specific equipment and software. (Hint: Use the acronym.)

4. Application [_____] describe the way an application should interact with users, store data, process data, and format reports.

5. System development can get sidetracked by feature [_____] .

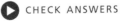 CHECK ANSWERS

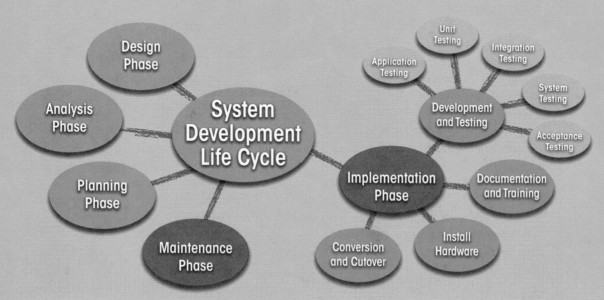

Implementation and Maintenance

SECTION **D**

AFTER THE PLAN for an information system is approved, it's time to start building it. During the implementation phase of the SDLC, an organization puts together the components for the new information system. After an information system is installed and tested, it enters the final phase of the SDLC—the maintenance phase.

FIGURE 10-37

IMPLEMENTATION PHASE

▶ **What happens during the implementation phase?** During the **implementation phase** of the SDLC, the project team supervises the tasks necessary to construct the new information system. The tasks that take place during the implementation phase can include any of those listed in Figure 10-37.

▶ **Does a new information system usually require new hardware?** As the implementation phase begins, programming languages, development tools, and application software needed for the new information system are purchased, installed, and tested to ensure that they work correctly.

Software testing can reveal problems that result from incompatibilities with existing hardware and software. These problems must be corrected before continuing with system development. Testing might also reveal bugs (errors) in the software, which must be corrected by the software publisher.

In addition to new software, the specifications for most new information systems require new hardware, which can either replace old equipment or supplement existing equipment. During the implementation phase, new hardware is purchased, installed, and tested to ensure that it operates correctly.

Implementation Phase
Activities:

✓ Purchase and install hardware and/or software

✓ Create applications

✓ Test applications

✓ Finalize documentation

✓ Train users

✓ Convert data

✓ Convert to new system

DEVELOPMENT AND TESTING

▶ **What's the next step in the implementation phase?** After hardware and software are set up and tested, the next step in the implementation phase depends on the software tools selected for the project.

583

When the software for an information system is created by using a programming language or application development tool, programmers must create and test all the new software modules. Chapter 12 provides more information about the programming process.

When an information system is constructed using commercial software, the software sometimes must be customized. **Software customization** is the process of modifying a commercial application to reflect an organization's needs. Customization might include modifying the user interface, enabling various security settings, selecting the menus that appear on the screen, and designing forms or reports.

▶ **How can the team ensure that a new information system works?** A rigorous testing process is the only way to make sure a new information system works. Different types of testing during the implementation phase help identify and fix problems before the information system is incorporated into day-to-day business activities.

▶ **What is application testing?** Application testing is the process of trying out various sequences of input values and checking the results to verify that the application works correctly. Application testing is performed in three ways: unit testing, integration testing, and system testing.

As each application module is completed, it undergoes **unit testing** to ensure that it operates reliably and correctly. When all modules have been completed and tested, **integration testing** is performed to ensure that the modules operate together correctly.

Unit testing and integration testing are usually performed in a test area. A **test area** is a place where software testing can occur without disrupting the organization's regular information system. A test area might be located in an isolated section of storage on the computer system that runs the organization's regular information system, or it might be located on an entirely separate computer system.

When a problem is discovered during unit testing or integration testing, the team must track down the source of the problem and correct it. Unit testing and integration testing are then repeated to make sure the problem is corrected, and no new problems were introduced.

FIGURE 10-38

Unit, integration, and system testing ensure that applications work.

After unit and integration testing are completed, **system testing** ensures that all hardware and software components work together correctly. Figure 10-38 summarizes the three stages of application testing.

Unit testing ensures that each module of the application software works correctly.

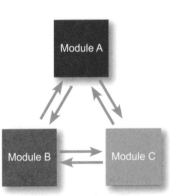

Integration testing ensures that all the modules work together correctly.

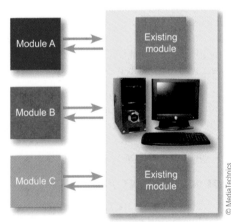

System testing ensures that new modules work with the rest of the system hardware and software.

DOCUMENTATION AND TRAINING

▶ What kinds of documentation does the project team create during the implementation phase? One of the most important tasks during the implementation phase is to make sure the information system is completely documented so that it can be used effectively and modified easily. The documentation for an information system can be broadly categorized as system documentation or user documentation.

System documentation describes a system's features, hardware architecture, and programming. The target audience for system documentation is programmers, designers, and analysts who might maintain the system on a day-to-day basis and implement modifications.

Much of the information required for system documentation is generated in the analysis and design phases of the SDLC. At the end of the implementation phase, these documents should be reviewed for accuracy because features sometimes change as a result of problems or opportunities encountered during implementation.

For system documentation, many project teams turn to automated applications that produce documentation from completed source code. These tools help the team retrofit the documentation to the actual system, which might differ somewhat from the original system specifications.

User documentation describes how to interact with the system to accomplish specific tasks. It includes a list of features and instructions for using them.

Both system and user documentation can be supplied in printed format, but the current trend is to supply documentation in digital format as electronic documents, online help, or hyperlinked HTML documents.

▶ How do employees learn how to use a new information system? In preparation for using a new information system, users generally need training on software use and data entry. Some users might also need training in hardware operation and backup procedures (Figure 10-39).

During training sessions, users learn how to interact with the interface, use the new system to perform day-to-day tasks, and find additional information in user manuals or procedure handbooks.

A **procedure handbook** is a type of user documentation that contains step-by-step instructions for performing specific tasks. It often takes the place of a lengthy user manual because in a large organization, an employee in a particular department usually performs specific tasks and does not need to know how all features of the system work.

FIGURE 10-39

Training sessions for a new information system can be conducted by members of the project team or outsourced to professional trainers.

10

CONVERSION AND CUTOVER

▶ What happens to data from the old system? The data for a new information system might exist in card files, file folders, or an old information system. This data must be loaded into the new system—a process called data conversion (Figure 10-40).

When converting data from an existing computer system to a new system, a programmer can write conversion software to read the old data and convert it into a format that is usable by the new system. Without such software, users would be forced to manually reenter data from the old system into the new system.

▶ How does a business switch to a new information system? **System conversion** refers to the process of deactivating an old information system and activating a new one. It is also referred to as a "cutover" or "to go live." There are several strategies for converting to a new system.

▶ **Direct conversion** means that the old system is completely deactivated and the new system is immediately activated. Direct conversion usually takes place during non-peak hours to minimize disruption to normal business routines. Direct conversion is risky, however, because if the new system does not work correctly, it might need to be deactivated and undergo further development or testing. In the meantime, the old system must be reactivated, and transactions that were entered into the new system must be re-entered into the old system.

▶ **Parallel conversion** avoids some of the risk of direct conversion because the old system remains in service while some or all of the new system is activated. Both the old and new systems operate in parallel until the project team can determine whether the new system is performing correctly. Parallel conversion often requires that all entries be made in both the new and old systems, which is costly in terms of time, computer resources, and personnel. Parallel conversion offers a good safety net in case a new information system fails to operate reliably or accurately.

▶ **Phased conversion** works well with large, modularized information systems because the new system is activated one module at a time. After the project team determines that one module is working correctly, the next module is activated, and so on, until the entire new system is operational. In a phased conversion, however, each module of the new system must work with both the old and new systems, which greatly increases the complexity and cost of application development.

▶ **Pilot conversion** works well in organizations with several branches that have independent information processing systems because the new information system is activated at one branch at a time. If the new system works correctly at one branch, it is activated at the next branch. To prepare for a pilot conversion, system developers must devise methods to integrate information from branches using the new system with information from branches still using the old system.

▶ When is the new information system formally "live"? A new or upgraded information system undergoes a final test called acceptance testing. **Acceptance testing** is designed to verify that the new information system works as required.

Procedures for acceptance testing are designed by users and systems analysts, and often include the use of real data to demonstrate that the system operates correctly under normal and peak data loads. Acceptance testing usually marks the completion of the implementation phase.

FIGURE 10-40

When converting data from a manual system to a computer system, the data can be typed or scanned electronically into the appropriate storage media. Even using scanners, this process can take a long time, require extra personnel, and be quite costly.

AP Photo/Ric Francis

MAINTENANCE PHASE

▶ **What happens during the maintenance phase?** The **maintenance phase** of the SDLC involves day-to-day operation of the system, making modifications to improve performance, and correcting problems. After an information system is implemented, it remains in operation for a period of time. During this time, maintenance activities ensure that the system functions as well as possible. Figure 10-41 lists the major maintenance activities for a typical information system.

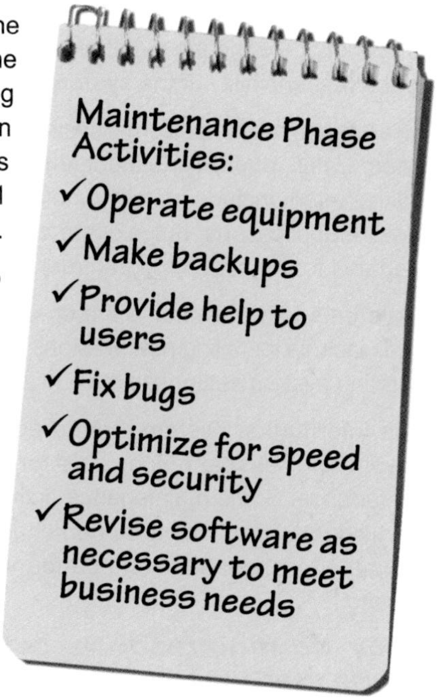

The term *maintenance phase* is a bit misleading because it seems to imply that the information system is maintained in a static state. On the contrary, during the maintenance phase, an information system is likely to undergo many changes to meet an organization's needs. Changes during the maintenance phase can include the following:

▶ Upgrades to the operating system and commercial software

▶ User interface revisions to make the system easier to use

▶ Application software revisions to fix bugs and add features

▶ Hardware replacements necessary to retire defective equipment or enhance performance

▶ Security upgrades (You'll find more on this topic in the next section of the chapter.)

▶ Hardware, software, or network adjustments to maintain and enhance quality of service

FIGURE 10-41

Maintenance Phase Activities:
✓ Operate equipment
✓ Make backups
✓ Provide help to users
✓ Fix bugs
✓ Optimize for speed and security
✓ Revise software as necessary to meet business needs

10

▶ **What is quality of service?** The term **quality of service** (QoS) refers to the level of performance a computer system provides. When quality of service is good, data flows swiftly through the system, software is easy and intuitive to use, and work is completed quickly and without error. When quality of service is poor, users experience long waits, software is clumsy to use, and information is difficult to find.

Three key concepts ensure good quality of service: reliability, availability, and serviceability. Computer systems are reliable when they can be counted on to function correctly. Availability refers to the ability of the system to be continuously accessible to all the people who use it. Systems exhibit serviceability when they are easily upgraded or repaired.

▶ **What are quality-of-service metrics?** A **quality-of-service metric** is a technique for measuring a specific QoS characteristic. Data for these metrics can be gathered by monitoring system performance and analyzing responses to user satisfaction surveys. Businesses use several QoS metrics, such as those described in Figure 10-42.

FIGURE 10-42

QoS Metrics

QoS Metric	Description
Throughput	Amount of data processed in a particular time interval
Accuracy	Number of errors occurring in a particular time interval for a particular function
Downtime	Amount of time a system is not available for processing
Capacity	Available storage space, number of users, number of connections, or number of packets
User levels	Number of users at peak, average, and low times
Response time	Time period between when a user initiates a request for information and when the request is fulfilled

▶ Who is responsible for system maintenance? In an information system that revolves around a mainframe computer or network servers, the task of operating the mainframe or servers on a day-to-day basis is usually the responsibility of the **system operator**.

The system operator performs system backups and data recovery, monitors system traffic, and troubleshoots operational problems. Additional responsibilities might include installing new versions of the operating system and software applications; but in some organizations, these responsibilities are delegated to a systems programmer.

A **systems programmer** is the operating system "guru," whose responsibilities include installing new versions of the operating system and modifying operating system settings to maximize performance.

In an information system structured as a LAN, a network manager or network specialist is responsible for day-to-day operations and system maintenance. Some maintenance activities might also fall on the shoulders of individual users, who are often charged with the responsibility of backing up their workstations and performing workstation installations of new software.

FIGURE 10-43

When you have questions about how to use an information system, first check the documentation. If you can't find an answer there, contact the help desk.

▶ Why do maintenance activities include user support? Even after in-depth training, employees sometimes forget procedures or have difficulty when they encounter a new set of circumstances. These employees turn to the IT department for help.

Many organizations establish a help desk to handle end-user problems. The **help desk** is staffed by technical support specialists who are familiar with the information system's software. Support specialists keep records of problems and solutions.

When you use an information system, you are likely to have questions. Your first source of information is your procedure handbook or user manual. It might be similar to the one in Figure 10-43 or it could be accessible online.

Help desk personnel have little tolerance for people who ask questions that are clearly answered in the documentation. You should not hesitate, however, to ask about procedures or problems that are not covered in the documentation.

Your questions can often promote much-needed modifications in the information system. For example, suppose you encounter a problem with an update procedure and contact the help desk. The help desk technician begins to troubleshoot the problem and soon realizes that it is caused by a programming error not caught during system testing. This bug is recorded in a bug report that is routed to the programming group, which can determine its severity and take steps to fix it.

▶ How long does the maintenance phase last? The maintenance phase is the longest SDLC phase and lasts until the system is retired. Although the analysis, design, and implementation phases of the SDLC are costly, for many organizations, the maintenance phase is the most expensive because it is the longest.

The maintenance phase often accounts for 70% of the total cost of an information system. As shown in Figure 10-44, maintenance costs follow a U-shaped curve—an information system requires the most maintenance at the beginning and end of its life cycle.

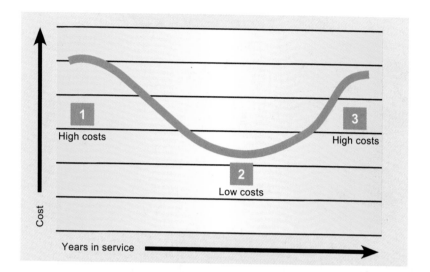

FIGURE 10-44

Maintenance Phase Costs

1. When a new information system first goes live, maintenance costs are high while programmers work out bugs and users clamor for support.

2. After most of the bugs are fixed and users become familiar with the information system, maintenance costs decrease.

3. As an information system nears the end of its useful life span, repair costs rise, and changing business practices begin to require modifications that are time consuming and expensive to implement.

▶ **When does the maintenance phase end?** The maintenance phase continues until an information system is no longer cost effective or until changes in the organization make the information system obsolete. It is not unusual for an information system to remain in operation for 20 years or more. Eventually, an information system's useful or cost-effective life nears a close. It is then time to begin the system development life cycle again.

QuickCheck   SECTION D

1. _____ testing ensures that a software module operates reliably and correctly, whereas _____ testing checks to make sure all the modules work with each other.

2. The target audience for _____ documentation is programmers, designers, and analysts.

3. A direct _____ is risky because if the new system does not work correctly, it might need to be deactivated to undergo further development and testing.

4. At the end of the implementation phase of the SDLC, users verify that the entire system works as specified, during a process called _____ testing.

5. During the maintenance phase, three key concepts ensure good _____ of service: reliability, availability, and serviceability.

 CHECK ANSWERS

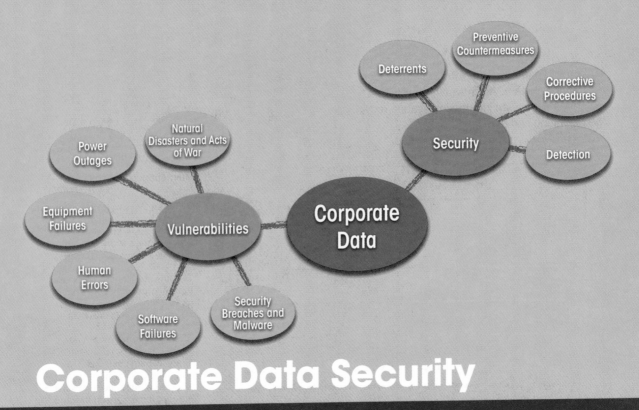

Corporate Data Security

THREATS AGAINST information systems are increasing. Corporations, government agencies, and other organizations are constantly shoring up their defenses to protect data and the people to whom it refers. In this security section, you'll learn about threats to corporate data and methods for protecting that data. You can then draw some informed conclusions about the risks you might face when data about you is stored in information systems and when you depend on information systems for key aspects of your lifestyle.

INFORMATION SYSTEM DATA VULNERABILITIES

▶ **What are the most common threats to the data stored on corporate information systems?** As with personal computers, common threats to corporate information systems include natural disasters, power outages, equipment failures, human errors, software failures, security breaches, acts of war, and malware. When disaster strikes the PC on your desktop, it is a major inconvenience—but just for one person. In contrast, threats to a corporate information system can affect thousands of people.

▶ **Natural disasters** can completely shut down a computer system, cut off service to customers, and potentially destroy the system completely. For example, when Hurricane Katrina tore through Louisiana, it left a swath of destruction in its wake. In many businesses, computer systems were drenched with rain and flood waters. During the storm, power outages knocked down several major Internet hosting services. Power remained out for weeks in some places, and businesses without generators scrambled to continue operating.

▶ **Power outages** can be caused by natural disasters, overloaded power grids, planned brownouts, and rolling blackouts. For example, the IT departments of many California businesses had to contend with rolling blackouts in the early 2000s when power grids in the area could not keep up with rising power demands.

590

▶ **Equipment failures** can occur in any hardware component of a computer system. The risk of failure increases as a hardware component ages, but failures can occur in brand-new hardware. Many device specifications include an **MTBF** (mean time between failures) rating. For example, an MTBF rating of 125,000 hours means that, on average, a device could function for 125,000 hours before failing. MTBF ratings are averages, however, so a server with a 125,000 MTBF rating might operate for only 10 hours before it fails, for example.

▶ **Human errors** are mistakes made by computer operators. Common errors within an information system include entering inaccurate data and failing to follow required procedures. Poorly trained computer operators were blamed for the biggest North American blackout in history, which left more than 50 million people without power in the summer of 2003 (Figure 10-45).

FIGURE 10-45

Human error was blamed for a blackout that cascaded from the Midwestern United States, across the Northeast, and into Canada.

James Patrick Cooper/Bloomberg via Getty Images

▶ **Software failures** can be caused by bugs or flawed software design. Flaws in critical software that controls air traffic or nuclear power plants can be deadly. Other bugs may cause security leaks that allow unauthorized access to corporate servers.

▶ **Security breaches** include stolen data, physical intrusions, and deliberate sabotage. In one of the most far-reaching security cases, hackers compromised the iTunes Store database containing customer credit card numbers and iTunes passwords. The number of customers whose data fell prey to the hackers was unknown, so it had to be assumed that everyone with a record in the database was vulnerable. iTunes customers were encouraged to change their passwords; and over the course of several months, banks were forced to notify millions of clients and issue new credit cards.

▶ **Acts of war** once affected only computer systems located on battlefronts. With a recent increase in terrorist incidents, however, civilian areas have become targets. Acts of war can cause physical damage to computer systems. Cyberterrorism can also cause damage, using viruses and worms to destroy data and otherwise disrupt computer-based operations, which now include critical national infrastructures such as power grids and telecommunications systems.

▶ **Malware** can damage just about any computer system. You might have experienced the nuisance of rooting out a virus from your personal computer. That inconvenience pales when compared to the potential effect of a virus on a corporate information system. The MyDoom worm, which spread through e-mail, infected Web sites and caused an estimated US$250 million in damage when it infected millions of computers worldwide.

INFORMATION SYSTEM DATA SECURITY

▶ **How is the data on corporate information systems protected from threats?** No computer system can be completely risk-free, but several proactive measures can protect information systems from threats. These measures can be grouped into four categories: deterrents, preventive countermeasures, corrective procedures, and detection activities.

FIGURE 10-46

Biometric identification methods, such as fingerprint and retinal scans, provide one line of defense against threats.

▶ Deterrents reduce the likelihood of deliberate attack. Physical deterrents, such as limiting access to critical servers, fall under this category. Common deterrents also include security features such as multi-level authentication, password protection, and biometric identification (Figure 10-46).

▶ Preventive countermeasures shield vulnerabilities to render an attack unsuccessful or reduce its impact. Firewalls that prevent unauthorized access to a system and encryption that makes stolen data indecipherable are examples of preventive countermeasures.

▶ Corrective procedures reduce the effect of an attack. Data backups, disaster recovery plans, and the availability of redundant hardware devices all are examples of corrective procedures.

▶ Detection activities recognize attacks and trigger preventive countermeasures or corrective procedures. For example, antivirus software detects viruses entering a system and can be configured to perform corrective procedures such as removing the virus and quarantining infected files. Theft or vandalism can be detected by periodic hardware inventories. The use of monitoring software to track users, file updates, and changes to critical systems can also help detect anomalies that indicate an intrusion or a threat.

▶ **Does a data center help minimize risks?** The hardware and software for most corporate information systems are housed in data centers. A **data center** is a specialized facility designed to hold and protect computer systems and data. Data centers include special security features, such as fireproof construction, earthquakeproof foundations, sprinkler systems, power generators, secure doors and windows, and antistatic floor coverings.

Data centers are designed to proactively reduce the risk of data loss that might occur as a result of a disaster. The best way to protect against risk is to avoid it altogether, and data centers can reduce or negate the effects of specific types of disasters.

In general, data centers are not located in earthquake, flood, or tornado prone areas. Data centers can be located in the basement of a building or even underground. Underground data centers provide protection against many natural disasters, such as storms, earthquakes, and forest fires, and they are not susceptible to extreme changes in surface temperature.

For maximum protection, some data centers are housed in former military bunkers, abandoned mines, or limestone caves. Some of the world's most secure data centers are listed in Figure 10-47.

10

FIGURE 10-47

Underground Data Centers

Bahnhof Pionen is located 100 feet beneath Stockholm, Sweden and sometimes called the "James Bond" data center.

Iron Mountain is located 220 feet underground in a limestone cave near Pittsburgh.

Smartbunker runs on wind power and is housed in a former NATO command bunker in the Lincolnshire Wolds, U.K.

InfoBunker is a 65,000 square foot data center built in a decommissioned Air Force bunker designed to survive a 20 megaton nuclear blast.

Data centers include equipment to keep computers functioning during power outages. Most areas experience occasional power failures or blackouts, which can be costly to organizations whose goal is to offer 24/7 coverage.

To avoid downtime, one of the most basic requirements for a data center is a supply of uninterrupted power from high-capacity, battery-operated uninterruptible power supplies and backup power generators. A data center must also protect and maintain its own power grid. For example, fuel tanks must be protected against explosions or fire, and batteries must be kept at room temperature for proper functioning.

Physical security is critical to data centers. Most data centers limit physical access using fingerprint identification systems, badges, or security guards. Steel doors divide the centers into secure areas. Motion detectors and automated alarm systems prevent unauthorized movement through the building. In addition, many data centers are located close to police and fire departments.

Conditions in a data center must be monitored at all times. Computerized detection systems monitor sensing devices that track temperature, humidity, water, smoke, fire, air flow, power levels, security systems, and many other metrics. Cameras can be placed in air ducts, under raised floors, and in computer system units to detect intruders, pests, or chemical leaks.

▶ **What if disaster strikes?** A particularly heavy rainfall in the United States Virgin Islands a few years ago caused massive water damage to the local driver's license offices. The computer system containing license data was soaked and the hard drive was damaged beyond repair. There were no backups. Residents were asked to appear in person at the license bureau so that government employees could re-enter license data. Episodes such as this one can be avoided when organizations create and implement a disaster recovery plan.

A **disaster recovery plan** is a step-by-step plan that describes the methods used to secure data against disaster and sets guidelines for how an organization will recover lost data if and when a disaster occurs.

Disaster recovery plans must deal not only with calamities such as the 9/11 World Trade Center collapse or the Tsunami that hit Japan in 2011; they also must take into account day-to-day events that could potentially cause data loss. Backup tapes can become corrupted, an employee might spill coffee onto the most critical storage device in the building, or a virus can slow down the network to the point that it's unusable.

A well-formulated disaster recovery plan should account for all kinds of trouble, from the most minor glitch to the most destructive disaster. Specifically, an enterprise-wide disaster recovery plan should:

▶ Ensure the safety of people on the premises at the time of a disaster

▶ Continue critical business operations

▶ Minimize the duration of a serious disruption to operations

▶ Minimize immediate damage and prevent additional losses

▶ Establish management succession and emergency powers

▶ Facilitate effective coordination of recovery tasks

A disaster recovery plan can mean the difference between an organization rebounding after a disaster or simply ceasing to exist. Disaster recovery plans are as critical to data security as data backups, firewalls, and password protection. As a key component of computer system management, disaster recovery is the focus of numerous publications and conferences (Figure 10-48).

CORPORATE IDENTITY THEFT

▶ **What is corporate identity theft?** In the corporate world, a brand symbolizes a company and its products or services. A brand includes a name, logo, trademark, and other visual elements. Brands are used on catalogs, store fronts, merchandise, letterheads, and Web sites to help build customer trust and confidence.

When a company's brand is used without authorization, the company has become a victim of identity theft. Corporate identity attacks can undermine customer confidence, overwhelm customer service, generate bad publicity, and result in lost revenues. With the escalation of online crime, corporate identity theft has become a major security threat.

▶ **How are corporate identities stolen?** The Internet makes it easy to steal corporate identities and use them for phishing scams and fake Web sites. The key to a phishing scam is an e-mail that looks like it originated from a legitimate company, such as Bank of America, PayPal, or Microsoft. It is not difficult for hackers to copy logos and other graphic elements from Web pages of legitimate sites and compile them into an official-looking e-mail message. Creating a fake Web site is also easy. Hackers

FIGURE 10-48

Publications such as the *Disaster Recovery Journal* help risk management professionals design and update disaster recovery plans.

can obtain a URL that's similar to one used by a legitimate company, perhaps by using a different country code or using .biz instead of .com. By copying and pasting a few graphics, the site looks legitimate, too.

▶ Why does corporate identity theft matter to consumers? Savvy consumers are on the lookout for phishing attacks and avoid clicking links embedded in e-mail messages. Unfortunately, other consumers unknowingly click fake links and divulge personal information. These unfortunate consumers in turn can become the victims of fraud and identity theft.

▶ What can companies do about fake sites and phishing scams? Preventing corporate identity theft is not really feasible. With current HTTP and HTML technologies, corporations have no way to lock down their branding elements, so hackers can easily misappropriate them.

Secure Web site identification has been in the works for many years, but a worldwide standard that is recognized and understood by consumers does not yet exist. Consumers will remain at risk until there is universal implementation of technology that verifies a Web site's legitimacy.

Companies can take steps to protect their customers and deal quickly with identity theft incidents. The American Management Association and other business advocates offer guidelines, such as those listed in Figure 10-49, to help corporations minimize the effects of identity theft.

FIGURE 10-49

Guidelines help corporations deal with identity theft.

10

▶ **Help customers report scams.** Provide a simple way for employees and customers to report phishing attacks that appear to originate from the company and fake versions of the corporate Web site.

▶ **Educate customers.** Let customers know what kinds of legitimate communications they can expect from the company. Avoid acclimatizing customers to e-mail notifications that can make them vulnerable to future attacks. Never send customers mass mailings that contain links to the company's site or ask them to send personal data as an e-mail reply. Instead, ask customers to connect to the company's site using their browsers and provide instructions for accessing a data collection form.

▶ **Manage URLs.** Make sure the company Web site is easy to find online. Keep the company URL simple so that users can access it directly, rather than through search engines or partner sites. Consider typical typographic errors that customers might make when typing the company URL. Try to reserve those URLs so that hackers can't take advantage of them. To minimize typographic errors, encourage customers to bookmark the company site by adding it to their Favorites lists.

▶ **Monitor domain name registration.** Keep up to date on the corporation's domain registration and periodically check for new registrations that might make unauthorized use of the company name or trademarks.

▶ **Be prepared.** Prepare for an attack before it happens by establishing relationships with law enforcement, ISPs, and others who can help locate and take down fraudulent sites.

QuickCheck

SECTION E

1. A(n) _____ rating of 125,000 hours means that, on average, a device could function for 125,000 hours before failing. (Hint: Use the acronym.)

2. A disaster _____ plan describes methods for securing data against disasters and sets guidelines for reconstructing lost data.

3. _____ procedures, such as data backups, can reduce the effect of a virus that spreads throughout corporate computers.

4. Some of the most secure _____ centers are located underground in old military bunkers and abandoned mines.

5. Corporate identity theft has become a major security concern because of increasing numbers of _____ scams and fake Web sites.

▶ CHECK ANSWERS

Issue: What's Wrong with Online Voting?

AMERICAN IDOL racks up more than 100 million votes each week, collected from text messages, dial-in calls, and Facebook links. You can vote online for Dancing With The Stars and Miss America; yet when it comes to voting in local or national elections, you're required to trek down to your local polling place and wait in line.

In the early days of the Internet, online voting looked easy; but the feasibility of an easy solution died with the advent of viruses, worms, bots, denial-of-service attacks, unauthorized intrusion attempts, and the growing threat of international terrorists. Computer scientists, systems analysts, security experts, and election officials now have a pretty good idea of the problems associated with online voting, but they disagree about the best solutions.

Whether manual or electronic, there are six basic requirements for a voting system (see box). Online voting meets some of these basic requirements better than current voting methods, but faces challenges in adequately fulfilling other requirements.

Online voting has several advantages. It is convenient. Voters can cast ballots from home or work, or even while on vacation. It is quick. Casting an online ballot doesn't require driving to a polling station and waiting in line.

Because of its advantages, online voting has the potential to attract net-savvy young voters who historically have voted in lower numbers than other segments of the population. It also simplifies the voting process for elderly and homebound voters. The convenience of online voting might also increase participation in local elections.

Online voting has the potential to decrease the number of ballots that are invalidated because of procedural problems, such as failing to completely punch out the chad on a ballot card, or checking more than one candidate on a paper ballot. Voting software can prevent voters from erroneously selecting more than one candidate and make sure that voters can revise their selections without invalidating their ballots.

Voter fraud includes voting multiple times, stuffing the electronic ballot box with ballots from nonexistent voters, and buying votes. To reduce voter fraud, voters must be identified to make sure they are eligible to vote and vote only once. When a person logs on to vote remotely, it is difficult to verify his or her identity. Passwords are not effective in controlling fraud because they can be shared and distributed. Biometric devices that offer more positive identification are not typically part of personal computer systems.

Online voting advocates point out, however, that traditional voting practices are also vulnerable to exploits such as disrupting polling places and stealing absentee ballots. Long lines at polling places produce something similar to online denial-of-service attacks.

Politically, skeptics of online voting are uncomfortable with its effect on voting demographics. Some Republican strategists are concerned about a sudden upswing in young voters—not a block of traditionally Republican supporters—who might take advantage of online polling. Democrats, on the other hand, have intimated that online voting would disproportionately increase the number of high-income voters because many economically deprived voters do not have access to a computer and an Internet connection.

For a democracy to function properly, its citizens should be confident that the electoral system is honest and works. Online voting presents some sticky technological and social challenges that must be resolved before it can be used with confidence.

BASIC REQUIREMENTS FOR DEMOCRATIC VOTING SYSTEMS

▶ Encourage and allow voters to register

▶ Provide voters with an easy-to-decipher ballot

▶ Allow voters to make their selections, review them, and revise them before casting their ballots

▶ Collect ballots and filter out those that are invalid or fraudulent

▶ Accurately tabulate votes from every valid ballot

▶ Allow officials to recount ballots if an election is challenged

Try It! Early enthusiasts of online voting envisioned it as a technological solution to the problems of representative democracy. They expected the rapid emergence of a new e-democracy in which citizens had a direct vote in every issue with the ease of dashing off an e-mail or logging on to a Web site. Here's your chance to explore the pros and cons of online voting from American Idol to high-stakes politics.

10

1. An online voting project called Secure Electronic Registration and Voting Experiment (SERVE) was initiated by the U.S. Department of Defense with a goal of offering online voting to overseas military personnel. The project was scrapped after experts in the Security Peer Review Group criticized its vulnerabilities. Read the report and list the five types of attacks that it identified.

2. Every year, *TIME* magazine holds a popular vote for the 100 most influential people. In 2009, the vote was hacked. Who was responsible for the hack and how did they do it?

3. A major worry about online voting is that people might be able to vote multiple times. The obvious solution would be to attach your Social Security number to your vote; however, that would violate the concept of secret ballots. A proposal called Pretty Good Democracy offers a solution to the "vote early, vote often" problem. What is it and do you think it will work?

> **INFOWEBLINKS**
>
> You can check the **NP2013 Chapter 10** InfoWebLink for updates to these activities.
>
> **W CLICK TO CONNECT**
> www.infoweblinks.com/np2013/ch10

4. Critics of current online voting technology make the point that national elections are different than picking the winner for American Idol or Dancing With The Stars. Since 2006, however, the country of Estonia has had an online voting option. To compare its voting protocol with reality show voting, use the Web to gather information for the table below.

	American Idol	Dancing With The Stars	Estonia
Voting platforms (texting, call-in, Web, etc.)			
Number of times you can vote			
Can you change your vote?			
What personal data is attached to the vote?			
Vote volume per election			
Examples of technical glitches			

What Do You Think?

ISSUE

1. Would you prefer online voting to voting at a polling place?

2. Do you think online voters would disproportionately vote for Republicans?

3. Should online voting be available only to specific groups, such as elderly voters and military personnel stationed abroad, who currently have trouble reaching polling places?

Information Tools: Recognizing Viewpoint

Information in newspapers, Web sites, blogs, and other sources is rarely 100% objective. No matter what the source, information is rarely presented in a way that is fair and balanced.

Rather than searching fruitlessly for unbiased information, it can be more practical to recognize the viewpoints of information at hand and sift through it for ideas and facts that can be corroborated as correct from other sources.

Biased material is not necessarily useless. For some projects, you might actively seek material that presents strong viewpoints. For example, when you want to compare and contrast divergent political viewpoints, you might actively look for biased material.

Information that is skewed toward a particular viewpoint can be classified as propaganda, misinformation, disinformation, or parody.

Propaganda

Information that is true, but selectively represented in a way that it encourages recipients to form certain opinions. In the old days, it was called "flim flam." Today it is called "spin."

Disinformation

False information that is disseminated with the deliberate intention of influencing policies or opinions. Examples include spam, fake viruses, and hoaxes.

Misinformation

Information that is unintentionally not true; a misstatement, gaffe, or error that isn't deliberate. Many urban legends fall into this category.

Parody

Humorous or satirical information that imitates or mimics a real event or original work, and is often disseminated to make fun of the subject.

Identifying biased information is not always easy. Viewpoints are sometimes subtle; and if they match your own views, you might not recognize them as biased. Here are some tips to help you detect viewpoint.

▶ Look for loaded words that evoke strong emotions, exaggerate, sensationalize, or vilify. Loaded words can help you uncover subtle viewpoints; positive words point to viewpoints that are supported.

▶ Look for evidence that the author is affiliated with a business or an organization that might affect his or her viewpoint. Skim the author's other publications (articles, blogs, Web site) and biographical information (Facebook, Wikipedia) for clues about his or her views.

▶ Consider if only one side of an issue is presented.

▶ Consider if the site's sponsor has a commercial, social, political, or other sort of agenda that would affect the viewpoint of information presented at the site.

▶ Look at other articles on the site. Sites tend to carry articles of similar viewpoints and some might more blatantly show their bias.

Try It! How is your "spin" radar? Can you spot viewpoints? Can you identify misinformation and distinguish it from propaganda and disinformation? Let's see if you can.

10

1 Watch each of the following YouTube videos and indicate whether it is propaganda, disinformation, misinformation, or parody.

   a. Medieval Help Desk with English Subtitles

   b. WWDC 2010 iPhone 4 Announcement

   c. Mac vs PC (Viruses)

   d. iPhone App Makes Popcorn!

2 Richard Stallman and the SIIA are at odds about an important digital issue. What is the issue and what are the two divergent viewpoints?

3 The Huffington Post has been labeled as a liberal-leaning news outlet. Many technology enthusiasts read its technology section, however, for information about the latest products and gadgets. Connect to the Huffington Post and read a technology article. Can you detect any evidence of bias in the article, and do any other elements on the page, such as advertising or links to other articles, reveal the site's bias?

4 How does Google's ranking system work? Use any search engine to look up "PigeonRank." How would you classify the information at this site?

5 Many people are not aware of their own bias; and when gathering facts, they tend to accept information that supports their biases and look for ways to refute data that doesn't. To find out if you have a bias that you're not aware of, go to the Project Implicit site and take a Demo Test. Which test did you take, and were the results what you expected?

6 In this world, there are enthusiastic Microsoft supporters and there are die-hard Apple fans. Even tech journalists have a hard time remaining unbiased or keeping their bias under wraps. Check out the online New York Times article *Microsoft Calling. Anyone There?* by Ashlee Vance. (If this article isn't available, look for similar articles on Vance's Web site.) What do you detect as his bias and why?

INFOWEBLINKS

You can check the **NP2013 Chapter 10** InfoWebLink for updates to these activities.

W CLICK TO CONNECT
www.infoweblinks.com/np2013/ch10

7 Technology columnists, innovators, and entrepreneurs influence not only consumers, but the entire direction of society. They have unique viewpoints that shape their work. They may even have a social, political, or economic agenda to promote. Look up biographies for the following computer-industry VIPs so that you can fill in the table below.

	Computer Industry Claim-to-Fame	Interesting Personal Fact	Viewpoint
John C. Dvorak			
Carly Fiorina			
Mitch Kapor			
Ray Kurzweil			
Tim O'Reilly			

Technology in Context:
Architecture and Construction

A CLUSTER OF HARDHATS study a dog-eared blueprint. Sun-bronzed laborers perch on a makeshift bench, munching sandwiches and waving to a group of carpenters hauling 2x4s onto a foundation. The sounds of hammers, shovels, and power tools fill the air from early morning through late afternoon. It is a typical construction site: an anthill of activity where a structure of some sort is eventually assembled—a house, a shopping mall, or a skyscraper.

Behind the scenes of this busy site, computer technology has added a high-tech flavor to construction projects with real-time interactive computer graphics, broadband wireless communications, distributed database management systems, wearable and vehicle-mounted computers, global positioning satellites, and laser-guided surveying systems.

Architects use computers to create blueprints. Contractors use computers for cost estimates and scheduling. Computers are even starting to appear on the job site, carried as handheld devices and embedded in construction equipment.

In the past, architects drew construction plans by hand on semitransparent film called vellum. To create a blueprint, they overlaid the vellum on special blue paper and then ran it through a machine that exposed it to intensified light and ammonia. Minor changes to a design were possible; but for major changes, architects often needed to create a new set of vellum drawings.

With the advent of computers and computer-aided design (CAD) software, architects realized they could be more productive—and make design changes more easily—by replacing their drafting tables with computers running CAD software, much as writers replaced their typewriters with computers running word processing software. Using plotters with wide print beds, architects are able to produce computer-generated blueprints similar to those they created at a drafting table.

Initially, architects used CAD software to create 2-D floor plans and elevations. Today architects use 3-D CAD software that offers a greatly expanded toolset.

Architects can begin with a simple 2-D floor plan, and then use CAD tools to draw interior and exterior walls, ceilings, and roofs. Standard building materials, such as doors and windows, can be selected from a list of clip-art objects and dragged into position with a mouse. Electrical, plumbing, and framing schematics can also be added.

Any elements of the drawing can be displayed or hidden—for example, when discussing the design with an electrical contractor, an architect can hide the plumbing details. These 3-D wireframe drawings with building, electrical, and plumbing elements included can be rotated and viewed from any angle.

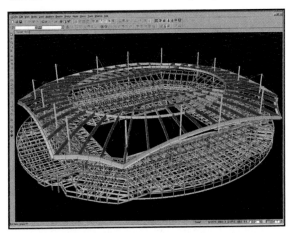

Inexpensive ink jet printers have replaced expensive first-generation plotters and give architects the option of printing in realistic color. Using 3-D CAD software, they can also apply textures and colors to convert wireframes into 3-D models that can be viewed from the inside or outside. Architects sometimes use an animated version of a 3-D model for virtual reality walkthroughs.

After an architect has completed the building plans, a contractor estimates the project's price tag by calculating the cost of materials and labor. Computerized spreadsheets, such as Excel, are a popular tool for cost estimates. Large contracting firms often use commercial software specifically designed for construction estimates.

Contractors are also responsible for scheduling the tasks in a construction project, such as excavating the building site, erecting the foundation, constructing the frame, assembling the roof, adding wiring and plumbing, and doing interior finish work. Large construction projects, such as malls and government buildings, can involve thousands of tasks and many subcontractors.

Computerized scheduling tools, such as Gantt charts, PERT diagrams, and WBS software, make it possible to plan and track each construction phase and break a project down into a series of tasks. For each task, planners enter its estimated duration and how it relates to other tasks. For example, drywall work that requires eight days depends on interior framing, electrical work, and plumbing being finished first. Given information about all the tasks in a project, planning software can create a master schedule showing both best-case and worst-case completion dates, and contractors can easily update the schedule based on actual construction progress.

© John Van Hasselt/Sygma/Corbis

At a high-tech construction site, computers can play several roles. A site supervisor can use a wireless handheld computer to view and update the construction schedule stored on a desktop computer at the contractor's main office. Rather than refer to a set of printed—and possibly outdated—plans, the supervisor can refer to up-to-date plans transmitted from the home office. A supervisor might even wear a hard-hat-mounted computer that collects multimedia data, such as video and sound, to document site inspections. A voice-activated microphone records the supervisor's comments and adds them to the digital video, which can be uploaded to a database in the contractor's main office.

Computers also play a role in guiding bulldozers during site preparation by using construction software developed at Ohio State University that works with a global positioning system (GPS). A GPS receiver is mounted on a vehicle that traverses the site. GPS

signals are collected and entered in the software program, which creates a map and a plan for site preparation. A wireless computer monitor mounted in each bulldozer's cab receives data from the software and displays it to the operator. The system allows construction crews to stake and grade a site with to-the-centimeter accuracy.

Computers embedded in robots are used extensively on large construction projects in Japan. These single-task robots perform specific jobs. For example, a concrete-task robot might lay forms, bend rebar, pour concrete, and screed the surface to a smooth finish. Other robots weld steel components, apply paint, or install tile. Single-task robots have been successful because they shield human workers from dangerous and difficult jobs, and tend to work faster and more consistently than humans. However, trained technicians are required to set up and monitor robot work.

Although construction robots are widely used in Japan, they aren't popular with contractors in many other parts of the world. Industry observers speculate that Japan's shortage of unskilled laborers differentiates it from countries where labor is readily available and relatively inexpensive. In the United States, for example, college students working in construction is a long-standing summer tradition—but one that might be changing. In a recent survey, students viewed construction work as dirty and undesirable and, out of 252 career choices, ranked it as 251.

Construction robots might help fill the labor gap in countries such as the United States, but potential barriers, such as union regulations, could discourage their use. Some observers question how building trade union agreements might affect construction site robots. According to one supervisor's worst-case scenario, "Millwrights will want to set up the device, electricians will want to fix the electronic controls, equipment operators will want to run it, cement finishers will want to adjust it, and laborers will be expected to clean it." The future of computer-powered robots at construction sites is still unclear and illustrates the controversies that sometimes surround technology as it filters into society and the workplace.

10

New Perspectives Labs

To access the New Perspectives Lab for Chapter 10, open the NP2013 interactive eBook and then click the icon next to the lab title.

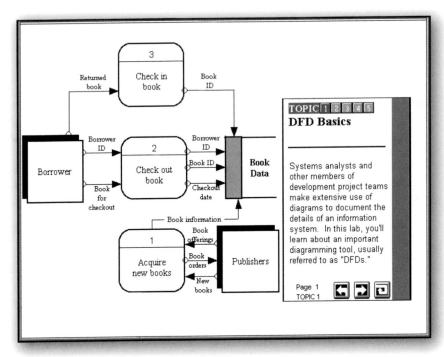

WORKING WITH DFDS

IN THIS LAB YOU'LL LEARN:

- The purpose of data flow diagrams (DFDs) in the system development life cycle
- How to read a leveled set of DFDs
- The meaning of each DFD symbol
- The differences between Gane/Sarson DFD notation and Yourdon/Coad DFD notation
- How to label data flows, entities, data stores, and processes
- How to create a context DFD
- How to "explode" a DFD to show additional levels of detail
- Why "black holes" and "miracles" indicate DFD errors

LAB ASSIGNMENTS

1. Start the interactive part of the lab. Make sure you've enabled Tracking if you want to save your QuickCheck results. Perform each lab step as directed, and answer all the lab QuickCheck questions. When you exit the lab, your answers are automatically graded and your results are displayed.

2. Use paper and pencil, graphics software, or a CASE tool to create a context DFD for a video rental store. Use Gane/Sarson notation. Remember that the store purchases as well as rents videos and DVDs.

3. Explode the DFD you created in Assignment 2 so that it represents the main processes and data stores for the video rental store. Make sure you label data flows, processes, entities, and data stores. Before you finalize your DFD, make sure it contains no black holes or miracles.

4. Convert the DFD you drew in Assignment 3 to Yourdon/Coad notation.

Key Terms

Make sure you understand all the boldfaced key terms presented in this chapter. With the NP2013 interactive eBook, you can use this list of terms as an interactive study activity. First, try to define a term in your own words, and then click the term to compare your definition with the definition presented in the chapter.

10

Acceptance testing, 586
Actors, 573
Ad hoc report, 561
Analysis phase, 571
Application development tool, 578
Application specifications, 581
Application testing, 584
Batch processing, 560
BI, 569
BPR, 569
Business, 556
CASE tool, 574
Centralized processing, 577
Change requests, 582
Class diagram, 573
Commit or rollback strategy, 560
CRM, 569
Data center, 592
Data flow, 572
Data flow diagram, 572
Data store, 572
Decision model, 562
Decision query, 562
Decision support system, 562
Decision support worksheet, 579
Design phase, 576
Detail reports, 560
Direct conversion, 586
Disaster recovery plan, 594
Distributed processing, 577
EAI, 569
EDI, 569
Enterprise information system, 559
ERP, 569
Exception report, 561
Executive information system, 562
Expert system, 564
Expert system shell, 564
External entity, 572
External information, 559
Feature creep, 582
Fuzzy logic, 564

Gantt chart, 570
Help desk, 588
Implementation phase, 583
Inference engine, 564
Info. engineering methodology, 570
Information system, 556
Integration testing, 584
Internal information, 559
JIT, 569
Joint application design, 567
Knowledge base, 564
Knowledge engineering, 564
Maintenance phase, 587
Management information system, 561
Managers, 557
Mission, 557
Mission statement, 557
MRP, 569
MTBF, 591
Neural network, 565
Nonprofit organization, 556
Object-oriented methodology, 570
OLTP system, 560
Online processing, 560
Operational planning, 558
Organization, 556
Organizational chart, 557
Parallel conversion, 586
PERT, 570
Phased conversion, 586
PIECES framework, 569
Pilot conversion, 586
Planning phase, 567
Procedure handbook, 585
Process, 572
Project Development Plan, 567
Project management software, 571
Quality of service, 587
Quality-of-service metric, 587
Request for proposal, 580
Request for quotation, 580
Scheduled reports, 561

Semi-structured problem, 558
Sequence diagram, 574
Software customization, 584
Strategic planning, 557
Structured methodology, 570
Structured problem, 558
Success factors, 571
Summary report, 561
System conversion, 586
System development life cycle, 566
System documentation, 585
System operator, 588
System requirements, 571
System Requirements Report, 572
System testing, 584
Systems analysis and design, 566
Systems programmer, 588
Tactical planning, 558
Test area, 584
TQM, 569
Transaction, 559
Transaction processing system, 559
Turnkey system, 578
UML, 573
Unit testing, 584
Unstructured problem, 558
Use case, 573
Use case diagram, 573
User documentation, 585
WBS, 570
Workers, 557

Interactive Summary

To review important concepts from this chapter, fill in the blanks to best complete each sentence. When using the NP2013 interactive eBook, click the Check Answers buttons to automatically score your answers.

SECTION A: _____ systems play a key role in helping organizations achieve goals, which are set forth in a(n) _____ statement. Computers can be used by people at all levels of an organization. Workers use information systems to produce and manipulate information. Managers depend on information systems to supply data that is essential for long-term _____ planning and short-term tactical planning.

Transaction _____ systems provide an organization with a way to collect, display, modify, or cancel transactions. These systems encompass activities such as general accounting, inventory tracking, and e-commerce. _____ information systems typically build on the data collected by a TPS to produce reports that managers use to make the business decisions needed to solve routine, structured problems.

A decision _____ system helps workers and managers make non-routine decisions by constructing decision models that include data collected from internal and external sources.

A(n) _____ system is designed to analyze data and produce a recommendation or decision based on a set of facts and rules called a(n) _____ base. These facts and rules can be written using an expert system shell or a programming language. A(n) _____ engine evaluates the facts and rules to produce answers to questions posed to the system. Using a technique called _____ logic, these systems can deal with imprecise data and problems that have more than one solution. If the rules for an expert system are not known, a neural _____ might be used to enable a computer to "learn" how to make a decision.

▶ CHECK ANSWERS

SECTION B: The process of planning and building an information system is referred to as systems _____ and design. The development process is supervised by an organization's Information Technology (IT) department, but the _____ team usually includes members from other departments as well. System development follows some type of system development _____ cycle (SDLC), which consists of several phases.

A project team can use one of several approaches to the system development process. For example, the _____ methodology focuses on the processes that take place in an information system. The information _____ methodology focuses on the data that an information system collects. The object-_____ methodology treats an information system as a collection of interacting objects.

A project begins with a(n) _____ phase in which a member of the IT department creates a Project Development Plan. The project team then proceeds to the _____ phase, with the goal of producing a list of requirements for a new or revised information system.

▶ CHECK ANSWERS

SECTION C: In the [＿＿＿＿＿＿＿＿] phase of the SDLC, the project team identifies potential solutions, evaluates those solutions, and then selects the best one. The team members might consider various levels of [＿＿＿＿＿＿＿＿] , such as scanning magnetic credit card strips instead of entering credit card numbers from a keyboard. The project team might also consider whether a(n) [＿＿＿＿＿＿＿＿] processing model would be better than a distributed processing model. Several [＿＿＿＿＿＿＿＿] technologies might provide connectivity solutions. Alternative software solutions for a project include the use of programming languages, application development tools, or commercial software. A(n) [＿＿＿＿＿＿＿＿] system might offer a complete hardware and software solution.

After the project team selects a solution, team members can then select specific hardware and software products to build the new information system. The project team might send out a request for [＿＿＿＿＿＿＿＿] , asking vendors to recommend a solution. As an alternative, the project team can send out a request for [＿＿＿＿＿＿＿＿] , which simply asks for vendor prices. After selecting hardware and software, the project team can develop [＿＿＿＿＿＿＿＿] specifications that describe the way the new information system should interact with the user, store data, process data, and format reports.

10

▶ CHECK ANSWERS

SECTION D: During the [＿＿＿＿＿＿＿＿] phase of the SDLC, the project team supervises the technicians who set up new hardware, install programming languages and other application [＿＿＿＿＿＿＿＿] tools, create and test applications, and customize software. The team also finalizes the system documentation and trains users. In this phase, three types of testing ensure that new software works correctly. [＿＿＿＿＿＿＿＿] testing is performed on each module, and then [＿＿＿＿＿＿＿＿] testing is performed to make sure that all the modules work together correctly. [＿＿＿＿＿＿＿＿] testing ensures that the software components work correctly on the hardware and with other, perhaps older, elements of the information system.

When application testing is complete, data is converted from the old system to the new one, users are trained, and the new system

goes live. Four types of information system go-live conversions are possible: direct, parallel, phased, or pilot. At the end of the conversion process, the information system undergoes a final test called [＿＿＿＿＿＿＿＿] testing, designed to assure the system's owner that the new system works as specified.

After testing and installation, an information system enters the [＿＿＿＿＿＿＿＿] phase of its life cycle. During this phase, a(n) [＿＿＿＿＿＿＿＿] operator performs backups, monitors system utilization, and troubleshoots operational problems. As users discover bugs, programmers must fix them. Ongoing user support from a help [＿＿＿＿＿＿＿＿] might also be required.

▶ CHECK ANSWERS

SECTION E: The most common threats to corporate information systems include natural disasters, power outages, equipment failure, human errors, software failures, [＿＿＿＿＿＿＿＿] breaches, acts of war, and malware. These threats can be handled in several ways. [＿＿＿＿＿＿＿＿] reduce the likelihood of deliberate attack. [＿＿＿＿＿＿＿＿] countermeasures shield vulnerabilities to render an attack unsuccessful. [＿＿＿＿＿＿＿＿] procedures reduce the effect of an attack. [＿＿＿＿＿＿＿＿] activities recognize attacks and trigger a

corrective response. To protect hardware, software, and data, corporate systems are often housed in a protective facility called a(n) [＿＿＿＿＿＿＿＿] center. Most companies have a disaster [＿＿＿＿＿＿＿＿] plan that describes how to secure data against disaster, reconstruct lost data, and restore normal operations after a disaster. Companies also have established policies that guard against corporate identity [＿＿＿＿＿＿＿＿] and protect personal data of employees and clients.

▶ CHECK ANSWERS

Interactive Situation Questions

Apply what you've learned to some typical computing situations. When using the NP2013 interactive eBook, you can type your answers, and then use the Check Answers button to automatically score your responses.

1. Suppose that you own a small bookstore located in a mall. Business seems to be declining, and you suspect that many of your former customers are now shopping at online bookstores. What can you do about declining sales? You realize that this problem falls into the category of a(n) [   ] problem, and you might not be able to solve it using the data supplied by your MIS.

2. Your friend just graduated and started work in a local pharmacy. She tells you about the pharmacy's computer system that warns of dangerous drug interactions by examining the patient's prescription record and sometimes asking the pharmacist to enter age and allergy information. The system that she has been describing sounds like a(n) [   ] system.

3. An article in your local newspaper describes a new airport security system as "a sophisticated facial-recognition system powered by advanced computer technology that learns on its own." This technology sounds like a(n) [   ] network.

4. As a member of the IT staff at a large corporation, you often hear about problems with the current information system. One recently discovered problem is that when an employee quits (or gets fired), sometimes the network manager is not notified, and the former employee continues to have access to company data over the Internet. Using the PIECES framework, you would classify this as a(n) [   ] problem.

5. Your county provides online access to property records. You simply enter the address of the property or the owner's name. However, each search seems to take longer than one minute. According to the PIECES framework, this delay would be classified as a(n) [   ] problem.

6. Your roommate works in the Data Entry department for a large corporation and has been asked to participate in a JAD session. When asked about it, you explain to your roommate that JAD stands for [   ] application design, and this probably means the corporation is working on a new information system.

7. You just started working in the IT department for a very small company that's developing a new information system. Your coworkers are trying to track down a discrepancy that resulted from a change in the name of a data field. Although you don't say it, you realize that such a problem would not have occurred if the project team had used [   ] tools. (Hint: Use the acronym.)

8. On your last job, you worked as an admitting clerk in a hospital. One day you were told to begin using the hospital's new information system. The next day, you were told to go back to using the old system until further notice. You suspect that these events occurred as a result of a failed attempt at a(n) [   ] conversion.

▶ CHECK ANSWERS

Interactive Practice Tests

Practice tests that consist of ten multiple-choice, true/false, and fill-in-the-blank questions are available in the NP2013 interactive eBook. Test questions are selected at random from a large test bank, so each time you take a test, you'll receive a different set of questions. Your tests are scored immediately, and you can print study guides that help you find the correct answers for any questions that you missed.

 CLICK TO START

Learning Objectives Checkpoints

Learning Objectives Checkpoints are designed to help you assess whether you have achieved the major learning objectives for this chapter. You can use paper and pencil or word processing software to complete most of the activities.

1. List ten information systems that you've used.

2. Describe how information systems help organizations fulfill their missions, deal with threats, and take advantage of opportunities.

3. Explain the differences between strategic, tactical, and operational planning. Provide an example of how a computer system might be used for each type of planning.

4. Explain the differences between structured, semi-structured, and unstructured problems. Provide an example of each type, and describe how an information system might contribute to solving the problems.

5. Using your own examples, discuss the ways in which an organization can respond to opportunities and threats.

6. Contrast and compare the characteristics of transaction processing systems, management information systems, decision support systems, and expert systems.

7. List the phases of the SDLC and the tasks that occur in each phase. Identify three development methodologies that systems analysts might use to complete the SDLC.

8. For each letter of the PIECES framework, create your own example of a problem that a systems analyst might discover in an obsolete information system.

9. List and briefly describe three tools used for project scheduling, and then list and describe four documentation tools used in the analysis phase of the SDLC. Draw a DFD showing the flow of data (ingredients) when you make a grilled cheese sandwich.

10. Explain the advantages and disadvantages of centralized processing and distributed processing.

11. List and describe four software alternatives that systems analysts might consider for a new information system.

12. Describe the five types of testing used during the implementation phase.

13. Use your own words to describe the advantages and disadvantages of direct, parallel, phased, and pilot conversions.

14. List and define at least four quality-of-service metrics.

15. List and describe eight threats that could cause information systems to fail.

16. Explain how organizations can protect the data stored on their information systems.

Study Tip: Make sure you can use your own words to correctly answer each of the purple focus questions that appear throughout the chapter.

10

Concept Map

Fill in the blanks to illustrate the hierarchy of SDLC phases.

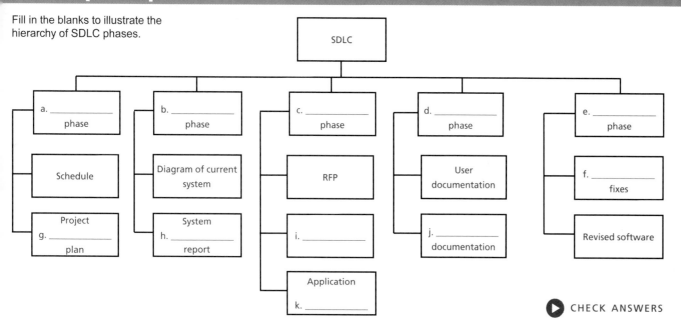

SDLC

a. _____ phase — Schedule — Project g. _____ plan

b. _____ phase — Diagram of current system — System h. _____ report

c. _____ phase — RFP — i. _____ — Application k. _____

d. _____ phase — User documentation — j. _____ documentation

e. _____ phase — f. _____ fixes — Revised software

▶ CHECK ANSWERS

11

Databases

Chapter Contents

Learning Objectives

After reading this chapter, you will be able to answer the following questions by completing the outcomes-based Learning Objectives Checkpoints on page 671.

1. What makes databases such an essential component of modern life?
2. Can databases be used to predict consumer behavior?
3. What are the basic components of a database?
4. Why are relationships a significant aspect of databases?
5. What's the difference between flat files and other database models?
6. What is the best software for creating and managing databases?
7. Is it possible to access databases using the Web?
8. What is the significance of field types in a database?
9. Why do errors creep into databases?
10. How do database designers use normalization to reduce data redundancy?
11. What role do sorting and indexing play in making databases more versatile?
12. Is it difficult to create reports from a database?
13. What is SQL?
14. How safe is the data in a database?
15. Have lawmakers kept up with technology by enacting laws and regulations pertaining to databases?
16. Can individuals take steps to protect their privacy when so much personal data is stored in corporate and government databases?

CourseMate

Visit the NP2013 CourseMate for this chapter's Pre-Quiz, Audio Overview and Flashcards, Detailed Objectives, Chapter Quiz, Online Games, and more labs.

Multimedia and Interactive Elements

When using the NP2013 interactive eBook, click the ▶ icons to access multimedia resources.

Apply Your Knowledge The information in this chapter will give you the background to:

- Decide if you can use a simple tool, such as a spreadsheet, for your own databases

- Create an efficient and effective database and then use it to organize, find, and report information

- Post database reports on the Web

- Formulate basic SQL queries

- Take steps to protect personal data that is stored on corporate and government databases

- Evaluate the pros and cons of proposals for using database technology in controversial applications such as profiling terrorists, exploring genetics, and predicting shopping habits

Try It!

HOW DOES "BAD" DATA GET INTO DATABASES?

Databases are everywhere and information about you is in many of them. You might wonder if that information is accurate. Data entry mistakes are easy to make, but a well designed database can prevent some common data entry errors. To start exploring databases, you can check the design of a database that's on most computers—the e-mail address book.

1. Start your e-mail program and access its address book function.

2. Use the menu bar or toolbar option to add an address or contact.

3. A typical address book stores data for each person in a record. The record is divided into fields, such as name and e-mail address. Many address books also store additional data such as phone numbers and physical addresses. How many fields does your address book provide?

4. Begin to fill in fields with data for one of your friends. Are the field names clearly labeled so you know what you're supposed to enter into them?

5. Does your address book divide the first name and last name into two fields or does it combine that data into one field?

6. Try entering the data for the Name field in all uppercase letters. When you move to the next field, does the database maintain the uppercase format? If necessary, go back and modify the field using an initial capital letter.

7. Try entering an e-mail address that does not contain an @ sign. Does the database accept e-mail addresses that are not valid?

8. Try entering invalid data in other fields. What happens if you enter an invalid state abbreviation, like OP?

9. It is not necessary to save the address you've entered. Close the address book. As you read Chapter 11, you'll discover the significance of field normalization, case sensitivity, and validity checks.

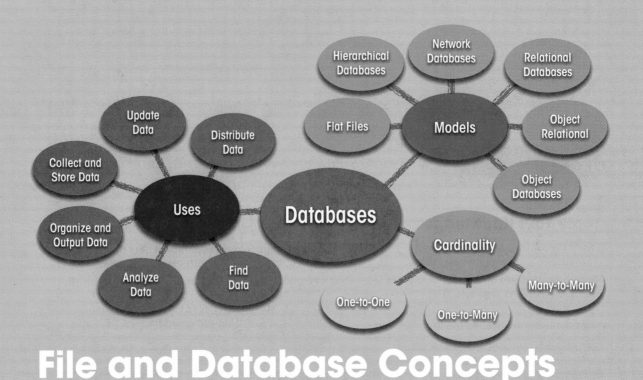

File and Database Concepts

DATABASES ARE AN ESSENTIAL aspect of modern life. Most businesses could not function without them and they are the backbone of popular Internet services such as iTunes, Facebook, Classmates, and eBay. Section A begins the chapter with an overview of databases and the many ways they are used today.

DATABASE BASICS

▶ **What is a database?** In the broadest definition, a **database** is a collection of information. Today, databases are typically stored as computer files. A database can be a simple personal list, such as your address book, or it can be a massive list, such as New York City telephone numbers. Databases can even incorporate several lists. For example, the database for an e-commerce site, such as Amazon.com, includes inventory lists and customer lists.

▶ **How is database information used?** The tasks associated with creating, maintaining, and accessing the information in databases are referred to as data management, file management, or database management. Databases can be used in a variety of ways, from a simple tool for collecting and tracking data, to a comprehensive source for making decisions and predicting future trends.

▶ Collect and store data. A database is a collection of data, but that collection grows as additional data is obtained. Data can be collected and entered manually or electronically. Information can also be removed from a database when it is no longer needed. Keeping a database lean can speed up searches and conserve storage space.

Historical data can be valuable; so rather than deleting it, old data can be moved to an archive. As a consumer, you should be aware that records can remain in databases and archives years after transactions have been completed, your name has been "removed," or your records are designated as "inactive" (Figure 11-1).

FIGURE 11-1

Database data that is no longer current is normally moved to an archive, which can be stored on a hard drive, secondary server, or tape. High-volume archives can be stored in a tape silo containing thousands of data tapes and a tape robot that pulls tapes off the shelves and loads them into a tape drive.

❱ **Update data.** One of the primary database management activities is keeping data up to date by entering current addresses, inventory quantities, and so on. As with collecting data, updates can be made manually or electronically.

Data entry errors can result in database inaccuracies, which are not always easy to correct. Horror stories about data entry errors abound, including individuals—very much alive—whose records were mistakenly marked "deceased" and victims of identity theft who had trouble restoring their credit ratings. Organizations that maintain databases should be held accountable for data accuracy.

❱ **Organize and output data.** The data in a typical database is stored in no particular order. New data is appended to the end of the file because it is too cumbersome to insert it in, say, alphabetical order, then rearrange all the records that come after it. Reports created with this jumble of raw data would not be particularly useful. To make data into a more suitable report, it can be organized in a variety of ways. It can be alphabetized, placed in numeric order, grouped, and subtotaled.

Database output is easy to organize and reorganize without actually rearranging the physical data on the disk. A database can be configured so that a librarian can extract a list of patrons with overdue books organized by date, while at the same time a student can look for a list of books written by Elizabeth Peters. The same database can be configured to print envelopes for a library fund-raiser in order by ZIP code to take advantage of cost-saving bulk mail rates.

❱ **Distribute data.** Databases, combined with mail merge and other computerized technologies, offer efficient ways to distribute information to customers, employees, the press, government agencies, and other companies. Your monthly electric bill is generated from the power company's database. That recall notice you received about the braking system in your six-month-old car, your monthly bank statement, and your class schedule for next semester all are generated from databases.

FIGURE 11-2

Digital databases are easier to store than paper records, but records in digital format are also easier to steal, copy, and misuse.

Unfortunately, databases also generate mountains of Publishers Clearing House mailings and an irritating amount of v1agr*a spam that lands in your e-mail Inbox. Today's digital databases are much more portable than old-fashioned paper-based databases, but the convenience of digital formats makes computer databases easier to misuse (Figure 11-2).

David Ellis/Getty Images

Spammers, junk mailers, and telemarketers pay only a fraction of a penny for each name on a mailing list or call list. Millions of records can be easily copied, sent over the Internet, and stored on an external hard drive, a USB flash drive, or a DVD. The legal system has yet to iron out details regarding database ownership and under what conditions it is allowable to share database data.

❱ **Find data.** Databases make it easy to locate information. You can use an online library card catalog to find books. A pharmacist can check a pharmaceutical database for drug interactions before filling a prescription. A computer technician can check a manufacturer's database to find the part number for replacing your computer's fried hard drive.

In the software chapter, you read about several ways to locate data in a database. Query languages offer a set of commands to help you formulate a search such as *Select from MusicCollection where Artist = 'Elvis'* that finds all the songs performed by Elvis Presley in your MP3 music collection. Natural query languages allow you to search by asking questions such as *What songs did Elvis perform?* You can also query by example using a fill-in form, like the one in Figure 11-3.

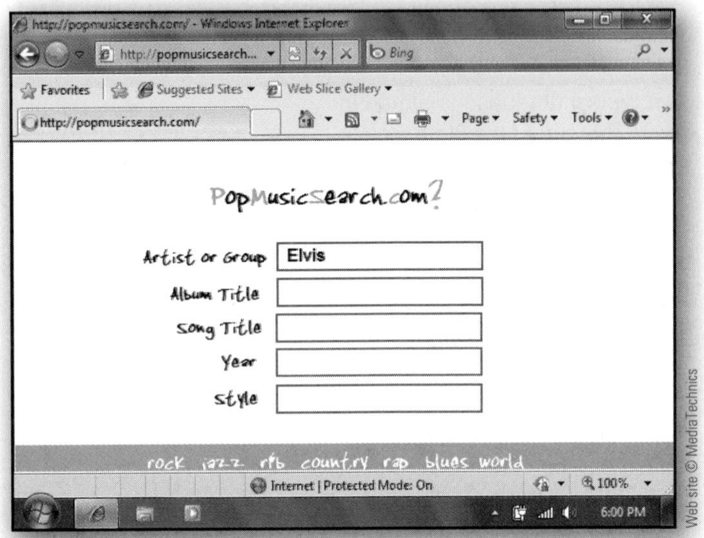

Web site © MediaTechnics

FIGURE 11-3

A query-by-example interface displays a form and formulates a query based on what the user enters.

▶ **Analyze data.** Databases include certain facts as raw data, such as names, addresses, bank balances, prices, and inventory quantities. Analyzing this data using statistics and other interpretive tools can produce information that is not readily apparent from simply looking at raw data.

For example, a nationwide chain of bookstores issues discount cards and tracks books purchased using each card. An analysis of sales data shows that customers who purchase self-help books typically purchase other similar books within six months. Nowhere in the database does it explicitly state "self-help book purchasers tend to buy additional self-help books." This conclusion is new information that can be gleaned from the raw data. Techniques for data analysis include data mining and OLAP.

▶ **What is data mining?** **Data mining** refers to the process of analyzing existing database information to discover previously unknown and potentially useful information, including relationships and patterns. The data accessed by data mining and other analysis techniques is often stored in a **data warehouse**, which is a repository for data from more than one database. Data from operational databases—those used for daily transactions—is transferred to a data warehouse where it can be combined with data from other databases to enhance the data set.

Data mining can reveal relationships. For example, an analysis of over 10 million policies and accident claims in the Farmers Insurance Group database revealed a relationship between age, marital status, second car ownership, sports car ownership, and accident claims. Married baby boomers who owned a full size car or minivan in addition to a sports car tended to make far fewer claims than younger, single sports car owners. As a result of the data analysis, lower insurance rates were offered to sports car owners who fit the low-risk profile.

A more complex type of data analysis can reveal sequences of events that predict future trends and patterns. **Predictive analytics** refers to a branch of data mining that focuses on predicting future probabilities and trends. It makes use of statistical algorithms, neural networks, and optimization research to discover patterns in data. For example, researchers might use predictive analytics to predict customer behavior, unmask terrorists, forecast storm paths, or determine genetic susceptibility to certain diseases.

Data mining and predictive analytics are sometimes criticized for finding relationships, patterns, and trends when none actually exist. You could, for example, use data mining to look for trends in lottery numbers and locations. Suppose that data mining reveals that October's winning numbers always include more even numbers than odd ones, and were purchased at convenience stores. Unhappily, probability theory would tell you that the pattern is an anomaly and won't help you predict next week's winning numbers. The misuse of data mining is sometimes called data dredging or data fishing.

▶ What is OLAP? One of today's most advanced data analysis methods, **OLAP** (online analytical processing), allows decision makers to look for relationships between multiple data dimensions. It is a technology used in the context of business intelligence and decision support systems that helps decision makers by providing timely, accurate, and relevant information for business decisions.

To understand how OLAP works, imagine an employee database for an international corporation. A manager might use OLAP to look for trends in employee performance. The analysis includes several dimensions, including location, revenue generated by each employee, attrition rates, and employee satisfaction. OLAP might show that although sales seem to be fairly good, the North American sales force is becoming dissatisfied and some employees are looking for jobs elsewhere.

To analyze and mine complex data sets, decision makers sometimes use **executive dashboard software**, which provides tools for formulating OLAP queries and displaying results visually (Figure 11-4).

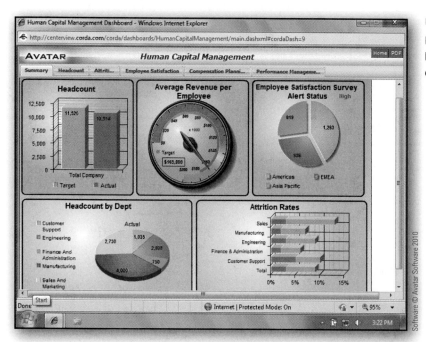

FIGURE 11-4

Executive dashboard software helps decision makers visualize data from complex data sets.

DATABASE MODELS

▶ **What is the underlying structure of a database?** Computer databases evolved from manual filing systems. A filing cabinet full of folders and papers would be classified as an **unstructured file** because every document has a unique structure and contains different kinds of data.

In a box of unstructured documents, you could find old receipts, photos, product brochures, and handwritten letters. The electronic equivalent to this jumble of information might be the collection of documents and graphics stored at a Web site.

In contrast to a collection of dissimilar information, library card catalogs and Rolodexes would be classified as structured files. A **structured file** uses a uniform format to store data for each person or thing in the file. The focus of this chapter is on databases that are constructed with structured files because they constitute the majority of databases used in business, e-commerce, and government activities.

Structured files can be used in different ways to build databases. The underlying structure of a database is referred to as a **database model**. Figure 11-5 lists basic database models.

Some of these models are becoming obsolete, whereas other models are just beginning to develop a track record. Understanding the characteristics of each model will help you determine which type of database is right for your needs, and understand why certain types of databases are popularly deployed for various business and organizational applications.

▶ **What's the simplest way to store data?** The simplest model for storing data is a **flat file** that consists of a single, two-dimensional table of data elements. Each row in the table is a record, and each column of the table is a field. Computer databases display records as rows in a table or as forms, as shown in Figure 11-6.

FIGURE 11-5

Database Models

▶ Flat file
▶ Hierarchical database
▶ Networked database
▶ Relational database
▶ Dimensional database
▶ Object database
▶ Object-relational database

FIGURE 11-6

Records can be displayed as rows in a table or as forms.

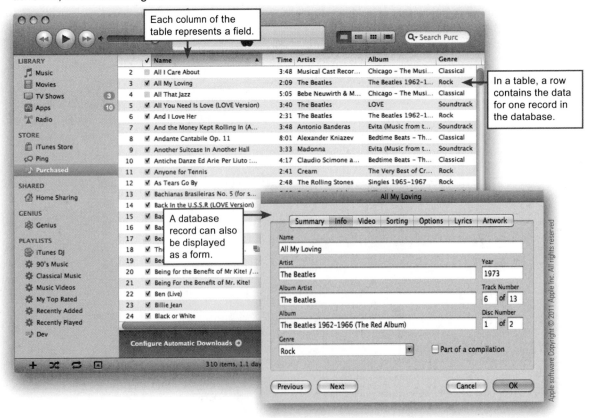

A **field** contains the smallest unit of meaningful information, so you might call it the basic building block for a structured file or database. Each field has a unique **field name** that describes its contents. For example, in an iTunes playlist, the field called Name holds the name of a song, the Time field holds the song length, the Artist field holds the name of the performer, the Album field holds the name of the album that the song came from, and the Genre field holds the type of song.

A field can be variable length or fixed length. A **variable-length field** is like an accordion—it expands to fit the data you enter, up to some maximum number of characters. A **fixed-length field** contains a predetermined number of characters (bytes). The data you enter in a fixed-length field cannot exceed the allocated field length. Moreover, if the data you enter is shorter than the allocated length, blank spaces are automatically added to fill the field. The fields in Figure 11-7 are fixed length. The underscores indicate the number of characters allocated for each field.

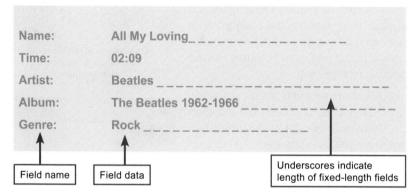

FIGURE 11-7

When setting up a database, the length of text fields should be adequate to store the longest names or titles. The Time field can be short because the longest tracks are 60 minutes or less, which can be expressed in the format MM:SS, where MM is minutes and SS is seconds.

In the world of databases, a **record** refers to a collection of data fields. You're already familiar with several types of records, such as student records, medical records, and dental records. Each record stores data about one entity—a person, place, thing, or event. For example, a data record stored in an iTunes playlist contains fields of data pertaining to a digital music track.

The template for a record is referred to as a **record type**. It contains field names, but no data. Creating record types is part of the design process that lets database designers specify the information needed to complete each record. A record type, similar to a blank form, is usually shown without any data in the fields. A record that contains data is referred to as a **record occurrence**, or simply a record (Figure 11-8).

FIGURE 11-8

A record type (left) is simply a list of fields, whereas a record occurrence (right) contains data for a particular entity. In this case, the entity is a track called "All My Loving" on the album *The Beatles 1962-1966*.

Record Type

| Name |
| Time |
| Artist |
| Album |
| Genre |

Record Occurrence

Name	All My Loving
Time	02:09
Artist	Beatles
Album	The Beatles 1962-1966
Genre	Rock

▶ How are flat files used? Flat files are the foundation for simple databases, such as an e-mail address book, an iTunes playlist, or the addresses for a mail merge. It is also the model used for spreadsheets. With a flat file, you can search for, update, group, and organize records.

Each record in a flat file, however, is an independent entity and no relationships can be established between records. For example, you can't set up links between all of The Beatles' songs in your iTunes playlist. If you are listening to "A Hard Day's Night," you can't automatically link to The Beatles' next most popular top ten song.

▶ Why would a database need to keep track of relationships? In database jargon, a **relationship** is an association between data that's stored in different record types. Relationships are important because there are associations among the real-life things that database records represent.

Let's use a fictional music store called Vintage Music Shop as an example. For this business, there are relationships such as between customers and the goods they purchase, and between an album and the song tracks it contains. Although you can work with an iTunes playlist without establishing relationships, other databases, such as the one used at Vintage Music Shop, are more efficient if relationships can be defined.

An important aspect of the relationship between record types is cardinality. **Cardinality** refers to the number of associations that can exist between two record types. For example, a Vintage Music Shop customer can place more than one order. The reverse is not true, however. A particular order cannot be placed jointly by two customers. When one record is related to many records, the relationship is referred to as a **one-to-many relationship**.

In contrast, a **many-to-many relationship** means that one record in a particular record type can be related to many records in another record type, and vice versa. For example, an album contains many song tracks. At the same time, a track could be included on several different albums. George Harrison's song "Something" was included in The Beatles' *Abbey Road* album and the greatest hits release, *The Beatles 1*.

A **one-to-one relationship** means that a record in one record type is related to only one record in another record type. This kind of relationship is rare in the world of databases. It is sometimes used to conserve disk space when an item of information will not be stored for every record in the database.

For example, the marketing director at Vintage Music Shop sometimes wants to include a description of an album in the database, but only for historically notable albums. If a Description field is included in the Albums record type, it will be empty for most records. Empty fields take up space on the disk, so it's not desirable to have fields that will most likely be blank. Creating another record type, called Album Description, allows this data to be stored efficiently. The Album record and its description record would have a one-to-one relationship.

The relationship between record types can be depicted graphically with an **entity-relationship diagram** (sometimes called an ER diagram or ERD). Figure 11-9 shows ERDs for one-to-many, many-to-many, and one-to-one relationships.

FIGURE 11-9

An entity-relationship diagram depicts each record type as a rectangle. Relationships and cardinality are shown by connecting lines.

One-to-many relationship
One customer can order many albums.

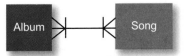

Many-to-many relationship
One album contains many tracks, and a track can be included on several different albums.

One-to-one relationship
An album has only one description.

KEY TO ERD SYMBOLS

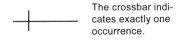

The crossbar indicates exactly one occurrence.

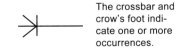

The crossbar and crow's foot indicate one or more occurrences.

▶ What kinds of databases track relationships?

Except for flat files, other database models allow you to track relationships. The way database models work with relationships is a key to their differences. A **hierarchical database** allows one-to-one and one-to-many relationships, linked in a hierarchical structure (Figure 11-10).

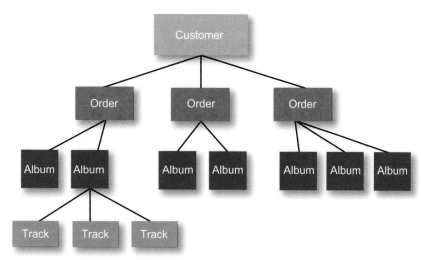

FIGURE 11-10

In this hierarchical database, Customer, Album, Track, and Order are record types. All of the relationships are one-to-many.

A **network database** uses a mesh-like structure to offer the additional capacity to define many-to-many relationships (Figure 11-11).

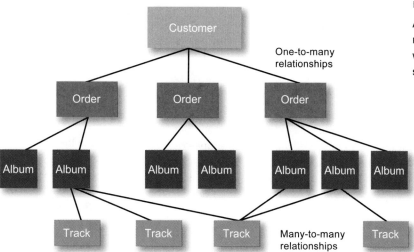

FIGURE 11-11

A network database allows many-to-many relationships as well as one-to-many relationships between record types.

Although hierarchical and network databases offer lightning quick searches and utilize a minimum amount of disk space for storage, they are rarely used today for business, consumer, and other mainstream database applications. Instead, they remain in use only for specialized applications.

Windows uses a hierarchical database to store Registry data that keeps track of the software and hardware configuration of your PC. The DNS system that keeps track of Internet addresses uses a network database structure. Outside of such specialized applications, databases built on hierarchical and network models have been replaced by relational or object databases.

TERMINOLOGY NOTE

A network database does not have any relation to computer networks; it is *not* a special kind of database designed for use on LANs or the Internet.

▶ **What's a relational database?** A **relational database** stores data in a collection of related tables. Each **table** is a sequence of records, similar to a flat file. All the records in a table are of the same record type. Each row of a table is equivalent to a record. Each column of the table is equivalent to a field. Most relational databases contain several tables. For example, the Vintage Music Shop's database uses six tables to store data, as shown in Figure 11-12.

FIGURE 11-12

Vintage Music Shop stores data in six tables.

ALBUM DESCRIPTION

Cat#	Description

TRACKS

Cat#	TrackTitle	Track Length	TrackSample

ORDER DETAILS

OrderNumber	Cat#	Qty	DiscountPrice

ORDERS

OrderNumber	CustomerNumber	TotalPrice	OrderDate

CUSTOMERS

CustomerNumber	FirstName	LastName	Street	City

ALBUMS

Cat#	Album	Artist	Release Date	In Stock	Value
LPM-2256	G.I. Blues	Elvis Presley	10/01/1960	4	20.00
7499-2	Between the Buttons	Rolling Stones	02/06/1967	1	13.99
LSP-246	Blue Hawaii	Elvis Presley	10/01/1961	5	50.00
N16014	Surfin' Safari	Beach Boys	10/29/1962	8	18.95

In a relational database, relationships are specified by joining common data stored in records from different tables. Figure 11-13 illustrates a one-to-many relationship between data in the Albums table and data in the Tracks table.

FIGURE 11-13

A relationship in this database shows that "Blue Suede Shoes," "Frankfort Special," and "Wooden Heart" are all tracks from the *G.I. Blues* album.

ALBUMS

Cat#	Album	Artist	Release Date	In Stock	Value
LPM-2256	G.I. Blues	Elvis Presley	10/01/1960	4	20.00
7499-2	Between the Buttons	Rolling Stones	02/06/1967	1	13.99
LSP-246	Blue Hawaii				
N16014	Surfin' Safari				

The Cat# LPM-2256 links records in both tables that refer to Elvis Presley's album *G.I. Blues*.

TRACKS

Cat#	TrackTitle	Track Length	TrackSample
LPM-2256	Blue Suede Shoes	104	BlueSuede.mp3
LPM-2256	Frankfort Special	132	FrankSpec.mp3
LPM-2256	Wooden Heart	163	WoodenHE.mp3
7499-2	Ruby Tuesday	197	RubyT.mp3

▶ **What's the advantage of a relational database?** In a relational database, each table is essentially independent, but tables can be joined for a particular task as required. Relationships can be added, changed, or deleted on demand, making this database model very flexible.

The relational database model's flexibility is a major factor in its use for the majority of databases that handle everyday query and reporting needs of businesses, government agencies, and organizations. It is also the database model supported by many consumer-level database products, such as Microsoft Access.

▶ **What's a dimensional database?** A **dimensional database**, sometimes referred to as a multidimensional database, organizes relationships over three or more dimensions. Each field is contained within a cell that can be accessed directly from a query or from following a relationship. Dimensional databases are an extension of the relational database model, but tables are stacked in addition to being linked side by side. One way to visualize the dimensional database model is as a three-dimensional cube (Figure 11-14).

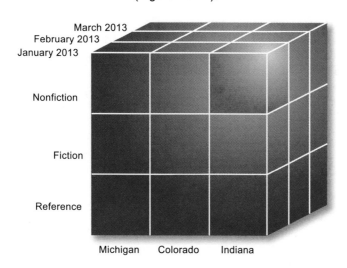

FIGURE 11-14

A data cube represents data in multiple dimensions. This data cube has three dimensions: months, states, and book categories.

The red cube represents data for nonfiction books sold in Indiana in January 2013.

Compared to a relational database with complex queries based on relationships and joins, a dimensional database offers a simpler way to visualize data and formulate queries. Dimensional databases are easy to maintain and efficient to use because data is stored in the same way as it is viewed.

Formulating and populating a dimensional database requires more expertise than formulating and populating a relational database. Consequently, dimensional databases are most often deployed for data analysis and decision support systems in which data from operational databases is moved into a dimensional data warehouse before being queried by managers.

▶ **What's an object database?** An **object database**, also referred to as an object-oriented database, stores data as objects, which can be grouped into classes and defined by attributes and methods. The Programming chapter covers object-oriented terminology in detail; but in the context of object databases, a class defines a group of objects, such as customers or albums.

Classes are described by attributes and methods. The attributes for an object are equivalent to fields in a relational database. For example, a class called Orders might have attributes such as OrderNumber, OrderDate, CustomerNumber, and OrderedAlbums.

A method is any behavior that an object is capable of performing. A method called CheckInventory can be defined for this class. Its job is to make sure the album is in stock.

▶ **What are the advantages of object databases?** Object databases excel in representing objects that have slightly different attributes, which is the case in many real-world business applications. Suppose that Vintage Music Shop accepts phone orders and Web orders.

These two types of orders differ slightly because an e-mail address is used to communicate with Web customers, whereas a telephone number and order clerk name need to be recorded for customers who order by phone. A relational database would require two record types, but an object database can be set up so that the Orders class has two derivative classes: one for Web customers and one for phone customers. Figure 11-15 illustrates classes, derivative classes, and methods in an object database.

FIGURE 11-15

An object database can easily store data about different types of orders. A class called Orders holds data and methods common to all types of orders. A derivative class called Phone Orders inherits all the characteristics of Orders, but it has attributes and methods unique to orders placed by telephone. Web Orders is a derivative class that has attributes and methods unique to orders placed over the Web.

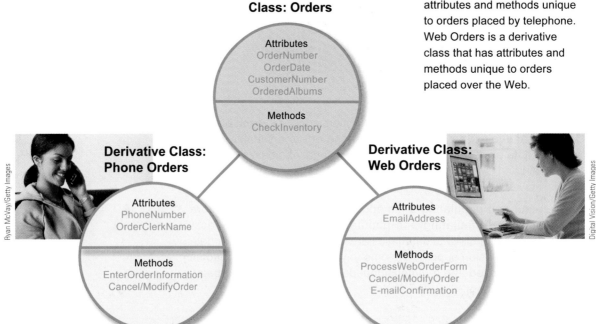

The object database model is newer than the relational model and has not yet gained a substantial foothold in mainstream database applications. Its advocates, however, cite advantages over rival database models, including the idea that object databases best reflect real-world entities and relationships.

▶ **What's an object-relational database?** The term **object-relational database** is used to describe a variety of technologies that combine object-oriented and relational concepts. The object-relational database model has been described as an attempt to add object-oriented characteristics to tables.

Basically, an object-relational database is organized as one or more tables, just as in a traditional relational database. Object-relational databases, however, have the flexibility to store unique types of data and program code necessary to access that data.

To understand the distinction between relational databases and object-relational databases, suppose you restructure your iTunes playlist as a table in a relational database containing fields for the song title, artist, time, and so on. The database does not actually contain the .m4p data for the song, but it probably contains the name of the computer file that holds the song. When you select a song to play, the database doesn't play it. Instead, the file name is passed to your iTunes jukebox, which plays the song.

In contrast, you could use an object-relational database to store the actual digital data for songs in a field called SongFile. Your database could also hold a routine called PlaySong. If you select the database record for "Yesterday," for example, the database uses its PlaySong routine to play the data stored in the SongFile field, so there is no need to use external music player software (Figure 11-16).

Most of today's relational database tools offer object-oriented features. For example, the popular database query language SQL, which you'll learn about later in the chapter, can be used to define custom functions to process the data in a database. However, object-relational hybrids tend not to support a full set of object-oriented characteristics. The distinction is somewhat technical. Suffice it to say that database models are still evolving as the best elements are blended and optimized to meet the needs of today's complex database applications.

FIGURE 11-16

A relational database sends a file name to an external player (top), but an object-relational database can store the song data and the routine to play it.

11

Relational Database

TRACKS

Title	TrackName
Yesterday	Yesterday.m4p

Yesterday.m4p

iTunes Jukebox

Object-relational Database

ALBUMS

Title	SongFile	PlaySong
Yesterday		Do while SongFile Check(bitrate) Open(audioport)

QuickCheck   SECTION A

1. Online [_____] processing allows decision makers to look for relationships between multiple data dimensions.

2. The simplest model for storing data is a(n) [_____] file that consists of a single two-dimensional table.

3. A(n) [_____] can be used to diagram the associations between data that is stored in several record types. (Hint: Use the acronym.)

4. A(n) [_____] database stores records in a collection of tables that can be joined by common data fields.

5. The terms *class*, *attribute*, and *method* apply to [_____] databases.

▶ CHECK ANSWERS

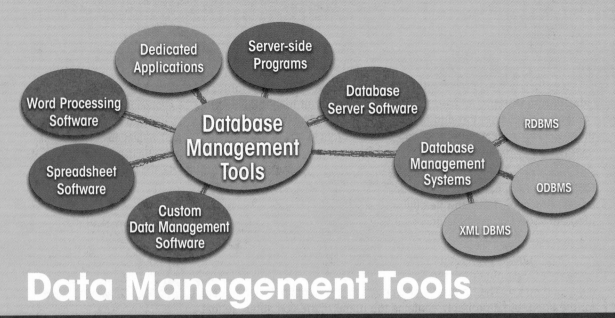

Data Management Tools

ONE OF THE FIRST decisions to make when creating a database is what type of data management tools to use. Different tools are designed for different uses. Section B describes the different types of tools available and explains how to decide which one best suits your needs.

DATA MANAGEMENT SOFTWARE

▶ **Are simple data management tools available?** Yes. The simplest tools for managing data are dedicated applications for specific data management tasks, such as keeping track of appointments or managing your checking account.

Although these tools are easy to use, they don't generally allow you to create new record types because the record types are predefined. To use one of these tools, you simply enter your data. The software includes menus that allow you to manipulate your data after entering it.

▶ **How about a simple, generic tool that allows me to define a file structure?** Most spreadsheet and word processing software packages feature simple tools that allow you to specify fields, enter data, and manipulate it. For example, your word processing software probably allows you to maintain data as a set of records, as shown in Figure 11-17.

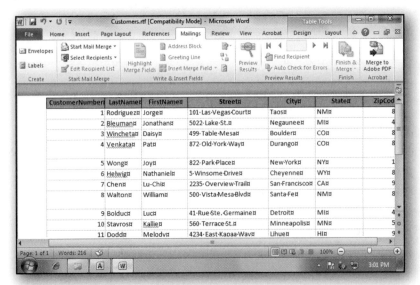

FIGURE 11-17

Microsoft Word allows you to create a table of information, such as a mailing list, which you can edit, sort, search, and print. In addition, you can merge data from the table with a template letter to create form letters, mailing labels, and envelopes. ▶ Access your digital textbook to learn how to use Microsoft Word to create mailing lists and mail merges.

▶ **Can I use spreadsheet software for databases?** Most spreadsheet software also includes basic data management features. It's quite easy to create simple flat files using a spreadsheet.

Depending on the spreadsheet software, it may be possible to sort records, validate data, search for records, perform simple statistical functions, and generate graphs based on the data. Figure 11-18 illustrates Microsoft Excel data management functions applied to a family's health records.

11

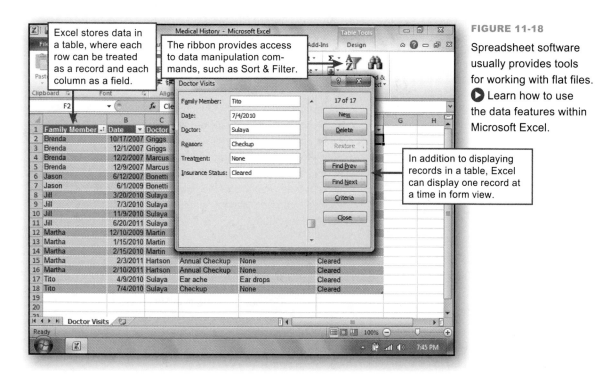

FIGURE 11-18

Spreadsheet software usually provides tools for working with flat files. ▶ Learn how to use the data features within Microsoft Excel.

Simple file management tools provided by word processing and spreadsheet software are popular for individuals who want to maintain flat files that contain hundreds, not thousands, of records. These tools work well for a simple address book, an inventory of household goods, a record of health care costs, and a variety of other simple lists.

These simple tools do not, however, offer database capabilities for establishing relationships between different record types, and they are not powerful enough to maintain the large volume of records required for business information systems.

▶ **Can I create my own data management software?** It is possible to simply enter data as an ASCII text file, and then use a programming language to write routines to access that data. Custom software can be created to accommodate flat files and other database models.

Custom data management software has the advantage of being tailored to the exact needs of a business or an individual. This advantage is offset, however, by several disadvantages. Custom software requires skilled programmers. The development time for each module can be lengthy and costly. In addition, programmer efforts are sometimes redundant because similar modules are often required for different data files. For example, programmers who write a report routine for one data file might have to repeat their efforts a few weeks later for a different data file.

Poorly designed custom software can result in **data dependence**—a term that refers to data and program modules being so tightly interrelated that they become difficult to modify. Imagine a database in which programs and data all exist in one large file! It would be impossible to access the data while editing any of the programs. Furthermore, changing the file structure in any way might make the programs unusable.

Modern database software supports **data independence**, which means separating data from the programs that manipulate data. As a result, a single data management tool can be used to maintain many different files and databases. In addition, standard search, sort, and print routines continue to function, regardless of changes to field names or record structure. Figure 11-19 further explains data dependence and independence.

FIGURE 11-19

Data independence is a design concept based on the idea that databases are most flexible when programs that manipulate a database are not too tightly tied to the structure of fields, records, calculations, and reports.

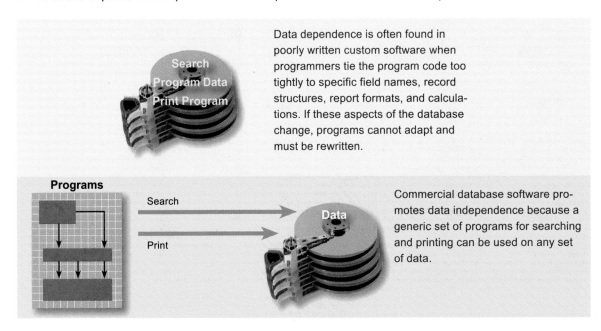

Data dependence is often found in poorly written custom software when programmers tie the program code too tightly to specific field names, record structures, report formats, and calculations. If these aspects of the database change, programs cannot adapt and must be rewritten.

Commercial database software promotes data independence because a generic set of programs for searching and printing can be used on any set of data.

▶ **What's the best data management tool?** The best tool depends on several factors. When selecting a data management tool, consider its cost, versatility, and ease of use (Figure 11-20).

FIGURE 11-20

Data Management Tools

Tool	Cost	Versatility	Ease of Use
Dedicated software, such as an address book	Inexpensive shareware available for simple applications; dedicated software for business applications can be costly	Normally dedicated to a single type of database	Easy; minimal setup required because fields are predefined
Word processing software	Most consumers have word processing software	Best for simple flat files, such as mailing lists	Easy; uses an interface familiar to most users
Spreadsheet software	Most consumers have spreadsheet software	Best for simple flat files that involve calculations	Easy; uses an interface familiar to most users
Custom software	Expensive development and programming time	Very versatile because programs can be tailored to any data	The programming can be difficult, but the final result may be easy to use
Database software	Basic shareware database software is inexpensive; high-end database software can be expensive	High-end packages provide excellent versatility	High-end database software often has a steep learning curve

DATABASE MANAGEMENT SYSTEMS

▶ **What kinds of tools are specifically designed for creating and manipulating databases?** The term **DBMS** (database management system) refers to software that is designed to manage data stored in a database. Each DBMS specializes in one database model, but some DBMS software offers versatility by dealing with a variety of models and data.

▶ **XML DBMS**: Optimized for handling data that exists in XML format. (You'll learn more about XML later in the chapter.)

▶ **ODBMS** (object database management system): Optimized for the object database model, allowing you to store and manipulate data classes, attributes, and methods.

▶ **RDBMS** (relational database management system): Allows you to create, update, and administer a relational database. Most of today's popular RDBMS software also provides the capability to handle object classes and XML data, making it unnecessary to purchase a separate ODBMS or XML DBMS.

▶ **Which DBMS should I use for my projects?** Today most database projects are implemented with a relational database management system. The RDBMS package you choose, however, depends on the scope of your project, the number of people who will simultaneously access the database, and the expected volume of records, queries, and updates.

Entry-level RDBMS software, such as Microsoft Access, is a good fit for small businesses and individuals whose data can't be efficiently handled as a flat file spreadsheet. An entry-level DBMS includes all the tools you need to manipulate data in a database, specify relationships, create data entry forms, query the database, and generate reports, as shown in Figure 11-21.

> **TERMINOLOGY NOTE**
> An ODBMS is also referred to as an OODBMS (object-oriented database management system).

11

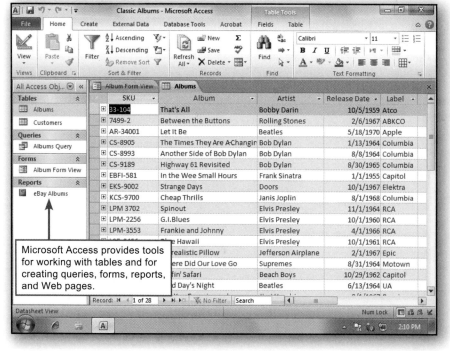

Microsoft Access provides tools for working with tables and for creating queries, forms, reports, and Web pages.

FIGURE 11-21

An entry-level DBMS usually includes all the tools you need to manipulate data in a database. ▶ Learn how to work with tables in a Microsoft Access database.

▶ **Do DBMSs support network access to databases?** If an entry-level DBMS is located on a network, it is possible for multiple users to access the database at the same time. As shown in Figure 11-22, each workstation uses database client software to communicate with the DBMS. **Database client software** allows any remote computer or network workstation to access data in a database.

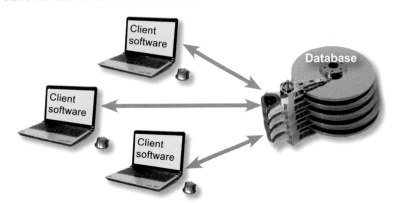

FIGURE 11-22

Multiple users can access a database using client software.

An entry-level DBMS that resides on a network server might be able to handle many simultaneous searches. However, these DBMSs are limited in their ability to deal with problems that arise when multiple users attempt to update the same record at the same time. This limited multiuser capability might be able to handle, for example, a civic center ticketing system operated by a box office clerk. It would not be sufficient, however, to handle the volume of simultaneous transactions for Ticketmaster's 6,700 retail ticket center outlets, 19 telephone call centers worldwide, and online Web site.

In situations with many users who make simultaneous updates, it is usually necessary to move to database server software, such as Oracle Database, IBM DB2, Microsoft SQL Server, or Oracle MySQL Server.

Database server software is designed to manage billions of records and several hundred transactions every second. It provides optimum performance in client/server environments, such as LANs and the Internet. It can also handle a **distributed database**, in which a database is stored on several computers, on multiple networks, or in different geographical locations. As shown in Figure 11-23, database server software passes query requests from client software to the database and sends query results back to the client.

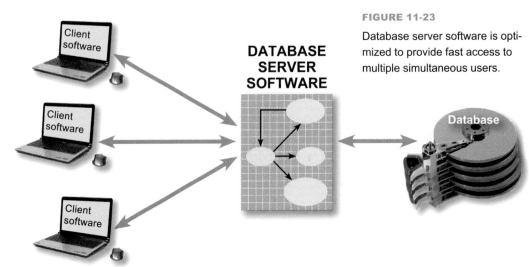

FIGURE 11-23

Database server software is optimized to provide fast access to multiple simultaneous users.

DATABASES AND THE WEB

▶ **Is it possible to access a database over the Web?** The Web allows access to many databases. When you shop at an online store, for example, the photos, descriptions, and prices you see are pulled from the merchant's database and displayed as Web pages. More direct database access is offered by online card catalogs, such as the one offered by the U.S. Library of Congress. A database also provides the foundation for online access to course registration systems, yellow pages, real estate listings, movie reviews, flight schedules, and a host of other information.

The Web provides both opportunities and challenges for accessing the information in a database. Obviously, with its global reach, the Web provides an opportunity for many people to gain access to data from multiple locations. Web access is constrained, however, by the stateless nature of HTTP and the necessity to provide access by using a browser as client software. Providing access to databases over the Web requires some tricks. It does not, however, require special databases or special DBMSs.

▶ **What's the simplest way to provide Web access to a database?** A technique called **static Web publishing** is a simple way to display the data in a database by converting a database report into an HTML document, which can be displayed as a Web page by a browser.

Static publishing provides extremely limited access to a database because it creates a Web page that essentially displays a snapshot of your data at the time the report was generated. Data on the Web page cannot be manipulated, except to be searched in a rudimentary way by the Find feature of your Web browser.

The advantages of static publishing include security and simplicity. Your data remains secure because you have not provided direct access to your database, so unauthorized users cannot change your data. Static publishing is simple because most entry-level DBMS software includes a menu option that allows you to easily produce an HTML page from a database report, as shown in Figure 11-24.

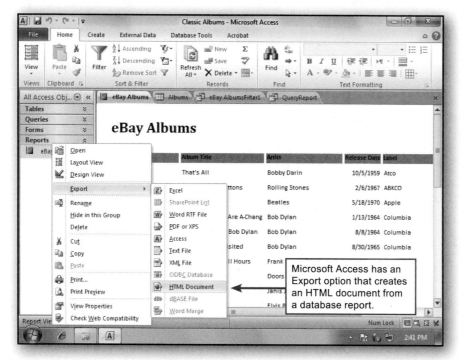

Microsoft Access has an Export option that creates an HTML document from a database report.

FIGURE 11-24

Many entry-level DBMSs include an easy way to turn a report into an HTML document that you can post as a Web page. ▶ Learn how to generate an HTML report from a Microsoft Access database.

▶ What if I want to provide access to current data? Each time regular customers access the Vintage Music Shop site, they see Web pages tailored to their music preferences. Country music fans, for example, see descriptions of Nashville classics and a list of discount albums by their favorite artists. Obviously, these pages cannot be the result of static publishing. They are created by a **dynamic Web publishing** process that generates customized Web pages as needed, or "on the fly."

Dynamic Web publishing relies on a program or script, referred to as a **server-side program**, that resides on a Web server and acts as an intermediary between your browser and a DBMS.

In the Vintage Music Shop example, a server-side program reads a cookie from the customer's computer to find the unique number assigned to the customer. The server-side program then uses the customer number to generate a query, which is sent to the database server software. This software accesses the database to locate the customer's music preferences and favorite artists.

The server-side program then asks the database server software to locate all the specials that apply to this customer's preferences. A list of applicable albums, descriptions, and prices is sent back to the Web server, where it is formulated as an HTML document and sent to the browser.

The architecture for dynamic publishing requires a Web server in addition to database server software, a database, and a browser, as shown in Figure 11-25.

FIGURE 11-25

Dynamic Web publishing requires several components, including a browser, a Web server, database server software, and a database.

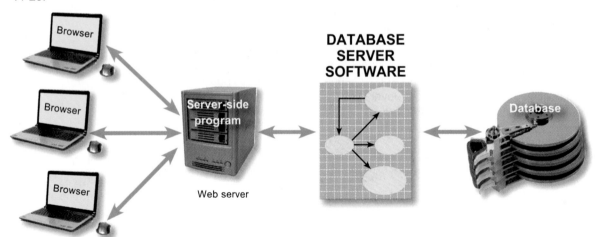

▶ How complex are server-side programs and scripts? Server-side programs and scripts range from a few simple lines of code to full-blown programs containing pages of code. Server-side scripts are coded using scripting languages such as ASP, PHP, Ruby, Python, Java, and ColdFusion Markup Language. These scripts can be executed by software that is installed on the server.

Servers can also process CGI programs. CGI (Common Gateway Interface) is a standard for processing information gathered from clients by a Web server. CGI programs are also referred to as CGI applications or CGI scripts and can be written in a variety of programming languages, including BASIC, C++, Perl, and Java.

Server-side programming requires familiarity with HTML and computer programming, so it is quite a bit more complex than setting up a Facebook page, creating a database, or configuring a local e-mail account.

▶ Is it possible to add to and update database records over the Web?

In several situations, such as making an e-commerce purchase or registering for a social networking site, it is important for people to use a browser to add or update records in a database. For example, the process of ordering merchandise at Vintage Music Shop creates a new order record, changes the InStock field in the Albums table, and creates a customer record for first-time customers. These dynamic database updates require an architecture similar to that used for dynamic Web publishing, plus the use of HTML forms.

An HTML form can collect data, such as a customer name and address, or it can collect the specifications for a query, such as a search for Hank Williams albums. The data collected by the form is sent from your browser to the Web server, which forwards it to the database server.

Most forms are created using the HTML <form> tag and <input> tag. Figure 11-26 illustrates an HTML document with <input> tags that collect a user's first name, last name, and e-mail address. It also shows the Web page form that is displayed in your browser.

FIGURE 11-26

An HTML document (top) produces a form (lower-right) when displayed by a browser.

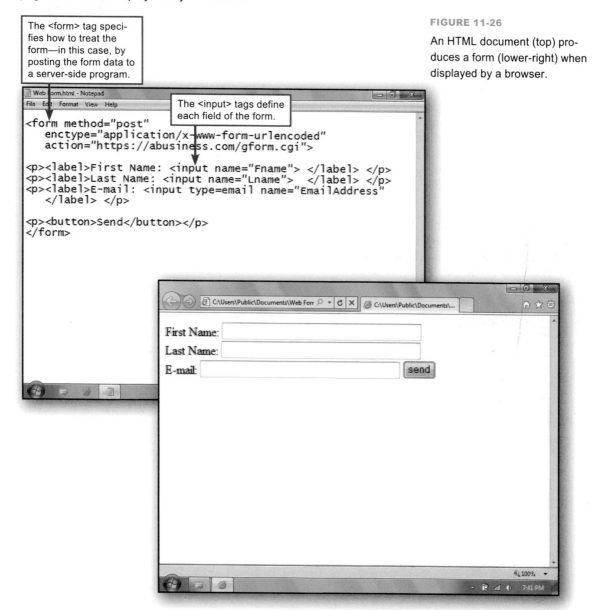

The <form> tag specifies how to treat the form—in this case, by posting the form data to a server-side program.

The <input> tags define each field of the form.

```
<form method="post"
    enctype="application/x-www-form-urlencoded"
    action="https://abusiness.com/gform.cgi">

<p><label>First Name: <input name="Fname"> </label> </p>
<p><label>Last Name: <input name="Lname">  </label> </p>
<p><label>E-mail: <input type=email name="EmailAddress"
    </label> </p>

<p><button>Send</button></p>
</form>
```

First Name:
Last Name:
E-mail: send

▶ So how does it all work? The process of sending data to a database requires several data handoffs. Data that originates from a form that you filled out in your browser is sent to a server-side script, then to a database server. The server-side script can tell the database server to validate the data before adding it to the database. The script can also create an HTML page that lets you know if the process was successfully completed.

Suppose that you use the form from the previous page to subscribe to a social networking site. Figure 11-27 tracks the data you enter as it flows from your browser to the social networking site's database.

FIGURE 11-27

A server-side script can collect user input, send data to a database, and create an HTML page containing data from the database.

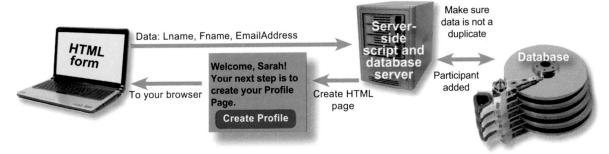

XML

▶ How does XML relate to the Web and databases? XML is a markup language that allows field tags, data, and tables to be incorporated into a Web document. It was developed in response to several deficiencies that became apparent as HTML gained widespread use. For example, suppose you are interested in speeches given by Martin Luther King, Jr. Entering his name in a search engine produces thousands of entries, including MLK biographies, streets and schools named after the famous civil rights leader, historic locations relating to the civil rights movement, and so on.

Wouldn't it be nice if King's speeches were stored in HTML documents that identified their content as speeches and their author as Martin Luther King, Jr.? XML provides tags that can be embedded in an XML document to put data in context, as shown in Figure 11-28.

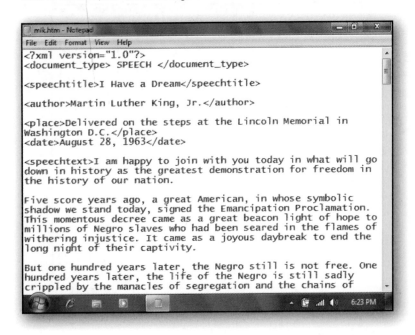

FIGURE 11-28

A document with XML tags allows you to make a targeted search for author = Martin Luther King, Jr. and document_type = SPEECH.

How is XML used today? One of XML's most positive contributions to data management is the potential to add context to the information contained in a widely diverse pool of documents on the Web. Although it is easy to see how XML tags might make the free-form documents currently on the Web much easier to manage, today XML is more often used for structured data.

XML can be used to specify a standard structure of fields and records, such as SportsML and Chemical Markup Language, for storing data that can be accessed from a browser. Using this standard structure, data entered into an XML document can be identified by field names. Figure 11-29 provides an example of an XML document that contains data similar to that in Vintage Music Shop's Albums table.

11

FIGURE 11-29

This XML document contains data that looks similar to the fields and records from a table of a relational database.

Can I search the data in an XML document? Yes. Access to XML data is provided by XML query engines, such as XPath and XQuery. Direct access to structured data like that shown in Figure 11-29 above, however, requires knowledge of its location, access rights, and a list of field names. Therefore, like many relational databases, access to structured data in XML documents is typically provided by some type of client software designed specifically to accept queries, access the data, and return results. XML clients can be offered as browser plug-ins.

What are the pros and cons of using XML for storing data? Storing data in an XML document offers several advantages. It exists as a document in human-readable format. It is also portable so that it can be easily accessed from virtually any computer platform—PCs, Macs, Linux computers, mainframes, and even handheld devices. All that's required on the platform is an XML-enabled browser, such as Internet Explorer or Firefox.

XML documents are not, however, optimized for many operations you would customarily associate with databases, such as fast sorts, searches, and updates.

To get the best out of XML and relational databases, some experts recommend storing data in a relational database, managing it with RDBMS software, and using server-side software to generate XML documents for exchanging data over the Web.

Some RDBMSs include features that allow a database server to receive queries in the form of XML commands. After receiving a query, the database compiles the results and uses XML to format the data into a Web page, as shown in Figure 11-30.

FIGURE 11-30

Manipulating XML Data with an RDBMS

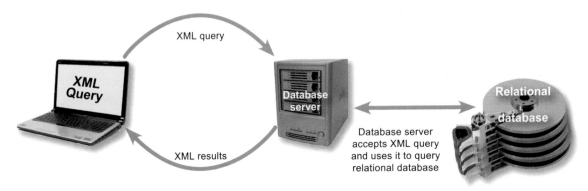

As you can see, many techniques exist for storing, accessing, and displaying the data from databases. Individuals can use simple tools to create personal databases, such as address books. Corporate database managers, however, need to be familiar with more complex tools used to distribute data over networks and the Web. Sometimes more than one database management tool has the potential to work for a specific application. Now that you've had an introduction to the options, you should be able to evaluate when and how to use them.

QuickCheck

SECTION B

1. Most of today's word processing and spreadsheet software offers tools for managing simple flat files containing fields and records. True or false? [_____]

2. Modern database software supports data [_____], which means keeping data separated from the program modules that manipulate the data.

3. To access the data in a database from a remote computer or network workstation, you can use database [_____] software.

4. ASP, PHP, Ruby, and Java are used to write [_____]-side scripts.

5. [_____] is a markup language that allows field tags, data, and tables to be incorporated into a Web document. (Hint: Use the acronym.)

 CHECK ANSWERS

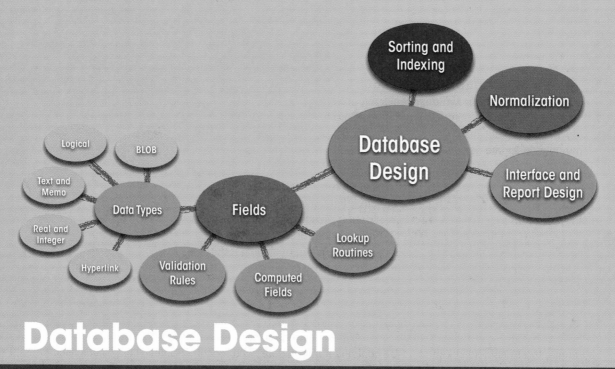

Database Design

SECTION **C**

THE KEY to an effective database is its initial design. In a well-designed database, data can be flexibly manipulated to produce timely, meaningful, and accurate information for decision making. Bad database design can lead to messy databases, lost records, and inaccurate data. Section C looks at databases from the perspective of the database designer and describes how to create an efficient structure for a relational database.

DEFINING FIELDS

▶ How does a database designer know what data to store? The term **database structure** refers to the arrangement of fields, tables, and relationships in a database. The first step in structuring a relational database is to determine what data should be collected and stored. To do so, a database designer might begin by consulting users and studying the current filing system to compile a list of available data as well as any additional data necessary to produce on-screen output or printed reports.

If you are designing the database structure for Vintage Music Shop, for example, you would probably recognize that data such as the album title, artist name, release date, catalog number, record label, quantity in stock, value, discount price, and album cover photo should be collected and stored.

After the database designer determines what data to store, the next step is to organize that data into fields. It is usually easy to break data into fields just by using common sense and considering how people might want to access the data. Any data that people would want to search for, sort on, or use in a calculation should be in its own field (Figure 11-31).

First Name * Gilbert   MI * B.

Last Name * Grape

Gilbert B. Grape   Grape, Gilbert B.

FIGURE 11-31

When a field contains an entire name, it is difficult to individually manipulate the first name, last name, and middle initial. A more flexible design provides separate fields for each part of the name.

633

▶ What makes each record unique? Although two people might have the same name or two paychecks might contain the same amount, a computer must have some way to differentiate between records. A **primary key** is a field that contains data unique to a record. Designers commonly designate fields such as CheckNumber, SocialSecurityNumber, TelephoneNumber, and PartNumber as primary keys.

▶ How does a database designer know what data types to use? The data that can be entered into a field depends on the field's data type. From a technical perspective, a **data type** specifies the way data is represented on the disk and in RAM. From a user perspective, the data type determines the way data can be manipulated. When designing a database, each field is assigned a data type.

Data can be broadly classified as numeric or character. As you learned in earlier chapters, character data contains letters, numerals, and symbols not used for calculations. Numeric data contains numbers that can be manipulated mathematically by adding, averaging, multiplying, and so forth. As an example, the Price field in Figure 11-32 contains numeric data, which can be added to the prices for other albums to calculate a total price when a customer buys more than one album.

FIGURE 11-32

Numeric data can be used for calculations.

Price [$70.00]

```
INVOICE
Qty  Album Title      Price

1    That's All       $70.00
1    Surfin' Safari   $10.00
1    Blue Hawaii      $18.00

     Total            $98.00
```

There are several numeric data types, including real, integer, and date. Database designers assign the **real data type** to fields that contain numbers with decimal places—prices, percentages, and so on.

The **integer data type** is used for fields that contain whole numbers—quantities, repetitions, rankings, and so on. Database designers use the integer data type unless the data requires decimal places because real numbers require more storage space.

As you might expect, the **date data type** is used to store dates in a format that allows them to be manipulated, such as when you want to calculate the number of days between two dates.

The **text data type** is normally assigned to fixed-length fields that hold character data—people's names, album titles, and so on. Text fields sometimes hold data that looks like numbers, but won't be mathematically manipulated. Telephone numbers, Social Security numbers, ZIP codes, and item numbers are examples of data that looks numeric, but is normally stored in text fields.

A **memo data type** usually provides a variable-length field into which users can enter comments. For example, the Vintage Music Shop database might contain a memo field for storing comments about a particular album, such as "*Where Did Our Love Go* was The Supremes' first hit album."

The **logical data type** (sometimes called a Boolean or yes/no data type) is used for true/false or yes/no data using minimal storage space. For example, a database designer might define a logical field called OrigCov, which would contain a Y if an album includes the original dust cover.

Some file and database management systems also include additional data types, such as BLOBs and hyperlinks. A **BLOB** (binary large object) is a collection of binary data stored in a single field of a database. BLOBs can be just about any kind of data you would store as a file, such as an MP3 music track.

The **hyperlink data type** stores URLs used to link directly from a database to a Web page. For example, data stored in a hyperlink field of the Vintage Music Shop database could provide a link to a musician's Web site. Figure 11-33 summarizes the most commonly used data types in today's databases.

FIGURE 11-33

Commonly Used Data Types

Data Type	Description	Sample Field	Sample Data
Real	Numbers that include decimal places	DiscountPrice	9.99
Integer	Whole numbers	Qty	5
Date	Month, day, and year	OrderDate	9/30/2013
Text	Letters or numerals not used for calculations	Name ZipCode	Gilbert 49866
Logical	Data that can have one of two values	InStock	Y
Memo	Variable length comment field	Condition	Some wear on album cover
BLOB	Binary data	SampleTrack	[An MP3 file]
Hyperlink	URLs	MusicianWebSite	www.bobdylan.com

▶ **How does a database handle computations?** When a customer looks for an album at Vintage Music Shop's Web site, three pieces of pricing information are provided. The first is the value. The second is the discounted price that Vintage Music Shop offers. The third is the amount of money a customer will save by purchasing the album through Vintage Music Shop.

The Albums record type, however, contains only two pieces of pricing information: Value and DiscountPrice. The third piece of information—the amount of money a customer saves by purchasing through Vintage Music Shop—is a computed field.

A **computed field** is a calculation that a DBMS performs during processing, and then temporarily stores in a memory location. An efficiently designed database uses computed fields whenever possible because they do not require disk storage space. Figure 11-34 illustrates how a computed field produces the amount saved with purchases at Vintage Music Shop's discount price.

TERMINOLOGY NOTE

A computed field works somewhat like a function in a spreadsheet; you set up a formula for the calculation, which is applied to compute the data.

FIGURE 11-34

Creating a Computed Field

Value	$47.00
DiscountPrice	$45.00

The database includes a field containing the value and another field containing the discount price.

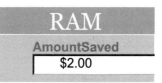

RAM

AmountSaved

$2.00

The amount in one field can be subtracted from the amount in the other field. The result is temporarily stored in a field in RAM and can appear on a screen or report.

▶ Can a database designer prevent people from entering inaccurate data? There's an old saying in the computer industry: "garbage in, garbage out." This adage is especially true when dealing with databases. The information produced by reports and processing routines is only as accurate as the information in the database. Unfortunately, data entry errors can compromise the accuracy and validity of a database.

When designing a database, it is important to think ahead and envision potential data entry errors. Most DBMSs provide tools that database designers can use to prevent some, but not all, data entry errors.

▶ Does uppercase make a difference? People who enter data into a database sometimes have difficulty deciding whether to use uppercase or lowercase characters. In a **case sensitive database**, uppercase letters are not equivalent to their lowercase counterparts. For example, in a case sensitive database, the artist name *Elvis* is not equivalent to *elvis*.

Inconsistent use of case can lead to several problems. A search for *elvis* will not produce records for *Elvis* or *ELVIS*. Furthermore, in a sorted or indexed list, *elvis* and *ELVIS* might not be grouped together.

Most DBMSs give database designers an option to turn case sensitivity on or off. Designers also might have the option to force data to all uppercase or all lowercase as it is entered. These techniques are not infallible solutions to the inconsistent use of case, but they can help to keep the data set more uniform.

▶ How about entering numbers? A data entry operator might enter a telephone number as 555-555-7777, (555) 555-7777, or 1-555-555-7777. When numbers are entered in different formats, it becomes difficult to produce nicely formatted reports or locate a particular telephone number.

To prevent inconsistent formatting, a database designer can specify a field format. A **field format** is a template that adds the correct formatting as data is entered. If someone attempts to enter data in the wrong format, the database can be set up to reject that entry or correct it. A telephone number field might use a field format such as the one shown in Figure 11-35.

FIGURE 11-35

A field format helps maintain consistent data by providing a structure for entering data into a field.

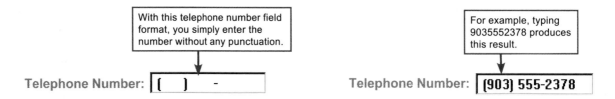

With this telephone number field format, you simply enter the number without any punctuation.

Telephone Number: [   ]   -

For example, typing 9035552378 produces this result.

Telephone Number: (903) 555-2378

▶ Can a database screen out typos? People who enter data sometimes make a mistake and press the wrong keys. Preventing every typographical error is not possible. However, it is possible to catch some of these errors by using field validation rules, list boxes, or lookups.

A **field validation rule** is a specification that the database designer sets up to filter data entered into a particular field. For example, the price of albums in the Vintage Music Shop database ranges from $0 (for promotions) to $800. No albums have a value greater than $1000. When intending to enter $19.98 in the value field, however, the omission of a decimal point could set the price of an album to $1998!

When designing the Vintage Music Shop database, a database designer can use a field validation rule to limit entries in the Value field to less than

$1000. If the DBMS receives a number such as 1998 in the value field, it displays a message requesting the correct price.

Another technique that prevents typographical and case sensitivity errors is to limit data entry to the items on a specified list. For example, the state abbreviation for Colorado might be entered as CO, Co, Colo, or VO if your fingers slipped. However, most database software allows database designers to specify a list of acceptable entries for each field. You are probably familiar with clickable lists of states, such as the one in Figure 11-36.

Database designers can also prevent entry errors by using lookup routines. A **lookup routine** validates an entry by checking data in a file or database table. For example, suppose that a Vintage Music Shop employee is entering new albums. It is important that each album has a unique Catalog Number (Cat#). When data is entered in the Cat# field, the database can use a lookup routine to search every existing record to make sure the new Cat# does not duplicate an existing Cat#.

NORMALIZATION

❯ How does a database designer group fields into tables?

A process called **normalization** helps database designers create a database structure that minimizes storage space and increases processing efficiency. The goal of normalization is to minimize **data redundancy**—the amount of data that is duplicated in a database. To normalize a database, one of the designer's main tasks is to decide how best to group fields into tables.

The first step to grouping fields is to get an idea of the big picture of the data. Groupings usually correspond to the physical items, or entities, that are tracked in the database. For example, Vintage Music Shop data is grouped into several tables: Albums, Tracks, Customers, Orders, and Order Details.

You might wonder why it is necessary to use three tables—Customers, Orders, and Order Details—to store data about an order. Why won't one table suffice? To answer this question, first take a look at the data relevant to each order in Figure 11-37.

FIGURE 11-36

Clickable lists are an easy way for users to enter data in a standard format.

FIGURE 11-37

A typical Vintage Music Shop order contains customer data and data about the merchandise being ordered.

If customer information and order information are grouped in the same table, each time Jorge Rodriguez places an order, his name, shipping address, billing address, telephone number, and e-mail address must be entered and stored. This data redundancy not only requires extra storage space, but also could lead to storing inconsistent or inaccurate data. The solution is to create separate tables for Orders and Customers, which can be related by including a CustomerNumber field in both tables, as shown in Figure 11-38.

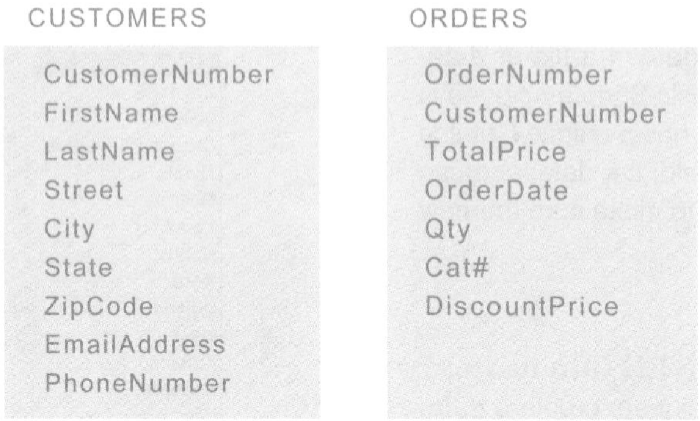

CUSTOMERS

CustomerNumber
FirstName
LastName
Street
City
State
ZipCode
EmailAddress
PhoneNumber

ORDERS

OrderNumber
CustomerNumber
TotalPrice
OrderDate
Qty
Cat#
DiscountPrice

FIGURE 11-38

Fields for each order are separated into two tables: one for customer information and one for order information. Information in these two tables can be linked using the CustomerNumber field. This field makes it easy to find all the orders for a specific customer.

Even after separating customer data from order data, the structure of the Vintage Music Shop database can be further improved. The Orders table in the previous figure allows customers to purchase only one album per order because the fields Cat# and DiscountPrice occur only once. Obviously, the Vintage Music Shop database should be able to handle orders for more than one album.

It might seem reasonable to provide several fields for the albums on an order. Perhaps they could be named AlbumNumber1, AlbumNumber2, AlbumNumber3, and so on. But how many fields should the database designer provide? If the designer provides fields for ordering ten albums, the database still cannot handle large orders for more than ten albums. Furthermore, if a customer orders fewer than ten albums, space is wasted by having empty fields in each record.

You might recognize that a one-to-many relationship exists between an order and the ordered items. That clue indicates that the database designer should separate the data into two tables, such as Orders and Order Details. These two tables are related by the OrderNumber field. Figure 11-39 illustrates how the Orders table is further normalized into two tables to store data more efficiently.

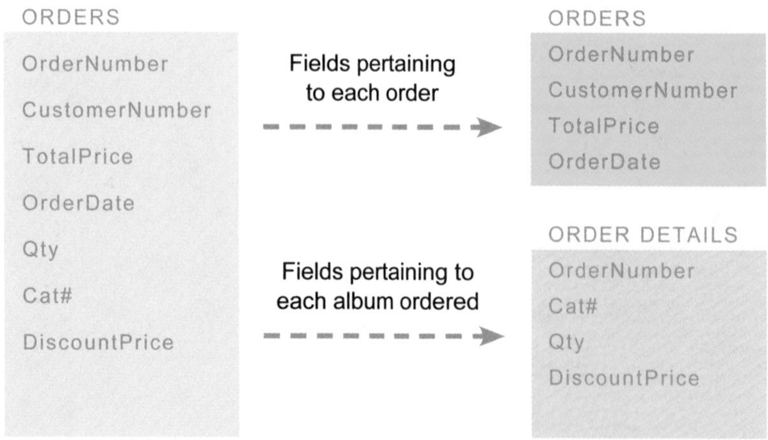

ORDERS

OrderNumber

CustomerNumber

TotalPrice

OrderDate

Qty

Cat#

DiscountPrice

Fields pertaining to each order

- - - - - - - - →

Fields pertaining to each album ordered

- - - - - - - - →

ORDERS

OrderNumber
CustomerNumber
TotalPrice
OrderDate

ORDER DETAILS

OrderNumber
Cat#
Qty
DiscountPrice

FIGURE 11-39

The fields pertaining to the ordered merchandise are further divided into two record types and related by the OrderNumber field.

ORGANIZING RECORDS

▶ **How are database records organized?** Records can be organized in different ways depending on how people want to use them. For example, Vintage Music Shop's customers will most often view the information in the Albums table by album title or artist name. The inventory manager usually wants the data sorted by quantity in stock so that it is easy to see which albums are overstocked. In contrast, the marketing manager is interested in the Value field, so that rare and expensive albums can be aggressively marketed. No single way of organizing the data accommodates everyone's needs, but tables can be sorted or indexed in multiple ways.

▶ **What happens when the data in a table is sorted?** A table's **sort order** is the order in which records are stored on disk. Sorted tables produce faster queries and updates because they take advantage of clever algorithms that quickly pinpoint records. In a sorted table, new records are inserted to maintain the order.

When no sort order is specified, new records are appended to the end of the file, resulting in a file that is not in any particular order. Queries and updates within an unsorted database are slow because the only algorithm for searching an unsorted table requires a sequential look at each record.

Most DBMSs use a sort key to determine the order in which records are stored. A table's **sort key** is one or more fields used to specify where new records are inserted in a table. A table can have only one sort key at a time, but the sort key can be changed. Changing a sort key can take a long time, however, because the process physically rearranges records on the disk. The database designer usually specifies the sort key for a database table at the time the database structure is created.

▶ **How is indexing different from sorting?** A database index can be used to organize data in alphabetical or numerical order. It is very similar to an index in a book that contains a list of keywords and pointers to the pages where they can be found. A **database index** contains a list of keys, and each key provides a pointer to the record that contains the rest of the fields related to that key. Figure 11-40 illustrates how an index works.

FIGURE 11-40

When arranged by date, *Blue Hawaii* is the second record in the index. The index file contains a list of keys and the record number (R#) that contains more information about the album released on that date. ▶ To see how indexing works, click this figure in your digital textbook.

INDEX

Index Order	Key Field	R#
1	10/01/1960	1
2	10/01/1961	3
3	10/29/1962	4
4	02/06/1967	2

ALBUMS

R#	Cat#	Album	Artist	Release Date	In Stock	Value
1	LPM-2256	G.I. Blues	Elvis Presley	10/01/1960	4	20.00
2	7499-2	Between the Buttons	Rolling Stones	02/06/1967	1	13.99
3	LSP-246	Blue Hawaii	Elvis Presley	10/01/1961	5	50.00
4	N16014	Surfin' Safari	Beach Boys	10/29/1962	8	18.95

Unlike a sort order, an index has no bearing on the physical sequence of records on disk. An index simply points to the record where the data can be found. The advantage of an index over a sort is that a table can have multiple indexes, but only one sort order. For example, the Albums table could be indexed by Album to facilitate searches for specific albums. The same table could also be indexed by Artist to facilitate searches using artist names.

Database tables should be indexed by any field or fields that are commonly used as search fields. The database designer normally creates indexes at the time the database structure is designed. Indexes can also be created at a later date, as needed.

DESIGNING THE INTERFACE

▶ Does a database designer have control over the user interface? The way that database queries, records, and reports appear on the screen depends on the user interface. An operating system provides some conventions for the user interface, such as dialog and button styles, but additional design decisions must be made for the database user interface.

Designing a database user interface can be a challenging task. If a company's database includes multiple tables used by many different people, a professional user interface designer usually creates and maintains the user interface. Large databases might even require a group of user interface designers.

The interface for smaller databases, such as those used by small businesses or individuals, is most likely created by the database designer. Some DBMSs include tools to create database interfaces. Others require separate tools for this task.

▶ What makes a good database interface? A well-defined user interface for a database should be clear, intuitive, and efficient. Take a moment to look at the data entry screen in Figure 11-41, and imagine that you are using the screen to finalize the purchase of several albums.

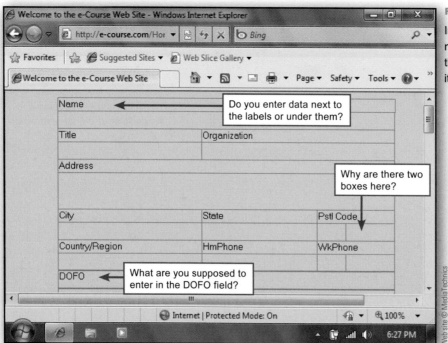

FIGURE 11-41

Imagine entering your own name and address using this on-screen form. Does it seem easy to use?

Using the data entry screen pictured on the previous page might be awkward because it does not follow good user interface design principles. The data entry fields seem out of order, and users might have difficulty discerning which entry box corresponds to each label. In addition, several fields have cryptic labels that don't provide good clues about the data you're supposed to enter.

To improve this database interface, a designer might consider the following principles:

▶ Arrange fields in a logical order beginning at the upper-left corner of the screen. The first fields should be those used most often or those that come first in the data entry sequence.

▶ Provide visual clues to the entry areas. An edit box, line, or shaded area can delineate data entry areas.

▶ Entry areas should appear in a consistent position relative to their labels. By convention, labels are placed to the left of the entry areas or above them.

▶ Provide a quick way to move through the fields in order. By convention, the Tab key performs this function.

▶ If all fields do not fit on a single screen, use scrolling or create a second screen.

▶ Provide buttons or other easy-to-use controls for moving from one record to another.

▶ Supply on-screen instructions to help ensure that data is entered correctly. Web databases can benefit from links to help pages.

Figure 11-42 contains an improved interface for the database in the previous figure.

11

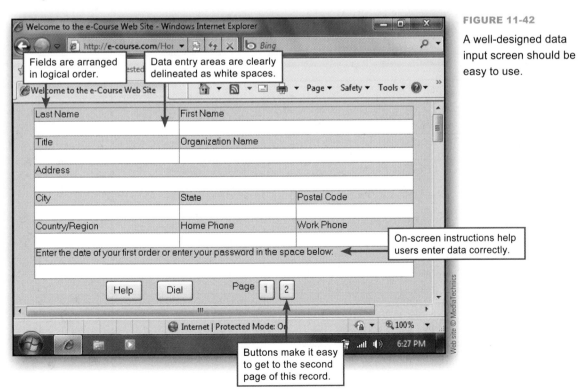

FIGURE 11-42

A well-designed data input screen should be easy to use.

DESIGNING REPORT TEMPLATES

▶ How can I display or print data as a formatted report?

A report is a printed or on-screen list of some or all of the data in a database. To create reports, most DBMSs include a **report generator**, which is a software tool for specifying the content and format for a database report. End users might use report generators, but more typically they are used by database designers.

A **report template** contains the outline or general specifications for a report, including such elements as the report title, fields to include, fields to subtotal or total, and report format specifications. The template does not, however, contain data from the database. Data is merged into the template when you actually run a report.

As an example, suppose that a manager at Vintage Music Shop wants to create a report that lists albums arranged by price. The manager can create a report template called AlbumPriceGroup, which specifies the following:

▶ The title of the report is Vintage Music Shop Albums by Price.

▶ The report contains data from the Albums table, arranged in four columns, with data from the DiscountPrice, Album, Artist, and InStock fields.

▶ The headings for the columns are Discount Price, Album, Artist, and Qty in Stock.

▶ The report is grouped by price.

These specifications would be used to produce a report similar to the one shown in Figure 11-43.

FIGURE 11-43

A report template contains the specifications to produce this report.

Report Date: 8/21/2013

Vintage Music Shop Albums by Price

Discount Price	Album	Artist	Qty in Stock
$9.00	Magical Mystery Tour	Beatles	3
$10.00	Surfin' Safari	Beach Boys	3
	Cheap Thrills	Janis Joplin	12
	Surrealistic Pillow	Jefferson Airplane	1
	One Day at a Time	Joan Baez	2
$14.00	Between the Buttons	Rolling Stones	1
$15.00	Let It Be	Beatles	2
	Abbey Road	Beatles	4
	Joan Baez	Joan Baez	1
$18.00	Chuck Berry's Golden Hits	Chuck Berry	1
	Strange Days	Doors	9

When a report is actually produced, it is based on the data currently contained in the database table. For example, the report on the previous page was produced on August 21st and includes albums that were stored in the database as of that date.

Now suppose that at the beginning of October, Vintage Music Shop receives a new shipment of vintage albums. The AlbumPriceGroup report template is used again to print a report on October 12th. This report, shown in Figure 11-44, follows the same format as the previous report, but includes the new albums.

FIGURE 11-44

This report uses the same template as the 8/21/2013 report, but different data.

11

Report Date: 10/12/2013

Vintage Music Shop Albums by Price

Discount Price	Album	Artist	Qty in Stock
$9.00	Magical Mystery Tour	Beatles	3
	In Person	Kingsmen	1
$10.00	Cheap Thrills	Janis Joplin	8
	About This Thing Called Love	Fabian	2
	One Day at a Time	Joan Baez	2
$14.00	Between the Buttons	Rolling Stones	1

▶ How does the database designer create effective report templates? The reports created by a report generator can be displayed, printed, saved as files, or output as Web pages. Some data management software also provides tools to output data as graphs, sounds, or graphics. The database designer can create templates for reports that effectively present information by observing the following guidelines:

▶ Supply only the information required. Too much information can make it difficult to identify what is essential.

▶ Present information in a usable format. For example, if subtotals are necessary for making a decision, include them. The people who use reports should not have to make additional manual calculations.

▶ Information should be timely. Reports must arrive in time to be used for effective decision making. Some decisions require periodic information— for example, monthly sales reports. Other decisions require ongoing information, such as current stock prices, that will be best satisfied by a continuous display.

▶ Information should be presented in a clear, unambiguous format and include necessary titles, page numbers, dates, page headers, labels, and column headings.

▶ Present information in the format most appropriate for the audience. In many cases, a traditional report organized in rows and columns is most appropriate. In other cases, graphs might be more effective.

LOADING DATA

▶ How is data loaded into database tables? After the design for the database structure is complete, it is time to load the database with an initial set of data. For example, before the Vintage Music Shop database went online, it was populated with data for all the albums in the inventory.

Data can be loaded into a database manually by using generic data entry tools supplied with the DBMS or by using a customized data entry module created by the database designer. Entering data manually can take a long time, however, and mistakes such as misspellings are common.

If the data exists electronically in another type of database or in flat files, it is usually possible to transfer the data using a custom-written conversion routine or import and export routines. A conversion routine converts the data from its current format into a format that can be automatically incorporated into the new database.

It takes some time and requires knowledge about database formats to write conversion routines; but for large databases, it's much quicker to convert data than to re-enter it manually. Converting data also results in fewer errors.

Some DBMSs provide built-in import and export routines that automatically convert data from one file format to another. An import routine brings data into a database. For example, if data was previously stored as a spreadsheet file, an import routine in Microsoft Access can be used to transfer data from the spreadsheet to an Access database.

In contrast, an export routine copies data out of a software package, such as spreadsheet software, and into the database. You would use either an import routine or an export routine to move data from one location to another, but not both.

QuickCheck   SECTION C

1. A primary [_____] contains data unique to a record, such as a Social Security number or ISBN.

2. A computed field is calculated during processing and stored temporarily in memory. True or false? [_____]

3. To filter data entered into a field, the database designer can set up a field [_____] rule.

4. Database designers use a process called [_____] to minimize data redundancy in a database.

5. In addition to storing records in sorted order, a database can be [_____] to produce a list of keys that can be used to alphabetize or otherwise organize the records.

▶ CHECK ANSWERS

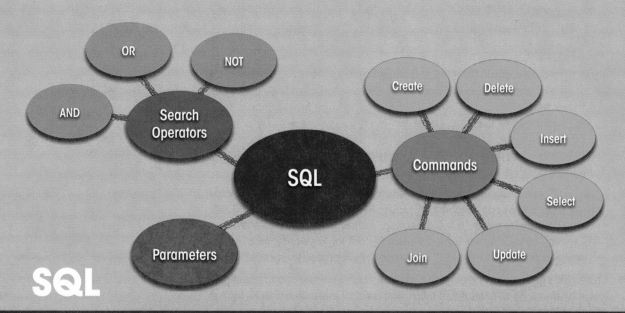

SECTION D

A LITTLE BACKGROUND

in query languages can help you understand the power and capabilities of databases. In Section D, you'll explore a database query language called SQL.

SQL BASICS

▶ How does a query language like SQL work? Query languages like **SQL** (Structured Query Language) work behind the scenes as an intermediary between the database client software provided to users and the database itself.

Database client software provides an easy-to-use interface for entering search specifications, new records, data updates, and so on. The client software collects your input, and then converts it into an **SQL query**, which can operate directly on the database to carry out your instructions, as shown in Figure 11-45.

FIGURE 11-45

Database client software provides database users with simple forms that can be used to enter search specifications or update data. Here a customer uses an online form to search for vintage Beatles albums in LP (long-playing 33⅓ rpm) format.

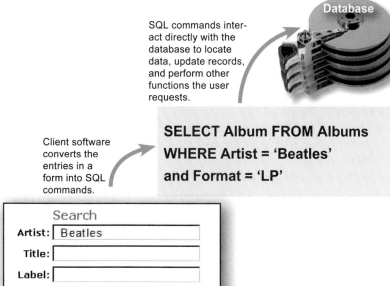

SQL commands interact directly with the database to locate data, update records, and perform other functions the user requests.

Client software converts the entries in a form into SQL commands.

SELECT Album FROM Albums WHERE Artist = 'Beatles' and Format = 'LP'

Form-based user interface

645

▶ **What does a simple SQL query look like?** An SQL query is a sequence of words, much like a sentence. For example, an SQL query that searches for a song called "Ruby Tuesday" in Vintage Music Shop's database might look like this:

SELECT TrackTitle FROM Tracks WHERE TrackTitle = 'Ruby Tuesday'

The SQL query language provides a collection of special command words called **SQL keywords**, such as SELECT, FROM, INSERT, and WHERE, which issue instructions to the database. Although the SQL examples in this section of the chapter use uppercase letters for keywords, most implementations of SQL accept either uppercase or lowercase keywords.

Most SQL queries can be divided into three simple elements that specify an action, the name of a database table, and a set of parameters. Let's look at each of these elements.

▶ **How does SQL specify the action that I want carried out in the database?** An SQL query begins with an action keyword, or command, which specifies the operation you want carried out. For example, the command word **CREATE** produces a new table in a database. Figure 11-46 lists some of the most commonly used SQL command words.

FIGURE 11-46

SQL Commands

Command	Description	Example
CREATE	Create a database or table	CREATE TABLE Album
DELETE	Remove a record from a table	DELETE FROM Tracks WHERE TrackTitle = 'Blue Suede Shoes'
INSERT	Add a record	INSERT INTO AlbumDescription (Cat#, Condition) VALUES ('LPM-2256', 'Mint condition; no visible scratches; original album cover')
JOIN	Use the data from two tables	SELECT FROM Albums JOIN Tracks ON Albums.Cat# = Tracks.Cat#
SELECT	Search for records	SELECT FROM Albums WHERE Artist = 'Beatles'
UPDATE	Change data in a field	UPDATE Albums SET DiscountPrice = 15.95 WHERE Cat# = 'LPM-2256'

▶ **How does SQL specify which table to use?** SQL keywords such as USE, FROM, or INTO can be used to construct a clause specifying the table you want to access. The clause consists of a keyword followed by the name of the table. For example, the clause FROM Tracks indicates that you want to use the Tracks table from Vintage Music Shop's database.

The command word **DELETE** removes a record from a table. An SQL query that begins with DELETE FROM Tracks means that you want to delete something from the Tracks table. To complete the query, you provide parameters that specify which record you want to delete.

How does SQL specify parameters? **Parameters** are detailed specifications for a command. Keywords such as WHERE usually begin an SQL clause containing the parameters for a command. Suppose that Vintage Music Shop's inventory manager wants to delete all the albums in the Vintage Music Shop database recorded by Bobby Darin. The parameter for the WHERE clause is Artist = 'Bobby Darin'.

DELETE	FROM Albums	WHERE Artist = 'Bobby Darin'
SQL command word	FROM clause specifies the table to use	WHERE clause specifies the field name and its contents

Now that you've learned the basic structure of an SQL query, take a closer look at the SQL for specific database tasks, such as adding records, searching for information, updating fields, organizing records, and joining tables.

ADDING RECORDS

How are records added to a database? Suppose you want to purchase an album from Vintage Music Shop's Web site. As a first-time customer, you fill out a form with your name, address, and so on.

The client software that you use collects the data you enter in the form and generates an SQL statement using the **INSERT** command, which adds your data to the Customers table of the Vintage Music Shop database. Figure 11-47 shows the Customer form, the SQL statement that adds the customer data to the database, and the data that is added to the Customers table.

FIGURE 11-47

Data from the Customer form is added to the database.

Customer form

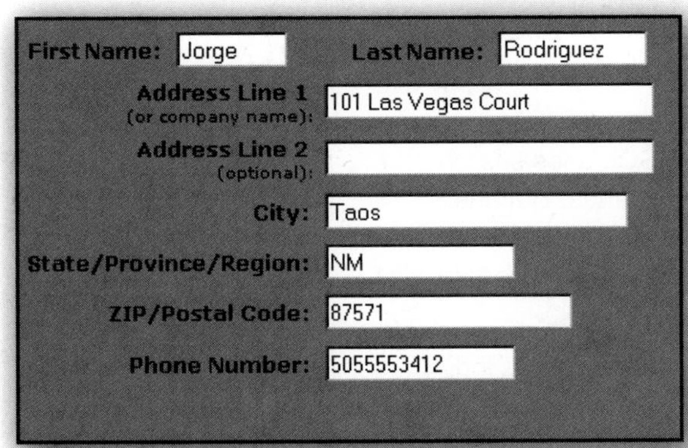

First Name: Jorge   Last Name: Rodriguez
Address Line 1 (or company name): 101 Las Vegas Court
Address Line 2 (optional):
City: Taos
State/Province/Region: NM
ZIP/Postal Code: 87571
Phone Number: 5055553412

SQL statement

INSERT INTO Customers (LastName, FirstName, Street, City, State, ZipCode, PhoneNumber) VALUES ('Rodriguez', 'Jorge', '101 Las Vegas Court', 'Taos', 'NM', '87571', '5055553412')

Customers table

LastName	FirstName	Street	City	State	ZipCode	PhoneNumber
Rodriguez	Jorge	101 Las Vegas Court	Taos	NM	87571	505-555-3412
Bleuman	Jonathan	5022 Lake St.	Negaunee	MI	49866	906-555-2131
Wincheta	Daisy	499 Table Mesa	Boulder	CO	80301	303-555-6902
Venkata	Patel	872 Old York Way	Durango	CO	81301	970-555-4438
Wong	Joy	822 Park Place	New York	NY	10023	212-555-9903
Helwig	Nathaniel	5 Winsome Drive	Cheyenne	WY	82003	303-555-3223
Chen	Lu-Chi	2235 Overview Trail	San Francisco	CA	94118	415--555-9001
Walton	William	500 Vista Mesa		NM	87504	505-555-1111
Bolduc	Luc	41 Rue				555-6487
	Kallie					

11

SEARCHING FOR INFORMATION

▶ **How do SQL queries carry out searches?** One of the most common database operations is to query for a particular record or group of records by using the **SELECT** command. Suppose you're looking for Jefferson Airplane albums. You fill in the Search box at the Vintage Music Shop site, as shown in Figure 11-48.

The database client software uses your search specification to create the SQL query:

SELECT Album, AlbumCover FROM Albums

WHERE Artist = 'Jefferson Airplane'

As a result of this query, the Vintage Music Shop Web page displays a list beginning with *Jefferson Airplane Takes Off*—the band's first album— and a photo of the album cover. Take a closer look at the parts of this query.

The phrase SELECT Album, AlbumCover specifies that the database should show you only the album title and cover. Until you confirm that this is the album you're interested in, it will not show you additional information, such as the price or list of tracks. FROM Albums tells the DBMS to search for the album in the Albums table. WHERE Artist = 'Jefferson Airplane' specifies that the record you want contains the data *Jefferson Airplane* in the Artist field.

▶ **Can SQL perform complex searches?** Yes. SQL uses search operators such as AND, OR, and NOT to form complex queries. Because search operators were originally the idea of mathematician George Boole, they are also referred to as Boolean operators. Let's see how they work in the context of SQL queries.

▶ **How does AND work in an SQL query?** AND (sometimes indicated by a + sign) is used when you want to retrieve records that meet more than one criterion. For example, suppose a customer wants to find all the albums by Jefferson Airplane, but wants to display only albums that are on sale for less than $10.00. You might enter something like Jefferson Airplane <$10.00 in the Vintage Music Shop search box. The database client creates an SQL query:

SELECT Album FROM Albums
WHERE Artist = 'Jefferson Airplane' AND
DiscountPrice < 10.00

In this example, a record is selected only if the Artist field contains *Jefferson Airplane* and the value in the DiscountPrice field is less than $10.00. If the discount price is $10.00 or more, the record is not selected. The AND operator specifies that both of the search criteria must be true for the record to be selected.

▶ How does OR differ from AND? Two variations of the OR operator exist. One variation, the inclusive OR, designates records that meet one criterion or both. The other variation, called the exclusive OR, designates records that meet one criterion or the other, but not both.

SQL uses the inclusive OR. A query such as

SELECT Album FROM Albums

WHERE Artist = 'Jefferson Airplane' OR

DiscountPrice < 10.00

produces all the Jefferson Airplane albums, regardless of price. It also produces any albums that are less than $10.00, regardless of the artist.

You can combine AND and OR clauses to formulate complex queries. For example, Jefferson Airplane became Jefferson Starship in 1974. If you'd like a list of Jefferson Airplane or Jefferson Starship albums for less than $10.00, you can use a query like the following:

SELECT Album FROM Albums

WHERE (Artist = 'Jefferson Airplane' OR Artist =

'Jefferson Starship') AND DiscountPrice < 10.00

Note the use of parentheses around the OR clause. Parentheses tell the DBMS to process this part of the query first. The placement of parentheses can change the results of a query, sometimes drastically. Compare the previous query to the following query:

SELECT Album FROM Albums

WHERE Artist = 'Jefferson Airplane' OR (Artist =

'Jefferson Starship' AND DiscountPrice < 10.00)

The query with parentheses around the OR clause returns albums by Jefferson Airplane or Jefferson Starship that are less than $10.00. The query with parentheses around the AND clause returns all albums by Jefferson Airplane, regardless of price, and any albums by Jefferson Starship that cost less than $10.00.

▶ How does NOT work in an SQL query? The NOT operator can be used to omit records from a search by specifying a not-equal relationship. For example, the following query returns all records in the Albums table where the Artist is not equal to *Jefferson Airplane*:

Select Album from Albums

WHERE NOT (Artist = 'Jefferson Airplane')

Sometimes NOT relationships are specified with a not-equal operator, such as <> or !=, depending on the specifications of the query language. For example, the following query returns the same records as one that uses the NOT operator:

Select Album from Albums

WHERE Artist <> 'Jefferson Airplane'

UPDATING FIELDS

▶ **Can I change the contents of a record?** You can change records in a database only if you have authorization to do so. At Vintage Music Shop's site, for example, customers do not have authorization to change album prices or alter the name of the songs on an album.

When a customer purchases an Elvis Presley *G.I. Blues* album, however, the number of *G.I. Blues* albums in Vintage Music Shop's inventory is reduced by one. To accomplish this update, one of the software modules in Vintage Music Shop's inventory system issues an **UPDATE** command:

> **UPDATE Albums**
>
> **SET InStock = InStock - 1**
>
> **WHERE Album = 'G.I. Blues'**

▶ **Is it possible to update a group of records?** In addition to changing the data in a single record, SQL can perform a **global update** that changes the data in more than one record at a time.

Suppose you're Vintage Music Shop's marketing manager, and you want to put all Rolling Stones albums on sale by reducing the DiscountPrice to $9.95. You could do it the hard way by searching for an Artist field that contains *Rolling Stones*, adjusting the DiscountPrice field for that record, and then looking for the next Rolling Stones album. However, it would be easier to change all the records with a single command.

> **UPDATE Albums**
>
> **SET DiscountPrice = 9.95**
>
> **WHERE Artist = 'Rolling Stones'**

Let's see how this command performs a global update. The UPDATE command means you want to change the data in some or all of the records. *Albums* is the name of the record type containing the data you want to change. SET DiscountPrice = 9.95 tells the DBMS to change the data in the DiscountPrice field to $9.95. WHERE Artist = 'Rolling Stones' tells the DBMS to change only those records where the artist name is *Rolling Stones*.

▶ **What are the limitations of the global UPDATE command?** Although the global UPDATE function is powerful, it works only for records that have similar characteristics—for example, all albums by the Rolling Stones or all albums produced in 1955. Custom programming is required to perform global operations on information that does not have any similar characteristics. Figure 11-49 provides an example.

FIGURE 11-49

Database designers can write modules that provide custom update capabilities.

Hard Day's Night
Blue Hawaii
Strange Days
Cheap Thrills
Yellow Submarine
Surfin' Safari
Blonde on Blonde
Dragon Fly
Rubber Soul
Anthem of the Sun

Vintage Music Shop's marketing manager picks ten albums each week to place on a special promotional sale. These albums have no common data that can be used to formulate a global UPDATE command.

Custom programming allows the marketing manager to simply submit a list of ten albums as a document. The module would "read" the document and issue an UPDATE command for each of the chosen albums.

JOINING TABLES

▶ How is data retrieved from more than one table at a time? Recall that the process of normalization creates tables that can be related by fields that exist in both tables. In SQL terminology, creating a relationship between tables is referred to as **joining tables**.

Suppose you want some information on Elvis Presley's *G.I. Blues* album. It would be nice to see not only the album name and cover, but also a list of the songs included on the album.

The songs, however, are not stored in the same table as the rest of the album data. The Albums table holds the album name, the artist's name, the release date, and other data about the album. The Tracks table holds the name of each song track, the track length, and an MP3 sample of the track. Both tables also contain a Cat# field.

Earlier in the chapter, you learned that a relationship can exist between Vintage Music Shop's Albums table and Tracks table, based on the data in the Cat# field, as shown in Figure 11-50.

FIGURE 11-50

Records in the Albums table and Tracks table both include a Cat# field. When the data in these fields is the same, the records refer to the same entity—in this case, an Elvis Presley album called *G.I. Blues*.

ALBUMS

R#	Cat#	Album	Artist	Release Date	In Stock	Value
1	LPM-2256	G.I. Blues	Elvis Presley	10/01/1960	4	20.00
2	7499-2	Between the Buttons	Rolling Stones	02/06/1967	1	13.99
3	LSP-246	Blue H				
4	N16014	Surfin'				

TRACKS

Cat#	TrackTitle	Track Length	TrackSample
LPM-2256	Blue Suede Shoes	104	BlueSuede.mp3
LPM-2256	Frankfort Special	132	FrankSpec.mp3
LPM-2256	Wooden Heart	163	WoodenHE.mp3
7499-2	Ruby Tuesday	197	RubyT.mp3

To take advantage of the relationship between these two tables, you first have to join the tables. Why? Remember that in a relational database, the tables are essentially independent unless you join them together. The SQL **JOIN** command allows you to temporarily join and simultaneously access the data in more than one table.

▶ How does the JOIN command work? A single SQL query can retrieve data from the Albums table and the Tracks table for Elvis Presley albums. To do so, however, requires some way to distinguish the data contained in each table. In the example, both tables contain a field called Cat#. How can you differentiate the Cat# field that belongs to the Albums table from the Cat# field in the Tracks table?

SQL uses dot notation to make this distinction. Albums.Cat# is the full specification for the Cat# field in the Albums table. Tracks.Cat# specifies its counterpart in the Tracks table.

When joining two tables, the convention is to use the full specification for table and field name. Figure 11-51 dissects an SQL query that joins two Vintage Music Shop tables.

FIGURE 11-51

The JOIN command links the Albums and Tracks tables to produce the album name, cover, price, and tracks for item number LPM-2256.

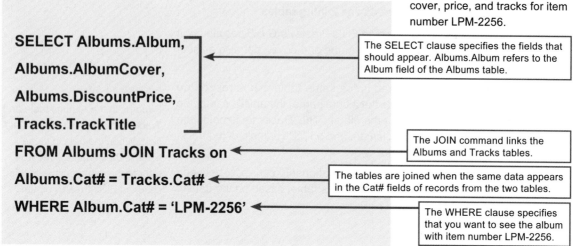

SELECT Albums.Album,

Albums.AlbumCover,

Albums.DiscountPrice,

Tracks.TrackTitle

The SELECT clause specifies the fields that should appear. Albums.Album refers to the Album field of the Albums table.

FROM Albums JOIN Tracks on

The JOIN command links the Albums and Tracks tables.

Albums.Cat# = Tracks.Cat#

The tables are joined when the same data appears in the Cat# fields of records from the two tables.

WHERE Album.Cat# = 'LPM-2256'

The WHERE clause specifies that you want to see the album with item number LPM-2256.

▶ **How extensive is SQL?** In this section, you were introduced to some of the most commonly used SQL commands, and you explored how they might be used in the context of an e-commerce music business. SQL is a very extensive and powerful language that can be used not only to manipulate data, but also to create databases, tables, and reports. Because SQL is one of the most popular database tools, many computer professionals consider SQL fluency an essential career skill.

QuickCheck

1. In search specifications, AND, OR, and NOT are examples of search operators, also called [   ] operators.

2. In SQL, the DATA command adds fields to a database. True or false? [   ]

3. To search for data in a specific field, you can use the SQL command [   ].

4. The SQL [   ] command can change the data in a specified field in one or more records.

5. In SQL, the JOIN command allows you to add fields to a database. True or false? [   ]

▶ CHECK ANSWERS

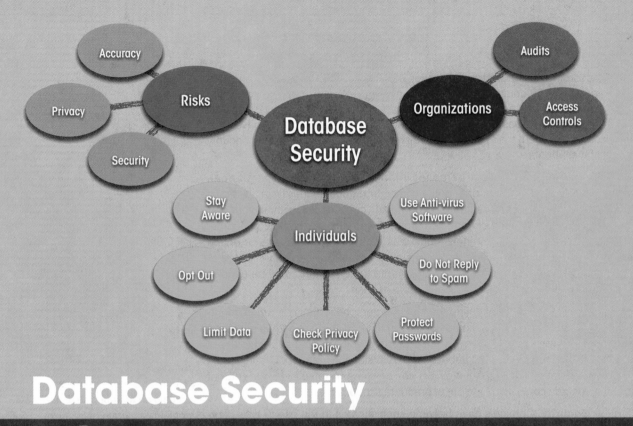

Database Security

IN THE PAST FEW YEARS, data for millions of people has been stolen, hacked, or simply gone missing. Consumers are alarmed that databases are so vulnerable. In Section E you'll learn why.

DATABASE VULNERABILITIES

▶ **How vulnerable are databases?** Databases are vulnerable to physical theft, hacking, and unauthorized access. A disk or tape containing a backup or an archive could be stolen. A notebook computer containing a database used by a field representative or teleworker can go missing. Hackers can gain unauthorized access to a database over the Internet or an unsecured wireless connection. Legitimate data entry personnel could make unauthorized copies, changes, and deletions.

The qualities that make databases efficient also make them vulnerable. Data stored in digital format is easy to copy, back up, store, and transmit. Although it would be impractical to steal millions of paper records from filing cabinets, to steal a digital database a criminal simply has to pocket a small backup drive or make a copy of the original database (Figure 11-52).

Electronic databases can be accessed over local area networks and the Internet, offering convenience to customers, clients, managers, and staff. Security holes can allow intruders to infiltrate computer systems housing databases, copy data, delete it, or change it.

When a database is illicitly copied, it is stolen but not missing, as it would be if a crook made off with the folders in a filing cabinet. The theft might not be discovered for days or weeks, if ever, and affected individuals are never warned that their identities are at risk.

▶ **How do database security breaches affect individuals?** There is hardly a person in America who is not in at least one computer database. Every time you fill out a survey, register to use a Web site, visit your doctor, use your credit card, or make a phone call, that information is stored somewhere in a database.

FIGURE 11-52

Database theft is all too common.

Fredrik Skold/Getty Images

According to the Electronic Frontier Foundation, the average American is in at least 50 commercial databases and the average Web user could be profiled in hundreds more. With personal data stored in so many databases and those databases at risk for being stolen or misused, citizens have valid concerns about their privacy, the validity of recorded data, and the security of their identities.

▶ **Privacy.** You expect personal information to remain confidential. However, when your data is in a computer database, there is a risk that it can be viewed by unauthorized individuals or distributed without your permission. Many people are concerned about misuse of medical records, but what about seemingly innocuous databases? Your local or online movie rental service probably has a list of the movies you've rented. A preferred customer card at your favorite supermarket could be used to collect data about the groceries you purchase.

▶ **Accuracy.** After accepting the fact that personal data is stored in countless databases, it would be comforting to know that the data is accurate. However, data entry errors, update errors, and hacking all add to doubt about the veracity of database data. A mistake in your credit rating could prevent you from purchasing a car or home. A mixup in your student records could keep you out of graduate school.

▶ **Security.** Criminals have become sophisticated in the use of bots, keyloggers, and redirection to access data stored on personal computers and in corporate databases. The data stored in a single database is often sufficient to provide a criminal with enough information to access your bank account or use your credit card. New trends in data aggregation and analysis make it possible to assemble a detailed picture of an individual's life with enough critical ID numbers and PINs to steal an entire identity and then run up debt, acquire a criminal record, and put a real person's life in shambles.

FIGURE 11-53

A bland but irritating spam that appears to originate from a legitimate air carrier might contain an opt-out clause that contains accurate data, such as your frequent flyer number. An average person reads this message and reasons, "If they have my frequent flyer number, it must be a legitimate site," and proceeds to enter his or her PIN, which gets sent directly to a hacker.

One worrisome development has been criminal database aggregation. Here's how it works. A hacker obtains a database containing moderately sensitive data, such as e-mail addresses and frequent flier account numbers. The list is sold to the highest bidder who devises a data-rich phishing attack, like the one in Figure 11-53, to gain even more data.

The hacker's database, which now contains e-mail addresses, frequent flyer numbers, and PINs, can be sold at a profit to another hacker who can devise other phishing schemes to gather even more data. Eventually, the database will contain a fairly complete dossier on its subjects, and it will be worth big bucks when sold to identity thieves.

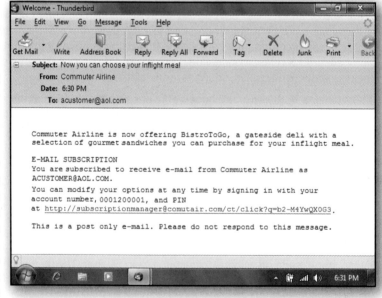

DATABASE SECURITY MEASURES

▶ Can databases be secured? Today's computers are under assault from hackers and natural disasters. Although no computer system can be 100% secure, system administrators can take steps to secure computer systems and the databases they contain. Security measures include encryption, access controls, data security policies, and intrusion monitoring.

▶ How does encryption secure a database? Although encryption cannot prevent a database from being lost or stolen, it can make the data it contains unintelligible to a hacker. It might seem that a prudent approach to database security would be encrypting the entire database and leaving it that way, but encrypted databases are not always practical.

Encrypted databases are less efficient than unencrypted databases because all or part of the database has to be decrypted for the query to locate information. The process of decrypting database information in response to a query increases the amount of time necessary to process each query.

Most active, operational databases are not encrypted while being used, but the data they contain can be encrypted before it is archived. Thieves who gain access to a database archive cannot make sense of the data if it is encrypted. Also, database data that's transmitted over the Web can be encrypted using encryption technologies such as SSL or SHTTP.

▶ What are access controls? An **access control** limits access to systems, such as computer databases. Access controls can block unauthorized users and limit activities of authorized users. IT professionals sometimes classify access controls as identification and authentication, authorization, and accountability.

▶ Identification and authentication determine who can access a database and the information it contains.

▶ Authorization defines what an authenticated user can do.

▶ Accountability tracks what a user did.

▶ How do organizations restrict access to databases? Basic security restricts physical access and network access to the computer that hosts the database. Physical access can be limited to authorized personnel by housing the computer in a locked data center. Online access can be limited by firewalls and passwords.

System administrators should be sure to change all default administrator passwords before opening the database to internal and external users. Most DBMSs ship with a standard administrator password. Hackers know it. Surveys show that as many as 25% of businesses never remember to change the default password, leaving their systems wide open to unauthorized access.

Security experts also recommend separating the server that hosts the database from the server that hosts publicly accessible services, such as Web pages. Database servers that supply information to Web servers should be configured to allow connections only from that Web server to prevent port-jumping exploits from unauthorized intruders.

11

▶ How does authorization help to secure databases?

Customers, clients, and even most employees who use a database have no need to change its structure by adding fields, changing field names, and setting keys. **User privileges** (also referred to as user rights or permissions) delineate what activities a user can perform within a database.

The lowest level privilege is read access, which allows a user to see the data, but not change it. Adding the update privilege allows a user to also change data in the database. Privileges can also be granted for deleting, adding, indexing, printing, and copying (Figure 11-54).

Data views provide additional security to databases. A **data view** establishes which fields and records a particular user is allowed to access. In a medical insurance database, for example, a customer service representative might be allowed to view an insured person's account, including the customer name and address; however, the treatment summary might display only dates and charges, not the nature of the treatment.

▶ How can policies help to secure databases?

A good set of policies decreases the risk of unauthorized access within the workplace, minimizes the chance of confidential data escaping from the workplace, and helps improve data entry accuracy.

A notebook computer is an easy target. Most thieves are after the hardware, but they might hit the jackpot if a computer contains a corporate or government database. To minimize vulnerabilities caused by employee inattention, organizations can formulate database use policies, such as prohibiting employees from removing sensitive data from the workplace.

Policies for retiring old equipment are also essential, and not just for computers. Modern office copier machines contain a hard disk, which stores images of every page that is copied. Removing and destroying storage devices from all discarded devices is a requirement for data security.

▶ What can monitoring accomplish?

A **database audit** is a procedure that monitors and records user activity within a database. In some instances, auditing can identify intruders before they can compromise a system. If an intruder breaches database security, an audit can help to identify the damage and correct it.

Database auditing tools can be configured to keep a record of who is accountable for changes to the database, gather general usage statistics, or investigate suspicious activity.

Tracking who makes changes in a database helps an organization maintain accountability, trace the source of errors, and make corrections. If a database has been compromised by a hacker, an audit report can be used to check recent changes to the database to make sure they are legitimate.

General usage statistics help database administrators maintain optimal performance, so that query response is quick even at peak usage times. Usage statistics gathered by LAN management software can also reveal abnormal usage patterns and alert system administrators to possible intrusion attempts.

FIGURE 11-54

A database administrator can limit the way individuals or groups access data. In this example, library patrons are given permission to read data in the Books table, but they cannot update, insert, or delete data from it.

If abnormal usage patterns become evident, database auditing tools can be configured to check specific types of database activity. For example, if a system administrator suspects that data is being surreptitiously deleted or changed, an audit can be set up to record any successful or unsuccessful deletions from tables in the database.

DATABASE SECURITY REGULATIONS

▶ **Is my government protecting me from database security breaches?** International e-commerce has made database security a global concern, and many countries have enacted laws to protect personal data stored on databases.

The European Union's Privacy Directive 95/46/EC and Canada's Personal Information Protection and Electronic Documents Act (PIPEDA) mandate that database breaches from accidental loss or electronic attack are disclosed, rather than swept under the carpet.

Although it leads the world in technology development, the United States has some of the weakest privacy regulations in the developed world. Its patchwork of laws regulates some types of databases, but not others.

▶ **Are government databases regulated?** The U.S. Privacy Act of 1974 requires government agencies to disclose to an individual the contents of his or her records. It places restrictions on how agencies can share an individual's data with other people and agencies.

The Act also requires agencies to follow "fair information practices" when gathering and handling personal data, and allows individuals to sue the government for violating its provisions. However, more recent legislation, such as the USA PATRIOT Act, relaxes some of the earlier rules governing the collection and use of data about U.S. citizens and visitors.

Seemingly reasonable steps to protect U.S. consumers have not yet been incorporated into comprehensive national database legislation. However, more than 40 states have established laws that require residents to be notified if their personal information is compromised by a database security breach.

FIGURE 11-55

U.S. laws that pertain to private-sector databases cover a patchwork of sectors, leaving loopholes where personal data is unprotected.

▶ **What about private sector databases?** Regulations in the private sector are, in many cases, less stringent than those imposed on the government.

Laws governing private sector databases (Figure 11-55) offer only spot coverage of specific types of data.

The Video Privacy Protection Act, passed in 1988, requires video stores to provide consumers with the opportunity to opt out from mailing lists that might be sold to other businesses.

The Health Insurance Portability and Accountability Act (HIPAA) of 1996 addresses the security and privacy of medical records. Medical records that include an individual's name, Social Security number, or other personal identification cannot be disclosed without consent.

The Gramm-Leach-Bliley Act of 1999 requires financial institutions to establish security standards that protect customer data from internal and external threats, including unauthorized access that occurs through networks and online systems. The law also contains an opt-out clause designed to protect consumer data from being sold or disclosed to third parties, though there are exceptions that allow even opt-out data to be shared.

WHAT INDIVIDUALS CAN DO

▶ What can I do to minimize my vulnerability to database security breaches? Even if businesses adhere to applicable database laws, consumers cannot be expected to understand the nuances for different types of databases and are therefore in the dark about their rights and responsibilities. Many consumer advocates are calling for comprehensive one-stop security-privacy legislation that applies to all databases.

In the meantime, what to do? You can't protect your personal data once you've released it, so the key to minimizing your risk is to be vigilant about the information you divulge.

▶ **Know when data is being collected.** Be aware of any activities that can possibly collect information about you for a database, such as registering to use a Web site, participating in a survey, submitting your resume to an online data bank, requesting a product rebate, participating in online discussion groups, clicking pop-up ads, and so on. Sometimes the gains aren't worth the risk or the potential nuisance of dealing with a deluge of junk mail.

▶ **Supply only the data that is required.** When asked for information, supply only what's required. Never divulge your Social Security number and be cautious about other personal information, such as your telephone number or address. When in doubt, you might consider using phony data.

▶ **Opt-out when possible.** Make sure you look for the opt-out button if you don't want your data distributed to third parties. Some Web sites have the opt-in button selected as the default; and if you don't want your data distributed, you will need to change to the opt-out status.

▶ **Protect your passwords.** Consider using a USB flash drive containing a portable password manager that stores strongly encrypted passwords and enters them when you want to access a password protected database or site. The flash drive can be removed from your computer when it is not in use to foil intrusion attempts (Figure 11-56).

▶ **Don't trade your privacy.** Be wary of offers for free services in exchange for personal information or permission to track your online footprints.

▶ **Use antivirus software.** Make sure your antivirus software is running and up to date. Use a personal firewall and pop-up blocker to protect your computer from unauthorized intrusions.

▶ **Do not reply to spam.** Never send personal information in response to an e-mail request that could be a phishing attack from an illegitimate source.

FIGURE 11-56

Portable password managers that you can use from a USB flash drive include:

▶ Siber Systems RoboForm2Go
▶ DobySoft KeyPass
▶ Open source KeePass
▶ Open source Password Safe

◗ **Before registering, check the site's privacy policy.** When a privacy policy exists, check it out—especially the part that explains whether your data might be shared with a third party (Figure 11-57). Even if the policy indicates that data will not be shared, don't assume the data will never be released. You'll have to weigh the sensitivity of the data and the dependability of the source to decide whether to supply the requested data.

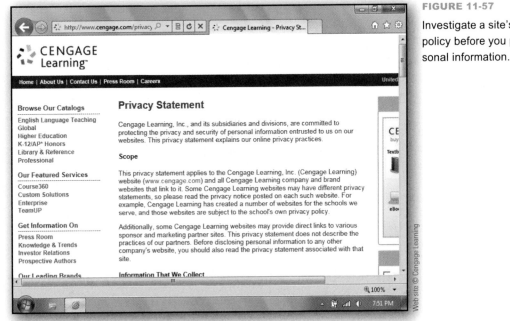

FIGURE 11-57

Investigate a site's privacy policy before you provide personal information.

11

QuickCheck

1. The qualities that make computer databases efficient also make them vulnerable to security breaches. True or false? [ ]

2. [ ] cannot prevent a database from being lost or stolen, but it can make the data it contains unusable.

3. Passwords, firewalls, and locked data centers are all types of [ ] controls that can prevent unauthorized use of a database.

4. A database [ ] is a procedure that monitors and records user activity within a database.

5. Individuals can minimize their vulnerability to database security breaches by looking for a way to [ ] -out so that data is not sent to third parties.

 CHECK ANSWERS

Issue: Can Computers Catch Terrorists?

SMOKE RISES OVER THE skyline. It could be New York, Oslo, Moscow, Mumbai, or any major city. The cause: a terrorist attack. As the survivors mourn the dead, they inevitably ask: Could this attack have been prevented?

Modern data analysis techniques are successfully deployed in the private sector to detect consumer fraud, assess home loan applications, and predict consumer buying patterns. If direct marketers can easily aggregate and analyze data from Web sites that you visit and public information in your Facebook profile, wouldn't it be just as easy to mine existing databases to uncover patterns in terrorist behavior, identify individuals who fit the pattern, and prevent them from carrying out terrorist activities?

Governments maintain vast databases. Surely a proper search of this data, combined with public sector data, such as Web site access, credit card use, travel history, e-mail messages, and telephone records, could produce a manageable list of potential terrorists.

This theory was put to the test when the founder of a data mining company trolled through a collection of data looking for people likely to commit acts of terror. His algorithm produced 1,200 names; five of them were hijackers in the September 11 attack.

What seems like a remarkable feat of predictive analysis, however, reveals several problems with data mining methodology. The analysis identified 1,200 potential terrorists, but only five of these individuals actually participated in a terrorist operation. The remaining 1,195 people did not carry out attacks. Nineteen terrorists were involved in the actual attack; data mining did not identify even a third of them.

Further, this data mining analysis was carried out after September 11, using hindsight information available about the attackers. Predicting who will carry out future attacks is more difficult because the targets and modus operandi are unknown.

"Terrorists can damage our country and way of life in two ways: through physical, psychological damage and through our own inappropriate response to that threat."

Charles Vest, co-chair of the committee investigating the role of technology in preventing terrorism

An algorithmic search for patterns in a collection of databases is an example of automated terrorist identification. Some degree of privacy is maintained because a machine, rather than a human analyst, searches the data.

To sort through machine-generated results and weed out false positives, however, a human analyst eventually has to view the data and all the personal details it includes. According to privacy advocates, this analysis subjects thousands of innocent civilians to intense scrutiny and potential loss of civil liberties.

Privacy advocates also fear that government data mining is susceptible to mission creep, a term that refers to projects that expand beyond their intended scope.

Data collected for homeland security might be used to identify other types of offenders, such as tax evaders, digital music pirates, or parents who are late on child support payments. Catching such individuals might be a worthy social goal, but it requires a considerable amount of government scrutiny into the lives of ordinary people.

Data mining could also be used to profile ethnic groups or harass individuals who contribute to organizations that oppose the policies of the dominant political party.

According to civil liberties advocates, government data mining is more dangerous than private sector analytics because the repercussions can be extreme. Government investigations can trigger IRS harassment, airport pat downs, and wiretaps, rather than a few irritating ads that pop up based on your profile in an online marketing aggregator's data warehouse.

Governments have a responsibility for the safety of their citizens, but societies have to remain vigilant to maintain the right balance between civil liberties and security.

Try It! Data mining is controversial, but it is an evolving technology that might have the potential to increase civilian security. Explore data mining firsthand to understand the issues.

1 As yet, there is not a fail-proof method for automatic terrorist identification. Suppose that a researcher devises an algorithm that is correct 99% of the time. For every 100 names it produces, one will be a false positive—someone who is not a terrorist. It will also miss one person who is a terrorist. If this algorithm is used to analyze the 308,745,538 people in the U.S., how many innocent people would be falsely identified as terrorists and how many real terrorists would go undiscovered?

2 People leave personal digital tracks whenever they make a purchase, take a trip, access their bank account, make a phone call, file an income tax return, stroll past a security camera, obtain a prescription, mail a package, apply for a loan, e-mail a friend, rent a video, or download music. Create a fictitious person and provide five examples of online activities he or she might perform that would look suspicious to a data mining algorithm, but are actually perfectly innocent activities.

3 After a flurry of post-9/11 controversies over data mining, privacy advocates were relieved to see articles in *Wired* magazine and several mainstream press sources citing a government-funded study on data mining that concluded it is not an effective tool against terrorism. Look through the executive summary for the 2008 study "Protecting Individual Privacy in the Struggle Against Terrorists: A Framework for Program Assessment." Find and copy the passage stating that data mining is not an effective tool for combating terrorism.

4 To find out how extensively your government is using data mining, you can go directly to the source. For example, in the U.S., the Department of Homeland Security Privacy Office issues an annual Data Mining Report to Congress. Read the most recent report. List and briefly describe the data mining projects that are operational.

5 Technology is increasing the amount and type of data that is available to data mining operations. Although data mining originally was designed to analyze text data, advances in facial recognition and translation provide multimedia input for data mining algorithms. You can test facial recognition systems at online sites that find celebrities with facial features similar to yours. Upload a photo (it doesn't have to be yours) at a celebrity look-alike site such as Picadilo.com, MyHeritage.com, or FaceDouble. Based on the accuracy of finding similar faces, how efficient would this system be for identifying a terrorist based on his or her photo?

INFOWEBLINKS

You can check the **NP2013 Chapter 11 InfoWebLink** for updates to these activities.

W CLICK TO CONNECT
www.infoweblinks.com/np2013/ch11

What Do You Think?   ISSUE

1. Should your government continue to develop and deploy data mining techniques designed to identify terrorists?

2. Are you concerned about your personal data being included in government data mining operations?

3. Do you think that governments should apologize and compensate individuals who are inappropriately harmed by data mining operations?

Information Tools: Vetting Anonymous

TWEETS, FORUM POSTINGS, and comments attached to online articles can be a gold mine of information. When you have a problem with a digital device, an online forum might offer advice on a quick "fix." When you want breaking eyewitness news as events unfold, there's no source like Twitter. And if you're interested in the other side of a story, look no further than the comments at the end of an online blog post or article.

The information from these sources is often difficult to verify. Many participants use pseudonyms, effectively making them anonymous. Let's take a look at the pros and cons of using these sources.

> You should be particularly careful about information on which you base personal activities such as treating illness, dieting, filing taxes, and troubleshooting digital or automotive equipment.

FORUMS

Forums allow participants to post questions to which other participants provide answers. Forums are popular sources for information when you are troubleshooting problems with digital devices, software, or automobiles. They also offer opportunities to discuss health, investments, diets, and a variety of other topics.

On technology topics, third-party forums sometimes address issues that are not acknowledged by online forums operated by equipment manufacturers and vendors.

When using information from forums to troubleshoot software, hardware, and connection problems, beware of misleading statements that could make problems worse.

Before you follow a complex set of instructions to tackle a technical problem, make sure the source is reliable and the solution seems technically plausible. Read comments and follow the discussion threads pertaining to suggested solutions; they can help you determine if the solution might work.

TWITTER

Twitter is like a river of information, continually flowing and ever changing. It is a premium source for information about what's happening right now.

Twitter posts broke the news of the Continental Airlines crash that became known as the Miracle on the Hudson, the 2008 earthquake in China, and Osama bin Laden's death.

But not everything on Twitter is legitimate. A group called Script Kiddies has managed to hack into several legitimate Twitter accounts and post false tweets; an attack on Ground Zero just before the 10th anniversary of 9/11, and a false report that President Obama had been assassinated in 2010.

These tweets originating from NBC News and Fox News appeared legitimate, but weren't—a reminder that even information with provenance that seems genuine may not be true.

Tweets often provide links to blog posts or Web sites containing more detailed information on an issue or topic. You can use standard techniques for checking the provenance of those sites.

COMMENTS

Provocative articles spawn commentary. That commentary is sometimes useful to readers and researchers because it reveals the scope of an issue and provides glimpses of its many facets.

Most sites that accept comments require participants to register and provide a valid e-mail address. However, that requirement does not prevent people from using screen names and throwaway e-mail accounts.

Commenters may have valid reasons for cloaking their identities, and their comments might be informative. Unless you can verify and cross-check the information, however, you should not accept it as authoritative.

Anonymous comments or those from sources that can't be properly verified should not be used as the basis for factual citations, but they can give you ideas and viewpoints that help you expand your research to encompass the full scope of a topic.

Try It! So what should you do with information that comes from an anonymous source or one cloaked in the secrecy of a screen name? Here's a chance to work with a few verification techniques.

1 Although forums are sometimes billed as "advice and recommendations from a community of experts," participants are not always experts and the advice offered is not always accurate. The first step to identifying the source of information is to click any links available to the user's profile. Select an article from a technology news source, such as Engadget or HuffPost Tech, that includes lots of comments. Click the picture and name links for three commenters, then fill in the following table, entering "NA" if the information is not available.

	Commenter 1	Commenter 2	Commenter 3
Commenter "Handle"			
Commenter Real Name			
Number of Posts			
General Quality of Posts			

2 Verifying tweets requires a twofold approach: gathering information on the tweeter, and triangulating the location and timing of the content. To see how it works, check out a technology Twitter feed. You can access tweets even without a Twitter account by googling *twitter search* and then using the Search box at the top of the screen. Enter *Cisco* to find information about the technology company that specializes in network equipment. Select a tweet that appears to come from an individual, then answer the following questions:

a. Does the tweeter provide a name, picture, and biography?

b. If you search for the tweeter's name in Google, do you find further clues to the person's identity?

c. What is the person's track record of blog posts, forum responses, or tweets?

d. Does the source have a large following on Twitter or an extensive network of friends on Facebook, LinkedIn, or Google+?

e. Can you determine where the source is located and if the location might be relevant to verifying the information (as in an eyewitness account)?

f. Are other sources reporting similar information?

g. If the information is a link or retweet, can you identify the original source?

h. Does the language of the message sound appropriate for the source?

3 When you're looking for a solution to a technical problem and you come across forum postings such as "I don't know" or "I've never tried this but...," you probably wonder why anyone would waste his or her time (and yours) with information that is totally useless. In addition to lame comments, online information sources are plagued by trolls and sockpuppets. Look for information about "trolls" and "sockpuppets" in Wikipedia. Make a list of characteristics that can help you stay alert for trolls and sockpuppets on Twitter feeds, forums, and other online sources.

Iwona Grodzka/Shutterstock.com

© Gabe Palmer/CORBIS

Technology in Context: Medicine

THE HEALTH CARE INDUSTRY was an early adopter of computer technology for traditional data processing applications, such as client billing and employee payroll. A computer's ability to process and store thousands of records helps reduce hospital administrative costs. Linking hospital billing to health insurance companies streamlines cumbersome manual procedures for submitting insurance claims. These behind-the-scenes applications do not, however, directly affect the quality of health care, where computer technology has now made a significant contribution.

Until recent years, paper charts dangled from the foot of every hospital bed and additional information was stored in thick file folders in nursing stations or the hospital's medical records department. Patient records include doctors' diagnoses, laboratory test results, medication schedules, and charts depicting a patient's vital signs.

The process of maintaining these paper-based records is time consuming and quite open to errors. Effective treatments might be dangerously delayed while a slip of paper that holds laboratory results wends its way through the hospital corridors. In a hospital where a patient's condition can change suddenly and unexpectedly, health care providers need instant and ubiquitous access to the information contained in the patient's record.

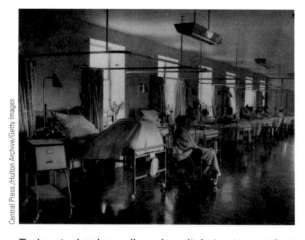

Today, technology allows hospitals to store patient records in computer databases that are instantly accessible to doctors, nurses, and other health care workers. A nurse can access a patient's record from a computer in the nursing station to check care instruc-

tions and enter vital statistics. Doctors can access a patient's record from an office or home computer to check progress, order tests, and make decisions when minutes count. Lab technicians can enter test results immediately into a patient's record.

Patient records tie into a comprehensive hospital information system (HIS) that integrates just about every aspect of hospital management. Even the hospital dietitian can access relevant parts of a patient's record to work out menus that fit a patient's dietary needs, while avoiding allergies.

According to technology pioneer Ray Kurzweil, "medicine is among the most knowledge-intensive professions." Most doctors agree that medicine has grown too complex to have all the answers "in their heads." Today, in just about every aspect of their practices, doctors use computer applications and Internet technologies.

At one time, doctors dictated the results of an examination or surgical procedure. The dictated notes were later transcribed into computer records by staff members. Today's technology allows doctors to enter this information directly into computerized patient records by typing or by dictating into a speech recognition system that digitally converts their comments into computer text.

The Internet supplies physicians with many informational and diagnostic resources. Health libraries provide online access to reference databases, such as MEDLINE and STAT!Ref. Doctors use drug databases to choose appropriate medications, avoid dangerous drug interactions, determine correct dosages, and print out prescriptions. One pediatrician says, "I use the computer to make sure the medicine will work with any other medicines the patient takes, the patient won't be allergic, and to check for warnings about certain foods or alcohol."

Hospitals are ideal candidates for wireless technologies because just about everything and everyone is on the move, including doctors, nurses, patients, and equipment. Overlake Hospital in Bellevue, Washington is a model of future wired, paperless hospitals. Nurses tote portable computer stations, physicians use voice recognition software to enter prescriptions, and bar coded patient wristbands help caregivers administer and track medications.

11

The Internet's ability to rapidly disseminate information worldwide makes it a crucial tool for tracking global health threats. During the H1N1 outbreak in 2009, Web sites maintained by the World Health Organization (WHO) and Centers for Disease Control (CDC) provided statistics on the spread of infection. They also kept doctors, researchers, and reporters up to date on efforts to identify the virus, develop a vaccine, and devise treatment options.

Many doctors use Internet technology to communicate with their colleagues by e-mail and send imaging data, such as X-rays, to specialists. Telemedicine uses communications links to supply medical services at a distance. It can be used to provide specialty medical services to rural patients, and allow medical personnel from several locations to collaborate on patient diagnosis and treatment.

Once limited to telephone consultations and fax transmission of paper-based patient records, today telemedicine takes full advantage of the Internet to transfer electronic patient records, still images, and even full motion video sequences. Images from diverse sources, such as X-rays, MRIs, and CT scans, stored in the standard DICOM (Digital Imaging and Communications in Medicine) format, can be easily transferred over the Internet and displayed using a single software package.

Computers have become an integral part of modern medical equipment. The use of X-rays was a huge medical breakthrough in the early 1900s, but X-rays capture only a two-dimensional image. A technology called CT (computed tomography) essentially assembles a series of X-ray images taken from slightly different angles. A computer works with the data to generate a three-dimensional image that can be rotated and viewed from any angle.

Computers, data, and telecommunications technology team up in a number of mobile medical devices that have revolutionized emergency medical services. An EMS worker describes a device used to monitor cardiac patients: "We can do a comprehensive 12-lead EKG at the scene and the computer inside the LIFEPAK 12 tells us what kind of arrhythmia we may be dealing with and even gives us suggestions for treatments."

Today, most patients want to be informed participants in their health care team. Patients use Web sites such as WebMD to find information on diseases, drugs, and treatment options. Doctors frequently recommend health-related Web sites and support groups to patients. Patients can gather information from these sites at their own pace and refer back to it as necessary. The availability of information on the Web reduces the need for doctors to make lengthy explanations that patients often cannot absorb or remember during an office visit.

The computer's use in medicine is not without potential pitfalls. Online patient records raise issues of confidentiality. Many patients are concerned about unauthorized access to their records by employers, human resources staff, and hackers.

The Health Insurance Portability and Accountability Act (HIPAA) requires insurance companies to protect the privacy of their policy holders from inappropriate use or disclosure. Insurance company employees are allowed to look at clients' personal health information only in the course of administering claims.

Insurance companies are not allowed to disclose personal health information to any other company or to a client's employer without permission. Insurance companies are, however, allowed to divulge information to government agencies if a serious threat to public health and safety exists. HIPAA also gives patients the right to amend incorrect or missing information in their records, and it allows clients to request a list of the disclosures.

The next time you're in a hospital or doctor's office, look around for computers. You're sure to find these essential tools used to improve the effectiveness of health care.

New Perspectives Labs

To access the New Perspectives Lab for Chapter 11, open the NP2013 interactive eBook and then click the icon next to the lab title.

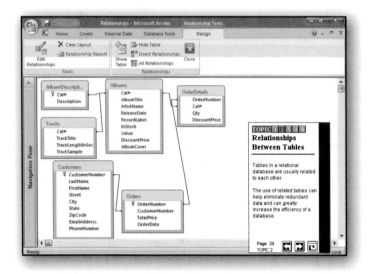

WORKING WITH DATABASE SOFTWARE

IN THIS LAB YOU'LL LEARN:

- How relational database software depicts data as tables, records, and fields
- How to use tables and forms to view data
- How to create a table
- How to use primary keys
- How to enter and edit data
- Why relationships between tables are so important
- How to sort data and create an index
- How to search for data
- How to set filters
- How to create queries
- How to view the SQL code for a query
- How to create a report
- How to modify a report in Design view

LAB ASSIGNMENTS

1. Start the interactive part of the lab. Make sure you've enabled Tracking if you want to save your QuickCheck results. Perform each lab step as directed, and answer all the lab QuickCheck questions. When you exit the lab, your answers are automatically graded and your results are displayed.

2. A friend wants to create a table to store information about a collection of old books. List the fields you might include in the table to store information about the books. For each field, specify the field name, data type (text, numeric, date, etc.), and field length. Indicate the primary key(s), and describe how you would sort and/or index the data.

3. Use Microsoft Access or any available file or database management software to create the structure for the table you specified in Assignment 2. Enter at least ten records. Print a list of all your data.

4. Make a list of five queries that might be useful if your database had hundreds of records. Try these queries on your table. For each query, list the records that were selected.

5. Sketch a report on paper that uses some of the fields in your table. Make sure your report contains a title and headings for each field. Specify whether you would like to align your data at the right, center, or left of each column. Use your software to generate and print the report.

Key Terms

Make sure you understand all the boldfaced key terms presented in this chapter. With the NP2013 interactive eBook, you can use this list of terms as an interactive study activity. First, try to define a term in your own words, and then click the term to compare your definition with the definition presented in the chapter.

11

Access control, 655
BLOB, 635
Cardinality, 616
Case sensitive database, 636
Computed field, 635
CREATE, 646
Data dependence, 624
Data independence, 624
Data mining, 612
Data redundancy, 637
Data type, 634
Data view, 656
Data warehouse, 612
Database, 610
Database audit, 656
Database client software, 626
Database index, 639
Database model, 614
Database server software, 626
Database structure, 633
Date data type, 634
DBMS, 625
DELETE, 646
Dimensional database, 619
Distributed database, 626
Dynamic Web publishing, 628
Entity-relationship diagram, 616
Executive dashboard software, 613
Field, 615

Field format, 636
Field name, 615
Field validation rule, 636
Fixed-length field, 615
Flat file, 614
Global update, 650
Hierarchical database, 617
Hyperlink data type, 635
INSERT, 647
Integer data type, 634
JOIN, 651
Joining tables, 651
Logical data type, 634
Lookup routine, 637
Many-to-many relationship, 616
Memo data type, 634
Network database, 617
Normalization, 637
Object database, 620
Object-relational database, 621
ODBMS, 625
OLAP, 613
One-to-many relationship, 616
One-to-one relationship, 616
Parameters, 647
Predictive analytics, 613
Primary key, 634
RDBMS, 625
Real data type, 634

Record, 615
Record occurrence, 615
Record type, 615
Relational database, 618
Relationship, 616
Report generator, 642
Report template, 642
SELECT, 648
Server-side program, 628
Sort key, 639
Sort order, 639
SQL, 645
SQL keywords, 646
SQL query, 645
Static Web publishing, 627
Structured file, 614
Table, 618
Text data type, 634
Unstructured file, 614
UPDATE, 650
User privileges, 656
Variable-length field, 615
XML, 630
XML DBMS, 625

Interactive Summary

To review important concepts from this chapter, fill in the blanks to best complete each sentence. When using the NP2013 interactive eBook, click the Check Answers buttons to automatically score your answers.

SECTION A: A(n) [_____] is a collection of information, typically stored as computer files. The information it contains can be stored, updated, organized, output, distributed, searched, and analyzed. A filing cabinet full of folders and papers would be classified as a(n) [_____] file. A(n) [_____] file uses a uniform format to store data for each person or thing in the file. The simplest model for storing data is a(n) [_____] file that consists of a single, two-dimensional table of data elements. Each row in the table is a(n) [_____] , and each column of the table is a(n) [_____] . Each kind of record is referred to as a record [_____] . A record that contains data is sometimes referred to as a record [_____] . In databases, records can be related by one-to- [_____] relationships, one-to-many relationships, or many-to-many relationships. The number of associations that can exist between two record types is referred to as [_____] . Relationships can be depicted graphically by using [_____] -relationship diagrams. [_____] databases allow only one-to-many relationships. [_____] databases allow one-to-many and many-to-many relationships. [_____] databases exist as a series of tables that can be related by common fields. A(n) [_____] database organizes relationships over three or more dimensions. A(n) [_____] database stores data in objects that can be grouped into classes and defined by attributes and methods.

▶ CHECK ANSWERS

SECTION B: Flat files can be created and manipulated by using a variety of tools, including word processing and spreadsheet software. For databases composed of more than one record type, however, it is best to use a database management system, which is abbreviated as [_____] .

A(n) [_____] -level database management system typically handles many simultaneous searches, but has limited capability to deal with multiple simultaneous updates. Handling billions of records and performing hundreds of transactions every second requires database [_____] software.

The data in a database can be accessed over the Web. A simple process called [_____] Web publishing converts a database report into an HTML document, which can be displayed by a browser. More sophisticated [_____] Web publishing produces data from a database on demand. HTML forms not only provide search capabilities, but can also be used to add or modify data in a database with a Web browser. [_____] documents provide a Web-based data management tool that uses special tags as field names within a document.

▶ CHECK ANSWERS

SECTION C:

The first step in designing a relational database is to define its fields by specifying a field name and data type. Integer, date, and _____ data types are used for fields containing data that might be mathematically manipulated. The _____ data type is used for fixed-length fields containing text that is not intended to be mathematically manipulated. The _____ data type is a variable-length field for entering text. The _____ data type is used to store true/false or yes/no data. The _____ data type can be used to store URLs. The _____ data type is used to store binary data, such as MP3 files or graphics. When designing fields, a database designer can also include field formats, field _____ rules, and lookup routines to reduce data entry errors.

The number of tables in a database can be determined by a process called _____, which helps a database designer group fields into record types and avoid data redundancy. A database designer must also consider how to sort or index records. The _____ key for a table specifies the order in which records are stored and indicates where new records are inserted in a table. Indexing provides an alternative way to organize records, using a series of keys and pointers to temporarily arrange data without affecting the physical sequence of records specified by the sort order.

▶ CHECK ANSWERS

SECTION D:

SQL is a database query language that typically works behind the scenes as an intermediary between the database _____ software provided to users and the database itself. Although the specifications for searches and other database tasks are collected by easy-to-use graphical user interfaces, those specifications are converted into SQL _____, which can communicate directly with the database.

An SQL query contains SQL _____, such as SELECT, FROM, INSERT, JOIN, and WHERE, plus _____ that specify the details of the command. Records can be removed from a database using the SQL _____ command. Records can be added to a table using the SQL _____ command. To search for data, you can use the SQL _____ command. Changing or replacing the data in a field requires the SQL _____ command. SQL also provides a(n) _____ command that can be used to temporarily consolidate two tables so that data can be accessed simultaneously from both of them.

▶ CHECK ANSWERS

SECTION E:

Databases are vulnerable to theft, hacking, and unauthorized access. Although _____ cannot prevent a database from being lost or stolen, it can make the data it contains unusable. This security technique, however, is typically used for archived databases, rather than operational databases. Access controls can be used to restrict physical access to a database, limit user privileges, and regulate data _____ that establish which fields a particular user is allowed to access. Tracking database use is also an important security tool. If an intruder breaches database security, a database _____ can help to identify the damage and correct it. A patchwork of database security laws in the U.S. leaves loopholes that allow some types of personal data to be gathered, aggregated, and shared with third parties. Individuals can take steps to protect their personal data by vigilantly monitoring what information is released, using strong passwords, running security software, and becoming familiar with the _____ policy for sites that store personal data.

▶ CHECK ANSWERS

Interactive Situation Questions

Apply what you've learned to some typical computing situations. When using the NP2013 interactive eBook, you can type your answers, and then use the Check Answers button to automatically score your responses.

1. You're working for a company that's just getting started with a database project. Your supervisor wants "the most standard kind of database," so you recommend using [ ] database management software.

2. You are analyzing a company's customer and order information. Because each customer can place multiple orders, you know this is a(n) [ ] -to-many relationship.

3. You are designing a record type that holds customer information. You should use a(n) [ ] data type for the fields that hold information such as telephone numbers and Social Security numbers because although this data looks like numbers, you'll never need to use it to perform mathematical calculations.

4. You are creating a movie review database, and one field stores the "star rating" that a popular reviewer gave each movie. Movies are rated from one to four stars, so the Stars field is valid only if the number is between 1 and 4. To ensure that nobody enters a value below 1 or above 4, you can use a field [ ] rule to filter the data as it's entered into the table.

5. You want to print a professionally designed list of all the records in your database. To organize and format the list, you use a report generator to create a reusable report [ ].

6. You own a fly-fishing shop and maintain an inventory database that, along with inventory data, stores the

names of the wholesalers from which you buy each item. Hot Rod Wholesalers just changed its name to Northern Rod and Reel, so you need to update your database. The best way to accomplish this task would be to perform a(n) [ ] update that changes every instance of "Hot Rod Wholesalers" to "Northern Rod and Reel."

7. You are designing the database structure for a mail-order catalog company. You recognize that a many-to-many relationship exists between an order and the items listed on the order. That clue indicates that you should separate the data into two [ ] , one called Orders and the other called Order Details.

8. Your friend is working on some Web pages, and you notice that they contain tags such as <editor>Ella Ellison</editor> and <born>1960/05/26</born>.

   You surmise that your friend is using [ ] instead of HTML.

 CHECK ANSWERS

Interactive Practice Tests

Practice tests that consist of ten multiple-choice, true/false, and fill-in-the-blank questions are available in the NP2013 interactive eBook. Test questions are selected at random from a large test bank, so each time you take a test, you'll receive a different set of questions. Your tests are scored immediately, and you can print study guides that help you find the correct answers for any questions that you missed.

CLICK TO START

Learning Objectives Checkpoints

Learning Objectives Checkpoints are designed to help you assess whether you have achieved the major learning objectives for this chapter. You can use paper and pencil or word processing software to complete most of the activities.

1. List eight ways the information in a database can be used and applied.

2. Create a descriptive example that would help explain the concepts of data mining, data warehouses, predictive analytics, and OLAP to an average adult who has no technical expertise.

3. Define basic database terminology, such as fields, records, record types, record occurrences, and cardinality.

4. For each of the following pairs of record types, draw an ERD showing whether the relationship is one-to-one, one-to-many, or many-to-many:

   Author—Book   Person—Social Security number

   House—Mailbox   Musician—CD

5. Describe flat files and six other database models. Give examples that illustrate each model.

6. Explain the capabilities of various data management tools, such as commercial applications, word processing software, spreadsheet software, custom data management software, and database management software.

7. Use diagrams to explain different ways of providing Web access to the data in a database.

8. Provide five examples of data you would store in real, integer, text, logical, date, memo, BLOB, and computed fields.

9. List the techniques that a database designer can use to reduce data entry errors.

10. Using a real-world entity, like a comic book collection or a recipe file that can be stored in a database, divide the information into fields and record types. Explain the steps you need to take to normalize the data.

11. Using your own examples, explain the differences between sorting and indexing.

12. Describe how a database report template works. List five principles for creating effective report templates.

13. Imagine that you must access a library card catalog using SQL. Write an SQL query that you would use to search for any books by J. K. Rowling in a table called Books, where authors' names are stored in a field called AuthorName and book titles are stored in a field called Title.

14. Explain the extent to which encryption, user privileges, and audits can secure a database.

15. Describe the status of privacy legislation in your country, providing examples of relevant laws and regulations.

16. List the steps you can take to protect your privacy and identity when working with databases.

Study Tip: Make sure you can use your own words to correctly answer each of the purple focus questions that appear throughout the chapter.

Concept Map

Fill in the blanks to correctly represent the hierarchy of relationships among the database terms used in this chapter.

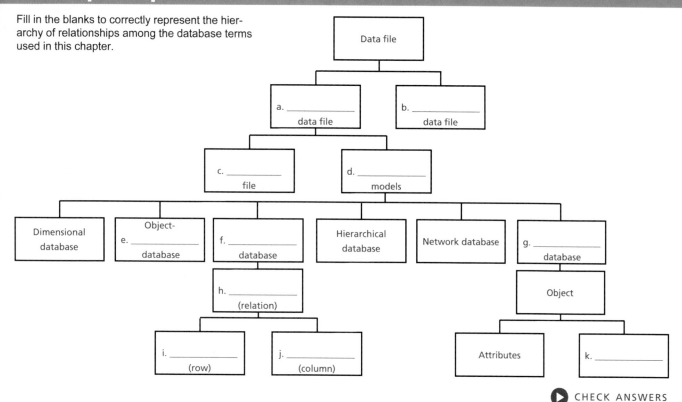

CHECK ANSWERS

12

Chapter Contents

INFOWEBLINKS

You'll find updates for chapter
material by connecting to the
NP2013 Chapter 12 InfoWebLink.

Ⓦ CLICK TO CONNECT
www.infoweblinks.com/np2013/ch12

Computer Programming

Learning Objectives

After reading this chapter, you will be able to answer the
following questions by completing the outcomes-based
Learning Objectives Checkpoints on page 741.

1. How many lines of code are in a typical computer
   program?

2. Do the activities performed by computer programmers
   differ from those performed by software engineers and
   systems analysts?

3. What's the best computer programming language?

4. What is a programming paradigm?

5. How is a computer program created?

6. What kinds of errors are discovered when programs
   are tested?

7. In addition to programming languages, what other
   tools do programmers use?

8. What is an algorithm?

9. What's the point of flowcharts, pseudocode, and structured English?

10. How do programmers make programs do things in the
    right order?

11. How does object-oriented programming work?

12. How does declarative programming work?

13. Is it easy to write Prolog rules?

14. What makes computer programs vulnerable to
    hackers?

15. How can programmers produce more secure code?

16. Can consumers take steps to avoid vulnerabilities that
    exist in software with code defects?

CourseMate

Visit the NP2013 CourseMate for this chapter's Pre-Quiz, Audio
Overview and Flashcards, Detailed Objectives, Chapter Quiz, Online
Games, and more labs.

Multimedia and Interactive Elements

When using the NP2013 interactive eBook, click the ▶ icons to
access multimedia resources.

Apply Your Knowledge
The information in this chapter will give you the background to:

- Read simple computer programs written in Pascal, Java, and Prolog
- Select programming tools appropriate for basic programming projects
- Read program flowcharts, pseudocode, and structured English

- Formulate algorithms
- Visualize objects and classes that might be used in object-oriented computer programs
- Take steps to avoid security problems that stem from software defects

Try It!

CAN I WRITE A SIMPLE COMPUTER PROGRAM?

Think about your favorite computer game. Chances are the program that makes it tick is huge and complex. Yet, all computer programs are based on simple ideas that are easy to grasp. Complete the following steps to try your hand at writing a program that produces a message based on the time of day.

Windows:

1. From the **All Programs** menu, select **Accessories**, then click **Notepad**.

2. When the Notepad window opens, type the following program:

```
REM Program to check time of day
@echo off
set time = %time%
echo %time%
if %time% lss 12 echo Good Morning!
if %time% gtr 12 echo Good Day!
pause
```

3. Save the program in your main user folder *C:\Users\Your Name* with the name *Greeting.bat*. Make sure you use bat as the file extension! Write down the full path (such as *C:\Users\Your Name*).

4. Click the **Start** button, point to **All Programs**, point to **Accessories**, and then select **Command Prompt**.

5. When the black Command Prompt window opens, make sure the Command Prompt lists your main user folder (i.e., *C:\Users\Your Name*). If you need to change it, type **CD** followed by the full path that you wrote down in step 3.

6. Type **Greeting** and press the **Enter** key. Your program should start, display the time, and then display "Good Morning!" or "Good Day!", depending on the time.

7. Close the Command Prompt window.

Mac:

1. From Finder's **Applications** menu, select the **Utilities** folder, and then double-click **Terminal**.

2. When the Terminal window opens, type **pico Greeting** and then press the **Enter** key.

3. In the blank entry area, type the following program (make sure you put spaces where indicated):

```
#!/bin/sh

TIMEOFDAY=$[ $(date +"%H")]

echo "TIME" $TIMEOFDAY

if [ $TIMEOFDAY -lt "12" ]; then echo "Good Morning!"

else echo "Good Day!" ; fi
```

4. To save your program, press **Ctrl-O** (hold down the Ctrl key while pressing O), press the **Enter** key, and then press **Ctrl-X**.

5. Back at the Terminal, type **chmod 755 Greeting** and then press the **Enter** key.

6. To run your program, type **./Greeting** and then press the **Enter** key.

7. Close the Terminal.

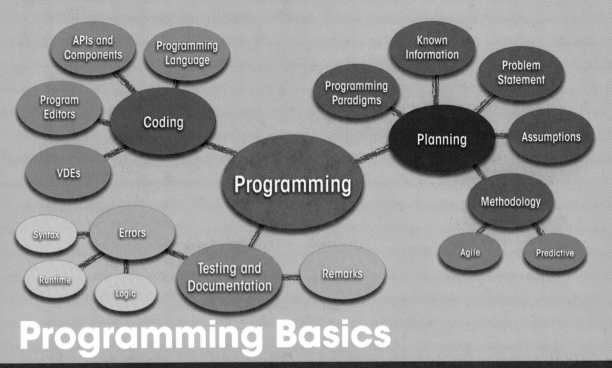

Programming Basics

SMARTPHONE APPS. Productivity software. Games. All the goodies on digital devices are powered by computer programs. What is programming all about? Section A introduces you to the programmer's world.

COMPUTER PROGRAMMING AND SOFTWARE ENGINEERING

▶ **What is program code?** As you learned in earlier chapters, a computer program is a set of step-by-step instructions that tell a computer how to solve a problem or carry out a task. The instructions that make up a computer program are sometimes referred to as **code**, probably because program instructions for first-generation computers were entered as binary codes.

Today, program code contains familiar English-like words. Figure 12-1 illustrates the code for a short program that converts feet and inches into centimeters.

FIGURE 12-1

A typical computer program consists of lines of code that tell a computer how to solve a problem or carry out a task. This program is written in a computer programming language called Pascal.

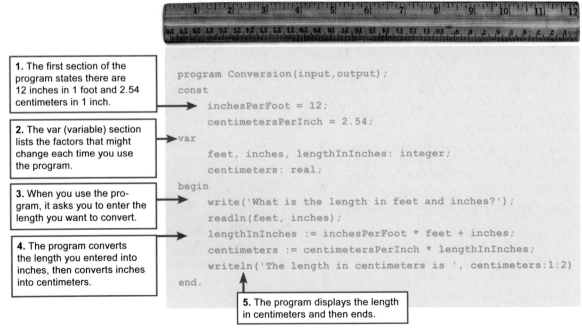

1. The first section of the program states there are 12 inches in 1 foot and 2.54 centimeters in 1 inch.

2. The var (variable) section lists the factors that might change each time you use the program.

3. When you use the program, it asks you to enter the length you want to convert.

4. The program converts the length you entered into inches, then converts inches into centimeters.

```pascal
program Conversion(input,output);
const
    inchesPerFoot = 12;
    centimetersPerInch = 2.54;
var
    feet, inches, lengthInInches: integer;
    centimeters: real;
begin
    write('What is the length in feet and inches?');
    readln(feet, inches);
    lengthInInches := inchesPerFoot * feet + inches;
    centimeters := centimetersPerInch * lengthInInches;
    writeln('The length in centimeters is ', centimeters:1:2)
end.
```

5. The program displays the length in centimeters and then ends.

A computer program is usually stored as a file and transferred into RAM when needed, but a computer program can also be embedded in computer hardware—in a ROM chip, for example. A computer program can exist as a single module that provides all the instructions necessary for a software application, device driver, or operating system. Alternatively, a computer program might consist of several modules that form a software application or operating system.

▶ How big is a typical computer program? Compared to commercial application software, the programs that you'll work with in this chapter are relatively tiny. Windows 7 contains more than 50 million lines of code. Even a typical cell phone contains over a million lines of code. Research has shown that, on average, one person can write, test, and document only 20 lines of code per day. It is not surprising, then, that most commercial programs are written by programming teams and take many months or years to complete.

▶ Who creates computer programs? Computer programs are developed by computer programmers (programmers for short) or software engineers. Computer programmers mainly focus on coding computer programs, whereas software engineers tend to focus on designing and testing activities (Figure 12-2).

© Thomas Barwick/Getty Images

▶ What's the difference between computer programming and software engineering? Computer programming encompasses a broad set of activities that include planning, coding, testing, and documenting. Most computer programmers participate to some extent in all of these phases of program development, but focus on the coding process.

Software engineering is a development process that uses mathematical, engineering, and management techniques to reduce the cost and complexity of a computer program while increasing its reliability and modifiability. It can be characterized as more formalized and rigorous than computer programming. It is used on large software projects where cost overruns and software errors might have disastrous consequences.

Some software engineering activities overlap with the systems analysis and design activities presented in Chapter 10. To distinguish between the two, remember that systems analysis and design encompass all aspects of an information system, including hardware, software, people, and procedures. In contrast, software engineering tends to focus on software development.

FIGURE 12-2

Although software engineers have the skills to design, code, test, and document software, they tend to focus on designing and testing activities. Software engineers approach these activities using formalized techniques based on mathematical proofs, computer science research, and engineering theory. For example, a computer programmer might code a search routine by simply instructing the computer to step through a list looking for a match. In contrast, a software engineer might consider several sophisticated methods for implementing the search, and select the one that provides the greatest efficiency based on the computer architecture and the data being processed.

12

PROGRAMMING LANGUAGES AND PARADIGMS

▶ **What is a programming language?** A **programming language**, or computer language, is a set of keywords and grammar rules designed for creating instructions that a computer can ultimately process or carry out. Most people are familiar with names of popular programming languages, such as BASIC, C, Pascal, Fortran, Java, and COBOL. But many other programming languages, such as 8088 assembly, FORTH, LISP, APL, and Scratch, remain relatively unknown to the general public.

The program you wrote at the beginning of the chapter to display a message based on the current time was written either in DOS scripting language (Windows) or Bash shell script (Mac).

Just as an English sentence is constructed from various words and punctuation marks that follow a set of grammar rules, each instruction for a computer program consists of keywords and parameters that are held together by a set of rules.

A **keyword**, or command, is a word with a predefined meaning for the compiler or interpreter that translates each line of program code into machine language. Keywords for the Pascal computer language include WRITE, READ, IF...THEN, and GOSUB. The Greeting program you wrote used keywords such as ECHO, SET, IF, and PAUSE.

Keywords can be combined with specific **parameters**, which provide more detailed instructions for the computer to carry out. Keywords and parameters are combined with punctuation according to a series of rules called **syntax**, as shown in Figure 12-3.

FIGURE 12-3

An instruction for a computer program consists of keywords and parameters, formed into sentence-like statements according to a set of syntax rules.

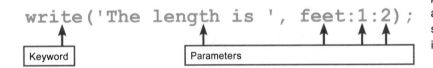

▶ **How are programming languages categorized?** Programming languages are categorized in several ways. They can be divided into two major categories: low-level languages and high-level languages. They are also categorized by generation and by paradigm.

▶ **What is a low-level language?** A **low-level language** includes commands specific to a particular CPU or microprocessor family. Low-level languages require a programmer to write instructions for the lowest level of the computer's hardware. Low-level languages include machine languages and assembly languages.

▶ **What is a high-level language?** A **high-level language** uses command words and grammar based on human languages to provide what computer scientists call a level of abstraction that hides the underlying low-level assembly or machine language. These languages are used to develop applications, games, and most other software.

High-level languages, such as BASIC, Java, Ada, and C, make the programming process easier by replacing unintelligible strings of 1s and 0s or cryptic assembly commands with understandable commands, such as PRINT and WRITE. High-level language commands eliminate many lines of code by substituting a single high-level command for multiple low-level commands (Figure 12-4).

FIGURE 12-4

A single high-level command does the work of multiple low-level commands.

High-level Pascal command

```
Total:=5+4
```

Low-level assembly commands

```
LDA 5
STA Num1
LDA 4
ADD Num1
STA Total
END
```

▶ **How did programming evolve from low-level to high-level languages?** The first computers were programmed without programming languages. Technicians rewired a computer's circuitry to prepare it for various processing tasks (Figure 12-5). Programming languages were very primitive at first, but they evolved through many generations into the computer languages of today.

Courtesy of IBM Corporate Archives

FIGURE 12-5

The idea of storing programs in computer memory paved the way for computer programming languages, which allowed a programmer to write commands and load them into the computer for execution.

12

▶ **What was the first generation of programming languages?** Machine languages were the first languages available for programming computers and, therefore, they are sometimes referred to as **first-generation languages**. In Chapter 1, you learned that a machine language consists of a set of commands, represented as a series of 1s and 0s, corresponding to the instruction set that is hard-wired into the circuitry of a microprocessor.

A machine language is specific to a particular CPU or microprocessor family. For example, the machine language that is hard-wired into an Intel i7 processor includes many unique commands that are not wired into older PC-based Intel 8088 microprocessors. Although machine languages continue to work on today's computers, programmers rarely use machine languages to write programs.

▶ **What is a second-generation language?** An **assembly language** allows programmers to use abbreviated command words, called op codes, such as LDA for load, rather than the 1s and 0s used in machine languages. At the time assembly languages were first introduced, they were hailed as a significant improvement over machine languages, and came to be known as **second-generation languages**.

Like a machine language, an assembly language is classified as a low-level language because it is machine specific—each assembly language command corresponds on a one-to-one basis to a machine language instruction. An assembly language is useful when a programmer wants to directly manipulate what happens at the hardware level. Today, programmers sometimes use assembly languages to write system software, such as compilers, operating systems, and device drivers.

▶ **What is a third-generation language?** When high-level languages were originally conceived in the 1950s, they were dubbed **third-generation languages** because they seemed a major improvement over machine and assembly languages. Third-generation languages used easy-to-remember command words, such as PRINT and INPUT, to take the place of several lines of assembly language op codes or lengthy strings of machine language 0s and 1s.

Third-generation languages, such as COBOL and Fortran, were used extensively for business and scientific applications. Pascal and BASIC were popular teaching languages. C and its derivative languages remain popular today for system and application software development—for example, to develop Microsoft Windows and Linux.

Many computer scientists believed that third-generation languages would eliminate programming errors. Errors certainly became less frequent, and program development time decreased significantly. Programmers using third-generation languages still made a variety of errors, however, so computer language development continued to progress.

▶ **What is a fourth-generation language?** In 1969, computer scientists began to develop high-level languages, called **fourth-generation languages**, which more closely resemble human languages, or natural languages, than do third-generation languages. Fourth-generation languages, such as SQL and RPG, eliminate many of the strict punctuation and grammar rules that complicate third-generation languages.

Today, fourth-generation languages are primarily used for database applications. A single SQL command, such as SORT TABLE Kids on Lastname, can replace many lines of third-generation code, as shown in Figure 12-6.

FIGURE 12-6

A single command written in a fourth-generation language can replace many lines of third-generation code.

```
SORT TABLE Kids on Lastname

PUBLIC SUB Sort(Kids As Variant, inLow As Long, inHi As Long)
    DIM pivot   As Variant
    DIM tmpSwap As Variant
    DIM tmpLow  As Long
    DIM tmpHi   As Long
    tmpLow = inLow
    tmpHi = inHi
    pivot = Kids((inLow + inHi) \ 2)
    WHILE (tmpLow <= tmpHi)
        WHILE (Kids(tmpLow) < pivot And tmpLow < inHi)
            tmpLow = tmpLow + 1
        WEND
        WHILE (pivot < Kids(tmpHi) And tmpHi > inLow)
            tmpHi = tmpHi - 1
        WEND
    IF (tmpLow <= tmpHi) THEN
            tmpSwap = Kids(tmpLow)
            Kids(tmpLow) = Kids(tmpHi)
            Kids(tmpHi) = tmpSwap
            tmpLow = tmpLow + 1
            tmpHi = tmpHi - 1
        END IF
    WEND
    IF (inLow < tmpHi) THEN Sort Kids, inLow, tmpHi
    IF (tmpLow < inHi) THEN Sort Kids, tmpLow, inHi
END SUB
```

▶ **What about fifth-generation languages?** In 1982, a group of Japanese researchers began work on a fifth-generation computer project that used Prolog—a computer programming language based on a declarative programming paradigm, which is described in detail later in the chapter. Prolog and other declarative languages became closely identified with the fifth-generation project and were classified as **fifth-generation languages**.

Some experts disagree with this classification, however, and instead define fifth-generation languages as those that allow programmers to use graphical or visual tools to construct programs instead of typing lines of code. You'll learn more about visual programming environments later in the chapter.

▶ **What is the best programming language?** Hundreds of programming languages exist, and each has unique strengths and weaknesses. Although it might be possible to select the best language for a particular project, most computer scientists would find it difficult to agree on one all-around best language. The table in Figure 12-7 on the next page briefly describes some of the programming languages discussed in this chapter.

FIGURE 12-7 Selected Programming Languages

Ada: A high-level programming language developed under the direction of the U.S. Department of Defense and originally intended for military applications.

APL (A Programming Language): A scientific language used to manipulate tables of numbers.

BASIC (Beginner's All-purpose Symbolic Instruction Code): Developed by John Kemeny and Thomas Kurtz in the mid-1960s, BASIC is a simple, interactive programming language.

C: Developed in the early 1970s by Dennis Ritchie at Bell Laboratories, C is used today for a wide range of commercial software.

C++, **C#**, and **Objective-C**: Languages derived from C that provide object-oriented (OO) capabilities.

COBOL (COmmon Business Oriented Language): A procedural language developed in the early 1960s and used extensively for mainframe business applications.

CPL (Combined Programming Language): A language developed in the 1960s for scientific and commercial programming.

Eiffel: An advanced OO language developed in 1988 with syntax similar to C.

Fortran (FORmula TRANslator): One of the original third-generation languages; developed in the 1950s and is still used today for scientific applications.

Haskell: A non-procedural programming language named for the mathematician Haskell Brooks Curry.

Java: A C++ derivative developed by Sun Microsystems used extensively for Web-based programming.

LISP (LISt Processing): Developed in 1959 by famed artificial intelligence researcher John McCarthy, LISP is used for artificial intelligence applications.

Pascal: Named in honor of Blaise Pascal, who invented one of the first mechanical adding machines, Pascal is a third-generation language developed to teach students programming concepts.

PL/1 (Programming Language 1): A complex business and scientific language developed in 1964 by IBM that combines Fortran, COBOL, and ALGOL.

Prolog (PROgramming in LOGic): A declarative language developed in 1972 and used for artificial intelligence applications.

REALbasic (RB): A modern OO version of BASIC that works cross platform on Windows, Macs, and Linux.

RPG (Report Program Generator): An IBM programming platform introduced in 1964 for easily generating business reports.

Scheme: A dialect of LISP, used for computer research and teaching.

Scratch: A simple, visual programming language based on Smalltalk/Squeak and used for teaching.

SIMULA (SIMUlation LAnguage): Believed to be the first object-oriented programming language.

Smalltalk: A classic object-oriented programming language developed by Xerox researchers in 1980.

Visual Basic: A Windows-based software development kit created by Microsoft in the early 1990s and designed for developing Windows-based applications.

12

▶ **What is a programming paradigm?** In addition to being classified by level and by generation, programming languages can also be classified by paradigm. Programmers approach problems in different ways. Whereas one programmer might focus on the steps required to complete a specific computation, another programmer might focus on the data that forms the basis for the computation.

The phrase **programming paradigm** refers to a way of conceptualizing and structuring the tasks a computer performs. Quite a number of programming paradigms exist, and they are not mutually exclusive.

Some programming languages support a single paradigm. Other programming languages—referred to as **multiparadigm languages**—support more than one paradigm. Figure 12-8 provides a brief description of today's most popular programming paradigms. Sections B, C, and D of this chapter give you a detailed look at three classic paradigms: procedural, object-oriented, and declarative.

FIGURE 12-8

Programming Paradigms

Paradigm	Languages	Description
Procedural	BASIC, Pascal, COBOL, Fortran, Ada	Emphasizes linear steps that provide the computer with instructions on how to solve a problem or carry out a task
Object-oriented	Smalltalk, C++, Java, Scratch	Formulates programs as a series of objects and methods that interact to perform a specific task
Declarative	Prolog	Focuses on the use of facts and rules to describe a problem
Event Driven	Visual Basic, C#	Focuses on selecting user interface elements and defining event-handling routines that are triggered by various mouse or keyboard activities

PROGRAM PLANNING

▶ How does a programmer plan a computer program?
Suppose a group of market analysts—or even a group of hungry students—wants to determine which pizza shop offers customers the best deal. Problems you might try to solve using a computer often begin as questions—for example, "Which pizza place has the best deal?" But such questions might not be stated in a way that helps you devise a method for a computer to arrive at an answer.

A question like "Which pizza place has the best deal?" is vague. It does not specify what information is available or how to determine the best deal. Do you know the price of several pizzas at different pizza places? Do you know the sizes of the pizzas? Do you know how many toppings are included in each price? What does "best deal" mean? Is it merely the cheapest pizza? Is it the pizza that gives you the most toppings for the dollar? Is it the biggest pizza you can get for the $24.63 that you and your friends managed to scrape together? The programming process begins with a problem statement that helps you clearly define the purpose of a computer program.

▶ What is a problem statement? In the context of programming, a **problem statement** defines certain elements that must be manipulated to achieve a result or goal. A good problem statement for a computer program has three characteristics:

▶ It specifies any assumptions that define the scope of the problem.

▶ It clearly specifies the known information.

▶ It specifies when the problem has been solved.

Study Figure 12-9 and see if you can formulate a problem statement that is better than the initial vague question, "Which pizza place has the best deal?"

▶ What is an assumption? In a problem statement, an **assumption** is something you accept as true in order to proceed with program planning. For example, with the pizza problem, you can make the assumption that you want to compare two pizzas. Furthermore, you can assume that some pizzas are round and others are square.

To simplify the problem, you might also assume that none of the pizzas are rectangular—that is, none will have one side longer than the other. This assumption simplifies the problem because you need to deal only with the size of a pizza, rather than the length and width of a pizza. A fourth assumption for the pizza problem is that the pizzas you compare have the same toppings. Finally, you can assume that the pizza with the lowest cost per square inch is the best buy.

▶ How does known information apply to a problem statement? The **known information** in a problem statement is the information that you supply to the computer to help it solve a problem. For the pizza problem, the known information includes the prices, shapes, and sizes of pizzas from two pizzerias. The known information is often included in the problem statement as *givens*. For example, a problem statement might include the phrase, "given the prices, shapes, and sizes of two pizzas...."

Factors, such as price, shape, and size, are often treated as variables in computer programs. A **variable** represents a value that can change. For example, the price of a pizza can vary or change, depending on the pizza shop from which it is purchased, so PizzaPrice could become a variable in

FIGURE 12-9

Two pizza shops advertise special prices. Which one offers the best deal? Can you formulate a problem statement that describes the pizza problem?

the pizza program. In contrast, a **constant** is a factor that remains the same throughout a program. For example, the mathematical constant *pi* always has a value of 3.142.

Computer programmers think of variables and constants as named memory locations, equivalent to empty boxes where data can be temporarily stored while being manipulated by a computer program. In the Greeting program, %time% was a variable. The command `set time = %time%` put the value for the actual time into the %time% variable.

▶ **How can a problem statement specify when a problem is solved?** After identifying the known information, a programmer must specify how to determine when the problem has been solved. Usually this step means specifying the output you expect. Of course, you cannot specify the answer in the problem statement. You won't know, for example, whether VanGo's Pizzeria or The Venice has the best deal before you run the program, but you can specify that the computer should output which pizza is the best deal.

Suppose we assume that the best deal is the pizza with the lowest price per square inch. For example, a pizza that costs 5¢ per square inch is a better deal than a pizza that costs 7¢ per square inch. The problem is solved, therefore, when the computer has calculated the price per square inch for both pizzas, compared the prices, and printed a message indicating which one has the lower price per square inch.

You could write this part of the problem statement as, "The computer will calculate each pizza's price per square inch, compare the prices, and then print a message indicating which pizza has the lower price per square inch."

▶ **What's the problem statement for the pizza program?** You can incorporate your assumptions, known information, and expected output into a problem statement, such as the one in Figure 12-10.

▶ **Does the problem statement provide sufficient planning to begin coding?** Formulating a problem statement provides a minimal amount of planning, which is sufficient for only the simplest programs. A typical commercial application requires far more extensive planning, which includes detailed program outlines, job assignments, and schedules. Several software development methodologies exist to help program designers and coders plan, execute, and test software. Methodologies can be classified as predictive or agile.

A **predictive methodology** requires extensive planning and documentation up front. It allows little room for adaptation and change once specifications for the software have been completed in the design phase. Predictive methodologies are preferred for large software development projects involving more than ten developers, geographically dispersed development teams, and life-critical applications.

In contrast to predictive methodologies, an **agile methodology** focuses on flexible development and specifications that evolve as a project progresses. In an agile-driven project, for example, programmers might produce a subset of the entire project, show it to users, and then plan the next phase of development based on the feedback received. Agile methods seem best for projects with a small core of developers working at a single location.

Regardless of the tools used, when planning is complete, programmers can begin coding, testing, and documenting.

TERMINOLOGY NOTE

In the Mac program, TIMEOFDAY was a variable. The command TIMEOFDAY=$[$(date +"%H")] put the hour of the day into the TIMEOFDAY variable.

12

FIGURE 12-10

Pizza Problem Statement

Assuming that there are two pizzas to compare, that both pizzas contain the same toppings, and that the pizzas could be round or square, and given the prices, shapes, and sizes of the two pizzas, the computer will print a message indicating which pizza has the lower price per square inch.

PROGRAM CODING

▶ **How do I code a computer program?** The process of coding a computer program depends on the programming language you use, the programming tools you select, and the programming paradigm that best fits the problem you're trying to solve. Programmers can use a text editor, program editor, or VDE to code computer programs.

▶ **What is a text editor?** A text editor is any word processor that can be used for basic text editing tasks, such as writing e-mail, creating documents, or coding computer programs. Notepad, the accessory program supplied with Microsoft Windows, is one of the most popular text editors used for programming PCs. Text editors such as Pico and TextEdit are popular on Macs.

When using a text editor to code a computer program, you simply type in each instruction. The lines of code are stored in a file, which can be opened and modified using the usual editing keys.

▶ **What is a program editor?** A **program editor** is a type of text editor specially designed for entering code for computer programs. These editors are available from several commercial, shareware, and freeware sources. Features vary, but can include helpful programming aids, such as keyword colorizing, word completion, keyboard macros, and search/replace. Figure 12-11 illustrates the difference between a text editor and a program editor.

FIGURE 12-11

A text editor such as Notepad (top) allows programmers to enter lines of code using a familiar word processing interface. A program editor (bottom) offers tools more targeted to programmers.

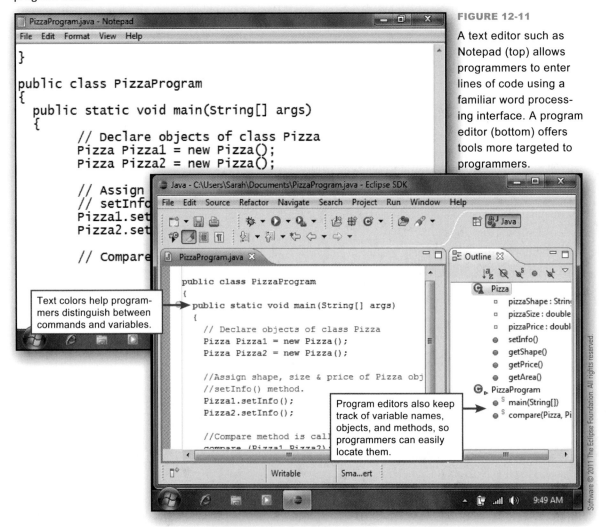

Text colors help programmers distinguish between commands and variables.

Program editors also keep track of variable names, objects, and methods, so programmers can easily locate them.

▶ **What is a VDE?** A **VDE** (visual development environment) provides programmers with tools to build substantial sections of a program by pointing and clicking rather than typing lines of code. A typical VDE is based on a **form design grid** that a programmer manipulates to design the user interface for a program.

By using various tools provided by the VDE, a programmer can add objects, such as controls and graphics, to the form design grid. In the context of a VDE, a **control** is a screen-based object whose behavior can be defined by a programmer. Frequently used controls include menus, toolbars, list boxes, text boxes, option buttons, check boxes, and graphical boxes. Figure 12-12 shows a form design grid and illustrates a variety of controls that can be added.

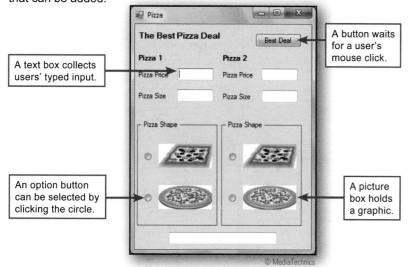

A text box collects users' typed input.

A button waits for a user's mouse click.

An option button can be selected by clicking the circle.

A picture box holds a graphic.

© MediaTechnics

FIGURE 12-12

A form design grid is an important part of a VDE. This form was designed for the pizza program using Visual Basic.

A control can be customized by specifying values for a set of built-in **properties**. For example, a button control can be customized for the pizza program by selecting values for properties such as shape, color, font, and label (Figure 12-13).

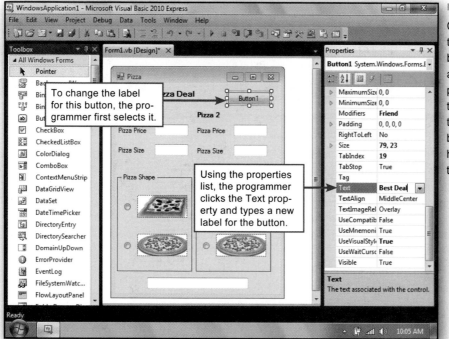

To change the label for this button, the programmer first selects it.

Using the properties list, the programmer clicks the Text property and types a new label for the button.

FIGURE 12-13

Controls, such as buttons, can be selected by a programmer from a properties list. Here a programmer is changing the text property of a button so that its label will be "Best Deal". ▶ Learn how to work with properties in a VDE.

In a visual development environment, each control comes with a predefined set of events. Within the context of programming, an **event** is defined as an action, such as a click, drag, or key press, associated with a form or control. A programmer can select the events that apply to each control. For example, a programmer might decide that pizza program users will be allowed to left-click either the Round or Square Pizza button in each Pizza Shape box. Users will not be allowed to right-click, double-click, or drag these buttons, however.

An event usually requires the computer to make a response. Programmers write **event-handling code** for the procedures that specify how the computer responds to each event. For example, if a user clicks an icon depicting a round pizza, an event-handling procedure might set a variable called pizzashape equal to round. When a user clicks the Best Deal button, another event-handling procedure must perform the calculations to determine which pizza is the best deal. Event-handling code is usually entered using a program editor supplied by the visual development environment. Figure 12-14 illustrates how event-handling code works.

FIGURE 12-14

The "Best Deal" event-handling code tells the computer what to do when users click the Best Deal button.

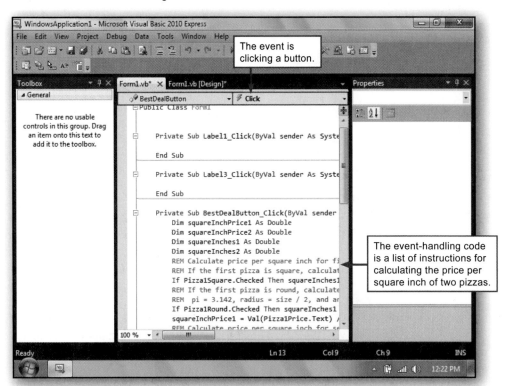

❱ Is a visual development environment better than an editor?

A programmer's choice of development tools depends on what is available for a particular programming language and the nature of the programming project. Microsoft Visual Basic was one of the first programming languages to feature a visual development environment. VDEs are not available for all programming languages, but they can be found for most of today's popular programming languages, including C++, C#, Java, REALbasic, and Prolog.

Text editors and program editors provide a fine toolset for programs with minimal user interfaces. Many so-called back-end applications, such as device drivers, middleware, and scripts embedded in HTML documents, require little or no user interaction and, therefore, can be created just as easily with an editor as with a visual development environment.

12

A visual development environment is a powerful tool for programming software applications for GUI environments, such as Windows, Linux desktops, Mac OS, and handheld apps. Most GUI applications are event-driven, which means that when launched, the program's interface appears on the screen and waits for the user to initiate an event by clicking a menu, dragging an object, double-clicking an icon, typing text, or touching the screen. The fact that the sequence of user actions cannot be predicted introduces a level of complexity that doesn't fit well with traditional programming languages, which tend to approach programs as a fixed sequence of procedures.

Visual development environments have spawned an approach to programming that is sometimes referred to as the **event-driven paradigm**, in which a programmer develops a program by selecting user interface elements and specifying event-handling routines. The programmer is never required to deal with the overall program sequence because the VDE automatically combines user interface elements and event-handling routines into a file that becomes the final computer program. This event-driven paradigm can significantly reduce development time and simplify the entire programming process.

PROGRAM TESTING AND DOCUMENTATION

▶ **How does a programmer know if a program works?** A computer program must be tested to ensure that it works correctly. Testing often consists of running the program and entering test data to see whether the program produces correct results. If testing does not produce the expected results, the program contains an error, sometimes called a bug. This error must be corrected, and then the program must be tested again and again until it runs error-free.

▶ **What can cause program errors?** When a program doesn't work correctly, it is usually the result of an error made by the programmer. A **syntax error** occurs when an instruction does not follow the syntax rules, or grammar, of the programming language.

For example, the BASIC command `If AGE = 16 Then "You can drive."` produces a syntax error because the command word `Print` is missing. The correct version of the command is `If AGE = 16 Then Print "You can drive."`. Syntax errors are easy to make, but they are usually also easy to detect and correct. Figure 12-15 lists some common syntax errors.

Another type of program bug is a **runtime error**, which occurs when you run a program. Some runtime errors result from instructions that the computer can't execute. The BASIC instruction `DiscountPrice = RegularPrice/0` produces a runtime error because dividing by 0 is a mathematically impossible operation that the computer cannot perform.

Some runtime errors are classified as logic errors. A **logic error** is an error in the logic or design of a program, such as using the wrong formula to calculate the area of a round pizza. Logic errors can be caused by an inadequate definition of the problem or an incorrect formula for a calculation, and are usually more difficult to identify than syntax errors.

▶ **How do programmers find errors?** Programmers can locate errors in a program by reading through lines of code, much like a proofreader. They can also use a tool called a **debugger** to step through a program and monitor the status of variables, input, and output. A debugger is sometimes packaged with a programming language or can be obtained as an add-on.

FIGURE 12-15

Common Syntax Errors

© Dex Images/CORBIS

▶ Omitting a keyword, such as THEN

▶ Misspelling a keyword, as when mistakenly typing PIRNT instead of PRINT

▶ Omitting required punctuation, such as a period

▶ Using incorrect punctuation, such as a colon where a semicolon is required

▶ Forgetting to close parentheses

▶ Do computer programs contain any special documentation?

Anyone who uses computers is familiar with program documentation in the form of user manuals and help files. Programmers also insert documentation called **remarks** into the program code. Remarks are identified by language-specific symbols, such as // in Java, or keywords, such as Rem in BASIC.

Remarks are useful for programmers who want to understand how a program works before modifying it. For example, suppose you are assigned to make some modifications to a 50,000-line program that calculates income tax. Your task would be simplified if the original programmer included remarks that identify the purpose of each section of the program and explain the basis for any formulas used to perform tax calculations.

A well-documented program contains initial remarks that explain its purpose and additional remarks in any sections of a program where the purpose of the code is not immediately clear. For example, in the pizza program, the purpose of the expression $3.142 * (size / 2) ^2$ might not be immediately obvious. Therefore, it would be helpful to have a remark preceding the expression, as shown in Figure 12-16.

> **TERMINOLOGY NOTE**
>
> Remarks are sometimes called comments and the process of adding remarks is sometimes referred to as commenting the code.

FIGURE 12-16

A series of remarks in a BASIC program can explain to programmers the method used to calculate the square inches in a round pizza.

```
Rem The program calculates the number of square inches
Rem in a round pizza using the formula pi r squared
Rem pi = 3.142, size / 2 = radius,
Rem and (size / 2) ^2 = radius squared
Rem SquareInches = 3.142 * (size / 2) ^2
```

PROGRAMMING TOOLS

▶ Where can I get programming tools?

Some programmers like to obtain programming tools a la carte by picking up a compiler from one Web site, selecting an interactive debugger from another Web site, and using any handy editor, such as Notepad. More typically, programmers download or purchase an SDK or IDE that contains a collection of programming tools.

▶ An **SDK** (software development kit) is a collection of language-specific programming tools that enables a programmer to develop applications for a specific computer platform, such as Windows PCs. A basic SDK includes a compiler, documentation about the language and syntax, and installation instructions. More sophisticated SDKs might also include an editor, a debugger, a visual user interface design module, and APIs. The components of an SDK are sometimes a hodgepodge of tools without consistent user interfaces for the programmer. For a more polished development environment, programmers turn to IDEs.

▶ An **IDE** (integrated development environment) is a type of SDK that packages a set of development tools into a sleek programming application. The modules in the application—editor, compiler, debugger, and user interface development tool—have a uniform set of menus and controls, which simplifies the programming process.

▶ Do I need components for my programming projects?
Every feature of a lengthy computer program is not necessarily created from scratch. A **component** is a prewritten module, designed to accomplish a specific task. For example, one component might provide spreadsheet capabilities, another component might provide encryption capabilities, and yet another component might provide some aspect of a Web service. Components can be incorporated into a program, saving days, weeks, or months of programming time.

▶ What's an API? In the context of computer programming, **API** is an abbreviation for application program interface or application programming interface. An API is a set of application program or operating system functions that programmers can access from within the programs they create.

The Windows API, for example, includes code for an assortment of dialog box controls familiar to anyone who uses a PC. The ability to browse through file folders is one element of the Windows API that might be useful in any application program that allows users to open or save files. APIs are usually supplied as part of an SDK.

▶ Do programmers use standard programming tools to develop computer games? Creating a computer game is a multifaceted project that includes creating a multiple-level virtual world, populating it with autonomous and user-controlled characters, providing characters with weapons and food, determining how characters interact with objects, adding sound effects, and keeping score (Figure 12-17).

FIGURE 12-17

Game development is a hot career field. Independent, or indie, game developers work on a freelance basis for game publishers or create their own games and market them as shareware. Commercial game developers collaborate with artists, animators, musicians, and even Hollywood stars to create arcade-style and adventure games for companies such as Electronic Arts, LucasArts, Nintendo, and Sony.

At the core of every computer game is a program that ties together the virtual game world, characters, weapons, and other objects. Most of these programs are written using standard SDK and IDE programming tools.

▶ What's the most popular programming language for game development? C, Java, and C++ are the most popular programming languages for commercial games. Serious game programmers universally learn those languages and Microsoft's Visual C++ is their IDE of choice. Microsoft's XNA framework is a set of popular tools for creating Xbox 360 games, and Objective-C is popular for creating apps for iPhones and iPads.

Although many independent game developers use C and C++, some indies prefer languages such as BASIC and Java. Popular IDEs and SDKs for these languages include GLBasic, REALbasic, Visual Basic, JCreator, Sun Java Studio Creator, and Eclipse.

12

▶ What other tools are handy for game programmers?

Computer games take place in virtual 3-D worlds populated by animated characters and objects that characters can pick up, move, open, and shoot. Game development requires several toolsets, such as those listed in Figure 12-18.

FIGURE 12-18

Game Programming Tools

Graphics Tools	On commercial game projects, artists usually create, render, and animate game objects using bitmap, vector, 3-D, and animation graphics software. For indies without artistic talent, 3-D animated characters can be obtained from freelance artists who peddle their creations on the Web at sites such as Animation Central. A type of special effects software called a particle renderer helps developers create explosions, flares, fog, and fairy dust.
Motion Tools	Pathfinder algorithms distributed as APIs map character routes, limiting them to valid paths and preventing them from walking through walls (unless they are magic users).
Audio Tools	Developers also use a variety of audio and sound software to record, edit, and mix sound effects for gun shots, explosions, footsteps, and so on. Even non-musicians can generate upbeat background music by using MIDI or tracker software. Tracker sound effects are popular for explosions, and original music produced by tracker software can give games added audio dimensions.
Game Play Tools	Commercially available artificial intelligence APIs and components can plug into programs to control the actions of autonomous, non-player-controlled monsters and foes. Physics APIs can tie into objects to make them respond with life-like realism to gravity, momentum, and collisions. Digital rights management (DRM) tools are also available to help game developers protect their creations from piracy and illegal copying.
Developer Packages	Microsoft's DirectX SDK contains APIs that are popular tools for game developers. It includes components for 2-D and 3-D drawing, game-play interfaces, network distribution, and multiplayer control.

▶ How can I learn computer programming?

You can learn the fundamentals of programming by taking a class or working with an online tutorial. As you gain fluency in a programming language, you can hone your skills by participating in an open source software development project. When you join, you'll be given a programming task by an online project manager. Your work will be reviewed by experienced members of the team who will help you meet the exacting standards of professional developers.

QuickCheck   SECTION A

1. [_____]-generation programming languages, such as C, COBOL, and Fortran, use easy-to-remember command words.

2. Computer programming [_____] include procedural, object-oriented, event-driven, and declarative.

3. A(n) [_____] methodology focuses on flexible program development and specifications that evolve as a project progresses.

4. To find errors in a computer program, programmers can use a software tool called a(n) [_____].

5. A(n) [_____] is a set of application program or operating system functions that programmers can access from within the programs they create. (Hint: Use the acronym.)

▶ CHECK ANSWERS

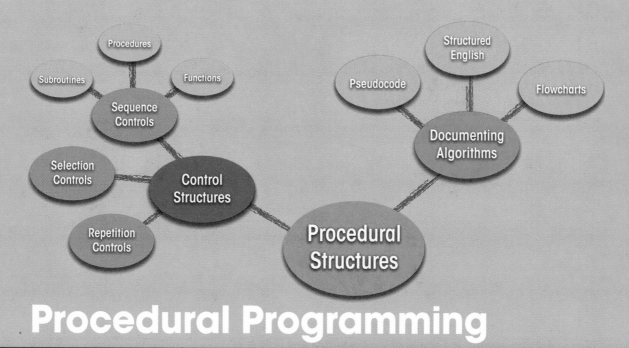

Procedural Structures
├── Control Structures
│   ├── Sequence Controls
│   │   ├── Procedures
│   │   ├── Subroutines
│   │   └── Functions
│   ├── Selection Controls
│   └── Repetition Controls
└── Documenting Algorithms
    ├── Structured English
    ├── Pseudocode
    └── Flowcharts

Procedural Programming

EARLY APPROACHES to computer programming were based on writing step-by-step instructions for the computer to follow. This technique is still in widespread use today and provides an easy starting point for learning what programming is all about. In this section, the examples are written in BASIC because it is one of the easiest programming languages to grasp.

ALGORITHMS

▶ **What is procedural programming?** The traditional approach to programming uses a **procedural paradigm** (sometimes called an imperative paradigm) to conceptualize the solution to a problem as a sequence of steps. A program written in a procedural language consists of self-contained instructions in a sequence that indicates how a task is to be performed or a problem is to be solved.

A programming language that supports the procedural paradigm is called a **procedural language**. Machine languages, assembly languages, COBOL, Fortran, C, and many other third-generation languages are classified as procedural languages.

Procedural languages are well suited for problems that can be easily solved with a linear, step-by-step algorithm. Programs created with procedural languages have a starting point and an ending point. The flow of execution from the beginning to the end of a program is essentially linear—that is, the computer begins at the first instruction and carries out the prescribed series of instructions until it reaches the end of the program.

▶ **What is an algorithm?** An **algorithm** is a set of steps for carrying out a task that can be written down and implemented. For example, the algorithm for making a batch of macaroni and cheese is a set of steps that includes boiling water, cooking the macaroni in the water, and making a cheese sauce (Figure 12-19).

TIP

This chapter presents some fairly technical material. You might want to consider taking a break between sections.

FIGURE 12-19

An important characteristic of a correctly formulated algorithm is that carefully following the steps guarantees that you can accomplish the task for which the algorithm was designed. If the recipe on a macaroni package is a correctly formulated algorithm, by following the recipe, you should be guaranteed a successful batch of macaroni and cheese.

▶ How do I write an algorithm? An algorithm for a computer program is a set of steps that explains how to begin with known information specified in a problem statement and how to manipulate that information to arrive at a solution.

Algorithms are usually written in a format that is not specific to a particular programming language. This approach allows you to focus on formulating a correct algorithm, without becoming distracted by the detailed syntax of a computer programming language. In a later phase of the software development process, the algorithm is coded into instructions written in a programming language so that a computer can implement it.

▶ How do I figure out an algorithm? To design an algorithm, you might begin by recording the steps required to solve the problem manually. If you take this route with the pizza problem, you must obtain initial information about the cost, size, and shape of each pizza. When the pizza program runs, it should ask the user to enter the initial information needed to solve the problem. Your algorithm might begin like this:

> **Ask the user for the shape of the first pizza and hold it in RAM as Shape1.**
>
> **Ask the user for the price of the first pizza and hold it in RAM as Price1.**
>
> **Ask the user for the size of the first pizza and hold it in RAM as Size1.**

Next, your algorithm should specify how to manipulate this information. You want the computer to calculate the price per square inch, but a statement like "Calculate the price per square inch" neither specifies how to do the calculation, nor deals with the fact that you must perform different calculations for square and round pizzas. A more appropriate set of statements for the algorithm is shown in Figure 12-20.

FIGURE 12-20

The algorithm for calculating the price per square inch must work for square pizzas as well as round ones.

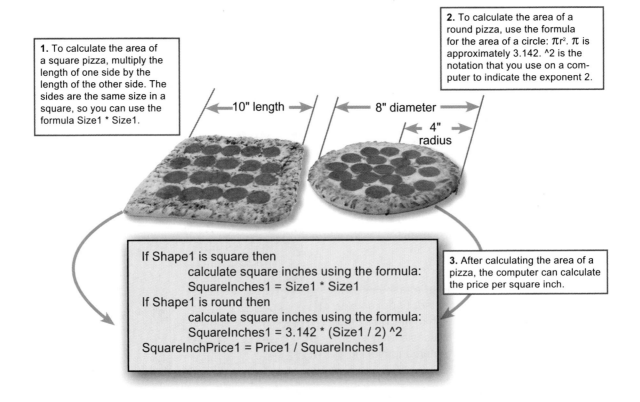

2. To calculate the area of a round pizza, use the formula for the area of a circle: πr^2. π is approximately 3.142. ^2 is the notation that you use on a computer to indicate the exponent 2.

1. To calculate the area of a square pizza, multiply the length of one side by the length of the other side. The sides are the same size in a square, so you can use the formula Size1 * Size1.

←— 10" length —→   ←— 8" diameter —→

|← 4" →|
radius

3. After calculating the area of a pizza, the computer can calculate the price per square inch.

```
If Shape1 is square then
        calculate square inches using the formula:
        SquareInches1 = Size1 * Size1
If Shape1 is round then
        calculate square inches using the formula:
        SquareInches1 = 3.142 * (Size1 / 2) ^2
SquareInchPrice1 = Price1 / SquareInches1
```

So far, the algorithm describes how to calculate the price per square inch of one pizza. It should specify a similar process for calculating the price per square inch of the second pizza.

Finally, the algorithm should specify how the computer decides what to display as the solution. You want the computer to display a message indicating which pizza has the lowest square-inch cost, so your algorithm should include steps like the following:

If SquareInchPrice1 is less than SquareInchPrice2 then display the message "Pizza 1 is the best deal."

If SquareInchPrice2 is less than SquareInchPrice1 then display the message "Pizza 2 is the best deal."

But don't forget to indicate what you want the computer to do if the price per square inch is the same for both pizzas:

If SquareInchPrice1 equals SquareInchPrice2 then display the message "Both pizzas are the same deal."

The complete algorithm for the pizza problem is shown in Figure 12-21.

FIGURE 12-21

The algorithm for the pizza problem, written in structured English, has five main sections.

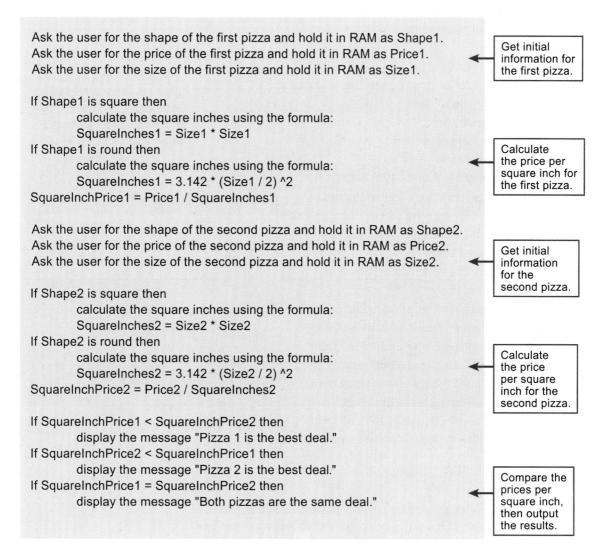

Ask the user for the shape of the first pizza and hold it in RAM as Shape1.
Ask the user for the price of the first pizza and hold it in RAM as Price1.
Ask the user for the size of the first pizza and hold it in RAM as Size1.

Get initial information for the first pizza.

If Shape1 is square then
    calculate the square inches using the formula:
    SquareInches1 = Size1 * Size1
If Shape1 is round then
    calculate the square inches using the formula:
    SquareInches1 = 3.142 * (Size1 / 2) ^2
SquareInchPrice1 = Price1 / SquareInches1

Calculate the price per square inch for the first pizza.

Ask the user for the shape of the second pizza and hold it in RAM as Shape2.
Ask the user for the price of the second pizza and hold it in RAM as Price2.
Ask the user for the size of the second pizza and hold it in RAM as Size2.

Get initial information for the second pizza.

If Shape2 is square then
    calculate the square inches using the formula:
    SquareInches2 = Size2 * Size2
If Shape2 is round then
    calculate the square inches using the formula:
    SquareInches2 = 3.142 * (Size2 / 2) ^2
SquareInchPrice2 = Price2 / SquareInches2

Calculate the price per square inch for the second pizza.

If SquareInchPrice1 < SquareInchPrice2 then
    display the message "Pizza 1 is the best deal."
If SquareInchPrice2 < SquareInchPrice1 then
    display the message "Pizza 2 is the best deal."
If SquareInchPrice1 = SquareInchPrice2 then
    display the message "Both pizzas are the same deal."

Compare the prices per square inch, then output the results.

12

EXPRESSING AN ALGORITHM

▶ What's the best way to express an algorithm? You can express an algorithm in several different ways, including structured English, pseudocode, and flowcharts. These tools are not programming languages, and they cannot be processed by a computer. Their purpose is to give you a way to document your ideas for program design.

Structured English is a subset of the English language with a limited selection of sentence structures that reflect processing activities. Refer to Figure 12-21 on the previous page to see how structured English can be used to express the algorithm for the pizza problem.

Another way to express an algorithm is with pseudocode. **Pseudocode** is a notational system for algorithms that has been described as a mixture of English and your favorite programming language.

Pseudocode is less formalized than structured English, so the structure and wording are left up to you. Also, when you write pseudocode, you are allowed to incorporate command words and syntax from the computer language you intend to use for the actual program. Compare Figure 12-22 with Figure 12-21 and see if you can identify some of the differences between structured English and pseudocode.

FIGURE 12-22

Pseudocode for the pizza program mixes some English-like instructions, such as display prompts, with programming commands, such as INPUT.

display prompts for entering shape, price, and size
input Shape1, Price1, Size1
if Shape1 = square **then**
      SquareInches1 ← Size1 * Size1
if Shape1 = round **then**
      SquareInches1 ← 3.142 * (Size1 / 2) ^2
SquareInchPrice1 ← Price1 / SquareInches1
display prompts for entering shape, price, and size
input Shape2, Price2, Size2
if Shape2 = square **then**
      SquareInches2 ← Size2 * Size2
if Shape2 = round **then**
      SquareInches2 ← 3.142 * (Size2 / 2) ^2
SquareInchPrice2 ← Price2 / SquareInches2
if SquareInchPrice1 < SquareInchPrice2 **then**
      output "Pizza 1 is the best deal."
if SquareInchPrice2 < SquareInchPrice1 **then**
      output "Pizza 2 is the best deal."
if SquareInchPrice1 = SquareInchPrice2 **then**
      output "Both pizzas are the same deal."

A third way to express an algorithm is to use a **flowchart**. A flowchart is a graphical representation of the way a computer should progress from one instruction to the next when it performs a task. The flowchart for the pizza program is shown in Figure 12-23 on the next page.

FIGURE 12-23

The pizza program flowchart illustrates how the computer should proceed through the instructions in the final program.

12

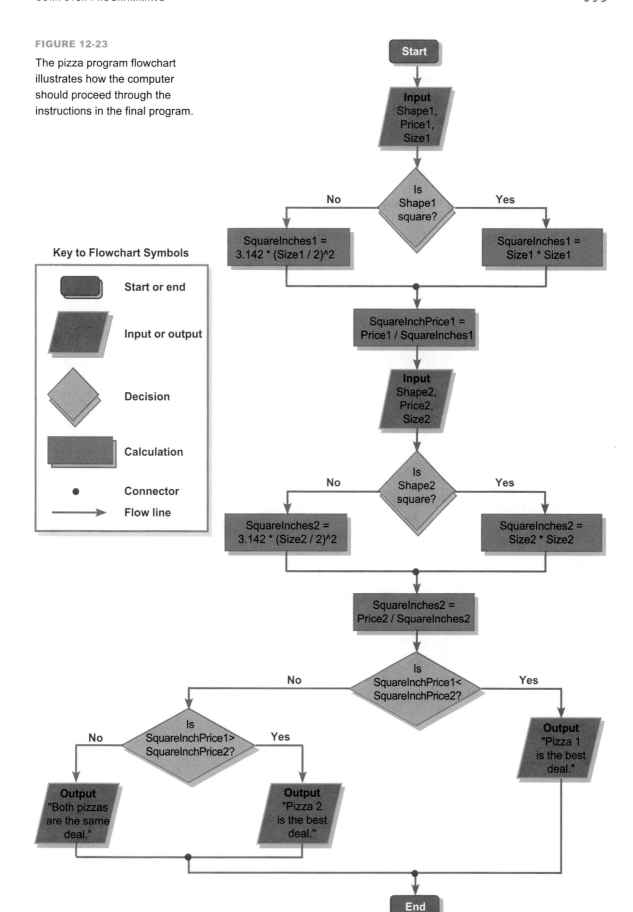

Key to Flowchart Symbols

Start or end

Input or output

Decision

Calculation

• Connector

→ Flow line

▶ How do I know if my algorithm is correct? Before finalizing the algorithm for a computer program, you should perform a **walkthrough** to verify that your algorithm works. To perform a walkthrough for a simple program, you can use a calculator, paper, and pencil to step through a sample problem using realistic test data.

For more complex programs, a walkthrough might consist of a verbal presentation to a group of programmers who can help identify logical errors in the algorithm and suggest ways to make the algorithm more efficient. Figure 12-24 illustrates how to check the pseudocode for the pizza program.

FIGURE 12-24

Pseudocode Walkthrough

display prompts for entering shape, price, and size
input Shape1, Price1, Size1
if Shape1 = square **then**
      SquareInches1 ← Size1 * Size1
if Shape1 = round **then**
      SquareInches1 ← 3.142 * (Size1 / 2) ^2
SquareInchPrice1 ← Price1 / SquareInches1

User asked to enter the first pizza's shape, price, and size
User enters square, $10.00, 12
The first pizza is square, so the computer should calculate:
*12 * 12 = 144 for SquareInches1*

The computer also calculates:
$10.00 / 144 = .069 for SquareInchPrice1

display prompts for entering shape, price, and size
input Shape2, Price2, Size2
if Shape2 = square **then**
      SquareInches2 ← Size2 * Size2
if Shape2 = round **then**
      SquareInches2 ← 3.142 * (Size2 / 2) ^2
SquareInchPrice2 ← Price2 / SquareInches2

User asked to enter the second pizza's shape, price, and size
User enters round, $10.00, 12
The second pizza is round, so the computer should calculate:
$3.142*(12 / 2)^2 = 113.112$ *for SquareInches2*

The computer should also calculate $10.00 / 113.112 = .088 for SquareInchPrice2

if SquareInchPrice1 < SquareInchPrice2 **then**
      output "Pizza 1 is the best deal."
if SquareInchPrice2 < SquareInchPrice1 **then**
      output "Pizza 2 is the best deal."
if SquareInchPrice1 = SquareInchPrice2 **then**
      output "Both pizzas are the same deal."

.069 < .088 so pizza 1 is the best deal

SEQUENCE, SELECTION, AND REPETITION CONTROLS

▶ **How do I specify the order in which program instructions are performed by the computer?** Unless you specify otherwise, sequential execution is the normal pattern of program execution. During **sequential execution**, the first instruction in the program is executed first, then the second instruction, and so on, to the last instruction in the program. Here is a simple program written in the BASIC programming language that outputs `This is the first line.`, and then outputs `This is the next line.`

```
Print "This is the first line."
Print "This is the next line."
```

▶ **Is there an alternative to sequential execution?** Some algorithms specify that a program must execute instructions in an order different from the sequence in which they are listed, skip some instructions under certain circumstances, or repeat instructions. **Control structures** are instructions that specify the sequence in which a program is executed. Most procedural languages have three types of control structures: sequence controls, selection controls, and repetition controls.

A **sequence control structure** changes the order in which instructions are carried out by directing the computer to execute an instruction elsewhere in the program. In the following simple BASIC program, a GOTO command tells the computer to jump directly to the instruction labeled "Widget." By performing the GOTO statement, the program never carries out the command `Print "This is the next line."`

```
Print "This is the first line."
Goto Widget
Print "This is the next line."
Widget: Print "All done!"
End
```

The flowchart in Figure 12-25 shows how the computer follows a series of sequential commands, and then jumps past other commands as the result of a GOTO command.

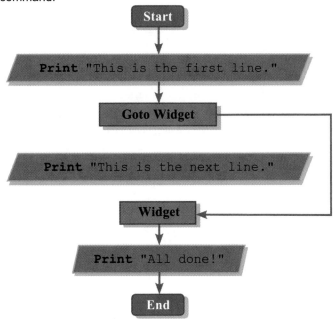

FIGURE 12-25

Executing a GOTO command directs the computer to a different part of the program. ▶ To see how a computer executes the GOTO command, start this animation in your interactive eBook.

Although it is the simplest control structure, the GOTO command is rarely used by skilled programmers because it can lead to programs that are difficult to understand and maintain.

In 1968, the journal *Communications of the ACM* published a now-famous letter from Edsger Dijkstra, called "Go To Statement Considered Harmful." In his letter, Dijkstra explained that injudicious use of the GOTO statement in programs makes it difficult for other programmers to understand the underlying algorithm, which in turn means that such programs are difficult to correct, improve, or revise.

Experienced programmers prefer to use sequence controls other than GOTO to transfer program execution to a subroutine, procedure, or function. A **subroutine**, **procedure**, or **function** is a section of code that is part of a program, but is not included in the main sequential execution path.

A sequence control structure directs the computer to the statements it contains; but when these statements have been executed, the computer neatly returns to the main program. Figure 12-26 shows the execution path of a program that uses the GOSUB command to transfer execution to a subroutine.

FIGURE 12-26

Executing a GOSUB command directs the computer to a different section of the program.

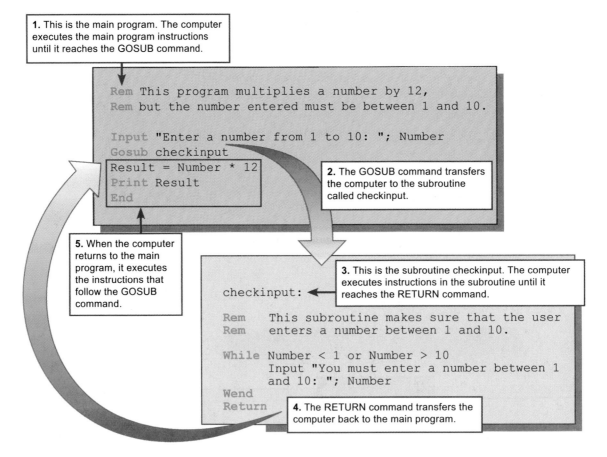

1. This is the main program. The computer executes the main program instructions until it reaches the GOSUB command.

```
Rem This program multiplies a number by 12,
Rem but the number entered must be between 1 and 10.

Input "Enter a number from 1 to 10: "; Number
Gosub checkinput
Result = Number * 12
Print Result
End
```

2. The GOSUB command transfers the computer to the subroutine called checkinput.

5. When the computer returns to the main program, it executes the instructions that follow the GOSUB command.

3. This is the subroutine checkinput. The computer executes instructions in the subroutine until it reaches the RETURN command.

```
checkinput:

Rem    This subroutine makes sure that the user
Rem    enters a number between 1 and 10.

While Number < 1 or Number > 10
      Input "You must enter a number between 1
      and 10: "; Number
Wend
Return
```

4. The RETURN command transfers the computer back to the main program.

▶ **Can the computer make decisions while it executes a program?** A **selection control structure** tells a computer what to do based on whether a condition is true or false. A simple example of a selection control structure is the IF...THEN...ELSE command.

The following program uses this command to decide whether a number entered is greater than 10. If the number is greater than 10, the computer prints `That number is greater than 10`. If the number is not greater than 10, the program performs the ELSE instruction and prints `That number is 10 or less`.

```
Input "Enter a number from 1 to 10: "; Number

If Number > 10 Then Print "That number is greater than
10."

Else Print "That number is 10 or less."

End
```

TERMINOLOGY NOTE

Selection control structures are also referred to as decision structures or branches.

Figure 12-27 uses a flowchart to illustrate how a computer follows commands in a decision structure.

FIGURE 12-27

On a flowchart, a diamond shape indicates a decision. ▶ Step through a decision structure using your interactive eBook.

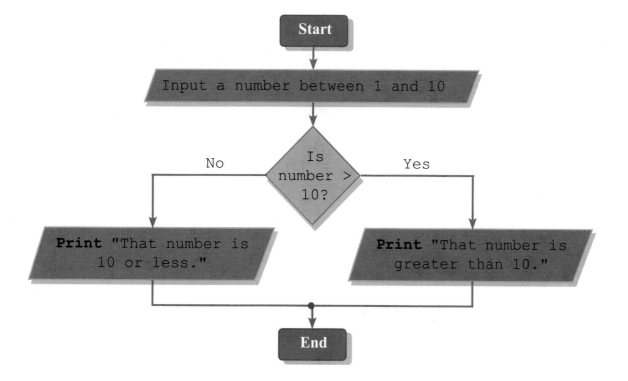

▶ Can a computer automatically repeat a series of instructions?

A **repetition control structure** directs the computer to repeat one or more instructions until a certain condition is met. The section of code that repeats is usually referred to as a **loop** or an **iteration**. Some of the most frequently used repetition commands are FOR...NEXT, DO...WHILE, DO...UNTIL, and WHILE...WEND.

The keyword FOR, DO, or WHILE marks the beginning of a loop. The keyword NEXT, UNTIL, or WEND (which means while ends) marks the end of a loop. The following simple BASIC program uses a FOR...NEXT command to print a message three times:

```
For N = 1 to 3
   Print "There's no place like home."
Next N
End
```

Follow the path of program execution in Figure 12-28 to see how a computer executes a series of commands in a repetition structure.

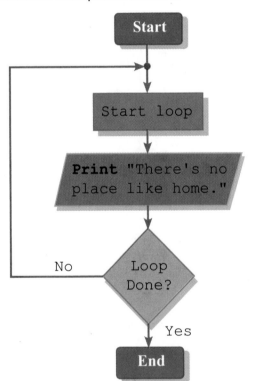

FIGURE 12-28

To execute a loop, the computer repeats one or more commands until some condition indicates that the looping should stop. ▶ Remember Dorothy in *The Wizard of Oz*? Watch how a computer would execute her "There's no place like home." loop.

To get a better idea of how a FOR...NEXT loop works, pretend that you're the computer executing the FOR...NEXT instructions below. You can use the box labeled N in the margin as a RAM location. As the computer, you would also have a screen on which to display output—use the Screen Output box. Now, walk through the loop.

```
For N = 1 to 3
   Print "There's no place like home."
Next N

End
```

1. As the computer, the first time you see the instruction `For N = 1 to 3`, you set N equal to 1. To do so, write the number 1 in the N box in the margin.

2. You would then execute the next instruction, `Print "There's no place like home."` To do so, write the phrase "There's no place like home." in the Screen Output box. (Hint: Write small; there's more to go in the Screen Output box.)

3. The instruction `Next` sends you back to the command `For N = 1 to 3`. Because this occasion is the second time you have executed this statement, put a 2 in the N box in the margin (you can erase the 1 that was there previously).

4. You must check whether the value in box N is greater than 3. Why? Because the command `For N = 1 to 3` means you can continue to loop only if N is 3 or less. N is only 2, so you can proceed.

5. Go to the next instruction, which is `Print "There's no place like home."` Write this sentence again in the Screen Output box.

6. Moving on, you reach the `Next` statement again, which sends you back to the `For` statement.

7. Continue by changing the value in the N box to 3. Check the N box to make sure it does not contain a value greater than 3. It doesn't, so continue.

8. The next line instructs you to `Print "There's no place like home."` Write this sentence again in the Screen Output box. The `Next` statement sends you back to the `For` statement. Increase the value in the N box to 4.

9. This time when you check whether the value in N is greater than 3, it is. That means the loop is complete, and you should jump to the statement past the end of the loop.

10. The next statement is `End`, so you've completed the program.

11. When your program is complete, the variable N should contain the number 4, and the Screen Output box should contain three lines of "There's no place like home."

N

Screen Output

12

▶ How do I use control structures to write a program? To
write the code for the pizza program, you use control structures, keywords, and syntax provided by your programming language. The completed pizza program, written in BASIC, is provided in Figure 12-29.

FIGURE 12-29

Each line of code for the pizza program consists of keywords and parameters.

```
Rem The Pizza Program
Rem This program tells you which of two pizzas is the best deal
Rem    by calculating the price per square inch of each pizza.
Rem Collect initial information for first pizza.
Input "Enter the shape of pizza 1:"; Shape1$
Input "Enter the price of pizza 1:"; Price1
Input "Enter the size of pizza 1:"; Size1

Rem Calculate price per square inch for first pizza.
Rem If the first pizza is square, calculate square inches by multiplying one side
Rem    by the other.
If Shape1$ = "square" Then SquareInches1 = Size1 * Size1
Rem If the first pizza is round, calculate the number of square inches where
Rem    pi = 3.142, size / 2 = radius, and (size / 2) ^2 = radius squared.
If Shape1$ = "round" Then SquareInches1 = 3.142 * (Size1 / 2) ^2
SquareInchPrice1 = Price1 / SquareInches1

Rem Collect initial information for second pizza.
Input "Enter the shape of pizza 2:"; Shape2$
Input "Enter the price of pizza 2:"; Price2
Input "Enter the size of pizza 2:"; Size2

Rem Calculate price per square inch for second pizza.
If Shape2$ = "square" Then SquareInches2 = Size2 * Size2
If Shape2$ = "round" Then SquareInches2 = 3.142 * (Size2 / 2) ^2
SquareInchPrice2 = Price2 / SquareInches2

Rem Decide which pizza is the best deal and display results.
If SquareInchPrice1 < SquareInchPrice2 Then Message$ = "Pizza 1 is the best deal."
If SquareInchPrice2 < SquareInchPrice1 Then Message$ = "Pizza 2 is the best deal."
If SquareInchPrice1 = SquareInchPrice2 Then Message$ = "Both pizzas are the same deal."
Print Message$
End
```

Lines that begin with Rem contain remarks that explain each section of the program. The computer does not execute the remarks.

Data is stored in variables, or memory locations, in RAM. The variable Shape2$ stores text, such as the word *round*. The $ indicates a text variable. Other variables, such as Price1 and Size1, store numbers; they do not include $ as part of the variable name.

PROCEDURAL LANGUAGES AND APPLICATIONS

▶ What are the most popular procedural languages? The
first programming languages were procedural. Fortran, developed by IBM in 1954, was the first widely used, standardized computer language. Its implementation of the procedural paradigm set the pattern for other popular procedural languages, such as COBOL, FORTH, APL, ALGOL, PL/1, Pascal, C, Ada, and BASIC.

In 1958, a group of European researchers created a new programming language, dubbed ALGOL, an acronym for ALGOrithmic Language. ALGOL was used for research applications and is the ancestor of several languages in widespread use today. CPL, created by Ken Thompson of AT&T Bell Laboratories, descended from ALGOL and evolved into the C language. Pascal, the popular teaching language created by Niklaus Wirth, was an important step in the development of Ada.

▶ What kinds of problems are best suited to the procedural approach? The procedural approach is best used for problems
that can be solved by following a step-by-step algorithm. One of the original problems tackled by computers was computing missile trajectories.

Missiles follow an arcing path called a trajectory. Aim too high or too low and the missile misses its target.

The factors that affect a missile's trajectory include the angle of the gun, weight of the missile, wind direction, wind speed, temperature, and distance to target. However, after these factors are known for a particular target, the calculation follows a simple mathematical algorithm. Therefore, the steps for calculating trajectories remain the same, regardless of the data.

To compute trajectories for missiles, you can simply plug in values and the computer follows the same steps to complete the task. Computing paychecks is similar; plug in the hours worked for each employee and the computer follows a set of steps to calculate earnings, taxes, and net pay. The concept that you can plug in values to a set of steps for completing a task is the key to understanding the kinds of problems that are best suited for the procedural approach.

The procedural approach has been widely used for transaction processing, which is characterized by the use of a single algorithm applied to many different sets of data. For example, in the banking industry, the algorithm for calculating checking account balances is the same, regardless of the amounts deposited and withdrawn. Many problems in math and science also lend themselves to the procedural approach.

▶ What are the advantages and disadvantages of the procedural paradigm? The procedural approach and procedural languages tend to produce programs that run quickly and use system resources efficiently. It is a classic approach understood by many programmers, software engineers, and systems analysts.

The procedural paradigm is quite flexible and powerful, which allows programmers to apply it to many types of problems. For example, although the programming example in this section worked only for round and square pizzas, it could be modified to handle rectangular pizzas, too.

The downside of the procedural paradigm is that it does not fit gracefully with certain types of problems—those that are unstructured or those with very complex algorithms. The procedural paradigm has also been criticized because it forces programmers to view problems as a series of steps, whereas some problems might better be visualized as interacting objects or as interrelated words, concepts, and ideas.

QuickCheck

1. A(n) [_____] is a set of steps for carrying out a task that programmers express in Structured English, pseudocode, or flowcharts.

2. COBOL, Fortran, and C are examples of programming languages used when working with the [_____] paradigm.

3. A selection control structure tells a computer what to do based on whether a condition is true or false, whereas a(n) [_____] control structure can change the order in which program instructions are executed.

4. A subroutine or procedure is a section of code that is part of a program, but is not included in the main execution path. True or false? [_____]

5. The section of a program that contains a repetition control is sometimes referred to as an iteration or a(n) [_____].

▶ CHECK ANSWERS

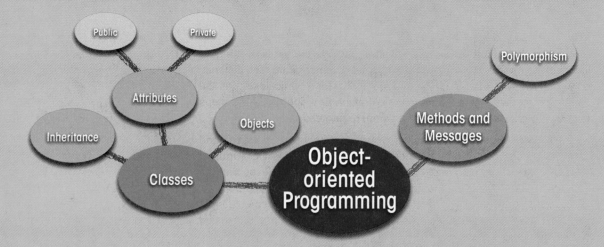

Object-oriented Programming

SECTION **C**

THE OBJECT-ORIENTED PARADIGM offers an alternative approach to step-by-step procedural programming. In this section, you'll find out what object-oriented programming is all about. Java is used for the examples in this section because it is one of today's most popular languages for implementing object-oriented programs.

OBJECTS AND CLASSES

▶ What is the basic focus of the object-oriented paradigm? The **object-oriented paradigm** is based on the idea that the solution for a problem can be visualized in terms of objects that interact with each other. In the context of this paradigm, an **object** is a unit of data that represents an abstract or a real-world entity, such as a person, place, or thing.

An object can represent a $10.99 small round pepperoni pizza. Another object can represent a pizza delivery guy named Jack Flash. Yet another object can represent a customer who lives at 22 W. Pointe Rd.

▶ What's the difference between an object and a class? The real world contains lots of pizzas, customers, and delivery guys. These objects can be defined in a general way by using classes. Whereas an object is a single instance of an entity, a **class** is a template for a group of objects with similar characteristics.

For example, a Pizza class defines a group of gooey Italian snacks that are made in a variety of sizes, crafted into rectangular or round shapes, and sold for various prices. A class can produce any number of unique objects, as shown in Figure 12-30.

CLASS: Pizza

Pizza objects

FIGURE 12-30

A class, such as the Pizza class, is a general template for a group of objects with similar characteristics.

▶ How do I define the classes I need to solve a problem?

When taking the object-oriented approach to a problem, one of the first steps is to identify the objects that pertain to a solution. As you might expect, the solution to the pizza problem requires some pizza objects.

Certain characteristics of pizzas provide information necessary to solve the problem. This information—the price, size, and shape of a pizza—provides the structure for the Pizza class. A class is defined by attributes and methods. A **class attribute** defines the characteristics of a set of objects. You will learn about methods, which define actions, later in this section.

Each class attribute generally has a name, scope, and data type. One class attribute of the Pizza class might be named pizzaPrice. Its scope can be defined as public or private:

▶ A **public attribute** is available for use by any routine in the program.

▶ A **private attribute** can be accessed only from the routine in which it is defined.

The pizzaPrice attribute's data type can be defined as double, which means that it can be any decimal number, such as 12.99. Figure 12-31 describes the data types most often used to describe class attributes.

TERMINOLOGY NOTE

The data types used to define class attributes are similar to the data types for defining database fields, but the terminology is slightly different.

FIGURE 12-31

Class Attribute Data Types

Data Type	Description	Example
Int	Integer whole numbers	10
Double	Numbers with decimal places	12.99
String	Multiple characters, symbols, and numerals	Square
Boolean	Limited to two values	T or F

OO programmers often use UML (Unified Modeling Language) diagrams to plan the classes for a program. The UML diagram in Figure 12-32 shows one possible way to envision the Pizza class.

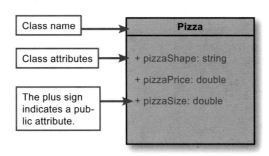

FIGURE 12-32

The core of a UML diagram is a box that contains information about a class.

How do I code a class when writing a program? Although a programmer usually completes the overall program plan before coding, jump ahead to take a quick look at the Java code for the attributes in the Pizza class. The first line of code defines the name of the class. Each subsequent line defines the scope, data type, and name of an attribute. The curly brackets simply define the start and end of the class.

```
class Pizza
{
  public string pizzaShape;
  public double pizzaPrice;
  public double pizzaSize;
}
```

INHERITANCE

How flexible are classes for defining different types of objects? The object-oriented paradigm endows classes with quite a bit of flexibility. For the pizza program, objects and classes make it easy to compare round pizzas to rectangular pizzas rather than just to square pizzas.

Suppose you want to compare a 10-inch round pizza to a rectangular pizza that has a length of 11 inches and a width of 8 inches. The Pizza class in Figure 12-32 on the previous page holds only one measurement for each pizza: pizzaSize. This single attribute won't work for rectangular pizzas, which might have a different length and width.

Should you modify the class definition to add attributes for pizzaLength and pizzaWidth? No, because these attributes are necessary only for rectangular pizzas, not for round pizzas. An OO feature called inheritance provides flexibility to deal with objects' unique characteristics.

What is inheritance? In object-oriented jargon, **inheritance** refers to passing certain characteristics from one class to other classes. For example, to solve the pizza problem, a programmer might decide to use a RoundPizza class and a RectanglePizza class. These two new classes can inherit attributes from the Pizza class, such as pizzaShape and pizzaPrice.

You can add specialized characteristics to the new classes. The RectanglePizza class can have attributes for length and width, and the RoundPizza class can have an attribute for diameter.

The process of producing new classes with inherited attributes creates a **class hierarchy** that includes a superclass and subclasses (Figure 12-33):

▶ A **superclass**, such as Pizza, is any class from which attributes can be inherited.

▶ A **subclass** (or derived class), such as RoundPizza or RectanglePizza, is any class that inherits attributes from a superclass.

FIGURE 12-33

The subclass attributes shown in blue text (pizzaShape and pizzaPrice) are inherited from the Pizza superclass. The attributes in red are unique to the subclasses. The plus sign indicates that these inherited attributes are public.

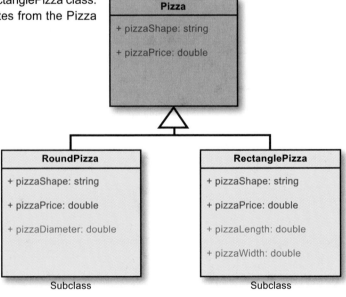

▶ **How do I code a subclass?** Java uses the `extends` command to link a subclass to a superclass. The statement `class RectanglePizza extends Pizza` means "create a class called RectanglePizza that's derived from the superclass called Pizza." Figure 12-34 contains the Java code that creates attributes for the RectanglePizza class.

```
class RectanglePizza extends Pizza
{
      double pizzaLength;
      double pizzaWidth;
}
```

FIGURE 12-34

Using the `extends` command, the RectanglePizza class inherits the pizzaShape and pizzaPrice attributes from the Pizza superclass. The pizzaLength and pizzaWidth attributes are unique to the RectanglePizza class.

METHODS AND MESSAGES

▶ **How does an OO program use objects?** An OO program can use objects in a variety of ways. A basic way to use objects is to manipulate them with methods. A **method** is a segment of code that defines an action. The names of methods end in a set of parentheses, such as compare() or getArea().

▶ **What can a method do?** A method can perform a variety of tasks, such as collecting input, performing calculations, making comparisons, executing decisions, and producing output. For example, the pizza program can use a method named compare() to compare the square-inch prices of two pizzas and display a message indicating which pizza is the best deal.

▶ **What does a method look like when it has been coded in Java?** A method begins with a line that names the method and can include a description of its scope and data type. The scope—public or private—specifies which parts of the program can access the method. The data type specifies the kind of data, if any, that the method produces.

The initial line of code is followed by one or more lines that specify the calculation, comparison, or routine that the method performs. Figure 12-35 illustrates the code for the compare() method.

FIGURE 12-35

Java Code for the compare() Method

The method title includes its scope and name. →

```
public compare(Pizza Pizza1, Pizza Pizza2)
{
        if (Pizza1.SquareInchPrice < Pizza2.SquareInchPrice)
           System.out.println("Pizza 1 is the best deal!");

        if (Pizza1.SquareInchPrice > Pizza2.SquareInchPrice)
           System.out.println("Pizza 2 is the best deal!");

        if (Pizza1.SquareInchPrice == Pizza2.SquareInchPrice
           System.out.println("The pizzas are the same deal!");
}
```

← The method manipulates pizza objects.

The body of the method contains statements that determine which pizza is the best deal and print the result.

▶ **What activates a method?** A method is activated by a **message**, which is included as a line of program code that is sometimes referred to as a call. For example, in a Java program, a line of code such as `compare(Pizza1, Pizza2)` produces a message used to activate or call the compare() method.

In the object-oriented world, objects often interact to solve a problem by sending and receiving messages. For example, a pizza object might receive a message asking for the pizza's area or price per square inch.

▶ **How do methods relate to classes?** Methods can be defined along with the class they affect. The getSquareInchPrice() method pertains to pizzas of any shape, so it can be defined as part of the Pizza class. To calculate the square-inch price, however, it is necessary to know the area of a pizza. That calculation can be achieved by defining a getArea() method.

The area calculation for round pizzas is different from the calculation for rectangular pizzas, so the getArea() method should become part of the RoundPizza and RectanglePizza subclasses, as indicated by the UML diagram in Figure 12-36.

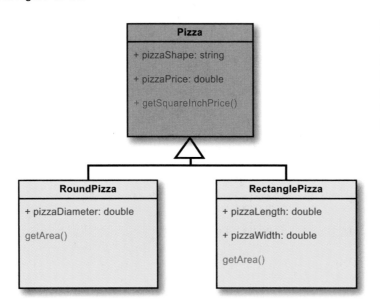

FIGURE 12-36

The getSquareInchPrice() method is defined as part of the Pizza class, whereas the getArea() method is defined within the RoundPizza and RectanglePizza classes.

▶ How does the getArea() method work? If you have been thinking ahead a bit, you might wonder how a programmer can define the getArea() method to perform two different calculations—one that calculates the area of a rectangle by multiplying its length times its width, and another that calculates the area of a circle using the formula πr^2. An object-oriented concept called polymorphism makes it possible to assign more than one formula to the getArea() method.

▶ What is polymorphism? **Polymorphism**, sometimes called overloading, is the ability to redefine a method in a subclass. It allows programmers to create a single, generic name for a procedure that behaves in unique ways for different classes.

In the pizza program, for example, both the RectanglePizza and RoundPizza classes can have a getArea() method. The calculation that getArea() performs is defined one way for the RectanglePizza class and another way for the RoundPizza class. Figure 12-37 illustrates how polymorphism allows subclasses to tailor methods to fit their unique requirements.

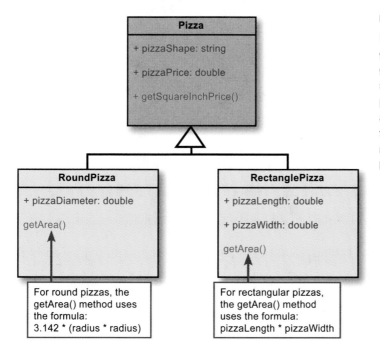

FIGURE 12-37

Polymorphism allows a programmer to define different getArea() methods for each subclass. When the completed program runs, pizza shapes are collected from the user and the corresponding getArea() method can be applied to calculate the area of a pizza.

▶ How does the code for the round getArea() method differ from the code for the rectangle getArea() method?
The code for the getArea() method defined in the RoundPizza class asks users to key in, or enter, the pizza's diameter. The method then divides the diameter by 2 to arrive at the radius. The value for the radius is used in the πr^2 calculation—3.142 * (radius * radius)—for the area of a circle.

The getArea() method defined in the RectanglePizza class asks users to key in the length of the pizza and then its width. This data is used in the calculation that multiplies length times width to produce the area of a rectangular pizza. Figure 12-38 illustrates the Java code for the getArea() methods. The lines that begin with // are remarks.

FIGURE 12-38

The getArea() Methods for Round and Rectangular Pizzas

```
getArea()

//Method to calculate the area of a round pizza
{
    pizzaDiameter = Keyin.inDouble("Enter the diameter of the pizza: ");

    radius = pizzaDiameter / 2;

    pizzaArea = 3.142 * (radius * radius);

}
```

```
getArea()

//Method to calculate the area of a rectangular pizza
{
    pizzaLength = Keyin.inDouble("Enter the length of the pizza: ");

    pizzaWidth = Keyin.inDouble("Enter the width of the pizza: ");

    pizzaArea = pizzaLength * pizzaWidth;
}
```

▶ What are the advantages of polymorphism? Polymorphism provides OO programs with easy extensibility and can help simplify program code. For example, if one of the pizzerias decides to get creative with pizza shapes, it would be easy to extend the pizza program to work with triangular pizzas. To extend the program, you would simply define a TrianglePizza class that includes attributes for pizzaWidth and pizzaHeight and tailor its getArea() method for calculating the area of a triangle.

The ability to tailor the getArea() method for round and square pizzas allows programmers to avoid complex logic and to simplify program code. As you can imagine, creating separate methods with unique names, such as getAreaRoundPizza(), getAreaRectanglePizza(), and getAreaTrianglePizza(), would add to the program's complexity and make it more difficult to extend the program for other pizza shapes.

OBJECT-ORIENTED PROGRAM STRUCTURE

▶ What does the completed pizza program look like in Java? So far in this section of the chapter, you have learned how objects and methods interact to solve the pizza problem. You know that the pizza program uses a Pizza class and two subclasses: RectanglePizza and RoundPizza.

You also know that these classes include the getSquareInchPrice() and getArea() methods to perform calculations that supply data for solving the problem. You should also remember that the compare() method is used to manipulate pizza objects to determine which is the best deal.

The classes and methods defined for the pizza program must be placed within the structure of a Java program, which contains class definitions, defines methods, initiates the comparison, and outputs results. Figure 12-39 provides an overview of the program structure.

FIGURE 12-39

Program Structure for the Pizza Program

Pizza Class Definition

Define Pizza as a class with attributes for shape and price. Define the getSquareInchPrice() method that collects input for the pizza price, then calculates a pizza's square-inch price.

RectanglePizza Class Definition

Define RectanglePizza as a subclass of Pizza with attributes for length and width. Define the getArea() method that collects input for the pizza length and width to calculate area.

RoundPizza Class Definition

Define RoundPizza as a subclass of Pizza with an attribute for diameter. Define a getArea() method that collects input for the pizza diameter, then calculates area.

Compare() Method

Compare the square-inch price of two pizzas and output results.

Main Module

Set up variables, create objects for Pizza1 and Pizza2, and activate the getArea(), getSquareInchPrice(), and compare() methods.

▶ **How does a Java program work?** The computer begins executing a Java program by locating a standard method called main(), which contains code to send messages to objects by calling methods.

For the pizza program, the main() method includes code that defines a few variables and then asks the user to enter the shape of the first pizza. If the shape entered is Round, the program creates an object called Pizza1 that is a member of the RoundPizza class. If the shape entered is Rectangle, the program creates an object called Pizza1 that is a member of the RectanglePizza class.

After the pizza object is created, the program uses the getArea() method to calculate its area. The program then uses the getSquareInchPrice() method to calculate the pizza's square-inch price.

When the calculations are complete for the first pizza, the program performs the same process for the second pizza. Finally, the program uses the compare() method to compare the square-inch prices of the two pizzas and output a statement about which one is the best deal.

Because it is not the goal of this section to teach you the particulars of Java programming, don't worry about the detailed syntax of the Java code. Instead, refer to Figure 12-40 to get an overview of the activity that takes place in the main() method for the pizza program.

FIGURE 12-40

Java Code for the Main Module of the Pizza Program

```
public static void main(String[] args)        1. Define arguments
  {                                               for main method.

      Pizza Pizza1;            2. Define variables used
      Pizza Pizza2;               in the main() method.
      String pizzaShape;

      pizzaShape = Keyin.inString("Enter the shape of the first pizza: ");
      if (pizzaShape.equals("Round"))     3. Collect input for the shape of the
        {                                    first pizza, then create an object
          Pizza1 = new RoundPizza();         called Pizza1 that belongs to the
        }                                    RoundPizza or RectanglePizza class.
      else
          Pizza1 = new RectanglePizza();

      Pizza1.getArea();            4. Use the getArea() and getSquare-
      Pizza1.getSquareInchPrice();    InchPrice() methods to calculate area
                                       and square-inch price for the first pizza.

      pizzaShape = Keyin.inString("Enter the shape of the second pizza: ");
      if (pizzaShape.equals("Round"))   5. Collect input for the shape of the second pizza,
          Pizza2 = new RoundPizza();       then create an object called Pizza2 that belongs
      else                                 to the RoundPizza or RectanglePizza class.
          Pizza2 = new RectanglePizza();

      Pizza2.getArea();            6. Use the getArea() and getSquareInchPrice() methods to
      Pizza2.getSquareInchPrice();    calculate area and square-inch price for the second pizza.

      compare(Pizza1, Pizza2);     7. Use the compare() method
  }                                   to determine which pizza is the
                                      best deal, then print results.
```

▶ **What happens when the completed pizza program runs?** When you run the pizza program, it looks for the main() method. This method displays an on-screen prompt that asks for the pizza's shape. The getArea() method displays a prompt for the pizza's diameter (for a round pizza) or the pizza's length and width (for a rectangular pizza).

A similar series of prompts appears for the second pizza. The program concludes when the compare() method displays a statement about which pizza is the best deal. The software tour for Figure 12-41 lets you see what happens when the OO pizza program runs.

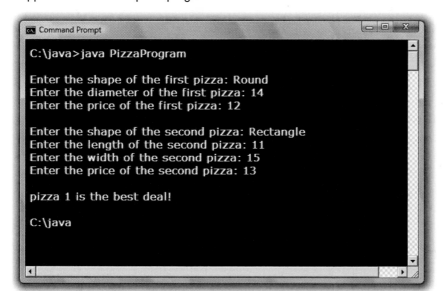

FIGURE 12-41

When the pizza program runs, on-screen prompts ask for the shape, size, and price of each pizza; then the program displays a message that indicates which pizza is the best deal. ▶ Watch the program run in your interactive eBook.

OBJECT-ORIENTED LANGUAGES AND APPLICATIONS

▶ **How did object-oriented languages originate?** Computer historians believe that SIMULA (SIMUlation LAnguage) was the first computer language to work with objects, classes, inheritance, and methods.

SIMULA was developed in 1962 by two Norwegian computer scientists for the purpose of programming simulations and models. SIMULA laid the foundation for the object-oriented paradigm, which was later incorporated into other programming languages, such as Smalltalk, C++, and Java.

The second major development in object-oriented languages came in 1972 when Alan Kay began work on the Dynabook project at the Xerox Palo Alto Research Center (PARC). Kay developed a programming language called Smalltalk for the Dynabook that could be easily used to create programs based on real-world objects. Smalltalk is regarded as a classic object-oriented language, which encourages programmers to take a pure OO approach to the programming process.

▶ **Which object-oriented languages are popular today?** As the object-oriented paradigm gained popularity, several existing programming languages were modified to allow programmers to work with objects, classes, inheritance, and polymorphism. The concept for the Ada programming language originated in 1978 at the U.S. Department of Defense. The first versions of Ada were procedural; but in 1995, the language was modified to incorporate object-oriented features.

A similar transformation took place with the C language in 1983, except that the object-oriented version earned a new name: C++. Hybrid languages, such as Ada 2005, C++, Visual Basic, Objective-C, and C#, give programmers the option of using both procedural and object-oriented techniques.

Java was originally planned as a programming language for consumer electronics, such as interactive cable television boxes, but evolved into an object-oriented programming platform for developing Web applications. Java was officially launched by Sun Microsystems in 1995 and has many of the characteristics of C++, from which it derives much of its syntax. Like C++, Java can also be used for procedural programming, so it is sometimes classified as a hybrid language.

Introduced in 2007, Scratch is one of the newest OO languages. Like Smalltalk, Scratch was designed as an easy-to-use starter language but has a modern GUI and built-in support for audio, graphics, and animation.

▶ What kinds of applications are suitable for object-oriented languages? The object-oriented paradigm can be applied to a wide range of programming problems. Basically, if you can envision a problem as a set of objects that pass messages back and forth, the problem is suitable for the OO approach.

▶ What are the advantages and disadvantages of the OO paradigm? The object-oriented paradigm is cognitively similar to the way human beings perceive the real world. Using the OO approach, programmers might be able to visualize the solutions to problems more easily.

Facets of the object-oriented paradigm can also increase a programmer's efficiency because encapsulation allows objects to be adapted and reused in a variety of different programs. **Encapsulation** refers to the process of hiding the internal details of objects and their methods.

After an object is coded, it becomes a "black box," which essentially hides its details from other objects and allows the data to be accessed using methods. Encapsulated objects can be easily reused, modified, and repurposed.

A potential disadvantage of object-oriented programs is runtime efficiency. Object-oriented programs tend to require more memory and processing resources than procedural programs. Programmers, software engineers, and systems analysts can work together to weigh the tradeoffs between the OO approach and runtime efficiency.

QuickCheck   SECTION C

1. In OO programming, a class is a template for a group of [_____] with similar characteristics.

2. OO programmers often use [_____] diagrams to plan the classes for a program. (Hint: Use the abbreviation.)

3. The process of passing certain characteristics from a superclass to a subclass is referred to as [_____].

4. In an OO program, getArea() would be called a(n) [_____].

5. The sample code for the object-oriented pizza program in this section of the chapter was written using the [_____] programming language.

 CHECK ANSWERS

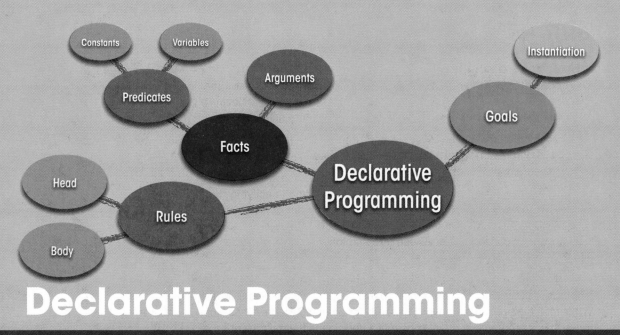

Declarative Programming

HOW CAN COMPUTERS make decisions and solve problems for non-numeric data, including words and concepts? Procedural programming languages, such as Fortran and COBOL, do not have the flexibility to deal efficiently with non-numeric data, so non-procedural languages were developed. This section explains a type of non-procedural programming that follows the declarative paradigm and gives you a little taste of the Prolog language.

THE DECLARATIVE PARADIGM

▶ **What is the declarative paradigm?** In earlier sections of this chapter, you learned that procedural programming focuses on a step-by-step algorithm that instructs the computer how to arrive at a solution. You also learned that the object-oriented approach emphasizes classes and methods that form objects. In contrast, the **declarative paradigm** describes aspects of a problem that lead to a solution.

Although the declarative paradigm might sound similar to the procedural paradigm, the procedural paradigm focuses on an algorithm that describes the solution, whereas the declarative paradigm focuses on describing the problem. Figure 12-42 summarizes these differences.

▶ **What are the building blocks for the declarative paradigm?** Many declarative programming languages, such as Prolog, use a collection of facts and rules to describe a problem. In the context of a Prolog program, a **fact** is a statement that provides the computer with basic information for solving a problem. In the pizza problem, for example, these facts might include:

A pizza has a price of $10.99, a size of 12 inches, and a round shape.

Another pizza has a price of $12.00, a size of 11 inches, and a square shape.

In the context of a Prolog program, a **rule** is a general statement about the relationship between facts. For example, the following rule is useful for solving the problem of which pizza is a better deal:

A pizza is a better deal if its square-inch price is less than the square-inch price of another pizza.

FIGURE 12-42

Paradigm Comparison

Procedural paradigm:
▶ Programs detail how to solve a problem
▶ Very efficient for number-crunching tasks

Object-oriented paradigm:
▶ Programs define objects, classes, and methods
▶ Efficient for problems that involve real-world objects

Declarative paradigm:
▶ Programs describe the problem
▶ Efficient for processing words and language

▶ How does a programmer plan a declarative program?

The core of most declarative programs is a set of facts and rules that describe a problem. The logic for the pizza program is very simple because the solution depends on a single factor: the lowest square-inch price.

Declarative programs with such simple logic don't require much planning. In contrast, programs that deal with multiple factors have more complex logic and often require planning tools, such as decision tables.

A **decision table** is a tabular method for visualizing and specifying rules based on multiple factors. As an example, suppose your decision to buy a pizza depends not just on its price, but on whether you can get it delivered and how soon it is ready. These three factors produce eight possible situations.

In which of those eight situations would you purchase a pizza? What if the best-priced pizza is ready in less than 30 minutes, but it can't be delivered? What if the best-priced pizza won't be ready for an hour? Figure 12-43 illustrates how a programmer might construct a decision table that describes all the rules pertaining to pizza prices, delivery, and time.

FIGURE 12-43

Decision Table

Lowest price?	Y	N	Y	N	Y	N	Y	N
Delivery available?	Y	Y	N	N	Y	Y	N	N
Ready in less than 30 minutes?	Y	Y	Y	Y	N	N	N	N
Buy it?	Y	Y	N	N	Y	N	N	N

PROLOG FACTS

▶ How does a programmer code facts?

Return to the simple problem of deciding which of two round or square pizzas is the best deal based on price per square inch. The first step in coding the program using Prolog is to enter facts that describe the prices, shapes, and sizes of two pizzas. The fact "The shape of a pizza is round." can be coded this way:

```
shapeof(pizza,round).
```

The words in parentheses are called arguments. An **argument** represents one of the main subjects that a fact describes. The word outside the parentheses, called the **predicate**, describes the relationship between the arguments. For example, the predicate shapeof describes the relationship between pizza and round. Figure 12-44 points out some important syntax details pertaining to capitalization and punctuation for Prolog facts.

FIGURE 12-44

A Prolog fact follows specific syntax rules.

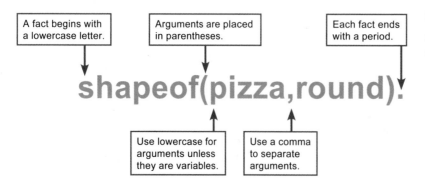

Although it might seem obvious that round describes the shape of a pizza, the predicate cannot be omitted. In many cases, the predicate can drastically change the meaning of a fact. For example, the facts in Figure 12-45 have the same arguments, (joe,fish), but the predicates give the facts very different meanings.

FIGURE 12-45

The predicate can drastically change the meaning of a fact.

hates(joe,fish).
Joe hates fish.

name(joe,fish).
Joe is the name of a fish.

playscardgame(joe,fish).
Joe plays a card game called fish.

12

For the pizza program, a series of facts can be used to describe a pizza:

```
priceof(pizza1,10).

sizeof(pizza1,12).

shapeof(pizza1,square).
```

Another set of similar facts can be used to describe a second pizza:

```
priceof(pizza2,12).

sizeof(pizza2,14).

shapeof(pizza2,round).
```

Facts can have more than two arguments. For example, a single fact can be used to fully describe a pizza:

```
pricesizeshape(pizza1,10,12,square).
```

Using a series of facts to describe a pizza has some advantages and some disadvantages over using a single fact. A single fact tends to make a program more compact, whereas multiple facts might provide more flexibility. The structure of a fact also affects the syntax for goals that produce information.

▶ **What is a goal?** The facts in a Prolog program are useful even without any rules. Prolog can manipulate facts in several ways without explicit programming. Each fact in a Prolog program is similar to a record in a database, but you can query a Prolog program's database by asking a question, called a **goal** in Prolog jargon. Suppose you have entered the following facts:

```
priceof(pizza1,10).

sizeof(pizza1,12).

shapeof(pizza1,square).

priceof(pizza2,12).

sizeof(pizza2,14).

shapeof(pizza2,round).
```

You can ask questions by entering goals from the ?- prompt. For example, the goal ?- shapeof(pizza1,square) means "Is the shape of pizza1 square?" Prolog searches through the facts to see if it can satisfy the goal by finding a match. If a match is found, Prolog responds with yes; otherwise, it responds with no.

This goal might seem trivial because you are working with a small set of facts, which are all visible on the screen. Many programs, however, contain hundreds of facts, which cannot be displayed on a single screen or easily remembered by a programmer.

Prolog allows you to ask open-ended questions by replacing constants with variables. A constant, such as pizza1, square, or 10, represents an unchanging value or attribute. In contrast, a Prolog variable is like a placeholder or an empty box, into which Prolog can put information gleaned from a fact. A Prolog variable begins with an uppercase letter to distinguish it from a constant. The argument Pizza is a variable, whereas pizza1 is a constant. The argument Inches is a variable, whereas 14 is a constant.

Prolog variables are handy tools for formulating open-ended goals. As an example, suppose you want to find the size of pizza2. You can obtain this information by using the variable Inches in the goal:

```
?- sizeof(pizza2,Inches).
```

Prolog looks for any facts that have sizeof as a predicate and pizza2 as the first argument. It responds with the actual value of the second argument:

```
Inches = 14
```

Much of the power and flexibility of the Prolog language stems from its ability to sift through facts trying to match predicates, compare constants, and instantiate variables. The screentour for Figure 12-46 demonstrates various Prolog goals.

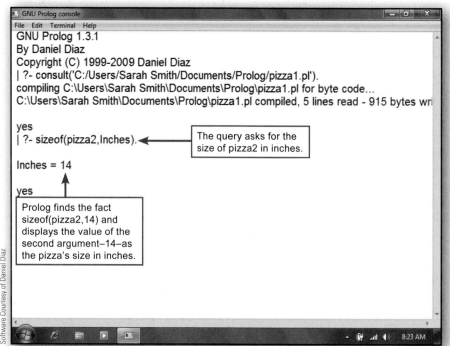

FIGURE 12-46

The ?- prompt allows you to work with a knowledge base by entering facts, rules, and goals. Suppose you have opened a knowledge base containing facts about two pizzas. You can enter goals to find their prices, sizes, and shapes. ▶ Go step-by-step through some goals for learning about the pizzas in this knowledge base.

▶ **What is instantiation?** Finding a value for a variable is referred to as **instantiation**. To solve the goal `?- sizeof(pizza2,Inches).`, a Prolog program looks for a fact that begins with `sizeof(pizza`....

When Prolog finds the rule `sizeof(pizza2,14).`, the program instantiates, or assigns, the value 14 to the variable Inches (Figure 12-47).

FIGURE 12-47

The number 14 is instantiated to the variable Inches.

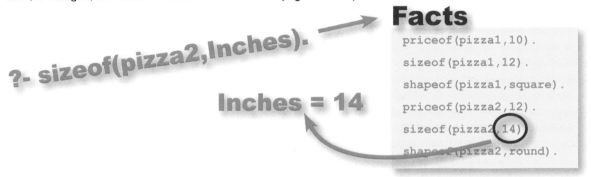

Instantiation can be used to produce information that is not implicitly stored in the database. Suppose you want to know the size of the round pizza. The knowledge base does not contain a fact like `sizeof(roundpizza,14).`; however, you can use a conjunction of two goals, as shown in Figure 12-48, to obtain the size of the round pizza.

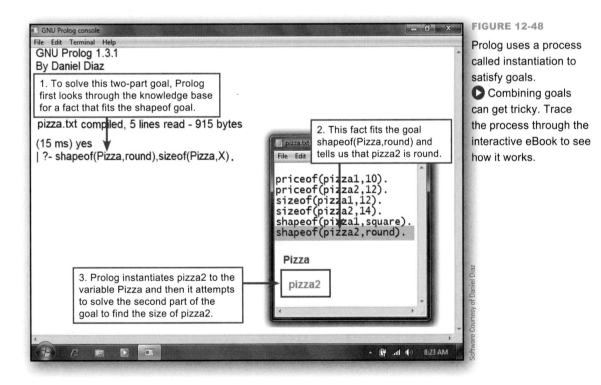

FIGURE 12-48

Prolog uses a process called instantiation to satisfy goals.
▶ Combining goals can get tricky. Trace the process through the interactive eBook to see how it works.

Instantiation is one of the keys to understanding how Prolog works. Unlike a procedural programming language, which is designed to step through a series of statements in a path prescribed by the programmer, Prolog can autonomously run through every possible instantiation, backtracking if necessary to deal with multiple variables.

PROLOG RULES

▶ How does a programmer code Prolog rules? The pizza program requires a rule that states, "A pizza is a better deal if its price per square inch is less than the price per square inch of the other pizza." Translated into Prolog code, this rule becomes:

```
betterdeal(PizzaX,PizzaY) :-

squareinchprice(PizzaX,AmountX),

squareinchprice(PizzaY,AmountY),

AmountX < AmountY.
```

FIGURE 12-49

Take a look at the logic behind this rule. A Prolog rule consists of a head, body, and connecting symbol, as described in Figure 12-49.

A Prolog rule consists of a head and one or more clauses that form the body of the rule.

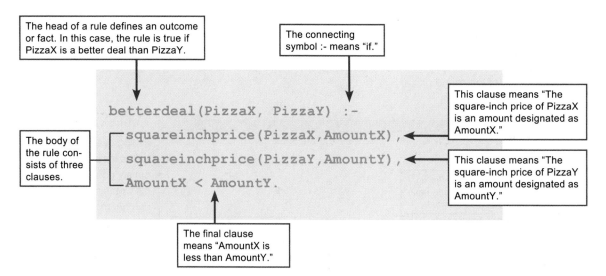

The head of a rule defines an outcome or fact. In this case, the rule is true if PizzaX is a better deal than PizzaY.

The connecting symbol :- means "if."

This clause means "The square-inch price of PizzaX is an amount designated as AmountX."

The body of the rule consists of three clauses.

This clause means "The square-inch price of PizzaY is an amount designated as AmountY."

The final clause means "AmountX is less than AmountY."

```
betterdeal(PizzaX, PizzaY) :-
    squareinchprice(PizzaX,AmountX),
    squareinchprice(PizzaY,AmountY),
    AmountX < AmountY.
```

▶ How do Prolog rules work? To understand how the betterdeal rule works, you'll need to perform a bit of magic to determine the price per square inch of each pizza. In the completed pizza program, the computer can calculate the square-inch price using a rule the programmer provides.

Because you don't yet have such a rule, temporarily assume that the square-inch price of the first pizza is .0694 (6.94 cents) and the square-inch price of the second pizza is .0779 (7.79 cents). These facts would be stated as:

`squareinchprice(pizza1,.0694).` and
`squareinchprice(pizza2,.0779).`

Now, suppose you enter the query `?- betterdeal(pizza1,pizza2).`, which translates to "Is pizza1 a better deal than pizza2?" Figure 12-50 illustrates how Prolog uses the betterdeal rule to answer your query.

FIGURE 12-50

Prolog executes the betterdeal rule.

Facts

```
priceof(pizza1,10).

sizeof(pizza1,12).

shapeof(pizza1,square).

priceof(pizza2,12).

sizeof(pizza2,14).

shapeof(pizza2,round).

squareinchprice(pizza1,.0694).

squareinchprice(pizza2,.0779).
```

Betterdeal Rule

```
betterdeal(PizzaX,PizzaY) :-

    squareinchprice(PizzaX,AmountX),

    squareinchprice(PizzaY,AmountY),

    AmountX < AmountY.
```

Query

```
?- betterdeal(Pizza1,Pizza2).
```

1. Prolog instantiates pizza1 to PizzaX and pizza2 to PizzaY.

```
betterdeal(pizza1,pizza2) :-

    squareinchprice(pizza1,AmountX),

    squareinchprice(pizza2,AmountY),

    AmountX < AmountY.
```

2. Prolog looks through the facts to find the squareinchprice for pizza1 and pizza2. These prices are instantiated to AmountX and AmountY, respectively.

```
betterdeal(pizza1,pizza2) :-

    squareinchprice(pizza1,.0694),

    squareinchprice(pizza2,.0779),

    .0694 < .0779.
```

3. The last line now contains a statement that is true—.0694 < .0779—which validates the rule and produces "yes" as a response to your query, "Is pizza1 a better deal than pizza2?"

12

▶ Does the order of rules affect the way a Prolog program runs? When coding programs in a procedural language, such as C, Pascal, or BASIC, the order of program instructions is critically important. For example, if you place input statements for pizza size and price after the code that calculates the price per square inch, the program produces an error because it has no numbers to use for the calculation. In contrast, the order or sequence of rules in a Prolog program is usually not critical.

▶ What does the complete pizza program look like in Prolog? The complete pizza program includes the facts that describe two pizzas and rules that describe the better deal, square-inch price, and area. Figure 12-51 contains the Prolog code for the entire pizza program.

FIGURE 12-51

The Complete Prolog Program

```
priceof(pizza1,10).
sizeof(pizza1,12).
shapeof(pizza1,square).
priceof(pizza2,12).
sizeof(pizza2,14).
shapeof(pizza2,round).
betterdeal(PizzaX,PizzaY) :-
    squareinchprice(PizzaX,Amount1),
    squareinchprice(PizzaY,Amount2),
    Amount1 < Amount2.
area(Pizza,Squareinches) :-
    sizeof(Pizza,Side),
    shapeof(Pizza,square),
    Squareinches is Side * Side.
area(Pizza,Squareinches) :-
    sizeof(Pizza,Diameter),
    shapeof(Pizza,round),
    Radius is Diameter / 2,
    Squareinches is 3.142 * (Radius * Radius).
squareinchprice(Pizza,Amount) :-
    area(Pizza,Squareinches),
    priceof(Pizza,Dollars),
    Amount is Dollars / Squareinches.
```

INPUT CAPABILITIES

▶ **Can I generalize the program for any pizzas?** A version of the pizza program that contains facts, such as `priceof(pizza1,10).` and `priceof(pizza2,12).`, is limited to specific pizzas that cost $10.00 and $12.00. The program can be generalized by collecting input from the user and storing it in variables or by asserting new facts at runtime.

▶ **How do I collect input from the user?** You can use read and write statements. Examine the following program code to see how a Prolog program collects user input, then take the screentour in Figure 12-52 to see how the program interacts with users when it is run.

> Prolog uses the write predicate to display a prompt for input.

> The read predicate gathers input entered by the user, then the assertz predicate creates a fact, such as priceof(pizza1,12).

```
write(user,'enter price of pizza1: '),
read(user,Price1), assertz(priceof(pizza1,Price1)),
write(user,'enter size of pizza1: '),
read(user,Size1), assertz(sizeof(pizza1,Size1)),
write(user,'enter shape of pizza1: '),
read(user,Shape1), assertz(shapeof(pizza1,Shape1)),
write(user,'enter price of pizza2: '),
read(user,Price2), assertz(priceof(pizza2,Price2)),
write(user,'enter size of pizza2: '),
read(user,Size2), assertz(sizeof(pizza2,Size2)),
write(user,'enter shape of pizza2: '),
read(user,Shape2), assertz(shapeof(pizza2,Shape2)),
```

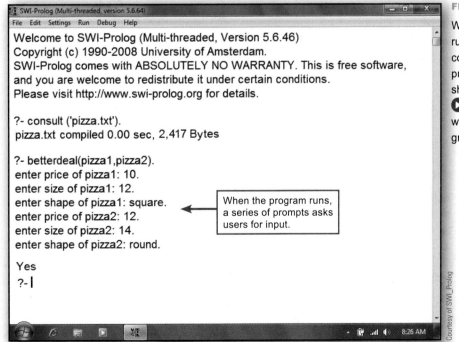

FIGURE 12-52

When the pizza program runs, read() predicates collect input for the prices, the sizes, and the shapes of two pizzas.
▶ See what happens when this Prolog program runs.

When the program runs, a series of prompts asks users for input.

DECLARATIVE LANGUAGES AND APPLICATIONS

▶ **What kinds of problems are suitable for the declarative approach?** As you have seen from the pizza example, it is possible to use a declarative language to solve a problem that involves calculations. However, problems that require intensive computation are not usually best suited for the declarative paradigm.

As a general rule, declarative programming languages are most suitable for problems that pertain to words and concepts rather than to numbers. These languages are a good choice for applications such as those listed in Figure 12-53.

▶ **What are the advantages and disadvantages of declarative languages?** Declarative languages offer a highly effective programming environment for problems that involve words, concepts, and complex logic. As you learned in this chapter, declarative languages offer a great deal of flexibility for querying a set of facts and rules. These languages also allow you to describe problems using words rather than the abstract structures procedural and object-oriented languages require.

Currently, declarative languages are not commonly used for production applications. To some extent, today's emphasis on the object-oriented paradigm has pushed declarative languages out of the mainstream, both in education and in the job market. Many aspiring programmers are never introduced to declarative languages, so they are not included in the languages evaluated for a specific project.

Declarative languages have a reputation for providing minimal input and output capabilities. Although many of today's Prolog compilers provide access to Windows and Mac user interface components, programmers are often unaware of this capability.

Although not in widespread use, declarative programming is popular in several niche markets. The U.S. Forest Service uses Prolog programs for resource management. Prolog programs are also used extensively in scientific research. The U.S. Department of Homeland Security experimented with a Prolog application developed to comb through social networking sites for terrorist activities. Finally, a growing trend is to incorporate Prolog modules with procedural and object-oriented programs to handle concept and language processing.

FIGURE 12-53

Examples of Applications That Are Suitable for Declarative Languages

▶ Databases that contain complex relationships— for example, a genealogy database used to trace ancestral lineage, or a street and highway database used for mapping routes

▶ Decision support systems that handle semi-structured problems—for example, a decision support system that helps determine tactics for military campaigns, or a system that helps planners efficiently allocate energy resources

▶ Expert systems that require analysis of multiple, interrelated factors—for example, an expert system that helps troubleshoot appliance repairs, or a program that translates documents from one language to another

QuickCheck   SECTION D

1. The declarative programming paradigm focuses on describing a(n) [_____], whereas the procedural paradigm focuses on algorithms that describe a(n) [_____].

2. In the Prolog fact location(balcony,H1), balcony and H1 are [_____], whereas location is referred to as the [_____].

3. A Prolog attribute can be a(n) [_____], such as round (with a lowercase r), or it can be a(n) [_____], such as Shape (with an uppercase S).

4. Finding the value for a variable while solving a Prolog goal is called [_____].

5. In a Prolog rule, the :- connecting symbol means [_____].

▶ CHECK ANSWERS

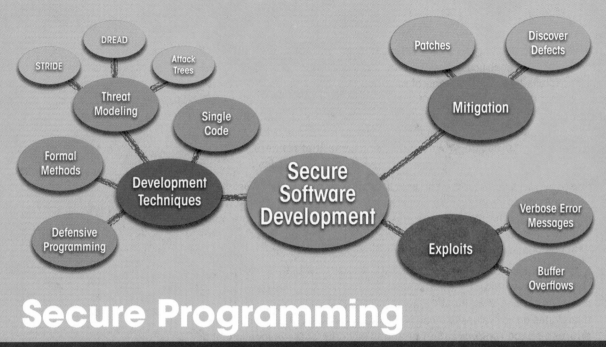

Secure Programming

HACKERS, CRACKERS, CYBERCRIMINALS, or black hats—no matter what you call them, their goal is to gain unauthorized access to information. The first line of defense in cyber security is computer programmers who create the applications, operating systems, and utilities that you use every day. Section E looks at program-level security vulnerabilities and what programmers can do to shore up security defenses.

BLACK HAT EXPLOITS

▶ What makes my computer vulnerable to attack? Viruses, worms, bots, malicious Web scripts, and other exploits creep into computer systems through security holes, but why do these holes exist?

Today's operating systems, utilities, and application software are full of defects that create security holes, which are exploited by black hats. Some of the most common software security defects include buffer overflows and verbose error messages.

▶ What is a buffer overflow? According to many experts, the most prevalent cause of security holes is program code that allows buffer overflows. A **buffer overflow** (also called a buffer overrun) is a condition in which data in memory exceeds its expected boundaries and flows into memory areas intended for use by other data. Figure 12-54 offers a simplified example of the problem.

FIGURE 12-54

A buffer overflow allows attackers to surreptitiously change the way a program works.

1. The programmer expects to collect a 2-byte state abbreviation as input for variable A. Variable B holds the address of the next instruction.

Variable A		Variable B		
		0	1	9

2. An attacker enters MI999. The 5-byte string overflows the buffer for variable A and spills over into variable B. Now variable B holds 999, which is not the correct address for the next instruction.

Variable A		Variable B		
M	I	9	9	9

3. When the program checks variable B to locate the next instruction, it goes to 999, where an attacker might have stored code for a virus, worm, bot, or malicious HTML script.

▶ **What causes buffer overflows?** Buffer overflows can be triggered by input specifically designed to execute malicious code. One of the first exploits to take advantage of buffer overflows was the Morris worm, which attacked the Internet in 1988. Since that time, Microsoft alone has disclosed hundreds of buffer overflow vulnerabilities in commonly used Windows components, such as Internet Explorer, Outlook, Plug and Play, the file decompression routine, and the routine that renders Windows Metafiles.

Sloppy C and C++ programming sets the stage for buffer overflows. C and C++, the two languages most commonly used for professional software development, offer little protection against buffer overflows. Commonly used routines, such as get() and strcpy(), from the standard C libraries perform no bounds checking and therefore allow buffer overflows.

▶ **Can buffer overflows be prevented?** Programmers can prevent buffer overflows by controlling pointers (or simply not using them), scrupulously checking input for suspicious characters, and placing strict boundaries on the values that can be stored in variables. A technique called **address space randomization** arranges key data areas in locations that are difficult for hackers to predict and target.

Some programming languages are less treacherous than C or C++. Languages such as D, Cyclone, Java, and C# offer a more structured programming environment in which pointers are less likely to go astray.

▶ **What is a verbose error message?** Applications fail for many reasons including hardware malfunctions, program bugs, and incompatibility with other software. Good programmers try to anticipate how a program might fail and include code to handle the failure as gracefully as possible. Often, the result is an error message displayed to the user.

When software is in developmental and testing phases, error messages can help programmers locate the source of errors if they contain information pertinent to the location of defective code and the state of variables. If those information-rich and verbose error messages remain when the software ships, hackers can use them to identify security vulnerabilities.

Some of the most common examples of verbose error messages appear during unsuccessful attempts to log in or access files. Those error messages, like the one in Figure 12-55, often give attackers information that makes break-ins easier.

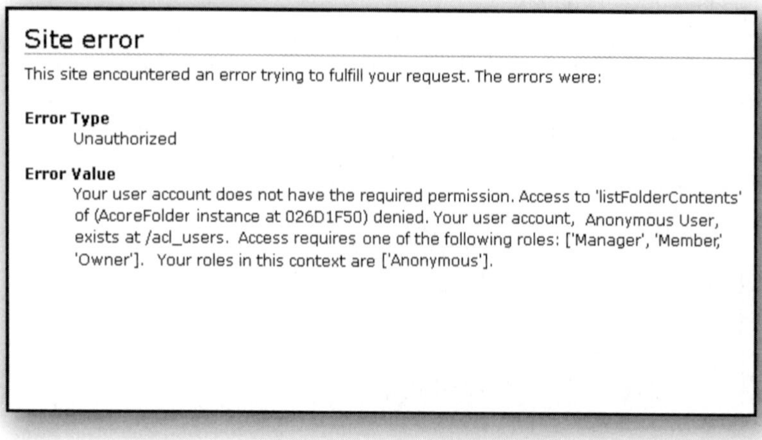

Site error

This site encountered an error trying to fulfill your request. The errors were:

Error Type
   Unauthorized

Error Value
   Your user account does not have the required permission. Access to 'listFolderContents' of (AcoreFolder instance at 026D1F50) denied. Your user account, Anonymous User, exists at /acl_users. Access requires one of the following roles: ['Manager', 'Member', 'Owner']. Your roles in this context are ['Anonymous'].

FIGURE 12-55

This verbose error message provides attackers with information about restricted access folder names and locations, as well as account names (Manager, Member, and Owner) that can gain access to these folders.

SECURE SOFTWARE DEVELOPMENT

▶ Is it possible to develop secure software? According to security experts, most software security problems can be traced back to defects that programmers unintentionally introduce in software during design and development. The general nature of the defects that open security holes is widely known and most can be eliminated.

Software security begins when program specifications are formulated. Techniques such as formal methods, threat modeling, attack trees, and defensive programming help programmers remain aware of security throughout the software development life cycle.

▶ What are formal methods? Formal methods help programmers apply rigorous logical and mathematical models to software design, coding, testing, and verification. Some software development methodologies incorporate formal methods, and organizations that use them tend to produce more secure software. Formal methods, however, add to the cost and time of software development, so they tend to be used only for life-critical systems, such as air traffic control and nuclear reactor control systems, where security and safety are crucial.

▶ What is threat modeling? Threat modeling (also called risk analysis) is a technique that can be used to identify potential vulnerabilities by listing the key assets of an application, categorizing the threats to each asset, ranking the threats, and developing threat mitigation strategies that can be implemented during coding. Threats can be categorized using a model like STRIDE as described in Figure 12-56.

FIGURE 12-56

STRIDE categories help software developers anticipate threats from attackers.

S poofing: Pretending to be someone else

T ampering: Changing, adding, or deleting data

R epudiation: Covering tracks to make attacks difficult to trace

I nformation disclosure: Gaining unauthorized access to information

D enial of service: Making a system unavailable to legitimate users

E levation of privilege: Modifying user rights to gain access to data

Some threats are more likely to occur than others, and some threats have the potential to cause more damage than others. As part of the threat modeling process, software designers can rank threats using the DREAD categories in Figure 12-57.

FIGURE 12-57

DREAD categories help software developers gauge the severity of threats.

D amage: How much damage can a particular attack cause?

R eproduce: Is this attack easy to reproduce?

E xploit: How much skill is needed to launch the attack?

A ffected: How many users would be affected by an attack?

D iscovered: How likely is it that this attack would be discovered?

▶ What is an attack tree? Attack trees offer another way to get a handle on potential threats. An **attack tree** is a hierarchical diagram of potential attacks against a system. The root of the upside-down tree-shaped diagram represents an attacker's ultimate objective, such as stealing passwords. The branches of the tree represent actions that attackers might take to achieve the objective.

By tracing paths through the attack tree, developers can discover which kinds of attacks are easiest, which are most difficult to detect, and which have the potential to cause the most damage. Figure 12-58 shows an attack tree for opening a safe.

FIGURE 12-58

Attack trees are used by security analysts in many fields. This diagram illustrates an attack tree that might be devised by a bank security officer examining the vulnerability of the bank vault.

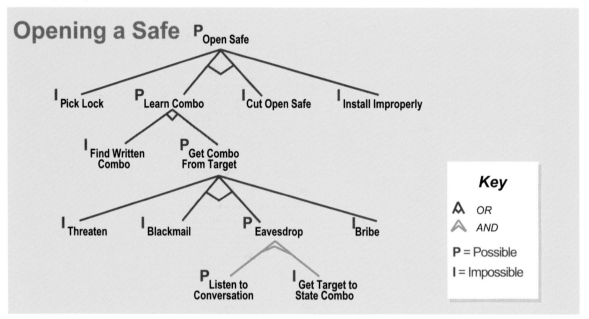

▶ What is defensive programming? **Defensive programming** (also referred to as secure programming) is an approach to software development in which programmers anticipate what might go wrong as their programs run, and take steps to smoothly handle those situations. It is analogous to defensive driving, which requires drivers to anticipate dangerous situations arising from adverse conditions or the mistakes of other drivers.

Defensive programmers anticipate ways in which their programs could be compromised by legitimate users, intruders, other applications, the operating system, or third-party security software. Avoiding code that allows buffer overflow is an example of defensive programming. Trapping program failures without displaying verbose error messages is another example. Techniques associated with defensive programming include:

▶ Source code walkthroughs. Open source software goes through extensive public scrutiny that can identify security holes, but proprietary software can also benefit from a walkthrough with other in-house programmers.

▶ Simplification. Complex code is more difficult to debug than simpler code. Simplifying complex sections of code can sometimes reduce a program's vulnerability to attacks.

▶ Filtering input. It is dangerous to assume that users will enter valid input. Attackers have become experts at concocting input that causes buffer overflows and runs rogue HTML scripts. Programmers should use a tight set of filters on all input fields.

▶ How does signed code help? **Signed code** is a software program that identifies its source and carries a digital certificate attesting to its authenticity. Its main advantage is to help users avoid downloading and running virus-infected or intrusive software. Signed code is wrapped in a sort of security blanket that contains the name of the software developer and ensures that the software will not run if even one bit of the source code is changed by a virus or any other factor.

Programmers who want to deliver signed code have to provide proof of their identity to a trusted third-party certification authority, such as VeriSign. Upon verification, the programmer is issued a code-signing utility and a certificate that can be used to sign any number of software products. To sign a product, the programmer uses the code-signing utility to encrypt the digital signature and program length. That encrypted information is incorporated in the product's executable file.

When a signed product is downloaded and launched, the encrypted signature is opened first, and the browser uses a client-side certificate validation routine to make sure the signature is valid and the program is the expected length before the actual product is opened and installed.

Signed certificates have been deployed for downloaded software, using a browser on the client end to verify the digital signature. Microsoft's Authenticode technology, for example, uses Internet Explorer as the verification client.

▶ Is signed code free of viruses? Signed certificates are not bulletproof. Fake certificates can be fashioned to look like the real ones and are likely to fool consumers who don't click the link to the certificate authority. Also, a signed certificate does not assure users that the original code was free of viruses or bugs. There is no third-party verification of the program's content, but programmers are unlikely to knowingly distribute infected code that could be traced back to its source through a signed certificate like the one in Figure 12-59.

FIGURE 12-59

A signed digital certificate identifies the source of a software program.

MITIGATION

▶ **What happens when vulnerabilities are discovered in products that have already shipped?** Despite defensive programming and other tactics for producing secure software, some defects inevitably remain undiscovered in products that end up in the hands of consumers. Some of those defects could be discovered and exploited by attackers.

To be fair, some exploits are caused by factors that didn't exist when a software product was in development. For example, features of a new operating system might interact with a product in such a way that previously secure code suddenly becomes vulnerable. When software bugs are discovered—especially if the bugs are being exploited by attackers—the programmer's remaining line of defense is to produce a bug fix, or patch.

▶ **What's up with all these patches?** In today's computing environment, patches seem to pop up like mushrooms after a spring rain. Computer users are encouraged to apply all available patches, and some software publishers such as Microsoft virtually force users to apply patches through an auto-update service.

To create a software patch, programmers first locate the source of the defect and make a judgment about its scope. Some patches require reworking an entire module, whereas small patches might affect just a few lines of code. Before being posted for users, patches should be thoroughly tested.

Patches can be supplied as complete files that simply overwrite an entire bad file with a more secure version. Patches can also be supplied as an inline code segment, which overwrites only a targeted section of code.

▶ **Are there steps consumers can take to mitigate security vulnerabilities that exist because of programming flaws?** You might remember seeing an error message like the one in Figure 12-60. The question "Do you want to debug?" could lead you to believe that you can simply correct program errors on your own. That is rarely the case. To debug software, you need access to source code or scripts. Even if those are available, as in the case of open source software, you would need programming expertise and knowledge of the application to locate the bug and fix it.

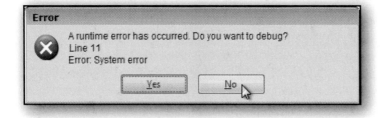

FIGURE 12-60

An error message that seems to offer an opportunity to fix a bug really isn't much use to most consumers.

Realistically, computer users have no control over software at the code level, but there are a few steps they can take to avoid security problems that stem from software defects:

▶ Select applications from software publishers with a good security track record.

▶ Watch for patches and apply them.

▶ Consider using open source software, which has been extensively reviewed by the programming community.

▶ And yes, keep your firewall and antivirus software deployed and up to date.

Security experts anticipate that buffer overflow and malicious script attacks may decline because social engineering exploits like phishing scams require much less technical expertise. Social engineering exploits pit attackers directly against consumers, and the techniques for fending off such attacks are typically out of the hands of programmers.

In addition to remaining vigilant to social engineering exploits, consumers should remain aware of the vulnerabilities related to software defects and factor that information into software purchase decisions.

12

QuickCheck   SECTION E

1. A(n) [_____] overflow is a condition in which data in memory exceeds its expected boundaries and flows into memory areas intended for use by other data.

2. To prevent hackers from guessing the location of critical program elements, programmers can use a technique called [_____] space randomization.

3. [_____] error messages can present attackers with information about the directory location of programs or files, the structure of a database, or the layout of the program in memory.

4. [_____] methods help programmers apply rigorous logical and mathematical models to the design of life-critical systems.

5. [_____] code produces a digital certificate, which identifies the source of a computer program but does not verify that the program code is free of viruses and other malware.

▶ CHECK ANSWERS

Issue: Too Violent to Sell to Kids?

A TEEN DIED from a stab wound inflicted by a friend who was described as obsessed with the game Mortal Kombat. A troubled teen in China jumped off a 22-story building after a marathon session playing World of Warcraft III. In Tennessee, two teenagers arrested for killing a motorist on Interstate 40 claimed they had been inspired by the game Grand Theft Auto: Vice City.

Real world teen violence has been linked to violent videogames by the news media, child advocacy groups, and several scientific studies. Some studies, however, found no evidence of a link. And far from an epidemic of teen violence that might be expected from a generation of children who grew up playing videogames, youth violence decreased by more than 50% between 1994 and 2007.

The debate about videogame violence started in 1976, when Exidy introduced a video console version of its Death Race arcade game. Players earned points by running over flocks of stick-figure gremlins.

The game's low res graphics were hardly realistic and a "kill" simply displayed an innocuous gravestone, yet the violent theme caused a public uproar and forced Exidy to pull the game from store shelves.

In 1992, the debate heated up when shoot-em-up games such as GameSpot's Mortal Kombat became the target of Congressional hearings. This generation of games depicted over-the-top, gory violence that usually ended in 2-D animated victims spewing blood in all directions.

To head off legislation that would restrict sales of violent videogames, the Entertainment Software Association formed the ESRB (Entertainment Software Rating Board), which doled out game ratings such as M, suitable for mature audiences, and E suitable for everyone.

These ratings did not satisfy many parents or child advocacy groups, and several states crafted legislation to keep violent games out of the hands of children. California passed a law in 2005 prohibiting the sale of violent videogames to minors. The law

"In some of these games, the violence is astounding. It also appears that there is no antisocial theme too base for some in the video-game industry to exploit."

Supreme Court Justice Alito concurring in BROWN v. ENTERTAINMENT MERCHANTS ASSN.

defined in detail elements that constitute a violent videogame. To conform to the law, violent videogame packaging was required to display a large "18" label. Selling a violent game to a minor could result in a fine up to US$1,000.

Even before the law was signed, videogame publishers mounted a legal challenge against it. The case moved through the court system and eventually reached the U.S. Supreme Court in 2011. California was joined by 11 other states that wanted to restrict videogame violence. They presented evidence from numerous studies linking videogames to real-world aggressive behavior and acts of violence.

Those who opposed the California law based their case on the First and Fourteenth Amendments, contending that the content of videogames is protected by principles of freedom of speech that protect books, plays, and movies.

The Supreme Court agreed, based in part on the notion that children have always been exposed to violent images when reading, for example, about Hansel and Gretel baking their captor in an oven, or watching Road Runner inadvertently blow himself up with a stick of dynamite. In a 7-2 decision, the Supreme Court tossed out the California law. Violent game sales to minors could no longer be prohibited.

Justice Alito agreed with the decision, but suggested that other legislation, more carefully crafted, might be acceptable. Alito was troubled by "the effect of exceptionally violent video games on impressionable minors, who often spend countless hours immersed in the alternative worlds that these games create."

Jason Della Rocca, former director of the International Game Developers Association, weighed in on the controversy, warning that videogames might be an easy scapegoat for problems that run deep within our society. "That's much easier than saying our society is messed up, people don't take care of each other, teachers aren't in control, there's rampant bullying, and there are no parents at home because they have to work two jobs."

Try It! Do you have an opinion about whether violent videogames encourage real-life violence? The issue might seem to have a simple answer, but it is one of those modern-day problems with a solution that erodes civil liberties, such as freedom of speech. You can explore various aspects of the issue through the following activities:

© iStockphoto.com/ryccio

1. Computer programmers are key members of the teams that create videogames. You might wonder if a simple, non-violent game can be compelling. See for yourself. Try your hand at designing a videogame using an online app such as Sploder.com or ChallengeYou.com.

2. Rating categories are assigned to videogames and to movies. How similar are the categories? Create a chart showing how the ratings match.

3. Exactly what is a violent videogame? You can look up California's definition by googling *Civil Code Section 1746-1746.5*. Would you say that this definition is detailed or general? Why?

4. Justices Thomas and Breyer disagreed with the Court's decision to throw out the California law that prohibited violent videogame sales to minors. You can find the full text of this decision by searching for *Brown v. Entertainment Merchants Association*. Read the first page of Thomas's dissent. Why does he believe that the California law was appropriate and should be upheld?

5. The Supreme Court threw out the California law based on the First and Fourteenth Amendments to the U.S. Constitution. The First Amendment includes wording about free speech. What part of the Fourteenth Amendment was critical to this case?

6. Find a study conducted within the last five years on the topic of real-life violence and videogame violence. Summarize the results of the study. Who conducted it? How was it carried out? Do you think the results are valid?

7. Optional: If you want to take a first-hand look at some of the most graphic videogames, check YouTube for *banned videogames*. On a scale of 1 to 10 (10 being close-your-eyes-cause-you-don't-want-to-watch), rate three of the banned games. Warning: This activity is optional because the images can be very offensive.

INFOWEBLINKS

You can check the **NP2013 Chapter 12** InfoWebLink for updates to these activities.

Ⓦ CLICK TO CONNECT
www.infoweblinks.com/np2013/ch12

ISSUE

What Do You Think?

1. Have you played violent videogames?

2. Do you believe that violent videogames contribute to teen violence?

3. Do you think that states might be able to craft legislation that limits violent videogame sales without eroding principles of free speech?

Information Tools: **Photo Forensics**

Digital tools make it easy to manipulate images. Many of the photos we see in magazines, newspapers, and online have been adjusted to improve color and contrast. But they can also be altered in ways that are intended to deceive viewers.

Some images are obviously fake. Just about everyone is familiar with tabloid cover photos with a celebrity's head pasted onto another person's body, and cosmetic ads airbrushed beyond believability.

Oprah's head on Ann Margret's body

Airbrushed skin

The top photo, supplied by the Iranian state media, was published in the New York Times and other newspapers before it was discovered that the photo had been doctored to conceal a malfunctioning missile (shown in the bottom unaltered photo). In the doctored photo, the third missile from the left was digitally added by cloning parts of the other missiles. Can you identify the cloned sections?

Although detailed photographic analysis is out of the hands of readers, most photo fakes are eventually unmasked. Before you base opinions on a dramatic photo or use an image to substantiate your own research, check Internet resources to make sure the photo is not a known fake.

According to researchers, most people can identify clumsy photo fakes by looking for body parts that seem out of proportion and cloned areas that repeat themselves within the image.

Savvy consumers understand that the faces and bodies depicted in ads are not always realistic, but they have different expectations about photojournalism and the photos published about world events.

Photos in mainstream news outlets affect our views and opinions of world events. Yet the photographs that record these events are sometimes manipulated to improve composition or convey a message.

To spot a fake photo, look for:

▶ Body parts that seem out of proportion

▶ Remnants of body parts, scenery, or objects removed from a photo

▶ Areas of lighting that seem brighter or darker than they should be

▶ Light and shadow that are not consistent for all objects in the photo

▶ Parts of the background or crowd that seem to be cloned duplicates

Try It! "If you can change photographs, you can change history." That quote from Hany Farid, a computer scientist specializing in digital forensics, contains a warning about the perils of digital photo manipulation. Here's your chance to find out how to uncover photo forgeries.

1. The Web site *www.fourandsix.com* has a "Photo Tampering throughout History" link with some surprising information about doctored photos, beginning with an iconic image of Abraham Lincoln. Look through the photo gallery and select the five photos you think are the most misleading and explain why.

2. It is surprisingly easy to edit digital photos using today's sophisticated graphics software. To see how it works, check out the YouTube video "Adobe Photoshop CS5: Content-Aware Fill Sneak Peek". List five of the items that were manipulated in the photo.

3. A Web site called TinEye bills itself as a reverse image search engine. Given any image, TinEye can find out where it came from and how it is being used. TinEye even finds modified versions of the image. Click the Goodies button and follow the Cool Searches link for some eye-opening examples of image modification. Then, upload an image of your own (or use an image that you select from the Web) to see what TinEye finds. Take a screenshot of your results. (Use the PrtScr or Print Screen key on a PC; use Command Shift 3 on a Mac.)

4. EXIF (Exchangeable Image File format) data can reveal information that helps to verify or unveil a photo's origins. Specialized software is needed to view all the EXIF data, but operating system utilities display some of the data. Select a photo stored in JPEG format and view its tags. On a PC, right-click the image, select Properties, and then select the Details tab. On a Mac, click File, click Get Info, and expand the More Info section. Which of the following are revealed?

   a. Date taken   c. Camera brand and model

   b. Date modified   d. Photographer

                        e. Place taken

5. A technique called error level analysis measures compression levels in JPEG images. In theory, images that have not been doctored will have consistent levels of compression across the entire image. Doctored images, however, may have areas that show different levels of compression.

   To see for yourself, connect to *errorlevelanaysis.com* and study the example. Next, upload an example of your own. Collect a screen image of the analysis. Use graphics software to change something on the original image. For example, you might superimpose a circle on it, or paste in a part from another photo. Upload it and collect a screen image. Did the analysis catch your modification?

6. When the eye cannot discern whether a photo is real or fake, photo detectives turn to computer science, mathematics, and physics. The same equations that are used to create light and shadows in 3-D rendered images can also be used to analyze the shadows in a suspicious photograph. Dartmouth researchers Kee and Farid conducted an analysis of a suspicious shadow in a frame of the 1962 Zapruder film of President Kennedy's assassination. Locate their research paper. What did they conclude? Was the film a fake or real?

12

Technology in Context: Agriculture

AGRICULTURE MIGHT SEEM like a low-tech enterprise, but many farmers are turning to technology for help managing their finances, crops, and livestock. Even home gardeners who need little more than a few seed packets and a hoe are digging into computer and Internet resources for tips on combating garden pests, growing spectacular roses, and producing a bumper crop of veggies.

Need to identify the pesky insect that's eating your tomatoes? Worried about the black spots appearing on your apple trees? Trying to figure out if that sprout is a flower or a weed? Many of your gardening questions are answered at sites sponsored by state and province extension services, the National Gardening Association, *Organic Gardening* magazine, and many more.

Computers first sprouted up on farms to take care of financial matters. Farming, like any business, is all about the bottom line—the profit that's left after paying for seed, feed, fertilizer, machinery, taxes, utilities, and labor. Tracking income and expenses provides essential information for analyzing ways to improve operations and generate more profit. To keep track of finances, farmers can use generic small-business accounting software, such as Quicken, or vertical market software designed especially for farming.

Farmers also use computers to maintain and analyze production records for crops and livestock. The Manitoba Milk Revenue Analyzer is an Excel spreadsheet template designed to help farmers pick the best dairy management scenario by analyzing factors such as feed costs and milk production levels. Cow Sense decision support software can help farmers improve cow herds and explore production, marketing, and financial alternatives.

How does a farmer decide whether to plant fields with soybeans, corn, or wheat? The Internet offers resources such as the Alberta Agriculture and Rural Development Web site where farmers can use an interactive crop cost calculator to compare profit potential for up to four crops. The calculator uses average market value for each crop and expected yield per acre based on the farm's growing zone. It produces a table that shows costs and estimated profit for each crop.

Suppose that a farmer decides to plant durum wheat. How much seed is needed? Too much seed is wasted money. Not enough seed produces scanty crops.

A Web-based seed calculator helps farmers decide how much seed is necessary to produce the desired plant population. It also provides instructions for calibrating the seeder so that it sows the correct amount of seed. And what if chickweeds are choking out the sunflower crop? Alberta's Agriculture Web site offers an expert system to determine the most effective herbicide.

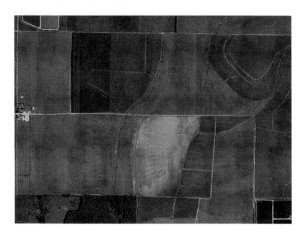

Farmers use the Internet to gather information about weather, market reports, farm equipment, loans, crops, and livestock. Lively discussions take place in "ag" chat groups, such as BackYardChickens, Crop Talk, and Hog Talk. Farmers subscribe to e-mail newsletters, such as Amber Waves, and tap government resources, such as the USDA (United States Department of Agriculture) Quarterly Hogs and Pigs report.

Farmers even use Twitter to publicize information about available produce. Chefs and gourmet grocers follow their favorite farmers' tweets to learn what's available so that they can obtain the freshest products for their customers.

The cutting edge of agricultural technology revolves around remote sensing, satellite imaging, geographical information systems, and global positioning systems. Remote sensing involves gathering information about an object without being in physical contact with it. For agriculture, two of the most often used remote sensing tools are satellite imaging and aerial photography.

Weather satellite images are readily available and help farmers decide the best days to plant and harvest crops. Topographical satellite images can help farmers analyze drainage patterns to prevent crops from being flooded. Other satellite images can be used for crop surveillance, such as looking for areas of low yield, drought, disease, and infestation.

A geographic information system (GIS) is a computer-based tool for storing data and creating layered maps of the earth's surface. A GIS can store data about many factors important to farmers, such as soil moisture, salinity, nitrogen levels, and acidity.

To collect data for a GIS, farmers use a GPS and a variety of monitoring devices. Throughout the growing season, farmers use GPSs to find specific locations in their fields where they record data from soil sampling and observations of weed growth, unusual plant stress, and growth conditions. They can enter this data into a GIS program, along with data from satellite images, to create maps that help them gauge where to plant, what to plant, and how to care for plants.

The experience of a North Dakota farmer illustrates how data from satellite images and GPS observations can be combined in a GIS to create valuable agricultural maps. The farmer was producing a bountiful harvest of sugar beets, but the crop's sugar content was low. The farmer enlisted the help of agriculture experts at a nearby university who obtained a satellite image of the fields that showed areas of high and low production.

The next step was to take soil samples—one every half acre. A handheld GPS was used to make sure samples were taken in an exact half-acre grid pattern. The satellite and soil sample data were then entered into a GIS, which showed that some areas of the field were low on nitrogen. The GIS produced

a map overlaid with a multicolored grid. Grid colors corresponded to the amount of nitrogen that should be applied for best production.

But how can the farmer apply these varying levels of nitrogen in each small area? GPS-equipped machinery is used to spread the correct amount of nitrogen in each area of the field. This selective fertilization, along with crop rotation to further even out nitrogen levels, increased the beets' sugar content and the farmer's income.

Applying detailed agricultural data collected with a GPS is called precision farming. Several specialized tools, such as GPS-equipped yield monitors, help farmers collect data on bushels per acre, wet and dry bushels, total pounds, acres per hour, acres worked, and grain moisture content. Yield monitors are usually installed on the combines that harvest crops. The collected data is recorded on a memory card for later analysis and mapping.

Although a variety of agricultural technologies are available, not all farmers embrace them with equal enthusiasm. Barriers to using technology such as computers, GISs, GPSs, and satellite imaging include cost, training, and concerns about reliability, privacy, and security.

The cost of obtaining satellite images, for example, has been the biggest deterrent to regular use of this data; the main barrier to the use of computers is simply a lack of expertise. Busy farmers might not have time to learn how to use even basic computer programs, and a fairly complex GIS database application can seem particularly daunting.

University and government agencies are targeting farmers with special extension courses on agriculture-specific software for accounting, livestock decision support, and crop management. The goal is to make these technology tools part of the legacy that will be handed down to the next generation of farmers.

AP Photo/Hays Daily News, Steven Hausler

12

New Perspectives Labs

To access the New Perspectives Lab for Chapter 12, open the NP2013 interactive eBook and then click the icon next to the lab title.

▶ USING A VISUAL DEVELOPMENT ENVIRONMENT

IN THIS LAB YOU'LL LEARN:

- How to use the basic tools provided by the Visual Basic VDE

- How to work with a form design grid

- How to select controls, such as buttons, menus, and dialog boxes, for the graphical user interface of a computer program

- The way that a visual development environment displays properties for a control

- How to set properties that modify the appearance and operation of a control

- About the variety of events that can affect a control

- How to add code that specifies how a control responds to events

- How to add a component to the Visual Basic toolbox, and then incorporate it into a program

- How to save and test a program

- How to compile a program and run the executable version

LAB ASSIGNMENTS

1. Start the interactive part of the lab. Make sure you've enabled Tracking if you want to save your QuickCheck results. Perform each lab step as directed, and answer all the lab QuickCheck questions. When you exit the lab, your answers are automatically graded and your results are displayed.

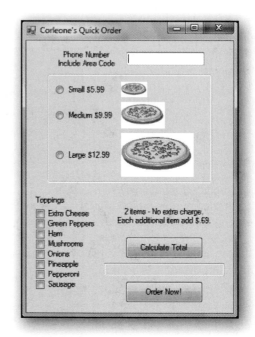

2. Draw a sketch of the main screen of your favorite word processing program. Identify five controls (such as menus, toolbars, lists, buttons, and scroll bars) provided by the programmer. Describe the external events (such as clicks, double-clicks, right-clicks, and mouseovers) to which each control responds.

3. Suppose you are preparing to write a program that calculates the number of calories you burn while exercising. The program requires users to enter their weight, the distance travelled, and the elapsed time in minutes from the beginning of the exercise to the end. Users should also be able to select from the following types of exercises: jogging, walking, swimming, and bicycling. After these calculations are entered, users should click a Calculate button to display the results of the calorie calculation. A Clear button should allow users to enter a new set of weight, distance, and time data. Sketch a form design grid like the one you used in the lab, and indicate where you would place each control necessary for this program's user interface.

Key Terms

Make sure you understand all the boldfaced key terms presented in this chapter. With the NP2013 interactive eBook, you can use this list of terms as an interactive study activity. First, try to define a term in your own words, and then click the term to compare your definition with the definition presented in the chapter.

12

Ada, 679
Address space randomization, 724
Agile methodology, 681
Algorithm, 689
API, 687
APL, 679
Argument, 714
Assembly language, 677
Assumption, 680
Attack tree, 726
BASIC, 679
Buffer overflow, 723
C, 679
C#, 679
C++, 679
Class, 702
Class attribute, 703
Class hierarchy, 704
COBOL, 679
Code, 674
Component, 687
Computer programming, 675
Constant, 681
Control, 683
Control structures, 695
CPL, 679
Debugger, 685
Decision table, 714
Declarative paradigm, 713
Defensive programming, 726
Eiffel, 679
Encapsulation, 712
Event, 684
Event-driven paradigm, 685
Event-handling code, 684
Fact, 713
Fifth-generation languages, 678
First-generation languages, 677

Flowchart, 692
Form design grid, 683
Formal methods, 725
Fortran, 679
Fourth-generation languages, 678
Function, 696
Goal, 715
Haskell, 679
High-level language, 676
IDE, 686
Inheritance, 704
Instantiation, 717
Iteration, 698
Java, 679
Keyword, 676
Known information, 680
LISP, 679
Logic error, 685
Loop, 698
Low-level language, 676
Message, 706
Method, 705
Multiparadigm languages, 679
Object, 702
Object-oriented paradigm, 702
Objective-C, 679
Parameters, 676
Pascal, 679
PL/1, 679
Polymorphism, 707
Predicate, 714
Predictive methodology, 681
Private attribute, 703
Problem statement, 680
Procedural language, 689
Procedural paradigm, 689
Procedure, 696
Program editor, 682

Programming language, 676
Programming paradigm, 679
Prolog, 679
Properties, 683
Pseudocode, 692
Public attribute, 703
REALbasic, 679
Remarks, 686
Repetition control structure, 698
RPG, 679
Rule, 713
Runtime error, 685
Scheme, 679
Scratch, 679
SDK, 686
Second-generation languages, 677
Selection control structure, 697
Sequence control structure, 695
Sequential execution, 695
Signed code, 727
SIMULA, 679
Smalltalk, 679
Structured English, 692
Subclass, 704
Subroutine, 696
Superclass, 704
Syntax, 676
Syntax error, 685
Third-generation languages, 677
Threat modeling, 725
Variable, 680
VDE, 683
Visual Basic, 679
Walkthrough, 694

Interactive Summary

To review important concepts from this chapter, fill in the blanks to best complete each sentence. When using the NP2013 interactive eBook, click the Check Answers buttons to automatically score your answers.

SECTION A: The instructions for a computer program are sometimes referred to as [   ]. Computer programmers focus on [   ] computer programs, but also plan, test, and document computer programs. In contrast, software [   ] tend to focus on designing and [   ] activities.

A computer programming language is a set of grammar rules and [   ] for creating instructions that can ultimately be processed by a computer. The first programming languages were low-level [   ] languages. Second-generation languages, called [   ] languages, allowed programmers to write programs consisting of abbreviated op codes instead of 1s and 0s. Third-generation languages provided programmers with easy-to-remember command words, such as PRINT and INPUT. Fourth-generation languages were designed to eliminate many of the strict punctuation and [   ] rules that complicated third-generation languages.

Some experts believe that [   ] languages, such as Prolog, constitute a fifth generation of computer languages. Other experts define fifth-generation languages as those that allow programmers to use graphical or visual tools to construct programs.

Before program code can be written, a programmer needs a clear problem [   ], which includes a list of assumptions, a description of known information, and a specification for what constitutes a solution. With a clear plan, a programmer can begin coding using a text editor, program editor, or [   ] development environment. A program is not complete until it has been tested to ensure that it contains no [   ] errors, logic errors, or runtime errors. All computer programs should include internal documentation in the form of [   ], which are explanatory comments inserted into a computer program along with lines of code.

▶ CHECK ANSWERS

SECTION B: A programming [   ] is a method that affects the way programmers conceptualize and approach a computer program. Every programming language supports one or more programming approaches. Languages such as COBOL and Fortran support a traditional approach to programming called the [   ] paradigm, which is based on a step-by-step [   ]. Various planning tools, such as structured English, [   ], and flowcharts, help programmers plan the steps for a procedural program.

Procedural languages provide programmers with a variety of [   ] structures for specifying the order of program execution. A(n) [   ] control structure directs the computer to execute one or more instructions, not coded as a simple succession of steps. A(n) [   ] control provides a choice of paths, based on whether a condition is true or false. A(n) [   ] control, or loop, repeats one or more instructions until a certain condition is met. The procedural paradigm provides a solid approach to problems that can be solved by following a set of steps. Procedural languages tend to produce programs that run quickly and use system resources efficiently.

▶ CHECK ANSWERS

SECTION C: The object-oriented paradigm is based on the idea that the solution to a problem can be visualized in terms of objects that [ ] with each other. An object is a single instance of an entity. Programmers can use a(n) [ ] as a template for a group of objects with similar characteristics. Classes can be derived from other classes through a process called [ ] . The set of superclasses and subclasses that are related to each other is referred to as a class [ ] . OO programmers often use [ ] Modeling Language diagrams to plan the classes for a program.

Objects interact to solve problems by exchanging [ ] , which initiate an action, process, or procedure. OO programmers can create [ ] to define what happens once an action is initiated. For flexibility, a concept called [ ] , or overloading, allows programmers to create a single, generic name for a procedure that behaves in unique ways for different classes. The OO paradigm allows programmers to hide the internal details of objects and their methods. This process, called [ ] , allows objects to be easily reused, modified, and repurposed.

▶ CHECK ANSWERS

SECTION D: Programming languages such as Prolog support the [ ] programming paradigm because they encourage programmers to describe a(n) [ ] rather than its solution. Prolog programs are typically based upon a collection of facts and rules. A Prolog fact begins with a(n) [ ] , such as shapeof, followed by a series of [ ] within parentheses, such as (pizza,round). Each Prolog rule has a(n) [ ] , which defines an outcome or fact, followed by the notation :-, which means "if." The body of the rule consists of one or more clauses that define conditions that must be satisfied

to validate the head of the rule. Prolog uses a process called [ ] to evaluate facts and rules to determine whether they are true. In Prolog jargon, a question or query to a program's database is called a(n) [ ] .

Declarative languages, such as Prolog, can be used for problems that require calculations, but those problems are typically better suited to [ ] languages. As a general rule, declarative languages are best suited for problems that pertain to words and concepts rather than numbers.

▶ CHECK ANSWERS

SECTION E: According to most experts, the primary cause of security holes is a(n) [ ] overflow, a condition in which data in memory exceeds its expected boundaries and flows into memory areas intended for use by other data. Hackers also use verbose [ ] messages to uncover security vulnerabilities. Developing secure software depends on rigorous software development techniques, such as [ ] methods, which generate proof that the program code meets listed requirements, and [ ] modeling that can be used to identify potential vulnerabilities to

security breaches. A technique called [ ] programming focuses on source code walkthroughs, simplification, and filtering input. [ ] code is a software program that identifies its source and carries a digital certificate attesting to its authenticity. Despite the best development efforts, code defects are sometimes found after products ship and must be remedied with [ ] . Consumers should remain aware of the vulnerabilities related to software defects and factor them into software purchase decisions.

▶ CHECK ANSWERS

12

Interactive Situation Questions

Apply what you've learned to some typical computing situations. When using the NP2013 interactive eBook, you can type your answers, and then use the Check Answers button to automatically score your responses.

1. A friend asks you for help writing a computer program to calculate the square yards of carpet needed for a dorm room. The statement "the living room floor is rectangular" is an example of a(n) [   ] . The length and width of the room are examples of [   ] information, which you can obtain as [   ] from the user.

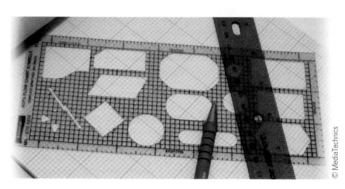

2. Continuing with the carpet example, you devise a set of steps, or a(n) [   ] , to solve the problem. You then use a programming language to write the [   ] shown below, which expresses the algorithm.

```
Input "Enter the width of the room in
   feet: "; width
Input "Enter the length of the room in
   feet: "; length
Print "Carpet needed:"
Print length*width & " square feet"
Print (length*width)/9 & "square yards"
```

3. Examine the code shown below. This program prints [   ] lines of text.

```
For n = 1 To 5
    Print "Loop number " & n
Next n
```

4. You've just joined a programming team that is developing a Java program for an earth-moving equipment vendor. The lead programmer shows you a UML with labels such as Cranes, Trucks, and Front-end Loaders. With your background in object-oriented programming, you can tell immediately that these are [   ] , which will be coded as a series of attributes, such as `private string manufacturer`.

5. While browsing through several programs posted online, you come across the following code and realize it is written using the [   ] programming language.

```
male(frodo).
male(mungo).
male(largo).
male(balbo).
female(berylla).
female(belladonna).
female(primula).
female(sella).
parents(mungo,berylla,balbo).
parents(frodo,primula,drogo).
parents(largo,berylla,balbo).
parents(sella,berylla,balbo).
brother_of(X,Y):-
    male(Y),
    parents(X,Mother,Father),
    parents(Y,Mother,Father).
```

 CHECK ANSWERS

Interactive Practice Tests

Practice tests that consist of ten multiple-choice, true/false, and fill-in-the-blank questions are available in the NP2013 interactive eBook. Test questions are selected at random from a large test bank, so each time you take a test, you'll receive a different set of questions. Your tests are scored immediately, and you can print study guides that help you find the correct answers for any questions that you missed.

CLICK TO START

Learning Objectives Checkpoints

Learning Objectives Checkpoints are designed to help you assess whether you have achieved the major learning objectives for this chapter. You can use paper and pencil or word processing software to complete most of the activities.

1. Provide a ballpark figure for the number of lines of code in an operating system such as Windows 7.

2. Describe how the jobs performed by computer programmers differ from the jobs performed by software engineers and systems analysts.

3. Create a diagram that shows how low-level and high-level languages relate to the five generations of computer languages.

4. Describe the differences between event-driven, procedural, object-oriented, and declarative paradigms. Provide at least one example of a language that supports each paradigm.

5. Describe the three elements of a problem statement. Provide examples within the context of the pizza problem.

6. List and describe three types of errors that are typically found when computer programs are tested.

7. List and describe at least eight tools other than programming languages that programmers use to create computer programs.

8. Define the term *algorithm* and explain how it relates to procedural programming.

9. Create a flowchart, structured English, and pseudocode to express the algorithm for tying your shoes.

10. Give an example of a sequence control structure, a selection control structure, and a repetition control structure.

11. Define the following terms associated with object-oriented programming: object, class, superclass, subclass, attribute, message, method, inheritance, polymorphism, and encapsulation.

12. Define the following terms associated with the declarative paradigm: fact, rule, predicate, arguments, goal, instantiation, and backtracking.

13. Write at least five Prolog facts that describe your relationships to members of your family.

14. Describe how buffer overflows and verbose error messages make computer programs vulnerable to hackers.

15. Create a sentence outline for Section E that focuses on techniques for secure programming.

16. List steps that consumers can take to avoid vulnerabilities that exist in defective software code.

Study Tip: Make sure you can use your own words to correctly answer each of the purple focus questions that appear throughout the chapter.

12

Concept Map

Fill in the blanks to show the hierarchy of programming paradigms described in this chapter.

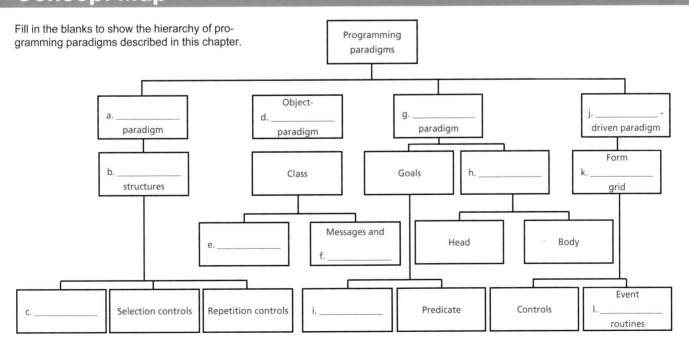

CHECK ANSWERS

GLOSSARY

3-D graphics A type of digital graphics format that displays a three-dimensional image on a two-dimensional space. 449

3-D graphics software The software used to create three-dimensional wireframe objects, then render them into images. 124

64-bit processor A microprocessor with registers, an address bus, and a data bus that holds 64 bits of data, in contrast to 32-bit processors that hold 32 bits of data. 68

AAC (Advanced Audio Coding) A file format that provides highly compressed audio files with very little loss of sound quality and is promoted by Apple on its iTunes Web site. 425

AACS (Advanced Access Content System) A digital rights management system that uses encryption to restrict access and copying content from optical media. 469

Abacus A manual calculator that consists of beads mounted on sticks inside a frame with each bead representing a specific quantity. 487

Absolute reference In a worksheet formula, cell references (usually preceded by a $ symbol) that cannot change as a result of a move or copy operation. 138

Acceptance testing The final phase of testing for a new information system, in which the system's new owner determines whether the system performs as required. 586

Access control Security measures that limit access to systems, such as databases. 655

Access time The estimated time for a storage device to locate data on a disk, usually measured in milliseconds. 77

Accounting software A category of software that includes accounting, money management, and tax preparation software. 126

ActionScript A scripting language used primarily to develop Flash applications and Web sites that include Flash media, such as Flash videos and animations. 372

ActiveX control A set of commands and components that can be used by programmers to add interactive features to Web pages. 373

Actors Object-oriented jargon for people who use an information system. 573

Ad hoc report A customized report (also called a demand report) generated as needed. 561

Ad-blocking software A type of software that prevents ads from appearing on your computer screen. 385

Ad-serving cookie A cookie installed by a marketing firm to track user activities on Web sites containing its ads. 400

Ada A high-level programming language developed by the U.S. Department of Defense and originally intended for military applications. 679

Adaptive utilities Utility software that alters a device's user interface to create an accessible environment for individuals with disabilities. 130

Address space randomization Also referred to as address space layout randomization (ASLR); a computer security technique in which program data is arranged in RAM according to an unpredictable arrangement, making it more difficult for hackers to locate key data and change it. 724

AES (Advanced Encryption Standard) An encryption standard that uses three separate key sizes and is based on the Rijndael encryption algorithm. 285

Agile methodology An approach to software development that produces programs in an incremental way, allowing specifications to evolve at each iteration. 681

AirPort A term used by some versions of Apple networking utilities to denote wireless or Wi-Fi connections. 263

Algorithm An abstract or general procedure for solving a problem, typically expressed as pseudocode, structured English, or a flowchart. 689

All-in-one computer A desktop computer form factor in which the system unit and touch screen are integrated into a single unit. 58

Alpha test One of the first phases of software testing, usually conducted by the software publisher's in-house testing team. 504

ALU (Arithmetic Logic Unit) The part of the CPU that performs arithmetic and logical operations on the numbers stored in its registers. 31

Always-on connection In the context of Internet access, a permanent connection, as opposed to a connection that is established and dropped as needed. 307

Analog data Data that is measured or represented on a continuously varying scale, such as a dimmer switch or a watch with a sweep second hand. 22

Analog hole Any device or technique that allows digital content to be copied legally or illegally from an analog device. 465

Analysis phase Tasks performed by the project team whose goal is to produce a list of requirements for a new or revised information system. 571

Analytical Engine A mechanical calculator designed by Charles Babbage that included memory and a programmable processor, and is widely regarded as the most important ancestor to modern computer design. 488

Android OS An open source operating system used primarily for handheld devices. 203

Anonymizer tools Software and/or hardware that cloaks the origination of an e-mail or Web page request. 11

Anonymous FTP A type of FTP access that requires no account on a server, but rather can be accessed using "anonymous" as the user ID. 336

Anonymous proxy service A server on the Internet that can be used to forward Web requests after cloaking the originating address for users who want to surf anonymously. 403

Antispyware Software that blocks spyware from entering a computer. 403

Antivirus software A computer program used to scan a computer's memory and disks to identify, isolate, and eliminate viruses. 167

API (application program[ming] interface) A set of application programs or operating system functions that can be utilized by a program. 687

APL The acronym for A Programming Language, a high-level scientific programming language used to manipulate tables of numbers. 679

Apple I An unassembled computer kit released in 1976 by Apple Computer Inc. for computer hobbyists. 496

Apple II A complete microcomputer system, developed by Apple Computer Inc. and introduced in 1978, that helped broaden the personal computer market beyond hobbyists. 496

Apple Lisa A personal computer system, developed and manufactured by Apple Computer Inc., that featured one of the first graphical user interfaces. 496

Apple Macintosh First released in 1984, it was one of the first commercially successful personal computers sold with graphical user interface software. 496

Application development tool Software, such as 4GLs, expert system shells, and component objects, that can be assembled into the applications software for an information system. 578

Application software Computer programs that help you perform a specific task such as word processing. Also called application programs, applications, or programs. 16

Application specifications A detailed description of the way that the software for an information system should interface with the user, store data, process data, and format reports. 581

Application testing The process of testing newly developed application software by running unit tests, integration tests, and system tests. 584

Apps Short for applications; popularly used to refer to applications available for the iPhone, iPad, and other mobile devices. 16

Argument In the context of Prolog programming, an argument describes a predicate and is enclosed in parentheses in a Prolog fact. 714

ASCII (American Standard Code for Information Interchange) A code that represents characters as a series of 1s and 0s. Most computers use ASCII code to represent text, making it possible to transfer data between computers. 24

ASF (Advanced Systems Format) Microsoft's proprietary container format for streaming digital multimedia; typically holds WMV and WMA files. 458

Assembly language A low-level computer programming language that uses simple commands and is translated into machine language by an assembler. 677

Assumption In the context of programming, a condition that you accept to be true, which often places limits on the scope of the programming problem. 680

Asymmetric Internet connection Any connection to the Internet in which the upstream speed differs from the downstream speed. 310

Asynchronous communications A communications mode, such as forums, e-mail, blogs, and tweets, in which participating parties do not have to be online at the same time. 332

Atanasoff-Berry Computer (ABC) An early electronic computer prototype that incorporated the use of vacuum tubes for data processing instead of mechanical switches. 489

Attack tree A hierarchical diagram of potential threats to a system used as one tool in creating more secure software. 726

Audio compression Techniques used to reduce the size of files that contain audio data. 424

Audio editing software A program that enables users to create and edit digital voice and music recordings. 121

Authentication protocol Passwords, user IDs, and biometric measures used to verify a person's identity. 34

Automatic recalculation A feature found in spreadsheet software that automatically recalculates every formula after a user makes a change to any cell. 138

AVI (Audio Video Interleave) A video file format, developed by Microsoft, that was once the most common format for desktop video on the PC. 458

B2B (business-to-business) An e-commerce exchange of products, services, or information between businesses. 385

B2C (business-to-consumer) An e-commerce exchange of products, services, or information between businesses and consumers. 385

B2G (business-to-government) An e-commerce exchange of products, services, or information between businesses and governments. 385

Backup A duplicate copy of a file, disk, or tape. Also refers to a Windows utility that allows you to create and restore backups. 222

Backup software A set of utility programs that performs a variety of backup-related tasks, such as helping users select files for backup, copying, and restoring. 226

Bandwidth The data transmission capacity of a communications channel. Digital signals are measured in bits per second; analog signals in Hertz. 251

Banner ad A type of advertisement typically embedded at the top of a Web page. 385

Bare-metal restore A process by which a backup is restored to a hard disk without first reinstalling the operating system and device drivers. 229

BASIC (Beginners All-purpose Symbolic Instruction Code) A simple high-level programming language that was popularized by Microsoft in the 1970s. 679

Batch processing A processing system that involves holding a group of transactions for processing until the end of a specified period of time. 560

Benchmarks A set of tests used to measure computer hardware or software performance. 70

Beta test A testing phase near the end of the software development process in which a software product is tested in real-world computer environments, often by end users. 504

BI (Business Intelligence) An integrated set of technologies and procedures used to collect and analyze data pertaining to sales, production, and other internal operations of a business in order to make better business decisions. 569

Binary number system A method for representing numbers using only two digits: 0 and 1. Contrast to the decimal number system, which uses ten digits: 0, 1, 2, 3, 4, 5, 6, 7, 8, and 9. 23

Biometrics The use of physical attributes, such as a fingerprint, to verify a person's identity. 34

Bit The smallest unit of information handled by a computer. A bit is one of two values, either a 0 or a 1. Eight bits constitute a byte, which can represent a letter or number. 23

Bitmap graphic An image, such as a digital photo, that is stored as a grid work of colored dots. 430

Bitrate A ratio such as 5:1 that indicates the ratio of compression that has been applied to a file. High compression ratios such as 35:1 indicate more compression so data can be contained in smaller files. 457

BitTorrent A peer-to-peer technology in which pieces of files are distributed to and from a collection of networked computers; used for distributing music and movies over the Internet. 337

BlackBerry OS The operating system software designed for handheld BlackBerry devices. 202

BLOB (binary large object) A collection of binary data, such as a graphic or audio clip, that is stored in a single field of a database. 635

Blog (Web log) A publicly-accessible personal journal posted on the Web. Blogs often reflect the personality of the author and are typically updated daily. 333

Blu-ray A high-capacity storage technology that stores up to 25 GB per layer on Blu-ray discs (BDs). 81

Blu-ray disc movie (BDMV) A file format used for storing high-definition video clips on Blu-ray discs. 458

Blue screen of death An error condition in which a PC "freezes" and displays a black screen (blue screen prior to Windows Vista); usually turning the computer off and turning it on again clears the error. 103

Bluetooth A wireless technology used in conjunction with standard Ethernet networks that allows data transfer rates between 200 and 700 Kbps up to a maximum range of 35 feet. 261

BMP The native bitmap graphic file format of the Microsoft Windows OS. 431

Boot disk A floppy disk or CD that contains the files needed for the boot process. 227

Boot process The sequence of events that occurs within a computer system between the time the user starts the computer and the time it is ready to process commands. 192

Bootstrap program A program stored in ROM that loads and initializes the operating system on a computer. 192

Bot An intelligent agent that autonomously executes commands behind the scenes. Sometimes used to refer to a remote access Trojan horse that infects computers. 164

Botnet A group of bots under the remote control of a botmaster, used to distribute spam and denial-of-service attacks. 164

BPR (Business Process Reengineering) A technique for improving a business by making radical changes to existing business procedures or organizational structure. 569

Break reminder software Software designed to signal users when it is time to take a break in order to avoid various repetitive-use and stress injuries. 541

Bridge A device that connects two similar networks by simply transferring data without regard to the network format. 267

Broadband A term used to refer to communications channels that have high bandwidth. 251

Broadcast flag A status flag inserted into the data stream of digital television to indicate whether it can be copied. 467

Brute force attack A method of breaking encryption code by trying all possible encryption keys. 37

BSD license (Berkeley Software Distribution) An open source software license patterned on a license originally used by the University of California. 160

Buffer overflow A condition that can be exploited by hackers in which data overflows its intended memory space to affect other variables; also called buffer overrun. 723

Business An organization that seeks profit by providing goods and services. 556

Button An on-screen graphical control that can be clicked to initiate an action or command. 190

Byte An 8-bit unit of data that represents a single character. 26

C A compiled procedural language that provides both high-level commands and low-level access to hardware. 679

C# A derivative of the C++ programming language developed by Microsoft. 679

C++ An object-oriented version of the C programming language. 679

C2C (consumer-to-consumer) An e-commerce exchange of products, services, or information between consumers; for example, online auctions. 385

Cable Internet service A type of Internet connection offered to subscribers by cable television companies. 316

Cable modem A communications device that can be used to connect a computer to the Internet via the cable TV infrastructure. 317

CAD software (computer-aided design software) A program designed to draw 3-D graphics for architecture and engineering tasks. 124

Capacitors Electronic circuit components that store an electrical charge; in RAM, a charged capacitor represents an "on" bit, and a discharged one represents an "off" bit. 72

Card reader A device that can be used to read and record data on solid state storage devices, such as flash memory cards. 84

Cardinality A description of the numeric relationship (one-to-one, one-to-many, or many-to-many) that exists between two record types. 616

Case sensitive A condition in which uppercase letters are not equivalent to their lowercase counterparts. 35

Case sensitive database A database in which uppercase letters are not equivalent to their lowercase counterparts. 636

CASE tool (computer-aided software engineering) Software that is used to summarize system requirements, diagram current and proposed information systems, schedule development tasks, prepare documentation, and develop computer programs. 574

CCD (charge-coupled device) One of the components in a digital camera that captures light from an image and converts it into color data. 433

CD (compact disc) An optical storage medium used to store digital information. CD-ROMs are read only. CD-Rs and CD-RWs can be used to record data. 81

Cell In spreadsheet terminology, the intersection of a column and a row. In cellular communications, a limited geographical area surrounding a cellular phone tower. 136

Cell references The column letter and row number that designate the location of a worksheet cell. For example, the cell reference C5 refers to a cell in column C, row 5. 137

Central processing unit (CPU) The main processing circuitry within a computer or chip that contains the ALU, control unit, and registers. 15

Centralized processing An information system design in which data is processed on a centrally located computer, usually a mainframe. 577

Change requests A formal, written request to add, delete, or change the features of an information system. 582

Channel conflict A situation in which computer vendors, from retail, wholesale, or mail-order channels, compete for customers. 508

Character data Letters, symbols, or numerals that will not be used in arithmetic operations (name, Social Security number, etc.). 24

Chat Interactive real-time person-to-person communication over a network. 331

Chief information officer (CIO) The highest-ranking executive responsible for information systems. 510

Chipmakers Companies that design and manufacture computer chips used in a wide variety of computer-related applications. 499

Ciphertext An encrypted message. 285

Circuit switching The method used by the telephone network to temporarily connect one telephone with another for the duration of a call. 253

CISC (complex instruction set computer) A general-purpose microprocessor chip designed to handle a wider array of instructions than a RISC chip. 69

Class In object-oriented terminology, a group with specific characteristics to which an object belongs. 702

Class attribute In the context of object-oriented programming, a class attribute defines a characteristic for the members of a class. Similar to a field in a database. 703

Class diagram A diagram that provides the name of each object, a list of the object's attributes, a list of methods, and an indication of the cardinality between objects. 573

Class hierarchy Like a hierarchical diagram, a class hierarchy is a set of related superclasses and subclasses defined within the object-oriented paradigm. 704

Click-through rate The number of times Web site visitors click an ad to connect to an advertiser's site. 385

Client A computer or software that requests information from another computer or server. 18

Client-side script Scripting statements embedded in an HTML document that are executed by a client's browser. 372

Cloud computing A type of computing in which local devices access applications that run on a remote server, where data can also be stored. 9

Cluster A group of sectors on a storage medium that, when accessed as a group, speeds up data access. 219

COBOL (COmmon Business-Oriented Language) A high-level programming language used for transaction processing on mainframe computers. 679

Code In the context of computer programming, code can be used as a noun to refer to the set of instructions that form a program, or as a verb that refers to the process of writing a program. 674

Code of ethics A set of guidelines designed to help professionals make on-the-job ethical decisions. 530

Codec Short for compressor/decompressor; a hardware or software routine that compresses and decompresses digital graphics, sound, and video files. 457

Color depth The number of bits that determines the range of possible colors that can be assigned to each pixel. For example, an 8-bit color depth can create 256 colors. 90

Color palette The selection of colors used in a graphic; also called color lookup table or color map. 438

COLOSSUS An early electronic computer prototype that used binary data representation and was used during WWII to decode messages encrypted by ENIGMA. 490

Command-line interface A style of user interface that requires users to type commands, rather than use a mouse to manipulate on-screen controls. 189

Commercial software Copyrighted computer applications sold to consumers for profit. 159

Commit or rollback strategy A procedure in transaction processing systems that will nullify, or roll back, a transaction if all the steps cannot be finalized or committed to. 560

Communications channel Any pathway between the sender and receiver; *channel* may refer to a physical medium or a frequency. 251

Communications port In the context of computer networking, a virtual location for data that arrives or leaves the device; common ports include 21 for FTP, 110 for e-mail, and 80 for Web data. 340

Communications protocol A set of rules that ensures the orderly and accurate transmission and reception of data. 252

Compiler Software that translates a program written in a high-level language into low-level instructions before the program is executed. 30

Component Prewritten objects or modules that programmers can customize and add to their own programs. 687

Compression ratio A ratio such as 5:1 that indicates the ratio of compression that has been applied to a file. High compression ratios such as 35:1 indicate more compression so data can be contained in smaller files. 457

Compute-intensive Refers to any task, problem, or product that is able to handle massive amounts of data and complex mathematical calculations. 19

Computed field A calculation that a DBMS performs during processing and then temporarily stores in a memory location. 635

Computer A device that accepts input, processes data, stores data, and produces output according to a stored program. 14

Computer engineer A computer professional who focuses on the design and development of computer hardware and peripheral devices. 512

Computer engineering A career that focuses on the design and development of computer hardware and peripheral devices. 514

Computer industry The corporations and individuals that supply computer-related goods and services to individuals and organizations. 498

Computer network A collection of computers and related devices, connected in a way that allows them to share data, hardware, and software. 8

Computer operator A computer professional who works directly with and maintains mainframe computers. 511

Computer professional Any person whose primary occupation involves one or more aspects of computer technology. 510

Computer program A detailed set of instructions that tells a computer how to solve a problem or carry out a task. 15

Computer programmer A person who designs, codes, and tests computer programs. 511

Computer programming The process of designing, coding, and testing computer programs. 675

Computer retailers Also called resellers; companies that sell computer-related products. 499

Computer salesperson A computer professional who sells computers and computer-related products. Also called a sales rep. 512

Computer science A career field that focuses on developing fast and efficient computers from their construction to their programming and operating systems. 514

Computer virus A program designed to attach itself to a file, reproduce, and spread from one file to another, destroying data, displaying an irritating message, or otherwise disrupting computer operations. 163

Computer worm A software program designed to enter a computer system, usually a network, through security "holes" and then replicate itself. 163

Concurrent-use license Legal permission for an organization to use a certain number of copies of a software program at the same time. 157

Confidentiality The obligation not to disclose willingly any information obtained in confidence. 526

Constant In the context of programming, a constant represents an unchanging value. In contrast, the data held in a variable can change. 681

Container formats File formats, typically for storing sound and video, that contain one or more types of data that is compressed using standard codecs. 458

Contract worker A computer professional who does not work directly for one company and often is paid by the job instead of a salary. 513

Control In the context of graphical user interfaces, a control is a screen-based object whose behavior can be specified by a programmer. 683

Control structures Instructions that specify the sequence in which a program is to be executed: sequence, selection, and repetition controls. 695

Control unit The part of the microprocessor that directs and coordinates processing. 31

Convergence In the context of technology, the melding of digital devices into a single platform that handles a diverse array of digital content, such as cell phones that also play digital music and display digital video. 9

Cookie A message sent from a Web server to a browser and stored on a user's hard disk, usually containing information about the user. 368

Copy protected Any digital rights management technology designed to prevent duplication of digital content; also referred to as copy prevention or copy restriction. 466

Copyright A form of legal protection that grants certain exclusive rights to the author of a program or the owner of the copyright. 156

Copyright notice A line such as "Copyright 2007 by ACME CO" that identifies a copyright holder. 156

CPL (Combined Programming Language) A programming language developed in the 1960s for scientific and commercial applications. 679

CPU (central processing unit) The main processing circuitry within a computer or chip that contains the ALU, control unit, and registers. 15

CPU cache Special high-speed memory providing the CPU rapid access to data that would otherwise be accessed from disk or RAM. 68

CREATE An SQL command that produces a new table in a database. 646

CRM (Customer Relationship Management) A technique for increasing profitability by improving the relationship between a company and its customers. 569

Cropping The process of selecting and removing part of an image. 436

Cryptographic algorithm A specific procedure for encrypting and decrypting data. 285

Cryptographic key A specific word, number, or phrase that must be used to encrypt or decrypt data. 285

CSS (Content Scramble System) A DRM technology designed to prevent unauthorized duplication of DVDs. 469

Data In the context of computing and data management, *data* refers to the symbols that a computer uses to represent facts and ideas. 15

Data bus An electronic pathway or circuit that connects the electronic components (such as the processor and RAM) on a computer's motherboard. 94

Data center A specialized facility designed to house and protect computer systems and data. 592

Data dependence The undesirable situation in which data and program modules become so interrelated that modifications become difficult. 624

Data flow On a DFD, a line with an arrow on the end, which indicates the direction in which data flows. 572

Data flow diagram (DFD) A diagram that illustrates how data moves through an information system. 572

Data fork An element of the Macintosh file system that comprises the part of the file that contains the text, audio, or video data; contrast with resource fork. 199

Data independence The separation of data from the programs that manipulate the data. 624

Data mining Analyzing data to discover patterns and relationships that are important to decision making. 612

Data processing An input-processing-output cycle that converts data into information. 6

Data redundancy Repetition of data within a database. 637

Data representation The use of electronic signals, marks, or binary digits to represent character, numeric, visual, or audio data. 22

Data store A filing cabinet, disk, or tape that holds data. On a DFD, usually represented by an open-ended rectangle. 572

Data transfer rate The amount of data that a storage device can move from a storage medium to computer memory in one time unit, such as one second. 77

Data type The characteristics of data that can be entered into a field in a data file; data types include character, numeric, date, logical, and memo. 634

Data view A mechanism typically applied to databases in which different forms or reports are displayed depending on a query, and can be customized for different categories of users. 656

Data warehouse A collection of information organized for analysis. 612

Database A collection of information that might be stored in more than one file or in more than one record type. 139, 610

Database administrator A person who supervises database design, development, testing, and maintenance. 511

Database audit A procedure that monitors or records user activity within a database, often for security purposes. 655

Database client software Software that allows any remote computer or network workstation to access data in a database. 626

Database index A file of keys and pointers used to display a list of database records organized according to the data in one or more fields. 639

Database model The underlying structure or category of a database, such as relational, hierarchical, network, or object. 614

Database server software Software that is designed to manage a large number of records and perform many simultaneous transactions. 626

Database software Software designed for entering, finding, organizing, updating, and reporting information stored in a database. 139

Database structure The arrangement of the fields, tables, and relationships in a database. 633

Date data type A data type that indicates that the data in a field represents a date. 634

DBMS (database management system) Application software that assists the user in manipulating, storing, and maintaining database files. 625

de Colmar's Arithmometer The first commercially successful, mass-produced mechanical calculator. 488

Debugger A programming utility that helps programmers test and correct a computer program. 685

DEC PDP-8 Built by Digital Equipment Corp. and introduced in 1965, the PDP-8 was the first commercially successful minicomputer. 494

Decision model A numerical representation of a realistic situation, such as a cash flow model of a business. 562

Decision query A question or set of instructions that describes the data that needs to be gathered to make a decision. 562

Decision support system (DSS) A computer system that allows decision makers to manipulate data directly, to incorporate data from external sources, and to create data models or "what-if" scenarios. 562

Decision support worksheet A comparison table used by a project team to evaluate solutions by assigning a score and a weight to each criterion. 579

Decision table A tabular method for listing rules and specifying the outcomes for various combinations of rules. 714

Declarative paradigm An approach to the programming process in which a programmer writes a program by specifying a set of statements and rules that define the conditions for solving a problem. 713

Decryption The process of converting ciphertext into plaintext. 285

Dedicated graphics Circuitry for graphics that is supplied on an expansion card rather than integrated into the main system board of a digital device. 91

Defensive programming An approach to programming that attempts to identify possible threats and proactively create code to avoid them; also called secure programming. 726

Defragmentation utility A software tool used to rearrange the files on a disk so that they are stored in contiguous clusters. 221

DELETE An SQL keyword that removes a record from a table. 646

Demoware Commercial software that is distributed free, but expires after a certain time limit and then requires users to pay to continue using it. 159

Design phase The process a project team uses for figuring out how to implement a new system. This phase is undertaken after the analysis phase is complete. 576

Desktop A term used to refer to the main screen of a graphical user interface that can hold objects such as folders and widgets. 189

Desktop computer A computer that is small enough to fit on a desk and built around a single microprocessor chip. 58

Desktop operating system An operating system specifically designed for use on personal computers, such as Windows 7 or Mac OS X. 188

Desktop publishing software (DTP) Software used to create high-quality output suitable for commercial printing. DTP software provides precise control over layout. 127

Desktop video Videos stored in digital format on a PC's hard disk or CD. 452

Detail reports Organized lists generated by a management information system (for example, an inventory list). 560

Device driver A type of system software that provides the computer with the means to control a peripheral device. 131

DHCP (Dynamic Host Configuration Protocol) A set of rules that allow network client computers to find and use the Internet address that corresponds to a domain name. 255

Dial-up connection A connection that uses a phone line to establish a temporary Internet connection. 312

Dialog box An element of graphical user interfaces that appears in a window and requests information, such as command parameters, from a user. 191

Dictionary attack A method of discovering a password by trying every word in an electronic dictionary. 36

Difference Engine A mechanical calculator design created by Charles Babbage that was to use steam power for fully automatic operation. It was never built. 488

Differential backup A copy of all the files that changed since the last full backup of a disk. 226

Digital audio Music or voice that has been digitized into files using sampling techniques; sometimes referred to as waveform audio. 422

Digital audio extraction The process of copying files from an audio CD and converting them into a format that can be stored and accessed from a computer storage device, such as a hard disk; sometimes referred to as ripping. 426

Digital camera A camera that takes and stores a digital image instead of recording onto film. 432

Digital certificate A security method that identifies the author of an ActiveX control. A computer programmer can "sign" a digital certificate after being approved. 373

Digital content Media content that is stored in digital format. 464

Digital data Text, numbers, graphics, or sound represented by discrete digits, such as 1s and 0s. 22

Digital divide A gap between those who have access to digital technologies and those who do not. 13

Digital revolution A set of significant changes brought about by computers and other digital devices during the second half of the 20th century. 4

Digital rights management (DRM) A set of techniques and technologies designed to discourage and prevent unauthorized duplication of digital content. 466

Digital signal processor Circuitry that is used to process, record, and play back audio files. 424

Digital video A series of still frames stored sequentially in digital format by assigning values to each pixel in a frame. 452

Digital watermark A digital rights management technology that inserts a hidden signal into multimedia content as an identifying marker that can be tracked or verified. 467

Digitization To convert nondigital information or media to a digital format through the use of a scanner, sampler, or other input device. 5

Digitizing tablet A device that provides a flat surface for a paper-based drawing and a "pen" used to create hand-drawn vector drawings. 446

Dimensional database A database often created for data analysis that has a more complex structure than a simple two-dimensional table. 619

Direct conversion The simultaneous deactivation of an old computer system and activation of a new one. 586

Directory In the context of computer file management, a list of files contained on a computer storage device. 206

Disaster recovery plan A step-by-step plan that describes the methods used to secure equipment and data against disasters, and how to recover from disasters. 594

Disc mastering The process of creating a CD or DVD by selecting all the files to be copied and then writing them in a single session. Contrast with packet writing. 219

Discovery mode The status of a Bluetooth device that is open for pairing. 261

Disk image A bit-by-bit copy of the contents of a disk created for backup, archiving, or duplication of data. 229

Disk partition An area of a hard disk created by dividing a large hard disk into several smaller virtual ones, such as when using two operating systems on a single computer. 205

Distributed database A database that is stored on different computers, on different networks, or in different locations. 626

Distributed processing An information system design in which data is processed on multiple workstations or servers. 577

DNS cache poisoning An exploit in which the DNS database is changed in such a way that a URL no longer connects to the correct Web site. 308

DOCSIS (Data Over Cable Service Interface Specification) A security technology used for filtering packets and maintaining customer privacy on cable Internet services. 317

Document formatting (1) The specifications applied to fonts, spacing, margins, and other elements in a document created with word processing software. (2) The file format, such as DOCX, used to store a document created with word processing software. 135

Document production software Computer programs that assist the user in composing, editing, designing, and printing documents. 125

Domain name Short for *fully qualified domain name*; an identifying name by which host computers on the Internet are familiarly known (for example, coca-cola.com). 307

Domain name server A computer that hosts the Domain Name System database. 308

Domain Name System (DNS) A large database of unique IP addresses that correspond with domain names. 308

DOS (Disk Operating System) The operating system software shipped with the first IBM PCs, then used on millions of computers until the introduction of Microsoft Windows. 201

Dot matrix printer A printer that creates characters and graphics by striking an inked ribbon with small wires called pins, generating a fine pattern of dots. 93

Dot pitch (dp) The diagonal distance between colored dots on a display screen. Measured in millimeters, dot pitch helps to determine the quality of an image displayed on a monitor. 90

Dot-coms A legacy term for companies formed mainly to offer goods and services online. 500

Download The process of transferring a copy of a file from a remote computer to a local computer's storage device. 18

Downstream speed The rate at which transmitted data flows from a host or server to a local computer (contrast with upstream speed). 310

Drawing software Programs that are used to create vector graphics with lines, shapes, and colors, such as logos or diagrams. 123, 446

Drive bays Areas within a computer system unit that can accommodate additional storage devices. 86

DSL (digital subscriber line) A high-speed Internet connection that uses existing telephone lines, requiring close proximity to a switching station. 314

DSL filter Devices that are commonly used to prevent interference from analog devices, such as telephones, that use the same line as DSL devices. 315

DSL modem A device that sends and receives digital data to and from computers over telephone lines. 315

Dual boot A computer that contains more than one operating system and can boot into either one. 198

Duplex printer A printer that prints on both sides of the paper in a single pass. 94

Duty cycle A measurement of how many pages a printer is able to produce per day or month. 93

DVD (digital video disc or digital versatile disc) An optical storage medium similar in appearance and technology to a CD but with higher storage capacity. 81

DVD authoring software Computer programs that offer tools for creating DVD menus and transferring digital video onto DVDs that can be played in a computer or standalone DVD player. 122

DVD image A series of files containing the data needed for a video DVD. The image is typically stored on a hard disk for testing before the image is transferred or "burned" to the DVD. 462

DVI (Digital Visual Interface) A standard type of plug and connector for computer display devices. 96

Dynamic IP address A temporarily assigned IP address usually provided by an ISP. 306

Dynamic RAM (DRAM) Random access memory that requires a power source to hold data; used as main memory on most computers. 72

Dynamic Web publishing A way of displaying data from a database as customized Web pages, which are generated as the page is sent to the browser. 628

E-commerce Short for *electronic commerce*, it is the business of buying and selling products online. 384

E-mail account A service that provides users with an e-mail address and a mailbox. 393

E-mail address An identifier that includes a user name, an @ symbol, and an e-mail server; used to route e-mail messages to their destination. 393

E-mail attachment A separate file that is transmitted along with an e-mail message. 398

E-mail client software Software that is installed on a client computer and has access to e-mail servers on a network. This software is used to compose, send, and read e-mail messages. 393

E-mail message A computer file containing a letter or memo that is transmitted electronically via a communications network. 392

E-mail server A computer that uses special software to store and send e-mail messages over the Internet. 392

E-mail system The collection of computers and software that works together to provide e-mail services. 392

EAI (Enterprise Application Integration) The use of networked software and databases for providing unrestricted sharing of data in an organization. 569

EBCDIC (Extended Binary-Coded Decimal Interchange Code) A method by which digital computers, usually mainframes, represent character data. 25

EDI (Electronic Data Interchange) The ability to transfer data between different companies using networks that enable companies to buy, sell, and trade information. 569

EEPROM (electrically erasable programmable read-only memory) A type of non-volatile storage typically used in personal computers to store boot and BIOS data. 74

Eiffel An object-oriented programming language with syntax similar to C. 679

Encapsulation An object-oriented technique in which the internal details of an object are "hidden" in order to simplify their use and reuse. 712

Encryption The process of scrambling or hiding information so that it cannot be understood without the key necessary to change it back into its original form. 285

Enhanced media player Handheld devices designed to play music, but with enhanced features, such as a browser and apps. 65

ENIAC (Electronic Numerical Integrator and Computer) An early electronic computer prototype that was designed for the U.S. Army for calculating trajectories and was completed in 1945. 491

Enterprise information system The use of one or more information systems that share data and typically provide information to hundreds or thousands of users who may be located in diverse locations. 559

Entity-relationship diagram (ERD) A diagram that graphically depicts relationships between record types. 616

Equipment manufacturers Companies that design and manufacture computer hardware and communication products. 499

Ergonomics The science of designing safe, comfortable, efficient machines and tools for human use. 537

ERP (Enterprise Resource Planning) A system of business management that integrates all resources of a business, including planning, manufacturing, sales, and marketing. 569

eSATA A standard for high-speed ports, plugs, and connectors typically used to connect external hard drives to computers. 96

Ethernet A popular network technology in which network nodes are connected by coaxial cable or twisted-pair wire. 257

Ethernet adapter A type of network interface card designed to support Ethernet protocols. 258

EULA (end user license Agreement) A type of software license that appears on the computer screen when software is being installed and prompts the user to accept or decline. 157

Event In the context of programming, an action or change in state, such as a mouse click, that requires a response from the computer. 684

Event-driven paradigm An approach to programming in which a programmer creates programs that continually check for, and respond to, program events, such as mouse clicks. 685

Event-handling code The program segment that instructs the computer how to react to events, such as mouse clicks. 684

Exception report A report generated by a management information system, listing information that is outside normal or acceptable ranges, such as a reorder report showing low-stock inventory items. 561

Executable file A file, usually with an .exe extension, containing instructions that tell a computer how to perform a specific task. 147

Executive dashboard software Software designed for managers that typically uses widgets to graphically display statistics relevant to business decisions. 613

Executive information system (EIS) A special type of decision support system that is designed to provide senior managers with information relevant to strategic management activities. 562

Expansion bus The segment of the data bus that transports data between RAM and peripheral devices. 94

Expansion card A circuit board that is plugged into a slot on a computer motherboard to add extra functions, devices, or ports. 95

Expansion port A socket into which the user plugs a cable from a peripheral device, allowing data to pass between the computer and the peripheral device. 95

Expansion slot A socket or "slot" on a PC motherboard designed to hold a circuit board called an expansion card. 95

Expert system A computer system incorporating knowledge from human experts, and designed to analyze data and produce a recommendation or decision (also called a knowledge-based system). 564

Expert system shell A software tool used for developing expert system applications. 564

Extended ASCII Similar to ASCII but with 8-bit character representation instead of 7-bit, allowing for an additional 128 characters. 24

External entity A person, organization, or device that exists outside an information system, but provides it with input or receives output. On a DFD, usually represented by a square. 572

External information Information obtained by organizations from outside sources. 559

Fact In the context of Prolog programming, a fact is a statement incorporated into a program that provides basic information for solving a problem. 713

Feature creep An undesirable occurrence during information system development when users, customers, or designers attempt to add features after the final specifications have been approved. 582

Field The smallest meaningful unit of information contained in a data file. 139, 615

Field format A specification for the way that data is displayed on the screen and printouts, usually using a series of Xs to indicate characters and 9s to indicate numbers. 636

Field name A name that identifies the contents of a field. 615

Field validation rule A specification that a database designer sets up to filter the data entered into a particular field. 636

Fifth-generation languages Either declarative languages, such as Prolog, or programming languages that allow programmers to use graphical or visual tools to construct programs. 678

File A named collection of data (such as a computer program, document, or graphic) that exists on a storage medium, such as a hard disk or CD. 15

File compression utility A type of data compression software that shrinks one or more files into a single file occupying less storage space than the files did separately. 442

File date The date that a file was created or last modified. 206

File extension A set of letters and/or numbers added to the end of a file name that helps to identify the file contents or file type. 204

File format The method of organization used to encode and store data in a computer. Text formats include DOCX and TXT. Graphics formats include BMP, TIFF, GIF, and PNG. 207

File header Hidden information inserted at the beginning of a file to identify its properties, such as the software that can open it. 207

File management utility Software, such as Windows Explorer, that helps users locate, rename, move, copy, and delete files. 214

File server A network computer that is dedicated to storing and distributing files to network clients. 279

File sharing The process of allowing access to document, photo, video, and other files from a computer other than the one on which they are stored. 275

File shredder software Software designed to overwrite sectors of a disk with a random series of 1s and 0s to ensure deletion of data. 220

File size The physical size of a file on a storage medium, usually measured in kilobytes (KB). 206

File specification A combination of the drive letter, subdirectory, file name, and extension that identifies a file (such as C:\Pictures\Photo.jpg); also called a path. 206

File system A method that is used by an operating system to keep files organized. 219

File tag In the context of Windows, a piece of information that describes a file. Tags, such as Owner, Rating, and Date Taken, can be added by users. 212

File-naming conventions A set of rules, established by the operating system, that must be followed to create a valid file name. 204

Firewall Software or hardware designed to analyze and control incoming and outgoing packets on a network, used to enhance security by filtering out potential intrusion attempts. 341

FireWire A standard for fairly high-speed ports, plugs, and connectors typically used to connect external storage devices, and for transferring data from cameras to computers. 96

First-generation computers Computers that used vacuum tubes to process and store data, such as UNIVAC. 492

First-generation languages Machine languages that were available for programming the earliest computers. 677

First-party cookie A cookie that is generated by the Web page that is shown in the browser. 401

Fixed Internet access Any Internet access service designed to be used from a fixed, non-portable location (i.e., dial-up, ISDN, DSL, and cable Internet service). 311

Fixed wireless Internet service High-speed, wide area Internet service alternative to cable and DSL that transmits data wirelessly using RF signals. 319

Fixed-length field A field in a data file that has a predetermined number of characters. 615

Flash A file format developed by Macromedia and marketed by Adobe that has become popular for animations on Web pages. 448

Flash cookie A cookie-like object that is created and used by the Adobe Flash Player; also referred to as a local shared object. 402

Flash video A popular video file format developed by Adobe Systems and used for Web-based video at sites such as YouTube. 458

Flat file A single file that is the electronic version of a box of index cards, in which all records use the same record format. 614

Floppy disk A removable magnetic storage medium, typically 3.5" in size, with a capacity of 1.44 MB. 80

Flowchart In software engineering, a graphical representation of the way a computer should progress from one instruction to the next when it performs a task. 692

Folder The subdirectories, or subdivisions of a directory, that can contain files or other folders. 206

Font A typeface or style of lettering, such as Arial, Times New Roman, and Gothic. 135

Footer Text that appears in the bottom margin of each page of a document. 135

Form design grid A visual programming tool that allows programmers to drag and drop controls to form the user interface for a program. 683

Form factor The configuration of a computer's system unit; examples include tower, mini-tower, and cube. 58

Formal methods Mathematically-based techniques for specifying and developing reliable and robust software or hardware. 725

Format shifting The process of converting media into a different file format to use it on a device other than the original one. 465

Formatting The process of dividing a disk into sectors so that it can be used to store information. 219

Formula In spreadsheet terminology, a combination of numbers and symbols that tells the computer how to use the contents of cells in calculations. 137

Fortran (FORmula TRANslator) The oldest high-level computer programming language still in use for scientific, mathematical, and engineering programs. 679

Fourth-generation computers Computers, such as today's personal computers, servers, and mainframes, that use a general purpose microprocessor for data processing. 494

Fourth-generation languages Programming and query languages, such as SQL and RPG, that more closely resemble human languages than did third-generation languages. 678

Fragmented files Files stored in scattered, noncontiguous clusters on a disk. 221

Freeware Copyrighted software that is given away by the author or copyright owner. 161

Front side bus (FSB) The data bus that carries signals between the CPU and RAM, disks, or expansion slots. 68

FTP (File Transfer Protocol) A set of rules for uploading and downloading files between a client computer and a remote server. 335

FTP client The computer or software that is used to access an FTP server and transfer files to it or from it. 336

FTP server A computer that stores and distributes files to remote client computers. 335

Full backup A copy of all the files for a specified backup job. 226

Fully justified The horizontal alignment of text where the text terminates exactly at both margins of the document. 135

Function (1) In the context of spreadsheet software, a built-in formula for making a calculation. (2) In the context of programming, a section of code that manipulates data, but is not included in the main sequential execution path of a program. 137, 696

Fuzzy logic A technique used by an expert system to deal with imprecise data by incorporating the probability that the input information is correct. 564

Game controllers Devices such as joysticks, wands, and steering wheels; used to control on-screen action in computer games. 88

Gantt chart A chart that depicts a project schedule by showing each task as a bar on the chart. 570

Gateway A network device that connects two dissimilar networks even if the networks use different protocols. 267

GIF (Graphics Interchange Format) A bitmap graphics file format, popularized by CompuServe, for use on the Web. 431

Gigabit (Gb or Gbit) Approximately 1 billion bits, exactly 1,024 megabits. 26

Gigabyte (GB) Approximately 1 billion bytes; exactly 1,024 megabytes (1,073,741,824 bytes). 26

Gigahertz (GHz) A measure of frequency equivalent to 1 billion cycles per second. 67

Global update In the context of databases, changing data in more than one record at a time (i.e., changing the due date in all the records). 650

Globalization A group of social, economic, political, and technological interdependencies linking people and institutions from all areas of the world. 12

Goal In the context of Prolog programming, a query that searches for an answer based on a set of Prolog facts and rules. 715

GPL (General Public License) A software license often used for freeware that insures it will be distributed freely whether in its original form or as a derivative work. 160

Gradient A smooth blending of shades of different colors, from light to dark. 447

Grammar checker A feature of word processing software that coaches the user on correct sentence structure and word usage. 134

Graphical user interface (GUI) A type of user interface that features on-screen objects, such as menus and icons, manipulated by a mouse. 189

Graphics Any picture, photograph, or image that can be manipulated or viewed on a computer. 123

Graphics card A circuit board inserted into a computer to handle the display of text, graphics, animation, and videos. Also called a video card or graphics board. 91

Graphics processing unit (GPU) A microprocessor dedicated to rendering and displaying graphics on personal computers, workstations, and videogame consoles. 91

Graphics software Computer programs for creating, editing, and manipulating images; types include paint software and drawing software. 123

Grayscale palette Digital images that are displayed in shades of gray, black, and white. 439

Grid computing system A network of computers harnessed together to perform processing tasks; distributed grids like the SETI@home project use ad hoc and diverse Internet connected computers; also see *cloud computing*. 334

Handheld computer A small, portable device such as a smartphone or enhanced media player that allows users to install apps and store data. 19

Handheld operating system An operating system used by a handheld device, such as a smartphone. 188

Handshaking A process where a protocol helps two network devices communicate. 252

Hard disk drive A computer storage device that contains a large-capacity rigid storage surface sealed inside a drive case. Typically used as the primary storage device in personal computers. 78

Hard disk platter The component of a hard disk drive on which data is stored. It is a flat, rigid disk made of aluminum or glass and coated with a magnetic oxide. 78

Harvard Mark I An early computer prototype also known as the ASCC (Automatic Sequence Controlled Calculator) developed by IBM that used decimal data representation rather than binary. 490

Hash value A number produced by a hash function to create a unique digital "fingerprint" that can be used to allow or deny access to a software application. 161

Haskell A functional programming language. 679

HDCP (High-bandwidth Digital Content Protection) A form of copy protection designed to prevent digital content from being transmitted over a DVI interface to a non-complying display device. 470

HDMI (High-Definition Multimedia Interface) A standard type of plug and connector for computer display devices. 96

Head crash A collision between the read-write head and the surface of the hard disk platter, resulting in damage to some of the data on the disk. 79

Header Text that is placed in the top margin of each page of a document. 135

Help desk Part of the Information Systems department designated to assist users experiencing problems with their computers or applications. 588

Hierarchical database A database model in which record types are arranged as a hierarchy, or tree, of child nodes that can have only one parent node. 617

High-level language A programming language that allows a programmer to write instructions using human-like language. 676

Hollerith Tabulating Machine A mechanical calculator first used in 1890 by the U.S. Census Bureau that used punch cards to store data and led to the creation of IBM. 489

Home computer system A personal computer designed for use with mainstream computer applications such as Web browsing, e-mail, music downloads, and productivity software. 60

Homegroup A feature of Windows 7 that quickly creates a peer-to-peer network for sharing files and printers. 278

Horizontal market software Any computer program that can be used by many different kinds of businesses (for example, an accounting program). 126

Hot-plugging The ability of a component, such as a USB flash drive, to connect to or disconnect from a computer while it is running; also referred to as hot-swapping. 97

Hover ad An advertisement, created using interactive Web tools such as DHTML, that appears on top of Web pages, sometimes obscuring parts of them. 385

HP webOS An operating system, formerly Palm webOS, designed for HP smartphones. 203

HTML (Hypertext Markup Language) A standardized format used to specify the layout for Web pages. 362

HTML conversion utility Utility software that converts documents, spreadsheets, and databases into HTML files that can be posted on the Web. 369

HTML document A plain text or ASCII document with embedded HTML tags that dictate formatting and are interpreted by a browser. 362

HTML forms An HTML document containing blank boxes that prompt users to enter information that can be sent to a Web server. Commonly used for e-commerce transactions. 371

HTML mail E-mail messages that contain formatting, such as bold and italics, by turning on the HTML mail function. 397

HTML script A series of instructions embedded directly into the text of an HTML document or a file referenced from an HTML document. 371

HTML tags A set of instructions, such as <B>, inserted into an HTML document to provide formatting and display information to a Web browser. 362

HTML5 The version of HTML that was in the final stages of the approval process as of 2012. 362

HTTP (Hypertext Transfer Protocol) The communications protocol used to transmit Web pages. HTTP:// is an identifier that appears at the beginning of Web URLs (for example, *http://www.fooyong.com*). 364

HTTP status code A code used by Web servers to report the status of a browser's request. The HTTP status code 404 means document not found. 365

HTTPS (Hypertext Transfer Protocol Secure) The protocol used to create secure connections for e-commerce by adding a layer of encryption. 390

Hub A network device that connects several nodes of a local area network. 267

Hyperlink data type A data type assigned to fields that store URLs used to link directly to a Web page. 635

Hypertext A way of organizing a collection of documents by assigning an address to each and providing a way to link from one address to another. 360

Hypertext link Also referred to as simply a link, an underlined word or phrase on a Web page that, when clicked, takes you to a designated URL. 361

IBM 360 An early third-generation computer that is widely regarded as the first general purpose mainframe. 494

IBM AS/400 IBM's most successful legacy minicomputer. 494

IBM PC An early, commercially successful personal computer system that featured a 4.77 MHz Intel 8088 processor, 64 KB RAM, and a floppy disk drive. Ancestor to today's PCs. 496

IBM PC XT An early, commercially successful personal computer system that included a hard disk drive. 496

ICANN (Internet Corporation for Assigned Names and Numbers) A global organization that coordinates the management of the Internet's domain name system, IP addresses, and protocol parameters. 309

Icon A graphical object, such as those that represent programs or folders on a computer desktop. 189

IDE (integrated development environment) A set of programming tools, typically including editor, compiler, and debugger, packaged into an application for creating programs. 686

Identity theft An illegal practice in which a criminal obtains enough information to masquerade as someone. 36

Image compression Any technique that is used to reduce the size of a file that holds a graphic. 440

IMAP (Internet Message Access Protocol) A protocol similar to POP that is used to retrieve e-mail messages from an e-mail server, but offers additional features, such as choosing which e-mails to download from the server. 394

Implementation phase A set of tasks performed with the supervision of a system development project team in which a new information system is constructed. 583

Incremental backup A backup that contains files that changed since the last backup. 226

Inference engine Software that can analyze and manipulate a knowledge base or expert system. 564

Information engineering methodology A method of developing an information system that focuses on data the information system collects before finding ways to process that data. 570

Information system A computer system that collects, stores, and processes information, usually within the context of an organization. 556

Information systems (IS or CIS) The career field or academic major that focuses on developing computer systems and networks for businesses. 514

Information technology (1) A degree program that focuses on the computer equipment and software used by businesses and organizations. (2) The use of computers and software to manipulate data. 514

Information technology industry (IT industry) Companies involved in the development, production, sales, and support of computers and software. 498

Infrared light A transmission technology that uses a frequency range just below the visible light spectrum to transport data. 259

Inheritance In object-oriented terminology, a method for defining new classes of objects based on the characteristics of existing classes. 704

Ink jet printer A non-impact printer that creates characters or graphics by spraying liquid ink onto paper or other media. 92

Input As a noun, the information that is conveyed to a computer. As a verb, to enter data into a computer. 15

INSERT An SQL keyword that adds a record to a table. 647

Instant messaging A private chat in which users can communicate with each other in real time using electronically transmitted text messages. 331

Instantiation A programming term that refers to the process of assigning a value to a variable. 717

Instruction cycle The steps followed by a computer to process a single instruction: fetch, interpret, execute, then increment the instruction pointer. 32

Instruction set The collection of instructions that a CPU is designed to process. 30

Integer data type A numeric data type used for fields that contain whole numbers. 634

Integrated audio Sound card circuitry that is built into the circuitry of a digital device, in contrast to the use of an add-on sound card. 424

Integrated circuit (IC) A thin slice of silicon crystal containing microscopic circuit elements such as transistors, wires, capacitors, and resistors; also called chips and microchips. 27

Integrated graphics Circuitry for graphics processing that is integrated into the mainboard rather than as an expansion card. 91

Integration testing The testing of completed modules of an application to ensure that they operate together correctly. 584

Intellectual property A legal concept that refers to ownership of intangible information, such as ideas. 12

Internal information Information obtained by an organization from its own resources, such as from accounting or personnel systems. 559

Internet The worldwide communication infrastructure that links computer networks using the TCP/IP protocol. 8

Internet backbone The major communications links that form the core of the Internet. 303

Internet forum An asynchronous online discussion in which participants post comments to discussion threads, which can be read at a later time by other participants. 332

Internet service provider (ISP) A company that provides Internet access to businesses, organizations, and individuals. 303

Interpreter A program that converts high-level instructions in a computer program into machine language instructions, one instruction at a time. 30

Intrusion In the context of computer security, the unauthorized access to a computer system. 339

Ionizing radiation A type of radiation that has sufficient energy to remove an electron from an atom and potentially cause tissue damage. 534

iOS The operating system used for iPhones. 202

IP (Internet Protocol) One of the main protocols of TCP/IP; responsible for addressing packets so that they can be routed to their destinations; IPv4 offers 32-bit addresses whereas IPv6 offers 128-bit addresses. 305

IP address Unique identifying numbers assigned to each computer connected to the Internet. 255

IT service companies A company that focuses on providing computer and network connections, repair, support, or other services to companies and consumers. 499

Iteration In the context of computer programming, a section of code that is repeated; also called a loop. 698

Jailbreak Making unauthorized changes to an iPod, iPhone, or iPad to get apps from a source other than the official iTunes App Store. 145

Java A platform-independent, object-oriented, high-level programming language based on C++, typically used to produce interactive Web applications. 679

Java applet Small programs that add processing and interactive capabilities to Web pages. 372

JIT (Just In Time) A manufacturing system in which the parts needed to construct a product are received at the assembly site only as needed. 569

Jitter Deviations in the timing of a digital signal that can interfere with communications, especially voice over IP. 332

Job search agent An automated program that searches one or more databases and notifies you when it finds a lead on a specific job type. 521

JOIN An SQL command that temporarily joins data from more than one table in order to allow simultaneous access to both tables. 651

Joining tables In SQL terminology, the act of creating a relationship between tables. 651

Joint application design (JAD) A widely accepted design technique that is based on the idea that the best information systems are designed when end users and systems analysts work together on a project as equal partners. 567

JPEG (Joint Photographic Experts Group) A format that uses lossy compression to store bitmap images. JPEG (pronounced "JAY-peg") files have a .jpg extension. 431

Kernel The core module of an operating system that typically manages memory, processes, tasks, and storage devices. 192

Keylogger A program, sometimes part of a Trojan horse, that records a person's keystrokes, saves them, and then sends them to a system administrator or remote hacker. 37

Keyword (1) A word or term used as the basis for a Web page search. (2) A command word provided by a programming language. 676

Keyword search The process of looking for information by providing a related word or phrase. 141

Keyword stuffing An unpopular practice of including a huge variety of keywords in the header of an HTML document in the hopes that a search engine will display it even when the content of the page is not relevant to the search. 377

Kilobit (Kbit or Kb) 1024 bits. 26

Kilobyte (KB) Approximately 1,000 bytes; exactly 1,024 bytes. 26

Knowledge base The collection of facts and rules obtained from experts that are incorporated into an expert system. 564

Knowledge engineering The process of designing rules, entering them into an expert system, and testing them. 564

Known information In a problem statement, information supplied to the computer to help it solve a problem. 680

Label In the context of spreadsheets, any text used to describe data. 136

LAN (local area network) An interconnected group of computers and peripherals located within a relatively limited area, such as a building or campus. 247

Lands Non-pitted surface areas on a CD that represent digital data. (See also *pits*.) 81

Laser printer A printer that uses laser-based technology, similar to that used by photocopiers, to produce text and graphics. 92

Latency The elapsed time it takes for a packet of data to arrive at its destination. 309

LCD display (liquid crystal display) Technology used for flat panel computer screens typically found on notebook computers. 90

Leading Also called line spacing, the vertical spacing between lines of text. 135

LED display (light-emitting diode display) Either a display device that uses LEDs to produce an image on the screen, or an LCD display that uses LEDs as backlighting. 90

Leibniz Calculator A mechanical calculator capable of performing the four arithmetic functions that helped develop the technology for the first commercially successful calculator. 488

Library In the context of Windows 7, a superfolder that contains pointers to various folders and files; examples include Documents, Pictures, and Videos. 217

Linear editing A video editing technique involving recording segments of video from one tape to another. 456

Link popularity A metric used by some search engines to rank the sites that are relevant to a query. 377

Linux An operating system that is a derivative of UNIX, available as freeware, and widely used for servers though it is also used on personal computers and workstations. 200

Linux distribution Usually a download that includes the Linux operating system, a Linux desktop, and other Linux utilities. 200

Linux platform A computer that is running the Linux operating system. 64

LISP (LISt Processing) A declarative programming language that excels at handling complex data structures, artificial intelligence projects, and very complex programs. 679

Local e-mail An e-mail system that requires users to install e-mail client software on their computer hard disk or flash drive; messages are held on a server until the client software downloads them to the local computer. 393

Local software Computer applications that are installed on and run from a local device, usually a computer hard drive. 7

Location-based software Applications that are able to access your current location using, for example, a smartphone's GPS or nearby LAN signals. 125

Logic error A run-time error in the logic or design of a computer program. 685

Logical data type A data type specifying that a field in a data file is used to store true/false or yes/no data. 634

Logical storage models Any visual or conceptual aid that helps a computer user visualize a file storage system. Also called a storage metaphor. 215

Lookup routine A validation process used by database designers to prevent data entry errors by searching for an entry such as a state abbreviation in a file or database table. 637

Loop The section of program code that is repeated because of a repetition control structure; also called an iteration. 698

Lossless compression A compression technique that is able to reconstitute all of the data in the original file; hence *lossless* means that this compression technique does not lose data. 440

Lossy compression Any data compression technique in which some of the data is sacrificed to obtain more compression. 440

Low-level language A programming language that requires a programmer to write instructions for specific hardware elements such as the computer processor, registers, and RAM locations. 676

MAC address (Media Access Control) A unique identifier similar to a serial number assigned to networking equipment at time of manufacture. 254

Mac OS The operating system software designed for use on Apple Macintosh computers. 197

Mac platform A family or category of Macintosh-compatible personal computers designed and manufactured by Apple Computer. 64

Machine code Program instructions written in binary code that the computer can execute directly. 30

Machine language A low-level language written in binary code that the computer can execute directly. 30

Magnetic storage A technology for recording data onto disks or tape by magnetizing particles of an oxide-based surface coating. 78

Mail order A type of retailing in which a merchant takes orders by telephone or from an Internet site, then ships orders by mail or other courier service. 507

Mainframe computer A large, fast, and expensive computer generally used by businesses or government agencies to provide centralized storage, processing, and management for large amounts of data. 18

Maintenance phase The day-to-day operation of an information system, including making modifications and correcting problems to insure correct operation. 587

Malicious software Any program or set of program instructions, such as a virus, worm, or Trojan horse, designed to surreptitiously enter a computer and disrupt its normal operations. 162

Malware Programs such as viruses, worms, and bots designed to disrupt computer operations. 162

MAN (metropolitan area network) A public, high-speed network that can transmit voice and data within a range of 50 miles. 247

Management information system (MIS) A type of information system that manipulates the data collected by a transaction processing system to generate reports that managers can use to make business decisions. 561

Managers People who make decisions about how an organization carries out its activities. 557

Manual calculator A device that helps solve mathematical calculations, but does not contain sophisticated built-in algorithms. 486

Manufacturer direct The selling of products by hardware manufacturers directly to consumers by means of a sales force or mail order. 507

Manufacturing technician A computer professional who participates in the fabrication of computer chips, systems, and devices. 512

Many-to-many relationship A relationship in which one record in a particular record type can be related to more than one record in another record type, and vice versa. 616

Mapping application An application that displays satellite, aerial, or street maps that can be used to locate places and get directions. 125

Mark-8 A microprocessor-based computer system, developed by Jonathan A. Titus in 1974, that helped lead to the development of personal computers. 495

Market share A company's share, or percentage, of the total market. 505

Marketing channels Marketing outlets such as retail stores or mail order for computer-related products. 506

Markup language A language that provides text and graphics formatting through the use of tags. Examples of markup languages include HTML, XML, and SGML. 362

Mass-mailing worm A worm that sends itself to every e-mail address in the address book of an infected computer. 163

Mathematical modeling software Software for visualizing and solving a wide range of math, science, and engineering problems. 126

Mathematical operators Symbols such as + - / * that represent specific mathematical functions in a formula. 137

Mechanical calculator A machine capable of implementing algorithms used to solve mathematical calculations. 488

Media content A term popularized in the context of multimedia that refers to music, movies, television shows, and books. 464

Megabit (Mb or Mbit) 1,048,576 bits. 26

Megabyte (MB) Approximately 1 million bytes; exactly 1,048,576 bytes. 26

Megahertz (MHz) A measure of frequency equivalent to 1 million cycles per second. 68

Megapixel 1 million pixels; expresses the resolution and quality of an image; usually used in reference to digital cameras. 434

Memo data type A data type that specifies that a field in a data file can contain variable-length text comments (also called a memo field). 634

Memory The computer circuitry that holds data waiting to be processed. 15

Memory card A small, flat, solid state storage medium, frequently used to store data on cameras and handheld devices. 84

Memory leak An undesirable state in which a program requests memory but never releases it, which can eventually prevent other programs from running. 187

Menu In the context of user interfaces, a list of commands or options often displayed as a list. 190

Menu bar A standard component of most graphical user interfaces that is displayed as a strip of clickable options, that in turn display a list of commands. 190

Message In the context of object-oriented programming, input that is collected and sent to an object. 706

Message header The section of an e-mail file that contains address, subject, and file attachment information. 392

Meta keyword A word that is included in the header of an HTML document in order to describe the document's contents. 377

Metafile In the context of graphics, a file that contains both vector and bitmap data. 447

Metasearch engine A search engine that searches other search engines. 380

Metasearch tool A program that performs broad-based Web searches, such as searching more than one job database at a time. 521

Method In the context of object-oriented programming, any action that an object can perform. 705

Microcontroller A special purpose microprocessor that is built into the device it controls. 20

Microprocessor An integrated circuit that contains the circuitry for processing data. It is a single-chip version of the central processing unit (CPU) found in all computers. 15

Microprocessor clock A timing signal that sets the pace for executing instructions in a microprocessor. 67

Microsoft Windows An operating system, developed by Microsoft Corporation, that provides a graphical interface. Versions include Windows 3.1, 95, 98, Me, NT, 2000, XP, Vista, and Windows 7. 194

Microwaves Electromagnetic waves with a frequency of at least 1 gigahertz; one type of channel for transmitting data over communications networks. 259

MIDI (Musical Instrument Digital Interface) A standardized way in which sound and music are encoded and transmitted between digital devices that play music. 427

MIDI sequence Digitally encoded MIDI music stored on a digital device, such as a computer or MIDI instrument. 427

MiFi A small, wireless router that connects to a cellular data network, creating a mobile Wi-Fi hotspot. 327

MIME (Multi-purpose Internet Mail Extensions) A standard for formatting non-ASCII messages so that they can be sent over the Internet, typically as e-mail messages. 398

MIMO (multiple input multiple output) A wireless communications device that uses an array of antennas to transmit data over more than one channel. 263

Mission An organization's goal or plan, which is reflected by the organization's activities. 557

Mission statement The written expression of an organization's goals and how those goals will be accomplished. 557

MITS Altair The first commercial microcomputer. It was based on the Intel 8080 processor and sold primarily to computer hobbyists. 495

Mobile app An application designed to be downloaded to a handheld device, such as a smartphone or tablet computer. 145

Mobile broadband High-bandwidth wireless technology that was developed for sending digital data over cell phone systems. 326

Mobile Internet access Any service that allows subscribers to access the Internet while on the go. 311

Modem A device that modulates and demodulates a signal; typically used to send data from a computer to the Internet over telephone, cable television, or satellite networks. 304

Module A component or part of a software program or office suite (e.g., a word processing module). 132

Money management software Software used to track monetary transactions and investments. 128

Monochrome bitmap A bitmap image that contains only the colors black and white. 437

Mouse An input device that allows the user to manipulate objects on the screen by clicking, dragging, and dropping. 88

MOV A multimedia file format, popular for digital videos, that works with QuickTime software. 458

MP3 A file format that provides highly compressed audio files with very little loss of sound quality. 425

MPEG (Moving Picture Experts Group) A family of highly compressed container file formats and codecs for digital multimedia; MPEG-1, MPEG-2, and MPEG-4. 458

MRP (Manufacturing Resource Planning) A business management technique in which an optimum manufacturing plan is generated based on a wide variety of data. 569

MTBF (mean time between failures) An estimate of the length of time a device will perform before it fails. 591

Multi-core processor A microprocessor that contains circuitry for more than one processing unit. 68

Multiparadigm language A programming language that supports more than one paradigm, such as object-oriented and procedural paradigms. 679

Multiple-user license Legal permission for more than one person to use a particular software package. 157

Multiprocessing The ability of a computer or operating system to support dual core processors or multiple processors. 186

Multitasking The ability of a computer, processor, or operating system to run more than one program, job, or task at the same time. 186

Multithreading A technology that allows multiple parts or threads from a program to run simultaneously. 186

Multiuser operating system An operating system that allows a single computer to deal with simultaneous processing requests from multiple users. 187

Music software A broad category of software that can be used to play, record, compose, or manipulate sound files. 121

Napier's Bones A manual calculator created by John Napier that could be used to perform mathematical calculations by manipulating numbered rods. 487

Narrowband A term that refers to communications channels that have low bandwidth. 251

Native file format A file format that is unique to a program or group of programs and has a unique file extension. 209

Native resolution The dimensions of the grid that holds LEDs in a flat-screen, LCD display device; the resolution at which an LCD offers the clearest display. 539

Natural language query A query formulated in human language, as opposed to an artificially constructed language such as machine language. 141

Netbook A scaled-down version of a standard clamshell-style notebook computer. Sometimes called a minilaptop. 59

Netiquette (Internet etiquette) A set of guidelines for posting messages and e-mails in a civil, concise way. 399

Network access points (NAPs) Internet nodes that link together different network service providers so that data can be transferred from one service provider to the other. 303

Network address translation (NAT) A security technique that allows a LAN to use one type of IP address for intra-network data and another type of address for data traveling to and from the Internet. 343

Network attached storage (NAS) Storage devices that are designed to be attached directly to a network, rather than to a workstation or server. 248

Network database A collection of physically linked records in a one-to-many relationship in which a member (child) can have more than one owner (parent). 617

Network device Any device, such as a gateway, hub, or router, that is used to broadcast network data, boost signals, or route data to its destination. 250

Network discovery A setting that when turned on allows a computer to see other computers on a network and to be seen by those other computers. 276

Network interface card Circuitry, often on an expansion card mounted inside a computer, that transmits and receives data on a local area network. Also called a NIC, network card, or network adapter. 250

Network service providers (NSPs) Companies that maintain a series of nationwide Internet links. 303

Network specialist/administrator A computer professional who plans, installs, and maintains one or more local area networks. 511

Networked peripheral A peripheral device that contains circuitry that allows it to be directly connected to a network, rather than connecting to a computer that transfers data to a network. 250

Neural network A type of expert system that uses computer circuitry to simulate the way in which the brain processes information, learns, and remembers. 565

Node In a network, a connection point; in a hierarchical database, a segment or record type. 250

Non-volatile Any electronic component that does not require a constant supply of power to hold data. 84

Nonlinear editing A digital video editing technique that requires a personal computer and video editing software. 456

Nonprofit organization Organizations with political, social, or charitable goals that are not intended to generate a profit. 556

Normalization The process of analyzing data to create the most efficient database structure. 637

Notebook computer A small, lightweight, portable computer that usually runs on batteries. Sometimes called a laptop. 59

Numeric data Numbers that represent quantities and can be used in arithmetic operations. 23

Object In an object database or OO programming language, a discrete piece of code describing a person, place, thing, event, or type of information. 702

Object code The low-level instructions that result from compiling source code. 30

Object database A database model that organizes data into classes of objects that can be manipulated by programmer-defined methods; also referred to as an object-oriented database. 620

Object-oriented methodology An approach to system development that regards the elements of a system as a collection of objects that interact with each other to accomplish tasks. 570

Object-oriented paradigm An approach to programming that focuses on the manipulation of objects rather than on the generation of procedure-based code. 702

Object-relational database A database that uses object-oriented and relational concepts. 621

Objective-C An object-oriented programming language that is based on C. 679

Octet One of four sections of an IP address. 255

ODBMS (object database management system) Database management software used to construct an object-oriented database. 625

Office suite A collection of productivity programs, typically word processing, spreadsheet, presentation, and database modules. 132

Offshoring The corporate practice of relocating production, manufacturing, or customer service to lower-cost overseas locations. 501

Ogg Vorbis An open source audio file format. 425

OLAP (online analytical processing) A system that consists of computer hardware, database software, and analytical tools that are optimized for analyzing and manipulating data. 613

OLTP system (online transaction processing system) Interactive online transaction processing methods that use a "commit or rollback" strategy to ensure accurate transaction processing. 560

One-to-many relationship A relationship in which one record of a particular type may be related to more than one record of another record type. 616

One-to-one relationship An association between database entities in which a record of one type is related to a record of another type. 616

Online backup services Space for backup data provided through a Web site. 223

Online employment service An online database of job opening announcements that spans many industries or just one specific industry. 520

Online processing An interactive method of processing transactions in which each transaction is processed as it is entered. 560

Online shopping cart A feature of e-commerce sites that stores information about items selected for purchase often by creating a cookie on a shopper's computer. 387

Op code Short for *operation code;* an assembly language command word that designates an operation, such as add (ADD), compare (CMP), or jump (JMP). 31

Open source An approach to developing and licensing software in which source code remains public so it can be improved and freely distributed. 12

Open source software Software that includes its source code, allowing programmers to modify and improve it. 160

Operand The part of an instruction that specifies the data, or the address of the data, on which the operation is to be performed. 31

Operating system The software that controls the computer's use of its hardware resources, such as memory and disk storage space. Also called OS. 16

Operational planning The scheduling and monitoring of workers and processes. 558

Optical fiber cable A high-bandwidth communications cable used for MANs and WANs. 251

Optical storage A technology that records data as light and dark spots on a CD, DVD, or other optical media. 81

Organization A group of people working together to accomplish a goal. 556

Organizational chart A diagram showing the hierarchy of workers in an organization. 557

Output The results produced by a computer (for example, reports, graphs, and music). 15

Outsourcing The corporate practice of using third-party contractors to supply raw goods, manufacturing, or services. 500

Overclocking Forcing a computer component, such as a microprocessor, to run at a higher speed than intended by the manufacturer. 71

P2P file sharing A practice in which individuals can obtain music, video, and other types of files from other users on a network; sometimes the files are shared without authorization from the copyright holder. 337

Packet A small unit of data transmitted over a network. 253

Packet loss A situation in which data bits are lost in transit, requiring them to be resent, which significantly increases the time required for an intact message to arrive at its destination. 332

Packet switching A technology used by data communications networks, such as the Internet, where a message is divided into smaller units called packets for transmission. 253

Packet writing The process of recording data to a CD or DVD in multiple sessions. Contrast with disc mastering. 219

Page layout The physical positions of elements on a document page such as headers, footers, page numbering, and graphics. 135

Paint software Software that creates and manipulates bitmap graphics. 123, 430

Pairing The process of establishing a link between two Bluetooth devices, usually through the exchange of passkeys. 261

PAN (personal area network) An interconnected group of personal digital devices located within a range of about 30 feet. 247

Paragraph alignment The horizontal position (left, right, justified, centered, for example) of the text in a document. 135

Paragraph style A specification for the format of a paragraph, which includes the alignment of text within the margins and line spacing. 135

Parallel conversion A type of system conversion in which the old computer system remains in service while some or all of the new system is activated. 586

Parallel processing The simultaneous use of more than one processor to execute a program. 69

Parameters (1) In the context of SQL, the specifications used to delineate a command by specifying a table or search keyword. (2) In the context of programming, a keyword or variable used to specify variations of commands. 647, 676

Pascal A high-level, procedural programming language developed to help computer programming students learn the structured approach to programming. 679

Pascaline An early mechanical calculator capable of performing addition, subtraction, division, and multiplication. 488

Password A special set of symbols used to restrict access to a user's computer or network. 35

Password manager Software that keeps track of sites at which a user has registered and the password that corresponds to each site. 40

Path A file's location specified by the drive on which it is stored and the hierarchy of folders in which it is stored. (See *file specification*.) 206

Payroll software Horizontal market business software used to track employee hours, calculate pay, and print pay checks. 126

PC platform A family of personal computers that use Windows software and contain Intel-compatible microprocessors. 64

PDF (Portable Document Format) A standard format for exchanging files that can be viewed using Adobe Reader software. 129

Peripheral device A component or equipment, such as a printer, that expands a computer's input, output, or storage capabilities. 56

Persistent HTTP connection The process of using the same TCP connection to handle multiple HTTP requests, such as for obtaining the text and then the graphics for a Web page; contrast to stateless protocol. 365

Person-to-person payment A method of e-commerce payment that uses an intermediary or third party such as PayPal to handle payment between a buyer and seller. 391

Personal computer A microcomputer designed for use by an individual user for applications such as Web browsing and word processing. 17

Personal computing A type of computing characterized by the use of standalone computers designed for single users. 7

Personal finance software Software geared toward individual finances that helps track bank account balances, credit card payments, investments, and bills. 128

PERT (Program Evaluation and Review Technique) A project management technique that displays interconnected events and task milestones on a timeline. 570

Pharming An exploit that redirects users to fake Web sites. 406

Phased conversion A type of information system conversion in which one module of a new information system is activated at a time. 586

Phishing An e-mail based scam that's designed to fool users into revealing confidential information. 37

Phoneme A unit of sound that is a basic component of words and is produced by speech synthesizers. 428

Photo editing software The software used to edit, enhance, retouch, and manipulate digital photographs. 123

Photosites In digital photography, each photosite is a single point in an image, equivalent to one pixel. 433

Physical storage model A representation of data as it is physically stored. 218

PIECES framework A concept developed by James Wetherbe to help identify problems in an information system. Each letter of PIECES stands for a potential problem (Performance, Information, Economics, Control, Efficiency, and Service). 569

Pilot conversion A type of system conversion in which a new information system is first activated at one branch of a multi-branch company. 586

Ping (Packet Internet Groper) A command on a TCP/IP network that sends a test packet to a specified IP address and waits for a reply. 309

Pipelining A technology that allows a processor to begin executing an instruction before completing the previous instruction. 69

Pirated software Software that is copied, sold, or distributed without permission from the copyright holder. 156

Pits Spots on a CD that are "burned" onto an optical storage medium to represent digital data. 81

Pixel interpolation A process that is used by graphics software to average the color of adjacent pixels in an image, usually when the image is enlarged. 436

Pixelated Describes the effect of increasing the size and thus decreasing the quality of an image. 436

Pixels Short for *picture element;* the smallest unit in a graphic image. Computer display devices use a matrix of pixels to display text and graphics. 90

PL/1 (Programming Language 1) A business and scientific programming language developed by IBM in 1964. 679

Place shifting The practice of accessing media from a remote location, such as over a network. 465

Plaintext An original, unencrypted message. 285

Planning phase The first phase of an information system development project with the goal of creating a Project Development Plan. 567

Plug and Play The ability of a computer to automatically recognize and adjust the system configuration for a newly added device. 97

Plug-in A software module that adds a specific feature to a system. In the context of browsers, a plug-in adds the ability to display or play various additional file formats. 367

PNG (Portable Network Graphics) A type of graphics file format similar to but newer than GIF or JPEG. 431

Point size A unit of measure (1/72 of an inch) used to specify the height of characters in a font. 135

Pointing device An input device, such as a mouse, trackball, pointing stick, or trackpad, that allows users to manipulate an on-screen pointer and other screen-based graphical controls. 88

Polymorphism In the context of object-oriented programming, the ability to redefine a method for a subclass. Also called overloading. 707

Pop-up ad A type of advertisement that usually appears in a separate window when you enter a Web site. 385

POP3 (Post Office Protocol version 3) A standard for retrieving e-mail messages from an e-mail server. 394

Port probe An exploit used by hackers to locate computer ports that can be used for surreptitious access; also called a port scan. 340

Portable computer Any type of computer, such as a notebook computer, that runs on batteries and is designed to be carried from one location to another; also called a mobile computer. 59

Portable Internet access Any type of Internet service, such as portable satellite, that can be moved from one place to another. 311

Portable software Software designed to be stored on a flash drive or CD, and that does not require installation before it is used. 151

PostScript A printer language, developed by Adobe Systems, that uses a special set of commands to control page layout, fonts, and graphics. 94

Power surge A spike in electrical voltage that has the potential to damage electronic equipment such as computers. 99

Predicate In a Prolog fact, such as likes(John, Mary), the predicate "likes" describes the relationship between the arguments in parentheses, such as (John, Mary). 714

Predictive analytics A branch of data mining that focuses on predicting future probabilities and trends using statistical algorithms, neural networks, and optimization research. 613

Predictive methodology The traditional approach to software development in which detailed specifications are created before coding begins. 681

Presentation software Software that provides tools to combine text, graphics, graphs, animation, and sound into a series of electronic "slides" that can be output on a projector, or as overhead transparencies, paper copies, or 35-millimeter slides. 142

Primary key A field in a database that contains data, such as a Social Security number, that is unique to a record. 634

Printer Command Language (PCL) A standard for formatting codes embedded within a document that specify how a printer should format each page. 94

Private attribute An attribute for an object, class, or record that can be accessed only from the program routine in which it is defined. 703

Private IP address An IP address that cannot be routed over the Internet. 343

Problem statement In software engineering, a concise summary of elements that must be manipulated in order to achieve a result or goal. 680

Procedural language Any programming language used to create programs composed of a series of statements that tell the computer how to perform a specific task. 689

Procedural paradigm An approach to programming in which a programmer defines the steps for solving a problem. 689

Procedure In the context of computer programming, a section of code that performs activities but is not included in the main sequential execution path of a program. 696

Procedure handbook Step-by-step instructions for performing a specific job or task. 585

Process A systematic series of actions that a computer performs to manipulate data; typically represented on a DFD by a rounded rectangle. 572

Processing The manipulation of data by a computer's microprocessor or central processing unit. 15

Product activation The process of becoming a registered user of a software product; the process might include entering a validation code to unlock the software. 161

Productivity software Software that helps people work more efficiently; traditionally word processing, spreadsheet, presentation, e-mail, and database software. 132

Professional ethics On-the-job actions and choices that reflect a person's values. 523

Program editor A programming tool, similar to a word processor, that provides specialized editing and formatting features to streamline the programming process. 682

Programming language A set of keywords and grammar (syntax) that allows a programmer to write instructions that a computer can execute. 29, 676

Programming paradigm A programming methodology or approach, as in the object-oriented paradigm. 679

Project Development Plan A planning document that is the final result of a planning phase and is reviewed and approved by management. 567

Project management software Software specifically designed as a tool for planning, scheduling, and tracking projects and their costs. 126, 571

Prolog A declarative programming language used to develop expert systems modeled after human thinking. 679

Properties The characteristics of an object in a program. 683

Proprietary information Financial and product data, procedures, or concepts created by an individual or organization that are not made public because they would aid the competition. 526

Proprietary software Software that carries restrictions on its use that are delineated by copyright, patents, or license agreements. 159

Protocol suite A group of protocols, such as TCP and IP, that work together. 305

Prototype An experimental or trial version of a device or system. 489

Pseudocode A notational system for algorithms that combines English and a programming language. 692

PSK (pre-shared key) A variation of WPA encryption protocol for wireless connections in which the encryption key used by the router is the same for all client computers that connect to the network. 271

Public attribute An attribute for an object, class, or record that can be accessed from any routine in a program. 703

Public domain software Software that is available for public use without restriction except that it cannot be copyrighted. 158

Public folder A predefined folder designed to hold files that can be shared over a network. 277

Public key encryption (PKE) An encryption method that uses a pair of keys; a public key (known to everyone) that encrypts the message, and a private key (known only to the recipient) that decrypts it. 286

Quality assurance specialist A computer professional who participates in alpha and beta test cycles of software. Also refers to a person who examines and tests computer chips and devices. 512

Quality of service (QoS) The level of performance that is provided by a computer system and measured by factors such as response time, downtime, and capacity. 587

Quality-of-service metric A technique for measuring a particular quality-of-service characteristic, such as response time. 587

Quarantined file A file suspected to be infected with a virus that antivirus software moves to a special folder to prevent accidental access to it. 169

Query A search specification that prompts the computer to look for particular records in a file. 141

Query by example (QBE) A type of database interface in which the user fills in a field with an example of the type of information that is being sought. 141

Query language A set of command words that can be used to direct the computer to create databases, locate information, sort records, and change the data in those records. 141

Query processor The component of a search engine that examines keywords entered by users and fetches results that match the query. 376

RAM (random access memory) Computer memory circuitry that holds data, program instructions, and the operating system while the computer is on. 72

Random access The ability of a storage device (such as a disk drive) to go directly to a specific storage location without having to search sequentially from a beginning location. 77

Rasterization The process of superimposing a grid over a vector image and determining the color depth for each pixel. 447

RAW In the context of digital graphics, a file that contains unprocessed image data directly from a digital camera's sensors. 431

Ray tracing A technique by which light and shadows are added to a 3-D image. 449

RCA Spectra 70 An early third-generation computer that was among the first to use integrated circuits for data processing. 494

RDBMS (relational database management system) Database management software used to create, update, and administer a relational database. 625

Read-only technology Storage media that can only be read from, but not recorded on. 82

Read-write head The mechanism in a disk drive that magnetizes particles on the storage disk surface to write data, or senses the bits that are present to read data. 78

Readability formula A feature found in some word processing software that can estimate the reading level of a written document. 134

Real data type A numeric data type used for fields that contain numbers with decimal places. 634

Real-time messaging system Technologies, such as instant messaging and chat, that allow people to exchange messages when they are online. 331

REALbasic A modern OO version of the BASIC programming language that works cross platform on Windows, Macs, and Linux. 679

Record In the context of database management, a record is the fields of data that pertain to a single entity in a database. 139, 615

Record occurrence A record that has been filled with data for a particular entity. 615

Record type The structure of a record, including the names, length, and data types for each field. 615

Recordable technology The devices and standards that allow computers to write data permanently on CDs and DVDs, but does not allow that data to be changed once it has been recorded. 82

Recovery disk A CD that contains all the operating system files and application software files necessary to restore a computer to its original state. 227

Recovery partition A section of a hard disk that contains the files necessary to restore a computer's hard disk contents to factory condition. 228

Registers A sort of "scratch pad" area of the microprocessor into which data or instructions are moved so that they can be processed. 31

Relational database A database structure that incorporates the use of tables that can establish relationships with other, similar tables. 618

Relationship In the context of databases, an association between entities that can be used to link records in more than one file. 616

Relative reference In a worksheet, a cell reference that can change if cells change position as a result of a move or copy operation. 138

Remarks Explanatory comments inserted into lines of code in a computer program. 686

Remote Access Trojan (RAT) A type of Trojan horse that provides a "backdoor" into a computer for remote hackers to transmit files, snoop, run programs, and launch attacks on other computers. 163

Rendering In graphics software, the process of creating a 3-D solid image by covering a wireframe drawing and applying computer-generated highlights and shadows. 449

Repeater A network device that can boost signals and retransmit them to extend the coverage area of a network. 267

Repetition control structure A component of a computer program that repeats one or more instructions until a certain condition is met (also called loop or iteration). 698

Repetitive stress injury (RSI) An injury that occurs from overuse over a period of time. 536

Report generator The component of a data management environment that provides a user with the ability to design reports. 642

Report template A predesigned pattern that provides the outline or general specifications for a report. 642

Request for proposal (RFP) A document sent by an organization to vendors to solicit proposals; it specifies the problem that needs to be solved and the requirements that must be met. 580

Request for quotation (RFQ) A document sent by an organization to vendors requesting a formal price quotation on a list of hardware and/or software. 580

Reserved words Special words used as commands in some operating systems that may not be used in file names. 205

Resolution dependent Graphics, such as bitmaps, in which the quality of the image is dependent on the number of pixels constituting the image. 436

Resource A component, either hardware or software, that is available for use by a computer's processor. 185

Resource fork A storage characteristic of Mac OS that creates a file containing a description of the data stored in an accompanying raw data file. 199

Response rate In relation to display technology, response rate is the time it takes for one pixel to change from black to white then back to black. 90

Restore The process of copying files from a backup back to a computer's hard disk. 222

Restore point Data stored about the state of files and the operating system at a given point in time, then used to roll back the computer system to that state. 228

Rewritable technology The devices and standards that allow users to write data on a storage medium and then change that data. 82

RF signals (radio frequency signals) Data that is broadcast and received via radio waves with a transceiver. 259

Ribbon An element of the user interface popularized by Microsoft Office 2007 that presents users with multiple tabs instead of menus at the top of the application window. 190

RISC (reduced instruction set computer) A microprocessor designed for rapid and efficient processing of a small set of simple instructions. 69

RJ45 connector A square plastic cable connector that resembles an oversized telephone connector, and is used to connect Ethernet devices. 251

ROM (read-only memory) Refers to one or more integrated circuits that contain permanent instructions that the computer uses during the boot process. 74

ROM BIOS A small set of basic input/output system instructions stored in ROM. 74

Root directory The main directory of a disk. 206

Rooting A process that enables users to gain root access to Android mobile devices with the purpose of overcoming limitations imposed by mobile service providers. 145

Rootkit Software that conceals running processes; used by hackers to disguise security breaches and break-ins. 165

Routable IP address A network address that can be routed over the Internet; contrast to private IP address. 343

Router A device used to make wired or wireless connections and route data to its destination on a network. 250

RPG (Report Program Generator) A programming language used to generate business reports. 679

Rule In the context of Prolog programming, a rule is a general statement about the relationship between facts. 713

Run-length encoding (RLE) A graphics file compression technique that looks for patterns of bytes and replaces them with messages that describe the patterns. 440

Runtime error An error that occurs when a computer program is run. 685

Safe Mode A menu option that appears when Windows is unable to complete the boot sequence. By entering Safe Mode, a user can gracefully shut down the computer, then try to reboot it. 105

Sampling rate The number of times per second a sound is measured during the recording process. 423

Satellite Internet service A high-speed Internet service that uses a geosynchronous or low-earth orbit satellite to send data directly to satellite dishes owned by individuals. 318

Satellite modem A device that connects a computer to a satellite for purposes of accessing the Internet. 318

Scanner A device that converts a printed image into a bitmap graphic. 432

Scheduled reports Reports such as monthly sales summaries that follow a fixed format and are produced according to a preset timetable. 561

Scheme A dialect of LISP, used for computer research and teaching. 679

Schickard's Calculator An early mechanical calculator consisting of a series of gears and spokes representing numerical values. 488

Scratch A simple-to-use visual programming language based on Smalltalk/Squeak and used to teach programming. 679

Screen resolution The density of the grid used to display text or graphics on a display device; the greater the horizontal and vertical density, the higher the resolution. 91

SDK (software development kit) A collection of language-specific programming tools. 686

Search and Replace A feature of document production software that allows the user to automatically locate all instances of a particular word or phrase and substitute another word or phrase. 133

Search engine indexer The component of a search engine that reviews the Web pages brought back by a crawler and creates pointers to them so that they can be quickly accessed. 376

Search operator A logical search operator such as AND, OR, and NOT that helps form complex queries. 379

Search terms The words entered into a search engine or database to form a query. 378

Second-generation computers Computers that use transistors for data processing and storage instead of vacuum tubes. 492

Second-generation languages Assembly languages that followed machine languages. 677

Sectors Subdivisions of the tracks on a storage medium that provide storage areas for data. 219

Secure connection An Internet connection that encrypts data transmitted between your computer and a Web site. 389

Security software Any software package that is designed to protect computers from destructive software and unauthorized intrusions. 162

Security specialist A computer professional who analyzes security threats, implements solutions, and develops policies and procedures to protect computer equipment and data. 511

Security suite A software suite containing modules to protect computers against viruses, worms, intrusions, spyware, and other threats. 166

SELECT An SQL keyword that queries for a particular record or group of records from a table. 648

Selection control structure A component of a computer program that tells a computer what to do, depending on whether a condition is true or false (also called decision structure or branch). 697

Semi-structured problem A problem for which a general procedure has been established, but that requires some degree of discretionary judgment to arrive at a solution. 558

Semiconducting materials (semiconductors) Substances, such as silicon or germanium, that can act as either a conductor or an insulator. Used in the manufacture of computer chips. 27

Sequence control structure A programming construct that alters the order in which instructions are executed. 695

Sequence diagram A tool used by a project team that depicts the detailed interactions that take place within an information system. 574

Sequential access A characteristic of data storage, usually on computer tape, that requires a device to read or write data one record after another, starting at the beginning of the medium. 77

Sequential execution The computer execution of program instructions performed in the sequence established by a programmer. 695

Serial processing Processing data one instruction at a time, completing one instruction before beginning another. 69

Server A computer or software on a network that supplies the network with data and storage. 18

Server operating system A type of operating system, sometimes called a network operating system, that provides management tools for distributed networks, e-mail servers, and Web hosting sites. 187

Server-side program A program or scripting statement that resides on a Web server and acts as an intermediary between a user's browser and a DBMS. 628

Server-side script Scripting statements that are executed by a Web server in response to client data. 372

Service pack A collection of patches designed to correct bugs and/or add features to an existing software program. 152

Setup program A program module supplied with a software package for the purpose of installing the software. 146

Shared resources Hardware, software, and data that is available over a network to authorized users. 248

Shareware Copyrighted software marketed under a license that allows users to use the software for a trial period and then send in a registration fee if they wish to continue to use it. 159

Shrink-wrap license A legal agreement printed on computer software packaging, which becomes binding when the package is opened. 157

Signed code Program code that has an associated digital certificate identifying the programmer; used to reduce susceptibility to malware. 727

SIMULA (SIMUlation LAnguage) Believed to be the first object-oriented programming language. 679

Single-user license Legal permission for one person to use a particular software package. 157

Single-user operating system A type of operating system that is designed for one user at a time using one set of input devices. 187

Site license Legal permission for software to be used on any and all computers at a specific location (for example, within a corporate building or on a university campus). 157

Slide rule A manual calculator invented by William Oughtred that uses John Napier's logarithms to perform complex engineering and scientific calculations. 487

Smalltalk A classic object-oriented programming language. 679

Smartphone A cellular phone that has a high resolution color screen, a browser, and the ability to run apps. 65

Smileys Text-based symbols used to express emotion. 399

SMTP (Simple Mail Transfer Protocol) A communications protocol used to send e-mail across a network or the Internet. 394

Sniffing In the context of computer hacking, a technique that uses packet sniffer software to capture packets as they are sent over a network. 37

Social media Online Web sites and services, such as Facebook, Twitter, and LinkedIn, that help users create content and share it with others. 10

Socket A communication path between two remote programs. 364

Software The instructions that direct a computer to perform a task, interact with a user, or process data. 15

Software as a service A cloud computing model in which consumers access applications using a browser; usually fee based. 330

Software customization The process of modifying a commercially available software application to meet the needs of a specific user or organization. 584

Software engineering The process of developing software using systematic mathematical, engineering, and management techniques. 515

Software installation The process by which programs and data are copied to the hard disk of a computer system and otherwise prepared for access and use. 143

Software license A legal contract that defines the ways in which a user may use a computer program. 157

Software publishers Companies that produce computer software. 499

Software update A section of code or a program module designed to correct errors or enhance security on an already installed software product. 152

Software upgrade A new version of a software product containing new features and designed to replace the entire earlier version of the product. 152

Solid state drive A data storage device that utilizes erasable, rewritable circuitry. 85

Solid state storage A technology that records data and stores it in a microscopic grid of cells on a non-volatile, erasable, low-power chip. 84

Sort key A field used to arrange records in order. 639

Sort order In a database table, the order in which records are stored on disk. 639

Sound card A circuit board that gives the computer the ability to accept audio input from a microphone, play sound files, and produce audio output through speakers or headphones. 424

Source code Computer instructions written in a high-level language. 29

Source document A file containing the HTML tags or scripts for a Web page. 363

Spam Unsolicited e-mail typically sent as a bulk or mass-mailing and often used for fraudulent or deceptive marketing. 404

Spam filter Software that identifies unsolicited and unwanted e-mail messages and blocks them from the recipient's Inbox. 404

Specific absorption rate A measure of the amount of RF energy that is absorbed by the body; used to indicate the levels of radiation emitted by cell phones and other devices. 536

Speech recognition The process by which computers recognize voice patterns and words, then convert them to digital data. 428

Speech synthesis The process by which computers produce sound that resembles spoken words. 428

Spelling checker A feature of document production software that checks each word in a document against an electronic dictionary of correctly spelled words, then presents a list of alternatives for possible misspellings. 134

Spelling dictionary A data module that is used by a spelling checker as a list of correctly spelled words. 134

Spreadsheet A numerical model or representation of a real situation, presented in the form of a table. 136

Spreadsheet software Software for creating electronic worksheets that hold data in cells and perform calculations based on that data. 136

Spyware Any software that covertly gathers user information without the user's knowledge, usually for advertising purposes. 164

SQL A popular query language used by mainframes and microcomputers. 645

SQL keywords A collection of command words that issue instructions to an SQL database. 646

SQL query A command created using SQL database client software that operates directly on the record in a database. 645

SSID (service set identifier) A code that identifies a network containing wireless connections and is attached to every packet that travels on that network. 269

SSL (Secure Sockets Layer) A security protocol that uses encryption to establish a secure connection between a computer and a Web server. 390

Stateless protocol A protocol, such as HTTP, that allows one request and response per session. 368

Static IP address A permanently assigned and unique IP address, used by hosts or servers. 306

Static Web publishing A simple way to display the data in a database by converting a database report into an HTML document. 627

Statistical software Software for analyzing large sets of data to discover patterns and relationships within them. 126

Storage The area in a computer where data is retained on a permanent basis. 15

Storage density The closeness of the particles on a disk surface. As density increases, the particles are packed more tightly together and are usually smaller. 77

Storage device A mechanical apparatus that records data to and retrieves data from a storage medium. 76

Storage medium The physical material used to store computer data, such as a floppy disk, a hard disk, or a CD-ROM. 76

Store-and-forward A technology used by communications networks in which an e-mail message is temporarily held in storage on a server until it is requested by a client computer. 394

Stored program A set of instructions that resides on a storage device, such as a hard drive, and can be loaded into computer memory and executed. 16

Strategic planning The process of developing long-range goals and plans for an organization. 557

Streaming audio An audio file format that allows the audio clip to begin before the file is entirely downloaded. 426

Streaming video An Internet video technology that sends a small segment of a video file to a user's computer and begins to play it while the next segment is being sent. 459

Strong encryption Encryption that is difficult to decrypt or "break" without the encryption key. 285

Structured English Vocabulary and syntax used by systems analysts to concisely and unambiguously explain the logic of a process. It is limited to words defined in a data dictionary and to specific logical terms such as IF...THEN. 692

Structured file A file that consists of a collection of data organized as a set of similarly structured records. 614

Structured methodology A method of developing an information system that focuses on the processes that take place within the information system. 570

Structured problem A problem for which there exists a well-established procedure for obtaining the best solution. 558

Style A feature in many desktop publishing and word processing programs that allows the user to apply numerous format settings with a single command. 135

Subclass In object-oriented programming, a subclass is derived from a superclass and inherits its attributes and methods. 704

Subdirectory A directory found under the root directory. 206

Submenu A user interface element that emerges after a menu is selected to offer additional options. 191

Subroutine A section of code that performs activities or manipulates data but is not included in the main sequential execution path of a program. 696

Success factors System requirements that also serve as an evaluation checklist at the end of a development project. 571

Summary report A report generated by a management information system that combines or groups data and usually provides totals, such as a report of total annual sales for the past five years. 561

Superclass In object-oriented programming, a superclass can provide attributes and methods for subclasses. 704

Supercomputer The fastest and most expensive type of computer, capable of processing trillions of instructions per second. 19

Surge strip A device that filters out electrical spikes that could damage computer equipment. 100

SVG (Scalable Vector Graphics) A graphics format designed specifically for Web display that automatically resizes when displayed on different screens. 448

Switch A network device that sends data to a specific address instead of broadcasting it over an entire network. 267

Symbian An operating system typically used on mobile phones and open to programming by third-party developers. 202

Symmetric Internet connection Any connection to the Internet in which the upstream speed is the same as the downstream speed. 311

Symmetric key encryption An encryption key that is used for both encryption and decryption of messages. 286

Synchronization The process of updating files so they are the same on two devices; can be used for backup or to update addresses, etc. 225

Synchronous communications A communications mode, such as VoIP, in which participants must be online at the same time. 332

Syntax In the context of programming languages, syntax refers to the grammar rules that create valid program statements. 676

Syntax error An error that results when an instruction does not follow the syntax rules, or grammar, of the programming language. 685

Synthesized sound Artificially created sound, usually found in MIDI music or synthesized speech. 427

System board The main circuit board in a computer that houses chips and other electronic components. 28

System conversion The process of deactivating an old information system and activating a new one. 586

System development life cycle (SDLC) The series of phases that outlines the development process of an information system. 566

System documentation Descriptions of the features, hardware architecture, and programming of an information system written for programmers, designers, and analysts who maintain the system. 585

System operator The person responsible for the day-to-day operation of a computer—usually a mainframe or supercomputer. 588

System palette A selection of colors that are used by an operating system to display graphic elements. 439

System requirements (1) The minimum hardware and operating system specifications required for a software application to operate correctly. (2) Criteria for developing a successful information system, which are typically compiled into a Systems Requirements Report at the conclusion of the analysis phase of the SDLC. 155, 571

System Requirements Report A report generated at the conclusion of the analysis phase of the SDLC by a project team that has studied a system and determined the system requirements. 572

System software Computer programs, such as an operating system or utility software, that help the computer carry out essential operating tasks. 16

System testing The process of testing an information system to ensure that all the hardware and software components work together. 584

System unit The case or box that contains the computer's power supply, storage devices, main circuit board, processor, and memory. 57

System utilities Utility software that diagnoses and repairs disk errors, corrupted files, and other software or hardware problems. 130

Systems analysis and design The process of planning and building an information system. 566

Systems analyst A computer professional responsible for analyzing requirements, designing information systems, and supervising the implementation of new information systems. 511

Systems programmer The person responsible for installing, modifying, and troubleshooting the operating system of a mainframe or supercomputer. 588

Tablet computer A small, portable computer with a touch-sensitive screen that can be used as a writing or drawing pad. 65

Tactical planning Short- or near-term decisions and goals that deploy the human, financial, and natural resources necessary to meet strategic goals. 558

Taskbar A graphical user interface element usually displayed near the bottom of the screen to help users launch and monitor applications. 190

Tax preparation software Software used to help individuals or businesses calculate annual state and federal taxes. 128

TCP (Transmission Control Protocol) The protocol within TCP/IP that is responsible for establishing a data connection between two hosts and breaking data into packets. 305

TCP/IP (Transmission Control Protocol/Internet Protocol) The primary protocol suite for transmitting messages over the Internet. 305

Technical support specialist A computer professional who provides phone or online help to customers of computer companies and software publishers. 511

Technical writer A person who specializes in writing explanations of technical concepts and procedures. 512

Telecommuting The act of using available technologies, such as computers, telephones, and the Internet, to work from home or another off-site location. 513

Test area A portion of a computer system where software testing can occur without disrupting an organization's regular information system. 584

Text data type A data type used for fixed-length fields that hold character data such as people's names or CD titles. 634

Text-to-speech software Software that generates speech based on written text that is played back through a computer's sound card. 428

Thesaurus A feature of documentation software that provides synonyms. 134

Third-generation computers Computers characterized by using integrated circuits instead of transistors or vacuum tubes for data processing. 494

Third-generation languages Programming languages, such as FORTRAN, BASIC, and COBOL, that followed assembly languages and provided English-like keywords. 677

Third-party cookie A cookie that is generated by an ad or an entity other than the Web page that is shown in the browser. 401

Threat modeling A component of defensive programming that helps programmers identify ways in which their programs might be compromised; also called risk analysis. 725

Thunderbolt A high-speed expansion port typically used to connect external storage devices to a computer. 96

TIFF (Tagged Image File Format) A bitmap image file format with a .tif extension that automatically compresses the file data. 431

Time shifting The practice of recording digital content for later playback. 465

TLS (Transport Layer Security) An update of the Secure Sockets Layer (SSL) protocol for encrypting data before it is transmitted over a network. 390

Toolbar A component of graphical user interfaces that displays icons representing tools, commands, and other options. 190

Top-level domain A major domain category into which groups of computers on the Internet are divided, such as com, edu, gov, int, mil, net, and org. 307

Touch screen A display device that accepts input from being touched with a stylus or fingertip. 89

Tower case A desktop computer form factor that stores the system board and storage devices in a tall system unit with detached display and keyboard. 58

TQM (Total Quality Management) The process by which an organization analyzes and implements ways to improve the quality of its products and/or services. 569

Traceroute A network utility that records a packet's path, the number of hops, and the time it takes for the packet to make each hop. 310

Tracing software Software that locates the edges of objects in a bitmap graphic and converts the resulting shape into a vector graphic. 447

Trackpad A touch-sensitive surface on which you slide your fingers to move the on-screen pointer. 89

Tracks A series of concentric or spiral storage areas created on a storage medium during the formatting process. 219

Transaction An exchange between two parties that can be recorded and stored in a computer system. 559

Transaction processing system (TPS) A system that keeps track of transactions for an organization by providing ways to collect, display, modify, and cancel transactions. 559

Transceiver A combination of a transmitter and a receiver used to send and receive data in the form of radio frequencies. 259

Transcoding The process of converting audio and video files from one digital format to another, such as converting an MOV file into a Flash video file. 458

Transistors A computer processing technology created by Bell Laboratories in 1947, characterizing second-generation computers, which replaced vacuum tubes for data processing. 492

Trojan horse A computer program that appears to perform one function while actually doing something else, such as inserting a virus into a computer system or stealing a password. 163

True Color bitmap A color image with a color depth of 24 bits or 32 bits. Each pixel in a True Color image can be displayed using any of 16.7 million different colors. 438

Turnkey system A complete information system that consists of both hardware and commercial software. 578

Tweet A short message, sometimes called a microblog, posted on Twitter. 333

UML (Unified Modeling Language) A tool for diagramming a set of object classes. 573

Unicode A 16-bit character-representation code that can represent more than 65,000 characters. 25

Uninstall routine A program that removes software files, references, and registry entries from a computer's hard disk. 153

Unit testing The process of testing a completed application module to make sure that it operates reliably and correctly. 584

UNIVAC The first commercially successful digital computer. 491

UNIX A multiuser, multitasking server operating system developed by AT&T Bell Laboratories in 1969. 200

Unstructured file A file that contains data, but that is not in a structured format of fields and records. 614

Unstructured problem A problem for which there is no established procedure for arriving at a solution. 558

Unzipped Refers to files that have been uncompressed. 150

UPDATE An SQL keyword used to alter the values in a database record. 650

Upload The process of transferring a file from a local computer to a remote computer over a LAN or the Internet. 18

UPS (uninterruptible power supply) A battery-backed device designed to provide power to a computer during blackouts, brownouts, or other electrical disruptions. 100

Upstream speed The rate at which data is transmitted from your home computer to the Internet. 310

URL (Uniform Resource Locator) The address of a Web page. 361

USB (universal serial bus) A high-speed bus commonly used for connecting peripheral devices to computers. 96

USB flash drive A portable solid state storage device nicknamed "pen drive" or "keychain drive" that plugs directly into a computer's USB port. 85

USB hub A device that provides several auxiliary USB ports. 96

Use case Tasks performed by an actor in an information system. 573

Use case diagram Documentation of the users of an information system and their functions. 573

User documentation Descriptions of how to interact with an information system or program, including instructions on use, features, and trouble-shooting. 585

User ID A combination of letters and numbers that serves as a user's "call sign" or identification. Also referred to as a user name. 34

User interface The software and hardware that enable people to interact with computers. 189

User privileges A set of assigned rights that specify what data is accessible to a particular user on a network or on a database. 655

Utility software A type of system software provided by the operating system vendor or third-party vendors that specializes in tasks such as system maintenance, security, or file management. 129

Vacuum tube An electronic device that controls the flow of electrons in a vacuum and represents binary data; used in the construction of first generation computers. 492

Value A number used in a calculation. 136

VAR (value-added reseller) A company that combines one product with additional hardware, software, and/or services to create a system designed to meet the needs of specific customers or industries. 508

Variable A named storage location that is capable of holding data, which can be modified during program execution. 680

Variable-length field A field in a data file that can expand to accept any number of characters up to a maximum limit. 615

VDE (visual development environment) Programming tools that allow programmers to build substantial parts of computer programs by pointing and clicking, rather than entering code. 683

Vector graphic An image generated from descriptions that specify the position, length, and direction in which lines and shapes are drawn. 444

Vertical market software Computer programs designed to meet the needs of a specific market segment or industry, such as medical record-keeping software for use in hospitals. 126

VGA (Video Graphics Array) A screen resolution of 640 x 480. 96

Video capture The process of converting analog video signals into digital data stored on a hard drive. 455

Video editing software Software that provides tools for capturing and editing video from a camcorder. 122

Videogame console A computer specifically designed for playing games using a television screen and game controllers. 17

Viewing angle width The angle at which you can clearly see the screen image from the side. 90

Virtual keyboard A keyboard that is displayed on a touch screen and used for input on smartphones and tablet computers. 89

Virtual machine Software that creates an operating environment that emulates another computer platform; as an example, Parallels Desktop creates a virtual PC on an Intel Macintosh computer. 198

Virtual memory A computer's use of hard disk storage to simulate RAM. 73

Virtual private network (VPN) A network connection that typically carries encrypted data over the Internet to and from a remote access server. 345

Virus definitions A group of virus signatures used by antivirus software to identify and block viruses and other malware. 168

Virus hoax A message, usually e-mail, that makes claims about a virus problem that doesn't actually exist. 166

Virus signature The unique computer code contained in a virus that security software uses to identify it. 167

VisiCalc First released on the Apple II, VisiCalc was the first electronic spreadsheet. 496

Visual Basic An event-driven programming environment in which the programmer uses forms to lay out the screen components of a program; components are defined by properties and BASIC program code. 679

VOB (Video Object) An industry-standard video format for standalone DVD players. 458

Voiceband modem The type of modem typically used to connect a computer to a telephone line. 313

VoIP (Voice over Internet Protocol) Hardware, software, and protocols used to make telephone-style calls over the Internet. Also referred to as Internet telephony. 331

Volatile A term that describes data (usually in RAM) that can exist only with a constant supply of power. 72

Walkthrough In the context of programming, a method of verifying that an algorithm functions properly when using realistic test data. 694

WAN (wide area network) An interconnected group of computers and peripherals that covers a large geographical area, such as multiple branches of a corporation. 247

WAP (Wireless Access Protocol) A communications protocol that provides Internet access for handheld devices. 325

Waterfall SDLC A series of phases that outlines the development process of an information system where each phase is a discrete step in the development process. 566

WAV An audio file format with a .wav extension that was Windows' original "native" sound format. 425

Wavetable A set of pre-recorded musical instrument sounds in MIDI format. 427

WBS (work breakdown structure) A project management tool based on a hierarchical structure of tasks and deliverables. 570

Weak encryption Encryption that is relatively easy or simple to decrypt without the encryption key. 285

Web Short for *World Wide Web*; an Internet service that links documents and information from computers located worldwide, using the HTTP protocol. 8

Web 2.0 A group of new and innovative ways to use the Web, such as for social networking, blogging, and wikis. 361

Web 3.0 A group of technologies including cloud computing that extend the ways in which the Internet and Web can be used. 361

Web application Application software that is accessed and used from within a browser. 143

Web browser A program that communicates with a Web server and displays Web pages. 361

Web bug A small graphic on a Web page that installs cookies designed to track your online activities. Also known as a clear GIF. 403

Web cache A collection of Web pages and associated graphics that have been accessed and are temporarily stored locally to speed up subsequent access to them. 365

Web crawler The component of a search engine that autonomously visits Web sites collecting Web page data that will be indexed and available for searching. 375

Web page Information displayed by a Web browser that's produced from an HTML document or generated on the fly from data in a database. 361

Web palette A standard selection of colors that all Internet browsers can display; also called a Web-safe palette or browser palette. 439

Web portfolio A hypertext version of a resume containing links to Web sites of former employers or schools. 519

Web search engine A program that uses keywords to find information on the Internet and returns a list of links to relevant documents. 374

Web server A computer that listens for queries from Web browsers and transmits HTML documents over the Internet. 361

Web site A Web address that holds a collection of information identified by a common domain name, such as *www.cnn.com*. 361

Web site designer A computer professional who creates, tests, posts, and modifies HTML documents and other data for a Web site. 511

Webcam An inexpensive digital camera that attaches directly to a computer and creates a video by capturing a series of still images. 454

WebM A multimedia container format designed for HTML5 projects. 458

Webmail An e-mail system that allows users to access e-mail messages using a browser. 393

WEP (Wired Equivalent Privacy) An encryption algorithm used to protect data on Wi-Fi networks. 271

What-if analysis The process of setting up a model in a spreadsheet and experimenting to see what happens when different values are entered. 136

Whistleblowing The disclosure by an employee of confidential information that relates to some danger, fraud, or other illegal or unethical conduct connected with the workplace. 532

Wi-Fi An Ethernet-compatible wireless connection that uses 802.11a, b, g, and n standards. 262

Wi-Fi adapter A type of network interface card that includes a transmitter and a receiver using Wi-Fi protocols. 264

Wi-Fi hotspot The geographical area in which you can connect to a Wi-Fi signal, such as a Wi-Fi equipped campus or coffeehouse. 322

Wiki Software that allows users to collaborate to create, change, and link Web pages. Used for applications such as Wikipedia and open source project management. 333

WiMAX A fixed wireless Internet service based on Ethernet protocols with a range of 30 miles and a transmission speed of 70 Mbps. 319

Window An element of graphical user interfaces that is rectangular in shape and displays the controls for a program or a dialog box. 189

Windows Explorer A file management utility included with most Windows operating systems that helps users manage their files. 216

Windows Phone 7 A mobile operating system designed by Microsoft for mobile phones and other handheld digital devices. 203

Windows Registry A group of files on Windows computers that is used by the operating system to store configuration information about hardware and software. 228

Wireframe A representation of a 3-D object using separate lines, which resemble wire, to create a model. 449

Wireless access point A network device that connects several devices of a local area network by broadcasting signals to any device with compatible Wi-Fi cards. 267

Wireless ad-hoc protocol Wireless connections in which devices broadcast directly to each other instead of to a central access point. 262

Wireless encryption A security measure for networks containing wireless connections that scrambles data transmitted between network devices. 270

Wireless encryption key The basis for scrambling and unscrambling the data that travels over a wireless connection. Sometimes called a network security key. 271

Wireless infrastructure protocol Wireless connections in which devices communicate through a central access point. 262

WMA (Windows Media Audio) A file format with a .wma extension that is promoted by Microsoft and provides highly compressed audio files with very little loss of sound quality. 425

Word processing software Computer programs that assist the user in producing documents, such as reports, letters, papers, and manuscripts. 133

Word size The number of bits that a CPU can manipulate at one time, which is dependent on the size of the registers in the CPU, and the number of data lines in the bus. 68

Word wrap The ability of word processing software to automatically sense the right margin and stream text to the next line. 133

Workers People who perform the tasks necessary to carry out an organization's mission. 557

Worksheet A computerized, or electronic, spreadsheet. 136

Workstation (1) A computer connected to a local area network. (2) A powerful desktop computer designed for specific tasks. 17

WPA (Wi-Fi Protected Access) A method for encrypting data transmitted over wireless connections. 271

Xerox Alto An early personal computer prototype developed by Xerox Corp. that featured, among other things, a graphical user interface that became influential in the development of the Apple Macintosh. 496

XHTML A markup language very similar to HTML, but more customizable. 362

XML (eXtensible Markup Language) A document format similar to HTML, but that allows the Web page developer to define customized tags, generally for the purpose of creating more interactivity. 630

XML DBMS A database management system that provides authoring and query tools for designing and managing collections of XML documents. 625

Z3 An early electronic computer prototype designed by Konrad Zuse that was the first to incorporate the use of binary numbers for data representation. 490

Zipped Refers to one or more files that have been compressed. 150

Zombie A computer that has been compromised by malware that allows it to be controlled by a remote user. 164

INDEX